KT-573-709

Contents

Contributors:

History of the Cinema
Written by Annette Kuhn
Research by Paul Kerr
Stars by James Donald
Italy and Neo-Realism by Geoffrey Nowell-Smith

Genre
Written by Christine Gledhill
The musical by Andy Medhurst
Film noir by Jane Root

Authorship
Written by Pam Cook

The history of narrative codes
Written by Annette Kuhn

Film narrative and the structuralist controversy
Written by Sheila Johnston

Extract Information
Compiled and written by Jane Root,
Terry Staples and Lez Cooke

PAM COOK has published several articles on women and cinema
and is now the Associate Editor of the *Monthly Film Bulletin*.

JAMES DONALD is a lecturer at the Open University and a former
editor of *Screen Education*.

CHRISTINE GLEDHILL is in charge of film study materials at BFI
Education and is the editor of a forthcoming anthology on
women and melodrama in film.

SHEILA JOHNSTON is a freelance journalist and writer.

PAUL KERR is the editor of the BFI Reader in Film Studies, *The
Hollywood Film Industry* (Routledge and Kegan Paul,
forthcoming).

ANNETTE KUHN is the author of *Women's Pictures: Feminism
and Cinema* (Routledge and Kegan Paul, 1982).

ANDY MEDHURST is research fellow in British Film History at the
University of East Anglia.

GEOFFREY NOWELL-SMITH is head of BFI Publishing.

JANE ROOT is the author of *Pictures of Women* (Routledge and
Kegan Paul, 1984) and is now researching the Channel 4
programme *About Television* and writing the book to
accompany the series.

TERRY STAPLES is a teacher and freelance writer and researcher,
and also programmes children's seasons at the National Film
Theatre.

Introduction

This is a book about cinema – the different ways in which it has been described, defined and discussed in film theory and criticism, and the implications of those discussions for film education. It is also a valuable historical document, tracing the shifts in debates over a particular period – roughly, from the mid-60s to the late 70s – in which Film Studies underwent a radical transformation in response to general social and cultural changes. The introduction of theories of ideology influenced by structuralism and psychoanalysis, for example, which still appears shrouded in mystery to many, is here placed in its historical context in order to make it more accessible. The collision of these new ideas with more traditional ways of approaching cinema (through authorship and genre for instance), is addressed from a perspective which is both critical of the wholesale incorporation of difficult, often obscure theories, and sympathetic to the enlivening effects of theory on a mainly empiricist film culture. The central premise of the book is that cinema is kept alive not just through systems of production, distribution and exhibition, but also through the circulation of debates which provide the cultural context in which it can flourish.

The Cinema Book is itself part of the process of debate, and is intended to provoke discussion. Each of the five main sections – History, Genre, Authorship, History of Narrative and Narrative and Structuralism – is separately authored by writers who argue from their different perspectives on film theory and criticism. Each section stands on its own, but a system of cross references indicates where the reader might look to find certain questions discussed differently, or elaborated upon, in other sections.

Something needs to be said about the development of the project, which has taken over five years to complete, and was itself transformed in that time. *The Cinema Book* began life as a catalogue of the film study extract material held by the British Film Institute Film and Video Library, selected over the years by the BFI Education Department to facilitate the teaching of film. The existing Extract Catalogue was in the form of an unwieldy set of duplicated documents dating back to the inception of the extract collection in the early 60s. The intention was to update these documents, expanding on the teaching categories which had informed extract selection, and showing how extracts could be used in the context of these categories. It soon became clear that this would entail the larger task of charting the history of the arguments covered in each category. Rather than a catalogue of extracts, the book became an account of the Education Department's involvement in the shifting terrain of Film Studies over a certain period. Nevertheless, the shape of the final product has to a great extent been determined by the extract collection, which is geared mainly towards Hollywood cinema and inevitably reflects the changes in selection criteria during that period. Certain discussion areas could only be updated within the limits of the collection. This is particularly obvious in the History section, where gaps in the collection meant that some important historical developments could not adequately be covered; and in the Authorship section, where the work of certain directors is dealt with specifically in terms of the films available in extract form. In the latter case, the emphasis is on showing how the work of the director in question has figured in authorship debates, rather than providing an auteurist chronology. In general, the presentation of film education debates in the book reflects the dynamic process of historical change and does not pretend to offer a definitive or prescriptive guide to Film Studies.

This precept has informed the book's structure, which is intended to be open to many different kinds of reader. Those wishing to concentrate on specific aspects of cinema history may confine themselves to one or two sections or sub-sections, while the reader with more general interests can range freely backwards and forwards across all sections. Teachers wishing to use the extract collection in their classes will find a complete list of available extract material at the back of the book. This includes plot synopses of each film title and incorporates italicised descriptions of the contents of each extract. In the body of the book at the end of the discussion sections are tinted boxes containing selected extracts which may be useful in illustrating discussion points, and for those who prefer to use the original teaching categories to guide them, these are reprinted, in updated form, after Extract Information. In addition, an index is provided for those who need to find information in a hurry.

It is hoped that the book will provide a useful and stimulating resource for teachers, students and the growing numbers of film enthusiasts with an interest in cinema history and film theory. *The Cinema Book* makes its appearance during British Film Year, and during a transition period for British cinema generally. A history of debates in British film culture could not be more timely.

Pam Cook
May 1985

Special Notes

Abbreviations

In showing the credits of individual film extracts we have adopted the following abbreviations:

p.c   production company
p   producer
d   director
sc   scriptwriter
ph   photography
ed   editor
a.d   art director
m   music

Technical features

The technical features of each film extract are placed directly after the credits, for example:

> **The Jazz Singer** (USA 1927 *p.c* –
> Warner Bros; *d* – Alan Crosland;
> st + sd b/w 12)

This data indicates that the film is available with sound and in silent form, is black and white and runs for 12 minutes. Alternative data, sd col scope 18, indicates that the film has sound, is colour and CinemaScope (widescreen) and runs for 18 minutes. All film extracts are available in 16 mm for hire in the UK only.

Address all bookings for film extracts to:

Film and Video Library
81 Dean Street
London W1V 6AA

tel: 01-437 4355

A provisional phone booking is recommended, followed by written confirmation, preferably on an official order form.

History of the Cinema

Introduction

In quantitative terms, a great deal of critical work has been done on the history of cinema from a variety of perspectives: aesthetic, economic, sociological, industrial, technological, authorial, to name but a few. Much of this work, however, has tended to take as given both its methods and its object, with the result that its partiality has rarely been noticed by its exponents. Each approach is generally taken to be entirely adequate to the task of describing what happened when, and debate is often reduced to controversy over conflicting evidence in the search for a final, incontrovertible truth. Thus, in the search for cinematic 'firsts' predominant until very recently in histories of cinema (the first close-up, the earliest example of matchcutting, and so on), the question of *why* the development of the close-up is actually important, or *how* it came to be so, remains unasked, lost in the controversy over who did what first. Clearly the desire for total historical accuracy, based as it is on the notion that there exist neutral facts which are unchanging, can rarely, if ever, be satisfied. After all, different versions of the same 'facts' will place emphasis on different aspects, since these versions are themselves caught up in history, circumscribed by time and place. Rather than a static and self-defeating search for objective 'truth', then, historical enquiry might better be seen as a process of sifting and reorganising different kinds and orders of information to produce new interpretations. This is not to discount the value of empirical data, but to be aware that it does not exist in an abstract and unmediated form.

One of the ideas taken for granted by traditional histories is that the development of cinema can be accounted for in terms of a few 'great' innovative masterpieces which demonstrate the medium's progression towards aesthetic perfection. In this scenario, a few 'great men' (e.g. D. W. Griffith) are seen to be responsible for this progression, and the contributions of other early cineastes, which may well call into question the idea of a simple chronological 'advance', are ignored. Moreover, when a 'Great Tradition' is set up in this way, students of cinema history are encouraged to see themselves as privileged heirs to a cultural heritage which is quite separate from, and more valuable than, that of ordinary filmgoers.

Another idea which has held sway is that films can be seen as direct reflections of developments in society, as though modern historians can sweep away their own preconceptions and see the films 'as they really were then'. However, the more

Kinetoscope parlour

one thinks about the ways in which repeated viewings of films in different contexts transform their meanings, the less it becomes possible to conceive of a transcendental 'first viewing' which can offer the possibility of a transparent, objective look at cinema history.

So it can be seen that traditional histories of cinema have often constructed the field in highly selective ways which have none the less largely been accepted as natural. Once this naturalness is questioned, it becomes clear that such partiality has consequences which are not necessarily desirable, and can lead to a blocking of the potential of history to analyse and explain, rather than simply describe. For example, the overwhelming bias, in spite of an apparent diversity of approach, towards describing cinema history as a chronological sequence of progressions towards ever more perfect forms occludes complex relationships between social structures, institutions and forms which do not necessarily operate chronologically. When analysis of these relationships is attempted, it becomes difficult to see them as non-problematic, as simple facts 'already there' for the historian to take up. Indeed, history can be seen in terms of a conflict between competing ideological constructions, or representations of the world.

A history which seeks to explain the complex interrelationships between the multiple, and often contradictory, elements at work in cinema would need to pay attention to the different constructions available, regarded as mutually exclusive by traditional approaches. Arguably, this would lead to an entirely different conception of the field of cinema history which would see it as far more diverse and more differentiated than at present. The preservation – and indeed the non-preservation – of certain films in archives, and the availability of films for distribution

and exhibition have largely been determined (and, indeed restricted) by conventional developmental historical models. And our conceptions of the relationship of film texts to cinema history have been similarly determined: films are seen to exemplify only those characteristics validated by a certain method. For example, some films are considered simply as 'evidence' of developments within the industry: thus *The Jazz Singer* (1927) is widely cited as cinematic evidence for the advent of sound in Hollywood and the pioneering of sound technology in the studios by Warner Bros, rather than considered for its ideological or aesthetic significance. On the other hand, another early sound film, *Scarface* (1931), has been seen as demonstrating how sound technology had a retroactive, rather than progressive, effect on film form because it inhibited camera movement and privileged the use of certain kinds of continuity editing based on filmed dialogue (the shot/reverse-shot and eyeline match), which had consequences for the development of a certain form of narrative cinema, the 'classic realistic text' (→ HISTORY OF NARRATIVE: *The classic narrative system*, p. 212; NARRATIVE AND STRUCTURALISM: *The classic realist text*, p. 242). The adoption by the studios of synchronous as opposed to other types of sound has also been seen as emerging from, and exerting influence upon, this historical matrix.

These two approaches, using similar empirical evidence, construct directly opposed views of a certain period in cinema history. The first assumes a series of chronological developments towards aesthetic and technological perfection; the second attempts a more complex analysis which takes into account industrial and ideological factors and their relationship to film language, eschewing simple chronology. From this perspective, films are regarded as both the outcome of, and as exerting their effects on, a certain cinematic institution at a particular place and time: in this case, film technology and the Hollywood studio system in the late 1920s and early 1930s. A third approach, perhaps best exemplified by the *Cahiers du Cinéma* collective text on John Ford's *Young Mr. Lincoln* (→ AUTHORSHIP: *Discursive activity*, p. 189), has attempted to analyse the relationship between a number of conflicting factors, historical, political, economic, ideological, authorial, generic and institutional, in a single film text, moreover a 'marginal' text not considered worthy of the Great Tradition favoured by traditional histories. *Cahiers'* analysis produced a 'reading' of *Young Mr. Lincoln* which constructs history as an arena of conflicting interests, and film texts as constantly open to re-interpretation from different historical perspectives, rather than tied forever to the immediate context.

Arguably, then, the question of what constitutes a history of cinema is now open to debate, as is the question of how to define the relationship of film texts to their conditions of production (understood in the widest sense of a matrix of contributing factors). The nature and extent of the influence of conditions of production on particular films can only tentatively be explored here, but the need to pay attention to such influences in the process of constructing cinema history is all too often ignored.

The American film industry

Film technology and the early film industry

In 1891 Thomas Edison took out patents on two new processes, the Kinetograph and the Kinetoscope. In spite of such precautions, however, Edison underestimated the economic potential of these inventions and failed either to secure foreign rights or effectively to exploit the domestic market. In 1893, a Kinetoscope Company was set up independent of Edison to retail 'Kinetographic' material and coin-operated Kinetoscope machines, both of which Edison agreed to manufacture for a price. In the same year, Edison opened what was perhaps the first purpose-built production studio, at a cost of some $700, a sum that was soon recovered by charging $200 for every Kinetoscope sold.

The first films to flicker inside the Kinetoscopes featured such exotica as boxers, ballerinas and bears, ran only a fragment of a single reel (about 50 feet, less than a minute, on average), and were watched by individual consumers in the comfort of their own homes. In 1894, however, the first Kinetoscope parlour opened in New York's Broadway, and a new company – the Kinetoscope Exhibition Company (KEC) – was set up to exploit an exclusive contract with Edison to exhibit his films.

Realising that greater profits could be made if more than one customer could watch a film at any one time, the KEC introduced a projection process, the Panoptikon, and other companies employing similar processes also began to appear in the mid-1890s. Among the earliest of these companies were Mutoscope in America and Lumière Brothers in France. In 1896 Lumière's Cinématographe and Mutoscope's American Biograph were both exhibited in New York, and the machines – rather than the material which passed through them – were clearly the main attraction. Indeed, Edison and his competitors made most of their money in these early years not from their films, which were sold outright, but from the cinematographic equipment for which they held the patents. The films themselves functioned in fact as little more than inducements to customers considering the purchase of Kinetoscopes, and it was for this reason that Edison was reluctant to develop film projectors.

Once available, though, projectors enabled vaudeville theatres to use single-reel motion pictures as top-of-the-bill novelties or as popular 'chasers' at the beginning and end of each advertised programme. As exhibition outlets began to multiply, cigar stores, pawn shops and small restaurants were converted into Nickelodeons, and film studios were increasingly in demand. By the early years of the twentieth century

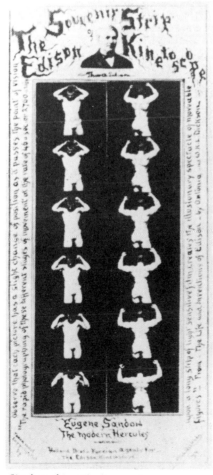

Single reel 'exotica'

A Country Girl's Seminary Life and Experience – Edison's New York studio

film production was already being regularised. Film audiences grew, new companies like Essanay, Kalem, Selig, Pathé and Méliès were set up and Edison attempted to reinforce his monopoly of the market by issuing a series of suits against his competitors for infringement of patent rights.

Meanwhile, industrial expansion widened the gap between production and exhibition, and the need for some sort of liaison was exploited by distributors operating 'film exchanges', buying, or later leasing, films from producers and selling, or later renting, them to exhibitors. At first rentals were set not in accordance with studio expenditure or cinema returns but simply in proportion to purchase price, cinema size and/or film footage. By the turn of the century, however, larger films of between 250 and 400 feet (4–6 mins) were becoming increasingly common, and by 1905 the standard length of a film was between 800 and 1000 feet (13–16 mins). As average footage increased, pricing became more complex and by 1907 more than 125 film exchanges, each with their own idiosyncratic pricing arrangements, had come into existence to serve the seven or eight thousand Nickelodeons in operation.

To stabilise an expanding industry and at the same time safeguard their control of it, the then largest production companies – Biograph, Essanay, Kalem, Lubin, Méliès, Pathé, Selig and Vitagraph – agreed in 1908 to become Edison licensees in the Motion Picture Patents Company (MPPC, also known as the 'Trust'). Henceforth, film producers and exhibitors alike would be required to pay licence fees to the Trust in order to purchase their patented equipment – for the projectors, cameras and raw film stock.

In 1910 the Trust had extended its technological monopoly into the institutions of the industry by entering the field of distribution with the formation of the General Film Company, an MPPC subsidiary: this constituted the earliest example of vertical integration in the history of the film industry (→ *The studios*, p. 10). The General Film Company proceeded to buy up film exchanges at such a rate that by the following year only one of the former exchanges remained independent. With this single exception, General Film became the sole film distributor in the USA. By this time profits in the film industry were already enormous: in 1910, American cinemas were attracting 26 million people a week. However, this very success effectively discouraged most MPPC members from experimenting with new modes of production, distribution or exhibition, which contributed to the MPPC's ultimate downfall.

Perhaps the most prolific, and certainly the most profitable of the MPPC production companies at this period was Vitagraph. Organised in 1897 with capital of $1,000, by 1912 Vitagraph had accumulated a gross income of $6 million. At that time the company had a staff of 400 actors,

Theda Bara – Fox's box-office attraction, aka 'Arab Death'

'Vitagraph girl' Florence Turner

actresses, executives and technicians, and was producing about 300 films a year. Vitagraph's success was probably at least partly due to a recognition that technological monopolies and even domination over distribution were no longer sufficient guarantees of long-term economic survival. The company consequently began to invest in longer films and familiar faces, pioneered the production of films of more than two reels (about 30 mins) and assembled an impressive array of popular contract performers, among them the 'Vitagraph Girl', Florence Turner, and John Bunny, star of *The Pickwick Papers* (1912). Nevertheless *The Pickwick Papers*, which was longer than the average MPPC product, was actually released by General Film in three separate parts: and, like previous prestige productions from Vitagraph (*A Tale of Two Cities* and *Vanity Fair*, for instance), was essentially filmed vaudeville and did not contribute to the development of a specific 'language' for cinema (→ HISTORY OF NARRATIVE: *Early cinema*, p. 208).

The MPPC's virtual monopoly in film production and distribution was gradually undercut by the formation of independent companies. Moreover, in 1912 the MPPC was brought to court on anti-Trust charges, and by 1915 the General Film Company had been dissolved. Two years later the Trust itself was finally outlawed by the Supreme Court. The abolition of the MPPC was not, however, a case of independent companies overcoming a monopoly, nor was it merely a matter of the legislature enforcing 'free enterprise'. Rather, one kind of industrial monopoly simply superseded another. The Trust, more or less secure in its monopoly of film technology and film distribution, failed to exploit the cinematic potential of longer films and star performers. Thus, while General Film still considered films to be little more than 1000 foot reels of celluloid merchandise, the independents were beginning to exploit various additional selling points or 'production values'. In this context, box-office attractions assumed paramount importance.

Box-office attractions

In 1910 Carl Laemmle lured the famous 'Biograph Girl' to his Independent Moving Picture Company and took the hitherto unprecedented step of revealing her real name, Florence Lawrence, to her fans. In 1914 William Fox, who had entered film production two years before with the formation of a studio-subsidiary, Box Office Attractions, went one better by tempting director Frank Powell away from Biograph. Powell fabricated a new star persona for his first Fox film: the star was Theda Bara and the film was *A Fool There Was* (1915). Fox needed box-office attractions in order to outmanoeuvre the MPPC, and the combination of a mysteriously exotic star and a melodramatic plot provided exactly the publicity Fox had

required. Indeed, Fox himself was largely responsible for that publicity: the very name Theda Bara was a suggestive anagram of 'Arab Death', and rumours were leaked to the press of Bara's 'parents' being a French artist and his Arabian mistress, and of her childhood spent under the shadow of the Sphinx, while stories were circulated of the star's smoking in public and burning incense in private and even of conducting interviews with reporters in her boudoir.

By this time, more and more licensee producers were going independent in order to exploit the flexibility of 'feature length' films, and more and more licensee exhibitors were building or converting special film theatres. One of the directors at Biograph, for example, whose 1911 two-reeler *Enoch Arden* was released by the studio in two parts, and whose four-reel film of the following year, *Judith of Bethulia*, Biograph refused to release at all, left the Trust to work for an independent production company, Reliance-Majestic. There he began work on an ambitious adaptation of Thomas Dixon's bestseller, *The Clansman*. That director was D. W. Griffith, and the film was *The Birth of a Nation* (1915).

The original budget for *The Birth of a Nation* was $40,000, but Griffith was allowed to expand the project to twelve reels and an estimated total cost of $110,000. To protect his investment in the film, Harry Aitken – President of Majestic's parent company – formed the Epoch Producing Corporation and decided to exploit the film's extravagant length and budget by releasing it as an unprecedented cinematic event. Prints were hand-tinted, and orchestral accompaniment commissioned and composed to synchronise with the on-screen action. Wherever the film was exhibited white-robed horsemen were employed to gallop up and down the nearest streets and publicise every screening. Seat prices in New York, where the film was premièred, were increased from the usual 10–25 cents to an astounding two dollars. Following its première, *The Birth of a Nation* was 'roadshowed' across the major American cities in the larger first-run theatres. Finally the film was released to independent distributors, and broke box-office records wherever it played. Louis B. Mayer, for instance, who operated a string of theatres in New England, made more than $50,000 from the film and with this bought Aitken's old Culver City Studio, which was later used by MGM. Estimates of the film's total earnings are notoriously unreliable, varying from 5 to 50 million dollars, but it seems certain that by 1916 a million tickets had been sold in New York alone. The film was first approved and then condemned by the National Board of Censorship; this, while barely affecting the number of screenings permitted, certainly increased the considerable publicity generated around the film. Griffith

invested the bulk of *The Birth of a Nation*'s profits in his next project, *Intolerance* (1916), and, of a budget estimated at $1.9 million, Griffith advanced almost a million himself. The film was considerably less successful than its predecessor however, and it virtually bankrupted Griffith. To finance the film Griffith had formed the Wark Producing Corporation and the investors behind this endeavour included a number of Wall Street financiers. In seeking aesthetic independence from the Trust studios, Griffith instead walked into the hands of the economic empires of Morgan and Rockefeller, whose domination of the industry would be cemented ten years later with the coming of sound (→ AUTHORSHIP: *D. W. Griffith*, p. 137).

As roadshow releases and regional releases began to compete for domestic distribution and exhibitor earnings, the economic necessity of a national network of distribution became increasingly apparent. In 1914 the first such network, Paramount Pictures Corporation, was set up: it released 104 films a year to its members' circuits. To supply this amount of product Adolph Zukor and Jesse Lasky merged their production units to form Famous Players-Lasky and, to ensure that the films they produced and distributed were all actually exhibited, Famous Players-Lasky introduced the policy of 'block booking' whereby exhibitors wishing to screen a particular film would be forced to book, unseen, an entire package which included that film. Famous Players-Lasky assembled a roster of 'stars' including Mary Pickford, Douglas Fairbanks, Gloria Swanson, Fatty Arbuckle, William S. Hart, Norma and Constance Talmadge as well as 'name' directors like Cecil B. DeMille, Griffith and Mack Sennett. With the collapse of competition from the European film industry during the First World War, Paramount escalated its annual output to 220 films for almost 5000 cinemas. To counter Paramount's increasing stranglehold over exhibition, 27 of America's largest first-run cinemas combined in 1917 to form their own 'independent' distribution network, the First National Exhibitors Circuit (FNEC). During the following year, the FNEC lured Charlie Chaplin away from Mutual and Mary Pickford away from Paramount with offers of million-dollar contracts, and themselves entered into film production.

Chaplin's early film career highlights a period of 'struggle for control' in American cinema, a struggle in which stars became important economic assets. At Keystone Chaplin was aesthetically and economically restricted, and he subsequently moved to Essanay and a salary of $1,250 a week, where he produced fifteen films, most of them two-reelers. In 1915, the year in which General Film was dissolved, Essanay expanded Chaplin's two-reel *Burlesque on Carmen* to four reels. The collapse of the Trust itself immediately elevated the economic value of the stars as box-office attractions, and Chaplin left Essanay for Mutual and a weekly salary of $10,000. At Mutual Chaplin perfected the persona of the Tramp which he had developed at Essanay, and made a further twelve films – including *Easy Street*, *The Vagabond* and *The Pawnshop* – before leaving for First National with an eight-film million-dollar contract. Like Essanay before it, Mutual soon collapsed without Chaplin, who was at this time probably the biggest box-office draw in the United States (→ HISTORY OF NARRATIVE: *Early cinema*, p. 208).

The origins of the studio system

By 1921 First National was linked to some 3,500 film theatres in the United States, and in 1922 added a production studio to its already extensive distribution and exhibition holdings. Recognising the threat to Paramount's profits, Zukor began by buying up cinemas himself, and by the end of 1926 had acquired a controlling interest in more than a thousand theatres. As Paramount expanded from production through distribution to exhibition, First National responded by increasing its investment in production and distribution; the industry was becoming characterised by vertical integration (→ *The studios*, p. 10), dominated by Carl Laemmle's Universal, William Fox's Fox Film Corporation, Zukor's Paramount, the exhibitors First National and, in 1924, a fifth group, Metro-Goldwyn-Mayer – which combined Marcus Loew's cinema chain, Metro's film exchanges and the production units of Goldwyn and Mayer. As inter-company competition became increasingly fierce, film publicity and production values became crucially important in attracting both independent exhibitors and audiences to studio-specific productions. Thus while the bulk of the packages of film distributed by these companies were of similar budgets and scales, each studio also produced occasional 'specials', often for roadshow release, and boasting huge investments, large crews and costs and impressive sets and settings. These included *The Covered Wagon* (Paramount/Famous Players-Lasky, 1923), *The Lost World* (First National, 1924), *Foolish Wives* (Universal, 1924), and *Sunrise* (Fox, 1927).

All four of these films exploited special effects and/or elaborate sets and settings and were released as exceptional cinematic events. *The Lost World*, for example, was one of the first full-length features to use animated models, *The Covered Wagon* was the first epic western, *Foolish Wives* was a fourteen-reel blockbuster, while *Sunrise* employed the largest single set since *Intolerance*, covering an area of a mile long and half a mile across. *The Covered Wagon* cost $350,000 and netted $1.5 million. *Foolish Wives* cost $1,400,000 and almost broke Universal. *Sunrise* cost even more. The emphasis of these specials was on literary sources – *The Covered Wagon*

Universal's elaborate set for *Foolish Wives*

for instance, was adapted from a popular novel by Emerson Hough, *The Lost World* based on a Conan Doyle story, *Sunrise* on Sudermann. These were all films based on stories already familiar to the general public which also featured the studio's biggest stars and highest paid directors.

Meanwhile other companies with less capital found it increasingly difficult to compete with the vertically integrated majors. United Artists, for instance, which had been founded in 1919 by four of the industry's best paid employees – Pickford, Fairbanks, Chaplin and Griffith – was only a distributor, lacking either studios or cinemas of its own and rising to major status only in the 1950s in the wake of anti-Trust judgements. Universal, with limited capital and only a small number of cinemas, was also frustrated in its efforts to expand. Similarly, Warner Bros, a minor but prosperous production company, found itself with neither distribution nor exhibition outlets, and so decided in

1925 to acquire the ailing Vitagraph with its national network of film exchanges.

Sound and the studio system in the 1930s

In 1926 Warner Bros, in combination with Western Electric, a subsidiary of the American Telephone and Telegraph Co. (AT&T), founded the Vitaphone Corporation to make sound films and market sound equipment, and in October 1927 Warners released *The Jazz Singer*. Capitalising on the success of the 'first talkie' Warners acquired and equipped for sound the First National exhibition circuit. AT&T's corporate rival RCA swiftly responded by setting up its own sound subsidiary, RKO. By 1930, then, the film industry was an oligopoly in which five vertically integrated companies, that is, five companies with holdings in production, distribution and exhibition, dominated the American market: Warner Bros, Loews-MGM, Fox, Paramount and RKO. Three smaller companies or 'minors' – United

Artists, Universal and Columbia – lacking exhibition outlets of their own, had to rely on the independent cinemas.

Of the 23,000 theatres operating in 1930 the majors controlled only 3,000 but these accounted for almost three-quarters of the annual box-office takings in the US. The majors produced only 50% of the total output of the industry, but this figure represented 80% of the 'A' films exhibited in the first-run theatres. And while the 'flagship' cinemas of each chain boasted blockbusters like *King Kong* (1933) the second-run cinemas thrived on less ambitious genre pictures like those of Warners and Universal. The coming of sound postponed for a while the effects of the Depression on the film industry, but eventually a combination of reduced receipts and increasing overheads hit the industry hard. In 1931 Warner Bros lost $8 million, Fox $3 million and RKO $5.5 million. In 1933 Paramount went into bankruptcy with a $21 million deficit, while RKO and Universal were thrown into receivership. Even MGM, the only major company not to go into debt, saw its profits plunge from $10 million in 1930 to $1.3 million three years later. Audience attendance, which had been estimated in 1929 at more than 80 million a week, fell to less than 60 million in 1932. The common stock value of the majors fell from a high of $960 million in 1930 to $140 million in 1934. To meet the crisis, President Roosevelt's New Deal administration passed a National Industrial Recovery Act (NIRA), encouraging 'fair competition' in the film industry as in other industries. A Code of Fair Competition for the Motion Picture Industry was ratified as law in 1933, and anti-Trust cases against the oligopoly were suspended in return for the signing of minimum wage and maximum hour agreements and the right to collective bargaining for employees. One of the consequences of the Depression for exhibition practices was the development of the 'double bill', developed as an 'added attraction' during the Depression, and allowed by the Code as fair competition. In 1935 the Supreme Court revoked NIRA but by then the industry was too firmly reorganised to be adversely affected.

Censorship

As early as 1895 an innocuous short, *Dolorita in the Passion Dance*, was removed from an Atlantic City Kinetoscope to appease local authorities. Two years later another film, *Orange Blossoms*, was closed by court order in New York as 'offensive to public decency'. As the number of Nickelodeons multiplied, a variety of pressure groups, including Churches, reform groups, police and press, began attempting to exert influence on the new medium of cinema. These pressures were institutionalised in the formation of state censorship boards with the objective of outflanking possible extra-industrial 'interference' in the content of films. The

Motion Picture Patents Company combined in 1909 with a self-appointed social research organisation to form the first National Board of Censorship.

The NBC, subsequently renamed the National Board of Review, employed rather uncertain censorship principles in relation to the films it reviewed. *The Birth of a Nation* (1915), for instance, was initially approved by the Board, only to have that approval revoked when the film met with criticism from liberal newspapers and anti-racist organisations. The MPPC, which was responsible for the production of almost two thirds of the films made in the US, agreed to submit all its films to the Board for pre-release inspection, but the independent States' Rights system entitled individual states to impose their own censorship. In 1915 the production company of *The Birth of a Nation* took the Ohio State censor to the Supreme Court for alleged infringement of constitutionally guaranteed free speech. However, the Supreme Court dismissed the case, on the grounds that motion pictures were a 'business pure and simple' and thus not entitled to First Amendment protection.

... 'business pure and simple'

With the collapse of the Trust and the emergence of the vertically integrated companies in the early 20s, the need for a new national industry-appointed censorship board became increasingly pressing. In 1921 the National Association of the Motion Picture Industry (NAMPI), a consortium of representatives of the major companies, adopted a 13-point code to serve as a yardstick for the production and exhibition of films. NAMPI's code proscribed certain kinds of subject matter – illicit love, nakedness, undue violence, vulgarity and so on – but lacked the means effectively to enforce its proscriptions. A series of scandals during the next two or three years – involving Mary Pickford in an apparently fraudulent divorce testimony, Fatty Arbuckle in a rape and murder trial, and director William Desmond Taylor in a murder case – provided the excuse the industry needed: in 1922 Will Hays, President Harding's Postmaster General, was invited by the majors to head the Motion Pictures Producers and Distributors of America (MPPDA).

Since state censorship boards were

becoming increasingly influential, Hays launched a fierce campaign under a 'free speech' banner aimed at defeating demands for film censorship legislation. At the same time, to offset press criticism and opposition from educational and religious organisations, the majors began to increase the output of films for 'women and children', and film-makers like Erich von Stroheim found themselves at the mercy of censors both in the studio and at the Hays office. Stroheim complained bitterly about interference on *Foolish Wives*: 'My ears have rung with their united cry: "It is not fit for children!" Children! Children! God, I did not make that picture for children.' After several unsatisfactory years in which the MPPDA published lists of 'Don'ts' and 'Be Carefuls', Hays together with Martin Quigley (publisher of the trade paper *Motion Picture Herald*) introduced a revised Production Code, which was adopted by the industry in 1930 and under whose terms every film made by members of the MPPDA would be censored by a Studio Relations Committee both in script and pre-release film form.

While the majors tended, at least at first, to accommodate the Code, independent productions occasionally exceeded its provisions. One such production was Howard Hughes's *Scarface* (1932), directed by Howard Hawks, which was alleged to contain scenes of hitherto unprecedented violence. On its submission to the Hays office dozens of cuts were demanded and, knowing that without Hays's approval most theatres would refuse to screen the film, Hughes compromised and agreed to several of them. Hays then granted the film a licence, but several local censorship boards still refused to allow *Scarface* to be shown. Hughes sued these censors and as a result of the publicity that the case (which Hughes in fact won) received, the film was a huge box-office success. These events were instrumental in ensuring that the Hays office rather than the local or national legislatures became arbiter of American film content: it was to remain so for more than two decades.

At first the studios conformed to the provisions of the Production Code, but falling attendances at film theatres during 1932 and 1933 led to the deployment of more 'daring' material, and the very adverse publicity such films received increased their box-office earnings. Mae West was one of the principal targets of the moral crusades, and indeed after *She Done Him Wrong* (1933) West became a symbol of everything the Code condemned. Meanwhile, however, Paramount grossed $2 million during the first three months of the film's release. The Catholic Church mobilised its forces, threatened the majors with mass picketing of Paramount's theatres, and formed the Legion of Decency. In 1934, under pressure from the Legion, the MPPDA abolished the Studio Relations Committee and replaced it with the more powerful Production Code

Administration (PCA). By the end of the year, the impact of the Production Code on the American cinema had become apparent. The PCA followed production from the script stage through to the final editing. 'The new regulatory structure made a changed woman of Mae West ... the title of her latest film *It Ain't No Sin* was transformed to *Belle of the Nineties* and her scintillating repartee and sexual independence were toned down considerably' (Stanley, 1978, p. 196).

In 1935, partly in order to placate the PCA, a number of studios began a cycle of 'prestige' literary adaptations, which included Warner Bros' *A Midsummer Night's Dream* (1935), Fox's *The Informer* (1935), and Goldwyn's *Stella Dallas* (1937). According to *Fortune*: 'It is generally conceded by leaders in the industry that productions like *A Midsummer Night's Dream* ... would have been unthinkable even ten years ago, and that Hays's national publicity grapevine, reaching several millions of the "best people" who attend movies infrequently has been the chief factor in making them possible' ('The Hays Office', in Balio, 1976, p. 311). But while prestigious Oscar-winning films like *A Midsummer Night's Dream* and *The Informer* were being made, the studios were also engaged in producing film series and genres that could accommodate the Code and be 'fit for children'. Partly as a result of such pressure, Warner Bros revised their gangster films to explicitly condemn gangsterism: in 1935 emphasis moved from the gangsters themselves to the G-men who gallantly battled against them. Once the Code's provisions had entered cinematic currency, in fact, they informed both the style and the content of the genres themselves.

For more than two decades the PCA was responsible for reviewing some 95% of the films exhibited in the US. Indeed, as long as the industry remained vertically integrated, the power of the PCA remained virtually unchallenged. Finally, however, in 1952 the Supreme Court extended the protection of the First Amendment to the film industry. The case in point centred on Roberto Rossellini's *The Miracle*, which had been deemed 'blasphemous' by the Legion of Decency. While Howard Hughes continued to offend the censors with his exploitation of Jane Russell in 3D for RKO, United Artists released a string of independent productions with 'controversial' and hitherto unpermitted subject matter. The link between the Catholic Church and the movie industry had remained intact as long as profits were high, but anti-Trust, the rise of television, and the growth of the art cinema and drive-in circuits fuelled Hollywood's hostility toward restraints, which were no longer economically viable.

The film which best illustrated – and indeed also influenced – these changes is Elia Kazan's *Baby Doll* (1956). The film received PCA approval, despite its portrayal of an unconsummated marriage between a child-wife and a middle-aged, sexually frustrated man. The Legion of Decency promptly condemned the film's 'carnal suggestiveness' as morally repellent both in theme and treatment, and Catholic cinemagoers were instructed to forego the film and picket the theatres in which it was shown (→ AUTHORSHIP: *Elia Kazan*, p. 155).

Such action may have reduced the film's potential audience, but it also prompted an outcry from other religious bodies and Civil Liberties groups against the Church's encroachment on individual freedoms. Late in 1956 the Production Code was revised, and in the following year the Legion of Decency expanded its film classification system. Finally in 1968 a National Motion Picture Rating System was introduced, and the PCA was replaced by the Code and Rating Administration, which operates a system based on labelling films as suitable for specific audiences.

Mae West in *It Ain't No Sin* censored to *Belle of the Nineties*

Sources

Robert C. Allen, 'William Fox presents *Sunrise*', *Quarterly Review of Film Studies* vol. 2 no. 3, August 1977.

Tino Balio (ed.), *The American Film Industry*, Madison, University of Wisconsin Press, 1976.

Phil Hardy (ed.), *Raoul Walsh*, Edinburgh Film Festival, 1974.

Ephraim Katz, *The International Film Encyclopaedia*, London, Macmillan Press, 1980.

Anthony Slide, *The Big V : a history of the Vitagraph company*, Metuchen N. J., Scarecrow Press, 1976.

Robert Stanley, *The Celluloid Empire : a history of the American movie industry*, New York, Hastings House, 1978.

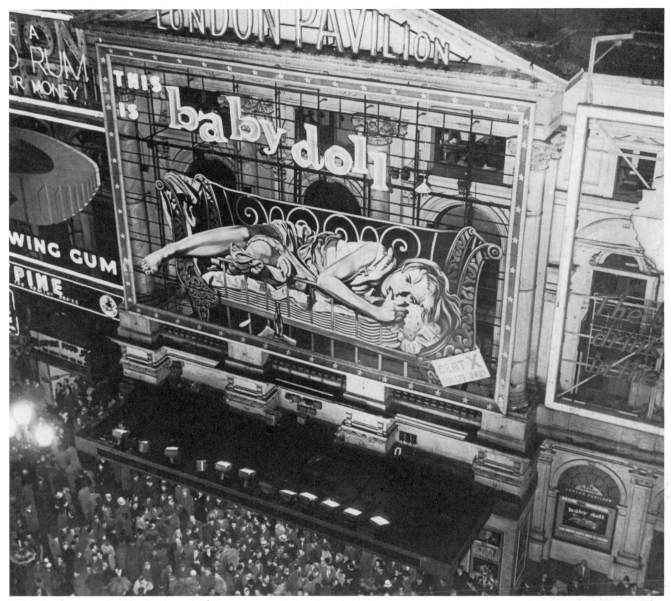

Baby Doll – condemned by the Legion of Decency

The Pickwick Papers (USA 1912 *p.c* – Vitagraph; *d* – Larry Trimble; st b/w 13)

A Fool There Was (USA 1915 *p.c* – Fox Film Corporation; *d* – Frank Powell; st b/w 16)

The Birth of a Nation (USA 1915 *p.c* – Epoch Producing Corp/Reliance-Majestic; *d* – D. W. Griffith; st b/w 12 + 12)

Intolerance (USA 1916 *p.c* – Wark Producing Corp; *d* – D. W. Griffith; st b/w 10 + 13)

Charlie Chaplin's Burlesque on 'Carmen' (USA 1916 *p.c* – Essanay; *d* – Charles Chaplin; st b/w 15)

The Pawnshop (USA 1916)/**The Vagabond** (USA 1916)/**Easy Street** (USA 1917) *p.c* – Mutual; *d* – Charles Chaplin; st b/w 5, 4 + 5; compiled together)

Hearts of the World (USA 1918 *p.c* – Griffith Inc; *d* – D. W. Griffith; st b/w 28)

Foolish Wives (USA 1921 *p.c* – Universal; *d* – Erich von Stroheim; st b/w 11)

The Covered Wagon (USA 1923 *p.c* – Paramount/Famous Players-Lasky; *d* – James Cruze; st b/w 9)

The Lost World (USA 1924 *p.c* – First National; *d* – Harry Hoyt; st b/w 16)

Sunrise (USA 1927 *p.c* – Fox Film Corporation; *d* – F. W. Murnau; st mu. sd b/w 12 + 16)

The Jazz Singer (USA 1927 *p.c* – Warner Bros; *d* – Alan Crosland; st + sd b/w 12)

King Kong (USA 1933 *p.c* – RKO; *d* – Ernest B. Schoedsack/Merian C. Cooper; sd b/w 16)

Scarface (USA 1932 *p.c* – Hughes Production; *d* – Howard Hawks; sd b/w 14)

Belle of the Nineties (USA 1935/**I'm No Angel** USA 1934 *p.c* – Paramount; *d* – Leo McCarey/Wesley Ruggles; sd b/w 5 + 12; compiled together)

A Midsummer Night's Dream (USA 1935 *p.c* – Warner Bros; *d* – Max Reinhardt/William Dieterle; sd b/w 12)

G-Men (USA 1935 *p.c* – Warner Bros; *d* – William Keighley; sd b/w 16)

The Informer (USA 1935 *p.c* – RKO; *d* – John Ford; sd b/w 14)

Stella Dallas (USA 1937 *p.c* – Goldwyn Productions; *d* – King Vidor; sd b/w 14)

Baby Doll (USA 1956 *p.c* – Newtown/Elia Kazan; *d* – Elia Kazan; sd b/w 17)

THE STUDIOS

Introduction

The apotheosis, economically and stylistically, of Hollywood cinema is usually considered to be the years of ascendancy of the 'studio system', when the film industry flourished as an oligopoly: when, in other words, the production of films was dominated almost entirely by a small number of vertically integrated companies – companies with controlling interests in the distribution and exhibition, as well as in the production, of films. The start of this stage in the development of the Hollywood film industry can be set at around 1930, when – as a consequence both of the Depression and of the financial demands on the studios of the coming of sound – a number of film production companies had gone to the wall, leaving the field open for domination by the 'majors' – companies which for various reasons managed to weather the economic vicissitudes of the time. The end of this period of oligopoly in the film industry may be dated precisely at 1948, when an anti-Trust suit filed against the majors in 1938 was finally settled, and vertical integration in the film industry outlawed.

Between 1930 and 1948, the Hollywood film industry was dominated by a hierarchy of eight companies. The 'Big Five' – Warner Bros, RKO, 20th Century-Fox, Paramount and MGM – were completely vertically integrated: they owned distribution companies and chains of film theatres as well as the means of production of films. The 'Little Three' – Universal, Columbia and United Artists – were not vertically integrated, but are usually included among the majors because their films had access to the first-run theatres owned by the Big Five. During the period of mature oligopoly, the eight majors controlled 95% of all films exhibited in the USA. The 1950s saw a decline in the studio system, which was undoubtedly hastened both by the rise of television in competition with cinema, and also by the deleterious effects on the film industry of the communist 'scare', in the form of the activities within Hollywood of the House Un-American Activities Committee, and the consequent blacklisting of large numbers of creative and technical personnel.

The study of the economic organisation of the film industry may be justified on a variety of grounds, ranging from an interest in its various modes of production, to a concern with the relationships between particular forms of organisation of film production, distribution and exhibition, and the films which were, on the face of it at least, the reasons for the industry's existence. If films are to be used in the latter way, however, some thought has to be given to the nature of the relationship between film texts and their immediate contexts. As Mae Huettig argues, there is a connection between the form taken by the film and the mechanics of the business,

even if the connection is somewhat obscure ('The motion picture industry today', in Balio, 1976). How might this be considered when looking at the Hollywood studio system as a particular form of economic organisation of film production?

One way of approaching this question is to look both at the economic organisation and also at the production relations (the ways in which the work involved in making films was organised) characteristic of studios, in order to draw out the implications for the nature of their products, the films themselves. On the side of economic organisation, for example, the nature and provenance of capital investment in the film industry between 1930 and 1948, and also vertical integration, can be seen to

The Public Enemy – simple sets and low-key lighting

have important consequences. The enormous investment required to equip studios and film theatres for sound, in combination with the effects of the general recession in the US economy in the late 1920s and early 1930s, led the industry to seek outside financial backing, usually from Eastern banking groups. During the early 1930s, all the major companies in fact underwent extensive financial reorganisation, which eventually led to the domination of some of the studios by these outside sources of finance. One of the consequences of this was to reinforce the majors' dependence on vertical integration, for their assets – the collateral against which they obtained financial backing – were chiefly in the form of real-estate: by the mid-1940s, about two-thirds of the majors' total capital was invested in film theatres. It has in fact been suggested that in this context the production of films by the majors was no more than a means towards

the primary objective of maintaining the property value of film theatres.

In this situation, the balance of power in determining the nature of the product lay largely on the side of the 'front office' – the industry's businessmen, rather than its creative personnel. The demand was for films that would secure financial return from exhibition. A 'good picture' in these terms was one which had access to first-run theatres, and hence combined production values with a certain degree of predictability. The emphasis was clearly not on the side of experimentation in film form and content.

The relations of film production characteristic of the studio system may also be examined in the light of the industry's

overall economic organisation. As part of the reorganisations which took place in the major companies in the early 1930s, the studios began to organise production increasingly on an 'assembly line' basis. The main features of this form of organisation of production are highly developed divisions of labour and hierarchies of authority and control, and detailed breakdown of tasks: the industrial model for this form of organisation is, of course, the mass production of commodities. Since the studio system was geared increasingly to the production of a constant flow of films to supply film theatres, there was an impetus towards organising film production along mass production lines. This resulted in a high degree of demarcation of skills, and a breakdown of the overall production process into small parts dealt with by different groups of workers. This development is evident also in the increased tendency for workers to be employed directly by the studios and kept on studio payrolls: a characteristic not only of technicians, but also of creative personnel, as the 'contract system' for actors indicates. All this was undoubtedly instrumental in the unionisation of the film industry which took place around the mid-1930s, a trend which probably itself served to consolidate the effects on the industry of the division of labour and the breakdown of tasks.

The overall impetus of these developments in the economic organisation and production relations of the Hollywood film industry is clearly in the direction of standardisation of the product, film. And indeed, during the period of the studio system's ascendancy, at least two forms of product standardisation may be observed. First of all, the 1930s and 1940s are commonly regarded as the golden years of the classic Hollywood text: of films, that is, marked by a highly specific type of narrative structure combined with a circumscribed range of cinematic expressions of narrative (→ HISTORY OF NARRATIVE: *The classic narrative system*, p. 212). Secondly, during this period, film genres – such as the gangster film, the western and the musical – were developed and refined to what is now regarded as their classic forms: genre films, which are of course a means of securing standardisation, may be regarded as guarantors of a reliable return of investment (→ GENRE: *What is genre criticism?* p. 58).

But at the same time, the studio system also contained a certain degree of internal contradiction, relating largely to the nature of film production and exhibition. Films cannot be totally standardised: they must differ from one another, to some extent at least, in order to attract the paying public. The studio system consequently embodied a series of tensions manifest, for example, in various struggles between creative personnel – directors in particular – and the front office, the business side of the industry, as well as in conflicts and disputes over the content, editing and marketing of individual films. If 'the production of films, essentially fluid and experimental as a process, is harnessed to a form of organisation which can rarely afford to be speculative . . .' (Huettig, in Balio, 1976, p. 238), then the Hollywood studio system in its maturity as an oligopoly, and the products of the system, were marked by these temporary – and contradictory – conflicts of interest.

Sources

Harry Braverman, *Labor and Monopoly Capital*, New York, Monthly Review Press, 1974.

Mae D. Huettig, 'The motion picture industry today', in Tino Balio (ed.), *The American Film Industry*, Madison, University of Wisconsin Press, 1976.

Robert Stanley, *The Celluloid Empire: a history of the American movie industry*, New York, Hastings House, 1978.

Warner Bros

Introduction

Warner Bros is probably best known as the studio that introduced sound to cinema. Warners, which started in the 1920s as a small family-owned film production company, in 1925 signed an agreement with Western Electric to develop a sound system. The famous talking picture *The Jazz Singer* was released in 1927, and in 1928 the company further consolidated its position by acquiring the First National film theatre circuit, a large studio in Burbank, and several prominent stars. In the same year, Warners made a net profit of more than $17 million, a record high for the film industry at that time. The momentum of this success carried the company through the following year, but by 1931 the effects of the Depression began to make themselves felt: between 1931 and 1934, the company's losses were of the order of $13 million. Warners' response to the crisis set it apart from the other major studios, and was an important factor in its economic recovery during the later 1930s.

The rationalisations made at Warner Bros during the early 1930s involved the adoption of 'assembly line' film production methods, rigid adherence to production schedules, and low budgets. During his time as head of production at Warners (between 1931 and 1933), Darryl F. Zanuck assumed much of the immediate responsibility for implementing the new regime. Throughout the 1930s, the studio was able to maintain a regular annual output of about sixty films, and unlike most of the majors managed to survive the Depression without losing managerial and financial control to Wall Street.

Warners and 'studio style'

As Edward Buscombe has pointed out, studio style is a term which occasionally crops up in film criticism, but in a loose way. While, for example, MGM went in for large-budget costume drama and later, musicals, and Paramount had a taste for raciness and decadence (Buscombe, 'Walsh and Warner Bros', 1974, p. 52), the products of Warner Bros are commonly held as embodying studio style in a particular marked way, combining certain genres (the gangster movies, the backstage musical, and later romantic adventure films) with a characteristic visual style (low-key lighting, simple sets), and a kind of populism in key with the studio's rather downmarket image.

But how is the identification of a particular style or set of styles within a studio to be explained? What, in other words, is the relationship between the 'house' and the 'style'? On the one hand, the fact that Warner Bros films are so often remembered exactly as Warner Bros films rather than, say, as films by their individual directors may be explained in terms of the tendency inherent in the studio's institutional structure to subordinate individuals to the

organisation. But the ways in which production was organised may well, in turn, be considered in relation to the economic restrictions impinging on the studio:

'Sets at Warners were customarily bare and workmanlike . . . The scale of a film could be judged by its budget, and in 1932 the average production cost per feature at Warners was estimated at $200,000, lowest of the majors except for Columbia ($175,000): MGM by comparison, averaged $450,000' (Campbell, 'Warner Bros in the 30s', 1971, p. 2).

These economic conditions, it may further be suggested, had certain aesthetic or stylistic consequences. They can certainly explain the relative simplicity of the settings of many Warner Bros films – of the action melodramas and gangster films in particular and the low-key lighting which

The Roaring Twenties – Warners' gangster genre

did much to conceal the cheapness of the sets, as well as the repetitions from film to film of financially successful formulae. (*The Public Enemy*, 1931, for example, was made in only 16 days at a cost of $151,000.) It has also been argued that something less easily observable than economic restrictions may also have been instrumental in its populism during the 30s – its use of working-class characters in films, and also the concern with social problems of the day. The notion of studio style, then, may incorporate an ideological as well as an economic component.

Warners and genre

The genre for which Warner Bros is perhaps most famous is the gangster film. In 1931, Darryl F. Zanuck announced a series of films whose subject matter would be drawn from contemporary newspaper stories. This is the inspiration behind both

Little Caesar (1931) and *The Public Enemy* (1931), and the commercial success of these films served to determine studio policy throughout the rest of the decade. Gangster films, it was clear, made money.

From the box-office success of the 'exposé' films emerged a style of 'critical social realism'. Campbell (1971) argues that the success of these films is attributable to the fact that Depression disillusion made Warners' predominantly working-class audiences receptive to attacks on the established power structure of American society. But it seems equally likely that the audiences were attracted by the action and violence in many of these films. Indeed, after the institution of the Production Code Administration (← *Censorship*, p. 7) some of Warners' more violent films were subjected to criticism from within the industry, and pressure was put on the studio to concentrate more on the enforcement of the law and less on the deeds of criminals. Warner Bros' response was to produce a cycle of films in which the central characters are federal agents rather than gangsters: these include *G-Men* (1935) and *Racket Busters* (1938).

The social conscience of Warner Bros

Within its economic and ideological conditions of operation, Warner Bros' studio policy has often been equated with a particular politics – that of President Roosevelt's Democratic New Deal. Indeed, one Warners advertisement of 1933 made this association quite explicit:

'Watch this industry turn over a New Leaf ... In the New Year ... With our New President ... And this New Deal ... New Leaders ... New Styles ... New Stars ...' (quoted in Campbell, 1971, p. 34).

It has sometimes been suggested that the studio's embrace of a relatively radical political stance is directly related to its financial and managerial independence from outside bodies. Whilst Warners had been forced to borrow from the banks in order to expand into exhibition and invest in sound, by 1933 the three surviving Warner brothers still owned 70% of the preferred stock in their company. Consequently during the 30s Warner Bros, along with Columbia and Universal, was not subject to direct interference from Wall Street (Buscombe, 1974, p. 53).

Within the framework of the overall capitalist economy and the specific industrial enterprise of cinema, Warner Bros as a studio was relatively independent of the Rockefeller/Morgan banking empires and was able in the short term to produce whatever films both it and its audiences wanted. Buscombe concludes that this economic indpendence is not unconnected with the fact that Warner Bros made a number of pictures which were notably to the left of other Hollywood products (Buscombe, 1974, p. 53). Certainly a considerable number of early 30s Warner Bros productions were explicit about their endorsement of Roosevelt and

the New Deal; indeed, several of the studio's films in that period even borrowed the National Recovery Administration's Eagle insignia for their credits and employed it in the choreography of its musicals (e.g. *Footlight Parade*, 1933). Buscombe points out, for instance:

'The famous "Forgotten Man" sequence of *Gold Diggers of 1933* (1933) derives from Roosevelt's use of the phrase in one of his speeches ... Pictures like *I Am a Fugitive from a Chain Gang, Black Legion, Heroes for Sale, Black Fury, A Modern Hero, 20,000 Years in Sing Sing, They Won't Forget,* and *Confessions of a Nazi Spy* to mention only the best known, all testify to the vaguely and uncertainly radical yearnings which the studio shared with the New Deal' (Buscombe, 1974, p. 54).

Warners' social conscience may also be seen at work in the studio's productions of World War II: indeed, Buscombe (1974) has argued that Warner Bros was the first Hollywood studio to throw its whole weight behind Government policy on the war. In place of Warners' earlier social criticism (which had to be dropped for the duration to maintain morale) came a crudely patriotic affirmation of the American way of life and an attack on pacifism, isolationism and, of course, Nazism (e.g. *Sergeant York*, 1941).

Warners and authorship

In 1944, Warner Bros released *To Have and Have Not*, a film which may be read as a typical example of a Warners' wartime

attempted to sort out the various contributing strands of the film, which he describes as 'a Hollywood genre movie (species: "adventures in exotic location") clearly conceived (by the studio at least) as a starring vehicle for Bogart, adapted from a novel by Hemingway, scripted by William Faulkner and Jules Furthman, and specifically indebted to at least two previous movies (*Morocco* and *Casablanca*) and perhaps a third (*Across the Pacific*) ...' (Wood, 'To Have (Written) and Have Not (Directed)', 1973).

While Wood isolates the studio as itself a 'contributor', he is wary of crediting it with more than a minor role. Thus while acknowledging, for example, that the lighting in *To Have and Have Not* is easily identifiable as Warners-style, Wood adds that the overall style is also 'the perfect visual expression of the essential Hawksian view'. At the same time, however, he argues that the film is marked not only by its studio provenance but also by its kinship with a certain genre: film noir. If this is the case, then *To Have and Have Not* embodies some of the tensions of authorship and studio style.

Similar problems arise when the work of another of Warners' contract directors, Raoul Walsh, is looked at in terms of authorship (→ AUTHORSHIP: *Raoul Walsh*, p. 176). Given the way in which production was organised at Warner Bros, once Walsh became a contract director he was obliged to work with contract crews and casts within the studio hierarchy, on projects that could capitalise both on recent

They Drive by Night – Warners' socio-political conscience

film with its implicit anti-isolation argument. But at the same time, it was directed by one of the studio's contract directors, Howard Hawks, who subsequently came to be regarded as an important *auteur* in his own right (→ AUTHORSHIP: *Howard Hawks*, p. 179). Interestingly enough, in the light of the tendency for the concept of studio style to dominate in discussions of Warner Bros films, Robin Wood has

financially successful formulae and also on the inclination and aptitudes of the rest of the contract staff. Discussing *The Roaring Twenties* and *They Drive by Night* Buscombe suggests:

'These films are typical of the studio for which they were made; to such an extent that one must call into question the simple notion of Walsh as an *auteur* who directed the style and content of his pictures.

Firstly, in working for Warner Bros Walsh was obliged to use the stars which the studio had under contract. So, *The Roaring Twenties* had Bogart and Cagney, *They Drive by Night* Bogart and George Raft . . . One can't say exactly that Walsh was forced to make gangster pictures because he had to use these stars, for they weren't the only ones available on the Warner lot. But stars and genre were, particularly at Warners, mutually reinforcing. Because the studio had Bogart, Cagney and the rest under contract they made a lot of gangster pictures; and because they made a lot of gangster pictures they had stars like this under contract' (Buscombe, 1974, p. 59).

Apart from the determining effects on Walsh's work of stars and genres, however, the character of the films' production units may also be of some importance. Thus the 'social content' of *The Roaring Twenties* (1939) and *They Drive by Night* (1938) might have something to do with the sociology of the studio's personnel:

'Mark Hellinger, who produced *The Roaring Twenties*, was a Broadway reporter in the 20s and 30s, covering New York crime stories. Jerry Wald, who helped write *The Roaring Twenties* and *They Drive by Night*, came from Brooklyn and worked with Walter Winchell on *The Graphic* in New York. Robert Rossen, who co-wrote *The Roaring Twenties* came from the East Side in New York, where his early experiences turned him to the left politically' (Buscombe, 1974, p. 60).

Sources

Edward Buscombe, 'Walsh and Warner Bros', in Phil Hardy (ed.), *Raoul Walsh*, Edinburgh Film Festival, 1974.

Russell Campbell, 'Warner Bros in the 30s: some tentative notes', *The Velvet Light Trap* no. 1, June 1971.

Russell Campbell, 'Warners, the Depression and FDR', *The Velvet Light Trap* no. 4, Spring 1972.

John Davis, 'Notes on Warner Bros' foreign policy 1918–1948', *The Velvet Light Trap* no. 4, cit.

James R. Silke, *Here's Looking at You, Kid; 50 years of fighting, working and dreaming at Warner Bros*, Boston, Little, Brown and Co., 1976.

Robin Wood, 'To Have (Written) and Have Not (Directed)', *Film Comment* vol. 9 no. 3, May/June 1973.

Nick Roddick, *A New Deal in Entertainment: Warner Brothers in the 1930s*, London, BFI, 1983.

The Public Enemy (USA 1931 *p.c* – Warner Bros; *d* – William Wellman; sd b/w 16)

The title sequence brings together a number of gangster stereotypes, recalling for Warners' audience the range of images of the city criminals the cinema was accumulating. Warners were not simply exploiting a genre for its sensational (in this case violent) potential but were also committed to situating that crime socially. Thus it could be argued that the prologue to the film, 'To honestly depict . . . rather than glorify' is not only a gesture to the demands for moral self-censorship by the Hays Code, it is also a statement of Warners' 'social conscience' ideology. In the first part of the extract the sequence depicting milling streets, the 'montage' of prohibition activities and particularly, the one-minute-long shot consisting of tracks, pans overlaid with continuous sound of the city streets, until the camera cuts to two boys coming out of the saloon, is on one level an example of a virtuoso performance of early sound cinema, but on another level it represents Warner Bros' social realist aesthetic.

The second part exemplifies Warners' populist ideology in the way the film looks to socio-economic factors as the source of crime, seeing the gangsters' rise to success as a result of the introduction of Prohibition. A number of traditional motifs inherent in the gangster genre, such as the use of clothes to indicate increasing success and power, are combined with an emphasis on the gangsters' working-class roots to link economic deprivation with the development of crime.

Little Caesar (USA 1930 *p.c* – Warner Bros; *d* – Mervyn Leroy; sd b/w 11)

The film deals with the relationship of the Italian immigrant community to the growth of organised large-scale racketeering in the Chicago underworld. In the context of Warners' populist ideology, the extract shows the ending of the film in which one of the gangsters is eliminated by the gang when he tries to 'go straight', thus confirming the film's fatalistic view of the relationship between social deprivation and crime.

G-Men (USA 1935 *p.c* – Warner Bros; *d* – William Keighley; sd b/w 16)

Warner Bros' response, partly, to pressure from the Hays Code was the revamping of the gangster genre in the mid 1930s. Suddenly the central character was no longer the social outcast, the gangster, but the G-Man, the federal agent. The G-Men films retained many of the features of the earlier gangster-centred ones, but the iconography of the genre changed from an emphasis on the tools of the gangsters' trade (the card game, the hatted man, the nightclub, the rifles) to the procedure of detection. In this extract, for instance, we see the minute details of the police investigation – concealed camera, fingerprint powder, and the care with which they respond to typewriters, telexes, etc. as offering clues.

Racket Busters (USA 1938 *p.c* – Warner Bros; *d* – Lloyd Bacon; sd b/w 20)

In *Racket Busters*, as in *G-Men*, the focus is on the police rather than the racketeers and the credits claim the film is 'based upon official records'. Also as in *G-Men* and *Each Dawn I Die* authenticity is created by the use of newspaper headlines, a documentary touch reinforced by the occasional documentary-style sequence, as in the street market. A characteristic Warners scene is the confrontation between the mobsters and the private enterprise truck drivers. It could be argued that the early populist sentiments of Warners were being gradually transformed into a moral crusade against crime, and that consequently the original commitment of the studio to situate crimes in a social context had been dropped. The studio's liberal reformism was forced to change with the times.

In the final section of the extract the gangsters are defeated by Skeet's personal call to end the strike on the grounds that there is a need for unionised labour which will unite worker and management against the gangsters for the maintenance of law and order, apparently setting the seal on Warners' move away from populism.

I Am a Fugitive from a Chain Gang (USA 1932 *p.c* – Warner Bros; *d* – Mervyn Leroy; sd b/w 20)

This extract begins with a scene in a factory, and is emphatic about the dehumanisation such work brings: 'Your duty is to your job', work is a 'drab routine, cramped, mechanical'. Warners' social realist aesthetic is visible in its observation of Depression America and its effect on the people; in one image we find a pawnshop full of *Croix de Guerre* medals; and as the hero of the film is sentenced, the shout goes up, 'They're the ones who should be in jail', which could be seen as a clarion call for Warners' New Deal politics. The documentary influence on this social realist style is apparent in the montage (reminiscent of 'March of Time' newsreels) of maps and trains, and later in the extract, of the prisoners' picks and calender pages. In the jail the horn sounds the same as that of the factory at the beginning of the film; an 'expressive' use of sound characteristics of Warners' early sound films. However, it could →

also be argued that the focus is presented in individualistic terms in that they are shown to be the result of accidental circumstances rather than political or economic factors.

Gold Diggers of 1933 (USA 1933 *p.c* – Warner Bros; *d* – Mervyn Leroy; sd b/w 20)

The 'Remember My Forgotten Man' number is an unusual example of direct social comment in a musical – at the time it was considered to be in very poor taste. The numbers were staged by Busby Berkeley, and here he uses a social panorama with, at times, almost 'realist' touches. An interesting example of a combination of the backstage musical and social realist form.

Sergeant York (USA 1941 *p.c* – Warner Bros; *d* – Howard Hawks; sd b/w 12 + 10)

Made shortly before Pearl Harbor, *Sergeant York* tells the 'true' story of a man who had made the headlines some years earlier. The real York, a national hero after his war service in 1917, had been offered a considerable sum to sell his story to Jesse L. Lasky of Famous Players-Lasky at the end of the war, but declined the offer then, and once more in 1930. He finally agreed in 1940 to an adaptation on condition that he could supervise the entire production in every detail from casting through to advertising.

'Of all the films of the period *Sergeant York* (July 1941) deals most directly with the problems of the country on the eve of the new war . . . To dispel any uncertainty concerning the film's message, Warners quoted the real York in their advertising: "By our victory in the last war, we won a lease on liberty, not a deed to it. Now after 23 years, Adolf Hitler tells us that lease is expiring

and, after the manner of all leases, we have the privilege of renewing it or letting it go by default." *Sergeant York*'s popularity (it was the top-grossing film of 1941) suggests that it dealt with questions which deeply concern the country' (Campbell, 1972, p. 29).

The Roaring Twenties (USA 1939 *p.c* – Warner Bros; *d* – Raoul Walsh; sd b/w 9)

The Roaring Twenties, like other Warners' gangster films, makes an implicit connection between social deprivation and crime, with Cagney's taxi-driver hero returning from the war to find his job gone and attempting to set up his own business as a taxi operator. This is, argues Buscombe, an example of the small-scale entrepreneurial capitalism which remains the ideal of most Warners' films of the period (Buscombe, p. 56). The extract demonstrates the documentary, sociological approach to the creation of the gangsters and their life-style, characteristic of Warners' 30s gangster films: e.g. the tommy-gun as an invention of World War I; the set-piece montage of gang warfare – the raid on a rival warehouse and narrow escape; the conflict between the gangster-by-default, for whom gangsterdom is the only available means of business, represented by Eddie, and the psychotic gangster, George, over the function of violence in their operations; the heroine, whose classy femininity is the object of the gangster hero's sexual desire and social aspirations and who, as a consequence, is unobtainable, unlike the faithful gangster's moll, Panama; the role of the lawyer, who for social reasons or personal weakness gets involved with the mob but ultimately crosses the gang leader by virtue of his superior knowledge of how the system

works; the gangster's life-long and faithful friend who goes down with him in his fall.

They Drive by Night (USA 1940 *p.c* – Warner Bros; *d* – Raoul Walsh; sd b/w 23)

An example of Warner Bros' crime/ thriller melodrama with elements of social comment. Warners' relative financial independence from East Coast financiers perhaps made it easier for the studio to make films which, within the capitalist film industry and by the standards of other Hollywood products, were fairly radical in terms of subject matter. The first part of the extract demonstrates the socio-political concerns of such films: the Fabrini brothers are seen as victims of capitalist exploitation from various directions – loan sharks like Farnsworth, crooked and unscrupulous haulage agents like Mike Williams, and the effects of piece-work resulting in dangerous over-loading and lack of sleep causing accidents. The independent truckers operating within this economic context co-operate to protect each other from the exploiters (e.g. in the cafe the truckers work together to conceal the presence of Joe and Paul from Farnsworth). Ultimately, the dominant ideology is re-established and any radicalism recuperated, in that Joe Fabrini's problems are solved on an individual basis by his take-over of Ed Carlsen's trucking business, and so effectively he is able to rise above the problems of his fellow truckers. The second part of the extract develops the crime/melodrama element of the film in a film noir style; the lighting and the use of music in this section is relevant to discussion of the treatment of the femme fatale stereotype, here played by Ida Lupino, in film noir.

Columbia Pictures

Introduction: Columbia's populism
Columbia, one of the 'Little Three' majors, began in 1920 as a Poverty Row company, CBC, named after the initials of its three founders, Harry Cohn, Joe Brandt and Jack Cohn. In 1924, the company was renamed Columbia Pictures, and by the end of the decade had acquired a production studio of its own and was already operating a national distribution network. In 1932 Joe Brandt was bought out by the Cohn brothers and his place on the voting trust taken by Attilio Giannini, an unorthodox banker who was also a supporter of President Roosevelt's New Deal, anathema to the Wall Street establishment. Harry Cohn replaced Brandt as President of the company – becoming the only movie mogul to be simultaneously President, pro-

duction head and principal shareholder of a studio. In his role as production head, Cohn instituted the hitherto unknown practice of shooting film scenes out of sequence to ensure maximum economy, and in general, the company operated under rigid cost controls.

Throughout the 1930s, Columbia, like United Artists and Universal, supplied the cinemas owned by the 'Big Five' (MGM, Fox, Warner Bros, RKO and Paramount) with low-budget supporting features for double bills, with running times of only seventy minutes or so, few – if any – stars, and little or no prestigious production values. Around 70% of Columbia's annual output of fifty to sixty pictures were in fact in this 'B' category. Columbia's continued solvency during the early 1930s, when so many other studios went bankrupt, is partly to be explained by the fact that the

company was not itself encumbered by empty film theatres, while at the same time it enjoyed access to cinemas owned by the larger majors.

Columbia, like Warner Bros, is often regarded as an exponent of New Deal-type populism, evidenced in particular in the films of the studio's sole *auteur*, Frank Capra (see below). Columbia's populism is perhaps explicable partly in terms of the company's history – its Poverty Row origins and its backing by the maverick banker Giannini – and by the fact that exactly half of the Hollywood Ten were actually employed at Columbia during the 1930s (Buscombe, 'Notes on Columbia Pictures Corporation', 1975, p. 78; the Hollywood Ten was a group of radical directors and screenwriters who were imprisoned in the early 1950s for alleged communist subversion of the industry). Although it is clearly

Capra – Columbia's *auteur* – at work with the cast of *You Can't Take It with You*

impossible to determine whether or not there was any deliberate policy of favouritism at Columbia towards the New Deal or left causes, it is perhaps significant that screenwriter Garson Kanin and actress Judy Holliday, both of whom worked at Columbia in the 1940s, were listed as 'subversives' in Red Channels, a compilation of 'radical names' by supporters in the film industry of the House Un-American Activities Committee. Indeed, *Born Yesterday* (1950), based on a play by Kanin and starring Holliday was extensively picketed on its release by the association of Catholic War Veterans (Cogley, 'The mass hearings', in Balio, 1976). Although it seems unlikely that there was a concerted communist effort at the studio, its economic structure and encouragement of 'freelancers' might well have facilitated the employment of radicals where the more careful vetting of employees by studios with large numbers of long-term contracts might not.

Capra and populism
Although the bulk of Columbia's productions during the 1930s were low-budget 'B' features, the studio occasionally invested in more expensive films. One such was the comedy *It Happened One Night* (1934), directed by Frank Capra. This film was enormously successful, won Columbia its first Oscars, and led the company to supplement its 'B' feature productions with more prestigious films. After *It Happened One Night*, Capra signed a six-film contract with Columbia at $100,000 per film plus 25% of profits, and was given increasingly larger production budgets. In 1936 Capra directed *Mr. Deeds Goes to Town*, which examines the unacceptable face of capitalism (in the form of anti-New Dealers) and portrays its hero as a charitable tycoon, loaning out his wealth to dispossessed farmers to give them a fresh start.

The success of Capra's films has been

such that the director and the company are often equated, which has tended in fact to reduce studies of the studio to studies of Capra as an *auteur*. It may be argued, however, that Capra's films and the populism which characterises them might be related not simply to Capra's personal 'vision' or to the director being 'in touch' with America, but also to the economic and ideological structures of Columbia itself.

Stars at Columbia
'Though Columbia had contract players of its own (for example Jack Holt, Ralph Bellamy or, in westerns, Buck Jones and Charles Starrett), they could not compare in box-office appeal with the stars of bigger studios. Columbia could not afford the budgets which bigger stars would have entailed. On the other hand it could never break into the big-time without them. Harry Cohn's solution to this vicious circle was to invite successful directors from other studios to make occasional pictures for Columbia, pictures which would have stars borrowed from other studios. Careful planning permitted short production schedules and kept costs down to what Columbia could afford . . . Thus a number of big-name directors came to work at Columbia during the later 1930s, often tempted by the offer of being allowed to produce their own films' (Buscombe, 1975, p. 80).

One of Columbia's 'more expensive productions', with 'bigger stars' and a 'big name producer-director' was Howard Hawks's *His Girl Friday* (1939) starring Cary Grant and Rosalind Russell with Ralph Bellamy in a supporting role. Grant, like Gable in *It Happened One Night* and Cooper in *Mr. Deeds Goes to Town*, was a star from outside the studio. It was in fact a not uncommon practice in the industry to rent the stars of one studio to another. The lending studio generally received about 75% more than the star's salary to compensate for its temporary

loss. The borrowing studio enjoyed the advantage of the star's services without incurring the cost of a long-term contract. Perhaps something of the appeal of those Columbia films which combined its own contract players with outside stars was exactly the pleasure of seeing familiar faces in unfamiliar settings: Cary Grant, for instance, without the costume and décor with which he was associated at Paramount. Columbia's practice of bringing in outside stars (and also directors and writers) for large-budget productions would, of course, tend to militate against any deliberate or unitary political stance (for instance, on the New Deal) within the studio or its productions.

While most of Columbia's contract performers were character actors like Ralph Bellamy, the studio occasionally succeeded in signing up a little-known actor or actress before he or she became too expensive, 'grooming' him or her for stardom itself. By the end of the 1930s the policy of bringing in outside stars and directors and paying them percentages was proving an important part of Columbia's economic

Rita Hayworth . . . 'the fourth most valuable property in the business' . . . in *Gilda*

Columbia 'rents' big-name stars – Cary Grant and Rosalind Russell in *His Girl Friday*

strategy, and certain stars (such as Cary Grant) returned to Columbia again and again. However, one thing the studio lacked in comparison with the other majors was a star it could claim to have created and developed for itself. By 1937, Columbia had only one female star under contract, Jean Arthur: but Arthur's resistance to publicity and her allegedly 'unglamorous' image encouraged Columbia to invest in another. Rita Hayworth, a little-known Fox employee, provided Columbia with its opportunity, and she was signed for a seven-year contract. She was at first restricted to Columbia's 'B' features, cast in a succession of cheap musicals and melodramas, but after 1941 played a number of singing and dancing roles opposite Fred Astaire, Gene Kelly and other borrowed stars. By the mid-1940s Hayworth was established, in Cohn's words, as 'the fourth most valuable property in the business' (quoted in Kobal, 1977, p. 198).

With the release of *Gilda* in 1946 Rita Hayworth's name became a household word: the film was a massive success at the box office, making $3 million for Columbia on its initial release. It may be argued that the combination of the Hayworth femme fatale and musical personas, and the combination of genres – the bleakness of film noir with the décor and choreography of the musical – permitted publicity for the film to be widely spread – from pin-ups in magazines to recordings of Hayworth's (albeit dubbed-over) songs on the radio.

Columbia and the decline of the studio system

1946, when *Gilda* was released, was a peak year for the American film industry in general, as well as for Columbia. However, it was in this same year that the first judgements in the anti-Trust case concerning the majors' monopoly of the film industry were handed down. Columbia was immediately and dramatically affected by the consequent legislation. The prohibition on block booking gave the 'Little Three' equal access with the 'Big Five' to non-affiliated film theatres. The decline in total picture output from the late 1940s meant that even the affiliated theatres needed more first grade films than the Five could supply. The three smaller studios, a large part of whose films had previously been relegated to the bottom half of double-feature programmes, found themselves able to bid for screen time in first-run theatres as equals of the bigger majors. Columbia was consequently able to expand its production of 'first class' films.

The industry-wide recession that followed anti-Trust legislation was due not only to the dismantling of the vertically integrated structures of the 'Big Five', however, but also to the rise of television, the effects of the anti-Communist scare within the film industry, and probably changing social trends in general. Columbia, not having been fully vertically integrated during the period of oligopoly (← p. 10), was in a relatively good position to survive the recession, since after divorcement they found the theatres more

open to their product than before. But survival also depended on the studio's ability to differentiate its product from its rivals – who were no longer only the other studios, but television as well.

One of several strategies Columbia embarked upon in the face of fierce competition from television in the early 1950s was the adaptation of established successes, either from the best-sellers lists or from Broadway hits. *Born Yesterday* (1950) is an example of the latter policy, and Columbia paid a million dollars for the rights to Garson Kanin's play, as well as contracting Judy Holliday, its original star, to repeat her role as Billie Dawn. By this time, while the majors were being forced to reduce their assets, selling off theatres and making contract players, technicians and other employees redundant, Columbia had assembled a stable (albeit modest) of contract actors which could be economically drawn upon (as William Holden and Broderick Crawford were for *Born Yesterday*, relatively inexpensively to off-set other expenditures such as, in this case, on the screenplay). *Born Yesterday* turned out to be the top box-office draw of the year for Columbia and earned the studio an estimated $4 million as well as winning Judy Holliday an Academy Award.

Columbia and television
While expensive adaptations of Broadway successes and best-sellers form obvious examples of the studio's attempts to sell its products, Columbia was also the first of the eight majors to enter television

production. Unable to afford excursions into wide screen, or Cinerama, Columbia chose around 1950 to invest some of its still very limited resources in the formation of a television subsidiary, Screen Gems (the first of the majors to follow Columbia's lead, Warners Bros, did not act until 1955). Thus Columbia, more than any of its competitors, was able to produce films which both related to, and also to some extent differed from, contemporary trends in television drama. For instance, when *The Big Heat* (1953) was released, a police series, *Dragnet*, was at the top of the American television ratings: Columbia was quick to exploit the trend. The violence and eccentricity of the characters in *The Big Heat*, however, illustrates how Columbia combined its exploitation of trends in television with a differentiated content. This proved a particularly important strategy for Columbia in the wake of the relaxation of censorship in the film industry after 1951.

By the mid-50s, with television becoming increasingly popular and cinema attendance dropping, the need to differentiate cinema product from the filmed television episodes that Hollywood was itself beginning to produce had become increasingly urgent. Two 1955 Columbia releases reveal how the studio attempted to weather the crisis. Both films were made in Technicolor and CinemaScope – technologies obviously unavailable to small-screen, black-and-white television transmitters – and boasted the kind of production values that television could not hope to afford. In 1955, the first western television series made by one of the Hollywood majors – Warner Bros' *Cheyenne* – appeared on the American networks. Screen Gems was not slow to follow suit, while Columbia's film division produced *The Man from Laramie*, one of their relatively rare 'A' feature westerns. The film's use not only of colour, wide-screen and location cinematography, but also its

violence, differentiated it successfully from its small-screen competitors.

Sources
Edward Buscombe, 'Notes on Columbia Pictures Corporation, 1926–41', *Screen* vol. 16 no. 3, Autumn 1975.
John Cogley, 'The mass hearings', in Tino Balio (ed.), *The American Film Industry*, Madison, University of Wisconsin Press, 1976.
Michael Conant, 'The impact of the Paramount Decrees', in Tino Balio (ed.), *The American Film Industry*, cit.
Tom Flinn, 'Letter', *The Velvet Light Trap* no. 11, Winter 1974, p. 62.
John Kobal, *Rita Hayworth: the time, the place and the woman*, London, W. H. Allen, 1977.
Rochelle Larkin, *Hail Columbia*, New Rochelle, N.Y., Arlington House, 1975.
Robert H. Stanley, *The Celluloid Empire: a history of the American movie industry*, New York, Hastings House, 1978.

Mr. Deeds Goes to Town (USA 1936 *p.c* – Columbia; *d* – Frank Capra; sd b/w 20)

The extract is taken from the end of the film and illustrates the way in which the narrative is resolved in favour of populism, validating Mr. Deeds as a populist hero whose qualities of innate goodness and common sense mark him off from 'the enemy': the patronising intellectuals who are isolated from the common people. Mr Deeds wins his case by virtue of his knowledge of the grass roots and small-town values, whereas the villainous intellectuals rely upon abstract ideas. Buscombe (1975) has suggested that this populism was characteristic of Columbia's output at this time.

The resolution of the narrative could be described as 'utopian', since all the characters (except the lawyer) are finally united in their support of the populist values of rural America. The ending seems to parody itself, raising the question of whether the apparent project of the film to validate populist ideology can be taken seriously (→ AUTHORSHIP: *Frank Capra*, p. 169).

The Big Heat (USA 1953 *p.c* – Columbia; *d* – Fritz Lang; sd b/w 13)

The film deals with the violence and sadism of a gang of racketeers, and their effect on a policeman who pursues the gang in a relentless quest to avenge his wife's death. The police series was a popular form on television at that time, and this film was probably an attempt to capitalise on that success while providing something more sensational than TV could offer; hence the excessive brutality running through the film, illustrated in the extract by the gangster Vince's (Lee Marvin) violence towards

women. It has been argued (Flinn, 1974) that *The Big Heat* owes more to studio style than to either film noir genre conventions or the authorship of Fritz Lang (→ AUTHORSHIP: *Fritz Lang*, p. 123).

The Man from Laramie (USA 1955 *p.c* – Columbia; *d* – Anthony Mann; sd col scope reduced to standard 12)

During the 1950s cinema capitalised upon its potential for spectacle as it began to lose its audiences to the new medium of television. The western offered the possibility of panoramic views in wide screen and colour, location shooting rather than studio sets, and sensationally violent content, none of which TV could match (→ GENRE: *The western*, p. 66). In spite of being in standard ratio, the extract illustrates some of those strategies that cinema used to differentiate itself from TV output of the time.

My Sister Eileen (USA 1955 *p.c* – Columbia; *d* – Richard Quine; sd col scope reduced to standard 10 + 10)

An example of cinema's exploitation of its potential for spectacle in its attempt to win back audiences from the new medium of television. In spite of the standard ratio, the extracts, which comprise two of the film's dance numbers, indicate some of the ways in which choreographer Bob Fosse's distinctive style meshed with cinema's need to differentiate itself from TV's small screen.

The Lineup (USA 1958 *p.c* – Columbia; *d* – Don Siegel; sd b/w 18)

A Columbia film with origins more specifically in the small screen, *The*

Lineup was a spin-off from a television series. Don Siegel, who had directed the pilot episode of the television version, was hired to direct the film, which was made in black-and-white with a cast of relative unknowns. In this case the difference between the source (the TV series) and the spin-off was that the former had focused on the police while the latter concentrated on the gangsters: television at this time would certainly have prohibited such a focus. Siegel's film exploits this relative licence accorded the cinema by including scenes of some violence (→ AUTHORSHIP: *Don Siegel*, p. 141).

Anatomy of a Murder (USA 1959 *p.c* – Columbia; *d* – Otto Preminger; sd b/w 8)

Anatomy of a Murder also exploits restrictions placed on the content of television programmes, dealing in this instance with a 'delicate' subject – rape – with a certain amount of frankness. The film's director, Otto Preminger, had already made a number of films independently (released through United Artists) and successfully outmanoeuvred the declining censorship powers of the Production Code Administration, even releasing some of them without the PCA seal of approval (← *Censorship*, p. 7). The director's record in this respect may well have attracted Columbia to the project of *Anatomy of a Murder*, since it was the only studio never to register with the PCA. Preminger, moreover, had a reputation for bringing in films under budget (→ AUTHORSHIP: *Otto Preminger*, p. 153).

20th Century-Fox

Introduction: The Fox Film Corporation
The Fox Film Corporation, which was founded in 1914, took its first steps towards 'major' status in 1925 when William Fox, the owner of the company, embarked on an ambitious programme of expansion, investing in a sound process and acquiring chains of film theatres. In 1927 Fox controlled, very briefly, the production studios of Fox and MGM, Loew's and Fox's theatre chains, one third of First National and other assorted holdings. This ambitious industrial programme was paralleled by attempts to enhance the prestige of Fox productions and the company made a number of 'specials', often adapted from Broadway hits and best sellers. Two such blockbusters, *Seventh Heaven* (1926) and *What Price Glory* (1926), both of them big-budget adaptations of plays, had been successful at the box-office, and Fox needed further major successes of this kind in order to offset excessive outlays incurred from production budgets and acquisitions of real estate.

This is the context within which Murnau's *Sunrise* (1927) was produced. Indeed it has been argued that *Sunrise* should been seen exactly as,

'an integral part of one of the most carefully orchestrated and ambitious bids for power and prestige in the history of the American cinema, and in large measure *Sunrise*'s historical significance is to be found in its relation to other Fox films that were equally part of William Fox's truly grandiose scheme to control the movie industry' (Allen, 'William Fox presents *Sunrise*', 1977, p. 237).

The film cost more than $1.5 million to make and included one of the largest sets ever constructed in the history of the cinema, a section of a city, complete with elevated trains and streetcars, constructed over an area a mile long and half a mile wide on the Fox studio lot (Lipkin, '*Sunrise*: a film meets its public', 1977).

By the end of the 1920s, however, William Fox had dangerously overstretched the company with big-budget productions of this kind, as well as by his ambitions for expanding. In 1930 he was ousted from the board and in the following year the Fox

Film Corporation made a loss of more than $5 million. In 1933 a combination of reduced receipts and increasing overheads forced Fox to place its theatres into receivership: in 1934 the company with two studios and a comprehensive national distribution network valued at $36 million had an annual earning power of only $1.8 million. Meanwhile Darryl F. Zanuck, former production head at Warner Bros had set up a small independent unit without studio space of its own, 20th Century Pictures. In 1935 the Fox Film Corporation announced a merger with 20th Century: henceforth, with Zanuck as head of production, the company would be known as 20th Century-Fox.

20th Century-Fox and its stars
When Zanuck took over production at 20th Century-Fox, the studio possessed two highly valuable assets, Will Rogers and the seven-year-old Shirley Temple. Charles Eckert has suggested that Temple was an asset to the Fox studios in that they held a monopoly on her star image, and were able to use that monopoly to control the distributors' choice of films. According to Eckert, the enormous commercial success of Shirley Temple's films – including, for example, *The Littlest Rebel* (1936) – has to do, in part, with their expression of a New Deal 'ideology of charity' (Eckert, 'Shirley Temple and the House of Rockefeller', 1974).

Even more successful than Temple however, in 20th Century-Fox's first year at least, was Will Rogers. Darryl F. Zanuck himself regarded a Rogers vehicle *Thanks a Million* (1935) as the film that made 20th Century-Fox. By 1936, moreover, Zanuck was already expanding 20th Century-Fox's small stable of stars with performers like Tyrone Power and Sonja Henie. But Zanuck's small stable of talent could not compete with the likes of MGM or Warners and so he made his screenplays his stars. The studio's success during this period, then, is perhaps not attributable solely to the success of its players.

Politics and the studio
20th Century-Fox's increasing commercial success during the latter half of the 1930s is commonly attributed on the one hand

to the appeal of certain stars contracted to the studio and on the other to the fact that its films expressed a characteristic and attractive political philosophy, which Charles Eckert characterises as 'opportunist':

'When one takes into account Fox's financial difficulties in 1934, its resurgence with Shirley Temple and its merger with Twentieth Century under the guidance of Rockefeller banking interests, one feels that the least that should be anticipated is a lackeying to the same interests that dominated Hoover and Roosevelt' (Eckert, 1974, p. 18).

In other words the 'line' taken up in 20th Century-Fox's productions of the later 1930s was basically pro-Republican. It has been suggested, for example, that the 1939 Fox production *Young Mr. Lincoln* constitutes a Republican offensive against the New Deal (see *Cahiers du Cinéma* collective text on John Ford's *Young Mr. Lincoln*; → AUTHORSHIP: *Discursive activity*, p. 189).

Fox's political 'opportunism' may not, however, be quite as straightforward as this argument would suggest. How, for example, is *The Grapes of Wrath* (1940) to be explained? The production of *The Grapes of Wrath* was made possible when in May 1939 Zanuck acquired the rights to Steinbeck's novel for an unprecedented $70,000 – the third largest amount ever paid for such rights in film history up to that time. In the 1938/39 financial year 20th Century-Fox was the third most successful studio in Hollywood (after MGM and Warners) and two of their 1938/39 releases reached the top ten box-office grossers list. This success prompted a decision by Fox executives to produce more 'A' pictures – including *The Grapes of Wrath* (→ AUTHORSHIP: *John Ford*, p. 184).

Rebecca Pulliam argues that the film represents, in fact, not a Republican but a Roosevelt/Democratic/New Deal perspective and explains this with reference to Zanuck's experiences in the early 30s at Warner Bros. As at Warners, Zanuck's primary interest and influence was on the screenplay.

'The screenplay for *The Grapes of Wrath* was contractually bound to preserve the theme of Steinbeck's book. Zanuck stated his impression of the book's theme as "... a stirring indictment of conditions which I think are a disgrace and ought to be remedied". Left-wing groups feared that he had bought the book to shelve it and see that it was never filmed. The large California growers were strongly against its production and threatened Zanuck with legal suits. The studio believed that the film might never be released in California' (Pulliam, '*The Grapes of Wrath*', 1971, p. 3).

Zanuck hired a private investigating firm to authenticate the novel's assertions and, having satisfied himself, refused to be thwarted by the Hays Office: 'If they ... interfere with this picture I'm going to take

Sunrise – an ambitious set for a prestige production

The Littlest Rebel – 'black characters . . . geared toward southern "taste"'

full-page ads in the papers and print our correspondence.' *The Grapes of Wrath* took seven weeks and cost $800,000. At its preview the first three rows of seats were reserved for executives of the Chase National Bank, the financial backer of 20th Century-Fox – and also, ironically, one of the institutions which controlled the land companies responsible for forcing the dispossessed farmers portrayed in *The Grapes of Wrath* from their land. Although the film did well commercially, it was not a massive box-office success. But it was perhaps more important to 20th Century-Fox that the company won from it the prestige and acclaim that had eluded it during the 1930s: *The Grapes of Wrath* won two Oscars. The film may therefore be regarded as marking the company's move from the economic security associated with earlier pro-Republican vehicles to the aesthetic prestige associated with its productions of the 1940s.

20th Century-Fox and the decline of the studio system
In the immediate post-war years 20th Century-Fox embarked on a series of 'serious', 'realistic' crime films employing semi-documentary devices and often including newsreel footage of the kind Fox had made famous with their *March of Time* newsreels (← *Warner Bros*, p. 11). *The House on 92nd Street* (1945), for

instance, includes just such a sequence: the film was produced by Louis De Rochemont who had, in fact, launched and supervised the *March of Time* series. In 1948 20th Century-Fox followed the De Rochemont documentary style thrillers with *Cry of the City* which combined the latter's grittiness with the characteristics of the contemporary film noir. More important, perhaps, than either style or subject matter in these bleak urban thrillers was Fox's decisive move to location shooting which prepared the studio for the westerns, musicals and spectaculars which were to follow the anti-Trust decision, and the advent of competition from the small screen and 'live' studio drama.

In the wake of the 1948 anti-Trust decision, declining audiences, and increasing competition from television, Fox's first response was to reduce production budgets. In 1947 the average cost of a full-length Fox feature was about $2,400,000; by 1952 films were regularly being produced at less than half that amount, since location shooting actually proved cheaper than studio shooting. Both *Broken Arrow* (1950) and *The Gunfighter* (1950) illustrate such economies. They serve at the same time to illustrate the ways in which the end of vertical integration in the film industry affected not only the studios but also stars and genres, in that both films concern the activities of ageing western stereotypes –

the 'veteran scout' and the 'retired gunfighter' (→ GENRE: *The western*, p. 66).

In 1952 Fox finally signed the Consent Decree agreeing to divorce its exhibition chain from its production/distribution apparatus in accordance with anti-Trust laws. The company could no longer guarantee the screening of its films simply by controlling first-run theatres. Moreover, by the early 1950s the celebrated 'social realism' of Fox's crime genre was hard to distinguish from innumerable TV crime series such as *Dragnet*. The company's response was to employ bigger, brighter stars – like Marlon Brando (*Viva Zapata!*, 1952), Marilyn Monroe (*River of No Return*, 1954, and *The Seven Year Itch*, 1955), Jane Russell (*The Revolt of Mamie Stover*, 1956), Monroe and Russell together (*Gentlemen Prefer Blondes*, 1953), and specifically cinematic technologies – colour and CinemaScope (*Carmen Jones*, 1954) Technicolor and CinemaScope (*River of No Return*, 1954). *The Seven Year Itch*, in fact, employs an explicit send-up of TV in the 'dumb blonde' character of advertising model Marilyn Monroe, who makes her living by modelling for an advertising company in toothpaste commercials.

Sources
Robert C. Allen, 'William Fox presents *Sunrise*', *Quarterly Review of Film Studies* vol. 2 no. 3, August 1977.
Charles Eckert, 'Shirley Temple and the House of Rockefeller', *Jump Cut* no. 2, July/August 1974.
Editors of *Cahiers du Cinéma*, 'Collective text on John Ford's *Young Mr Lincoln*', *Screen* vol. 13 no. 3, Autumn 1972.
Steven N. Lipkin, '*Sunrise*: a film meets its public', *Quarterly Review of Film Studies*, cit.
Roy Pickard, *The Hollywood Studios*, London, Frederick Muller, 1978.
Rebecca Pulliam, '*The Grapes of Wrath*', *The Velvet Light Trap* no. 2, August 1971.
John Howard Reid, 'The best second fiddle', *Films and Filming* vol. 9 no. 2, November 1962.
Tony Thomas and Aubrey Solomon, *The Films of 20th Century-Fox: a pictorial history*, Secaucus N.J., Citadel Press, 1979.

Sunrise (USA 1927 *p.c* – Fox Film Corporation; *d* – F. W. Murnau; st mu. sd b/w 12 + 16)

Extract 2 in particular illustrates the ambitious set-up of this prestige production. In the scene between husband and wife on the lake, for example, Fox went to the trouble of shooting on location and constructing a village set on the edge of a real lake. The trolley-ride, too, shows the trouble the studio went to, by using deep-focus and long takes to indicate continuity and authenticity, to present the scene as realistically as possible. The demands of realism make an interesting contrast with the 'expressionist' techniques

characteristic of Murnau's style in his early films.

The Littlest Rebel (USA 1936 *p.c* – 20th Century-Fox; *d* – David Butler; sd b/w 11)

It has been argued that the Southern box-office was of paramount importance to Hollywood in the 1930s, and that the depiction of black characters had to be geared towards Southern 'taste' to ensure the film's success. These films romanticise the South of the Civil War. They play up paternalistic notions of chivalry and gracious living, into which blacks are accommodated as loyal family retainers or Uncle Tom figures,

or by offering comic relief. Antebellum myths and values define the essential features of the genre. This construction involves, on the one hand, the portrayal of the Southern white family as a kind of aristocracy, and on the other hand, the incorporation of black plantation life in terms of white entertainment: e.g. the folksiness of song and dance routines, the quaint humour of the blacks which conveys an image of lovable but simple childlikeness. A point for discussion would be the way in which Shirley Temple's star persona (as one of the studio's hottest properties at that time) meshes with this appeal to an audience of white liberals, and, indeed, →

RKO Radio Pictures

Introduction

RKO, a creation of the Rockefeller-backed Radio Corporation of America (RCA), was formed at the beginning of the era of sound in cinema. RCA had patented its own sound-on-film system – Photophone – in conjunction with its radio subsidiary NBC. In response to Warner Bros' experiments with sound, RCA acquired its own theatre circuit, Keith-Albee-Orpheum, and a film production company, FBO. Together these groups formed the new company RKO Radio Pictures. The studio's earliest productions, were, predictably enough, dominated by dialogue-heavy comedies and musicals.

Although the company enjoyed modest financial success in its first few years of operation, the directors were not completely satisfied, and so in order to increase production capacity and distribution outlets, Pathé, with its 60-acre studio, was purchased, and in 1931 David O. Selznick immediately instituted 'unit production', a system whereby independent producers were contracted to make a specific number of films for RKO entirely free from studio supervision, with costs shared by the studio and the producer, and distribution guaranteed by RKO. Despite a series of administrative reorganisations and policy changes within the company in subsequent years, RKO's most famous pictures – including *King Kong* (1933) and *Citizen Kane* (1941) – were nearly all produced in this way.

Selznick was also partially responsible for the construction of the Radio City Music Hall, the world's largest motion picture house. It was felt that exhibition at Radio City would secure solid New York openings for RKO films. But this strategy proved extremely expensive, and by the end of 1932 Selznick was gone and RKO had made a net loss in that year of more than $10,000,000. Selznick's replacement was Merian C. Cooper, who had been acting as Selznick's adviser on evaluating future projects. One of the first films they had

6,200-seat Radio City Music Hall – the world's largest motion picture house

agreed upon had been *King Kong* (1933). After much opposition from the studio's New York office, the film was made (at a cost of more than $650,000) and finally opened at Radio City and the Roxy. In four days it had grossed $89,931. It was the perfect film for RKO's Radio City Music Hall – for which it made a great deal of money and publicity. In 1930 RKO had announced its own inauguration as 'The Radio Titan' with full page advertisements in the trade press, and *King Kong*, too, was launched with a massive wave of publicity.

1933, the year of *King Kong*'s release, also saw the first teaming of Fred Astaire and Ginger Rogers in the film *Flying Down to Rio*. Almost immediately Astaire and Rogers became RKO's biggest stars of the decade. It is significant that as musical stars they were eminently exploitable on radio. In *The Gay Divorcee* (1934) and *Top Hat* (1935) the two stars epitomise the

sophisticated musical comedy tradition that RKO had made its own, combining leisurely playboy and/or heiress plots with spectacular big white sets in art deco styles especially appropriate for the ornate decor of Radio City Music Hall and RKO's first run theatres.

After 1937, when George Schaefer became production head at RKO, some of Selznick's ideas – including unit production – were revived. Schaefer claimed that he intended to concentrate the studio's energy on the production of a few big features that would hopefully prove to be big moneymakers as well. Thus prestige productions, often produced and directed by independents, were encouraged (for example *Bringing Up Baby*, 1938, directed by Howard Hawks), and RKO continued its musical comedy traditions with films like *Dance, Girl, Dance* (1940), also by an outside director, Dorothy Arzner (→ AUTHOR-

→ detracts from the presentation of the racial issues of the Civil War by supporting nostalgic antebellum myths of the South.

The Grapes of Wrath (USA 1940 *p.c* – 20th Century-Fox; *d* – John Ford; sd b/w 10)

The extract offers an example of the treatment of populist ideology and the family generally associated with the director John Ford, and could usefully raise the question of the director's contribution to the ideological meaning of the film in relation to changes in studio policy during the 1930s and 40s (→ AUTHORSHIP: *John Ford*, p. 184).

Cry of the City (USA 1948 *p.c* – 20th Century-Fox; *d* – Robert Siodmak; sd b/w 10)

The extract offers a useful example of the combination of a documentary style with the characteristics of film noir adopted by the studio in the 1940s when it began to produce bleak urban thrillers and to move to cheaper location shooting rather than studio shooting.

The Gunfighter (USA 1950 *p.c* – 20th Century-Fox; *d* – Henry King; sd b/w 11)

A western much admired by Robert Warshow for its combination of greater realism with traditional western themes. The film marks a change in the depiction

of the western hero in its story of a weary itinerant gunman (Gregory Peck), target for every small-time sharp-shooter, and wanting to settle down. In the extract, the gunfighter is provoked by an upstart in the saloon.

Broken Arrow (USA 1950 *p.c* – 20th Century-Fox; *d* – Delmer Daves; sd col 10)

As well as the stylistic and aesthetic changes brought about by Fox's move to economise during the 1950s, the extract indicates a shift in the conventions of the western genre towards a sympathetic understanding of the Indian as operating within the codes of his own culture (→ GENRE: *The western*, p. 66).

King Kong – grossed $89,931 in four days

SHIP: *Howard Hawks*, p. 179; *Dorothy Arzner*, p. 198).

But the most famous production at RKO under Schaefer's supervision is undoubtedly *Citizen Kane* (1941). There can, perhaps, be no better test-case of the importance of industrial determinants than *Citizen Kane*. Pauline Kael has devoted a book to the film, most of which is concerned with deciding between Orson Welles, the director, and Herman J. Mankiewicz, its screenwriter, as the film's *auteurs* (→ AUTHORSHIP: *Orson Welles*, p. 132). Kael's starting point, however, is her insistence that *Citizen Kane* was not an ordinary assignment, and she goes on to argue:

'It is one of the few films ever made inside a major studio in the United States in freedom – not merely in freedom from interference but in freedom from the routine methods of experienced directors. George J. Schaefer, who, with the help of Nelson Rockefeller, had become president of RKO late in 1938, when it was struggling to avert bankruptcy, needed a miracle to save the company, and after the national uproar over Orson Welles's *The War of the Worlds* broadcast, Rockefeller apparently thought that Welles – the wonder boy – might come up with one, and urged Schaefer to get him' (Kael, 1971, pp. 1–2).

Shooting on the film officially began in July 1940 and was completed in October: a twelve-week shooting schedule and a budget of $700,000 were at this period extraordinarily low for RKO prestige productions. Before *Citizen Kane* opened, Schaefer was summoned to New York by Nicholas Schenck, the president of the board of Loew's Inc., the MGM parent company that controlled the distribution of MGM pictures, and offered $842,000 if he

would destroy the negative and all the prints. The reason for the offer was the well-founded suspicion that Welles and Mankiewicz had modelled the characters of Kane and Susan Alexander on the publisher William Randolph Hearst and the actress Marion Davies. Kael quotes from the trade press of the time: 'The industry could ill afford to be made the object of counter-attack by the Hearst newspapers' (pp. 3–4). When Schaefer refused Mayer's offer, the Hearst press launched a tirade of front page denunciations of RKO and its employees, while banning all publicity of RKO pictures. RKO's usual theatrical showcase – the Radio City Music Hall – retracted its offer to screen *Citizen Kane*, and other first-run cinemas proved equally reluctant. Eventually, Warner Bros opened the film – Schaefer was by this time threatening to sue the majors on a charge of conspiracy – but it was too late and it was rapidly withdrawn from circulation to be reissued only in the late 1950s on the art cinema circuit.

Although Kael's analysis is of the authorial contributions of Welles and Mankiewicz, she does emphasise how different the whole feeling of *Kane* would be if it had been made at MGM instead of at RKO, and discusses the collaborative work that went into the film:

'Most big-studio movies were made in such a restrictive way that the crews were hostile and bored and the atmosphere was oppressive. The worst aspect of the factory system was that almost everyone worked beneath his capacity. Working on *Kane*, in an atmosphere of freedom, the designers and technicians came forth with ideas they'd been bottling up for years; they were all in on the creative process ... *Citizen Kane* is not a great work that sud-

denly burst out of a young prodigy's head. It is a superb example of collaboration' (Kael, 1971, p. 62).

By 1942, with heavy losses, prestige again began to be seen as a less urgent priority than profits, and Charles Koerner was appointed under the slogan 'showmanship instead of genius'. Double features and low budgets became the new rule. After Koerner's death in 1946, Dore Schary was appointed his successor. Schary in his turn attempted to revive certain practices of the Selznick period, and once more RKO went upmarket, co-producing a number of films with independent production companies like Goldwyn (*The Best Years of Our Lives*, 1946), Liberty (*It's a Wonderful Life*, 1947), International Pictures (*The Stranger*, 1946), and John Ford's Argosy (*Fort Apache*, 1948, *She Wore a Yellow Ribbon*, 1949, and *Wagon Master*, 1950).

In 1948 Howard Hughes acquired a controlling interest in RKO for just under $9 million, and within a matter of weeks Schary, together with 150 other RKO employees, had been sacked. In 1949 RKO signed a Consent Decree agreeing to divorce its exhibition arm from its production/distribution apparatus, in accordance with the Supreme Court's anti-Trust decision. In 1955 the company was sold to General Teleradio, a television production company; the RKO Hollywood studios had been acquired by Desilu in 1953.

RKO and studio style

Unlike MGM with its lavish family melodramas and musicals, or Warner Bros with its gangster films, or Universal with its horror films, RKO is rarely associated with any specific style or genre: indeed, it is often suggested that RKO is an example of a studio without a style:

'One problem was that no movie mogul had ever attached himself to RKO's banner – as did Louis B. Mayer at MGM, Harry Cohn at Columbia, and Darryl F. Zanuck at 20th Century-Fox ... RKO's ownership was for the most part anonymous – just like the movies it put out. Today a large audience remember the famous RKO productions, but few associate them with RKO. Its roster of stars are still household words – Katharine Hepburn, Ingrid Bergman, Fred Astaire, Robert Mitchum and Cary Grant – but in time there would be other studios with which they would become more closely identified. Even the famous films, *Citizen Kane*, the Fred Astaire musicals, *The Informer*, Val Lewton horror shows, *King Kong* and *Gunga Din* – give RKO no recognisable image: the range of styles was so large, so miscellaneous, and RKO's interest in sustaining any single style or genre (with the exception of the Astaire musicals) so short-lived, that the movies blur rather than blend together' (Merritt, 'RKO Radio: the little studio that couldn't', 1973, pp. 7–8).

One of the reasons for RKO's lack of any

identifiable 'brand image' may be not so much the fact that the company lacked its own 'moguls' as the very number of such men who attached themselves to the studio, reversing its production policies and stylistic commitments so often that no overall house style ever had the opportunity to become established.

RKO and genre: the film noir cycle

Although the number and diversity of the executive regimes at RKO obviously inhibited the development of an easily recognisable studio style, the studio nevertheless did sustain one genre over a period of several years during the middle and late 1940s: the 'low-key' film noir (→ GENRE: *Film noir*, p. oo). Ron Haver associates the development of this genre at RKO with the work there of writers Daniel Mainwaring, John Paxton, and Charles Schnee, and directors Nicholas Ray, Jacques Tourneur and Edward Dmytryk ('The mighty show machine', 1977).

At the same time, by 1944 Charles Koerner's emphasis on low-budget, atmospheric thrillers had almost entirely replaced George Schaefer's prestige pictures

Arzner's *Dance, Girl, Dance* an example of RKO's investment in the women's picture

and musical comedies. RKO made $5 million net in 1944, and the film noir became a formula product for the studio until the end of the decade. These films featured players like Robert Mitchum and Robert Ryan, Jane Greer and Audrey Totter – all of them popular but none of them quite ranking with the stars of RKO's rival studios. In 1947, however, RKO's brief period of post-war profitability was punctured by losses of $1,800,000, but the studio's commitment to low-budget, low-key film-making continued.

As long as the popularity of the genre continued, losses could be attributed, at

least in part, not to overspending but to declining audiences. 1946, after all, was the peak box-office year in the history of the American film industry; at the end of the war it had to face competition from television and alternative leisure activities.

RKO's 'B' pictures

As well as the 'prestige' films produced under its various regimes, RKO also usually had a production programme of 'B' pictures – low-budget movies designed as second features on double bills. If the 'B' production units were economically restricted, they did have a degree of aesthetic and ideological independence from the front office that prestige pictures were often denied. An interesting case in point is provided by the films made under the aegis of Val Lewton, *Cat People* (1942) in particular. By 1942 it had become obvious that the Schaefer 'prestige' policy was not paying dividends at the box-office. In 1940 the studio had lost almost half a million dollars and by 1942 had sunk $2 million in debt. The Atlas Corporation's Floyd B. Odlum bought shares from RCA and Rockefeller until he had acquired a con-

trolling interest in RKO. Schaefer was fired and the more businesslike Ned Depinet replaced him as head of RKO. In 1942, Depinet's Vice President in charge of Production, Charles Koerner, set up a number of 'B' units at the studio, and Val Lewton was assigned to head one of them. Lewton's contract stipulated that he was to produce only horror films, that budgets were not to exceed $150,000, that shooting schedules were not to exceed three weeks, and that running times were to average about seventy minutes. Within these limits, however, Lewton had relative freedom: he was able to select and contract

Cat People (above) filmed on the *Magnificent Ambersons* set (below)

a stable core of creative personnel, functioning as an independent production unit in much the same way as the units producing prestige pictures in the Selznick era. Editors (and later directors) Mark Robson and Robert Wise, scriptwriter DeWitt Bodeen, secretary Jessie Ponitz, cinematographer Nicholas Musuraca, art directors Albert D'Agostino and Walter Keller, and director Jacques Tourneur all worked together for several years in this way.

Budgetary restraint coupled with generic convention encouraged Lewton's unit to economise on labour and lighting costs by employing low-key effects. Furthermore, studio-wide set budgets, imposed by the War Production Board, limited expenditure on sets to $10,000 per picture, which meant that where possible existing sets were re-dressed rather than new sets being built. The unit's first production, *Cat People*, was completed in three weeks at a cost of $134,000, and on its initial release grossed more than $3 million, saving RKO from a second bankruptcy in a year of several big box-office disasters, which included *The Magnificent Ambersons*.

Sources

John Davis, 'RKO: a studio chronology', *The Velvet Light Trap* no. 10, Fall 1973.

Ron Haver, 'The mighty show machine', *American Film* vol. 3 no. 2, November 1977.

Pauline Kael, *The Citizen Kane Book: raising Kane*, London, Secker and Warburg, 1971.

Paul Kerr, 'Out of what past? Notes on the 'B' film noir', *Screen Education* 32/33, Autumn/Winter 1979/80.

Russell Merritt, 'RKO Radio: the little studio that couldn't', *Marquee Theatre*, University of Wisconsin Extension Television Centre, 1973.

Tim Onosko, 'RKO Radio: an overview', *The Velvet Light Trap* no. 10, cit.

Gerald Peary, 'A speculation: the historicity of King Kong', *Jump Cut* no. 4, Nov/Dec 1974.

Joel Siegel, *Val Lewton: the reality of terror*, London, Secker and Warburg/BFI, 1972.

King Kong (USA 1933 *p.c* – RKO
Radio; *d* – Ernest B. Schoedsack/Merian
C. Cooper; sd b/w 16)

The extracts shows one of the climactic moments of the film when King Kong wreaks havoc in New York, capturing Fay Wray and climbing the Empire State Building, and provides a good example of the ambitious special effects on which the studio were banking to make the film a success.

Dance, Girl, Dance (USA 1940 *p.c* –
RKO Radio; *d* – Dorothy Arzner;
sd b/w 20)

An example of RKO's investment in the women's picture, that is, films featuring strong female protagonists, directly mainly at a female audience, offering a critical perspective on male values from a female point of view. Generally a despised or underrated genre, at least critically, the women's pictures of the 1930s and 1940s were nevertheless box-office successes, featuring popular stars, and obviously thought of as 'bankable' by the studios.

The Magnificent Ambersons (USA 1942
p.c – RKO Radio; *d* – Orson Welles;
sd b/w 12)

Russell Merritt has usefully described the industrial atmosphere of this film's production and is cautious about privileging Welles' role as genius-victim

as so many film histories have done. Instead he situates it in a moment midway between the ousted 'prestige policy' and unit production system of Schaefer, and the economics and 'showmanship' of Koerner (Merritt, 1973, p. 18).

The Magnificent Ambersons was 'slashed from two hours to eighty-eight minutes so that it would fit on a double bill' (Haver, 1977, p. 30) and Koerner replaced the absent Welles and the ousted Mercury Theatre units with 'second unit crews, . . . and then released it on a split bill with a Lupe Velez Mexican Spitfire comedy' (Merritt, 1973, p. 20). It is important to emphasise, however, that *The Magnificent Ambersons* was never, even under Schaefer, autonomous of economic and industrial determinants. It was based on Booth Tarkington's Pulitzer prize-winning novel, starred Tim Holt, a familiar RKO western performer, and was a melodrama about the decline of the aristocracy, reminiscent of the previous year's production of *The Little Foxes* (→ AUTHORSHIP: *Orson Welles*, p. 00; *William Wyler*, p. 00).

Cat People (USA 1942 *p.c* – RKO
Radio; *d* – Jacques Tourneur;
sd b/w 15)

'The wreck of *The Magnificent*

Ambersons may have been taken as one monument to the Koerner regime; but from its ashes rose another: the famous cycle of Val Lewton's *Cat People*, sometimes actually filmed on the abandoned *Ambersons* sets' (Merritt, 1973, p. 18).

The *Ambersons* staircase, in fact, was to become a central icon in *Cat People* – re-dressed sets were considerably cheaper than purpose-built ones. And the fact of having to re-dress and disguise such sets encouraged an attention to detail often absent from more expensive production. The 'bus' sequence in this extract is a useful illustration of an extremely (cost) effective and remarkably expressionist approach to concealing economies. The use of low-key lighting, low-angle camerawork, heightened sound effects and so on – animation, shadows in the swimming pool scene, silence in the walking scene – indicate the aesthetic potential in such economic imperatives. And the minute detail with which the Lewton unit were able to invest their films (see, for instance, the ash on the apron in this extract) bears witness to the continuity and relative cohesiveness of the low-budget unit production system.

Universal

Introduction
Universal was a relatively minor studio, one of the 'Little Three' companies (the others being Columbia and United Artists) which lacked their own theatres and depended for exhibition outlets on the cinema circuits of the 'Big Five' (Warner Bros, RKO, Fox, Paramount and MGM), the vertically integrated majors. The company established itself in the 1920s under the ownership of Carl Laemmle and adapted its studio to sound production relatively early: by 1930, all of its releases were 'talkies'. However, by this time the recession which affected the entire film industry had forced Universal to re-examine its approach to film production. Laemmle decided to make fewer pictures, but 'of the highest excellence that the resources of Universal City could achieve' (quoted in Pendo, 'Universal's Golden Age of horror', 1975, p. 155).

In 1930 Carl Laemmle Jr, who had been put in charge of the studio by his father, began a series of horror films, which became Universal's speciality in the early 1930s, with the production of *Dracula* and *Frankenstein*. In the first few years of the decade, however, the effects of the Depression made themselves felt particularly keenly at Universal, the studio's output decreased substantially, and during an

industry-wide strike the studio actually closed down for several months. In 1931 film budgets were cut, production schedules shortened and static 'dialogue' shooting emphasised at the expense of expressionist visual styles. In 1933, despite Laemmle Sr's ambitions, the company entered a two-year period of receivership. The studio was re-established, after some administrative reorganisation, at the end of the decade.

However, by the mid-1940s Universal was once again in economic difficulties. The studio's financial welfare was resting somewhat precariously on Deanna Durbin and on Abbott and Costello; their pictures, while still profitable, were not doing as well as in the past (Alan Eyles, 'Universal and International', 1978).

Universal's response to this situation was to attempt to attract major stars to the studio by giving them a percentage of the profits from their films, and simultaneously to increase budgets, thereby attracting a number of independent producers. The company also merged its distribution activities with the independent production company, International. This reorganisation was finalised in November 1946, when it was announced that all 'B' film units would be shut down immediately, whether in production or not. From then on, all Universal films were to be prestige pictures and absolutely no 'B' or cheap

films would be produced. What would happen, however, to 'B' films – rather than units – already in production? While Universal was in no position, economically, simply to abandon 'B' films in production, low-budget films were redundant because, with the banning of block booking, they would henceforth have to be sold individually. *The Killers* (1946) and *Brute Force* (1947), therefore, are examples of 'B' project given 'prestige' treatment on very slim budgets in order to attract buyers.

Universal, studio style and genre
Universal's output of the early 1930s is identifiable primarily with a single genre, horror, though they did make *All Quiet on the Western Front*. A consideration of Universal films of the period thus calls for an examination of the intersection of genre and studio style within a set of industrial determinants. A variety of explanations have been put forward for Universal's specialisation in the horror genre. Stephen Pendo, for example, argues:

'Depression audiences wanted the escapist entertainment which horror provided . . . Universal's contribution was to assemble the best and most imaginative technicians – cameramen, directors, make-up artists, set designers and special effects men available. Many of them had graduated with horror from the classic German silent film school' (Pendo, 1975, p. 161).

Thus, it is implied, Universal's output would be predisposed, because of the contributions of some of the studio's personnel, to the expressionism characteristic of the visual style of horror movies. In Universal's case, too, the existence of certain types of stars in the studio's stable – Boris Karloff and Bela Lugosi in particular – would serve to reinforce the existing tendency to concentrate on this genre. Lugosi, for example, had played horror roles on the stage and had also appeared in silent horror films for Universal. Moreover, once horror films were identified as Universal's genre, stars of this type would tend to be employed at the studio. Furthermore, as a minor studio which needed to establish a certain kind of 'product identification' in order to sell its films to the exhibition circuits controlled by the majors, Universal particularly needed to develop a generic area of its own.

The dominance of horror films in Universal's output of the early 30s has also been explained in terms of the transition from silent to sound cinema – that the visual style of such films enabled the move to sound to take place as economically as possible. As far as individual films are concerned, *Dracula* (1931) illustrates this argument quite well. Production on the film was begun in 1930 as part of Universal's intended move into pictures 'of the highest excellence'. The desire to make such pictures involved attempting to recapture the visual qualities of silent cinema which were considered in some quarters to be under threat from sound cinema with its temporary immobilisation of the movie camera. In *Dracula* there is consequently a great deal of mobile framing and only a minimal use of sound. The film's relative 'silence' served to increase the chilling atmosphere. There is an emphasis too on 'night' and 'outdoor' sequences with tracking shots concentrating on actors and props rather than on sets.

In *Frankenstein* (1931) the camera is considerably less mobile than in *Dracula*, and there is far more dialogue. However, *Frankenstein* compensates for lack of camera movement with use of low angle shots and expressionist sets. But at the same time, this film was intended to be the first of a series , and is consequently less of a prestigious production than *Dracula*: 'With an eye towards sequels, the finish was reshot so that Baron Frankenstein escaped a fiery death – a fortunate change . . . *Frankenstein* was an outstanding success. This convinced Universal even more that horror pictures should henceforth be an integral part of its production schedule' (Pendo, 1975, p. 157). (→ GENRE: *The horror film*, p. 99).

Universal in the 1950s and 1960s

After the 1948 anti-Trust decision (← *The studios*, p. 10) which put an end to the industry's monopolistic practices of block booking and blind selling, Universal could no longer be guaranteed exhibition of its films, and so returned to its earlier practice of providing an easily identifiable studio style and subject matter. After the late 40s Universal's output was dominated by several genres: thrillers like *Brute Force* (1947), *The Killers* (1946) and *Touch of Evil* (1958); melodramas like *Letter from an Unknown Woman* (1948), *All That Heaven Allows* (1955) and *Written on the Wind* (1956), and westerns such as *Winchester 73* (1950), *Bend of the River* (1952) and *The Far Country* (1954). The combination of such specialisation with reduced receipts and competition from television had a dramatic effect on the quantity of Universal's annual output. In 1950, for instance, Universal only released two major productions, *Winchester 73* and *Harvey*, both of which featured James Stewart: the studio was able to present stars like Stewart because of its offering them a percentage of the profits from its films. Such stars were central to Universal's success at this time. One of the

Touch of Evil – big stars attracted by percentage of profits

Universal's horror output – *Dracula* and *Frankenstein*

independent directors who worked at Universal during this period was Orson Welles, whose *Touch of Evil* was released in 1958. The film was shot in 1957 when Welles had been away from Hollywood for nearly ten years. According to Joseph McBride:

'Charlton Heston agreed to appear in a Universal police melodrama, thinking that Welles had been signed to direct it, when actually he had only been signed as an actor. The studio, undaunted by Welles's pariah status in Hollywood, then asked him to direct . . . he accepted with alacrity, and received no salary as writer or director. He never read the source novel, Whit Masterson's *Badge of Evil*, but found the studio's scenario "ridiculous" and demanded the right to write his own . . . Nonplussed by the result, the studio called it *Touch of Evil* . . . and slipped it into release without a trade showing' (McBride, 1972, p. 131).

There are, however, conflicting accounts of how Welles came to direct *Touch of Evil*:

'*Newsweek* reported that Welles had been offered the film as a sop for a character role he had played previously at Universal. Charlton Heston has said he suggested Welles as director after reading the film's uncompromising script . . . but producer Albert Zugsmith . . . tells still another story. According to Zugsmith, Welles had come to Universal in the late 50s in need of money to pay tax debts . . . and Welles offered to direct the "worst" script the producer had to offer – the Paul Monash adaptation of Whit Masterson's novel, *Badge of Evil* (Naremore, 1978, p. 177).

What is possibly most interesting about the film in relation to its studio provenance, however, is the degree to which it has been seen to depart from the Universal norm of the period. Perhaps because Welles's films tend to offer themselves up immediately to an auterist analysis (→ AUTHORSHIP: *Orson Welles*, p. 132), the marks of the studio are either ignored, or seem particularly difficult to determine, in relation to *Touch of Evil*.

It may, however, be significant that in 1958 Universal recorded $2 million worth of losses, and that since the mid-50s space in the Universal studio lot had been regularly rented out to television production companies. Furthermore, while *Touch of Evil* was being made, 'trade papers were filled with rumours of sweeping changes within the Universal hierarchy, including reports that the film division would fold altogether in order to save their second arm, Decca records' (Naremore, 1978, p. 176).

Perhaps it was industrial indecision which permitted the 'ridiculous' (Welles's word) project of *Touch of Evil*? But the presence in the film of Marlene Dietrich, Dennis Weaver, Zsa Zsa Gabor, Joseph Cotten, Akim Tamiroff, Mercedes McCambridge, Janet Leigh, Charlton Heston and Welles himself may also suggest that *Touch of Evil* is a final example of Universal's ability to attract big stars by offering them a percentage of the profits from its films. Henceforth almost all Universal features were to be made with an eye toward future television scheduling.

By 1959 when Universal sold its studio lot to MCA, its westerns and melodramas were being undercut by competition from television. The studio's new owners divided film production into expensive blockbusters (e.g. *Spartacus*, 1960) on the one hand and small (often made-for-TV) movies such as *The Killers* (1964) on the other.

Sources

Tino Balio, 'A mature oligopoly: 1930–1948', in Balio (ed.), *The American Film Industry*, Madison, University of Wisconsin Press, 1976.

Allen Eyles, 'Universal and International', *Focus on Film* 30, June 1978.

Michael G. Fitzgerald, *Universal Pictures: a panoramic history in words, pictures and filmographies*, New Rochelle, N.Y., Arlington House, 1977.

Charles Higham, *The Films of Orson Welles*, Berkeley, University of California Press, 1970.

Joseph McBride, *Orson Welles*, London, Secker and Warburg/BFI, 1972.

James Naremore, *The Magic World of Orson Welles*, New York, Oxford University Press, 1978.

Stephen Pendo, 'Universal's golden age of horror', *Films in Review* vol. 26 no. 3, March 1975.

Robert Stanley, *The Celluloid Empire: a history of the American movie industry*, New York, Hastings House, 1978.

Dracula (USA 1931 *p.c* – Universal; *d* – Tod Browning; sd b/w 10)

Frankenstein (USA 1931 *p.c* – Universal; *d* – James Whale; sd b/w 7)

The Killers (USA 1946 *p.c* – Universal; *d* – Robert Siodmak; sd b/w 12)

Brute Force (USA 1947 *p.c* – Universal; *d* – Jules Dassin; sd b/w 20)

Letter from an Unknown Woman (USA 1948 *p.c* – Universal; *d* – Max Ophuls; sd b/w 18)

The Far Country (USA 1954 *p.c* – Universal; *d* – Anthony Mann; sd col 20)

All That Heaven Allows (USA 1955 *p.c* – Universal; *d* – Douglas Sirk; sd col 20 + 20)

Written on the Wind (USA 1956 *p.c* – Universal; *d* – Douglas Sirk; sd col 15)

Touch of Evil (USA 1958 *p.c* – Universal-International; *d* – Orson Welles; sd b/w 14)

The Killers (USA 1964 *p.c* – Universal; *d* – Don Siegel; sd col 10)

Spartacus (USA 1959–60 *p.c* – Universal; *d* – Stanley Kubrick; sd col standard reduced from scope 25)

Technology

Introduction

Much of what has been written about the history of cinema attributes the invention and implementation of new cinematographic technologies to a combination of individual enterprise and aesthetic destiny. According to this approach, the film director, camera operator or technician initiates the improvement of intransigent machinery, whilst the film medium itself evolves irresistibly towards an ultimate 'total' cinema. This teleological model tends to suggest that technological advances occur only when they are necessary in order to solve aesthetic problems. More often than not, the aesthetic in question has been realism.

Deep-focus cinematography, for instance, is commonly associated with the work of a single Hollywood cinematographer, Gregg Toland, and with a certain 'unmanipulated' mode of cinematic realism. Indeed both the defenders and the detractors of deep-focus tend to share the assumption that its defining characteristic is an increased verisimilitude in the film image. Thus André Bazin, perhaps the foremost polemicist on behalf of deep-focus cinematography, has described how it '. . . brings the spectator into a relation with the image closer to that which he enjoys with reality . . .' (→ NARRATIVE AND STRUCTURALISM: *Bazin*, p. 224). Furthermore, in a discussion of the use of deep-focus in *Citizen Kane*, Bazin suggests that:

'Whereas the camera lens, classically, had focused successfully on different parts of the scene, the camera of Orson Welles takes in with equal sharpness the whole field of vision contained simultaneously within the dramatic field. It is no longer the editing that selects what we see, thus giving it an *a priori* significance, it is the mind of the spectator which is forced to discern . . . the dramatic spectrum proper to the scene' (Bazin, 'Cinematic realism and the Italian school of the liberation', 1972, p. 28).

In much the same way, Charles Barr has applauded the way in which the wide screen increases the spectator's freedom (Barr, 'CinemaScope: before and after', 1974). The suggestion is that the more we see on screen – the deeper the focus, the wider the screen, and so forth – the more 'realistic' cinema becomes. Similar arguments have also been made on behalf of sound (stereo is more 'realistic' than mono) and colour (three-colour Technicolor is more 'realistic' than two-colour). It may, however, be argued to the contrary that technological transitions have often involved – initially at least – the adoption of apparently non-realist aesthetic strategies, until such time as the innovation in question has entered general cinematic currency. Edward Buscombe has suggested, for example, that both sound and colour were originally associated, in the

American film industry, with that least realistic of genres, the musical (Buscombe, 'Sound and color,' 1978). Indeed, rather than recognising an all-embracing trend towards realism in cinema, it seems that some kind of movement between product differentiation and the eventual appropriation of such differentiation by prevailing cinematic orthodoxy has been the model for much of cinema's aesthetic development. According to this model, new technologies derive, in part at least, from a desire to differentiate cinema from other media and forms of entertainment, and from the attempts of individual studios to distinguish their own output from that of their competitors. Thus moving pictures are distinct from still images, and widescreen forms (like CinemaScope) are distinct from small-screen (television in particular). Similarly, six-reel films are distinct from one-reelers, talking pictures are distinct from silent films, colour is distinct from black-and-white, deep-focus from shallow-focus and low-key lighting from high-key. This cycle of differentiation and appropriation can be seen at work through various technological developments in cinema. Thus once the initially 'non-realist' mobilisation of sound (for instance, its use at first in musicals), became taken for granted, it was replaced by other innovations – Technicolor, deep-focus, CinemaScope.

However, if the differentiation/appropriation/new differentiation cycle is of some help in understanding the technological and aesthetic history of cinema without recourse to concepts of realism, it is by no means a sufficient explanation. New technologies have tended to be introduced only when the film industry as a whole, or a specific section of it, has been engaged either in expansion or in self-defensive retrenchment. The development of sound, for instance, supported Warner Bros' bid for major status, Technicolor helped Hollywood out of the Depression, and deep-focus reinforced the 'ideology of realism' and re-established the aesthetic respectability of cinema. Similarly, widescreen formats, Cinerama and 3D were all part of the American film industry's response to the audience-stealing appeal of television.

Furthermore, the economic influences on technological innovation provided an opportunity for a new 'technological rent' for patents, and also new monopolies such as, in the early years of the century, the Motion Picture Patents Company. With the coming of sound, Warners' Vitaphone and RKO's Photophone struggled for technological supremacy, while Technicolor and Eastman Color later fought for a monopoly over colour, and CinemaScope successfully overcame competition from VistaVision and other wide-screen processes. Finally, the scale of investment in studio and film theatre conversions necessitated by most technological innovations has often forced the industry to seek new sources of finance. Sound brought AT&T (Western Electric) and RCA (RKO Photophone) into the industry whilst 20th Century-Fox in introducing CinemaScope were forced to rely on the capital of the Chase Manhattan Bank and other Rockefeller-controlled organisations.

Economics alone, however, cannot explain the development and adoption of new technologies. Such innovations may open up new aesthetic opportunities and may even create new audiences – drive-ins for the youth market, sound for the consumers of vaudeville, deep-focus for the 'cultivated' middle classes, for example. Technological innovations can offer the spectator not simply 'a relation with the image closer to that which he enjoys with reality', but more subtly a celebration of the production values, codes and conventions of cinema itself.

Sound

The sound era of cinema is generally dated from the release of *The Jazz Singer* in 1927 – although this was neither the first sound feature nor the first 'talking' film. Attempts to give film a 'voice' were being made from the very beginnings of cinema: in fact Thomas Edison's main reason for encouraging his assistant W. K. L. Dickson to develop the Kinetograph was that he hoped it would complement the Edison Phonograph. In 1895 Edison introduced his Kinetophone, a mechanism which piped in a musical accompaniment to the ears of the viewer peering through the peep-holes of the Kinetoscope. The device was unsuccessful with the public and it was eighteen years before Edison tried again. Probably the earliest and certainly the cheapest and most common of the many methods of adding sound to silent films involved the placing of actors, musicians and noise-making machines directly behind the screen. This practice was employed as late as 1915 in special roadshow presentations of *The Birth of a Nation* (← p.5). Meanwhile, the most prestigious productions – which in the 1920s were those shown in the lavish picture palaces – had the benefit of orchestral accompaniment while even the smallest of cinemas from the days of the Nickelodeon until the advent of sound employed improvising pianists. Film-makers like Griffith and Chaplin even went so far, when budgets and schedules allowed, as respectively to commission and compose their own scores to be performed in careful synchronisation with the films themselves.

The unreliability of 'live' accompanists and developments in radio and electronic research together led to experiments in 'photographing' sound directly on to film, the first patent for such a process being issued as early as 1900. The advent of sound in cinema, however, provides an excellent illustration of the fact that technologies are not necessarily implemented as soon as they become available. The American Telephone and Telegraph Company (AT&T) and the Radio Coporation of America (RCA) both conducted experiments in sound cinema from the early years of the century, but executives in the film studios were unwilling to make changes in an already profitable industry. The major film companies were all listed on the Stock Exchange and in 1926 the total capital invested in the industry exceeded $1.5 billion. A move to sound would involve vast expenditure in re-equipping studios and theatres and retraining casts and crews all for a commodity for which there could hardly be said to be a demand. The film industry was thus not, for the most part, keen to move from silent to sound production.

Earliest links with sound

At Warner Bros, however, the situation was somewhat different. Although by 1925 Warners had built up a relatively prosperous production company, the bulk of the audiences for their films was the clientele of small independent theatre circuits and neighbourhood film theatres, and it was becoming increasingly difficult to compete with the opulent picture palaces of the vertically integrated companies (← *The studios*, p. 10). If, however, Warners could afford to equip their studios with sound, which the company hoped would in the long run provide an economically viable alternative to the pit orchestras in the theatres controlled by their rivals – they might at last be able to compete with them. In the event, Wadill Catchings, an investment banker with Wall Street's Goodman Sachs Company, was so impressed with Warners' cost accounting and strict budgetary control that he agreed to finance the company through a period of carefully planned expansion. With Catchings appointed to Warners' board of directors, the company acquired the ailing Vitagraph Corporation with its fifty film exchanges, a worldwide distribution system, and a Hollywood radio station equipped by Western Electric.

In May 1925, Harry and Jack Warner witnessed a demonstration of Western Electric's sound system and, intrigued by the possibilities it presented, a deal between the two companies was negotiated. In April of the following year, the two companies co-founded the Vitaphone Corporation to make sound films and market sound equipment. In August, Vitaphone presented its first sound feature,

Don Juan. *Don Juan* itself boasted a synchronised musical accompaniment throughout, but it was the eight 'Vitaphone preludes', including recorded concerts and a filmed speech by Will Hays, that greatly impressed audiences. At this point, the Fox Film Corporation decided to join the move to sound, and with the acquisition of their own sound system began to produce sound newsreels under the Movietone banner. In January 1927, Warner Bros followed its earlier success with the release of *The Jazz Singer*: although this film was more of a 'singing' than a 'talking' film, the brief improvised dialogue sequences included the prophetic

production companies and Wall Street that were to last for many years.

The advent of sound briefly curtailed the possibilities of mobile framing only recently established in silent cinema. The new sound cameras were enclosed in sound-proof booths which had to remain virtually immobile during shooting. The immobilisation of the camera also put an end to the use of the directorial megaphone during shooting, and this led to time-consuming rehearsals. Actors at first had to be grouped around concealed microphones, and for some time the hitherto customary close-up was almost abandoned as shots became longer and cuts fewer.

far from bankrupt, being engaged rather in a carefully planned expansion. Gomery rejects the more orthodox approach by advancing an economic theory of technological innovation, which posits that 'a production process is introduced to increase profits in three systematic phases: invention, innovation and diffusion' (Gomery, 'The coming of the talkies', 1976). More recently Edward Buscombe has argued that sound was invented primarily as a means to increase the productivity of vaudeville performers and theatre musicians and that the availability of a new 'technological rent' – the monopoly of a new technology and thus a new commodity – was what attracted Warner Bros to sound technology (Buscombe, 'Sound and color', 1978).

The Jazz Singer – 'Warners proved the commercial viability of the sound movie'

words 'You ain't heard nothin' yet'. By the following spring, all the majors were busily engaged in equipping studios for the transition to sound, and the Vitaphone system was rapidly revised. On both *Don Juan* and *The Jazz Singer* the 'soundtrack' had been recorded on discs whose playing time equalled the running time of one reel of film. Because the disc-synchronisation process was rather unreliable, it was soon replaced by sound directly on film.

By the end of 1930 Warner Bros not only entirely controlled its former rival, First National, but had also boosted its own assets from $5 million in 1925 to $230 million. Western Electric had quickly secured contracts with all the existing production companies, while AT&T's rival, RCA, responded in 1928 by creating a wholly-owned integrated company of its own, Radio-Keith-Orpheum (RKO) to exploit its own Photophone sound system. On several occasions over the next decade RKO threatened AT&T with anti-Trust action because of the latter's virtual monopoly over the sound market, but by 1943 some 60% of all equipment in the industry was in fact being supplied by RKO. As had been expected, sound boosted production costs – to an average $375,000 per film in 1930 as against less than $80,000 a decade earlier. The conversion to sound cost the industry an estimated $500 million and established alliances between the major

Despite constant improvements in sound quality, especially at the 'prestige' end of the market, the next decisive innovation in sound came only with the introduction after World War II of magnetic tape. Later, stereophonic sound accompanied the wide-screen movies of the 1950s, and the acquisition of the major film companies by multi-media conglomerates during the 1960s led to the exploitation of other electronic and musical systems such as Quadrophonic sound, Sensurround and Dolby sound. Sound tracks which in the early 1930s had consisted only of dialogue and musical accompaniment could, in the 1970s, be mixed from eight and even sixteen tracks.

Film history had usually explained the coming of sound in terms of individual enterprise and technological evolution. Patrick Ogle, for instance, has attributed the development of sound systems to a combination of 'gradualism' on the one hand and, on the other, 'relatively unexpected breakthroughs, often wrought by technology or personnel suddenly injected into the motion picture milieu' (Ogle, 'Development of sound systems', 1977). Lewis Jacobs (1968) argues that Warner Bros' impending bankruptcy was responsible for the innovation of sound – an argument which is brought into question by recent evidence, assembled by Douglas Gomery, that Warner Bros was at the time

The Jazz Singer (USA 1927 *p.c* – Warner Bros; *d* – Alan Crosland; st + sd b/w 12)

This extract was chosen to illustrate a moment of technological change, when Warner Bros decided to augment their adaptation to a successful Broadway drama, *The Jazz Singer*, with some Vitaphone musical sequences including lines of improvised dialogue. In fact they were using a technique – sound-on-disc – that Edison and others had already experimented with, but either lacked economic motives or capital to develop further. Warners proved the commercial viability of the sound movie at a time when the industry was in the doldrums, and so motivated the development of sound-on-film systems which founded sound cinema proper.

Apart from the historical background, the consequence of the introduction of sound for acting styles is illustrated by the contrast between the heavily emphasised gesture and mime of the opening and closing sequences, and the central sequence in which the power of speech and the necessity of improvisation confronts the actors with totally different demands on their acting styles. (NB Projection should be at sound speed throughout.)

The Public Enemy (USA 1931 *p.c* – Warner Bros; *d* – William Wellman; sd b/w 16)

The first part of the extract illustrates the way in which the studio attempted to negotiate the transition to synchronised sound recording. The tracking shot which reveals the working-class Chicago streets has a dubbed soundtrack, while the conversation between the two boys has synchronised sound, necessitating an immobile camera. Although we may experience the scene as continuous, the transition is marked by a cut which signals the difference between the two recording techniques.

Colour

Unlike sound, which was taken up by the entire film industry within a few years, colour took more than thirty years from its commercial introduction to fully dominate the industry.

Like sound, however, colour has been associated with the cinema in one form or another from the earliest years of the medium: as early as 1896, for example, teams of women were employed to hand-colour films, frame by frame. As films increased in length and the number of film prints soared and hand-colouring became less practicable, Pathé Frères patented a device for stencilling prints according to simple colour correspondences. At the same time in America less expensive tinting and toning processes converted black and white images to colour chemically. By the time of the transition to sound, this process was a long-standing tradition for the more prestigious productions. However, as soon as the sound-on-disc device was replaced by the recording of sound directly on to film, tinting and toning were discontinued because it became evident that the process affected the quality of the soundtrack. It was eventually decided that post-production conversion of black and white images to colour was less sensible than actually filming with colour stock.

The principle of colour photography had been introduced in the 1850s and demonstrated in 1861 by the Scottish physicist James Clerk Maxwell. The cinematic process that first successfully employed those principles – Kinemacolour – was exhibited in 1911. This process, which made use of a red and green filter through which black and white frames could be projected, was a considerable commercial success. Nevertheless these 'additive' colour processes had several drawbacks, and were soon superseded by other two-colour methods such as Kodachrome (1915), a 'subtractive' process in which colour images were formed directly in the film rather than indirectly on the screen. In 1922, Technicolor also introduced a two-colour process; but the limited effects of the two-colour systems hardly justified their expense, and in 1932 it was replaced by Technicolor's superior three-colour format. Technicolor was able to capitalise on the coming of sound by offering a process that had no adverse effect on the sound track. By means of combining superior print quality with patent control, Technicolor continued to dominate the American colour movie market for three decades.

At first, the two-colour process proved insufficiently attractive to the majors to induce them to experiment with it, and so Technicolor began to produce shorts of its own and also to provide MGM and Warner Bros with Technicolor supervisors when the two companies began their own series of colour shorts and introduced short colour sequences into primarily black and white films. Finally, in 1929, Warner Bros released two 'all colour, all talking' features – *On with the Show* and *Gold Diggers of Broadway*, the first results of a twenty-feature contract Jack Warner had signed with Technicolor. At the beginning of the new decade, when the industry began to feel the effects of the Depression, the majors, unable to withdraw from their commitment to sound, chose instead to reduce their interest in colour cinematography, and the musical – the genre with which colour had been most closely associated – was briefly considered to be 'box-office poison'. Undaunted, Technicolor invested a further $180,000 in their three-colour process, and instead of entering the market themselves, offered exclusive contracts to two independent production companies – Walt Disney and Pioneer Films. Disney acquired exclusive rights for colour cartoons and released a series of 'Silly Symphonies' which won critical acclaim, Academy Awards and massive box-office returns. Meanwhile Pioneer, after experimenting with three-colour shorts and sequences, released the first three-colour feature, *Becky Sharp*, in 1935. When *Becky Sharp* proved only a modest commercial success, Pioneer's executives joined forces with another independent producer, David O. Selznick, and under the banner of Selznick International absorbed Pioneer's eight-feature contract with Technicolor. There followed a string of three-colour successes from Selznick International: *The Garden of Allah* (1936), *A Star Is Born* (1937), *The Adventures of Tom Sawyer* (1938) and *Gone with the Wind* (1939).

By the time the economic viability of

COLOUR IN THE 40S

She Wore a Yellow Ribbon (USA 1949 p.c – Argosy Pictures; d – John Ford; sd col 26)

Under Capricorn (USA 1949 p.c – Transatlantic Pictures; d – Alfred Hitchcock; sd col 15)

COLOUR IN THE 50S

Rancho Notorious (USA 1952 p.c – Fidelity Pictures/RKO Radio; d – Fritz Lang; sd col 20)

Shane (USA 1952 p.c – Paramount; d – George Stevens; sd col 20+20)

Gentlemen Prefer Blondes (USA 1953 p.c – 20th Century-Fox; d – Howard Hawks; sd col 15)

Carmen Jones (USA 1954 p.c – 20th Century-Fox; d – Otto Preminger; sd col 10)

My Sister Eileen (USA 1955 p.c – Columbia; d – Richard Quine; sd col scope reduced to standard 10+10)

All That Heaven Allows (USA 1955 p.c – Universal-International; d – Douglas Sirk; sd col 20+20)

Written on the Wind (USA 1956 p.c – Universal-International; d – Douglas Sirk; sd col 15)

Oh! For a Man (USA 1957 p.c – 20th Century-Fox; d – Frank Tashlin; sd col scope 6)

Rio Bravo (USA 1959 p.c – Armada; d – Howard Hawks; sd col 18)

COLOUR IN THE 60S

Sergeant Rutledge (USA 1960 p.c – John Ford/Warner Bros; d – John Ford; sd col 16)

Wild River (USA 1960 p.c – 20th Century-Fox; d – Elia Kazan; sd col scope or standard 10)

The Birds (USA 1963 p.c – Alfred Hitchcock/Universal-International; d – Alfred Hitchcock; sd col 18)

The Haunted Palace (USA 1963 p.c – Alta Vista; d – Roger Corman; sd col scope reduced to standard 20)

Marnie (USA 1964 p.c – Geoffrey Stanley Inc/Universal-International; d – Alfred Hitchcock; sd col 20+20)

The St. Valentine's Day Massacre (USA 1967 p.c – Los Altos/20th Century-Fox; d – Roger Corman; sd col scope 18)

Coogan's Bluff (USA 1968 p.c – Universal; d – Donald Siegel; sd col 20)

Sweet Charity (USA 1968 p.c – Universal; d – Bob Fosse; sd col 25)

Easy Rider (USA 1969 p.c – Pando Company; d – Dennis Hopper; sd col 15)

COLOUR IN THE 70S

Student Nurses (USA 1970 p.c – New World Pictures; d – Stephanie Rothman; sd col 15)

Loving (USA 1970 p.c – Brooks Ltd; d – Irvin Kershner; sd col 13)

Dirty Harry (USA 1971 p.c – Warner Bros/Malpaso; d – Donald Siegel; sd col 15)

Klute (USA 1971 p.c – Warner Bros; d – Alan J. Pakula; sd col scope 20)

Shaft (USA 1971 p.c – MGM/Shaft Productions; d – Gordon Parks; sd col 19)

Blacula (USA 1972 p.c – American International Pictures; d – William Crain; sd col 12)

Two-Lane Blacktop (USA 1972 p.c – Universal/Michael Laughlin Enterprises; d – Monte Hellman; sd col 20)

Cleopatra Jones (USA 1973 p.c – Warner Bros; d – Jack Starrett; sd col 12)

Mandingo (USA 1975 p.c – Dino De Laurentiis; d – Richard Fleischer; sd col 14)

Technicolor was established, World War II, the shrinking world market for films, and reduced budgets and production schedules curtailed the expansion of colour cinematography for some time. While in 1935 it was estimated that colour added approximately 30% to production costs – which then averaged about $300,000, in 1949 this figure had fallen to 10% while the average costs of American 'A' features had risen to about $1 million. In 1948, *Variety* estimated that colour could add as much as 25% to a feature film's financial return, but this was not sufficient to cover additional production costs. In 1940, only 4% of American features were in colour. By 1951, this figure had risen to 51% but in 1958 had fallen to 25%, as a result of shrinking budgets and the emergence of the black-and-white TV market. By 1967, however, the TV networks having turned to colour broadcasting, the percentage rose once more to 75%, and in 1976, 94%.

Deep-focus

Deep-focus cinematography is characterised by a film image of some depth from foreground to background, in which all the components of the image are in sharp

The Best Years of our Lives – deep focus and realism

focus. This style of film making is commonly associated with certain Hollywood films of the 1940s. Patrick Ogle dates its emergence at around 1941, and argues that its development was influenced by a matrix of cinematic and non-cinematic factors, such as the rise of photojournalism and social realist and documentary film movements during the 1930s, and the availability of new kinds of film stock, lighting equipment and lenses. According to this argument, cinematographers at this period were attempting to duplicate on film the perspective and foreground-background image size relationships seen in picture magazines. Since the normal focal length of a 35 mm still camera is (relatively speaking) half that of the 35 mm motion picture camera, most still camera pictures take in an angle of view twice as wide as that taken in by a movie camera filming the same event from the same distance. In order to reproduce the effects of still photographs, cinematographers had to use what, in motion picture terms, were considered unusually wide angle lenses. (Ogle, 'Technological and aesthetic influences upon the development of deep-focus

cinematography', 1977).

In the mid-1930s improved arc lights – which, because of noise and flicker problems, had been virtually abandoned in favour of incandescents better suited to panchromatic film stock and sound filming – were introduced specifically, at first, for Technicolor cinematography, which demanded high levels of lighting. In the latter half of the decade, however, faster film stocks became available, and while many cinematographers chose to underdevelop their footage in order to maintain the soft tones and low contrast levels they had been used to, a few opted for the possibilities of increased crispness and depth of field. In 1939, a new emulsion type was introduced which reproduced both sound and image more clearly and crisply than ever before, and, at the same time, new lens coatings were produced which resulted in improvements in light transmissions of more than 75% under some conditions. This more efficient use of light led to better screen illumination, image contrast, and sharpness of focus for both colour and black-and-white cinematography ($\rightarrow$ *Lighting*, p. 30). Although this conjunction of powerful point source arc lights, fast

film emulsions and crisp coated lenses were necessary preconditions for deep-focus cinematography, they were by no means sufficient. According to Ogle, for deep-focus to develop as it did, a number of essentially aesthetic choices and creative syntheses had to occur. The aesthetic in question is cinematic realism, which Ogle defines as 'a sense of presence' similar to that experienced by spectators in the theatre, in that the viewer is provided with 'visually acute high information imagery that he may scan according to his own desires without the interruptions of intercutting . . .'. This argument echoes Bazin, for whom deep-focus brought the spectator into a relation with the image closer to that which s/he enjoyed with reality ($\rightarrow$ NARRATIVE AND STRUCTURALISM: *Bazin*, p. 224). For Ogle, deep-focus cinematography as a recognised visual style first came to critical and public attention with the release of *Citizen Kane* (1941), though it had certainly been practised before. Although not obviously realistic in style, *Citizen Kane* manifested an unprecedented depth of field in the scene photographed, which led a contemporary reviewer to

claim that it produced '. . . a picture closely approximating to what the eye sees . . . The result is realism in a new dimension: we forget we are looking at a picture, and feel the living, breathing presence of the characters' (*American Cinematographer*, May 1941, p. 222).

Although Ogle disagrees that the human eye sees in deep-focus, he believes the sense of realism celebrated by the reviewer consists in deep-focus cinematography's tendency towards long duration sequences, avoidance of cut aways and reaction shots, the employment of a relatively static camera, and the use of unobtrusive editing – once again echoing Bazin.

Avoiding an argument based on technological determinism, Ogle insists that deep-focus could never have emerged without the timely creative input of Gregg Toland, William Wyler, John Ford and Orson Welles, and indeed, without certain production conditions. He considers that *Citizen Kane*, for example, 'constituted a major coming together of technological practice with aesthetic choice in an environment highly conducive to creativity' ($\leftarrow$ *RKO Radio Pictures*, p. 20).

Against Ogle's account, however, it has been argued (Williams, 'The deep-focus question', 1977) that neither technological practice nor aesthetic choice are independent of ideological and economic choices and practices, as Ogle's analysis suggests; moreover, realism is not simply an aesthetic but also an ideology, an 'ideology of the visible'. The importance of deep-focus cinematography for film criticism lies in its encapsulation of issues concerning economics and technology, aesthetics and ideology. An economic imperative might be detected, for instance, in the industry's need to mark a difference, a new kind of product; and part of the aesthetics of deep-focus may well have emerged from the cinematographers' desire to assert their 'creative' status in the industry hierarchy.

La Grande illusion (France 1938 *p.c* – Réalisations d'Art Cinématographique; *d* – Jean Renoir; sd b/w 11)

La Règle du jeu (France 1938 *p.c* – La Nouvelle Edition Française; *d* – Jean Renoir; sd b/w 9 + 10)

Stagecoach (USA 1939 *p.c* – Walter Wanger Productions; *d* – John Ford; sd b/w 13)

Citizen Kane (USA 1941 *p.c* – RKO; *d* – Orson Welles; sd b/w 25)

The Little Foxes (USA 1941 *p.c* – RKO/Goldwyn; *d* – William Wyler; sd b/w 15 + 16)

The Magnificent Ambersons (USA 1942 *p.c* – RKO; *d* – Orson Welles; sd b/w 12)

The Best Years of our Lives (USA 1942 *p.c* – Goldwyn; *d* – William Wyler; sd b/w 22)

Rotating Edison's 'Black Maria' . . . and lighting advances at his New York studio

Elaborate and expressionist lighting on the set of *Foolish Wives*

Lighting

While the technologies of sound, colour and deep-focus are relatively well-researched areas of film scholarship, comparatively little work has been done on the history of film lighting, a history which has both influenced and been influenced by various other film technologies. In the 1890s the major source of illumination for shooting film was sunlight. Sets were built and filmed on outdoor stages with muslin diffusers mounted on wires and various kinds of reflectors employed to adjust the levels of brightness and to reduce obtrusive shadows. The first film studio, Edison's 'Black Maria', built in 1893, had its walls covered in black tarpaper and its stages draped in black cloth; its roof opened to adjust sunlight, and the whole building could be rotated to maximise daylight. Only occasionally did early films employ artificial lighting effects: in 1899 D. W. Griffith's camera operator Billy Bitzer installed some 400 arc lights in order to film an indoor boxing match. By 1905 several studios including Biograph and Vitagraph, had equipped themselves with Cooper-Hewitt mercury vapour lamps.

At first the Cooper-Hewitt lamps were used only sparingly in order to supplement the diffuse sunlight which filtered through studio roofs. Only around 1910 did supplementary light from arc floodlights on floor stands begin to be added. These lights permitted more distinct facial modelling and separation of actors from their backgrounds, as well as offering the possibility

of simulating 'directed' lamp or window light with far greater precision than the diffused vapour lights that had preceded them. For some time, however, all that was expected of film lighting was an adequately exposed negative and an evenly diffused light, preferably flat, bright and shadowless. Rudolph Arnheim in his book *Film as Art* has remarked: 'In the early days any auspicious light effect was avoided, just as perspective size alterations and overlapping were shunned. If the effects of the lighting sprang to the eye too obviously in the picture, it was considered a professional error' (Arnheim, 1971, p. 72). How then did film lighting, as a meaningful element of *mise en scène*, develop? Barry Salt has suggested that the main thrust in the development of lighting interior scenes in American films was the change to overall use of directional artificial light and its application separately to actors and to sets, though he offers no explanation as to why this change took place (Salt, 'Film style and technology in the 40s', 1977). Another historian, Charles W. Handley, has argued that it was inter-company competition between members of the Motion Picture Patents Company and independent producers which encouraged camera operators to introduce carbon arc floodlights and spotlights and so differentiate their own sets and stars from others (Handley, 1954).

For whatever reason, by 1915 lighting for illumination was gradually being replaced by lighting for dramatic effect, and

Klieg spotlights were becoming normal in studio practice:

'Light becomes atmosphere instead of illumination, coming naturally from some window, lamp, or doorway, it illuminates the centre of the picture and the people standing there with a glow that in intensity, in volume, or in variety of sources has some quality expressive of the emotion of the scene' (Contemporary review, quoted in MacGowan, 1965, p. 169).

Peter Baxter argues that during this crucial period for the American film industry, when its industrial organisation was consolidated, the expressive potential of lighting, its ability to achieve dramatic 'effects' was harnessed to a naturalist aesthetic which paralleled developments in commercial American theatre at the time (Baxter, 'On the history and ideology of film lighting', 1975, p. 97). By 1918 the conventions of lighting (revelation and expression) which were to dominate Hollywood production up to the present day were more or less established: lighting should never be so artificial or abstract as to disconcert the cinema audience. Its potential for abstraction became subordinated to the representational codes characteristic of seventeenth-century Dutch painters – Rembrandt in particular; in other words, it was given source and direction. In 1930 a cinematographer wrote:

'In a well photographed picture the lighting should match the dramatic tone of the story. If the picture is a heavy drama . . . the lighting should be predominantly sombre. If a picture is a melodrama . . . the lighting should remain in low-key but be full of strong contrasts. If the picture is, on the other hand, a light comedy . . . the lighting should be in a low-key throughout. For two reasons: first, to match the action, and secondly, so that no portion of the comedy action will go unperceived' (Milner, 'Painting with Light', 1972, p. 96).

As the Klieg lights came into general use so too did three-dimensional rather than painted sets, and sunlight was finally eliminated altogether from studios. The 1920s saw the gradual conventionalisation of the use of stronger and weaker arc floodlights functioning as key (hard, direct light), fill (soft, diffused light filling in the shadows cast by key lighting) and back lighting. The coming of sound, however, called forth a new range of technological demands, and 'restricted to small sets and with his camera static, the cinematographer . . . began casting about for light sources that would not be restricted, as were his cameras, by the noise they created' (Handley, 1954). Humming carbon lights were replaced by silent Mazda tungsten incandescent lamps, and the hard light of the arcs was considerably softened by the more diffused incandescents. Incandescent lights were also better suited to the panchromatic stock which began to replace orthochromatic in 1928. By 1931, however, improved carbon arcs had been introduced to provide the high-key bright light necessary for the new two-colour Technicolor process. In the latter half of the 1930s, the brightly-lit look was further encouraged by the successful introduction of three-colour Technicolor. Arc lights were too powerful for monochrome work, and pre-sound Mazda incandescents were still used. By the end of the decade, however, the arrival of faster Technicolor film stock allowed a reduction in lighting power requirements for colour cinematography (← *Deep-focus*, p. 29) and the modern arc lights began to be used in black-and-white production also, in preference to old-fashioned incandescents (Ogle, 1972). The move to more economical location filming after World War II was encouraged by war-developed technology like the Colortran, a relatively lightweight and mobile source which required fewer lighting units and involved a cruder use of fill lights. Until the late 1940s, studio lighting was either low-key (for film noir) or high-key (for deep-focus cinematography). But the codes of 'dramatic lighting' which had been established much earlier, and which demanded that lighting should be subordinated to aesthetic coherence, continued to dominate Hollywood production.

However, the ideology of aesthetic coherence was not the only factor governing the development of lighting conventions and technology. Some studios, for instance, worried by high electricity bills, sought to economise by using the lowest possible lighting levels and automated machinery which would reduce manning requirements (Salt, 1977; Handley, 1954). As with other cinematic technologies, their development (or, in some cases, such as 3D, non-development) is often uneven rather than chronologically linear, due to pressure from a variety of sources, economic and institutional as well as aesthetic and ideological.

Sources

Rudolph Arnheim, *Film as Art*, Berkeley, University of California Press, 1971.
Charles Barr, 'CinemaScope: before and after', in Mast and Cohen (eds.), *Film Theory and Criticism*, New York, Oxford University Press, 1974.
Peter Baxter, 'On the history and ideology of film lighting', *Screen* vol. 16 no. 3, Autumn 1975.
André Bazin, 'An aesthetic of reality: cinematic realism and the Italian school of the liberation', in Hugh Gray (ed. and trans.), *What is Cinema?* Vol. 2, Berkeley, University of California Press, 1972.
André Bazin, 'The evolution of film language', in Peter Graham (ed.), *The New Wave*, London, Secker and Warburg/BFI, 1968.
David Bordwell and Kristin Thompson, *Film Art*, Reading, Massachusetts, Addison-Wesley, 1979 (82–84).
Edward Buscombe, 'Sound and color', *Jump Cut* no. 17, April 1978.
Evan William Cameron (ed.), *Sound and the Cinema*, New York, Redgrave Publishing Co, 1980.
J. Douglas Gomery, 'The coming of the talkies: invention, innovation and diffusion', in Tino Balio (ed.), *The American Film Industry*, Madison, University of Wisconsin Press, 1976.
Benjamin B. Hampton, *History of the American Film Industry*, New York, Dover Press, 1970.
Charles W. Handley, 'History of motion picture studio lighting', *Journal of the SMPTE* vol. 63, October 1954.
Lewis Jacobs, *The Rise of the American Film*, New York, Teachers College Press, 1968.
Gorham A. Kindem, 'Hollywood's conversion to color: the technological, economic and aesthetic factors', *Journal of the University Film Association* vol. 31 no. 2, Spring 1979.
James Limbacher, *Four Aspects of the Film*, New York, Brussell and Brussell, 1969.
Kenneth MacGowan, *Behind the Screen: the history and techniques of the motion picture*, New York, Delta, 1965.
Roger Manvell (ed.), *The International Encyclopaedia of Film*, London, Michael Joseph, 1972 (pp. 29–32).
Victor Milner, 'Painting with light', *Cinematographic Annual I* (1930), New York, Arno Press, 1972.
Patrick L. Ogle, 'Development of sound systems: the commercial era', *Film Reader 2*, January 1977.
Patrick L. Ogle, 'Technological and aesthetic influences upon the development of deep-focus cinematography in the United States', *Screen Reader I*, London, Society for Education in Film and Television, 1977.
'Photography of the month', *American Cinematographer*, May 1941.
Barry Salt, 'Film style and technology in the 40s', *Film Quarterly* vol. 31 no. 1, Fall 1977.
Christopher Williams, 'The deep-focus question: some comments on Patrick Ogle's article', *Screen Reader I*, cit.
Stephen Neale, *Cinema and Technology*, London, BFI/Macmillan, 1985.

Hearts of the World (USA 1918 *p.c* – Griffith Inc; *d* – D. W. Griffith; st b/w 28)

Foolish Wives (USA 1921 *p.c* – Universal; *d* – Erich von Stroheim; st b/w 11)

Sunrise (USA 1927 *p.c* – Fox Film Corporation; *d* – F. W. Murnau; st mu.sd. b/w 12 + 16)

Dracula (USA 1931 *p.c* – Universal; *d* – Tod Browning; sd b/w 10)

The Scarlet Empress (USA 1934 *p.c* – Paramount; *d* – Joseph von Sternberg; sd b/w 11)

The Informer (USA 1935 *p.c* – RKO Radio; *d* – John Ford; sd b/w 14)

Citizen Kane (USA 1941 *p.c* – Mercury Productions/RKO; *d* – Orson Welles; sd b/w 25)

The Little Foxes (USA 1941 *p.c* – RKO/ Goldwyn; *d* – William Wyler; sd b/w 15 + 16)

The Maltese Falcon (USA 1941 *p.c* – Warner Bros; *d* – John Huston; sd b/w 9)

Double Indemnity (USA 1944 *p.c* – Paramount; *d* – Billy Wilder; sd b/w 20)

Rancho Notorious (USA 1952 *p.c* – Fidelity Pictures/RKO; *d* – Fritz Lang; sd col 20)

Shane (USA 1952 *p.c* – Paramount; *d* – George Stevens; sd col 20 + 20)

River of no Return (USA 1954 *p.c* – 20th Century-Fox; *d* – Otto Preminger; sd col scope + standard 10)

Written on the Wind (USA 1956 *p.c* – Universal-International; *d* – Douglas Sirk; sd col 15)

Touch of Evil (USA 1958 *p.c* – Universal-International; *d* – Orson Welles; sd b/w 14)

Sergeant Rutledge (USA 1960 *p.c* – John Ford/Warner Bros; *d* – John Ford; sd col 16)

The Haunted Palace (USA 1963 *p.c* – Alta Vista; *d* – Roger Corman; sd col scope reduced to standard 20)

The Beguiled (USA 1970 *p.c* – Universal/ Malpaso; *d* – Donald Siegel; sd col 20)

The Way We Were (USA 1973 *p.c* – Rastar Productions; *d* – Sydney Pollack; sd col scope 10)

Soviet agit-prop ship

The Soviet cinema: industry and aesthetics

Until 1907 the only film companies operating in Russian market were foreign, and the domestic market was dominated by the likes of Lumière Brothers and Pathé. In 1907, however, the first Russian production company, Drankov, was set up in competition with the foreign films and film companies which nevertheless continued to flourish in Russia until the outbreak of World War I and the consequent collapse of the import boom. By 1917 there were more than twenty Russian film companies exploiting a steadily expanding home market, whose output consisted mainly of literary and dramatic adaptations, and costume spectaculars. This situation was suddenly and radically changed by the October Revolution. Veteran directors, actors and technicians emigrated as a period of violent transition totally disrupted normal conditions of production. The new Bolshevik government saw film as a vital tool in the revolutionary struggle, and immediately set about reconstructing the film industry to this end. On 9 November, 1917, a centralised film subsection of the State Department of Education, Narkompros, was set up. This centralisation was resisted at first by the private sector, which boycotted the State-sanctioned films, and even went so far as to destroy precious raw film stock. Lack of supplies of equipment and new film stock made production very difficult for the emerging revolutionary cinema, but nevertheless, by the summer of 1918 the first agit-trains (mobile propaganda centres) left for the Eastern front, specially equipped to disseminate political propaganda through films, plays and other media to the farthest corners of Russia.

The transition from entrepreneurial to State control of film production, distribution and exhibition proved a slow and difficult process, with post-war famine and continuing political and military conflict postponing the revival of the industry until the early to middle 20s. By 1920 Soviet film production had dwindled to a trickle, but in 1921 when Lenin's New Economic Policy encouraged a cautious short-term return to limited private investment releases rose from 11 in 1921 to 157 in 1924. The resumption of imports in the early 1920s following the restabilisation of the economy allowed profits to be ploughed back into domestic production, and, as film equipment and stock resurfaced, the several Soviet studios by then in existence began to expand to pre-Revolution proportions. In 1922, Goskino, the State Cinema Trust, was established as a central authority with a virtual monopoly over domestic film production, distribution and exhibition in Russia, although certain companies retained a degree of independence, and film industries in the more distant republics were allowed some autonomy from Moscow and Leningrad. Studios were set up in the various regions, such as VUFKU in the Ukraine, while others, Mezhrabpom-Russ for example, expanded in mergers with private industry. In 1923 a special propaganda production unit, Proletkino, was formed specifically for the production of political films in line with party ideology. Until 1924, films remained conventional in style, apparently untouched by the explosion of avant-garde experiment transforming the other arts in post-Revolutionary Russia. Then in 1925, when the industry was allowed an increased aesthetic independence in the wake of a Politburo decision endorsing State non-intervention in matters of form and style in the arts, the new Soviet cinema entered its most exciting and formally adventurous period.

By the mid-1920s all the production units including Goskino (renamed Sovkino in 1925), Proletkino, Kultkino, Sevzapkino and Mezhrabpom-Russ, had begun to assemble their own personnel – directors, cinematographers, editors and so on, as well as performers. Vsevolod Pudovkin worked at Mezhrabpom, Sergei Eisenstein at Sovkino, Alexander Dovzhenko at VUFKU, for example. During this period, cinema came into productive collision with the energetic theoretical and artistic activity taking place in the other arts. The work of poet Vladimir Mayakovsky and theatre director Vsevolod Meyerhold, for example, profoundly influenced the early work of Eisenstein, whose avant-garde film experiments were accompanied by an impressive body of theoretical writings which are still influential today (→ AUTHORSHIP: *Sergei M. Eisenstein*, p. 203). In the wake of the 1925 Politburo decision, Eisenstein was commissioned by the Central Committee to produce a film commemorating the 1905 revolution. This film, *Battleship Potemkin*, was premiered at Moscow's Bolshoi Theatre, an indication of its industrial prestige. But despite a relatively positive critical response, the film's domestic release was relegated to Russia's second-run cinemas and its foreign sales delayed until pressure from influential writers, journalists and party officials induced Sovkino to send it to Berlin. Subsequently it was a huge international success, reflecting small credit on the conservative policies of the Soviet film industry at that time. *Battleship Potemkin*'s success heralded a series of ambitious and expensive productions. In 1926 Mezhrabpom-Russ released Pudovkin's *Mother*, another prestigious film which, like *Battleship Potemkin*, exceeded average budget allowances. By 1927 all the major production units were engaged in equally extravagant and prestigious projects in order to celebrate the tenth anniversary of the 1917 Revolution.

The Jubilee films

The impulse to produce the best, as well as the first, of the tenth anniversary films resulted in a race involving Esfir Shub and Eisenstein at Sovkino and Pudovkin at Mezhrabpom-Russ. Pudovkin won with the release of *The End of St. Petersburg*. Almost simultaneously, however, Sovkino completed two films recreating Russia's pre-revolutionary history entirely from archive footage – *The Great Road* and *The Fall of the Romanov Dynasty*. Both were directed by Shub, who had been trained as an editor at Sovkino (→ AUTHORSHIP: *Esfir Shub*, p. 206). Production schedules and budgets were adjusted across the board for these Jubilee celebrations. At Sovkino, for example, Eisenstein and his collaborators were ordered away from production on *The General Line* (later retitled *The Old and the New*) to produce *October*.

The last of the Jubilee films, *October* was not in fact released until 1928. The delayed release was due in part to the film's reliance on recent Soviet history, which by the late 1920s was the subject of intense ideological scrutiny and rewriting in the wake of Trotsky's expulsion from the Party. In the event, *October* was extensively re-edited, and references to the role of Stalin's political opponents in the revolution eliminated. The film was finally released in March 1928 to a hostile reception from the party leadership, who objected to its experimental style as 'formalist'. Simultaneously, the first All-Union Party Congress on Film Questions concluded that in future all fictional films should be accessible to the mass audience. The Congress ruled that film-makers should cease to employ formalist devices and seek instead to emphasise socialist content along strict party lines. This resolution has been seen as marking the beginnings of official sanction for a certain artistic method, that of socialist realism, which was to dominate Soviet cinema until after Stalin's death.

Emergence of socialist realism

In the words of the 1928 Congress resolution: 'the basic criterion for evaluating the art qualities of a film is the requirement that it be presented in a form which can be understood by the millions' (quoted in Katz, 1980, p. 1076). On completing *October* Eisenstein returned to the unfinished *The General Line* and decided to simplify his experimentations to a level more easily understood by a general audience, choosing objects like a bull, a tractor and a cream separator to symbolise the transition from primitive farming to mechanised modern agriculture, though he did not abandon his montage experiments. *The General Line* was symptomatic also of the transition to centralised control of film production: indeed, its title was changed to *The Old and the New* because the original title was criticised for implying that the film had received official sanction which, for all its extensive re-editing on Stalin's orders, it never actually achieved. *Earth* was similarly symptomatic: its controversial poetic lyricism was condemned as 'counter-revolutionary' and 'defeatist', though it managed to escape outright prohibition (→ HISTORY OF NARRATIVE: *Soviet cinema of the 1920s*, p. 218).

Other projects managed to sidestep, if not altogether escape, the aesthetic consequences of the directives of the 1928 Congress by producing or selling films at some geographical distance from the metropolitan centres of power in the Soviet Union. The Vertov Unit's experimental *Man with a Movie Camera* (1929) was produced at VUFKU in the Ukraine, for instance. Vertov had been sacked by Sovkino in early 1927 and ordered to leave Moscow, in some measure no doubt because his work was regarded as overly formalist. With his editor wife Elisaveta Svilova and cameraman brother, Mikhail Kaufman (Kino-Eye's Council of Three), Vertov made his way to the Ukraine. Between 1926 and 1928 VUFKU was

engaged in an embargo on all Sovkino films, and employed the exiled Vertov on condition that his first project would be to complete the film *The Eleventh Year*, which was to have been Vertov's contribution to Sovkino's celebration of the tenth anniversary of the October Revolution. Once this film was finished Vertov embarked on another ambitious project, *Man with a Movie Camera*, whose formal extravagance marks it off from others in the 1920s 'City' cycle of films, exemplified by Kaufman's *Moscow*, Ruttmann's *Berlin*, Cavalcanti's *Rien que les heures* and Vigo's *A propos de Nice*. Vertov continued his imaginative experiments after the advent of sound, but then gradually faded away after Stalin's consolidation of power.

Stalin's decrees under his first Five Year Plan led to increased production of documentaries in support of its industrial objectives, and in 1930 Sovkino was dissolved and replaced by Soyuzkino, an organisation directly supervised by the Politburo's Economic (rather than as previously, the Education) Department. In future Soyuzkino, under Stalin's appointee Boris Shumyatsky, was to function in close correspondence with Proletkino. It also officially adopted the resolution of the 1928 Congress in determining its aesthetic policy. After a brief transition period in which some interesting sound experiments emerged (e.g. Vertov's *Enthusiasm*, 1931), the coming of sound in 1930 combined with government-imposed restrictions on form and content encouraged an increasing realism of dialogue and character. Musicals and literary adaptations dominated the film industry's output, though there was also a spate of historical biopics celebrating the achievements of Lenin and Stalin. Eisenstein's first sound film *Alexander Nevsky* (1938) was made during this period, after a campaign by Shumyatsky to discredit and humiliate the director which involved hostile government interference in the production of *Bezhin Meadow*, and finally abandonment of the project. Only after a painful confession in which he was forced to renounce his film was Eisenstein assigned another important production, the patriotic *Alexander Nevsky*, intended to strengthen Russian national identity in the face of the growing threat from Nazi Germany. In 1938 Shumyatsky was sacked, though there was no change in policy as a result. The administrative reshuffling in the film industry which followed, combined with the outbreak of World War II, led to a reduction in film output and a revival of the documentary. During the war film industry personnel were evacuated from Moscow to remote parts of the USSR, and feature film production gave way to morale-boosting political propaganda in the form of documentary material gathered from the fronts. *Alexander Nevsky*, which had been made as implicit anti-fascist propaganda, was withdrawn in

Dziga Vertov with camera crew

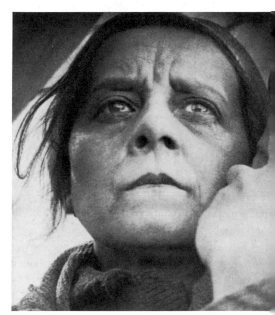

Pudovkin's prestige production – *Mother*

1939 in the wake of the German-Soviet Pact. In 1940 Eisenstein, having emerged from disgrace for his formalism in 1938, was appointed artistic head of Mosfilm, the revamped Soyuzkino, and in 1945 won the Stalin Prize for Part I of *Ivan the Terrible*. The following year Eisenstein began work on a sequel, but Part II met with none of the support that had greeted Part I, and its release was postponed for a decade. During the Cold War period Stalinist repression reached its highest level, repudiating the faintest hint of formalism as deviation from Socialist realism, and several films were banned outright. It was only in 1956, three years after Stalin's death, that the effects of Khrushchev's denunciation of some aspects of Stalinism allowed a gradual withdrawal from the aesthetic orthodoxies of the Cold War years and a return to a more 'poetic' cinema. Chukhrai's *Ballad of a Soldier* is an illustration of this liberalisation. However, Khrushchev's enforced retirement in 1964 and the reintroduction of State controls in the film industry under the auspices of the Cinematography Commission of the USSR Council of Ministers resulted in another retreat to prestige literary adaptation and 'safe' historical reconstructions, until the late 1960s, when an international co-production programme resulted in a broadening of scope (e.g. Akira Kurosawa's *Dersu Uzala*, 1975). In spite of a recent trend towards decentralisation of production, all foreign and domestic films are still carefully vetted for their suitability for general release.

Sources

David Bordwell and Kristin Thompson, *Film Art*, Reading, Massachusetts, Addison-Wesley, 1979 (pp. 306–309).

Ephraim Katz, *The International Film Encyclopaedia*, London, The Macmillan Press, 1980 (pp. 1074–1079).

Jay Leyda, *Kino: a history of the Russian and Soviet film*, London, George Allen and Unwin, 1973.

Battleship Potemkin (USSR 1925 *p.c* – Sovkino; *d* – Sergei M. Eisenstein; st b/w 11)

Mother (USSR 1926 *p.c* – Mezhrabpom-Russ; *d* – Vsevolod Pudovkin; st b/w 12)

The End of St. Petersburg (USSR 1927 *p.c* – Mezhrabpom-Russ; *d* – Vsevolod Pudovkin; st b/w 16)

The Great Road (USSR 1927 *p.c* – Sovkino and The Museum of the Revolution; *d* – Esfir Shub; st b/w 20)

The Fall of the Romanov Dynasty (USSR 1927 *p.c* – Sovkino and the Museum of the Revolution; *d* – Esfir Shub; st b/w 20)

October (USSR 1928 *p.c* – Sovkino; *d* – Sergei M. Eisenstein and Grigori Alexandrov; st b/w 13)

New Babylon (USSR 1929 *p.c* – Leningrad Studio of Sovkino; *d* – Grigori Kozintsev and Leonid Trauberg; st b/w 18)

The General Line (The Old and the New) (USSR 1929 *p.c* – Sovkino; *d* – Sergei M. Eisenstein and Grigori Alexandrov; st b/w 12)

Earth (USSR 1930 *p.c* – VUFKU; *d* – Alexander Dovzhenko; st b/w 13)

The Ghost that Never Returns (USSR 1929 *p.c* – Sovkino; *d* – Abram Room; st b/w 12+15)

Man with a Movie Camera (USSR 1929 *p.c* – VUFKU; *d* – Dziga Vertov; st b/w 20)

The Childhood of Maxim Gorky (USSR 1938 *p.c* – Children's Film Studio; *d* – Mark Donskoy; sd b/w 11)

Ivan the Terrible Part I (USSR 1943–44 *p.c* – Mosfilm; *d* – Sergei M. Eisenstein; sd b/w 15)

Ballad of a Soldier (USSR 1959 *p.c* – Mosfilm; *d* – Grigori Chukhrai; sd b/w 15)

Italy and Neo-Realism

A national cinema, in the full sense of the term, is not just the national production registered in a particular country but a cinema which in some way signifies itself to its audiences as the cinema through which that country speaks. By this token the Italian Neo-Realism of the late 1940s and early 50s was a quintessentially national cinema. Neo-realist films represented only a small proportion of box-office takings on the home market and their claim to signify on behalf of the nation was bitterly contested within Italy – not least by the Italian government itself. But the critical reputation acquired by Neo-Realism, in Italy and abroad, and the unequivocal way in which the films developed a national and popular subject-matter, meant that for many years 'Italian cinema' meant the neo-realist production of Rossellini, De Sica, Visconti, etc., and other forms of film-making in Italy, however commercially successful, were relegated to a secondary role.

Italian Neo-Realism was the product of the Second World War and the defeat of Italian and German fascism. Ideologically it arose from the need, widely felt throughout Italy and most clearly articulated among intellectuals of the left, to break with the cultural heritage of fascism and in particular with rhetorical artistic schemata which seemed to bear no relation to life as it was lived. Industrially, the conditions for the emergence of the neo-realist cinema were provided by the economic breakdown that followed the Allied invasion and the collapse of the Mussolini regime in 1943–45.

The Italian cinema had a long if not always distinguished history. Like many European national industries it had a flourishing period just before the First World War, before the Americans established their stranglehold on the world market. Of particular significance were the giant historical spectaculars (e.g. *Cabiria*, 1914) which reputedly impressed both Griffith and Eisenstein and which for many years functioned as a model, for some, of what the Italian cinema should once again become and, for others, of what it should avoid. The coming of fascism in 1922 affected the Italian cinema at first very little. But throughout the 20s the industry was in economic and cultural decline, which the coming of sound at the end of the decade only aggravated. Having at first adopted more or less *laissez-faire* policies, the government took steps from about 1926 onwards to remedy the decline. The purpose of the intervention was not to create a distinctively 'fascist' cinema, but simply an 'Italian' one, which would be economically and culturally self-sufficient. Though a number of patriotic and pro-fascist features were produced, overt propaganda was confined mainly to the newsreels. After a brief period of experimenting with the 'art film', encouragement was given principally to the

development of efficient studio production and out of this there emerged a steady stream of comedies and dramas which were designed to compete successfully, at least on the home market, with their Hollywood equivalents. To ensure that this would be possible, various protectionist measures were introduced, in the form first of quotas and then of import restrictions; these culminated in 1938 in a situation where the films from the 'major' Hollywood studios could not be seen in Italy at all, whereas those from the 'minors' could. In December 1941, with America's entry into the war, the importation of Hollywood films ceased entirely.

Although fascism had a firm grip on economic and political life, its ability to secure popular consent was much less certain. Whereas in the 1920s, when the fascists were struggling to consolidate their power, they did enjoy the active support of sections of the population; after 1930 when that power had been consolidated fascist rule became something of an empty shell, receiving little more than a formal and grudging obeisance on the part of the population at large. Political opposition, crushed in 1926, began to revive in clandestine conditions from the mid-30s onwards. Intellectually, opposition and the seeds of a national renewal began to develop within the ranks of the fascist organisations themselves. When war came, this opposition was to transfer itself to the ranks of the Resistance. For the cinema, key centres of the oppositional culture out of which the neo-realist aesthetic was to develop were to be found in the government-sponsored film school, the Centro Sperimentale (founded 1935) and in the Cine-GUF or fascist university film societies.

In July 1943, Allied troops invaded Sicily. Mussolini was deposed by an internal coup, rescued by a German commando unit and restored to nominal power as head of a puppet republic based in the northern resort town of Salò. One of the more bizarre acts of this puppet regime was an unsuccessful attempt to transfer the headquarters of the Italian film industry from Rome, where the grandiose film studios of Cinecittà had been opened in 1937, to the relative safety of Venice. When the Allies entered Rome in June 1944, they found the studios deserted but intact, and turned them into a refugee camp.

The final defeat of the German forces in Italy in April 1945 left the country liberated but also under Allied military occupation pending an official transition to civilian government. The Italian film industry was saddled with a control commission dominated by American trade representatives (in military uniform), whose main objective was the reopening of the Italian market to American films. Within the Italian industry a sharp divide emerged between the exhibitors, who made common cause with the Americans in their eagerness to fill the cinemas with

The desperate search for the stolen bike – Zavattini/De Sica's *Bicycle Thieves*

the Hollywood films of which the public had been deprived during the war, and the producers (supported in this by the British on the commission), who wanted import restrictions at least for the time it would take to reconstruct the indigenous industry.

It was during this immediately post-war period, before the dismantled Italian film industry had been restructured in monopolistic form, that the neo-realist cinema was able to establish itself and to achieve a modest box-office success. This was also a period of political and social ferment, in which a radical cultural project such as that of Neo-Realism could enjoy a lot of political goodwill among the groupings that had emerged from the Resistance and in which a public could be found for an art which sought to reflect immediate reality in simple terms. Neo-Realism survived so long as these conditions lasted; when they began to change what survived was no longer Neo-Realism.

Aesthetically the 'realism' of the neo-realist movement consisted principally of a commitment to the representation of human reality. This commitment could not and did not translate itself into any precise technical or stylistic prescriptions. In so far as there were prescriptions for a specifically realist practice, these tended to be dictated by (or rationalisations of) material conditions and often to lead into contradictions. Thus a preference for visual authenticity (coupled with the non-

availablity of studio space) led to a lot of scenes being shot on location, both indoors and outdoors, and also to the use of non-professional actors. But a necessary corollary of this was that sound almost always had to be dubbed or post-synchronised (which was standard Italian practice for imported films anyway), and the dubbing was generally done, not by the people whose faces appeared on the screen, but by professionals. Visual style and that of the sound-track were thus regularly at odds with one another, with the former aspiring to a strong form of realism and the latter merely mimicking ordinary dramatic illusionism. If this contradiction was to be avoided – as, for example, in Visconti's *La terra trema* (1947), where the Sicilian fisherfolk speak their own lines in their native dialect – others would be generated. Thus in *La terra trema* the use of a dialect which most audiences would find incomprehensible breaks the dramatic illusion and imposes the need for a commentary; for commercial release on the home market the distributors in fact reverted to dubbing the film back into standard Italian. It is also noticeable that there is no consistency of camera and editing techniques in films of the neo-realist movement. The long-held deep-focus shot singled out by André Bazin as a distinguishing feature of Neo-Realism as well as of the style of Wyler and Welles, is not in fact very common. The incidence of cutaways and other elements of the editor's stock-in-trade is quite high, even in the films of Ros-

sellini which Bazin found stylistically so exemplary. For *Germany Year Zero* (1947), Rossellini shot the dramatic action of the film in the studio in Italy, set against back-projected material filmed on location in Berlin.

Neo-Realism in fact comprised a number of tendencies, which differed in their conception of realism as well as politically and in other ways. For a while these differences were masked, but with the break-up of the united anti-fascist 'front' and a political realignment imposed by the Cold War, the aesthetic differences also came to the fore. The disintegration of the movement in the early 50s also coincides with the successful re-establishment of a commercial industry, supported by a centre-right Christian Democrat government, able to produce popular films in competition with the Americans. Although the political left continued for some years to promote the idea of a national cinema based on neo-realist ideals, the idea that this cinema was a homogeneous entity and that it was, or could be, the true and only 'national cinema' became increasingly hard to sustain. By the end of the 1950s Neo-Realism had effectively disappeared, giving way to a mixture of 'art' and 'genre' films, some of which (e.g. 'underworld' pictures) contained a certain neo-realist heritage.

The core of original Neo-Realism – most typically represented by the work in tandem of director Vittorio De Sica and scriptwriter Cesare Zavattini (e.g. *Bicycle Thieves*, 1948, and *Umberto D*, 1951) – was a strongly humanist and reformist impulse. In Zavattini's conception, the honest portrayal of ordinary life would be sufficient to create a bond between audience and film such that the protagonist would display his or her inherent humanity and the audience would grasp the nature of the circumstances which had to change if that humanity was to display itself more fully. The preferred narrative mode was realist in the sense that fictional events were portrayed as if they were real and without the sort of dramatisation which would draw attention to their fictional character. Except in the immediately post-war period, when ordinary life was experienced in quite dramatic terms, the ordinariness and lack of drama of neo-realist films of this type gave them on the whole little appeal at the box office.

Flanking the humanists, on their left as it were, stood the Marxist tendency – represented for example by Luchino Visconti and Giuseppe De Santis. For the Marxists, a descriptive portrayal of ordinary life was not sufficient to convey a proper understanding of the circumstances to be struggled against. Increasingly the realism favoured by these film-makers came to be either contaminated by melodrama (rather splendidly in the case of De Santis' *Bitter Rice*, 1949) or reinterpreted in the light of Marxist aesthetic theory to become a 'critical realism' which

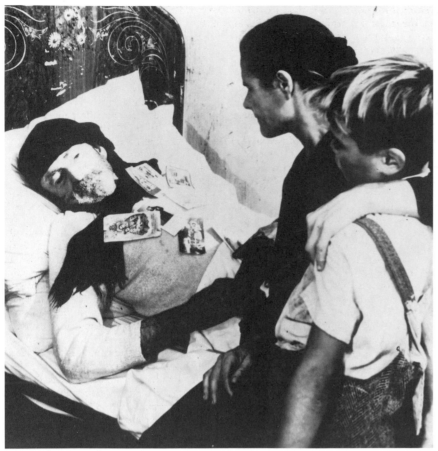

Death of a patriarch – Visconti's *La Terra Trema*

was avowedly non-naturalistic. The high point of this tendency comes with Visconti's *Senso* (1954), which is a costume picture that offers a highly dramatised figuration of personal and class conflict in a nineteenth-century Risorgimento setting. The political-aesthetic justification for such a radical change from the style of *La terra trema* was to be found in the debate about realism going on in Marxist circles in Italy where the *Prison Notebooks* of Antonio Gramsci had recently been published and the ideas of Georg Lukács were also beginning to circulate. An equally important consideration, however, was the change in the structure of the industry and in audience expectations. As well as being 'realist' in the Lukácsian sense of producing a narration that captures historical truth, *Senso* (starring Farley Granger and Alida Valli) was designed as a high-class entertainment film with export as well as home-market potential.

While the majority of the neo-realists remained aligned with the political left, where they were to be joined by a second wave of Italian film-makers such as Francesco Rosi and Pier Paolo Pasolini, there also existed tendencies which were either non-aligned or specifically aligned with Christian Democracy. The anti-fascist front, which had comprised all the democratic parties during and after the Resistance, broke up in 1947/48, leaving the Christian Democrats (the Catholic

Fellini's *La Strada* – the circus comes to town

party) at the head of a centre-right government, with the Socialists and Communists in opposition on the left and monarchist and neo-fascist parties on the right. Of the major neo-realist film-makers, Roberto Rossellini was the only one to throw in his lot squarely with the Christian Democrats, but other Catholic film-makers such as Federico Fellini sheltered within the same politico-cultural space and there also developed a generically Catholic form of sub-Neo-Realism which produced dramas of guilt and redemption. Although melodramatic in conception, these films borrowed many of the trappings of Neo-Realism, particularly in the choice of humdrum settings and an emphasis (Catholic, however, rather than left-reformist) on the nobility of poverty.

The case of Rossellini deserves treatment on its own. During the early part of the war, Rossellini had made feature films about the war and service life which were government-backed though not excessively fascistic in ideology. After the fall of Mussolini in 1943, he joined the anti-German Resistance and made the first Resistance feature, *Rome Open City*, in 1945. *Rome Open City* tells the story of a priest and a Communist partisan which ends with the partisan being tortured to death while the priest is forced to look on, and the priest then being shot. While the film celebrates Catholic–Communist unity in resistance to the Germans, its focus is spiritual rather than political and it is the priest rather than the partisan who is the real hero.

Rome Open City was followed by two other films about war and its aftermath, *Paisà* (1946) and *Germany Year Zero* (1947), which belong within the neo-realist mainstream, even though their existential Catholic tone is untypical of the movement as a whole. But with the series of films that he embarked on with Ingrid Bergman beginning with *Stromboli* (1949), and even more with his film about St. Francis (*Francesco, giullare di Dio*, 1950), Rossellini distanced himself emphatically from the rest of Neo-Realism. Not only is the spirituality even more prominent, but the address of the films is toward European and American audiences, rather than toward Italy itself. As a commercial ploy this was not successful – none of the films was a great box-office success and *Stromboli* was mangled by RKO for American release. But the choice of direction is significant since it mirrors the political priorities of the Christian Democrat government which was committed both to the Atlantic alliance and to Western European integration; it was also a deliberate repudiation of the 'national-popular' cultural strategy promoted by the Communists and supported by the rest of the left.

This political break with the rest of the neo-realist movement, however, did not mean that Rossellini should no longer be considered as a neo-realist in the aesthetic sense. Indeed the case has been made, most notably by André Bazin, that Rossellini was the truest neo-realist of all. For Bazin, Neo-Realism was an advance on conventional literary realism in that it was less constructed and, thanks to the camera, the film artist could work with immediate reality, filtering it through his/her consciousness, without having to impose an artificial purposive form on it. Bazin found this immediacy – an immediacy of things in themselves and an immediacy of the intervening consciousness – in Rossellini's films, far more than – for example – in the films of Visconti, which he judged realistic only in the conventional literary and theatrical sense. In a celebrated passage, defending Rossellini's *Journey to Italy* (1953) from its Lukácsian critics in Italy, Bazin wrote:

'With classical and with traditional realist art forms, I would say, the work of art is constructed like a house, of bricks or cut stone. There is no reason to question the usefulness of houses and their possible beauty, or the suitability of bricks for their construction, but it may be agreed that the reality of the brick lies less in its [physical] composition than in its shape and strength. One would not define it as a piece of clay and its mineral origin is irrelevant; what matters is the convenience of its volume. The brick is an element of the house, and this is already implicit in appearances themselves. Similarly the cut stones that make a bridge. They fit perfectly to form an arch. But blocks of stone scattered in a ford are and remain stones; their reality as stone is not altered by the fact that, by jumping from one to another, I can use them to cross the stream. If they provisionally performed the task of a bridge, this is due to the fact that I have been able to complement the accident of their layout with my own inventiveness and to perform the motion which, without modifying their nature or appearance, has provisionally given these stones a sense and a use' (Bazin, 'Défense de Rossellini', 1962, p. 157).

Although the metaphor (as he himself admitted) is a bit stretched, Bazin here hits on a quality that other critics too have felt to be present in many of Rossellini's films from *Paisà* onwards, and especially in *Europe '51* (1952) and *Journey to Italy*. The films give evidence of an *ad hoc* construction in which bits of the external world which happen to be there, together with reactions solicited from the actors/characters from the events of the filming/scenario, are fused together in an apparently unpremeditated way. It is not only the director but the spectator too who is being asked to 'make sense' by hopping over the stepping stones. Although Rossellini's films have their own forms of contrivance, including a strong dramatic push towards a moment of spiritual illumination, and sometimes bend reality towards their purposes, it is also often the case that the film is bent to submit to elements of reality which stand outside, or in the way of, the film-makers' intentions and plans. Politically fairly conservative, Rossellini was in this respect artistically extremely radical, and has since come to be recognised as such.

Once it had so visibly split, aesthetically and politically, there was no way that Neo-Realism was going to be reconstituted. The Italian cinema that followed the neo-realist phase of the late 40s and early 50s was very different in character. Neo-realist directors continued to make films, but with very few exceptions these films were not neo-realist. The revived commercial cinema which grew up alongside Neo-Realism was extremely eclectic. It had room for the occasional prestige production from Visconti or Fellini, but its staple was genre films. These genres included comedies and dramas of a type which had flourished under fascism in the 30s and had been temporarily eclipsed in the immediately post-war years. They also included fantasy and costume pictures, generally low-budget, which engaged the talents of such masters of the genre as Riccardo Freda, Mario Bava and Vittorio Cottafavi. Along with the dramas of Raffaello Matarazzo and others, these became the Italian popular cinema, which lasted until the cinema ceased to be the major popular art. By comparison Neo-Realism must be rated a popular cinema that might have been.

Sources
André Bazin, *Qu'est-ce que le cinéma?* Vol. IV, Paris, Éditions du Cerf, 1962; also in Gray (ed. and trans.), *What is Cinema?* Vol. II, Berkeley, University of California Press, 1971, p. 99.
José Luis Guarner, *Roberto Rossellini*, London, Studio Vista, 1970.
Geoffrey Nowell-Smith, *Visconti*, London, Secker and Warburg/BFI, 1967; rev. ed. 1973.
Sam Rohdie, 'A note on Italian cinema during fascism', Screen vol. 22 no. 4, 1981.

Paisà (Italy 1946 *p.c* – Organisation Films International/Foreign Film Productions; *d* – Roberto Rossellini; sd b/w 20)

Vivere in pace (Live in Peace) (Italy 1947 *p.c* – Lux Pao; *d* – Luigi Zampa; sd b/w 12)

La terra trema (Italy 1947 *p.c* – Universalia; *d* – Luchino Visconti; sd b/w 20)

Stromboli (Italy 1949 *p.c* – Be-Ro Film; *d* – Roberto Rossellini; sd b/w 20)

Umberto D (Italy 1952 *p.c* – Dear Films; *d* – Vittorio De Sica; sd b/w 10)

La signora senza cammelie (Italy 1953 *p.c* – Produzioni Domenico Forges Davanzati/ENIC; *d* – Michelangelo Antonioni; sd b/w 12)

La strada (Italy 1954 *p.c* – Ponti-De Laurentiis; *d* – Federico Fellini; sd b/w 9)

The New Wave in French cinema

The New Wave (*Nouvelle Vague*) blossomed for a brief period in the history of French cinema – between 1959 and 1963 – when certain historical, technological and economic factors combined to enable some young film-makers to influence French cinema temporarily in diverse ways. Commentators on the New Wave have tended to focus on the film-makers, ignoring the combination of factors which permitted them to work in the way they did. Roy Armes, for example, attributes the development of a New Wave of film-making to the emergence of a new generation of critics-turned-film-makers. According to Armes, at the beginning of the 1950s

'. . . the French cinema presented, on the surface at least, a rather depressing and moribund scene. No new director of the first rank had emerged . . . since 1949 and the veteran directors were showing their first signs of lassitude. Experiment was rare and the newcomers of the 40s were moving towards big-budget films and international co-productions . . . But beneath the surface things were stirring. Young critics under the guidance of André Bazin were laying the foundations of a new approach, particularly in *Cahiers du Cinéma*' (Armes, 1970, p. 7).

Another critic, James Monaco, begins more cautiously with the term 'New Wave' itself, admitting that, like most such critical labels, it resists easy definition. According to Monaco, the term was first used by Françoise Giroud in 1958 to refer to a 'youthful' spirit in contemporary cinema, but it swiftly became a synonym for the avant-garde in general. For Monaco himself, however, the term refers much more specifically to the work during a certain period of five film-makers – Truffaut, Godard, Chabrol, Rohmer and Rivette – who shared a common film intellectual background influenced on the one hand by Henri Langlois, founder of the *Cinémathèque Française*, and on the other by André Bazin, co-founder of the film magazine *Cahiers du Cinéma*:

'Astruc sounded the call; Langlois provided the material; Bazin supplied the basic architectonics. In the pages of *Cahiers du Cinéma* in the 1950s, Truffaut, Godard, Chabrol, Rohmer and Rivette argued out a new theory of film' (Monaco, 1976, p. vii).

This theory hinged on two crucial propositions: the first was that of individual authorship in cinema, the *politique des auteurs* (→ AUTHORSHIP: *The 'politique des auteurs'*, p. 134); the second was that of cinematic genre, of creative conventions in film language. Although simple enough, these ideas seemed at the time perverse, and indeed they served a polemical function in the context of critical attitudes in currency at the time. The New Wave directors have been considered as a unitary group, therefore, largely on the grounds of their common intellectual background. The five film-makers isolated by Monaco, for example, had all written for *Cahiers du Cinéma*, and even other directors associated with the New Wave who had not been critics had usually learned about cinema as consumers rather than as producers: of all the major film-makers of the New Wave, only Alexandre Astruc, Roger Vadim and Louis Malle had any previous experience in the film industry.

Armes and Monaco are thus able to explain the New Wave aesthetic in terms of film criticism, pointing to a critical response to French cinema of the 1940s – a cinema of classical virtues, literary scripts, smooth photography, elegant décor. These virtues had been repeatedly attacked by Truffaut, among others, in the pages of *Cahiers du Cinéma*. By contrast, the aesthetic of New Wave cinema was improvisational (unscripted), and its photography and editing were far less mannered than its predecessors. The fragmented style of many New Wave films thus came in part as a response to the cohesiveness of 'quality' French cinema. Apparent improvisations in camera technique (the long take, the freeze frame) editing (the jump cut) dialogue, plot and performance were all deployed because cinema was seen for the first time not as a neutral form through which something else (literature or 'reality') could be transmitted, but as a specific aesthetic system, a language in itself.

Why was this aesthetic initiative undertaken when it was? One of the New Wave directors, François Truffaut, has described how 'at the end of 1959 there was a kind of euphoric ease in production that would have been unthinkable a couple of years earlier' (interview with Truffaut, in Graham, 1968, p. 9). According to Durgnat:

'The invention of fast emulsions led to low budgets, minimum crews, location work and "independent" finance. These new styles in aesthetics and production accompany new thematic perspectives . . . Commercially, the *raison d'être* of the New Wave was a renewal of tone and theme (the industry was already speaking of a "*crise des sujets*") and the cheapness of the films' budgets' (Durgnat, 1963, pp. 3–4).

During the 1950s, the film industry in France had been very closed. However, when Roger Vadim's film *And Woman was Created* (1956) was a commercial success despite its low budget, the industry did open its doors for a while to low-budget productions, encouraging a climate of experimentation (→ AUTHORSHIP: *French film-making context*, p. 134). The New Wave constituted an attempt to make saleable films cheaply through reduced shooting schedules, the use of natural locations, day and night shooting out in the streets, and the employment of small units. The New Wave may in fact be compared with Italian Neo-Realism in this respect, since both operated under similar material constraints (← p. 36). However, the influence of television is also apparent in New Wave cinema in a way it could not be in Neo-Realism. 'A certain kind of reportage and "direct" camera (shooting with a hand-held camera; an acting style closer to the interview than the theatre) came into fashion . . .' (Siclier, 'New Wave and French cinema', 1961, p. 117).

One of the few writers who has dealt in any depth with the economic, ideological

And Woman was Created – a commercial success with Brigitte Bardot

Influence of 'all things American' in
A bout de souffle

and political underpinnings of the New Wave is Terry Lovell. She offers an outline of the characteristic qualities of New Wave film-making:

'The lack of any social dimension is one of the most notable features of the typical New Wave film. Its heroes are neither personally or socially integrated, and are dissociated from their social roles. These are,

in any case, difficult or impossible to identify. They are marginal men, disaffected intellectuals, students and in one case (Rohmer's *Sign of the Lion*), a rather high-class tramp. Interest centres exclusively on immediate face-to-face relations. They have no family ties that are apparent, and on the whole, no political affiliations: action is for its own sake, having no further end, arbitrary and motiveless. There are no social antecedents of action, only emotional and volitional. There is no point of contact between the individual and society, nor are these anomic lives placed in any broader context within which they can be understood. The milieu of the individual exhausts the film's compass . . .

. . . This stands in marked contrast to the naive realism of the films of the 1940s and 1950s. Stylistic and technical innovations are equally marked. In addition to new cadres of directors and actors, certain cameramen and other technical experts emerged, and were specifically associated with New Wave films' (Lovell, 'Sociology of aesthetic structures', 1972, pp. 341-342).

Lovell goes on to describe a number of the social conditions underlying the existence of the New Wave: the advent of Gaullism, peace in Algeria, the post-war economic miracle, and a crisis in the role of the French intellectual. However, she places greater emphasis on determinants relating more immediately to cinema and the film industry, including:

'the huge influx of American films upon

the market immediately after the war, in the circumstances in which the American allies were also liberators. This influx may have something to do with the near-obsession with all things American and especially with American movies, which the New Wave evidenced so strongly in both its films and in its critical judgements' (Lovell, 1972, p. 343).

Another significant feature of the industrial context of the New Wave, according to Lovell, is the horizontal structure of the French film industry – in contrast with the vertical integration of the American industry (← *The studios*, p. 10) – and the fact that State intervention in French film production is greater than in any other non-socialist country. She concludes however, that:

'such conditions, being relatively stable over time, cannot explain the emergence of the New Wave. More proximate causes relate to the crisis in the industry in the 1950s. The history of the French film industry is a history of crises. After the war the Blum Byrnes agreement resulted in a flood of American films, with which a war-damaged indigenous industry could not compete. The 1949 Temporary Aid Law was ameliorative, but the situation remained precarious. Many well-established directors were unable to work, or did so at a much reduced rate. Clair, Autant-Lara, Becker, Duvivier and Carné had each directed only one film between 1945 59. The opportunity structure for film personnel was extremely poor. This

Les Quatre cents coups (The 400 Blows) (France 1958 *p.c* – Les Films du Carosse, SEDIF; *d* – François Truffaut; sd b/w 20)

'When I was shooting *Les Quatre cents coups* I was horrified to see that my budget – about £20,000 – had gone up to £25,000. I got into a panic, and felt I had involved myself in something that would not easily make a profit. But once it was finished the film more than paid for itself, what with the Cannes Film Festival and sales abroad. In the USA alone it was bought for £35,000' (Interview with Truffaut, in Graham, 1968, p. 9).

In 1958 Truffaut was banned from the Cannes Film Festival for his violent denunciation of festivals and his uncompromising attitude to most of the films shown there. The following year *Les Quatre cents coups* was the official French entry at Cannes and Truffaut won the Best Director award. James Monaco has pointed out that the film's 'instant critical and commercial success not only afforded Truffaut considerable artistic independence right from the beginning of his career, but also made it much easier for other *Cahiers* critics turned film-makers to finance their own projects; at least a modicum of success

for the new movement in film was assured' (Monaco, 1976, p. 13).

A bout de souffle (Breathless) (France 1959 *p.c* – SNC; *d* – Jean-Luc Godard; sd b/w 20)

In early 1959 Jean-Luc Godard offered four scripts to film financier Georges de Beauregard, one of which was the screenplay of *A bout de souffle*. Beauregard accepted the script and on a very small budget (400,000 francs) Godard shot and edited the film between 17 August and 15 September. The film finally premièred in Paris on March 16 1960 and was a considerable critical and small-scale commercial success. According to the Chronology in *Focus on Godard*, Beauregard eventually recouped more than 150 million francs on his investment (p. 21). Although Godard directed, scripted and edited the film, it was based on an idea by François Truffaut, and Claude Chabrol was artistic supervisor – typical of the way in which the *Cahiers* group collaborated on their early films, an aesthetic factor but also an economic one. *A bout de souffle* is dedicated to Monogram Pictures, a Hollywood 'B' movie studio of the 1930s and 40s, and, in James Monaco's words 'it is a film about film

noirs' (Monaco, 1976, p. 120). In this extract the sequence of the police pursuit of Michel's car, the shooting, and the poster of Humphrey Bogart all refer to the conventions of the American gangster film/thriller, but at the same time these references could have the function of easing the film into an international market. Jean Seberg, who plays Patricia, had recently starred in Preminger's *Saint Joan* and here plays an 'American in Paris' role which would also be familiar to the international audience.

This extract is from the beginning of the film, including the dedication to Monogram and continuing with Jean-Paul Belmondo's attempt to model himself on Humphrey Bogart. We first see him reading a comic, wearing a hat and smoking a cigarette very much in the hard-boiled Hollywood mould. Behind him his silhouette in a shop window echoes images from low-budget film noirs of the 1940s. Later in the extract we see Belmondo in front of a poster for *The Harder They Fall* stroking his lip Bogart-style. The construction of the narrative in this sequence is characteristically inconsequential, consisting of fragmented monuments from a petty →

situation was exacerbated from the point of view of new entrants by the policy of using well-known actors and directors, in adaptations of literary works to prestige productions, aimed at the foreign market. (It is interesting that it was precisely these films with which the New Wave competed. They tended to have a cool reception in France initially, followed by success abroad, and a renewed interest at home). Union regulations were formidable, though loosely enforced.

The crisis in the cinema tradionally and misleadingly associated with the advent of television came late in France, and can be dated almost precisely at 1957. At the same time, "quality films" were waning in their success. The old formula was failing, and the result was a widespread openness to innovation. The success of Vadim's *And Woman was Created* let loose the flood' (Lovell, 1972, pp. 345–346).

Lovell concludes that in spite of the considerable critical, theoretical and aesthetic achievements of the French New Wave:

'At the structural level, it resulted in little change. Controls were if anything tighter than they had been previously. Initial capital requirements, for instance, for a film were raised out of all proportion to increased costs, in order to deter ill-considered ventures. Union requirements were more strictly enforced. The net result was merely that a generation of film-makers were able to force an entry into a moribund industry, without in any way changing its structure so as to make it any easier for future generations' (Lovell, 1972, pp. 346–347).

Although the French New Wave is thought of as a national movement, it also had some distinctly international traits. It could be argued that its self-conscious references to Hollywood were an attempt to provide effective competition for the American films which threatened to invade French cinema screens, and at the same time made inroads into the American home market itself. Moreover, New Wave films made explicit reference to other national and international film movements: Italian Neo-Realism, for example, and European art cinema, which, although primarily deployed for aesthetic reasons, could help their insertion into other European markets. A number of New Wave films were European co-productions: *Le Feu follet* was a French-Italian co-production, *La Guerre est finie* was French-Swedish, *Pierrot le fou* was French-Italian as was *Adieu Philippine*. The looseness of the plots of these films – as of other productions of this period – together with the often minimal and desultory dialogue, the fragmented scenes and shots, may perhaps have made them more easily understood by foreign audiences, who would also probably recognise the familiar Parisian and/or Mediterranean locations. It may even be argued that the geographical locations of New Wave films correspond to a tourist's view of France in general and of Paris in particular – the café (*La Peau douce, A bout de souffle, Bande à part, Masculin/Féminin*), the airport (*Une Femme mariée, Bande à part*), Paris streets at night (*Les Quatre cents coups, La Peau douce, A bout de souffle, Une Femme mariée, Bande à part, Masculin/Féminin*, etc.), sun-drenched summer in the countryside (*Pierrot le fou*). And, of course, the New Wave had its own easily recognisable 'stars' – Jean-Paul Belmondo in *A bout de souffle* and *Pierrot le fou*, Jeanne Moreau in *Jules et Jim*, Jean-Pierre Léaud in *Les Quatre cents, coups* and *Masculin/Féminin* – whose international familiarity might ease the films' insertion into both domestic and foreign markets.

Sources
Roy Armes, *French Cinema since 1946*, Vol. 2, London, A. Zwemmer Ltd., 1970.
Royal S. Brown (ed.), *Focus on Godard*, Englewood Cliffs N.J., Prentice-Hall, 1972.
Raymond Durgnat, *Nouvelle Vague: the first decade*, Loughton, Essex, Motion Publications, 1963.
Peter Graham (ed.), *The New Wave: critical landmarks*, London, Secker and Warburg/BFI, 1968.
Terry Lovell, 'Sociology of aesthetic structures and contextualism', in McQuail (ed.), *Sociology of Mass Communications*, Harmondsworth, Middlesex, Penguin, 1972.
James Monaco, *The New Wave*, New York, Oxford University Press, 1976.
Jacques Siclier, 'New Wave and French cinema', *Sight and Sound* vol. 30 no. 3, Summer 1961.

criminal milieu – stealing a car, taking money from a girlfriend's purse, being pursued by two motor-cycle cops and, later, two plainclothes men. The dialogue is both perfunctory and perverse: 'It's nice in the country . . . I like France a lot' says Belmondo to camera as he drives a stolen car through the provinces.

Adieu Philippine (France 1961–62
p.c – Unitec France/Alpha Productions/Rome-Paris Films/Euro-International Films; *d* – Jacques Rozier; sd b/w 12)

Director Jacques Rozier had already worked in television (and made several short films), which may help explain the laboured parody of television commercials to which a long episode is devoted. According to Roy Armes:

'The circumstances of production and distribution, which resulted in the film's waiting two years for release, have given it an undeserved reputation of an unacknowledged masterpiece. Rozier exceeded his budget and failed to meet completion dates, taking a year to complete the film, including five months spent recovering the film's improvised dialogue for post-synchronisation' (Armes, 1970, p. 178–179).

For Armes the film's 'chief qualities are its youthful vitality, and the improvised *cinéma-vérité* style of the language, characters and settings', while its weaknesses are largely those of construction: 'it is a disjointed and often somewhat incoherent telling of what is in essence a simple story . . .' (p. 179). It was precisely these qualities of narrative disjuncture which attracted film theorist Christian Metz, who subjected *Adieu Philippine* to a syntagmatic analysis (→ NARRATIVE AND STRUCTURALISM: *Metz*, p. 229).

Bande à part (France 1964
p.c – Anouchka Films/Orsay Films; *d* – Jean-Luc Godard; sd b/w 14 + 8)

Bande à part is a feature-length film shot in twenty-five days. Godard has described how such restraints can be creative:

'I always like to have a balance between the shooting of a film and its financing, between the budget and the subject . . . It's in that vein that I shot the film in twenty-five days. I always like to impose restraints on myself. I never agree with the conditions my producers set up, simply because these are never the right conditions with respect to the film's subject' (interview with Godard in Brown, 1972, pp. 41–42).

Godard's description of his mode of production echoes that of 1940s American films. To achieve the necessary 'balance' Godard set up his own production company, Anouchka Films. *Bande à part* is based on a *série noir* novel *Fool's Gold*, and is another example of Godard's critical interest in and capitalisation on the American cinema, specifically here the musical and gangster genres. In Extract I the three characters – Arthur, Odile and Franz – are sitting in a café with little to say. Then they dance to a record on the juke box in a tribute to the non-narrative choreography of the Hollywood musical. Their dance – or rather the music for their dance – is repeatedly interrupted by a voice-over commentary on the characters: 'It is time to open another parenthesis and describe our characters' feelings'. Outside in the night-time streets of Paris we see Odile and Arthur drive past a *Nouvelle Vague* nightspot. There is another similarly self-conscious moment somewhat later in the extract when they observe a boy with an unhappy expression on the metro and consider different 'readings' of that expression according to alternative fictional contexts – the package he is holding is either a teddy bear or a bomb.

Ealing Studios – on street location

The British Film industry

Ealing Studios

In 1929 a company called Associated Talking Pictures was set up to exploit the advent of cinematic sound in Britain. In 1931 the company built its own sound-equipped studio in Ealing and by 1936 some sixty films had been made there, about half of them by ATP, the rest by various independents. In the financial year 1937–38, however, extravagant over-production took its toll, forcing several studios to close down. The government responded to the crisis with a revised quota system to protect and promote British films, but American production companies were quick to exploit loopholes in the quota legislation. MGM, for instance, set up a British studio at Borehamwood making films for Anglo-American audiences with American stars and creative staff, British technicians and facilities and 'transatlantic' subjects. The first of three such MGM productions of the period was *A Yank at Oxford*; on its release MGM's Borehamwood production head, Michael Balcon, whose hopes of making high-quality Anglo-American films for the world market had been frustrated, resigned, and by the end of the year replaced Basil Dean who had retired after running ATP since its inception. Ealing Studios Limited, which had previously been no more than a holding company for ATP's studio lot, became a production company and ATP was quietly phased out.

During the 1940s Britain produced an annual average of forty feature films: of these Ealing studios provided about five. To maximise profits, Ealing and its rivals would obviously benefit from an arrangement with one of the three major cinema circuits – ABC, Odeon and Gaumont-British. By 1941 Odeon and Gaumont-British were both owned by J. Arthur Rank, who controlled 70% of Britain's studio space as well as being the biggest single domestic distributor. In 1944 Rank signed an agreement with Ealing guaranteeing the screening, as top of the bill attractions, of all its features as well as providing 50% of the company's finances. In 1952 Rank increased its financial interest to 75%, but in 1955 the relationship came to an end, and the studios at Ealing were sold to the British Broadcasting Corporation (BBC). Television had been encroaching on cinema audiences for some years and the advent of commercial television

proved a major setback to Rank and Ealing. Ealing struggled on as a production company until 1959, operating from MGM's Borehamwood premises.

This sketch of the history of Ealing Studios is taken from the work of two writers on the history of Ealing, Charles Barr (1977) and John Ellis (1975). While Barr concentrates on the atmosphere of the studio and the attitudes of its personnel, Ellis examines its economic and institutional structures. Barr begins his book with analysis of an example of what he sees as the studio's characteristic product. This analysis explores the analogy between the world of the film and the world of Ealing. The film in question is *Cheer Boys Cheer* (1939), which concerns the competition between a small family brewery and a large impersonal beer factory. The two firms are called Greenleaf and Ironside and, Barr argues, these names and firms stand not only for England and Germany but also for Ealing and Rank/MGM. The relation between the stories told on the screen and the experiences of the studio itself is a central theme of Barr's book.

Barr establishes that Ealing, like Greenleaf, was 'a small production centre' with 'the air of a family business, set on the village green' (Barr, 1977, p. 6). Ealing, Barr suggests, exemplifies one of the two choices for the film industry in post-war Britain, the small business; the other, collaboration with the Americans, Barr sees as epitomised by Borehamwood.

In attempting to trace the relation between the stories told on the screen and the experience of the studio itself, Barr is aware of the problems of a simple 'reflection' thesis in which the films act as a mirror for England, or for the studio. And he admits that 'the celebration of the little man, of the small-scale enterprise, is a traditional theme not confined to Ealing or to England; one need only refer to Frank Capra's Hollywood comedies of the thirties' (Barr, 1977, p. 6). Clearly, an equation which simply revises the traditional slogan: 'film reflects society', to read: 'film reflects studio' is somewhat problematic. Nevertheless, attention to industrial determinations can throw considerable light on the aesthetics of a studio's products, and not only at a level of analogy or internal reference. John Ellis, in an article on Ealing ('Made in Ealing', 1975) has attempted to provide such economic and organisational data.

Ellis's emphasis is on the economics, technology and industrial organisation of Ealing. He establishes that the studio's average of five films per year were all 'A' features almost all with 'U' certificates, running some 80 or 90 minutes each and costing between £120,000 and £200,000 with the comedies averaging out at about £160,000. Each film would take about 8 to 10 weeks to shoot with an average of about two minutes screen time completed every day. Ealing had its own pre-production and post-production departments at the studio including scripting and advertising as well as having access (between 1944 and 1955) to Rank's laboratories. The studio employed about 400 people and Ellis cites figures which support Michael Balcon's contention that at Ealing 'the most important work is done before and after a film goes on the floor' (quoted in Ellis, 1975, p. 93). Under Balcon's leadership studio production was stabilised with a contract staff of about 50 who constituted Ealing's 'creative élite' of directors, producers, editors, scriptwriters and cinematographers, protected by a system of internal staff promotion and a regular 'round table' discussion of present and future projects at which all 'creative' personnel could have a say (→ AUTHORSHIP: *Ealing Studios*, p. 160). Director Alexander Mackendrick has since commented: 'We weren't paid much but we had the advantage of being very free' (interview in *Positif* no. 92, 1968), but the extent of that freedom seems to have depended to a large extent on the agreement of the staff's attitudes with those of Balcon, who had clear ideas about the boundaries within which the studio should work: 'Nothing would induce us to do anything against the public interest just for the sake of making money' (quoted in Ellis, 1975, p. 123). Ellis argues that the extremely tight production conditions had precise effects, and describes Ealing's overall aesthetic as a combination of bland studio lighting, short takes and static camera shots, little or no reliance on 'atmospheric' music and an unsual emphasis on dialogue and performance – and thus on scripting and casting, both pre-production elements. Location sequences were kept to an economic minimum unless, of course, they cost less than sequences shot in the studio. Thus in *The Lavender Hill Mob* a scene originally scripted for Victoria Station was rewritten for Northolt Airport at 'a tenth of the price' (quoted in Ellis, 1975, p. 98).

With the signing of the 1944 Rank-Ealing agreement, the studio was able to step up its production schedule and resume its pre-war policy of assembling a stable roster of contract staff while mapping out a path along which the company could profitably travel in the years to come. Charles Barr identifies the period until 1943 with the war films, and the period after 1947/48 with 'Ealing comedies', arguing that the films produced in the interval between these periods 'cover a greater

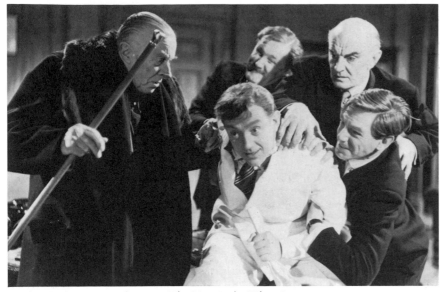

Made in Ealing's pinnacle year – *The Man in the White Suit*

range than before or since' (Barr, 1977, p. 50). Following Ellis, it might be argued that industrial conditions determined such a variety. A film like *Dead of Night* (1945) explores the possibilities of an unfamiliar (to Ealing) genre and, as an anthology, allows several apprentice talents to be tried out at less than feature length. But *Dead of Night* was an isolated experiment for Ealing. The studio consequently retreated to the cosy, familiar, rational, domestic world of the comedies. In Barr's terms 'Ealing became typed as the safe, respectable, 'U'-certificate British cinema par excellence' (Barr, 1977, p. 58). Why did Ealing fail to follow up the experiment of *Dead of Night*, which was by no means a commercial disaster? One possible explanation is Balcon's admission in an interview than 'none of us would ever suggest any subject, whatever its box-office potential, if it were socially objectionable or doubtful. We want to achieve box-office success, of course, but we consider it our primary task to make pictures worthy of that name' (quoted in Barr, 1977, p. 58). Yet if this is true how did the 'horrific' *Dead of Night* ever slip through Ealing's self-censorship? Barr has argued that the supernatural nature of the film's subject sanctions its ideologically 'doubtful' content, while its episodic form functions to guarantee that those very elements remain at the level of suggestions.

If *Dead of Night* represents a closed avenue for Ealing, *The Lavender Hill Mob* (1951) and *The Man in the White Suit* (1951) are examples of the path the studio did choose to follow, that of comedy. 1951 was a pinnacle year for Ealing, as for the British film industry as a whole. Between 1942 and 1951 no one came in as a director from outside the studio, and a stable core of contract players and creative personnel transformed it into the cinematic equivalent of a repertory theatre company. In 1951 British censorship regulations were relaxed and the 'X' certificate was intro-

duced. But in 1952 the Rank-Ealing agreement was revised, and only three years later terminated. Attendances at film theatres were falling off sharply, film production costs were spiralling and American companies were finding it easier than ever before to exploit the British market. Moreover, in 1952 the BBC finally achieved its ambition of national television transmission, and in the following year some two million TV sets were tuned in to watch the Coronation. The cinema circuits could compete only by offering feature-length Technicolor coverage of the same event some weeks later.

In this period of low receipts and increasing competition from both television and American cinema, other film companies responded by exploiting subjects unavailable to television (e.g. Hammer and the horror film), thus differentiating their products from those of the competition. Ealing, too, had either to change its production values radically or to cease production. In the end the company took the latter course.

Sources

Charles Barr, *Ealing Studios*, London, Cameron and Tayleur/Newton Abbot, David and Charles, 1977.

John Ellis, 'Made in Ealing', *Screen* vol. 16 no. 1, Spring 1975.

Dead of Night (UK 1945 *p.c* – Ealing Studios; *d* – Robert Hamer (*The Haunted Mirror*); sd b/w 15)

The Lavender Hill Mob (UK 1951 *p.c* – Ealing Studios; *d* – Charles Crichton; sd b/w 10)

The Man in the White Suit (UK 1951 *p.c* – Ealing Studios; *d* – Alexander Mackendrick; sd b/w 18)

Hammer Productions

Hammer Productions Limited was first registered as a film company in 1934, but soon after disappeared for almost a decade. In the wake of a shortlived exhibition quota imposed by protectionist postwar legislation (the Dalton Duty, 1947–48), Hammer's controlling company, Exclusive Films was 'encouraged by the ABC cinema circuit to supply low-budget supporting features . . . [and] . . . this was the impetus for reforming Hammer' (Eyles, 1973, p. 22). Very rapidly it became company policy to produce films which could 'capitalise on subjects and characters that were pre-sold to the public either through radio and television or via myth and legend' (Pirie, 1973, p. 26). Adaptations of recent BBC radio programmes proved a particularly reliable and profitable source and a cycle of low-budget 'B' feature quota quickies was launched, featuring such familiar radio characters as Dick Barton, PC 49 and The Man in Black.

Between 1948 and 1950 Hammer moved its production base several times from one large country house to another. The decision to use country houses rather than studios was determined by cost factors, and it proved to be one of the company's most important policy decisions, for it gave the films a distinctive style and put them in the ideal position to recreate historical/mythical subjects. In 1951 Hammer finally settled at Bray in Berkshire, in a large building which housed the company until 1968. Also in 1951 Hammer negotiated an agreement with an independent American producer, Robert Lippert, which guaranteed a 20th Century-Fox release for their product in return, among other things, for Hammer's agreement to employ American stars in leading roles to ease their films into the US market. For almost four years Hammer produced 'B' films starring American actors such as Zachary Scott, Paul Henreid and Cesar Romero, with the result that American studios began to see the benefits of low-budget British production of supporting features. But when the Americans withdrew from this arrangement around 1954, Hammer, like the rest of the British film industry found themselves in a critical position.

'. . .An industry observer might very well have written Hammer off . . . Bray Studios lay miserably empty for twelve months apart from a series of featurettes and one particularly dreary 'B' feature . . . If the 1954 films had failed or had had only a routine success it is not impossible that the whole course of British film history might have been very different' (Pirie, 1973, p. 27).

Characteristically, Hammer negotiated this crisis by changing their production policy as the structure of the industry and the expectations of the audiences changed. In the mid-1950s there were a number of such changes for the company to exploit. At the beginning of the decade there existed three main cinema circuits in Britain – Odeon, Gaumont-British and ABC. Rank owned both Odeon and Gaumont-British and had an agreement with Ealing. ABC, who already had a long-standing agreement with Hammer, may have decided that a degree of differentiation from Rank's Ealing comedy 'family audiences' policy was worth attempting (← *Ealing Studios*, p. 43). Since the relaxation of British film censorship and the introduction of the 'X' certificate in 1951, Rank had only very rarely exhibited 'adults only' films. Indeed, only one 'X' was screened in Rank cinemas in 1956, and only fourteen in the entire decade. ABC, on the other hand, showed more than fifty 'X's in the 1950s, many of which came from Hammer. The mid-1950s also saw an expansion in the black-and-white television industry, with each new TV licence 'costing' approximately 100 cinema attendances a year (Limbacher, n.d., p. 15). Hammer's decision to exploit colour and 'X' certificate material at this point set them on the road to success. The house at Bray provided the perfect location for the period of intensive production and expansion that followed. At Bray, Hammer became

'... a production company utterly unlike anything that the British cinema had previously known. There is a very slight echo of Ealing in the structure that emerged, but perhaps the most obvious analogy is with one of the small Hollywood studios of the 1930s and 40s like Republic or Monogram; for almost overnight Hammer became a highly efficient factory for a vast series of exploitation pictures made on tight budgets with a repertory company of actors and a small, sometimes over-exposed series of locations surrounding their tiny Buckinghamshire estate' (Pirie, 1973, p. 42).

This set-up combined with a continuity of personnel at all levels throughout the company enabled Hammer to produce a distinctive and professional product at low cost. Anthony Hinds, a producer and prolific screenwriter at Hammer, has summarised the studio's aesthetic/economic policy with the slogan 'Put the money on the screen' (quoted in *Little Shoppe of Horrors* no. 4, p. 40). Certainly, in the 1960s, when Hammer's budgets averaged at about £120,000 per film, £15,000 or even £20,000 would be spent on sets and décor, with additional amounts on lighting, Technicolor and occasionally wide screens. Scripts, on the other hand, were much less expensive, deriving as they did almost entirely from radio, television, theatre, published works, myth, legend and, of course, other films.

Hammer's move into the horror cycle for which they became famous was by no means simple, though it was certainly facilitated both by the economic and industrial conditions just described, and by the social climate of Britain in the 50s (Pirie, 1980). The decision was helped by

the peculiar attributes of the company's set-up at Bray:

'... the studio was a partial anachronism, out of time and out of place. All the other small self-contained British studios run by production companies were in the process of closing down or selling out to television ... But in a way, it was the very old fashioned nature of the production set-up at Bray which made it so ideal as a focal point for Hammer's recreation of its own horrific version of nineteenth-century Europe. Bray could present the past because it was the past' (Pirie, 1980, p. 13).

And, paradoxically, American financial interests in the British film industry also contributed to the success of Hammer's choice of the British gothic novel tradition as a source of inspiration. Pirie has described how

'By the 1950s production in Hollywood had become so costly that Britain became a viable filmmaking centre for low-cost production. One of the advantages for American producers was that they could in this way spend some of the money earned from distribution in Britain which the Anglo-American Agreement of 1948 prohibited them from converting from pounds into dollars ...' (Pirie, 1980, p. 4).

According to this Agreement, American companies could only take an annual amount of £17 million out of Britain. There were, however, ways round this

Productions, p. 162) made Hammer an attractive investment for American companies and allowed the American film industry to secure an economic foothold in Britain. For a while Hammer profited enormously from this kind of arrangement, but the bubble was to burst when the Americans eventually pulled out, leaving the British film industry in a great many difficulties (→ *British social realism 1959–63*, p. 47). But perhaps the most influential factor was the company's ability to capitalise on the situation when their luck broke with the success of *The Quatermass Xperiment*. In 1954, like Ealing ten years before, Hammer were being forced to experiment to find a new product and a new market. One 1954 production was the studio's first film in Technicolor, *Men of Sherwood Forest*. Another film, much more successful, was an experiment with a new genre – horror: *The Quatermass Xperiment* (1955) combined the then unfamiliar territory of horror with the science fiction elements which Hammer had already explored in films like *Spaceways* (1952). Moreover, the eccentric spelling of the word 'experiment' in the title capitalised upon the film's 'X' certificate while also functioning as ready-made publicity. Furthermore, it was an adaptation of an already very successful BBC serial, first broadcast in July and August of 1953. 'The film opened at the London Pavilion

The Quatermass Xperiment – 'X' certificate

prohibition, co-production of films or co-ownership of facilities among them. It was, for instance, the loan capital of the National Film Finance Corporation which paid for the production of *The Curse of Frankenstein* (1957) but the film was distributed by Warner Bros. Similarly, the Eady Levy, which returned a proportion of box-office takings to the production companies of the respective best grossing British films, was so slack in defining nationality that American subsidiaries or partnerships could easily profit from it. The 'Britishness' of films set in the Victorian period and featuring a decadent aristocracy (→ AUTHORSHIP: *Hammer*

on Friday 26 August 1955 with Hammer's fortunes at their lowest ebb and immediately began breaking box office records both here and subsequently in America' (Pirie, 1973, p. 28).

After the unexpected success of *The Quatermass Xperiment*, Hammer commissioned another science fiction script as well as a *Quatermass* sequel. Pirie points to the relationship between the themes that Hammer (and in due course many other film companies) began to approach in 1956, and the political events in the country during those crucial twelve months (Pirie, 1973, p. 31). On the very day that the greatest British anxiety movie

Taste the Blood of Dracula – marked the decline of Hammer horror

of all, *Quatermass II* (1956), followed *X – The Unknown* (1956) into production at Bray, a headline in *The Times* read 'Giant H-Bomb Dropped'. Both films received 'X' certificates in Britain and were distributed as adult entertainment: once again the title *X–The Unknown* simultaneously exploited and re-emphasised its certificate. In the same year, 1956, the Production Code of the Motion Picture Association of America was revised and relaxed, which widened the market for Hammer's product in the United States. Nevertheless, for Hammer to survive the demise of the double bill it was necessary for the studio to shake off their 'B' feature reputation and explore entirely new generic avenues: to do this, however, they needed the American market. Hammer was thus encouraged to continue employing American actors in leading roles: Dean Jagger as the Professor in *X–The Unknown*, for example, and Brian Donlevy as Quatermass.

Pirie argues in *A Heritage of Horror* that it is easy to underestimate the aesthetic and economic risk Hammer were taking in 1956 when the decision was made to elevate horror to a privileged role in their production hierarchy. 'By the time *Quatermass II* finished filming in July 1956 Hammer had more or less finalised plans for a complete change in their output . . . No less than ten projects were abandoned in 1956' and in their place 'Hammer embarked on their most significant and ambitious venture so far, *The Curse of Frankenstein* which went into production at Bray on 19 November' (Pirie, 1973, p. 38), and enjoyed enormous international success.

'*Dracula* went into production at Bray about a year after the shooting of *The Curse of Frankenstein*, in November 1957 . . . While the *Frankenstein* film had been made on behalf of Warners, the new *Dracula* was sponsored by Universal, the same American studio which had fathered the whole horror movie tradition in Hollywood during the 1930s with Karloff and Lugosi . . . The final seal was set on Hammer's new status in the summer of 1958 when *Dracula* began to register its enormous success all over the world. Universal announced at this point that they would turn over to Hammer the remake rights of their entire library of horror movies' (Pirie, 1973, p. 43).

Sir James Carreras, then head of Hammer, has explained the studio's initial interest in the horror genre (rather than in sci-fi) as the result of a realisation that there had never been a *Frankenstein* or a *Dracula* in colour. Colour certainly differentiated Hammer's remakes from Universal's monochrome horror films, but this in itself was not enough. At this time, Universal's copyright expressly forbade imitation of the make-up and the neck bolts of the earlier *Frankenstein*, and for similar reasons on *Dracula* (1957) (retitled *Horror of Dracula* in the US to avoid confusion with the original) Hammer's sets were designed so as to be as unlike those in the American version as possible.

It has been estimated that between them *Dracula* and *The Curse of Frankenstein* grossed more than $4 million. That two such inexpensive films could be such a gigantic success was due in part to the

interest of the American market. It also meant that sequels, spin-offs and so on were bound to follow. Eventually, having received the rights to remake Universal's entire horror library, and finally released from the copyright problems that had plagued the productions of *Dracula* and *Frankenstein*, Hammer embarked on a series of adaptations of Universal's 1930's tales of the supernatural. The proven success of previous entries in the series prompted Rank to reconsider its virtual embargo on Hammer horror films, and *The Mummy* (1959) was released in Britain not by ABC but by Rank's Odeon circuit. *The Mummy* reunited Peter Cushing and Christopher Lee for the first time since *Dracula* and proved a considerable success.

Another Rank release, *The Brides of Dracula* (1960), was Hammer's response to Christopher Lee's unwillingness to be typecast as Dracula, a role which he had played in 1957 but was not to repeat until 1965. Thus, according to Pirie (1973), Hammer were forced into the position of having to find some way of making a *Dracula* movie without Dracula. The absence of Count Dracula encouraged Hammer to compensate by adding ingredients to the formula: the brides themselves, for instance, provided an increased sexual component. However, even before 1960 Hammer were obviously aware of the need to vary the formula of the vampire myth. Once an audience has grasped the basic elements of the vampire hunters' artillery – stake, crucifix, strong daylight, communion host – the plot could all too easily subside into a succession of shopping lists. So Hammer carefully elaborated the paraphernalia and in doing so were able to persuade the audiences of the late 50s that this time evil might just triumph (→ GENRE: *The horror film*, p. 99).

In 1968, Hammer received the Queen's Award for industry for having brought in £1½ million from America over three successive years. However, 1968 was probably the last year in which Hammer could be certain of obtaining American distribution for its films. *The Devil Rides Out* (1968) was in fact advertised under the name of Dennis Wheatley – upon whose novel it was based – rather than that of Hammer Productions. By this time American finance had more or less abandoned the British film industry to its fate.

'Hammer, who were still in an extremely good box-office position, found it at once necessary to fix up deals with British, as opposed to American companies, in order to secure regular finance. Distribution in America was still guaranteed, but in return the British companies who were themselves in trouble began to insist that Hammer use their own studio space rather than Bray, to make the films. Consequently, after much deliberation, Hammer were forced to sell Bray to a property company in 1968' (Pirie, 1973, pp. 47–48).

Having finally been forced by 1969 into vacating Bray, some of the company's confidence in the horror genre was lost with the studio. *Taste the Blood of Dracula* (1969) was advertised with the tongue-in-cheek slogan 'Drink A Pint of Blood A Day' and its deviation from formula requirements proved unpopular at the box-office. Once again Hammer tried hard to differentiate their product from television: the film opens with Roy Kinnear, a familiar TV comedian, being confronted with the horrific Technicolor Count Dracula, an opening which illustrated the complicated rituals Hammer utilised to re-invest their Count Dracula character with life at the start of each film in the series. This was the fourth Hammer Dracula film and, at the end of the third, the Count had fallen hundreds of yards from the battlements of his own castle to be impaled on a sharp cross. The resurrection of the Count from absolute death to life is one of the key ingredients of the series. Indeed, one film, *Dracula, Prince of Darkness* (1965) took almost half its length to effect the Count's reappearance.

Following the financial failure of *Taste the Blood of Dracula* (1969), which had compensated for the absence of Peter Cushing with other box-office attractions such as violence and sexuality, Hammer were uncertain as to the future of the horror genre. At the end of the 1960s the company vacillated between EMI-Elstree and Rank-Pinewood, the exhibition circuits ABC and Odeon, and between straightforward horror and self-parody. With a change of management at Hammer in the early 1970s and encouragement from Warners, Hammer decided to bring the Dracula story up to date with films such as *Dracula AD 72, Dracula is Dead and Well and Living in London*, and *The Satanic Rites of Dracula. The Satanic Rites*

of Dracula (1973) reunited Cushing and Lee, injected a number of controversial contemporary issues – such as property speculation and political corruption – and included a characteristic Hammer scene, with Van Helsing being interviewed by a television reporter. All these elements were unable to generate an audience in the UK large enough to convince American distributors that the film was worth releasing in the USA. In the same year American and British audiences were watching *The Exorcist*, beside which *Dracula* was apparently all too ordinary. Once the American horror and sci-fi cycles were under way in the mid-1970s, films like *The Omen* (1976) and *Star Wars* (1977) were being produced in the same studios and with the same facilities that Hammer had employed. Meanwhile, Hammer returned to the source of their original success – the television spin-off. In 1972/73, for instance, Hammer released *Mutiny on the Buses, That's Your Funeral, Love Thy Neighbour* and *Nearest and Dearest*. None of these ever appeared on the American circuits. Since the late 1970s, Hammer's horror film production has virtually ceased, and is now confined mainly to television series.

Sources

Allen Eyles et al (eds.), *The House of Horror: the complete story of Hammer films*, London, Lorrimer, 1973.

James L. Limbacher, *The Influence of J. Arthur Rank on the History of the British Film*, Dearborn, Michigan, Henry Ford Centennial Library, n.d.

Little Shoppe of Horrors no. 4, April 1978.

George Perry, *The Great British Picture Show*, London, Hart-Davis MacGibbon, 1974.

David Pirie, *A Heritage of Horror: the English gothic cinema 1946–1972*, London, Gordon Fraser, 1973.

David Pirie, *Hammer: a Cinema Case Study*, London, BFI Education, 1980.

British social realism 1959–1963

Nearly 15 years ago Alan Lovell described the British cinema as an almost totally unknown quantity, pointing to the lack of a framework for discussion as partly responsible.

'There is no model for an examination of a particular cinema over a period of time. Or, to be more precise, there is not a model which doesn't dissolve into a discussion of particular artists with a few general remarks about the context they worked in' (Lovell, 1969, p. 1).

And in the same year Peter Wollen argued that 'the English cinema ... is still utterly amorphous, unclassified, unperceived' (Wollen, 1972, p. 115). Recently there have been signs that this situation is changing. Critical work on British cinema has emerged which attempts to reconcile history and industrial conditions of production with aesthetics in interesting and productive ways (e.g. Charles Barr's writing on Ealing studios, ← p. 43, or recent feminist work on the little-known 1940s Gainsborough melodramas in *BFI Dossier 18*). Perhaps, then, the critical impasse which has traditionally existed in relation to British cinema, and has contributed to its reputation as stylistically mediocre, is finally breaking down.

Lovell (1969) provides a tentative historical analysis to explain what he perceives as the aesthetic under-development of British cinema: an 'art' cinema dominated by the Griersonian ethic of documentary in the service of propaganda; an entertainment cinema hamstrung by notions of 'good taste'; and a 'New Wave' of critics-turned-film-makers (the Free Cinema movement) forced by exclusion from the feature film industry to make documentaries. This diagnosis of the stultifying effects of a prevailing social realist aesthetic hostile to formal experiment is shared by other critics. John Hill, for example, writing about the group of social realist films made around 1959–63, sees them in similar terms as emerging from the documentary prerogative in both commercial and non-commercial film-making, and 'the insulation of British culture from European modernism in the 1920s and 1930s at the very time that the "documentary spirit" was achieving its hegemony across the arts' (Hill, 'Ideology, economy and the British cinema', 1979, pp. 130–131). However, Hill points to the complex nature of the relationship between the aesthetic prejudices and procedures internalised by film-makers and film audiences alike and the final products, the films themselves. He argues that the British social realist movement related not only to an internalised aesthetic ideology but also to an external economy. Recognising that it constituted part of a particular response to the development of post-war British capitalism, he is careful also to specify both the social formation and historical context in

---

The Quatermass Xperiment (UK 1955 *p.c* – Hammer; *d* – Val Guest; sd b/w 21)

X – The Unknown (UK 1956 *p.c* – Hammer; *d* – Leslie Norman; sd b/w 7)

Quatermass II (UK 1957 *p.c* – Hammer; *d* – Val Guest; sd b/w 19)

The Curse of Frankenstein (UK 1957 *p.c* – Hammer; *d* – Terence Fisher; sd col 9)

Dracula (UK 1957 *p.c* – Hammer; *d* – Terence Fisher; sd col 16)

The Hound of the Baskervilles (UK 1959 *p.c* – Hammer; *d* – Terence Fisher; sd col 16)

The Mummy (UK 1959 *p.c* – Hammer; *d* – Terence Fisher; sd col 20)

The Brides of Dracula (UK 1960 *p.c* – Hammer; *d* – Terence Fisher; sd col 14)

The Damned (UK 1961 *p.c* – Hammer; *d* – Joseph Losey; sd b/w scope 19)

The Evil of Frankenstein (UK 1963 *p.c* – Hammer; *d* – Freddie Francis; sd col 13)

Dracula, Prince of Darkness (UK 1965 *p.c* – Hammer; *d* – Terence Fisher; sd col scope 23)

Fanatic (UK 1965 *p.c* – Hammer/Seven Arts; *d* – Silvio Narizzano; sd col 18)

The Plague of the Zombies (UK 1966 *p.c* – Hammer; *d* – John Gilling; sd col 24)

The Devil Rides Out (UK 1967 *p.c* – Hammer; *d* – Terence Fisher; sd col 20)

Taste the Blood of Dracula (UK 1969 *p.c* – Hammer; *d* – Peter Sasdy; sd col 21 + 16)

The Satanic Rites of Dracula (UK 1973 *p.c* – Hammer; *d* – Alan Gibson; sd col 15)

which the movement developed, and the industrial and institutional foundations upon which it was built. But he emphasises that the movement, far from simply expressing social attitudes or a response to the economic climate, actively contributed to that response 'which was likewise refracted through the particular context and struggles of the British film industry and its cinematic conventions' (Hill, 1979, p. 129). During this period, British cinema was in the process of being redefined and reorganised. Hill discusses several aspects of this transformation, including the advent of commercial television, 'X' certificates, the dis-integration of the American majors and the impetus towards independent production, and the role of the National Film Finance Corporation. A wish to turn the tide of cinema's decline led to a certain 'openness' to new ideas which permitted 'a possibility of innovation . . . subject to the demands of financial success' (Hill, 1979, p. 132). This combination of factors, then, enabled a group of socially-committed directors to put into practice their aspirations, to produce a popular cinema which would re-connect with the traditional working-class rather than provide escapist fantasies for its audience. The space given to those aspirations, however, lasted just as long as they proved to be commercially viable.

Alan Lovell provides another explanation for the short-lived success of the social realist movement. He argues that the *Sequence* film magazine critics who became independent Free Cinema filmmakers in the 1950s (Linday Anderson and Karel Reisz for example), together with ex-theatre directors (such as Tony Richardson)

'. . . were forced into documentary because of the basic situation of the British film industry at that time. The feature industry was difficult to enter because it was contracting under the pressure of television and changing leisure habits. The documentary industry was conversely expanding as a result of increased industrial sponsorship for films . . . And once this generation made the break into the feature industry it created feature films within the Social Documentary genre' (Lovell, 1969, p. 8).

Lovell concludes that once the 'Free Cinema aesthetic' had acquired the status of a genre, it could no longer license innovation. John Hill also suggests that the social realist movement may have destroyed itself through becoming 'conventional' and hence delegitimising its claims to realism. Lovell's epitaph on the British social realists – that because of the lack of a clear analysis of the situation in British cinema at the time they became prisoners of the very situation they had criticised – is echoed in Hill's suggestion that the critique of commerce implied in social realist cinema exemplified a liberal humanist culture that was itself in crisis. The financial failure of Anderson's *This*

1959 Academy Awards for *Room at the Top*

Sporting Life signalled more or less the end of the movement and a return to 'entertainment' films, which, Hill argues, tells us something of the limits of the challenge that had been made to the industry. The control apparently given to the directors was circumscribed by a system in which the real control rested with the Rank-ABC monopoly of distribution and exhibition, which gave them the right to define what was 'entertainment' and what was not (Hill, 1979, p. 132).

However, Hill and Lovell perhaps over-emphasise the influence of the documentary/Free Cinema tradition on the aesthetics and ideology of social realist cinema. Another critic has attributed the social realist aesthetic to new developments in literature and theatre:

'If we look at the development of the newer style in features, we find the trail-blazer is Jack Clayton's *Room at the Top*, based on a best-selling novel. It wasn't *Momma Don't Allow* that brought Tony Richardson into the directorial chair of *Look Back in Anger*; it was the fact that he had directed the play on the London stage. While the partisans of Free Cinema were directing stage plays and TV commercials, the new wave arose in response to the work of artists in other media. Far from originating a new documentary approach, the impulse came from the plays of John Osborne, Keith Waterhouse and Willis Hall, Wolf Mankowitz and Shelagh Delaney, novels by John Braine and Alan Sillitoe, Stan Barstow and David Storey, and a new generation of actors, like Albert Finney, Rita Tushingham, Rachel Roberts, Tom Courtenay, Richard Harris and Ronald Fraser' (Durgnat, 1970, p. 129).

According to this argument, the 'transparency' of the social realist aesthetic

not only resided in cinema's alleged ability to reproduce reality unmediated but also in its apparent ability to transmit, without adversely transforming, literary texts. And most important to this aesthetic was a notion of 'quality' grounded in the established artistic status of British literature and theatre.

Whatever its origins, the brief flowering of British social realism testifies to Hill's argument that as a movement it must be seen in the context of the British film industry of the time, although he tends to under-estimate the influence exerted on this situation by American capital. In 1959, according to Michael Balcon, 'you couldn't run a studio in the way Ealing was run – certainly not in this country, and perhaps nowhere in the world' (quoted in *Sight and Sound*, Summer/Autumn 1959, p. 133). Balcon was speaking as the newly-appointed chairman of Bryanston Films, a confederation of sixteen independent producers and production companies, financed by the producers themselves as well as by the distributors British Lion and by Lloyds Bank, Alliance Film Studios and Rank Laboratories, and releasing through British Lion. British Lion was modelled on the American Company, United Artists, and like United Artists lacked an exhibition circuit of its own. American financier Walter Reade's presence on the British Lion Board was part of a campaign to secure showings of British films in the United States, for without exhibition back-up they would be unlikely to make a profit in the domestic market. According to George Perry (1974) at this time 'up to 90% of the films made in Britain derived their financing at least in some part from American sources' (p. 215). However, this financial interest was likely to be withdrawn as

Finney and Roberts's *Saturday Night and Sunday Morning*

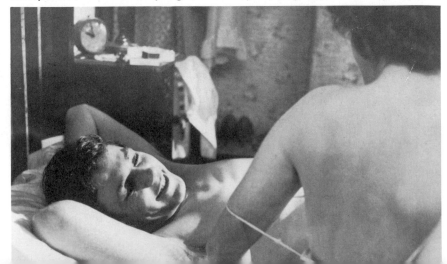

soon as production conditions in Hollywood improved, with disastrous effects for the British industry. When this eventually happened, British cinema in general, and the social realist movement in particular, were suddenly and radically affected.

One of the most important independent companies linked to Bryanston was Woodfall. Formed by playwright John Osborne and Tony Richardson, one of the co-founders of Free Cinema, the company was dedicated to British social realism. Bryanston Films themselves were financed by American moneymen like Walter Reade, the NFFC and theatrical impressarios like Harry Saltzman and Oscar Lewenstein. This theatrical connection was important to Woodfall: not only were

Osborne, Richardson, Saltzman and Lewenstein all identified with it, but many of the company's screenplays and performances derived from Royal Court Theatre successes. In the early 1960s, however, Reade withdrew from British Lion, Harry Saltzman left Woodfall for the James Bond series and Bryanston began producing blockbusters for the American market. In 1963, British social realism, as a coherent movement, was abruptly brought to an end (→ AUTHORSHIP: *Free Cinema and British social realism*, p. 147).

Sources

Sue Aspinall and Robert Murphy (eds.) *BFI Dossier 18: Gainsborough Melodrama*, London, BFI, 1983.
Michael Balcon, Interview in 'In the picture',

Sight and Sound vol. 28 no. 3/4, Summer/Autumn 1959, p. 133.
Raymond Durgnat, *A Mirror for England: British movies from austerity to affluence*, London, Faber and Faber, 1970.
John Hill, 'Ideology, economy and the British cinema', in Barrett, Corrigan, Kuhn and Wolff (eds.), *Ideology and Cultural Production*, London, Croon Helm, 1979.
Alan Lovell, *The British Cinema: the Unknown Cinema*, London, BFI Education Dept. Seminar Paper, 1969.
George Perry, *The Great British Picture Show*, London, Hart-Davis, MacGibbon, 1974.
Alexander Walker, *Hollywood, England: the British film industry in the 60s*, London, Michael Joseph, 1974.
Peter Wollen, *Signs and Meaning in the Cinema*, London, Secker and Warburg/BFI, 1969, revised edition 1972.

Room at the Top (UK 1959 *p.c* – Remus; *d* – Jack Clayton; sd b/w 14)

Both Alexander Walker and Raymond Durgnat suggest a direct relationship between British society of the late 1950s and films like *Room at the Top*. Thus, for Durgnat, 'hints of disquiet about the time of Suez (1956), led rapidly to *Room at the Top* (1958) and *Look Back in Anger* (1959). Their success established another, and continuing mood of uneasiness . . .' (Durgnat, 1970, p. 13). Walker argues that working-class anti-hero Joe Lampton's envy in *Room at the Top* was the same feeling that swept the post-war Labour government to power, and was immediately recognised by the audience that went to movies. However, Walker also points to the influence of box-office concerns and the attempt to attract international audiences, citing as evidence the casting of international star Simone Signoret and the use of the American rather than the English pronunciation of the word 'brassière' (Walker, 1974, p. 46). In its desire to have this international appeal, Walker argues, the film plays down Joe's social origins and the class conflict in favour of the clash of generations and an emphasis on Joe's sexuality, and this is what won it its large audiences. John Hill had also noted that the social realist films' attitude to class was less a positive affirmation than a displacement of it to make way for the generalised category of the 'social problem' (Hill, 1979, p. 129).

In the case of *Room at the Top*, the combination of class, youth and sex with a best-selling literary source was an innovation in British cinema and proved to be enormously successful. The film took two of the 1959 Academy Awards (for Neil Paterson's screenplay and Simone Signoret's performance), made Laurence Harvey into an international star, and introduced Jack Clayton to full-length feature film-making.

Saturday Night and Sunday Morning (UK 1960 *p.c* – Woodfall; *d* – Karel Reisz; sd b/w 11)

Since 1960 several critics have attempted to explain the unexpected box-office success of *Saturday Night and Sunday Morning*. Albert Finney's performance as Arthur has often been cited as responsible. Harry Saltzman, the film's producer, has said 'People's identification with Finney, especially young people and working young people, was total. Of course it was well directed and acted, and a very well-written film, but it was this empathy people had for the character which was more responsible than anything else for the business it did' (quoted in Walker, 1974, p. 88), and director Karel Reisz agrees that 'in a metaphorical way Arthur embodied what was happening in England' (quoted in Walker, 1974, p. 85).

Woodfall and Bryanston made more than half a million pounds from the success of *Saturday Night and Sunday Morning*. But that success may have been due to more than the popular appeal of the Arthur Seaton character. Walker's argument is that its success resulted, at least to some extent, from the truculent tone which marked it as different from other films in the genre. This truculence is apparent in the 'workbench soliloquy' at the beginning of the film in which Arthur's attitudes are spoken in some detail: 'Don't let the bastards grind you down. That's one thing you learn. What I'm out for is a good time. All the rest is propaganda' (quoted in Walker, 1974, p. 83).

For its language and frank representation of sex and violence, the film received an 'X' certificate from the censor, and was even banned outright in one country. But despite the box-office value of such measures *Saturday Night and Sunday Morning* very nearly did not get the chance to do any business at all. According to Alexander Walker, the bookers refused to show it in their

cinemas, and only the unexpected failure of a Warner Bros film at their West End showcase cinema, plus the advantage to the cinema of at last playing a British film and gaining quota credit, allowed the film to open. The first week's business was so phenomenal as to cause an instantaneous turn-round in the popularity of the film-makers vis-à-vis the film industry (Walker, 1974, p. 88).

A Taste of Honey (UK 1961 *p.c* – Woodfall; *d* – Tony Richardson; sd b/w 11)

Soon after *Saturday Night and Sunday Morning* opened it was announced that Harry Saltzman was leaving Woodfall. Walker quotes Saltzman to the effect that the parting of the ways was over the filming of *A Taste of Honey*, which he felt was too provincial to appeal to an international market (Walker, 1974, p. 91).

Shelagh Delaney's play *A Taste of Honey* was acquired for adaptation at a price of £6,000, a project which Woodfall had been unable to get Bryanston to finance until the breakthrough of *Saturday Night and Sunday Morning*. The director, Tony Richardson, having just returned from a frustrating trip to America where he had directed Delaney's play on Broadway, determined that no sets would be built for *A Taste of Honey*, and that it would be entirely shot on location. His experience of directing *Sanctuary* for 20th Century-Fox in Hollywood had been less than happy. For *A Taste of Honey* the unit was entirely based in Fulham, with the top floor of a derelict house being used as the 'rooming house' and the rest as production offices for Woodfall. An unknown actress, Rita Tushingham, played the central role; Richardson rejected an offer from American financiers to back the film if Audrey Hepburn played the part.

Stars

The Hollywood star machine

Although film studies has only recently begun to address the theoretical questions raised by stars, the fascination of film stars for both intellectual and popular audiences goes back a long way. A report on *The Film in National Life* by the Commission on Educational and Cultural Films in 1932 observed:

'A fellow of an Oxford college no longer feels an embarrassed explanation to be necessary when he is recognised leaving a cinema. A growing number of cultivated and unaffected people enjoy going to the pictures, and frequent not merely the performances of intellectual film societies, but also the local picture house, to see, for instance, Marlene Dietrich' (p. 10).

Apart from the visceral pleasures of looking at a Dietrich, stars have also provided a useful point of reference for intellectuals' speculations around popular culture. Thus Simone de Beauvoir (1960) has used Brigitte Bardot as a scalpel with which to dissect the anxieties of French bourgeois masculinity in the 1950s, and Norman Mailer (1973) has worked over the image of Marilyn Monroe to bolster his mythologising of the American dream.

The broad range of more popular writing about stars can seem overwhelming – from histories by journalists like Alexander Walker, to gossip, hack hagiographies and salacious muckraking. Until recently, though, there seemed to be little inclination by film theorists to engage with the topic (see Dyer, 1979), a sign, perhaps, of the gulf between theory and popular experience, but more significantly of the difficult problems posed for the academic study of film, at whatever level, by the phenomenon of stardom. The circulation, reception and cultural currency of stars cannot be explained convincingly by exclusively textual, sociological or economic forms of analysis. More expansive conceptions of the various 'machineries' of cinema seem a step in the right direction. But in the end, as figures which (like 'Robinson Crusoe', 'Mata Hari' or 'Margaret Thatcher') condense a number of ideological themes, stars have a currency which runs beyond the institution of cinema. They require an analysis capable of explaining the resilience of these images which we pay to have haunt our minds (see Nowell-Smith, 'On the writing of the history of cinema', 1977, p. 12) – an account which must attend to both industrial and psychic processes.

Such concerns do seem to have sparked off the present flurry of academic interest. Work is developing in two main areas. One is the very diverse body of film analysis inspired by, and contributing to feminist and gay politics. To begin with, much of this work was concerned with the appropriation of certain stars (Katharine Hepburn, Bette Davis) as figures for posi-

tive identification, as in Molly Haskell's *From Reverence to Rape* (1974); alternatively, it offered a critical diagnosis of 'stereotypes of women' or, as in Joan Mellen's *Big Bad Wolves* (1978), of male Hollywood stars as images of American patriarchy. Richard Dyer's (1979) attempt to give a firmer theoretical grounding to such concerns has provoked a lively debate in which his attempt to combine sociological and semiological approaches has been challenged by critics drawing on a psychoanalytically-oriented feminist theory (see Cook, 'Star Signs', 1979/80; Gledhill, 1982).

The other, so far subsidiary, area of work has followed the renascence of more theoretically informed historical writing on the cinema. This has emphasised, on the one hand, the material determinants of film production and distribution (the political economy of Hollywood, court actions and patents wars, real-estate deals and zoning agreements) and, on the other hand, the constitution of the codes of classic narrative film. So far only a couple of articles directly concerned with stars have been produced (see deCordova, 'The emergence of the star system', 1982; Staiger, 'Seeing stars', 1983) but there are clearly intriguing possibilities for developing work which studies stars as both marketing devices for selling films and simultaneously as organising presences in cinematic fictions.

The Hollywood System

'Mass culture', according to Roland Barthes, 'is a machine for showing desire. Here is what must interest you, it says, as if it guessed that men are incapable of finding what to desire by themselves' (Barthes, quoted in Mazzocco, 'The supply-side star', 1982). What is involved, Barthes suggests, is some investment by us, the punters, which involves not conscious choice but a repertoire of unconscious processes. The object in which we make that investment is always provided for us – some would say imposed on us – by the 'machine' of culture. This machine involves not just the bricks and mortar of Hollywood studios and chains of cinemas, but also certain cultural orientations and competences (shared languages, for example, and shared conceptions of time, personality and aesthetic value) and the psychic processes whereby we enter culture and negotiate shifting, insecure positions within it.

The implications of this argument are that, in investigating the phenomenon of stardom, we are not just dealing with a person or an image with particular characteristics (talent, beauty, glamour, charisma, etc.) but with a rather complex set of cultural processes. The interesting question is not so much, 'what is a star?' as, 'how do stars function – within the cinema industry, within film narratives, at the level of individual fantasy and desire?' In considering their production, circula-

tion and reception, for example, John Ellis has suggested a preliminary definition of a star as 'a performer in a particular medium whose figure enters into subsidiary forms of circulation and then feeds back into future performances' (Ellis, 'Star/industry/image', 1982, p. 1). This indicates that, from the film industry's perspective, the purpose of disseminating star images so widely is to draw audiences back into the cinema. Anne Friedberg takes a similar approach, but indicates some of the complexities implied by terms like *performer, figure* and *circulation*. 'The film star is . . . a particular commoditised human, routed through a system of signs with exchange value' (Friedberg, 'Identification and the star', 1982, p. 47). The concepts of commodities, signs and exchange value suggest a model in which a homology might be established between the circulation of the star image in a circuit of exchange value which produces profit (production, distribution, exhibition) and its circulation in a circuit of semiotic use value (performance, publicity and spectatorship) which produces pleasure. Just as a commodity is defined as having both exchange value (it can be bought and sold) and use value, so the two circuits of stardom are separable only analytically. For the profit to be realised, there must be at least a promise of pleasure; enjoyment of the star has to be paid for.

This simple model, based on a conventional account of the elements of the cinema industry, can be fleshed out in a number of ways. It provides a useful peg on which to hang more detailed historical studies; it can be used to organise the empirical research produced within conflicting perspectives; and it can provide a reasonably accessible focus for some of the theoretical debates. Here I shall just indicate some possible lines of development.

Production/performance

What does a star contribute to the production of a Hollywood movie? Talent, glamour, and charisma – 'that little bit extra' – might provide the terms for one answer, but they probably indicate what has to be explained rather than explain it. Richard Dyer has suggested a model that seems to offer a more useful starting point by indicating the sort of labour done by the star (*Teachers' Study Guide 1*, 1979, p. 18). To begin with, there is a person who constitutes the raw material to be transformed into an image or product – hence talent schools, dialogue coaches, beauticians, dazzling blond hair, nose jobs and, in Clark Gable's case, a new set of teeth. This product is both a form of capital, owned either by the studio or the individual, and also a form of raw material which, through further labour, is incorporated into another product, the film, which is sold in a market for a profit.

What distinguishes stars from other performers is that, apart from their input of labour (i.e. their acting), their 'image' gives

'The Biograph Girl' (Florence Lawrence) – early movie star . . . and Marilyn Monroe – 'mythologising the American dream'

them an additional value. This is important in two ways. On the one hand, it can be used to attract financial backing for a film and, on the other, it provides a signal for exhibitors and audiences that this will be a particular type of film. The two aspects are closely related. Investors will only back a film that seems likely to make a profit. Hence Hollywood's task within the cinema industry has been to provide high quality product that is both predictable enough and, at the same time, novel enough to attract and satisfy audiences. In 1927, for example, the Wall Street stockbrokers Halsey, Stuart and Co. insisted that stars, despite their high salaries, are an integral part of this process.

'In the "star" your producer gets not only a "production" value in the making of his picture, but a "trademark" value, and an "insurance" value, which are very real and very potent in guaranteeing the sale of this product to the cash customers at a profit' ('The motion picture industry as a basis for bond financing', 1976, p. 179).

In the earliest years of Hollywood, producers saw things differently. When films were hired out by the foot and nickelodeon audiences still paid for the novel experience of seeing pictures that moved, players remained anonymous. Most histories suggest that stars were introduced as a marketing device by independent producers trying to challenge the monopolistic stranglehold of the Patents Trust, formed by the equipment manufacturers (← HISTORY: *Film technology and the early film industry*, p. 4). Janet Staiger (1983) has cast some doubt on this account, suggesting closer links to developments within the theatre. But whatever the details, it is clear that stardom, along with narrative and the classical Hollywood style, became institutionalised during the second decade of the century. It would be interesting to explore

the affinities in this period between the organisation of these narratives around the position of the spectator and the psychology of novelistic character, the development of the continuity style, and the role and presentation of the star on screen (→ HISTORY OF NARRATIVE: *The classic narrative system*, p. 212).

Stars can also provide a useful way into an understanding of Hollywood's shifting political economy. Interesting topics from this point of view might include the crisis provoked in the 1920s by the economic power of stars like Pickford, Fairbanks and Chaplin, especially when they formed United Artists (see Balio, 1976); the unionisation of Hollywood players, from freelance stars to extras, in the Screen Actors Guild set up in 1933 during Hollywood's economic blizzard (see Ross, 1941); the contracts and work patterns imposed on their stables of stars by the oligopolistic Big Five studios from the mid-20s until the early 40s; the collapse of that system under pressure from anti-Trust suits, independent studios and newly aggressive Hollywood agents; and the bargaining power of stars in the subsequent era of packages, deals and independent production companies (see Pirie, 'The deal', 1981; Maltby, 'The political economy of Hollywood', 1982).

What such accounts of stars as labour cannot reveal is their specific contribution to a film in terms of performance (i.e. how they 'represent' a particular character). One approach to this question considers the clusters of connotations already associated with a star and how these create resonances for the audience watching not just Lorelei Lee *but also* Marilyn Monroe, not just Wyatt Earp *but also* Henry Fonda. Richard Dyer discusses the relationship between character and star image, pointing out that star image or persona may either 'fit' the fictional character or work to produce a disjuncture which may have

ideological significance (Dyer, 1979, p. 148). Thus the star image carries powerful cultural connotations which both exceed the fictional codes of character and identification and work to bind us into the fictional world of the film. John O. Thompson ('Screen acting and the commutation test', 1978) has suggested that one way of understanding how these cultural connotations work in relation to specific film performances is to use a commutation test. This device simply asks, what would happen if Lorelei Lee in *Gentlemen Prefer Blondes* were played not by Monroe but by, say, Jayne Mansfield or Gloria Grahame, or Wyatt Earp in *My Darling Clementine* not by Fonda but by John Wayne or Gary Cooper? This would enable us to separate out connotations specific to the star from those specific to the fictional character, and helps to explain the elusive and relatively unanalysed notion of 'star presence' or 'charisma'. However, there remains an argument about whether the star figure can be seen as *mediating* pre-existing social meanings, as a sociological approach would have it, or whether it works, together with other cinematic codes, to *produce* apparently coherent meaning from unstable and contradictory material (see Cook, 'Star signs', 1979/80). It has been argued that the erotic play of the 'look' around the female star figure in classic Hollywood cinema is an integral part of the narrative drive towards closure and the reinstatement of equilibrium (Mulvey, 'Visual pleasure and narrative cinema', 1975). This argument uses psychoanalytical concepts to address the question of the fantasy relationship between spectators and film and the role of the star in that relationship (see also Cook, 'Stars and politics', 1982; Friedberg, 'Identification and the star', 1982). Whether the emphasis be sociological, semiotic or psychoanalytical, though, the appeal of the star cannot be understood solely in the context of production and performance.

Distribution/publicity

Although less glamorous than Hollywood production and less familiar than cinema exhibition, distribution has always been at the heart of the organisation and profitability of the film industry. This is where the star's 'trademark' value and 'insurance' value come in: they embody the distributor's promise to the exhibitor of both the audience guaranteed by the familiar presence of the star and also the novelty appeal of a new vehicle.

But more important than this trade promotion, from our point of view, is the use of stars in advertising films to the public. As we have seen, John Ellis (1982) sees stars primarily as a marketing device, as an 'invitation to cinema'. This appeal is manufactured not solely by the industry's promotional and advertising machinery, but also more diffusely through fan magazines, through feature articles, news items and reviews in the press, and so forth. All these play upon the central paradoxes of stardom: that stars are both ordinary and glamorous, both like us and unlike us, both a person and a commodity, both real and mythical, both public and intimate. These dualities seem to work in two ways. They draw us into the cinema, where we can be in the presence of a more complete (moving, talking) image of the star. At the same time, that performance is never somehow enough and helps to fuel again our insatiable curiosity about what the star is 'really' like – hence the cycle of fandom, gossip and scandal. This view of stardom is also fostered by Hollywood's own representations of the phenomenon – most notably, perhaps, in *A Star Is Born* (see Dyer, '*A Star Is Born* and the construction of authenticity', 1982).

Exhibition/spectatorship

Consumption of a star's performance in a film has two aspects: paying your money and watching the film. This spectatorship is by no means a passive activity: what it involves is the most complex and hotly disputed question in the whole study of stars. Nor is it the end point of the circulation of a star, although the production-distribution-consumption model may suggest that it is. Indeed, there would be a good case for starting not with the return on capital invested in film production, but with the unquantifiable returns on our emotional investments in these pleasurable images. The pleasure derived from those moments of erotic contemplation of the spectacular figure of the star constantly threatens' to spill over, to exceed the bounds of narrative which work to regulate our desires (see Mulvey, 1975). Indeed, for some spectators this excess may well overturn the delicate balance between static image and narrative flow on which classic Hollywood cinema rests (→ NARRATIVE AND STRUCTURALISM: *Narrative*

and audience, p. 242). The 'management', or containment of excess, successful or not, represents one of the ways in which Hollywood cinema attempts to hold spectators in place as consumers of its product, drawing them in with the promise of fulfilment of forbidden desires played out in the safety and secrecy of a darkened chamber. And it is generally agreed that these fantasies are awakened in ways that tend to sustain existing social definitions and relations of power.

How does this work when you or I sit watching a movie in the cinema? Here there is considerably less unanimity. Partly this involves different conceptions of the relationship between narrative and spectator. Do the structure of the narrative and presentation of bodies (especially women's bodies) on the screen implicitly address a 'masculine' spectator? If so, where does that leave the women in the audience? What is involved in identifying with a star? Can star images be read in 'subversive' ways by oppressed groups, and thus appropriated in their construction of social identities? (see Clarke, Merck and Simmonds, 1981; and 'Doris Day case study', 1982). These are just some of the questions; the debates continue.

Studying stars

One reason for including work on stars in courses of film study has been that, as an integral part of the machinery of Hollywood, they provide an accessible way into an analysis of its political economy, the organisation of the narratives it produces, and the relationship between the two. A more problematic, often troubling aspect of studying stars is our own fascination with them, which can prove disturbing of apparently objective academic analysis. We do not fully understand these pleasures. We may think them too embarrassingly banal for serious academic study. Equally, we may be reluctant to put them under the microscope for fear they may dissolve or reveal a darker side we had only dimly and uneasily perceived. Not surprisingly, these hesitations can provoke resistance to what are, in any case, undeniably difficult theoretical questions. So what may appear at first glance an attractively straightforward topic turns out to be anything but. Here we are studying the disregarded processes of popular culture and our own place within them – with no pat academic routines to provide a compensating sense of balance. That is what can make a study of stars so compelling. That cultivated and unaffected Oxford don back in the 30s would no doubt have been able to chat lucidly about what was on show at the intellectual film society. He may have found it harder to theorise his fascination with Dietrich.

References

Tino Balio, *United Artists: the company built by the stars*, Madison, University of Wisconsin Press, 1976.

Roland Barthes, quoted in Robert Mazzocco, 'The supply-side star', *New York Review of Books*, 1 April 1982.
Simone de Beauvoir, *Brigitte Bardot and the Lolita Syndrome*, London, André Deutsch/Weidenfeld and Nicolson, 1960.
Jane Clarke, Mandy Merck and Diana Simmonds, *BFI Dossier no. 4: Move Over Misconceptions: Doris Day reappraised*, London, BFI Publishing, 1981.
Jane Clarke, Mandy Merck and Diana Simmonds, 'Doris Day case study', in Gledhill (ed.), *Star Signs: papers from a weekend workshop*, London, BFI Education, 1982.
Commission on Educational and Cultural Films, *The Film in National Life*, London, 1932.
Pam Cook, 'Star signs', *Screen* vol. 20 no. 3/4, Winter 1979/80.
Pam Cook, 'Stars and politics', in Gledhill (ed.), *Star Signs*, cit.
Richard deCordova, 'The emergence of the star system and the bourgeoisification of the American cinema', in Gledhill (ed.), *Star Signs*, cit.
Richard, Dyer, *Teachers' Study Guide 1: The Stars*, London, 3F1 Education Advisory Service, 1979.
Richard Dyer, *Stars*, London, BFI, 1979.
Richard Dyer, '*A Star is Born* and the construction of authenticity', in Gledhill (ed.), *Star Signs*, cit.
John Ellis, 'Star/industry/image', in Gledhill (ed.), *Star Signs*, cit.
Anne Friedberg, 'Identification and the star: a refusal of difference', in Gledhill (ed.), *Star Signs*, cit.
Christine Gledhill (ed.), *Star Signs*, cit.
Halsey, Stuart and Co., 'The motion picture industry as a basis for bond financing', in Balio (ed.), *The American Film Industry*, Madison, University of Wisconsin Press, 1976.
Molly Haskell, *From Reverence to Rape*, New York, Holt Rinehart and Winston, 1974.
Norman Mailer, *Marilyn*, London, Hodder and Stoughton, 1973.
Richard Maltby, 'The political economy of Hollywood: the studio system', in Davies and Neve (eds.), *Cinema, Politics and Society in America*, Manchester, University of Manchester Press, 1982.
Patrick McGilligan, *Cagney: the actor as auteur*, South Brunswick/London, A. S. Barnes/Tantivy, 1975.
Joan Mellen, *Big Bad Wolves: masculinity in the American film*, London, Elm Tree Books, 1978.
Edgar Morin, *The Stars*, New York, Grove Press, 1960.
Laura Mulvey, 'Visual pleasure and narrative cinema', *Screen* vol. 16 no. 3, Autumn 1975.
Geoffrey Nowell-Smith, 'On the writing of the history of cinema: some problems', *Edinburgh Magazine* no. 2, Edinburgh Film Festival, 1977.
David Pirie, 'The deal', in Pirie (ed.), *Anatomy of the Movies*, London, Windward, 1981.
Murray Ross, *Stars and Strikes*, New York, Columbia University Press, 1941.
James F. Scott, *Film – the Medium and the Maker*, New York, Holt, Rinehart and Winston, 1975.
Janet Staiger, 'Seeing stars', *The Velvet Light Trap* no. 20, Summer 1983.
John O. Thompson, 'Screen acting and the commutation test', *Screen* vol. 19 no. 2, Summer 1978.

Bogart's off-screen image?

The characteristic Bogart persona in *To Have and Have Not*

JAMES CAGNEY

The Public Enemy (USA 1931 *p.c* –
Warner Bros; *d* – William Wellman;
sd b/w 16)

This was the film that made Cagney
a star and the role which provided the
model for the way in which he is
generally remembered (though he was
only a gangster in a quarter of his films).
The extract emphasises two 'Cagney'
characteristics, his working-class
background and toughness (seen in the
representation of the stockyards, beer
parlours etc.) and his brusque,
dismissive attitude towards women (the
film includes a now notorious scene in
which Cagney thrusts a grapefruit in
Mae Clark's face). The extract also
offers an early example of the Cagney
persona's relationship with his mother,
which was to become explicitly neurotic
in later films (e.g. *White Heat*, 1949).

G-Men (USA 1935: *p.c* – Warner Bros;
d – William Keighley; sd b/w 15)

Although in this extract Cagney is
seen on the 'right' side of the law for a
change, the emphasis is still on his East
Side background, his competence and
competitiveness (the shooting gallery),
his nervousness and impatience (desire
for a transfer to New York), his ease
with men (the card game) and unease
with women (the embarrassed meeting
with Margaret/Kay McCord.) The
orthodox explanation for Cagney's
conversion from criminal to lawman is
the pressure of Hays Code censorship,

but Patrick McGilligan points out that
Cagney had himself begun to change his
persona two years earlier (McGilligan,
1975, p. 57).

Each Dawn I Die (USA 1939 *p.c* –
Warner Bros; *d* – William Keighley;
sd b/w 10)

The good/bad Cagney persona is
crucial to the plot of *Each Dawn I Die*,
in which he plays a crusading journalist
wrongly imprisoned after being framed
for drunken driving. He epitomises the
downtrodden 'little guy' who refuses to
stay down. Patrick McGilligan has
described this aspect of Cagney as
follows: 'He was hard times and bad
luck but spit-grin-and-fight-back'
(McGilligan, 1975, p. 184).

The Roaring Twenties (USA 1939 *p.c* –
Warner Bros; *d* – Raoul Walsh;
sd b/w 9)

This extract illustrates the two 'types'
of gangster generally represented in the
genre: the gangster by default, for
whom gangsterdom is the only available
means of making a living – represented
by Cagney – and the psychotic gangster
– represented by Humphrey Bogart (in
The Public Enemy Cagney had
incorporated both these characteristics
into a single persona). Ironically, this
was to be Cagney's last gangster role for
more than a decade; he returned to the
genre in *White Heat* (1949) as a
psychotic gangster. Meanwhile Bogart
dominated the roles of good/bad anti-
hero protagonists throughout the 40s.

The alleged tendency for stars to
embody social types, discussed by
Richard Dyer (1979), is worth discussing
here.

HUMPHREY BOGART

The Maltese Falcon (USA 1941 *p.c* –
Warner Bros; *d* – John Huston;
sd b/w 9)

Edgar Morin in his study *The Stars*
(1960), has attempted to isolate the
stars' historic significance – and
significations – by attending to specific
roles and genres in specific periods.
Bogart, for instance, he associates with
film noir, a genre which, he argues,
'secularised' stardom and made
stereotypes increasingly ambiguous.
This was an era of good/bad
protagonists of which Bogart is Morin's
example:

'Humphrey Bogart in *The Maltese
Falcon* (1941) incarnates the new
synthesis which the crime film (film noir)
is to spread over the whole American
screen. The crime film suppresses the
opposition of the odious ex-gangster
and the good-policeman-arbiter of
justice, proposing instead a new
confused and confusing type . . . half
good, half bad . . .' (Morin, 1960,
pp. 25–26).

Bogart's image embodies this shift: in
the 30s, in films like *Racket Busters*
(1938) and *The Roaring Twenties* (1939)
he was an archetypal gangster. In the 40s
he was cast as the private eye of *The
Maltese Falcon* and *The Big Sleep* (1946) →

Rebel hero and method actor, Brando made up for *On the Waterfront* . . . and poised animal-like in *A Streetcar named Desire*

and as the American interventionist hero of *Casablanca* (1942) and *To Have and Have Not* (1944). Throughout these films Bogart provided a continuity of voice, gesture, movement, costume and even world view: the cigarette, the pulled back lip, the gravelly voice, the trenchcoat, the sentimental sarcasm. His gestural repertoire was minimal but accumulated a maximum expressiveness on the level of generic conventions: the cupping of a cigarette, the lisp, the meditative tugging of an earlobe, the squint, the grimace, the tightening of the lower lip over the teeth. The specific attributes of Bogart's persona take on different meanings (within limits) across different films suggesting that star images consist of multiple contradictory elements which can be mobilised differently according to context (see Dyer, 1979). In the extract from *The Roaring Twenties*, for instance, Bogart's George is a violent, distrustful gangster characteristic of the roles the actor often assumed in gangster films in the 1930s. These same characteristics feed into the role of Sam Spade in *The Maltese Falcon* (see the sequence in the extract in which Bogart's Spade suddenly knocks Lorre/Cairo out and neither men trust each other for all their actions to the contrary). The film also employs the earlier Bogart persona's aggressive self-confidence and relish of violence – see, for instance, Bogart's gangland boss in *Racket Busters* dedicated to taking over the Truckers Association and impervious to the attempts of the Special

Prosecutor to stop him.

Racket Busters (USA 1938 *p.c* – Warner Bros; *d* – Lloyd Bacon; sd b/w 20)

The Roaring Twenties (USA 1939 *p.c* – Warner Bros; *d* – Raoul Walsh; sd b/w 9)

They Drive by Night (USA 1940 *p.c* – Warner Bros; *d* – Raoul Walsh; sd b/w 23)

High Sierra (USA 1941 *p.c* – Warner Bros; *d* – Raoul Walsh; sd b/w 14)

To Have and Have Not (USA 1944 *p.c* – Warner Bros; *d* – Howard Hawks; sd b/w 20)

The Treasure of the Sierra Madre (USA 1947 *p.c* – Warner Bros; *d* – John Huston; sd b/w 11)

MARLENE DIETRICH

The Scarlet Empress (USA 1934 *p.c* – Paramount; *d* – Josef von Sternberg; sd b/w 11)

Discussing approaches to star study which see the director–star relationship as complementary, Richard Dyer summarises different versions of the Dietrich–Sternberg duality. Marjorie Rosen sees the Dietrich–Sternberg films as the 'canonization' of Dietrich 'as the von Sternberg ideal'. Claire Johnston, on the other hand, sees these films not as promoting a male ideal of the feminine but as proposing a denial of the female. Sternberg dresses Dietrich in masculine clothing, a masquerade which

indicates the absence of man, and simultaneously negates and recuperates that absence so that the image of the woman becomes merely the trace of her exclusion and repression. Both these views correspond to Sternberg's own statement, 'In my films Marlene is not herself. Remember that, Marlene is not Marlene. I am Marlene . . .' (quoted in Dyer, 1979, p. 179). Molly Haskell, however, has placed Dietrich in a category of women stars who successfully resist the stereotypes they are supposed to embody. Her resplendent beauty, or 'charisma', transcends her role as a projection of male dreams, an idea echoed by Tom Flinn. Laura Mulvey attempts to theorise the Dietrich–Sternberg relationship as projecting the voyeuristic fantasies of the male director, seeing the star figure as a formal element in those fantasies. These arguments differ as to where responsibility for producing meaning lies – with director or star. On the one hand, Dietrich is seen as an empty vehicle for Sternberg's erotic formalism, and on the other, her star charisma transcends all attempts to objectify her. Dyer suggests that it might be productive to view the films in a more complex way as revealing the tensions and contradictions in the star – director relationship (Dyer, 1979, p. 180).

In the extract Dietrich is clearly employed as part of Sternberg's *mise en scène*. Her veil, for instance, is one of several aspects increasing the haziness of the image and lavish detail of the décor.

Marlene Dietrich – part of the Sternberg's *mise en scène* in *The Scarlet Empress*

Rancho Notorious (USA 1952 *p.c* –
Fidelity Pictures/RKO; *d* – Fritz Lang;
sd col 20)

Touch of Evil (USA 1958 *p.c* –
Universal/International; *d* – Orson
Welles; sd b/w 14)

MARLON BRANDO

A Streetcar Named Desire (USA 1951 *p.c*
– Group Productions; *d* – Elia Kazan;
sd b/w 10)

Marlon Brando is associated with two
traditions: the 'rebel hero' and Method
acting, both of which are clearly evident
in this extract, which includes the trunk-
searching scene described by James F.
Scott thus:

'In *Streetcar* Brando evidently built
the part around his sense of Stanley
Kowalski's animal aggressiveness.
Sometimes this is innocently canine, as
when his incessant scratching of back
and belly remind us of a dog going after
fleas. But the Kowalski character is also
destructive, as we are told in Brando's
use of the mouth: he chews fruit with
loud crunching noises, munches up
potato chips with the same relentless
jaw muscles, washes beer around in his
mouth and then swallows it with
physically noticeable gulps. These two
Brando-generated metaphors come
together in the scene where Kowalski
rummages through Blanche's trunk, his
clawlike hands burrowing furiously and
throwing velveteen dresses and fake fur
back over his shoulders with fierce

determination. These apparently
insubstantial bits of stage business
prepare us for the climactic scene in
which Kowalski, having worked havoc
upon Blanche's wardrobe, at last
destroys the woman herself, devouring
her little illusions of Southern gentility'
(Scott, 1975, p. 249).

The details Scott detects in Brando's
performance are clearly those of
Method acting, but their connotations
are also those of the rebel – 'the surly
proletarian who suspects every smell of
middle-class decorum'. Indeed, the
casting of this film with Method-trained
Brando as the proletarian Kowalski and
British repertory actress Vivien Leigh as
Blanche DuBois reveals the class
association of different schools of
acting. Brando's performance suggests
an authenticity which contrasts
dramatically with the apparent
artificiality of Leigh's DuBois, although
both styles are in fact equally mannered.
Richard Dyer has suggested that
Method acting, for all its claims to
authenticity, reveals a sexist ideological
bias since the characteristics of
disturbance and anguish on which it
places such value are reserved for men,
while women represent the repression of
those values (Dyer, 1979, p. 161).

Last Tango in Paris (Italy/France 1972
p.c – P.E.A. Cinematografica (Rome)/
Les Artistes Associés (Paris); *d* –
Bernardo Bertolucci; sd col 17)

E. Ann Kaplan has criticised this film
on the grounds that its star, Brando,

prohibits the film from achieving that
criticism of its main characters which it
attempts. Kaplan describes the film's
intentions as a critique of two types of
film styles – 1950s American and French
New Wave – which she associates
respectively with 'Hemingway-tough
male dominance and anguish, and chic
and "modern" irresponsibility and
permissiveness', and which correspond
to Brando's 'method-ism' and Jean-
Pierre Léaud's 'modernism'. Richard
Dyer summarises Kaplan's argument:

'Brando – as image (the
reverberations of *A Streetcar Named
Desire* and *On the Waterfront* still
remaining) and as performer (the
compelling interiority of the Method) –
is so powerful that "it was logical for
people to take Brando's consciousness
for the consciousness of the film". Since
Brando's view – a hatred of "the false
middle-class way of being" which is
taken out on women – becomes
identified as the truth about the
character and the film, the seemingly
anti-sexist intentions of the latter are
overturned by the (very complexly)
sexist attitudes of the former' (Dyer,
1979, p. 142).

Dyer points out that *Last Tango in
Paris* represents a specific case in which
the star persona can be seen as the
ultimate source of truth about a
character, and cautions that character is
established in multiple ways.

Contradictions for Fonda's star image – sexual tomboy in *Walk on the Wild Side* and middle-class radical in *Tout va bien*

Viva Zapata! (USA 1952 *p.c* – 20th Century-Fox; *d* – Elia Kazan; sd b/w 10)

On the Waterfront (USA 1954 *p.c* – Horizon; *d* – Elia Kazan; sd b/w 15)

The Godfather (USA 1971 *p.c* – Alfran Productions; *d* – Francis Ford Coppola; sd col 19)

JANE FONDA

Walk on the Wild Side/Barbarella (USA 1962/France/Italy 1967 *p.c* – Famous Artists/Marianne Productions (Paris)/ Dino De Laurentiis (Rome); *d* – Edward Dmytryk/Roger Vadim; sd b/w 9/sd col 1)

Richard Dyer takes Jane Fonda as a test case for his approach to 'rebel' stereotypes and concludes with a cautious speculation that her rebelliousness does not lie in a simple rejection of dominant values, but might better be understood 'not only in the reconciliation of radicalism and feminism with Americanness and ordinariness but also in her ability to suggest (as a tomboy) redefinitions of sexuality while at the same time overtly reasserting heterosexuality' (Dyer, 1979, p. 98).

Dyer identifies *Walk on the Wild Side* as one of Fonda's films which illustrates how crudely her sex appeal was often constructed. 'She was often photographed in a manner that vulgarised rather than beautified her body. Her bottom, in particular, was focused on – in the early scenes' (Dyer, 1979, pp. 81–83), from which this extract was taken. Despite this emphasis on sexuality, the 'tomboyism' that Dyer points to is central to *Walk on the Wild*

Side. Indeed, Dyer notes that all her most successful roles up until *Klute* (1971), including *Cat Ballou* (1965) and *Barbarella* (1967) were basically tomboys.

The way in which Fonda's image reconciles apparently oppositional characteristics (described by Dyer above) is integral to *Barbarella*. For Dyer, an 'indelible Americanness has been an important element in her later career, which, with its French sex films and radical politics, has in substance been the antithesis of all-Americanness' (Dyer, 1979, p. 78). *Barbarella* is perhaps the most famous of those sex films. In spite of its exploitation of 'kinky' eroticism associated with European sex cinema, Fonda was seen by many critics as retaining her all-American morality nevertheless (Dyer, 1979, p. 87).

Klute (USA 1971 *p.c* – Warner Bros; *d* – Alan J. Pakula; sd colscope 24)

Having argued that Fonda's image is organised around elements of eroticism, radicalism, all-Americannism, 'tomboyism' etc., Dyer (1979) suggests that 'not till the time of *Klute* (1971) did the elements of the image come together in a certain dynamic tension' (p. 77). Thus, for instance, Fonda's earlier 'sexy' roles (in French erotic films, deep South melodramas and so on) are simultaneously invoked and inflected in feminist terms by her performance as a prostitute in *Klute*. Dyer points out, however, that

'What is not clear is whether the role does cut free from the exploitative quality of the earlier image, or whether the latter contributes to reducing the radical potential of the character . . . It

depends how the audience member reads these films, what sort of interest in or knowledge of Fonda s/he has' (p. 84).

The tension between such elements in Fonda's films in general and *Klute* in particular is negotiated by her acting skills, and she won an Oscar for her performance. She has developed the naturalistic style characteristic of contemporary American cinema and in *Klute* employs many of its devices – interrupted speech, hesitation, mumbling, tics and other techniques that give an air of improvisation to the performance (Dyer, p. 89).

Tout va bien (France/Italy 1972 *p.c* – Anouchka Films/Vicco Films (Paris)/ Empire Films (Rome); *d* – Jean-Pierre Gorin, Jean-Luc Godard; sd col 9 + 13)

Dyer (1979) argues that Fonda's adoption of radical politics since the late 60s raises sharp contradictions for her star image (p. 89). The political issues are obfuscated by the overriding presence of the extraordinary star persona, a point also made by Godard and Gorin in their film *Letter to Jane* (1974). This argument suggests that the star is a sign inevitably imbued with reactionary values, and this proposition is tested in *Tout va bien*, particularly in the scene, shown in Extract 2, where Susan (Fonda) and Jacques (Yves Montand), both middle-class radicals, are shown doing the same work as the strikers. Dyer argues that this exploration of class issues is absent from her American 'radical' films (e.g. *Julia*, 1977, *Coming Home*, 1978) and is only possible because the Godard/Gorin film is far removed from Fonda's actual situation and public (Dyer, 1979, p. 90).

Genre

History of genre criticism

Introduction

While literary genre criticism has a long history – going back to Aristotle (Buscombe, 'The idea of genre in the American cinema', 1970; Pye, 'Genre and movies', 1975) – it was introduced into Anglo-Saxon film criticism comparatively recently, in the mid-60s and early 70s. In cinema itself, generic forms were one of the earliest means used by the industry to organise the production and marketing of films, and by reviewers and the popular audience to guide their viewing. In this respect, genres – like stars a decade later – emerged from the studio system's dual need for standardisation and product differentiation. The genres, each with its recognisable repertoire of conventions running across visual imagery, plot, character, setting, modes of narrative development, music and stars, enabled the industry to predict audience expectation. Differences between genres meant different audiences could be identified and catered to. All this made it easier to standardise and stabilise production (← HISTORY: *The studios*, p. 10).

These industrial associations account for the late entry of the cinematic genres into film criticism, which, in its attempt to divest itself of its literary or sociological heritage, sought to demonstrate the presence of individual artists (*auteurs*) *despite* rather than in relation to industrial conditions. Genre conventions in Hollywood cinema had, of course, been remarked by film criticism before genre itself became a theoretical issue. But here the term 'convention' was used pejoratively, referring to the second-hand meanings and stereotypes associated with mass production which militated both against the personal expression of the artist and the authentic portrayal of reality. When *auteur* criticism took on the cause of Hollywood cinema it was committed to reproducing the author as 'artist' in what was largely genre product. In Colin McArthur's view (1972) this meant sifting the 'irrelevancies brought to particular works' by studio personnel and genre conventions in order to lay bare the core of thematic and stylistic motifs peculiar to the film-maker (→ AUTHORSHIP: *Nicholas Ray*, p. 139).

The relationship of genre and *auteur* criticism will be pursued later. Important to note here is that cinematic genre criticism grew out of the growing dissatisfaction with *auteur* analysis of Hollywood product which, Tom Ryall (1978) argues, 'tended to treat popular art as if it were "high culture"' (→ AUTHORSHIP: *Auteur theory and British film criticism*, p. 147).

Seminal to this work of reassessment were essays written in different contexts in the 50s by André Bazin on the western ('The western, or the American film *par excellence*', and 'The evolution of the western', 1971) and by Robert Warshow ('The gangster as tragic hero', and 'Movie chronicle: *The Westerner*', 1970), focusing on two genres which were central to early genre cricitism's concern with popular art (→ *The western*, p. 64; *The gangster/crime film*, p. 85).

In the 60s Laurence Alloway wrote an influential piece in *Movie* ('Iconography of the movies', 1963) and mounted and wrote an introductory booklet to an important season at the Museum of Modern Art in New York, *Violent America: the movies 1946–64* (1971). His approach was rigorously uncompromising in its insistence on formulae and ephemera as the basis of the popular Hollywood cinema claimed as the product of great 'artists' by the auteurists. In the early 1970s several articles on genre appeared in the British journal *Screen*, and three books were produced concentrating on the two genres central to the debate – *Horizons West* (Kitses, 1969), *Underworld USA* (McArthur, 1972) and *The Six-Gun Mystique* (Cawelti, 1971) – and here for a while the theoretical debates around genre stopped. As *auteur* theory was challenged by the emphasis of cinesemiotics on the text itself as the site of production of meaning and author and spectator positions (→ NARRATIVE AND STRUCTURALISM: *Introduction*, p. 222; *Narrative and audience*, p. 242), so the specificities of genre were lost in the general concern with narrative and processes of signification.

Meanwhile, in the 70s interest shifted from the western and gangster genres which had dominated the 60s, to exploration of film noir. This was a generic category used by film criticism rather than the industry. It demarcated a body of films which could be explored in the new terms being introduced into Anglo-Saxon criticism from the French journal *Cahiers du Cinéma*. Under the influence of a revival of interest in Marxist aesthetics, *Cahiers du Cinéma* was detaching itself from its championship of Hollywood *auteurs*; it suggested a system of categorisation that would discriminate between those films whose formal organisation reinforced their manifest ideological themes, and those which through a process of fracture and disjuncture exposed ideological contradictions (→ AUTHORSHIP: *Cahiers' Category 'e'* p. 172). Under this rubric a whole range of Hollywood films, which auteurism had virtually been unable to place, could be reappropriated for critical validation (→ *Film noir*, p. 93). In the late

70s in response to the intervention of psychoanalysis and feminism into film theory, melodramas were seen to provide excellent material for the investigation of these interests. As in the case of film noir, a neglected, if not despised, area of Hollywood production was brought into critical view (and feminist film theory has since taken up the even lower-rated women's picture as an adjunct to work on melodrama), but little in these investigations took the issues of genre theory itself much further. Exceptional in this respect was an American study by Will Wright, *Six-guns and Society* (1975), which attempted a structuralist analysis of the western (→ NARRATIVE AND STRUCTURALISM: *Lévi-Strauss*, p. 232). In the preliminaries to his analysis of the western itself Wright attempts to adapt Lévi-Strauss's concept of myth to an explanation of how genre conventions represent problems and shifts in social meanings – in how a society communicates with itself. However, the book's concentration on an individual genre begs the question of how genre itself operates in cinema.

Two recent studies have in different ways attempted to revitalise work on the question of genre. Tom Ryall's *Teachers' Study Guide* (1978) on the gangster film sets out to analyse the work and debates of the 60s and 70s, clarifying the main issues, and to relocate these in relation to post-68 questions about ideology and signification. In so doing he attempts to indicate how genre criticism can be useful to the student of film. Stephen Neale's monograph, *Genre* (1980), rather than historicising such debates (a task taken on by Paul Willemen in his short introduction), attempts to recast them, conceptualising genre in terms of linguistic and psychoanalytic theory. Before looking more closely at these ideas, however, it is necessary to ask precisely what are the questions posed by a genre approach to the cinema.

What is genre criticism?

Tom Ryall (1978) distinguishes genre criticism from the two approaches dominant at the time of its development: auteurism, and an earlier tradition which saw films as providing social documents. He sees as a central concern of genre criticism the relationship between the art product, its source and its audience. Both *auteur* and 'social document' approaches use a linear model of this relationship, privileging artist or social reality as the originating source of the art product, which, representing their expression, is then consumed by its audience. In contrast, Ryall suggests, the model offered by genre criticism is triangular, with art product, artist and audience as three equally constituting moments in the production of the text – a view which posits a dynamic and mutually determining relationship between them. The basis of this equality lies in the way the conventions of genre operate. They provide a framework of structuring rules, in the shape of patterns/forms/styles/structures, which act as a form of 'supervision' over the work of production of film-makers and the work of reading by an audience. As a critical enterprise genre analysis, which looks for repetitions and variations between films rather than originality or individuality, was developed as a more appropriate tool for understanding popular cinema than authorship theories. Following the structuralist intervention and revival of Marxist aesthetics, genre analysis enables film criticism to take account of conditions of production and consumption of films and their relationship to ideology. Thus Ryall places his original triangle – film/artist/audience – in two concentric circles, the first representing the studio, or particular production institution – the film's immediate industrial context – and the second representing the social formation – here American society, western capitalism – of which the film industry and cinematic signification are a part. Whereas the triangular model displaces the notion of a single originating source, the concentric circles displace an earlier Marxist linear model used to account for historical and social determination – in which the base is seen as unproblematically reflected in the superstructure. In this reconceptualisation art and society are not opposed to each other as two abstract and discrete entities; rather art is understood as one of the social practices in which society exists. Ryall's model, then, attempts to grasp the range of determinants – historical, economic, social, cinematic, aesthetic, ideological – involved in the production of meaning in the cinema, without foreclosing on the question of which element dominates in any given instance (→ NARRATIVE AND STRUCTURALISM: *Narrative and audience*, p. 242).

Ryall's conceptual models enable us to establish the general ground of genre criticism. When we move from this overall project to the particularities of how it works, however, we confront many of the problems which have dogged genre criticism in the cinema. While the existence of the major genres is in some ways a self-evident fact, the business of definition and demarcation is less clear-cut. Description gets tangled up with evaluation, both of which snag on the problem of historical change – new films often deny accepted definitions and appear to the genre critic to mark a decline from 'classic' examples. The problem of evaluation reappears in the need for genre criticism to sort out its relation to auteurism and the relative weight it gives to the play of conventions compared to the work of the author in the

production of particular genre films. The understanding of genre formulae and conventions as a form of cultural tradition poses the problem of how to conceptualise the relation between cultural and other social practices and the ideological roles of the different genres; and this involves consideration of the studio system as part of this relationship. Finally, given that film theory has more recently focused on the production of meaning across all texts, and through all cinematic strategies (→ NARRATIVE AND STRUCTURALISM: *Introduction*, p. 222) we have to ask what pertinence genre criticism can have to this project.

Genres: problems of definition

Work on individual genres sooner or later comes up against the problem of where one genre stops and another begins. Much early genre criticism concentrated on producing accounts of defining characteristics for particular genres. To do this the critic must start out with at least a provisional notion of what constitutes the genre. Andrew Tudor points succinctly to the problem in this:

'To take a genre such as the "western", analyse it, and list its principal characteristics, is to beg the question that we must first isolate the body of films which are "westerns". But they can only be isolated on the basis of the "principle characteristics" which can only be discovered from the films themselves after they have been isolated' (Tudor, 1974, p. 135).

The danger here is that the 'provisional notion' crystallises around certain films or a certain period of genre production as a prescriptive 'essence'. Earlier developments then become an 'evolution' towards a 'classic' moment and later deviations constitute decline or decadence. This is very clearly indicated in the work of the two founding critics of genre study of film, André Bazin and Robert Warshow: both wrote seminal pieces about the western, but both picked on different films from different periods as classic examples of the essence of the genre (→ *The western*, p. 64). At issue here is the place of *differentiation* within the type in genre analysis. Looking to historically discarded literary genres such as Elizabethan revenge tragedy or Restoration comedy as models, Robert Warshow saw repetition rather than differentiation as providing the aesthetic force of a genre:

'For a type to be successful means that its conventions have imposed themselves upon the general consciousness and become the accepted vehicles of a particular set of attitudes and a particular aesthetic effect. One goes to any individual example of the type with very definite expectations, and originality is to be welcomed only in the degree that it intensifies the expected experience without fundamentally altering it' (Warshow, 1970, pp. 129–130).

Laurence Alloway (1971), on the other hand, writing in the context of late 60s developments in genre theory, resists the

The Searchers – 'the western . . . the American film *par excellence*'

The Big Sleep – gangster/crime film with contract star Bogart

Scarface – gangster as tragic hero?

temptation to establish 'classic' timeless dimensions in popular forms. He insists on the transitional and emphemeral character of any particular period of genre production. Rather than attempting definitive accounts of particular genres or genre films he talks about 'cycles, runs or sets', so drawing attention to the shifts and differences which constitute 'internal successive modifications of forms'. Colin McArthur's study of the gangster film (1972) extends this view of differentiation within particular forms to the problems of demarcating one form from another. He argues that one must talk about the gangster/thriller, because the limits of each form are fluid, constituting a spectrum with an infinite number of gradations. He describes the forty-year development of this sprawling genre as 'a constantly growing amoeba, assimilating stages of its own development' (p. 8). A more recent contributor to this debate, Anthony Easthope ('Notes on genre', 1980) has suggested the usefulness of Tzvetan Todorov's argument that a specific genre should be understood as an abstract, theoretical and provisional structure, incarnated in specific examples, but itself transformed by each new production so 'any instance of a genre will be *necessarily* different' (p. 40). Stephen Neale's work similarly argues against attempts to define genres as discrete, strictly differentiated and fixed systems in which the critic searches across the range of cinematic codes for relationships of repetition representing rigid rules of inclusion and exclusion. Neale's position, discussed more fully below, emphasises the role of 'difference' in generic production (see also Vernet, 'Genre', 1978).

However, even with a flexible model, empirical assumptions will enter any discussion of specific genres. If these are to be rigorously founded the critic must decide which of the cinematic codes are pertinent to the definition of a particular genre. In his survey of the early development of British genre criticism, Tom Ryall identifies three broad sets of terms used to net the constituents of individual genres: socio-historical actuality, thematic/ideological constructions deriving from history and iconography or visual imagery.

Iconography

The notion of iconography was perhaps particularly influential in the work of the 60s and early 70s on genre because it offered a parallel course to the one already laid out by the *auteur* validation of Hollywood films. If to literary minds their plots were corny and the dialogue banal this was because the literary critic had no language to cope with cinema as a visual medium. Auteurism developed the notion of *mise en scène* to fill this gap; genre critics turned to iconography. Ed Buscombe (1970), for instance, argued forcibly that it was in terms of iconography – rather than, for example, narrative structure or rhythm – that the dynamic of particular genres

should be specified: 'Since we are dealing with a visual medium we ought surely to look for our defining criteria at what we actually see on the screen . . .' (p. 36). Whereas *mise en scène* provided the means of materialising the author's personal vision, the notion of iconography gave life to the conventions of generic production, investing them with historical and cultural 'resonances' which, put to work in new combinations and contexts, could produce new articulations of meaning. By iconography Buscombe meant recurrent images, including the physical attributes and dress of the actors, the settings, the tools of the trade (horses, cars, guns, etc.). Colin McArthur (1972) makes a similar categorisation for the gangster/thriller, attributing to these icons a degree of formal organisation – a 'continuity over several decades of *patterns* of visual imagery' (p. 24, our emphasis). Although iconography was undeniably 'visual', McArthur in a later unpublished BFI seminar paper, 'Iconography and iconology' (1973), located it in the 'profilmic arrangements of sign-events'. In other words it was not produced by specifically filmic codes but was taken up and transformed by cinema from cultural codes already in circulation, a point returned to below.

Crucial to the functioning of such iconic conventions is the cumulative knowledge and expectation of the audience:

'In *Little Caesar* (1930) a police lieutenant and two of his men visit a nightclub run by gangsters. All three wear large hats and heavy coats, are grim and sardonic and stand in triangular formation, the lieutenant at the front, his two men flanking him in the rear. The audience knows immediately what to expect of them by their physical attributes, their dress and deportment. It knows, too, by the disposition of the figures, which is dominant, which is subordinate' (McArthur, 1972, p. 23).

This knowledge provides the ground on which the 'popular' in the commercial cinema attains its dynamic, the means by which significance, art, is produced sometimes without the artist; for accretions of the cinematic past in generic convention generate a set of expectations in audiences and these provide, as Bourget has suggested, opportunities for their disruption, postponement or displacement; disturbances not necessarily attributable to individual film-makers (Bourget, 'Social implications in Hollywood genres', 1977).

Buscombe has given a celebrated example of iconography at work in his account of the opening of *Guns in the Afternoon*:

'Knowing the period and location, we expect at the beginning to find a familiar western town. In fact, the first few minutes of the film brilliantly disturb expectations. As the camera moves around the town, we discover a policeman in uniform, a car, a camel, and Randolph Scott dressed up as Buffalo Bill. Each of these images performs a function. The figure of the policeman conveys that the law has become institutionalised; the rough and ready frontier days are over. The car suggests, as in *The Wild Bunch*, that the west is no longer isolated from modern technology and its implications. Significantly, the camel is racing against a horse; such a grotesque juxtaposition is painful. A horse in a western is not just an animal but a symbol of dignity, grace and power. These qualities are mocked by it competing with a camel; and to add insult to injury, the camel wins' (Buscombe, in Grant, 1977, p. 44).

Of course, it could be argued that while the genre allows for the introduction of the car into a western under pressure from the industry to mine relatively unworked aspects of its relation to the historical west – in this case the closing of the frontier – only the touch of the baroque sensibilities of a Sam Peckinpah could have dreamed up the camel. However, it is the accumulated tradition of the western that allows

Shane – the western 'talking about America's agrarian past' . . .

a camel to produce so forceful a shock and sense of estrangement (→ *Genre and authorship*, p. 62).

It can be seen from these examples that while iconography is manifested in visual terms it contains considerably more than simple visual imagery – dress connotes character, the three gangsters formation will initiate certain movements in plot, and so on. Moreover, in particular visual motifs iconography focuses a wide range of social, cultural and political themes which are part of the currency of the society for which it works. The art criticism of Erwin Panofsky was often cited by critics looking for a visual rather than literary heritage to illuminate cinematic conventions. Colin McArthur (1973) argues that the iconography of the western or ganster films carries cultural meanings which are 'read' by contemporary western audiences in much the same way that an ordinary Frenchman of the thirteenth century could 'read' Chartres Cathedral and that a seventeenth-century Venetian could 'read' Francesco Maffei's painting of Judith of Bethulia. This aspect of iconography provided the source of some debate with *auteur* critics, and the ground on which the genre critics attempted to argue a more subtle relation between socio-historical actuality and particular genres (→ *Genre: history and ideology*, p. 61).

Iconography dominated genre study as long as the western and gangster genres remained the focus of empirical interest – perhaps because of its capacity to mediate between historical traditions and particular cinematic forms. However despite its basis in visual imagery, iconography fails to take account of the finer detail of visual style – camera movement, lighting, editing, for example. Nor does it deal with patterns of narrative structure. And while it enabled the critic to infer action and character attributes in a film's play of meaning, the shift of interest into new generic areas

– film noir, or melodrama for instance – found the 'iconographical programmes' which seemed appropriate to the western or gangster film restricting, so that the notion of genre was often displaced in favour of visual style or dramatic modality (see Place, and Harvey, in Kaplan, 1978). A further problem was the tendency of the focus on iconography to produce taxonomies which, while they provided the underlying structure of individual genres and were an extremely useful empirical tool for collating the range of cultural knowledge such genres assumed, could offer little illumination of any particular example beyond its membership of a particular genre (see Ryall, 1978, pp. 13 and 24–26). Thus genre criticism would often turn back to authorship to account for individual films, and both Jim Kitses and Colin McArthur provide authorship case studies, though qualified ones, to follow on their seminal accounts of the western and gangster/thriller genres respectively (→ *Genre and authorship*, p. 62).

The problems of an iconographical approach to genre were displaced by the British appropriation of semiotics and structuralism in the 70s, which seemed to offer a totalising account of the production of meaning in the cinema. However, semiotics and structuralism tend to work at an asbtract, formal level, and while they may explain how iconography functions, the iconographical programmes worked out by the earlier genre critics provide an empirical base for locating particular genres and a means of tracing the historical and cultural traditions which give them their social dimension. Later writing on melodrama, for instance – a genre with very fluid boundaries, many sub-generic offshoots and a complex relation to other forms and traditions – has, arguably, suffered from the absence of such empirical groundwork in its frequent lack of precision.

Genre: history and ideology

The foregoing discussion of iconography has already broached the question of the relation of cinematic genres to historical traditions and cultural conventions. This dimension was important to the evaluation of Hollywood genre films in terms of popular rather than high art. In the case of the western and gangster these connections could be traced to historical actuality itself:

'... the western and the gangster film have a special relationship with American society. Both deal with critical phases of American history. It could be said that they represent America talking to itself about, in the case of the western, its agrarian past, and in the case of the gangster film/thriller its urban technological present' (McArthur, 1972, p. 18).

While it is evident that for these genres at least history provides basic subject matter and many aspects of form, the question that confronts genre study is how the relation of history to fiction is to be understood. McArthur's notion of a society 'talking to itself' suggests less a search for historical reconstruction or, in the case of the gangster film, reflection, than what Tom Ryall calls the 'social perception of historical actuality'. This shifts the focus from historical 'fact' to ideology; here, as Tom Ryall (1978) suggests, the historical raw material of a genre is perceived in terms of a network of thematic constructions – for instance, Jim Kitses' (1969) analysis of the history of the west in American consciousness as a conflict between the themes of Garden versus Wilderness (→ *The western*, p. 64).

At issue here is the relation of socio-historical reality and cultural and aesthetic convention. On the one hand, as Colin McArthur (1972) points out, our ideas about the American west or Prohibition are as likely to be gleaned from the cinema as from history books. On the other, Robert Warshow has argued that once historical reality is taken up in an aesthetic process, aesthetic determinations take over: genre films refer not to historical reality but to other genre films and they evolve according to the rules of generic production:

'Moreover, the relationship between the conventions which go to make up such a type and the real experience of its audience or the real facts of whatever situation it pretends to describe is only of secondary importance and does not determine its aesthetic force. It is only in an ultimate sense that the type appeals to its audience's experience of reality; much more immediately, it appeals to previous experience of the type itself: it creates its own field of reference' (Warshow, 1970, pp. 129–130).

Neither of these positions confront the problem of determining *what* meanings are being circulated. However, together they raise interesting questions about the interplay between ideologies and aesthetic conventions in the construction of 'social

... and the gangster film – 'its urban technological present' – *Machine Gun Kelly*

perceptions of history'. Judith Hess ('Genre film and the status quo', in Grant, 1977) starts from the position that generic convention, as a product of formulaic repetition for a capitalist-financed studio system, can only produce meanings in support of the status quo. Genre films drew audiences and were financially successful 'because they temporarily relieved the fears aroused by a recognition of social and political conflicts' (p.54). They did this by encouraging 'simplistic solutions – the adherence to a well-defined, unchanging code, the advocacy of methods of problem solving based on tradition' (p. 55). Clearly behind such a view of the working of convention in the cinema is the assumption that films address the problems of the real world directly, and provide solutions on a realisable level. Genre films are indictable because they construct reality according to outworn, reactionary conventions. An opposite view, in relation to the gangster film, is put by Robert Warshow, who argues that the popularity of this genre rests not in its official solution to a social problem – 'crime does not pay' – but its ability to provide at an imaginative level a quite different response to American society:

'. . . the importance of the gangster film, and the nature and intensity of its emotional and aesthetic impact, cannot be measured in terms of the place of the gangster himself or the importance of the problem of crime in American life . . . What matters is that the experience of the gangster *as an experience of art* is universal to Americans' (Warshow, 1970, p. 130, original emphasis).

'. . . the gangster speaks for us, expressing that part of the American psyche which rejects the qualities and demands of modern life, which rejects 'Americanism' itself . . . the gangster is the 'no' to that great American 'yes' which is stamped so big over our official culture and yet has so little to do with the way we really feel about out lives' (Warshow, 1970, p. 136).

For Warshow, generic convention is distinct from the social reality on which it feeds, thus allowing the possibility of ideological criticism. The aesthetic compulsion of generic repetition then suggests, as it were, a neuralgic point – 'there is something more here than meets the eye'.

The emergence in the late 60s of a concern with the workings of ideology in cinematic forms found a progressive potential for genre in the requirement for differentiation at the commercial as well as aesthetic level – the *difference* being precisely what draws the audience back into the cinema for the pleasure of repetition, and what makes 'the same' perceptible (← HISTORY: *The studios*, p. 10). Jean-Loup Bourget (1977) argues that 'wherever an art form is highly conventional, the opportunity for subtle irony or distanciation presents itself all the more readily' (p. 62).

The concept of radical reading – suggesting that generic conventions allow

meanings to be constructed against a film's ideological grain – introduces a further problem in the task of relating genres to socio-historical reality: the question of whether the meanings we construct for a genre are those understood by the audience who went to see the films when they first appeared, or those which belong to a contemporary perception of both socio-historical and cinematic actuality. This means respecting the historical conditions of production and consumption (see Ryall, 1978, pp. 11–12) and drawing on the understanding given us by semiotics of the potentially multiple meanings of any signification and our dependency on particular cultural contexts for specific readings.

Genre and industry
So far discussion has focused on how authorial concerns and socio-historical reality have been seen as caught up in the interplay between aesthetic structures and their audiences – arguably producing something far removed from either social actuality or a director's intentions. It remains to consider the place of this activity in the film industry and the wider institution of cinema. While history has often been posed as a source of a genre's subject matter, and social or psychic reasons credited with maintaining an audience's interest in a particular genre, the economic organisation of the film industry along the lines of commodity production is cited as the reason for the existence of genres themselves. As the market for entertainment is notoriously difficult to predict and control, profit is dependent on the successful identification and capture of particular audiences. Generic production grew out of the attempt to repeat and build on initial successes. The studio system developed to facilitate such production: 'each genre had its regular scriptwriters, sometimes on a yearly contract, its directors, its craftsmen, its studios' (Metz, 1974, p. 122). Tom Ryall (1978) describes how 'the standardisation of product obliged by the economic necessities of large scale industrial production led to particular studios concentrating on particular genres' (p. 4). And Ed Buscombe ('Walsh and Warner Bros', 1974), argued that at Warner Bros 'stars and genre were . . . mutually reinforcing' (p. 59) – the presence of Cagney and Bogart on contract there favoured production of gangster films and vice versa. Moreover if a studio spent a lot of money acquiring a star or another sort of 'generic asset' – e.g. an elaborate western townscape or nightclub set – the cost could be spread over extended periods of production and returns maximised against capital outlay.

It was not only production that was organised along generic lines. Distribution and exhibition sought to market films and attract audiences by mobilising a set of expectations through advertising and promotional gimmicks, while film journalism

and critical reviewing perpetuated generic divisions by working within generic expectations and assumptions.

In this context it has been argued that any study of Hollywood or the studio system must be a study of genre. The problem, however, is not to identify the economic rationale for genres, but to know what such knowledge tells us about this particular aspect of cultural production. Tom Ryall argues that it indicates one set of constraints in the production context of film-making which must be taken into account but not accorded sole determination over the end products. This context, particularly in an entertainment industry, is not and cannot function monolithically. Not only is product differentiation an economic necessity, but:

'. . . the production personnel of a film will include a number of people whose practices fall under the general rubric of "the creative", e.g. directors, scriptwriters, actors, actresses, designers and so on. A corpus of individuals whose ideology of film will inevitably differ from that of those whose primary allegiance is to a Wall Street finance house. Any description of the Hollywood system will have to take account of the many different often contradictory, tendencies which jostle with each other during the production of a film' (Ryall, 1978, p. 32).

More recently Stephen Neale (1980) has tried to extend the purchase of industrial consideration on genre by utilising the concept of cinematic institution or machine developed by Christian Metz and Stephen Heath amongst others, and taking a cue from Ryall's references to generic marketing and reviewing practices. In this perspective the industry is seen not so much as an economic or manufacturing system, but rather as a social institution constituted in a number of discursive practices which include both production and consumption. Genres are not simply the outcome of a certain kind of studio organisation but involve the consolidation in the spectator of a set of viewing orientations, expectations, positions. Behind this lies an attempt to provide a more dialectical model of the relation between industry, text and audience and to conceptualise it as a *process* rather than a series of reflections between a number of discrete, fixed and static positions. This reconceptualisation of the film industry as cinematic institution prepares the ground for Neale's interest in locating genre within a general, psychoanalytic theory of narrative (see below, p. 63).

Genre and authorship
Having outlined the different ways in which genre criticism was established it remains to consider how its relation to authorship was conceived after its initial challenge to this tradition. Only Laurence Alloway appeared to accept the total displacement of the author by generic convention, arguing that collective authorship

and diffusion of responsibility are the actual working conditions of Hollywood and that authorship is therefore much less appropriate than genre theory in analysis of the American cinema:

'The rhetoric of art discussion tends to require . . . personal authorship and a high level of permanence, criteria not easily satisfied in the popular cinema . . . reflex homage to personal originality too often makes us dismiss as aesthetically formulaic a negligible film that may be an interesting, valid, even original development within the convention' (Alloway, 1971, p. 60).

At the other extreme is the view that while indubitably genre conventions exist, their productivity is dependent on the animating power of an author:

'. . . if genre exists as a distinct quantity it is in terms of a repertoire of stock situations, selected from the events of the American frontier, that are themselves unspecific, ambiguous and intrinsically without meaning . . . neither a structure of archetypal patterns and myths nor of history is sufficiently precise to constitute a genre, nor do recurrent locations, clothes and props do more than signal a temporal and geographical context for a film' (Collins, 'Genre: a reply to Ed Buscombe', 1970, pp. 74–75).

Thus history and myth are mediated through the obsessions of the author to animate the conventions of the western with a power attributed by Buscombe and others to the genre itself.

Most genre criticism, however, avoids the extremes of either of these positions, positing a relation between genre convention and authorial concerns which in different ways could be beneficial to the latter. In one view there can be a coincidence between genre and author which enables the director to use its conventions as a kind of shorthand, enabling him or her to go straight to the heart of his/her concerns and express them at a formal level through the interplay of genre convention and motif – a common view, for instance, of the relation between John Ford and the western. In another view the author works in tension with the conventions; attempting to inflect them, so as to express his/her own vision in the differences set up between the expected playing out of the convention and the new twists s/he develops – a vision expressed in counterpoint (see McArthur, 1972, p. 17; → AUTHORSHIP: *The auteur theory*, p. 137). A third view posits genre as a beneficial constraint which provides a formal ordering and control over the drive to personal expression, preventing its dissolution in an excess of individualism and incomprehensibility, but at the same time capable of containing a certain nonnaturalistic dimension – the theatricality or expressionism of a baroque sensibility. Colin McArthur argues such a position in relation to Jules Dassin, whose work within the apparent greater freedom of European cinema he sees as inferior to his

earlier Hollywood productions.

Finally it remains to note that authorship was often the only recourse for genre critics who wanted to move from discussing the constituents and functioning of the genre itself to discussing their operation in particular films. If genre films could not be evaluated against some presupposed definitive model, then their particularity had to be netted by overlaying another grid, and authorship was the obvious one to hand. Both the major book studies of genres that culminated the first phase of genre study, *Horizons West* and *Underworld USA*, devoted their second halves to looking at individual genre films categorised by author. Thus the question of the place of the author did not disappear. Moreover the difference in *Underworld USA* between the chapters on John Huston and Nicholas Ray suggest that genre and author codes do have different weight in different cases and that these distinctions may parallel those between *auteur* and *metteur en scène* (→ AUTHORSHIP: *The politique des auteurs*, p. 119).

Genre: redirections in the 80s

Both Tom Ryall (1978) and Stephen Neale (1980) imply in their respective assessments of the first 'wave' of genre criticism the need to place genre within a more 'totalising' theory of cinema. Tom Ryall draws on the concepts of 'cultural production' and 'reading' as a means of shifting genre criticism from the circular and taxonomic tendencies of its earlier phase. The notion of *cultural production* places film making as one more practice in a 'network of social practices which constitute a social formation' (p. 24). It therefore stands in dynamic relationship to these practices, overlapping with them, mediating them, participating in a shared body of cultural knowledge or group of discourses, while at the same time operating within its own history and productivity. In this perspective film making is in the business of producing or reproducing and circulating varieties of pleasure and cultural meaning. Access to cultural meaning is through the activity of *reading*, understood as the mobilisation of a particular set of conventions and audience expectations. Genre study for Ryall, then, becomes the 'elaboration of perceived meaning where the individual film is tied to its generic roots on the basis of the reading process' (p. 26). The point is not to allocate particular films to their respective genres, but to investigate the implications of our being able to do this at all. Such an examination of how and why the perceived meanings of a film are produced in particular contexts are not tied to the specific text, but can pull back to look at the social motivations and expectations that governed its production, marketing and consumption.

For Stephen Neale, Ryall's approach, although giving valuable insight into the way genre can be reconceptualised, is not totalising enough. Film-makers and audience, history, industry, and society still retain a degree of discreteness and autonomy, confronting each other as a series of dichotomies rather than in dialectic process. For Neale, any aspect of film must be understood in terms of the social process of cinema as a whole. Working within a psychoanalytic framework, this must in turn be understood in terms of the role of signification in producing and

My Darling Clementine – Wyatt Earp . . . 'an agent of eastern expansion into the west'

regulating subjectivity. Here subjectivity is understood not as a discrete and fixed identity, but involves three basic propositions. First, that the subject is driven by the desire to repeat a past pleasure that can never be attained because something can only be perceived as the same through a gap of difference. Second, that identity is always conferred from the position of another – a 'you' is essential to the meaning of 'I'. All signification repeats this basic pattern, constructing inter-personal subject positions which speaker and addressee must fill in order for signification to take place. Third, that in consequence of one and two, an autonomous and stable identity can never be attained; rather subjectivity is a *process*, in which individuals move in and out of positions constructed for them in the various discourses which constitute society (→ NARRATIVE AND STRUCTURALISM: *Narrative and audience*, p. 242).

In this perspective genres have to be seen as specific modes of the narrative system, which function to exploit and contain the diversity of mainstream cinema. As components of the cinematic machine they represent 'systems of orientations, expectations and conventions that circulate between industry, text and subject' (p. 19). Above all genres work on the terrain of repetition and difference which it is the work of narrative to regulate. Neale is at pains here to stress repetition and difference as a *relation* rather than as distinct elements. There can be no difference except in so far as it emerges from repetition and, vice versa, it is only the element of difference that allows repetition to become visible.

Genres, then, are not discrete systems, consisting of a fixed number of listable items and separated out from the rest of cinema, but 'constitute specific variations of the interplay of codes, discursive structures and drives involved in the whole of mainstream cinema' (p. 48). In order to locate the 'specific variation' of a particular genre we have to know how narrative organises the codes and discourses which are its material. Narrative is 'a process of transformation of the balance of elements that constitute its pretext; the interruption of an initial equilibrium and tracing of the dispersal and refiguration of its elements' (p. 20). Generic specification starts therefore with a consideration of the way in which equilibrium and disruption are articulated. Difference between genres occurs in the particular discourses invoked, the particularity of emphasis on and combinations of elements that are shared with other genres – for instance the relative placing and relations between the discourses of law and heterosexual love are what differentiate the melodrama from the film noir, not the exclusivity of one kind of discourse to one genre. Such different emphases and relations between different discourses produce different positionings of the subject. Genre specification can

therefore be traced in the different functionings of subjectivity each produces, and in their different modes of addressing the spectator.

Neale's intervention into genre criticism represents an attempt to reorientate the task of genre specification in order to achieve a greater flexibility in demarcation – for instance the emphasis on the relation of repetition and difference allows for the textual productivity of overlaps and contradictions – and a greater sense of how genre may draw on other forms of cinematic signification. As it stands, his account operates at a highly abstract level, the specification of discourses appearing no easier than the categorisation of icons, and often relying on an already established iconographic base as clues to their presence.

References

Lawrence Alloway, *Violent America: the movies 1946–64*, New York, Museum of Modern Art, 1971.
André Bazin, 'The western, or the American film *par excellence*' and 'The evolution of the western' in Hugh Gray (ed. and trans.), *What is Cinema?* Vol. 2, Berkeley, University of California Press, 1971.
Jean-Loup Bourget, 'Social implications in Hollywood genres', in Grant (ed.), *Film Genre: Theory and Criticism*, Metuchen, N.J., Scarecrow Press, 1977.
Edward Buscombe, 'The idea of genre in the American cinema', *Screen* vol. 11 no. 2, March/April 1970.
Edward Buscombe, 'Walsh and Warner Bros', in Hardy (ed.), *Raoul Walsh*, Edinburgh Film Festival, 1974.
John Cawelti, *The Six-Gun Mystique*, Bowling Green, Ohio, Bowling Green University Popular Press, 1971.
Richard Collins, 'Genre: a reply to Ed Buscombe', *Screen* vol. 11 no. 4/5, July/October 1970.
Anthony Easthope, 'Notes on Genre', *Screen Education* no. 32/33, Winter/Spring 1979/80.
Barry Grant, (ed.), *Film Genre: Theory and Criticism*, cit.
Judith Hess, 'Genre film and the status quo', in Grant (ed.), *Film Genre: Theory and Criticism*, cit.
E. Ann Kaplan, (ed.), *Women and Film Noir*, London, BFI, 1978.
Jim Kitses, *Horizons West*, London, Secker & Warburg/BFI, 1969.
Colin McArthur, *Underworld USA*, London, Secker & Warburg/BFI, 1972.
Colin McArthur, 'Iconography and iconology', London, BFI Education seminar paper, 1973.
Christian Metz, *Language and Cinema*, The Hague, Mouton, 1974.
Stephen Neale, *Genre*, London, BFI, 1980.
Douglas Pye, 'Genre and movies', *Movie* no. 20, 1975.
Tom Ryall, *Teachers Study Guide No. 2: The Gangster Film*, London, BFI Education, 1978.
Andrew Tudor, *Theories of Film*, London, Secker & Warburg/BFI, 1974.
Marc Vernet, 'Genre', in *Film Reader* 3, 1978.
Robert Warshow, 'The Gangster as tragic hero', and 'Movie Chronicle: *The Westerner*', in *The Immediate Experience*, New York, Atheneum Books, 1970.
Will Wright, *Sixguns and Society: a structural study of the western*, Berkeley, University of California Press, 1975.

The western

Introduction

Arguably the western represented the starting point of genre criticism in Britain, contributing to the popular culture debate evidence of the capacity of Hollywood formula films to produce works of significance and value. In the 60s discussions of genre mostly used the western as their chief example, and were less interested in the critical problems of the notion of genre itself than they were in demonstrating the value of western films.

Alan Lovell characterised the critical context of this debate in the following way:

'For Anglo-Saxon critics, the western is typical of most of the vices of the mass media. It is endlessly repetitive, utterly simple in form and expresses naive attitudes. For French critics, the western contains nearly all the things they most admire in the American cinema, its directness, its intelligence, its energy, its formal concerns' ('The western', 1967, p. 93).

This work of reclamation reflected its British context in the struggle to deflect, sometimes by incorporating, a Leavisite literary tradition, and in its concern to argue via the western for the place of Hollywood films in education. Two main concerns can be traced: the first, the status of the western as popular art and the capacity of such forms to handle questions of value and morality; and the second, the contribution of convention to great films or the work of great directors (see Hall and Whannel, 1964, Ch. 4).

The western and history

A key notion in the validation of the Hollywood western has been its relation to history and to national cultural motifs. As we are repeatedly told, the material of the western is drawn from a brief period in the winning and settling of the American frontier:

'... Hollywood's West has typically been from about 1865 to 1890 or so ... within its brief span we can count a number of frontiers in the sudden rush of mining camps, the building of railways, the Indian wars, the cattle drives, the coming of the farmer. Together with the last days of the Civil War and the exploits of the badmen, here is the raw material of the western' (Kitses, 1969, p. 8).

Although a widespread anti-mass media view of the western was that it travestied the West, only a few serious approaches to the genre attempted to found their arguments on its historical truth. The French critic, Jean-Louis Rieupeyrout, argued enthusiastically that the pleasures of the western derive from its reconstruction of the adventures of the frontier. He had spent much time researching the sources of individual western films and considered that proof of authenticity should change condescending attitudes to the form. However the potential naivety of his notion of

... 'the raw material of the western' – cattle drives in *My Darling Clementine* ...

... and the building of railways and crossing of frontiers in *Iron Horse*

historical reflection is mitigated by his accepting as historical sources secondary elaborations in oral folklore, and newspaper journalism, so that an imaginative response to frontier tales becomes part of the fabric of history (Rieupeyrout, 'The western: a historical genre', 1952). The majority of commentators, however, have been concerned with either the contribution of history to the thematic structure and narrative functioning of the western, or with the transformations performed by successive fictionalisations of the West.

The problem of relating history and the western has been posed in different ways. One form of the question is to ask why this particular brief stretch of history is capable of sustaining such a wide range of cultural elaboration over so long a period. Two answers emerge. One, from the perspective of cultural history, argues that the conditions of existence in the West put into particularly sharp focus and provided imagery for a deep-seated ideological tension in America's view of itself and of progress – a tension axed around the conflicting ideals of unfettered individualism and community values represented in opposing views of the West as Desert or Garden. The second, looking for greater socio-economic precision, argues that within these narrow geographic and temporal boundaries assembled an exemplary cross-section of social types, representing a range of economic and social interests in struggle and caught in a variety of activities eminently susceptible to the kind of narrativisation that can illuminate the underlying play of historical forces.

From such approaches arises a second way of posing the history/western question, i.e. the relation of fictionalised history not simply to the past it represents, but to the contemporary audiences for whom it is constructed. While some critics see the genre as crucially linked to the American problem of national identity (see Kitses, 1969) and imply the enduring viability of a set of representations produced out of a particular historical experience for succeeding generations, others argue for greater historical determinism, attempting to link different phases of western production to changes in economic and ideological conditions (Wagner, 'The western, history and actuality', 1961; Wright, 1975), or even to particular political leaders in power (French, 1973).

For critics in the first category a crucial factor is the precise moment in the conquering of the West that the western takes up – a moment critical in the formation of America as a nation, balanced between the past and the future, 'when options are still open' (Kitses, 1969, p. 12). Most critics agree that the fact that this moment of choice is past intensifies its possibility for ideological elaboration. Options closed off by history and a developing social order can safely be reopened, nostalgically indulged, judged and closed off again (see Pye, 'Genre and history', 1977/78; Warshow, 'Movie chronicle: *The Westerner*', 1970).

The implication that the western is specific to American culture and history raises the question of the genre's almost universal appeal and its production in different cultural contexts, e.g. the Italian westerns made between 1965 and 1975. Rieupeyrout (1952) deals with this problem by assuming a universal fascination with enacted history. Bazin (1971) side-steps it by asserting a mythic dimension through which the western finds in frontier history sympathetic material for reworking older and more universal themes. Other critics assert the importance of the movement westward and of America itself for older European nations, the 'idea of the West' having dominated western civilisation since classical times (Kitses, 1969, pp. 8–9).

Founding fathers

Most influential in Anglo-Saxon criticism of the western were André Bazin's two essays, 'The western, or the American film *par excellence*', and 'The evolution of the western' (1971), and Robert Warshow's 'Movie chronicle: *The Westerner*' (1970), all written in the 50s. Both writers were concerned with defining the essence of the western film in order to locate its cinematic and cultural significance. They examine the development of the genre and attempt to determine its outer boundaries, so that they can distinguish acceptable transformations from violations. At the centre of their investigations stands a 'classic example' against which they evaluate earlier and later developments. Writing, however, from different perspectives and in different cultural contexts both their choice of example and their estimation of the value of the western differ.

André Bazin

As a celebrated proponent of cinematic realism (→ NARRATIVE AND STRUCTURALISM: *Bazin*, p. 224) Bazin's account of the genre's realism is surprisingly oblique as he steers round the obvious pitfalls of a naive view of the relationship between the western and history:

'... the relations between the facts of history and the western are not immediate and direct, but dialectic. Tom Mix is the opposite of Abraham Lincoln, but after his own fashion he perpetuates Lincoln's cult and memory' (Bazin, 'The western, or the American film *par excellence*', 1971, p. 143).

Between history and cinema a process of mythologising has taken place.

'Those formal attributes by which one normally recognises the western are simply signs or symbols of its profound reality, namely the myth. The western was born of an encounter between a mythology and a means of expression . . .' (p. 142).

For Bazin myth is an idealisation of historical reality; the historical and sociological conditions of the West permit imaginative elaborations dealing with fundamental realities that exceed the particular moment, replaying in contempor-

Stagecoach – Bazin's classic western mythologising history

ary form metaphysical and moral dramas that recur throughout the history of cultural expression. The particular myth that Bazin elaborates is 'the great epic Manicheism which sets the forces of evil over against the knights of the true cause' (p. 145), at the centre of which is the woman posed as representative of the good. This myth is demanded by the actual sociological conditions of the West and the role of women in the conquering and civilising of the frontier, but it both points back to earlier cultural forms, for instance the courtly romance, and also works through problems of the ambiguous relation of law and social justice, or morality and individual conscience, endemic to civilisation itself.

For Bazin the ideal example of this mythologising of history is *Stagecoach* (Ford, 1939) made in a brief period (1937–40) in which the western arrived at its classic peak, that 'ideal balance between social myth, historical reconstruction, psychological truth, and the traditional theme of the western *mise en scène*' ('The evolution

of the western', p. 149). Against this classical achievement Bazin poses the post-war emergence of the 'superwestern' which under pressure to deal with serious themes appropriate to the times, and self-conscious of its own history, effectively treated the western as 'a form in need of a content', stepping outside the parameters of its own concerns to bring in 'aesthetic, social, moral, psychological, political or erotic interest, in short some quality extrinsic to the genre and which is supposed to enrich it' (p. 151). *High Noon* (1952) and *Shane* (1952) are examples of this tendency. However, Bazin argues, the traditional western did not die, but continued to be nourished at its popular base, in the 'B' westerns churned out in great numbers during the 50s, e.g. *The Gun-fighter* (Henry King, 1950), or by older directors whose experience in western traditions was not to be deflected by new trends, e.g. *The Big Sky* (Howard Hawks, 1952). The 50s also produced a group of newer directors who managed to make a class of western which, while developing a more contemporary flavour, did not break with the spirit of the true western, a class which Bazin termed 'novelistic', and characterised by their lyricism and their sincere rather than patronising approach to the form, e.g. *Johnny Guitar* (Nicholas Ray, 1954), *Bend of the River* and *The Far Country* (Anthony Mann, 1952 and 1954).

Robert Warshow

Like Bazin, Warshow, writing in 1954, sets out to define the essence of the western and like Bazin he sees its value in its capacity to handle moral ambiguity in traditionally epic terms. However, while Bazin writes from a Catholic/existentialist perspective and locates the struggle between good and evil as informing history itself, Warshow

is concerned with the aesthetic realisation of ideological conflicts attendant on the development of twentieth-century American capitalism. His concern, as for many writers on the western since, is the relation of the individual to society, the westerner rather than the western. Warshow defines the western hero in relation to the same problematic which, he argues, produced the gangster as tragic hero. The latter's acquisitive urge and inevitable defeat represents 'the "no" to that great American "yes" which is stamped so big over our official culture and yet has so little to do with the way we really feel about our lives' (Warshow, 'Movie chronicle: *The Westerner*', 1970, p. 136). However, while the gangster's desperate need to prove himself drives him from one bout of activity to another, the westerner is self-contained, knows his worth, and needs only to be able to live by his code. In this respect he represents a type of hero, of individualism, not realisable in twentieth-century society. In these terms the historical West is important only in as much as it is *past* – 'Where the westerner lives it is always about 1870 – not the real 1870, either, or the real West . . .' (p. 141) – and in so far as the material it offers the cinema, 'the land and the horses', provide a 'moral openness'. In the western guns are carried openly rather than secretly as in the gangster film, forcing the hero into moral self-responsibility. The other crucial aspect of this hero for Warshow is his relation to violence. Unlike the opportunism of the gangster, the Westerner's violence is a statement of his being, and he waits for the quintessential moment in which to express this (p. 140).

For Warshow then, the central problem of the western is individual *masculine* identity and the violence necessary to its expression. His conception of the place of women in the western is the antithesis of Bazin's, for whom woman is the object of a metaphyiscal struggle between good and evil. In Warshow's account the role of women is associated with the establishment of community and the necessary qualifications of individualism and violence brought by the civilising of the frontier. Prior to this moment 'the West, lacking the graces of civilisation, is the place "where men are men": in western movies, men have the deeper wisdom and women are children' (p. 138).

The western's move from primitivism to full maturity Warshow cautiously attributes to a deeper realism – more in terms of philosophical outlook and the ageing of the stars than in terms of historical truth. The western grows up when it foregoes its innocent romanticism and recognises the tragic limitations of the frontier ethos, as for instance in Henry King's *The Gunfighter* (1950). However, when the impulse to realism breaks totally with this ethos and the code of the westerner for the sake of a '"reinterpretation" of the West as a developed society' we arrive at a different genre, social drama for which the western setting is irrelevant except as a backdrop. *High Noon* (1952) provides an example of this kind of breakdown. Warshow also identifies an opposite tendency away from realism towards an aesthetic embalming of western conventions in response to their mythological and cinematic potential. Here Bazin's exemplum, *Stagecoach* (1939) and Ford's later *My Darling Clementine* (1946) stand accused.

Alan Lovell: the western's formal history
Both Bazin and Warshow define the essence of the western and choose their classic examples with scant reference to the historical development of the genre, basing their judgements on their own

of *Billy the Kid* in 1930 (Lovell, 1967, p. 97). For Lovell, the history of the western over the next twenty years can be understood in terms of the working of these elements into a coherent formal structure. From this perspective *My Darling Clementine* (1946) becomes the classic centre of the genre. In this film the narrative is structured by the revenge theme, which is itself integrated into the historical theme of civilising the West, as the hero's quest for personal revenge is translated into the establishment of law and order for the nascent township of Tombstone, under the influence of the heroine schoolteacher from the East (→ AUTHORSHIP: *John Ford*, p. 184).

Although not all these elements necessarily recur in every western since *Clemen-*

From this position Lovell goes on to argue against the assumed naivety of the pre-war westerns, and against the attribution of a precocious progressivism to the so-called adult westerns of the 50s – sympathetic treatment of the Indian for instance may be less a contemporary concern with racial questions than an exploration of ambiguous attitudes to the coming of civilisation to the West which are contained in the structure of the genre. However, Lovell does not deny that 50s westerns also bear the marks of the prevailing climate of ideas or of the influx of a post-war generation of new and more cinematically conscious directors. But rather than a transformation of the genre, this represents 'the imposition of a new sensibility on the old forms', and Lovell

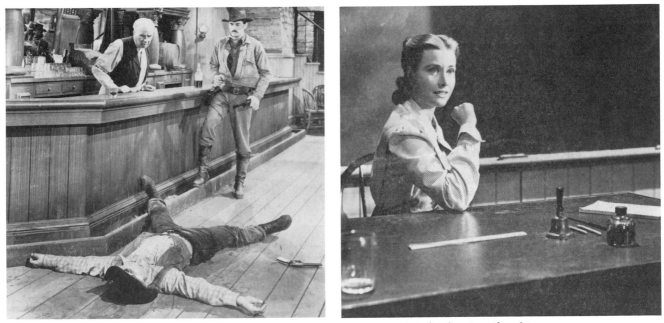

The Gunfighter – the tragic western hero (male) exists outside of social values and civilised society (female)

respective metaphysical and ideological concerns. Alan Lovell ('The western', 1967) sought a more objective way of establishing the parameters of the genre by examining its formal history. Such an attempt, he argues, must take account of the themes and forms introduced into the western through its *source materials* and of how it combined, displaced or transformed these in its movement towards establishing a coherent and stable structure. Lovell defines four principal elements which contributed to the formation of the western genre: 1) a structure drawn from nineteenth-century popular melodramatic literature, involving a virtuous hero and wicked villain who menaces a virginal heroine; 2) 'an action story, composed of violence, chases and crimes appropriate to a place like the American West in the 19th century'; 3) the introduction of the history of the migration westwards and the opening of the frontier signalled in such films as *The Covered Wagon* (1924) and *The Iron Horse* (1924); and 4) the revenge structure, which was present by the time

tine, the structural balance identified in that film, Lovell argues, is determining in the genre's subsequent development. Against frequent assertions that 50s westerns broke with their primitive past to become more adult, sophisticated and individualised Lovell argues for the continuity between pre- and post-war westerns, positing a tradition that runs from *My Darling Clementine* (1946) through *The Gunfighter* (1950) to *Guns in the Afternoon* (1962), and citing the shared characteristics of *The Left-Handed Gun* (1958), often seen as one of the 'more modern' westerns, and *My Darling Clementine*. From this perspective, shifts in emphasis in the genre become interesting not in terms of breaks with a classic past but rather in terms of significant differences produced in relation to a maintained continuity. Thus *The Oxbow Incident* (1943), maligned by Warshow for its illegitimate concern with problems of social organisation in the West, becomes interesting for its recasting of familiar elements in a darker, more pessimistic tone.

argues that 'part of the fascination of the western in the 50s results from the confusions caused when this . . . comes into contact with the traditional forms of the genre' (p. 101). It is then arguable that some of these films are simply confused, but that others such as *Guns in the Afternoon* (1962) or *The Tall T* (1957) demonstrate the productive power of genre confronted with 'new sensibility'.

Jim Kitses: Horizons West
Jim Kitses' book (1969) on the western and western directors represents an attempt to deepen knowledge of the genre by consciously confronting, in its influential first chapter, many of the problems of generic criticism exhibited in earlier writings on the subject, namely prescriptiveness, the task of relating the western to history and the problem of understanding it as myth. Whereas Alan Lovell tackles the problem of arbitrary prescriptiveness by describing the history of a central tradition, Kitses attempts a synchronic and structural account of the genre's basic elements.

Thus he takes account of the genre's complex historical and socio-cultural inheritance in order to propose, rather than a central model, 'a loose, shifting and variegated genre with many roots and branches' (p. 17), which can account for films made at any period. History, in his account, is not the record of the genre's development but what has made the genre so fruitful.

Kitses sees history as contributing to the western in two ways. First, it provides the national cultural tradition in which the western is rooted and to which it speaks, and secondly, in a narrower sense, it offers as 'raw material' that brief historical span which covers the opening of the American frontier, 1865–1890.

For a definition of the particular cultural tradition underlying the western Kitses turns to Henry Nash Smith's seminal study, *Virgin Land*. Citing a range of political and cultural output, Nash Smith identifies as central to America's national consciousness an ambiguous attitude to the West, torn between the symbols of Garden and Desert. Several commentators have seen this ambiguity as providing much of the thematic preoccupations of the western (see Lovell, 1967; McArthur, 'The roots of the Western', 1969). Under the master opposition, Wilderness/Civilisation, Kitses elaborates a series of antinomies which together represent a 'philosophical dialectic, an ambiguous cluster of meanings and attitudes that provide the traditional/thematic structure of the genre' (p. 11). The shift in meanings from the top to the bottom of each set of oppositions – the Wilderness starting with the Individual and Freedom and ending with Tradition and the Past, while Civilisation starts with the Community and Restriction and ends with Change and the Future – demonstrates both the flexibility of the structure and the ideological tension which it embodies. While the structure animates many forms of cultural activity, the use of frontier history in the western brought it into particularly acute focus, for the period was placed 'at exactly that moment when options are still open, the dream of a primitivistic individualism, the ambivalence of at once beneficent and threatening horizons still tenable' (p. 12). A third factor in the genre's appropriation of frontier history was that it had already been reworked in folkloric and mythic terms. Kitses attempts to differentiate the varieties of meaning attendant on the concept of myth, and to distinguish between a mythic dimension frequently attributed to twentieth-century popular culture, and the tales of gods and heroes handed down through oral traditions from classical and medieval times. While the western does not represent myth in the latter sense, it 'incorporates elements of *displaced* (or corrupted) myth on a scale that can render them considerably more prominent than in most art' (p. 14). Such incorporation takes place through the western's particularly

varied inheritance from the popular literary forms in which frontier history was first reworked. Following Northrop Frye's definition of archetypes, Kitses argues that different literary modes are characterised by types of hero and patterns of heroic action. Central to the western was the mode of romance 'which insisted on the idealisation of characters who wielded near-magical powers' (p. 15), and provided . . . 'the movement of a god-like figure into the demonic wasteland, the death and resurrection, the return to a paradisal garden' (p. 20).

Wilderness vs. civilisation – the community buries its dead in *The Searchers*

However, the incursion of morality play, melodrama, revenge tragedy into the tradition together with the input from wild west shows and cracker-barrel humour meant that the western could develop within different modes and draw on a rich and complex profusion of mythic and archetypal elements. Finally the cultural resources of the western are enriched cinematically by the repertoire of visual iconography most frequently commented on in generic studies (e.g. Buscombe, 'The idea of genre in the American cinema', 1970; Collins, 'Genre: a reply to Ed Buscombe', 1970).

Thus Kitses provides an account of the western as a four-part structure: 1) frontier history, 2) the thematic antinomies of Wilderness/Civilisation; 3) archetype, and 4) iconography. Contrary to argument that a non-prescriptive genre criticism must be limited to description (see Ryall, 'The notion of genre', 1970), Kitses sees in the conceptual richness of the western genre a potential source of value, capable of realisation in the hands of 'the artist of vision in rapport with the genre' (p. 20). The peak of authorial westerns, however, is dependent on the structure produced by a particular social, cultural and formal history, a structure, moreover which includes the existence of the large popular

audience who supported the development of the 'mass production at the base' which in turn 'allows refinement and reinvigoration' at the peak (p. 21). Thus, 'the western is not just the men who have worked within it . . . an empty vessel breathed into by the film-maker' (p. 26) but represents a vital structure 'saturated with conceptual significance' (p. 21).

Will Wright

Will Wright's much debated intervention (1975) in discussion of the western (see Frayling, 1981) sought to shift the loose-

ness of its validation in terms of general moral or archetypal themes, cultural or psychological conflicts. He insists first that the significance of the western must be located in its appeal to contemporary popular audiences, which are subject to historical change, and secondly that it must be treated as an aspect of communication, subject to the rules that govern the production of symbolic meaning. He calls on the structural linguistics of Saussure and Jakobson and the structural anthropology of Lévi-Strauss to support his argument that all human endeavour is an effort to communicate meaning. In Wright's view the work of myth or mass culture is not to achieve emotional expression of problems arising elsewhere, in the psyche or cultural climate, but itself contributes to them through the forms of knowledge it produces. Thus in the cinema the western myth 'has become part of the cultural language by which America understands itself' (p. 12). What interests Wright in structuralism is its promise of a methodology for understanding scientifically how social communication works. Where he differs from the structuralists is in his retention of a sociological concern to analyse what meanings are produced in particular societies in given historical periods. What he is attempting then is to make content analysis more rigorous (p. 10).

In approaching the western from this standpoint Wright starts out from a number of basic premises. First, integrating Lévi-Strauss's view of primitive myth with Kenneth Burke's narrative theory, Wright contends that modern societies, despite the apparent authority of science, history and literature, still have recourse to myth as a means of producing knowledge of and order in the world. Second, he argues that western films represent industrially produced stories made from mythic material already in social circulation which are amenable to the same, if liberalised, kind of analysis that Propp used on the Russian oral folk-tale or Lévi-Strauss on the myths of tribal peoples (→ NARRATIVE AND STRUCTURALISM: *Propp*, p. 234; *Lévi-Strauss*, p. 232). Third, he asserts that because analysis of the western as myth stresses the social and historical (rather than formal, authorial or industrial) production of meaning, its mythic significance can only be found in what the mass of people went to see. The 'classic' westerns are those most popular in the period in which the genre achieves clear definition and contours, not examples chosen in terms of a schema already constructed in the critic's mind, whether generic, cultural or authorial. Box-office popularity is in its turn an indicator of the 'meanings viewers demand of the myth' (p. 12). Wright therefore confines his structural analysis to those westerns which grossed $4,000,000 dollars or more. From these films he seeks to derive the 'communicative structure of the western' (p. 12), and from shifts in the structure over the decades to reveal a pattern of change and development 'corresponding to changes in the structure of dominant institutions' (p. 14).

Wright's final premise is that the history of the American West supplies the western with appropriate material for the production of myth. This it does in two main ways. First it furnished a dramatic concatenation of social types and actions productive of the kinds of oppositions from which, in Lévi-Straussian terms, myth is made; and second, these character types and actions were capable of carrying the meanings and shifts in meaning which could make sense of the social conflicts dominant in American society at any one time (p. 6).

The meaning of the myths circulated by the western is located in two basic structures: one of binary oppositions in which its characters are placed; and another, the organisation of these characters' functions into narrative sequences. Here Wright uses the Proppian notion of 'character function' – which he interprets as a single action or attribute referring to roles performed in the plot – as a link between Lévi-Straussian oppositions and an argument mounted by the philosopher, Arthur Danto, that any narrative sequence, in so far as it describes a change in an initial state of affairs, also includes an explanation of it. In the *explanatory* function of narrative, combined with the *representative* function of the characters, Wright finds the power of the western myth to provide 'a conceptual response to the requirements of human action in a social situation' (p. 17). On this basis Wright proceeds to categorise the plots of westerns in terms of their constituent 'character functions' and the way character functions are organised into narrative sequences and narrative sequences into plots.

Wright's final task is to provide 'an independent analysis of the social institutions of America and demonstrate the correlation between the structure of the western and the structure of those institutions' (p. 130). This is not a relation of direct causation. Wright argues, however, for institutional determination on the way individuals live their lives, a determination which may be in conflict with the cultural traditions and values of a society, because institutional requirements tend to change more rapidly. This then produces 'a conceptual dilemma ... for the people of the society' to which a myth such as the western speaks. Drawing on social analysts such as Kenneth Galbraith, Jürgen Habermas, and C. B. MacPherson (a somewhat heterogeneous grouping of authorities), he argues that 'the classical western plot corresponds to the individualistic conception of society underlying a market economy', that 'the vengeance plot is a variation that begins to reflect changes in the market economy', and that 'the professional plot reveals a new conception of society corresponding to the values and attitudes inherent in a planned, corporate economy' (p. 15).

The language of reflection here indicates the weak link in Wright's conception of the social function of myth: cultural production and social institutions confront each other as discrete entities, the influence of box office returns providing the only explanation as to why film-makers should provide audiences with the cultural models of social action necessary for their survival as institutions change. Moreover, the predominance of 'myth' in his analysis necessitates excluding many aspects of the film-making and reading process that intervene between the institutional needs of society and the finished film. This leads to a view of genre cinema as essentially conservative. For Wright assumes that, in its reliance on a structure of binary oppositions, 'myth depends on simple and recognisable meanings which reinforce rather than challenge social understandings' (p. 23). Works by individual artists, however, construct more complex, realistic and unique characters, which are not amenable to analysis by binary opposition. Thus the 'social action' proposed by any particular phase of a genre is seen as adapting to institutional demands rather than resisting them or exploring their contradictions.

Gender and sexuality in the western

Disagreement may arise over the place of woman in the western, but most commentators assume its address to a male problematic and a male audience. For instance, John Cawelti in *The Six-Gun Mystique* (1971) argues that the western speaks to adolescent or working-class males about 'the conflict between the adolescent's desire to be an adult and his fear and hesitation about the nature of adulthood' and 'the tension between a strong need for aggression and a sense of ambiguity and guilt about violence' which the working-class male feels in relation to the authority of corporation America (p. 82 and p. 14).

In very different terms, Raymond Bellour has argued (see *Camera Obscura* 3/4, 1979) that the western depends upon 'a whole organised circuit of feminine representations (the young heroine, the mother, the saloon girl, the wife, etc.) without which the film cannot function (p. 88). For Bellour the western is a variation of the classic Hollywood narrative text (→ HISTORY OF NARRATIVE: *The classic narrative system*, p. 212) which, in line with the nineteenth-century novel, centres on the symbolic figure of the woman as source of

Johnny Guitar – the western offering female hero figures

Ritual and tradition in *My Darling Clementine*

the disruption that sets going a narrative trajectory of male desire and its ultimate resolution in heterosexual couple formation.

Feminist response to the dominance in the western of a male-defined problematic has taken two forms. Jacqueline Levitin has attacked the western for the circumscribed roles it gives women. ('The western: any good roles for feminists?', 1982). She analyses their function in catalysing the choices that face the hero, and the narrative contortions undergone by those exceptional westerns which attempt to support a female hero – for instance *Johnny Guitar*. She also suggests that the historical West offered opportunities for greater freedom and social power for women, as well as potential female hero figures, which are transformed and traduced in the process of producing patriarchal fiction. In this respect she argues that the history of the West provides material which could be colonised by feminism. The problem in her account is the assumption that all that is required is greater historical accuracy; she seems to ignore the work of fantasy and fiction at play in the childhood memories she cites of identification with the male hero, and the problems of finding forms that will fulfill this task for women.

The question of the female audience and the western is taken up by Laura Mulvey in a consideration of how women deal with the male system of spectatorship she had analysed in 'Visual Pleasure and Narrative Cinema' (1975) (→ NARRATIVE AND STRUCTURALISM: *Narrative and audience*, p. 242). Mulvey draws on Freud for an argument both about how the western relates to the male oedipal scenario and about the trans-sexual identification of women with

male heroes described by Levitin. In both cases what she sees at work is a fictional indulgence of the fantasy of omnipotence belonging to the pre-oedipal phase, experienced by both boys and girls, before the socially required gender positions are taken up. This phase is characterised by narcissism, allowing for object-choices and identifications based on similarity rather than difference, so that boys and girls are able to take up one another's positions. This forms the basis of trans-sexual identification. Despite its hypothetical freedom from social categorisation, Mulvey notes that the pre-oedipal phase is nevertheless conceived in traditionally 'masculine' terms – as active, phallic. For the boy the oedipal passage into 'manhood' requires forsaking the fantasy of omnipotence, submission to sexual difference ('masculinity') through the castration scenario, and the channelling of his desire towards the woman positioned within the couple, marriage. For the girl passage through the oedipal phase requires not merely channelling active desire towards the correct goal, but forsaking it altogether by taking up the feminine position traditionally conceived as 'passive'. However because of the relative weakness of the castration scenario for women, the 'active' fantasies of the non-gender specific pre-oedipal phase are never entirely repressed.

The western serves the pre-oedipal fantasies of the gendered audience in two distinct and gender-specific ways. If, as Bellour suggests, the oedipal resolution of 'couple formation' is the implicit goal of every western, the 'not marriage' choice, Mulvey argues, is also central to its agenda. The indulgence of this male fantasy, involving a disavowal of the feminine sphere, frequently leads in the western to a splitting of the hero:

'Here two functions emerge, one celebrating integration into society through marriage, the *other* celebrating resistance to social demands and responsibilities, above all those of marriage and family, the sphere represented by woman' (p. 14).

In the first option 'the fiction "marriage" sublimates the erotic into a final closing social ritual'. In the second the male spectator is offered 'a nostalgic celebration of phallic, narcissistic omnipotence . . . difficult to integrate exactly into the oedipal drama' (p. 14) – the hero rejects the woman and rides alone into the sunset.

However the dominance of the male hero, and role of woman as a signifier in a male scenario in this as in most genres does not, Mulvey argues, mean the films do not address the female spectator. They do so through the mechanism of trans-sex identification in which pre-oedipal 'active' and narcissistic fantasising, never finally repressed in women, is given cultural outlet and reinforcement by the logic of narrative grammar, which 'places the

reader, listener or spectator *with* the hero' (p. 13).

'In this sense Hollywood genre films, structured around masculine pleasure, offering an identification with the *active* point of view, allow a woman spectator to rediscover that lost aspect of her sexual identity, the never fully repressed bed-rock of feminine neurosis' (p. 13).

From this perspective it could be argued that in the western female pleasure may be derived from its offering to women identification with a male figure asserting desire in pre-oedipal terms, the male fantasy of self-sufficiency serving women's own ambivalence towards the 'correct' feminine position.

Male spectators and the western
In his book *Genre* (1980) Stephen Neale touches briefly on the question of spectatorship and the western from the masculine perspective. Laura Mulvey had argued in 'Visual pleasure and narrative cinema' (1975) that the role of the male hero for the male spectator is that of an ideal ego, through whose gaze the spectator gains symbolic possession of the female body placed as the central spectacle in the fiction. Neale is interested in Paul Willemen's qualification of this argument ('Voyeurism, the look and Dwoskin', 1976) in which he points out that in the Freudian scenario the scopophilic instinct (the drive to look) is in the first instance 'auto-erotic', taking as its object the subject's own body. If the cinema can be seen as pleasuring such formative desires, then the male body can be 'a substantial source of gratification for a male viewer' (Willemen, 1976, p. 43). Mulvey had suggested that the narrative function of the hero acts in part as a deflection of such desires in so far as they threaten the social taboo against homosexuality. Neale takes this further, arguing that the spectator's gaze at the male hero is legitimated, 'rendered "innocent"', because in following his actions eroticism is deflected into the hero's pursuit of the woman, who constitutes an ideologically acceptable sexual object. What interests Neale here is the way the western plays on this ambiguous production of male hero as an object for the spectator's gaze. He argues that many of the structural antinomies of the western, described by Kitses, can be set in opposition around the way the hero's body is represented, 'opening a space for . . . the male as privileged object of the look' (p. 58). Thus the opposition Law/Outside Law can be set up in the way the body of the hero, 'through the codes of dress, comportment, movement, adornment' (p. 58), relates to those of Indian, outlaw, townspeople, farmers, elaborated through similar codes; or in the dynamic oscillation between natural landscape and township, realised in the play of 'light, texture, colour' over the male figure, and in the pace and rhythm of his movements. For Neale, the drama of the western revolves around

its exploration of various modes of the inscription of Law on the human body. Since it is the hero who engages with the Law, the Father/Son relationship dominates the scenario, and the western can be said to be 'about' the male half of the oedipus trauma (p. 59).

Italian westerns
Finally the representation of sexuality and gender identity in the western received a revealing inflection in the decade of Italian production of what became known as the 'spaghetti western' – 1965–1975 – a period associated most strongly with the names of directors Sergio Leone and Sergio Corbucci, and the American star Clint Eastwood, whose fame was made by the Dollars Trilogy. Little serious work has been done on how the popularity of this sub-genre affects the demarcation of the western *per se*, although Christopher Frayling (1981) has attempted a pioneering work of archival research on this phenomenon in which he mounts an argument that Leone's films, at least, represent a critique of Hollywood's reconstruction of the West and its meanings. The films clearly mark a challenge to the dominance of Hollywood over genre production, complicating the question of the relation of genre motifs to the culture which produced them, and demonstrating the work of translation and transformation that goes on between cultures, especially in the cinema. Anglo-Saxon critics of the period were appalled at what they saw as a travesty of the traditional western and its time-honoured values. Behind the outrage at what was considered gratuitous violence and sexual sado-masochism can be sensed an unease about the production of a more rampant, less romanticised expression of masculine identity. On the whole it is the Eastwood/Leone Dollars Trilogy through which this period of production has entered film studies, and the films are liable to be discussed as much in terms of the Eastwood image and how it speaks to a post-68, 'post-feminist' crisis in male identity as in terms of its contribution to and development of western traditions. Currently critics and industry seem agreed that the era of large-scale and popular production of westerns is over.

References
André Bazin, 'The western, or the American film *par excellence*', and 'The evolution of the western', in Gray (ed. and trans.) *What is Cinema?* vol. 2, Berkeley, University of California Press, 1971.
Raymond Bellour, 'Alternation, segmentation, hypnosis: interview with Raymond Bellour', in *Camera Obscura* no. 3/4, 1979.
Ed Buscombe, 'The idea of genre in the American cinema', *Screen* vol. II no. 2, March/April 1970.
John Cawelti, *The Six Gun Mystique*, Bowling Green, Ohio, Bowling Green University Popular Press, 1971.
Richard Collins, 'Genre: a reply to Ed Buscombe', *Screen* vol. II no. 4/5, July–October 1970; reprinted in Nichols (ed.) *Movies and Methods*, Berkeley, University of California Press, 1976.
Christopher Frayling, 'The American western and American society', in Davies and Neve (eds.) *Cinema, Politics and Society in America* Manchester, Manchester University Press, 1981.
Christopher Frayling, *Spaghetti Westerns: cowboys and Europeans from Karl May to Sergio Leone*, London, Routledge and Kegan Paul, 1981.
Philip French, *Westerns*, London, Secker and Warburg/BFI, 1973.
Stuart Hall and Paddy Whannel, *The Popular Arts*, London, Hutchinson Educational, 1964.
Jim Kitses, *Horizons West*, London, Secker and Warburg/BFI, 1969.
Jacqueline Levitin, 'The western: any good roles for feminists?', *Film Reader* no. 5, 1982.
Alan Lovell, 'The western', *Screen Education* no. 41, September/October 1967.
Colin McArthur, 'The roots of the western', *Cinema* (UK) no. 4, October 1969.
Laura Mulvey, 'Afterthoughts on "Visual pleasure and narrative cinema" inspired by *Duel in the Sun*', *Framework* no. 15/16/17, Summer 1981.
Stephen Neale, *Genre*, London, BFI Publishing, 1980.
Douglas Pye, 'Genre and history: *Fort Apache* and *Liberty Valance*', *Movie* no. 25, Winter 1977/78.
Jean-Louis Rieupeyrout, 'The western: a historical genre', *Quarterly of Film Radio and Television*, vol. 3, Winter 1952.
Tom Ryall, 'The notion of genre', *Screen* vol. II no. 2, March/April 1970.
Jean Wagner, 'The western, history and actuality', in Henri Agel (ed.), *Le Western*, Paris, Lettres Modernes, 1961.
Robert Warshow, 'Movie chronicle: *The Westerner*', in *The Immediate Experience*, New York, Atheneum Books, 1970.
Paul Willemen, 'Voyeurism, the look and Dwoskin,' *Afterimage* no. 6, 1976.
Will Wright, *Sixguns and Society: a structural study of the western*, Berkeley, University of California Press, 1975.

My Darling Clementine (USA 1946 *p.c* – 20th Century-Fox; *d* – John Ford; sd b/w 14)

At the centre of this romantic western (typifying Bazin's 'classical' form and period of the genre) is the figure of Wyatt Earp. Thematically, this hero, cattleman-cum-town marshall, represents the rugged individualism of the frontier consciousness, assured in male company and as an agent of legal justice, but uneasy as a member of the burgeoning white community and especially in the company of women.

Structurally, the figure is an agent of eastern expansion into the West, pacifying Indian and destroying outlaw. In the extract, the positive qualities of the West are expressed in conditions of early settlement through community life, crackerbarrel wit, dance and music, all characteristic qualities of John Ford's authorship (→ AUTHORSHIP: *John Ford*, p. 184).

In the same way that the West is seen in its negative and positive aspects, so too is the East. The schoolteacher, Clementine, provides positive elements such as education and stability, seen as necessary to the utopian promise of western settlement, elements which are celebrated in the extract's final scene at the dance in the shell of the new church under the sign of the Stars and Stripes. The negative elements – vice and decadence – are embodied in the figure of the consumptive Doc Holliday, expressed in the extract through the 'noirish' lighting of the scene in which he appears.

The extract also provides evidence of structural oppositions, not least between Chihuahua, woman of the West, bearer of an overtly-coded glamorous sexuality and a figure of fun, and Clementine, woman of the East, sedate, unattainable sexually and socially. Indeed, the coded signs of class difference are notably matched in signs of racial difference between the two women.

As an agent in the transformation of positive eastern values into the West, and the ejection of all negative values from the West, Earp's centrality is clear. Interestingly, despite the essential nature of that agency to the narrative and ideological project of the film, the figure's unease is evident. This phenomenon can be viewed as presaging generic shifts in the role of the gunfighter, authorial developments in Ford's view of America as well as exemplifying the characteristic laconic liberalism of the star persona of Henry Fonda.

Johnny Guitar (USA 1954 *p.c* – Republic; *d* – Nicholas Ray; sd col 11)

Johnny Guitar is an example of the 50s baroque western (c.f. *Rancho Notorious*) which deviated in significant ways from the conventions of the earlier romantic form: for example, in its representation of a stylised landscape and décor contrasting the ornate interior of Vienna's place (hanging chandelier, grand piano, red-suffused lighting) and the dark, windswept, barren exteriors. An impulse toward myth and melodrama is also revealed in the central conflict between the two female adversaries.

The mythic dimension can be seen in the frenzied performance of Mercedes McCambridge as Emma, whose black widow's weeds lead the mob of settlers and townspeople. Elements of melodrama emerge from the treatment of Vienna as a central agent in the fortunes of the partly-criminalised all-male group. In the extract, her isolation →

from both these groups can be identified in the action (the quietness as she lights the lamps and sits at the piano) and in the organisation of spatial relations during the scene of the search, during which the contrast of her white dress with the predominant blacks and reds around her is notable. It is here, too, that the coded social and sexual antagonisms between the two monumental female adversaries can be located.

The extract also demonstrates the significant displacements affecting the conventions of the western when the protagonists are female. The most revealing displacement is the marginalisation of male action as the dramas of gunfighters/outlaws and settlers/ranchers alike are subordinated to the central female conflict (→ AUTHORSHIP: *Nicholas Ray*, p. 139).

Cowboy (USA 1957 *p.c* – Phoenix; *d* – Delmer Daves; sd col 14)

This is a romantic western replete with recurrent plot strategies and familiar iconic references. The film traces the intitiation of an eastern greenhorn (Harris) into the culture of the West, specifically the cattle trail and the life of cowboy. In the extract the rhythm of working life, with its daily routines rooted in the passing of the sun and the seasons, and the cameraderie of the male team are celebrated. Harris's intitiation is represented both comically (false starts at bronco-busting, treating saddle sores with whisky, eating haunches of Indians, for example) and tragically (the death at the campfire). The play between the comic and the dramatic modes is paralleled in the character relationship between the initiate and the 'man of the West' (Reece). The tension in their relationship derives from Reece having taken Harris on the trail unwillingly, in return for a loan; in the extract this is expressed in scenes in which Reece's apparently harsh treatment of the novice Harris is played off against shots which indicate his respect for Harris's resilience. The film's sanction of Reece's authority – and, thereby, the celebration of the West over the comic refinement of the East – is shown in scenes depicting Reece's humanity, from which Harris's absence (e.g. during Doc Bender's tired gunfighter/marshall testimony) or marginalisation (e.g. during Reece's speech about enclosures) is marked. This procedure serves to validate a romantic view of western expansion, accommodating rather than contrasting the harshness and dangers of life on the trail. It also accounts for the merely vestigial references to pacified Indians, sexually-available women and the constraints of urban living, none of

which can have an authorised place in the all-male, itinerant, working group which represents the ideal western life-style.

The Wonderful Country (USA 1959 *p.c* – D.R.M.; *d* – Robert Parrish; sd col 13)

In westerns set in frontier townships, a common structure (following Kitses' model of antinomies) is the 'taming of the wilderness' through the imposition of eastern law and the agency of the marshall/lawman (c.f. *Destry Rides Again*, *My Darling Clementine* and *Rio Bravo*).

In contrast, westerns centring on the figure of the gunfighter/outlaw typically form a journey-structure in which the hero drifts or is chased from town to town (c.f. *Butch Cassidy and The Sundance Kid*, *The Gunfighter* and *The James Brothers*). In one strand of such westerns, the figure of the gunfighter takes on a more ambivalent role as an agent of Western expansion.

Representative of this strand, *The Wonderful Country* features Brady (Robert Mitchum) as the unsettled protagonist forced to travel between two cultures, American and Mexican. Exceptionally, the film plays explicitly with ideas of national culture and identity. The title is both an ironic commentary on, and, finally, affirmation of, a national identity as the hero seeks a role in either culture before reluctantly 'choosing' America.

In the extract, the ambivalance of the hero is connoted ironically by a use of costume, confusing the two national cultures, which also underlines the spatial separation of Brady from the military party and its elaborate rituals. The display of cultural acceptance is interrupted twice by Brady, once in attempting to refuse a liaison offered by Ellen and again in an act of spontaneous violence resulting in a gunfight killing. Brady's actions put him beyond the pale of the authorised social order; it is notable that his ejection results from individual action and expression of sexuality.

The woman's role exceeds western conventions, since Ellen's sexuality is both a threat to the hero's tenuous security in America and a critical comment on the hypocricy of the nation's authorised culture. In this respect, Ellen resembles the femme fatales of film noir.

The extract's visual style also demonstrates the connections between the two cultures in parallel night-time scenes of eating and leisure, contrasting the veiled power structure of the American scenes with the explicitly brutalised power relations of the Mexican scenes.

Ulzana's Raid (USA 1972 *p.c* – Universal; *d* – Robert Aldrich; sd b/w 20)

This is an example of a cavalry western with a characteristic chase structure, challenges to authority as the all-male group is gradually depleted in running battles, and a final victory over the savage enemy.

Ulzana's Raid is distinctive in three ways. First, the enemy raid is pointedly motivated by reaction to white injustice on the Indian reservation, and the resulting excessive brutality of the raid is grounded in a materialistic analysis of Indian culture after white subjugation. This strand is represented in the figure of Ke-Ni-Tay/Luke, an Indian scout and brother-in-law to the offending Ulzana. Ke-Ni-Tay straddles two cultures, informed by one but committed by contract ('I signed the paper') to another. In the extract, he provides the explanation for the otherwise unfathomable consequences of the Indian attack on the galloper and the settler mother and son, and the subsequent torture of the settler father, Rukeyser. This component therefore remains rooted in the representation of the Indian-as-savage, but substantially qualifies and accounts for the conditions that produce the savagery. In this sense, the film offers a corrective to the previous cycle of pro-Indian liberal films (e.g. *Little Big Man* and *Soldier Blue*).

Second, the scenes of attack and the product of torture are uncharacteristically represented graphically, deploying codes of suspense and surprise in a form appropriated from the gothic horror film. The film is therefore representative of both the increased stylisation of the western film of the period (c.f. spaghetti westerns) and the mutation of the western genre into horror and sci-fi during the 1970s.

Third, the film is a supreme example of play with an audience's generic expectations, notably in the attack on the wagon when the galloper's shooting of Mrs. Rukeyser, his suicide and the abandonment of the boy offend all expectations of masculine heroism in the western and confound audience expectations of the Indians' actions. Similarly, Rukeyser's tragic under-estimation of the Indians' capacity ('No drunk Indian's gonna take my farm from me!') is brutally punished through the trick of the bugle call, a reflexive, almost parodic, comment on audience familiarity with western conventions. The pleasure of such moments registers the exemplary role of *Ulzana's Raid* as an economic, non-nostalgic example of the final commercial days of the western genre.

Melodrama

Introduction: problems of definition

The study of melodrama as a cinematic genre is a recent development still in its early stages. It achieved public visibility in 1977, when the Society for Education in Film and Television commissioned papers for a study weekend, some of which were subsequently published in *Screen* and *Movie* in the UK and in *The Australian Journal of Screen Theory*. Around this time and since a spate of articles has appeared in British, French and American film journals and interest in the genre has been extended to work on television, particularly soap operas.

The British foundations of this work were laid in two very different contexts. In 1972 a small independent film journal, *Monogram*, opened a special issue on melodrama with a detailed and seminal account of the historical sources and aesthetics of the 'great Hollywood melodramas of the 50s', written by Thomas Elsaesser as part of a project of re-evaluating the American cinema. Then in 1974, *Spare Rib*, a general interest magazine for the Women's Movement, published a review by Laura Mulvey of Fassbinder's *Fear Eats the Soul* in which she used the film's acknowledged homage to Douglas Sirk's *All That Heaven Allows* to argue a case for feminist interest in the genre. Elsaesser's and Mulvey's contributions represented two very different approaches to melodrama, and dominant film theory and feminist work co-exist uneasily on this terrain.

One major source of difficulty in the ensuing debate is the diversity of forms that are gathered under the heading of melodrama. Until the 70s the term hardly existed in relation to the cinema except pejoratively to mean a 'melodramatic' and theatrical mode which manipulated the audience's emotions and failed aesthetically to justify the response summoned up. The film industry used the category to denote dramas involving the passions – hence crime melodrama, psychological melodrama, family melodrama. Closely related are two further categories, the women's film and romantic drama. To these, film critics have added the maternal melodrama and the argument that most American silent cinema should be considered as melodrama, with the work of D. W. Griffith constituting a virtual subset of its own. Ascription of literary and theatrical sources is equally diverse, running from Greek tragedy, through the bourgeois sentimental novel, Italian opera to Victorian stage melodrama. In the face of such confusion arguments that melodrama constitutes a 'mode' or 'style' crossing a range of different periods and forms are persuasive. However this does not evade the problem of generic definition, for recent writers on melodrama are united in seeking to trace in it the convergence of capitalist and patriarchal

Gardener/fantasy hero of women's romantic fiction in *All That Heaven Allows*

The Girl finds the body of her dead fiancé in *Hearts of the World*

structures, a project which requires historical, cultural and formal specificity. The categories set out above belong to particular phases of generic production and particular socio-historic circumstances – although with considerable overlapping and transformation of material between them.

Lack of generic specificity may arise in part from the fact that interest in melodrama first entered film criticism via the channels of *mise en scène* and the *auteur*. Criticism from this standpoint (e.g. *Movie*) saw in the work of Ray, Minnelli, Ophuls and Preminger a transformation of banal and melodramatic scripts through the power of authorial vision expressed in *mise en scène*. Later, post-68 film criticism which re-evaluated Hollywood in terms of

ideological textual analysis looked to *mise en scène* for a formal play of distanciation and irony. The work of Douglas Sirk was discovered around 1971 and lined up alongside Ophuls and Minnelli, preparing the ground for the central place occupied by melodrama in debates on ideology and film aesthetics during the 70s, and at the same time allowing more critical space to the role of generic convention (see Halliday, 1971; Willemen, 'Distanciation and Douglas Sirk', 1971). These beginnings in *mise en scène* and ideological criticism account for the tendency of much writing on melodrama to focus on the 50s family melodramas made by a small number of *auteurs*, Minnelli, Ophuls, Ray, Preminger, Sirk (e.g. Schatz, 1981). This contrasts with the constitution of film noir as a critical category which led to the greater visibility of a corpus of non-authorial works. On the other hand, more recent work on the women's film, which is not so predicated on preceding film critical traditions, has allowed a much wider range of titles to emerge.

Early feminist investigation of Hollywood had dismissed much of the work validated by auteurism as enshrining a male viewpoint on the world which was oppressive to women. However, Molly Haskell's (1979) influential chapter on the women's film of the 30s and 40s drew attention to a whole area of submerged and despised production, featuring domestic or romantic dramas centred on female protagonists played by stars valued by the Women's Movement. Critical work on melodrama has tended to elide the women's film with the family melodrama. Only feminists have drawn attention to the women's film as a category of production aimed at women, about women, drawing on other cultural forms produced for women often by women – e.g. women's magazine or paperback fiction – and to raise questions about the aesthetic and cultural significance of this gender specification.

Theorising family melodrama

While on the surface appearing far removed from the western and gangster, genres whose plots are often rooted in actual historical events, the family melodrama is nevertheless frequently defined as the dramatic mode for a historic project, namely the centrality of the bourgeois family to the ascendancy and continued dominance of that class. For example, Geoffrey Nowell-Smith ('Minnelli and melodrama', 1977) argues that 'melodrama arises from the conjunction of a formal history proper (development of tragedy, realism, etc.), a set of social determinations, which have to do with the rise of the bourgeoisie, and a set of psychic determinations which take shape around the family' (p. 113). This description places melodrama within a network of different concerns, the relationship between which is at issue according to the theoretical and political commitments of the writer.

One problem that emerges is the relation between the socio-historical conjuncture that gives rise to a particular form and its subsequent aesthetic development and history. Another set of problems are introduced in the meeting of Marxism and feminism, which offer competing notions of patriarchy, capitalism and bourgeois ideology, sex and class as key terms for the analysis of the family in melodrama. When Freudian psychoanalysis is brought to bear on melodrama interesting tensions are produced between the application of those ideas in film theory and in feminism. The feminist emphasis on the problem of the construction of femininity in patriarchal culture introduces questions of gender in

Sunrise – 'silent cinema forced into melodramatic mode'

relation to both the industrial and aesthetic constitution of a form: what, for instance, is the relation between specific audiences and the forms produced in their name? How is the male oedipal scenario – so often cited as the bedrock of classic narrative cinema and frequently the explicit subject matter of 50s melodramas – to be understood in forms which offer an unusual space to female protagonists and 'feminine' problems, and are specifically addressed to a female audience?

The question of gender is also a factor in the argument as to whether melodrama is better considered as an expressive code rather than a genre and as to whether it can be considered 'progressive' or not. The taxonomies that arise out of genre analysis bring into focus iconographic motifs, themes, and situations which have a material or structural force in feminist analysis of women's lives, but which in *mise en scène* analysis produce metaphorical significance on behalf of patriarchy. Similarly, ironic distanciation or disruption at the level of style may seem progressive in giving the spectator, both male and female, access to 'structures of feeling' normally closed off, but do little to shift the

social relations between the sexes represented at the level of plot and character. Such shifts of emphasis characterise the complexities of the melodrama debate.

Thomas Elsaesser: melodrama as a problem of 'style and articulation'

Writing in 1972, Elsaesser's approach draws on the 60s concern to validate Hollywood through *mise en scène* analysis and the post-68 interest in irony, distanciation and ideological criticism, reworking both in the context of his own concerns with aesthetic affect ('Tales of sound and fury', 1972). Much of Elsaesser's article is concerned to counter the conventional relegation of the form for its blatant use of 'mechanisms of emotional solicitation' (p. 8). He counteracts this view from two main directions. First, he seeks to show how the aesthetics of melodrama as a popular and commercial form give access to truths about human existence denied to more culturally respectable forms such as European art cinema. Second, he seeks to demonstrate how it is possible under certain social and production conditions for the melodrama to be ideologically subversive.

In common with other critics Elsaesser establishes melodrama as a form which belongs to the bourgeoisie. In its first manifestations – which Elsaesser cites as the eighteenth-century sentimental novel and post-Revolution romantic drama – it constituted an ideological weapon against a corrupt and feudal aristocracy. The bourgeois family's struggle to preserve the honour of the daughter from despotic and unprincipled aristocrats marked a contest over space for private conscience and individual rights. Elsaesser identifies certain features in early bourgeois melodrama as important to its later developments: the capacity of the eighteenth-century sentimental novel and romantic drama to make individual conflicts speak for a society which, he argues, lies in the popular cultural tradition it inherited, leading from the medieval morality play to music-hall drama, the most significant aspect of which was its 'non-psychological conception of the *dramatis personae*' (p. 2); and formal devices such as ironic parallelism, parody, counterpoint and rhythm. Another significant feature is the siting of the struggles of individualism in the family. For Elsaesser the family is not, except in early forms of melodrama, important in itself as a political institution; rather, through the highly-charged formal motifs of melodrama, it provided a means of delineating social crises in concretely personalised and emotional terms.

These constituents of the melodrama – its non-psychological conception of character and formally complex *mise en scène*, its containment of action within the family and consequent emphasis on private feeling and psychic levels of truth – enable Elsaesser to construct the family melodrama of the 50s as the peak of Hollywood's achievement. According to Elsaesser's argument, by the time melodrama was taken up in the cinema it was already saturated with significance beyond the specific socio-historical conditions that gave rise to it. He therefore looks to cinematic history to illuminate how the strategies of melodrama are realised in film. He argues that in the beginning all silent cinema was forced into a melodramatic mode – not simply because of its temporal closeness to Victorian popular forms (see Fell, 1974, and Vardac, 1949), but because the requirements of expression outside verbal language fortuitously pushed the medium into modes which favoured a melodramatic world-view. While the coming of sound meant the dominance of the verbal register and a consequently different dramatic mode, the development of new technologies in the 50s – colour, wide screen, deep-focus, crane and dolly – often in the hands of German directors with backgrounds in Expressionism, made a complex visual *mise en scène* again possible, in which the spoken word would be submerged as only one strand in a musical counterpoint.

Coincident with the development of the technology for such a dramaturgy was the popularisation of Freudian psychoanalysis in America in the 40s and 50s. The family reappears as a site of dramatic action, though in a far different ideological context from its heroic stance in the emergence of melodrama as a bourgeois form. The domestic melodrama provides not the exterior spaces of the western or urban gangster film to be conquered by a hero, who, in search of oedipal identity can express himself in action, but a closed self-reflexive space in which characters are inward looking, unable to act in society (p. 10).

Not only does the location and mores of the family reduce the scope for dramatic action, but the characters themselves, in line with the melodramatic tradition, are unaware of the forces that drive them. The intensity and the significance of the drama, then, is not carried in what the characters say, or in the articulation of inner struggle as in tragedy: rather it is the *mise en scène* of melodrama, providing an 'aesthetics of the domestic', that tells us what is at stake. The 'pressure generated by things crowding in on the characters ... by the claustrophobic atmosphere of the bourgeois home and/or small town setting' (p. 13) is intensified through the demand of the 90-minute feature film for compression of what may be far more expansively expressed in its literary sources. There is, Elsaesser argues, a sense of 'hysteria bubbling all the time just below the surface' and a 'feeling that there is always more to tell than can be said' (p. 7).

Elsaesser draws on Freudian concepts for the interpretation of *mise en scène*, arguing that the aesthetic strategies of 50s melodrama function similarly to Freud's dream-work. Sometimes this is a matter of the stock characters' lack of self-awareness producing an explicit form of displacement at the level of the plot:

'... the characters' behaviour is often pathetically at variance with the real objectives they want to achieve. A sequence of substitute actions creates a kind of vicious circle in which the close nexus of cause and effect is somehow broken and – in an often overtly Freudian sense – displaced' (p. 10).
In other cases it functions

'... by what one might call an intensified symbolisation of everyday actions, the heightening of the ordinary gesture and a use of setting and décor so as to reflect the character's fetishist fixations' (p. 10).

This account provides the basis of Elsaesser's argument that in the hands of gifted directors and at the right historical moment it can be used to critique the society it represents. Key terms here are pathos and irony. The externalisation of feelings and reactions into décor, gesture and events objectifies and distances emotions, producing pathos or irony 'through a "liberal" *mise en scène* which balances different points of view so that the spectator is in a position of seeing and evaluating contrasting attitudes within a given

framework ... result[ing from] ... the total configuration and therefore inaccessible to the protagonists themselves' (p. 15). Thus melodrama can suggest causes beyond individual responsibility, to be found on a 'social and existential level' (p. 14).

The melodramatic aesthetic gains its social force in a circular movement of displacement: while capitalist society creates psychic problems which become acutely focused in family and sexual relations, so events within the family are displaced outwards into the *mise en scène* indicating forces that exceed specific family conditions. From this position Elsaesser suggests that the shift in 50s Hollywood from the linear trajectory of the active hero conquering the spaces of the West or the city, to the impotent hero trapped within a domestic interior and confined by the codes of behaviour appropriate to the family, indicates a shift in the ideological conditions obtaining under post-war advanced capitalism. The melodramatic form had come full circle from its initial championing of individual human rights via the bourgeois family's struggle against a feudal aristocracy to a later critique of the ideology of individualism in which the bourgeois family becomes the site of the 'social and emotional alienation' consequent on a corrupt individualism and the failure of the drive to self-fulfilment (p. 14).

The major distinction between Elsaesser's position and the work that followed later lay in his use of Freud and Marxism. While noting the rich potential of Freudian subject matter for Hollywood melodrama and assuming rather than analysing the oedipal hero as dominating the form, it is on the formal mechanisms of a Freudian 'dream-work' that Elsaesser bases his argument for the rich and complex significance of the melodrama's *mise en scène*. And what he takes from Marxism is not so much a classical definition of class relations as a notion of alienation translated into existential terms. Consequently, his arguments do not analyse nor distinguish between class and gender relations in Hollywood melodrama, beyond the displacement of one into the other, 'the metaphysical interpretation of class conflict as sexual exploitation and rape' which, according to Elsaesser, dominates the form throughout its history (p. 3). This means that the question of how a female protagonist may affect plot structures or the trajectory of the hero's oedipal drama remains unexamined. Furthermore the emphasis on melodrama as 'form' and '*mise en scène*' neglects questions which generic specifications would have raised; for instance, the distinctions and relations between the women's film, romantic drama, family melodrama – questions important to an understanding of the place of women in melodrama. Issues of class and gender, but particularly of gender, were to figure in the next stage in the emerging debate about melodrama.

Sex and class in melodrama

Later work on melodrama was to prise Elsaesser's groundbreaking work away from its metaphorical and existential proclivity for *mise en scène* analysis. What followed was either a more sociological approach to its subject matter (see Kleinhans, 'Notes on melodrama and the family under capitalism', 1978; French, 1978), which understood the family as a political institution and site of real oppression, particularly for women; or work influenced by the development of feminist film theory which produced accounts of the social or sexual *positions* made available in the narrative to protagonists and spectators. Here *mise en scène*, rather than being metaphorically resonant, was seen as *symptomatic*, indicating the 'return of the repressed', or insoluble contradictions.

Central to the debates that emerge in these reassessments of melodrama is the significance of the bourgeois family as a product of patriarchy and capitalism. At issue here is how the social relations of capitalist production – class – articulate with the social relations of capitalist/patriarchal *re*production – the family. Once the bourgeoisie stops rising it is no longer easy to see in it a direct symbolisation of class struggle – as is argued of the eighteenth-century sentimental novel or post-Revolution romantic drama, for instance. However, the family is felt to be related to class at an ideological level. On the one hand, it seems to operate as a transclass institution; on the other, it reproduces individuals as class subjects. The family, however, does not simply secure class subjects; it also produces sexed individuals. Arguably the neuralgic point for debates around cinema melodrama is the interrelation of sex and class. In this respect Freud and Marx compete to provide the terms of analysis of the family; according to which authority is given more emphasis, the family is viewed as the site of sexual repression (Nowell-Smith, 1977; Mulvey, 'Notes on Sirk and melodrama', 1977/78) or of displaced socio-economic contradiction (Kleinhans, 1978). From Freud is taken the oedipal drama, particularly the moment of castration and repression; from Marxism the concept of the division between productive and personal life, in which the contradictions inherent in the alienated labour of capitalist production are supposed to be compensated for within the family, where, however, they are merely displaced (see Kleinhans, 1978).

Geoffrey Nowell-Smith and the male oedipal crisis

Geoffrey Nowell-Smith (1977) locates melodrama as a bourgeois form by distinguishing its address from that of classical tragedy. Whereas tragedy does not depict the class to which it is addressed, the social relations depicted in melodrama

presume authority to be distributed 'democratically' among heads of families rather than vested in kings and princes. Thus 'the address is from one bourgeois to another bourgeois and the subject matter is the life of the bourgeoisie'. While this apparent egalitarianism avoids questions about the class exercise of power, the relation between social power and gender becomes potentially more visible – less a question of the symbolisation of one by the other (see Elsaesser, 1972) than of their articulation together. The paternal function becomes crucial in establishing both the right of the family to a place in the bourgeois social hierarchy and, through the mechanism of inheritance, the property relations which underpin this position. The problem for the family is the possible failure of the father to fulful this function suitably, together with the risky business of raising the son into a patriarchal identity in order that he may take over his property and his place within the community. One root cause of such possible failure is the confinement of sexual relations within the family – evoking the oedipal drama – and the problematic position of women there.

However while Nowell-Smith makes the relations of power, gender and sex more visible he still leans towards a masculine construction of melodrama. Like Elsaesser, he distinguishes melodrama from the western in the way it closes down on potential social action and turns inward for its drama. Although he does not make the home an existential space, it becomes simply the arena of the 'feminine' characterised by passivity and negativity. Feminist film theory had argued that representation of the 'feminine' as positive, rather than 'non-male', was impossible within the framework of classic Hollywood narrative. Nowell-Smith draws on such arguments to deal with the 'feminine' presence in melodrama. While acknowledging it frequently figures female protagonists he argues that 'masculinity' still constitutes the only knowable heroic norm, so that acute contradictions are involved in the production of active female characters. The space allowed female characters, while it cannot represent femininity, facilitates an exploration of problems of male identity.

From here Nowell-Smith goes on to give an account of melodrama as a patriarchal form, taking the oedipal drama (more literally than does Elsaesser) as its subject matter. 50s Hollywood melodrama is structured in terms of conflict between the generations, in which the son has to accept his symbolic castration by the father before he can take up his place in the patriarchal and bourgeois order, proving himself, by becoming both an individual and like his father, capable of reconstituting the family unit for the next generation (p. 116).

Like Elsaesser, Nowell-Smith draws on Freud for an understanding of the mech-

anisms of melodramatic narrative and *mise en scène*. However, rather than concepts elaborated in *The Interpretation of Dreams*, Nowell-Smith deploys Freud's account of a childhood fantasy, the 'family romance', and his theory of conversion hysteria. The family romance provides the means of understanding the melodrama as being both about the family, foregrounding female characters, and about patriarchal identity. In the family romance the child questions its parenthood, exploring through the question 'Whose child am I?', or 'would I like to be?', different family arrangements. Thus the structure allows differential and even taboo sexual relations to be explored, reorganised and eventually closed off in the final resolution of a reconstituted family to which melodrama is committed.

However, Nowell-Smith argues, such resolution is consequent on castration and therefore on repression; for fiction this means an initial laying out of the problems, entry into the fantasy, which, nevertheless cannot be articulated explicitly. This leads Nowell-Smith to the notion of *mise en scène* as 'excess' – a 'too much' of music, colour, movement which indicates not simply a heightening of emotion but a substitution for what cannot be admitted in plot or dialogue, a process for which Freud's theory of 'conversion hysteria' provides an analogy (p. 117). From a perspective that views classic Hollywood in terms of the 'classic realist text' (→ NARRATIVE AND STRUCTURALISM: *The classic realist text*, p. 242), such 'hysterical moments' can be seen as a breakdown in realist conventions, where elements of the *mise en scène* lose their motivation and coherence is lost. Such moments of breakdown cannot be done away with by a 'happy end' but represent the 'ideological failure' of melodrama as a form, and so its 'progressive' potential.

Chuck Kleinhans: melodrama and real life

Chuck Kleinhans's 'Notes on melodrama and the family under capitalism' (1978) offers a different perspective. A Marxist-feminist sociology of the family, rather than Freudian theories of sexuality, provides the premise of his arguments: 'Since bourgeois domestic melodrama emerges with the ascension of capitalism, and since it deals with the family, it makes sense to look at the family under capitalism to better understand melodrama' (p. 41). He characterises the social relations of capitalist production in terms of a split between 'productive' work and personal life now confined to the home – the sphere of reproduction. The alienation of the labour process within capitalist forms of production is disguised and compensated for in the notions of personal identity and happiness supposed to be found in the family – a bourgeois conception of 'people's needs' shaped by the ideology of individualism. At the same time women and children are marginalised outside production and confined to the home, while women become responsible for providing the fulfilment that capitalist relations of production cannot – a need whose source lies outside the family and therefore cannot be achieved. 'This basic contradiction forms the raw material of melodrama' (p. 42).

Kleinhans argues that, in the piling on of domestic conflict and disaster, in its concentration on 'the personal sphere, home, family, and women's problems' (p. 42) and its closeness to real life, melodrama deals more directly than many other genres with themes and situations close to its audience's experiences. In so doing its function is similar to that of the family itself, displacing social contradiction, working through the problems of keeping the family intact at the cost of repression and women's self-sacrifice. In these terms melodrama is a profoundly conservative form. Its penchant for ambiguity, far from providing an ironic critique of bourgeois society, disperses critical focus among a number of possible readings. In *All That Heaven Allows*, for instance, the unsuitability of Cary's second marriage to her gardener is equally and indifferently a problem of class, of age, of life-style – thus attenuating the film's purchase on its subject matter. For Kleinhans these films are symptomatic – indicating the strategies of bourgeois ideology for evading structural problems. They are not, however, instances of ideological breakdown or aesthetic radicalism and it is only analysis from quite a different position to that of the film which can reveal its project.

Laura Mulvey: the two voices of melodrama

Laura Mulvey's (1977/78) contribution shifts the emphasis away from melodrama as a 'progressive' genre by reinserting questions about the place of women both in the subject matter of melodrama and in its conditions of production and consumption. While sharing some of Kleinhans's concerns, her feminist perspective produces a very different intervention. Kleinhans sees the family as a product of capitalist social relations residing in the split between 'productive' and 'reproductive' life: patriarchy does not enter as a term in his analysis, and, as with Elsaesser, the question of gender specificity in melodrama disappears.

For Mulvey however, it is in patriarchy that the pertinent and irresolvable contradictions lie. For her the notion that melodrama exposes contradictions in bourgeois ideology by its failure to accommodate the 'excess' generated by its subject matter (see Nowell-Smith, 1977) fails to understand either the degree to which family and sexual relations are constituted as contradictory or the role of melodrama in providing a 'safety valve' for them. Drawing on Helen Foley's view (about Aeschylean tragedy) that 'over-valuation

of virility under patriarchy causes social and ideological problems which the drama comments on' (p. 54), Mulvey argues that 'ideological contradiction is the overt mainspring and specific content of melodrama, not a hidden, unconscious threat' (p. 53). Consequently *mise en scène* can no longer be the means of privileged critical access to progressive interpretation, but rather, in 50s Hollywood melodrama, represents the specific aesthetic mode which distinguishes it from tragedy, working overtime to carry what the limited stock figures of bourgeois melodrama cannot consciously be aware of, 'giving abstract emotion spectacular form' (p. 55). Thus Mulvey closes off the notion of a formal subversiveness being inherent in the melodramatic mode.

Instead, she looks to the production conditions of melodrama and its relation to its imputed female audience, whose material and cultural conditions of existence the form, despite the 'symbolic imbalance' of narrative structures, was forced to acknowledge: it is, after all, the patriarchal need for co-existence with women that produces the crisis melodrama seeks to alleviate. Because she insists on the real contradictions of patriarchal ideology for women, rather than their metaphorical significance for men, Mulvey begins to show how melodrama can both function for patriarchal ends, bringing about a narrative resolution of its contradictions, and at the same time perform a quite different function for women: offering the satisfaction of recognising those contradictions, usually suppressed (p. 53).

This view leads Mulvey to distinguish

between those films which are 'coloured by a female protagonist's dominating point-of-view' and those which deal with male oedipal problems by examining 'tensions in the family, and between sex and generations' (p. 54), constructing the hero as Elsaesser's and Nowell-Smith's victim of patriarchal society. Sirk, she argues, worked in both traditions, his independently produced *Tarnished Angels* and *Written on the Wind* conforming to the second pattern, his work for Ross Hunter at Universal, who specialised in women's pictures (see *All That Heaven Allows*), belonging to the first. Women's pictures, variously known in the trade as 'weepies', 'sudsers', 'four handkerchief pictures', etc., were tailored to the female matinée audience, generally deriving from

Ron and Cary under the 'golden rain tree' in *All That Heaven Allows*

women's magazine fiction or novelettes, and had a tangential relation, yet to be fully explored, to the family melodrama derived from the bourgeois novel. These films are characterised by an attempt to reproduce the woman's point-of-view as central to the narrative, and if there is subversive excess in melodrama, this is where Mulvey locates it. Whereas the patriarchal mode of melodrama is able to produce some form of readjustment of its values, some reconciliation between the sexes, the attempt to entertain the woman's point-of-view, to figure feminine desire, produces narrative problems of an order impossible to tie up, except in the fantasies of women's magazine fiction. In *All That Heaven Allows*, Cary, a widowed mother of two, past child-bearing age, is able to unite with her younger, employee lover only when a last minute accident renders him bedridden and incapable. However, such a fantasy, while resolving certain of the narrative's contradictions, touches on 'recognisable, real and familiar traps, which for women brings it closer to daydream than fairy story' (p. 56).

Progressing the debate: patriarchy and capitalism

Two major and interlinked areas of debate emerged from Mulvey's and Nowell-Smith's interventions. The first concerns the 'obscured dialectic between class politics and sexual politics, bourgeois ideology and the patriarchal order' (Pollock, 'Report on the weekend school', 1977, p. 106); the second the question of whether gender difference can be said to have aesthetic consequences in fictional structures.

Griselda Pollock: the repressed feminine

Griselda Pollock (1977) takes up the first issue in a consideration of what precisely is repressed in the oedipal moment. She notes a confusion in discussion of melodrama as to whether its representation of the family signifies an interrogation of bourgeois family relations, or the displacement of contradictions found in bourgeois social relations, or both. Behind this lies an issue about the primacy of patriarchal or of capitalist relations – of sex or class determination. Pollock wants to argue the necessity of thinking of the family, and the place of women within it, as a product of both in dialectical articulation together. In this respect she sees both Nowell-Smith (1977) and Mulvey (1977/78) as in danger of 'reifying sexuality outside the social formation', arguing that 'the contradictions which *All That Heaven Allows* exposes are between different social positions, not just irreconcilable desires or the sexuality of women' (p. 110). Taking issue with the view that femininity in patriarchal culture is unrepresentable because unknown and unknowable, Pollock argues that femininity can be produced only as specific social positions. In Western society the social position of mother is crucial to the perpetuation both of capitalist social relations and patriarchal dominance, demanding the subjugation of female sexuality in social and cultural life. From Pollock's perspective the women's point-of-view movies and male oedipal dramas have one thing in common: the relocation of the woman as mother, a position that, while fathers may disappear, be rendered silent or impotent, dominates the conclusion of these films.

However, such relocation faces the problem of 'the extraordinary and disruptive role played by the woman's uncontained, withheld or frustrated sexuality in the dynamic of the narrative' – which includes 'female sexuality outside familial roles' (p. 111) and the continued sexuality of mothers. This leads Pollock to posit the 'repressed feminine' as the key to understanding melodrama. In her terms the 'feminine' represents a psycho-sexual position, hypothetically available to either sex, but foregone and repressed in the reproduction of sons in the patriarchal, masculine position and daughters as mothers. What is important here is that femininity is understood not simply as an empty, negative, passive space, but something positively 'lost' in the construction of the social and sexed subject positions necessary to patriarchal, bourgeois society. Although Pollock does not do so, the fantasy of the family romance could be invoked here to explain the patriarchal function of both women's film and male family melodrama. In one of its forms it allows the child to disown the father and fantasise the mother's independent sexuality with another man. This, for the male child in particular, allows both an exploration of incestuous desire and identification with the female position; for the female child, it allows a refusal of the repression required for the confinement of female sexuality to reproduction.

Taking up Mulvey's (1977/78) 'safety valve' theory of melodrama, Pollock goes on to suggest that many of the contradictions exposed in 'progressive' analysis of melodrama are in fact ones which patriarchal and bourgeois culture can contain. And this is as true of the women's picture tradition as of the male family melodrama; the woman's point-of-view in *All That Heaven Allows* is not in the last analysis what is disruptive. Cary in fact is offered as a passive spectator of her own fate, quite in line with patriarchal ideology, whereas in *Home from the Hill*, on the surface a male melodrama, the figure of the woman, totally robbed of point-of-view, holds nevertheless enormous control in the disposition of narrative events.

Pollock's intervention in the debate constitutes a useful appraisal of its theoretical assumptions. She attempts to construct terms in which the women's picture and family melodrama can be thought through together in terms of a problematic which embraces the dialectic of sex and class. However, attractive as Pollock's conception of the source of potential disruption in melodrama might be, the notion of the 'feminine position' outside of patriarchal and bourgeois social relations is highly abstract, and not much further forward in providing a sense of the articulation of sex and class which she demands.

Christian Viviani: class and sex in the maternal melodrama

Christian Viviani ('Who is without sin?', 1980) is concerned with 'woman' as an already culturally coded figure capable of mobilising audience response towards new conceptions of social organisation. He attempts an analysis of the ideologies reworked in a sub-set of Hollywood melodrama which appears to effect a passage between its Victorian forms, epi-tomised in the work of Griffith, and the women's film – a sub-set which Viviani dubs 'the maternal melodrama'. His analysis of this sub-genre in the 30s deals with the transformation of European, Victorian themes under pressure from New Deal ideology. In this, the role of woman as mother is pivotal, suggesting something of the way issues around female sexuality and maternity can be dramatised as a displacement or resolution of class issues (see Elsaesser, 1972). Viviani's contention is that as a fictional mode, melodrama seeks to move its audience emotionally by an appeal to everyday feelings and experiences which are then magnified in intensity through a complexity of baroque incident and coincidence. The fallen mother is a figure who can readily summon up such feelings, particularly for the male audience for whom she carries a charge of oedipal eroticism. At the same time, the sexual transgression of the mother is capable of evoking not only a moral but a class register, for the variations in moral attitude to her speak different class ideologies.

The dramaturgical structure on which this is based, and which was adopted by Hollywood from the European Victorian stage, involved

'a woman [who] . . . separated from her child, falls from her social class and founders in disgrace. The child grows up in respectability and enters established society where he [*sic*] stands for progress . . . The mother watches the social rise of her child from afar; she cannot risk jeopardising his fortunes by contamination with her own bad repute. Chance draws them together again and the partial or total rehabilitation of the mother is accomplished, often through a cathartic trial scene' (p. 7).

This basic structure could be organised ideologically according to two different codes of judgement, one moral, the other social. For the European-influenced and smaller cycle, the woman's fall 'was traceable to her adultery, committed in a moment of frenzy and expiated in lifelong maternal suffering' (p. 6). In Hollywood this vein represented a female equivalent to Warshow's 'gangster as tragic hero' (→ *The gangster/crime film*, p. 86). Although still morally condemned, the heroine's descent into the 'more realistic, more tawdry or desperate ambiance of music halls and furnished rooms', marked an opposition to the permanence of the bourgeois household, 'veritable ideal of this thematic, totally impregnated by Victorian morality' (p. 8). Her fate of 'anonymity and silence' was the opposite of the tale favoured by Hollywood of success and rise to fame. However, though admitting its potentially critical slant on European aristocratic moral codes, Viviani argues that this cycle looked decidely reactionary from the perspective of the New Deal:

'Heroines who are submissive, resigned,

sickly, even naive . . . defenceless, lacking in energy or decisiveness were hardly good examples for the movie-going public of 1932 and 1933 who needed to be mobilised to face the economic crisis. The direct lineage of *Madame X* was an uncomfortable reminder of an earlier state of mind which had led to the Wall Street crash' (pp. 9–10).

As America became more isolationist and nationalistic the moral codes of the maternal melodrama shifted gear. The

rural society in the name of the 'pantheistic philosophies of Thoreau and Whitman'. In the American maternal melodrama of the 30s, epitomised by *Stella Dallas* (1937), the motif of maternal sacrifice is rearticulated in relation to themes closer to American society of that time: 'prejudice, education, female understanding, the "good marriage" of the children' (p. 10). In this context moral sin is replaced by social error and a new kind of heroine can emerge whose sacrifice is less dumb acquiescence

woman's loss due to a man's lack of conscience and show her reconquering her dignity while helping her child re-enter society thanks to her sacrifices. It is a clear metaphor for an attitude America could adopt in facing its national crisis' (p. 14).

The figure of the mother could effect such ideological work because of the powerful emotions she calls on in the viewer, producing 'an illusion destined to mobilise the public in a certain direction, an illusion that transposed the anguish of an era, an illusion . . . knowingly grounded in eroticism' (p. 16). By implication the power of such eroticism to effect displacement or resolution of class difference lies in the flexible class definition of the woman. On the one hand, this is dependent on familial and sexual placing, transgression of which produces the woman in the position of outcast. On the other, ideologies of maternity and femininity – e.g. the woman sacrifices self for child, or acts out of true love for a man – can be utilised to argue for an ideological shift in the moral balance of power between different class forces.

Feminist approaches to the female protagonist

Laura Mulvey's essay 'Visual pleasure and narrative cinema' has been seminal in suggesting the role the figure of woman plays in patriarchal fiction (→ NARRATIVE AND STRUCTURALISM: *Narrative and audience*, p. 242). Her concern there, as she has since explained it (see 'Afterthoughts', 1981), was to examine the masculinisation of spectator position and identification in classic Hollywood cinema. However, as she herself argued in 'Notes on Sirk and melodrama' (1977/78), a female protagonist at the centre of the narrative disturbs this structure. This view has led to work by feminists on the possible aesthetic consequences of gender difference. Pam Cook's 'Duplicity in *Mildred Pierce*' (1978) argued that *Mildred Pierce* represented a mixed genre film in which the male voice of film noir combated the female voice of the women's film. Barbara Creed (1977) considered the narrative consequences of the generic necessity of the women's melodrama (in her terms any melodrama that supports a central heroine) to produce the figure of the woman as leading protagonist. She investigated the differences between the narrative structures developed to cope with a female protagonist and those which characterise most other genres. The problem the melodramatic structure faces is one of producing drama while conforming to social definitions of women in their domestic roles as wives and mothers (Creed, 'The position of women in Hollywood melodramas', 1977, p. 28).

From a small group of women's pictures she derives a typical narrative structure capable of supporting a central feminine protagonist 'which involves a pattern of female role transgression; the entry of an

Stella Dallas – 'maternal sacrifice . . . as a means to upward mobility and social hope'

foundations of such a shift had been laid in the work of Griffith, who had performed the necessary transposition from a European aristocratic urban milieu to an American, petit-bourgeois and rural one, which both bore the brunt of an ideological criticism (as for instance in *Way Down East*, 1920), but was capable of regeneration. New Deal ideology, according to Viviani, 'is incarnated halfway between city and country' (p. 12), and it is the figure of woman with her culturally given connection to nature, who can facilitate this incarnation, which both castigates 'the residue of an outworn morality' hung on to by the idle city rich and the rigidity of

to an inevitable and remote fate than a struggle to survive in a society whose values need correcting:

'Integrated into the world of work, she unconsciously participates in the general effort to bring America out of the crisis; she is set up as an antagonist to a hoarding, speculating society, repository of false and outworn values' (p. 12).

Her child becomes a stake in this regeneration, not taken away from the mother as in the European cycle, but given up 'to insure him an education, a moral training that only a well-placed family can give him' (p. 13).

'These films recount the tale of a

Mildred Pierce – melodrama and film noir in conflict

exceptional male; marked change in the heroine's point-of-view; suffering and sacrifice; and, finally, her acceptance of a more socially desirable role' (p. 28). She goes on to show how in the three women's pictures she studied the discourse of the doctor is used to bring the transgressing woman's viewpoint into line with the accepted codes of feminine behaviour. For Creed, the displacement of the female protagonist's dilemma into *mise en scène* and into a range of other characters, far from combating an ideology of individualism, simply restates her problem in terms of other people's needs – reproducing a scenario in which the woman does not speak, but is spoken for (p. 29). Like Kleinhans, she sees melodrama as interesting for the questions which an analysis constructed elsewhere – by Marxism or feminism – can show it touching on but not able to ask. Whereas in Kleinhans's case there are questions of capitalist relations of production and class, Creed suggests that the unspoken question of women's melodramas is to do with the taboo subject of female sexuality.

Melodrama and the status quo

Most accounts of melodrama in literature and cinema, including those discussed above, agree on one thing: that in its post-Revolutionary bourgeois forms the boundaries of the field in which it operates are those of the established social order as lived in everyday domestic terms. For instance, Stephen Neale (1980) argues that whereas in most other genres the establishment of law and order is the object of the narrative, melodrama focuses on problems of living within such order, suggesting not 'a crisis of that order, but a crisis within it, an "in-house" rearrangement' (p. 22).

Jean-Loup Bourget ('Faces of the American melodrama', 1978) presents the same

idea in ideological rather than moral terms: '. . . America after questioning the myth of progress, urbanisation and socialisation, is content with a rhetorical question and at the end of the story reinstates the same belief' (p. 32). Elsaesser concretises these generalities in an acute description of the *mise en scène* of the domestic, arising from an account of *Hilda Crane*, which, he argues, 'brings out the characteristic attempt of the bourgeois household to make time stand still, immobilise life and fix forever domestic property relations as the model of social life and a bulwark against the more disturbing sides in human nature' (p. 13). Thomas Schatz (1981) in a recent survey of 50s melodramas notes the paradoxical narrative function of marriage and the family, which provides both dramatic conflict and resolution. Of *Young at Heart* he argues:

'. . . We have seen the central characters as either victimised by or utterly hostile to the existing social-familial-marital system, but somehow romantic love and parenthood magically transform familial anxiety and despair into domestic bliss' (p. 229).

The necessity for melodrama of producing dramatic action while staying in the same place gives it a characteristically circular thematic and narrative structure – many cinematic melodramas start out from a flashback so that their end literally lies in their beginning. And it gives melodrama a characteristically ambiguous modality and address, which has given rise to different interpretations. Bourget, writing about the romantic dramas of 40s Hollywood, describes their hesitation between, on the one hand, a heavy-handed moralistic realism, operating in parable-like fashion in support of the bourgeois family, and on the other, the disbelief of

whimsy, of escape offered by 'romance'. Stephen Neale, writing from a psychoanalytic perspective, describes this ambiguity of melodrama as a form of pathos to do with the narrativisation of desire, which, by its very nature, can never be fulfilled (Neale, 1980, p. 30).

While these accounts vary in the degree to which they see subversive potential within, or despite, such constraints, they are alike in concentrating on formal analysis of the genre. Only a feminist interest in the relation of the films to the lives of their audience has suggested that the formal ambiguity within which the genre works is neither simply a meretricious ploy to soak the drama for all the pathos it's worth without confronting serious issues, nor a mass medium's attenuation of the tragic vision, but provides a structure that relates to the material conditions of women's lives.

What appears as the affect of form in one critical context, is given a material reality in another. This observation is not quite the same as noting the 'real life' occurrence of events that seem exaggerated or absurd in the films. Links between the form and the lives of the presumed female audience are commonly made by industry, establishment critics and feminists. The audience for women's films and melodramas is most often characterised as composed of frustrated housewives, oppressed by the duties of motherhood and marriage, by sexual frustration and lost fantasies of romantic love. In this view, the women's films and melodramas of the 40s and 50s gave cultural expression to these frustrations, offering in vicarious outlets escapist fantasy, rage, or sublimation. In the words of Molly Haskell (1979), the films represent 'soft-core emotional porn for the frustrated housewife'.

What the industry and Marxist feminism have in common is an implicit view of the housewife's life and the emotions it calls forth as being narrow, circumscribed, petty, boring, frustrated, etc. Critics, and many of the directors and writers involved in these films, regard them with contempt or mild patronage, looking for value in what can be made of the situations in terms of the 'human condition'. Hence the great interest in the notion of the form's power lying in its capacity to subvert its content. Recent work on melodrama, however, has ceased to look for textual progressiveness. This is partly due to the displacement of *mise en scène* by a psychoanalytically construed concept of narrative as the key to a film's ideological operation. In this view classic narrative functions precisely to engage with 'difference' – whether social, sexual, or unconscious – but always from the reassuring perspective of 'the same' to which everything is returned at the end. From quite a different approach, the notion of progressive reading has become suspect because of the formalism that constitutes meaning textually, without reference to the reading situation and practices of actual audiences. Further work on melodrama and the women's film has been pursued predominantly by feminists, proceeding in two main directions: one a formal, narrative/discourse orientated approach; another, frequently focusing on TV soap opera, an audience orientated approach. The former is concerned to analyse the work performed by narrative structure and the process of enunciation when a female protagonist is posited as subject of desire and discourse rather than its object – see Lea Jacobs, 'Censorship and the Fallen Woman cycle' forthcoming, and Mary Ann Doane, 'The "woman's film"', 1983. The latter traces a homology between the ambiguous modality of melodrama, its circular structure, and the contradictions within which women's lives are constructed. The women's film and melodrama provide fictional structures and forms of pleasure which reproduce a 'female' subject, and at the level of the text some of the material conditions in which women live (see Modleski, 'The search for tomorrow in today's soap operas', 1979, and Brunsdon, 'Crossroads: notes on soap opera', 1981.). In these terms the duplicitous complexity with which Kleinhans charges *All That Heaven Allows* – where the displacement of problems to do with class, age, sexuality into female problems of personal relations renders them simply confusing   is not so much a question of ideological poverty in the analysis of class, or age, etc., but of the difficulty of mapping the 'question of femininity', of women's issues, across other social definitions.

References

Jean-Loup Bourget, 'Faces of the American melodrama. Joan Crawford', *Film Reader* 3, 1978.

Charlotte Brunsdon, '*Crossroads*: notes on soap opera', *Screen* vol. 22 no. 4, 1981.

Pam Cook, 'Duplicity in *Mildred Pierce*', in Kaplan (ed.), *Women in Film Noir*, London, BFI, 1978.

Barbara Creed, 'The position of women in Hollywood melodramas', *Australian Journal of Screen Theory* no. 4, 1977.

Mary Ann Doane, 'The "woman's film": possession and address', in Doane, Mellencamp and Williams (eds.), *Re-Vision: Essays in Feminist Film Criticism*, Frederick MD, AFI Monograph Series, University Publications of America/AFI, 1983.

Barbara Ehrenreich, *The Hearts of Men*, London, Pluto Press, 1983.

Lotte Eisner, *Murnau*, London, Secker and Warburg, 1973.

Thomas Elsaesser, 'Tales of sound and fury: observations on the family melodrama', *Monogram* no. 4, 1972.

John Fell, *Film and the Narrative Tradition*, Norman OK, University of Oklahoma Press, 1974.

Brandon French, *On the Verge of Revolt*, New York, Ungar, 1978.

Jon Halliday, *Sirk on Sirk*, London, Secker and Warburg/BFI, 1971.

Molly Haskell, *From Reverence to Rape*, Harmonsworth, Penguin, 1979.

Lea Jacobs, 'Censorship and the Fallen Woman cycle', in Gledhill (ed.), *Studies in Melodrama and the Women's Film*, London, BFI, forthcoming.

Ann Kaplan, 'Mothering, feminism and representation: the maternal in melodrama and the women's film from 1910 to 1940', in Gledhill (ed.), *Studies in Melodrama and the Women's Film*, cit.

Chuck Kleinhans, 'Notes on melodrama and the family under capitalism', *Film Reader* 3, 1978.

Tania Modleski, 'The search for tomorrow in today's soap operas', *Film Quarterly* vol. 33 no. 1, 1979.

Laura Mulvey, 'Fear Eats the Soul', *Spare Rib* no. 30, 1974.

Laura Mulvey, 'Notes on Sirk and melodrama', *Movie* no. 25, 1977/78.

Laura Mulvey, 'Afterthoughts on "Visual pleasure and narrative cinema" inspired by *Duel in the Sun*', *Framework*, no. 15/16/17, Summer 1981.

Stephen Neale, *Genre*, London, BFI, 1980.

Geoffrey Nowell-Smith, 'Minnelli and melodrama', *Screen* vol. 18 no. 2, Summer 1977.

Griselda Pollock, 'Report on the weekend school', *Screen* vol. 18 no 2, Summer 1977.

D. N. Rodowick, 'Madness, authority and ideology in the domestic melodrama of the 1950s', *The Velvet Light Trap* no. 19, 1982.

Thomas Schatz, *Hollywood Genres*, New York, Random House, 1981.

Nicholas Vardac, *From Stage to Screen: theatrical method from Garrick to Griffith*, Boston, Harvard University Press, 1949.

Christian Viviani, 'Who is without sin? The maternal melodrama in American film 1930–39', *Wide Angle* vol. 4 no. 2, 1980.

Paul Willemen, 'Distanciation and Douglas Sirk', *Screen* vol. 12 no. 2, Summer 1971.

Linda Williams, 'Something else besides a mother: *Stella Dallas* and the maternal melodrama', in Gledhill (ed.), *Studies in Melodrama and the Women's Film*, cit.

A Fool There Was (USA 1914 *p.c* – The Box-Office Attractions Company; *d* – Frank Powell; st b/w 10)

This film plays on a typical theme of nineteenth-century stage melodrama – the disaster that besets a respectable family when its head falls prey to fashionable vamp (a stereotype instituted in Theda Bara's role here, and which made her a star). The extract provides an example of early film melodrama style utilising a static camera, lack of close-ups and natural light sources. Viewed from the perspective of 50s family melodramas this can be seen as a lack of technological development; or it can be understood as the continuity, even fulfilment, of certain nineteenth-century theatrical traditions (see Vardac, 1949). Melodramatic effects, for instance, are produced by the crosscutting between pathetic scenes of the wife with her angelic daughter or in church, and the scenes of dissolution at the vamp's apartment or of despair in the husband's home, wrecked through his squandering time and money on his mistress and drink. The husband himself becomes the site of a struggle between two representations of women: the wife, who hearing of the vamp's desertion declares 'If he is as you say my place is with him', and the dark-haired sexual woman. Melodramatic expression is carried, as in the theatre, by furnishing and fittings – a chaise longue, a card table, half-empty bottles and glasses, costume – the wife's squashed down hat, the furs and silky gowns of the vamp, and significant gesture – the vamp's stare which drives the wife from her husband's arms. The climax of this extract utilises the staircase which was to become a standard feature of a cinematic rhetoric in the expression of melodramatic confrontation (see *Rebel Without a Cause, The Little Foxes, The Magnificent Ambersons, Written on the Wind*). Here, the husband is tempted to return to wife and daughter until the vamp appears in her nightdress at the top of the stairs to drive them away, causing the husband to collapse, his hand reaching through the banister in a gesture of helpless appeal. The necessary reliance on natural light is turned to theatrical affect by lighting schemes exploiting the dramatic conflict of darkened rooms pierced by shafts of light as curtains and blinds are drawn or closed. And a substitute for the play of light and shade is found in the wreaths of incense that swathe the vamp in her apartment, evoking an atmosphere of decadence and mystery.

Hearts of the World (USA 1918 *p.c* – Artcraft/D. W. Griffith Productions for the Allied Governments; *d* – D. W. Griffith; st b/w 28)

Nicolas Vardac (1949) and John Fell (1974) have argued that the cinema, rather than originating an entirely new art form, constituted a summation of long-developing trends in the nineteenth-century novel, theatre and painting, pointing to the increasing pictorialisation of the verbal arts, to the point that stage melodrama and spectacle sought to eliminate dialogue, concentrating on action, tableau-like *mise en scène*, crosscutting, lighting effects and the mandatory, spectacular 'sensation scene'. Vardac in particular stresses the apparently contradictory combination of realism and romance in these trends, the effort being to achieve as realistic and spectacular a rendering of the romantic and melodramatic as possible. This accounts perhaps for Griffith's paradoxical status as the father both of cinematic melodrama and realism. His theatrical inheritance can be seen in the staging of spectacular battle scenes, crosscut with intimate →

Rebel Without a Cause – Jim (Dean) seeking masculine identity

Hearts of the World – Griffith's stress on pictorial values

domestic scenes; stress on pictorial values and the influence of Victorian genre painting is present in the use of circular iris for poignant scenes of tenderness and farewell (for instance when The Boy parts from his young brother) or wavy, 'cinemascope' framing for the advancing enemy columns; the influence of stage melodrama appears in the archetypal, non-individualised roles (The Girl, The Boy), in the detail of domestic interiors and in the central, pathetic role of the young girl whose innocence and suffering provides a moral index of the actions of men. This reaches its climax in plot structure and pictorial *mise en scène* when the enemy's ultimatum falls on The Girl's projected wedding day and, deranged by events, she wanders with her wedding dress in her arms over the smoke-filled battlefield, finally to spend her wedding night by the body of her dead fiancé. The search for realism can be seen in location shooting in France and in the development of continuity editing and the use of close-ups which allows for an intimate and naturalistic style of acting – for instance the changes of expression that play across Lillian Gish's face as she realises her mother is dead, passing from panic to a stony stare of derangement.

Sunrise (USA 1927 *p.c* – Fox Film Corporation; *d* – F. W. Murnau; st b/w 12 + 16)

The plot of this film is typical of nineteenth-century domestic melodrama, involving the temptations held out to a young farmer, living happily with his wife and child, by a city vamp, who consumes his small financial resources, and finally suggests murdering his wife. Much of the iconography of the domestic melodrama is there: the oil lamps, soup bowls, peasant bread and chequered tablecloth signifying domestic virtues; conflicting representations of femininity – the wife

and mother with blonde hair pulled back flat in a bun, associated with traditional peasant country life, the sexual woman in silky garb, black bobbed hair, smoking, jitterbugging and associated with the modern city; the moon and mists over the marshes as the site for the young farmer's succumbing to the murder plot. This iconography contributes to the extreme moral polarities between which the man is pulled, and which are intensified by the non-individualisation of the characters, designated only as The Man, The Wife, The Woman from the City, etc.

While much of the film's iconography, melodramatic structure and *mise en scène* looks back to nineteenth-century theatrical melodrama, it also looks forward in its style to the full development of cinematic melodrama. Most notable is, first, the influence of German Expressionism which Murnau brings to Hollywood, particularly in the distorted perspectives of the interior sets, the stereotyping of The Woman from the City, the dramatisation of typography in the intertitles that spell out the murder plot, the split screen, superimpositions and dissolves that link the woman and the city; second, Murnau's development of the moving camera, which led Bazin to put him on the side of the realists. Arguably, however, the moving camera (for instance to bring the young farmer to the City Woman on the marshes) and the long-take, deep-focus, tracking shot which allows us to travel with the young couple on the trolley from lakeside to city is part of the externalisation of emotion into cinematic *mise en scène* which Elsaesser (1972) describes as the hallmark of fullblown Hollywood melodrama in the 40s and 50s.

Finally, the film's use of sound marks its transitional status. For while it utilises a synchronous soundtrack, it fulfils the nineteenth-century melodramatic ideal of reducing dialogue

in favour of music and pictorial *mise en scène*, adding only a few expressive sound effects.

Rebel Without a Cause (USA 1955 *p.c* – Warner Bros; *d* – Nicholas Ray; sd col scope 24)

This film takes up issues of concern to Eisenhower's America – the problem of youth, of middle-class suburban conformity, of definitions of masculinity (see Ehrenreich, 1983) – and plays them out within a melodramatic *mise en scène*. In this respect it stands between the social problem picture and family melodrama. In so far as it falls into the category of family melodrama we find a clear delineation of the bourgeois, oedipal problem described by Geoffrey Nowell-Smith (1977) – the son's need to find his masculine identity, 'to be both himself and at home' – complicated by a failure of the 50s father to provide the necessary patriarchal stature against which the son can test himself (see also *Written on the Wind*). For David Rodowick (1982) paternal inadequacy enacts the ideological 'failure' of melodrama as a form in the 50s, when the necessary affirmative conclusion involves a return to a social and sexual order shown to be so palpably problematic in the body of the film. Peter Brooks's argument (1976) that melodramatic rhetoric forces language to reveal meaning in excess of what can be socially signified suggests how the *mise en scène* of this film invests a contemporary social problem with melodramatic demands and desires. This is clearly announced in the opening credits in which the music, colour, scope and Dean's self-dramatising play with the monkey and adoption of a foetal position draws from the problem of teenage delinquency its melodramatic potential, linking desire for meaning with oedipal regression. The 'chickie-run' in the second part of the extract is only one of several set-piece 'action tableaux' in →

this film, which turn teenage ritual into melodramatic theatre, externalising the demand for meaning in dramatic action and expressive *mise en scène*. The apparent 'openness' of landscape in this scene, in which the teenagers construct the possibility of meaningful action, is belied by the rest of the film in which the only field of action is the home or the school, and the only source of satisfaction the construction of meaningful family relations. In this respect Nowell-Smith's (1977) invocation of the Freudian 'family romance' as the motivating fantasy of family melodrama is literalised in the film. Thus despite the gang heroics, the neuralgic centre of the chickie-run lies in moments such as Plato's fantasy of his long-standing friendship with Jim in which building on a chance question of Judy's he constructs his image as an ideal father figure. The narrow terrain of possible action is dramatised in the third part of the extract when Jim returns to his home to a family row with his father and mother about the right course of action following Buzz's death, enacted, classically, on the staircase, the narrowness of Jim's choices externalised in the constriction of his figure by the dark brown verticals of banister, door frame mouldings and curtain folds. Finally, melodramatic enactment is carried in the improvisatory, yet theatrical acting style used in the film, which in the case of James Dean is pushed to excess and retrospectively draws on his melodramatic star image.

Stella Dallas (USA 1938 *p.c* – Goldwyn Productions; *d* – King Vidor; sd b/w 14)

This is a classic and much debated women's film, so designated because of its central woman protagonist, its 'feminine' subject matter and its address to a female audience. These features overlap with the melodramatic mode in so far as domestic subject matter, family relations, and the expression of 'feelings' are seen as both sources of the melodramatic and belonging to the feminine province. In this context, and given the cultural ghetto in which the women's film till recently existed, the melodramatic becomes a pejorative designation, associated with tearjerking pathos and sentimentality, provided frequently by the presentation of women as victims of their circumstances or nobly self-sacrificing. Christian Viviani ('Who is without sin?', 1980) has described a shift in the articulation of the maternal self-sacrifice theme in 30s Hollywood when, under pressure of New Deal ideology, the motif of the mother's fall and degradation gave way to her energetic attempts at recovery, providing a more up-beat ending. It is

this spirit that motivates *Stella Dallas* where the motif of maternal sacrifice is called on to collaborate in the portrayal of the family as a means to upward mobility and social hope. Stella's 'failing' is not so much the utilisation of her charms to catch a rich man as a means of escaping her depression-oppressed family, but her refusal to tone her ambitions and life-style in with those of her upper-class husband or to suppress her sexuality once a mother, and then later allowing her bonding with her daughter to replace conjugal relations. Stella's punishment is the crushing realisation that her lack of financial and social capital will hinder the possibility of a 'happy', upwardly mobile marriage for her daughter. She therefore proves her superior motherhood by deliberately alienating her daughter to make such a marriage possible, and thereby loses for ever the relationship which motivates the sacrifice.

The debate about the film is how to understand the implications of the ending. Does it represent the punishment of the erring mother, or is it more contradictory? Arguments that this is the case point to the difference in the maternal sacrifice theme when played out in a women's film. The first part of the extract offers an interesting example of this, where Laurel is entranced with the 'good taste' and economic well being of the Morrison household to the detriment of Stella's goodhearted vulgarity. The scene is played out through women's magazine iconography – the dressing-table, mirror, cold-cream and hair bleach – and the activities of the 'feminine' world. However this iconography does not simply dramatise the problem of female upward mobility; it also plays on the dependency of such mobility on the right appearance, a rightness that has little to do with the real underlying relations between mother and daughter.

This suggests a second twist to the maternal sacrifice theme offered by the women's film. Ann Kaplan has argued ('Mothering, feminism and representation', forthcoming) that the mother/daughter bond characteristic of the women's film is potentially threatening to patriarchal social and sexual relations. This, Kaplan argues, gives a special meaning to the film's ending when Stella is forced to accede to the sacrifice of the bond so that her daughter can enter heterosexual monogamy and contribute to social progress, while she herself is reduced to mere spectatorship, outside the scene of action. However, Linda Williams gives a different inflection to the ending by concentrating on its address to a female audience ('Something else besides a mother', forthcoming). Williams argues

that the multiple identification through which the 'feminine' is constructed in the film means that the female audience identifies with the contradictions of Stella's position itself. The only possible unifying point of identification is Stephen Dallas, who, however, is totally lacking in 'spectatorial empathy'. The audience stand-in at this point is Helen Morrison, the only person to recognise Stella's sacrifice, and who purposefully includes Stella into the scene patriarchy would exclude her from by leaving the wedding parlour curtains open. We *see* Stella's patriarchal placement, but *feel* the loss of mother and daughter to each other.

Written on the Wind (USA 1956 *p.c* – Universal-International; *d* – Douglas Sirk; sd col 15)

This film was central to the rediscovery of melodrama in the early 70s, when a revaluation of Douglas Sirk pointed to the ideological critique operated by his ironic *mise en scène* on 50s middle-class America.

Its plot enacts a typical family melodrama in which the constriction of its range of action is reinforced by the circularity of its flashback structure and the hopeless, limited and incestuous channels for its protagonists' desires locked as they are within the bourgeois patriarchal family. Behind the son's impotence, of which he learns at the beginning of this extract, lies the father's failure as patriarch (see also *Rebel Without a Cause*), further manifested in the excessive, misdirected desire of his daughter, expressed here in the displacement of her desire for Mitch into her active pursuit of a lower-class petrol pump attendant. In this respect the plot foregrounds the interconnection of class and sexuality which Elsaesser and others contend is central to melodrama, class struggle being enacted as a problem of desire, in which female sexuality plays an ambiguous but central role (see Pollock, 1977).

The play of class and sex is carried in the iconography of the film – all the signs of conspicuous bourgeois consumption of the Hadley mansion, the oil pumps working incessantly against the skyline, the contrasting colours and costume of the conflicting couples – particularly reds associated with Marylee (sports car, flowers, negligée) and the cool green twinsets of Lucy. Such use of décor, costume and consumer goods is typical of Hollywood family melodrama, as is also the use of the space of hallway and landings where characters cross paths, eavesdrop, exchange confidences, malicious innuendo or accusations (see *The Magnificent Ambersons*, *Rebel Without A Cause*). Climactic here is the staircase →

Written on the Wind – sexual iconography in the oil pumps

used as the site of final confrontation or denouncement. Overlaying 50s melodramatic plot structure and iconography is the special injection of Sirkian irony into its excessive *mise en scène*; his play with cliché (the nodding mechanical horse and grinning child that confront Kyle at the moment he believes himself impotent); an obsessive play with mirrors (Mitch's entrance with a drunken Kyle over his shoulder is first caught in a hallway mirror), screens and windows (Marylee looking through her window panes to the policeman and the petrol pump attendant), and above all an expressionist use of colour, which breaks with realist conventions for the sake of wresting ironic contrasts from objects and faces (the harsh lighting and make-up on Lucy's and Mitch's faces as they attempt to sooth Kyle at the country club, where the palm court music is also in striking contrast to the extremities expressed by Kyle).

Sirkian *mise en scène* can also be read in terms of the repression so often said to provide melodrama with its outbreaks of expressive excess, which in turn draws its audience into the emotional drama rather than putting them at a critical distance. The breaking out of repression at the level of plot, florid *mise en scène* and crosscutting typical of melodramatic style is epitomised in this extract in the scene where the Hadley father falls to his death while Marylee dances wildly and erotically to blaring pop music in her bedroom. The extract as a whole exemplifies the extension of 'musical counterpoint' so crucial to nineteenth-century theatrical melodrama into visual and aural *mise en scène* (see Elsaesser, 1972).

All That Heaven Allows (USA 1955 *p.c* – Universal-International; *d* – Douglas Sirk; sd col 20+20)

One of Sirk's women's pictures, the film concerns a middle-American bourgeois family for whom the death of the father poses a problem in the now available sexuality of the mother. Her rejection of the suitably respectable,

middle-aged Harvey for her young gardener not only threatens the life-style and values of her children, but the social identity of the family and of the bourgeois community. The film plays out the family crisis from the woman protagonist's point-of-view, focusing on her conflicting desires. The themes of romance and renunciation which produce the heroine's crisis and mark the film's ending similarly pull the film into the women's picture category.

The opening of the first extract sets the small-town, middle-American context and signals women's picture concerns with its pan from whitewood church spire to the arrival of Sarah returning crockery to Cary. Ron Kirby, the gardener, is introduced as the fantasy hero of women's fiction – tall, dark, self-contained, at work in the background but attentive, gentle, yet authoritative. He is romantic because 'different' – in his style of masculinity (his work with nature), in age, in social class, and above all in his appreciation of the codes of romantic women's fiction: the golden rain tree 'can only thrive where there is love'. Music supports the motif of romance, which the Sirkian *mise en scène* takes up and pits against family melodrama themes in the shot of Cary caught in her mirror, the golden rain tree twig beside her and her children crowding in behind, the clash of harsh and warm colours signalling either the conflicting demands about to ensue, or operating an ironic critique of the genre, depending on one's critical perspective.

The second part of this extract broaches the crisis which the women's film constructs for its heroine: the conflict between her maternal role and personal and sexual desire. Here the conflict is overlaid by class, for Ron offers an escape into the realm of the personal, truth to self, from the realm of class status, represented by her dead husband's world. The romantic hero offers the possibility of unifying the two divided sides of a woman's life, represented in signs and symbols drawn from women's magazines and fiction: the 'natural', personally converted barn

with roaring log fire, the man who speaks firmly what the heroine wants yet is compelled to resist – 'home is where you are' – the shared concern over the restored Wedgwood teapot. The register is self-consciously melodramatic as Sirkian *mise en scène* foregrounds the symbolic dimension of the transaction, its setting and surrounding objects.

The first part of the second extract focuses issues of family melodrama in the scandal caused by Cary's and Ron's presence at the country club, centred on Cary's sexual and class status, and her ensuing confrontation with her son, shot in typical Sirkian fashion with Cary's face caught in the window frame lit by the lurid red of a setting sun, and screens and shadows dividing mother and son. This continues with the play of rainbow-coloured light on mother's and daughter's faces when Kay rushes up the stairs after quarrelling with her boyfriend about her mother. A quintessential Sirkian irony occurs in the second part when the children's Christmas present, a TV set, is triumphantly unveiled by the salesman – 'all the company you want, right there on the screen; drama, comedy . . .' – and Cary's face is caught in the screen, miserable with the news of Ned's impending departure abroad and Kay's engagement.

The critical question raised by the film is whether Sirkian *mise en scène* distances the audience, to ironise the smug, bourgeois world of Eisenhower's middle America (see Willemen, 1971) or whether, as in Chuck Kleinhans's (1978) argument, the film works with mystificatory ambiguity, providing a range of reasons for the failure of Cary and Ron's relationship, none of which are conclusive, or, as in Mulvey's (1977/78) view, the placing of a female character as main protagonist in a family melodrama distorts the genre's 'safety valve' function for patriarchy, raising, in a way very recognisable to female audiences, the problems and questions of women's desire. Feminist critics might want to ask, is the desire that romance feeds ironised along with Eisenhower's America?

The gangster/crime film

Introduction

Until the emergence of genre criticism, writing on the gangster/crime film was divided between censorship issues and journalistic accounts of the historical phases and thematic and iconographic features of the genre and its various sub-genres. Until the 70s, Warshow's 'The gangster as tragic hero' (1970) was almost the sole attempt to deal with the aesthetic and ideological significance of this enormously popular and endlessly proliferating genre, supported by a somewhat different, more generalised approach in Lawrence Alloway's *Violent America* (1971), which concentrated on the depiction of violence. It was not until the arrival of one of the founding texts of genre criticism, Colin McArthur's *Underworld USA* (1972), that we find in Tom Ryall's words, 'a systematic attempt to define the genre, and to indicate the achievement within it of a selection of notable *auteurs*' (see Ryall, *Teachers' Study Guide 2*, 1979, p. 14).

Insight into the reasons for this early neglect can be gleaned from Andrew Tudor's account of the genre in *Image and Influence* (1974) where he compares it unfavourably with the western, characterising the 'urban nightmare' so often attributed to the gangster film as a 'brutal universe . . . mechanistic, [offering] little in the way of social and emotional riches' (p. 201). This says much about what the western contributed to establishing genre criticism as a way of talking seriously about popular culture:

'Unlike the western there is no code governing the violence, no set of rules for the regulation of this war of all against all' (p. 201).

A feminist perspective might suggest that what is at stake here is the too naked expression of a certain form of male heroics. The gangster's 'self-interested individualism is totally unfettered . . . It is the cowboy's world but without his integrity and without his sense of character' (p. 202).

Clearly one problem that confronted early genre criticism in relation to the gangster film was its seemingly symbiotic relation to contemporary events as circulated in a sensational press rather than to an already mythologised history. As Andrew Tudor puts it:

'. . . the construction of the genre was almost contemporaneous with the construction of the events themselves. . . It was stimulated by the late 20s boom in publicity for gangster activities. The fame of Capone and the notorious St. Valentine's Day massacre of 1929 created a storm of publicity. Quick to see the possibilities, the studios reacted, and on the crest of this wave came Mervyn LeRoy's *Little Caesar*' (pp. 196–197).

Another related problem confronted by film criticism was the extreme fragmentation of the genre, whose 'classic' period

Little Caesar – a reaction to contemporaneous events in the 1930s

Roaring Twenties – Cagney arrested in the warehouse raid

lasts, according to most accounts, only three years. Thomas Schatz (1981) argues that,

'because of their overt celebration of the gangster-hero and their less-than-flattering portrayal of contemporary urban life, these films were as controversial as they were popular, and threats of censorship, boycott, and federal regulation forced the studios to restructure the gangster formula by the mid-30s. Consequently . . . its narrative formula was splintered into various derivative strains . . .' (p. 82).

These can be enumerated in terms of various cycles, phases and sub-genres: the G-Man cycle, private eye thrillers, film noir, police movies, detective mysteries, crime melodramas and so on. The mythic coherence which could be attributed to the western and which supported claims that it connected with long established traditions was difficult to establish for the

gangster/crime film with its seemingly opportunistic shifts and turns according to changes of the physiognomy of crime and law enforcement in America – Tudor cites, for instance, the lack of anything like the 'Garden-Desert thesis' for the gangster film (p. 196). A succinct account of how changes in 'the reality of American crime' surface in generic change can be found in Colin McArthur's *Underworld USA* (1972, pp. 64–65).

For early criticism the apparently close relation between generic change and contemporary reality encouraged notions of 'reflection'. This was made all the easier by the association of the classic gangster film with the Warner Bros Studio, widely known for its 30s 'social issue' movies, and with the development of sound by that studio, again popularly understood as an instrument of realism. This supposed realism contributed and still contributes to recurring 'moral panics' about the effects of the films' violence, glorification of the criminal and misogyny on young audiences, and consequently the history of the genre has been interlaced with censorship problems. Beyond this, early work on the genre was much concerned with tracing the appearance of different cycles and sub-genres in terms of social sources, subject matter and dominant conventions, much of which is taxed with problems to do with periodisation, cycle demarcation and definition and ultimate origins (see Whitehall, 'Crime Inc.', 1964; French, 'Incitement against violence', 1967/68).

Warshow: the gangster film as an experience of art

In this context Warshow's seminal 'The gangster as tragic hero' (1970) attempted to break the grip of readings of gangster films as if they reflected or were accountable to historical or sociological renderings of American contemporary reality:

'. . . the importance of the gangster film, and the nature and intensity of its emotional and aesthetic impact, cannot be measured in terms of the place of the gangster himself or the importance of the problem of crime in American life. Those European movie-goers who think there is a gangster on every corner in New York are certainly deceived, but defenders of the "positive" side of American culture are equally deceived if they think it relevant to point out that most Americans have never seen a gangster. What matters is that the experience of the gangster *as an experience of art* is universal to Americans' (p. 130, original emphasis).

In Warshow's view the data of social reality are reorganised to produce a reality of the imagination whose referential field is other gangster films rather than the 'real world'.

McArthur: the gangster/thriller as iconography

Writing on the gangster film produced as part of, or since, the emergence of genre studies, has generally taken Warshow's argument as its starting point. Most notable within the first category was Colin McArthur's *Underworld USA* (1972), one chapter of which was concerned to lay out the basic unity of the genre's iconography, which he understands as 'the continuity over several decades of patterns of visual imagery, of recurrent objects and figures in dynamic relationship' (p. 23). These stable iconographic elements can be divided into three categories (see Ryall, 1979):

1. The physical presence, attributes and dress of the actors and actresses and the characters they play.
2. The urban milieux in which the fiction is played out.
3. The technology at the character's disposal, principally guns and cars.

These elements recur consistently, in spite of shifts between different phases or subsets of the genre. As Ryall argues, McArthur's iconographical approach enables him to produce a flexible, dynamic account of the genre, whereas Warshow's attachment to the 'rise and fall' narrative freezes the genre at an early point in its development (p. 18). Ryall outlines McArthur's categorisation of the following phases or cycles:

1930s
– the 'classic' gangster film (*Little Caesar, The Public Enemy, Scarface*)
– the FBI film (*G-Men, Bullets or Ballots*)
– the 'social background' film (*Angels with Dirty Faces, Dead End*)
1940s
– the film noir (*The Big Sleep, The Maltese Falcon*)
– the 'police documentary' (*The House on 92nd Street*)
– the morally-oriented gangster film (*Force of Evil*)
1950s
– the syndicate film (*Murder Inc., New York Confidential*)
– the historical reconstructions (*Al Capone, Machine Gun Kelly*)
1960s
– the 'forties thriller' reprised (*Warning Shot, The Moving Target*).
To these we might now add:
Late 1960's/1970s
– the 'police movie' (*Dirty Harry, Magnum Force*)
– film noir reprised (*Chinatown, Marlowe, Klute*)
1980s
– the 'classic' gangster film reprised (*Scarface*)

The gangster film and ideology

McArthur's book constituted a ground-breaking exercise in making visible and delineating the genre. Two major problems remained: one, to offer a convincing analysis of the relationship of the genre to reality which would also account for generic change; the other, to extend the account of the aesthetic and imaginative reach of the genre beyond the limitations of the classic moment as in Warshow, or of a concentration on iconography at the expense of all the other elements in a film production, both cinematic and extra-cinematic (←*Iconography*, p. 60). The debates about ideology and aesthetics which superseded generic criticism (←*Genre: history and ideology*, p. 61) would seem to have ideal material in the gangster film, but on the whole recent studies of the genre have not chosen this route, preferring to elaborate the genre's formal development in terms of production histories – studios, censorship, technologies, etc. – or in terms of narrative and cinematic codes. Ideological readings tend to be sensitive to textual appraisals of what Warshow describes as the obverse of the American dream, the 'urban nightmare'. In this respect the gangster/thriller is most often poised between the western on the one hand and the horror film on the other.

Warshow (1970), having rescued the gangster from reductionist 'realist' readings, had to go on to define and defend the significance of this perverse 'creature of the imagination'. The loss of tragedy to American culture is the cornerstone of Warshow's argument. American capitalism claims to eliminate tragedy from human experience by making individual happiness the ostensible goal and rationale of all its social arrangements. This ethos in turn destroys the conditions for the production of tragic art, which depends on a social order which subordinates the fate of the individual to 'a fixed and supra-political . . . moral order or fate' (p. 127). However, if banished from 'official ideology', the 'tragic sense' does not disappear, because of fundamental contradiction between the ideals of equality and individualism, and the ambiguous nature of happiness when conceived in terms of 'success'. Happiness as success not only pitches the individual against others, inviting his or her downfall, but breeds its obverse, a 'sense of desperation and inevitable failure' (p. 129). This, argues Warshow, is 'our intolerable dilemma: that failure is a kind of death, and success is evil and dangerous, is ultimately – impossible' (p. 133). The gangster film enables this dilemma to be played out and resolved in a way that its message is both 'disguised' and involves the minimum of distortion:

'. . . the gangster is the 'no' to that great American 'yes' which is stamped so big over our official culture and yet has so little to do with the way we really feel about our lives' (p. 136).

The notion that the gangster film represents 'the modern sense of tragedy' is frequently assumed and will be returned to later. Similarly the link between the gangster film and capitalist ideology has been elaborated by many critics. For some, the problems posed by the contradictions of capitalism open onto wider philosophical issues to do with appearance, reality, the individual and society, self-assertion and death.

The formal history of the gangster/crime film

Jack Shadoian (1977) has offered one of the more interesting developments of the Warshow thesis. In place of iconography he utilises the idea of 'structure' as the form's unifying principle. His deployment of this concept in relation to other cinematic codes such as narrative, *mise en scène*, lighting, etc., enables him to mount an interesting history of the way the necessities of generic and formal change produce shifting possibilities of pleasure and meaning. Less successful perhaps are his occasional attempts to link these shifts back to political and social realities of the time.

Shadoian's thesis is that the basic structure of the gangster/crime film is 'ready-made for certain kinds of concerns' (p. 3). Along with Warshow and several other commentators since who see the fictional gangster as 'a product of advanced urban civilisation', Shadoian argues that these concerns arise out of the contradictions of the 'American dream' in the context of industrialism and post-industrial corporate capitalism – for instance 'between America as a land of opportunity and the vision of a classless, democratic society' (p. 5) – contradictions which come to a head in the gangster film in the drive to suc-

Angels with Dirty Faces – the 'social background' film

cess, 'the urge for it, the fear of it, the consequences that both having it and not having it entail' (p. 5).

The structure that emerged with the classical gangster film carried these contradictions with it. The legal and social status of the criminal produced a figure, the gangster, outside and opposed to society, who 'violates a system of rules that a group of people live under' (p. 3). The position of the hero as outside but related by conflict and violence to society produces a perspective from which that society must be viewed; in this way 'meanings emerge, whether deliberately or not, about the nature of society and the kind of individual it creates' (p. 3). In this respect the gangster differs from the western 'outlaw'; in the west society – civilisation – has yet to be constructed and fought for. The gangster/crime film speaks to the 'American Dream' at a different stage.

From his starting point in the formal and aesthetic working of the genre, Shadoian moves on to a flexible account of its ideology in which the personal, psychic and political intertwine. Central to his analysis is its construction of the contradictions of capitalism as the simultaneous summoning and restriction of desire. Above all the gangster/crime film deals with desire confronted by constraint. It pits 'basic human needs in opposition to a world that denies them' (p. 119). 'The

gangster', says Shadoian, 'is a creature who wants, and although he shares this trait with characters in other genres, the degree of his compulsion is probably unique' (p. 14).

In Shadoian's analysis gangster/crime film develops towards inward and existential examination of human existence in modern American corporate society, accompanied by the increasing formalisation of the genre, and indeed of cinema itself. He discerns, for instance, a shift from the use of the gangster outside as a means of gaining a new perspective on society to a film noir concern, expressed in an increasing use of 'symbol, metaphor and allusion', with the nature of society itself, in which the distinction between gangster and society, and society and self becomes confused and a new 'flavour of guilt and atonement' replaces the 'amorality, cynicism and self-confident' behaviour of the classic gangster hero (p. 120).

The formal history of the genre illuminates this shift. The 'classic' gangster took off from a known public fascination with real criminals, already being processed by sensational journalism. The films quickly diverged from reality, while maintaining a realist address. They were, in Shadoian's terms, travelogues and documentaries into alien territory – the world of the gangster, whose otherness became increasingly marked by stylisation which prepared the ground for the genre's transformation when the combined forces of censorship, the passing of the Depression, the logic of generic renewal and sophistication, made the gangster's heroic rise and near tragic fall no longer a viable structure. *The Roaring Twenties* and *High Sierra* stand nostalgically poised between the world of the classic gangster offering 'resonant myths of defeat that echoed with heroic,

positive reverberations' and the more pessimistic world of film noir where 'views of freedom and possibility narrow' (p. 59). In the 50s the existential confusion of film noir shifts into a new organisation of the basic structure of gangster versus society. 'If noir scrambled the terms of the opposition, the 50s inverts them' (p. 211). In the era of affluence crime and corporate capitalism are equated, an equation which not only inverts the 'classic' gangster's position as outsider, but also the struggle celebrated by the western, in which civilisation is attained by overcoming primitivism and savagery. In the 50s gangster film, the evils of civilisation can only be purified by a reversion to instinctive actions and emotions. In this period, the gangster has gone the farthest in achieving control, reason, logic, and precision and has consequently lost contact with his real self more than others. Within the overall structure of the gangster film, then, 'when the gangster ... becomes that which he used to oppose, the genre finds his substitute, one who can assume his former function' (p. 214). The hero who will combat society as crime in the name of the American dream is one who has to detach himself from society. If he is a policeman, since the force is incorporated into crime, he must 'act independently of the machinery'. This process of detachment involves the hero being 'restored to his fundamental drives, his basic instincts' (p. 212), and occurs only through the agency of violence, the re-assertion of desire once embodied in the gangster.

With the end of the 60s and entry to the 70s, Shadoian argues that the genre, in line with the overall development of cinematic codes, reaches a point of sophistication and self-referentiality that makes the shift towards modernism inevitable. The unfeasibility of representational storytelling forces the genre into evasive strategies such as replaying stories from the past, or creating characters and heroes 'who can scarcely be defined as human' at all (p. 291). A further consequence of this shift is an increase in violence and the creation of 'highly aggressive fictions that have little regard for facts' (p. 291). Use of colour and the dominance of *auteurs* further heightens violence and anti-realism. Violence in this sense has to be understood aesthetically:

'The brutalisation of the audience, which took on systematic form in the 50s, has detached itself from urgent content and become an aesthetic factor with its own logic of communication. It has become the genre's core experience, and its ultimate statement' (p. 8).

Studio, technology and style
The emergence of the gangster film as a distinct genre in the 30s, and its reputed realism and contemporaneousness, has often been associated with the consolidation of the Warner Bros Studio, which produces many of the 'classic' titles. Nick Roddick (1983) explores the association of

Warners in the 30s with the 'social con-science' movie, arguing that there exists 'a certain similarity between American social history and the themes produced by Warners during the 1930s' (p. 65) (←HISTORY: *The studios*, p. 10).

The studio system was developed as a means of rationalising production in relation to the market; 'there was an identifiable audience need to be met, and the studio system was designed to meet it economically – and therefore as profitably – as possible' (p. 10). The major studios set out to produce clear and differentiated identities to avoid duplication of effort, specialising in 'a particular kind or style of film' (p. 8).

The development of sound, in which Warners played a large part and which contributed to its studio identity, shifted Hollywood production generally in the direction of realism and away from fantasy and the exotic. Warners followed the route of realism and contemporaneity with a heavy emphasis on what can be loosely designated 'social problem' pictures, although Roddick points out that only just under one third of Warners 30s output dealt with contemporary American society and 'the vast majority bear little or no immediate social message' (p. 73). Nevertheless Warners did consciously identify themselves with the New Deal. The question is what such identification could mean ideologically or aesthetically. Warners, a more emphatically 'family' business than any of the other majors, was also 'the most tightly run, economical and streamlined of the big five during the 1930s' (p. 22). Yet while Warners were geared to 'a mass-production system', what they were producing for consumption was, quite consciously, 'art'. The relationship of their films to the real world, Roddick argues,

'. . . was not a direct one: it was an aesthetic one. What is more, the terms in which the films are discussed in the studio memos – structure, balance, impact, pacing, credibility – are terms which are basically concerned with the artistic, not the physical nature of the product. Even in cases where financial considerations are clearly the origin of the memo, the aim is always to get the best effect in the most economical way. The criterion remains, in the final instance, artistic. How else is "the best effect" to be designated?' (p. 25).

With a liberal leaning towards contemporary issues, a pressure towards realism increased through a heavy investment both of capital and identity in sound, and an equal pressure towards maximising use of studio space and avoidance of costly location work, the implicit aesthetic problem for Warners was how to turn reality into drama and narrative. As Roddick points out a tradition already existed in the fiction of Balzac, Dickens and their derivatives for the association of social realism and crime, an association made vivid in the 30s as gangsterism, and potential social breakdown consequent upon prohibition

and the Depression, hit the newspaper headlines. Crime movies, then, 'provided a potentially perfect formula for fulfilling [Warners'] early talkie policy of realistic and at the same time popular entertainment' (p. 77). Not only did they give 'a dramatic focus to fairly ordinary problems or aspirations – poverty, unemployment, sexual inadequacy, alienation, ambition, greed – by making them criminal motives' (p. 77), they also offered in the criminal 'a hero whose anti-social individualism could speak to the contradictions of capitalist ideology, be romanticised and identified with by the audiences of the small-town and neighbourhood theatres' (p. 99) to which the gangster films were directed.

Roddick identifies two levels of production in Warners' output of contemporary pictures in the 30s. While the more directly 'social problem' pictures ranged across genres, taking in crime thrillers, gangster films, newspaper films, and were, because of their importance to the studio's corporate image, 'allocated top writers, major stars and comparatively large budgets . . . [and were] road-shown in the major theatres with strong promotional campaigns guaranteeing them longer than usual runs' (p. 78), the consolidation of the 'classic' gangster film itself was a more tightly generic and economical affair. Such films,

'. . . were relatively cheap to make, since they used contemporary dress, sets (seedy restaurants, backroom offices and hotel rooms) and exteriors that rarely if ever called for anything other than the standing sets of the backlot. Additionally, once the formula was perfected – as early, basically, as 1931 – the scripting and pre-production process was ideally suited to Warners' streamlined studio methods' (p. 99).

They were also extremely popular, and clearly provided an economic and an aesthetic base to the more prestigious productions. Eventually, it would seem, the aesthetic force of generic convention displaced the foregrounding of social issues in Warners' crime movies, which came to be seen rather as 'mystery melodramas' (p. 82).

In considering the ideological significance of studio policy, Roddick is concerned to dispel either a too radical, or too recuperative view of Warner's social realism. He cites Hans Magnus Enzensberger's comment on advertising – 'that it is not the creation of a false need, but the false meeting of a real need' (p. 8) – in order to suggest the contradictions inherent in the consolidation of studio style and genre as a means of 'manipulating' the market. The liberal ideology of the studio bosses, the commitment of studio style to a 'hard-hitting' realism, meant in Roddick's view that inevitably, 'in tackling the symptoms, Warners should tackle some of the causes' for instance of the Depression or fascism (p. 74). The limitations of what could be done were set both by the contradictions of liberalism's

attempts to make capitalism work and by the demands of fiction. Social responsibility, economic self-interest, and the demand for narrative resolution made it a *sine qua non* 'that a film which tackled a problem had to offer a solution, even if the real-life problem seemed likely to remain unsolved for some time to come' (p. 66). Nevertheless 'the contradictions of American society in the 1930s were the material on which the studio drew, [if] not something it necessarily set out to highlight' (p. 66). If the studio by its very nature and situation could not produce social change, its product was a medium through which indirectly a need for change could be registered.

Thomas Schatz's chapter on the gangster film in *Hollywood Genres* (1981) follows the general line pursued by Warshow, Shadoian and Roddick, and offers some interesting elaborations on the latter's concern to trace the interplay of studio, technology, aesthetics and ideology. Sound, he argues, not only effected a decisive shift towards realism, but was the catalyst for the consolidation of the crime film as a staple of the studio's output, contributing much to its aesthetic formalisation. Warners' experimental *The Lights of New York* (1928),

'. . . demonstrated that sound effects and dialogue greatly heightened the impact of urban crime dramas. As later films would confirm, synchronous sound affected both the visual and editing strategies of gangster movies. The new audio effects (gunshots, screams, screeching tyres, etc.) encouraged film-makers to focus upon action and urban violence, and also to develop a fast-paced narrative and editing style' (p. 85).

Similarly the gangster persona itself – with his propensity for asserting his individual will through violent action and self-styled profiteering – offers an ideal figure for cinematic narrative elaboration. 'The fact that his assertiveness flaunts social order even heightens his individuality' (p. 86).

Like other writers, Schatz argues that the aesthetics of the genre organise a range of meaning around the gangster hero of far greater imaginative power than the attempts of censorship bodies to assert against him the values of the status quo. One good reason for this perhaps is that the gangster speaks, if contradictorily, for the status quo, for its buried underside as well as its affirmative goals. As Schatz comments, 'the urban lone wolf's brutality and antisocial attitudes in Hollywood films are simply components of an essentially positive cultural model – that of the personable and aggressive but somewhat misguided self-made American man' (p. 84). It is therefore perfectly possible, when the Hays Code intervenes, to shift the role of hero from gangster to cop and maintain the same expressive style: 'Cagney as gangster in *The Public Enemy* is basically indistinguishable from that of Cagney as government agent in *G-Men* . . .

Lights of New York – new technology helped shape the gangster genre

He may be advocating a different value system in each role, but his self-assured swagger, caustic disposition, and violent demeanour are basic to each' (p. 84). Clearly part of this continuity is to do with the star, and several commentators (e.g. McArthur, 1972) have noted the importance of the stars of these films – Cagney, Robinson, Bogart, Muni, etc. – to the consolidation of the genre's conventions.

Schatz sees the ideological significance of the classic gangster film as stemming from an interplay of such aesthetic factors with the conditions of production and consumption of genre, to which the studio had to submit. Once a business is mounted in the field of entertainment, promulgation of safe ideologies is complicated by the technical and aesthetic requirements of the 'product':

'Despite the film industry's avowed efforts to support the status quo ... filmmakers and audiences were cooperating in refining genres that examined the more contradictory tenets of American ideology' (p. 95).
For,

'... camerawork, editing, dialogue, characterisation, and even the star system work together to engage our sympathy for the criminal. So from a technical (as well as thematic) standpoint, the gangster-hero functions as an *organising sensibility* in these films, serving to offset the other characters' naive moralising and to control our perception of his corrupt, Kafkaesque milieu' (p. 93).

In this respect the death of the hero is not a sop to the various pressure groups that concerned themselves with the morality of Hollywood. It is an aesthetic and ideological necessity, which recognises both sides of the contradiction that provides the dynamic of the genre. The appeal of the gangster is his ability to grasp those

goals for which the status quo says we should strive despite the minimal options it offers. 'For a brief time, at least, the gangster is on top of his own pathetically limited world' (p. 89). The strength of this appeal qualifies the apparent endorsement of social order of the genre's ending; paradoxically the gangster's 'very death is the consummate reaffirmation of his own identity' (p. 90).

The necessity of this ending has the same formal force as 'the romantic embrace which resolves the musical comedy, or the gunfight which resolves the western' in maintaining 'a narrative balance between the hero's individuality and the need for social order' (p. 90). But it is *balance* that is arrived at, not the elmination of one side of the contradiction in favour of the other. (This accounts perhaps for critical unease with more recent variants of the genre, with what is often seen as the proto-fascist police movie exemplified in the Eastwood Dirty Harry series, in which the cathartic end in death is denied.)

The death of the gangster: tragedy or melodrama?

For most critics the moralistic intentions behind many of the gangster films' tacked-on endings of retribution are far outweighed by the imaginative necessity of the hero's death. It is this – the inevitability and mode of the gangster's death – which permits critics' frequent appeal to tragedy as a justification for taking the genre seriously (in much the same way as the western claims prestige as epic). As Steve Jenkins (1982, p. 44) suggests, the death of the gangster is qualitatively different from death in other genres. Death comes with an inevitability that precludes suspense, often arbitrarily, and always with finality. The gangster dies at the hand of fate, isolated, and yet a public spectacle. What

makes this death appear tragic is variously defined. Jenkins, noting that the gangster's death generally ends the film, offers the suggestive comment that 'the genre concentrates on the progress of an *individual male* character ...' (p. 44, our emphasis). As we have seen Warshow finds the ending tragic because its rise and fall structure contains within it the failure of a struggle for individual self-assertion with which we identify, but which we also know society cannot allow. Schatz pursues an indentification of the tragic in the gangster film by looking for the gangster's tragic flaw, which he isolates as 'his inability to channel his considerable individual energies in a viable direction' (p. 88). However he immediately qualifies this by suggesting society is itself partly responsible, 'in that it denies individual expression and provides minimal options to the struggling, aggressive male from an inner-city, working-class background' (p. 89). Shadoian in claiming that the gangster film offers a 'tradition of popular tragedy in film' cities the 'combination of hubris, social fate and moral reckoning' (p. 15) in the gangster's story, arguing that *Little Caesar* is to the gangster film what *Oedipus Rex* is to Greek tragedy. Crucial to his argument is the gangster's choice of his fate, and the awesomeness of his overthrow.

What is interesting here is the need to rediscover the tragic and the sense that it has to be redefined in 'modern' terms. It is also notable that the designation, tragedy, is applied almost exclusively to the 'classic' gangster films of the 30s with their clear rise and fall structure. Shadoian goes so far as to suggest that the interaction of the needs provoked by the Depression with a cinema still in its 'age of innocence' was productive of a tragic catharsis in the classic gangster film denied to later phases of the genre. However, melodrama, closely related to tragedy, may provide a different understanding of the conflicts and violence which make the gangster's death seem tragic.

Robert Heilman (1968) and Peter Brooks (1976), have both discussed the relationship between tragedy and melodrama. Heilman's concern is to preserve the category of tragedy from its frequent, mystifying reduction to melodrama. Awesomeness of fate, even if chosen, does not by itself define the tragic hero. What is crucial is his internalisation of conflict, his coming to awareness of division within and of his own responsibility. Brooks seeks to historicise the distinction by suggesting that the two forms belong to different sets of historical socio-economic and cultural circumstances. Following a somewhat similar line to Warshow, Brooks argues that tragedy belongs to a social hierarchy, organised around the monarchy and church, which integrates individual lives to a transcendental, sacred order, embracing the forces of good and evil. Brooks, like Heilman, sees our identification with the hero's coming to self-awareness, his introspective contemplation of his internal divisions, as the source of tragedy's lesson. The downfall itself relates back to communal sacrificial rites, and is a mechanism for catharsis rather than insight.

However, with the destruction of traditional social hierarchies bringing to an end the transcendental sacred order, the problem arises of how to found a new ethical order; how to prove the existence of good and evil and find the means for their expression within a secular framework and in a way that would satisfy the ethical and psychic needs of the new bourgeois 'individual'. For Brooks, melodrama attempts to do this by finding a new moral order 'occulted' within individual lives lived in an everyday, ordinary world. Thus, melodramatic rhetoric seeks to 'infuse the banal and the ordinary with the excitement of grandiose conflict' (p. 40). Good and evil can only be grasped as features of personal life; thus 'they are assigned to, they inhabit persons who indeed have no psychological complexity but who are strongly characterised' (p. 16). What such rhetoric entails is a 'victory over repression', which is 'simultaneously social, psychological, historical and conventional' (p. 41). Such victory means saying – asserting – what social and verbal constraints do not permit to be said; it means forcing language beyond its limitations as a symbolic system to yield fullness of meaning and identity to speakers and audience in moments of 'ringing identification' (p. 42).

The gangster/crime film can be understood in terms of the ethical-psychic terms offered by Brooks. We have already noted Shadoian's 'the gangster is a creature who wants'. Schatz also suggests the primal nature of the gangster's self-assertion: 'destiny may kill him, but the intensity of the hero's commitment to his fate indicates that power and individuality are more important than a long life' (p. 94). The gangster/crime film provides a context in which the desire for power and acquisition can be named and asserted against all the codes that would control and repress it.

Nevertheless such desire cannot overthrow the social order. As Brooks comments:

'The ritual of melodrama involves the confrontation of clearly identified antagonists and the expulsion of one of them. It can offer no terminal reconciliation, for there is no longer a clear transcendent value to be reconciled to. There is, rather, a social order to be purged, a set of ethical imperatives to be made clear' (pp. 16–17).

This inability to move beyond the bourgeois world is found in the gangster/crime film. For instance Shadoian observes that,

'. . . the genre offers no alternative to the American way of life. America's political, social and economic flaws are not hidden, but the system, in principle, is never

Marked Woman – Bette Davis takes the witness stand

seriously argued with' (p. 11).

The capacity of the genre to transmute the values of society and gangster allow a critique of society to emerge. However, 'upper-middle, middle-class, or prole heroes continue in the same system after convulsing it. In the end they act on behalf of its *ideal* nature' (p. 11).

In this context the function of the tableau-like endings of gangster films noted by Steve Jenkins can be set in a wider perspective:

'At the moment of the gangster's death these [female] characters are placed in opposition to the representatives of the law in a recurring tableau-like representation of the significance of that death . . . By placing the dead gangster between the law (man) who stands over the body, and the woman, who often kneels by it or cradles the dead man's head, the distinction is clearly made between the official "meaning" of the death (public enemy dealt with) and its resonance for the audience's emotional investment in the character, the spectator's interest in the gangster's human qualities, which is developed through the woman's romantic interest' (pp. 47–48).

Clearly from Brooks's account of the melodramatic, both sets of meanings carry weight. The distance of the genre from tragedy may be responsible for the poverty of the 'official' meaning: 'nor is there, as in tragedy, a reconciliation to a sacred order larger than man. The expulsion of evil entails no sacrifice . . . There is rather confirmation and restoration' (p. 32). Melodrama's fundamental manichaeism discerned by Brooks may also account for the apparent division in the hero which leads some critics to label him a tragic figure. Schatz, for instance, argues that 'the ultimate conflict of the gangster film . . . involves contradictory impulses within the gangster himself' (p. 85). But his account of this conflict hardly suggests the introspection and coming to self awareness

of the tragic hero:

'This internal conflict – between individual accomplishment and the common good, between man's self-serving and communal instincts, between his savagery and his rational morality – is mirrored in society . . .' (p. 85)

More appropriate perhaps is Brooks's contention that if the melodramatic protagonist be conceived as 'theatre for the interplay of manichaeistic forces, the meeting place of opposites, and his self-expressions as nominations of those forces at play within himself – himself their point of clash – the role of character as a purely dramaturgic centre and vehicle becomes evident' (p. 101).

Charles Eckert, in 'The anatomy of a proletarian film: Warners' *Marked Woman*' (1973/74), has offered a different evaluation of the relation of melodrama and realism in the gangster film. The search for a 'moral occult' in his view is less a need to re-find categories of good and evil than to impose a displacement of the origin of social conflict in class. Drawing on Lévi-Strauss's theory that,

'. . . a dilemma (or contradiction) stands at the heart of every living myth . . . The impulse to construct the myth arises from the desire to resolve the dilemma; but the impossibility of resolving it leads to a crystal-like growth of the myth through which the dilemma is repeated, or conceived in new terms, or inverted . . .' (p. 18)

Eckert contends that the melodrama of the gangster film displaces the class conflict which is at the centre of much of its Depression/ Prohibition originated material into a series of oppositions of ethics – the good life versus the wrong; of region – the rural small-town versus the city; and of life-style – the snobbish rich versus the true proletarian. While the 'realist' scenes of *Marked Women* dealing with the problems of the prostitute/witnesses 'attempt to conceptualise the dilemmas that the women face' (p. 17), the

crucial question, why the poor are poor, is displaced into the oppositions floated by the melodrama, which themselves achieve resolution in the figure of the gangster in whom melodrama discovers the villain, an exploiter characterised less by his role as capitalist than by his sadism. In Eckert's terms, then, ethical conflict framed as a 'moral occult' is the mystified means of reconciliation to the status quo. What are occulted are the 'real conditions of existence' – the social relations and forces of production.

References
Lawrence Alloway, *Violent America: the Movies 1946–64*, New York, *Museum of Modern Art*, 1971.
Peter Brooks, *The Melodramatic Imagination*, New Haven and London, Yale University Press, 1976.
Charles Eckert, 'The anatomy of a proletarian film: Warners' *Marked Woman*', *Film Quarterly* vol. 27 no. 2, Winter 1973/74.
Philip French, 'Incitement against violence', *Sight and Sound* vol. 37 no. 1, Winter 1967/68.
Robert B. Heilman, *Tragedy and Melodrama*, Seattle, University of Washington Press, 1968.
Steve Jenkins, *The Death of a Gangster*, London, BFI Education, 1982.
Alan Lovell, *Don Siegel: American Cinema*, London, BFI, 1975.
Colin McArthur, *Underworld USA*, London, Secker and Warburg/BFI, 1972.
William Park, 'The police state', *Journal of Popular Film* vol. 6 no. 3, 1978.
Nick Roddick, *A New Deal in Entertainment: Warner Bros in the 1930s*, London, BFI, 1983.
Tom Ryall, *Teachers' Study Guide 2: The Gangster Film*, London BFI Education, 1979.
Jack Shadoian, *Dreams and Dead Ends*, Cambridge, Massachusetts, MIT Press, 1977.
Thomas Schatz, *Hollywood Genres*, New York, Random House, 1981.
Andrew Tudor, *Image and Influence*, London, Allen and Unwin, 1974.
Robert Warshow, 'The gangster as tragic hero', in *The Immediate Experience*, New York, Atheneum Books, 1970.
Richard Whitehall, 'Crime Inc', *Films and Filming*, vol. 10 nos. 4/5/6, January/February/March 1964.

Scarface (USA 1932 *p.c* – Caddo Company; *d* – Howard Hawks; sd b/w 14)

Loosely based on the Capone story, *Scarface*, along with *The Public Enemy* and *Little Caesar*, has contributed to the definition of the 'classic' gangster film, exhibiting a rise and fall structure and many of the iconographic and thematic elements later developed in the genre. The gangster hero in these films is depicted as a paradoxical figure, at once representing the worst in society and the best in his striving towards the goals of the American dream: wealth, individualism, success, power. All the iconographic elements of the genre are visible: cars, guns, hats and coats, back-room gangsters and brash front-men. The emphasis on consumerism, particularly clothes, indicates increasing wealth and status: for example lapel flowers, smoking jackets, handkerchiefs, the array of shirts and the interior sprung mattress shown to Poppy. Poppy herself is part of Camonte's success, for in the gangster film accession to gang leadership is often won by taking the leader's girlfriend.

Also demonstrated here is the extravagant violence of these early films which provoked attacks from censorship bodies. Here it is exemplified in the total destruction of the restaurant (c.f. *The St. Valentine's Day Massacre*, 1967, where this incident is repeated), and by the introduction of the machine gun. Socio-economic explanation of the gangster is suggested in Camonte's gleeful wave at the Cook's sign, 'The World is Yours'.

If the film is more violent than its two 'classic' contemporaries, however, it is also more comic – and indeed, Robin Wood (1981) identifies *Scarface* as one of Hawks's comedies. Here the antics of Angelo juggling between the telephone and a stream of hot water are used to counterpoint the destruction of the restaurant. In this context the figure of

Scarface is offered as an innocent primitive and much of the comedy in the film comes from this – for example Camonte's reply to Poppy's suggestion that his flat is 'kind of gaudy': 'Isn't it though? Glad you like it.'

G-Men (USA 1935 *p.c* – Warner Bros; *d* – William Keighley; sd b/w 15)

This extract exemplifies a second phase in the development of the gangster genre in which the gangster hero is replaced by a new protagonist, the crime fighter. This development was at least partly determined by the revision of the Production Code in 1934 and its criticism of films glorifying gangsters; in 1930 films like *The Public Enemy* had been able to circumvent such criticisms by providing moral epilogues but by 1935 this was no longer adequate. Nevertheless, much of the genre's iconography is here indistinguishable from earlier gangster films like *Little Caesar*: for example, the hat-wearing card players, office and nightclub locations, the gunman and coffin, Cagney's persona and acting style, unchanged in the shift from gangster to cop, the bank robbery, the East Side milieu. The second section of the extract celebrates police technology (in this respect anticipating the police procedure sub-genre of the late 40s and 50s), for example the concealed camera, fingerprint equipment, typewriters, telex, microscopes, etc., all of which are employed in the painstaking search for Leggett.

The Roaring Twenties (USA 1939 *p.c* – Warner Bros; *d* – Raoul Walsh; sd b/w 9)

This extract demonstrates a number of gangster film motifs: the documentary *March of Time* style; sociological explanation of the gangsters and their lifestyle, characteristic of Warners' 30s gangster films (see *The Public Enemy*); the set-piece montage of

gang warfare; the raid on a rival warehouse and narrow escape; the conflict between the gangster for whom crime is a matter of material survival, represented by Eddie, and the psychotic gangster, George; the heroine, whose classy femininity is the object of the gangster's sexual desire and social aspiration but who is unobtainable, in contrast to the gangster's faithful moll, Panama (see *Scarface, The Public Enemy, Portrait of a Mobster*); the role of the lawyer, who for social reasons or personal weakness gets involved with the mob but ultimately crosses the gangster leader by virtue of his superior knowledge of how the system works; the gangster's lifelong and faithful friend who goes down with him in his fall (see *Portrait of a Mobster*).

On the other hand the film also signals the shift from the 'classic' gangster film and G-Men cycle towards film noir, in what Shadoian calls its 'ambiguously elegiac perspective' on the gangster motifs. In this respect the authorship of Walsh is significant in that his other crime melodramas for Warners, *They Drive by Night* and *High Sierra*, also exhibited a noir dimension. Here it is exhibited in the expressionist architecture and lighting of the warehouse raid, and in the unsocially motivated cynicism, and psychotic violence of George (→AUTHORSHIP: *Raoul Walsh*, p. 176; ←HISTORY: *Warner Bros*, p. 11).

Underworld USA (USA 1960 *p.c* – Globe Enterprises; *d* – Samuel Fuller; sd b/w 22)

This extract exemplifies both the syndicate cycle of gangster films which dominated the genre in the 50s and the themes and preoccupations of Samuel Fuller. This intersection of *auteur* with genre was facilitated by Fuller's setting up his own 'independent' production company – Globe Enterprises (→ AUTHORSHIP: *Samuel Fuller*, p. 171).→

Chinatown – film noir reprised in the 1970s

Dirty Harry – Eastwood as isolated psychotic cop

Features typical of the gangster film are the parallels drawn between the organisations of FBI and the underworld; the relationship between gangsterdom and big business which is fully developed in the syndicate movie; brutal realistic violence often performed in startling ways – for instance, Gus gives chewing gum to the Mencken child and then runs her down; the roles of the subsidiary characters, for example Gus, the emotionless gunman, and Cuddles, the moll, who sees through the values of both underworld and revenge motivation of the hero. Finally, while in plot terms the film belongs to the syndicate cycle, there are elements which also suggest the influence of film noir, and its transformation in the emergence of the police movie in the 60s. The emphasis on night-time shooting, with seedy, urban, shadow-infested locations, is reminiscent of film noir, while the isolation of the hero who belongs neither to police nor underworld but has an investigative primitive role, a revenge motif and an ambiguous if not callous attitude to women, looks back to the noir private eye and forward to the lone crusading cop, exemplified in the Dirty Harry series. The role of the family has also been transformed through the impact of film noir, from the incestuous clannishness of the classic gangster film to its unobtainability and delineation as object of victimisation or source of the hero's betrayal – a theme which continues into the 60s police movies.

Consideration of the intersection of genre and *auteur* raises the question how far Tolly's inability to acquire a family is indicative of Fuller's growing pessimism about American society or how far it is due to the influence of the noir thriller. A similar issue is raised about the characterisation of Tolly, who is both sympathetic yet by virtue of his

psychotic behaviour – e.g. his use of Cuddles's love-making to get information from her – distanced from us: is this noir-influenced characterisation, an element in Fuller's world-view, or a response by both genre and *auteur* to the 50s 'crisis of American individualism'?

Dirty Harry (USA 1971 *p.c* – Warner Bros/Malpaso; *d* – Don Siegel; sd col 15)

Dirty Harry is a big-budget 70s police thriller using as its central protagonist the psychotic policeman in place of the psychotic gangster of earlier decades. It is both representative of the police movie sub-genre and of the work of its director, Don Siegel, who had also directed earlier psychotic gangster pictures – e.g. *Baby Face Nelson* (1957), *The Lineup* (1958). It also marks the collaboration between Eastwood and Siegel and the inception of the Dirty Harry character, whom Eastwood continues periodically to revive. The film, then, marks an interesting interplay between genre, author and star (→ AUTHORSHIP: *Don Siegel*, p. 141).

William Park (1978) has described the police movie as a union of psychological melodrama and observation of social conditions. The cop hero is both isolated and a representative American Everyman, positioned between black and hispanic minorities on the one hand and Wasps on the other. Having worked his way up through the force he despises middle-class liberalism and its conscience-ridden advocacy of civil liberties; on the other hand he works with a black or hispanic partner – here, Chico. He lives alone, has no private life and is up against a source of corruption which is unseen but penetrates even the precinct. The cop hero fights corruption on all sides motivated by an idealistic moral anger which justifies his breaking

all laws, except the policeman's taboo against taking a bribe.

Siegel himself contributed to the development of this character in *Coogan's Bluff* (1968) and *Madigan* (1968), the former marking the effective transposition of Eastwood's 'Man With No Name' from its enormous popularity in Spaghetti Westerns to a contemporary American urban setting, in which the cynical policeman confronts an obstructive, short-sighted police bureaucracy. Here Harry is up against the liberalism of the Mayor whose vote-seeking allegiance to civil rights means he cannot identify, let alone act against evil when it confronts him. Alan Lovell (1975) has noted the 'gothic' dimension to the construction of the villain, Scorpio, who is isolated, sadistic and sexually perverted. This element seems quite removed from the journalistic strand of the movie which deploys the hunt/chase structure to incorporate elements of social observation – e.g. signs of social tension in the use of blacks and symbols of protest movements (Scorpio's peace badge buckle).

The union of melodramatic structure and signifiers of political minority opposition has produced conflicting ideological assessments of the police movie-sub-genre, the Dirty Harry character and this film. For instance Harry's confrontation with the black bank-robber parallels Scorpio's sadistic games later in the film such as the burying of Anne Mary Deacon. Hero and villain are both isolated loners and Harry displays both sadism and voyeuristic tendencies. The issue is how far this parallel suggests a critique of Harry's attitudes and how far it exemplifies a cynicism on the part of the film in which there is small choice between fascism and madness.

Film noir

Introduction

'Whoever went to the movies with any regularity during 1946 was caught in the midst of Hollywood's profound postwar affection for morbid drama. From January through December deep shadows, clutching hands, exploding revolvers, sadistic villains and heroines tormented with deeply rooted diseases of the mind flashed across the screen in a panting display of psychoneuroses, unsublimated sex and murder most foul.'

This article from a 1947 *Life* magazine quoted in *Hollywood Genres* (Schatz, 1981, p. 111) is revealing not only for the way in which, at a time when the genre was still young, it manages to touch on many of what were later to be seen as the essential elements of film noir, but also for the high moral tone it adopts towards 'panting', 'morbid drama'. At a time when few popular American films were taken seriously, concern about the explicitness of the sexuality and, curiously in the light of later work, the 'realism' of the violence of noir, amounted to moral panic. Critics' dislike was compounded by economic snobbery: the low budgets and 'B' film status of many film noirs was seen as *a priori* proof that the films were 'trash'. Within this framework the noir films by emigrés whose earlier work was considered 'art' were seen as particularly lamentable. As documented in Stephen Jenkins's book (1981), it became an English and American critical truism to decry Fritz Lang's decline into the production of what Gavin Lambert, for instance, saw as mere 'workmanlike commerce' (p. 2).

The major period of noir production is usually taken to run from *The Maltese Falcon* in 1941 to *Touch of Evil* in 1958. Even after this time, however, British and American critics failed to take film noir seriously. As Paul Schrader comments, 'For a long time film noir, with its emphasis on corruption and despair, was considered an aberration of the American character. The western, with its moral primitivism, and the gangster film, with its Horatio Alger values, were considered more American than the film noir.' Schrader goes on to suggest that the fundamental reason for the neglect of noir was the importance of visual style to the form: 'American critics have been traditionally more interested in theme than style .. it was easier for the sociological critics to discuss the themes of the western and the gangster film apart from stylistic analysis than it was to do for the film noir' (Schrader 'Notes on film noir', 1972, p. 13).

In France the situation was very different. Initially, interest focused on the links between noir films and the writing of the 'hard-boiled' novelists such as Chandler, Hammett, Woolrich, Cain and McCoy, who all either wrote screenplays or source novels for noir films. The phrase film noir itself derives from the *série noire* books – mainly translations of the above-named American writers. Interestingly, it seems that this examination of writers as one of the sources for film noir became, in Britain and America, a method of ascribing respectability – see, for example, Jenkins's comments on the overvaluation of the role of the literary Hammett in histories of film noir compared with the contribution of, for example, Woolrich (Jenkins, 'Dashiell Hammett and film noir', 1982, p. 276).

Equally relevant to the French context was the rise of authorship theories known historically as the *politique des auteurs*. The re-evaluation of noir films by particular directors, especially Lang, Huston, Ray, Fuller and Aldrich, involved a new depth of investigation and, especially, a close examination of *mise en scène*. The basic aim of such studies was, however, the tracing of continuities across careers rather than the lateral investigation of work produced in particular periods and production contexts. The most interesting questions about noir do not concern the marks of directorial difference. Rather, the crucial issue, as phrased by Silver and Ward, is that of 'cohesiveness': the wide influence of noir *across* the work of different directors and genres. Silver and Ward take a random sample of seven film noirs and note that 'different directors and cinematographers, of great and small technical reputations, working at seven different studios, completed seven ostensibly unrelated motion pictures with one cohesive visual style' (Silver and Ward, 1981, p. 3).

Although it is generally accepted that crime and criminal acts provide the basis for the majority of noir films and the noir style (see Durgnat, 'The family tree of film noir', 1974) the influence of noir spreads beyond the gangster/thriller genres influencing melodramas, horror films, detectives, even (although this would not be universally agreed) westerns and musicals. Indeed, Schrader has suggested that noir can be seen as touching 'most every dramatic Hollywood film from 1941 to 53' (Schrader, 1972, p. 9).

Categories and definitions

Given the potential expansiveness of the term, noir demanded both a theoretical system which could pin down what it was that made noir noir, and criticism which examined its generic marks and investigated the structural, thematic and visual systems integral to the whole series of films. Before work on defining the crucial elements of noir and an examination of their workings could begin, however, preliminary attempts were made to categorise those films which seemed central to noir.

The first book-length study of noir (Borde and Chaumeton, 1955) began this work by mapping out various recurrent themes within noir (violence, crime, psychological emphasis) and relating these to particular films. This in turn provided the basis for Durgnat's eccentric and amorphous 'Family tree of film noir' (1974) which listed nearly 300 films under headings such as 'Psychopaths', 'Gangsters', and 'Middle-Class Murder'. The latter category was sub-divided into lists including 'Corruption of the Not-So Innocent Male' (e.g. *Double Indemnity*, *The Postman Always Rings Twice*); 'Woman As Heroic Victim' (e.g. *Rebecca, Gaslight*) and 'Mirror Images' (e.g. *Rebecca, The Woman in the Window*). Durgnat's article, written in 1970, was influential in mapping the territory but it pointed up the need for more rigorous and specific definition – for many, his inclusion of films like *2001* was mere provocation.

Paul Schrader touches on what he sees as some of the recurring visual marks of noir – the majority of the scenes lit for night, rain-drenched streets, doom-laden narration, compositional tension rather than action and a fondness for oblique lines and fractured light. Generally appreciative of Durgnat's categorisation, Schrader suggests that the family tree is structured around a halting of the upwardly mobile thrust of the 30s. 'Frontierism has turned to paranoia and claustrophobia. The small-time gangster had made it big and sits in the mayor's chair. The private eye has quit the police force in disgust, and the young heroine, sick of going along for the ride is now taking others for a ride.' Writing more historically than Durgnat, Schrader identifies an intensification of this downward movement as the noir period continues and categorises noir temporally by sub-dividing it into three main periods. These are: *Wartime 1941–46* (characterised by 'the private eye and the lone wolf ... studio sets and more talk than action', e.g. *The Maltese Falcon, Gilda, Mildred Pierce*), *Post-War Realistic 1945–49* ('crime in the streets, political corruption and police routine' and 'less romantic heroes', e.g. *The Killers, Brute Force*) and finally *Psychotic Action and Suicidal Impulse 1949–53* ('the psychotic killer as active protagonist, despair and disintegration', e.g. *Gun Crazy, D.O.A., Sunset Boulevard*) (Schrader, 1972, pp. 11–12).

Both Durgnat and Schrader state that they do not see film noir as a genre. Instead, Schrader suggests that it should be seen as a period or movement similar to German Expressionism or Italian Neo-Realism. Critics of this use of the term claimed that unlike the quoted movements noir did not involve an overt, or even implicit, commitment to a political/aesthetic programme and that to imply that it did misrepresented the divergent attitudes of noir film-makers and noir's precise industrial production context.

Janey Place (with Peterson, 'Some visual motifs of film noir', 1974; 'Women in film noir', 1978) also uses the term 'movement' and justifies her use of it in some depth.

Corruption of the not-so-innocent male in *Double Indemnity*

The fantasy woman comes to life in *Woman in the Window*

She claims that 'unlike genres, defined by objects and subjects, but like other film movements, film noir is characterised by a remarkable homogeneous visual style with which it cuts across genres' (Place, 1978, p. 39). In the earlier article Place and Peterson attempt to identify the elements of this 'consistent thread'. They outline the difference between the dominant 'high-key lighting style' which eliminates 'unnatural' shadows on faces and gave 'what was considered to be an impression of reality' and noir's chiaroscuro 'low-key lighting' which eschews softening filters and gauzes and 'opposes light and darkness, hiding faces, rooms, urban landscapes – and by extension, motivations and true character – in shadow and darkness'. The night scenes integral to film noir would, in the 'blanc' style, have been shot 'day for night'

with special filters. A central element of the noir look, however, was the high contrast image and jet black (rather than blanc grey-black) skies given by 'night for night' shooting. Place and Peterson go on to describe noir's *mise en scène* 'designed to unsettle, jar, and disorient the viewer in correlation with the disorientation felt by the noir heroes'. Typically, they argue, noir is distinguished by the use of 'claustrophobic framing devices' which separate characters from each other, unbalanced compositions with shutters or banisters casting oblique shadows or placing grids over faces and furniture, 'obtrusive and disturbing' close-ups juxtaposed with extreme high-angle shots which make the protagonist look like 'a rat in a trap.' Overall, the visual style of noir as described by Place and Peterson

amounts to a disorientating anti-realism which exists in opposition to the harmonious 'blanc' world of the realist film.

Place's insistence on the distinguishing character of the visual style of the noir is challenged in an article by James Damico ('Film noir: a modest proposal', 1978). Arguing against the view of noir as movement and for it as a genre, Damico claims that the visual style of noir is actually an iconography. He suggests that the common denominator of noir films is their narrative structure and proposes a model by which film noirs may be isolated, objectified and their examination facilitated.

'Either because he is fated to do so by chance, or because he has been hired for a job especially associated with her, a man whose experience of life has left him sanguine and often bitter meets a not-so-innocent woman of similar outlook to whom he is sexually and fatally attracted. Through this attraction, either because the woman induces him to it or because it is a natural result of their relationship, the man comes to cheat, attempt to murder, or actually murder a second man to whom the woman is unhappily or unwillingly attached (generally he is her husband or lover), an act which often leads to the woman's betrayal of the protagonist, but which in any event brings about the sometimes metaphoric, but usually literal destruction of the woman, the man to whom she is attached, and frequently the protagonist himself' (Damico, 1978, p. 54).

While Place's and Damico's respective use of the terms 'movement' and 'genre' is closely argued in relation to their individual stress on either visual style or narrative structure, other writers have used them differently, or have opted instead for 'series', 'cycle' or 'sub-genre'. Subsequent authors have not automatically accepted Damico's contention that his schema provides an alternative reading of noir which is in opposition to accounts stressing visual style. For example, Paul Kerr's article on the industrial context of the 'B' film noir unproblematically includes both Place and Damico in a general introduction to the genre's characteristics (Kerr, 'Out of what past?', 1979/80, p. 49). Sylvia Harvey, meanwhile, offers a useful synthesis within a framework which accepts visual style as the most fundamental aspect of noir. The defining contour of genre, Harvey suggests, is dissonance: 'the sense of disorientation and unease' produced by 'that which is abnormal and dissonant' (Harvey, 'Woman's place: the absent family of film noir', 1978, p. 32).

The historical specificity of film noir
Underlying all these different attempts at categorisation of noir lies the issue of its historical specificity. How did it become so dominant in Hollywood for more than twenty years, touching (one might almost say consuming) almost every genre whilst retaining a specific visual and narrative

structure? What caused it to decline? And if, as this line of questioning suggests, there was a relationship between historical period and the stylistic and thematic elements of noir, how should this relationship be characterised?

Before dealing with how various theorists have answered these questions it is important to signal the debate about the delineation of the genre's historical period. Following Schrader, most critics have understood the major period of noir to fall between *The Maltese Falcon* in 1941 and *Touch of Evil* in 1958 (Schrader, 1972, p. 8), although the search for immediate precursors has been a popular academic occupation (e.g. Flinn, who claims in 'Three faces of film noir', 1972, that the 65-minute 'B' movie *Stranger on the Third Floor* is the earliest film noir). This strictly time-bound view is, however, implicitly challenged by some listings. Durgnat's family tree lists several titles made outside of the 1942–58 period, including several more usually seen as precursors, such as Warner Bros gangster films. A more complex challenge to Schrader's time limits comes from Silver and Ward (1981), whose book includes synopses of later films which were clearly influenced by noir, often to the point of intentional *hommage*. The genesis of films like *Klute*, *Hustle*, *Body Heat* and Schrader's own *American Gigolo* was provocatively prefigured by his comment that 'as the current political mood hardens, filmgoers and film-makers will find the film noir of the late 40s increasingly attractive' (Schrader, 1972, p. 8). These later films may be better described as 'film *après* noir', as suggested by Larry Gross (Gross 'Film *après* noir', 1976), but this merely recasts, rather than eliminates, questions about the relationship between noir and its specific historical configuration.

Industry and aesthetics

Borde and Chaumeton comment briefly on the influence of German Expressionism, which they see as transmitted chiefly through the agency of emigré directors Lang and Siodmak, but then go on to say that noir is better understood as a 'synthesis' of 'the brutal and colourful gangster films' made by Warner Bros, the horror films associated with Universal and the 'detective fiction shared by Fox and MGM'. They also identify in the genre the 'inexhaustible sadism' of animation, the 'absurdity and casual cynicism' of American comedy and the influence of certain realist and/or social commentary films, notably LeRoy's *I Am a Fugitive From a Chain Gang* (Borde and Chaumeton, 'Sources of film noir', 1978, p. 63). Rather than helping to explain why a synthesis in the form of noir should have taken place during the 40s and 50s, the diversity of their sources tends to obscure the issue. They do make it clear, however, that noir grew from within the American as well as

Spider woman Norma Desmond traps her prey in *Sunset Boulevard*

European industries.

Schrader's account stresses the historical time limits of genre, but does little to explain the industrial context for the 'halting of 30s optimism' except to speculate that the end of the war and Depression freed the industry from the task of 'keeping people's spirits up' (Schrader, 1972, p. 9). His combination of a listing of sources (to which others have added *Citizen Kane*) linked to a vague statement of post-war gloom can be seen as the most dominant paradigm for understanding the industrial/aesthetic context for noir.

Paul Kerr challenges the generality of such accounts, suggesting a re-examination of the conjuncture between 'a primarily economically determined mode of production known as "B" film-making' and what were primarily ideologically defined modes of 'difference' known as the film noir (Kerr, 1979/80, p. 65). More specifically, Kerr argues that some of the stylistic features of noir such as night for night shooting, disorientating lighting and camera angles and the generation of tension through editing and short bursts of extreme violence, were direct results of economic factors such as the desire to thwart union restrictions and use stock footage. Furthermore, production took place in the context of the need to demonstrate a clear difference from the realism of 'A' films, with which the 'B' noirs were paired in double bills. Kerr's account goes on to examine the decline of noir, which he relates to various technical developments, such as Technicolor, which were the products of an ideological pressure for increased verisimilitude, and changes in the economic structure of the industry, particularly the anti-monopoly Bill of Divorcement which contributed to the end of the double bill (Kerr, 1979/80, pp. 56–65).

Genre and social context

Kerr's article is explicitly written as a counter-attack on the series of books and articles which have dealt with the wider social/economic/political configurations of the noir period. Again, Borde and Chaumeton (1978) offer a fairly typical account. They suggest the influence of 'vulgarised' psychoanalysis in America and the publicity given to crime. While both of these form recurring elements in noir narratives, Borde and Chaumeton's comments lack historical specificity. A more detailed and influential account of noir's social context can be found in Colin McArthur's *Underworld USA* (1972). McArthur notes that 'it is useless to try to align the wholly fictitious events of the thriller with actual events', but then goes on to speculate on the reasons for the emergence of the thriller as film noir. These 'speculations' include the aftermath of the Depression, the war and the Cold War and the 'general mood of fear and insecurity' produced by an uncertain future. 'It seems reasonable to suggest', he continues, 'that this uncertainty is paralleled in the general mood of malaise, the loneliness and angst and the lack of clarity about the characters' motives in the thriller'. McArthur also cites the misogyny associated with 'the heightened desirability and concomitant suspicion of women back home experienced by men at war' and the horrors of Auschwitz and Hiroshima, which he sees echoed in a shift from 30s gangsters overtly concerned with the social origins of crime to noir thrillers such as *Dark Corner*, 'a cry of loneliness and despair in a sick world' (McArthur, 1972, pp. 66–67).

These speculations are suggestive, but McArthur offers few clear suggestions as to how they are actually articulated in the texts. Furthermore, there is a paradox in

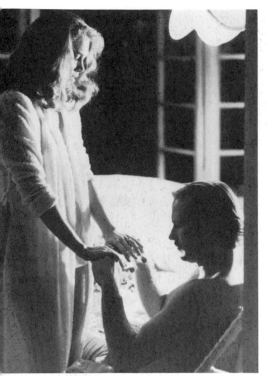

Body Heat – film *après* noir

his positing a relationship between the social/psychological formations of a particular period and angst, a term which is a-historical. Given the point in the development of critical theory at which the study was undertaken, it is perhaps inevitable that McArthur falls back on auteurist notions to explain the connection between these events and the texts. It was, he suggests, the 'sour and pessimistic sensibilities' of directors such as Lang, Siodmak, and Wilder, 'forged in the uncertainty of Weimar Germany and decaying Austria–Hungary', which provide the vital link between film noir and America in the 40s and 50s.

The connection between 'post-war gloom' and the 'meaninglessness', 'depression' and 'angst' of noir became almost *de rigeur* in critical analyses. Perhaps the most extreme examples linking an apparently angst-laden period and noir via the agency of *auteurs* comes in the articles about noir and Existentialism. Robert G. Porfirio ('No way out', 1976), for example, attempts to connect French existentialist philosophy to noir through 'hard-boiled' writers, especially, and dubiously (see Jenkins, 1982) Hammett and Hemingway. Writing about the Flitcraft parable, for instance, included in the novel *The Maltese Falcon* was taken from but omitted from the film, Porfirio claims it reveals that 'Spade is by nature an existentialist, with a strong conception of the randomness of existence.' Porfirio's analysis implicitly depends upon making an unproblematic leap between the historical configurations within which Existentialism developed in France and the 'world' that exists within the noir texts.

Women in film noir

A very different approach to the historical context of noir can be seen in the feminist writing collected in *Women in Film Noir* (1978). Making a decisive attempt to shift discussion away from angst, these writers concentrate on the structuring role of patriarchal ideology within the texts. Their interest in noir comes from an understanding of the period of its growth as one of social and economic transition following the disruption of the war years, producing problems for male power and control, and a concern to analyse the genre's treatment of women. Kaplan, for instance, notes that:

'The film noir world is one in which women are central to the intrigue of the films, and are furthermore usually not placed safely in ... familiar roles ... Defined by their sexuality, which is presented as desirable but dangerous, the women function as an obstacle to the male quest. The hero's success or not depends on the degree to which he can extricate himself from the women's manipulations. Although the man is sometimes simply destroyed because he cannot resist women's lures, often the world of the film is the attempted restoration of order through the exposure and then destruction of the sexual, manipulating woman' (Kaplan, 'Introduction', 1978, pp. 2–3).

In contrast to the seamless, unproblematic assimilation of Existentialism by the noir text assumed by Porfirio's article, these feminist analyses emphasise the text as a site of contradiction. Thus, rather than searching for symbolic truths residing statically within the text, many of the writers (e.g. Gledhill, Johnston and Cook) are concerned to discern structural relationships which they then rework through conceptual frameworks provided by Marxist and psychoanalytically influenced feminism. Gledhill, for instance, says that to understand the significance of film noir for women

'It would be necessary to analyse the conjecture of specific aesthetic, cultural and economic forces; on the one hand the on-going production of the private eye/thriller ... on the other, the post-war drive to get women out of the workforce and return them to the domestic sphere; and finally the perennial myth of woman as threat to male control of the world and destroyer of male aspiration – forces, which in cinematic terms, interlock to form what we now think of as the aberrant style and world of film noir' (Gledhill, '*Klute 1*', 1978, p. 19).

Gledhill's analysis of film noir is based on examination of a series of structural elements which open up contradictions around the ambiguously placed noir women. Her 'five features' of noir are: the investigative structure of the narrative which 'probes the secrets of female sexuality within patterns of submission and dominance (p. 15); flashbacks and voice-overs which can sometimes open up a tex-

Klute – a shift in the nature of the noir detective hero

tual gap between a male narrator and the woman he is investigating, as in *Gilda*; a proliferation of points-of-view, with, typically, a struggle between men and women; unstable characterisation of the heroine, who is likely to be a treacherous femme fatale; and the sexualised filming of this heroine, who is also enmeshed in the contradictory visual style of noir.

This last point is expanded by Place ('Women in film noir', 1978). Working from the basis provided by her earlier work with L. S. Peterson (1974), Place examines the visual motifs through which two archetypcal women – the spider woman and the nurturing woman – are articulated. Writing about the spider woman, Place comments that 'the sexual woman's dangerous power is expressed visually' and details her inconography: long hair, cigarette smoke as a cue for immorality, a habitat of darkness and, perhaps most importantly, a domination of composition, camera movement and lighting which seems to pull 'the camera (and the hero's gaze with our own) irresistibly with them as they move' (Place, 1978, p. 45). Despite her apparent power, the femme fatale 'ultimately loses physical strength' and is actually or symbolically imprisoned (p. 45). For Place, however, this visual and narrative containment is not what is retained from noir. Instead, it is the power of the femme fatale that we remember, 'their strong, dangerous and above all exciting sexuality' (p. 37).

Place's analysis signals the importance in these analyses of the different emphases placed on the recuperative potential of noir – i.e. on the extent to which the text is able to contain and mask the social contradic-

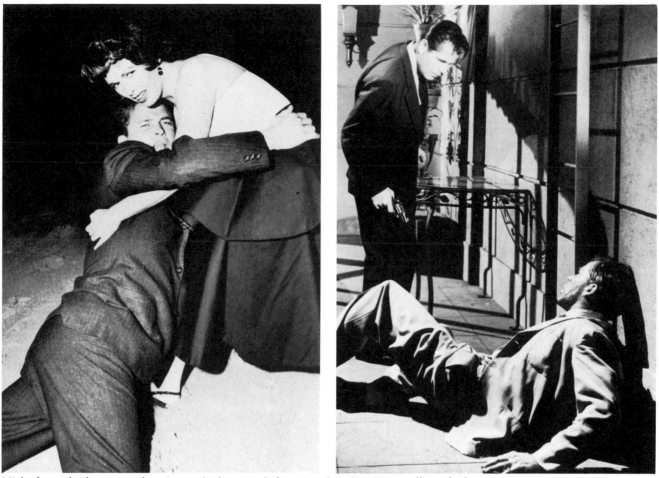

Night for night shooting and menacing shadows mark the noir style in *Kiss Me Deadly* and *The Big Heat*

tions structured into its narrative and visual systems. Here is considerable divergence between theorists. Unlike Place, and Dyer ('Resistance through charisma', 1978), who argues for Gilda/Rita Hayworth's 'resistance through charisma' to textual and ideological containment in *Gilda*, Pam Cook offers a reading of *Mildred Pierce* in which the film's textual organisation works to suppress the noir heroine's discourse 'in favour of that of the male', with Mildred finally designated guilty by the Law and returned to a safe, subordinate domestic situation (Cook, 'Duplicity in *Mildred Pierce*', 1978). Gledhill's examination of *Klute*, an example of what has been described as 'film *après* noir', discerns a similar final positioning for a different, but equally equivocal heroine – redefinition, yet again, as guilty (Gledhill, '*Klute* 2', 1978). These feminist analyses makes a provocative intervention into critical debates about film noir, which have generally been characterised by a masculine perspective on the part of critics and a concentration on the existential dilemmas of the noir hero.

References

Raymond Borde and Etienne Chaumeton, *Panorame du Film Noir Americain*, Paris, Les Editions de Minuit, 1955, reprinted in part as 'Sources of film noir', *Film Reader* 3, 1978.

Pam Cook, 'Duplicity in *Mildred Pierce*', in Kaplan (ed.), *Women in Film Noir*, London, BFI, 1978.

James Damico, 'Film noir: a modest proposal', *Film Reader* 3, 1978.

Raymond Durgnat, 'The family tree of film noir', *Cinema* (UK), August 1970, reprinted in *Film Comment* vol. 10 no. 6, November/December 1974.

Richard Dyer, 'Resistance through charisma: Rita Hayworth and *Gilda*', in Kaplan (ed.), *Women in Film Noir*, cit.

Tom Flinn, 'Three faces of film noir', *The Velvet Light Trap* no. 5, Summer 1972.

Christine Gledhill, '*Klute* 1: a contemporary film noir and feminist criticism', and '*Klute* 2: feminism and *Klute*', in Kaplan (ed.), *Women in Film Noir*, cit.

Larry Gross, 'Film *après* noir', *Film Comment* vol. 12 no. 4, July/August 1976.

Sylvia Harvey, 'Woman's place: the absent family of film noir', in Kaplan (ed.), *Women in Film Noir*, cit.

Stephen Jenkins, *Fritz Lang: the image and the look*, London, BFI, 1981.

Stephen Jenkins, 'Dashiell Hammett and film noir', *Monthly Film Bulletin* vol. 49 no. 586, November 1982.

Claire Johnston, '*Double Indemnity*', in Kaplan (ed.), *Women in Film Noir*, cit.

E. Ann Kaplan, 'Introduction', in Kaplan (ed.), *Women in Film Noir*, cit.

Paul Kerr, 'Out of what past? Notes on the 'B' film noir', *Screen Education* no. 32/33, Autumn/Wnter 1979/80.

Colin McArthur, *Underworld USA*, London, BFI/Secker and Warburg, 1972.

J. A. Place and L. S. Peterson, 'Some visual motifs of film noir', *Film Comment* vol. 10 no. 1, January/February 1974.

J. A. Place, 'Women in film noir', in Kaplan (ed.), *Women in Film Noir*, cit.

Robert Porfirio, 'No way out', *Sight and Sound* vol. 45 no. 4, Autumn 1976.

Thomas Schatz, *Hollywood Genres*, New York, Random House, 1981.

Paul Schrader, 'Notes on film noir', *Film Comment* vol. 8 no. 1, Spring 1972.

Alan Silver and Elizabeth Ward (eds.), *Film Noir*, London, Secker and Warburg, 1981.

Double Indemnity (USA 1944 *p.c* – Paramount; *d* – Billy Wilder; sd b/w 23)

Barbara Stanwyck's performance as Phyllis Dietrichson in *Double Indemnity* represents one of the most powerful and disturbing noir portraits of a femme fatale – the destructive, duplicitous woman who transgresses rules of female behaviour by luring men with the promise of possessing her sexually and then using them for her own, murderous, ends. Immensely successful despite early studio qualms about the 'appropriateness' of a thriller with such a dark heroine, the film had a substantial effect on later noirs.

The extract begins after the renowned double entendre-filled first meeting →

between bored housewife Phyllis and insurance salesman Walter Neff. Neff's voice-over delivers a classically hard-boiled, retrospective description of events which is, as we see at the end of the extract, dictated into an office machine for the benefit of Keys, Neff's father figure and in Johnston's analysis 'signifier of the patriarchal order' ('*Double Indemnity*' 1978). Discussing narration in her essay on *Klute* (1978), Christine Gledhill comments that for the audience 'the temporal separation of the moment of telling and the event told lead to something of a dislocation between what they observe and the storyteller's account of it. This aspect is intensified in that the storyteller is often proved wrong by subsequent events and may even be lying' (p. 16). In the extract, Neff's voice-over suggests that he despises Phyllis and wants to be rid of her while the audience knows that this is not the case. Later that evening, Phyllis arrives at his apartment. As Claire Johnston points out, yet again a gap is created, this time between image and voice-over. 'The voice-over suggests an appointment which the image denies: "it would be eight and she would be there"' (Johnston, 1978, p. 105).

During this meeting at his appartment, Phyllis is identified visually and through the voice-over with the darkness in the apartment and with the rain. During the whole scene he is softly lit, while at certain moments the chiaroscuro low-key lighting makes her appear jewel-hard. Most crucially, the interaction between Phyllis and Neff is both sexual and violent. The real moment of sexual catharsis in the extract is not the first kiss, but the embrace which follows Neff's commitment to help her kill her husband. The importance of the intention to do violence to Mr. Dietrichson is outweighed by the sadistic eroticism between the two of them: he grips her shoulders so hard that she tells him he is hurting her, while he tells her that 'I don't want you to hang, baby.'

The second part of the extract is from the end of the film. The death of the transgressive woman – in a narrative which closely adheres to Damico's (1978) ideal noir structure-does not end the film. With Phyllis's death, the gap between retrospective narration and image can be resolved into a present. The trajectory of *Double Indemnity* follows the shattering of the primal friendship between Keys and Neff and the imperilling of the smooth workings of the insurance system (and the patriarchal order it represents) by Neff's involvement with the world of women. In particular, Phyllis concretised Neff's unacknowledged desire to 'buck the

system' by testing the fallibility of Keys and, in Johnston's analysis, the Law he represents. The elimination of her and her challenge to the patriarchal order means that the film can finish with a brief re-establishment of the homo-erotic relationship between Keys and Neff, signified by their affectionate ritual with Neff's last cigarette.

The Big Heat (USA 1953 *p.c* – Columbia; *d* – Fritz Lang; sd b/w 13)

As the extract begins Debbie, girlfriend of the sadistic gangster Vince, is mixing cocktails in Vince's opulent apartment. Already the transgressive nonconformism that will lead to her downfall is clear: she laughs at the way Vince and his friends respond to Lagana, their boss and parodies Vince's commands to her. This separates her from the gangsters and links her with the honest cop Bannion, estranged from the self-satisfied fellow officers earlier in the film.

Although the shots of Bannion stopping outside the car-wrecking lot where he goes to get information hint at the iconography of the police procedural film, a genre that co-existed alongside the film noir, the *mise en scène* inside the yard and its tiny office is peculiarly noir. A series of barely illuminated forms cast bewildering shadows. The human occupants are the grotesquely fat and callous owner, who sucks on a coke bottle in an infantile manner, and his scared, crippled secretary. After Bannion leaves she calls to him through the wire which surrounds the yard: wire which stretches upwards above their heads and out of the frame. As they talk and she gives him the information he needs, a series of increasingly tightly framed shot/reverse-shots superimpose the wire alternately on her and Bannion's faces, ending with his bleak gaze through the wire, as though Bannion, once a gentle, home-loving detective, now has the marks of the noir underworld branded upon his face. The extent of Bannion's descent from the bland overlit suburbia he occupied at the beginning of the films is underlined by a brief tender scene with his child. Outside the door, however, the dark passage with its angular shadows reminds us of the more ambiguous status that Bannion, now a vigilante rather than a policeman, occupies.

It is important to point out, however, that *The Big Heat* is not only concerned with the changing status of Bannion. Although Colin McArthur's (1972) influential examination of the film suggests that Bannion's tragic fall 'carries the weight of thematic interest' in the film (p. 78), it could be argued that interest rests with both Bannion *and* Debbie. Jenkins, for example, has

suggested that the centre of Fritz Lang's work is sexual difference rather than fate or destiny, thus shifting emphasis away from the trajectory of the noir hero towards more complex readings of Lang's film noirs (Jenkins, 1981).

Kiss Me Deadly (USA 1955 *p.c* – Parklane Pictures; *d* – Robert Aldrich; sd b/w 18)

Kiss Me Deadly was made comparatively late in the noir cycle and represents its most extreme and psychotic vision. Unlike some earlier films, the noir world of *Kiss Me Deadly* is not a sub-stratum of society into which the protagonist gradually and inexorably slips. Mike Hammer, a seedy private detective who specialises in providing evidence in divorce cases, is already part of that world when the film begins, and the anti-realist noir style is therefore present from the very first frames in the night-for-night shooting of the road, with its white lines emphasised almost to the point of abstraction, while the half-naked body of the hysterical, running woman is disturbingly segmented by the framing. This is accompanied on the soundtrack by the noise of her frenzied breathing and followed by the credits, which arrive, disconcertingly, in reverse.

Mike Hammer, unlike earlier noir heroes (e.g. Sam Spade), is an entirely unsympathetic character: morose, violent and stupid.

Narrative and *mise en scène* mark him as a man trapped by forces beyond his control – see, for example, the powerful and unsettling framing of the staircase shots at the beginning of the second extract. These elements, especially when linked to the extreme violence of the film, have allowed *Kiss Me Deadly* to be seen as a prime example of 'existential' noir. At the same time, the film is useful for discussion of the sexual dissonances of noir. In the extract, Hammer's encounters with three different women are all marked by female sexual aggressiveness. Lily Carver (Gaby Rogers), who in the second part of the extract makes an explicit play for Hammer, causes world destruction at the end of the film through rampant 'female' acquisitiveness coupled with a desire to look at the forbidden. Velda (Maxine Cooper), meanwhile, is given a position of power from which she criticises both Hammer and the entire trajectory of the film (in her speech about his pursuit of 'the great whatsit' half-way through the narrative). It could be argued that the occurrence of this speech criticising the male quest right at the centre of the film produces a radical disjuncture in a genre predicated upon such a quest.

The horror film

Introduction

Horror films have had comparatively little serious discussion, and only in the second half of the 70s was the genre put on the agenda of film studies. From 1935 to the late 40s accounts of Local Authority bannings of 'H' films and of reports on their harmful social effects, especially on children, proliferated in the British trade press. The 50s witnessed renewed panic around the spectacular international success of a native development of the genre by the Hammer studio (→ AUTHORSHIP: *Hammer Productions*, p. 162; ← HISTORY: *Hammer Productions*, p. 44) and British film journals carried articles on the psychology of the genre. Quite distinct was the French response; during the 50s and 60s French journals located the genre within the category of the 'fantastique' and made links with surrealism, as well as investigating the new British contribution largely ignored at home. Then in the late 60s two books appeared by Carlos Clarens and Ivan Butler arguing for the horror film as art, pointing to the long literary tradition of 'the art of terror', and chronicling a history of the genre in the cinema. These groundbreaking contributions were followed in the early 70s by a spate of books on both sides of the Atlantic devoted to the monsters and stars of the horror film, offering historical and psychological studies. Anglo-Saxon journals in the mean time devoted space to 'special effects' and returned again to the question of social/psychological significance of the 70s boom in horror with violence, frequently against women. In the late 70s/early 80s feminists mounted public protest at the perpetuation of a wide-spread cultural misogyny by such films.

The titles of the 70s horror film books reveal the emergence of a cultist knowledge stored up over the decades by the closet horror film addict. Robin Wood in a recent attempt to theorise the genre has commented on this characteristic:

'The horror film has consistently been one of the most popular and, at the same, time, the most disreputable of Hollywood genres. The popularity itself has a peculiar characteristic that sets the horror film apart from other genres: it is restricted to aficionados and complemented by total rejection, people tending to go to horror films either obsessively or not at all. They are dismissed with contempt by the majority of reviewer-critics, or simply ignored' (Wood, 'Introduction', 1979, p. 13).

This attribute of the horror film's popularity is further illustrated by the number of specialist journals devoted to its different aspects – *Midi-Minuit Fantastique, Twilight, Cinefantastique* (US), *The Horror Elite, L'Ecran Fantastique, Vampyr, Little Shoppe of Horrors*, etc. All this attests to the special relationship of the horror film with its 'aficionados' which early on became the centre of critical attention and arguably inhibited theoretical elaboration of the genre. Frequently the form is identified by industry and critics alike as aimed at the 'youth market' or 'adolescents of whatever age' (see Evans, 'Monster movies: a sexual theory', 1973; Kapsis, '*Dressed to Kill*', 1982; Wood, 1979).

However the relegation of the horror film was not solely a result of critical disdain for its supposed audience. Other factors arose from its mixed heritage and development in a wide range of different forms and cultures, which appear to defy coherent categorisation. Historical approaches demonstrate a heterogeneity of inputs and developments rather than the integrated evolution of generic tradition attributed to the western or gangster film – e.g. Universal's gothic horror films of the 30s; German Expressionism; 50s science fiction monster movies; Hammer horror in the UK; Corman's Poe cycle; the onset of the psychological thriller with *Psycho* (1960), all cited in T. J. Ross's introduction to *Focus on the Horror Film* (1972). A tension remains between older European traditions and Hollywood, producing the problem of relating the forms which developed in the European art cinema in terms of the 'fantastique' or supernatural (see Clarens, 1968) and the formation of a popular Hollywood genre. As with melodrama the origins of the horror film looked back to European literary traditions – the Victorian gothic novel for instance – and a central strand of the genre has retained its mythical European location, 'Transylvania'. This heterogeneity is increased by the input of two European movements, German Expressionism (see Eisner, 1969), and surrealism, the former often cited as indispensable to the 'horror style' of Hollywood, the latter arguably more influential on European developments in the work of, for instance, Franju or Dreyer, or 'Europeanised' directors in Hollywood such as Polanski. Some critics attempt to get round this impasse by defining the horror film in terms of its aesthetic effect – its intention to horrify. Andrew Tudor (1974) argues, for instance, that the heritage from German Expressionism was important because 'the style itself is capable of infecting almost any subject matter with its eerie tone . . . the sense of mystery, of lurkers in the shadows is the constant factor' (p. 208). However, the mechanics of the horror movie did not provide the material for the elaboration of the existential/moral dramas central to early attempts to regain classic Hollywood for serious critical consideration. For example, both Andrew Tudor, who writes mainly about gothic horror, and Brian Murphy, who deals with 50s science fiction monster movies, agree that the genre offers a 'never-never land' governed by absolutely inflexible laws:

'. . . men turn into werewolves only but always on nights of the full moon;

Pregnant with suspense and the supernatural – Polanski's *Rosemary's Baby*

vampires always dislike garlic, cast no reflection in mirrors, and can be destroyed only by having their hearts pierced with a wooden stake; and it is the nature of Frankenstein's monster that he can never be destroyed . . . horror's never-never land is bearable because it is so entirely rational' (Murphy, 'Monster movies', 1972, p. 34).

The gothic mode in particular, with its self-referentiality, refused elaboration in more social terms. Thus several commentators have argued (Ross, 1972, Tudor, 1974) that of all the genres the horror film shows least connection with American history, thereby cutting it off from a major source of legitimation. This, added to the rigid simplicity of the horror film's conventions, deprives it of the resonances that inform and deepen, for example, the western or gangster film (Tudor, 1974). As a result, and compounding the problem, the directors and stars of the horror movie have generally been unable to escape the pejorative implications of cultism and failed to win acclaim as *auteurs* of the cinema.

The chief route to cultural legitimation, therefore, has been through popular anthropological or Freudian/Jungian reference, which assumes 'inside us a constant, ever-present yearning for the fantastic, for the darkly mysterious, for the choked terror of the dark' (Clarens, 1968, p. 9). As the capacity of religion and its attendant enemies to fill this need receded with the advance of rationalism and technology in the nineteenth century, the simultaneous discovery of the unconscious and the cinema released a new source of imagery for 'rendering unto film . . . the immanent fears of mankind: damnation, demonic possession, old age, death, in brief the nightside of life' (Clarens, 1968, p. 13, Butler, 1970, pp. 15–16). For Clarens this symbolic approach to the horror movie provides clear, normative boundaries. Thus *Psycho* and its imitators are rejected because, 'in Jungian fashion, I feel more compelled to single out and explore the visionary than the psychological' (p. 13). Similarly he excludes much European work because it uses horror as

. . . 'the normal aspect of nature that turns abnormal' . . . *The Birds*

a means rather than an end in itself. This emphasis leads him to speculate that the horror movie declines in the late 60s when horror ceases to be clothed in mythic forms. Other critics have turned to the notion of aesthetic affect as a source of evaluation. So, for example, distinctions are drawn between the horror produced by suggestion – the terror of the unimaginable – and the guignol effects of things seen. The former is often associated with the European tradition, or the New (and Europeanised) Hollywood of Polanski and others, while the latter is identified as the Hollywood gothic or more recent 'splatter' movies:

'Sublime terror rests in the unseen – the Ultimate Horror. Things seen, fully described, explained, and laid to rest in the last reel or paragraph are mere horrors, the weakest of which are the merest revulsions over bloodshed and dismemberment . . .' (Rockett, 'Perspectives', 1982, p. 132).

Ivan Butler identifies the promise of 'too much' – the production of expectations that cannot possibly be rendered in visual terms – as a major aesthetic problem of the horror film, and dissociates his claims for the genre as art from any tendency towards 'beastliness for its own sake'. These attempts to establish both the boundaries of the genre and a basis for its evaluation have not gone unchallenged. David Pirie's book (1973), largely about the horror films produced in the 50s and 60s by the English production company Hammer, argues that

the aesthetics of gothic horror are based on the act of showing rather than on suggestion. And in a more recent study Charles Derry (1977) has charted not only the emergence of three distinct sub-genres in the decades following *Psycho* (1960), but has traced their historical predecessors in the 'classic' horror movie and other genres. From this preliminary investigation of critical approaches to the horror movie a broad distinction emerges between those seeking predominantly psycho-sociological explanation of the genre – what it represents for its audiences – and those attempting to analyse the aesthetic affects offered to the audience by the play of the genre's conventions.

Psycho-sociological explanation

The problem facing all such accounts is to explain the meaning of the monster, or of the threat that produces the horror. 'Normality' is our everyday commonsense world – in more recent interpretations, the world of the dominant ideology, sanctioned by the established authorities. As suggested above, approaches to this problem via the notion of reflection have been thwarted by the horror film's lack of historical or social context, although where the genre borders on science fiction political readings become possible. The outcropping of mutant monsters in 50s horror/science fiction films are frequently understood as reflecting a 'doom-centred, eschatological fear' provoked by Cold War politics and the nuclear deterrent, which yet relied on the scientist and 'co-operation with the military' for protection (see Murphy, 1972, pp. 38–39). Ernest Larsen ('Hi-tech horror', 1979) argues in similar vein that those horror films which take up aspects of the disaster movie – for instance *Alien* (1979) and *Dawn of the Dead* (1978) – 'advance . . . the notion that modern technology is so overwhelming that it

tends to obliterate any possibility of its liberatory use . . . science has, as the hand-maiden of capitalism, created an uncontrolled monster' (p. 30).

Such readings suggest that traditional sources of horror in the unknown or the supernatural are less potent to the post-World War II Western audience than the horrors that society has already perpetuated and seems in some scenarios likely to exceed – horrors often referred to as the 'American nightmare'. Such a premise provides the basis for at least two of Charles Derry's (1977) sub-generic categories for the modern horror film, though, in his account, the forms they take derive from cinematic history. Thus he distinguishes first, 'the horror of personality', inaugurated by *Psycho*, where the horror, rather than projected in a monster and so distanced and externalised, is now seen to be 'man' himself. Such a source of horror requires not supernatural or pseudo-scientific but psychological explanation, and represents a response to the escalation of violence, mass killings and the Kennedy assassination of the early 60s. The *Dr. Jekyll and Mr. Hyde* series, Hitchcock's 40s psychological thrillers, and film noir have all contributed to the generic realisation of this popular obsession. The second sub-genre Derry labels 'the horror of Armageddon', which in continuity with the 50s science fiction mutant monster cycle, and exemplified by *The Birds* (1963), deals with a 'normal aspect of nature [that] turns abnormal', resulting in 'a struggle that is obviously ultimate, mythical and soul-rending' (p. 50). Such films Derry sees as representing a 'modern, cataclysmic corner of our everyday fears' traceable to anxiety about the spread of totalitarian, automaton-like political regimes and the threat of nuclear warfare. Their narratives are articulated in three major themes, proliferation, besiegement and death, the first

Dawn of the Dead – 'science has . . . created an uncontrolled monster'

and the last of which serve to demarcate this cycle from another closely-related one, the disaster movie. Derry's final category is 'the horror of the demonic', which reverts to the presence of evil forces as a time-honoured explanation of the horror of the world, thereby suggesting the possibility of a moral order in the wings. While Derry's cataloguing of the conventions and strategies of these sub-genres and his sensitivity to cinematic and generic traditions illuminate the development of the horror movie, his appeal to eruptions of violence in society to explain its existence tends to assume a relationship between films and society in which the former directly reflect the latter rather than mediating or representing it.

The notion of the 'nightmare' opens up a different and more common approach to understanding the horror film through popular Freudianism and anthropology. Concepts of the unconscious, of repression, of the cinema as an analogy for dreaming displace the literalism of the 'reflection' thesis. With varying degrees of sophistication they are used to explain the monster as that which must be excluded, or repressed, so that the Western drive towards technological progress and world domination can proceed. According to this view, the threat is neither external to society, nor to the cinema. Rather the horror movie represents a medium in which the underside of the 'normal' world makes its appearance in a play of fantasy and ritual. Notions of the primordial, the tribal, figure centrally in this scenario, and sexuality is a key component. Depending on the politics of the writer this perspective leads to a view of the horror film as adaptive (Evans, 1973), symptomatic (Kennedy, 'Things that go howl in the id', 1982; Snyder, 'Family life and leisure culture in *The Shining*', 1982), or potentially progressive (Williams, 'American cinema in the 70s: family horror', 1980/81; Wood, 1979). Walter Evans, for example, works on the commonly attributed youth of the audience for horror to advance the view that the gothic horror film's appeal is to 'those masses in American film and TV audiences who struggle with the most universal and horrible of personal trials: the sexual traumas of adolescence'. In a later account he argues that monster movies 'respond to a deep cultural need largely ignored in Western society . . . the need for rituals of initiation' (Evans, 'Monster movies and rites of initiation', 1975, pp. 124–125).

Harlan Kennedy, on the other hand, uses the terminology of the 'unconscious' and 'id' to explain the recent resurgence of werewolf movies in terms of atavistic throwbacks manifested in political behaviour. Watergate and the facts and imagery of Vietnam which are now beginning to receive popular circulation, the guilty conflation of the Vietcong abroad and the Indians at home, the 'wolf-like features of Richard Nixon', all point in the American

cinema of the 80s to an obsession with the horror of the split personality.

The impulse displayed here to explain the modern horror film in terms of a specifically American crisis of conscience is characteristic of many recent accounts of the genre. Rather than political traumas, many writers focus on the American 'way of life' as symptomatic of the distortions and repressions consequent on the development of American capitalism. Consumerism is identified as a prime symptom, behind which stands middle-class life, or the family and patriarchal social relations as sources of horror – for example *Night of the Living Dead* (1968), *The Hills Have Eyes* (1977), *Communion* (1976), *Martin* (1976). Stephen Snyder (1982), for example, argues in relation to *The Shining* (1980), *The Texas Chainsaw Massacre* (1974), *Burnt Offerings* (1976) and *Halloween* (1978) that 'the notion of . . . (middle-class) life as tantamount to the world of horror has been mushrooming'. This location of horror in the home is symptomatic of a 'network of anxieties . . . often realised in terms of the troubling insatiateness which underlies the structure of American family life' (p. 4). Rather than a 'Watergate syndrome', Snyder identifies in the American 'collective psyche' a 'leisure culture syndrome' (p. 5), in which 'traditional masculine values of conquest coupled to a mindless consumerism', threaten to unhinge 'our sanity' (p. 4). Tony Williams (1980/81) takes this argument further, seeing the family as a key institution for the production of individuals in the social roles required for the perpetuation of the – patriarchal – state and therefore itself an instrument of repression and supported by other apparatuses of oppression, the church, the police, etc. The source of horror, then, is not so much in the family's economic role but in the monstrous reactions which inevitably erupt against its repressiveness when fantasy attempts to obliterate what cannot be changed by political means. In the terms of William's argument, the horrors of Vietnam are not perpetrated by werewolf-like authorities. Vietnam simply provides the opportunity for a re-enactment of the monstrous fantasies engendered within the heart of the repressive patriarchal family.

Robin Wood: the return of the repressed

The most sustained discussion of the horror film in such terms has been provided by Robin Wood in his introduction to a booklet *American Nightmare* produced to accompany a season of horror films at the Toronto Festival of Festivals (1979). Wood attempts to provide a teleological account of the post-*Psycho* American horror film as the appropriation and reworking of European traditions in popular cultural forms relating to the American way of life. Wood's analytical apparatus, drawing on Marcusean Freud, combines the notion of ideology as a form of social conditioning

with a view of the unconscious as the receptacle of energies repressed by the patriarchal family. Citing Gad Horowitz's distinction between basic and surplus repression, Wood argues that 'surplus repression' in Western civilisation occurs in the production of individuals conditioned to be 'monogamous, heterosexual, bourgeois, patriarchal capitalists' (Wood, 1979, p. 8). What is repressed is sexuality, in its fullest, polymorphous sense, in the interests of producing narrowly defined gender roles, and the strictly functional deployment of the individual's creative energy. The tensions consequent on such repression and the threatened return of the repressed are siphoned off 'through the projection onto the Other of what is

The Shining – 'the family . . . patriarchal social relations as sources of horror'

repressed within the Self, in order that it can be discredited, disowned, and if possible, annihilated' (p. 9). Exploiting the analogy of cinema and dream, and its degraded status as escapist entertainment, the horror movie is able to escape both inner and outer censor to explore in the figure of the monster – a stand-in for 'The Other' – the nature of the sexual energies repressed and denied.

'One might say that the true subject of the horror genre is the struggle for recognition of all that our civilisation *re*presses and *op*presses: its re-emergence dramatised, as our nightmares, as an object of horror, a matter for terror, the 'happy ending' (when it exists) typically signifying the restoration of repression' (Wood, 1979, p. 10).

Significant here is not escape *from* the real world, but what is escaped *into*. The distance from the 'reality' evoked by fantasy makes radical criticism of that world possible. In fact the centre of energy in the horror film, as most commentators point out, is the monster: 'the definition of normality in horror films is in general boringly constant'. It is rare for the monster not to be treated sympathetically, for . . . 'central to the effect and fascination of horror films is their fulfillment of our nightmare wish to smash the norms that oppress us' (p. 27). From this basis Wood goes on to deal with the American form's development. While normality has always, in the horror film, been represented by the 'heterosexual, monogamous couple, the family, and the social institutions (police, church, armed forces) that support them' (p. 26), and often defined in terms of dominant American stereotypes, even when the action takes place in Europe, the monster and its associates were, in the early period of gothic horror, conceived as foreign. Wood argues that this represents for the early horror film a mechanism of 'disavowal' while at the same time allowing horror to be located in a 'country of the mind'. The various phases of the horror film – e.g. the Val Lewton cycle of the 40s, the extra-terrestrial invaders or mutant monster of the 50s – can, then, be seen as 'the process whereby horror becomes associated with its true milieu, the family . . . reflected in its steady *geographical* progress towards America' (p. 29). In post-*Psycho* movies the *Doppelgänger* is not a foreign phenomenon but integral to the psychic life of the American family.

Wood argues for the potential progressiveness of the horror film in the focus of its destructiveness and its ambivalence toward the 'monsters' who destroy.

'While by definition the monster is related to evil . . . horror films . . . are progressive precisely to the degree that they refuse to be satisfied with this simple designation – to the degree that, whether explicitly or implicitly, consciously or unconsciously, they modify, question, challenge, seek to invert it' (Wood, 1979, p. 23).

In Wood's view this ambivalence offers the possibility of a challenge to 'the highly specific world of patriarchal capitalism' (p. 23). The pleasures such films offer their makers and audiences is the release of repressed energies and the destruction of those social norms which demand the repression in the first place. Opposed to this progressive, or 'apocalyptic' strand in the horror films is the 'reactionary wing', defined in its designation of the monster as nothing but evil. This strand confuses repressed and aberrant sexuality with sexuality itself, its ideological project being the reinstatement of repression in the name of normality, supported by a Hollywood version of Christianity. Such films serve the dominant ideology by allowing some release of repressed energies only to rename them evil and cynically justify their further repression.

Horror as affect

The approaches discussed above share a belief in the possibility of understanding

Night of the Living Dead – bringing it all back home

the horror film in terms of historically and culturally specific meanings already in circulation in the society which has produced them. Notions derived from anthropology and psychoanalysis such as the 'collective unconscious', 'repression', the 'id', the 'interpretation of dreams' support readings of the hermetic, self-referential fantasy world of the horror film as the working through in 'irrational' imagery of material lodged in the unconscious, material not to be found in the epics of history or social contemporary reality which provide the more intellectually acceptable explanations of the western or the gangster film. The advent of 'personal politics' in the 70s, and the socio-historical critiques of the family and sexuality provide a theoretical, if controversial, grounding to claims for the social relevance of the horror film.

However, the horror film has also been

Halloween – trick or treat

approached in terms of what it *does* to the audience, rather than what it *represents*. The significance of the horror film is not so much in the content released through its symbolic imagery – primitive fears, repressed energies, etc. – but the way it plays on insecurities as to the basis and adequacy of rational explanation. The audience goes to horror films not only to see things to be feared, or that have been repressed, but to experience fear, to explore the outer limits of knowledge, and of cinematic represention itself.

W. H. Rockett (1982) argues that the horror film has to manoeuvre delicately between the contradictory needs of the aesthetic territory it inhabits. In an epistemological and cultural universe dominated by an Aristotelian logic the overriding compulsion of representation is to produce order by demonstration, showing an action's origins, development and ultimate consequences. The horror film attains the dimensions of terror to the extent that it can resist the Aristotelian compulsion to 'open the door, and show what is behind it'.

Terror relies on convincing the audience of the fallibility of the logic we assume governs the world. To achieve this the horror film makes the audience oscillate between terror (of uncertainty), horror and revulsion (both at things ultimately glimpsed or shown) and finally relief. It can achieve this through a play with off-screen space, or with space hidden in the frame, 'to emphasise what we do not see', or by breaking not simply the 'fixed laws of Nature' but one or more of the laws of the horror film . . . which the '"fixed laws" aficionados of the genre have come to believe in with a almost religious fervour' (p. 133). Moreover, although the horror film may be compelled to open the door, to show the audience something of what is behind, the oscillation between the reassurance of suspended disbelief and the experience of terror is maintained by the door being closed again, to produce further uncertainty. Finally, Aristotelian closure may be denied if the monster's destruction is left in question. However Rockett's description of this fine balance rests on a judgement of value: those horror films which go for quick sensation and show all and more fall victim to the Aristotelian logic and fail to reach the sublimity of terror. Terror depends, however, on the existence of the ground rules which are to be questioned; implicitly it also depends on the Aristotelian gullibility or debased tastes of the audience that sustains them.

The post-structuralist approach

Stephen Neale in his monograph on genre (1980) attempts to elucidate the horror film's form and address in relation to its circulation in critical discourse – an attempt, in other words, to account for all the work described so far. A major distinction between his approach and those discussed above is the place he finds for so-called anti-realist, anti-Aristotelian or 'progressive' elements *within* the embrace of classic narrative cinema, where they play their part in the contradictory functioning of the dominant ideology. Neale's position derives from the link Lacanian psychoanalysis makes between the oedipal scenario consequent on the child's confrontation with sexual difference and 'castration', and the functioning of language. This link knits together three dimensions of human experience. First, desire is haunted by lack, depends on it for its existence and continuation and in the Freudian/Lacanian scenario is primarily about repossessing the plenitude and unity experienced in infancy with the mother. Second, structural linguistics state that in language there are no positive terms; meaning arises in the gap, the difference, between terms. Third, while castration inaugurates desire and compels the child to separate from the mother and enter the symbolic order, achieving individual identity in language, language itself institutes in the subject a splitting of identity: 'I' achieves its meaning only in relation to an implied 'you'. The patriarchal subject then is one driven to construct an illusory identity, unity, coherence on a foundation of lack, difference, separation. In this context the unconscious is not so much a receptacle for repressed contents which in a liberated society would emerge comfortably into the light of day (see Wood, 1979, and Williams, 1980), but a consequence of the human subject's endeavour to construct meaning out of difference, for any attempt to possess the object of desire through coherent, full representation also calls into play its opposite, its founding lack (→ NARRATIVE AND STRUCTURALISM: *Narrative and audience*, p. 242).

According to this perspective the activity of representation is a fetishistic process, which seeks to disavow lack by instituting presence elsewhere (e.g. in the cinema the fetishisation of the star's hair or clothing, producing a perfection which obscures the 'castration' threat of female sexuality). However, as Neale argues, the fetishistic substitute implicitly acknowledges its instituting lack, involving a play on the motif of presence/absence and a 'splitting of belief' in the subject – 'I know very well this is so, and yet . . .'. From the psychoanalytic perspective, then, the pleasures and fascinations of classic narrative cinema arise out of its capacity to play on these contradictions – especially as they centre on sexual difference – while at the same time it preserves the integrity of subjective identity outside the contradictions that found it. The fetishism of cinematic representation takes place on three interrelated levels. First, following Christian Metz, Neale argues that the fascination of the cinematic image itself derives from its play of presence and absence – we know that the events and figures we watch on the screen are not really there, yet we believe we grasp them in some way more real than life. Second, the function of classic narrative structure is to command 'the viewer's adherence to a coherent and homogeneous diegesis'. In other words the fetishism of fiction has to be supported by the production of the conditions in which the audience will accept the make-believe, will be willing to suspend disbelief, accept the fiction as a 'real world', and so support the reality-effect of classic Hollywood. Finally, further and specific 'regimes of credence' – conventions of verisimilitude – are produced by the different genres.

In this context Neale sees the horror film as bound up with fetishism in an over determined way. For a start, in the body of the monster it addresses directly the question of sexual difference and castration. But also, in relation to the foregoing discussion, its fetishistic fictionality is trebled in that it deals in areas pre-defined as pertaining to imagination, fantasy, subjectivity. Genres like the gangster, war film or western, focusing questions of law/disorder, derive their regimes of credence from discourses and codes defined as 'nonfiction' – e.g. newspaper reporting, sociology, historical documentation. The horror film, on the other hand, dramatises questions about the definition of the 'human' and the 'natural' against the concept of the 'unnatural/supernatural'. The order it refers to is metaphysical, its narrative disequilibrium produced in the disjunction between the 'real' world and the 'supernatural'. The narrative quest of the horror film then is to find that discourse capable of solving this disjunction, explaining events (Neale, 1980, p. 22). Given that the discourses mobilised by the horror film are 'characterised as representing not factual reality but poetic or psychological realities' the 'kinds of legitimating documents and references employed . . . will tend to be ancient texts, parapsychological treatises, myths, folklore, religion' (p. 37).

Clearly the maintenance of verisimilitude, the 'splitting of belief' in the audience, is harder for fantasy genres like the horror film, hence the requirement for 'rigorous conventionalisation' noted by some of its critics, and its cultural marginalisation as fodder for adolescents and children. At the same time the cinematic work involved in making credible an avowedly fictional world produces the particular brand of fetishistic fascination – with special effects and so on – exhibited by the cinephilia of the aficionados. Accepting that the neuralgic point of nar-

The Texas Chainsaw Massacre – is the monster always male?

rative in the horror film is sexual difference, and that its successful suspension of disbelief produces affects – horror, anxiety, fear – 'linked to the problematic of castration' (p. 39), the horror film, Neale argues, engages the spectator directly in the play of fetishism. This is taken further in the materialisation of the monster. While the fascination with the monster brings the spectator close to the source and terror of desire and close to the truth of his condition as a patriarchal subject, the fetishistic structure of cinematic narrative ensures that the monster also acts as a displacement of this lack:

'Hence the monster may represent the lack, but precisely by doing so it in fact functions to fill the lack with its own presence, thus coming to function as a fetish simultaneously representing and disavowing the problems of sexual difference at stake' (Neale, 1980, p. 44).

This happens in two ways. First, in the narrative search for the means of controlling the 'play of the monster's appearance/disappearance', in order to contain the lack in place of which the monster appears. Second, in the emphasis the horror film puts on the 'appearance' of the monster, the special effects used both to make the

Peeping Tom – the heroine rejects the terrified victim/monster image

Dressed to Kill – woman is 'responsible for the horror that destroys her'

monster terrifying and convincing and to highlight the key moments of its first appearance or birth, and of its destruction. From this investment in the fetishistic moment Neale concludes, against the 'horror by suggestion' critics, that it is essential for the genre that the monster is physically materialised.

Neale elaborates further the significance of the monster in relation to sexual difference. The monster is defined as monstrous in relation to notions of masculinity and feminity. However these categories intersect with and are complicated by definitions of the 'monstrous' versus the 'human'. On the one hand, the notion of the 'human' does not recognise sexual difference, producing homogeneity in place of heterogeneity. On the other, the monster is rarely without human traits. Its heterogeneity, then, could be seen as a displaced instance of the sexual difference for which it acts as a fetish: the monster's

consequently double heterogeneity 'functions to disturb the boundaries of sexual identity and difference' (p. 61). Nevertheless, Neale goes on to speculate, since the monster is frequently given male gender and woman is his victim, his desire for the woman – whether lustful or homicidal – could be understood as representing the horror that female sexuality produces for the male subject in the castration scenario.

In Stephen Neale's account, then, the violence and sexual ambiguity of the monster, whether gothic creature or deranged psychotic, the hovering of the horror film around the abnormal and taboo, far from representing a release of the repressed and a challenge to the patriarchal status quo, simply offers a fetishistic feast in acknowledgement and perpetuation of the perversity on which patriarchy is founded, the simultaneous fascination with and, disavowal of, female sexuality: 'The horror film is concerned . . . not only with curi-

osity, knowledge and belief, but also, and crucially, with their transgressive and '"forbidden" forms.' From this, he argues, arises the dominance of religious, or religio-scientific forms of explanation within the horror film, and of critical accounts of the genre 'rooted in mysticism and other forms of irrationalism' (p. 45).

Feminism and the horror film

Several commentators on the horror film have pointed out the role of woman as victim – a role treated with increasing viciousness as the sexual violence of recent cycles increases. Stephen Neale's account of the monster from a Lacanian psychoanalytic perspective suggests that its association with sexual difference and the castration scenario makes it a representation of female sexuality itself. However, the interpretative consequences of this argument have recently been challenged in Linda Williams' reintroduction of the question of the woman's 'look' into psychoanalytic accounts of the mechanisms of classic narrative structure ('When the woman looks', 1983). Accepting the notion of the voyeuristic nature of cinematic pleasure in which the woman's look is denied in order to secure the safe identification of a male audience with the male hero's gaze at the objectified female, and accepting also that the horror film makes a special play with the relations of looking, knowledge and desire, Linda Williams offers a different system of interpretation, submitting the Lacanian scenario to the empirical realities of female sexuality: *women are not castrated*, a fact that a symbolic system found on such a notion has to negotiate somehow.

The interest of the horror film for Linda Williams is that it provides an exception to the general denial of the woman's look in the cinema, for a central moment of these films is the gaze of the heroine at the monster. On one level, the woman is punished for daring to look; instead of the mastery that is conferred on the male gaze the act of her looking paralyses the woman and enables the monster to master the looker. However, Williams goes on to question the meaning of the woman's look, and of her relation to the monster, arguing that the power of the monster lies not in its castration, but in its sexual difference from the 'normal male':

'In this difference he is remarkably like the woman in the eyes of the traumatised male: a biological freak with impossible and threatening appetites that suggest a frightening potency precisely where the normal male would perceive a lack' (Williams, 1983, p. 87).

To ground this re-reading of sexual difference, Williams interrogates the notion of woman as a 'castrated version of the man'. Drawing on Susan Lurie's 'Pornography and the Dread of Woman' (1980), she argues that the mother's traumatic representation of sexual difference to the male child lies in her *not* being castrated: she does not possess a penis, yet is not mutilated, thus suggesting a totally other, non-phallic potency. Similarly 'the monster is not so much lacking as he is powerful in a different way' – as is, for example, the vampire. This then leads Williams to argue that the woman's look at the monster

'is more than simply a punishment for looking, or a narcissistic fascination with the distortion of her own image in the mirror that patriarchy holds up to her; it is also a recognition of their similar status, as potent threats to a vulnerable male power' (Williams, 1983, p. 90).

This re-reading of the castration scenario then enables Williams to account for several features of the classic horror film: the 'vindictive destruction of the monster', the frequent sympathy of the female characters for the plight of the monster, their similar constitution 'as an exhibitionist object by the desiring look of the male', the frequent weakness of the male heroes, and 'the extreme excitement and surplus danger when the monster and the woman get together' (p. 90).

This is clearly a reading against the grain of a dominant view of how female sexuality is represented, a reading made easier by the gothic horror film's use of mythical figures. The coming of the psychological thriller in the 60s, however, with its abandonment of mythic monsters and its self-conscious Freudianism, make the possibilities of such subversive reading more problematic. *Peeping Tom* (1959) which along with *Psycho* (1960) inaugurated the cycle is, according to Williams, exceptional in that it offers 'a self-conscious meditation on the relations between a sadistic voyeur/subject and the exhibitionist objects he murders', for what the woman sees at the moment of confrontation is not the monster but her own reflection literally distorted in the concave mirror he holds up to her. The film marks a break in 'the history of the woman's look

in the horror film' in that it constructs a heroine who refuses to recognise herself in the mirror: 'she sees it for the distortion it is and has the power to turn away, to reject the image of woman as terrified victim and monster proffered by the male artist' (p. 93). The cost of such a breakthrough, however, is a simultaneous refusal of 'the only way patriarchal cinema has of representing woman's desire': Helen can resist because she is without sexual desire herself. *Psycho*, and the cycle it inspired, including the recent controversial *Dressed to Kill* (1980), display no such self-consciousness about the structures they operate. These films reduce the gap between woman and monster, so eliminating that flash of sympathetic recognition which in gothic horror suggests the 'possibility of a power located in her very difference from the male' (p. 96).

In the modern psychological thriller/horror film 'the monster who attacks, looks like and, in some sense, *is* a woman' and we are asked to believe 'that the woman is both victim and monster', for she is 'responsible for the horror that destroys her' (p. 93). For Williams the twenty years between *Psycho* and *Dressed to Kill* has seen an intensification of this shift so that 'the identification between woman and monster becomes greater, the nature of the identification is more negatively charged and women are increasingly punished for the threatening nature of their sexuality', to the point that, in the recent spate of 'women-in-danger' exploitation films and 'video nasties', the psychopathic murderer is rarely seen: the body of the female victim is the only visible horror in the film.

References

Ivan Butler, *Horror in the Cinema*, London, A. Zwemmer, 1970.
Carlos Clarens, *Horror Movies: an illustrated survey*, London, Secker and Warburg, 1968.
Charles Derry, *Dark Dreams: a psychological history of the modern horror film*, London, Thomas Yoseloff, 1977.
Lotte Eisner, *The Haunted Screen: Expressionism in the German cinema and the influence of Max Reinhardt*, London, Thames and Hudson, 1969.
Walter Evans, 'Monster movies: a sexual theory', *Journal of Popular Film* vol. 2 no. 4, Fall 1973.
Walter Evans, 'Monster movies and rites of initiation', *Journal of Popular Film* vol. 4 no. 2, Fall 1975.
Robert E. Kapsis, '*Dressed to Kill*', *American Film* vol. 7 no. 5, March 1982.
Harlan Kennedy, 'Things that go howl in the id', *Film Comment* vol. 18 no. 2, March/April 1982.
Ernest Larsen, 'Hi-tech horror', *Jump Cut* no. 22, November 1977.
Susan Lurie, 'Pornography and the dread of woman', in Laura Lederer (ed.), *Take Back the Night*, New York, William Morrow and Co., 1980.
Brian Murphy, 'Monster movies: they came from beneath the 50s', *Journal of Popular Film* vol. 1 no. 1, Winter 1972.
Stephen Neale, *Genre*, London, BFI, 1980.
Davie Pirie, *A Heritage of Horror: the English gothic cinema 1946–72*, London, Gordon Fraser, 1973.
W. H. Rockett, 'Perspectives', *Journal of Popular Film and Television* vol. 10 no. 3, Fall 1982.
T. J. Ross, 'Introduction', in Roy Huss and T. J. Ross (eds.), *Focus on the Horror Film*, Englewood Cliffs, N.J., Prentice-Hall Inc., 1972.
Stephen Snyder, 'Family life and leisure culture in *The Shining*', *Film Criticism* vol. 6 no. 1, Fall 1982.
Andrew Tudor, *Image and Influence: studies in the sociology of film*, London, Allen and Unwin, 1974.
Linda Williams, 'When the woman looks', in Doane, Mellencamp, Williams (eds.), *Re-vision: essays in feminist film criticism*, Frederick MD, AFI Monograph Series, University Publications of America AFI 1983.
Tony Williams, 'American cinema in the 70s: family horror', *Movie* no. 27/28, Winter 1980/Spring 1981.
Robin Wood, 'Introduction', in Britton, Lippe, Williams, Wood (eds.), *American Nightmare: essays on the horror film*, Toronto, Festival of Festivals, 1979.

The Cabinet of Dr. Caligari (Das Cabinett des Dr. Caligari) (Germany 1919 *p.c* – Decla-Bioscop; *d* – Robert Wiene; st b/w 11)

Nosferatu, eine Symphonie des Grauens (Germany 1922 *p.c* – Prana Film; *d* – F. W. Murnau; st b/w 10+20)

Dracula (USA 1931 *p.c* – Universal; *d* – Tod Browning; sd b/w 10)

Frankenstein (USA 1931 *p.c* – Universal; *d* – James Whale; sd b/w 7)

King Kong (USA 1933 *p.c* – RKO Radio; *d* – Ernest B. Schoedsack/Merian C. Cooper; sd b/w 16)

Cat People (USA 1942 *p.c* – RKO Radio; *d* – Jacques Tourneur; sd b/w 15)

Dead of Night (UK 1945 *p.c* – Ealing Studios; *d* – Alberto Cavalcanti/Charles Crichton/Basil Dearden/Robert Hamer; sd b/w 15)

Peeping Tom (UK 1959 *p.c* – Michael Powell (Theatre); *d* – Michael Powell; sd col 10)

Eyes Without a Face (Les Yeux sans visage) (France/Italy 1959 *p.c* – Champs Elysées Productions (Paris)/Lux (Rome); *d* – Georges Franju; st b/w 11)

The Birds (USA 1963 *p.c* – Alfred Hitchcock/Universal-International; *d* – Alfred Hitchcock; sd col 18)

The Tomb of Ligeia (USA 1964 *p.c* – Alta Vista; *d* – Roger Corman; sd col 10)

King Kong Versus Godzilla (Japan 1963 *p.c* – Toho; *d* – Inoshiro Honda/Thomas Montgomery (US version); sd col 23)

Rosemary's Baby (USA 1968 *p.c* – Paramount/William Castle; *d* – Roman Polanski; sd col 20)

Blacula (USA 1972 *p.c* – American International Pictures; *d* – William Crain; sd col 12)

Legend of the Werewolf (UK 1974 *p.c* – Tyburn; *d* – Freddie Francis; sd b/w col 18)

Don't Look Now (UK/Italy 1973 *p.c* – Casey Productions (London)/Eldorado Films (Rome); *d* – Nicholas Roeg; sd col 15)

The musical

Introduction

The musical has only recently received its share of serious critical attention. A tone of incredulous disdain still tends to prevail, even though the claims of other genres have long since been accepted. As Jane Feuer put it, 'Westerns might now be seen as a conflict between chaos and civilisation, but Fred Astaire remained ineffable' (Feuer, 1982, p. vii). Feuer's use of the past tense shows that this situation is changing; musicals are increasingly coming under investigation for their ideological projects, their relationship to social moments and their orchestration of structures of pleasure. This survey of critical approaches to the genre is organised thematically to avoid following a cramped chronology, but first it is worth sketching in some details of the place within British film culture of this apparently uniquely American genre.

Musicals have been produced by almost every nation that produces films. Yet the musical has come to be seen as synonymous with Hollywood, indeed, as embodying what we may think of as the virtues or vices of classical Hollywood cinema. Thus the attitude towards the genre displayed by any given period or tendency of film criticism is characteristic of that particular criticism's attitudes towards Hollywood as a whole. For British film culture, particularly in its rare self-assertive moments, the musical is Hollywood writ large.

John Grierson's much-discussed puritan streak, for example, reveals itself when in 1929 he writes of trying to come to grips with the new, in his eyes vulgarised, sound cinema. Banal adventure stories were bad enough, but with 'musical comedies, musical dramas and the like . . . there indeed I am lost . . . I am constitutionally against love-howls . . . They may have their place, but it is in the exclusively women's theatres which men may know to avoid. These, I regret to say, do not as yet exist' (Grierson, in Hardy (ed.), 1981, p. 33).

The unofficial successor to Grierson's position was Roger Manvell, whose response to the Hollywood musical is less one of bristling incomprehension than of patronising approval. While the musical could never satisfy Manvell's criteria of value for defining cinematic art, he was willing to grant it a position as the best of entertainment (a lower but equally mystificatory category). The musical is made to stand for the most typical Hollywood product, the best musicals being among Hollywood's 'genuine bursts of fantasy' (Manvell, 1946, p. 83). Precisely what is meant by fantasy is never fully explained, but the word serves as a counterbalance to the equally ill-defined 'realism' – and whereas the latter is the true vehicle for the moral seriousness and high cultural values which Manvell erects as prerequisites for Art, the fantasy of the musical can on its

An American in Paris – 'the ultimate wedding of popular and elite art'

own (inferior) terms demonstrate cinema's potential for serving up satisfying diversions. In his later book *The Film and the Public*, Manvell inflects the notion of musical-as-epitomising-Hollywood into a crude version of cultural anthropology:

'The essence of the American musical is the spirit it evokes – the mystique of the American way of life. The best musicals have the vitality of a nation which has no inhibitions when it comes to singing about the heartaches and happiness of contemporary life, or laughing at its own absurdities or glamourising the sheer love of sex and material success' (Manvell, 1955, p. 174).

The couplet musicals/Hollywood (and its unstated inverse, realism/British cinema) was thus sufficiently established to ensure that when the successive waves of post-war cinephiles (e.g. *Sequence*, *Movie*) intervened in British film culture they seized upon the musical as illustrative of the superiority of American cinema. (It may be worth adding that since it was the twin thrust of cinema and popular music that achieved American cultural dominance over Britain, the form which coupled the two was perhaps inevitably a central icon within those hegemonic discourses.) The critical project which served as the impetus and vehicle for this cultural shift hinged upon notions of authorship in popular cinema, so that the musical began to be mobilised in the interests of constructing the 'world view' of an *auteur* such as Minnelli. Clearly, a genre so devoted to sensuous detail in *mise en scène* held polemical value for critical projects committed to celebrating style as an index of personalised authorial vision.

Facts, fans and fetishes

More than any other genre, with the possible exception of the horror film, the musical not only attracts excesses of fan enthusiasm but also caters for that enthusiasm with a plethora of secondary texts. Hundreds of picture books exist solely to present the Hollywood musical as a series of fetishised memories, reproducing the same litany of 'facts' that common sense

deems to be the history of the genre. Confirming, or rather dominating these written texts are the stills, privileged objects for our rapturous nostalgia. These vary as little from book to book as do the narrative histories. A kneeling, pleading Al Jolson leads on to an overhead shot from a Busby Berkeley number, although the Berkeley image as a still appears merely decorative geometry when denied the lubricious mobility of the prowling camera. Then the Fred and Ginger stills, frozen bliss on polished floors, followed by Jeanette MacDonald and Nelson Eddy (often subverted by a coyly satirical caption), Dorothy and pals off to see the Wizard, and the inescapable icon of Gene Kelly halfway up *that* lamp-post. Hereafter the nostalgia dims a little, with images of the increasingly anonymous dance numbers from mid-50s Broadway transfers, then a brief flourish for the leaping youths of *West Side Story*, Barbra Streisand in full flow, and a mountain-top Julie Andrews.

The register of discourse in these picture books is exemplified by breathless tabloid paragraphs such as:

'1952 saw *Singin' in the Rain*. Occasionally everything goes right. A young kid still in her teens named Debbie Reynolds . . . got the female lead. Donald O'Connor was around to do some of the best comic dancing ever. Comden and Green were at their wittiest. Kelly was there. The result? A gentle spoof, with the best singing, best dancing ever . . .' (Cohen, 1984, p. 44).

This extract is interesting for the way it reproduces the same set of assumptions that the Hollywood musical itself has striven to disseminate – it describes nothing more or less than putting on a show. Success is won by chance, talent and spontaneity; any notion of industry, economics or labour is effaced; the joy of performance is its own reward, its own celebration.

Such re-articulation of the musical's own ideological projects is not confined to fan books. Consider this, from an American University primer on Hollywood genres:

'Perhaps the genre's ultimate wedding of

Gold Diggers of 1933 – 'Remember My Forgotten Man'

popular and élite art occurs in the "American in Paris" ballet, wherein Gershwin's music, French painting, Kelly's modern dance and ballet, and Minnelli's *mise en scène* coalesce into nearly twenty minutes of musical and visual perfection' (Schatz, 1981, p. 219).

The only difference is one of vocabulary. The predominant, common sense notion of the genre's history is reaffirmed (no matter that Stanley Donen called the Kelly ballets, in retrospect, 'objectionable . . . sort of horseshit . . . something of a wart' (Donen, quoted in *Movie* no. 24, p. 32), the notion which also fits exactly with the industry's image, given that the 'American in Paris' ballet also closes the celebratory compilation film *That's Entertainment* (1974). The history of the genre as presented in these secondary texts becomes self-fulfilling prophecy. The musical is a genre where the recirculation of images (whether in prose, still images or film extracts) plays an essential role in activating the full social resonances of the films. Rather than confirm or challenge estimations of particular films, then, the primary task for any critical theory of the genre is to try to undercut the self-congratulation connoted by those discourses of entertainment which dazzle by their very simplicity.

The politics of energy
Interrogating the mythologies of the genre and its surrounding discourses demanded a new, musicals-specific critical approach. Probably the most influential article in this respect has been Richard Dyer's 'Entertainment and utopia' (1977), which sets its sights firmly on the most intractable problem of all, the precise structural and cultural function of the genre's founding notion, entertainment.

Dyer's crucial insight is to identify the utopian sensibility at work in entertainment, a sensibility that even colours our commonsense understanding of the term:

'Two of the taken-for-granted descriptions of entertainment, as 'escape' and as 'wish-fulfilment, point to its central thrust, namely, utopianism. Entertainment offers the image of "something better" to escape into, or something we want deeply that our day-to-day lives don't provide. Alternatives, hopes, wishes, these are the stuff of utopia, the sense that things could be better, that something other than what is can be imagined and maybe realised' (Dyer, 1977, p. 3).

He then breaks down the central shaping sensibility into five categories – energy, abundance, intensity, transparency and community – which he traces through three different but representative musicals, noting, for example, the energy in *On the Town*'s 'New York, New York', the intensity in *Gold Diggers of 1933*'s 'Remember my Forgotten Man' and the abundance in *Funny Face*'s 'Think Pink'. All five categories will occur in every musical, with their varying degrees of emphasis providing one way into a comparative analysis within the genre. Furthermore, Dyer relates the categories to specific social needs or problems (rather than to any metaphysical questions, which would pluck the texts from history) showing how, for example, the musical's utopian vision of abundance would have special force at times of widespread poverty.

Already, then, we have reached the complex question of how politically to regard the genre's utopianism. Dyer seems to suggest that by mobilising utopian notions the musical runs the risk of setting into play truly radical aspirations which cannot be recuperated through the strategies of closure and resolution employed by standard classical narrative. This is an important point, since it raises for analysis the way in which the formal structures of musicals militate against the operations of classical narratives.

The issue of how the musical reconciles production numbers with narrative is to be found at all levels of critical approaches to the genre. The common-sense histories present the issue as one of generic evolution: earlier musicals were 'non-integrated' (in backstage musicals, for example, the numbers remain signalled *as* numbers, distinct from the narrative), while later the genre became 'integrated' (i.e. the numbers arise organically from the

narrative). In Dyer's critique, on the other hand, the numbers/narrative conflict becomes the site where the escape of non-recuperable utopianism is likely to occur.

Leo Braudy also stresses the energy embodied in dance as the key aspect of the genre, the element of the textual system most likely to offer an 'opposition to the artifices of tradition, social formality, and high art of all kinds', arguing that the energies of dance may not be confined to individual liberation, but may 're-invigorate and reform the stodgy society against which its rebellion had first taken shape' (Braudy, 1976, p. 139).

The problem with these readings of the utopianism of the genre is that faced by all ideological readings of popular fiction: that is, how far can they be taken? There is a specific problem with the musical, which is so heavily dependent for its success on non-representational signifiers (see Dyer, 1977) that it can never be reduced to a single 'meaning' readable in ideological terms. A danger remains of too whole-heartedly accepting the utopian potentiality of the genre, of confusing textual hint with achieved political reality. Jane Feuer illuminates this problematic point:

'Musicals are unparalleled in presenting a vision of human liberation which is profoundly aesthetic. Part of the reason some of us love musicals so passionately is that they give us a glimpse of what it would be like to be free. We desperately need images of liberation in the popular arts. But the musical presents its vision of the unfettered human spirit in a way that forecloses a desire to translate that vision into reality. The Hollywood version of utopia is entirely solipsistic. In its endless reflexivity the musical can offer only itself, only entertainment, as its picture of utopia' (Feuer, 1982, p. 84).

The strategies of paradox
Feuer's critique of the utopian reading of the genre relates closely to her central thesis on the musical, which she sees as founded on a basic paradox: that it is committed to attempting the recreation of the immediacy of live performance while always remaining a secondary mediation, a recording of an actuality. She sees this commitment as underlying the stress on community identified by Dyer, since musicals attempt to compensate for their inevitable alienation from spontaneous communal experience by obsessively centring their narratives on the search for the perfect community. Culturally and historically specific, the musical is mass art, yet it always seems to be trying to pass itself off as a folk art (the mode of cultural production where producer and consumer are one), striving to represent on screen the type of integrated community which has been rendered untenable off screeen by the very technological, economic and social forces which created the climate of existence for cinema itself.

Gigi – 'thank heaven for little girls'

Meet Me in St. Louis – 'a seething nexus of repressions and neuroses'

The most typical narrative and spectacular strategies employed by the genre can thus be traced back to reverberations engendered by this instigating self-reflective paradox between the technology needed to produce musical numbers (engineering, in Feuer's terms) and the illusion that such numbers arise narratively from chance and spontaneity (here Feuer adopts Lévi-Strauss's term, *bricolage*):

'Engineering as the mode of production of the Hollywood musical is cancelled by a content relying heavily upon *bricolage*. We lose all sense of calculation lying behind the numbers and we gain as a bonus the aura of absolute spontaneity. The number may appeal as 'folk' art while taking full advantage of the possibilities technology gives 'mass art' (Feuer, 1982, p. 7).

Similarly, the illusion of amateurism (anyone can sing or dance, it just happens) effaces the strain and labour that really goes into singing and dancing professionally.

The genre's persistent formal strategy for recreating community is, says Feuer, the elimination of theatrical space. Such space has to be first present and then eliminated, since (another paradox) to have never had it would destroy the conceit that the genre is reproducing the immediacy of live performance. Where other kinds of narrative film seek to achieve a 'third person' reported story, the musical hopes (always a folorn hope) to re-establish the directness of 'first person' live entertainment. Hence even musicals without theatrical setting to eliminate (unlike backstage films) will often impose proscenium arch-like *mise en scène* on to their ostensibly 'natural' setting, as in *Top Hat*, or, supremely, *Meet Me in St. Louis*. Richard Dyer's notion of intensity is pertinent here, since that too is an attempt to regain first-person directness. The particularly devoted affection felt for certain stars of this genre can also be read in this light.

Feuer also notes the recurring formal device whereby films with theatrical settings place the cinematic audience in the space/place of the onscreen theatrical audience, thus binding the former into the implied communal satisfaction of the latter. A shot of a performer on stage from behind two or three rows of audience heads is followed by a cut to just the performer:

'We are, as it were, lifted out of the audience we actually belong to (the cinema audience) and transported into another audience, one at once alive and more ghostly. And, in the cut to a closer shot, since the internal audience retreats into offscreen space, the performance can be truly 'all for us' (Feuer, 1982, p. 28).

The pleasure mobilised by the resulting illusion of intimacy, intensity and community is the principal mechanism by which the musical seeks to mask its own workings, its own inescapable crux of paradoxes. Our pleasure increases, for example, if we see rehearsals for a number and then the number itself, so that the final number is more than just filmed song and dance for us, since we both know the 'work' behind the number and enjoy its 'ineffable' spectacle. But we are never allowed to see on screen the rehearsals behind the onscreen rehearsal.

If Feuer's thesis represents the most coherent attempt to take on the musical *as* musical, it remains only to survey the way in which other critical traditions have dealt with the musical as evidenced in various long-standing critical debates.

Authorship and the musical

The clearest awareness of the inapplicability of traditional auteurism is displayed by Paddy Whannel:

'The musical film represents the clearest challenge to *auteur* criticism, not only because it most obviously depends upon the division of labour between highly specialised talents (and studio departments) but also because its roots include pre-existing styles of song and dance, concepts of entertainment and the more immediate sources of an adapted story or play . . . Musicals are not so much made by an author, but rather emerge out of a network of contending forces' (Whannel, '*My Sister Eileen*', 1977, p. 58).

Nevertheless, the language of auteurism surfaces frequently in writing about the musical, even if the fiction of directorial authorship cannot be sustained; thus the producer Arthur Freed is accredited with possessing 'unique vision' (Schatz, 1981, p. 204). A more fruitful area of enquiry is the role played by stars in the genre, given the potency, noted above, that star images tend to have in musical films. Richard Dyer has discussed Judy Garland in this context, focusing on both the construction of authenticity as a shaping force in her work and in musicals generally, and on her position within the textual readings practised by a particular social subculture (Dyer, '*A Star Is Born* and the construction of authenticity', 1982). More conventional but still perceptive studies have also been done on Astaire and Rogers (Croce, 1972), Gene Kelly (Hirschorn, 1974), and Al Jolson (Sarris, 'Al Jolson', 1977).

Two directors are worth individual mention, one because of his central identification with the genre (Vincente Minnelli), one because of the way in which his admirers have tried to deal with his rather odd foray into the genre (Howard Hawks). These two cases are discussed in the section on musical extracts below.

Contextual and ideological approaches

If the musical remained for too long 'ineffable', that can be traced back to the lack of criticism relating musical texts to their historical and social moment of production. A pioneering essay in this respect was Mark Roth's discussion of Warner Bros musicals of the early 1930s in relation to the political and economic situation of America at that time. Talking of Busby Berkeley numbers in terms of 'escapism from the Depression' had become a lazy truism, but Roth provides the specificity of detail and accuracy of comment to flesh out such shorthand and make such analysis a viable proposition with regard to the musical (Roth, 'Some Warners musicals and the spirit of the New Deal', 1981). Two years earlier, Michael Wood's perceptive, albeit reductive book *America in the Movies* (1975) discussed the difference between the choreographic styles of Astaire and Kelly in relation to shifts in American life between the 1930s and 1950s. Compare a standard, banal account of the differences which asserts that the styles differ 'for reasons that have as much

Seven Brides for Seven Brothers – 'dance
... bringing the eccentric into society'

to do with their different musical personalities as with the genre's evolving narrative sophistication' (Schatz, 1981, p. 207) and in which history does not exist beyond a predetermined aesthetic teleology, with Wood's intriguing account of Gene Kelly, who

'suggests fantastic skill edged with uncertainty ... He is a portrait of America before the plague of locusts which came in the shape of Hiss, Korea, the Rosenbergs, McCarthy and the rest ... But part of his appeal is a touch of strain and even faint fear, an air of scenting locusts on the wind ...' (Wood, 1975, p. 164).

This account is rather over-reliant on a simple, reflective relation between text and society, but it at least opens up the musical for the contextual discussion given to other Hollywood genres.

Leo Braudy draws further parallels between American dominant ideologies of the 1950s and the changes that decade saw in the musical – *Seven Brides for Seven Brothers* 'makes dance into another way of bringing the eccentric into society, forcing him to mind his manners and accept society's values' so that dance is 'domesticated to the vision of family, Thanksgiving dinners, and children' (Braudy, 1976, p. 159). A useful recent article examines the working through of various ideological structures in three Gene Kelly musicals (Telotte, 'Ideology and the Kelly-Donen musicals', 1984).

Robin Wood chose a musical as his test case for addressing the issues he felt challenging him from developments in post-1968 ideological criticism, finding that *Silk Stockings* did benefit in some ways from such criticism, but that (and perhaps particularly because of its genre) the film could not 'be justly evaluated on purely ideological grounds' (Wood, 'Art and ideology', 1981, p. 68). Two long undervalued ideological analyses of individual musicals need to be mentioned here. First, Richard Dyer's article on *The Sound of Music*, which remains probably the best application of his critical method applied to an individual film, and Andrew Britton's reading of *Meet Me in St. Louis* (Britton, 'Meet Me in St. Louis', 1977). The latter sets the film in cultural,

psychoanalytical and ideological contexts, arguing that not far beneath the surface of this manifest project of celebrating small-town life lies a seething nexus of repressions and neuroses. In its analysis of the relation to be found between production numbers and narrative, and in its stress on the centrality of energy, it bears some resemblance to other strands in criticism of the genre, but it differs in linking the film with elements of Gothic literature and the horror film, centring on the Halloween sequence.

Probably the most important branch of ideological criticism of the musical is that based on sexual politics. The genre's emphasis on spectacle organised around the female body; its reliance on strong female stars; its often presumed address to a female, or at least feminine, audience; its almost total adherence to heterosexual romance as a narrative instigator; all these provide fertile ground for feminist and sexual-political critiques. The less sophisticated examples of this criticism can be overly concerned with a simplistic content analysis, informed by a notion of 'positive' or 'negative' images of women; for example a feminist attack on *Gentlemen Prefer Blondes* which pays little attention to issues of genre, industry or the subtler questions of textual pleasure (Turim, 'Gentlemen consume blondes', 1976). Especially instructive is a 1973 article where two male authors, smitten with liberal guilt, attempt to portray all Hollywood musicals as part of a male chauvinist plot. Their concern to right past wrongs leads to bizarre value judgements such as calling Fred Astaire 'a vulgar, wise-cracking lowbrow' (Patrick and Haislip, 'Thank heaven for little girls', 1973, p. 23). As an example of misplaced male breast-beating, this article is difficult to better.

Transcending the level of content analysis to provide one of the most incisive articles on a single musical is Lucy Fischer's essay on *Dames* (Fischer, 'The image of woman as image: the optical politics of *Dames*', 1976). Coining the useful phrase 'optical politics', Fischer concentrates on the ideological elements of visual signifiers, enabling her to avoid simply seeking out 'positive' images. Her feminist critique of Busby Berkeley's *mise en scène* remains an uncompromising attack on those who would excuse his voyeuristic stategies under the aestheticised rubric of 'surrealist'.

Psychoanalysis as a critical method has as yet made little headway into discussions of the musical – Dennis Giles's 'Show-making' written in 1977, (1981), remains a comparatively isolated attempt to apply Freudian psychoanalysis directly to the genre. In Rick Altman's words, 'where others have pointed up the important parallel between making the show and making the couple, Giles moves directly to the sexual level' (Altman, 1981, p. 85). It could be argued, however, that Andrew Britton (1977) makes more convincing use

of psychoanalytic concepts by relating the musical's psycho-sexual motifs to tensions in society. Giles's essay, though provocative, perhaps remains too deeply enmeshed in purely Freudian readings.

References
Rick Altman (ed.), *Genre: The Musical*, London, BFI Publishing/Routledge and Kegan Paul, 1981.
Leo Braudy, *The World In a Frame: what we see in films*, New York, Anchor, 1976.
Andrew Britton, 'Meet Me in St. Louis: Smith, or the ambiguities', *Australian Journal of Screen Theory* no. 3, 1977.
Daniel Cohen, *Musicals*, Greenwich, Connecticut, Bison Books, 1984.
Jim Cook, 'On a Clear Day You Can See Forever', *Movie* no. 24, 1977.
Arlene Croce, *The Fred Astaire and Ginger Rogers Book*, New York, Galahad Books, 1972.
Jerome Delameter, *Dance in the Hollywood Musical*, Ann Arbor, UMI Research Press, 1981.
Stanley Donen, interview in *Movie* no. 24, 1977.
Richard Dyer, 'The Sound of Music', *Movie* no. 23, 1976/77.
Richard Dyer, 'Entertainment and utopia', *Movie* no. 24, 1977.
Richard Dyer, 'A Star Is Born and the construction of authenticity', in Gledhill (ed.), *Star Signs*, London, BFI Education, 1982.
Thomas Elsaesser, 'Vincent Minnelli', in Altman (ed.), *Genre: The Musical*, cit.
Jane Feuer, *The Hollywood Musical*, London, BFI Publishing, 1982.
Lucy Fischer, 'The image of woman as image: the optical politics of *Dames*', in Altman (ed.), *Genre: The Musical*, cit.
Denis Giles, 'Show-making', in Altman (ed.), *Genre: The Musical*, cit.
John Grierson, in F. Hardy (ed.), *Grierson on the Movies*, London, Faber, 1981.
Clive Hirschorn, *Gene Kelly: a biography*, Chicago, Henry Regnery, 1974.
John Kobal, *Gotta Sing, Gotta Dance: a pictorial history of film musicals*, London, Hamlyn, 1971.
Roger Manvell, *Film*, Harmondsworth, Penguin, 2nd ed., 1946.
Roger Manvell, *The Film and the Public*, Harmondsworth, Penguin, 1955.
Robert Patrick and William Haislip, 'Thank heaven for little girls', *Cineaste* no. 6, 1973.
Mark Roth, 'Some Warners musicals and the spirit of the New Deal', in Altman (ed.), *Genre: The Musical*, cit.
Andrew Sarris, *The American Cinema*, New York, Dutton, 1968.
Andrew Sarris, 'Al Jolson', *Film Comment*, September/October 1977.
Thomas Schatz, *Hollywood Genres*, New York, Random House, 1981.
J. P. Telotte, 'Ideology and the Kelly-Donen musicals', *Film Criticism* vol. 8 no. 3, 1984.
Maureen Turim, 'Gentlemen consume blondes', *Wide Angle* no. 1, 1976.
Paddy Whannel, 'My Sister Eileen', *Movie* no. 24, 1977.
Michael Wood, *America in the Movies*, London, Secker and Warburg, 1975.
Robin Wood, 'Art and ideology: notes on *Silk Stockings*', in Altman (ed.), *Genre: The Musical*, cit
Robin Wood, *Howard Hawks*, London, BFI Publishing, rev. ed., 1981.

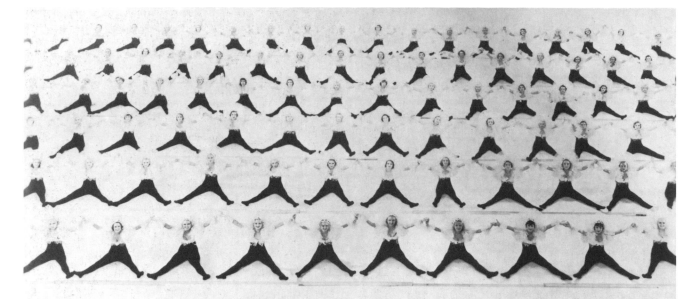

Dames – musical as 'spectacle organised around the female body'

Top Hat (USA 1935 *p.c* – RKO; *d* – Mark Sandrich; sd b/w 25)

Like all the Astaire-Rogers films, this can be profitably considered in terms of its sexual politics, the ideology of the perfect romance. *Top Hat* offers a particularly pure example of the way in which heterosexual desire in the musical 'occupies a central as opposed to a secondary or peripheral place in the discursive ensemble . . . its presence is a necessity, not a variable option' (Neale, 1980, p. 23).

The two couple-dances in this extract could, with appropriate caution, be analysed in terms of the significatory potential of non-representational signs, for although, as Dyer says, the methodology for any such reading remains particularly undeveloped (Dyer, 1977, p. 4), a clear difference between these dances is perceptible.

'Isn't This a Lovely Day' offers a rare pleasure in mainstream cinema – the couple as equals. It is the courtship dance which has the same structural function in all Astaire-Rogers films, as the antagonistic couple forget their personal animosity in the joy of shared dancing. The dance is in one respect Astaire's pursuit of Rogers, but it never becomes an oppressive celebration of male prowess. The star personas of the couple are a contributing factor – Astaire is not the conventional macho hero, Rogers is never the demure feminine heroine. In this dance their equality is further reinforced by Rogers' 'masculine' clothes (dress being one of the key non-representational signs). The dance becomes a mutual game, the couple's joy further multiplied by the realisation that each knows the rules of the other's game. Once again, this is a reading of non-representational signs, in

this case gesture. The setting is 'rural' (in the park) as opposed to the glossy interiors that serve as the space for the later dances in each of their films, and they end by shaking hands rather than kissing. They remain equal in dance (whatever the relative skills of the performers) as long as signifiers of conventional romance are avoided.

The different complexion of the second couple-dance, 'Cheek to Cheek', indicates the importance of non-representational signs. Now the dancers are in evening dress, Rogers' dress a particularly elaborate 'feminine' creation. The setting is the nightclub, interior glamour as opposed to pastoral outdoors. The style of dancing has changed, traditional gender roles are as strongly reinforced here as they were unnecessary earlier; aspirations to the balletic have replaced the previous informality. The couple's steps are now organised around his dominance ('leading' is the appropriate dance term) where they had been identical or humorously competitive. If 'Cheek to Cheek' reinforces the terms of classical Hollywood romance, then 'Isn't This a Lovely Day' at least suggests an alternative, perhaps utopian view, of romance based on equality.

This shift from dislike to mutual discovery to conventional romance recurs not only throughout this and other Astaire-Rogers films, but throughout most musicals, comedies and romances in Hollywood production. The Astaire-Rogers relationship has assumed mythic status as an ideal of the ideology of romance, so that the responsibility of analysis lies with teasing apart the contradictions in that ideology. In their progression from side-by-side to cheek-to-cheek, these

films clearly close down more egalitarian possibilities. However, the existence of the earlier dances of mutual discovery (and the initial meeting/quarrelling scenes, such as the one that opens this extract) raises the question of whether subversive moments can escape eventual narrative recuperation.

Gold Diggers of 1933 (USA 1933 *p.c* – Warner Bros; *d* – Mervyn LeRoy; sd b/w 20)

Discussion of the 1930s musical usually sets up Busby Berkeley and Fred Astaire as contrasting poles. In the simplistic teleological version of the genre's history it is Astaire's intimacy which is acclaimed as advancing the musical towards its later integrated and 'realistic' modes, while Berkeley becomes a dead end of baroque spectacle, an efflorescence in a vacuum. Berkeley's aesthetic is perceived as wholly self-referential, perfected quickly so that thereafter it could only develop further in on itself, retreating into self-parody and insular camp. A later Berkeley film like *The Gang's All Here* (1943) might amaze on a first viewing with its Freudian fruit salad of symbolic outrage, but it soon stands revealed as seduced by its own abstractions, self-referential to the point of cancelling itself out.

For Leo Braudy, Berkeley's 'attitude towards individuals is that of a silent film director, iconographic and symmetric'; Braudy also points up the crucial distinction between Berkeley's and Astaire's roles in their films – Berkeley the 'non-participating choreographer-director', Astaire the 'dancer-choreographer himself . . . a participant' (Braudy, 1976, p. 142). To

Gentlemen Prefer Blondes – 'Ain't There Anyone Here for Love?'   *Sweet Charity* – 'Hey, Big Spender'

put it simply, Berkeley contributed a great deal to the use of movement in cinema, but almost nothing to dance (see Delamater, 1981).

Gold Diggers of 1933 (choreographed by Berkeley) is one of the musicals Richard Dyer singles out for analysis in 'Entertainment and utopia'. He sees the relationship between numbers and narrative as particularly problematic in this film, given its explicit narrative concern with the effects of the Depression:

'The thrust of the narrative is towards seeing the show as 'solution' to the ... problems of the characters; yet the non-realist presentation of the numbers makes it very hard to take this solution seriously ...' (Dyer, 1977, p. 8).

This is clearly the case with the 'Shadow Waltz' – one of Berkeley's more fanciful set-pieces, yet interestingly atypical in its relative lack of overt sexual symbolism. While the female body is as usual the raw material for aesthetic composition and scopic concentration, the end result is, for Berkeley, a little tame, even prim. With the exception of one shot of reflected legs, the *mise en scène* is not directly voyeuristic. This is perhaps not unrelated to the number's slight straining after European high cultural values (it is, after all, a waltz).

Dyer's argument is less convincing in relation to 'Remember My Forgotten Man', although this number is a prime example of his categories of intensity and – all the more powerful because inflected negatively – community. It, too, is not typical Berkeley, nor even typical of the whole genre, in being direct social comment, worlds away from the same film's 'Petting in the Park' or any of the Astaire love ballads. It was

certainly read as aberrant by some critics in the 1930s:

'I can take most war films cheerfully on the chin, but I want none of them in musical comedies, where they certainly do not belong. For downright offensiveness and bad taste, that last reel wins the Croix de Garbage' (quoted in Roth, 1981, p. 55).

Precisely why seriousness and social awareness were thought so incompatible with a musical rendering, even so early in the genre's history, is an intriguing question. Certainly 'My Forgotten Man' shows that the attempt could be brought off, indeed the number now strikes us among Berkeley's most impressive, demonstrating his undeniable mastery in the orchestration of space, spectacle and editing without the usual stress on fetishistic voyeurism.

Gentlemen Prefer Blondes (USA 1953 *p.c* – 20th Century-Fox; *d* – Howard Hawks; sd col 15)

Because of its director, there have been many attempts to accommodate this film within an auteurist framework. All have faced severe problems, with Andrew Sarris going so far as to omit the film completely from his entry on Hawks in *The American Cinema* (1968). Robin Wood relegates it to the 'Failures and Marginal Works' chapter of his book on Hawks, deeming it not 'meaningful', lacking in 'satisfactory unity', bereft of any 'firm positive centre' – all, taking into account Wood's critical framework at that time, highly pejorative remarks (Wood, 1981, p. 171).

Equally, standard histories of the genre have found it something of a rogue text. Its sexual knowingness, brashness and indebtedness to vaudeville traditions make it difficult to

set alongside the balletic pretensions of the 1950s Kelly or the aestheticised ideals of 50s Minnelli. It quite literally clashes. Its use of Monroe and Russell, however, bring it into line with the increased use of sexual stereotyping that has often been seen as typical of Hollywood production later in the decade.

A third dominant approach has been to read it in terms of its particular inflection of the Monroe star persona, though this can raise just as many problems as attempting to manoeuvre it into the 'Hawksian canon'. Perhaps a new way into the text, more precisely into its sexual politics (signalled as important by the unusual absence of any even remotely attractive male characters) is through the critically neglected role of Jane Russell.

This extract contains one of the most extraordinary numbers in any Hollywood musical. Russell self-parodically pouts 'Ain't There Anyone Here for Love?' against the heaving backdrop of the American Olympic team. These men, clad in fetching flesh-coloured shorts, perform what appear to be flamboyantly masculine exercises in fact used as chorus-girl gyrations. The number can be taken as a striking example of the tensions of homoeroticism in Hawks's films, but it is also a generic parody – casting Russell as Dick Powell in an inverted Berkeley production number.

Quite how one reads the courtroom number is open to debate. A legitimate case could be made for mounting a critique of its fetishistic exploitation of Russell, or for enjoying her manipulation of the various legal, social and sexual codes and institutions ranged against her. As with the previous →

number, as indeed with so many musical texts, the choice of reading must be considered in terms of how one regards the interpretation of non-representational signs, and of how much weight one places on the potential escape of reputedly subversive energies before the recuperation of narrative closure. Russell is narratively subordinated into marriage, but the privileged images of the film, one could argue, are her capture of the courtroom and her cry of 'Doubles, anyone?' to the bulging narcissists of the Olympic team. Notions of authorial control, star persona, generic specificity and cultural context would all have to be considered in any such analysis.

Sweet Charity (USA 1968 *p.c* – Universal; *d* – Bob Fosse; sd col 25)

By the late 1960s, the moment of production of this film, the musical was in most respects stranded by shifts in industrial practice and cultural sensibility. The traditional audiences of cinema were largely captured by television, and the mainstream musical could hardly be expected to redirect itself towards the new youth market – since that market's preferred musical entertainment had little to do with Irving Berlin or Rodgers and Hammerstein. The Elvis Presley films were an attempt to combine the old cinematic practice with the new musical practice, but they functioned largely as objects for fan adoration. Hollywood was deceived by the great success of *The Sound of Music* into investing in other expensive musicals, such as *Sweet Charity*, which flopped badly.

Despite its commercial failure, however, *Sweet Charity* has been seized upon by devotees of the musical, and, more importantly, Bob Fosse has been hailed as the new saviour-*auteur* of the genre. Recognised as a major choreographer in earlier films like *The Pajama Game* (1957), Fosse clearly directs dance in a distinctive and immediately recognisable way (see Delamater, 1981, for an analysis of the Fosse style). 'Hey, Big Spender' has taken its place in the nostalgic repertory of Hollywood musical numbers. But to obtain a perspective on *Sweet Charity* beyond the authorial and adulatory, the film must be considered in terms of its historical moment.

'Hey, Big Spender' is memorable for reasons that go beyond talent – it is the most sexually direct musical number since the heyday of Berkeley. And it can be so because of relaxed censorship laws – moreover it *needs* to be so to receive the description 'adult' intended to attract a late 1960s audience. (Fosse was to capitalise on such social nuances again with *Cabaret*, 1972, Hollywood's

first foray into decadent chic.) 'If They Could See Me Now', however, is of a different register. Editing trickery apart (and the film can be dated now by the self-congratulatory flashiness of the editing), this number is a throwback to vaudeville. The film is trying to have it both ways – the so-daring sleaze of 'Big Spender' and the old-fashioned barnstorming of 'If They Could See Me Now'. The use of top hat and cane in the latter clearly marks it as an attempted tribute to earlier musical styles, but the effect is muddled.

Sweet Charity was also acclaimed for introducing a central star performance reminiscent of the genre's classic period (see especially Kobal, 1971). Shirley MacLaine does, indeed, perform a creditable impersonation of a musical star, but she is indulged by Fosse (especially in 'If They Could See Me Now') to an extent undreamed of in, say, the 1940s musical. The very notion of a old-style musical star functioning in the late 60s seems anachronistic. MacLaine's one register is the relentless projection of being lovable – difficult to bring off in any text, and floundering in misplaced energy in *Sweet Charity*, where Fosse's determination to be modern is uppermost. The jagged, mannered stylisation of a number like 'The Aloof' cannot co-exist with the gushing warmth of MacLaine without resulting in a seriously ruptured text.

On a Clear Day You Can See Forever (USA 1970 *p.c* – Paramount; *d* – Vincente Minnelli; sd col 17)

With Minnelli's musicals (as that very phrase shows) issues of authorship occupy the centre of critical discussion. *On a Clear Day . . .* could also be approached in terms of its place within a declining genre (like *Sweet Charity*) or consideration of Barbra Streisand's star persona, but its chief interest is as a Minnelli-text (see Cook, 'On a Clear Day You Can See Forever', 1977).

Thomas Elsaesser's classic account of Minnelli suggests that all the director's films, of whatever genre, 'aspire to the condition of the musical' and goes on to assert that

'Minnelli's films are structured so as to give the greatest possible scope to the expansive nature of a certain vitality (call it 'will', or libido) – in short, to the confrontation of an inner, dynamic reality and an outward, static one . . . What characterises the Minnelli musical is the total and magic victory of the impulse, the vision, over any reality whatsoever . . .' (Elsaesser, 'Vincente Minnelli', 1981).

The confrontation referred to is of course best embodied in the numbers/narrative tension, with the numbers bearing the victorious magic. Minnelli

films like *The Pirate* (1948), *Yolanda and the Thief* (1945), and *Brigadoon* (1954) are usually produced as evidence to clinch the case. What makes *On a Clear Day . . .* so interesting, not only as a Minnellian text but also for the genre as a whole, is that there are no 'numbers' as such. In the extract, what would usually be a grand dramatic visualisation of Streisand's love ballad is rendered as a variety of interior monologue.

On a Clear Day . . ., like most musicals, strives to attain an ideal, utopian world. This world is not, however, the ideal romance of *Top Hat*, the perfect show of *Gold Diggers of 1933*, the mythicised New York of *On The Town*, or even the dream village of *Brigadoon* – it is purely abstract, wholly internalised, a utopian state of mind. Thus *On a Clear Day . . .* has a distinct, seductive appeal to certain theories of the genre, in that it can be posited as a transcendent soaring conclusion to the genre's striving after the ideal – and the film's narrative resolution can only aid such a reading. It comes at virtually the close of Minnelli's career, so it is perfectly suited to round off that particular authorial narrative. At this point, however, the theoretical pretence breaks down, and we are left with something resembling Prospero's-last-speech-is-Shakespeare's-farewell-to-the-theatre criticism transposed from Stratford to Hollywood.

In such writing about Minnelli's musicals as with all dedicated auteurist criticism, the pleasure of the text is the central issue – but the text in question is the body of films that make up the authorial super-text. The individual film is valued according to how well it can be moulded to fit into that wider text. Thus in terms of the musical and Minnelli, certain films receive what might strike uninitiated viewers as undue attention. *The Pirate*, *Yolanda and the Thief* and *Brigadoon* were all commercial failures, none of them has an important place within popular and fan histories of the genre, but all three are indispensable to academic criticism of the musical.

On a Clear Day . . . follows this pattern, perhaps even more strongly, since it is virtually incomprehensible to viewers not immersed in Minnelli – certainly it is liable to strike them as miscast (a film posited on delicacy of touch and intellectual audacity of conception is seriously hampered by the presence of such an abrasive star as Streisand) and confused. For the Minnelli-watcher, though, it is liable to prove deeply satisfying. If nothing else, the film shows how far the musical has come from its once unassailable position as socially central definer and dispenser of mass entertainment.

Authorship and Cinema

Introduction

Debates about authorship in both the production and consumption of film have occupied a privileged position in film studies since the 1950s, when the French journal *Cahiers du Cinéma* formulated the *politique des auteurs*. Basically a polemical critical strategy aimed at the 'quality' French cinema and the critical writing that supported it, the *politique* proposed that, in spite of the industrial nature of film production, the director, like any other artist, was the sole author of the finished product. This proposition has been appropriated, attacked and reformulated in many different ways, and its continuing relevance to critical debates is some indication of the value of *Cahiers'* initial polemic.

Historical and political changes, particularly since May 1968, brought about a radical re-thinking of the underlying assumptions of traditional *auteur* study of cinema, and an assault on the ideology of the artist as sole creator of the art work. In spite of this assault, *auteur* study has not been destroyed, but rather transformed: from a way of accounting for the whole of cinema into a critical methodology which poses questions for film study, and for cultural practices in general. The history of this transformation is traced in this section.

The question of authorship and its application to the industrial context of cinema has often been presented and argued a-historically, for example by American film critic Andrew Sarris, who reformulated *Cahiers' politique* as the '*auteur* theory', transforming the original polemic for a new cinema of *auteurs* into a critical method for evaluating films (mostly Hollywood films, some European art cinema) and creating a pantheon of 'best directors' which is still effective in

much film criticism today. It can be seen from many film courses (and from many cinema programmes) that the notion of the 'great director' is still important to the way cinema is learned and understood. Recognising the marks of 'greatness' can be a source of pleasure for some spectators watching the film, in the same way as recognising the elements of genre can be a source of pleasure as well as knowledge. These pleasures are used in the marketing of films to attract audiences by offering the possibility of using their specialist knowledge of cinema.

All too often the critical assault on authorship has refused to recognise the force of these pleasures, and the importance of taking them into account, finding itself in the impasse of a puritanical rejection. A historical approach helps us out of that impasse because it attempts to show how and why *auteur* theory emerged and was transformed, beginning the work of understanding different critical attitudes to cinema, the different pleasures we get from it, and how they change with history. Evaluative categories which are often assumed to be universal, such as the 'great director', or the 'good film' can be shown to be historically specific and open to debate.

In the last decade film theory has appropriated concepts from structural linguistics, semiology and psychoanalysis to question the underlying assumptions of *auteur* theory such as 'coherence', 'self-expression' and 'creativity'. These debates are by no means closed. The history of *auteur* theory itself makes it difficult to hold to established positions: it is hoped that the problems raised in the following pages will stimulate discussion of many different aspects of film study and invigorate the authorship debate itself.

Authorship in art cinema

Cinema as art or commodity?

Before the *politique des auteurs* emerged in France in the 1950s traditional film criticism (largely sociological) assumed that the industrial nature of film production prevented a single authorial voice making itself heard (or seen) in film. For some critics this meant that cinema could not be regarded as art: a commodity product at the service of the laws of the capitalist economy, it could do no more than reflect the ideology of the capitalist system. For others, cinema only achieved the status of art when a film or body of films could be seen as the expression of certain intentions carried out by an individual person, who was an artist by virtue of his or her struggle against the industrial system of production to attain control of that process of production in order to express his or her personal concerns. Few artists achieved this empirical control; Carl Dreyer is an example of a film director whose career can be seen to be defined by his uncompromising insistence on control of production: his status as one of the great artists of cinema resides as much in the intransigence of his position vis à vis the film industry as in the aesthetic quality of the relatively small number of films he was able to make (see Nash, 1977). Moreover, the 'butchering' of many of these films by 'uncomprehending' (commercially motivated) distributors is seen as further evidence of the fundamental antagonism between art, or the interests of the artist, and the interests of commodity production. The artist is conceived of as a solitary isolated figure struggling for creative autonomy against the interference of outside bodies.

The artist as creative source

The ideology which located the individual artist as the source of true creativity can be traced back to historical shifts which have radically changed the position of the artist in society. Before the Renaissance the artist was seen as a craftsman producing useful objects: God was the locus of creativity rather than man. When creativity was extended to painters and poets the divine gift of inspiration and genius was re-located in the artist, who was directly dependent upon the patronage of the ruling class. A division emerged between craftsman, or artisan who produced for consumption, and artist whose innate genius presented a potential challenge to the assumptions of the prevailing social order. However, the artist's autonomy was limited by his or her dependence upon the patronage of the ruling class.

The emergence of the capitalist com-

A Hitchcock hoarding – important in marketing

modity economy changed the traditional relationship of the artist to society from direct dependence upon the patronage of a clearly-defined group to indirect dependence on a large, anonymous group which was always expanding, i.e. the market. This shift produced a new conflict: on the one hand the artist was now 'free' to exploit the market to sell the results of his or her labour to the highest bidder; on the other hand the Romantic notion of 'artistic genius' resisted the forces of the market in the interests of artistic autonomy in opposition to 'commercial, socially conformist art' (see Murdock, 'Authorship and organisation', 1980).

In a capitalist economy art is a commodity subject to the laws of the market: the division between mass-produced culture and art proper merges with the distinction between craftsman and artist to marginalise the artist from society. Since artistic activity cannot be totally rationalised according to the laws of profitability governing commodity production, if it is to survive at all it can only do so through state intervention in the form of subsidies, in which case the artist is guaranteed a minority prestige status, subsidised by a society of which only a tiny part represents his or her audience. The minority status of art can be seen to perform a double function: to guarantee critical approval for those who control it (the subsidising agencies), and to provide a safe, licensed space for artistic activity, necessarily marginalised. This marginalisation effectively neutralises the potentially critical voice of the artist in society.

The practice of attributing cultural products back to the name of an individual artist performs an important function in the process of commodity production, ensuring that a product is marketed in a particular way, as 'art' rather than 'mass production', and consumed by a particular knowledgeable audience. In practice, however, the distinction is far from clear-cut: art is constantly appropriated by popular culture, and vice versa. Thus it could be argued that the status of any cultural product as art (or otherwise) depends less on its intrinsic aesthetic value, or indeed on any intrinsic property, than on the way it is taken up and exploited by the laws of the market.

The function of authorship in cinema

The distinction between 'art' and 'commercial product' has its own history within the history of cinema, and can be seen to perform different functions at different moments. In the early days of Hollywood, for instance, the enormous commercial potential of cinema was recognised, and the rush to exploit that potential meant that innovation and experiment were held at a premium. The early Hollywood industry was in a relatively open state, and copyright laws were minimal, so much pirating took place. The practice of marking a film with the logo of its production company grew up as a way of protecting the rights of the company over the film, but the logo could also function as a mark of authorship, and hence as a guarantee of artistic value. The artistic experiments which emerged from Hollywood in this period were greatly admired by Russian and European avant-garde film-makers. In Hollywood itself, the films were marketed as exceptional cinematic events: their status as art was part of their commodity value, and the mark of the presence of the 'artist' (Griffith's logo, Chaplin's 'Tramp' persona) performed a function in the marketing process. (← HISTORY: *Early film industry*, p. 6).

There is, however, a danger in reducing the concept of authorship to the status of a simple function (see Foucault, 'What is an author?' 1979). As the history of *auteur* study of cinema shows, the idea of author-

Chaplin's 'Tramp' persona in *Modern Times*

ship can be taken up in many different ways. It could be argued, for instance, that after the coming of sound the idea of film as art gave way in Hollywood to the idea of entertainment, although a place was reserved for prestige productions which were usually literary adaptations. In this case the creative source of the film was taken to be the writer of the original work rather than the director. As the strength of the major studios grew, producers and stars became more important in the marketing process than directors. At the time of the emergence of the *politique des auteurs*, then, the idea that a Hollywood film could be related back to the intentions of an individual director in the same way as it was in the case of films which fell into the category of art cinema, had an important polemical impetus. It attempted to break down the barrier between art cinema and commercial cinema by establishing the presence of artists in the apparently monolithic commodity production of Hollywood. Although the idea of the director as artist was prevalent in writing on art cinema, it was not important to writing on Hollywood at that time.

In the wake of *auteur* theory's polemic for popular cinema, and the anti-auterist politics which followed May 1968, art cinema has become unfashionable in film criticism. It has also declined in economic importance, and its distribution and exhibition is on the whole restricted to a small art house and film society circuit. Yet it is possible to argue that its importance and influence in some form or other on cinema in general is increasing rather than waning. It would be interesting to look at contemporary Eastern European cinema, for instance, or at New German cinema in terms of their relationship with art cinema. And New Hollywood cinema (e.g. Altman, Penn, Coppola) owes much to the erstwhile enemy of Hollywood, art cinema. Significantly, in some recent Hollywood cinema the director's name has once again become important in marketing: hoardings advertise 'Samuel Fuller's *The Big Red One*' and 'John Carpenter's *Hallowee'n*' alongside '*Don Giovanni*: a film by Joseph Losey' and '*Kagemusha*: an Akira Kurosawa film'. It could be argued that art cinema is suffering from critical neglect at a time when the division between art cinema and popular cinema is breaking down generally.

Authors in art cinema

Tracing the history of the emergence of art cinema after World War II, David Bordwell gives a cogent account of the ways in which art cinema differs from classic narrative cinema (Bordwell, 'The art cinema as a mode of film practice', 1979). He sees the loose narrative structure of art cinema as motivated by a desire for realism, i.e. an attempt to represent 'real' problems in 'real' locations, using psychologically complex characters to validate the drive towards verisimilitude: social, emotional and sexual problems are reflected in individual characters, and only become significant in so far as they impinge upon the sensitive individual.

This drive towards realism seems incompatible with the idea of a creative artist as source of meaning in art cinema: the artist's voice is intrusive and disrupts verisimilitude. Yet, Bordwell argues, art cinema specifically uses authorship to unify the film text, to organise it for the audience's comprehension in the absence of clearly identifiable stars and genres. Art cinema addresses its audience as one of knowledgeable cinemagoers who will recognise the characteristic stylistic touches of the author's oeuvre. The art film is intended to be read as the work of an expressive individual, and a small industry is devoted to informing viewers of particular authorial marks: career retrospectives, press reviews and television programmes all contribute to introducing viewers to authorial codes.

In art cinema, then, the informed, educated audience looks for the marks of authorship to make sense of the film rather than to the rambling story of the characters, who are often aimless victims rather than controlling agents. Audience identification shifts from characters to author: the audience is often given privileged information over the characters (e.g. the device of the 'flash forward') which strengthens identification with the author. Although apparently at odds with the realist project of art cinema, this controlling authorial discourse provides the final guarantee of 'truth' for the audience: if the realism of locations and character psychology represents the world 'as it is', the authorial discourse can be said to confirm the essential truth of the individual's experience of that world. This textual organisation differs from that of the 'classic realist text' (→ *Documentary*, p. 190; NARRATIVE AND STRUCTURALISM: *Classic realist text*, p. 242). However, the dominance of authorial discourse is by no means secure in art cinema – Bordwell sees the art film in terms of a shifting, uneasy relationship between the discourses of narrative, character and author. In this way art cinema maintains hesitation and ambiguity rather than the resolution of problems: the essential ambiguity of life reflected in art (→ HISTORY OF NARRATIVE: *Art cinema*, p. 216).

If, as Bordwell argues, art cinema can be established as a distinct mode, different from classic Hollywood or the modernist avant-garde, there are none the less interesting areas of overlap. Some 'classic' films (e.g. Sirk, Ford or Lang) display affinities with art cinema, and it is possible to argue that Hitchcock's films emphasise the narrational process and authorial discourse and problems of point-of-view in much the same way as the art film does. On the other hand, some modernist film-making has taken up and extended art cinema strategies beyond its own limits (Dreyer, Resnais, Straub/Huillet) and in some cases has begun to question it (Godard). One interesting way of approaching art cinema might be in terms of its relationship to, or difference from other modes of film-making. For instance, while it could be argued that contemporary Hollywood cinema owes much to art cinema, conditions of production are different in Hollywood, so that Hollywood art films represent a complex transformation of the codes of art cinema (see Neale, 'New Hollywood Cinema', 1976).

INGMAR BERGMAN

If, as Bordwell (1979) argues, one of the principles of art cinema that distinguishes it from classic narrative cinema is the marked presence of the author/artist as organising source of a film or group of films, so that the author becomes a kind of protagonist in the drama, a point of identification for the knowledgeable viewer, then it is possible to argue that traditional film criticism has responded to art cinema in its own terms, by supporting the relationship of complicity between artist/director and critic. The task of the critic is to be more knowledgeable than the ordinary, fairly knowledgeable viewer, to pass on his or her insights to this viewer on the assumption that s/he aspires to the privileged status of author and critic. This identity between author, critic and audience set up by traditional film criticism supports the circulation of art films as 'serious', 'intellectual' cinema, minority fare as opposed to mass entertainment.

It could be argued that the transformation of traditional *auteur* analysis of films since 1968 makes it difficult to take it seriously now. However, the name of the director-as-author is increasingly important in marketing film, and while theoretical film criticism may have abandoned straightforward *auteur* analysis, much of the criticism in 'quality' newspapers and film journals is still devoted to the idea of the director as artist. Since it seems that the function of the author/artist at one time limited to art cinema is extending to popular commercial cinema too, and the name-of-the-artist can perform the function of attracting a large, knowledgeable audience (rather than the minority audience of art cinema proper) for commercial cinema, then a study of art cinema in terms of authorship could offer useful information about the viewer's pleasure in recognising the marks of authorship in cinema in general. Art cinema could provide a means of critical entry into commercial cinema, not in terms of the confirmation of traditional *auteur* analysis, but in the interests of understanding the relationship between art cinema and commercial cinema in order to question the conventional division between 'art' and 'entertainment'.

In spite of the basic polemic of *auteur*

Isolation of the artist/victim in Bergman's *Sawdust and Tinsel*

theory in favour of popular cinema, Ingmar Bergman retained a place in the pantheons of *auteur* critics (see Wood, 1969), and many of the critics writing for *Cahiers du Cinéma* in the 1950s and 60s admired the formal strategies of art cinema. Its influence can be seen in the films of the *Nouvelle Vague* (French New Wave), and the films of Jean-Luc Godard, for example, show a shift away from the desire to explore the formal possibilities offered by art cinema to an interest in using the strategy of montage to criticise it. In Britain, *Movie* magazine included critical (but supportive) accounts of art films as well as Hollywood movies during the 1960s (see Cameron, '*About These Women*', 1972). However, these approaches tended to remove films and directors from their historical context in the interests of defending films as an art in its own right. A different approach is taken by Maria Bergom-Larsson in *Ingmar Bergman and Society* (1978). She writes from a position informed by a post-1968 awareness of the political and ideological function of cinema and film criticism, attempting to place Bergman historically in Swedish culture and ideology, and to read the films in terms of the director's preoccupation with the myths of his society. Although she retains the idea of the director as the organising source of his films, the emphasis on history and ideology enables her to break with the idea of the 'great artist' and to produce a convincing critique of Bergman's position which is illuminating for art cinema in general. She concentrates on ideological content rather than formal strategies, but her approach could usefully be combined with Bordwell's to discuss Bergman's films in the context of art cinema.

Maria Bergom-Larsson argues that the place of the artist in society has shifted radically from centre stage to the wings: serious critical art has lost its social function, artists cannot make a living from their work, and art is now increasingly subsidised by State intervention. Although taxes are paid by everyone, only a minority is in a position to enjoy art. The artist has two alternatives: to refuse the marginalised position allotted to artists and organise with other artists to make a political intervention into society; or to accept the futility of artistic production and continue to work entirely for his or her own sake, a retreat from politics into solipsism. By his own account, this last route is the one taken by Bergman, and many of his films take the predicament of the artist as their central theme. The consequences of this decision to adopt a position of isolated individualism are that the individual can only be seen as a victim of social forces: unable to play a positive role in society, s/he experiences social change as traumatic, a threat to emotional and psychological security. Many of Bergman's characters are shown to be caught in the conflict between the inner emotional world and the menacing outer world of society, often depicted in a state of violent upheaval. One of the most important aspects of social change has been in the area of sexuality and the family: the changing status of women is also regarded as a problem by Bergman, and provides the third major theme of his films, one that has been widely discussed by feminist film critics (see Steene, 'Bergman's portrait of women: Sexism or suggestive metaphor', 1979).

Sawdust and Tinsel (Sweden 1953 *p.c* – Sandrew Productions; *d* – Ingmar Bergman: sd b/w 15)

Bergman has used the metaphor of the circus to characterise the position of the artist in society as one of risk: the artist puts his or her life on the line for the chance amusement of others. In this film the clown, Frost, represents the suffering artist-victim, treated with derision by the uncomprehending spectators. Failure of communication between artist and audience emphasises the former's tragic isolation. In the extract, which is a story told in flashback, Frost is unable to communicate this anguish to his wife Alma, or to the audiences of soldiers.

Frost's humiliation has a sexual dimension: Alma's sexual antics for the benefit of the soldiers are depicted as a threat to his manhood. Not only is he unable to communicate his anguish, he is unable to control Alma or to rescue her from the humiliating situation. Only when he finally collapses in despair does Alma recognise his suffering and take up the position of anxious mother towards him. The depiction of woman-as-mother is a recurring image in Bergman's films and has been taken as a positive representation of woman by some critics.

In terms of art cinema, the flashback sets up an interesting relationship between cinema audiences and film. It is treated non-realistically, and the symbolic use of image and sound intensifies the tragedy of Frost's predicament, encouraging the cinema audience to identify with him rather than the uncomprehending audience of soldiers in the film: by responding to the 'expressive' use of film language in the flashback they are able, like the author of the film, to understand Frost's suffering. The flashback is introduced by the voice-over of one of the characters in the film, but it could be argued that Bergman's authorial 'voice' takes over the scene, marked in the 'expressive' *mise en scène*, and confirming identification between Frost, Bergman as artist, and the viewer.

The Seventh Seal (Sweden 1957 *p.c* – Svensk Filmindustri; *d* – Ingmar Bergman; sd b/w 10)

Bergman has commented that the increasing isolation of the artist in society was partly a result of the divorce of art from the Church (see Bergom-Larsson, 1978). When the artist was part of a creative collective and all art was in the service of God the artist had no need to question the function of art or his own place in the world; Truth was guaranteed. The modern artist, by contrast, has no guarantees, either of universal Truth or of his own place in the world: his life has been put at risk.

In the film the Knight and his Squire faced with a constant struggle with the figure of Death represent the doubters and searchers who have lost the security of their faith in God, and are consequently condemned to a precarious existence in a world where meaning can no longer be taken for granted. The strolling players, on the other hand, do not experience life as hostile; indeed, the jester and his family perform in the service of God and so succeed in escaping both the suffering of life and the cruelty of death. The jester's vision of the Virgin Mary is a source of joy rather than threat to him.

In terms of art cinema, the extract illustrates the preoccupation with myth and symbols which can be found in the work of several directors (for example, Fellini and Antonioni). Symbols perform several functions in art cinema: they indicate that the self-enclosed world of art is separate from the 'real' world; they present an element of difficulty to the art cinema audience, which is encouraged to think, to recognise and decode signs, rather than follow the narrative; and they maintain a level of unresolved ambiguity in the film, the principal strategy employed by art cinema to indicate that art cannot provide any final truths.

Wild Strawberries (Sweden 1957 *p.c* – Svensk Filmindustri; *d* – Ingmar Bergman; sd b/w 18)

A consistent theme in Bergman's work is that of the family (see also *The Seventh Seal*, 1957, and *The Silence*,

1963, and recent television work e.g. *Scenes from a Marriage*, 1974). The family is defined by Bergman as authoritarian and patriarchal, strictly dividing the roles of men and women so that men are confined to the public sphere of work, technology, intellect, etc., and women to the private sphere of family, pleasure, sexuality and emotion. Bergman sees this patriarchal family as dehumanising, particularly for men, and seems to offer a criticism of the family at one level (see Bergom-Larsson, 1978). He accepts, however, the place allotted to women and sees the values associated with femininity as more 'natural'. It is arguable that this leads to idealise the role of woman-as-mother, seeing it as both refuge and salvation for men dehumanised by patriarchy. The link between women and reproduction is crucial to Bergman's world-view, so that he sees social change in the area of sexuality (e.g. abortion) which might free women from their place in the family as problematic for men (e.g. *Persona*, 1966). The image of woman in Bergman's films is, it could be argued, the locus of male problems with sexuality, although some critics have responded to that image as a positive or progressive representation.

This film examines the effect of the patriarchal family on a father who has become successful in social terms as an eminent doctor. His success is only a mask, however, and the film sets out to reveal that behind the distorted mask lies a 'real human being' (cf. *Sawdust and Tinsel*, 1953).

The extract illustrates the flash-back dream device through which the truth about his life is revealed to the protagonist, Isak Borg. The use of flash-back and dream to represent subjective states of mind is characteristic of art cinema. In this film they function as an interruption into 'everyday reality': Borg's car journey to collect his accolades is presented as less important than his journey into the inner recesses of his mind. Truth is seen to reside in this inner, emotional world rather than in the public world.   →

...LLINI

...well (1979) has identified the ...neo-realist films as early exam-p... ...rnational art cinema. From this perspective the career of Fellini is particularly interesting, since it moves from a short period of collaboration with neo-realist directors like Roberto Rossellini and Alberto Lattuada, through their acknowledged influence in Fellini's early films, to be a fully-fledged, personal art cinema in which the basic principles of Neo-Realism are reversed.

When Fellini began directing films in 1950, the social and economic conditions which produced Italian Neo-Realism had already changed considerably. Neo-Realism had offered an 'objective' look at society at a time when anti-facist struggles were important in Italy (see Cannella, 'Ideology and aesthetic hypothesis', 1973/74). After the Second World War, with the break-up of the fascist dictatorship and improving economic conditions the social criticism and analysis of Neo-Realism gave way to a personal art cinema in which subjective states of mind were more important than objective social conditions. If Neo-Realism saw its characters in the context of society, art cinema sees society mediated through its characters, who are represented as individuals rather than social types. If the neo-realist director tried to be as inconspicuous as possible, allowing the material to speak for itself, the art cinema director inserts his or her own discourse between the audience and the subject matter of the film (← HISTORY: *Italian Neo-Realism*, p. 36; NARRATIVE AND STRUCTURALISM: *Bazin*, p. 224).

Fellini is often compared with Ingmar

Reminiscent of Chaplin's 'Tramp' persona – Gelsomina in Fellini's *La strada*

Bergman (see Rosenthal, 1976). Although the two directors share common themes, their treatment of them differs radically. Fellini's 'personal' cinema contains a strong autobiographical element; although Bergman can be seen to 'speak through' his characters he is never directly autobiographical. Fellini's films often take up a non-intellectual, even anti-intellectual position, whereas Bergman is concerned with the problematic position of intellectuals in society. If Fellini identifies with 'wise fools', the outcasts of society as offering insight and truth, Bergman identifies with the alienated intellectual, another kind of social outcast.

References
Maria Bergom-Larsson, *Ingmar Bergman and Society*, London, Tantivy/Swedish Film Institute, 1978.

David Bordwell, 'The art cinema as a mode of film practice', *Film Criticism* vol. 4 no. 1, 1979.

Ian Cameron, '*About These Women*', in *Movie Reader*, London, November Books, 1972, p. 100.

Mario Cannella, 'Ideology and aesthetic hypothesis in the criticism of Neo-Realism', *Screen* vol. 14 no. 4, Winter 1973/74.

Michel Foucault, 'What is an author?' *Screen* vol. 20 no. 1, Spring 1979.

Graham Murdock, 'Authorship and organisation', *Screen Education* 35, Summer 1980.

Mark Nash, *Dreyer*, London, British Film Institute, 1977.

Stephen Neale, 'New Hollywood cinema', *Screen* vol. 17 no. 2, Summer 1976.

Stuart Rosenthal, *The Cinema of Federico Fellini*, London, Tantivy Press, 1976.

Birgitta Steene, 'Bergman's portrait of women: sexism or suggestive metaphor', in Erens (ed.), *Sexual Stratagems: the world of women in films*, New York, Horizon Press, 1979.

INGMAR BERGMAN (*continued*)
The Silence (Sweden 1963 *p.c* – Svensk Filmindustri; *d* – Ingmar Bergman; sd b/w 12)

Bergman's ambiguous response to the breakdown of the patriarchal family can be seen in this film. The two sisters Anna and Ester are obsessed with the death of their father, which has cast them adrift. They respond to this in different ways; Anna exploits her active sexual desires, while Ester turns her aggression against herself. Both are depicted as perverse and doomed, condemned to a sterile existence in the midst of a society in a state of collapse. It is arguable that the isolation of the protagonists is represented as both necessary and self-destructive: the audience is offered two positions from which to judge events, one of acceptance of necessity, or one of moral disgust (art cinema's 'ambiguity').

The film was made at a time when political debate among Swedish intellectuals about Sweden's internal affairs, and about the United States' involvement in Vietnam was growing. By 1963 Bergman occupied a top

position within the Swedish cultural establishment and resisted as a 'political vogue' all criticism of that establishment (see Bergom-Larsson, 1978). His resistance to politics can be seen in *The Silence*: the two sisters remain remote from the political upheavals in the world outside as do most Bergman characters. On the other hand, the violence of the external world erupts in the inner world too, in the personal relationships and obsessions of the protagonists.

It has been argued that Bergman's representation of women changes in the films made after 1960. The woman-as-mother figure changes to an image of woman as anguished, tortured subject, taking over the role of the male protagonists in the earlier films. After 1960, Bergman begins to 'speak through' his female characters, offering them as a central point of identification for the audience, which has led some critics to see his later work as offering a progressive view of women as strong, and a shift from a male to a female perspective (see Steene, 1979).

FEDERICO FELLINI
La strada (Italy 1954 *p.c* – Ponti-De Laurentiis; *d* – Federico Fellini; sd b/w 9)

An echo of Neo-Realism can be seen in the subject matter of this film: the destruction of child-like innocence by a brutal and uncomprehending world. However, Fellini treats the subject entirely in terms of human relationships, so that the film is a celebration of lost innocence rather than a criticism of social attitudes.

The character of Gelsomina is reminiscent of Charlie Chaplin's 'Tramp' persona: potentially subversive, or at least critical of conventional society, it is offered as a point of identification for the audience, although the essential ambiguity of art cinema is maintained since both characters are represented as 'essentially human', and the audience is simply asked to recognise 'the human condition'.

Gelsomina is an outcast, a child-like innocent whose view of the world is untouched by adult cynicism. In a later →

For a new French cinema: the 'politique des auteurs'

The *politique* was signalled by Alexandre Astruc's 1948 article 'The birth of a new avant-garde: la caméra-stylo', calling for a new language of cinema in which the individual artist could express his or her thoughts, using the camera to *write* a world-view, a philosophy of life. Astruc was writing as a left-wing intellectual and film-maker in post-war France, where the extreme social fragmentation and isolation of the left after the war resulted in the need for reconstruction and stabilisation formulated in individual rather than political or collective terms. Furthermore, during the war the Americans had developed lightweight 16mm cameras which made possible film-making in small groups as opposed to the methods of studio production in Hollywood or France and this, combined with the growth of television, made the possibility of wider access to the means of production seem real and immediate. Moreover, after World War II French intellectuals and film-makers were able to see those Hollywood films which were previously unavailable at the Cinémathèque in Paris. Against this background of contradictory historical circumstances, the European intellectual tradition which saw the artist as a voice of dissent in society took on a polemical force in film criticism (see Buscombe, 'Ideas of authorship', 1973)

The film-makers and critics who subsequently wrote for *Cahiers du Cinema* were committed to questions of form and *mise en scène* and to the necessity for a theoretical analysis of the relationship of the artist and the film product to society, rather than to the untheorised political commitment of other journals of film criticism in France at the time, notably *Positif* (see Benayoun, 'Le roi est nu', 1962). So the *politique des auteurs* emerged in opposition not only to established French film criticism with its support for a 'quality' cinema of serious social themes, but also to the untheorised committed political criticism of the left, which ignored the contribution of individuals to the process of film production (see Truffaut, 'A certain tendency of the French cinema', 1976).

André Bazin

It is sometimes tempting to dismiss the *politique des auteurs* as a simple manifesto for individual personal expression, which is why it is important to understand the historical and political context (the upheaval of left-wing politics in the 1950s, the Cold War, anti-Stalinism) from which it emerged. It could be argued that these historical and political roots account for the ongoing debate around auteurism in film criticism through the 60s and up to the present day. It was the status of personal feelings within left-wing cultural struggle that was at stake in the early formulations of the *politique* in the pages of *Cahiers* and in its relationship to the film-making practice of the *Nouvelle Vague* (the French New Wave), and although this polemic was often lost in the process of appropriation, it remains relevant to present-day arguments in film theory (see Hess, 'World view as aesthetic', 1974).

Within *Cahiers* itself the debate about the *politique* was equally strong. The shift towards the film-maker/director as the organising source of meaning in the film was resisted by André Bazin, who believed that the film-maker should act as a passive recorder of the real world rather than manipulator of it – a contradictory position, given his admiration for Hollywood directors such as Orson Welles and Alfred Hitchcock. There were political implications in the disagreement: Bazin's notion of society as based on the interdependence of individuals and social forces was at odds with the idea of a society of conflict and opposition espoused by many of *Cahiers'* younger writers. At the same time Bazin criticised the notion that a body of work could be ascribed to an individual *auteur* as though the individual was not part of society and history, subject to social and historical constraints (see Bazin, 'La politique des auteurs', 1968). Bazin argued for a sociological approach to film which would take into account the historical moment of production. However, when it came to his own analysis of the work and directors he thought important, his position often led him into a critical impasse (→ NARRATIVE AND STRUCTURALISM: *Bazin*, p. 224).

Bazin's criticism of the *politique* was perceptive: the evaluation of films according to the criterion of the 'great director' who transcended history and ideology was the least productive aspect of the *politique des auteurs*, together with the importance given to the critic's personal taste that went with it.

'Auteurs' *vs.* 'metteurs en scène'

Closely linked to this discussion about the

---

film, *Giulietta degli spiriti* (1965), Giulietta Masina plays a similar role as a naive housewife whose personal vision of the world, expressed in fantasy, dominates the film and acts as a criticism of a corrupt and sterile society. The image of woman as a potential critical force in this film bears comparison with that in Ingmar Bergman's films.

In terms of art cinema, the protagonists of *La strada* are aimless: no one knows where 'the road' leads. This is illustrated in the extract by Gelsomina's apparently positive decision to leave Zampanò and go home. As soon as the small band appears, however, she arbitrarily decides to follow them.

Otto e mezzo (8½) (Italy 1962/63 *p.c* – Cineriz; *d* – Federico Fellini; sd b/w 14)

The film which marks Fellini's movement into an autobiographical cinema in which his own fantasies and childhood memories are explicitly worked through. The film is presented through the eyes of its central male character, Guido, a film director, who has been taken to represent Fellini himself. The film might be said to entirely express the point-of-view of its author, with whom the audience is asked to identify. It could be compared with *Giulietta degli spiriti*, in which, it has been argued (Bordwell, 1979), Fellini's authorial discourse is displaced by the fantasies of the central female protagonist.

Guido might also be taken to represent the 'artist-victim', a recurring figure in Ingmar Bergman's work also. Whereas he is entirely at the mercy of his subjective obsessions however, the artist-victim in Bergman's films suffers because of his relationship, albeit alienated, from society. Guido bears some resemblance to Isak Borg in *Wild Strawberries*: his success is a mask which hides his inner inadequacy.

Guido's inadequacy is manifested on one level in sexual impotence, and in his relationship to women in general. It is arguable that Fellini's use of surrealism and fantasy enables the audience to take a distance on Guido's obsessions and criticise them, and, by implication, the social forces that give rise to them (e.g. the Catholic family). A question would be whether these formal strategies, characteristic of art cinema, invite the audience to think about the films, or encourage it to accept their underlying preconceptions.

status of the individual artist in artistic production was the distinction the *auteur* critics made between an *auteur* and a *metteur en scène* (→ p. 126). The idea of *mise en scène* (the staging of the real world for the camera) was central to the interest in form and cinematic language that many *Cahiers* critics shared, but their notion of the individual artist as primary source of meaning in film led them to make a distinction between those directors who simply directed (who had mastered the language of cinema) and those who were true *auteurs*, in the sense that they put forward a coherent world-view in their films and manifested a uniquely individual style. Again Bazin differed: a film's *mise en scène* should efface individual style to allow the inner meaning to shine through naturally so that the spectator could come to his or her own conclusions without being manipulated (→ NARRATIVE AND STRUC-TURALISM: *Bazin*, p. 224). Bazin's emphasis on the transparency of cinematic language was at odds with many *Cahiers* critics' interest in the possibility of manipulating the language of cinema to express the director's personal concerns. Bazin's argument comes close to eliminating human intervention in the process of production altogether (see Wollen, '"Ontology" and "Materialism" in film', 1976).

This defence of formalism against notions of transparency (film as window-on-the-world) and realism (film expressing the truth of reality) remained important to the *Cahiers* critics even through the reassessments that took place in that journal during the 1960s under the impact of structuralist theory (→ NARRATIVE AND STRUC-TURALISM: *Introduction*, p. 222). The structuralist attack on humanism and personal expression was to have major repercussions for the *politique* and for the centrality of the individual artist within it. None the less, the basic argument that the director of a film should be considered an important source of meaning in that film remains relevant to debate in film studies, though the terms of the debates have changed.

Politique des auteurs: style and theme

JEAN RENOIR

Renoir's film-making career spanned more than 40 years; he worked in many different production situations and is now considered one of the great film-artists, whose films display a consistency of cinematic style and thematic concerns which remain constant through the years. He was a major influence on New Wave film-makers (e.g. François Truffaut) and a favourite *auteur* of André Bazin because of his subtle use of *mise en scène*, a style based on absence of montage, deep-focus photography and fluid camera movement, exemplifying the transparency of style which Bazin argued could most effectively reveal the essence of the real world for the spectator. Equally, Renoir's humanist view of

'Natural man . . . flouts polite conventions' in Renoirs *Boudu sauvé des eaux*

Boudu sauvé des eaux (France 1932 *p.c* – Michel Simon/Jean Gehret; *d* – Jean Renoir; sd b/w 11)

Renoir's consistent interest in the idea of 'natural man' is manifest here in the person of Boudu, who flouts polite conventions and is restless and disruptive within the bourgeois milieu of the man who saves him from drowning. This concern with the positive anti-social values of the anarchic outsider can be traced as a theme throughout Renoir's work, but since this film was made in the 1930s during his involvement with left-wing politics, it is equally relevant to place this concern within the context of French cinema of the time and to take into account the collaboration between Renoir and Michel Simon (Boudu). Simon co-produced the film under the banner of his own production company, while Renoir wrote and directed. The character of Boudu, the anarchic renegade in opposition to petit-bourgeois values is in many ways a vehicle for Simon who was often associated with such roles (e.g. in Jean Vigo's *L'Atalante*, 1934).

In terms of Renoir's characteristic *mise en scène* the film uses deep-focus photography and moving camera to indicate a coherent space which the camera reveals, disclosing people and objects as if by accident. Bazin saw Renoir's use of camera movement to integrate actors and space as exemplary of a style which captures reality for the spectator, the camera acting as an 'invisible guest' at the scene to be filmed.

Le Crime de Monsieur Lange (France 1935 *p.c* – Oberon; *d* – Jean Renoir; sd b/w 12)

A film made directly out of Renoir's

political commitment to the Popular Front and its ideas of the unity between white-collar and labouring workers against capitalist businessmen and employers. The idea of unity in a common cause, here represented by the workers' co-operative, is central to much of Renoir's work, whether that cause be war (*La Grande illusion*), art (*French Can-Can*), or social change as in the case of this film. Contradictions arise and are resolved by group solidarity and mutual caring, but the continued existence of the problem boss Batala, can only be resolved by extreme and violent action. Lange must become a hero (like Arizona Jim) and kill the villain, placing himself outside the law for ever. It could be argued that a dark note of irony overshadows the 'happy ending'. Lange sacrifices himself (and Valentine) for the co-operative, and finally a group of workmen help them to escape. The co-operative survives at the expense of individual sacrifice.

In terms of *mise en scène*, Renoir characteristically creates a coherent and identifiable space, centred on the courtyard where all communal discussion and action take place. Individual workers move between the courtyard and their work-places in the block, and the fluidity of movement of the actors between on-screen and off-screen space, combined with a naturalistic use of sound makes the interaction between individuals and group and the sense of solidarity especially convincing. However, the 'Arizona Jim' sub-plot, with its emphasis on fiction and fantasy, seems to work against the realism of Renoir's style, thus complicating the overall meaning of the film and its endorsement of Popular Front ideology.

the world expressed in the way he integrated actors with objects and space coincided with Bazin's interest in the way cinema could be used to express the relationship between individuals and society as one of mutual interdependence (see Bazin, 1971).

While these stylistic and thematic concerns can certainly be seen in Renoir's work, it is also evident that history (the 30s Popular Front in *Le Crime de Monsieur Lange*, the impending Second World War in *La Grande illusion*) and different production situations (the American Renoir) also had an impact on the films and, it could be argued, should be taken into account in any study of Renoir as an *auteur*. While *auteur* study sometimes allows us to understand films better by detecting the director's concerns over a body of work, it should not obscure questions of history and ideology as equally important determining factors, not only on the films but on the way we read them.

La Grande illusion – Renoir's concern with class differences

La Grande illusion (France 1937 *p.c* – Réalisations d'Art Cinématographique; *d* – Jean Renoir; sd b/w 11)

The context of war is used to work through Renoir's concern with class and racial differences and human affinities. The aristocrat, the bourgeois, the intellectual and the 'common man' have different attitudes and manners. War is said to make them all equal, but the French aristocrat de Boeldieu has more in common with von Rauffenstein, his German enemy, than with his fellow Frenchmen. His solidarity with them is based on patriotism and a 'gentlemanly' sense of generosity which causes him to sacrifice himself so that they may escape successfully. Renoir's sympathy for the aristocrats and their doomed way of life is evident in his treatment of their relationship in the extract: a characteristic humanism. Yet it is arguable that the scene appears contradictory, undermining humanism by putting blatantly fascist remarks in the mouth of von Rauffenstein, and raising the question of how far sympathy for individual human beings can be maintained when the primary struggle is against fascism. The idea of 'unity in a common cause' is more complex and contradictory here than in *Le Crime de Monsieur Lange*, manifested in the differences between characters and a greater fragmentation of space. However, Renoir's *mise en scène*, the use of deep-focus, long takes and sideways and panning shots, can be seen as realistic, depicting a world fragmented by war into which death, loss and fear are constantly erupting. This *mise en scène* seems to endorse the film's central pacifist theme, emerging from the policies of the Popular Front at the time.

La Règle du jeu (France 1938 *p.c* – La Nouvelle Edition Française; *d* – Jean Renoir; sd b/w 9 + 10)

A further exploration of social differences, this time in the context of a house party where the love-intrigues of high-society guests are mirrored by parallel activities among the servants. An extremely complex film in which contradictions are raised and left unresolved. Renoir uses the theatrical conventions of farce to explore the extent to which personal relationships, and by extension social structures, are based on pretence, accident and misunderstanding. The idea of 'social cohesion' is brought into question as it becomes clear that social unity is illusory, based on an acceptance of deceit.

If the stability of the status quo is based on illusion and deceit, who has the greatest vested interest in maintaining the illusion? The upper classes, evidently; but they cannot totally control events, much as they try. A servant's sexual jealousy can cause chaos in the system. The film reflects Renoir's growing concern with the opposition art (artifice) vs. life (reality), and the overlapping of the two. In terms of his relationship with the Popular Front, he has returned to his bourgeois roots in the subject matter of his film, but his treatment of the theme is lucid and detached. Extract 1 shows the hunt as a metaphor for the exploitative power of the upper classes. The apparent naturalism of the *mise en scène* is offset by the incident in which the Marquise sees her husband and his mistress through binoculars, and misreads what she sees. The audience knows what is happening, the Marquise misreads the scene because of her subjective position.

This disjuncture between objectivity and subjectivity shows Renoir's awareness that appearances are deceptive. The misunderstanding shown in Extract 1 eventually leads to the chaotic chase and conflict depicted in Extract 2, in which conflict of interests is paramount and pretence is seriously disturbed. The question remains: does Renoir's humanism, his concern for each of his characters and their vested interests, obscure the serious social questions about class differences that the film raises?

Renoir's interest in theatrical conventions, and in acting, relevant to all his work, is particularly important in this film, where it becomes part of the thematic structure.

This Land is Mine (USA 1943 *p.c* – RKO Radio; *d* – Jean Renoir; sd b/w 15)

Made during Renoir's period in the US, he co-wrote, co-produced and directed this film under the auspices of RKO, who also provided the facilities for Welles and *Citizen Kane*. We can assume that Renoir had considerable artistic control, although it is interesting to see how the context of a Hollywood studio production and actors affected the film, which looks quite different from his earlier work.

Nevertheless the theme is familiar: a community divided by war, misunderstandings and deception. The demands of Hollywood narrative can be seen in the use of a central character through whose maturing consciousness the problems are resolved, and a touch of American Freudianism can be discerned in the relationship between Albert and his possessive mother. The studio sets look strangely constricting in relation to the characters compared with

→

Today's viewers, used to the static realism of television programmes, may find Renoir's *mise en scène* excessive, even melodramatic.

Renoir made over 35 films between 1924 and 1961. Any serious attempt to approach his work as an *auteur* would need to look carefully at as many of these films as possible. His work is used here to discuss one aspect of the *politique des auteurs*: the use of the name *Jean Renoir* as a means of classifying and evaluating films according to the assumed presence of a consistent personal vision or world-view. This auteurist approach could be questioned by a consideration of Renoir's work in the context of the 1930s Popular Front, which affected a whole generation of French film-workers, and the different production conditions he met in America (see Fofi, 'The cinema of the Popular Front in France, 1934–38', 1972/73; Rivette and Truffaut, 'Renoir in America', 1954).

French Can-Can – homage to the French Impressionist painters

the real locations used in previous extracts. How then do these factors: the use of stars as central protagonists, the psychological realism of the Hollywood narrative, the conditions of studio production, combine to affect the place of this film within the 'Renoir oeuvre' constructed by *auteur* study? The theme of war, collaboration and resistance is characteristic, but the director's point-of-view may have been affected by different conditions of production. Renoir was criticised for his attempt to make a propaganda film about the Nazi occupation which gave a less blatantly heroic view of occupied France.

The Woman on the Beach (USA 1947 RKO Radio: *d* – Jean Renoir; *p.c* – sd b/w 22)

Another example of Renoir's American work, again for RKO. The film is almost entirely dominated by the requirements of the film noir genre as it developed in post-war USA. In contrast with earlier extracts, the narrative problems are here internalised in terms of individual psychology, projected against a dream-like expressionist set. The film seems most relevant to later Renoir, with its theme of solitude and formalised *mise en scène*.

'It was a story quite opposed to everything I had hitherto attempted. In all my previous films I had tried to depict the bonds uniting the individual to his background. The older I grew, the more I had proclaimed the consoling truth that the world is one; and now I was embarked on a study of persons whose sole idea was to close the door on the absolutely concrete phenomena which we call life . . .' (Renoir, 1974).

How then was Renoir's perspective changed by the experience of working in post-war America? Certainly the

expressive use of montage, and fragmentation of space would not have found approval from Bazin. When seen as a transition to later Renoir, as *auteur* study prescribes, it seems less strange. But despite Renoir's words above claiming his own point-of-view is expressed in the film, the conditions of Hollywood production, and the generic conventions of film noir could be said to have as much claim on the final product as Renoir's authorial 'voice'.

French Can-Can (France/Italy 1955 *p.c* – Franco London Film/Jolly Film; *d* – Jean Renoir; sd col 16)

Made after his return to Europe, an example of mature Renoir in which the relationship between art (artifice) and reality (life) is developed and explored. Although the film pays homage to the Impressionist painters and the popular theatre of turn-of-century France in its use of colour photography, music and spectacle, it is pessimistic about the potential of art to change anything. Dangland's belief in the importance of the Can-Can as art has the quality of an obsession imposed as a repressive discipline on the girls he employs, whom he also exploits. Since he labours under such extreme financial difficulties and is always on the verge of bankruptcy and imprisonment, his involvement with the theatre seems perverse, and his final exhortation to Nini that the artist must dedicate himself *totally* to his/her art seems to be an argument for 'art for art's sake'. This cynical view of the relationship between art and life contrasts sharply with earlier films such as *Le Crime de Monsieur Lange*, and the use of a single central character (Dangland) as a focus for identification tends to obscure contradictions arising from the subject matter (such as that

between the pleasurable aspects of the Can-Can as spectacle, and the repression/distortion/exploitation of the female body on which it depends).

Le Caporal épinglé (The Vanishing Corporal) (France 1961 *p.c* – Films du Cyclope; *d* – Jean Renoir; sd b/w 15)

Interesting to compare with *La Grande illusion*. Thematically it has many of the same preoccupations. But whereas in *La Grand illusion* the struggle against fascism is given real importance, in this film the urge to escape, the concern with 'freedom', is seen as a human obsession, a perversity in the face of the obvious advantages in staying in prison, opting out of the struggle.

Human perversity is shown in this scene from the end of the film: the sombre funeral procession which the escapers join appears bizarre in the context of war which values life so cheaply, and in the train the over-friendliness of the drunken German to the Frenchmen makes a mockery of human relationships, and threatens their safety. The Corporal and his friend admire the trouble-free life of the peasant couple, yet they themselves are perversely driven to return to Paris and give up the comradeship that the war has provided, each going their separate ways. The comic emphasis and use of sentimentalised characters barely obscures the implications that human impulses exist in their own right, irrespective of social realities. The will to escape takes on the aspect of a childish game, and at the end of the film the question remains – what is there left to fight for? Considered in the context of Renoir's earlier films made with the Popular Front, the question takes on added poignancy.

FRITZ LANG

It is possible, as we have shown in the case of Renoir, to see an author's work as a whole in terms of a linear development of themes and style (e.g. from early Renoir to mature Renoir, although critical opinion may differ on the relative merits of 'early' or 'late'). Thus Renoir falls into the category of the *auteur* as artist in critical writing about his work, a view which is supported to a great extent by the concerns of that work and his own pronoucements on it. From this perspective, the artist/*auteur* is the sole source of meaning, transcending history, both in terms of conditions of production and the conditions in which the film is seen by different audiences.

The career of Fritz Lang is similar to Renoir's in many ways: he worked as scriptwriter and director in the German film industry in the 1920s and 1930s, leaving to go to Hollywood in 1935, where he

Expressionism in the geometric *mise en scène* of Lang's *Metropolis*

Destiny (Der müde Tod) (Germany 1921 *p.c* – Decla-Bioscop; *d* – Fritz Lang; st b/w 20)

Lang's first major film as a director, and an example of his use of Expressionist motifs, such as the obsession with allegory and myth as a framework for representing individuals overpowered and destroyed by the repressive forces of a hostile world. The extract shows the Expressionist *mise en scène* which creates an enclosed imaginary world in which human figures are overpowered by the huge sets (Petley, 1978). However, the film is not totally pessimistic about the fate of individuals. If human desire ultimately cannot prevail against Destiny, here represented by Death, it is nonetheless shown to be entirely motivated by the need to resist such a cruel and inevitable fate.

Dr. Mabuse der Spieler: I – Der grosse Spieler/Ein Bild der Zeit (Germany 1921 *p.c* – Ullstein-Uco Film/Decla-Bioscop/ Ufa; *d* – Fritz Lang; st b/w 10 + 10)

Lang began his career by writing scripts for detective films and never lost his interest in this genre as a medium for expressing a critical view of society. Expressionist art is full of representation of evil, supernatural figures who attempt to control events but are ultimately controlled by them, and Mabuse is one of these. But the film does not entirely condemn him: the police are also subject to the movement of events, and while Mabuse and the policeman von Wenk struggle against each other they are both at the mercy of a hostile world. Thus it could be argued that Lang attempts to create a position for the spectator from which to criticise the social system which produces such manipulative monsters.

Extract 1 shows Mabuse's manipulation of the Stock Exchange illustrating one aspect of his exploitation of the laws of capitalism. This exploitation is then directly linked to his manipulation of 'the look' in the theatrical spectacle: the audience in the night-club is fascinated by Carozza's performance, and this enables Mabuse to pick out his victim Hull with his binoculars. The scene seems to provide a commentary on the erotic fascination with looking, so important to pleasure in the cinema (see Jenkins, 1981).

Dr. Mabuse der Spieler: II – Inferno Ein Spiel von Menschen unserer Zeit (Germany 1921 *p.c* – Ullstein-Uco Film/ Decla-Bioscop/Ufa; *d* – Fritz Lang; st b/w 13)

Characteristically, the power-crazed Dr. Mabuse tries to control the destiny of others, here by using disguise and hypnosis to lead his enemy Inspector von Wenk to his death. *Dr. Mabuse* can be seen as an early example of a theme central to all Lang's work: the danger of trusting appearances. However, Mabuse's apparently supernatural powers do not make him omnipotent: his attempt to kill von Wenk is foiled, indicating that he is as much at the mercy of events as his victims. Mabuse's fantasies of himself as superman finally brings about his destruction.

Die Nibelungen: II – Kriemhilds Rache (Germany 1923–24 *p.c* – Decla-Bioscop/ Ufa; *d* – Fritz Lang; st b/w 20)

Die Nibelungen is a film based on the orginal saga, which describes the destiny of the hero Siegfried. The form of the legend allows Lang to explore his concern with the individual pitted against Fate, but in Part II the innocent Siegfried is replaced as protagonist by

his revengeful widow Kriemhild, whose destructive obsession brings about chaos, manifested in the *mise en scène* by a tension between geometric composition and the fluid movement of actors within the frame. Kriemhild's unnatural rigidity and manic gaze emphasise her transformation into the manupulative monster who is ultimately defeated by her obsession. It is possible to see her as a forerunner of the American Lang's femmes fatales · women as destructive and violent erotic forces created by a violent male-dominated society.

Metropolis (Germany 1926 *p.c* – Ufa; *d* – Fritz Lang; st b/w 15, 13 + 10)

Expressionism is usually seen as an artistic movement arising out of the economic reconstruction of Germany after the First World War. A so-called 'agrarian mysticism' was manifested in a revulsion against city life and the dehumanising exploitation of technology by capital. While it would be wrong to characterise this idealism as proto-fascist, certainly the Expressionist emphasis on the irrational and the primitive could in some cases seem like a retreat into mysticism (see Petley, 1978). It is interesting here to compare Expressionism with Futurism, which saw itself as a revolutionary modernist movement committed to the enormous potential for social change offered by technological advances. Somewhere between the humanism of Expressionism and the anti-humanism of Futurism lies *Metropolis*: a criticism of the manipulative capitalist system which both oppresses the people and transforms them into a monstrous destructive power. The irrational resurgence of the masses is not entirely endorsed by the film however: rather →

The 'Kammerspiel' film – a new psychological realism in Lang's *M*

had a prolific career except for a brief period of blacklisting in the 1950s (see Bogdanovich, 1968, p. 83). His work is generally divided by critics into 'early' and 'late', German and American, and critical opinion differs as to the relative merits of each.

In discussion of the *politique des auteurs*, Lang's work is interesting because it demonstrates how authorship can be traced across apparently totally different sets of films, such as German and American Lang, to confer the status of art on commercial cinema. Lang's American films have been described as artistically inferior to those he made in Germany. *Cahiers du Cinéma* (e.g. no. 99, 1959) was interested primarily in Lang's American work as part of their polemic for a reassessment of American cinema in general, and they were responsible for rescuing Lang's American films from the dismissive category of routine commercial production to which they had been relegated, tracing a consistent world-view through them, and a consistent use of Expressionist *mise en scène* which had its roots in the German films.

There are problems with locating a director's work so firmly within a particular artistic movement like German Expressionism. Firstly, the use of a term borrowed from painting tends to locate the film as art rather than commodity production, endorsing the notion of self-expression and obscuring the numerous processes involved in producing a film (see Petley, 1978). Secondly, the term 'Expressionist' can be used to cover such a variety

they are seen as victims of a manipulative system, and the destruction of the machines by the workers does not bring about the destruction of that system itself (see Kracauer, 1947). The re-introduction of a formalised geometric *mise en scène*, broken up during the scenes of revolution, testifies to the re-establishment of order. Beneath this final resolution lies a question: 'But who now holds the power?' It is arguable that the abstract expressionist *mise en scène* allows this critical space to open up: it represents social structures topographically, so that each of the characters is seen to inhabit an ideological position rather than appear as a coherent psychological entity. The final resolution could be seen as ironic rather than positive, offering the audience the possibility of a critical perspective (see Johnstone, 1977).

M (Germany 1931 *p.c* – Nero Films; *d* – Fritz Lang; sd b/w 16)

This film marks an aesthetic turning-point in Lang's work, which can be placed historically. The post-war boom in which Expressionism had flourished

came to an end, and a new psychological realism emerged in the 'Kammerspiel' film, supported by the introduction of sound which made it possible for individual psychology to be represented through characters' speech. The fragmentation of society came to be reflected in the tormented individual psyche. 'M', like the protagonist's of Lang's later American films, is a victim of the tension between his desires and a hostile, destructive environment.

The world is divided between two organisations: the police and the criminals. 'Normality' is the state of uneasy equilibrium between them which is disturbed by the irrationality of the child-murderer, and which must be restored at all costs. When 'M' defends himself in a long speech which has little effect on criminals or police, we are made aware of the limitations of a so-called rational society which relies on repression to maintain normality. 'M''s challenge to society takes the form of an individualistic struggle against his fate: in Lang's view such a struggle can reveal the mechanisms of the system, but it can never defeat it. It is the individual who is ultimately defeated, and the rational,

hierarchical organisation which survives. Yet it is arguable that this makes clear that the underside of normality is a destructive drive which allows its victim no pity and will tolerate no questioning. In arousing the spectator's compassion for 'M', Lang also makes it possible to criticise the structures upon which normal society rests. Another argument suggests that Lang sees an alternative to the individual's self-defeating struggle in the organisation of the community into social action (see Lusted, 1979).

Rancho Notorious (USA 1952 *p.c* – Fidelity Pictures/ RKO Radio; *d* – Fritz Lang; sd col 20)

Lang's career in Hollywood began c.1935 when he fled from an offer by Goebbels to become Head of the German film industy. He seems to have had less freedom in the Hollywood studio system than in Germany, and suffered some interference in his projects. His Expressionist style and interest in the psychological thriller format were well-suited to the studio system, and in general he collaborated on scripts and controlled the sets for his

Rancho Notorious – in which Lang uses 'Brechtian' distancing strategies

of formal practices of film-making that it becomes meaningless. However, the value of placing Lang's work historically within German Expressionism is that as an author he can be shown to be working within a specific historical and cultural moment (see Johnston, 1977). Also, Expressionism itself is generally regarded as a movement which arose quite directly out of social change in Europe at the turn of the century: Expressionist artists attempted to express this changing, fragmented world and the alienated place of the individual within it. In Germany Lang used Expressionism to explore his interest in social criticism, an interest which can be directly related to an historical moment. However, the 'modernist' momentum behind the German Expressionist movement and the artistic experiments which flourished in the post-war boom of the early 1920s in Germany cannot be directly mapped onto Lang's work in Hollywood. Rather, his American films show the way in which a director's social and artistic concerns are transformed by different production contexts (← HISTORY: *German Expressionism*, p. 32).

References

Alexandre Astruc, 'The birth of a new avant-garde: la caméra-stylo', *Ecran Français* no. 144, 1948, trans. in Peter Graham (ed.), *The New Wave*, London, Secker and Warburg/BFI, 1968.
André Bazin, 'La politique des auteurs', *Cahiers du Cinéma* no. 70, April 1957, trans. in Peter Graham (ed.), *The New Wave*, cit.
André Bazin, *Jean Renoir*, Paris, Editions Champ Libre, 1971.
Robert Benayoun, 'Le roi est nu', *Positif* no. 46, June 1962.
Peter Bogdanovich, *Fritz Lang in America*, London, Studio Vista, 1968.
Edward Buscombe, 'Ideas of authorship', *Screen* vol. 14 no. 3, Autumn 1973.
Cahiers du Cinéma no. 99, September 1959. Special issue on Fritz Lang.
Goffredo Fofi, 'The cinema of the Popular Front in France, 1934–38', *Screen* vol. 13 no. 4, Winter 1972/73.
John Hess, 'World view as aesthetic', *Jump Cut* no. 1, May/June 1974; no. 2, July/August 1974.
Steve Jenkins (ed.) *Fritz Lang: the image and the look*, London, British Film Institute, 1981.
Claire Johnston, *Study Unit 10: Fritz Lang*, London, BFI Education Dept., January 1969, revised 1977.
Siegfried Kracauer, *From Caligari to Hitler: a psychological history of the German film*, Princeton, Princeton University Press, 1947.
David Lusted, *Study notes for the slide set from 'The Big Heat'*, London, BFI Education Dept., June 1979.
Julian Petley, *British Film Institute Distribution Library Catalogue 1978*, London, BFI, 1978.
Jean Renoir, *My Life and my Films*, London, Collins, 1974; trans. Norman Denny.
Jacques Rivette and François Truffaut, 'Renoir in America', *Sight and Sound* vol. 24 no. 1, July/September 1954.
François Truffaut, 'A certain tendency of the French cinema', *Cahiers du Cinéma* no. 31, January 1954, trans. in Bill Nichols (ed.), *Movies and Methods*, Berkeley, University of California Press, 1976.
Peter Wollen, '"Ontology" and "Materialism" in film', *Screen* vol. 17 no. 1, Spring 1976.

films. None the less, his interest in social criticism and formal experiment (he was much influenced by Bertolt Brecht, with whom he collaborated on *Hangmen Also Die*, 1943) had to come to terms with the demands of genre, and although the political climate of America in the 1930s and early 40s was reasonably sympathetic to these interests, in the 1950s Lang found himself blacklisted for a short period.

Rancho Notorious can be seen as an example of the intersection of these conflicting interests. The film was a re-working of the Western revenge genre in terms of 'Brechtian' strategies, (i.e. fragmented episodic narrative, use of songs to break into the story-line) all intended to distance the audience from the spectacle. Completely recut by the studio, much of the film's self-reflexiveness became subservient to the demands of narrative and the psychology of the vengeful hero. Yet the extract shows Lang's interests breaking through: the hero is a detective figure following a trail of clues; obsessed with revenge, he is transformed into a monster with a manic stare; Marlene Dietrich as femme fatale foregrounds the obsessional nature of the masculine desire that creates her as fetish-object; and the abstract, stylised *mise en scène* recalls Lang's Expressionist beginnings.

The Big Heat (USA 1953 *p.c* – Columbia; *d* – Fritz Lang; sd b/w 13)

Made during a difficult period in Lang's American career, this film is primarily a genre piece: a police thriller. However, it is clear that Lang's interests coincided very well with the genre. Bannion is fighting the racketeers who control the city administration, he becomes obsessed with revenge after his wife's death, and becomes involved in the corrupt and destructive underworld with its deformed and distorted figures (the femme fatale is one of these products of a diseased world). As with all Lang's American films, the question remains whether his view of the individual's struggle with society is pessimistic, or whether he sees a way out of the impasse in organised community action (see Lusted, 1979).

Beyond a Reasonable Doubt (USA 1956 *p.c* – RKO Radio; *d* – Fritz Lang; sd b/w 15)

Lang's last film in America, sometimes thought to be the most definitive statement of his preoccupations. The hero, Tom Garrett, becomes caught between two opposing organisations: the opponents of capital punishment, and the law. He attempts to manipulate one on behalf of the other, becoming obsessively caught up in the masquerade and his wish to beat the system. The result is a schematic, abstract film in which, it can be argued, identification with the characters is impossible: instead the spectator comes to recognise the inhumanity of a system reflected in the increasing inhuman obsessions of the central protagonist. The abstraction of the geometric compositions, the minimal schematic narrative, all combine to produce a bleak criticism of a ruthless, hostile society which can be pushed to its limits but never overcome, except, perhaps, by organised community action. Interestingly again, the world of the burlesque and its exploitation of women's bodies provides one important aspect of Lang's social criticism.

The politique des auteurs: 'auteurs' and 'metteurs en scène'

The distinction between *auteur* and *metteur en scène* introduced by *Cahiers* critics was intended to support the idea of a cinema of personal vision, defined in terms of the presence of a true *auteur*. Like much of the polemic behind the *politique*, it drew attention to significant factors which had not been considered before, and raised questions which are still unresolved in film criticism.

The term *mise en scène* refers to the staging of events for the camera, but can also be used loosely to mean the formal organisation of the finished film, the 'style' in which the film-maker expresses his or her personal concerns. Sometimes the film-maker masters the *mise en scène* competently, but the overall meaning expressed is not his or her own, in which case s/he qualifies as a *metteur en scène* rather than a true *auteur*. In *auteur* study these criteria provide one way of evaluating 'good' and 'bad' films, and 'good' and 'bad' directors.

The distinction *auteur/metteur en scène* led to some unfortunate evaluations by film critics, and to some critical pantheons which would not hold up today (→ *The auteur theory*, p. 137). It had its roots in the historical division between 'art' and 'entertainment' (← *Art cinema*, p. 114) which had previously prevented cinema from being taken seriously. Part of the 'scandal' created by the *politique* was caused by its application of such criteria to popular American cinema, generally thought of as mass entertainment reproducing dominant ideology and incompatible with the interests of art.

ALFRED HITCHCOCK

For the *Cahiers auteur* critics Hitchcock was the classic *auteur*: a master of cinematic *mise en scène* who created an unmistakable and homogeneous world-view, controlling the audience so that they were completely at the mercy of his intentions. Hitchcock's habit of making a personal appearance in his films contributed further to the myth, but more than this his world-view is intimately bound up with the mechanisms of cinematic language and the relationship of spectator to film. Many of Hitchcock's films deal with the act of looking or spying, given a centrality which transcends the plot, so it can be argued that a narrative of human psychology emerges in which characters and cinema audience are involved in a play of exchange of looks. This drama of exchange opens up a scene of obsession, guilt, paranoia and phobia in which author, characters and audience are all implicated, but which Hitchcock as author ultimately controls (see Wollen, 'Hitchcock's vision', 1969).

It was this aspect of Hitchcock's work, interpreted as raising serious questions of morality, which intrigued and influenced many *Cahiers* critics and film-makers, especially Chabrol, Rohmer and Truffaut, whose films contain many direct references to Hitchcock (see Truffaut, 1968).

The *Cahiers* approach was echoed by Robin Wood in Britain, who argued that Hitchcock's work not only explored important moral dilemmas through its obsessional characters, but included the audience in the drama, forcing them to acknowledge previously unrecognised moral ambiguities in themselves (see Wood, 1977). More recently Raymond Bellour, writing under the influence of French structuralist criticism, has used Hitchcock's work to demonstrate the closed structure, in formal and ideological

---

Blackmail (UK 1929 *p.c* – John Maxwell; *d* – Alfred Hitchcock; sd b/w 10)

Hitchcock worked in Britain until 1940, and his films of this period are important in many ways, not least for their relationship with other British films (see Smith, 'Conservative individualism: a selection of English Hitchcock', 1972). Influenced by his period in Germany where he encountered German Expressionism, they show a desire to experiment with the possibilities of cinematic language. He began directing films at a time of technological change (the transition to sound) when the opportunities for experiment within the film industry were still open, and in contrast to much of the British cinema made at this time, his films can be seen to work against the conventional notions of realism which have dominated mainstream British cinema.

The extract shows an experimental use of montage editing (cutting shots of the dead man's arm against shots of the heroine's legs as she walks home after the murder, building to the climax of the landlady's scream when she discovers the body) and of the zoom-in for dramatic effect. This device both depicts Alice's subjective state of mind and engages the specator's emotions, a strategy found in much of Hitchcock's work. Hitchcock's symbolic use of the 'act of looking' can be seen in the use of pictures which return the looks of the guilty protagonists: the jester looks mockingly at Frank, and the policeman looks sternly at Alice.

Alice can be seen as one of Hitchcock's earliest guilty aberrant females (cf. *Under Capricorn, Psycho, The Birds, Marnie*) and in the extract sound is used expressively to stress her guilt. The emphasis on the word 'knife' could be compared with the montage stabbing sequence in the shower in *Psycho*, to show a similar concern with the obsessional state of mind of the murderer.

Foreign Correspondent (UK 1940 *p.c* – Walter Wanger Productions; *d* – Alfred Hitchcock; sd b/w 8)

Between 1935 and 1938 Hitchcock made a cycle of thriller films which established him as England's 'great director'. He moved to the US in 1939 and this was his second film made there. Not generally regarded as a major Hitchcock film it nevertheless provides an example of transition between his English and American work, particularly in the use of comedy and parodied English stereotype characters, which both crosses and interrupts the forward drive of the narrative characteristic of the thriller genre. Looking forward to later work, note the use of apparently innocent objects to suggest threat or problem (e.g. the mass of umbrellas shot from above as the assassin escapes; the windmills which become a significant feature in the plot; the errant derby belonging to the comic Englishman which leads to a vital clue). Thus the author and the spectator share a joke initiated by the former, at the expense of, and for the pleasure of the latter. It could be argued that this play with the spectator is central to all Hitchcock's films.

Mr. and Mrs. Smith (USA 1941 *p.c* – RKO Radio; *d* – Alfred Hitchcock; sd b/w 7)

Hitchcock's interest in the relationship between couples, which he portrays as perverse, can be found in most of his films. Often the couple is yoked together unwillingly, or under difficult circumstances, united by a sexual desire which is bound to be frustrated. The extract shows the workings of male desire in its worst light: in order to reconcile himself with his wife, the hero must spy on and pursue her, disrupt her plans to marry another man, causing everyone concerned acute embarrassment. Beneath the comedy lies the darker side of personal relationships: the sado-masochism of the male/female relationship, the overturning of social and moral codes under the impact of sexual desire, and the consequent prevalence of paranoia, which seems to be totally justified in Hitchcock's world view.

Shadow of a Doubt (USA 1943 *p.c* – Universal; *d* – Alfred Hitchcock; sd b/w 23)

One of Hitchcock's themes in which *Cahiers* critics (including Bazin) were particularly interested was the 'double' relationship between characters in which guilt was transferred from one to

Blackmail – Hitchcock working against conventional notions of realism

terms, of the classic Hollywood text (Bellour, 'Hitchcock, the enunciator', 1977; → NARRATIVE AND STRUCTURALISM: *Narrative and audience*, p. 244).

Many of Hitchcock's films use the detective or spy genre as a pretext for exploring the predatory aspects of human behaviour, be it in a sexual or a political context. Moreover, it has recently been argued, using psychoanalytical concepts which attempt to go beyond 'Hollywood Freud', that Hitchcock's work is exemplary of a cinema in which voyeurism and scopophilia (the drive to look) is manipulated in such a way that the male gaze (of author, characters and spectators) predominates, thus raising the question of the subordinate place of the figure of woman in Hollywood cinema. Victim and predator may seem at some points to be interchangeable in Hitchcock's work but ultimately, the argument goes, the drama is resolved in favour of the male and at the expense of the female, confirming patriarchal ideology. Hitchcock's work is seen as drawing attention to that ideology, at the same time as representing its apotheosis. (see Mulvey, 'Visual pleasure and narrative cinema', 1975). Hitchcock's interest in

the other (see Bazin, 'Hitchcock versus Hitchcock', 1972). One character takes on the features of another so that the question of a fixed identity attributable to one person becomes problematic: examples from Hitchcock's films would be *Strangers on a Train*, *Psycho*, and *Vertigo*, although the theme appears in some form in all of his work. The concept is particularly disturbing when the relationship is between members of the same family, as in *Psycho*, where the identities of mother and son are fused and in conflict. It is rarely explicitly recognised, however, that this doubling of identities introduces a perverse sexual element into the narrative, and it is often this very perversity which motivates events.

In this film Hitchcock uses two different genres to underline the splitting of the characters' identities: the thriller/film noir, to which the psychopathic killer belongs, and the small-town melodrama, locus of the 'nice' family into which he intrudes. Hitchcock was particularly fond of the thriller genre because of its potential for dramatising the splitting of identity theme, and he has objected to the fact that Hollywood produced so many 'women's pictures', the category into which the small-town melodrama conventionally falls. Thus the trouble in the superficially nice family, trouble represented by Young Charlie and her fantasies of excitement is given another disturbing dimension by the introduction into the scene of her 'double' and namesake, Uncle Charlie, visitor from another world.

The extract is taken from the beginning of the film and shows the formal differences between the two genres, the evil of Charlie the killer clearly out of true with the image of him held by the family, and by Young Charlie in particular, who is looking for excitement. The sense of unease, and even impending chaos, established in these opening scenes is characteristic of Hitchcock's work.

Under Capricorn (USA 1949 *p.c* – Transatlantic Pictures; *d* – Alfred Hitchcock; sd col 15)

By this time Hitchcock's international reputation was well established. He co-produced many of his films of this period, and arguably had sufficient control in Hollywood to do as he wished. In 1948 he experimented with long takes in *Rope*, only cutting when the film itself ran out and had to be replaced. This produced 10 minute-long takes which were unusual in Hitchcock's *mise en scène*, since the long take generally excludes the shot/reverse-shot point-of-view technique for which he is well known, and which forms the basis of his narrative suspense. *Under Capricorn* is also a deviation from the usual Hitchcock method, employing long takes and moving camera usually associated with realism, and very little shot/reverse-shot, in a totally unrealistic manner. It could be argued that Hitchcock uses the moving camera in such a way as to draw attention to it *as a camera*, reminding the spectator that s/he is not actually

present on the scene in the same way as the director. An example from the extract would be the long pan around the room from table to door, a gratuitous camera movement. The scene in which Henrietta comes down the staircase dressed for the ball, watched by the two men, demonstrates an interesting use of the movement of a tracking shot into a close-up of the ruby necklace held behind Sam's back, which, we see, he hurriedly hides. This shot replaces the conventional 'reaction shot' which would show his feelings from the expression on his face. It might be interesting to discuss how this substitution of shots affects the meaning of the scene, if at all, and what sort of position is created for the spectator in relation to the characters. It is, of course, characteristic of Hitchcock to emphasise small gestures in this way to create a sense of unease which cannot be easily explained, and the acute social embarrassment caused by Sam's intrusion in the ball sequence, and Henrietta's flight is also typical.

Psycho (USA 1960 *p.c* + Shamley; *d* – Alfred Hitchcock; sd b/w 13)

It has been noted that in Hitchcock's films the spectator is often held in a state of anxiety which may or may not be resolved by the narrative (in *The Birds* for instance it is arguable that it is not). This *'mise en scène* of anxiety' is played out on many levels in the film not least in the sexual relationships between characters. It has been argued recently (see Mulvey, 1975) that Hitchcock's →

the drama of looking is not only reflected in his choice of the investigative thriller genre as a form of expression: he is considered a master of the classic point-of-view shot structure in which a shot of a character looking at something is followed by a shot of what they are looking at. This shot/reverse-shot structure has been identified as a basic element of continuity in Hollywood narrative cinema (→ HISTORY OF NARRATIVE: *Classic narrative system*, p. 212) and Hitchcock uses it frequently to build up narrative suspense.

The *Cahiers auteur* critics who championed Hitchcock saw him as the major exponent of cinema at its purest. They liked the manipulation of the language of editing in Hitchcock's films because it corresponded to their own interests as film-makers, and because the world view expressed was that of the isolated individual trapped in a hostile world not of his or her own making, an alienation manifested in Hitchcock's use of the fragmentation of montage editing. More recent theoretical work, by Laura Mulvey for example, has attempted to reassess Hitchcock's films in terms of ideology rather than the criteria of the 'purely cinematic',

Hitchcock directs the famous shower scene in *Psycho*

thus beginning to place the work of this *grand auteur* within history.

In order to establish Hitchcock as a true *auteur* the critic must be able to trace the development of a consistent theme, expressed in a style which is perfectly suited to that theme, across all his films. Those films which don't fit the critic's construction of

Hitchcock's world view are either ignored, or treated as minor or flawed works. These gaps and inconsistencies can provide the basis of a challenge to traditional *auteur* study by drawing attention to its partiality of approach, and to the need for a historical analysis to explain those films considered uncharacteristic.

films organise the play of looks between characters and cinema audience in terms of the dominance of the male (heterosexual) gaze, i.e. that the relationship between male and female characters is a struggle based on dominance and subordination in which the former finally dominates the latter, thus neatly resolving the narrative in favour of patriarchal ideology (see below, NARRATIVE AND STRUCTURALISM: *Narrative and audience*, p. 244). This account is very useful in discussion of the ideological implications of Hitchcock's films, especially in *Psycho*, where fear and guilt is induced in the female protagonist by the investigatory looks of male characters, and her inability to escape these looks places her in a subordinate and vulnerable position. The notorious attack in the shower, not included in the extract, could also be seen in terms of an attempt to link the 'look' of the camera and of the audience with the aggression of the stabbing, thus reducing the female protagonist to the status of object rather than subject: the female transgressor is not, as she thought, in command of her own destiny, the power of the 'look' is taken from her (the image of Marion's dead, unseeing eye is significant in this respect) and she is fixed as an object.

However, it could also be argued that the question of sexuality is complicated in *Psycho* by the fact that both Marion and Norman have male *and* female characteristics. Like many of Hitchcock's heroines (see *Blackmail*, *Marnie*, *The Birds*) Marion, a woman,

attempts to cross conventional sexual divisions by becoming active rather than passive, by becoming a thief in order to get what she wants. Similarly, although Norman Bates, voyeur, is male, and his 'look' at Marion could be assumed to be male, as a killer he is bi-sexual (part mother/part son), and this sexual ambiguity (we never know which part is dominant) is unresolved at the end, even though it is 'explained' by the psychiatrist. What kind of fantasy/pleasure is evoked for the spectator when the edges of 'male' and 'female' sexual categories are blurred?

In the extract Marion is the object of a variety of looks (from male characters, and from the camera) yet she is also a subject looking (her eyes are emphasised and there are point-of-view shots). An important question then is how meaning is to be constructed from this exchange of looks.

The Birds (USA 1963 *p.c* – Alfred Hitchcock/Universal; *d* – Alfred Hitchcock; sd col 18)

Melanie Daniels, like many Hitchcock heroines, takes destiny into her own hands and pursues Mitch Brenner, reversing the conventional male/female roles. In doing so she brings the bird attack onto the Bodega Bay Community, culminating in her own symbolic 'rape' by the birds. The extract compares with *Psycho* in that it shows the independently curious woman, an active subject, as the object of violent aggression and punishment. The theme of aggression is manifested on the level

of *mise en scène* in the use of montage, low-angled shots, and a composition of characters within the frame based on disequilibrium.

There is a classic Hitchcockian use of point-of-view as Melanie moves towards the stairs and the attic door, which could be seen to serve a double function: to build suspense from the rhythm of shot/reverse-shot, and to emphasise Melanie's subjectivity through point-of-view before she is reduced to an object in the attic. After the bird-rape when Melanie regains consciousness, she looks straight into camera and defends herself against its 'look', equating it with an act of aggression.

Hitchcock's interest in mixing genres can be seen, as the romantic melodrama becomes a science fiction horror story in which the untroubled surface of a community and a family is radically disturbed.

Marnie (USA 1964 *p.c* – Geoffrey Stanley Inc/Universal; *d* – Alfred Hitchcock; sd col 20+20)

Marnie, like Marion in *Psycho* (and other Hitchcock heroines) threatens the social order: not only is she a compulsive thief who steals large sums of money from her employers but she is a mistress of disguise, changing her identity at will to avoid being caught. This double problematic (aggression and masquerade) it could be argued is particularly threatening to a society in which men control the exchange of money and the place of women.

Foreign Correspondent – the mass of umbrellas which mask the escape of the assassin

Characteristically Hitchcock develops the explicitly sexual aspect of this problem through the relationship of dominance and subordination between Marnie and Mark Rutland: Marnie is an object of desire for Mark *because* she is a threat. Mark's compulsive desire to master the problem provides the central drive of the narrative, and as usual in Hitchcock's films the characters are shown to be the victims of their own desires so that the narrative resolution (Mark brings about Marnie's 'cure') is profoundly ambiguous. Both protagonists are in the grip of their compulsions, but Mark's go unexamined. The 'problem' is displaced on to the female character: she *is* the problem to be solved through the narrative. It has been argued that Hitchcock's films epitomise the construction of the place of woman in patriarchal society as the locus of male problems and fears (Mulvey, 1975).

Extract 1 provides an illustration of this argument: in the first part the camera tracks the figure of the woman in such a way as to mark her as an object of curiosity: we see what she does but we are denied her face. We watch as she substitutes one identity for another, washing black dye from her hair. Curiosity and suspense build up until the shot in which she lifts her head and looks straight into the camera. The moment is explicitly erotic and marked as transgression: the rule, 'Don't look at the camera' is broken since Marnie exchanges looks with the audience. Arguably, her subjective desire is

explicitly marked as a threat.

The second part shows the relationship between Mark and Marnie in which he tries to pin her down by interpreting her nightmare as she mocks his attempts. Clearly 'Hollywood Freud', this section none the less points up Mark's obsessional involvement with curing and rehabilitating Marnie: fitting her into his world and possessing her.

Extract 2 shows Hitchcock's characteristic treatment of his obsessional protagonists, and the formal strategies he uses to encourage audience identification with the characters' subjective states (→ HISTORY OF NARRATIVE: *Classic narrative system*, p. 212).

Topaz (USA 1969 *p.c* – Universal; *d* – Alfred Hitchcock; sd col 20)

An example of later Hitchcock, a political thriller. The male protagonist finds himself drawn into a world which is dangerous and difficult to make sense of. In the extract, suspense is built up by the spectator's identification with Devereux, who watches events from a distance, is involved but unable to control them. It could be argued that the 'look' of Dubois' camera at secret documents echoes Hitchcock's constant preoccupation with the forbidden gaze and the desire to see and that the whole drama in the extract is built around 'getting a look' at something forbidden. This is reflected in the *mise en scène* by the obsessional play of looks around the briefcase which is fetishised by the repeated shots which focus on it as an

object of desire, endowing it with excess meaning. The 'play of looks' seems to have become almost abstract, a formalist game, in spite of the political context of the film. Politics is another MacGuffin, a red-herring, a hollow pretext for Hitchcock's preoccupations (see Truffaut, 1968).

Frenzy (UK 1972 *p.c* – Universal; *d* – Alfred Hitchcock; sd col 15)

The extract shows the behaviour of another guilty Hitchcock protagonist under threat of discovery, this time given a 'black' twist characteristic of the later work. The psychopathic killer goes to enormous lengths to protect himself from being found out: perhaps a metaphor for Hitchcock's view of the place of the spectator as secret voyeur in the cinema? Certainly suspense is built around this central problem of discovery. Characteristically the woman's body, now fixed with rigor mortis, is the problem for the psychopath, and it could be argued that the fragmentation of the *mise en scène* draws attention to the underlying fantasy of the cutting up of the woman's body (cf. *Psycho*). One question is how far the *mise en scène* sets up spectator identification with the guilty protagonist and his fear of being found out.

JOHN HUSTON

'It seems significant that attempts to trace a consistent pattern in Huston's work should lead one chiefly to an awareness of *absences*' (Wood, 'John Huston', 1980).

Wood, until recently a confirmed auteurist, is expressing a dissatisfaction with Huston's work which is shared by many *auteur* critics. While a pattern can be traced through his films, such a pattern reveals no marked development nor any complexity of relationship between films. His personal concerns are heterogeneous rather than consistent, although Wood sees his preoccupation with a central, isolated male protagonist as a continuing pessimistic theme. Huston's *mise en scène*, however, fails to express this theme as an *auteur*'s should: it is a decorative flourish rather than a coherent artistic statement. Huston is merely a *metteur en scène*.

Wood's argument echoes that of the *Cahiers auteur* critics, to whom the *metteur en scène* was inferior to the *auteur* because his or her work lacked the inspiration, the personal expression, to create a world-view proper. Although they could discern a consistent thematic in the films of John Huston, there was no consistency of style, even though he often produced, wrote and directed his films. Arguably, it is precisely this lack of a coherent personal vision which makes the *metteur en scène* more interesting in some respects than the *auteur*: by removing the author from the centre of the work a number of other factors can be discovered to be at work in the film, and the critic would need to look further than the presence of authorial intentions to analyse the source of meaning, to

The train transformed into coffin in the fantasy sequence in *Freud*

history, for example, or to production conditions (← HISTORY: *The studios*, p. 10). The very unevenness of Huston's work invites another form of analysis than *auteur* study. By making the distinction *auteur/metteur en scène* the *Cahiers* critics highlighted one of the problems of the *auteur* approach: the attribution of a film's meaning to the intentions of an individual director who transcended history.

References

André Bazin, 'Hitchcock versus Hitchcock', in Albert J. LaValley (ed.), *Focus on Hitchcock*, Englewood Cliffs, N. J., Prentice-Hall, 1972.

Raymond Bellour, 'Hitchcock the enunciator', *Camera Obscura* no. 2, Fall 1977.

Edward Buscombe, 'Walsh and Warner Bros', in Phil Hardy (ed.), *Raoul Walsh*, Edinburgh Film Festival, 1974.

Laura Mulvey, 'Visual pleasure and narrative cinema', *Screen* vol. 16 no. 3, Autumn 1975.

V. F. Perkins, *Film as Film: understanding and judging movies*, London, Penguin, 1972.

John Smith, 'Conservative individualism: a selection of English Hitchcock', *Screen* vol. 13 no. 3, Autumn 1972.

François Truffaut, *Hitchcock*, London, Secker and Warburg, 1968.

Peter Wollen, 'Hitchcock's vision', *Cinema* (UK), June 1969.

Robin Wood, *Hitchcock's Films*, London/New York, Zwemmer/A. S. Barnes, 1965, reprinted 1969, 1977.

Robin Wood, 'John Huston', in Richard Roud (ed.), *Cinema: a critical dictionary* Vol. 1. London, Secker and Warburg, 1980.

The Maltese Falcon (USA 1942 *p.c.* – Warner Bros; *d* – John Huston; sd b/w 9)

Although Huston both directed and wrote this film, it could be argued that its interest lies less in his authorship than in other elements which contribute to its meaning. It was adapted from a Dashiell Hammett novel and is in the film noir genre; the production company was Warner Bros, whose relative economic independence as a studio enabled them to engage in some radical projects in the 1930s and 40s (Buscombe, 'Walsh and Warner Bros', 1974). Humphrey Bogart worked with Huston on many films in which the less favourable aspects of his image were represented (as Dobbs in *The Treasure of the Sierra Madre*, as Allnut in *The African Queen*, for instance); the film also pushes the complexities of its narrative to extremes. In a sense it could be said to be *about* all these elements: narrative, *mise en scène*, genre, stars, character, studio production, rather than any single coherent authorial theme, although the general debunking of heroism and the placing of men and women at the mercy

of their fate rather than in control of it might be said to be typical of Huston's work.

The Treasure of the Sierra Madre (USA 1947 *p.c* – Warner Bros; *d* – John Huston; sd b/w 11)

An example of Huston's use of Humphrey Bogart as a character actor. Dobbs can be seen to represent a corruptible version of the 'Huston hero': the non-conforming individualist. Huston's interest in corrupt, imperfect men has been noted by Robin Wood as his central theme, and the pessimism identified by Wood is illustrated in this extract from the end of the film (Wood, 1980).

Moulin Rouge (UK 1952 *p.c* – Romulus; *d* – John Huston; sd col 20)

Huston directed, produced and co-wrote the film, which nevertheless, like *The Maltese Falcon*, shows more concern with the formal properties of *mise en scène* than with creating a world-view. Indeed the film, as the extract shows, tries rather to recreate *a world*, specifically in the use of colour,

composition and spectacle to reconstruct the Toulouse Lautrec prints. On the level of theme, the banal drama of the disfigured artist seem sentimental and moralistic: the human drama takes second place to the dramatic spectacle of the *mise en scène*. V. F. Perkins (1972) has argued that this lack of coherence between style and theme is a serious flaw, leading to a pretentiousness of style.

Freud (Freud – The Secret Passion) (USA 1962 *p.c* – Universal-International; *d* – John Huston; sd b/w 10)

Much admired by Huston supporters for its depiction of its central male protagonist, Freud, as a flawed imperfect character, a victim of his obsessional urges. In the extract, Freud's search for the truth from his patient leads to her final hostile rejection of him: a characteristically pessimistic touch from Huston. The director's interest in a highly formalised *mise en scène* is demonstrated in the hypnosis-induced fantasy sequence.

The politique des auteurs: 'auteurs' and studio

WILLIAM WYLER

André Bazin, in his assessment of William Wyler as 'the Jansenist of *mise en scène*' argues for the value of a *mise en scène* 'defined by its own absence', a 'style without style' which allows the spectator to perceive the world presented by the film as directly as possible, without human intervention (Bazin, 1980). Wyler was probably the best director to use in support of Bazin's argument for the transparency of film, i.e. the ability of cinema to reproduce a place for the spectator as close as possible to his or her relationship to 'reality'. For Bazin, this 'reality' consisted of the harmonious integration of objects in time and space; this was the way, according to him, that the human eye perceived the real world: as a unity. Deep-focus photography made it possible for film to reproduce this relationship (→ NARRATIVE AND STRUCTURALISM: *Bazin*, p. 224).

There is a tendency among critics of Bazin to reduce his philosophy to that of a naive realism which sees film as a 'window on the world'. However contradictory, his arguments remain useful in raising questions for *auteur* analysis of film. In relation to his assessment of Wyler's work, for instance, what are the implications of an auteurist analysis (i.e. one that returns to the director as source

of meaning) which depends upon the critic establishing a 'lack of style'? How can the *auteur* be identified as present by an argument which depends precisely on his absence? This raises a crucial question for auteurism itself (one which will be raised again): how precisely do we identify the marks of authorship in a film or body of films?

In view of this contradiction in Bazin's position it could be argued that Wyler's work is most interesting as a product of the Hollywood studio set-up in the 1930s and 40s. Unlike Welles, for instance, Wyler seems to have been quite at home in the context of studio production, and his films exhibit a range of production values and genres, and a range of contributions from stars, writers, technicians and others, which combine to make a 'studio product' rather than works of 'artistic genius'. This provides a different basis for approaching Wyler's films since it can be argued that it is this multiplicity of contributions which makes up the 'style' that Bazin's analysis suppresses.

It is also, incidentally, this auteurist approach which leads some critics to dismiss Wyler's films outright as 'atrophied' and 'studio-bound', and, significantly, too bound to the melodrama genre, conventionally associated with the 'women's film', a much maligned phenomenon (see Petley, 1978). For these critics, Wyler is simply a cog in the studio machine, reproducing the respectable middle-class

The Little Foxes – sympathy for Regina alienated by deep-focus?

ideology of the studio heads (in particular Samuel Goldwyn). A closer examination of the melodramas in terms of the contradictions they work through might encourage a reassessment of Wyler's films. (←GENRE: *Melodrama*, p. 73).

The Little Foxes (USA 1940–41 *p.c* – RKO-Goldwyn; *d* – William Wyler; sd b/w 15+20)

Bazin praises the fact that the cinematic adaptation of the Lillian Hellman play is faithful to the original text; paradoxically it is also 'one of the most purely cinematic works there is' (Bazin, 1980).

The crux of Bazin's argument is that Wyler has retained the theatrical setting of the play ('the dramatic architecture'), using the elements of cinematic *mise en scène* (static camera, depth-of-field, the minimum of cuts, and re-framing) to construct extra meaning. Each of these cinematic elements emphasises the dramatic tension inherent in the scene: the criminal immobility of Regina (Bette Davis) in the face of her husband's imminent death, illustrated in both extracts.

The film can be seen to be a studio production, manifested in the carefully constructed sets, costume, and the use of a repertory of actors. Samuel Goldwyn was an independent producer who had a respectable critical reputation as a producer of 'quality' films with serious overtones. Many of his films were adaptations of literary or theatrical works, and *The Little Foxes* is an adaptation of a play by a writer (Lillian

Hellman) with a serious intellectual reputation. There is a level on which the Regina character acts as a criticism of the bourgeois values which the other protagonists exemplify. At the same time she is represented as repressed and 'unnatural', and the criticism gives way to the liberal humanist values represented by the dying husband, played by Herbert Marshall, the focus for audience identification. However, the tragic overtones surrounding Bette Davis as Regina ensures that contradictions are not finally closed off. On one level the film is a family melodrama, a 'women's picture' (written by a woman, centred on a female protagonist, addressed to a female audience). It is arguable that the values supported by *The Little Foxes* are those of humanism and self-sacrifice, asserted at the expense of the 'independent woman', a conflict of values typical of the family melodrama (← GENRE: *Melodrama*, p. 78) Much of Extract 2 is taken up with establishing Regina as a strong and ambitious woman who will stop at nothing (not even murder) to get what she wants. The breakdown of her relationship with her dying husband is attributed to her lack of human qualities and compassion, her precise, cerebral detachment, her

predatory manipulative nature. Her success in getting what she wants is presented negatively, since she loses her daughter's love and is finally left alone. Some questions might be raised about the ideological nature of this treatment.

Both extracts are relevant to discussion of Bazin's argument about realism and deep-focus photography, and Wyler's 'styleless style'. It could be argued however, that far from allowing the spectator to scan the scene at will, deep-focus is used precisely to manipulate the audience: to alienate sympathy from Regina, for instance.

The Best Years of Our Lives (USA 1946 *p.c.* – Goldwyn; *d* – William Wyler; sd b/w 20)

It has been argued that the techniques of deep-focus, long takes and re-framing as deployed here are particularly suited to social realism, revealing the events staged for the camera as though they were in 'real space', encouraging a position of tolerant understanding in the spectator, who is confronted with a series of 'serious social problems': the crippling effects of war on body, mind and spirit which threaten to disturb the normal social order (see Bazin, 1980).

In the first part of the extract, these problems are expressed in the *mise en* →

ORSON WELLES

The myths surrounding Welles's 'larger-than-life' personality, his turbulent relationship with the film industry and his struggles for artistic control have contributed to a general critical consensus which ascribes all meaning in the films to Welles himself. The fact that Welles not only directed, but wrote and acted in most of them, has contributed to this view, and Welles himself has supported it.

'. . . Theatre is a collective experience, but cinema is the work of a single man, the director . . .

. . . You've got to have all your helpers, all the necessary collaborators; it's a collective endeavour, but in essence a very personal outcome, much more than the theatre to my mind, because film is something dead, a band of celluloid like the blank sheet on which you write a poem. A film is what you write on the screen . . .' (Welles, quoted in *Study Unit no. 9*, 1977, p. 26).

In the context of 1940s Hollywood studio production, this view perpetuates the myth of the lone individual struggling against the dictates of a monolithic commercial organisation, the industry, which is interested in profit rather than 'art' (← *Authorship in art cinema*, p. 114). The idea that cinema is produced in the same mode as writing (which also occurs in Astruc's argument for the 'caméra-stylo', p. 119) is hardly tenable in the context of Hollywood studio production, where precisely 'writing' (the script) is a separate area of work, generally placed lower in the hierarchy than that of the director.

Nevertheless, because of Welles's persistent struggle against the interference of the industry his films are an interesting example (compared with Wyler's, for instance) of cinema authorship at a time when the studio system in Hollywood was still very strong, and studio control over the process of production was such that the contribution of the director was often effaced altogether. However, as Welles himself was aware, that contribution was dependent on other factors than the presence of 'genius' and 'personal vision'. '. . . If I were producer-director, if I had a financial interest in the production, it would all be different. But my services are hired and on salary alone I was at the mercy of my bosses . . .' (ibid.)

The legend of Orson Welles (his dazzling artistic virtuosity which could not survive in the philistine world of Hollywood, condemning him to wander from country to country, working when and where he could) has by and large determined the way in which his work has been approached by critics. Even when it has provoked bitter controversy (see Kael, 1971), that work is seen in terms of authorship, rather than in historical terms for its place in the development of studio technology, for instance, or as an indication of the politics of 1930s and 1940s Hollywood. Welles came to the film industry from radical theatre and radio, a political and aesthetic background which clashed rather than merged with the prevailing ideology of the studio system. His films were markedly different from other studio products of the time in that they combined the techniques of deep-focus photography, wide-angled lenses, upward-tilting shots, lighting from below, long tracking shots and sets with ceilings in a new way which went against the grain of the prevalent realist aesthetic.

WILLIAM WYLER (*continued*)
scène in the spatial relationship between characters: the break-up of male camaraderie is emphasised by the use of deep-focus to show Fred (Dana Andrews) in the background, alienated from the group in the foreground, and in the sense of distance between Al (Fredric March) and Fred.

In the second part of the extract, these problems are resolved in the conventional Hollywood manner: through love, marriage and the stabilisation of the heterosexual couple. Deep-focus is here used to emphasise unity and balance.

The film has been much praised, as Wyler's best work with Goldwyn, as an exemplary piece of social realism, and for its 'classical' technique, courtesy of photographer Gregg Toland. It is rarely discussed in terms of ideology, however, as a 'post-war reconstruction' film exemplifying the need for individual courage, perserverance and self-sacrifice in peace-time as well as war. Something of a departure for Goldwyn, it is less concerned with the aspirations of the middle class, and more with class itself as a problem, giving the film an edge of social criticism.

According to Bazin, the *mise en scène* of *The Best Years of Our Lives* corresponds to the 'geometry of normal vision', allowing the spectator to 'see everything' and to 'choose to his liking'. It is questionable whether the film actually does allow for this democratic participation, or whether viewers today would see its stark geometric *mise en scène* as realistic.

Citizen Kane (USA 1940 *p.c* – Mercury Productions/RKO *d* – Orson Welles; sd b/w 25)

Citizen Kane is regarded by many as an example of Welles's artistic genius; he produced, co-wrote, acted in and directed the film – an apparently classic case of cinema authorship. In spite of the fact that Welles has acknowledged the importance of photographer Gregg Toland's contribution, and others have insisted that scriptwriter H. J. Mankiewicz is the real author of the film (see Kael, 1971), *Citizen Kane* retains its reputation as the first Wellesian masterpiece, a stylistic *tour de force*.

Stylistic virtuosity is indeed one of the primary pleasures the film offers, not least for the way it plays with the conventions of Hollywood cinema (the personal biography genre, the *March of Time* newsreels) to produce something which looks quite different from other films of the period. Bazin hailed *Citizen Kane* as inaugurating a new period in cinema: a break with the 'expressive montage' of Russian cinema, and the shot/reverse-shot editing of American narrative films in the 1930s, in favour of the democratic realism of deep-focus photography (Bazin, 1978). The extract illustrates the variety of cinematic techniques used in the film, employed by Welles for symbolic rather than realistic effects: deep-focus photography, low-angled shots and the constructed ceilings made necessary by depth-of-field, wide-angle shots, overlapping dialogue and whip-pans in the marriage sequence. In the second part, deep-focus photography combines with an experimental use of shot/reverse-shot, sound and lighting to symbolise the increasing distance and alienation between Kane and his wife Susan.

Kane himself is the kind of hero/villain who recurs in Welles's films. Welles's politics, emerging from the Popular Front of the time, ensure that the film is on one level critical of Kane, his will to power and inevitable moral decline (see *Study Unit no. 9*, 1977). However, the film's basis in melodrama gives its theme a tragic dimension: Kane is a villain almost in spite of himself, a tragic hero caught in contradictions he cannot control. Kane was loosely based on William Randolph Hearst, a newspaper tycoon with massive interests in the film industry. The legal action taken by Hearst failed to prove the connection, but it delayed the release of the film and made it difficult for RKO to find bookings, so they never allowed Welles such artistic control again (← HISTORY: *The studios*, p. 21).

Citizen Kane is interesting from a number of perspectives: as part of the Welles oeuvre; for its technical virtuosity, made possible by the studio technology of the time; in relation to the power politics of the Hollywood industry; and for its enduring place in critical pantheons, in spite of its box-office failure.

The Magnificent Ambersons (USA 1942 *p.c* – Mercury Productions/RKO; *d* – Orson Welles; sd b/w 12)

Citizen Kane was something of a critical success, but it was not commercially successful. Welles had a

Citizen Kane – the first Wellesian masterpiece

development of deep-focus photography at this point in cinema history. For this reason they can be useful in testing Bazin's argument (→ NARRATIVE AND STRUCTURALISM: *Bazin*, p. 224) and to test the assumptions of *auteur* theory by looking at Welles's work in terms of its tension with the studio system and the industry of 1940s Hollywood.

References

André Bazin, 'William Wyler or the Jansenist of *mise en scène*', in Christopher Williams (ed), *Realism and the cinema*, London, Routledge and Kegan Paul/British Film Institute, 1980, pp. 36–52.

André Bazin, *Orson Welles: a critical view*, London, Elm Tree Books, 1978; trans. Jonathan Rosenbaum.

Stephen Heath, 'Film and system: terms of analysis', *Screen* vol. 16 no. 1, Spring 1975; no. 2, Summer 1975.

Pauline Kael, *The Citizen Kane Book*, London, Secker and Warburg, 1971.

Julian Petley, *British Film Institute Distribution Library Catalogue 1978*, London, BFI, 1978, pp. 119–122.

Peter Wollen, *Study Unit no. 9: Orson Welles*, London, BFI Education Dept., January 1969, reprinted October 1977.

This difference was not noted by Bazin, who admired the films of Orson Welles if anything more than those of Wyler – surprisingly, since those films depend above all on the techniques of 'expressive montage' that Bazin was arguing against, and Welles's style can hardly be called 'self-effacing' (see Bazin, 1978). All his films have a distinctive *mise en scène*, which represents a recognisable world view (see the interview in *Study Unit no. 9*, 1977). It is difficult to see how Welles's films correspond to Bazin's ideas about the 'democratic' realism offered by the

similar production set-up for *The Magnificent Ambersons* at RKO (i.e. his own company of actors and the superb technical resources of the studio) but the studio took a much greater part in supervising the film to make sure that this time it recouped their investment (← HISTORY: *RKO Radio*, p. 22).

The film's central figure is once again an egocentric male protagonist whose arrogance finally causes his downfall. The story concerns the disintegration of an aristocratic American family under pressure of social change, but the social dimension was submerged by the studio's insistence on emphasising the melodramatic elements of the film, and cutting it accordingly.

Welles's style, which consists of a combination (or rather, conflict) of opposing strategies, such as moving camera vs. static camera, close-up vs. long takes, light vs. dark, whispering vs. shouting, gives the world created in the film a sense of turmoil and upheaval. Again it is fragmentation and contradiction that dominate rather than unity; however, this fragmentation, manifested in the behaviour of the protagonists and the disintegration of the family and its traditions, is not only characteristic of Welles's 'world-view': it is prevalent in Hollywood cinema of the 40s, particularly in the film noirs (← GENRE: *Film noir*, p. 93).

Touch of Evil (USA 1958 *p.c* – Universal-International; *d* – Orson Welles; sd b/w 14)

It is arguable that Welles's best films were made in Hollywood, where he had the resources of the studios at his disposal. Other arguments, suggested above, indicate that his relationship with the studios was turbulent, and that the films reflect this relationship. His output of films is small and he has many uncompleted projects, a symptom of the mutual distrust with which director and studio regarded one another. In the context of Hollywood production values, the demands of narrative, genre, the star system, the need to produce commercially viable products (commodities), the baroque world and flamboyant style of Welles's films may seem monstrously self-indulgent, asserting the value of 'art' against 'commerce'. Yet, it can be argued, it is this *excess* of style which pushes against the limits of Hollywood studio production, threatening to overturn them and therefore revealing them *as* limits (see Heath, 'Film and system: terms of analysis', 1975; → *Discursive activity*, p. 189).

Touch of Evil was directed by Welles after an absence from Hollywood lasting ten years. The film ran into problems with its production company Universal-International, who gave Welles *carte blanche* throughout the shooting, then prevented him from completing the cutting, and cut some of it themselves.

The extract illustrates Welles's excessive style manifested in extreme camera angles and violent fragmentation of shots, light/dark contrasts typical of expressionist *mise en scène*. Excess is also marked in the extensive use of tracking camera which

underlines the obsessional 'tracking' of Quinlan (Welles) by Vargas (Charlton Heston). The sense of a perverse, nightmarish world is emphasised by the *mise en scène*, and by the way Vargas is shown struggling to follow and cavesdrop on Quinlan, a struggle with which the spectator is encouraged to identify, but which, because of its marked perversity, brings the relationship between the two men into question. Although Quinlan is depicted as evil and must be exposed by Vargas, it could be argued that Welles pushes at the limits of the conventions to question the narrative resolution, implicating the spectator in questions of moral ambiguity.

Welles's stylistic and thematic concerns were fairly consistent, especially in those films he made in Hollywood (from which the extracts are taken). It might be productive, therefore, to compare the Hollywood films with films he made outside of the Hollywood production system to test the notion that 'artistic freedom' is only possible outside the 'constraints' of commodity film production.

The politique des auteurs and the French New Wave

The New Wave covers a brief period in French cinema history from 1959 to around 1964, when certain historical, technological and economic factors combined to enable some young film-makers to influence French cinema temporarily in very diverse ways (← HISTORY: *French New Wave*, p. 40). The cinema industry in France in the 1950s was economically shaky: when Roger Vadim's film *And God Created Woman* (1956) was a commercial success in spite of being made on a low budget, the industry opened its doors, temporarily, to low-budget production. Technological developments contributed to keeping costs low and enabled film-makers to experiment with light-weight, cheaper equipment and stock. Many young film-makers started out as critics, concerned with attacking the 'quality' films of Clément, Delannoy, Clouzot etc. which made up the established French art cinema, hence the polemical emphasis in *Cahiers* on popular American cinema and its *auteurs*.

At this point in time, then, it suddenly became possible for a group of young French film-makers to experiment with expressing their personal concerns on film, to become *auteurs* in their own right. They admired the technical skill and the personal vision of the great Hollywood directors: much of their work is in homage to them. At the same time they wanted to experiment with new cinematic forms in opposition to the established genres and stereotypes. They borrowed widely from the rich traditions offered by the great moments of cinema, giving them a new immediacy made possible by technological and economic developments. The New Wave took cinema out of the studio and into the streets, celebrating its new-found possibilities (see Bordwell and Thompson, 1979, p. 318).

As might be expected, this cinema of experiment and change could not continue to be commercially successful, and by 1964 the backers had seen enough failures to make them more cautious. The experimental flowering died for the most part. Some film-makers were absorbed into the industry; a few survived, to continue to make films which have influenced world cinema and whose directors have, like their mentors, achieved the status of *auteur* in the eyes of the critical establishment (see Kinder and Houston, 1972, p. 181).

The economic and ideological context in which the French New Wave emerged is discussed elsewhere (← HISTORY: *French New Wave*, p. 40). Between 1959 and 1965 the work of the New Wave directors was particularly interesting in relation to the *politique des auteurs* and its defence of popular American cinema.

JEAN-LUC GODARD

Godard has continued to be the most radically experimental and the most politically aware of the New Wave directors, constantly raising new problems which are

---

A bout de souffle (Breathless) (France 1959 *p.c* – SNC; *d* – Jean-Luc Godard; sd b/w 20)

One of the first New Wave films to be financially successful. It was Godard's first feature: he scripted, directed and edited, but there was collaboration with Chabrol and Truffaut, and with cameraman Raoul Coutard. New Wave film-makers often worked together, although they each had very different positions and developed in different directions. The film can be seen as a homage to Hollywood, but it is arguable that the mixing of Hollywood conventions with those from other cinemas allows space for critical distance as well as the pleasures of recognition.

The plot is based on the conventions of the American gangster movie, and the 'hero' Michel (played by Jean-Paul Belmondo) models himself on Humphrey Bogart, whose image on movie posters appears throughout this film. The references to other films, and to other popular forms like comics or newspapers, is a strategy employed by Godard to show that film is a multiple system, that it is made up of influences from other arts. It is not simply a question of filling the film with 'in-jokes', although this is certainly part of the pleasure in watching it, but of bringing diverse elements into conflict.

The *Cahiers* critics also admired Italian Neo-Realism, and it could be argued that the documentary style of the film conflicts with the Hollywood stereotypes to reveal the conventional nature of both: neither can be seen as embodiments of 'truth'. However, the hand-held moving camera appears to support the romantic ideology of 'individual freedom' which underpins many New Wave films, and the philosophy of the *politique des auteurs*.

Michel is a nihilistic anti-hero whose fascination with 'things American' – not only cinema but his independent American girlfriend – leads to his betrayal and death. He is also characteristic of the aimless protagonists of European art cinema (← *Authorship and art cinema*, p. 114).

The low-budget, experimental quality of the film (natural lighting, natural sound and fast-moving hand-held 35 mm camera) combined with use of real locations, acts as a critical juxtaposition with Hollywood studio production. At this stage Godard tries to encourage a critical reaction from the audience without losing the pleasurable fantasies that cinema offers.

Bande à part (France 1964 *p.c* – Anouchka Films/Orsay Films; *d* – Jean-Luc Godard; sd b/w 14+8)

The title refers to a group of renegade outsiders, thieves who prey on bourgeois society, but are doomed, of course, to failure. Based on a popular American thriller, the plot has been stripped down to its basic elements as part of Godard's strategy of 'de-naturalising' narrative structures for the audience, arguably preventing direct involvement or identification.

Nevertheless the spontaneity (almost child-like innocence) of the protagonists is extremely seductive, and is celebrated on one level by the film. Again, the self-conscious mixing of genre conventions has the effect of denaturalising them. For example, in Extract 1, the romantic isolation of the characters is set against their dance, which is an explicit reference to the American musical. Arguably, Godard allows the spectator to celebrate, enjoy *and* criticise traditional pleasures offered by cinema.

Extract 2 shows the way that Godard reduces the conventions of the thriller genre to their most schematic elements: in this case a climactic 'shoot-out' from which all tension is removed. The narrative conventions appear banal because of Godard's ironic treatment of them: they are revealed *as* conventions. By showing that conventions are not eternal or universal Godard poses the possibility of changing the combinations to produce new meanings. It could be argued that this is the value of his work on film language itself, which is more highly developed in later films.

Une Femme mariée (France 1964 *p.c* – Anouchka Films/Orsay Films, *d* – Jean-Luc Godard; sd b/w 13)

Godard uses a banal plot (this time a melodrama of the affair between a bourgeois mother/housewife and her actor-lover) to raise questions about cinematic language and social conditions.

The film plays with sound and image disjunctures, visual and verbal signs, subjective monologues and documentary-style images, positive and negative photographic images to reveal the interrelationship of different language systems, and the way they come together to make up cinema. He takes the different systems apart and re-combines them to create new meanings, for example, through the use of visual/verbal puns, not just an intellectual exercise but a productive activity similar to that of modern poets.

The 'heroine's' fragmented interior

Godard's reference to the American musical in *Bande à part*

both formal, to do with cinematic and other kinds of language, and political, to do with transforming existing social structures (see Williams, 'Politics and production', 1971/72).

As one of the *Cahiers* critics who argued polemically for the artistic value of popular cinema, he made films which not only reflected those concerns, but had far-reaching implications for film-making as well as theoretical film criticism. His films constantly refer outside themselves to other films, other traditions, using this method of extra-textual reference and quotation to bring together apparently incompatible ideas and forms to contradict and conflict with each other. Arguably, it is this process of questioning and transformation that makes Godard such an important 'modern' director. During the events of 1968 Godard, like many intellectuals, became politicised and his film-making practice changed. The pre-1968 films are discussed here in the historical context of the French New Wave and its relationship to the *politique des auteurs* (→ *Structuralism and British film criticism*, p. 167); *Authorship and counter-cinema*, p. 192).

monologues are also a kind of poetry which reflect her status as woman/housewife/consumer rather than try to present her as a psychologically coherent character. The sequence of lovers in bed is important not only as an explicit reference to another New Wave film, *Hiroshima, Mon Amour*, but also in its use of the fade-out to fragment narrative. The representation of female sexuality in the film raises questions about the place of women in Godard's work.

Pierrot le fou (France/Italy 1965 *p.c* – Rome-Paris Films; *d* – Jean-Luc Godard; sd col scope 15)

Another adaptation from a popular novel, in which Godard fragments the narrative fiction in order to raise questions which throw the romantic aspirations of the protagonists into perspective. The debt to Hollywood is evident in the use of the gangster film convention of the couple in retreat from a hostile society, but the film uses various formal strategies to question that notion. Its protagonists are doomed, by the conflict between their inner desires and the violence and corruption of society, to destruction. Godard uses CinemaScope and colour to emphasise the seductive nature of their dream of an idyllic paradise. Social reality constantly interrupts the idyll, however, (see the 'Vietnam playlet' in the extract) and the protagonists are driven back into society, which finally kills them. In spite of Godard's evident ambiguity towards politics at this stage, the film looks forward to the explicitly political concerns of later work.

The extract illustrates the film's central theme of the escape of the young couple away from civilisation, and Godard's strategy of fragmenting the narrative, juxtaposing written texts with film image. Godard has often been accused of a puritanical distrust of the seductive potential of the cinematic image: here, Scope and colour emphasise the lush beauty of the fantasy island, while written texts constantly intrude to 'jog' the spectator out of the fiction in the direction of politics.

The film's basic romanticism is conservative in many respects: for example, in the representations of Marianne as instinctual and Ferdinand as 'the thinker', and in the anarchism of Ferdinand's final gesture of self-destruction: the only alternative, it would seem, to Utopianism.

Masculin-Féminin (France/Sweden 1966 *p.c.* – Anouchka Films/Argos Films (Paris) Svensk Filmindustri/Sandrews (Stockholm); *d* – Jean-Luc Godard; sd b/w 10)

Masculin-Féminin looks forward to later Godard in which political questions are raised more directly. The problem presented here is the relationship between the 'personal' and the 'political'. The hesitant, tentative relationship between two young people (a young man involved in Communist Party politics and a woman involved in herself and pop music) is used as the basis for an enquiry into sexual relationships and the representation of sexuality.

The narrative is divided into sections, or 'acts', indicating Godard's growing interest in Brecht's theories of 'epic' theatre and the use of tableaux to break up narrative fiction to allow the spectator to stand back critically from

time to time. Note the use of the 'interview' sequence to break down identification with characters.

The extract is interesting in terms of Godard's development towards a rigorous theoretical style in which camera movement, long takes and editing are used in an abstract manner to foreground and question the language of cinema, and the use of this strategy of abstraction to attempt to place the spectator in a critical position vis-à-vis the film (and its protagonists), breaking down identification and therefore raising the question of pleasure, a question to which Godard was constantly to return as a political priority (as it was indeed for Brecht also).

In the context of the New Wave, Godard's use of Jean-Pierre Léaud could be compared with the different use of that actor by François Truffaut (see below). In the 'interview' sequence Paul answers that 'la tendresse' is the most important thing in his life: a reference to Truffaut, who had become associated with this expression, and to Léaud's appearance in Truffaut's films. This 'extra-textual' reference, a form of quotation, has the effect of emphasising the fact that Léaud is an actor, that an actor is a 'sign' whose meaning can change according to different contexts, and that Godard is using Léaud as sign in a different way from Truffaut. The difference is significant, since Godard's project is, increasingly, to criticise notions of human spontaneity and freedom, whereas Truffaut is often concerned to celebrate them, and mourn their loss.

FRANÇOIS TRUFFAUT

Truffaut's critical writing for *Cahiers du Cinéma* in the 1950s was passionate and flamboyant, denouncing established French cinema in favour of the technical expertise, inventiveness and 'personal vision' of certain Hollywood films (Hawks, Walsh, Fuller, Ford and above all Hitchcock) and of 1930s French cinema (Renoir in particular). Truffaut's polemical article 'A certain tendency of the French cinema' (1954) was important in marking the critical shift towards the *politique des auteurs* by the *Cahiers* critics. Yet Truffaut's importance as a polemical critic does not seem to be carried over into his films. Unlike Godard, who has constantly tested and developed his critical and theoretical ideas with an intellectual toughness which has allowed him to grow and change, Truffaut seems to have remained locked within a conservative romantic ideology (which is indeed one strand within the auteurist position). He is one of the New Wave directors who has

Catherine ... the destructive force in the *Jules et Jim* relationship?

survived, founding his own production company. Don Allen says:
'The word 'revolutionary' might be applied to Truffaut in two senses only. First because he was committed to the violent destruction by spectacular critical attacks of what he judged bad; secondly, and more literally, because 'revolution' for him has implied turning the wheel back to his cinematic golden age, the 30's. The cinema which Truffaut advocates is firmly based on the best characteristics of this period, and in particular on the *total authorship* and consequent directional

freedom of such lyrical film creators as Jean Renoir and Jean Vigo' (Allen, 1974, p. 13).

French cinema of the 1930s, the films of Alfred Hitchcock, and the American 'B' picture are the main influences on Truffaut's work, which remains within the conventions of narrative cinema.

References

Don Allen, *François Truffaut*, London, Secker and Warburg/BFI, 1974.
David Bordwell and Kristin Thompson, *Film Art: an introduction*, Reading, Massachusetts, Addison-Wesley, 1979.
Marsha Kinder and Beverle Houston, *Close-up: a critical perspective on film*, New York, Harcourt Brace Jovanovich, 1972.
François Truffaut, 'A certain tendency of the French cinema', *Cahiers du Cinéma* no. 31, January 1954, trans. in Bill Nichols (ed.), *Movies and Methods*, Berkeley, University of California Press, 1976.
Christopher Williams, 'Politics and production', *Screen* vol. 12 no. 4, Winter 1971/72.

Les Quatre cents coups (The 400 Blows) (France 1959 *p.c* – Les Films du Carosse, SEDIF; *d* – François Truffaut; sd b/w 20)

The series of films Truffaut made with Jean-Pierre Léaud playing Antoine Doinel (as a boy, then growing up into an increasingly conformist young man) are thought to be based loosely on his own life. Truffaut himself endorses this view, and of course he also acts in some of his films.

There are contradictions within this (auto-)biographical mode which could be explored. Jean-Pierre Léaud/Antoine Doinel may 'stand for' François Truffaut, but other factors intrude to complicate any simple idea of self-expression. *Les Quatre cents coups*, for instance, owes much to Jean Vigo's film *Zéro de conduite*, and the use of camera movement to capture 'real space' is reminiscent of 1930s Renoir films. In the late 1950s and early 60s films about young people were prevalent; in fact several of the New Wave film-makers were working in this genre. It could be argued that Léaud/Doinel 'represents', therefore, much more than 'Truffaut'.

Truffaut's interest in the theme of individual freedom and spontaneity is manifested in the opposition between scenes on location in Paris, where the camera is constantly moving, tracking and panning, and closed interior scenes where the camera is predominantly static. Motion is used to represent freedom (Antoine and René are constantly running) and stasis to represent confinement, a structural polarisation which runs through the film. Arguably, the presence of structure questions the idea of absolute freedom, since it is only in opposition to

confinement that freedom exists (see Kinder and Houston, 1972). This is the question that underlies the final shot of the film: a freeze-frame in which Antoine, free at last from reform school, is left totally alone: the *reductio ad absurdum* of romantic/anarchistic positions.

Jules et Jim (France 1965 *p.c* – Films du Carosse, SEDIF; *d* – François Truffaut; sd b/w scope reduced to standard 12)

Truffaut's concern with exploring the complexities of the idea of individual freedom is worked through in *Jules et Jim*. The representative of spontaneity here is a woman, and the effects of her behaviour are reflected in the triangular relationship between herself and the two men rather than in any resistance to social institutions, as in *Les Quatre cents coups*.

Catherine, played by Jeanne Moreau, represents the primitive forces which are both the source of creative activity (art) and the impulse behind mindless, nihilistic destruction. The social background is that of the bohemian intellectual spirit in Paris before World War I, fragmented and shattered by the war and the rise of fascism. Jules and Jim have a peaceful and productive rapport which is transformed when Catherine enters their lives, never to be regained. She represents the freedom they desire, which ultimately destroys them and their relationship.

In the extract, the disruptive force of Catherine's wild and instinctual impulses is manifested in her unease in her marriage to Jules, reflected in the use of a restless, wandering camera and the constant motion of the protagonists. The effects of displacing the

contradictions inherent in the idea of individual freedom on to a female character is, it could be argued, to create her as a monster who constantly threatens the apparent stability of the male world. Jules and Jim are the victims of their own self-destructive fantasies, but the film does not explore the extent to which Catherine is also the victim of those fantasies.

La Peau douce (France 1964 *p.c* – Films du Carosse, SEDIF; *d* – François Truffaut; sd b/w 10)

One of Truffaut's preoccupations (shared by other New Wave film-makers) was with the institution of marriage and the problem it presents for men, a theme central to many Hollywood films also. *La Peau douce* owes much to Hitchcock (e.g. *Vertigo*) in its portrayal of a man trapped and destroyed by his desires. Like most Truffaut heroes, Pierre Lachenay looks for freedom, which is conceived entirely in terms of the options offered by bourgeois society, in this case an obsession with a young and beautiful mistress as a way out of a sterile marriage.

The film can be seen in terms of Truffaut's debt to American cinema, especially the work of Hitchcock, and of his view of male sexuality as constantly under threat, manifested in the use of a weak obsessive hero destroyed by his own fantasies. In this respect the extract could be usefully compared with Claude Chabrol's *La Femme infidèle* to show contrasting treatment of the same theme, and with Agnès Varda's *Le Bonheur* – a view of male fantasies from a woman's perspective (the only woman director in the French New Wave).

The auteur theory

Andrew Sarris and American film criticism

Andrew Sarris was writing film criticism in the late 1950s when America was emerging from a period of Cold War politics, which partly explains why he took up the *Cahiers politique*'s argument against social realism. The argument was, inevitably, transformed by being transplanted into American culture, but was in many ways similar to that of the original *politique des auteurs*, directed against established criteria of film criticism (see Murray, 1975).

Post-war American film criticism (exemplified perhaps by the writing of James Agee) had been primarily sociological, asserting the value of social realism. The best films, it was argued, were those 'quality' productions which dealt with serious social issues: this was how the 'art' of film was described. Yet at the same time, the 1940s and 1950s in Hollywood had produced a vast number of popular entertainment films in general dismissed by critics because of their blatant commercialism, which was considered incompatible with artistry and seriousness. In the 1950s Hollywood began to sell old movies to television, which made it possible for many people to review and reassess the earlier work of those directors considered to be at their peak in the 1950s.

In the late 1950s and early 1960s Andrew Sarris wrote film criticism for small magazines like *The Village Voice* and *Film Culture*, the locus of much debate and polemic. Ironically, at the same time as he began arguing for the *auteur* theory and popular American cinema, that cinema and its 'mass audience' was beginning to decline and many of his friends were involved in actively opposing it through their film-making practice (in 1961 the New American Cinema Group published in *Film Culture* a 'revolutionary manifesto' for a new independent cinema in opposition to Hollywood). After the repressive Cold War period of the 1950s, a general cultural shift in American society in the 1960s towards the greater intellectual freedom established a climate in which polemical writing could flourish. Sarris's critical polemic was directed against social realism in favour of formal concerns, against 'serious art' in favour of the 'art of popular cinema'. It had a double impetus: towards bringing forward Hollywood films as worthy of critical consideration, and towards using the director as a criterion of value (as opposed to the star, the screenwriter or the producer). It could be argued that this emphasis on the role of director and on formal concerns was linked with the decline of the Hollywood studio system and the growth of small-scale production facilities which allowed greater individual access to facilities for production: many artists in America had begun experimenting with 16 mm film after the war for

instance. Thus some of the social conditions which gave rise to the French *politique des auteurs* also contributed to the emergence of the *auteur* theory in America. Although Sarris was not a filmmaker he came into contact with the French New Wave at the Cannes Film Festival in 1961 and spent a year in Paris in 1962 watching old Hollywood films at the Cinémathèque. He was the editor of the English language version of *Cahiers du Cinéma* published in London and New York, and was certainly responsible for introducing the *politique des auteurs*, translated as the *auteur* theory and elaborated into a system of evaluating and classifying Hollywood cinema. In *The American Cinema* (1968) Sarris was to establish a critical pantheon which graded directors according to the extent to which their personal vision transcended the hierarchical system within which they worked. Earlier, in 'Notes on the *auteur* theory in 1962', he clarified his version of the *auteur* theory, which, he emphasised, was not prescriptive. It was a means of evaluating films *a posteriori* according to the director's technical competence, the presence of a distinct visual style, and an interior meaning which arose precisely from the tension between the director (*auteur*) and the conditions of production with which he or she worked. At this stage *auteurs* were not limited to American cinema, but later (in *The American Cinema*, 1968) Sarris elaborated his 'theory' (which might better be called a rationalisation) in terms of Hollywood cinema in particular, and some other great directors who were said to have influenced those working in Hollywood. Sarris never denied the importance of recognising both social conditions and the contributions of other workers besides the director in the production process, but he claimed that in the case of great directors, they had been lucky enough to find 'the proper conditions and collaborators for the full expansion of their talent'. Nevertheless, he rarely, if ever, mentions 'collaborators' and manages to summarise the career of Orson Welles without mentioning Gregg Toland, Herman J. Mankiewicz or production conditions at all. One of Sarris's most vocal opponents, Pauline Kael, devoted *The Citizen Kane Book* (1971) to the refutation of his theory that the director alone was the *auteur* of a film.

The basis of Sarris's argument in 1962 was the conviction that although it was impossible to deny the importance of history (the social conditions of production) in understanding any work of art, it was equally important not to reduce the work to its conditions of production. Recognition of the contribution of individual personal concerns was important therefore as part of the argument against a sociological criticism which saw film as a direct reflection of 'reality', without human mediation. To this extent he took issue with André Bazin (←p. 119) as well as with

contemporary American film criticism.

Another important strand of his argument was the polemic for the recognition of the artistic achievements of popular Hollywood cinema.

'After years of tortured revaluation, I am now prepared to stake my critical reputation, such as it is, on the proposition that Alfred Hitchcock is artistically superior to Robert Bresson by every criterion of excellence, and, further, that, film for film, director for director, the American cinema has been consistently superior to that of the rest of the world from 1915 through 1962. Consequently, I now regard the *auteur* theory primarily as a critical device for recording the history of the American cinema, the only cinema in the world worth exploring in depth beneath the frosting of a few great directors at the top' (Sarris, 1962, p. 130).

In his introduction to *The American Cinema* (1968) Sarris develops this polemic on behalf of popular cinema even further, classifying Hollywood in terms of its directors, and in terms of a hierarchy, running from 'pantheon directors' (the best) down to 'miscellaneous' (the least distinguished). Like any pantheon, Sarris's classifications are questionable, subject to differences of personal taste and historical change. None the less, it can be argued that the assumptions underlying the polemic (that there are 'good' and 'bad' directors, 'good' and 'bad' films, and that these evaluations can be accounted for simply in terms of the *auteur* theory) are an important element in the way that we look at films. Part of the pleasure in criticising films is to be able to discern what is 'good' and what is 'bad', and it is easy to forget that these judgements are both subjective and culturally specific. The *auteur* theory, in so far as it privileges one area of cinema over others, and the director over other determining factors in the process of production, encourages the acceptance of these ideological assumptions as natural rather than open to question. Rather than accepting Sarris's categories then, (and it is surprising how far they have continued to hold good for most *auteur* criticism in film studies) they can be used to provoke questions. For example: what is the value of assessing the quality of a film according to the consistency of its 'world-view'? Does it matter *which* world-view is being presented?

Auteur theory: 'pantheon directors'

D. W. GRIFFITH

Sarris argued that the history of American cinema could be written in terms of its great directors:

'Very early in his career, Griffith mastered most of the technical vocabulary of the cinema, and then proceeded to simplify his vocabulary for the sake of greater psychological penetration of the dramatic issues that concerned him ... The debt that all film-makers owe to D. W. Griffith defies calculation. Even before *The Birth of a Nation*, he had managed to synthesize the dramatic and documentary elements of the modern feature film' (Sarris, 1968, p. 51).

According to this argument, history could be explained through the actions of a few 'great men', and indeed, this is the way Griffith is usually regarded. His film career spanned the history of the industry from its beginnings to the introduction of sound, and in that time he had struggled with an increasingly monolithic studio system for the right to artistic control over his films. He was credited with developing a specifically cinematic language, which was to become the basis of American narrative film through skilful editing together of panning shots, extreme long-shots, full screen close-ups and judicious use of split screen, dissolves, iris and other masking devices. This cinematic vocabulary was, of course, available to other film-makers working at that time, but Griffith's world-wide reputation among critics and film-makers as a pioneering artist of the cinema arose from the way in which he combined these elements to produce profoundly moving epic statements about history and

Intolerance – Griffith's historical tableau

the men and women who were caught up in it despite themselves. He was not afraid to embark on extravagant experiments and broke away from the studios in 1914 when his extravagance apparently became too much for them, and he began to produce, write and direct his own films (← HISTORY: *Box office attractions*, p. 5; Petley, 1978, pp. 81–85).

His skill in editing and experimental flair, although closely tied to narrative, was influential on film-makers all over the world. The montage tempo of *Intolerance*, for instance, was admired by the cinematic avant-gardes in France and Russia for the way it managed to convey abstract ideas and feelings, taking the language of cinema much further than the one or two-reeler

The Birth of a Nation (USA 1915 *p.c* – Epoch Producing Corp; *d* – D. W. Griffith; st b/w 12 + 7)

Griffith's first major independent production after several smaller-scale experiments with narrative and montage. Large-scale epic production was not confined to Griffith: it was a feature of both the contemporary American and Italian cinema (Petley, 1978, p. 81). None the less, the scale of the production envisaged by Griffith, his reputation for being intractable, and the controversial subject matter, discouraged investment from traditional sources, so that Griffith had to finance and distribute the film independently.

The Birth of a Nation is not only important in relation to the development of Hollywood narrative cinema, but also in terms of its ideological implications, which can be seen to be linked with its narrative structure. The combination of epic historical spectacle and family melodrama forms the basis here (as in other films) of a humanist ideology dedicated to individual freedom and the resolution of all contradictions of class, race and sex in terms of an ideal unity (see Extract 2). The racist Ku Klux Klan can be seen to represent unity (i.e. unity of whites against the emancipated blacks) which gives an ideological perspective on the value placed on family unity, and on the unity of the couple, in this film and other Griffith films. *The Birth of a Nation* was based on a racist novel, *The Clansman*, and its racist content has been the subject of

much controversy.

Griffith's development of cinematic narrative and spectacle, his use of the combination of the two genres, historical epic and melodrama, demonstrate a particular use of narrative fiction films as powerful, moving political propaganda. When compared with contemporary Russian cinema (Eisenstein and Pudovkin, for example), in spite of cross-fertilisation ideological differences emerge. If the epic quality of *The Birth of a Nation* encourages us to forget the way it elides and suppresses contradictions because of its spectacular dimension, it can be argued that the Russians exploited cinematic strategies in order to *produce* contradiction and criticism: a very different view of the function of art, and the artist, in society (→ *Soviet cinema of the 1920s*, p. 203).

Intolerance (USA 1916 *p.c* – Wark Producing Corp; *d* – D. W. Griffith; st b/w 10 + 13)

Intolerance is considered to be a virtuoso work: those cinematic strategies which Griffith had been developing in earlier films come together here to form a complex combination of technique and spectacle.

The narrative structure is based on the intercutting of four different stories illustrating social intolerance and its effects at different historical periods. Apart from the difficulty the spectator may have in following four separate plots, the variety of technical devices contributes to the overall effect of

complexity which gives the film the quality of an historical tableau, or tapestry, in which detail is ultimately less important than the movement of history itself. How far can this effect be attributed to the intentions of Griffith himself? The translation of traditional material (the Modern Story is borrowed directly from popular melodrama, for instance) into a sophisticated, innovative cinematic language can be seen as a high-point in Griffith's development of the multiple-plot narrative, or as a breakthrough in the silent cinema of this period. It was a time of technical innovation generally, in Hollywood and the rest of the world, and this film influenced film-makers in France and Russia. The Russians in particular admired its use of montage editing to bring together different stories and themes, and to manipulate the spectator's emotions, although it is unlikely that they would have subscribed to the theme of democracy based on individual freedom (see Bordwell and Thompson, 1979, p. 159, pp. 307–308).

Extract 1 shows the strategy of intercutting between different (though related) stories, with the use of titles to link two stories thematically. It can also be used to demonstrate Griffith's use of the stylised forms of melodrama to engage the spectator's sympathy and emotions through pathos. Acting styles could be compared with others from different production contexts (e.g. contemporary German, French and Russian cinema). →

comedies and dramas produced within the studios (see Bordwell and Thompson, 1979, pp. 293–298). Griffith's films were also different for the way they dealt with the great epic themes of history and civilisation, investing cinema with a prestige generally denied it in relation to the other arts; at the same time he tried to reach the widest possible audience by using popular forms such as melodrama to convey the 'humanity' of his characters. This combination of the epic and the personal, of history and melodrama, became the basis of classic Hollywood narrative cinema (→ HISTORY OF NARRATIVE: *Early cinema*, p. 208).

While there is no doubt that the exploitation of cinema's potential for spectacle and emotional involvement in Griffith's films was instrumental in establishing the artistic reputation of silent American cinema throughout the world, it is doubtful whether this great step forward can be entirely put down to Griffith himself, as Sarris's argument (and others) would suggest. Griffith's work was made possible by a combination of historical, economic and ideological factors which a traditional *auteur* analysis such as Sarris's ignores.

Auteur theory: 'the far side of Paradise'

NICHOLAS RAY

Sarris introduces Section II of *The American Cinema* thus:

'There are the directors who fall short of the pantheon either because of fragmentation of their personal vision or because of disruptive career problems' (Sarris, 1968, p. 83).

It could be argued that this second section is potentially more interesting than that of the 'Pantheon Directors' because it raises the question of how far the idea of 'personal vision' can be maintained in the context of Hollywood studio production. For many *auteur* critics Ray was the supreme example of the artist whose vision transcended conditions of production; for others he was the opposite, a Hollywood hack.

The extremes of critical positions in the debate surrounding Ray's films match the extreme differences between those films, and the inconsistencies within many of them. It could be said that the violence of their themes reverberates on the level of form so that they test the limits of the Hollywood system of representation.

This, together with the myths surrounding Ray's dramatic conflicts with the Hollywood studio hierarchy at times in his career, combines to produce an image of Ray as the archetypal Romantic Artist, in a continual state of crisis vis à vis the world (← *Orson Welles*, p. 132).

The overall sense of crisis and fragmentation which characterises Ray's work, its 'unevenness', paradoxically has made it possible for *auteur* critics to construct it as an oeuvre, seeing in its moments of perception and insight a unified personal vision (see Perkins, 'The cinema of Nicholas Ray', 1972). Thus such radically different films as *They Live by Night* (1948), *Rebel Without a Cause* (1955) and *Johnny Guitar* (1954) can all be seen as manifestations of a theme of almost mythic dimensions:

'. . . Moral crisis and salvation, a thirst for liberty, the clash of the individual and society, and the beauty of those ideals which men and women will pursue past all discretion to the point of their own annihilation' (Wilmington, 'The years at RKO: Part I', 1973, p. 46).

Sarris's call for a sense of proportion in relation to Ray's work, and his hint that

---

D. W. GRIFFITH (*continued*)

Extract 2 shows the lavish (and expensive) mounting of spectacle for which Griffith was notorious, and the use of rapid, rhythmic montage editing for dramatic effect.

Hearts of the World (USA 1918 *p.c* – Griffith Inc; *d* – D. W. Griffith; st b/w 28)

A combination of documentary and melodrama, this film's theme is the destructive effect of war on family and personal relationships. The scenes of war are spectacular, as usual in Griffith's films, but in general the film underwrites the necessity of defending democracy and individual freedom by dwelling on the drama of personal suffering.

Some documentary footage was used, and the war provides the background to the drama, so that the film works as powerful humanist propaganda. Scenes of love, caring and happiness in the family and between the Boy and Girl are dwelt upon: this innocence is shattered by the war, and the Girl in particular (played by Lillian Gish) is forced to come to maturity through personal suffering and unhappiness, a characteristic which became part of her star persona. In the extract the suffering imposed on the family and the couple by the mobilisation order and the devastation of war is taken to almost grotesque lengths when the Girl, distraught after the destruction of her village, finds the Boy unconscious on the battlefield and lies down beside him.

NICHOLAS RAY

They Live by Night (USA 1948 *p.c* – RKO Radio; *d* – Nicholas Ray; sd b/w 6)

Ray's first film for RKO, which at that time was in the 'progressive' hands of Dore Schary. Ray came from radical community theatre into post-war Hollywood; this is probably the only project he was able to film as he wished. The film, which belongs loosely in the sub-film noir category 'gangster couple on the run', is a sympathetic portrayal of the illusion of freedom cherished by the two young protagonists, forced to live outside the law and trying to realise their own desires from their position as outsiders. This attempt brings them into conflict with the system which they are seeking to escape and which ultimately destroys them. The romanticism of the couple cannot be denied: their innocence and playful naiveté might seem absurd, were it not for the fact that it is opposed to a hostile and threatening social system which allows no room for romantic fantasy. Meaning resides in this play of oppositions: from the point-of-view of the lovers, normality appears grotesque, yet their innocence is also unreal, and we know that they are doomed (cf. *You Only Live Once*, *Bonnie and Clyde*, *Pierrot le fou*). Ray returned to the theme of rootless young persons again (in *Rebel Without a Cause, Knock on any Door*) often depicting them at odds with social institutions such as the family or the legal system. The extent to which this theme in itself can be regarded as critical

of American society provides an interesting area for debate: what is the role of genre, or narrative, for instance, in articulating such criticism? How far is social criticism possible within the Hollywood system of representation?

On Dangerous Ground (USA 1951 *p.c* – RKO Radio; *d* – Nicholas Ray; sd b/w 15)

They Live by Night spent two years in the vaults of RKO Studios before being released. Howard Hughes arrived at the Studios, demanding personal approval on everything in the production process: consequently, Ray often found himself with uncongenial projects (*A Woman's Secret, Born to be Bad* – two of Ray's 'bad' films from this period).

At the end of the 1940s Ray was reunited with his sympathetic producer John Houseman and regained some of the control he had lost. He worked on the script of *On Dangerous Ground*, which can be seen as a development of preoccupations in *They Live By Night*, looking forward to later films.

The protagonists of this film are victims of a destructive society, mirrored in their own violence. *Mise en scène* and editing (Sarris has called Ray's style 'kinetic') emphasise conflict and fragmentation, which is not seen as exclusive to city life, but has spread to the country too: the brutality of the cop Jim Wilson is seen as the effect of a social system built on repression of human desires. Characteristically, Ray depicts social repression as one of the root causes of psychological →

it might be productive to look at the films from the point of view of Ray's relationship to the industry (Sarris, 1968, p. 107) is perceptive. The fragmentation of the director's world-view can be seen as the result of contradictory elements which emphasises the *difference* between each film rather then their similarity, differences which can be attributed to their place in history.

Ray's film career can be roughly divided into four phases: the years at RKO Studio (1948–1952); an independent phase between 1954 and 1958; an 'epic' period (1961–63) and a final phase in which he rejected Hollywood completely, working in Europe and latterly in New York on underground, experimental projects. His 'best' films are generally thought to belong to the first two phases, although there are several 'bad' films there too; placing the films in their production context enables those evaluations made according to the criteria of the *auteur* theory to be reassessed.

They Live by Night – a theme critical of American society?

disturbance, but the psychologically disturbed hero was a common feature in Hollywood of the 1950s across many genres, as was the film's theme in which the hero policeman makes a journey from the urban landscape of the police thriller/film noir to the pastoral haven of the American countryside (cf. *The Asphalt Jungle*). In this film the haven or sanctuary is fraught with danger, perversion and a sense of loss.

The Lusty Men (USA 1952 *p.c* – Wald/Krasna Productions; *d* – Nicholas Ray; sd b/w 15)
This film, his last in black and white, was made at the end of Ray's 'apprenticeship' with RKO, and as Mike Wilmington points out, he was surrounded by so many excellent collaborators that it is not easy to single out his contribution ('The years at RKO: Part II', 1973/74, p. 35).

All these RKO films might be regarded as 'work in progress': they are stylistically very different, even when a consistent Ray thematic can be detected in them. Yet all of Ray's oeuvre displays this stylistic inconsistency, manifesting a willingness to experiment and explore the limits of cinematic language. Victor Perkins ('The cinema of Nicholas Ray', 1972) constructs a coherent unified *auteur* from this experimental principle. Another argument might construct the Ray oeuvre as the site of multiple contributions, constantly shifting, in which the contribution of Nicholas Ray is sometimes dominant, sometimes not, according to the specific historical moment in which each film was produced, and the different contexts in which it is received, which might produce different 'readings'.

In terms of Ray's treatment of genre, the thematic opposition between disorder (rootlessness) and normality (stability) is here transposed on to the rural setting of the rodeo film, a sub-genre of the western. An opposition is drawn between 'rodeo' (male: rootlessness/isolation) and 'home' (female: stability/family), both terms seen as incompatible. Typically, the obsessions of the characters in the fiction, their inability to control their impulses, drive the narrative forward, and ultimately the problem is resolved through death.

In comparison with other Ray films, the muted (almost realistic) *mise en scène* gives this film a rigour and certainty of style which differs from the 'experimental' excess which characterises Ray's oeuvre overall. Nonetheless, it can be argued that it occupies a pivotal place in that oeuvre, looking back to the concerns of earlier films and forward to *Johnny Guitar*. The strength of Susan Hayward's portrayal of Louise Merrit is interesting in this respect. She seems to be the first of Ray's 'strong' heroines, to be developed in splendid ambiguity in *Johnny Guitar* (see Haskell, 1974), a film considered by some to be Ray's personal statement against the McCarthy witch-hunts (see Kreidl, 1977).

Johnny Guitar (USA 1954 *p.c* – Republic; *d* – Nicholas Ray; sd col 10)
Kreidl (1977) describes *Johnny Guitar* as a political western with a female hero, an anti-McCarthy parable made during self-imposed exile in Spain. Certainly the film's theme of a disenchanted outsider who returns home to find a

land ravaged by hatred, distrust and revenge which he must find the strength to resist is both characteristic of Ray's work and appropriate to Cold War America.

Kreidl argues that Ray is more clearly the sole author of *Johnny Guitar* than of *Rebel Without a Cause*, which was a collaborative effort. It seems Ray had a high degree of control over the production: the film was made in Spain away from the scrutiny of Hollywood executives, and Ray was an investing co-producer. His 'signature' can be seen in the symbolic use of colour to code the different characters, the exploitation of the wide screen through horizontal composition, and the expressive use of sets and décor.

V. F. Perkins (1972) also emphasises the importance of décor and *mise en scène* as an expression of Ray's recurring preoccupations. He points to the division in *Johnny Guitar* between 'upstairs', Vienna's private, feminine retreat, and 'downstairs', the public, masculine, violent world where she must shed her femininity to survive.

Indeed, the political themes of the film are partly worked through in terms of the characters' sexuality: in order to resolve the unhappy situation Johnny Guitar must become stronger, more masculine, which in turn allows Vienna's 'true' femininity to emerge. Vienna's oscillation between masculinity and femininity has been seen by feminist critics as both offering the possibility of a positive role for women in the western (e.g. Haskell, 1974), and more negatively as a symptom of the way the genre activates women's predisposition to trans-sexual identification only to finally replace

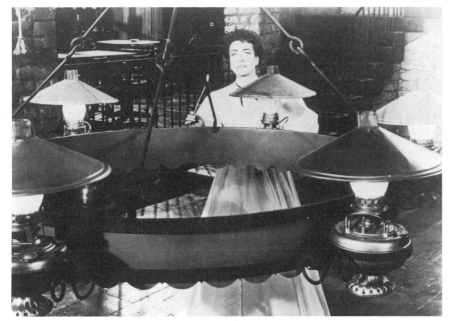

Johnny Guitar – positive roles for women in the western?

them, albeit uneasily, in the feminine position (← GENRE: *Gender and sexuality in the western*, p. 69).

Rebel Without a Cause (USA 1955 *p.c* – Warner Bros; *d* – Nicholas Ray; sd col scope 24)

The box-office success of *Johnny Guitar* led to Ray's return to America and the offer from Warner Bros to direct a film in the new 'youth movie' genre. Kreidl (1977) traces the different conditions and contributions which affected the final product, in his view a collaborative venture representing the way in which Ray preferred to work. None the less, Kreidl considers this Ray's finest work, and finds it ironic that its international success rests largely on the presence of James Dean, whose performance as Jim Stark is exemplary of Hollywood 50s Method acting.

Kreidl argues that the film breaks with the classic Hollywood narrative tradition, and points to Ray's characteristically dislocated *mise en scène* combined with horizontal composition to exploit the potential of CinemaScope (see Extract 1a). He sees the upside-down shot and the tilted camera used in the family confrontation scene (see Extract 1c) as code-breaking in the context of Hollywood emerging from the Cold War.

V. F. Perkins (1972), however, sees these strategies in classical terms as the perfect representation of Ray's ideas, projecting the world as he and his angry, alienated characters experience it. For Perkins the Chicken Run (see Extract 1b) represents Ray's world view in microcosm: life as a meaningless, chaotic journey towards death, unless one stops to question it, as Jim Stark

does, in order to find an alternative.

The James Brothers (The True Story of Jesse James) (USA 1956 *p.c* – 20th Century-Fox; *d* – Nicholas Ray; sd col scope reduced to standard 10)

In 1955 *Rebel Without a Cause* was a huge commercial success, enabling Ray to work in Hollywood at a time when CinemaScope and colour (the film industry's answers to television) were increasingly important. These developments in CinemaScope and colour in the 1950s contributed to the emergence of a new kind of super-western, (spectacular in style, and dealing with psychological themes) of which *The James Brothers* is one (← GENRE: *The western*, p. 64).

Like many of Ray's films, *The James Brothers* is regarded both as a hack-work and a masterpiece. The genre components are strong, but Ray's concern might be seen in the treatment of the outlaw band as both alienated from and trapped by the society it opposes. The violence within the gang is matched by the violence which society uses against the threat that the outlaws represent to capitalism (in the form of the railroad and the banks).

While Ray's sympathies can be seen to lie with the renegade outlaws, his use of *mise en scène* to depict the violent confrontations between them and the established social order suggests an interest in social conflict itself, an interest which can be traced throughout his work. Ray's '*mise en scène* of violence' could be compared with other westerns of this period to discuss different treatments of these common themes of violence and social unrest.

Auteur theory: 'expressive esoterica'

DONALD SIEGEL

In 1968 Sarris categorised Siegel as one of the unsung directors with difficult styles or unfashionable genres or both (p. 123) and described his oeuvre thus:

'Siegel's style does not encompass the demonic distortions of Fuller's, Aldrich's, Losey's, and, to a lesser extent, Karlson's. Siegel declines to implicate the world at large in the anarchic causes of his heroes. Nor does he adjust his compositions to their psychological quirks. The moral architecture of his universe is never undermined by the editing, however frenzied, (Sarris, 1968, p. 137).

The implication is that while Siegel's films manifest a consistent theme (the anarchic individual at odds with the social order) the structural austerity of his style represents containment rather than disruption or formal excess. The aforesaid theme is frequently found in Hollywood narrative cinema, and a comparison between Siegel's films and those of Nicholas Ray (see above) raises the question of the role of *mise en scène* in producing different interpretations of basic ideological material. While Ray's *mise en scène* manifests turmoil and upheaval in the structural organisation of the film itself, Siegel's direction, by contrast, uses montage to emphasise containment and order with schematic economy. This stylistic economy often makes it difficult for the critic to separate out Siegel's personal concerns from the generic concerns of the low-budget action film with which he worked for much of his career, and on which his reputation rests. For instance, the theme of the psychotic outlaw hero compelled to transgress social norms is present in much Hollywood cinema of the 1940s, 50s and 60s, particularly in thriller and western genres (cf. Fritz Lang, Nicholas Ray). While other directors can be seen to use these genre elements in the interests of social criticism, Siegel uses them to construct a view of society in which 'good' is indistinguishable from 'evil', justifying the individualism which motivates the violent actions of its protagonists. The spectacle of violence is an essential component of the action film, both as a source of pleasure for the audience and as a problem to be resolved by the narrative. Often violence triggers off a chain of events which can only be resolved through violence, and it could be argued that Siegel sees violence and its repression as inseparable elements in the maintenance of social stability, rather than as symptoms of a diseased social order.

Writing about Siegel's work in 1975, and with the benefit of hindsight, Alan Lovell offers a different perspective on the director from Andrew Sarris. Lovell criticises his own earlier attachment in the first version of his book (1968) to the combination of *auteur* theory and structural anthropology which was thought to offer a way out of the subjectivism of traditional *auteur* study. This auto-critique is used as the basis for a historical analysis of the changes affecting film theory, and Hollywood cinema itself, in the intervening years. Changes which, in Lovell's view, necessitate a complete rethinking of the analytic methods brought to bear on film study. Lovell's historical, descriptive approach is in sharp contrast to his, and Sarris's, 1968 evaluation of Siegel's work. From a post-structuralist perspective (→ *The passing of auteur-structuralism*, p. 183) he calls for a critical position on authorship which will take note of the social nature of all artistic production:

'The production process of particular films has to be related to the general production situation, available artistic forms, ideological meanings, intended audiences. The director works within this situation and he can do little to change it' (Lovell, 1975, p. 12).

In arguing for a consideration of the ideological meanings at work in particular films in terms of the conjunction of a

Children/gangsters in 50s reconstruction of 30s gangster movie – *Baby Face Nelson*

Baby Face Nelson (USA 1957 *p.c* – Fryman-ZS for United Artists; *d* – Don Siegel; sd b/w 8)

Siegel's films of this period show a consistency of style and thematic concern which it is possible to link with later films, in spite of the fact that they were made for different production companies. It is, however, difficult to establish whether this consistency derives from genre conventions, authorship concerns, or both. *Baby Face Nelson* is one of the series of reconstructions of 30s gangster movies characteristic of the genre in the late 50s (compare, for instance, Corman's *Machine Gun Kelly*, 1958, for different authorial concerns in the same genre). The psychotic, anarchistic protagonist who is a threat not only to normal society but also to organised crime is an essential element of the genre. Equally, the narrative can be seen to depend upon a central character who is the locus of contradictions, and whose function in the narrative is to cause problems which threaten the stability of social institutions, so that the resolution of the problem must be his elimination. A comparison with other films of this period in the same genre might point to the presence of different authorial concerns. Some of Siegel's own variations on the conventions might be identified as: the connection made between the gangsters and children (note the playground setting in this extract, and the hero's name 'Baby Face') and the use of prohibitive roadsigns to indicate imminent transgression of the law. Both of these motifs occur in other films directed by Siegel: however, they might also be

identified as intrinsic to the gangster genre (← GENRE: *The gangster film*, p. 86).

The Lineup (USA 1958 *p.c* – Columbia; *d* – Don Siegel; sd b/w 18)

This extract shows similar preoccupations to *Baby Face Nelson*. The psychotic protagonist, Dancer, is seen in apparently tranquil surroundings at the ice-rink. In the context of normal activities of play and leisure, the process of scrutiny whereby Dancer and The Man recognise each other takes on additional menacing force; the ordinary people around them are oblivious to the potential violence in their midst. When Dancer does lose control, killing The Man by exploiting the fact that he is crippled, escaping in a violent car chase, attempting to use a child as a cover for his escape, turning on his mentor (Julian) and killing him, his psychosis appears as the other side of normal human behaviour, a threat which must be eliminated if society is to continue.

The relationship between Julian and Dancer, the former more rational, mature, and the latter irrational, anarchic, echoes that between Sue and Nelson in *Baby Face Nelson* and that between Charlie and Lee in *The Killers* (1964). Relationships such as this in which one member of a couple contains and/or restrains the potential violence of another, less stable member, is common to this (and other) genres within the action film category (e.g. the western). An interesting area for investigation might be the function of episodes of excessive and spectacular violence in relation to the implied perversity of these couples, and its development in the

more recent 'buddy movies'. In Siegel's films the violence which unites these couples seems to function as a displacement for the 'perverse' desires which mark his protagonists off from 'normal' society, represented by the heterosexual family unit.

The Killers (USA 1964 *p.c* – Universal; *d* – Don Siegel; sd col 10)

Many of the preoccupations outlined above are developed in this film, made at a time when Siegel's reputation was well established and he was moving into bigger productions and different projects. At the same time, as Alan Lovell points out, Hollywood film production was shrinking, particularly in the area of modestly-budgeted productions, and Siegel's film work was interspersed with television work. *The Killers* was made for television, but considered too violent to be shown, and manifests the economy of construction typical of Siegel's style. However, critics have pointed out moments of obscurity and incoherence in the narrative (motivations left unexplained) which they consider make this film less impressive than, for example, *The Lineup* (see Lovell, 1975). In this context, a comparison with the Hemingway story, and the earlier film *The Killers* (1946) directed by Robert Siodmak, might be useful. The shift in emphasis in the Siegel film away from the victim towards the killers themselves and their relationship (again one of mentor and pupil) has interesting consequences: it is the intellectual curiosity about the motivations of their victim which initiates the narrative, and finally destroys the killers. The fact that

variety of different determining elements, Lovell comes close to positing as a critical method the 'conjunctural analysis' proposed by work on British cinema discussed below (→ *Ealing Studios*, p. 160).

Lovell divides Siegel's work into three phases: apprentice years (1946–53); development of distinctive themes and style (1954–59); and extension and changes in theme and style (1959–) as he gained artistic control. But he goes on to emphasise that the reconstruction of the Siegel oeuvre is complicated by forces outside the director's control: changes in the American film industry which transformed Hollywood cinema from a highly profitable economic enterprise into a declining form of popular entertainment (Lovell, 1975, p. 30). Lovell's analysis rings particularly true in the context of the present rapid decline of the traditional system of production, distribution and exhibition of films under the impact of new technology.

The Killers – Siegel's preoccupation with psychotic protagonists and extreme violence

motivations remain unclear and the narrative enigma is unresolved on one level means that in this film the problem of 'the irrational' is not solved in the way that it is in earlier films. We are left with the nihilistic image of the killer Charlie in the throes of a violent death as the money scatters over the street.

The treatment of killer-couple in this extract parallels that in *The Lineup*: again the concept of childhood is used to contrast the psychotic infantilism of gangsters (note Lee's obsessional playing with objects in this extract) with the vulnerability of 'normal' children (in the Blind School). Here the psychotic protagonists have a superficial veneer of normality (they are dressed like business executives) but violence constantly threatens to erupt (note the gratuitously violent attack on the blind woman). As in other Siegel films, the psychotic protagonists stand in opposition to 'normal', caring society, and to the organised criminal gang, from a position of extreme individualism. While Siegel himself stresses his lack of sympathy with such characters his continuing interest in them raises the question of his own position, or world-view.

The Killers seems to occupy an interesting place in Siegel's oeuvre, indicating the beginnings of a fragmentation on the levels of form and content under the impact of changing conditions of production in the film industry, and changing social mores in America in the 1960s.

Madigan (USA 1968 *p.c* – Universal; *d* – Don Siegel; sd col scope reduced to standard 20)

In *Madigan* the changes in production

values indicated above can be seen quite clearly. A police film in the 'action' category, it demonstrates the ways in which the genre was developed partly to attract audiences away from television. Cinema censorship was relaxed so that more extravagant violence and more explicit sex were introduced: note the spectacular violence in the first part of the extract, and the suggestion that Benesch's sexuality is perverse. The second part of the extract shows Madigan's own sexual problems with his wife, drawing a parallel between psychotic killer and detective which runs through the film (Benesch uses Madigan's gun to kill) and which is opposed to the liberal humanism represented by the Police Commissioner.

Siegel's preoccupations (in so far as they can be separated out from the conventions of the genre) have also developed. The existence of the perverse psychotic Benesch, who represents the breakdown of moral and social order, is seen as a justification for the extreme individualism of Madigan's behaviour, as is the inadequacy of correct police procedure to cope with this social breakdown. Madigan is a victim of society in the process of disintegration, and the failure of liberalism to come to terms with it, two sides of the same coin.

The opposition drawn between an obsessional cop and the assumed alliance between perverse morality and liberalism is further developed in the films featuring Siegel's collaboration with star Clint Eastwood, resulting in a cynical justification of those obsessional qualities in the service of the law which could be seen as a departure from the earlier films.

Coogan's Bluff (USA 1969 *p.c* – Universal; *d* – Don Siegel; sd col 20)

The beginning of the Siegel/Eastwood collaboration, in which the 'macho' elements of Eastwood's star persona came together with Siegel's interest in the 'maverick' cop as antidote to a disintegrating liberal society, to produce a self-reflective film full of ironic references to its own premises.

The fact that Coogan himself comes from Arizona and represents certain 'unfashionable' virtues associated with the western, such as stoicism, individualism, courage, is a constant source of reference in the film, which is set in the degenerate urban society of New York (degenerate = alternative drug culture). This is also a reference to Eastwood's rise to stardom in westerns, apparently a parodic reference, but the Eastwood image is eventually validated in opposition to society's decadence and liberalism. 'Alternative' society is also apparently parodied (note the disco scene in the extract) but the homicidal violence which underlies it, and the assumption that it has its roots in corruption and psychosis (Linny Raven and Ringerman) establishes it as a threat to society against which the confused liberalism of Julie, the probation officer, is inadequate (viz her naive trust in Coogan in the extract).

Coogan's methods are not totally validated by the narrative; in many ways he is the mirror reflection of the decadence he is fighting. However, the power of Eastwood's star presence in validating the conservative values represented by Coogan must be taken into account, particularly since they are opposed to 'inferior', 'feminine' values,

→

Auteur theory: film as commodity product

ROGER CORMAN

Sarris places Corman in his 'Oddities, One-Shots, and Newcomers' category, although he lists as many as twenty-five films directed by Corman between 1955 and 1967, many of which represent a consistent contribution to a genre (for instance, the Poe cycle of horror films and the gangster films). Apart from its value as a polemical 'scandalisation' category, this section – which includes Charles Laughton, Howard Hughes and Ida Lupino – perhaps best demonstrates the contradictions inherent in an *auteur* theory which depends upon a conception of an individual personal vision transcending conditions of production and material. Behind Sarris's summary dismissal of Corman's work seems to lie the implication that he fails to produce 'high art' from popular culture, and so falls short of being a true *auteur*.

There have been many attempts to reclaim the status of *auteur* for Corman (e.g. Will and Willemen, 1970; Wheeler Dixon 'In defense of Roger Corman', 1976) It is possible to argue, however, that Corman's resistance to the criteria imposed by Sarris's *auteur* theory (such as 'art' and 'good' films) makes it possible to question the basic premises of those criteria.

'Meaningful coherence'

Auteur theory enables the critic to impose unity in retrospect on a body of films produced in a variety of production set-ups. This unity is attributed to the presence of the director as the essential source of meaning, across different genres, studios, etc. The director as *auteur* is therefore opposed to Hollywood production conditions, and it is from this *relationship of opposition* that true authorship arises, distinguishing 'art' from 'mass entertainment'.

Corman's films cannot be fitted into this formation, since they remain firmly linked to the production set-up of low-budget 'exploitation' films in Hollywood in the 1950s, and rather than displaying any tension or opposition, seem to revel in their own 'trashiness'. Meaning seems to emerge directly from *conditions of production* rather than the director's personal vision. The profit motive, the need to make 'a quick buck' is so dominant that the *auteur*'s intentions seem to recede in the face of this assertion of film as commodity product, and coherence seems to reside rather in genre conventions and production values (→ *The passing of auteur-structuralism*, p. 183).

'Popular cinema as art'

Auteur theory demands that popular entertainment cinema be taken seriously: to take the work of a Hollywood director seriously is to take seriously the materials and conventions with which he or she works, to put popular cinema on a level with art.

The 'exploitation' material with which Corman works depends upon ripping off, and often parodying, more up-market expensive productions. Since it does not

---

DONALD SIEGEL (*continued*)
represented by Julie, Linny Raven and Ringerman. It could be argued that the film reflects upon the process of posing schematic oppositions in this way, looking for some middle ground in its constant play with the notion of 'pity', associated with the colour red, and Julie. Julie's compassion is questioned for its naive liberalism, but it also seen as an antidote to Coogan's 'hard', masculine values and his resistance to social change.

The extract is useful in demonstrating the ways in which certain aspects of Eastwood's star persona mesh with Siegel's developing concern with the maverick loner, the development of the police film in relation to the permissive culture of America in the 1960s, and Siegel's ambivalent response to these changes.

The Beguiled (USA 1971 *p.c* – Universal; *d* – Don Siegel; sd col 20)
'*The Beguiled* is the best film I have done, and possibly the best I will ever do. One reason that I wanted to do the picture is that it is a woman's picture, not a picture for women, but about them. Women are capable of deceit, larceny, murder, anything. Behind that mask of innocence lurks just as much evil as you'll ever find in members of the Mafia. Any young girl, who looks perfectly harmless is capable of murder. There is a careful unity about the film, starting with the first frame. We begin with black and white and end with black and white; we start with Clint and the mushrooms, and end with them; we start with Clint practically dead and end with him dead. The film is rounded,

intentionally turned in on itself' (Siegel, quoted in Lovell, 1975, p. 59).

As an 'art' film, *The Beguiled* can be seen as exceptional in the context of Siegel's work as a whole; it is none the less, like all of his films, the product of a number of contradictory elements. Some of these are: the incorporation of the 'art' movie into Hollywood film production in the 1970s, together with the notion of the director as artist (partly in response to the *auteur* theory); the collaboration between Siegel and Eastwood which led to the foregrounding of the most misogynist fantasies of both (cf. Eastwood's *Play Misty for Me*) and explicitly raises the question of the representation of male and female sexuality in Siegel's work in general, and in the action film in particular; the unstable conditions of production in Hollywood at this time which made it possible to make an a-typical, formally adventurous film, albeit strictly on a one-off basis. Formally adventurous though it may be, it can be argued that the fantasy it represents is central to Siegel's work and Eastwood's star persona; a paranoid fantasy of sexual relationships in which perversity and psychosis are placed within an all-female society which is destructive and threatening.

Dirty Harry (USA 1971 *p.c* – Warner Bros; *d* – Don Siegel; sd col 15)
As an example of a big-budget 70s police thriller with a psychotic villain and a potentially psychotic hero, *Dirty Harry* brings together many of the strands in Siegel's work discussed above, looking back to earlier films (*Baby Face Nelson, The Lineup, Madigan,*

Coogan's Bluff) in its treatment of genre, but displaying a more coherent grasp of the contradictions inherent in the society against which the hero sets himself.

The familiar opposition and parallels between the outsider cop, the psychotic killer and the liberal politicians remain, but they are complicated by the inclusion in this film of a social awareness which takes into account contradictory questions of race, sex and class which makes simple oppositions impossible. Harry is seen to recognise this when, at the end of the film, having finally killed the villain after obsessively hunting him down, he acknowledges his own futile isolation by throwing away his police badge.

The extract shows Siegel's development into big-budget production, one element of which is the presence of Eastwood playing Harry. It also demonstrates historical changes in the gangster police film. Notable in the context of Siegel's works is the process of scrutiny (cf. *The Lineup*) employed alternately by the killer and by Harry; the confrontation between Harry as a renegade cop and the Mayor as liberal politician; the confrontation between Harry as lone 'enforcer' (complete with magnum gun) and the black bank robber with whom he plays a sadistic and violent game, reflecting his cynical and nihilistic position. However, it could also be argued that the film carries the individualistic, 'macho' elements of the Eastwood persona to almost extreme limits, arguably allowing for criticism of the conservative ideology it represents by verging on parody.

b/w, CinemaScope, unknown actors and cheap sets characterise *Machine Gun Kelly*

take Hollywood seriously itself, and overtly displays this lack of seriousness, it is difficult to reconcile with the demands of the *auteur* theory to evaluate films as 'good' or 'bad'. Bad acting, bad direction are the hall-marks of exploitation films, and, it has been argued, their strength. They cannot be considered 'classic' works; indeed, they refuse the notion of classicism (→ *Stephanie Rothman*, p. 199).

'The critic's role'
Sarris stresses that authorship is discerned retrospectively by the critic, who looks closely at a film or a body of films to abstract the essence of the *auteur*. The role of the critic is one of contemplation and reassessment, and in this context authorship theory attempts to break with the ideology of mass production of films for immediate consumption by a paying audience. Exploitation films are precisely produced for immediate consumption (the drive-in circuit in America) and their value is assumed to be exhausted when they cease to make money. The disposable

ROGER CORMAN
Machine Gun Kelly (USA 1958 *p.c* – AIP; *d* – Roger Corman; sd b/w 15)

Before directing this film, Corman had made at least seventeen films for the exploitation market with the production company AIP (American International Pictures), all cheaply made using 'sensational' material and saturation booking to exploit all the potential markets. In the case of this film, the company was cashing in on the 1950s cycle of ganster movies (often remakes of 1930s films: cf. Siegel's *Baby Face Nelson*) popular with young people on the drive-in circuits.

Low budget production values can be discerned in the extract in use of black and white CinemaScope, unknown actors and cheap sets. David Will argues that the film resembles a comic strip (Will and Willemen, 1970, p. 73) but goes on to say that, like pop artist Lichtenstein, Corman redefines the 'validity of the lowest forms of commercial cinema' (p. 74). However, the production conditions in which Corman works are very different from those of a painter. His collaboration with a team or writers, technicians and actors can be seen from a glance at his filmography. Before attributing to him the status of artist therefore, the contributions of R. Wright Campbell (script) and Floyd Crosby (photography) in particular would have to be considered. One reason why Corman's work does not fit easily into Sarris's *auteur* theory is that the process of commodity production militates against the attribution of authorship to a single source. In this context the reconstruction of a body of films under the name 'Corman' privileges one element of the production process at the expense of others which may equally contribute to meaning in films.

An auterist construction of this film as a Corman work finds his personal concerns in the treatment of its gangster protagonist. Kelly is a pathological hero. In Corman's world 'heroism' is by definition a pathological state (cf. *The St. Valentine's Day Massacre*) which precludes any 'normal' relationships. However, the pathological hero is also a feature of the gangster genre: the 'Corman variation' on the genre can be seen in the bleak pessimism of this film, which implies that the only possible resolution is the complete destruction of society as it exists in order to rebuild from scratch.

The Haunted Palace (USA 1963 *p.c* – Alta Vista; *d* – Roger Corman; sd col scope reduced to standard 20)

By 1960 both Corman and AIP had become well-established. Corman himself became a major international director whose films opened international film festivals and were the subject of articles in European critical journals. The series of horror films known as the Poe Cycle reflect this change in their more expensive production values, slicker style, and use of more respectable literary source material. *The Haunted Palace* comes towards the end of the cycle, which finished with *The Tomb of Ligeia* (1964).

Critical renown and respectability do not, however, affect the basically commercial nature of the films, which continue to revel in their own conventions. Typical elements of the horror genre illustrated in the extract include the theme of black magic which undermines and is opposed by the community; the rational man of science who believes himself able to explain everything; the 'good' woman as victim; and the themes of psychic possession and physical deformity. The 'Corman variation' on the conventions can be seen in the atmosphere of decadence and social decay; the opposition between civilised manners and aggressive primitive desires in one pathological individual; an obsession with death and the past; and an all-pervasive sense of doom and despair. In terms of *mise en scène* the contributions of art director Daniel Haller and cameraman Floyd Crosby, both regular collaborators with Corman, are important. Haller is noted for his ability to make cheap sets look expensively mounted, and Floyd Crosby for his fluid camerawork. The importance of actor Vincent Price to this horror cycle should also be stressed.

The Tomb of Ligeia (USA 1964 *p.c* – Alta Vista; *d* – Roger Corman; sd col scope reduced to standard 10)

The basic elements of the genre are present in the form of the decaying aristocratic society; the possession of a person by supernatural forces; and the inclusion of a dream sequence to indicate the preoccupation with primitive desires repressed by society.

Auteur critics have seen Corman's interests in the concern with the past, the return of the repressed, the divided pathological hero tortured by the past and death, and with female sexuality as a potential force for the destruction of →

Themes of psychic possession and physical deformity in Corman's *Haunted Place*

A Cormanesque line-up in *The St. Valentine's Day Massacre*

existing society. In this film the 'hero', Fell, is destroyed in Ligeia's arms in the final apocalyptic blaze which concludes the narrative.

The treatment of female sexuality in this film could be seen in relation to Corman's general interest in strong, destructive female figures, and is interesting as a precedent for many of the films later produced by Corman for his own production/distribution company, New World Pictures, which has built up a reputation for producing films with a 'feminist' bent in exploitation packaging (see Morris, 'Introduction to New World Pictures', 1974; 'Interview with Roger Corman', 1975).

In the context of Corman's work the use of popular Freudian psychology should also be noted. In one sense it is 'camped up' as part of the commodity film package but it is also powerfully and seriously used in the scene in which Rowena is hypnotised, and in her dream. It could be argued that the audience is made aware of the process of manipulation, and then invited to participate in that process.

The St. Valentine's Day Massacre (USA 1967 *p.c* – Los Altos/20th Century-Fox; *d* – Roger Corman; sd col scope 18)

An example of Corman's move into big-budget production. An interesting comparison could be made with the low-budget *Machine Gun Kelly*, to discuss different production values, and with other historical reconstruction

gangster films such as *Portrait of a Mobster, Bloody Mama, Bonnie and Clyde*.

The film has a semi-documentary framework and taking up from the announcement in the opening legend that 'every character and event herein is based on real characters and events', the film's voice-over commentary gives biographical facts about each character as he appears. It is arguable that this device, together with emphasis on myth and ritual in the film works to produce an epic sense of the inevitability of Fate, which has often been seen as fundamental to the gangster genre. Will argues, however, that this film is different in that violent action is employed by Corman to reveal the rules and rituals of the gangster's world, rather than as a defining characteristic of that world (Will and Willemen, 1970, p. 75). Corman's own interest in, and respect for, the conventions of the genre have been seen in the use of colour and Scope (i.e. the plush red velvet of Capone's 'boardroom', suggesting his power and the extent of his aspirations; the use of Scope to suggest domination of space and territory). Capone himself is a monstrous, distorted psychopathic figure in the tradition of the genre, and of Cormanesque heroes. The extreme violence portrayed in the flashback (shot with red filter) elevates violence to the level of ritualistic exchange between the gangs, drawing a parallel between the gansters and American big business.

ideology of 'trash' exploitation films seems to be incompatible with the notion of the discerning critic analysing and evaluating films according to their status as classic works (see Nowell-Smith, 'Six authors in pursuit of *The Searchers*', 1976).

It is arguable that Sarris's *auteur theory* reached an impasse with Corman's work. By virtue of its own criteria of value it excluded discussion of film as commodity product, and it was precisely this discussion which was brought to bear against traditional auteurism in later, post-structuralist film theory.

References

James Agee, *Agee on Film: reviews and comments by James Agee*, London, Peter Owen Ltd., 1963.

David Bordwell and Kristin Thompson, *Film Art: an introduction*, Reading, Massachusetts, Addison-Wesley, 1979.

Wheeler Dixon, 'In defense of Roger Corman', *The Velvet Light Trap* no. 16, Fall 1976.

Molly Haskell, *From Reverence to Rape*, New York, Holt, Rinehart and Winston, 1974.

Pauline Kael, *The Citizen Kane Book*, London, Secker and Warburg, 1971.

J. F. Kreidl, *Nicholas Ray*, Boston, Twayne Publishers, 1977.

Alan Lovell, *Don Siegel: American Cinema*, London, British Film Institute, 1975.

Gary Morris, 'Introduction to New World Pictures', *Bright Lights* vol. 1 no. 1, Fall 1974.

Gary Morris, 'Interview with Roger Corman', *Bright Lights* vol. 1 no. 2, Spring 1975.

Edward Murray, *Nine American Film Critics*, New York, Frederick Ungar, 1975.

The New American Cinema Group, 'The first statement of the group', *Film Culture* no. 22/23, Summer 1961.

Geoffrey Nowell-Smith, 'Six authors in pursuit of *The Searchers*', *Screen* vol. 17, no. 1, Spring 1976.

V. F. Perkins, 'The cinema of Nicholas Ray', in Cameron (ed.), *Movie Reader*, London, November Books, 1972.

Julian Petley, *BFI Distribution Library Catalogue 1978*, London, BFI, 1978.

Andrew Sarris, 'Notes on the *auteur* theory in 1962', *Film Culture* no. 27, Winter 1962/63.

Andrew Sarris, *The American Cinema: directors and directions 1929–1968*, New York, Dutton, 1968.

David Will and Paul Willemen, *Roger Corman: the millenic vision*, Edinburgh Film Festival, 1970.

Mike Wilmington, 'Nicholas Ray: the years at RKO: Parts I and II', *The Velvet Light Trap* no. 10, Fall 1973; no. 11, Winter 1973/74.

Auteur theory and British cinema

The British critical context: Movie

The British authorship debate, as it emerged in the magazine *Movie*, was formulated rather differently because of historical factors specific to British culture. British critical tradition had its roots in an art criticism which stressed the importance of the critic's personal taste in assessment of works of art; a literary criticism which stressed the social and moral function of art, and the importance of the author's unified world-view as a criterion of value; a general cultural resistance to industrial modes of production geared to entertainment rather than art; and a Marxist social criticism which regarded mass media as essentially manipulative and dangerous, to be counteracted by the insights of a critical élite. This tradition was challenged by the 'popular culture debate' in the 1950s and 60s, in which film criticism played an active part (see Lovell, 1975; Rohdie, 'Review: *Movie Reader, Film As Film*', 1972/73).

These contradictory strands came together in the film criticism of the magazines *Sequence* and *Sight and Sound* with their dismissal of much Hollywood cinema as unworthy of serious critical attention and emphasis on European art cinema as a cinema of personal vision and integrity. Some of the critics who wrote for these magazines were also film-makers unable to find work in the contracting British film industry and forced to work as independents (Lovell, 1969).

At the time the New Wave was developing in France (← p. 134) the British film-making tendency, which came to be known as the Free Cinema movement, appeared, committed to the idea of 'personal vision' which was at the root of the *politique des auteurs*, but without its emphasis on popular American cinema. Later many of the Free Cinema film-makers became established in the British industry (e.g. Lindsay Anderson, Karel Reisz) carrying this commitment with them (← HISTORY: *British social realism 1959–63*, p. 47).

At this stage in British film criticism authorship in cinema had been stressed in opposition to the industrialised mass production of Hollywood entertainment films: this argument assumed that art cinema produced most 'good' films, and Hollywood produced mostly 'bad' films because it was controlled by capital, whose interests it reproduced. In this context the magazine *Movie* appeared in 1962 with an energetic attack on these defensive critical positions and on British cinema itself for its lack of style and imagination (see Perkins, 'The British cinema', 1972). *Movie* writers compared the mediocrity of British cinema with the technical expertise of Hollywood and put the former down to a cultural context which precluded the possibility of British directors achieving

any artistic control. They pointed to the climate of critical opinion which ignored questions of form and demanded 'quality' pictures with serious social themes, and to the lack of British *auteurs* with their own personal style. They argued that *how* a film put over its theme was indistinguishable from *what* it attempted to say, emphasising detailed analysis of *mise en scène* as the primary critical approach, because it was in the formal organisation of film that meaning was to be found, not in society itself. This emphasis on formal analysis was the link between *Cahiers'* *politique des auteurs* and *Movie's* *auteur* theory, but *Movie* critics lacked the film-making context of the New Wave which gave *Cahiers* its polemical force. They also lacked the strong national cinema, Hollywood, which lent strength to Andrew Sarris's arguments. This situation led them to look for a model towards a great popular cinema which was, paradoxically, in a state of decline.

Movie's attack on British cinema for its lack of inventiveness, based as it was on an auteurist position which saw only that style and personal vision were absent, now seems misplaced. It failed to analyse the economic, social and ideological factors underlying the British production context and, by looking towards Hollywood as a model, paradoxically supported the domination of British film production by the American industry. The concentration on the formal organisation of the film text itself at the expense of other forms of analysis led to a reinforcement of some of the least productive aspects of the *auteur* theory: the 'good' film as the coherent, non-contradictory expression of the director's personal vision and the task of evaluation given to the perceptive critic whose insights marked him/her off from the ordinary viewer. However, *Movie's* championing of the *auteur* theory and popular Hollywood cinema at this point had far-reaching effects on British film criticism, initiating debates which still continue. Its contribution to film education has been considerable; many *Movie* writers were teachers engaged in debate about the status of film studies in schools and universities, concerned to establish film as a serious object of study on the level of other arts such as literature and music. Their support of Hollywood as a cinema of *auteurs* was important to this struggle.

Free Cinema and British social realism

The critical tradition against which *Movie* directed its attack (i.e. *Sequence* and *Sight and Sound* critics and the film-makers who emerged from Free Cinema) had also defined itself in opposition to current values in British cinema. Critics such as Lindsay Anderson and Karel Reisz argued in the pages of *Sequence*, and later in *Sight and Sound*, for a 'new' cinema which would discard outmoded artifice in favour of the simplicity and freshness of personal observation of everyday reality. In 1947

Anderson criticised Rossellini's *Paisà* for its lack of personal statement and in 1955 condemned *On the Waterfront* for its flashy excesses of style, for masking its right-wing ideology with a display of technical tricks. In this article Anderson described his view of the artist:

'The directors whom Tony Richardson would be more justified in castigating are surely those false creators with professional talent beyond the ordinary, with heavyweight pretensions, but without equivalent honesty, insight or sensibility who undertake significant subjects only to betray them. It is less a question of 'dominating' one's material than of being truthful about it' (Anderson, 'The last sequence of *On the Waterfront*', 1955, p. 130).

Although as socialists these writers were interested in popular cinema as a means of reaching a large audience, they positioned

Look Back in Anger – criticised for its lack of feeling for cinema

themselves against the artificiality and stereotypes of Hollywood, which they saw as conformist, in favour of a personal poetic observation of reality, an affectionate look which respected its material enough to avoid distortion. In this approach meaning was an essence which pre-existed the film, brought to life by the director with the minimum of interference. The *Movie* critics argued against this that meaning was inseparable from form (*mise en scène*) and that only through close attention to the cinematic language specific to each film could meaning be *deduced*, constructed after the event.

As co-founders of Free Cinema, Lindsay Anderson, Karel Reisz and Tony Richardson made 'personal' documentaries on 16mm (e.g. *O Dreamland*, Anderson, 1953; *Momma Don't Allow*, Reisz/Richardson, 1955) during the fifties until the industry opened up to the production of the social realist films of the 1960s. For a brief period they were able to resist the monopoly of large-scale production set-ups in order to maintain artistic autonomy (see Hill, 'Ideology, economy and the British cinema', 1979). The Woodfall Group, formed by John Osborne and Tony Richardson in 1958 to make a film of the successful stage play by Osborne, *Look Back in Anger*, was criticised in *Movie* for its commitment to a social realism which put lofty themes before a feeling for cinema (see Perkins, 'The British cinema', 1972).

As Alan Lovell points out the Free Cinema/*Sequence* current emerged out of specific social and historical factors and disappeared for similar reasons:

'The impact was not a sustained one. Under the pressure of a situation that neither its aesthetic nor its economic and social analysis of the cinema could properly cope with, the Free Cinema/*Sequence* position was modified into one simplified diagram of the cinema, a mixture of Marxist and liberal attitudes – art is personal expression, personal expression is extremely difficult with a capitalist economic system, the artist's position is a very difficult one in our society' (Lovell, 'Free Cinema', 1972, p. 158).

When the Free Cinema/*Sequence* film-makers moved into the feature film industry in the 1960s they took with them this combination of 'personal expression' and the need for a sense of social responsibility. Their unwillingness to compromise may account for the small number of films they actually made and the fact that those films now seem to belong to a particular moment in British film culture. It could be argued that *Movie*'s attack on British social realist films of the 60s and on British film culture in general for its lack of style and *auteurs* fails to analyse its historical context. The very absence that *Movie* deplored has opened the way to critical investigation of British film history which reconstructs it in other terms than those which demand the presence of *auteurs* as a criterion of value (→ *British cinema: auteur and studio*, p. 160).

LINDSAY ANDERSON

Although Lindsay Anderson is acknowledged to be one of the most active and influential of British film directors he has directed few feature films in the last 20 years, which makes it difficult to establish him as a cinema *auteur*. Anderson's œuvre covers his critical writings for *Sequence* and *Sight and Sound*, sponsored promotional films, work in the theatre as producer, director and actor, television commercials and films made with the Free Cinema movement, besides his feature films, (see Lovell and Hillier, 1972). Conventionally, *auteur* theory would look for a consistent world-view across all this work and indeed it would be possible to detect a continuity of thematic

Public school life in *If . . .*

and stlyistic concerns (i.e. a committed left-wing view of British society and an interest in questions of artistic forms). However, those concerns have made it difficult for Anderson to work consistently within the British film industry, which has only periodically been open to aesthetic innovation, and those feature films he has made often seem confused and contradictory rather than homogeneous. Lovell argues that in the context of an entrenched bias towards realism in British cinema the production of non-naturalistic films within the British feature film industry constitutes a major achievement and this is perhaps the most productive way to understand the significance of Anderson's work (see Lovell, 'Brecht in Britain', 1975/76).

As one of the most active members of the Free Cinema movement, Anderson argued for the freedom of the film-maker to make personal statements through his or her films, that those statements should act as a commentary on contemporary society and should reflect the commitment of the film-maker to certain basic values for which he or she should be prepared to fight. Anderson's 'basic values' might be described as a kind of militant liberal humanism which saw the weaknesses of liberalism in its lack of commitment rather than in its theoretical or political position.

The aesthetics of Free Cinema were basically those of documentary reportage; however, it is arguable that they were never simply documentary. The use of sound-image disjunctions in Anderson's *O Dreamland* (1953) is an example of the way that the documentary mode was often transformed into personal commentary. Although the documentary strand of Free Cinema seems to feed directly into British social realism, the 'freedom of personal expression' strand did not and many of the Free Cinema directors, including Anderson, who moved into the industry found themselves at odds with it. Anderson's interest in surealism and in broadly Brechtian ideas taken from British theatre can be

seen in all his feature films and could be said to differentiate them from 'mainstream' British social realism. Those interests are perhaps most clearly identifiable in *If . . .* (1968) and *O Lucky Man!* (1973), albeit in a sometimes confused and contradictory way.

If . . . (UK 1968 *p.c* – Memorial Enterprises; *d* – Lindsay Anderson; sd b/w and col 14)

Co-produced and directed by Anderson, the film is interesting both in the context of Anderson's work as an explicit, if not entirely coherent, expression of his personal concerns and as a break with the naturalism of British social realism.

The film combines fantasy and social satire in a critique of public school life and mores and was explicitly influenced by Jean Vigo's *Zéro de conduite*. Anderson admired Vigo, Humphrey Jennings and John Ford as personal film-makers who combined their own concerns with a sincerity and honesty of style.

The film was made in colour and black and white and although this was primarily due to economic pressures it works to add greater stylisation to the film, which is concerned with the power of the imagination and its place in political action. It could be argued that the effect of this stylisation is to give the spectator a critical distance on the events in the film, denying the pleasure of identification in favour of a more intellectual perception. The extract illustrates the influence of surrealism on the film, representing Anderson's interest in repressed desires and their return in the form of destructive fantasies, and in the role of fantasy in political action.

The Entertainer – 'promotion for home-grown British produce'

Reconstructing the working class 'ethnographically' – *A Taste of Honey*

TONY RICHARDSON

A co-founder of the Free Cinema movement, Richardson was active in radical theatre, especially as a producer, and worked with John Osborne to produce *Look Back in Anger, The Entertainer* and *Luther*. When the British film industry opened up temporarily in the late 1950s his theatrical experience and film-making experience in Free Cinema made it possible for him to move into feature film production in 1958 under his own production banner – Woodfall Films (← HISTORY: *British social realism 1959–63*, p. 49).

In their polemic for recognition of the great *auteurs* of Hollywood cinema *Movie* critics attacked what they called 'the Woodfall answer' to the stalemate situation in the British film industry for its lack of cinematic flair and imagination (Perkins, 1972). Indeed, at first glance the films produced by Woodfall do seem constricted by their origins in the contemporary British theatre and novel, and by an over-earnest commitment to social realist themes. However, in the context of the project of Free Cinema they display significant differences from the rest of the British social realist films of the period. It is debatable whether Richardson manages to produce a personal statement through his films in the way that Anderson and Reisz have, but his films are interesting for the way they indicate the interrelationship between film and the other arts in Britain at this period.

The Entertainer (UK 1960 *p.c* – Woodfall/Hollis; *d* – Tony Richardson; sd b/w 10)

The presence of John Osborne as scriptwriter and Laurence Olivier heading the cast in this film adaptation of Osborne's stage success is an indication of the cross-fertilisation process between theatre and cinema which was prevalent in many British films of this period. This process, plus the social realist project of taking social questions seriously, added prestige to film production and caused it to be seen as art in contrast to television and popular American cinema. Indeed, the films could be seen as promotion for home-grown British produce as opposed to Hollywood fare as well as a polemic for the necessary social commitment of the artist.

The theme of the film, carried over from John Osborne's play, evokes the moral decay of Britain against the background of the deterioration of the popular art of music-hall, and asks where social criticism might come from in the future. It is not simply an adaptation of the play, however, but tries to raise questions about the critical function of art in the context of cinema too.

The extract offers an illustration of Richardson's early commitment to social satire and to film as an art form. In terms of the *auteur* theory it stands as an example of the British films *Movie* critics were arguing against (i.e. a 'quality cinema' of serious social themes lacking true *auteurs*).

A Taste of Honey (UK 1961 *p.c* – Woodfall; *d* – Tony Richardson; sd b/w 11)

Again an adaptation (of Shelagh Delaney's stage play), produced, directed and co-scripted by Richardson for his own company Woodfall Films, this film is an interesting contrast to *The Entertainer* because it was shot entirely on location and therefore looks less theatrical.

In the context of British social realism the film seems to fall into the category (or genre) 'youth movie' and is interesting for its use of a female protagonist as the youthful alienated heroine and its concern with the problems of female and homosexual sexuality in the context of the family. In terms of Richardson's roots in Free Cinema the film approaches the freer sexual mores of the 1960s through its working-class protagonists, who are mostly depicted as comic-grotesque, except perhaps for the heroine and her black boyfriend. Free Cinema was concerned with reconstructing the working class 'ethnographically'; however, this was from the point-of-view of the middle-class intellectual film-maker whose personal statement and social commitment were embodied in the film. In this film the element of personal statement is less easily identifiable with the result that social criticism is subordinated to the realist project of confirming for the audience what it already knows to be true.

KAREL REISZ

Reisz co-directed *Momma Don't Allow* (1955) with Tony Richardson and made *We Are the Lambeth Boys* (1959) both as part of the Free Cinema project; and the concerns expressed in these films can be detected in his first feature film *Saturday Night and Sunday Morning* (1960) although somewhat transformed by the context of British social realism.

In an interview published in *Cinéma International* in 1967, Reisz described his style:

'The style in which you make a film reflects faithfully what you have to say; there are no two ways of saying the same thing. The way you hold the camera reveals exactly what you have chosen to reveal. In my case, it's a question of filming based much more on observation than on abstraction. This implies a tendency to use the camera in the most simple way; I want the people in front of the camera to feel very free in their movements, instead of having to change places for the camera, that is in terms of the camera' (p. 690).

This formulation echoes the polemical writing of Lindsay Anderson and the commitment of the Free Cinema film-makers to personal observation, social commitment and sincerity of style. In terms of theme, Reisz's later films, such as *Morgan a Suitable Case for Treatment* (1966) and *Isadora* (1968), show a preoccupation with unconventional individuals, often artists or intellectuals, at odds with a restricted and unsympathetic society. It is difficult to see a direct connection with Free Cinema here. Although Reisz shared the basic principles of Free Cinema, it is arguable that his personal concerns moved away from those principles in a way that Anderson's, for instance, did not.

References

Lindsay Anderson, 'The last sequence of *On the Waterfront*', Sight and Sound vol. 24 no. 3, January/March 1955.

Lindsay Anderson, '*Paisà*', Sequence no. 2, Winter 1947.

John Hill, 'Ideology, economy and the British cinema', in Barratt, Corrigan, Kuhn and Wolff (eds.), *Ideology and Cultural Production*, London, Croon Helm, 1979.

Raymond Lefèvre and Roland Lacourbe, *Trente Ans de Cinéma Britannique*, Paris, Editions Cinéma 76, 1976.

Alan Lovell, *The British Cinema: the Unknown Cinema*, London, BFI Education Department Seminar Paper, 1969.

Alan Lovell, 'Brecht in Britain: Lindsay Anderson', *Screen* vol. 16 no. 4, Winter 1975/76.

Alan Lovell, *Don Siegel: American Cinema*, London, BFI, 1975.

Alan Lovell, 'Free Cinema', in Lovell and Hillier, *Studies in Documentary*, London, Secker & Warburg/BFI, 1972.

Victor Perkins, 'The British cinema', in Cameron (ed.), *Movie Reader*, London, November Books, 1972.

Karel Reisz, Interview, *Cinéma International* no. 16, 1967.

Sam Rohdie, 'Review: *Movie Reader, Film as Film*', Screen vol. 13 no. 4, Winter 1972/73.

Rebelling against bourgeois society – *Morgan a Suitable Case for Treatment*

Saturday Night and Sunday Morning
(UK 1960 *p.c* – Woodfall; *d* – Karel Reisz; sd b/w 11)

Adapted from the novel by Alan Sillitoe and scripted by him, this film marks an important moment in Reisz's career, since it was an unprecedented box-office success. Reisz respected the principles of Free Cinema in attempting to reconstruct with maximum authenticity and minimum distortion the daily life of a young working-class man in conflict with his provincial background. However, the film departed from Free Cinema in its use of the strategies of narrative fiction to 'get inside' the psychology of its central protagonist.

'In *We are the Lambeth Boys* I had tried to analyse only the relationship of some adolescents to society. The documentary form imposed limits on me and it was difficult to show the personal ties binding a boy to his mother, to his fiancée, to his friends. By contrast, the fiction film allowed me to do this and, through the characters in Alan Sillitoe's book, I discovered what might have been the private life of these "Lambeth Boys"' (quoted in Lefèvre and Lacourbe, 1976, p. 279).

As an example of British social realism this film belongs to the 'youth problem' genre prevalent in the 1950s and 1960s; Albert Finney's portrayal of a rebel anti-hero, engaged at times with his society yet alienated from it, has often been taken to account for the success of the film (← HISTORY: *British social realism 1959–63*, p. 48).

Reisz's concerns can be seen in the treatment of Arthur's critical view of his society. The working-class male protagonist, whose problems are represented in sexual as much as class terms, is set against a provincial industrial background which he seeks to escape because of its narrow restrictive moral codes, recalling Free Cinema's middle-class view of working-class life: Arthur's virility is closely linked to his desire to change the conditions of his existence.

Morgan a Suitable Case for Treatment
(UK 1966 *p.c* – Quintra; *d* – Karel Reisz; sd b/w 14)

This film began as a TV play: another example of the close relationship between film and other media in British cinema at this time. Although Reisz has moved away from his background in Free Cinema an element of social criticism remains: Morgan's 'madness' enables him to see what is wrong with the world.

The film illustrates the kind of dramatic situation that John Osborne's *Look Back in Anger* introduced into English drama – the young male protagonist whose rebellion against bourgeois society pushes him towards madness. In terms of Reisz's work, there is a development away from the social realist format of *Saturday Night and Sunday Morning* towards fantasy and surrealism. The sexuality of the hero is a continuing theme; however, his sexual competence is in question here. Morgan's impotence is in sharp contrast to the virility of Arthur, the working-class rebel hero of *Saturday Night and Sunday Morning*, though ultimately they are both depicted as victims of their society.

Movie and mise en scène analysis

Although each *Movie* critic writes about film from a different perspective (see Perkins, 'A reply to Sam Rohdie', 1972/73) they share an approach to film criticism which can be traced back to a British tradition of literary criticism, best exemplified perhaps by the journal *Scrutiny*, especially contributors such as F. R. Leavis, L. C. Knights and Denys Thompson, and the debate about the value of mass culture in which it was engaged (see Filmer, 'Literary criticism and the mass media', 1969). The 'popular culture debate' hinged upon an opposition between traditional high art and popular mass culture. For some critics, the former was capable of providing moral insights for the perceptive reader, while the latter, because it was mass produced for the entertainment of a passive popular audience, could do no more than reproduce the status quo. Cinema, as part of the mass media, was thought to preclude the possibility of individual statements because of its industrial mode of production and was placed in the category of popular culture (see Collins, 'Media/Film Studies', 1981). During the early 60s left-wing critics began to question the inferior status given to the mass media, arguing that it was not a monolithic phenomenon and that it offered the possibility of reaching a mass audience in a way that high art, which was only available to a privileged minority, did not. As a result of this debate Hollywood, the mass cinema par excellence, began to be reassessed. The *auteur* theory, which insisted that statements from individual directors were possible even in the Hollywood system of commodity production, performed an important function at this point in the attempt to break down resistance to mass art. At the same time, methods of film analysis were carried over from the literary criticism tradition. This tradition emphasised the 'organic' relationship of form to content and close analysis of the text as a means of discovering the themes and values embedded in it.

Movie's approach based on detailed attention to form merged quite well with that strand of the *Cahiers' politique* which saw analysis of *mise en scène* as a way of discovering an author's themes or moral values. Some confusion exists about the term *mise en scène* in film criticism, partly because it is imported from theatre and partly because of its collapse into *auteur* theory, where it came to mean 'style' or 'formal conventions'. Strictly speaking, *mise en scène* refers to the practice of stage direction in the theatre in which things are 'put into the scene', i.e. arranged on the stage (see Bordwell and Thompson, 1979, p. 75). When applied to film, it refers to whatever appears in the film frame, including those aspects that overlap with the art of the theatre: setting, lighting, costume, and the behaviour of the figures. By this definition the term does not include specifically cinematographic qualities such

as photographic elements, framing and length of shot, camera position, and movement, or editing. In formal analysis of film, then, *mise en scène* analysis is only one important area demanding attention. By extension from theatre to cinema, the term has come to mean the director's control over what appears in the frame, the way the director stages the event for the camera. *Cahiers du Cinéma* took this a stage further by making an evaluative distinction between *auteur* and *metteur en scène* in which the latter would be concerned simply with the craft of staging events for the camera rather than with organising the whole film according to a personal vision (← p. 126).

While *Movie* critics subscribed to the *auteur* theory as an evaluative method, their concept of *mise en scène* was broader than *Cahiers*' and referred to the overall formal organisation of films, their 'style'. *Movie*'s brand of *mise en scène* analysis is based on a deductive method whereby detailed description of films is seen to provide evidence to criticism, a method which sees film criticism as a practical activity rather than as a theoretical project. *Movie*'s attachment to this form of *mise en scène* analysis and *auteur* theory at the expense of other approaches seems to have led it into a critical impasse. By virtue of its own criteria of value (i.e. criteria of classicism, such as the 'organic unity' of a given film or body of films) it was forced to resist the impact of historical change, whether this was manifested in new film-making practices which did not embody classical unity and coherence or in new critical theories, e.g. Godard, or Soviet cinema (see the exchange of views between the *Movie* critics in 'Movie Differences', *Movie Reader*, 1972, p. 19, and again in 'The Return of Movie', *Movie* no. 20, Spring 1975, p. 1). Indeed, it could be argued that the combination of a deductive empirical method and *auteur* analysis cut many *Movie* writers off from engaging with more general political and ideological questions.

One of the oldest debates in film criticism is between the advocates of the art of *mise en scène* (e.g. Bazin, ← p. 119) and the advocates of the art of editing (e.g. Eisenstein, → p. 203) a debate which has tended to polarise issues rather than open up discussion of the interrelationship between the two methods of construction (see Henderson, 'The long take', 1976). Without collapsing the different positions of the *Movie* critics into the Bazinian world-view, it is possible to trace in some of their arguments a preference for a cinema of *mise en scène* untroubled by obtrusive editing or camera movements and a predilection for a classic cinema which eschews blatant formal effects in favour of a style which is adequate or equivalent to content. *Movie*'s pantheon (see *Movie Reader*, 1972) is headed by the great classic Hollywood directors, Alfred Hitchcock and Howard Hawks, closely

followed by a range of directors whose styles, the overall composition of their films, are seen by *Movie* to be entirely compatible with their themes or values. By this criterion they are judged to be true *auteurs*.

Movie can be credited with initiating a critical debate in Britain about the artistic value of popular cinema; it is however debatable whether its basic critical preconceptions were very different from those of *Sight and Sound* against which it argued; it simply applied these values to a different body of films – Hollywood rather than art cinema. Since its return in 1975 it has attempted to come to terms with the different questions raised for British film criticism by structuralism and semiology (→ p. 167; NARRATIVE AND STRUCTURALISM: *Introduction*, p. 223) and with the contradictions raised for its own critical position by the New Hollywood cinema.

JOSEPH LOSEY

Two articles on the films of Joseph Losey in *Movie Reader* provide different examples of *Movie*'s critical method based on *mise en scène* analysis and *auteur* theory.

Paul Mayersberg writing on *The Damned* starts with a close analysis of the opening sequence of the film, from which he proceeds to deduce Losey's symbolism (themes or values). He supports the analysis by reference to other Losey films in which he traces similar values, then returning to close analysis of *The Damned* to find other themes which in turn he relates to other Losey films, in a constant movement from the particular to the general. Mayersberg points to the importance of *mise en scène* as a conveyor of meaning in Losey's work.

'In his use of décor as an element in the construction of his movies Losey has no equal in the cinema. He and [Richard] Macdonald devise a setting that will characterise the person associated with it: the white simplicity of the psychiatrist's room in *The Sleeping Tiger*, the angrily contrasted surface textures of Stanford's flat in *Time Without Pity* conveying the moody violence of the man, the nudes in Bannion's flat [in *The Criminal*] which give the appearances of luxury, but are in reality no more than a grandiose extension of the pin-ups on the walls of the prison cells. . .' (Mayersberg, 'Contamination', 1972, p. 74).

Charles Barr's article ('*King and Country*', 1972, p. 75) also uses close analysis of the film to indicate his dissatisfaction with its 'cerebral' quality, nevertheless acknowledging that its schematic formal beauty articulates with logical precision the hopelessness of its theme. Barr makes reference not only to other Losey films but to other Hollywood films, and to Shakespeare's *King Lear*, to show how *King and Country* differs both from standard British films and from other anti-war films.

Both these approaches move from the

Losey links a rigid criminal code with big business in *The Criminal*

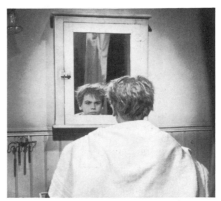

Innocent but deadly – *The Boy with Green Hair*

specific (the film text) to the general (other film texts), constructing the *auteur*'s personal values from analysis of single films and tending to ignore historical factors like

The Criminal UK 1960 *p.c* – Merton Park Studios; *d* – Joseph Losey; sd b/w 20)

Losey's career began in American radical theatre in the 1930s. His work as a theatre director was influenced by Russian theatre and by the theory and practice of Piscator and of Brecht with the Berliner Ensemble, about which he wrote several articles. He collaborated closely with Brecht on a theatre production of *Galileo Galilei* just before directing his first feature film *The Boy With Green Hair* in 1947 and has acknowledged the Brechtian influence not only on this film but on his work in general.

Losey's cinema is primarily intellectual. In an interview in *Image et Son* no. 202 he described his wish to stimulate thought in the audience (p. 21) through the use of an abstract *mise en scène* which encourages critical distance rather than emotional involvement and identification with characters (p. 25). In the context of Brecht's ideas, the 'cerebral' quality that Charles Barr objects to in *King and Country* can be seen to form the basis of Losey's work. Barr's resistance to the 'alienation effect' is perceptive and perhaps symptomatic of a critical approach which distrusts any signs of formal excess which might disturb the balance of form and content.

Because of his left-wing views Losey was blacklisted by the House Un-American Activities Committee and came to England in 1951, where he had some difficulty at first in finding work because of restrictions on the number of foreign directors allowed to work in Britain (see Roud, 'The reluctant exile', 1979). After completing several low-budget productions in between directing commercials for television, he had a success with *Blind Date* (1959) which led to a larger budget for *The Criminal*, a

story about prison life and organised crime which attracted Losey because he saw a parallel between the rigid criminal code and the organisation of big business. The film was not a success in Britain, but when it opened in Paris in 1961 French critics acclaimed the film as a masterpiece and Losey as a great director. It was largely due to the support of the French critics that Losey's reputation as an international *auteur* was established, making it possible for him to gain a measure of artistic control over his projects.

The Damned (UK 1961 *p.c* – Hammer/Swallow; *d* – Joseph Losey; sd b/w scope 19)

The expatriate Losey worked for Hammer Studios on this science fiction film: an unlikely partnership which resulted in one of the most pessimistic of all Hammer's post-war science fiction films, revolving around an insane government plot to preserve contaminated children from the outside world and a woman-hating teenage gang leader who stumbles on the results.

The Damned is staple Hammer diet: sensational science fiction full of violence, but it also manifests Losey's characteristic use of *mise en scène* and his political concerns. Some of Losey's preoccupations can be seen in the parallel drawn between the obsessional government scientist, Bernard, and the mindless violence of gang leader, King, and in the opposition drawn between Bernard the scientist, preoccupied with death, and Freya the artist, dedicated to life. The use of the innocent but deadly children to represent the contradictions between absolute purity (non-contamination) and the corruption of the system which has brought them into being is reminiscent of Losey's first film *The Boy With Green Hair* (1948).

Eva (**Eve**) (France/Italy 1962 *p.c* – Paris Film/Interopa Film; *d* – Joseph Losey; sd b/w 17)

The critical success of *The Criminal* in France established Losey's artistic reputation and caused Jeanne Moreau to suggest his name as a director of *Eva*. The production laboured under constant difficulties: disagreements between Losey and the producers over the script, Moreau and Losey both ill, the producers pushing Losey to complete the film. The music Losey wanted (Miles Davis and Billie Holliday) was unobtainable and the producers forced him to cut the film drastically to keep costs low, finally making further cuts without his consent (see Rissient, 1966, pp. 129–30).

In spite of these difficulties, the film is considered to be one of Losey's most important, both in its conception and its theme. Carefully structured in a prologue, three acts and an epilogue, it deals with an impossible relationship between a strong independent woman and a puritanical working-class Welshman who assumes his right to dominate her and is finally destroyed by his obsession. The film contrasts two characters from different societies to point up contradictions in the notion of sexual liberation. The portrayal of Eva by Jeanne Moreau is cold and detached and her 'independence' is established simply by her ability to control her own sexuality and to humiliate Tyrian through it. The interaction of class and sexual struggle in the film is interesting in relation to British films of this period which also attempt to deal with the subject of changing social values.

Accident (UK 1967 *p.c* – Royal Avenue, Chelsea; *d* – Joseph Losey; sd col 20)

Losey collaborated with Harold Pinter on the scenario of *The Servant* in

conditions of production, or even the director's known interests and ideas. In the late 60s some British Marxist structuralist film critics took *Movie* to task for its resistance to general theoretical and political questions and for the emphasis placed on the critic's interpretation of the films rather than on more 'objective' criteria. It could be argued that Mayersberg and Barr evaluate Losey according to their own personal taste and that a more objective approach would have been to place Losey in his historical context. However, it should be remembered that *Movie*'s attempt to validate Losey as a cinema *auteur* was part of their attack on British cinema for its lack of style. Losey had difficulty finding work in Britain after he was blacklisted in America, a fact which *Movie* saw as symptomatic of the stalemate situation in the British film industry at that time.

1963, which again took up the themes of sexuality, class and relationships of domination and subordination in the confrontation between master and servant. Pinter's concern with using the suggestive possibilities of language to make apparently normal situations seem strange and full of hidden menace meshed well with Losey's precisely structured *mise en scène* to create a nightmarish world of corruption in which the characters are turned in on themselves, obsessed with their own destruction.

Accident, their second collaboration, also deals with a closed world: an academic community, compulsively claustrophobic, in which class and sexual tensions erupt, disturbing the narrative continuity of the film. Discontinuities of time and place in the construction of the film contribute to a 'strangeness' which is intended to alienate the spectator, much as the central protagonists of all Losey's films feel themselves to be alienated, displaced in a world which imposes its rules upon them, destroying their individuality.

The studied formalism of this film, combined with the highly mannered performances from the actors, is typical of Losey's later work. The themes of the closed community with its stifling moral code and of class and sex struggles as destructive and self-defeating recur in all his films. The role of the mysterious Anna as a catalyst, or agent of destruction, takes up the recurring theme of the dangerous, sexually emancipated woman in Losey's work (e.g. Jeanne Moreau in *Eva*, 1962, Monica Vitti in *Modesty Blaise*, 1966, Melina Mercouri in *The Gypsy and the Gentleman*, 1957, Micheline Presle in *Blind Date*, 1959).

OTTO PREMINGER

The *Movie* critics' approach to *auteur* analysis generally, but not always, depended upon a form of deductive criticism which *a posteriori* reconstructed the *auteur* by abstracting personal themes and style from the films themselves. This reconstructed *auteur*, in so far as it consisted of meanings inscribed only in the director's oeuvre and not elsewhere (e.g. in biographies or interviews) bore no necessary resemblance to the actual person who directed the films, although of course it always shared the same name. It was a construction built by the critic and in this sense *Movie*'s *auteur* analysis was different from a more romantic auteurist approach which celebrates the presence of a visionary artist at the centre of the work. However, the disadvantage of this approach is that it places primary importance on the film itself and the relationship of the critic to it: the film is removed from its historical context and the critic's interpretation is privileged. This interpretation can be challenged by others but in general the subjectivity of the critic remains unquestioned: his or her task is to pass on insights and interpretations to the reader. One way of demonstrating the difference between *Movie*'s critical approach and the approaches the *Movie* critics rejected is to look at examples of these approaches and

Woman as enigma in Preminger's *Laura*

how they each construct an *auteur*. In the case of Otto Preminger for instance, there are clearly defined differences between the popular myth of the man himself (temperamental, intolerant autocrat – see Crawley, 'Vot you mean, ogre?', 1980) Preminger's own account of his relationship to the Hollywood film industry (see Pratley, 1971) and *Movie*'s *auteur* analyses of some of his films (see Perkins, 'Why

Preminger?', 1972). Each one of these accounts represents not only a different way of describing Otto Preminger, but also a different idea of where the truth of the matter (the 'essential' Otto Preminger) is to be found.

An interview article in *Films Illustrated* (January 1980) begins by laying out the myth of Preminger as a tyrant, a myth which it sees perpetuated by the popular press (and Billy Wilder!). In the course of the interview the interviewer comes to know Preminger and his career better, so that by the end he has discovered the 'real' Otto Preminger: a liberal human being quite different from the popular myth. The investigator goes behind the image to find the truth.

The Cinema of Otto Preminger (1971) by Gerald Pratley is also based on interviews. However, its project is one of serious academic criticism, an attempt to evaluate Preminger as a great artist. In this account Preminger's struggle for independence from the major Hollywood studios is seen as the struggle of the artist for freedom of expression, a freedom which is impossible within the hierarchical organisation of the studio system. Preminger's films are seen as reflections of this struggle for self-expression: because he asserts complete control over every aspect of the film-making process, includ-

ing distribution, then the films remain indisputably his, true reflections of what he wants to express.

The *Movie* critics' approach is different in that they start from the films themselves; nevertheless they reconstruct a 'Preminger' which has something in common with both the above and they are also concerned with finding the 'truth of the matter'. Preminger is a key *Movie auteur*

Mitchum and Monroe on the *River of
No Return*

because of his formal restraint, his lucidity,
and because his visual style displays an
equivalence between form and content
characteristic of classic Hollywood
cinema. This balance, or harmony
between form and content is basic to the
detached, liberal world-view which *Movie*
ascribes to Preminger.

One of the advantages of looking at different ways of constructing an *auteur* is
that it enables us to see that the *auteur* is,
precisely, a construction, and that different constructions (different readings)
are possible, no one construction bearing
the truth in preference to another. While
one account taken on its own may tell us
quite a lot about a body of films, several
accounts used comparatively could tell us
more about the films *and* throw light upon
the critical preconceptions of the *auteur*
theory. Another advantage is that popular
forms of critical writing generally considered to be too journalistic for serious
academic study can be seen to be equally,
if not more, influential on our thinking
about films as the academic critical writing
with which we are more familiar in studying films.

As with many *auteurs*, Preminger's
work is generally divided into two periods:
a first period between 1931 and 1952,
which covers the single film he directed in
Vienna and the stormy years spent as a
contract director and producer for 20th
Century-Fox, and a second period from
1953 to the present, which covers his work
as an independent producer/director following the consent decree of 1951 (the
anti-Trust laws) (← HISTORY: *The studios*,
p. 10). In this second period, the mid-1960s
saw a decline in Preminger's reputation,
only temporarily relieved by *Such Good
Friends* (1971). In spite of this unevenness,
however, *auteur* analysis looks for consistency in Preminger's oeuvre, whether
this can be defined heroically in terms of
a constant and dedicated struggle by
Preminger the man against all forms of
censorship, or in terms of a consistent
moral attitude discernible in the films
themselves.

Laura (USA 1944 *p.c* – 20th Century-
Fox; *d* – Otto Preminger; sd b/w 9)

In an interesting article 'From *Laura*
to *Angel Face*' (1972, p. 44) Paul
Mayersberg argues that Preminger's
early films show a preoccupation with
certain types of women which can be
seen to recur throughout his work.
Choosing ten out of the sixteen
American films of this period he
attempts to show that this
preoccupation manifests a continuity
which is all the more surprising in that
Preminger was not in a position to
choose his scripts. What emerges from
Mayersberg's investigation of women in
Preminger's work is the discovery of a
basic moral problem: the status, or
value of truth and knowledge in the
abstract. His protagonists, believing
themselves to be rational and in control
of themselves, find that they are in fact
at the mercy of events and their own
desires. The realisation enables them to
change, or, when it does not, the results
are often tragic.

This problem is certainly central to
Laura. Laura herself is an enigmatic
figure whose image changes according to
the shifting point-of-view of other
characters. The detective, Mark,
previously a rational man, finds himself
seduced by the enigma and in danger of
losing his detached perspective: this
almost leads to his death.

The extract illuminates this
preoccupation with balance and
detachment. Mark is played by Dana
Andrews who subsequently often played
the role of the apparently detached,
rational observer whose world-view is
threatened (see *Beyond a Reasonable
Doubt*, 1956, *Night of the Demon*,
1957). The representation of woman as
enigma in *Laura* is, it could be argued,
more central to film noir than to
Preminger's work in general (← GENRE:
Film noir, p. 96).

Angel Face (USA 1952 *p.c* – RKO
Radio; *d* – Otto Preminger; sd b/w 17)

Preminger's last film before going
independent. He was borrowed from
20th Century-Fox by RKO and,
according to him, given considerable
freedom by Howard Hughes to do as he
wanted on this film.

A good companion piece to *Laura*
because of the central relationship
between the sceptical male protagonist
(Robert Mitchum) and the beautiful but
dangerous young woman (Jean
Simmons) by whom he is seduced. This
type of female character is prevalent in
much Hollywood cinema (in thriller,
detective and film noir genres
especially): the duplicitous woman,
beautiful on the surface but basically
evil and dangerously seductive precisely
because of this double-edged quality (see

Kaplan, 1978). In the context of
Preminger's work, the duplicitous
woman threatens to make the male lose
his rational perspective. (See, however,
Such Good Friends, 1971, in which this
relationship is reversed.)

River of No Return (USA 1954 *p.c* –
20th Century-Fox; *d* – Otto Preminger;
sd col scope and standard 20)

The move to independent production
gave Preminger control over the entire
production process.

'Being an independent producer
indicates a change which I am convinced
will go much further than it has so far,
which developed during the last few
years, the change from mass production
by major studios to individual
productions. Today, independent
producers (like myself, Kazan, Wallis,
Kramer) produce a picture like we
produce plays on broadway, which
means selecting a subject, having a
screenplay written, casting it, being
autonomous; it is the individual's
authority and his responsibility. He
stands and falls with the success of this
one picture. There is no supervision from
any front office, there are no alibis that
we used to have. . .' (Preminger, 1956,
quoted in Pratley, 1971, p. 97).

However, *River of No Return* was
made for 20th Century-Fox, to whom
Preminger owed several films under his
contract. It provided him with the
opportunity to use the new
CinemaScope lenses and the wide-screen
format adapted well to his preference
for a *mise en scène* which employed long
takes rather than abrupt cuts. For
Preminger, CinemaScope and long takes
allowed the audience to contemplate the
scene, whereas cutting disturbed them.
This view of the potential of
CinemaScope is to some extent shared
and developed by Victor Perkins (1972)
and Charles Barr (see 'CinemaScope:
before and after', 1974) and is relevant
to the kinds of *mise en scène* analysis
employed by *Movie* critics.

Preminger's 'objectivity' might be
seen in the opposition between two
different ways of life, represented in the
struggle between Robert Mitchum and
Marilyn Monroe (uncompromising
moral rectitude versus moral
pragmatism). The extract shows how
this struggle is resolved in favour of
Robert Mitchum, raising the question of
how far 'objectivity' is possible in classic
narrative cinema, where the narrative
ending works to resolve opposing views.

Carmen Jones (USA 1954 *p.c* – 20th
Century-Fox; *d* – Otto Preminger;
sd col scope reduced to standard 10)

As an independent producer
Preminger developed a reputation for
dealing with 'controversial' subjects: →

sexuality (e.g. *Bonjour Tristesse*, 1957), race (e.g. *Carmen Jones, Porgy and Bess*, 1959) and drugs (*The Man with the Golden Arm*, 1955) some of which led to battles with the censorship bodies of the American film industry. *Carmen Jones*, however, although it figures an all-black cast, is not in itself about race. It belongs to an interesting and little investigated American genre: the black musical (cf. *Cabin in the Sky*, 1943).

As Paul Mayersberg points out ('Carmen and Bess', 1972) the film is primarily concerned with the theme of freedom, one of Preminger's preoccupations, exemplified by the tension between anarchic freedom and military rigidity. The musical film is particularly adept at articulating 'utopian' themes of freedom and self-expression, and Preminger says of this film:

'This was really a fantasy, as was *Porgy and Bess*. The all-black world shown in these films doesn't exist, at least not in the United States. We used the musical-fantasy quality to convey something of the needs and aspirations of coloured people. Later, I moved into objective reality with *Hurry Sundown*. . .' (quoted in Pratley, 1971, p. 11).

Anatomy of a Murder (USA 1959 *p.c* – Columbia; *d* – Otto Preminger; sd b/w 8)

In the context of Preminger's oeuvre, this film is interesting for its return to the theme of *Laura*: the central protagonist, a lawyer (James Stewart), finds himself involved in a situation in which the 'truth' is very hard to establish and is in this film called into question by the narrative resolution. The jury finds Lieutenant Mannion (Ben Gazzara) not guilty, but the truth of the matter remains undecided, and the lawyer finds himself 'hoist by his own petard' when his clients disappear without paying his fee.

The film is interesting in the context of Preminger's work because the enigma revolves around the female protagonist (Lee Remick) and the question of whether or not she was raped. Her guilt or innocence is central to the narrative and remains undecided (cf. *Laura*).

The credits for the film are attached to the extract because they are designed by Saul Bass, one of the most famous of Hollywood's graphic designers, who collaborated with Preminger on many of his independent productions. The contribution of credit sequences is usually overlooked in film analysis, although they can play a large part in 'setting the scene' for the audience.

ELIA KAZAN

Movie 19 (Winter 1971/72) is devoted to a study of Kazan's career and provides an interesting introduction to his work which consists of a lengthy interview and extensive bio-filmography as well as detailed critical analysis of several films.

One reason why this detailed knowledge of the man, his background and ideas should be seen to be important in this case could be the assertively personal quality of Kazan's films and the extent to which they seem to manifest the changing concerns and attitudes of a man clearly caught up in, and acutely aware of changing historical circumstances. There is a strong autobiographical thread in Kazan's work: unlike Preminger, he cannot be said to have a 'detached' view of the world; like Losey, he is aware of the need to formulate a political position and engage the audience in critical activity. He differs from both of them in that he inscribes himself, as a human being rather than as an artist, across his work. This aggressive

artist to society and to politics, and of the individual to history.

Because of his roots in left-wing radical theatre of the 1930s in America, where questions of form and content, of style and politics, of art and society were constantly debated, the influence of social realism, naturalism and agit-prop can be seen throughout his films, providing a sometimes uneasy mixture with classic Hollywood narrative cinema; an uneasiness which it might be productive to explore rather than to dismiss. Similarly, Kazan's growing interest in psychoanalysis and sexuality is often represented as a disturbing force intruding with some violence into a social order which retains its balance precariously. This mixture of politics and sexuality in Kazan's work attracted French critics, as did the acknowledged influence of John Ford (see Tailleur, 1971; Ciment, 1974). The response of English critics, as noted above, has been more ambiguous. Interestingly, the contributors to *Movie 19* are split between those who find his work

Kazan humanising political questions – *Wild River*

self-display has caused some English critics to distrust his films, seeing in its 'flashy excesses of style' (see Anderson, 'The last sequence of *On the Waterfront*', 1955), an over-emphasis on the individual's role in history, or a vulgarity of expression (Robin Wood) which betrays the function of the 'true' artist: to educate with restraint, without rhetoric (Wood, 'The Kazan problem', 1971/72).

A different argument might be that it is precisely the unevenness, the emotional excess which characterises Kazan's work which makes it interesting, raising questions about the relationship of art and the

uneven, lacking balance and restraint (Robin Wood, V. F. Perkins) and those who find this unevenness the symbolic expression of Kazan's world-view (Jim Hillier, Michael Walker).

References

Charles Barr, 'CinemaScope: before and after', in Mast and Cohen (eds.), *Film Theory and Criticism*, New York, Oxford University Press, 1974.

Charles Barr, '*King and Country*' in Cameron (ed.), *Movie Reader*, London, November Books, 1972.

David Bordwell and Kristin Thompson, *Film Art: an Introduction*, Reading, Massachusetts, Addison-Wesley, 1979.

The revolutionary figure with whom
Kazan identified – *Viva Zapata!*

Ian Cameron (ed.), *Movie Reader*, cit.
Michel Ciment, *Kazan on Kazan*, London,
    Secker & Warburg/BFI, 1974.
Richard Collins, 'Media/Film studies', in
    Gledhill (ed.), *Film and Media Studies in
    Higher Education*, London, BFI Education,
    1981.
Tony Crawley, 'Vot you mean, ogre?', *Films
    Illustrated* vol. 9 no. 101, January 1980.
Paul Filmer, 'Literary criticism and the mass
    media, with special reference to the cinema',
    in Wollen (ed.), *Working Papers on the
    Cinema: Sociology and Semiology*, London,
    BFI Education Department, 1969.
Brian Henderson, 'The long take', in Nichols
    (ed.), *Movies and Methods*, Berkeley,
    University of California Press, 1976.
Jim Hillier, '*East of Eden*', *Movie* no. 19,
    Winter 1971/72.
E. Ann Kaplan (ed.), *Women in Film Noir*,
    London, British Film Institute, 1978.
Raymond Lefèvre, Interview with Joseph
    Losey, *Image et Son* no. 202, February 1967.
Paul Mayersberg, 'Carmen and Bess', in
    Cameron (ed.), *Movie Reader*, cit.
Paul Mayersberg, 'Contamination', in
    Cameron (ed.), *Movie Reader*, cit.
Paul Mayersberg, 'From *Laura* to *Angel Face*'
    in Cameron (ed.), *Movie Reader*, cit.
V. F. Perkins, '*America, America*', *Movie*
    no. 19, cit.
V. F. Perkins, 'A reply to Sam Rohdie', *Screen*
    vol 13 no. 4, Winter 1972/73.
V. F. Perkins, *Film as Film: understanding and
    judging movies*, London, Penguin Books,
    1972.
V. F. Perkins, 'Why Preminger?', in Cameron
    (ed.), *Movie Reader*, cit.
Gerald Pratley, *The Cinema of Otto Preminger*,
    London/New York, A. Zwemmer/A. S.
    Barnes, 1971.
Pierre Rissient, *Losey*, Paris, Editions du
    Cinéma, 1966.
Richard Roud, 'The reluctant exile', *Sight and
    Sound* vol. 48 no. 3, Summer 1979.
Roger Tailleur, *Elia Kazan*, Paris, Editions
    Seghers, 1971.
Michael Walker '*Splendor in the Grass*', *Movie*
    no. 19, cit.
Robin Wood, 'The Kazan problem', *Movie*
    no. 19, cit.

A Streetcar Named Desire (USA 1951
p.c – Group Productions; *d* – Elia
Kazan; sd b/w 10)

An example of Kazan's collaboration
with Tennessee Williams: he directed
two movies from Williams's plays (*A
Streetcar Named Desire*, and *Baby Doll*)
and directed several for the stage
throughout the 50s. It was independently
produced, and manifests Kazan's roots
in radical theatre. The ideas about
acting which emerged from the Actors'
Studio, co-founded by Kazan in 1948,
can be seen in Brando's performance as
Stanley, which is given value because of
its directness and immediacy in relation
to the mannered, 'dishonest' acting style
of Vivien Leigh (Blanche). A conflict, or
tension is set up between 'honesty'
(realism) and 'hypocrisy' (artifice), a
tension which can be seen throughout
Kazan's work. In this particular case
Kazan's populist politics can be
identified in the value placed upon
Stanley's virile working-class persona:
his violence seems to be justified in the
face of Blanche's social pretensions. The
extreme 'femininity' of Vivien Leigh's
performance has the effect of feminising,
and (in this film) devaluing the middle
class. One way of approaching the film
is in terms of the way that race, class and
sexuality interact to reinforce certain
class positions and identifications for the
audience, and the contribution of acting,
gesture and *mise en scène* to this
process. How, for instance, does the
power of Brando's performance affect
the way the audience views the sadism
and brutality of the Stanley Kowalski
character and mitigate our response to
Blanche as his victim? Is it conceivable
that the sexual and racial roles could be
reversed? The problem of Kazan's
'excessive' style raised by some *Movie*
critics could be discussed in terms of the
director's intentions to disturb, or move
his audience.

Viva Zapata! (USA 1952 *p.c* – 20th
Century-Fox; *d* – Elia Kazan;
sd b/w 10)

In 1951–52 Kazan became directly
involved in the proceedings of the House
Un-American Activities Committee by
giving testimony to the Committee
against some of his colleagues and critics
have seen a direct relationship between
these events and the films Kazan went
on to make in the 1950s. Certainly
Kazan has characterised his own
position as antagonistic to any party line
and in favour of intellectual freedom,
while still retaining his left-wing
sympathies, and insists that the films he
made during and after his testimony
were more explicitly left-wing.

Kazan worked closely with John
Steinbeck on the script; they were both
interested in the revolutionary figure of
Zapata, and Kazan seems to have
identified with him directly:

'... the figure of Zapata was
particularly attractive to me, because
after he got all the power that comes
with triumph, he didn't know what to
do with it or where to put it or where
to exert it. He felt about things as I was
beginning to feel about my own
situation. So all these three things – the
fact that he was extremely colourful and
interesting, the fact that he represented
a left position that was anti-
authoritarian, and the fact that in some
way he related to my life story, at that
point in my life – were reasons why I
became so interested in the subject'
(quoted in Ciment, 1974, p. 89).

The extract demonstrates the way
Kazan uses the crosscutting editing
technique basic to Hollywood narrative
cinema, combined with music, to create
intense excitement, involving the
spectator in a process of identification
with Zapata and his peasant supporters.
Comparison with *A Streetcar Named
Desire* raises the question of Kazan's
manipulation of audience response
through editing and *mise en scène*.

On the Waterfront (USA 1954 *p.c* –
Horizon/Columbia; *d* – Elia Kazan;
sd b/w 15)

After Darryl F. Zanuck cut *Man on a
Tightrope* (1953) without his
permission, Kazan insisted on cutting
rights on this film and following its
success he became an independent
producer with absolute rights on all his
projects.

The central theme of individual
conscience and social responsibility has
been seen as an attempt by Kazan to re-
establish his political integrity after
giving evidence to the House Un-
American Activities Committee: Kazan
characterises all his films of this period
as emerging from a desire to question
himself and the world around him.
Indeed, the narrative of *On the
Waterfront* arguably revolves around
the idea of the difficulty of taking up
political positions. Lindsay Anderson
(1955) is one critic who sees the ending
of the film as validating right-wing
individualist politics, a view which
perhaps fails to take the whole film into
account. Nevertheless, a problem
remains with the use of narrative and a
central heroic figure to raise political
questions: a problem which runs
through much of Kazan's work. Terry
Malloy is the central charismatic
character with whom the audience is
intended to identify, rejecting with him
the other available positions offered by
the other characters (or, indeed, any
which might not be offered). The extent
to which Brando's performance
strengthens this identification,

overcoming any questions we may have about the film's political stance, is an interesting point for discussion. In relation to *A Streetcar Named Desire*, for instance, there are important differences between Stanley Kowalski, characterised as essentially masculine and embodying a virile immigrant strength which arguably represents the New America, and Terry Malloy, a character who exists precisely in order to question those values, but finds himself unable to discard them completely, since he must become a man.

The relationship between Terry and Edie Doyle (Eva Marie Saint) represents the problem posed in sexual terms: the softness and passivity embodied in Edie (her 'feminine' virtues) are also to be found in Terry (he is a sexually ambivalent character in this respect). These 'feminine' qualities of caring and tenderness are to some extent validated by the film, as is illustrated by the meeting between Terry and Edie in the first part of the extract. However, they are qualities associated with passivity, and Edie rejects them in Terry because the political struggle against the union bosses requires 'masculine' toughness. To a certain extent she also rejects her own traditionally 'feminine' role by becoming more politically active after the death of her brother. Terry is required to 'become a man' in the struggle for freedom, and the extent to which political struggle is identified with 'masculine' qualities, particularly in this film, but also in Kazan's work in general, is an interesting issue.

Baby Doll (USA 1956 *p.c* – Newtown Productions; *d* – Elia Kazan; sd b/w 17)

This is Kazan's other filmed version of a Tennessee Williams play and is interesting as an early example of a more explicit expression of sexuality on the screen which emerged in America during the late 1950s and the 1960s. In spite of pressure from the Catholic Legion of Decency, Kazan refused to make any changes and persuaded Warner Bros that the notoriety would help sell the picture. The gigantic sign which advertised the film, showing Carroll Baker in a crib sucking her thumb, is now legendary (← HISTORY: *Censorship*, p. 7).

Kazan shared Williams's obsession with the crumbling way of life in the South and with the idea of the virile immigrant-outsider who acts as force for change and rejuvenation. Kazan wanted Brando to play this role, but he refused. Characteristically, the political questions are represented in terms of sexual problems: Archie Lee's inability to fulfill his side of the marriage agreement in material terms is explicitly linked with his sexual frustration and Baby Doll's arrested development.

Baby Doll is the first of Kazan's films in which blacks from time to time act as a chorus, commenting on the whites' behaviour (see also *A Face in the Crowd*, 1957, *Wild River*, 1960). However, Kazan has said that he intended to portray the bigoted white Southerners sympathetically (if comically) in this film and sees it as the beginnings of a more liberal position in his work.

In terms of *mise en scène*, the opposition white/black is striking and was intended to represent symbolically the death of the old South in the face of new blood: the immigrants and the blacks. White is associated with femininity and weakness, black with masculinity and strength (see interview with Kazan, *Movie* no. 19, p. 9).

The use of the opposition between blonde woman and dark man here can be compared with its use in other Kazan films (Eva Marie Saint vs. Marlon Brando in *On the Waterfront*, Lee Remick vs. Montgomery Clift in *Wild River*). Kazan's complex version of the 'dumb blonde' stereotype is embodied in the performance of Carroll Baker as Baby Doll: arrested sexual development combined with material acquisitiveness. At the same time she has much in common with other Kazan heroes, in particular those represented by Marlon Brando and James Dean, a continuity underlined by the similarity of their acting styles emerging from the Method acting developed by the Actors' Studio.

A Face in the Crowd (USA 1957 *p.c* – Newtown Productions; *d* – Elia Kazan; sd b/w 17)

Kazan worked closely with writer Budd Schulberg on the script which was adapted from a Schulberg short story. The film is a mixture of authentic realism (in the location scenes, the choice of some Nashville natives as actors and in the journalistic format) and psychological fantasy in its portrayal of Lonesome Rhodes's tragic downfall.

In the context of Kazan's work, the extract illustrates the portrayal of the left-wing intellectual (played by Walter Matthau) as basically impotent, the relationship between personal relationships and political beliefs (i.e. the perverse attraction between Marcia and Lonesome Rhodes) and the distinction drawn between surface appearances and underlying reality, here played out in the tension between what the public sees and what goes on behind the scenes. The theatrical metaphor is apt, given Kazan's background in the theatre and his interest in Method acting

as a style most suitable for directly and truthfully expressing the character's innermost feelings.

Wild River (USA 1960 *p.c* – 20th Century-Fox; *d* – Elia Kazan; sd col scope or standard 10)

The film which perhaps shows most clearly Kazan's debt to John Ford in its humanising of political questions, its nostalgia for those values inevitably threatened by progress and its lyrical approach to its subject.

Kazan had been fascinated by Roosevelt's New Deal policies, particularly in the context of the Tennessee Valley Authority, where he spent a lot of time when he was a communist in the 1930s: he describes the film as the story of his love affair with the people of Tennessee and New Deal policies (see Ciment, 1974).

The basic conflicts in the film are between city and country, intellectual and uneducated, bureaucracy and traditional values, manifested in the relationship between the southern Garth family and the Tennessee Valley Authority Agent (Montgomery Clift) who tries to move them off their island, becoming deeply involved with them in the process.

The central relationship between Carol (Lee Remick) and Chuck (Montgomery Clift) evolves around the river, and the extract raises issues about the use of the woman to represent 'the natural', the qualities which the intellectual bureaucrat feels he is lacking, to which he is attracted, but of which he is also afraid, because he must prove himself as a man (cf. *On the Waterfront*). The *mise en scène* depends on wide screen and long takes, which seems to support the validation of 'natural qualities' projected by the film, although Kazan has suggested that the absence of montage editing was forced on him by the aesthetics of the CinemaScope shape and that the style of the film was not intentional (Ciment, 1974, p. 122).

The Stars Look Down – pre-war propaganda for nationalisation of the coal industry

Auteurs in British cinema

CAROL REED

The film career of Carol Reed is interesting because it spans thirty-five years of the British film industry, years in which his status as a British *auteur* seem assured, until his artistic decline in the 1960s. The distinction between *auteur* and *metteur en scène* is often invoked in relation to his work, which could be used in comparison with that of Michael Powell, for instance, to open up discussion of authorship in British cinema, a discussion which has

barely begun. Reed's reputation as a distinguished *metteur en scène* seems to rest on the evidence of a few films from his total production and a few privileged moments in some films which can be seem to epitomise the 'essence' of his style: the concern with employing cinematic *mise en scène* to emphasise social and psychological conflict.

Reed's uncertain status in the history of British cinema might be attributed to specific historical factors rather than to a lack of 'personal vision'. He had close working relationships with writers such as Edgar

Wallace and Graham Greene, both of whom profoundly influenced his career and whose contributions are arguably more important than Reed's to some films (e.g. *Our Man in Havana*, 1959, an adaptation of Greene's novel).

Although he is often identified as a director of thrillers and spy films, he directed more than thirty films in many different genres. The two study extracts are taken from films considered to be among his best, from the beginning of his career when he showed such promise and from the point when he began to decline.

The Stars Look Down (UK 1939 *p.c* – Grafton; *d* – Carol Reed; *sd* b/w 9)

Carol Reed's cinema career began at a time when the British film industry was gaining strength in the 1930s. He directed for Ealing Studios and for Gainsborough, but also worked independently and later produced and directed his own projects.

In terms of the influences on Reed's work: the 1930s saw the birth of Grierson's documentary cinema, which had some influence on the feature films produced at the time. This film, an adaptation of an A. J. Cronin novel, invites comparison with Griersonian documentary in its representation of class struggle in a small mining community. Graham Greene in a contemporary review compared the film favourably with Pabst's *Kameradschaft* (1931).

In the context of British cinema the film is interesting as pre-war propaganda for the nationalisation of the coal industry and against the dangers of private ownership. The conflict between the two male protagonists, Joe and David, both originally working-class, is one of ideas.

It is the position of David, who becomes a left-wing intellectual dedicated to the true interests of the miners, which is validated against that of the opportunistic, entrepreneurial Joe (cf. Ealing's *The Proud Valley*, 1939).

The character of Joe (opportunistic working-class man out for himself), is a stereotype which figures strongly in British cinema, calling to mind anti-heroes of the late 1950s and 1960s such as Joe Lampton (*Room at the Top*), Arthur Seaton (*Saturday Night and Sunday Morning*), and Vic Brown (*A Kind of Loving*).

Our Man in Havana (UK 1959 *p.c* – Kingsmead; *d* – Carol Reed; *sd* b/w scope reduced to standard 11)

Reed was at the peak of his stylistic achievement with *Odd Man Out* (1947) and went on to make three more films for which he is probably best remembered and which form the basis of his artistic reputation (*The Fallen Idol*, 1948, *The Third Man*, 1949, *Outcast of the Islands*, 1951). This was the period of his fruitful collaboration with novelist Graham Greene and producer Alexander Korda. On the basis

of this reputation he was able to move into bigger productions and made *Trapeze* in the USA in 1956, for instance, although it is generally recognised that the films he made after 1953 are not 'good' films, that is to say, they lack the mark of a 'true *auteur*'.

The reasons for this 'decline' may lie less with Reed the artist than with changes taking place in the British film industry in the 1950s. The shrinkage of the industry itself under the impact of television led to a small (and temporary) explosion of independent and experimental production whose interests merged with the new cinema of social realism heralded by *Room at the Top* in 1958 and *Look Back in Anger* in 1959 (← HISTORY: *British social realism 1959–63*, p. 48).

Our Man in Havana is interesting in that it was made at this point of historical change in the industry and, in terms of Reed's œuvre, marked a return to collaboration with Graham Greene which, together with his own masterly use of CinemaScope, might have proved his salvation had the time and place been different.

MICHAEL POWELL

'Let us not be afraid to use the words; for us, no doubt remains: the name of Michael Powell deserves a very high place among the greatest directors in the history of cinema. Among the most misunderstood also; for who, today, can cite a reasonable number of films made by the man who dared to sign *Peeping Tom*? And what a prestigious filmography! From the magnificent *The Thief of Bagdad* to the subtle *Black Narcissus*, from the celebrated *The Red Shoes* to the fabulous *The Tales of Hoffmann*, from the spellbinding *Gone to Earth* to the surprising *A Matter of Life and Death*, all works capable of delighting the most fastidious of cinéphiles! Twenty-five films mark out this exemplary career given over entirely to the service of an art; twenty-five works, spread out over thirty years, through which Michael Powell proves himself beyond any possible argument as an authentic *auteur*, creator of a personal universe with clearly defined boundaries, always open to artistic innovations as to the most unconventional subjects, capable of making with the same good grace (and the same pleasure) a tale from *A Thousand and One Nights* or a simple propaganda piece commissioned by the British government!' (Lefèvre and Lacourbe, 1976, pp. 274–275).

These are the words of two French critics who have championed the cause of Michael Powell: their tone of hyperbolic excess is perhaps a symptom of the need to counteract the general hostility with which Powell's work has until recently been received (particularly by British critics). It also points to the limitations of traditional *auteur* theory itself in so far as it fails to account for the fact that the power of these films lies as much in their 'strangeness' in the context of British cinema as in their inherent aesthetic value or in the possibility of attributing them to the personal vision of one man.

British cinema: realism and the 'quality film'
In his article 'Art, culture and quality: terms for a cinema in the forties and seventies' John Ellis traces, through the (often contradictory) discourses of British film critics during the 1940s, the concern to build a national cinema based on the concept of the 'quality' film:

'The quality film has purpose, form, and morality. It is linked to a strong humanist perspective, stressing the importance of international understanding between the various cultures of mankind. Film has a particularly important role in promoting this understanding, through the fiction film of quality. This is a unified construction, harnessing technique to produce a flowing visual narrative which refuses to indulge in overstated emotionality. It is imperative that this film have a close and deep relation to reality, not only reproducing its surface, but touching the very spirit

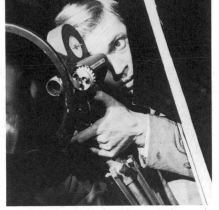

Peeping Tom – the film that went beyond the pale

of the real' (Ellis, 1978, p. 34).

Ellis's analysis reveals that while some Powell films were seen by critics to correspond to this definition, others were seen to resist it (viz. the description of *The Red Shoes*, p. 25) while others were reviled because they engage in a criticism of the basic tenets of the definition (viz. *A Canterbury Tale*, p. 42). The idea of the 'quality' film is found to depend upon the notion of the artist (be it scriptwriter, director or producer) as a central unifying force, dominating the multiple elements at work in the production process to produce a unified construction. If the film fails to conform to this definition, it is judged a 'bad' film, and the artist has failed in his task as defined by the critic.

The ideological function of criticism
An historical analysis of critical writing about the cinema can be used to show how definitions of authorship and concomitant evaluation of films as 'good' and 'bad', change in relation to different historical contexts. When value judgements are placed in their historical contexts they lose their appearance of truth or finality: instead they can be seen to perform a specific ideological function in relation to the cinema audience at a particular historical moment, defining what is 'good' and what

is 'bad' for them. Traditional *auteur* criticism can be seen to perform a similar function (see Lefèvre and Lacourbe above). Michael Powell's films have been met with a variety of contradictory critical responses, from outright condemnation (the case of *Peeping Tom* in Britain) to extravagant praise. When these films are seen in conjunction with critical writing about them, their changing status according to historical contexts becomes clear.

A traditional *auteur* analysis of Powell's work is complicated by the fact that many of the films were produced in collaboration with Emeric Pressburger, whom Powell met and worked with at London Films in 1938 and with whom he formed the independent production company, The Archers, in 1942 under the auspices of Rank. An *auteur* study of the work of Michael Powell should distinguish between the Powell/Pressburger films and the others (e.g. the 'Quota Quickies' on which Powell served his apprenticeship), which would raise historical questions about the changing structure of the British film industry, and its effect on the 'Powell œuvre'. In this way Michael Powell's work can be used to test some of the basic assumptions of the *auteur* theory: for example, that the *auteur* is the director of the film; or that meaning lies within the film itself, waiting to be found by the discerning critic.

References
Ian Christie (ed.), *Powell, Pressburger and Others*, London, BFI, 1978.
Ian Christie, 'The scandal of *Peeping Tom*', in Christie (ed.), *Powell, Pressburger and Others*, cit.
Brenda Davies (ed.), *Carol Reed*, London, BFI, 1978.
John Ellis, 'Art, culture and quality: terms for a cinema in the forties and seventies', *Screen* vol. 19 no. 3, Autumn 1978.
Raymond Lefèvre and Roland Lacourbe, *Trente Ans de Cinéma Brittanique*, Paris, Editions Cinéma 76, 1976.

Peeping Tom (UK 1960 *p.c* – Michael Powell (Theatre); *d* – Michael Powell; sd col 10)

Peeping Tom marked the end of Powell's career as a major British film director: significantly, perhaps, it was made at the moment of inauguration of the new wave of social realism in the British cinema of the 1960s. Powell's work is distinguished by a persistent *anti-realism*, which, at certain historical moments, it has been argued, stood in opposition to the prevailing aesthetic of realism in British film culture, an aesthetic founded on ideological notions of 'quality', 'sensitivity', 'seriousness' and 'good taste' (Ellis, 1978). Powell's films, more often than not, have been seen by critics as violating (by implication criticising) all their most hallowed canons. In the case of *Peeping Tom* they were unanimous as never before: the film went beyond the pale.

Ian Christie has traced the outraged response of contemporary reviewers to the film arguing that in their blanket rejection of it they accurately pinpointed its transgression, which was to draw attention to those basic mechanisms of cinema which it is the project of realism to efface. Some of these basic mechanisms are illustrated in the study extract: the projection of the home movie to a spectator in a darkened room; the manipulation of the spectator; the disturbing implications of voyeurism implicit in the situation (Christie, 'The scandal of *Peeping Tom*', 1978).

Another useful approach would be to place the extract in conjunction with a range of critical responses which construct the film in different ways, to show historical and ideological shifts in *auteur* analysis.

British cinema: auteur and studio

Ealing Studios

In his introduction to *Powell, Pressburger and Others* Ian Christie points out that *auteur* theory has had little to say about British cinema.

'During the last twenty years, there has been a certain symmetry between, on the one hand, the advance of *auteur* analysis as applied to American cinema, with a corresponding lack of attention to the industrial 'base' of Hollywood; and on the other hand, an almost exclusively 'industrial' conception of British cinema in terms of monopoly control, government subsidy and the like, with comparatively little attention paid to *auteurs*. Leaving aside the continued presence of a recognisably Griersonian discourse in British film criticism, the British cinema is constituted as a cinema of producers and production finance. If this seems too sweeping, consider that the only major studies of British cinema to be published within the last five years are two on Ealing Studios, one centring on Hammer and a biography of Alexander Korda' (Christie, 1978, p. 2).

This argument raises some interesting questions. Does *auteur* analysis automatically exclude analysis of the industrial 'base'? Certainly traditional *auteur* study tends to concentrate on the director as source of meaning at the expense of conditions of production. Conversely, analyses of conditions of production often fail to account for the director's contribution altogether. In the two studies on Ealing Studios mentioned by Christie, Charles Barr's *Ealing Studios* (1977) and John Ellis's 'Made in Ealing' (1975), both authors attempt to relate conditions of production to ideological readings of the films, with important consequences for *auteur* analysis. John Ellis traces in detail the nexus of working relationships and methods within the apparently homogeneous group known as 'Ealing', showing how the group's reputation for working together as a team, or 'family' was based on an hierarchical division of labour between 'creative workers' and technicians, with producer Michael Balcon retaining final control. Within this framework, members of the 'creative élite' consisting of producers, directors and scriptwriters collaborated in the early stages of preproduction, but Balcon's decisions were final. Robert Hamer, for instance, constantly found his projects vetoed because his concerns were significantly different from those of the studio. At production stage, too, requirements of time, space and money dictated certain shooting methods which produced a particular style of film: short takes and static shots. Some directors (Hamer again, and Mackendrick) who wanted to work differently found this very difficult. Rushes were viewed by the editor in consultation with Balcon rather than with the director, but final editing was done in collaboration

The Lavender Hill Mob – one of the Ealing Studios' mainstream productions

with the director, a situation which could lead to conflict, as it did on *Kind Hearts and Coronets* (Ellis, 1975, p. 103).

This historical analysis of the institutional framework within which the filmmakers worked reveals the contradictions underlying the prevailing view of the studio as a liberal and democratic working team; by showing how the concerns of some directors were in conflict with the studio's attempt to perpetuate an 'Ealing product' it begins to differentiate between films, arguing that the product cannot be seen as homogeneous. This approach suggests that the organisational structure of Ealing militated against the emergence of *auteurs*, though directors like Hamer and Mackendrick have been given that status in retrospect by critics.

In a later article 'Art, culture and quality' (1978) John Ellis shows how the formulation by critics of the relationship of 'artist' to film at a particular historical moment (Britain in the 1940s) was both hesitant and contradictory, caught between the project of creating a national 'quality' film in which the director is a central unifying force, and a concept of the director as an individual personality controlling the medium by the force of his/her preoccupations. This hesitancy about the relationship of artist to society, about the extent to which s/he should be held accountable or should be free to follow his/her own concerns, can be seen to run through British film culture (viz. Grierson's documentary movement and Free Cinema). The critics' response to those film-makers who have achieved artistic autonomy through independent production companies (Cineguild and Archers in the 1940s for instance) has been divided between admiration and outrage. Some Powell/Pressburger films positively

offended critics because they deliberately opposed the accepted definition of British cinema as 'quality' cinema, founded on notions of realism and good taste.

'Made in Ealing' describes how the hierarchial organisation and system of controls in operation at Ealing Studios under Michael Balcon both supported the project of producing a particular kind of 'quality' film and effectively prevented other, different projects from being realised. Ellis shows that the personal concerns and methods of working of some directors (notably Robert Hamer, but also to a certain extent Alexander Mackendrick and Thorold Dickinson) were generally at variance with the interests of the studio. In *Ealing Studios* Charles Barr argues along similar lines that there is a 'mainstream' Ealing (none the less important and interesting for being so) manifested mainly in the films of Basil Dearden and T. E. B. Clarke, and an 'oppositional' Ealing (the films of Robert Hamer and Alexander Mackendrick) which not only shows different concerns from the 'mainstream' but reflects critically upon it. Barr's reading of the Hamer and Mackendrick places them in their historical context, showing how they contradict and undermine the Ealing project in general while working within its different genres and stereotypes and how they indirectly reflect upon the frustrations experienced by those film-makers whose interests conflicted with those of the studio. *Auteur* analysis here has the advantage of differentiating between a body of films in such a way as to bring out contradictions, thus challenging dismissive critical accounts which stress the homogeneity of the films produced by Ealing. Barr combines several different forms of reading: ideological, historical and auteurist, to build up a complex and fascinating account of the work of Ealing studios which leads to a reassessment of those films in which *auteur* study plays an important part. By implication, a reassessment of British cinema in general is now not only possible but extremely important. Both Ellis and Barr concentrate on the conflicts between directors and studio head Michael Balcon, seeing the 'oppositional' films as a result of that conflict. However, there are other potentially critical voices in the film-making process – that of the writer, for instance. It should be possible to read some Ealing films in terms of multiple conflicting contributions, so that the director is not always seen as the major critical voice.

ROBERT HAMER

Ellis describes the relationship between Hamer and Ealing studios in terms of Hamer's antipathy to certain of the studio's fundamental values, which made his career there somewhat uneasy:

'His attitude to the studio was one of profound ambivalence: he left after *Kind Hearts and Coronets* to make *The Spider and the Fly* for Rank (edited by Ealing's Seth Holt), but then returned for several years. He existed at the extreme edge of, but still within, the community of ideas and assumptions which the studio held' (Ellis, 1975, p. 95).

The extent to which Hamer existed within the community of ideas and assumptions which the studio held is open to debate. In a detailed analysis of *Kind Hearts and Coronets* Charles Barr attempts to show the ways in which the film's complex and multi-layered structure works against the form of realism prevalent in the Ealing 'mainstream' to produce meanings which undermine its commonsense humanism and, more than this, inscribe a scenario of frustrated desire which comments both on British society itself and on Ealing's depiction of it. The dispute between Hamer and Balcon over the editing of the trial sequence is usually described in terms of different interests: Balcon wanted to emphasise the class aspects of the scene, Hamer was interested in the sexual aspects. This illustrates another point of conflict between Hamer and Ealing: the studio's attitude towards sexuality is generally recognised to have been repressive, linked to ideas of 'good taste' and 'quality' as hallmarks of British cinema, and to notions of sexuality which place women safely within the family and men in the public, cultural sphere (Ellis, 1975). Hammer is known to have been interested in sexual and psychological themes and Charles Barr makes a good case for his films as forming part of the 'underground current' in British cinema: the cinema of sex and violence which surfaces in the Gainsborough productions of the 1940s and in the films of Powell/Pressburger, burgeoning forth in Hammer productions a decade later. What is not yet

established, however, is the extent to which Hamer's films might be seen as a critique of petty bourgeois morality and the place of female sexuality within it. This would certainly be an important avenue of

investigation in an historical study of Hamer's work in the context of Ealing: an avenue tantalisingly hinted at by both Ellis and Barr.

Dead of Night – Ealing's last venture into the dark 'other world' of horror

Dead of Night (UK 1945 *p.c* – Ealing Studios; *d* – Robert Hamer (*The Haunted Mirror*); sd b/w 15)

John Ellis argues that the basic strategies of Ealing's realist cinema were closely linked to those of classic narrative cinema. Formal innovations were contained within a realist project which carried with it 'a certain mode of watching', encouraging the audience to recognise (or rather misrecognise) itself in the representation of full and finished characters, coherent entities living at the centre of society (Ellis, 1975, p. 107).

Ellis emphasises that this process of identification is complex and that Ealing managed to pose some real social problems in this mode. It is tempting to see Hamer's section of *Dead of Night, The Haunted Mirror*, as a metaphor for the process of recognition/misrecognition and as a criticism of it. The complacent middle-class hero finds the coherence of his own identity and then the ordered pattern of his life split and fractured by violent images from some mysterious past projected by the

mirror, images which gradually take him over and transform him into a madman, violently possessed by sexual jealousy. The Ealing image of the 'ideal hero', represented by Ralph Michael, could be said to be radically questioned by this film, distancing the spectator from the process of identification. The place of the woman in restoring the status quo could be discussed in relation to Ealing's representation of women. In a sense, Joan controls the narrative: she gives Peter the mirror, and her presence seems to dispel the 'other world'. Finally she defeats it by smashing the mirror.

The film can also be seen as a link with later developments in the British horror film, where a complacent social order is frequently disrupted by repressed forces (→ *Hammer Productions*, p. 162). After *Dead of Night* Ealing did not open the gate to the dark 'other world' again. Instead it accepted the terms of constraint on sexuality and violence which *The Haunted Mirror* implicitly criticises.

ALEXANDER MACKENDRICK

The status of *auteur* conferred upon Hamer and Mackendrick is justified in terms of readings of their films which reveal the tensions they display with all that Ealing represents. However, Ealing itself did not remain the same and the differences of inflection between the films of Hamer and Mackendrick are as much the result of the changing historical situation as of different personal concerns.

Mackendrick was active in Ealing from 1949 on; by the early 1950s the self-effacement of the individual in the Ealing community was consolidated and sexuality is more or less excluded from the films. The established order was now to be learned from, rather than questioned (see Barr, 1977). It is against this background that Mackendrick co-wrote and directed *The Man in the White Suit*.

The Man in the White Suit (UK 1951 *p.c* – Ealing Studios; *d* – Alexander Mackendrick; sd b/w 18)

Charles Barr sees the film as a critical statement about England 'governed by consensus' and about the relationship of opposition between the old and the new, between father and son (Barr, 1977, p. 134).

John Ellis (1975) provides a reading of the film which places it more centrally (less critically) with Ealing's output drawing on a description of the studio's 'creative élite' as a group of middle-class intellectuals who conceived of 'the people' in a certain way, as petty bourgeois shopkeepers and clerks rather than factory workers.

In this article Ellis criticises *The Man in the White Suit* for concentrating on individuals 'at the point of exchange' rather than workers 'at the point of production'. However, it could be argued that it is through this emphasis on 'the point of exchange' that the film is able to criticise the social relationships which 'mainstream' Ealing takes for granted: relationships between workers and bosses, between father and daughter, between men and women, as organised by capitalism – not necessarily a conscious criticism, however, since Mackendrick himself sees the film in psychological terms:

'I'd like to make another "hysterical comedy" like *The Man in the White Suit* which is my favourite film. A man lives in a social group. This group seems normal and he abnormal. Little by little you realise that it is he who is full of good sense. In a psychotic world, neurotics sometimes seem normal' (Interview in *Positif* no. 92, 1968).

Charles Barr analyses a scene from the film in which the heroine Daphne is asked to use her sexuality to get Sidney to change his mind, and responds by

making a point of putting a price on her services, a scene which is a good example of Mackendrick's use of comedy to make a critical statement about social relationships.

'Behind the mask of Ealing comedy, this seems to me to express a vision of the logic of capitalism as extreme as anything in Buñuel or Godard. For the metaphor of prostitution, compare Godard's *Two or Three Things I Know about Her*. In its seriousness and ruthlessness, in what it does with its comedy 'licence', it is, in case a reminder is needed, light years away from anything in the work of T. E. B. Clarke' (Barr, 1977, p. 142).

One might add about *The Man in the White Suit*: for the metaphor of the role of the intellectual in society, compare Godard's *Tout va bien*.

It could be argued that Daphne (Joan Greenwood) is a significantly different type of heroine from the ideal of femininity represented in 'mainstream' Ealing, although she necessarily remains within the terms of the stereotype. The character of Daphne tests the limits of the stereotype, much as *The Man in the White Suit* itself can be seen to rest the limits of the genre 'Ealing comedy'.

One way of exploring some of these questions about Mackendrick's relationship to Ealing might be to compare those films he made in Ealing with those he made after he left. It is arguable that the later films, while superficially different, show the same underlying structural and thematic concerns and the same critical intelligence: towards Hollywood and America in *Don't Make Waves* (1967) and towards the adult world in *A High Wind in Jamaica* (1965) and *Sammy Going South* (1963) (see Simpson, 'Directions to Ealing', 1977).

Hammer Productions

The approaches to Ealing Studios outlined above exemplify a form of analysis which attempts to locate films historically in terms of the multiple, often contradictory, elements which contribute to their meanings and so provides one way out of the impasse of traditional *auteur* study, which attributes meaning simply to the assumed intentions of the director. This kind of *conjunctural analysis* acknowledges the director's contribution, although it is not necessarily always the most important or the most helpful in understanding particular films. The conjunctural analyses of Ealing Studios above attempted to show how *auteurs* such as Hamer and Mackendrick emerged from specific conditions of production. The apparent similarities between Ealing and Hammer (← HISTORY: *Hammer Productions*, p. 44) and the fact

that Hammer was born as Ealing died, apparently giving life to that side of British cinema which Ealing 'suppressed'; psychology, sexuality and violence, suggests that a conjunctural analysis might also be useful in differentiating between the films produced by Hammer.

However, the most impressive critical account of Hammer to date, *A Heritage of Horror* (1973) by David Pirie, takes a traditional *auteur* approach in which Terence Fisher emerges as the Hammer director *par excellence*, creating his own world-view from basic studio material. Pirie argues that Fisher's Romantic vision (which he traces back to pre-Hammer productions) transforms even the most banal low-budget project (e.g. *The Devil Rides Out*) into a work of 'classic' distinction, making a qualitative difference between Fisher and other directors in much the same way as the *Cahiers* critics, and others, differentiated between *auteurs* and *metteurs en scène*.

By all accounts, Hammer directors seem to have had very little personal control over their films. They were employed on a freelance basis, had little to say about casting and scripts, and had to work strictly within the constraints of time, money and space imposed by low-budget commercial production. Under such conditions, the contributions of production workers other than the directors (such as the set designers, for instance) were important, especially in making cheap horror films look expensive. With this in mind, one might ask whether a traditional *auteur* approach is adequate to understanding Hammer's films.

TERENCE FISHER

One of the functions of the *auteur* theory is to bestow the status of art on apparently trivial material by showing how a director's œuvre displays a consistency of style, theme and structure which differentiates it from other work in the same genre, thus allowing us to look at it in a new way. *Auteur* study can be useful in critical re-assessment of areas of cinema history previously neglected or dismissed, such as British cinema for instance, opening up questions of pleasure which might otherwise be lost and which are not the same as those offered by genre study or study of production conditions.

The sensational, 'exploitation' projects with which Hammer studios made its name provide a good example of overtly popular, commercial material which outraged critics when it first appeared. One way to begin the work of reassessment would be to examine the historical reasons for the (temporary) unacceptability of this material to 'serious' British film criticism. Another way would be to give new value to the material by viewing it, as Pirie does, in the context of the literary tradition of Romantic poetry and Gothic writing in British culture. This perspective, combined with *auteur* analysis, allows Pirie to argue convincingly that Hammer produced a 'revolutionary kind of popular art' so that it comes possible to view the Hammer films as 'good' rather than 'bad', giving them the status of 'quality' films in retrospect. If Fisher's films remain within the bounds of the 'quality film', however, other Hammer films do not (e.g. *Taste the Blood of Dracula*), which suggests that Pirie's approach might not be applicable to the entire Hammer output.

Pirie takes the work of Terence Fisher as a test case: by establishing Fisher's status as an *auteur* he demonstrates that Hammer films are worthy of the serious critical attention so often denied to them. Significantly, he sees Fisher's art as that of a nineteenth-century story-teller, comparable to that of the best Gothic novelists, tracing in his films a coherent world-view based on a strict dualism, an ambiguity towards sexual excess and the body and a strong belief in the power of rational thought to overcome evil and corruption. It is interesting to speculate to what extent Fisher's work can be identified with the 'mainstream' Hammer product and how

Egyptian culture vs. British imperialism in Fisher's *The Mummy*

far his style and thematic concerns meshed with the interests of the studio. By all accounts Fisher and Hammer were in complete harmony, which was not the case with all their directors (see *Little Shoppe of Horrors* no. 4, April 1978).

Dracula (UK 1957 *p.c* – Hammer; *d* – Terence Fisher; sd col 16)

Fisher inaugurated Hammer's horror cycle with *The Curse of Frankenstein*, which was greeted with critical outrage when it appeared in 1957, but became a huge box-office success. Hammer were quick to capitalise on this success, and *Dracula* went into production about a year later. Pirie's detailed analysis of the film relates it specifically to Bram Stoker's novel, stressing its essentially British version of the legend and describing how Fisher's allusive style apparently meshed perfectly with the studio's concern to convey visually Dracula's sensuality and its effect on women (Pirie, 1973, p. 86).

The Mummy (UK 1959 *p.c* – Hammer; *d* – Terence Fisher; sd col 20)

Pirie attributes the *mise en scène* entirely to Fisher, although some of its 'pictorial sensuality' must be due to the work of designers (Pirie, 1973, pp. 57–58).

The violation of an Egyptian princess's tomb is the pretext for a revenge curse on a family of British archaeologists. A primary opposition set up in the film is a political one between British imperialism and Egyptian culture (viz. the conversation between Banning and the Egyptian in the extract) and the 'return of the repressed' theme centres here on the struggle between a 'primitive' culture and so-called civilisation. Compare this with similar struggles between primitive forces and scientific reason in the *Dracula* and *Frankenstein* films directed by Fisher for

Hammer. It might be argued that the dualism attributed to Fisher's world-view by Pirie is, rather, a requirement of the genre (← GENRE: *The Horror Film*, p. 100).

The Hound of the Baskervilles (UK 1959 *p.c* – Hammer; *d* – Terence Fisher; sd col 16)

Fisher's work is often admired for the precision with which he unfolds a narrative: he has been described as a master story-teller.

'(. . .) Some of the most completely successful of Fisher's films are those in which the lines are drawn with absolute clarity. This is amply demonstrated by a film like *The Hound of the Baskervilles*, where he uses Conan Doyle's plot to establish a stylish dialectic between Holmes's nominally rational Victorian milieu and the dark fabulous cruelty behind the Baskerville legend. The opposition is expressed within the first ten minutes of the film when he moves from the 'legend' with its strong connotations of the Hellfire Club and Francis Dashwood (the demonic noblemen torment a young girl) to the rational eccentricities of Baker Street' (Pirie, 1973, pp. 56–57).

The extract, which consists of this opening sequence, provides an interesting contrast with John Gilling's *The Plague of the Zombies* in which the hero/doctor is, unlike the 'Renaissance Man' Sherlock Holmes, as susceptible to the threat represented by repressed evil as the other chracters in the film.

The Brides of Dracula (UK 1960 *p.c* – Hammer; *d* – Terence Fisher; sd col 14)

In agreeing to direct this film for Hammer, Fisher laboured under the difficulties imposed by the absence of Christopher Lee as Count Dracula. *Dracula* (1957) had been an enormous success and in order to cash in on this, Hammer were forced to find a way to make a sequel without Count Dracula himself. In spite of these production constraints, Pirie identifies some characteristic Fisher touches, particularly in the film's finale (illustrated in the extract).

'The spirited climax sees Van Helsing in danger of succumbing after being bitten until, in a moment of puritanical strength, he purges the wound with a red hot iron and then uses the blades of an old windmill to make a moonlight cross which destroys the vampire. Sadly, this was the last appearance of Van Helsing in Hammer's repertoire for some time, but the figure of the scholar/scientist/poet/priest whose weapons are books and ritual formulae is never absent from Fisher's work for very long (next appearing as Professor Meister in *The Gorgon*) and owes much to Stoker's Dutch hero' (Pirie, 1973, pp. 88–89).

Note the implied lesbian sexuality in the extract; although only an oblique reference here, it was to reappear in more explicit form in later Hammer products, which became increasingly sensational. →

The agents of good spend a night in the Pentacle in *The Devil Rides Out*

TERENCE FISHER (continued)
Dracula, Prince of Darkness (UK 1965
p.c – Hammer; *d* – Terence Fisher;
sd col scope 23)

Pirie places Fisher's 'artistry' in this
film on a par with European art cinema,
evoking a comparison with Ingmar
Bergman – 'The detailed portrayal of
Dracula's re-birth in *Dracula, Prince of
Darkness* is a precise observation of a
religious (or anti-religious) ritual and on
this basis it might easily be compared on
a stylistic/thematic level with, say, the
mass in Bergman's *Winter Light*' – and
regretting that Hammer proceeded to
hand over the Dracula series to a
succession of directors. According to
Pirie, none of the subsequent films can
quite compare with Fisher's (Pirie, 1973,
pp. 89–93).

A different, perhaps more critical
treatment of the myth is offered by
Sasdy's *Taste the Blood of Dracula*
(1969).

The Devil Rides Out (UK 1967 *p.c* –
Hammer; *d* – Terence Fisher;
sd col 20).

Pirie evaluates this film as one of
Fisher's best, and places it in a
specifically English tradition of horror.
According to Pirie, Dennis Wheatley's
unremarkable novel is transformed by
Fisher and scriptwriter Richard
Matheson. Referring to the scenes
illustrated in the extract, Mocata's visit
to the Eaton household and the film's
climax in which the four agents of good
spend a night within the Pentacle
assailed by the forces of evil, he argues
that the subtle script combined with
Fisher's allusive and restrained *mise en
scène* produce a new and powerful
aesthetic masterpiece consistent with
Fisher's dualistic world-view (Pirie,
1973, pp. 60–64)

JOHN GILLING

Gilling's career as director with Hammer
was short and somewhat problematic: it
seems that he had differences with the producers, especially with Anthony Hinds,
who wrote many of the scripts for Hammer Productions under the name of John
Elder (see *Little Shoppe of Horrors* no. 4).
Gilling was himself a scriptwriter with an
enormous number of films to his credit for
British International Pictures, some of
which he had also directed.

His first directorial venture into horror
was *The Flesh and the Fiends* (1959) which
prompted Hammer to invite him to direct
for them for the first time (he had previously scripted a couple of their films).
The Shadow of the Cat (1960) has been
described as Gilling's masterpiece, and as
David Pirie (1973) points out it was significantly different from Hammer's 'normal'
style (epitomised by Terence Fisher), formally adventurous and evocative of Edgar
Allen Poe.

Gilling's reputation as an important
director of horror films derives from the
two films he made for Hammer about
Cornwall: *The Plague of the Zombies* and
The Reptile. In contrast to Fisher's work,
they are among the most deeply pessimistic
films that Hammer ever made. *The Plague
of the Zombies* raises questions about
'mainstream' Hammer (exemplied by the
work of Terence Fisher) and a different
kind of Hammer product in which the
formal and thematic concerns of the director can be seen to be different from, and
perhaps at odds with, the overall concerns
of the studio.

The Plague of the Zombies (UK 1966 *p.c*
– Hammer; *d* – John Gilling; sd col 24)

As indicated above, Fisher's
directorial style is basically within a
realist narrative tradition: he is often
described as a great story-teller, with an
economic style which relies upon the
setting up of tensions between schematic
oppositions (such as 'good' and 'evil')
and which resolves those tensions in
favour of 'good', which means reason
and science will prevail.

Gilling's style and concerns in *The
Plague of the Zombies* can be seen to be
significantly different from Fisher's: the
film is overtly surrealistic in form, using
shock effects, camera angles and dream
imagery to disturb the surface of the film
itself, producing a feeling of
disequilibrium which is never there in
Fisher's more cerebral treatments of the
genre. It could be argued that it is an
excess of form in Gilling's films which is
troubling and which makes them
peculiarly 'un-British' (in the sense that
David Pirie would describe the 'British'
manifestation of the Gothic horror
film).

The characters in Gilling's film do not
represent schematic oppositions:
certainly the scientist figure (played by
André Morell) is not the obsessional,
rational, 'objective' character
personified by Peter Cushing, who uses
knowledge as a defence against 'evil'.
Instead he is an agnostic, experimental
scientist who admits that there are areas
of thought and experience which defy
the tyranny of reason. For this kind of
character it is necessary to become
actively involved in these areas, risking
his rational objectivity.

Plague of the Zombies – shock effects and dream imagery disturb the surface of the film . . .

PETER SASDY

Sasdy, a Hungarian director who had worked for television, seems to have been interested in the potential for social criticism in the sado-masochistic themes of sexuality and violence on which the Dracula legend was based. In *Taste the Blood of Dracula* this potential was used to attack the hypocritical façade of the bourgeois Victorian family, in particular its hierarchical structure in which the word of the father was law. The family is split open as, under the spell of Dracula, the children become actively destructive of the old patriarchal order. Finally, the families decimated and the fathers dead at the hands of their children, Dracula himself must be destroyed if any form of new society is to emerge. But, in contrast to the treatment of Dracula in other Hammer films, his destruction is profoundly ambiguous in the light of this representation of him as a positive agent of liberation, and his return perhaps to be welcomed rather than feared.

References

Charles Barr, *Ealing Studios*, London, Cameron & Tayleur/Newton Abbott, David & Charles, 1977.
Ian Christie, 'Introduction', in Christie (ed.), *Powell, Pressburger and Others*, London, BFI, 1978.
Bernard Cohn, Interview with Mackendrick, *Positif* no. 92, February 1968.
John Ellis, 'Made in Ealing', *Screen* vol. 16 no. 1, Spring 1975.
John Ellis, 'Art, culture and quality: terms for a cinema in the forties and seventies', *Screen* vol. 19 no. 3, Autumn 1978.
Little Shoppe of Horrors no. 4, April 1978. Special issue on Hammer.
David Pirie, *A Heritage of Horror: the English gothic cinema 1946–1972*, London, Gordon & Fraser, 1973.
Philip Simpson, 'Directions to Ealing', *Screen Education* no. 24, Autumn 1977.

Taste the Blood of Dracula (UK 1969 *p.c* – Hammer; *d* – Peter Sasdy; *sd* col 16)

In contrast to Fisher's schematic treatment of the Dracula legend, Sasdy's version is based on a more complex conception of the implicitly destructive relationship of Count Dracula to 'normal' society. Sasdy is concerned with psychological and social rather than metaphysical themes and he bases them firmly on physical eroticism rather than spiritual values.

The film dwells on the implications of oral sexuality which underly the myth, making much of the blood-tasting rituals and the physicality of the process of vampirisation, and it presents these rituals as transgression of the bourgeois moral codes. The regression of the children to forbidden oral sexuality seems to be associated particularly with female sexuality and is seen as a positive force, since it is a source of energy which can be turned against the corrupt fathers and their decadent inversion of Catholic religious ritual (cf. Sasdy's next film *Countess Dracula*, 1970).

Sasdy's *mise en scène* is restrainedly surreal, stressing the fantasy aspect of eroticism and the destructive drives which underly it. The bourgeois façade of Victorian society is seen to be cracking open at the seams under the impact of all that it represses. *Taste the Blood of Dracula* goes far beyond the bounds of the standards of 'restraint' and 'good taste' set by Fisher's work and indicates some of the changes Hammer introduced into its products to maintain its audience (← HISTORY: *Hammer Productions*, p. 45).

Structuralism and auteur study

French intellectual context

The 'structuralist controversy' (as it has come to be known) emerged from the fierce debates raging among left-wing intellectuals in the universities of Paris during the mid-1960s. These debates caused reverberations in British intellectual life which are still felt today.

The year in which *Movie* first appeared (1962) was also the year of publication in Paris of anthropologist Claude Lévi-Strauss's *La Pensée sauvage* which included a critique of Jean-Paul Sartre's 'developmental' view of history and was to bring forward debates with far reaching effects in many disciplines: linguistics, literature, anthropology, history, sociology, art, music, psychoanalysis and, not least, philosophy and politics. In contrast to the Existentialists, Lévi-Strauss argued that history does not reveal the present as the necessary culmination of events in the past: rather, history offers us images of past societies which are structural transformations of those we know today, neither better nor worse. In this sense, modern 'man' is not so much a superior development of his antecedents as a complex amalgam of different historical levels which can be shown to co-exist in our modern minds (Leach, 1970). This view of 'man' as the result of the interaction of historical forces rather than occupying a position of superiority in relation to the past set in motion an intellectual shift which was to recast the problems posed by nineteenth-century thought and demand that they be looked at in a new way.

Structuralism, by drawing attention to the underlying sets of relationships both within and between cultural objects (or events), claimed that it was these relationships that should occupy the attention of the analyst rather than the search for some pre-existing essential meaning hidden behind the mask of language. Structuralism and the allied discipline semiology were a radical challenge to those empirical methods which took for granted as pre-given the objects of its analysis. However, as its critics were later to point out, structuralism itself fell into some of the ideological traps it was so anxious to avoid: the search for 'underlying structural relationships' often involved a reduction of those relationships to a fixed, static underlying structure, waiting to be revealed; and structures themselves were often seen as existing outside of time and place, outside of history. None the less, the fundamental challenge of structuralist thought remained, and in the intellectual climate of Paris took on a social and political dimension.

Political implications of structuralism

The Marxist philosopher Louis Althusser, one of the most influential writers to advocate the importance of structuralist theory for political philosophy and criticism (though he has denied that he is a 'structuralist'), has made an attempt to define the historical moment or 'conjecture' which made possible the development of this theoretical work in France (Althusser, 1969).

Althusser's ideas about ideology and representation were profoundly influential on British cultural theory, particularly the film theory of the journal *Screen*. He attempted to establish the 'relative autonomy' of ideology from the economic base of society, taking issue with the orthodox Marxist view that cultural artefacts were directly determined by economic factors on the grounds that such a view ignored the way in which the different elements of the social formation interact to affect one another at any given moment (→NARRATIVE AND STRUCTURALISM: *Narrative and audience*, p. 243).

Althusser's ideas formed part of a historical movement in which traditional disciplines such as philosophy, linguistics and literary criticism became increasingly politicised and in which theory was given an active role in determining political strategy and practice. Broadly speaking, the 'structuralist method' took issue with the notion that human beings could be conceived of as 'free' individuals in control of society. It argued, on the contrary, that while individuals ('man') might experience themselves as the origin and source of all meaning, action and history, and the world as an independent constituted domain of objects, in fact both individuals and objects were caught up in a system of structural relationships and it was this system that made the construction of a world of individuals and things, the construction of meaning, possible (Belsey, 1980).

The focus of attention for structuralist critics was language, but language as an activity of construction rather than as a mask for inner meaning which the critic could conjure up at will. Literary texts had certain reading practices built into them, some of which contributed to the process of reproducing capitalist relations of production, while others challenged or resisted that process. Classic realist fiction, the dominant literary form of the nineteenth century, addressed the reader as the central point from which the meaning of the text would emerge: the reader matched the author as the controlling source of the coherence and intelligibility of the text. Some twentieth-century modernist literary practices, on the other hand, were structured to produce contradiction rather than harmony and coherence, and these avant-garde texts challenged the central place given to author and reader in classic realism. Instead of a search for immanent meanings, intentions or causes, such texts demanded the abandonment of attempts to master and control meaning in favour of an activity of reading which can never exhaust the meaning of the text, but is rather a process of reading and writing in

which texts are constantly transformed. The structuralist impulse to displace universal categories such as 'man' and 'human nature' from their 'natural' place at the centre of the world and history has political implications, since an understanding of individuals and society as formed contradictorily rather than essentially or finally fixed provides the basis for theories of radical social transformation. However, the 'de-centred self' proposed by structuralism also posed problems for political action.

Ideology and the subject
It has been argued that structuralism was concerned from the beginning with the dissolution of the notion of 'man' as a full and original presence, the source of all meaning. Stephen Heath, for instance, one of the first British critics to write about structuralism in relation to literary criticism, argued that 'structure' should be understood as a process, or network of processes, whereby individuals are put in place in society and that language played an important part in 'calling up' individuals, thereby transforming them into 'subjects' in society (Heath, 1972, pp. 35–36).

This account of 'the subject', developed from Althusser (1971), implies that while individuals may experience themselves as possessing a consciousness which enables them to freely form the ideas in which they believe, in fact this experience is an *imaginary* or *ideological* one, based on misrecognition. The ideological construction of subjects as individuals free to exchange their labour is seen to be important to capitalist relations of production, which therefore seek to perpetuate it, using language as their means. Broadly speaking, then, ideology cannot be thought of as a set of ideas or thoughts which individuals can take up and discard at will. Rather, it consists in the material practices and representations within which the subject is inscribed and is largely unconsciously acquired. Returning to questions of authorship, while traditional criticism envisages the work of art as the expression of the intentions of the individual artist containing an identity which can be directly recovered by the critic, structuralism proposes that the 'author', far from controlling the meaning of the work, is an *effect* of the interaction of different texts, or discourses, which have their own autonomy.

Language as convention
Many critics of structuralism thought that it tended to rely on a rather mechanistic concept of the subject as a fixed structure, totally at the mercy of language. Later, when structuralism was displaced by semiotic analysis, Julia Kristeva and writers from the theoretical journal *Tel Quel*, principally concerned with modernist practices of writing which attempt to disturb the ideological construction of the subject as unified and coherent, drew on

psychoanalytic and linguistic theory to develop the concept that the subject itself is no more than the marks left by the process of intersection of different and conflicting texts. The 'I' which we use to designate our presence as individuals was seen as a convention, or code which was the result of the interaction of a number of codes, rather than a unified expression of the individuality of the person using the code. Moreover, this emphasis on the conventional nature of language enabled the semioticians to give language a material base in society and history, independently of individual language users, who inherited a set of institutional conventions without which they would not be able to communicate. These conventions predated the writer and continued to be readable in his or her absence (Culler, 1975). By evacuating the coherent, intentional subject from language in this way, semiotics hoped to bring into play new, revolutionary practices of writing which would mobilise unconscious desires as a force for social change.

The end of the Author
Structuralist and semiological criticism insisted that language functions independently of the Author: does the individual author then disappear? While the theoretical interventions of structuralism may have called into question some of the fundamental premises of traditional critical approaches, the influence of these ideas has been uneven, especially in Britain and the United States. Moreover, the sway of the Author remains powerful as a social institution and it would be utopian to assume that structuralism or new practices of writing could have achieved its annihilation. In France the structuralist intervention paved the way for radical changes in cultural practices, particularly in cinema after the political upheavals of May '68, when the attribution of individual authorship to films was attacked as part of an assault on traditional methods of production, distribution and exhibition. In Britain during the 1970s, the French ideas were influential in producing new theories and practices of cinema. Sylvia Harvey has argued that the importation of these ideas into British and American criticism occurred at the expense of the theoretical and political context which engendered them in France.

'Those ideas which, in France, were the product of a momentary but radical displacement, a critical calling into question of all the levels of the social formation, have become in Britain and the United States little more than a hiccup in the superstructures, a slight grinding of gears in that social machine whose fundamental mode of operating has not changed' (Harvey, 1978, pp. 1–2).

This argument tends to underestimate the extent to which cultural practices in Britain were affected by French theory and politics (the development of independent oppositional cinema during the 70s, for instance). The French debates are marked by a consciousness of their social, political and historical background which adds vigour and relevance to their arguments, a process of self-reflection which at its best takes nothing for granted. The transformation of those arguments by their insertion into Anglo-Saxon culture, and their different effects, have yet to be investigated.

Structuralism and British film criticism
It is perhaps significant that the first indications of the intervention of structuralist ideas into British film criticism should circulate around the work of Jean-Luc Godard, a French critic and film-maker whose ideas were profoundly affected by French structuralist thought and by the political events of May '68 in France. It is also significant that this discussion first appeared in the pages of *New Left Review*, since it is largely through the writings of a small but influential group of left-wing intellectuals that structuralism emerged in Britain. This emergence, in contrast to the French situation, has been slow and painful, symptomatic perhaps of an intellectual tradition which is firmly entrenched in empiricism and distrusts theoretical enquiry.

The beginnings of 'English cinestructuralism'
The debate between Robin Wood and Peter Wollen about Jean-Luc Godard in *New Left Review* no. 39, 1966 offers an opportunity to see a confrontation between one kind of critical approach developed in the pages of *Movie* (← p. 147), and a Marxist criticism influenced by structuralism which was to be developed in the journal *Screen* in the 1970s. It also offers an opportunity to see an early example of the way in which structuralist ideas 'seeped into' British film criticism, producing problems and contradictions. As Peter Wollen (pseud. Lee Russell) points out in his article, there is no simple opposition between his approach and that of Robin Wood, but there are important differences of emphasis which produce conflicting views of Godard's work and of the function of the artist in society.

A sense of tradition: Robin Wood
Wood isolates a single central theme in Godard's oeuvre around which all the other themes cohere: 'the sense of tradition'. Through detailed analysis of one scene in *Bande à part* he argues that Godard's view of contemporary society is a pessimistic one: seeing it as fragmented, lacking cultural tradition, the film-maker looks back nostalgically to a time when a relatively stable society enabled the great classical tradition (defined by Wood in terms of 'harmony') of art to appear. For Wood, Godard is a modern artist who constantly tries to resolve the problem of the

Les Carabiniers – Godard's bitter self parody ?

lack of stable cultural tradition by fabricating his own tradition, essentially personal rather than social. Even Godard's 'most savage statement of discontinuity' in *Les Carabiniers* is seen as bitter self-parody: his position is characterised as a tragic one. In Wood's view the relationship of form to content is perfectly equivalent; the style and structure of the films express Godard's tragic statement that the loss of tradition leads to the loss of personal identity and relationships.

It is possible to trace in Wood's approach to Godard's work a clear statement of the critic's own humanist concerns and it was this approach with which British Marxist film critics took issue. Nevertheless, the differences between Wood's and Wollen's approaches are not always clear-cut: the articles mark a historical point of transition rather than a break.

Unresolved contradictions: Peter Wollen
Lee Russell/Peter Wollen agrees that the issue of tradition is a 'key' one (rather than 'the essential one') but points to a difference of approach in his article which is more than a difference of opinion: it is 'a clash of world-views'.

Wollen begins, not with an inner theme, but with French society and politics: the social and historical context for Godard's work. He traces a set of structural oppositions running through the films: action vs. destiny, culture vs. society, art vs. tradition. These oppositions form unresolved contradictions in the films, they do not cohere to form an ideal unity. Indeed, the artist, in Wollen's view, far from being a central unifying force in society, is generally marginal to it, sometimes antagonistic, often simply indifferent. Wollen goes

on to criticise Godard's romantic individualistic position and the absence of politics in the films, an absence of which the filmmaker is aware and which he regrets. According to Wollen, Godard's way forward from his despairing view of society should be in the direction of politics, which is 'the principle of change in history'. A very different view of the artist and of art in society can be seen at work here. Far from transcending society with a unique and unifying personal vision, the artist is placed firmly within history: no longer the romantic 'outsider', his or her task is to contribute to social change through the critical activity of political film-making.

However, like Wood, Wollen retains a central place for Godard as *auteur* in this article and still subscribes to the critical method which depends upon bringing forward meanings hidden behind language. Nevertheless, it is possible to see the beginnings of a shift away from the notion of the *auteur* as originating source of the work towards the idea of the work as a set of contradictory relationships between structural elements which interact to *produce* the author's world-view rather than express it. Wollen is working towards a 'world-view' which is less that of a coherent totality, the expression of a pre-given set of ideas, than a collage of different positions transformed in the process of history. Underlying Wollen's arguments is a criticism of the relativism of subjective criticism and a desire to move towards a more rigorous objective method. At the same time, Wollen is careful to point out that he is writing from a particular position, which he elaborates in the course of the article. The subjectivity of the critic is not denied, but it is beginning to be called

Young Mr. Lincoln – proffered a rich text for the structuralist debate

into question.

Wollen was to revise his position on Godard in the light of his post-1968 films, developing his argument about thematic oppositions in Godard's work into a political strategy of film-making which would counter, or oppose, Hollywood cinema, and assessing his contribution as a political film-maker. The dualism of Wollen's structural criticism (elaborated in *Signs and Meanings in the Cinema*, 1969, 1972) came under attack with later developments in Anglo-Saxon film theory, as did his attempt to make an alliance between structuralism and *auteur* theory (→ *Auteur-structuralism under attack*, p. 179). But the problems in Wollen's arguments do not detract from the contribution they make to shifting the ground of British film criticism away from empiricism towards a different problematic: the relationship of science and theory to artistic practice and to politics.

Against interpretation: Alan Lovell
The methodological differences arising from the Wood/Wollen debate were elaborated in a later discussion between Robin Wood and Alan Lovell in *Screen* (March/April 1969 and May/June 1969). Lovell criticises Wood's selective approach: classification of an *auteur*'s films according to thematic resemblances, the choice of which, Lovell argues, is based on the critic's subjective system of values. The result is that certain films achieve the status of 'great art' entirely according to Wood's personal dispensation, his approval of certain moral values which he claims all great artists will express, irrespective of social, historical and cultural context. In order to break through this critical impasse, this subjective dogmatism in which the critic's values are validated by recourse to an absolute, transcendental system, Alan Lovell suggests

that criticism needs to become more objective by developing an analytic apparatus, part of which would be 'the *auteur* principle conceived as a search for the basic structure of an artist's work through examination of its recurrent features...' (Lovell, 'Robin Wood – a dissenting view', 1969, p. 54).

It should be descriptive rather than evaluative in intent, and collaborative in order to avoid the solipsism of the individual critic accountable only to her/himself. It should be provisional in nature, rather than assertive or evaluative.

Lovell argues for a descriptive, analytic approach against subjective interpretation, but in doing so he avoids a basic problem: the critic searching for basic structures is not simply an objective scientist; he or she is still engaged in the activity of reading and producing meanings and the question of subjectivity remains. Lovell's suggestion that criticism should be a social rather than a private activity does not come to terms with the troubling question of what the relationship of the 'private' and 'personal' to the social might be, a question which dogged most early structuralist writing.

In the revised edition of his booklet on Don Siegel (1975), Alan Lovell reformulated his position in the light of historical and theoretical changes which led him to believe that structuralism had failed in its original radical task of displacing the author as creator from the centre of the work, and called for more attention to the production conditions within which directors worked. The shift in Lovell's argument away from formalism toward social and ideological analysis of films is an indication of the general shift that took place in French and English structuralist criticism in the early 1970s. The shift defined itself against 'mechanistic' structuralism and posited a theoretical advance, a re-

reading of structuralist method which attempted to articulate a new relation between history, ideology and the author. The *Cahiers du Cinéma* collective text on John Ford's *Young Mr. Lincoln* (→ p. 189) is perhaps the best example of the process of self-criticism involved in this intellectual shift, which profoundly influenced the path of British film theory, particularly in the journal *Screen*.

Auteur-structuralism: Geoffrey Nowell-Smith
The 'English cinestructuralists' as they came to be called, after Eckert and Henderson (→ *Auteur-structuralism under attack*, p. 179), were not a homogeneous group. Though they shared a concern with developing materialist methods of analysis the use of structuralism differed from critic to critic. Indeed, the Marxist framework within which each critic worked was also very different and often contradictory. One of those approaches is represented by Geoffrey Nowell-Smith in his book on Visconti (1967) who states his intention of retrieving Visconti's work from the place assigned to it by traditional criticism:

'This does not mean exalting the later work at the expense of the earlier, but making it one's primary concern to consider the work as a whole, as the product of a single intelligence, and to seek out the connections between each film at whatever level they are to be found. In Visconti's case the connections are multifarious and can be traced in his choice of actors, his use of décors, his concern with certain historical questions and so on. The development of each film out of the problems posed by the last can also be easily demonstrated. But there are further links within his work which exists at a deeper level, less easily discernible and which are perhaps even more important ...' (Nowell-Smith, 1967, p. 9).

Nowell-Smith emphasises that he is not using *auteur*-structuralism to support the idea that every detail of a film is the sole responsibility of its author, the director, or as a mode of evaluating films as 'good' or 'bad'; rather it is a 'principle of method' around which the critic organises his or her work. 'The purpose of criticism becomes therefore to uncover behind the superficial contrasts of subject and treatment a structural hard core of basic and often recondite motifs' (Nowell-Smith, 1967, p. 10).

However, as Nowell-Smith demonstrates, *auteur*-structuralism is not so much an answer to the early excesses of the *auteur* theory as a problem in itself. In narrowing the field of enquiry to the internal formal and thematic analysis of the work it tends to ignore the possibility of historical changes affecting the basic structure, and the importance of non-thematic elements and *mise en scène*. Moreover, certain directors, of whom Visconti is one, cannot be discussed simply in structuralist terms because external factors of history and production are so important to their work. Nowell-Smith begins with a defence of *auteur*-structuralism which is radically questioned by the critical method he then chooses to adopt: discussion of Visconti's work not only in terms of its internal relationships, but in its social and historical context.

To characterise these early *auteur*-structuralist writings as theoretical failures would be to misunderstand the nature of theoretical enquiry which proceeds from problem to problem rather than looking for 'correctness' or immediate solutions. It would also be to underestimate the value of polemic in critical debate. Most of the *auteur*-structuralists reformulated their original positions, although the project of a materialist enquiry remained.

References

Louis Althusser, *For Marx*, Harmondsworth, Middx, Penguin Books, 1969; trans. Ben Brewster.

Louis Althusser, *Lenin and Philosophy and Other Essays*, London, New Left Books, 1971; trans. Ben Brewster.

Catherine Belsey, *Critical Practice*, London, Methuen, 1980.

Jonathan Culler, *Structuralist Poetics*, London, Routledge and Kegan Paul, 1975.

Sylvia Harvey, *May '68 and Film Culture*, London, BFI, 1978.

Stephen Heath, *The Nouveau Roman: a study in the practice of writing*, London, Elek Books, 1972.

Edmund Leach, *Lévi-Strauss*, London, Fontana, 1970.

Alan Lovell, 'Robin Wood – a dissenting view', *Screen* vol. 10 no. 2, March/April 1969.

Alan Lovell, *Don Siegel: American Cinema*, London, BFI, 1975.

Geoffrey Nowell-Smith, *Visconti*, London, Secker and Warburg/BFI, 1967; rev. ed. 1973.

Lee Russell/Peter Wollen, 'Jean-Luc Godard', *New Left Review* no. 38, September/October 1966.

Peter Wollen, *Signs and Meaning in the Cinema*, London, Secker and Warburg/BFI, 1969; rev. ed. 1972.

Robin Wood, 'Jean-Luc Godard', *New Left Review* no. 39, cit.

Robin Wood, 'Ghostly paradigm and HCF: an answer to Alan Lovell', *Screen* vol. 10 no. 3, May/June 1969.

Early structuralist film analysis

FRANK CAPRA

A good example of the difficulties posed by structuralist analysis occurs in the juxtaposition of two different approaches to the films of Frank Capra in *Cinema* no. 5: 'Frank Capra and the cinema of populism' by Jeffrey Richards, which considers Capra's work historically in the context of its relationship to American populism, and 'A structural analysis of *Mr. Deeds Goes to Town*' by Sam Rohdie, which attempts to separate out basic structural oppositions and to see how they interrelate with narrative structure and cinematic language to produce meaning. Richards' argument is that Capra brought his own Italian immigrant vision to the

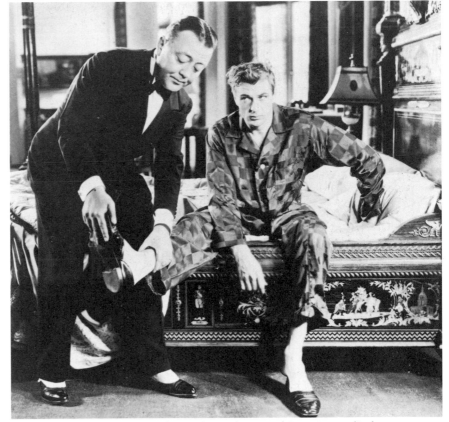

Mr. Deeds Goes to Town – the first and most famous of Capra's populist heroes

'fundamental principles which underlay American life from the Revolution to the New Deal'. Its analysis of populist ideology and history provides background information which offers a valuable filter through which to view Capra's films and to understand them better. However, Richards pays no attention to form or to differences between films which might show that there were contradictions in populism, or in Capra's version of it. Instead he assumes a transparent relationship in which a set of pre-given ideas are unproblematically reflected in the films, where they can be directly perceived by the viewer.

Structuralist/semiological criticism, on the other hand, argued for the importance of formal relationships and of the mediating function of language to an understanding of the way in which ideology works. According to this argument, ideology does not exist as a pre-given entity, but is deeply bound up with form, in effect, *produced* in and through language; thus there is no 'ideology' in the abstract, only systems of representation which work to produce ideology in specific and contradictory forms.

Sam Rohdie's article attempts to come to terms with a particular articulation of populist myth in one film using an approach based on textual analysis. He isolates the way in which the structural oppositions he identifies at work in the film (which are in fact identifiable in most American cinema) are reversed in this case to produce a resolution of the conflicts

opened up at the beginning of the narrative. The thematic structures of opposition are shifted in the course of the narrative to produce the dissolution of oppositions. The cinematic language employed also displays an oppositional structure which produces meaning (e.g. close-up vs. medium shot, soft-focus vs. sharp definition). Rohdie does not go much further than 'decoding' the oppositional structures, questioning the value of structuralism as a theoretical tool because it cannot deal with the powerful impact of the film, or the contributions of authorship, genre and the language of cinema itself to that impact. Indeed, it seems to provide a rather banal and reductive account of the way the film works.

The *Cahiers du Cinéma* analysis of *Young Mr. Lincoln* (→ p. 189) provides an interesting example of the extension of structuralist method to questions of authorship and genre. The analysis attempts to separate out precisely what is specific to Ford, to cinematic language and to ideology in the film. A comparison with *Mr. Deeds Goes to Town* seems productive because both films draw on American populist myth, but from different perspectives.

References

Jeffrey Richards, 'Frank Capra and the cinema of populism', *Cinema* (UK) no. 5, February 1970.

Sam Rohdie, 'A structural analysis of *Mr. Deeds Goes to Town*', *Cinema* (UK) no. 5, cit.

Structuralism, individualism and *auteur* theory

Structuralism, from its beginnings, posed itself against those forms of criticism which regarded the work of art as a closed, self-sufficient system in which the intentions of the author were to be found. In *La Pensée sauvage* (1962) anthropologist Claude Lévi-Strauss attacked Sartre's existentialist concept of the ego as consciousness, fully present to itself and freely able to create its own values. According to Lévi-Strauss, the final goal of the human sciences is not to constitute 'man' but to dissolve him. In a well-known remark about the language of myth he refuted the idea that 'man' could be conceived of as a 'language user', existing outside structures and therefore able to master and use them at will: 'We are not therefore claiming to show how men think in myths but rather how the myths think themselves out

in men and without men's knowledge' (quoted in Leach, 1970, p. 51).

Lévi-Strauss introduces the Freudian concept of the unconscious to explain the way in which (as he sees it) the human mind assimilates the deep structures which are seen to underpin all social organisation and forms of communication. In his attack on the notion of the individual self, Lévi-Strauss collapses individuality into a formulation of the human mind as a kind of 'collective unconscious' which assumes the universality of the structures he identifies. Individual myths, indeed all individual 'utterances' are different versions of these universal structures: emphasis is put upon the structures rather than on the utterances. This approach tends to be a-historical, denying the particularity of different kinds of utterance, and returns constantly to the presence of a structure hidden in the myth. It has been pointed out

that, like the critical tradition it is supposed to reject, it assumes the presence of an intention, whether this intention is shifted over to the side of the myth itself, or back to the 'human mind', conscious or unconscious.

In a radical re-reading of Freud, French psychoanalyst Jacques Lacan has also offered a challenge to the self-sufficiency of the individual subject, redefining the unconscious not as a deep well or reservoir of repressed thoughts or feelings, but as 'structured', indeed as 'structured like a language'. Far from being a place, Lacan argues, the unconscious is in fact a network of deep structural patterns in which our conscious thinking and discourse are intimately caught up, in the same way as the act of speech is transformed by the underlying linguistic structures (see Benoist, 'The end of structuralism', 1970). Freudian psychoanalysis does not attempt to recover the intention hidden behind each utterance, or to seek out the underlying structures, but by paying close attention to the relationship between the conscious discourse and what is absent from it (an absence marked by jokes, slips of the tongue, etc.) it attempts to throw light upon the structural activity which produced the discourse. According to Lacan ('The mirror stage', 1977) the individual self is not, as traditional ego-psychology would have it, a unified ego, but is constantly produced and transformed by the activity of the unconscious, a 'self' divided between the unconscious id and the conscious ego, which can never be captured or reconstituted as a coherent presence which transcends language and society (→ NARRATIVE AND STRUCTURALISM: *Narrative and audience*, p. 246).

The Marxist philosopher Louis Althusser drew on Lacan's theories when he attempted to reformulate Marx's concepts of identity and alienation into a 'theory of the subject': the unconscious network of structures which simultaneously held him or her in place, and produces the illusion of 'free men' (Althusser, 1971).

How does this sustained attack on 'individuality', 'presence' and 'intention', the attempted dissolution of 'man' relate to the principles of *auteur* study, which precisely depends upon the presence of an authorial (authoritative) voice as the prime source of meaning in the work? If the author/subject is constituted only in language, and a language is by definition social and independent of any particular individuality, then why does the author return, as it does in some structuralist accounts of film? The early work of Christian Metz, for instance, depends upon a literal application to cinema of the linguistic distinction between 'langue' and 'parole', defining cinema as a language without a 'langue', or underlying system of rules (→ NARRATIVE AND STRUCTURALISM: *Metz*, p. 229) a realm of pure performance or expression, which seems to confirm the idea of authorship in its con-

---

FRANK CAPRA

Mr. Deeds Goes to Town (USA 1936 *p.c – Columbia; d –* Frank Capra; sd b/w 20)

The extract is from the end of the film and provides a good example of the procedure of reversal which Rohdie's analysis identifies as basic to the resolution of contradictions in the film. It also demonstrates the influence of populist ideology on the film.

Richards argues that Mr. Deeds was the first and most famous of the Capra populist heroes, played by Gary Cooper, a popular archetype of the good American who fits the Lincoln prototype physically: tall, lean, slow-talking, while evoking for the audience the values of his other film roles in westerns. *Mr. Deeds Goes to Town* epitomises the confrontation between the populist hero and the intellectual: 'in no other (Capra) film is there such an onslaught on intellectuals'. This 'onslaught on intellectuals' can be seen in the sequence in which Mr. Deeds conducts his own defence, refuting the evidence of the experts who pronounce him insane. As a populist hero, he wins his case by virtue of common sense and knowledge of the people, as opposed to the abstract ideas of the experts.

The key role of the Capra heroine in restoring the hero's shattered confidence in human nature can be seen in Mary's passionate speech defending Deeds. Her declaration of love enables him to help himself, self-help being an important factor in populist mythology. According to Richards, the populist theme of 'good neighbourliness' is basic to Capra's work, asserting the values of the small community, co-operative enterprise and human friendship. It is these values which Mary defends in her speech and in her admission of love (a reversal of her previous cynicism) and on which

Deeds draws in his questioning of the witnesses from Mandrake Falls (his home town). They share a common language which is quite different from the language of the big city (viz. the play with the word 'pixillated' on which Mr. Deeds' fate rests). Richards reads this validation of populism directly from the film, equating it with Capra's authorial concerns.

Rohdie argues that the narrative opens by posing the opposition between town/country, sophisticated/naive, then proceeds to reverse these oppositions, producing a situation where 'country', 'naive' appear as good, honest, right-minded, indeed, sophisticated, until all the characters (except the lawyer) are united in the populist values of rural America; a utopian resolution, representing ideal unity.

The play of structural oppositions can be seen in the values assigned to different characters, who are given the status of stereotypes. Names are important in identifying those values, e.g. Longfellow Deeds (good deeds), Cedar (the 'oily' lawyer), Babe (the soft, sweet baby). The extract demonstrates the structural importance of the shifting of these oppositions. In order for the narrative resolution to take place, both Mary and Deeds must reverse positions: she must validate his values, reversing her own, and he must subscribe to her values (words and sophisticated argument) in order to save himself. Rohdie argues that the comedy of the film rests on the unmasking of the *town* and all it stands for in fakery, cynicism and inhumanity, by the *country*. Rohdie's structural analysis, despite his disclaimers, raises important questions for the kind of approach taken by Richards, which assumes the transparency of ideology and authorial intentions.

ventional sense. In the absence of a general 'langue' there is only the singular usage, and the language-user (the author) is free to express his or her intentions directly. Significantly, this notion of language as direct expression also appears in Astruc's 'The birth of a new avant-garde: la caméra-stylo' (1948), one of the earliest defences of the *politique des auteurs* (← 'Politique des auteurs', p. 119). It is hardly surprising, then, that *auteur*-structuralism was also caught in this dilemma: the attempt to re-define the *auteur* as a structure, an 'effect' rather than a punctual source of meaning in the film(s) none the less retained the notion of the underlying intention present in the basic structures, and therefore failed to displace conventional *auteur* theory (see Nowell-Smith, 'Cinema and structuralism', 1970).

The divided author

SAMUEL FULLER

Because of his anti-communism, Fuller has often been dismissed as a 'fascist' or an 'imperialist' film director. The value of an *auteur* study of his work is to show that his position is more ambiguous and contradictory than it appears. By looking at the way in which the basic thematic structures of his work shift from film to film it is possible to argue that the importance of Fuller's films lies in the questions that they raise for politics and for cinema.

The attraction of Fuller's work for structuralist critics seems to lie in the contradictions it produces. Its 'pro-Americanism' rests on an ambiguity towards American society and ideology; its 'pro-individualism' rests on a notion of the individual as profoundly divided and alienated from society. In this play of oppositions, the original unity of the work of art, and of the individual *auteur*, are displaced. Thus *auteur*-structuralism seemed to offer an alternative to the traditional *auteur* theory which celebrated the personal vision of the artist and to the unqualified support it gave to popular American cinema, whose values were increasingly coming under attack, particularly in France after the political events of May 1968 when many intellectuals became politicised. The works of those directors like Fuller whose films offered a criticism of traditional American values became important for polemical reasons. It is no accident that Fuller's name is closely linked with that of Jean-Luc Godard and that Brecht and Eisenstein are invoked in critical accounts of his work.

'Fuller's world is essentially dualistic: both war and marriage depend on a pair of partners, the self and other. Fuller explores his themes by breaking down the polarity of the two sides in war and by superimposing hate and love on the same pair. Thus the two basic situations for Fuller are those of the double agent and of the racially mixed marriage. In the first situation the protagonist is not clearly defined

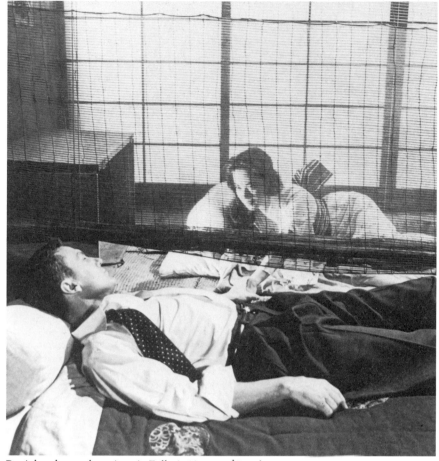

Racial and sexual tensions in Fuller's *House of Bamboo*

as being on one side or the other; he must live a complex dialectic of allegiance and treachery. In the second situation, relations of racial hatred and personal love are antagonistically combined within the same pair. This kind of thematic structure enables Fuller to explore the nature of American identity, vis-à-vis both the external enemy – Communism – and the internal divisions and hatreds which divide the country – especially race hatred' (Wollen, 'Introduction', 1969, p. 10).

Other accounts of Fuller's work also stress conflict and contradiction (e.g. Perkins, '*Underworld USA*', 1969, and Garnham, 1971, both characterise Fuller's themes as based on opposition) but see the *thematic* content expressed in *style*, which together reflect Fuller's moral values, or world-view. In contrast to these approaches, Peter Wollen is less interested in drawing out Fuller's moral values than in identifying the basic structures which make his work possible: the structures provide the basic raw material with which the director works to produce meaning, which is not necessarily attributable to the director's manifest intentions.

However, Peter Wollen still assumes an intention, conscious or unconscious, on Fuller's part, a set of 'personal concerns' which organise the basic structures and give them meaning. Indeed, it is difficult to imagine how the idea of intention might be totally dispensed with, without ignor-

ing entirely the contribution of individuals to the process of constructing meaning. What becomes clearer when comparing Wollen's approach with others is that the author's world view is a critical construction which changes depending on the point-of-view adopted by the critic.

References

Louis Althusser, *Lenin and Philosophy and Other Essays*, London, New Left Books, 1971; trans. Ben Brewster.

Jean-Marie Benoist, 'The end of structuralism', *20th Century Studies* no. 3, May 1970.

Nicholas Garnham, *Samuel Fuller*, London, Secker and Warburg/BFI, 1971.

Sylvia Harvey, 'Woman's place: the absent family of film noir', in Kaplan (ed.), *Women in Film Noir*, London, BFI Publishing, 1980.

Jacques Lacan, 'The mirror stage as formative of the function of the I', in Jacques Lacan, *Ecrits: a Selection*, London, Tavistock Publications, 1977; trans. Alan Sheridan.

Edmund Leach, *Lévi-Strauss*, London, Fontana, 1970.

Geoffrey Nowell-Smith, 'Cinema and structuralism', *20th Century Studies* no. 3, cit.

V. F. Perkins, '*Underworld USA*', in Will and Wollen (eds.), *Samuel Fuller*, Edinburgh Film Festival, 1969.

Sam Rohdie, '*House of Bamboo*', in Will and Wollen (eds.), *Samuel Fuller*, cit.

Peter Wollen, 'Introduction', in Will and Wollen (eds.), *Samuel Fuller*, cit.

Peter Wollen, '*Verboten!*', in Will and Wollen (eds.), *Samuel Fuller*, cit.

Verboten! – the aftermath of war

SAMUEL FULLER

House of Bamboo (USA 1955 *p.c* – 20th
Century-Fox; *d* – Samuel Fuller;
sd col 10)

Fuller began his career in movies as a
story and scriptwriter, directing his first
film in 1948 (*I Shot Jesse James*). His
early films were nearly all made for 20th
Century-Fox, in general quick cheap 'B'
features. Nicholas Garnham points to
the fact that in spite of the conditions
under which the films were made, Fuller
manages to achieve an extraordinary
consistency of style and theme. For
example, the preponderance of long-
takes in his films is unusual in low-
budget film-making, since economy
dictates the use of cutting and static
shots rather than risky, therefore
expensive, camera movements
(Garnham, 1971, p. 28).

At the same time Fuller's style is often
described as having the directness of
poster-art, a propagandistic quality
which is primitive and direct rather than
realistic, producing alienating shock-
effects, hence the constant evocation of
Brecht in relation to his work and the
acknowledged influence of Fuller's films
on the work of Jean-Luc Godard. This
didactic quality attracted the Marxist
structuralist critics, who were interested
in the ways in which cinematic language
could be put to political use.

Sam Rohdie ('House of Bamboo',
1969) points to a central problem in the
film as being one of identification. The
male protagonist, Eddie (Robert Stack),
is a double agent and most of the other
characters in the film pretend to be what
they are not. Thus the audience's
assumptions are constantly unsettled.
The problem of identification is worked
out in terms of racial and sexual
tension: between Eddie and the
Japanese Mariko and between this
couple and the male gang. For an
American public these tensions pose

problems of allegiance and national
identity (Rohdie, 1969, p. 29).

Fuller's films are often described as
the most violent in American cinema, a
violence translated into images rather
than appearing directly on the screen,
the violence of intellectual shock rather
than shocking exhibition of violence.
Rohdie argues that Fuller's 'assault on
the audience' is reinforced by 'a violence
of editing, colouring and the staging of
shots' (Rohdie, 1969, p. 40).

House of Bamboo is the last film
Fuller made for Fox before founding his
own production company, Globe
Enterprises, in 1956.

Verboten! (USA 1958 *p.c* – Globe
Enterprises for RKO; *d* – Samuel Fuller;
sd b/w 15)

Fuller had always wanted to make a
film of his war experiences and returned
to Europe to seek out people he met
during the war so as to get accurate
reconstruction. However, this film was
never realised, and *Verboten!* is only
partly a war film: it deals, like *Run of
the Arrow*, 1957, with the aftermath of
war.

Peter Wollen traces the paradoxical
themes in *Verboten!* – the tension
between Fuller's anti-war attitudes and
the increasing post-war involvement of
America in launching and waging wars
of conquest; an interest in the children
of war, orphaned and therefore in need
of 'foster parents' who will give them
the right guidance (cf. *China Gate*,
1957); the need for union between
violently opposed factions in order to
produce social stability (cf. *House of
Bamboo*, 1955, and *Run of the Arrow*)
(Wollen, '*Verboten!*', 1969).

Verboten! is very close to *House of
Bamboo* in its symmetrical structure of
infiltration and betrayal. Bruno has
infiltrated the American HQ and Franz
betrays the Werewolf (neo-Nazi)

Cultural politics and auteur theory

Cahiers' Category 'e'
The events of May 1968 heralded radical
changes in French film criticism which
were to have a profound effect on British
criticism too. Dissatisfied with its early
auteurist work, the French journal *Cahiers
du Cinéma* began a series of articles on
cinema, ideology and politics which drew
on the development of French structuralist
thought in politics, psychoanalysis and
literary criticism within the framework of
an explicitly Marxist approach. The project of this politicised film criticism was to
develop a new theory and practice of the
cinema and the fierce debates which followed (principally between *Cahiers du
Cinéma* and *Cinéthique*) were taken up in
Britain in the pages of the journal *Screen*,
which allied itself to this programme of

organisation to the Americans from the
inside. The hero's fiancée, Helga, is (like
Mariko) at the centre of the structure:
her friends and her brother are members
of the Werewolf organisation, her fiancé
is an American official. Arguably, it is
from this almost schematic play of
oppositions that ideological
contradictions emerge.

It is arguable that Fuller's pro-
Americanism is necessarily ambiguous,
and that this ambiguity is crystallised in
the figure of David, who speaks the
words of American democracy (viz. his
speech in the extract) which are also the
words of imperialism. David's
relationship to his wife and unborn child
is also imperialist. We can ask here how
Fuller makes the audience aware of this
ambiguity.

Underworld USA (USA 1960 *p.c* – Globe
Enterprises; *d* – Samuel Fuller;
sd b/w 22)

Described by Fuller as a 'quickie', the
original project was to make a film
about contemporary America showing
that crime does indeed pay. However,
the censor objected and Fuller was
unable to be as explicit about the subject
as he wanted.

As with many Fuller films, there is a
central tension between the 'hero' and
society, conceived as hostile, a
battleground. Fuller's view of his hero
(Tolly Devlin) is profoundly pessimistic:
he is a psychopath, the offspring of a
corrupt and brutal society. Also
pessimistic is the view of American
society as a totalitarian system
controlled by organised crime, against
which democratic action has little or no
effect. Tolly Devlin's motive for fighting
the syndicate is the individualistic one of
revenge and he never grasps the social
meaning of his actions, a theme
common to many Fuller films. In spite of
this, it is on social outcasts such as →

political and theoretical struggle when it emerged in a new form in 1971.

The period which followed the events of May 1968 in France also saw the proliferation of radical film-making groups dedicated to making political cinema and to mounting an attack on the existing structures of the film industry. Technological and economic developments made small-scale film production more viable and an increasing political awareness among filmmakers and film critics meant that the ideological function of Hollywood cinema came under scrutiny. Hollywood was seen as the principal agency of cultural imperialism in its domination of world cinema; for many people the task of revolutionary cultural struggle was to dismantle its hold on the popular imagination, to produce new, politically aware audiences. To this end, attention was

---

Tolly, Sandy and Cuddles that the democratic future of America depends and Tolly's perverse obsession with violent revenge is a bizarre reflection of American values of family loyalty and national identity. Similarly, the vulnerability of the family and personal relationships in the gangster/film noir genre (see Harvey, 'The absent family of film noir', 1980) gives the opportunity to introduce the recurrent Fuller theme of concern for 'children without parents', i.e. the future of America. Tolly himself is an orphan and is unable to acquire a 'family' in the course of the film.

Victor Perkins points to the political impulse behind Fuller's extreme individualism:

'The film ends on a zoom into a close up of Tolly's clenched fist. (This has been a visual motif throughout the film.) The propaganda purpose of Fuller's pictures is to instill into a democracy the vigour of his hero. The ideal would be a compromise between Tolly's individualism and the needs of society. But Fuller is not concerned with ideals. Instead the tension of equal and opposite forces, each dangerous and each salutary, maintains his world in its spectacularly perilous equilibrium' (Perkins, 'Underworld USA', 1969, p. 74).

By posing Tolly's psychotic individualism against the corrupt and brutal society which produced him, it can be argued that Fuller produced a devastating critique of his own society.

Arguably also Fuller's style, which is often described as 'propagandistic' or 'journalistic' (demonstrated in the extract in his use of the rhetoric of newspaper photographs, both literally – the headline announcing the Mencken child's death – or as a principle of construction – the shock cuts), is instrumental in producing this critique.

---

turned towards the question of how to find new structures, new forms to express new revolutionary content: the debates of the Russian Formalists, the ideas of Brecht became the models for film-makers and critics (see Harvey, 1978).

The refusal of dominant cinema also involved an attack on hierarchical production systems in favour of collective working methods and rejection of the idea that any individual should be enshrined as the author of a film. *Auteur* criticism, which focused on the director as central controlling presence, was seen as supporting the hierarchical division of labour and the individualist ideology of the dominant system. However, there was disagreement about how that system should be conceptualised. Critics were divided between those who argued for the necessity of building alternative structures 'outside' the dominant mode of production and those who argued for a theoretical concept of the dominant mode which would allow for intervention within it. The journal *Cahiers du Cinéma* did not subscribe to the notion of Hollywood as an ideological monolith and struggled to produce a theoretical conception of the commercial industrial system, and of the place of the director within it, which allowed more space for contradiction. In an influential editorial which appeared in *Cahiers du Cinéma* in the autumn of 1969 the editors proposed dividing films into seven categories 'a'–'g' according to whether they allowed the ideology a free passage, or whether they attempted to turn the ideology back upon itself to reveal the contradictions which it was the nature of ideology to efface. The fifth category 'e' was defined as those films which seem at first sight to belong firmly within the ideology, but which reveal on closer inspection that:

'An internal criticism is taking place which cracks the film apart at the seams. If one reads the film obliquely, looking for symptoms, if one looks beyond its apparent formal coherence, one can see that it is riddled with cracks: it is splitting under an internal tension which is simply not there in an ideologically innocuous film. This is the case in many Hollywood films, for example, which while being completely integrated in the system and the ideology end up by partially dismantling the system from within' (Comolli and Narboni, 1969, quoted in Harvey, 1978, p. 35).

Cahiers cited the films of John Ford, Carl Dreyer, and Roberto Rossellini as examples of this category and their subsequent analysis of Ford's *Young Mr. Lincoln* demonstrated the importance of the authorial sub-code in that film to the process of internal criticism. Thus films which appeared to be basically 'reactionary' (i.e. instruments of the dominant ideology) could, on re-reading, prove to be 'progressive' in so far as they produced a criticism of that ideology. *Cahiers du Cinéma* followed up its definitions of clas-

---

ses of films with analyses of individual texts (*Young Mr. Lincoln, Sylvia Scarlett, Morocco*) to demonstrate how they each challenged dominant ideology in specific ways. *Cahiers'* approach allowed for the possibility of progressive texts to be found in Hollywood cinema and it was this position which had most effect on the theoretical work of *Screen*. *Auteur* criticism in Britain began to look at the films of certain Hollywood directors in terms of the way they resisted dominant ideology, laying bare its operations. Those directors whose work seemed to offer a radical criticism of the system through manipulation, conscious or unconscious, of its language were the most important; their work was evaluated according to the extent to which it could be read as breaking with the traditional pleasures offered by mainstream cinema, which attempted to seduce the audience into losing itself in a self-contained fictional world, putting its doubts and questions aside (→ NARRATIVE AND STRUCTURALISM: *The classic realist text*, p. 242).

The 'progressive' auteur

DOUGLAS SIRK

One of the basic premises of post-68 resistance to Hollywood was that the project of mainstream cinema is illusionist; that is, that it attempts to create an illusion of reality on the screen in such a way that the spectator becomes totally absorbed in the spectacle and is prepared to accept the illusion as 'truth', at least for the time spent viewing the film. Any critical resistance is overcome and the ideology of mainstream cinema is accepted as 'natural'. This argument depends upon the idea that while all ideology is actually inconsistent, bourgeois ideology struggles to overcome its own inconsistencies. 'Progressive' cinema, then, can be defined as anti-illusionist, or anti-realist, in the sense that it works to produce these contradictions which bourgeois ideology attempts to efface. In order to do this it must work on the illusionist strategies of mainstream cinema to disturb the 'illusion of reality', to remind the spectator that the illusion is ideological rather than natural, that it can therefore be questioned. Not all non-realist films can be seen as progressive however: many Hollywood films are blatantly unrealistic, while still preserving the illusion of a coherent self-contained world which becomes imaginatively real for the period of watching. To qualify as progressive, a Hollywood film would have to be perceived as producing a criticism, at some level, of its manifest ideological project. A sub-text would be discernible which works against the grain of that project, denaturalising it.

The films of Douglas Sirk provide an opportunity to examine the influence of these ideas on British film theory. Sirk was a European left-wing intellectual with a background in art history and the German

Zu neuen Ufern – the trial of Gloria Vane

Written on the Wind – a criticism of the patriarchal American family

theatre of the 1920s and early 1930s. He was not only familiar with the debates about art and politics in the Soviet Union and Germany during that period: he had lived through the advent of the Third Reich and the consequent campaign against left-wing artists and intellectuals which signalled the demise of one of the most thriving periods in German theatrical history, a theatre of criticism and social commitment (see Elsaesser, 'Postscript', 1971). Sirk's theatrical productions owed much (formally at least) to the Expressionist emphasis on *mise en scène*, on the supremacy of gesture, light, colour and sound over the spoken word, which drew attention to the symbolic aspect of the stage-spectacle rather than its realism. At the same time he was interested in the controversial political dramas of Brecht and Bronnen, which were designed to shock the conventional, primarily middle-class German theatre audience. As the Nazi authorities interfered more and more with the running of the theatre, Sirk turned to the cinema, becoming a director for Ufa, since there was still considerable freedom for directors within the German film industry at that time (1934) (see Halliday, 1971, p. 35). His success was established with the melodrama *Schlussakkord* (1936), and continued with *Zu neuen Ufern* (1937), which shows explicitly Sirk's interest in the ideas of Brecht and Weill and in film as social criticism. Thus, before he moved to America in 1937, Sirk's theatrical productions and German films reveal the

Zu neuen Ufern (To New Shores)
(Germany 1937 *p.c* – Ufa; *d* – Detlef Sierck (Douglas Sirk); sd b/w 19)
  After the enormous success of *Schlussakkord*, Sirk's first full-blown melodrama, he went on to direct this film, which he describes as incorporating his interest in melodrama as a vehicle for encouraging social criticism in the audience and in characters who are uncertain about their aims in life and so find themselves going in circles – the 'tragic rondo' (see Halliday, 1971, pp. 47–48). Jon Halliday describes the film as a tough social criticism of the British ruling class and colonialism in nineteenth-century Australia (Halliday, 'Notes on Sirk's German films', 1971). The tragic, vacillating figure in this case is Sir Albert Finsbury, a weak British officer.
  The first part of the extract comprises a scene from the film which usefully demonstrates Sirk's interest in adapting Brecht–Weill for cinema. The trial of Gloria Vane (Zarah Leander) is introduced by an old woman singing a song about Paramatta (the women's prison in Australia to which Gloria is about to be consigned by a class-

prejudiced court) outside the courtroom; she has a large placard with a number of pictures on it: the camera passes from her to the courtroom where Gloria is sentenced, back out to the placard, whereupon a picture of Paramatta dissolves to Paramatta itself. This explicitly Brechtian strategy has the effect of drawing attention to the formal construction of the film and, some would argue, introducing a critical distance for the audience.
  The second part of the extract shows Sirk's interest, influenced by German Expressionism, in using *mise en scène* to create an independent, dream-like world on the screen entirely divorced from 'reality'. Sharp contrasts of light and dark combined with stylised acting and sets are an extension of the theatrical conventions of melodrama.

All That Heaven Allows (USA 1955 *p.c* – Universal International; *d* – Douglas Sirk; sd col 20+20)
  One of Sirk's women's pictures (← GENRE: *Melodrama*, p. 84), this film has been praised both as a critique of American bourgeois values (Halliday, '*All That Heaven Allows*', 1972) and as

a poignant working through of the contradictions faced by women in patriarchal society (Mulvey, 'Sirk and melodrama', 1977).
  The film presents events through the point-of-view of its central female protagonist, using the visual code of *mise en scène* to indicate her state of mind. This ironic use of *mise en scène* can either be read as an attempt by the director to comment on the conservative values supposedly adhered to in the melodrama's subject matter, or as part of the melodramatic convention in which stylised *mise en scène* is used to offer the audience privileged information over the characters (Elsaesser, 'Tales of sound and fury', 1972).
  In the family melodrama, it has been argued, dramatic conflict is engendered by working through the contradictions, particularly for women, of heterosexual monogamy and motherhood. *All That Heaven Allows* centres these problems in the point-of-view of its heroine, arguably producing problems for the classic Hollywood narrative which are out of the director's control. From this perspective, the film is less a 'progressive

extent to which he was able to transform the materials at his disposal in his own interests.

Sirk's first experience of Hollywood (between 1939 and 1949) was rather bleak (in common with that of many European emigré directors). Working as a contract scriptwriter for Columbia, he was consistently denied work as a director, in spite of successes with films made by independent producers. After a year spent in Germany in 1949, where he found the film industry more or less destroyed, he returned to America where he signed up as a director with Universal. After a few years he began to impose his own style and personal concerns on the material handed to him by producer Ross Hunter and others, in the form of sometimes 'impossible' scripts. He gradually gained more control over his projects and with the help of a sympathetic studio (Universal) and collaborators (photographer Russell Metty, scriptwriter George Zuckerman, producer Albert Zugsmith) a group of melodramas emerged which have been identified as characteristically Sirkian, showing the same interest in form and politics as his German theatre and film work, albeit less explicitly (see Halliday, 1971; Mulvey and Halliday, 1972; *Screen* special issue on Sirk, 1971).

The argument for Sirk as a 'progressive' *auteur* rests on the assumption that he was working as a director in uncongenial circumstances (Nazi Germany in the 30s, America in the 50s). His own political beliefs and interests as a left-wing intellectual were under attack, he was working in a hierarchical industrial situation and therefore did not have complete control over his projects, yet he managed to produce work which can be read as critical of the prevailing ideology at one level, not necessarily the most obvious one (see Willemen, 'Distanciation and Douglas Sirk', 1971). One problem with this argument is that the films chosen by critics to illustrate it (*Schlussakkord*, *Zu neuen Ufern* and *La Habanera* from the 30s, the Universal melodramas from the 50s) were all produced at a time when Sirk had considerable control over his projects (see Halliday, 1971, p. 35; Mulvey and Halliday, 1972, p. 109). Moreover, it is well known that he had several sympathetic collaborators within Universal studios, which makes it difficult to argue that Sirk was totally responsible for the 50s melodramas associated with his name. It has also been argued that it is the overt project of melodrama as a genre to act as a safety-valve, siphoning off ideological contradictions and deliberately leaving them unresolved (← GENRE: *Melodrama*, p. 81). From this perspective, Sirk would appear to have been less in tension with his material, producing a hidden, underlying criticism, than at one with it; any criticism of the prevailing ideology to be found in his work could therefore be seen as overt and, moreover, sanctioned by that ideology.

The argument for the 'progressivity' of Sirk's films raises important questions about the relationship of authorship to genre, of the director to the conditions in which he or she works and of how ideology is produced in films.

The 'deconstructive' auteur

FRANK TASHLIN

'Tashlin's modernity, then, rests not so much with his subject matter but with his radical break with the notion of an author communicating his personal "vision" or "truth" about his "world-view". In Tashlin's films reality is deconstructed, reactivated and re-produced' (Johnston and Willemen, 'Introduction', 1973, p. 6).

The Edinburgh Film Festival Book (1973) on Frank Tashlin introduces the concepts of film as text and author as producer into the British authorship debates. A text is defined as an open structure: while it has its own set of internal relationships it also relates outwards to other texts: this relationship is the one of *intertextuality* by which all texts form part of a network of other texts. Thus no film is a self-contained, organic whole, but many films, particularly those which conform to the model of the 'classic realist text' disguise their intertextuality and present themselves as closed and unified (NARRATIVE AND STRUCTURALISM: *The classic realist text*, p. 242). Willemen ('Tashlin's method') argues that Tashlin's 'modernity' resides in the way that he 'breaks' with the classic realist text and uses intertextuality as an active, structuring principle in his work. His films refer to other Tashlin films, either directly or indirectly; he quotes from other Hollywood films and genres and refers to the film production process itself; he brings together different types of visual discourse, like television programmes, comic books, animated films. The end result is a 'demystification' of the process of film production by drawing attention to its multiple, collective nature. But the true value of Tashlin's work lies in the way that all these elements are combined to form new structures: the method of *combination* is basic to Tashlin's comedy, which rests on the type of combination used, i.e. illogical, incongruous, breaking the laws of verisimilitude, therefore *deconstructive*.

The activity of combination is described as *bricolage* (after Lévi-Strauss), a process of assembly and dismantling in which the *bricoleur*, given a number of codes to play with, proceeds to combine them into original constructions; every *auteur* ends up with a construction not quite like anybody else's. Tashlin's difference from other directors lies in the fact that he draws an analogy between the way in which he constructs his films and the way in which the social reality of American consumer ideology is constructed. So Tashlin's work does not so much satirise 50s American consumer-orientated society, as has often been thought, as draw attention to its basic process of construction.

This account of Tashlin's method differs from conventional *auteur* study in several ways: the director is seen, not as a great artist, but as a producer of meaning working within an economic system

---

text' than a safety valve for painful ideological contradictions (see Mulvey, 1977).

Written on the Wind (USA 1956 *p.c* – Universal International; *d* – Douglas Sirk; sd col 15)

Sirk's theatrical background can be seen in the organisation of the *mise en scène*: strong primary colours, contrasts of dark and light, exaggerated acting and gestures combine to produce a world dominated by physical and psychological violence, marked by an emotional excess which threatens to overturn the stability of the established order. This film is a tragic melodrama, concentrating on male oedipal problems with the patriarchal order (see Mulvey, 1977).

Kyle Hadley (Robert Stack) is an example of one of Sirk's vacillating characters (cf. Cary in *All That Heaven Allows*, Sir Albert Finsbury in *Zu neuen Ufern*), but his hysterical response to his supposed sterility has also been identified as one of the basic motifs of tragic melodrama. The 'negative' destructive impulses of Kyle and his sister Marylee (Dorothy Malone) are played off against the 'positive' qualities of the 'good' couple, Mitch (Rock Hudson) and Lucy (Lauren Bacall) to produce a criticism of the patriarchal American family and the ideals of masculinity and femininity on which it depends. Marylee's orgiastic 'dance of death' shown in the extract explicitly draws a parallel between excessive female sexuality and the overthrow of the patriarchal order, a view of female sexuality as threat which is common in American cinema and which is arguably mobilised here in the interests of social criticism.

The symbolic use of colour in the *mise en scène* to refer to the values held by different characters is typical of melodramatic conventions, but could also be seen as a particular use of ironic commentary by the director in order to distance the audience from their emotional response and induce a critical awareness (i.e. a 'Brechtian' strategy which can undermine the pathos and catharsis characteristic of tragedy as a form).

Will Success Spoil Rock Hunter? – the construction of an attractive male form

employing a particular language; moreover, that language is not a personal, private ideolect, it is social, a set of codes available to anyone in a society at a given time. The director cannot transcend those codes, only re-work them to produce new meaning. As an attempt to identify the basic mechanisms of Tashlin's comedy this account goes some way towards providing the means for understanding the 'deconstructive' or subversive quality of his work and the pleasure it affords. However, the textual analysis which would demonstrate *how* the director is implicated in the film texts is missing; it is taken for granted that Tashlin's intentions coincide with those of the critic giving a 'deconstructive reading' of his work.

FRANK TASHLIN
Will Success Spoil Rock Hunter? (Oh! For a Man!) (USA 1957 *p.c* – 20th Century-Fox; *d* – Frank Tashlin; sd col scope 6)

'The construction of an attractive female form is an elaborate process, and proceeds along the same principles which underlie Tashlin's films' (Willemen, 'Tashlin's method', 1973, p. 129).

So, apparently, does the construction of an attractive male form. Film star Rita (Jayne Mansfield-archetypal constructed female form) attempts to build the diminutive Rock (Tony Randall) into an approximation to her 'better half', Bobo (Mickey Hargitay). But it is not only difficult and painful for 'real' people to live up to the ideal that society constructs for them, it can also destroy them. Tashlin's comedy produces a gap between the 'real' and the constructed ideal which provides both theatre of the absurd and a brilliant deconstruction of American society's view of what it takes to be a man or a woman. Spot the quotes, references and in-jokes. Does Tashlin's comic method, and the playing off of the 'real' against the 'ideal' work to provide a criticism of American ideology?

Love Happy (USA 1949 *p.c* – Lester Cowan Productions; *d* – David Miller; sd b/w 10+24)

Before becoming a director, Tashlin worked in Hollywood as an animator (for Disney, also on *Bugs Bunny*, etc.) and as a gagman and comedy scriptwriter. In 1948 he collaborated with Ben Hecht on the script of this Marx Brothers comedy.

The film would never be included in an *auteur* study of the Tashlin oeuvre; but in some ways it exhibits precisely those qualities of 'intertextuality' and concern with collaborative production which, it has been argued, were developed by Tashlin as a director. *Love Happy* provides an example of the screwball comedy which influenced Tashlin's later work; also an example of his contribution as scriptwriter (arguably most evident in the cartoonist's sensibility observable in the roof-top chase). Perhaps most important, it demonstrates the collaborative process which makes up a Hollywood film. Although Tashlin's contribution is important, so is that of the Marx Brothers, the director David Miller and, in the second part of Extract 1 particularly, the art director Gabriel Scognamillo.

The evacuation of the author

RAOUL WALSH
Structuralist criticism leads the critic away from conventional *auteur* criticism towards a consideration of other areas of cinema in an attempt to displace the *auteur* from the centre of the work. However, in the process the specificity of a particular director can be lost altogether (see Nowell-Smith, 'Cinema and structuralism', 1970). Structuralism at its best aims to understand the interaction of multiple structures in and between texts, seeing the *auteur* structure as one among many in any given film: it may or may not be dominant. Rather than dissolve the author altogether, a structuralist approach to film could determine the specific relationship of different authors to each film.

It is arguable that in the Edinburgh Film Festival book on Raoul Walsh (1974) which takes as its subject the *auteur* theory itself as much as the *auteur* Walsh (see MacCabe, 'Walsh an author?', 1975), Walsh is made to disappear (almost) completely. Apart from the first article by Peter Lloyd ('Walsh – a preliminary demarcation'), which treats the director in terms of conventional *auteur* theory, the other writers find him either enmeshed in the structures of the studio (Buscombe), or in the structures of the text (Willemen), or in the structures of patriarchal ideology (Cook and Johnston).

Ed Buscombe ('Walsh and Warner Bros') argues that the films directed by Walsh for Warner Bros between 1939 and 1951 are typical of the known general policy of the studio at that time, to such an extent that one must call into question the simple notion of Walsh as an *auteur* who dictated the style and content of his pictures. On the contrary, Walsh was obliged to make use of the stars and genres available at Warners to produce films which conformed to the studio product. Similarly, he was working with a group of left-wing producers and writers whose contributions must be taken into account. Buscombe surmises that these conditions of production must have been congenial for Walsh because he stayed with Warners until 1951; thus they were not so much 'constraints' as conditions which provided possibilities for good work in certain directions rather than others. The problematic absence in Buscombe's account is Walsh himself. Without analysis of film texts it is impossible to say what the director's contribution might have been. Did he simply reproduce the studio product as Buscombe seems to suggest? The presence of left-wing personnel on the studio production team could not guarantee a left-wing product and 'studio style', if it is to mean anything at all, must be composed of many contradictory elements since the studio itself presumably consists of shifting power relationships which change with history ← HISTORY: *Warner Bros*, p. 11).

Paul Willeman ('*Pursued:* the fugitive

Pursued – the fugitive subject

subject') examines the film *Pursued* closely, analysing its textual operation in terms of a network of shifting relationships between the formal signifiers in which the place of the subject of the discourse (the director) and of the audience (the reader of the text) is never fixed. Willemen displaces the linear form of communication which is generally assumed to exist between the subject of an utterance (the 'addresser') and the receiver of that utterance (the 'addressee') in favour of a concept of the film text constructed like a fantasy in which both 'subject' and 'reader' are dispersed across the network of overlaps and substitutions among the different characters. The effect is to deny the possibility of the full presence of the director/*auteur* as organising source; only the traces of his presence remain and this only in the interstices (i.e. gaps) of the text. Thus the author is to be found in the marks of interruption and incoherence; the subject, by definition, is always fading away.

If this argument seems somewhat reductive, taking Lacanian psychoanalytic theory to an extreme in order to demonstrate a primary truth, it nevertheless has the advantage of showing that conventional *auteur* theory, by unifying *auteur*, text and critic and constructing them in terms of intention and presence, is an ideological operation dedicated to smoothing over contradictions. In Willemen's construction, Walsh's specificity is dissolved into the specificity of the textual operation of the film: or rather, according to this argument, it precisely depends upon the specific *reading* given to any text(s) at any given moment.

Pam Cook and Claire Johnston ('The place of woman in the cinema of Raoul Walsh') argue that conventional *auteur* theory avoids coming to terms with the organisation of the film text and the way it mediates ideology; if ideology is described in analysis of film it is usually seen as an expression of the director's worldview rather than in terms of the structure of the film itself. They propose looking at Walsh as a 'subject within ideology, and, ultimately, the laws of the human order' and, specifically, at the film text in terms of the way it articulates the ideology of patriarchy, since it is this ideology which

The Roaring Twenties (USA 1939 *p.c* – Warner Bros; *d* – Raoul Walsh; sd b/w 9)

Peter Lloyd argues that Walsh's relationship with Warner Bros was ambiguous, in that his concern with individual personal action went against the grain of the studio's commitment to a 'socially conscious' cinema (Lloyd, 1974, p. 18).

Buscombe takes a different view. Having characterised Warners' studio product during the 1930s as the manifestation of the 'vaguely and uncertainly radical yearnings which the studio shared with the New Deal', he claims that Walsh's first three pictures for Warners fit squarely into this mould and that *The Roaring Twenties* makes a connection between social deprivation and crime which perfectly expresses New Deal ideology (Buscombe, 1974, p. 56).

These different readings of Walsh's Warner Bros' films raise the question of the relationship between director, studio and genre, and of how 'studio style', as opposed to the director's style can be distinguished.

They Drive by Night (USA 1940 *p.c* – Warner Bros; *d* – Raoul Walsh; sd b/w 23)

Buscombe argues that this film 'exemplifed perfectly both the strengths and limitations of Warners' radicalism' (Buscombe, 1974, p. 57). The desperation of the truck drivers is specifically linked to an economic insecurity deriving from mass unemployment in society at large, but the solution to this social problem is presented entirely in individual terms: 'George Raft eventually becomes the owner of his own haulage company and so insulates himself from the pressures which affect the mass below him' (Buscombe, 1974, p. 57).

It is interesting to speculate whether the 'individualism' noted by Buscombe can be seen as an indication of Walsh's contribution rather than the studio's. If the film can be described as 'ideologically radical', at least in terms of the New Deal, how does the figure of the independent woman (played by Ida Lupino), who acts on her desires and is ultimately destroyed by them, and who presents a serious problem to the hero of the film (George Raft) attaining his own desires, fit into this description? It could be argued that in this respect, this film

fits less with the studio product than with Walsh's work in general (cf. *The Revolt of Mamie Stover*).

High Sierra (USA 1941 *p.c* – Warner Bros; *d* – Raoul Walsh; sd b/w 14)

'The whole film in fact deals with people who are in various ways outcasts from society, and while Bogart's own alienation has a metaphysical dimension, the attempt to relate crime to social causes is a real one. There is every difference between this and the gangster films of the 40s and 50s, which tend to see crime as a manifestation of some purely psychological disturbance' (Buscombe, 1974, p. 57).

The 'metaphysical' dimensions of Bogart's alienation may have been contributed by John Huston, who co-scripted this film but was not a regular member of the team of writers with whom Walsh worked.

The film has a strong melodramatic element. The family Roy Earle (Bogart) meets represents an ideal for him: when the crippled daughter Velma is 'corrupted' he is shattered, left with a grotesque parody of a family in the moll Marie (Ida Lupino) and a stray dog, in the tradition of the 'absent family' of the thriller/film noir genre (see Harvey, →

defines a particular social place for women. The authors argue that the Hollywood system is of interest to feminist critics because the image of 'woman' that it presents is fetishistic, i.e. it endows this image with masculine attributes of power which efface woman's sexual difference, fixing her as the locus of male castration anxiety. In this system, woman is 'spoken' as a sign, as an object to be exchanged by men rather than the subject of desire (see Cowie, 'Woman as sign', 1978). However, because women are, in social reality, more than objects of exchange, the process of fixing 'woman' in place is problematic for the patriarchal order, which must constantly work to overcome the contradictions within itself. So the fetishistic system is seen to be relatively unstable: its contradictions can either be effaced, or exploited to draw attention to the system itself. The authors argue that Walsh's oeuvre can be read in this way as drawing attention to the patriarchal ideology within which it is placed: its interest lies precisely in the way it *presents* that ideology to the spectator rather than effacing it.

The text they choose to analyse, *The Revolt of Mamie Stover*, revolves around the problem of the exchange and circulation of money at a time of economic crisis: the Second World War. It is vital that women support the economy when men are absent, yet the very absence of men means that women threaten to take over the system of exchange rather than support

The Revolt of Mamie Stover – Mamie (Jane Russell) threatening to take control

it. In *The Revolt of Mamie Stover* women, in this case prostitutes, exemplified by the central character Mamie (played by Jane Russell) are exchanged like money, in the same way that Mamie's highly fetishised image is exchanged. The ideological problem that the narrative tries to resolve is that it is precisely the objects men need to exchange (money, women, images) which threaten to escape and take control of the system controlling their circulation. The function of the positive, independent woman image exemplified by Mamie/Jane Russell is to trigger the process of 'putting into place' by which the narrative contains this threat. The character's strength and independence is thus apparent rather than real, since she is a sign with a specific function in the narrative system. The 'symbolic order' of the narrative is seen to correspond to the symbolic order of patriarchy itself, in that both work to override contradiction by attempting to fix women in place, in the case of film by means of the codes of cinematic language. Because Walsh's films seem to present this problem quite explicitly in terms of the

power relationships between men and women and in terms of the struggle by men to keep control of the system of exchange and therefore of women, patriarchal ideology seeps through the very structure of the films, in the organisation of images and narrative, and rises to the surface.

In this account, Walsh the *auteur* is again displaced from centre stage to make way, this time, for ideology. Again, the problem of the specificity of the director's contribution is side-stepped in favour of more generalised concepts such as *narrative structure* and *patriarchal ideology*. Text, and director, are treated a-historically (see also Gledhill, 'Recent developments in feminist film criticism', 1978).

These three articles succeed in evacuating Walsh as *auteur*, as originating source of meaning of his films, from his work. At the same time they fail to deal with the question of precisely what Walsh's contribution to the production of meaning might be as director of a body of films.

References

Edward Buscombe, 'Walsh and Warner Bros', in Hardy (ed.), *Raoul Walsh*, Edinburgh Film Festival, 1974.

Pam Cook and Claire Johnston, 'The place of woman in the cinema of Raoul Walsh', in Hardy (ed.), *Raoul Walsh*, cit.

Elizabeth Cowie, 'Woman as sign', *m/f*, no. 1, 1978.

Thomas Elsaesser, 'Postscript', *Screen* vol. 12 no. 2, Summer 1971.

Thomas Elsaesser, 'Tales of sound and fury', *Monogram* no. 4, 1972.

Christine Gledhill, 'Recent developments in feminist film criticism', *Quarterly Review of Film Studies* vol. 3 no. 4, Fall 1978.

Jon Halliday, *Sirk on Sirk*, London, Secker and Warburg/BFI, 1971.

Jon Halliday, 'Notes on Sirk's German films', *Screen* vol. 12 no. 2, cit.

Jon Halliday, '*All That Heaven Allows*', in Mulvey and Halliday (eds.), *Douglas Sirk*, Edinburgh Film Festival, 1972.

Sylvia Harvey, *May '68 and Film Culture*, London, British Film Institute, 1978.

Sylvia Harvey, 'Woman's place: the absent family of film noir', in Kaplan (ed.), *Women in Film Noir*, London, BFI Publishing, 1980.

Claire Johnston and Paul Willemen, 'Introduction', in Johnston and Willemen (eds.), *Frank Tashlin*, Edinburgh Film Festival/SEFT, 1973.

Peter Lloyd, 'Walsh, a preliminary demarcation', in Hardy (ed.), *Raoul Walsh*, cit.

Colin MacCabe, 'Walsh an Author?', *Screen* vol. 16 no. 1, Spring 1975.

Laura Mulvey and Jon Halliday (eds.), *Douglas Sirk*, Edinburgh Film Festival, 1972.

Laura Mulvey, 'Sirk and melodrama', *Movie* no. 25, 1977.

Geoffrey Nowell-Smith, 'Cinema and structuralism', *20th Century Studies* no. 3, May 1970.

Paul Willemen, 'Distanciation and Douglas Sirk', *Screen* vol. 12 no. 2, cit.

Paul Willemen, 'Tashlin's method: an hypothesis', in Johnston and Willemen (eds.), *Frank Tashlin*, cit.

Paul Willemen, '*Pursued*: the fugitive subject', in Hardy (ed.), *Raoul Walsh*, cit.

'The absent family of film noir', 1980).

In terms of Walsh's oeuvre, the rejection of Velma by Roy occurs when it is clear to him that he has lost control of her. Although Velma is portrayed unsympathetically and it is Roy Earle's point-of-view that is offered for identification, the gangster's bitterness and isolation could be read as an indictment of his patriarchal attitude to women and of the very ideas he cherishes. It is characteristic of the genre that the stoicism, honesty and compassion of the gangster's moll, Marie, provide a primary focus of identification for the audience.

The Revolt of Mamie Stover (USA 1956 *p.c* – 20th Century-Fox; *d* – Raoul Walsh; sd col scope 20)

Cook and Johnston's argument about this film raises questions of the representation of female sexuality in Walsh's work in general and of how this representation cuts across the distinctions made by critics between, for example, Walsh's Warner Bros films and the others.

The extract depicts the opening of the film and the ways in which Mamie/Jane Russell is established as a threat (her 'look' directly into camera, etc.); central

sections of the narrative in which her 'image' is seen as part of a system of exchange controlled by men, and then as it threatens to slip out of the grasp of Jimmy/Richard Egan (that is, as Mamie is about to be totally economically independent and in control of the system of exchange); the resolution of the narrative in which Mamie is 'put in place' by Jimmy, a totally symbolic resolution because she is actually in a position economically to control most of the island. She gives up all her money and returns to home and family.

Discussion could take shape around the question of the 'distancing' devices in the film, e.g. the way in which Mamie's 'image' is seen to be controlled by men, apparently drawing attention to the workings of patriarchal ideology. The symbolic, arbitrary structure of the narrative resolution, by appearing totally unrealistic, could be said to raise the question of the problem of male control of women, and the 'fetishised' image of Jane Russell seems to emphasise her function in the film as a sign of 'phallic displacement', thus drawing attention to the 'positive woman' figure as a projection of male sexual anxieties.

Auteur-structuralism under attack

Signs and Meaning in the Cinema

Peter Wollen's defence of *auteur*-structuralism in *Signs and Meaning in the Cinema* (1969, 1972) is perhaps the most cogent argument for the retention of the *auteur* theory in some form or other and it remains relevant today because the problem of authorship and cinema remains, in spite of the attempts of some of the more reductionist and formalist developments of structuralist method to dissolve the *auteur* altogether into the generalities of other structures. The theoretical problems inherent in British *auteur*-structuralism have often been pointed out (Eckert, 'The English cinestructuralists', 1973; Henderson, 'Critique of cinestructuralism', 1973). Henderson's careful reading of Wollen's chapter on the *auteur* theory reveals the lack of theoretical foundation in *auteur*-structuralism and the empiricism underlying many of Wollen's rhetorical strategies. It also points to the fundamental incompatibility of the two critical approaches, which produces contradictions in the arguments which must finally destroy *auteur*-structuralism itself: that is, while *auteur* theory as it stands (and as it is retained by Wollen) rests on the principle that the subject is the producer of a unique or distinctive meaning, Lévi-Strauss's structural study of myth is founded upon the interchangeability of subjects in the production of meaning. Henderson's impressive demolition of *auteur*-structuralism is the prelude to a criticism of structuralism itself in the light of theoretical developments emerging from the French *Tel Quel* group and others which called for a new theory of textual operation and of the place of the subject in the process of production of meaning (Henderson, p. 33). None the less, as Henderson himself points out, it is only in the destruction of *auteur*-structuralism itself that the new question can be liberated. The value of *auteur*-structuralism resides in the problems it poses and the questions it provokes.

Wollen argues that *auteur*-structuralism provides a critical approach which can retain the impetus of the original *politique des auteurs* (i.e. to decipher the presence of authors in Hollywood film production as opposed to European art cinema) while avoiding its excesses by providing the more objective criteria of basic structures rather than subjective ones of personal taste. Structuralism allows the critic to define a core of repeated motifs in the director's oeuvre: however, it must also analyse the system of differences and oppositions which marks one film off from the others in the oeuvre, and which produce meaning in each film. It is not enough to reduce films to basic oppositional structures: the critic must also pay attention to the whole series of shifting variations within and between films. Different levels of complexity of combination mark the work of some directors as 'richer' than others. For Wollen, Ford's work is richer than Hawks's because Hawks's films can be summed up in terms of schematic sets of oppositions, whereas Ford's manifest many different and shifting levels of variation. It is interesting that Wollen retains the categories of 'good' and 'bad' films which structuralist method could, in theory at least, have dispensed with. In the first edition of his book Wollen discounts the importance of other contributions (such as those of the star or the studio) to the production of meaning in film: the *auteur*-structure, for him, is the primary or dominant one. Strangely, it is at this point of greatest tension between *auteur* theory and Lévi-Strauss's structuralism that Wollen calls on Lévi-Strauss and equates film with myth (Wollen, 1972, p. 105). For meaning in myth is indeed collectively produced: there is no place in myth for the individual language-user (→ NARRATIVE AND STRUCTURALISM: *Lévi-Strauss*, p. 232).

An important part of Wollen's polemic is his reformulation of *auteur* theory in terms of the *auteur* as unconscious catalyst rather than intentional presence, an argument he elaborates in the Postscript to the revised edition:

'*Auteur* analysis does not consist of retracing a film to its creative source. It consists of tracing a structure (not a message) within the work, which can then *post factum* be assigned to an individual, the director, on empirical grounds. It is wrong, in the name of a denial of the traditional idea of creative subjectivity, to deny any status to individuals at all. But Fuller, or Hawks or Hitchcock, the directors, are quite separate from "Fuller" or "Hawks" or "Hitchcock", the structures named after them, and should not be methodologically confused. There can be no doubt that the presence of a structure in the text can often be connected with the presence of a director on the set, but the situation in cinema, where the director's primary task is often one of co-ordination and rationalisation, is very different from that in the other arts, where there is a much more direct relationship between artist and work. It is in this sense that it is possible to speak of a film *auteur* as an unconscious catalyst' (Wollen, 1972, p. 168).

While there is clearly a tension at work here between the traditional notion of structure as present in the work (noted by Henderson) and a new formulation of the *auteur* as a 'fiction' in the text rather than as intentional subject, this new formulation precisely looks forward to the theory of meaning production that Henderson argues for. The *auteur* as catalyst can be read as one element in the play of assemblage of different elements which makes up the film text(s).

The auteur as structure

HOWARD HAWKS

A comparison of the different critical approaches to the work of Howard Hawks taken by Robin Wood in *Howard Hawks* (1968, 1981) and Peter Wollen in *Signs and Meaning in the Cinema* (1969, 1972) demonstrates basic differences in conceptualising the *auteur* theory and Hawks's place within it which illuminate the historical context for British *auteur*-structuralist criticism.

Both writers are concerned with the status of film as an art and its relationship to the other, established arts. Both use the *auteur* theory to support the contention that film does indeed deserve the status of 'art' rather than (or as well as) 'entertainment' by demonstrating that Hawks's work is on a par with the great classical tradition (which in Wood's case means Shakespeare, Bach, Mozart). While Wood supports this tradition in opposition to modernism, however, Wollen is primarily concerned, especially in the Postscript to the revised edition of *Signs and Meaning in the Cinema*, with a defence of modernism which attacks the roots of Wood's critical assumptions.

An intuitive artist: Robin Wood

Wood argues that art is defined by the extent of the artist's personal involvement with his material and not by the common distinction between 'art' and 'entertainment', which is virtually meaningless when applied to the classical tradition. The classical tradition is opposed to the modern tradition in that in the former the artist develops an already existing language rather than developing a new one. Hawks belongs in the classical tradition because he is totally unselfconscious; he does not draw attention to the forms he uses, therefore his work is ultimately unanalysable: the critic responds intuitively and spontaneously to the intuitive and spontaneous work that is the film. Although Hawks worked within many of the Hollywood genres, his personal vision transforms those genres; therefore he should be classified not according to genre, but according to his way of looking at the world. For Wood, his only limitation as an artist is his refusal to think of himself as such and his commitment to film as commercial entertainment. Hawks's masterpieces were produced in those moments when he was 'suddenly completely engaged by his material', when his 'intuitive consciousness' is fully alerted.

A structure of reversal: Peter Wollen

Wollen (p. 80) uses Hawks as a test-case for *auteur* theory. He is a director who is generally judged on the basis of his adventure dramas and found wanting. It is only by looking at the whole of his work, at the crazy comedies as well as the dramas, that a core of repeated motifs emerges which gives added dimension to the films and makes it possible for the critic to decipher a Hawks world-view through the play of oppositions and reversals between the dramas and the comedies. Wollen is critical of that world-view and supports his criticisms by differentiating between Hawks's work and that of Ford and Boetticher: they are all concerned with similar problems of heroism and masculinity, but the problem is articulated quite differently by each one. For Wollen, the strength of Hawks lies not in his spontaneous, intuitive artistry but in the systematic organisation of structural reversals throughout his work as a whole. Wollen does not subscribe to Hawks's values, as Wood appears to, but this does not prevent him from attempting to establish Hawks's status as an *auteur* on the basis of criteria which go beyond his personal taste as a critic.

Bringing Up Baby – anarchic woman and foolish male intellectual?

Scarface (USA 1932 *p.c* – Hughes Productions; *d* – Howard Hawks; sd b/w 14)

This film clearly belongs in the so-called 'classical' cycle of the gangster film in which the gangster hero is depicted as a paradoxical and schizophrenic figure, representing the worst in society and the best, in so far as he is striving towards the goals of the American Dream (i.e. wealth, individualism, success and power). In the context of Hawks's work, however, Robin Wood has identified *Scarface* as one of his comedies. Camonte is presented as an innocent primitive with whom we should sympathise rather than pass moral judgement. Much of the comedy resides in the way that the male characters are ridiculed (viz. the comic violence involving Angelo and Camonte's innocent enjoyment of his own bad taste). Wood pays close attention to Hawks's *mise en scène* to demonstrate how the audience is both drawn in to enjoy the gangsters' sense of complete freedom through violence, and yet distanced by the horror of it (Wood, 1968, p. 64). The combination of farce and horror makes the film truly disturbing, and it could be argued that Hawks here presents a complete reversal (and possible criticism) of the values he seems to justify in the dramas.

Wollen sees this opposition between the comedies and the dramas as vital. In the comedies the retrograde, Spartan heroism of the dramas is exposed to reveal their underlying tensions: the regression to infantilism and savagery and the sexual humiliation of the male (Wollen, 1972, p. 91). If in the dramas man is master of his world, in the comedies he is its victim. It is in this opposition that Hawks's value as an *auteur* is to be found, because it lends complexity to the representation of sexuality in his work as a whole.

Bringing Up Baby (USA 1938 *p.c* – RKO Radio; *d* – Howard Hawks; sd b/w 8)

Wood characterises Hawks's comedy thus:

'There is the extremeness of it, in the context of the light comedy genre: we are almost in the world of the Marx Brothers. There is the sexual reversal, the humiliation of the male, his loss of mastery, which makes the comedies an inversion of the adventure films. Finally, there is the *resilience* of the male, his ability to live through extremes of humiliation retaining an innate dignity' (Wood, 1968, p. 68).

He sees this film as based on the opposition between duty and nature, order and chaos, superego and id, the oppositions manifested in the struggle between the man and the woman in the progress from order to chaos and back to order again. The safety of David's world is shattered by Susan's anarchistic behaviour and can only be precariously rebuilt, leaving the spectator with an uneasy feeling that the male/female couple relationship will never be ideal. Wood points to the representation of the woman in this film as an anarchic, destructive natural force, dominating the weak and foolish male intellectual.

Wollen agrees that the comedies are the reversal of the dramas in that the hero becomes victim and that Hawks's comedy often centres around sex and role reversal (i.e. domineering women and timid, pliable men). The association of women with nature, and therefore with danger and disruption, is common to Hawks's films in general – although *Scarface* presents an interesting variation on this theme in that these primitive forces are represented by a male hero. Hawks generally keeps the male and female worlds strictly apart: when they are combined in one character (e.g. Tony Camonte) they lead to self-destruction.

The comedy in this film is again farcical, sadistic and destructive. It could be argued that Hawks undermines the ideology of male heroism only at the expense of putting forward a view of women which mirrors the fears and anxieties of men. Another argument might be that the use of structural oppositions and reversals in this work allows the ideology to be presented in a schematic form, thus inviting the audience to criticise it.

His Girl Friday (USA 1939 *p.c* – Columbia; *d* – Howard Hawks; sd b/w 19)

His Girl Friday is one of Hawks's mature comedies which works out the sets of oppositions outlined above in an extremely complex structural network using all the elements described by Wood and Wollen as specific to the comedies, but reversing many of them. A structural study of Hawks's work is useful for revealing the varied and shifting combinations of basic structures that are possible. Wollen argues that the greater the complexity of combinations the richer the work becomes.

The male world is again opposed to the female world, but this time amorality and irresponsibility lie with the former and the latter is associated with a desire for stability, home and family. Both worlds are controlled by men: the frenetic newspaper office by the unscrupulous Walter Burns (Cary Grant) and the home and marriage scene by the stolid, safe insurance salesman Bruce (Ralph Bellamy). Hildy (Rosalind Russell) is torn between the two: her 'feminine' qualities enable her to be critical of the moral chaos of the newspaper world but in the end, in an extraordinary reversal, she rejects marriage and respectability and takes her 'natural' place in that world as a 'newspaperman'.

Sergeant York – Alvin York (Gary Cooper) as 'natural' hero

Hawks vs. Ford

Both writers compare Hawks with Ford, arriving at totally different conclusions. Wollen sees Ford as going beyond the question of the value of individual action to society and to American history: but he does not simply validate those American values, he begins to question the movement of American history itself. Hawks, on the other hand, finds the solution to individual isolation in the camaraderie of the self-sufficient all-male group, cut off from society, history, and women, who are a threat to this male world.

For Wood, the comparison between Hawks and Ford reveals Hawks to be the more modern of the two artists because the idea of a stable social tradition is absent from his work. While Ford looks back nostalgically to lost values, Hawks deals with the problem of modern society by rejecting it, by creating his own world of personal loyalties in which an ideal society would be one in which the individual had maximum possible freedom from social constraints.

'Within the group, one feels an absence of *civilised* sensibility, but the strong presence of the uncultivated, instinctive

---

Hildy, played by Rosalind Russell, is an example of Hollywood's 'positive heroines' and of the use of this stereotype by Hawks. She holds her own in an exclusively male world and is critical of it. However, it is arguable that the 'positive heroine' only succeeds in Hawks's male world because she behaves like a man: her 'femininity' is negated. In the extract this sexual reversal is illustrated in terms of verbal language: in the first part Walter dominates Hildy and Bruce by his command of words and in the second part the situation is reversed when Hildy tells Walter off. Her verbal diatribe is the mirror image of his; similarly, her rugby tackle which brings down the Sheriff is 'heroic' in a masculine sense and heralds her final capitulation to Walter Burns' demands that she rejoin the male world of the newspaper. Nevertheless, Hildy's struggle to retain her own identity and the impossibility of that struggle produce an ironic commentary on the problems of sexual difference which is characteristic of Hawks's work.

Sergeant York (USA 1941 *p.c* – Warner Bros; *d* – Howard Hawks; sd b/w 12 + 10)

Apparently atypical of Hawks's work, this film nonetheless represents a validation of the virtues of individual heroism. Alvin York (Gary Cooper) is an ordinary man forced by circumstances (America's involvement in the First World War) to become a reluctant hero. While violence and heroism are against his principles, he sacrifices those principles for the sake of his country and discovers that he is, in fact, a 'natural' hero. This structure is similar to that of *His Girl Friday* and the values attached to home life and community, while initially opposed to those attached to war, are eventually

shown to be interchangeable with them. It could be argued that the reversal of oppositions in this film works to validate the ideology of individual heroism and patriotism.

To Have and Have Not (USA 1944 *p.c* – Warner Bros; *d* – Howard Hawks; sd b/w 20)

Harry Morgan (Humphrey Bogart) refuses to commit himself to help the French patriots escape until he finds himself directly and personally involved, and even then political action against fascism is justified in personal terms, so that the film appears less an anti-fascist statement than a validation of individual action against corrupt authoritarian forces. The first meeting between Slim (Lauren Bacall) and Harry is interesting because of the woman's self-assurance and insistence on meeting the man on equal terms. However, this is immediately undermined in the sequence in which Harry forces Slim to return the wallet she has stolen, thus asserting his mastery and control of her.

The uneasy relationship between Slim and Harry is characteristic of Hawks's work. Peter Wollen has pointed to the ritualistic quality of Hawks's male groups: one of the ways in which women enter the group is by learning the rituals, by acting like men. Slim's 'feminine', 'caring' qualities are rejected by Harry because they threaten his self-sufficiency. The only way she can help him is by subscribing to his code, in effect, by becoming 'masculinised'.

Robin Wood takes this film as a test-case for his view of the *auteur* theory. One of the arguments which critics of *auteur* study of films put forward is the collaborative nature of film production in Hollywood: the director's contribution is only one among many, and not necessarily the most important one. *To Have and Have Not* would

seem to support this view: it is a genre movie (i.e. 'adventures in exotic location') conceived by the studio (Warner Bros) as a starring vehicle for Bogart, adapted from a novel by Hemingway, scripted by William Faulkner and Jules Furthman and specifically indebted to at least two other films (*Morocco*, 1930, and *Casablanca*, 1942). Starting with his conception of Hawks's world-view, Wood looks carefully and in detail at all these possible contributions in order to establish that the film is in fact 'quint-essentially Hawksian' (Wood, 'To Have (written) and Have Not (directed)', 1976).

The Big Sky (USA 1952 *p.c* – Winchester Pictures; *d* – Howard Hawks; sd b/w 15)

The idea of love between men recurs in Hawks's films and has been explicitly acknowledged by him. It appears most clearly in the westerns and it could be argued that it is fundamental to this genre (← GENRE: *The western*, p. 66).

Robin Wood does not see the male relationships in Hawks's films as homosexual since they co-exist with, and often finally yield to, heterosexual love. For Wood, the love between men is an immature relationship which gives way in the progress of the hero to maturity and responsibility (i.e. hetero-sexuality and marriage).

Wollen, however, refers to 'the undercurrent of homosexuality' in Hawks's films which he sees as closely linked to the director's idealisation of the all-male group and rejection of women. Men are equals, whereas women are closely identified with nature and the animal world (cf. *Bringing Up Baby, Gentlemen Prefer Blondes*). Marriage, and the heterosexual relationship, is a threat to the integrity of the elite male group. →

sensibility that must underlie any valid civilisation: intuitive-sympathetic contact, a sturdily positive, generous spirit' (Wood, 1968, p. 92).

A feminist view

One might wish to question the value of any view of society in which the 'sturdily positive, generous spirit' does not extend beyond the male group to the other half of society: women. Women exist at the periphery of Hawks's male group, at the point at which it threatens to break down. It is this representation of 'woman' as a point of tension or anxiety in male society – in effect a troublesome question which refuses to go away – which has attracted the attention of feminist film critics to Hawks's work. Hawks's films appear to epitomise the workings of patriarchal ideology in the way that they

Gentlemen Prefer Blondes – one of Hawks' failures?

represent the 'otherness' of women as a threat which can only be resolved (uneasily) by the initiation of this 'other' into the codes of male society: in effect by recognising and then recuperating the 'otherness', the difference of women.

References

Richard Dyer, *Stars*, London, British Film Institute, 1979.

Charles Eckert, 'The English cinestructuralists', *Film Comment* vol. 9 no. 3, May/June 1973.

Molly Haskell, *From Reverence to Rape*, New York, Holt, Rinehart and Winston, 1974.

Brian Henderson, 'Critique of cinestructuralism, Part I', *Film Quarterly* vol. 27 no. 1, Fall 1973; 'Part II', *Film Quarterly* vol. 27 no. 2, Winter 1973.

Peter Wollen, *Signs and Meaning in the Cinema*, London, Secker and Warburg/BFI, 1969; rev. ed. 1972.

Robin Wood, *Howard Hawks*, London, Secker and Warburg/BFI, 1968; rev. ed. BFI Publishing, 1981.

Robin Wood, 'To Have (written) and Have Not (directed)', in Nichols (ed.), *Movies and Methods*, Berkeley, University of California Press, 1976.

Narrative plays an important role in resolving the complex network of 'perverse' relationships running through the film: the relationships between the two men, between the Indian woman and two white men (one sadistic, the other tender) and between the white men and Indian woman are resolved ambiguously and, it could be argued, in a somewhat arbitrary fashion. It could seem that Hawks's view of these relationships is at odds with the demands of narrative resolution. Hawks's particular inflection of the 'male love' theme seems to pose it in opposition to heterosexual love, as an ideal in contrast to the problems inherent in homosexuality, thus raising sexual difference itself as a problem.

Gentlemen Prefer Blondes (USA 1953 *p.c* – 20th Century-Fox; *d* – Howard Hawks; sd col 15)

This film is one of Hawks's comedies in which sexual role-reversal is predominant. Wollen points to the scenes of male humiliation (e.g. Jane Russell's song number in which the Olympic athletic team are reduced to passive objects) as an example of Hawks's comic strategy of reversals.

Wood sees this film as one of Hawks's failures: while all the essential elements are there, they do not fuse into a satisfactory coherent whole. However, Richard Dyer (1979) has argued that this lack of coherence is one of the most interesting aspects of the film: the 'lack of fit' between the different elements, in particular, what Dyer sees as the miscasting of Marilyn Monroe in the part of Lorelei, works to undermine the consistency of Hawks's world-view.

Of all the genres within which Hawks worked the musical seems the most unlikely: indeed *Gentlemen Prefer Blondes* is his only musical and is generally referred to as one of his

comedies. While viewing the film as a comedy is revealing in the context of his other work, it is interesting to speculate on his use of the musical numbers here to point up moments of extreme tension between the male world and the threat to it represented by the female. The 'excessive' nature of the musical numbers has been pointed out by Robin Wood, who finds them vulgar and crude. If, as Wood argues, *Gentlemen Prefer Blondes* represents a break in Hawks's work with his usual 'classical' style, it could be seen as one of the points at which the ideology of his world-view begins to fall apart at the seams, making it particularly useful for an ideological reading.

Rio Bravo (USA 1959 *p.c* – Armada; *d* – Howard Hawks; sd col 18)

Robin Wood argues that this film lies firmly within the tradition of the western, at the same time representing the most complete statement of Hawks's position that exists. Genre and director fuse perfectly.

'The action of *Rio Bravo* is played out against a background hard and bare, with nothing to distract the individual from working out his essential relationship to life. The virtual removal of a social framework – the relegating of society to the function of a *pretext* – throws all the emphasis on the characters' sense of *self*: on their need to find a sense of purpose and meaning not through allegiance to any developing order, but within themselves, in their own instinctual needs' (Wood, 1968, p. 39).

Wood points to the positive qualities of the male group in *Rio Bravo*, seeing in the relationships between the men a moral vision which confirms Hawks's 'spirit of generosity' (p. 48). Peter Wollen sees it slightly differently: the self-sufficient all-male group represents

an exclusive elite, imposing severe tests of ability and courage on its members (Wollen, 1972, p. 82).

Wollen's shift of emphasis makes Hawks's treatment of the male group seem oppressive rather than positive, particularly in relation to women, who never really become full members of the group however hard they try to prove themselves worthy (Wollen, 1972, p. 86).

Some feminist critics have defended Hawks's 'positive heroines' as strong female figures (e.g. Molly Haskell, 1974). However, it is arguable that Feathers (Angie Dickinson) is first recognised as a problem for the male hero, Chance (John Wayne), when she takes the initiative, and then recuperated as a threat when the hero conquers her, precisely confirming Hawks's view of the necessity for strong male heroes. In this context, the threat of male humiliation is expressed through the use of screwball comedy in the scene between Feathers and Chance at the end of the film. On the level of *mise en scène*, the exoticism of Feathers' room, the sharp contrasts between red and black, seem to reinforce her function as a sign of threat to the stability of Hawks's male world. It could be argued that Hawks takes John Wayne's star persona to an extreme point of stylisation, so that it almost becomes self-parody, undercutting the masculine values of stoicism and self-sufficiency normally associated with the western hero (← GENRE: *The Western*, p. 66).

Auteur study after structuralism

The passing of auteur-structuralism

British *auteur*-structuralism had attempted to bring together two apparently incompatible theories to resolve the problems inherent in both. On one hand, it tried to preserve a place for the individual in artistic production, generally retaining the notion found in the *politique des auteurs* of the artist as a potentially critical voice in society. On the other, it saw the individual as enmeshed in linguistic, social and institutional structures which affected the organisation of meaning: the individual was not a free human being in control of the work, whose conscious intentions could be simply retrieved or decoded by the critic. What could be decoded was an authorial system, not to be confused with a real author, which was only one code among many others and not always dominant (see Wollen, 1972). Nevertheless, *auteur*-structuralism, as a method of 'reading', still posited the *auteur*-code as dominant, since it rarely attempted to account for any other codes. So, while claiming to dissolve the *auteur* into a generality of codes, it continued to provide a partial analysis which maintained a place for the author, still seen as the director, at the centre of his/her work.

The contradictions inherent in *auteur*-structuralism created the need for new theoretical enquiry to deal with them. At the same time, the historical context in which *auteur*-structuralism first emerged had changed. In France after 1968 a new emphasis on art as political practice brought the idea of individual authorship into question. Also in question was the structuralist 'method' itself, in so far as it was used to decode an abstract, static code or system outside history and society. What was needed, it was argued, was a more dynamic concept of the text which took account of the processes within which it was constantly transformed.

The modernist answer: Peter Wollen

British film criticism produced diverse answers to the theoretical problems generated by *auteur* – structuralism. Peter Wollen argued for a bringing together of modernist art practice which drew attention to the text as a system of signs, and a theory of language (semiology) which would break with the functionalist approach which saw the work as the expression of thought or intention (Wollen, 1972). The work, he argued, generated meanings through an internal conflict of codes, independently of author or critic; it was a kind of 'factory where thought was at work': author and reader collaborated to produce different and conflicting meanings or interpretations, an activity which would always be 'work in progress' and could never provide a comprehensive, final or 'correct' meaning.

The pluralist answer: Ed Buscombe

Ed Buscombe suggested three possible ways out of the impasse of auteurism, all of which would displace the traditional notion of the *auteur*: a sociology which would attempt to understand how society makes sense of cinema; a theory which would examine the effects of ideology, economics and technology on the cinema; a history which would look at the language of cinema and the effects of films on other films (Buscombe, 'Ideas of Authorship', 1973).

The psychoanalytic answer: Stephen Heath

Stephen Heath argued that it was precisely this shift, or displacement of the idea of the individual *auteur* at the centre of the work that was in need of theorisation. (Heath, 'Comment on "The Idea of Authorship",' 1973). Close textual analysis, and the employment of psychoanalysis as a tool of analysis, would reveal not the presence of the author, but the play of the unconscious across a body of films and the ways in which the system of each particular film constructed a set of positions for the spectator which determined his or her relationship to the film.

The social answer: Alan Lovell

Alan Lovell insisted that film production was, like all artistic production, primarily social (Lovell, 1975). A film was the result of the interaction of all the elements in the production situation and available artistic forms, ideological meanings and intended audiences. The director had little control over these factors, therefore his or her intentions were less important than the effect of this interaction of multiple elements in the films, which was responsible for producing their ideological meanings.

These arguments seemed to signal the end, in theoretical film study anyway, of *auteur* study as it had been known. The shift of emphasis towards the text as the place where meaning was produced, and towards analysis of ideology militated against the classification of films under the name of an author/director. Some textual analysis continued to draw on the idea of an 'authorial code' which could be detected in individual films: this code was not important in itself however, except as part of the textual system. The question raised for film study by the death of *auteur*-structuralism (a death, it could be argued, implicit in its formation) was an awkward one: why study 'authorship' at all?

The answers outlined above were not without their own problems. Wollen's idea of the partial autonomy of textual operations and the collective process of reading did not entirely dispense with the problem of intentionality: at the same time it did not attempt to deal with the problem. On the other hand, Buscombe's pluralist approach which argued for attention to other methods of analysis besides that of *auteur* study, if it was formulated simply in terms of the adding together of different methods, seemed to avoid the problem of the author altogether since it did not come to grips with the organisation of all these different elements into a system of meaning. Moreover, recasting authorship in terms of its production by the 'textual system' rather than the other way about, as suggested by Heath, seemed to place too much emphasis on the text itself as a self-contained object outside the system of production and exchange in which films were marketed as commodity products. Geoffrey Nowell-Smith argued that the process of assemblage by which a film is put together to be marketed militated against the attribution of a single meaning to one intentional source: traditionally criticism works against the grain of this fragmentation of meaning and intention to recover the coherence of the text, which then entered into circulation as an object of use. From this perspective, authors and critics could not be seen simply as 'effects', dispersed across the textual system. It was precisely the authorial sub-code, or the fragmented marks of authorship, which enabled the critic to reconstruct a coherent *auteur*. There was no *necessary* fit between the process of commodity production and that of consumption, but neither should be seen as somehow escaping its place in the social formation (Nowell-Smith, 'Six authors in pursuit of *The Searchers*', 1976).

If the author-code can be seen, then, as one of the organising principles of coherence in the film which enables us to grasp meaning, to read it, the problem still remains of what methods to use to identify the marks of the author as distinct from the other elements. So, paradoxically, the post-structuralist debates about authorship and cinema, far from evacuating the problems, had the effect of drawing attention to questions of different methods of 'reading' films, and to the social function of criticism itself.

The many phases of authorship: auteur study today

The question raised by structuralism for film theory was 'why study authorship?', the answer to which can partly be found in the multiple problems *auteur* analysis raises for film criticism in general; the history of *auteur* criticism can be seen as the history of different methods of reading films, and of the shifting and complex relationship between spectator/critic and film. Different critical approaches to the work of an *auteur* can be brought together to demonstrate the historical specificity of 'authorship' as a category and the way in which different readings depend upon and produce different relationships between author, film and spectator. In study of Hollywood cinema in particular, *auteur* analysis can be posed against other approaches to the text (e.g. through genre, or industry) as a principle of opposition which goes against the grain of the industrial system. The difference between the critics' construction of the *auteur* and the real director's own assessment of his or her films helps to show that the *auteur* is indeed a construction, which cannot necessarily be related back to the intentions of a real person. This more complex, historical approach to authorship demonstrates the partiality of different methods of studying cinema, rather than posing one method as more adequate than others.

JOHN FORD

John Ellis has outlined the principles of an historical approach to studying authorship in 'Teaching authorship: Ford or fraud?' (1981). Ellis's approach is limited to a consideration of a director working within the Hollywood system over a long period whose status as an *auteur* in film criticism changes with history. Furthermore, the best kind of director for the purpose would be one whose own account of his work was decidedly not theoretical: interview material could then be used to point up differences between critics' and director's statements. The approach is based on the study of a wide range of critical texts and a large number of films all of which should show as many differences as possible: the

The beleaguered stagecoach community in Ford's classic – *Stagecoach*

The Informer (USA 1935 *p.c* – RKO Radio; *d* – John Ford; sd b/w 14)

This film was acclaimed by critics as a masterpiece when it first appeared because of its formal concerns (expressionism, a return to the imagery of silent cinema) and incorporation of serious social themes of hunger and unemployment in Ireland in the 1920s. Later it was to be condemned by the same criteria: as formally pretentious and approaching its theme with an over-serious sentimentality (see Anderson, 1981).

In terms of the Fordian system, Victor McLaglen is one of Ford's repertory of actors and the comic-grotesque quality of his performance, his weakness set beside his basic humanity, can be found in his performances in other Ford films. The IRA is described by Sarris as 'the ultra-Fordian community' (Sarris, 1976): comparison of its treatment here with Fordian communities in other films (e.g. the families in *My Darling Clementine*, the army in *She Wore a Yellow Ribbon* and *Sergeant Rutledge*) might illuminate the influence of Irish Catholicism on his work. Peter Wollen (1972) sees a development in Ford's career in terms of a shift in structural oppositions: from an identity between 'civilised versus savage' and 'European versus Indian' to their separation and final reversal so that in *Cheyenne Autumn* it is the Europeans who are savage, the victims who are heroes. How does *The Informer* fit into this pattern of

shifting antinomies? Does Wollen's structural model apply to the whole of Ford's work, or only to the westerns?

Ford made this film for RKO – the 'studio of his conscience . . . of his moral commitment to his material' (Sarris, 1976) as opposed to Fox, 'his bread and butter base' – and a comparison could be drawn with *The Grapes of Wrath* (Fox) to discuss how far differences might be attributable to studio policies (← HISTORY: *The studios*, p. 18). The prestige production of *The Informer* might be attributable to Ford's concern with taking on projects at this stage in his career which would further his reputation and give him more control: hence the collaboration with Dudley Nichols and the adaptation of a serious novel.

Stagecoach (USA 1939 *p.c* – Walter Wanger Productions; *d* – John Ford; sd b/w 10)

Critical opinion has generally been united over this film, hailing it as a 'classic', in spite of the fact that it is blatantly a genre piece with no 'artistic' pretensions: in fact, the western genre conventions completely submerge the origins of the film in a novel by Guy de Maupassant (turned into a western story by Ernest Haycox).

Wollen's structural antinomies (Civilised vs. Savage, European vs. Indian) are worked out in terms of the opposition between the savage Apache and the beleaguered stage coach

'community'. The community is riven with contradictions of class and sexuality between the various characters, but these contradictions are transcended by the primary opposition between Indian savage/American civilised values, allowing the extermination of the American Indian to be validated and celebrated. It has been argued that this view of American history is reversed and questioned in other Ford films (Wollen, 1972).

The landscape of Monument Valley has become a kind of stylistic signature in Ford's westerns, raising the question of how to identify the marks of authorship in relation to genre conventions.

Stagecoach has often been held up as an example of the classical art of narrative based on montage editing prevalent in Hollywood cinema of the 30s (see Bazin, 'The Evolution of the language of cinema', 1967). The extract provides an opportunity to look closely at the organisation of shots and the relationship between image and sound which provides the basis of this narrative system.

Although the film is clearly a genre piece, and also an example of 'classical' narrative cinema, it could be argued that it nonetheless deals with 'serious' questions (e.g. class, sexuality, race) as much as *The Informer* or *The Grapes of Wrath*, in spite of the fact that critics do not generally give it the status of a 'quality' film.

Beautiful imagery in Ford's prestige production *The Grapes of Wrath*

more 'unevenness' there is between texts and between films the easier it is to demonstrate that *auteur* study is an ideological project which attempts to unify and systematise. There are very few directors who would fulfil these requirements. John Ford is an obvious choice because of his veteran status in the Hollywood industry, his critical reputation as a monumental artist of the cinema and the ability of his films to engage the audience on many complex levels. Ford's relationship to the industry and to critical taste is complicated: his film-making career covers artistic experiments, genre films, studio product and independent productions; his critical reception has varied from Oscars to complete disdain. Moreover, many of his films take as their subject matter questions of imperialism, racism and sexism in American society and history: some of them (e.g. *Young Mr. Lincoln, Wings of Eagles*) seem to undermine their ostensible ideological message through their textual operations, raising the question of the viability of relating them back to the director's intention (or to any other intentional source).

This approach has the advantage of illuminating the notion of authorship as well as the work of the chosen *auteur* and,

The Grapes of Wrath (USA 1940 *p.c* – 20th Century-Fox; *d* – John Ford; sd b/w 10)

The film which established Ford's reputation as the great poet of American cinema, but one which it is, paradoxically, difficult to identify as belonging only to Ford without ignoring the contributions to the final product of, for example, Nunnally Johnson's adaptation of Steinbeck's novel, Gregg Toland's photography, not to mention producer Darryl F. Zanuck, as the partial approach of *auteur* study tends to.

In terms of the Fordian system, Ford's reputed populism could be detected in the depiction of the family as a community and the role of the mother in unifying the family. Arguably, however, this populism emerges as much from Steinbeck's concerns, or from New Deal ideology as from a Fordian system. Comparison with other Ford films (e.g. *Young Mr. Lincoln* → p. 189) and with other Hollywood populist films (e.g. Frank Capra's *Mr. Deeds Goes to Town* ← p. 170) could illuminate this question. Sarris argues that Steinbeck's criticism of American society is undermined by New Deal homilies (Sarris, 1976).

The structural opposition between wilderness (or desert) and garden identified by Wollen (1972) as the master antinomy in Ford's films is worked out here in terms of the opposition between the Arizona desert and the luxuriant promised land of California, which

proves to be less than ideal. The journey, or quest of the Joad family has been identified as part of Ford's thematic system: the search for the promised land involves a movement between desert and garden which changes in emphasis, and therefore in meaning, from film to film.

It is arguable that the film's aesthetically beautiful images, attributable to Ford and Toland, are in contradiction to the angry, critical words of Steinbeck and Johnson, a contradiction produced perhaps by Ford's desire to enhance his directorial career at this time with prestige productions (Sarris, 1976).

How Green Was My Valley (USA 1941 *p.c* – 20th Century-Fox; *d* – John Ford; sd b/w 10)

A lavish, prestige production which Ford took over from William Wyler in the early stages of preparation and which won six Academy Awards. The film draws attention to its literary origins in a novel by using the device of voice-over narration through which a central character (the boy Huw Morgan) remembers the past (Sarris, 1976, relates this strategy to the many writers-turned-director in the industry in the 1940s). The extract is from the opening of the film and illustrates the narrative flashback device, which is usual in Ford's work in general (see, however, *Sergeant Rutledge*, p. 188).

The film centres on family and

community, a thematic element in many Ford films, but here providing the entire motivation for the film. The combination of nostalgia for past values and the representation of the community as the location of positive values such as loyalty, discipline and gallantry has been identified by Robin Wood as Ford's major preoccupation (Wood, 1968). Whereas the fragmentation of the family in *The Grapes of Wrath* provides the basis for a criticism of social conditions, *How Green Was My Valley* seems to look back to the Depression as a time when social conditions destroyed family unity, the project of the film being to mourn its loss.

In terms of genre, the film belongs to a certain type of family melodrama prevalent in Hollywood in the 1940s (see Higham and Greenberg, 1968). Ford's films often use melodrama to move the audience and this film is one of the all-time great weepies, yet it also combines 'serious' political questions with a genre not usually valued highly for its seriousness.

My Darling Clementine (USA 1946 *p.c* – *20th Century-Fox; d* – John Ford; sd b/w 14)

After the Second World War Ford's reputation fell into something of a critical decline (see Sarris, 1976). This film was his second western in twenty years and did little to restore that reputation.

→

How Green Was My Valley – Ford's film mourning the loss of family unity

because of the emphasis on the process of reading, is able to confront questions of ideology, personal taste and politics in relation to film study. Since it is structured specifically around John Ford and his relationship to the Hollywood industry, however, and it seems as though Ford is the only director whose work could be utilised in this way, the problem remains of how to approach authorship with different directors and in other production situations. For example, the concept of authorship retained by Ellis is the one of *opposition* to the institutional structures of Hollywood (genre, industry): one question would be whether other institutional structures (e.g. New German Cinema, art cinema, independent cinema) bring into play different principles of authorship.

As Ellis points out, the attention given to different critical texts in his approach is not just a way of establishing relative differences between them: a marked distinction emerges between those accounts which assume the relationship between the director and his films is one of continuity of self-expression (e.g. Andrew Sarris, ← p. 137), and those which distinguish between the man Ford and the *auteur* construction 'Ford' (e.g. Peter Wollen, ← p. 168). In the first case, these readings,

It is arguable that the traditional conventions of the genre (action sequences, gun-fights) are displaced or transformed by the emphasis placed in this film on domestic activity; that is, on day-to-day activities of personal hygiene, dressing up, courting, going to church, etc., which represent the civilising forces which take over the desert/wilderness, transforming it into a cultivated garden.

Wollen (1972) sees the progress of Wyatt Earp (Henry Fonda) from 'nature' to 'culture' as relatively unproblematic compared with other Fordian heroes (e.g. Ethan Edwards in *The Searchers*). The scene in the barber-shop (illustrated in the extract) is seen by Wollen as symbolic of this progress: the barber 'civilises' the unkempt Earp, splashing him with honeysuckle scent, an artificial rather than a natural perfume, thus marking his transition from nomad to settled, civilised man, administrator of the law. However, it could also be argued that Earp's progress can only be measured against the decline of Doc Holliday (Victor Mature), which is seen in terms of the loss of an anarchic spirit which is the basis of poetry and subversive sexual energy. Moreover, Earp's bearing during his transformation remains stiff and unwieldy, even in the communal dance sequence. The transition from nature to culture is heavily marked as comic, and could be seen as more problematic than Wollen allows. Furthermore, the highly

stylised *mise en scène* (extreme perspectives, predominance of long-shots, and 'expressionist' lighting, i.e. dark/light contrasts) might offer the audience a critical distance both on the genre conventions and the narrative events.

The opposition between the two women, Clementine and Chihuahua, is also interesting in terms of the transition from nature to culture discussed by Wollen in relation to the central male character. This taming of energy is often depicted in Ford's films as necessary but regrettable, so that the films seem to question the 'progress' of history.

Fort Apache (USA 1948 *p.c* – Argosy Pictures; *d* – John Ford; sd b/w 20)

Sarris (1976) argues that the last two decades of Ford's career were the most vigorous in that 'he became fully his own man'. Contemporary critics, however, did not agree, and saw the late Ford as self-indulgent, relegating him to the status of an honoured has-been, now engaged in re-working tired old themes with the same stock company.

Peter Wollen's (1972) structural approach can be seen as an attempt to redress the critical balance. By looking for underlying patterns of shifting oppositions he was able to argue that the shifting pattern became more complex as Ford's work developed. *Movie*, following *Cahiers du Cinéma*, had declared its preference for Sam Fuller over Ford; in the mid-6os *Cahiers*

re-evaluated Ford, but only in terms of 'key' *auteur* films.

Wollen's approach provided the possibility of looking again at the whole of Ford's work, and not necessarily in terms of 'good' and 'bad' films, rather in terms of an underlying 'Fordian system'. Although this approach attempted to come to terms with the unevenness of Ford's work, with its differences and contradictions, Wollen himself deals mainly with westerns, which seem most amenable to analysis according to structural oppositions. The question still remains of how the more 'aberrant' works fit into the schema. Ford's work seems to resist schematic systematisation, which is what makes it so useful for a critical approach to *auteur* study.

This film was the first in a series of Cavalry westerns which demonstrated a changing attitude towards the American Indians in Ford's work (see *Stagecoach*, p. 184). However, it could be argued that this liberalised attitude in the films was less a political shift (on the part of Ford or anyone else) than a way of dramatising the conflict of values within the Cavalry community. Wollen may be right in pointing to a reversal between the oppositions savage (Indian) and civilised (European) in Ford's later work, but it is not a simple reversal in which the Indians take the place of the Europeans at the centre of the drama.

This film also marks the shift from Henry Fonda to John Wayne as the hero

combined with interview material, can be seen to perform a particular function in the construction of a persona which will contribute to the process of marketing the Ford commodity. The second kind of readings work against this by positing a 'Fordian system' which is the result of the critical activity of reading rather than the discovery of an expressive essence. In these terms, authorship study is posed as an operation of reading and criticism rather than the straight-forward consumption of the Ford commodity.

The difficulty of systematisation, the extent to which any attempt to construct a Fordian system falls short of the complete Ford oeuvre, can be shown by examining the ways in which Ford films contradict one another, undermining the possibility of attributing a set of positive values to Ford or 'Ford'. The use of star John Wayne, for instance, in many different and often contradictory roles, works against the idea of a Fordian world-view outside of history and change (and indeed, against the idea of a Wayne persona outside of history and change).

A comparison of films from the 30s indicates the extent of the differences and contradictions. *The Informer* and *Grapes of Wrath* appear as 'quality' films with

My Darling Clementine – and Chihuahua – the taming of the West

of Ford's films. The confrontation between Captain York (Wayne) and Lieutenant Colonel Thursday (Fonda) in the extract is useful for discussing the iconographical differences between the two stars as deployed in the Fordian system.

Ford's late westerns appear significantly different from other examples of the genre in 50s and 60s Hollywood, retaining Fordian set-pieces and a stylised *mise en scène* in the face of technological developments such as CinemaScope (← GENRE: *The western*, p. 66).

In the extract the women are seen as supporters of the Cavalry's values. The soldiers sing 'The Girl I Left Behind Me' and there are strains of 'She Wore a Yellow Ribbon' on the soundtrack. This use of music for dramatic and ideological effect is characteristic of Ford's work.

She Wore a Yellow Ribbon (USA 1949 *p.c* – Argosy Pictures; *d* – John Ford; sd col 27)

Wood (1968) identifies this film as one in which Fordian values are clearly marked. The Cavalry is seen to represent the ideal community built on traditions of loyalty, discipline, and allegiance to an established code of behaviour. Women and men alike must submit to this code.

Olivia Dandridge can be seen as a potential threat to the Cavalry traditions, mostly because of her

exuberant sexuality. In the second part of the extract the ageing Captain Brittles (John Wayne) and the high-spirited Olivia are both excluded from the military in spite of the fact that they both represent some of its highest values. It could be argued that the film questions on one level the rigidity of the military order (cf. *Fort Apache*).

The first part of the extract demonstrates the film's attitude towards the Indians as brutal savages in contrast to the 'civilised' values of the Cavalry (see also *Stagecoach* p. 184) and both parts show John Wayne in a role of 'father figure' which is significantly different from his persona in other Ford films (see *Stagecoach*; *Fort Apache*).

It could also be argued that Ford's Cavalry westerns are marked by an opposition between panoramic views of the western landscape and the closed, tight compositions of the more intimate sequences involving the Cavalry. If so, how does this work to affect the meanings produced by the films?

The Searchers (USA 1956 *p.c* – C. V. Whitney Pictures Inc; *d* – John Ford; sd col 32)

As John Ellis (1981) argues, Ford's work can be used to raise a wide range of questions about the ways in which films are produced and consumed and the critical methods employed to analyse cinema. *The Searchers* is a paradigmatic case: it has achieved the status of a key text in film studies for the possibilities it

offers as the site of different, often conflicting, analytical methods which work productively with and against one another (see *Screen Education* no. 17).

The film's perceived usefulness in different contexts can be partly ascribed to its problematic place in the Fordian oeuvre, which makes it necessary to look outside the film itself for an explanation of its 'lack of fit'. Critics are deeply divided in their evaluations. Anderson ('*The Searchers*', 1956), for example, denies that the film has any place in the humanistic world-view he defines as Ford's, while Wollen (1972) sees the film as perhaps Ford's most complex working-through of the opposition wilderness/garden which forms the basis of his work. For Wollen the complexity lies in the overlapping of these oppositions within and between characters, particularly between Ethan Edwards (John Wayne), a tragic hero torn apart by the divisions Indian/European, savage/civilised, nomad/settler, his 'opposite', Scar, the Indian chief with whom he shares many characteristics, his companion in the quest to find Debbie, part-Cherokee Martin Pawley, and the European family of home-steaders who represent the eventual transformation of wilderness into garden. This structural complexity enables the film to complicate, perhaps undermine, any simple progress from wilderness to garden, savage to civilised, which may be seen as its manifest ideological project. →

Sergeant Rutledge – anti-racism based on the myth of black supersexuality

serious intent: they seem more worthy of critical attention/approval than genre films such as *Steamboat Round the Bend* or even *Stagecoach*, partly because 'Fordian concerns' can be discerned more easily in them. Such a comparison raises quite directly questions of authorship, genre, industry and critical taste (i.e. what one expects from a 'good' movie). One of the positive aspects of *auteur* study employed to decode an underlying authorial system is, it could be argued, the

way in which it takes issue with critical notions of some films as more 'culturally respectable' than others. However, close analysis of film texts can point to the contradictions within them which seem to fragment or undermine any unifying discourse (e.g. *Wings of Eagles, Young Mr. Lincoln*).

In this way, Ellis argues, *auteur* study can be seen to raise a multitude of questions both for itself and for other critical methods. At the same time it can be revealed as a partial approach which ignores questions of the industry, except as a set of constraints or limitations on expressivity, or questions of production of meaning in film texts, except as the expression of the author's intentions. Looking at authorship as an activity of reading can raise the general question of criticism and its role in relation to film, for instance, by highlighting the way in which textual operations always tend to exceed or escape attempts to delimit their meanings by critical writing.

References

Lindsay Anderson, 'The Searchers', *Sight and Sound* vol. 26 no. 2, Autumn 1956, reprinted in Caughie (ed.), *Theories of Authorship*, London, Routledge and Kegan Paul/BFI, 1981.

Lindsay Anderson, *About John Ford*, London, Plexus, 1981.

André Bazin, 'The evolution of the language of cinema', in Gray (ed. and trans.), *What Is Cinema?* Vol. I, Berkeley, University of California Press, 1967.

Edward Buscombe, 'Ideas of authorship', *Screen* vol. 14 no. 3, Autumn 1973.

John Caughie, 'Teaching through authorship', *Screen Education* no. 17, Autumn 1975.

John Ellis, 'Teaching authorship: Ford or fraud?', in Gledhill (ed.), *Film and Media Studies in Higher Education*, London, BFI Education, 1981.

Stephen Heath, 'Comment on "The Idea of Authorship"', *Screen* vol. 14 no. 3, cit.

Charles Higham and Joel Greenberg, *Hollywood in the 40s*, London, Tantivy Press, 1968.

Alan Lovell, *Don Siegel: American Cinema*, London, BFI, 1975.

Geoffrey Nowell-Smith, 'Six authors in pursuit of *The Searchers*', *Screen* vol. 17 no. 1, Spring 1976.

Andrew Sarris, *The John Ford Movie Mystery*, London, Secker and Warburg/BFI, 1976.

Screen Education no. 17, Autumn 1975. Special issue on *The Searchers*.

Peter Wollen, *Signs and Meaning in the Cinema*, London, Secker and Warburg/BFI, 1972.

Robin Wood, *Howard Hawks*, London, Secker and Warburg/BFI, 1968; rev. ed. BFI Publishing, 1981.

For Wollen, then, Ford's particular inflection of material basic to the mythology of the western forms a sub-text or code which contradicts the genre's ideological bias, an analysis which can be used to challenge allegations that the film is racist. However, as John Caughie points out ('Teaching through authorship', 1975), even if it could be proved that a critique of racism was 'intended', the narrative resolution in which Debbie is returned to the white community and the 'natural order' restored at the very least removes the sting from the critique. Caughie also argues that the wilderness/garden opposition is supported by a sexual division in which men are active participants in the struggle towards civilisation and women passively represent the values for which they are fighting. It would seem, then, that the complexity noted by Wollen is not present at the level of sexist ideology.

Sergeant Rutledge (USA 1960 *p.c* – John Ford/Warner Bros; *d* – John Ford; sd col 16)

Wollen (1972) identifies a transition in Ford's work which equates 'non-Americans' (Irish, Indians, Polynesians, Negroes) with the traditional values of the American Dream which America itself has lost. It could be argued that this appropriation of other races in the service of 'American' values is imperialistic, to say the least. While the representation of the negro Rutledge is

often seen (see Ellis, 1981) to be a more liberalised view of the blacks than in Ford's earlier work (e.g. *Judge Priest*, 1934, *Steamboat Round the Bend*, 1935, *The Sun Shines Bright*, 1954), this 'liberalisation' seems to involve divesting Rutledge of both his blackness and sexuality, superimposing the values of courage and nobility associated with the American Cavalry and so producing Rutledge as a 'noble savage' figure who transcends racism. The position of the black soldier is never raised in terms of his relation to the American Indians, the white man's ideology is accepted and the Apache are unquestionably regarded as the enemy, the destruction of whom will enable the black soldiers to become free Americans.

The first part of the extract illustrates this contradiction between the humanitarian/civil-rights project of the film (seen in Rutledge's raised, clenched fists) and the superimposition of white values on the negro (seen in the defence of Rutledge by the humanitarian Mary Beecher and the ambiguous attitude of Lieutenant Cantrell, who clearly regards Rutledge as 'innocent'). The second part shows the opposition between the traditional values which Rutledge represents and the decaying of those values among the members of the court, here played comically, as though to emphasise Rutledge's idealisation.

John Ellis (1981) argues that the film produces a commentary on racism by taking the myth of black super-sexuality

as its central problem, displacing the myth in favour of the proposition that blacks are a-sexual; Rutledge becomes a human being only insofar as he foreswears his sexuality. This forswearing of sexuality in a higher cause can be traced in other Ford films (e.g. *My Darling Clementine, She Wore a Yellow Ribbon, Rio Grande*). According to Ellis, the film is only able to raise the problem of race and sexuality in this way because of its tightly coded narrative structure: the trial device enables commentary to be carried out at all points of ambiguity in the story, with returns from flash-backs to the cross-examination of witnesses. Thus multiple meanings are limited and controlled, and the film articulates its position against a certain kind of racism based on the myth of black super-sexuality. Ellis's account focuses on the way in which narrative structure contributes to the construction of meaning in the film, independently of the intentions of the author.

Authorship as 'discursive activity'

Auteur-structuralism had insisted that the author should no longer be thought of as a 'real' person existing independently of the films, the intentional source of meaning, and that a new formulation was required which located him or her as producer of meanings within the films themselves. One such formulation defined the authorial 'voice' as a code, or sub-code (e.g. Wollen, 1972), one of many codes which made up the films and which could be objectively defined by reference to the films in question. However, there still remained the problem of the status of the *auteur*-code; why should it be privileged over others, such as those of genre, or studio? Moreover, the emphasis on the film text as a set of objectively definable codes tended to stultify it, fixing meaning in a somewhat mechanical way. What was needed, it was argued (e.g. Heath, 'Comment on "The Idea of Authorship"', 1973; Nowell-Smith, 'Six authors in pursuit of *The Searchers*', 1976) was a theory of meaning production which understood the particular way in which each text worked to produce meaning: objective knowledge of the codes required to decipher meanings was not enough – a 'reading' of the text implied attention to the process of interaction of codes in producing a particular message. This notion of the text as the intersection of various codes stressed the multiplicity of codes at work in any utterance and hence the importance of recognising the effects of different texts upon one another (their 'intertextuality'). The author was not simply an objectively definable sub-code, but rather a 'discursive subject' identifiable as a 'speaker' in the text through the network of different discourses by which it is made up. This discursive subject did not reside in a single point-of-view or authorial position: it was produced in the interaction of discourses, and itself contributed to the production of meaning. It was the particular historical manifestation of a general set, or system of codes, of specific modes of writing (*écriture*) in circulation at any given moment in a given society. This concept of the 'discursive subject' had the advantage of constituting the subject as productive at the same time as determined by forces of history and language, thus avoiding more mechanical structuralist formulations of the 'subject structured by language'.

The idea of the author as discursive subject, produced by the film text defined as a network of discourses, offered a more flexible account of the relationship between text and reader in which the latter, while clearly now seen as equally responsible with the author (if not more so) for constructing meanings, was also caught in history and society. Thus different readings would produce different, historically specific meanings, and the text was no longer seen as a finished, complete object: it was transformed by, and accumulated meanings in, the historical process of reading. The reader's codes intersected the codes in the text, of which the authorial code was one, to produce meaning (see Brewster, 'Notes on the text "Young Mr. Lincoln"', 1973).

Cahiers du Cinéma's 'John Ford'

This idea of 'text' as constituted by the interaction of different historically specific codes provides the context for the collective text by the editors of the French film journal *Cahiers du Cinéma*: 'John Ford's *Young Mr Lincoln*' (1972). After 1968 *Cahiers* reformulated its position on authorship and cinema, producing a programme of work which would approach cinema as an ideological system and a table which classified films according to the relationship each film held with the dominant ideology. The fifth category in the table referred to those films which seemed at first sight to be caught within the dominant ideology, but on closer inspection were revealed to be cracking apart under the tension of internal contradictions (← *Cahiers*' Category 'e', p. 172). A 'symptomatic' reading would reveal the contradictions and demonstrate the extent to which the film dismantled the ideology from within.

Cahiers' symptomatic reading of *Young Mr. Lincoln* attempted to uncover cracks in the system of the film, disjunctures between the different codes which made up the text, specifically between the generic framework of the film (the 'early life of the great man' genre), its fictional sub-codes (the 'detective story' plot superimposed on the genre) and the Fordian authorial sub-code. According to *Cahiers*' argument, while the generic code allowed the film to present Lincoln (against historical evidence) as the great reconciler, in accordance with the ideological product of the film to promote a Republican victory in the American Presidential election of 1940, this code was contradicted by others at work in the film: the detective-story plot which made Lincoln ambiguously both the 'bringer of the truth' and the involuntary puppet of the truth, and the Fordian sub-code (working in parallel to the detective story) which identified Lincoln with his dead mother and dead ideal wife (vehicle of the truth of the community) at the same time as presenting him as implementer of the truth of the community. These two codes work against the depiction of Lincoln as the 'great reconciler', turning him into a kind of monster. In order to implement their symptomatic reading, *Cahiers* employed a code of psychoanalytic decipherment which also worked, in parallel with the detective-story code and the Fordian sub-code, against the 'early life of the hero' generic code to subvert the manifest ideological project of the film.

There are several problems inherent in this analysis: for instance, *Cahiers* do not establish the 'ideological project' of *Young Mr. Lincoln* except by reference to Darryl F. Zanuck's intentions, largely ignoring the role played by political and economic factors. Moreover, their use of psychoanalysis as a tool of decipherment tends to remove the film from its historical and political background: thus their reading of the generic code and its ideological motivation in this film can be seen to give it too much importance, leading to an underestimation of the importance of the Fordian system in the film. These problems point to an interesting contradiction: while attempting to displace the author (Ford) as intentional source of the film, the *Cahiers* analysis ends up by confirming the importance of the Fordian authorial system to *Young Mr. Lincoln* and by implication the continuing relevance of *auteur* analysis in the study of American cinema.

Stephen Heath's 'Touch of Evil'

In his analysis of *Touch of Evil* ('Film and system: terms of analysis', 1975) Stephen Heath also, like *Cahiers du Cinéma*, approaches the film as a textual system, as a narrative product which opens up problems and contradictions in order to resolve them, to re-establish stability in the final resolution of tensions. Heath is primarily concerned with the way in which different codes, different 'orders of discourse' cross the text in an activity which 'constructs the ideological subject'. The work of the narrative is seen as the 'setting in place' of this subject which is both author and reader of the text. One of the analytical tools used is, again, psychoanalysis, employed here to unravel the unconscious workings of language and ideology which cut across and resist the systematic coding of the narrative. Heath's close analysis of the textual system of *Touch of Evil* (influenced by Roland Barthes' *S/Z*: → NARRATIVE AND STRUCTURALISM: *Barthes*, p. 238) does not refuse other, more traditional kinds of reading, but attempts to displace them and so bring them into question. He recognises the historical and institutional factors which have contributed to producing 'Orson Welles' as the author of the film, immediately recognisable in its distinctive style. His analysis, however, is interested in the author as 'an effect of the text', in so far as that effect is significant in the production of the filmic system of *Touch of Evil*. Heath disperses Welles-as-author across the system of the film: 'Welles' is produced as a kind of fiction in the text, one fiction among others. Heath's choice of a film directed by Orson Welles seems to confirm his notion of the author as a fiction: Welles appears as an actor in this film as he does in most of the films he directed; thus he is, self-evidently, part of the fiction. Yet Heath doesn't quite deal with the power and significance of Welles's presence as author/actor. Quinlan/Welles's first appearance in the film is marked as the colossal entry of a great 'star' into the narrative (supported by the

Touch of Evil – Welles' distinctive style and presence as actor/star

effects of Welles's distinctive cinematic style). This marking of the 'star presence' exceeds the fiction of the film, referring outwards to other films, other acting roles, i.e. to the industry itself. It does not just signify in the system of *Touch of Evil*, it seems to disturb that system, to unbalance the organisation of the narrative codes. It is this disturbance of, or opposition to the narrative system of 'classical' cinema which, in much traditional *auteur* criticism, indicates the presence of the authorial voice. By demonstrating that this 'voice' is produced by the film's textual system Heath avoids constructing Welles as external, intentional source of meaning;

however, by presenting the authorial discourse as 'an effect of the text' his reading implies that there is no general Wellesian system (verifiable by reference to other Welles films), only a Wellesian discourse produced by this film, *Touch of Evil*. The production of this discourse, moreover, is seen primarily in terms of formal strategies which do not include extra-textual references to history, politics or economic factors which might play some part in determining those textual strategies. Thus, Heath's construction of Welles as discursive subject in some ways confirms Romantic notions of the artist's 'freedom of expression'.

Touch of Evil (USA 1958 *p.c* – Universal International; *d* – Orson Welles; sd b/w 14)

Conventional *auteur* analysis has seen the heavily-marked style of Welles's films as a sign of the presence of a great artist and has pointed to the existence of Wellesian themes beneath the 'superficial' detective-story framework of *Touch of Evil* (e.g. Bazin, 1978). Welles himself understands the film as an expression of his hatred of police abuse of power, and identifies himself with the point-of-view of Vargas, who destroys the evil Quinlan. Heath (1973), however, argues for an understanding of the way the textual system works to produce 'Welles as Author-artist', seeing this production as part of the ideological project of the text. The extract provides a focus for these different approaches to authorship. It demonstrates Welles's distinctive style (in the play with image and sound, in the use of moving camera and 'strange' camera angles) and his presence as actor-star (in the form of Quinlan). It also provides a useful

metaphor which might illuminate the kind of reading Heath is proposing: it is taken from the end of the film, and shows Vargas tracking Quinlan in order to destroy him. The destruction of the crooked cop Quinlan is a prerequisite of the resolution of the narrative, but also, by implication, the destruction of the 'authorial voice' must be achieved if textual stability is to be restored, since it was the friction of this discourse with the narrative system that (according to Heath) opened up problems and contradictions in the text. The tracking-down and pinning-down in death of Quinlan/Welles could be seen as a metaphor for the resolution of the excesses of the authorial discourse and a victory for 'classic' narrative. If this (rather fanciful) interpretation holds, then the ending of *Touch of Evil* produces Welles-the-artist as a tragic figure, pilloried and destroyed by the Hollywood system, thus supporting the myth to which Welles and his admirers have traditionally subscribed.

Authorship and documentary

The development of theories of authorship as discursive activity took place in conjunction with theories of narrative, in particular the narrative organisation of Hollywood films. These theories attempted to provide an analysis of mainstream narrative cinema which recognised its status as a commodity product, furthering the interests of capitalist relations of production, without presenting it as an ideological monolith, a non-contradictory reflection of those relations. The theory of the 'classic realist text' (→ NARRATIVE AND STRUCTURALISM: *The classic realist text*, p. 242) delineated a narrative model against which specific Hollywood films could be measured to indicate the degree of ideological closure of each particular text. The 'realism' of the classic realist text did not reside in its transparency, or the illusion it offered of 'a window on the world', but in its overall narrative organisation, seen as a drive towards the resolution of contradictions which finally offered the spectator the imaginary satisfaction of a position of transcendence, or omnipotence through identification with a third-person metadiscourse which put all the other discourses of the text in place, and was understood as 'truth' rather than as ideology. In this way the classic realist text masked its own contradictions, presenting itself as (finally) a coherent unity. The many contradictory discourses which made up the text were organised into a hierarchy, and one discourse (the impersonal one of the ideological status quo) was given dominance. Analysis of Hollywood films which paid attention to the contradictory discourses which those films attempted to unify could provide an important means of 'de-naturalising' the ideology of the classic realist text. The discourse of the author, for instance, personal rather than impersonal, could be seen to be in contradiction with the third-person narrative discourse, disrupting its drive towards resolution and coherence (see *Young Mr. Lincoln* and *Touch of Evil* above).

While it could be argued that this 'text', if it exists at all, does not exist outside the traditional Hollywood system of production, which has now more or less collapsed, it provides a useful model for differentiating the realist strategies of other kinds of film, which may not work on the same narrative principles, but nonetheless aim to 'naturalise' ideology by presenting it as truth.

The documentary film differs from Hollywood narrative film in that it does not 'present' ideology through narrative organisation (although most documentaries use narrative in some form or other). It is primarily a rhetorical form which both offers the audience information and attempts to put forward an argument, to persuade the audience to think in a certain way, to do something, to accept the argument. It achieves this by presenting the

Nightcleaners – challenging conventional forms of agit-prop cinema

truth of its argument as self-evident, unified and non-contradictory. Most often, an authoritative voice-over commentary is used to frame and contain the images which are seen as unmediated recordings of the 'real world'. Both commentary and images come over as neutral, as third-person discourses which guarantee their own 'truth'. It could be argued that the codes of classic Hollywood cinema and the codes of rhetorical documentary prevalent in television programmes and advertising provide the dominant modes of reading film in our society.

Since documentary usually has a 'serious' purpose (to argue, persuade) and a social function (to educate people), the point-of-view of the individual film-maker is seen as subservient to the social purpose. There are few *auteurs* in documentary cinema: those that there are (such as Dziga Vertov, Joris Ivens, Walter Ruttman, Humphrey Jennings) pose a problem for the documentary mode by inscribing themselves as 'speakers' in their films, as political subjects (Vertov, Ivens) or as artists (Ruttman, Jennings).The 'truth' of the film's argument is brought into question by an insistence on the presence of more than one discourse, more than one voice in the film, re-introducing the question of subjectivity which the documentary mode attempts to efface. 'Truth' is shown to be constructed and therefore open to argument.

Political film-making has traditionally relied on the documentary mode, posing itself in opposition to the Hollywood system of production and to the stereotypical forms of Hollywood cinema. Documentary films can be made cheaply and quickly, apparently without interference, and are seen as presenting the 'truth' in opposition to the 'lies' of Hollywood. In this argument, film becomes the instrument of political struggle, which is captured through realist images which present the world as it 'really is', rather than as constructed in the process of film-making. By effacing the contradictory elements at work in constructing and presenting its argument, the traditional documentary mode removes the argument from its social and political context of struggle.

References

André Bazin, *Orson Welles: a critical view*, London, Elm Tree Books, 1978.

Ben Brewster, 'Notes on the text "*Young Mr. Lincoln*" by the editors of *Cahiers du Cinéma*', Screen vol. 14 no. 3, Autumn 1973.

Editors of *Cahiers du Cinéma*, 'John Ford's *Young Mr. Lincoln*', Screen vol. 13 no. 3, Autumn 1972.

Stephen Heath, 'Comment on "The Idea of Authorship"', Screen vol. 14 no. 3, Autumn 1973.

Stephen Heath, 'Film and system: terms of analysis', Screen vol. 16 no. 1/2, Spring/Summer 1975.

Claire Johnston and Paul Willemen, 'Brecht in Britain: the independent political film', Screen vol. 16 no. 4, Winter 1975/76.

Geoffrey Nowell-Smith, 'Six authors in pursuit of *The Searchers*', Screen vol. 17 no. 1, Spring 1976.

Peter Wollen, *Signs and Meaning in the Cinema*, London, Secker and Warburg/BFI, 1972.

Nightcleaners (UK 1975 *p.c* – Berwick Street Collective; sd b/w 10+1?)

Nightcleaners can be seen as a film which attempts to reintroduce contradiction into the form of the political documentary. In doing so, it seems to challenge the basic assumptions of that form and to set up an entirely different relationship between film and political struggle, and between film and audience. Initially intended as a campaign film on behalf of the struggle of the women office cleaners to organise and unionise, it began as a *cinéma-vérité* documentary, which was then transformed by the film-makers (the Berwick Street Collective) at the editing stage into a film which radically questioned the conventional forms of agit-prop cinema. It could be argued that the campaign was lost in the process and indeed the film was badly received by the Women's Movement, particularly by many of the women who were involved in the cleaners' campaign and by the militant left who saw film as primarily an instrument in economic political struggle.

The film introduces contradiction on two levels; the level of film language and representation and the level of the organisation of discourses within the film. Both levels interact to constitute the film as a process of learning, for the people involved in its making as well as for the audience. The problem of understanding resides not only in the events depicted (the nightcleaners' campaign, problems of sexuality and class) but also in the language used to depict it (the editing of documentary images and sound). On the level of representation, images of the nightcleaners are reworked, editing is foregrounded, sound is de-synchronised to draw attention to the language of film as a constructive element and to the work of the film-makers in the process of construction. An analogy is drawn between the work of the film-makers and the work of the cleaners.

On the second level, the relationship between the different discourses in the film is presented as a shifting pattern of antagonisms and alliances from which the viewer has to produce his or her own critical reading of the struggle. There is no 'dominant discourse' that represents the 'truth' for all the others. The different discourses have been identified as: the nightcleaners; women's liberation; the film-makers (as makers of the film, not as 'authors'); the employer; the spokeswoman of the nightcleaners (May Hobbs); the unions; observers; the discourse of sexism which pervades all these other discourses in a fragmentary manner. Thus the film could be said to present itself as a political issue, rather than as a vehicle for political issues (see Johnston and Willemen, 'Brecht in Britain: the independent political film', 1975/76).

This analysis of *The Nightcleaners* has the advantage of illuminating the formal strategies at work in the film, which is difficult to read and can appear formidable and alienating. However, it slides over the question of the hierarchical status of the authorial point-of-view of the film-makers by collapsing it into the idea of 'work on the film' (editing, etc.), giving it equal status with the 'work of the cleaners' and the viewer's 'work of reading'. While the film refuses the authority of a voice-over, the discourse of the authors is heavily marked in its formal organisation and, it could be argued, determines to a large extent the way in which the film can be read. It refuses a 'transparent' (realist) reading entirely, for instance, and it could be argued that the images of working women are highly sentimentalised and manipulative. In spite of the apparent project of the film to refuse a dominant discourse or point-of-view, the authorial discourse can be seen to act as an overarching discourse against which the truth of the other discourses is measured, effectively appropriating the real political struggle of the nightcleaners. →

Authorship and counter-cinema

Cahiers' Category 'e' (← p. 172) was influential on British *auteur* criticism, which began to look at the work of certain Hollywood directors for the way in which it 'dismantled' or criticised prevailing ideology. But to many in post-68 France these 'radical readings' of Hollywood texts appeared formalist; what was needed was not simply a deconstruction of ideology, but a fundamental restructuring of the industrial system of production, distribution and exhibition from which a new, revolutionary cinema could emerge, not only political in content, but *made politically* (see 'The Estates General of the French cinema', 1972/73). This refusal of industrial, hierarchical methods of working was accompanied by a rejection of individual authorship. Many newly-politicised film-makers formed small independent groups dedicated to collective working methods, skill-sharing and to producing films for a small and specific political audience. Jean-Luc Godard joined with other young Maoists to form the Dziga-Vertov Group during this period; Vertov's name was mobilised less as an authorial inspiration than for his practice, his battle to produce a cinematic language adequate to express the 'truth' of class struggle.

This emphasis on the need for a totally new *practice* of cinema was to be influential on the growth of independent filmmaking in Britain during the 1970s. But initially it emerged here as a discussion of what *forms* this new cinema should adopt

A bout de souffle – Belmondo/Bogart drawing attention to Hollywood codes

and was expressed, perhaps surprisingly, in quite conventional auteurist terms.

This formalist emphasis had a polemical force as a theoretical intervention into the prevailing assumptions of British independent political cinema, which was primarily documentary and realist. Jean-Luc Godard's work was taken up by Peter Wollen as exemplary of what a materialist oppositional cinema, a 'counter-cinema', might be (→ HISTORY OF NARRATIVE: *Counter-cinema*, p. 220).

JEAN-LUC GODARD

In his Postscript to the revised edition of *Signs and Meaning in the Cinema* (1972) Wollen argued that since Hollywood provided the dominant codes with which films are read, it was only in confrontation with Hollywood that anything new could be produced and that it was in the work of Godard that this kind of confrontation, interrogation and criticism could be found. In 'Counter-Cinema: *Vent d'est*' (1972) he took this argument a stage further by

---

A bout de souffle (Breathless) (France 1959 *p.c* – SNC; *d* – Jean-Luc Godard; sd b/w 20)

This is Godard's first feature film and the one he likes least. Made in the context of the early French New Wave, it was based on an idea by François Truffaut and it is possible to see in the film's celebration of an individual freedom which transcends social relations a theme which is central to Truffaut's work rather than Godard's. In later films Godard was to question this idea of the criminal/outsider as 'free'.

At this stage, Godard's films remained within the Hollywood narrative conventions, resisting any political analysis of that cinema. The verbal and visual references to Hollywood seem to act more as a *hommage* than a criticism, although it could be argued that the strategy of 'quotation' and 'punning' has the effect of drawing attention to the Hollywood codes, offering the audience an added pleasure of recognition.

The character of Patricia is a play on the femme fatale of Hollywood's film noir, a representation of the figure of the woman as enigmatic and deceptive which recurs throughout Godard's work and seems to be part of his distrust of

the deceptive quality of images in general. 'Woman' and 'image' are often conflated as the site of the problem of representation: however, the problem is posed differently in later films, which attempt to question the construction and circulation of the image of woman in society.

Masculin-Féminin (France/Sweden 1966 *p.c* – Anouchka Films/Argos Films (Paris) Svensk Filmindustri/Sandrews (Stockholm); *d* – Jean-Luc Godard; sd b/w 10)

Lee Russell/Peter Wollen has noted and criticised the ambiguity towards politics in Godard's early films, but it is also possible to see those films as an unsatisfactory search for a cinematic form in which to discuss politics, a search which became acute in the mid-1960s when the political pressures became intense and opposition to the Vietnam war was a key political issue. In *Masculin-Féminin* the problem of politics and representation is seen in terms of the male protagonist's dilemma: Paul (Jean-Pierre Léaud) is caught between the 'masculine' world of party politics and the 'feminine' world of pop culture and consumerism. Both are inadequate in themselves: the

politics of the French Communist Party are depicted as repressive and unable to come to terms with questions of art or sexuality, while the pop culture world depends for its appeal on a stultifying relationship between producer and consumer. Paul's attempt to unite the positive virtues of both fails and he ends up alone, alienated from both.

The division represented here between the male and female worlds has recurred in different forms throughout Godard's work. He seems to accept the conventional social division which places women on the side of nature, instinct and consumption and man on the side of culture and production (and, by implication, politics). Although he is able to draw attention to the way in which consumer society uses images of women, he does not seem to radically question the social construction of these images.

Weekend (France/Italy 1967 *p.c* – Comacico/Copernic/Lira Films; *d* – Jean-Luc Godard; sd col 10)

1966 seems to have been a year of despair for Godard in his search for politics and form – in *Made in USA* he rejected the forms of Hollywood cinema as inadequate to the task of raising

Godard accepts the conventional divisions between men and women in *Masculin-Féminin*

elaborating on those values of 'orthodox' cinema with which Godard's 'counter-cinema' took issue and evaluating his work up to 1972 in terms of its increasing opposition to, or break with, Hollywood cinema. Wollen argues that Godard's method of *negation*, or contrast, enables him to produce a revolutionary materialist cinema which takes account of 'Hollywood-Mosfilm' (Godard's term for 'bourgeois capitalist cinema') while working to criticise it. For Wollen, the value of

this method is that it creates questions and disagreements in Godard's films, setting up a different relationship between spectator and films from that of traditional cinema, which he characterises in terms of *narrative coherence* and *identification*, the generation of pleasures which aim to satisfy the spectator rather than to change him or her. However, Wollen criticises Godard's rather puritanical rejection of the fantasy pleasures offered by mainstream cinema and argues that a

'revolutionary' cinema must address itself to the specific relationship between pleasure, entertainment, fantasy, ideology and science produced in film.

The article illustrates some of the advantages and disadvantages of *auteur-*structuralism as a critical method. It reduces all Godard's films to a set of formal strategies of opposition and suggests that those strategies are always present in Godard's work, increasingly since 1968, evaluating films according to the presence (or not) of these strategies. While Wollen's account illuminates Godard's films belonging to a certain period between 1968 and 1972 and evaluates their importance as political cinema, it does not take account of the influence of history on those films; instead it holds them up as an ideal practice of materialist film-making. Moreover, in his attempt to establish Godard as an exemplary counter-cinema *auteur*, Wollen ignores the fact that *Vent d'est* was made by the Maoist Dziga-Vertov collective of which Godard was only one member.

This approach seems even more limited when Godard's pre-1968 and post-1972 work is taken into account. It could be argued that the value of Godard's work lies precisely in its evident sensitivity to historical and political change. While similar concerns can be traced through all his films and later video work, the ways in which those concerns shift and change bear testimony to the fact that the film-maker is caught up in history and changing

political questions directly because its fictional forms represented politics as fantasy, 'out there' on the screen rather than as part of the spectators' lives. In *Deux ou trois choses . . .* he investigated the possibilities of documentary style and a fragmented, episodic structure, referring explicitly to Brecht and his theory of 'distanciation' or 'alienation'. In 1967 he began to collaborate with Maoist militants and became interested in *cinéma-vérité*. The films made in this period show an intense desire to resolve the problem of representation and politics by casting about for many different solutions, none of which are found to be adequate. *Weekend* is perhaps the most desperate of all of them in its total disillusionment with French society, which is conceived of as monolithically bourgeois, brutalised by its own consumer ideology. In the face of the total insensitivity of this society, violence and brutality are seen to be the only solution. Godard uses surrealist images and montage to call into question the violence of bourgeois society and the bland images of art cinema by which it represents itself. The justification of violence and instinctive action which appears in this film recurs throughout Godard's work. Although

with hindsight it seems politically regressive (revolutionaries eat the bourgeoisie!), in the context of French left politics just prior to 1968, where the demand for guerrilla action in response to imperialist wars and the violence of bourgeois society was increasing, its political nihilism is perhaps more understandable.

Characteristically, Godard foregrounds the problems of finding a political language. The use of direct address to the camera/spectator in the extended quotations from Frantz Fanon suggests the desire to communicate directly with an audience which shares the political frame of reference of the speakers, unlike Corinne and Raymond, who represent the bourgeois audience, bored and uncomprehending. It was this 'uncomprehending bourgeois audience' that Godard was to leave behind in the aftermath of 1968 when he abandoned 'normal' cinema. He also left behind any critical acclaim his New Wave films had accrued.

Godard's increasing politicisation did not prevent him from continuing to question the means of representing politics: arguably, the mixture of fiction, direct address to the camera, use of stars, extended quotation and theatre

of the absurd allows the spectator to criticise the political discourse (provided that the spectator shares the political frame of reference of the film).

British Sounds (UK 1969 *p.c* – Kestrel Productions for London Weekend Television; *d* – Jean-Luc Godard; sd col 10)

Of the many contradictory political tendencies that participated in May 1968 in France, it was Maoism, or rather the European form of it developed by Althusser, which provided the focus for Godard's preoccupations. European Maoism stressed the importance of personal struggle in the ideological sphere, and a commitment to the Third World which provided an appropriate form for the expression of hatred of consumer society (see MacCabe, 1980). At the same time, it held that all ideological struggle should remain an open question to be solved by a combination of practical experiment and theoretical reflection. It was this emphasis which informed Godard's film-making practice in this period, but equally important was the decision to abandon traditional methods of working and commit himself to collaborative work. The Dziga-Vertov →

Weekend – disillusionment with bourgeois French society

conditions of production which can be seen to affect his work. Wollen's account deals with a period in which the ideas of structuralism, semiology and psycho-analysis, combined with a cultural politics emerging from the events of May 1968, explicitly informed Godard's work. It is questionable whether the strategies identi-fied by Wollen could be effective outside that particular context. His argument about Godard is linked to a polemic for the necessity of developing a new, opposi-tional film-making practice and was

influential on subsequent debates about independent political cinema in Britain.

Godard and history
Godard himself has insisted that the politi-cal upheavals of 1968 in France repre-sented for him not so much a break with the past as the possibility of developing the ideas he was already formulating (see MacCabe, 1980). He had already col-laborated with Maoist militants on some films when in the immediate aftermath of 1968 it became possible for him as a film-

maker to commit himself to engaging in totally new methods of work. Although his Maoism waned with the disintegration of French Maoism in 1972, the commitment to alternative methods of work has remained, a heritage of 1968. However, in Godard's case those alternative methods have not remained the same. There are evident differences between the films emerging from his collaboration with Gorin and others in the Dziga-Vertov Group in 1969–70 and after the dissolution of the group in 1972. In 1974 he set up his

group was formed as a collaborative enterprise: on *British Sounds* and *Pravda* Godard worked with Jean-Henri Roger and they were joined on *Pravda* by Paul Burron. The importance of this decision was that it attempted to posit film-making as a genuinely collective process, so that it should no longer be a question of attributing the film to a single creative individual, but of recognising the interplay of different and contradictory voices. The 'correct' voice (of Maoism) was set into conflict with other ideological voices so that the films provoked question and argument, thus setting up a new relationship between film and audience. However, that audience was not the traditional cinema audience: it was an audience born of May 1968 and specific to it. The conjunction of politics, theory and cultural practice gave the concepts of structuralism, semiology and psychoanalysis an unprecedented political force, and Godard was among many young intellectuals who took them up as tools in their revolutionary struggle (cf. *Le Gai Savoir*).
    The films made by the Dziga-Vertov group in this period are preoccupied with the question of setting up a new, non-synchronous relationship between

image and sound: the film screen becomes 'a blackboard offering a concrete analysis of a concrete situation'; the ideological struggle is seen in terms of establishing a new relationship with the audience by interrogating the basis of film language, the organisation of images and sounds. It seems that Godard had gone some way towards finding his 'form of the political': the despair of the pre-1968 films (← *Weekend*) and the rejection of existing forms and politics was displaced into the political task of combatting oppression at every level of experience.
    The extract deals specifically with the plight of women in capitalist society. The politicisation of Godard's representation of women is evident in the feminist and Marxist-Leninist discourses which are set over (and separated from) the image of the woman's naked body. It could be argued, however, that this image, however resolutely unexploitative, presents the woman's body as an enigma, uses it as the locus of the problem for the male, a representation not very different from Godard's earlier work.
    British Sounds was made in

collaboration with Ken Loach and Tony Garnett's production company Kestrel Films, which resulted in a strange mixture of Godard's cultural revolutionist politics and British Trotskyism. The film was subsequently banned by London Weekend Television, who had commissioned it.

Tout va bien (France/Italy 1972 *p.c* – Anouchka Films/Vicco Films (Paris)/ Empire Films (Rome); *d* – Jean-Luc Godard/Jean-Pierre Gorin; sd col 9 + 13)
    Godard had collaborated with the young Maoist Jean-Pierre Gorin before the formation of the Dziga-Vertov group (on *La Chinoise*). Together they made the last four Dziga-Vertov films before releasing *Tout va bien* and *Letter to Jane* under their own names. Godard has always insisted that his contribution to these films was largely technical, eighty per cent of the ideas coming from Gorin.
    The Dziga-Vertov group had found its justification for ideological struggle in the political audience which it addressed in its films: by 1972 that audience was fast disappearing. *Tout va bien* was an attempt to reconstitute an audience by returning to mainstream

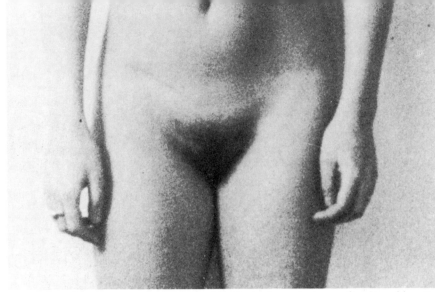

British Sounds – the woman's body – used by Godard – as the locus of male problems?

own production company away from Paris in the French Alps with Anne-Marie Miéville: the films and television programmes they produced show a further shift of concern towards the investigation of the relationship between the personal and the political. Even more recently Godard has returned to using fictional forms and stars in his film projects – e.g. *Sauve qui peut (la vie)* (*Slow Motion*), 1980.

In the light of history Godard's work can be seen to show a continuing preoccupation with theory and politics, with the language of cinema and the circulation of images in society, and with formulating new languages to express revolutionary questions, although the form of those preoccupations constantly changes, some-times quite radically. One of the lessons of May 1968 which seems to have remained with Godard has been the idea of cinema as *social practice*: that is, a political commitment to bringing cinema into relationship with people's everyday lives, a different relationship from that of 'normal' cinema-going, which depends for its continuing commercial success on the fact that it is divorced from (an escape from) day-to-day existence. Such a commitment involves changing the traditional ways in which films are produced, distributed, exhibited and consumed. A productive way of looking at Godard's films would be in terms of this idea of social practice, in terms of their political, historical and social context and the way they pose prob-

lems for certain kinds of critical analysis, such as traditional *auteur* study. Godard's work is exciting because it is capable of raising a multitude of questions about cinema and politics. The particular combination of theory and practice in the films, the fact that they manifest the extent to which the film-maker is caught up in history rather than being consciously in control of his work, makes it difficult to apply traditional critical criteria to that work, although this has been done (see Perkins, 1972; Harcourt, 1974). The aggressive 'intertextuality' of Godard's films, that is, the way in which they break with classical unity of forms to assert their critical, dialectical relationship with other films, other texts, other ideas and historical situations, makes them a vital part of discussion about strategies for cultural politics (← *Politique des auteurs: Jean-Luc Godard*, p. 134).

References

'The Estates General of the French cinema, May 1968', *Screen* vol. 13 no. 4, Winter 1972/73.
Peter Harcourt, *Six European Directors*, Harmondsworth, Middx, Penguin, 1974.
Colin MacCabe, *Godard: Images, Sound, Politics*, London, Macmillan/BFI, 1980.
V. F. Perkins, *Film as Film: understanding and judging movies*, Harmondsworth, Middx, Penguin, 1972.
Peter Wollen, *Signs and Meaning in the Cinema*, London, Secker and Warburg/BFI, 1972.
Peter Wollen, 'Counter-cinema: *Vent d'est*', *Afterimage* no. 4, Autumn, 1972.

cinema: to convince a non-militant audience of the necessity to investigate questions of subjectivity and class through an investigation of the language of image and sound. The Maoist emphasis on the primacy of the political which characterised the Dziga Vertov films is still there, but not as a starting point, rather as something that needs to be demonstrated.

The return to commercial cinema involved the use of stars and narrative and the mechanisms of identification, which earlier Dziga-Vertov group films had rigorously refused. Rather than simply accepting the terms of commercial cinema however, the film poses them as a problem, attempting to investigate those terms and the institutional logic which determines them in relation to the conditions of its own production.

Tout va bien has been described as a 'Brechtian experiment' because of its attempt to disrupt identification between the camera and spectator: the movement of the camera is clearly marked (mainly in travelling, or tracking shots, but also in the organisation of *mise en scène* and framing) so that the spectator is made aware of the limitations of his/her point-

of-view. The rupture of identification is said to lead the spectator to a political understanding of the forces operating in his/her life. However, in spite of this strategy of disruption, Susan (Jane Fonda) and Jacques (Yves Montand) seem to act as representatives in the film of the post-1968 audience to which it was addressed; indeed, the character played by Jane Fonda comes to provide the central focus for the political message of the film (i.e. the validation of random violence as the solution to political paralysis). It could be argued that by using the star as a point of recognition in this way, the film asks the spectator to identify with a leftist position which is seen to be outside criticism and analysis, unlike the other political positions represented in the film.

Extract 1 provides an example of the way in which the film poses as its central problem the question of understanding and knowledge. The incomprehension of Susan and Jacques in the face of the strike could be seen to represent the audience's incomprehension and their separation from the lived experience of the workers. The long tracking shot from left to right and back reminds the

audience of the work of 'reading' and analysis involved in understanding images. Finally, the comic treatment of the boss's monologue provides a critical distance on his political position.

Extract 2 concentrates on the process of learning involved in understanding. As representatives of the audience, Susan and Jacques begin to understand the workers' struggle in terms of contradiction (for instance, the women workers' discussion of sexism at work and women's work in the home). The discussion between Susan, Jacques and the workers is not only about learning to understand, but about the problem of finding a language with which to talk about the struggle. The language of the unions is rejected, as was that of the boss in Extract 1, while the position of the leftist strikers is, it could be argued, validated.

For the most part, the status of Jane Fonda and Yves Montand as stars remains unquestioned by the film. However, when Susan and Jacques are shown doing the work of the strikers, it has the effect of reminding the audience that they are both played by stars who would not normally play such roles, thus inviting a critical response to the rules of commercial cinema.

Counter-cinema and cultural practice

The idea of counter-cinema, as it was elaborated by Peter Wollen (1972) and taken up subsequently by certain strands within British film theory, was influenced by the debates about revolutionary cultural struggle in France during the 1960s which became particularly fierce after the events of May 1968. At the centre of the debate (which has a long history within Marxist ideas) was the reformulation of the Marxist concept of ideology initiated by the French philosopher Louis Althusser, which attempted to recast the relationship between the economic base of society and the art, the cultural artefacts which society produces (the 'superstructure') (→ NARRATIVE AND STRUCTURALISM: *Narrative and audience*, p. 242). Traditionally, Marxist theories of commodity production had not really come to terms with the difference between artistic products and commodities except to see the former as reflecting the ruling ideology in their modes of production and in their forms, although some writers, such as Lukács, argued that certain forms (i.e. the nineteenth-century novel) articulated the historical and social forces which ideology attempted to efface (see Harvey, 1978; Lovell, 1980). Crudely speaking, this position can be identified in certain arguments about cinema which reject the products of the dominant system as ideologically contaminated in favour of a political cinema which would overthrow the prevailing ideology and reveal social relations as they really are. From this perspective, documentary forms are often thought to offer a more truthful account of social reality than the stereotypes of mainstream Hollywood cinema, which are seen as the carriers of a false, distorting ideology (← *Authorship and documentary*, p. 190). Linked with this argument is the idea that subordinate classes or oppressed groups have their own ideology which is inherently different, i.e. more truthful, and naturally in opposition to the prevailing ideology. Such a position seems to suggest that subordinate groups or classes somehow escape the prevailing ideology and that once they acquire access to the means of production the truth of their oppression can be directly spoken.

Against this idea of ideology as a system of lies belonging to, and perpetuated by, the ruling class, Althusser proposed a new formulation which presented it as 'a system of representations' within which all men and women live, which is acquired unconsciously rather than consciously and is therefore indispensable to the existence of all societies. Moreover, rather than being simply reflected in society's cultural artefacts, it was produced through the complex interaction of social, historical, economic and institutional forces in a highly mediated, uneven and contradictory manner, which meant that it was, in fact, 'relatively autonomous' from the economic base. The difficulties in this theory have been documented elsewhere

(→ NARRATIVE AND STRUCTURALISM: *Narrative and audience*, p. 242): in the context of arguments about cultural practice, Althusser's concept of the ruling ideology saw it as achieving a rather precarious dominance as a result of the struggle between different and conflicting ideologies in society, none of which held the 'truth' (a privilege Althusser reserved for 'science'). Cultural artefacts could be seen as the site of such conflicts: in certain circumstances a work would be produced so riven with contradictions that the ruling ideology's dominance would be seriously threatened, if not completely overturned (← *Cahiers*' Category 'e', p. 192). So, according to this argument, cultural products should not be seen as sealed containers of ideology, ruling or otherwise; rather,

Wanda – documentary style used to challenge Hollywood's depictions of women

they were fractured and imperfect, open to criticism, and most important, to political intervention, which could exploit the gaps and inconsistencies produced by the contradictions in ideology.

Althusser's more complex formulation of the role played by ideology in perpetuating the existing social order and its status as 'relatively autonomous' from the economic base placed great importance on language and systems of representation as part of the machinery whereby ruling orders attempted to maintain their dominance. By the same token, great importance was also placed on the role of theory, and therefore of intellectuals, artists and other cultural workers, in dismantling this ideological machinery in the interests of social change through the interrelated activities of criticism and cultural practices. The idea of counter-cinema, then, was an attempt to define how a theoretical materialist cinema, adequate to the task of confronting dominant ideology on its own terrain, that of representation, might develop. Through this strategy of confrontation the means whereby cinema traditionally held spectators in the security of

a willing 'suspension of disbelief' (→ NARRATIVE AND STRUCTURALISM: *Narrative and audience* p. 242) could be transformed into a new, more actively questioning relationship. If mainstream cinema worked to reinforce the existing social order by inviting spectators to put their 'knowledge' of harsh social realities temporarily to one side, then counter-cinema should interrogate the strategies which sustained this imaginary captivation (such as identification and narrative coherence) in order to produce new 'knowledge' which would lead to analysis and understanding.

Feminism and counter-cinema

It has been argued that for a feminist analysis of cinema the idea of counter-cinema has considerable advantages (Johnston, 'Women's cinema as counter-cinema', 1973).

The Women's Movement has always assumed the importance of mobilising the media in the interests of political struggle, arguing that while images of women are central to society's perpetuation of its economic and ideological system women themselves are almost totally excluded from the process of production of those images: the virtual absence of women film directors in all the major film industries (with notable exceptions in some European countries) is an indication of this. Feminists have attempted to struggle against this contradiction on several fronts: by organising film-making collectives outside the industry; by lobbying for equality within the industry and the unions; and by insisting on the importance of women's creative contribution to the arts in general. In the early 1970s these disparate areas of activity began to come together through the organisation of women's film festivals in America and Britain, and in the emergence of a feminist film criticism which took as its subject the manipulation of images of women by the media and saw the writing of a feminist history of cinema which would challenge the exclusion of women from the conventional histories as a priority (e.g. the now defunct American journal *Women and Film*). The underlying assumption of this criticism was that Hollywood cinema was a major vehicle for the economic and ideological oppression of women. A different, but allied position argued that a woman's point-of-view was essentially different from, and therefore naturally opposed to, the prevailing ideology.

The search began for alternative 'positive' images of women which would counteract their negative portrayal by the male-dominated media industries, leading to the development of a 'women's cinema'

Dorothy Arzner directing *Working Girls*

which would express the lived experience of women's oppression. For the most part, this cinema took up the forms of documentary and *cinéma-vérité* as more truthful than the language of Hollywood, but another strand of the argument stressed the suppression of women's creativity in male-dominated society, seeing its return as a positive voice in that society through an essentially female art and looking towards art cinema or the avant-garde to provide the vocabulary for an alternative women's film culture. The idea of a feminist counter-cinema, however, differed in starting from the principle that the conceptions of women prevalent in society, perpetuated in the language of mainstream cinema and the pleasures it offered, had to be confronted: the idea of a separate autonomous 'woman's art' ran the risk of confirming the marginal place allotted to women in society. According to this view, existing social categories of 'femininity' and 'women's language' could not be straightforwardly adopted by feminists: they had to be dismantled and reconstructed through an understanding of the way ideology and language worked to

produce them in specific historical contexts. It was argued that the theoretical advances of semiology and psychoanalysis in film studies could be implemented to bring about this understanding (see Johnston, 1973).

This argument led to a consideration of the ways in which the work of women directors within industrial systems of production could be seen to manipulate the codes of mainstream cinema to challenge prevailing conceptions of femininity. Drawing on post-structuralist developments of the *auteur* theory (← *Cahiers'* Category 'e', p. 192) it was possible to argue that while women film directors working in the industry were clearly enmeshed in its institutional structures and available codes, they could potentially use

its language (consciously or unconsciously) to dismantle the prevailing ideology. Hollywood's stereotypical images of women, for instance, could be parodied in such a way that the meanings conventionally attached to them were disengaged and their ideological construction revealed (→ *Stephanie Rothman*, p. 199). This critical activity could not be seen as essentially feminist, however, nor even totally conscious, reflecting the intentions of the woman director: instead, it emerged from the process of opposition itself, in the contradictions produced by the clash of the different preoccupations of the woman director and the prevailing ideology.

This argument, then, saw feminist film theory and practice developing on three interdependent fronts: theoretical analysis of the way in which mainstream cinema constructed the place of woman in the texts of particular films; critical analysis of the work of women directors within the industry, and the extent to which that work could be seen as an intervention into the prevailing ideology; and a feminist film-making practice which would interrogate and demystify that ideology (i.e. a

'revolutionary counter-cinema'). During the 1970s feminist film criticism in Britain debated the issues raised by the idea of women's cinema as counter-cinema and the problems it posed as a prescriptive strategy for both criticism and film-making practice (see Cottringer, 'Representation and feminist film practice', 1978), a debate which continues to flourish as questions of sexuality and ideology increasingly encroach upon the traditional bastions of film history, education and criticism.

Women directors in Hollywood

One of the first tasks undertaken by feminist film criticism was that of rewriting the history of cinema to include the contribution of women film-makers, notably missing from traditional *auteur* pantheons. This new history quickly revealed the virtual absence of successful women directors within the Hollywood industry and, perhaps more surprisingly, the relatively small number of women who had worked independently in documentary and avant-garde cinema. Although the development of lightweight equipment and cheap film stock after the Second World War seemed to promise wider access to the means of production, the absence of women from the independent sector too seemed to suggest that ideological and economic factors played a greater part than technology in determining the place of women in cinema's history. In the case of Hollywood, feminist film criticism found that although women had worked as editors and scriptwriters, and of course as stars, very few ever made it to positions of power as directors or producers. One of the major contributions of feminist film history has been to draw attention to the hierarchical conditions of production and the ideological bias which have militated against the possibility of women having any significant control over the meanings produced by the industry (see also Benton, 1975). Sometimes this discovery has led to an overvaluation of the work of those women directors who managed to survive and a tendency to construct their films as positive feminist statements, or as feminist 'art', as in the case of Dorothy Arzner (e.g. Peary, 'Dorothy Arzner', 1974).

A different approach, developed from the counter-cinema argument, insisted that the writing of a history of the cinema to include the contribution of women directors would have to recognise that a simple chronology which 'redressed the balance' in favour of female *auteurs* would not be enough: what was required was a theoretical understanding of the complex relationship between ideological, technological and institutional factors which precisely made it impossible for positive feminist statements to emerge from the Hollywood system of production (see Johnston, 'Dorothy Arzner: critical strategies', 1975). A history of women's cinema did not simply already exist to be unearthed:

it would have to be constructed. The contributions of women working within the Hollywood system could only be assessed in terms of the institutional structures of that system, and its ideological machinery: to suggest that the woman director's 'voice', or point-of-view, could somehow bypass or transcend those structures was to remove it from the context of historical struggle. This approach, once again drawing on post-structuralist theories of authorship, saw the woman director's point-of-view as a *discourse* produced by the interaction of the many discourses which combined to make up the film text, rather than a pre-existing intention or world-view (← *Authorship as 'discursive activity'*, p. 189). In classic Hollywood cinema the male discourse was almost invariably dominant (→ NARRATIVE AND STRUCTURALISM: *The classic realist text*, p. 242; Mulvey, 'Visual pleasure and narrative cinema', 1975). Potentially, though, the woman director's discourse from its subordinate place in the hierarchy of discourses in the text could be seen to work in opposition to the naturalised dominant male discourse to produce textual contradictions which would de-naturalise the working of patriarchal ideology (← *Cahiers' Category 'e'*, p. 192). From this perspective Dorothy Arzner's films could be characterised as sites of conflicting interests at work, which produced a criticism of prevailing myths of feminity, rather than as the statements of a feminist *auteur* who was conceived of as the intentional source of meaning in the film(s) (see Cook, 'Approaching the work of Dorothy Arzner', 1975).

DOROTHY ARZNER

In order to understand how Dorothy Arzner's films can be seen as working in opposition to the ideology of classic Hollywood cinema it is important to ask first of all how that cinema has traditionally constructed the place of woman. One answer produced by feminist film theory is that woman has been constructed as spectacle, as an object of male fantasy and as 'spoken by' that cinema rather than speaking in it (← *The Revolt of Mamie Stover*, p.178). While this particular construction, it is argued, attempts to fix the place of woman as controlled and contained by the dominant male discourse, it produces an image of woman which is paradoxically characterised in terms of excess and transgression: 'woman', it seems, constantly threatens to escape suppression, the subordinate place assigned to her. This contradiction within patriarchal ideology produces momentary gaps in representation into which the woman's discourse can insert itself, 're-writing' the dominant discourse, making it appear 'strange' (see Johnston, 1975), thus calling it into question so that it no longer reigns supreme: the woman's critical discourse takes over as the structuring principle of the film(s). In the process, the conventions

Dance, Girl, Dance – Arzner reworking genre conventions?

of classic Hollywood cinema (genre, narrative, iconography) are 'de-naturalised' or disturbed to reveal and question the way they construct a place for woman (see Cook, 1975). Through feminist re-readings of this sort the traditional relationship of imaginary fascination between mainstream cinema and its audience can be transformed in the interests of critical analysis. The problems with this kind of 'radical reading' of Hollywood films have been pointed out elsewhere (← *Cahiers du Cinéma's 'John Ford'*, p. 189). Clearly an approach based on textual analysis does not tell us much about the actual conditions of production and reception of Arzner's films in the 30s and 40s: in that sense it attempts to construct these films as contradictory texts without recourse to a traditional historiography. However, by focusing on the activity of 're-reading' and 're-writing' (→ NARRATIVE AND STRUCTURALISM: *Barthes*, p. 238), it does raise important questions about the nature of dominant ideology and the possibility of feminist intervention within it by asking 'how might a "feminist discourse", as opposed to an autonomous "women's art" be conceived?' Dorothy Arzner disclaimed any feminist intention on her part: a re-reading of her work can show that meaning is not necessarily fixed according to the author's intentions, and that a film text can accumulate meanings through different readings at different historical moments. Thus films with no immanent political content can be used to raise political questions in a different context.

Dorothy Arzner began her career in Hollywood in the 1920s typing scripts. After the First World War the film industry was fairly open and she soon became an editor and scriptwriter. She was given her first directorial assignment by Paramount in 1927 and went on to direct several comedies and dramas in the category of the women's picture. Although many women worked as editors and writers in Hollywood few became directors: however, to understand the nature of Arzner's extraordinary achievement it would be necessary to look at the structure of the industry at that time and the way it affected her work. She claims to have had considerable freedom on her projects (see Peary and Kay, 'Interview with Dorothy Arzner', 1975); at the same time she was publicised as a woman director and was limited to the women's picture, a fact which raises important questions about the status of women in the Hollywood industry during the 20s and 30s. There are significant differences between the films she directed before the coming of sound and those she made afterwards, and again between the films she directed for different studios. The unevenness of her work, and the difficulty of assimilating it to a coherent oeuvre as *auteur* study prescribes, seems to confirm the proposition put forward by a theoretical analysis of her films: that any challenge to the prevailing ideology they may offer presents itself in the form of symptoms rather than as a direct statement (see Cook, 1975).

STEPHANIE ROTHMAN

In 'Women's cinema as counter-cinema' (1973), Claire Johnston argued for a new women's cinema which would confront the ideology of mainstream cinema by developing the means to challenge its depiction of reality. By interrogating the conventions of Hollywood, the iconography and stereotypes whereby it attempted to fix myths of women as natural and universal, a dislocation could be brought about between sexist ideology and the language used to perpetuate it which would provide the basis for strategies of subversion.

This argument drew on *Cahiers'* Category 'e' (← p. 192) and on post-structuralist versions of *auteur* theory which challenged the idea of the director as intentional source of meaning, redefining it in terms of the unconscious pre-occupations which could be decoded in the formal play of film texts and which were often outside the control of the director concerned (← *Signs and Meaning in the Cinema*, p. 192). Johnston took issue with the idea that mainstream cinema was monolithically closed to intervention by women film-makers, arguing that the work of these few women directors who had managed to build up a consistent body of work in the Hollywood system was of interest to feminists precisely because of the ways in which their unconscious pre-occupations could be seen to turn sexist ideology on its head, manipulating the codes of mainstream cinema in order to criticise it. Johnston used Dorothy Arzner and Ida Lupino as examples of women directors whose work manifested an internal criticism of mainstream ideology.

The context for feminist discussion of

Knucklemen – suffering under patriarchy

Rothman's work is slightly different, though still emerging from the counter-cinema arguments. Rothman is a contemporary film-maker, a film school graduate and a feminist, working in 1970s Hollywood. The break-up of the classic Hollywood system of production and its mass audience after the Second World War led to the growth of independent production and distribution companies, one of which was Roger Corman's New World Pictures, founded in 1970. Through this company, which was initially geared to fast, low-budget production, Corman offered many young film-makers, including Rothman, the chance to direct within the Hollywood industry (← *Roger Corman*, p. 144). New World Pictures developed a reputation for dealing with serious political themes within the format of 'exploitation' film production (i.e. cheap re-makes of more up-market productions in order to make a quick profit), acquiring a name as something of a feminist studio because of its promotion of the 'positive heroine' stereotype (see Hillier and Lipstadt, 1981). However, in spite of the apparent potential of this situation for a declared feminist like Rothman, it is arguable that the exploitation film depends for

---

DOROTHY ARZNER

Dance, Girl, Dance (USA 1940 *p.c* – RKO *d* – Dorothy Arzner; sd b/w 18)

Dance, Girl, Dance was the personal project of Erich Pommer, the former head of Germany's Ufa Studio, then in exile in Hollywood: he had conceived, cast, and started shooting the film and called in Dorothy Arzner to replace another RKO director. She re-worked the script and sharply defined the central conflict as a clash between the artistic inspirations of Judy (Maureen O'Hara) and the commercial, gold-digging Bubbles (Lucille Ball). It is a mixed-genre film combining the conventions of the chorus/working-girl film (backstage musical) and the sophisticated romantic comedy. It is arguable that this combination produces a particularly acute contradiction in the film between, on the one hand, an image of woman as spectacle, and on the other, as the subject of her own desires, both of which are seen to be ultimately controlled by men. The film has been seen as playing with the generic

conventions to point up this contradiction, using irony and parody to bring ideology to the surface of the film in its *mise en scène* (see Johnston, and Cook, 1975). For instance, it has been argued that genre conventions are re-worked to displace the male discourse and focus on the woman's point-of-view; the scene in which Judy turns on and interrogates the burlesque audience is particularly striking in this context. The film uses class stereotypes to point up differences in Judy's and Bubbles' aspirations: however, these class differences seem to be transcended by the similarities between the two women's problems within patriarchal society.

The same argument sees the 'happy ending' of this film as ironic, pointing up the power structures within which male-female relationships exist under patriarchy. Rather than attribute this irony entirely to Arzner, the film might be discussed in the context of the ironic endings characteristic of the women's picture (← GENRE: *Melodrama*, p. 78).

STEPHANIE ROTHMAN

Student Nurses (USA 1970 *p.c* – New World Pictures; *d* – Stephanie Rothman; sd col 13)

The first of Rothman's major films for Corman's New World studio, made in the 'student nurse' genre that Corman is said to have invented. Working in the sexploitation, soft-porn genre produced mainly for male audiences, Rothman introduces several jarring notes which seem to be incompatible with the generic project. Her use of strategies such as parody and mixed styles could be seen to work to criticise the underlying pre-conceptions of sexploitation material, bringing them to the surface and exposing their sexism.

On another level, like many New World films, the film deals explicitly with social issues such as abortion, here presented from the perspective of the women characters and questioning masculine attitudes to female sexuality in a manner which would seem to be incompatible with the demands of sexploitation films. However, it might→

its success upon the image of woman as spectacle, as the object of male fantasy, just as much as classic Hollywood. A feminist statement emerging from exploitation cinema could not therefore simply appear naturally, it would have to be constructed through the manipulation (conscious or unconscious) of the exploitation codes in order to create new meanings which counter the myths of male fantasies. Rothman often parodies the codes of exploitation genres to expose their roots in male fantasies and it is this use of formal play to criticise male myths of women which has interested many feminists and which, it has been argued, places Rothman's work in the tradition of women's counter-cinema (see Cook, '"Exploitation" films and feminism', 1976). Rothman is also of interest to feminists because for a short period she owned her own company (with husband Charles Swartz), Dimension Films, thus achieving an unusual level of control within the Hollywood industry. The company was dissolved in 1974 and Rothman has since gone back to writing scripts (see Terry Curtis Fox, 'Fully Female', 1976).

Women directors outside Hollywood: art cinema

Initially, the counter-cinema argument was directed at the illusionist organisation of codes in classic Hollywood cinema (see Wollen, 1972). In its feminist application the argument was extended to include European art cinema, which, it was argued, was at least as open to the invasion

of ideology as Hollywood cinema because it employed a more naturalistic language (see Johnston, 1973). If the codes and stereotypes of Hollywood cinema could be manipulated to de-naturalise the prevailing ideology, this process was much more difficult in art cinema because of the absence of obvious iconography: the conventions of art cinema were 'naturalised' in its attempt to achieve verisimilitude (also ← *Art cinema*, p. 114; → HISTORY OF NARRATIVE: *Art cinema*, p. 216).

However, some feminist criticism has seen in art cinema a potential form of expression for women artists (see Martineau, 'Subjecting her Objectification', 1973). The dominant system of commodity production prevents women from making any significant contribution, blocking or censoring their self-expression, and denying women's subjectivity. In art cinema, it is argued, the artist's voice is able to transcend the industrial mode of production, allowing women's true creativity to return as a revolutionary force in a spontaneous upsurge of anger and desire. From this perspective, revolutionary art is primarily seen in terms of a subjective, individual response to oppression and women's art appears as pure self-expression, somehow uncontaminated by dominant ideology: it doesn't offer a direct challenge to that ideology, but rather, by virtue of its total marginalisation by male-dominated society, it has the potential to destroy it completely.

In contrast to this view, the counter-

A New Leaf – how far can comedy work to displace dominant ideology?

cinema argument insisted that it was only through confronting and challenging the dominant forms that a revolutionary women's cinema could be constructed. This argument influenced feminist independent cinema in Britain during the 1970s (see Mulvey, 'Feminism, film and the avant-garde', 1979). In spite of the prescriptive basis of the counter-cinema argument (see Cottringer, 1978) its value lies in its emphasis on the need to construct a feminist perspective in opposition to the dominant masculine one, rather than on the essentially revolutionary nature of the woman's point-of-view.

STEPHANIE ROTHMAN (continued)
also be argued that abortion is just one more sensational element in a genre which depends for its existence on the exploitation of women's bodies as objects of erotic contemplation.

Knucklemen (Terminal Island) (USA 1973 *p.c* – Dimension Films; *d* – Stephanie Rothman; sd col 17)

This is an example of a film made by Rothman for her own production company, Dimension Films, continuing in the tradition of exploitation films. It can be argued that Rothman works on the action-sexploitation genre to challenge the pleasures it usually offers its audience, and so create new meanings out of basically uncongenial material. The question then is, how far is it possible to undermine such material, or does the use of it inevitably support the status quo? Comparison with other exploitation films could indicate how far the film's potential commercial audiences might be expected to perceive the feminist criticism of exploitation genre conventions.

The first part of the extract shows the two opposing camps – the one

hierarchical and patriarchal, the other exploring the feasibility of a new social order in which notions of sharing and community, group discussion and responsibility are proposed. This section also establishes the conventions of the action-sexploitation genre.

In the second part, the bee-stinging sequence exemplifies a sadistic reversal of conventions which parodies male fantasies. Joy's exit from the pool, for example, is a parodic reversal of normal strip-tease procedure. Another generic reversal can be seen in the fact that it is the women's knowledge and ingenuity in turning the island's resources to their own use which eventually brings about the take-over by the radical group of the enemy camp. Many exploitation films employ the positive heroine stereotype as a mirror of the male (i.e. as physically aggressive) and one would expect the action genre in particular to validate this stereotype. In this film, the new social order is based on a division of labour which gives men and women equal but different roles, arguably questioning the patriarchal system in which women are seen as mirror-images of the male (← *Howard Hawks*, p. 181).

ELAINE MAY
A New Leaf (USA 1970 *p.c* – Paramount/Aries/Elkins Productions; *d* – Elaine May; sd col 18)

It is arguable that some genres are more appropriate for social criticism than others (← *Douglas Sirk*, p. 173; GENRE: *Melodrama*, p. 73) and certainly comedy offers possibilities for satire that women directors working in Hollywood have been able to use in their own interests (e.g. Mae West, *Dorothy Arzner*, ← p. 198, *Stephanie Rothman* ← p.199; also ← *Howard Hawks*, p. 181; *Frank Tashlin*, p. 175).

Elaine May worked for some time with Mike Nichols in a satirical cabaret act. She wrote the script for this, her first feature film, which is interesting for its comic work on Hollywood's sexual stereotypes, using ironic verbal humour and reference to 30s comedies (also ← *Frank Capra*, p. 169).

The first part of the extract sets up the male hero, whose point-of-view dominates the film, and who is presented as a parody on the playboy stereotype (arguably also a send-up of Walter Matthau's usual image).

The second part illustrates the ruthlessness with which May takes the

NELLY KAPLAN

Nelly Kaplan worked as assistant to the French experimental film director Abel Gance before becoming a director in her own right in 1961. There has always been a strong art cinema tradition in France (see Neale, 'Art cinema as institution', 1981), closely linked to a surrealist movement concerned with the liberating force of unconscious desires and fantasy, which has always been interested in anti-realist formal strategies and often looked to Hollywood cinema as a source of inspiration. This inscription of elements of Hollywood across the terms of French art cinema could be said to undermine the realism characteristic of art cinema in general. While art cinema usually presents prevailing myths of women as natural and universal, surrealism embraces the conventions of Hollywood entertainment cinema, such as narrative and genre, and so is able to draw attention to the process of construction of the myths.

The surrealist tradition at work in Kaplan's films has meant that they have been taken up in different ways by feminist critics. Some have responded to the idea of woman as embodying magical powers, possessing insights which will ultimately destroy patriarchal society (see Martineau. 'Interview with Nelly Kaplan', 1973). Others have seen in Kaplan's particular use of surrealist formal strategies a way of criticising the myths of women which art cinema is seen to support and thus a way of undermining the expectations of the audience of that cinema. In this view, the value of Kaplan's films lies in the way the two traditions (of art cinema and surrealism) are brought into conflict to produce contradictions (see Johnston, 'Introduction to interview with Nelly Kaplan', 1973).

La Fiancée du pirate – women's art?

References

Sarah Benton, *Patterns of Discrimination against Women in the Film and Television Industries*, London, Association of Cinematograph Television and Allied Technicians, 1975.

Pam Cook, 'Approaching the work of Dorothy Arzner', in Johnston (ed.), *Dorothy Arzner: towards a feminist cinema*, London, British Film Institute, 1975.

Pam Cook, '"Exploitation films" and feminism', *Screen* vol. 17 no. 2, Summer 1976.

Anne Cottringer, 'Representation and feminist film practice', in Cowie (ed.), *Catalogue British Film Institute Productions 1977–1978*, London, BFI, 1978.

Terry Curtis Fox, 'Fully female', *Film Comment* vol. 12 no. 6, November/December 1976.

Sylvia Harvey, *May '68 and Film Culture*, London, BFI, 1978.

Jim Hillier and Aaron Lipstadt, *BFI Dossier no. 7: Roger Corman's New World*, London, BFI, 1981.

Claire Johnston, 'Women's cinema as counter-cinema', in Johnston (ed.), *Notes on Women's Cinema*, London, Society for Education in Film and Television, 1973.

Claire Johnston, 'Dorothy Arzner: critical strategies', in Johnston (ed.), *Dorothy Arzner: towards a feminist cinema*, cit.

Claire Johnston, 'Introduction to interview with Nelly Kaplan', in Johnston (ed.), *Notes on Women's Cinema*, cit.

Terry Lovell, *Pictures of Reality*, London, BFI, 1980.

Barbara Martineau, 'Subjecting her Objectification', in Johnston (ed.), *Notes on Women's Cinema*, cit.

Barbara Martineau, 'Interview with Nelly Kaplan', in Johnston (ed.), *Notes on Women's Cinema*, cit.

Laura Mulvey, 'Visual pleasure and narrative cinema', *Screen* vol. 16 no. 3, Autumn 1975.

Laura Mulvey, 'Feminism, film and the avant-garde', *Framework* no. 10, Spring 1979.

Steve Neale, 'Art cinema as institution', *Screen* vol. 22 no. 1, 1981.

Gerald Peary, 'Dorothy Arzner', *Cinema* (USA) no. 34, Fall 1974.

Gerald Peary and Karyn Kay, 'Interview with Dorothy Arzner', in Johnston (ed.), *Dorothy Arzner: towards a feminist cinema*, cit.

Peter Wollen, 'Counter-cinema: *Vent d'est*', *Afterimage* no. 4, Autumn 1972.

Peter Wollen, 'The two avant-gardes', in Hardy/Johnston/Willemen (eds.), *Edinburgh '76 Magazine: Psychoanalysis/Cinema/Avant-Garde*, Edinburgh Film Festival, 1976.

stereotypes and obsessions of Hollywood cinema to extremes, for example, the breast-fetish of the 1950s; the stereotype of the dumb female incompetent; the convention of the romantic duologue against the sunset. In the context of the counter-cinema argument (← p. 196), it is debatable whether, in this case, the satirical play with stereotypes and conventions displaces the prevailing ideology in favour of the woman's critical point-of-view, or whether it allows the status quo to remain intact by encouraging a cynical, rather than critical, distance in the audience.

NELLY KAPLAN

La Fiancée du pirate (France 1969 *p.c* – Cythère Films; *d* – Nelly Kaplan; sd col 20)

The extract illustrates Kaplan's use of anti-realist strategies in the surrealist tradition (e.g. the theme of witchcraft as potentially subversive of bourgeois society and the emphasis on fantasy as an expression of suppressed anti-social desires; the refusal of narrative resolution in favour of contradiction). While these surrealist elements could be regarded as progressive, it might also be argued that Kaplan has simply embraced the surrealist tradition, in which women are free spirits vested with magical powers, where she might have interrogated it.

The film presents its characters as stereotypes, often using parody to produce a criticism of bourgeois attitudes to sexuality. There is an interesting use, illustrated in the second part of the extract, of a thematic reversal which both reveals and parodies the workings of myth, when Marie, the witch, burns the 'village', thus reversing the usual procedure (cf. *Knucklemen* p. 201). Although Kaplan is a committed feminist, the film poses problems for some feminists because of its unsympathetic portrayal of the village women, who are seen as avaricious and hypocritical, and Irene, Marie's lesbian employer, who is presented as totally exploitative both economically and sexually. Arguably, Kaplan's use of surrealist strategies to alienate and distance the audience has the effect of focusing sympathy on the central character, Marie, thus validating spontaneous individual action rather than organised feminist resistance.

AGNÈS VARDA

Agnès Varda began her directorial career in the context of the French New Wave (← *Politique des auteurs* p. 134). Her husband, Jacques Demy, was a New Wave film director whose primary interest was in re-working the conventions of the Hollywood musical to point up its 'utopian' qualities. It might be suggested that this interest in utopian fantasies informed Varda's first film *Le Bonheur*, where it takes on a specifically feminist inflection.

Besides its interest in Hollywood, the French New Wave owed a considerable amount to the European tradition of art cinema. Although film-makers such as Godard, Truffaut and Chabrol looked first to Hollywood for inspiration, others, such as Alain Resnais looked towards art cinema and women film-makers like Marguerite Duras and Chantal Akerman can also be seen to emerge from this tradition. Little critical work exists so far on art cinema and its transformation by the New Wave directors, which has allowed unsympathetic critics to dismiss it rather too easily.

Varda's films seem to lean more towards the art cinema strand of the New Wave than the Hollywood strand. However, just as it would be simplistic to think of the films of Godard, Truffaut and Chabrol as dependent upon the Hollywood codes rather than critical of them, Varda's films cannot be seen as lying unproblematically within the art cinema tradition. It could be argued that she is interested in investigating the basic processes by which cinematic images captivate the audience, which would place her in the avant-garde tradition within art cinema rather than in the counter-cinema tradition of Godard (see Wollen, 'The two avant-gardes', 1976).

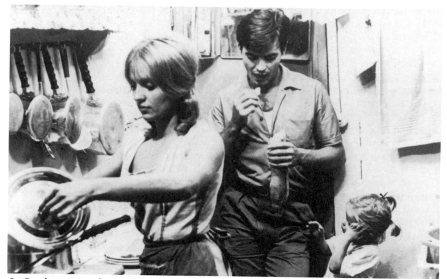

Le Bonheur – 'perfect wife'. . .

. . . and 'perfect' mistress

Le Bonheur (France 1965 *p.c* – Parc Films/Mag Bodard; *d* – Agnès Varda; sd col 11)

Varda was the only woman director to work within the New Wave and this film could be interestingly compared with early films of Godard and Truffaut for the way it questions the romantic point-of-view of its male protagonist, who conceives of 'freedom' in bourgeois terms. The theme of freedom and the impossibility of attaining it is central to many early New Wave films, but the problem is usually presented entirely from the male protagonist's viewpoint, which is validated (e.g. Michel in *A bout de souffle* ← p. 134; Jules and Jim in *Jules et Jim* ← p. 136). It is arguable that Varda undermines that viewpoint by showing that it rests on an image, or myth of woman which is oppressive.

Although the film presents a romantic fantasy of love and marriage, it places that fantasy as male and shows how it controls the production of images for women to identify with. This is illustrated in the extract by the treatment of the wedding preparations, the taking of photographs after the ceremony and the images of motherhood at the reception, all of which are seen to be caught up in a process of image-making at the same time as they present an ideal image of happiness. As François, the husband, makes love to his mistress, shots of his wife shopping with the children provide an ironic commentary on his idea of happiness. It could be argued that Varda attempts to take a distance on the male point-of-view and open it up to criticism.

BARBARA LODEN

Wanda (USA 1970 *p.c* – Foundation for Film-makers; *d* – Barbara Loden; sd col 15)

The film was made independently on 16mm and is interesting as an example of the convergence of a documentary style associated with 16mm production with Hollywood genre conventions (in this case the thriller).

For this reason, *Wanda* bears comparison both with *cinéma-vérité* women's films and with Hollywood films depicting positive heroines (e.g. *Howard Hawks* ← p. 181). Here, the central female protagonist is presented in a situation of extreme oppression as the ultimate victim of capitalist/sexist society. The question is whether this use of the realist documentary mode challenges the depiction of women in Hollywood cinema, or simply reinforces the heroine's oppression as 'a fact of life'.

Authorship in different contexts

Soviet Cinema in the 1920s: the assault on art

The period immediately following the Bolshevik Revolution in Russia is often thought of as a 'golden age' in which the old conservative academic order was swept away, albeit temporarily, to make way for an explosion of critical and artistic talent. Theory and practice came together in all the arts in an unprecedented way, feeding into the cinematic experiments of Eisenstein, Kuleshov, Pudovkin, Vertov and others, and influencing artistic movements throughout the world. In the absence of detailed information about this extraordinary period (much of the critical material and many of the films are not available) it is not surprising that the Soviet cinema of that time has often been characterised in terms of the artistic achievements of a few great directors, of whom Eisenstein is generally seen as the greatest because of his impressive and prolific output of theoretical writings and the technical virtuosity of his films. And clearly, in the face of such evidence, it would be difficult to deny Eisenstein's monumental stature in the history of world cinema, as both theorist and filmmaker. However, this recognition often leads us to forget that his pioneering work, like that of other Soviet artists of the period, was precisely made possible by historical events, and, indeed, finally curtailed by them.

For some years prior to 1917, the predominantly representational traditions of Russian painting had been under attack from young artists interested in the abstract forms emerging from European modernist movements like Cubism and Futurism. Immediately before the Revolution Russian Suprematism, with its emphasis on technique, line, colour, and the evacuation of fixed meanings, laid the foundations for Constructivism: the post-revolutionary movement which was to combine technology, science and art in the interest of a brave new vision of society in which artists and intellectuals would work side by side with other workers (see Enzensberger, 'Osip Brik', 1974).

After 1917 a new emphasis on art as a social product geared towards the needs of the proletariat gave modernist ideas an unprecedented social and political relevance. Iconoclastic abstraction, the hallmark of the 'pure' avant-garde, gave way to the idea of art as production, as labour. The artist's function was like that of an engineer: to bridge the gap between artistic creation, engineering and design.

This transformation of modernist ideas by the demands of revolution influenced the new Soviet cinema of the 1920s and the theoretical debates which surrounded it. Film, because of its technological base, its industrialised mode of production, and the process of assembly, or montage by which it was put together, fitted in perfectly with the idea of art as production, and the artist as technician. Both Lenin and Stalin recognised the propaganda potential in cinema's ability to reach illiterate mass audiences and in 1919 nationalisation of the film industry was decreed. Because of the severe economic problems in post-revolutionary Russia it was not until 1922 that the film industry really found its feet. A central co-ordinating company, Goskino, was formed which eventually controlled the whole Russian industry with state finance, though certain companies retained separate identities (Petley, 1978, p. 30).

In spite of the Soviet cinema's later arrival on the scene in comparison with the other arts, it was just as much caught up in the debates. Many artists and intellectuals were interested in cinema as a medium for expressing revolutionary struggle in a way which would move audiences to identify with that struggle and their ideas fed into the new theories of the film-makers themselves. These debates have been documented elsewhere (see Wollen, 1972; Petley, 1978; *Screen* Winter 1971/72). In the context of discussion about authorship, a tension existed between those who believed in the value of formal experiment and the manipulation of film material in order to shock or move the audience, and those who preferred to let the original material 'speak for itself' as far as possible. In the former case, the degree of personal intervention by the film-maker would be greater, manifested in an authorial style. In the latter, personal intervention would be minimised: in a sense, the film would be authored by the Revolution. Although by no means clear cut, this distinction can be seen in the different approaches of Eisenstein and Vertov, and in the debates about the relative merits of 'played' and 'unplayed' films (→ *Esfir Shub*, p. 206). Its roots can be found in the Constructivist arguments which saw the function of art as serving the interests of the proletariat and the artist as first and foremost a technician.

The Soviet debates about authorship were part of a much wider discussion, specific to a particular historical period, about the role of art in society. None the less, they are echoed in authorship debates of other periods (e.g. Bazin's disagreements with the *politique des auteurs* ← p. 119) although they rarely take on the social and political relevance given them by the context of post-revolutionary Russia.

They surfaced again briefly in post-68 France, where the desire among many film-makers and critics to build a new, revolutionary practice of cinema occasioned renewed interest in the ideas of the Russian Formalists, among others (see Harvey, 1978). The theories of the Soviet film-makers were once again urgently debated; in the anti-auteurist climate of post-68 France attention was focused on the differences of approach between the film-makers rather than their individual artistic achievement. The theories of Eisenstein, for example, were opposed to those of Vertov and discussed in terms of the contribution they made to a materialist theory of cinema. Moreover, those theories were given equal status with their films, and were valued not only in their own right but for the extent to which they might be integrated into a new theory. The films themselves were seen as emerging from the movement of history, rather than as the statements of 'great artists'.

In spite of the wholesale assault on individualism which provided the background for his work, it is difficult not to see Eisenstein's contribution to the Soviet cinema debates as profoundly significant, or not to see him as the first, and perhaps the greatest, major film theorist. But his achievements cannot easily be separated from the context in which they were formed, the context of the Bolshevik Revolution and its effects on all the arts in Russia (→ HISTORY OF NARRATIVE: *Soviet cinema of the 1920s*, p. 218).

SERGEI M. EISENSTEIN

After several years as an engineer, Eisenstein began his artistic career in 1920 as a set designer at the new Proletkult Theatre in Moscow, which, under the supervision of actor-director Meyerhold and the influence of other artists such as poet Mayakovsky and painters Malevich and Tatlin, was seen as simultaneously a vehicle for political propaganda and a laboratory for avant-garde experiment. Art was to be a branch of production in the service of the Revolution and this new movement was to be called Constructivism.

So the early influences on Eisenstein's thinking were the anti-realist ideas of Meyerhold, which drew on the fantastic, the marvellous, the popular and the folkloric, looking towards circus and pantomime for inspiration. The human body was seen as a machine, rather than as a vehicle for the expression of inner emotions: gesture was of primary importance. In his theatrical work Eisenstein brought together many diverse forms, from American slapstick comedy to the mime of the *commedia dell'arte*, using traditional stereotypes to satirise the capitalist bourgeoisie. He called his method 'the montage of attractions', thus drawing attention to the work of construction involved, rather than to his own 'creative artistry'. He envisaged the theatre as a large gesture expressing all the rage of oppressed people and, drawing on the ideas of Freud and Pavlov, began to develop his theories in the direction of agit-prop, in the form of an aggressive assault on the audience which would shock them into political awareness. And in its attempt to reach its audience, the people of Russia, the theatre took to the streets and to the factories themselves, actively seeking out those it wished to influence (Wollen, 1972).

Eisenstein's ideas about the emotional

The 'Odessa steps' sequence in Eisenstein's *Battleship Potemkin*

Battleship Potemkin (USSR 1925 *p.c* –
Goskino; *d* – Sergei Eisenstein;
st b/w 11)

After the success of *Strike*, Eisenstein
was commissioned by the appointed
jubilee committee to direct a film to
celebrate the abortive 1905 Revolution,
which became *Battleship Potemkin*.
Eisenstein took the Potemkin mutiny as
the central metaphor for the Revolution.

Eisenstein worked closely with
cameraman Tisse on the film and the
famous 'Odessa steps sequence', which
the extract comprises, required radically
new filming techniques to put the
director's ideas into practice (see Leyda,
1973, p. 195). The editing was planned
in advance and the film was
photographed accordingly. The
principle behind the cutting was the
editing together of disparate images to
produce new ideas, which would emerge
from the collision itself rather than the
individual images. This idea has much in
common with theories of counter-
cinema (← p. 196) and with the
linguistic theories which influenced
much structuralist work on cinema (→
NARRATIVE AND STRUCTURALISM, p. 222).

The 'Odessa steps sequence' is an
example of Eisenstein's agitational
cinema, using montage to build a
tension which finally provokes a violent
emotional response. It is also interesting
as an attempt to make history itself the
motivating force of the action, rather
than individual men and women. If the
Revolution speaks through the
combination of images, however, the
staging of events still clearly rests with
Eisenstein. Later he would be heavily
criticised for this manipulative approach
to his material.

October (USSR 1927 *p.c* – Sovkino; *d* –
Sergei Eisenstein/Grigori Alexandrov;
st b/w 17)

Another anniversary film,
commissioned to celebrate the tenth
anniversary of the October Revolution
along with a number of others (→ *Esfir
Shub*, p. 206), it combined actual
newsreel with scenes of reconstruction
to dramatise the events leading up to the
Bolshevik Revolution in 1917. However,
it was never actually shown in the
Jubilee because the Government
objected that no distinction had been

made in the reconstruction between the
contributions made to the Revolution by
different and opposed factions (see
Leyda, 1973, p. 238). The film had to be
re-cut and *October* was released in 1928.

The film marks Eisenstein's move
towards a more intellectual cinema, in
which 'reason' would be infused with
fire and passion (Petley, 1978, p. 33).
However, he had not abandoned his
attempts to manipulate the emotions
of the audience. In the extract, sympathy
for the Bolshevik revolutionaries is
aroused by the depiction of the
bourgeoisie as sadistic grotesques. The
use of stereotypes to represent the
bourgeois women is sharply contrasted
with the innocence of the young
revolutionary girl killed on the bridge
and the image of the dead horse adds a
surrealistic touch. The 'extended time'
of this sequence, achieved through
editing, creates a mounting emotional
tension while at the same time offering
the audience time to think about the
outrage visited upon the proletariat by
the military, and the sharp social and
class divisions implied by the raising of
the bridge.

October – 'agitational art'

The General Line – purely cinematic language?

power of montage led him towards film as the apotheosis of his method. His first film *Strike* (1924) brought together violently conflicting ideas in a succession of sketches which attempted to intensify the expression of class feeling and aggressive social protest, mobilising the language of cinema in the interests of political poster-art. Drawing on Kuleshov's ideas about montage editing (see Petley, 1978, pp. 34–35), Eisenstein attempted to transfer his theatrical ideas into specifically cinematic form. He also incorporated many of Vertov's ideas (see Petley, 1978, pp. 37–38), although he was basically hostile to the documentary tendency of Vertov's work.

Like Kuleshov, Eisenstein rejected orthodox stage acting in favour of 'typage'. The actor had no independent existence, except as an element of *mise en scène*. He or she represented simple stock types which would be immediately recognisable by the audience: there was no place for expression of individual personality or acting style.

In Wollen's view, the theatrical/agitprop influences on Eisenstein's films began to fall away after *October* (1927) as he began to develop a more 'purely cinematic' language, and his later films lack the agitational force characteristic of *Strike* and *October*. As Wollen points out, this development was implicit in the terms of his theory to some extent, but it also owed a great deal to the historical and political shifts in Russia at that time (Wollen, 1972).

References

'Documents from *Novy Lef*', *Screen* vol. 12 no. 4, Winter 1971/72. Special issue on Russian Formalism.

Maria Enzensberger, 'Osip Brik: selected writings', *Screen* vol. 15 no. 3, Autumn 1974.

Sylvia Harvey, *May '68 and Film Culture*, London, BFI, 1978.

Jay Leyda, *Kino: a history of the Russian and Soviet film*, London, Allen and Unwin, 1973.

Julian Petley, *British Film Institute Distribution Library Catalogue 1978*, London, BFI, 1978.

Peter Wollen, *Signs and Meaning in the Cinema*, London, Secker and Warburg/BFI, 1972; Ch. 1.

The General Line (Old and New)
(USSR 1929 *p.c* – Sovkino: *d* – Sergei Eisenstein/Grigori Alexandrov; st b/w 12)

The collaboration between Eisenstein, Alexandrov and Tisse continued with this film, which is interesting as a development of Eisenstein's ideas about 'tonal' or 'sensual montage'. The film was edited in such a way as to bring out the underlying associations between images, a method which would make the emotional reverberations of the image the dominant form of associations between ideas. The deepest emotional responses of the audience would be engaged in this process: they would be involved in the intensity of the drama of the organisation of the film itself, as well as the emotional drama depicted on the screen (Leyda, 1973, p. 265).

Eisenstein's use of musical terminology to describe his method in this film (see Petley, 1978, p. 34) indicates how close he had come to simulating the effect of sound entirely through the counterpointing of visual and audio images. Indeed, Extract 2 shows the use of montage editing to create the illusion of sound and provides a useful example of pre-sound cinema (→HISTORY OF NARRATIVE: *Soviet cinema of the 1920s*, p. 218).

Ivan the Terrible: Part I (USSR 1945 *p.c* – Alma Ata Studios; *d* – Sergei Eisenstein; sd b/w 15)

In the 1930s Eisenstein became caught up in political and historical upheavals over which he had no control and which shattered his life. He visited Western Europe, the USA and Mexico and returned to Russia to be faced with a changed political and cultural atmosphere which was hostile to his ideas. Party control was rigid, there was a standard requisite ideology, and many of the artistic and academic 'stars' of the 1920s had been discredited. Eisenstein began working in isolation as a theorist and lecturer: arguably, his theories continued to run counter to the main lines of Stalinist aesthetics (see Wollen, 1972). His later theories were dominated by the idea of 'synesthesia': a way of combining all the different elements of cinema (actors, music, light, landscape, colour and motion) into an integral whole by a single idea. Eisenstein's continuing interest in the grotesque and in caricature can be seen in the strange, distorted costumes he designed for this film and in the extreme stylisation of decor and acting style. Although the film is markedly 'theatrical' it lacks the agitational quality of the earlier films (← *Battleship Potemkin*, *October*, p. 204).

Peter Wollen argues that, unlike Brecht, Eisenstein was prevented from developing an artistic language of rational political argument because of his obsession with the emotional impact of cinema, a legacy from the intellectual context within which he worked (Wollen, 1972). However, it could also be argued that Eisenstein's preoccupation with the relationship between rational argument and emotional response is one of the most useful aspects of his theory for discussion of political cinema.

Ivan The Terrible; Part 1 – Eisenstein's 'played' film   *The Fall of the Romanov Dynasty* – Esfir Shub's 'unplayed' film

ESFIR SHUB

In the programme of production of films which reconstructed Russia's revolutionary history it was quite common for filmmakers to use existing newsreel footage and re-edit it as part of a new film. Many films combined fiction and documentary newsreel in order to lend the reconstruction authenticity. However, the intention was not so much to give a realistic reflection of events in conventional documentary manner; the debate about the relative merits of the 'played' and 'unplayed' film between Eisenstein and Vertov had more to do with the search for a cinematic language which could convey the 'truth' of the spirit of the revolution (see 'Documents from Novy Lef', *Screen*, Winter 1971/72, pp. 74, 83–90).

The distinction between the 'played'

and the 'unplayed' film depended upon the degree of deformation of the material from which the film was composed. Eisenstein's films were 'played' in the sense that he manipulated his material in order to affect the audience, thus introducing a strong personal element. Vertov's films were 'unplayed' in so far as they remained true to the original material, minimising personal intervention. This distinction between 'played' and 'unplayed' was by no means hard and fast. Shub's films, for instance, could be said to be 'unplayed' in that they depended upon a painstaking reconstruction of original newsreel material. On the other hand, they were also 'played' because the extent of her own personal intervention was considerable: she re-edited her material according to a principle of montage of attractions

intended to engage the emotions of the audience. The original newsreel material could be said to contain an element of 'play' also, for example, in 'candid camera' shots where the subjects photographed are caught unawares by the camera.

Shub's films are generally placed on the side of the 'unplayed' and are seen as relatively unauthored. However, since the meaning of those films arises entirely from the editing process, she could be said to be, as the editor, solely responsible for those meanings. An interesting question arises of how far her own interests as a woman in post-revolutionary Russia coincided with the historical analysis she brought to bear on her material, and how far the editing process allowed her a degree of ironic play with that material.

Fall of the Romanov Dynasty (USSR 1927 *p.c* – Sovkino and the Museum of the Revolution; *d* – Esfir Shub; st b/w 20)

This film is an example of Shub's pioneering work in the development of reconstructed documentary. She put enormous energy into researching and collecting her material, often a difficult task given the poor condition and fragmentary nature of the newsreel clips. By editing the pieces together according to a system of juxtaposition of connecting images she was able to achieve effects of irony, absurdity and pathos which few of the pieces had intrinsically. Through this editing technique she gave Russia's history and its progress towards socialist reconstruction great emotional power.

Although her work was held up as an

example of pure 'factography' (clearly by its very nature it could never aspire to the visual stylistic flourishes of Eisenstein, Vertov and others) there is a level of playful irony in the films which could be seen as characteristic of Shub's approach.

The Great Road (USSR 1927 *p.c* – Sovkino and the Museum of the Revolution; *d* – Esfir Shub; st b/w 20)

This was Shub's October anniversary film, for which she combed minutely through all the newsreels made in the ten years between 1917 and 1927. She found that those newsreels did not in themselves provide a record of how the country had been transformed into a new socialist state: she had to reconstruct that process herself by re-editing the original newsreel material.

In the debate about the relative ideological and aesthetic merits of the 'played' and the 'unplayed' film, Eisenstein's *October* was compared unfavourably with Shub's documentary montage reconstruction. It was thought that Eisenstein let his world-wide reputation as a 'great' director interfere with his relationship to his material, while Shub's films resolutely refused to deviate from the task of representing historical truth. Yet it can be argued that Shub's montage techniques are just as emotionally manipulative as Eisenstein's, involving a high degree of personal intervention on her part. The played/unplayed debate raised acutely the question of the place of individual contributions to historical materialist analysis and to the process of history itself.

History of Narrative Codes

Introduction

In spite of the fact that the history of cinema may be approached in a variety of ways, most accounts have been dominated by an emphasis on cinematographic technology or on contributions made by individual *auteurs*. Such a focus on matters strictly external to the films themselves tends to deflect attention from specific questions concerning the nature and implications of variations and developments in the 'language' of cinema. However, such attention ideally calls for close scrutiny of numerous films, which presents a number of problems to the film historian. In particular, many early films have been lost, while those remaining in existence are rarely easily accessible for viewing. Nevertheless, work in this field is increasingly being undertaken. One of the most interesting aspects of this research is its concern to trace the process through which, by the 1930s and 1940s, a highly specific mode of cinematic representation had become dominant. In the 1930s, the cultural ascendancy of narrative cinema was complete, and a particular set of cinematic codes through which film narratives were constructed and articulated was already quite firmly in place. Noël Burch has called this set of codes the Institutional Mode of Representation (IMR) (Burch, 1980/81). The IMR could be said to consist basically of conventions of *mise en scène*, framing, and in particular of editing, by means of which coherent narrative space and time are set up and fictional characters individuated in ways which both engage, and are imperceptible to, the spectator.

Crucial in this process is the organisation of shots in a film according to the rules of continuity editing. Perhaps the foremost effect of continuity editing is to efface the moment of transition between shots, with the result that the spectator is caught up in the film to such an extent that disbelief is suspended, and s/he is swept along with the story, unaware of the artifice of the means of representation. It is commonly accepted that this 'zero point of cinematic style' enjoyed its apotheosis in the Hollywood cinema of the 1930s and 1940s, the era of the 'classic' narrative system (see Bordwell and Thompson, 1979).

But all-powerful though the Institutional Mode of Representation may seem even today, its dominance is in no way historically inevitable. Like all representations, the IMR exists within a particular social and historical context, and in other circumstances modes of cinematic representation might well have developed differently. The dominance of the IMR may therefore be regarded as contingent – the outcome of struggles within the cinematic institution between different modes of representation. That there is indeed nothing inevitable or final about this dominance may be demonstrated simply by pointing to the existence of many other forms of cinema. For example, narrative films made in the early years of the medium, before the IMR was fully established, look very different from narrative films of the 'classic' era. Moreover, throughout the entire history of cinema alternative approaches to cinematic representation have co-existed alongside the Institutional Mode. Avant-garde and experimental cinema, 'art' cinema and various counter-cinemas, for instance, all relativise the dominance of the IMR.

Early cinema

Film form and film narrative

Right from its beginnings – around 1895 – cinema was dominated by fictional narrative representations of one kind or another. During the first twenty to twenty-five years of its existence, the new medium was marked by a degree of experimentation with various approaches to the telling of stories on film. By about 1919, what Noël Burch has called the era of 'primitive cinema', a period during which a film language was in the process of construction, was at an end. Apart from some further refinements during the 1920s, the Institutional Mode of Representation was more or less in place.

The cinematic codes of narration observable in films made before about 1920 may be regarded as constituting a prehistory for the more limited codes characterising the IMR. The 'primitive' mode of representation is different from the IMR, and as film language it has its own specificity. At the same time, it may be regarded also as bearing the embryo of the IMR. This is not necessarily either a contradictory or a teleological argument: early cinema certainly embodied, within its specific codes, potential modes of cinematic representation other than that which emerged ultimately as dominant. The highly circumscribed set of codes which came to dominate mainstream narrative cinema from around the mid-1920s onwards may be regarded as a visible outcome of the social, historical and industrial conditions in which the films were produced. The IMR, then, is not an inevitable, nor is it even the only logical development from the codes of early cinema. The specific character of the IMR is highlighted by an exploration of its embryonic existence within the codes of narrativity of primitive cinema. However, primitive cinema is also of interest in its own right as a mode of representation.

Figs 1a, b, c

The earliest films were usually very short: the 'one-reeler', with a running time of about ten minutes, predominated until around 1912 or 1913 (←HISTORY: *Early film industry*, p. 3). Most of these short films were narratives of one kind or another, which means that the nature of fictional situations set up and developed in them was to some extent determined by their brevity. Often, therefore, stories are simple vignettes or straightforward action narratives, with little scope for complexity of characterisation, subplot, and so on. This point also has implications for the cinematic articulation of the stories for the construction and composition of individual shots and the relationship set up between shots.

The tableau

The very earliest narrative films typically consisted of a small number of shots, each one constituting a separate 'scene'. In each scene, action is played out in long shot or medium long shot, head on, with static framing, and frequently unfolding through a single take. Action tends also to be restricted to a narrow plane of depth and takes place well within the bounds of the film frame, offscreen space being implied only in simple exits and entrances. Here the individual shot/scene or sequence shot operates very much as a kind of moving tableau: indeed the debt of primitive cinema to modes of representation characteristic of contemporary popular theatre has frequently been acknowledged. An entire film may consist of a succession of such tableaux, edited together without links of continuity, and sometimes separated from one another by written intertitles which explain the action. Since in this form of primitive cinema a whole scene may unfold in one single panoramic take, there exists the possibility that small, but narratively significant, details might be overlooked by the audience, so that there may be some general difficulty in discerning what is actually going on in the story. In Edwin S. Porter's film *The Great Train Robbery* (1903), for instance, a lengthy single-take scene in which passengers in a train are held up and robbed contains an enormous amount of information which it is quite easy to miss (*figs. 1a, b, c*). This may be a greater problem, however, for the present-day viewer, used to entirely different modes of cinematic narration, than it was for the contemporary film spectator.

The panoramic frontal tableau is commonly regarded as the most 'elementary' mode of narration in early cinema, and indeed by 1905 or so it was already breaking down. It nevertheless remained as an element in later films, though usually in combination with more 'advanced' forms of cinematic narration, for a number of years. Certain marks of the tableau were still quite commonplace, for example, in interior sequences, while action shot outdoors for the same film is usually more fluid in its composition and uses offscreen space and action in depth. The relatively late film *The Pickwick Papers* (1912) includes a number of the defining features of the tableau film, and even such a pioneering director as D. W. Griffith at this period retained some tableau-like compositions in his films, *The Lonedale Operator*

Fig 2

(1911) for example (*fig. 2*). The difference between *The Lonedale Operator* and *The Pickwick Papers* is interesting, however, in that whereas in the Griffith film the 'tableau' shots are usually relatively short, forming only a part of any particular

scene, *The Pickwick Papers* looks back in a sense to earlier forms and contains a number of tableau shots which are also entire scenes. Changes or 'developments' within the codes of early film narrative were not necessarily chronologically linear.

The Organisation of Shots
Immediately beyond the simple series of tableau sequence shots of primitive cinema come developments in film language which pivot on the relationships between individual shots and on the methods of linking scenes together. If narrative may be defined as the recounting of a series of fictional events which are linked temporally and spatially, in cause-effect relationship, then in a narrative film it is in the linking together of shots and scenes through editing, that the movement forward of the narrative takes place (see Bordwell and Thompson, 1979). Apart from being among the most important of the specifically cinematic codes, editing is crucial to the process of narration in fiction film.

In the primitive tableau film, editing consists of nothing more than joining together autonomous shots/scenes, without either spatial or temporal continuity. The earliest editing in early cinema consists firstly of simple temporal/spatial match cuts (see Bordwell and Thompson, 1979, p. 168) and secondly of crosscutting between two or more simultaneous, but spatially separated, actions. *The Great Train Robbery*, considered to be advanced for its date (1903), contains one virtual match cut, while the much later but relatively 'primitive' *The Pickwick Papers* contains, in a 13-minute extract, only two matches on action. Matchcutting on action is used early and to good effect in Cecil Hepworth's 1905 film *Rescued by Rover*, in which a coherent narrative space is constructed in the editing of sequences in which the canine hero seeks out a kidnapped baby and then guides the infant's distraught father back to the kidnapper's lair (*figs. 3a, b, c*).

The Great Train Robbery includes an early example of what was to become one of the defining features of action cinema – crosscutting for suspense: in this instance in the section of the film depicting the rescue of the telegraph operator and the gathering of the posse while bandits make off with the loot. In crosscutting, narrative time is typically extended by the device of cutting between implicitly simultaneous actions taking place in different locations. This convention rapidly became well established, so that, for example, by 1911 in *The Lonedale Operator* suspense is effectively generated through well-paced crosscutting between as many as four different locations (*figs. 4a, b, c, d, e*). It is perhaps significant that crosscutting had already been established for a number of years before it seems to have been used regularly for any purpose other than generating suspense. In the 1915 film *A Fool There Was*, crosscutting functions

Figs 3a, b, c

both to set up a contrast of character and also to emphasise the poignancy of a melodramatic situation, in a sequence in which a virtuous wronged wife seeks out her drunken husband. This sequence is intercut with shots of the vamp who has led the husband astray setting out simultaneously for the same destination. If it is typical, this relatively late example of crosscutting for melodramatic effect suggests that the cinematic narration of pure action developed somewhat earlier than the means for constructing anything other than the crudest of characterisations.

Characterisation
Characterisation is a cornerstone of narrative whose human agents are represented as motivated by traits of personality or individual psychology. This was not as a rule true of the earliest film narratives, which tended to be constructed around action (as for example *The Great Train Robbery*). In these films, the characters are invariably subordinated to narrative action and at their most complex are usually little more than stereotypes (see Burch, 1978/79). Alternatively, characters may be endowed with qualities already familiar to audiences from sources external to the film itself, as in literary adaptations like *The Pickwick Papers*. But in *The Great Train Robbery* we know the bandits are villains only because of their

Figs 4a, b, c, d, e

tions of physiognomy, and members of both the bandit gang and the posse wear black clothes. Partly because of the anonymity of its characters, it may be difficult for a present-day audience to 'read' this film.

Characterisation, it may be argued, demands a mode of representation by means of which narrative agents can be individuated. In terms of cinematic narrative, this calls for procedures for directing the spectator's gaze, for example to facial expressions and gestures. Although the close shot was apparently in regular use by around 1912, its function in cinematic narration did not at this point relate exclusively to characterisation, nor indeed was the close shot the only device used for directing the gaze of the spectator to significant detail.

Probably one of the earliest examples of the close shot in the history of cinema is the medium close-up of a man facing camera and firing a gun which appears at the end of *The Great Train Robbery* (*fig. 5*). But because this shot is outside the film's narrative system, its function in the fiction, if any, is not altogether clear. Close shots used in this 'emblematic' manner were, it has been suggested, something of a mark of films made around this period (Burch, 1978/79). They certainly also occur in *Rescued by Rover* (1905) made two years after Porter's film. The close shot does not acquire a motivating function in the fiction unless it is integrated within the overall cinematic narration. This integration is a somewhat later development, one which again appears initially in the sphere of action rather than characterisation. In *The Lonedale Operator* (1911), for example, there appears a close-up of a wrench which the heroine has convinced the villains is a gun (*figs. 6a, b*). This cut-in shot directs attention to a significant detail of the story, whilst simultaneously offering an explanation that constitutes a resolution of one of the strands of the film's narrative action. It is interesting that, despite the existence of this precedent, Griffith made a film in the following year, *The Musketeers of Pig Alley*, in which a crucial item of narrative detail (the heroine being slipped a Mickey Finn) is embedded in a 'busy' tableau shot and could be quite easily missed. Even at this stage, then, the close shot probably remains something of an 'experimental' device.

The fact that cinema had by this time developed other means of pointing up detail – notably the mask and the iris – may have contributed to this apparently uneven usage of the close shot. Unlike the close shot, however, these devices were never really incorporated in the Institutional Mode of Representation even though they appeared with some regularity right into the 1920s. With these devices the spectator's attention is guided by the masking off of 'irrelevant' areas of the screen, or by 'irising-in' to a detail. The mask and the iris were in fact frequently used in conjunc-

Fig 5

Figs 6a, b

Fig 7

tion with close shots, and by the mid-1910s both were mobilised not only in the field of narrative action but also in the service of characterisation. *Intolerance* (1916) contains close-ups, notably of women's faces, masked so as to fill the illuminated area of the screen (*fig. 7*). Such close-ups, by showing facial expressions, serve to reveal emotions, and to some extent individual personality traits, of the characters. By the 1920s, the cinematic articulation of characterisation was well-developed in other respects (e.g. *Foolish Wives*, 1921).

Spectator engagement

The direction of attention to significant detail, and the construction of individual characters by means of close shots, suggests a rather different relationship between spectator and narrative than is

actions: they commit a crime, therefore they are villains. No distinction is made between individuals in the gang, nor is there any of that iconography of character which was soon to mark the western as a film genre (←GENRE: *The western*, p. 64). Thus it is difficult to distinguish the bandits from the posse, because there are no shots in the main body of the film sufficiently close to reveal individual distinc-

implied by the frontal panoramic view of tableau film. It suggests a greater degree of spectator involvement, or identification with what is unfolding on screen; that certain strategies of cinematic narration may 'engage' spectators more than others; and that there was already, before 1920, a tendency for cinematic strategies which evoked spectator engagement to be taken up and developed while more 'distanced' modes of narration were being dropped. The process of engagement operates not only through the framing of shots, however, but also through the way they are edited together. The chase sequence in *The Lonedale Operator*, for example, is cut for maximum suspense: even in this relatively early film some measure of identification or, perhaps better, sympathy with the heroine is already set up, so that the spectator has no doubt about which side s/he is on. The tension generated in the chase sequence solicits the spectator's involvement in the narrative. In Griffith's subsequent films the melodramatic element is further developed in crosscutting for

suspense as, for example, in scenes in *The Birth of a Nation* which show a log cabin being attacked and besieged. Nevertheless, it seems that strategies of spectator involvement developed quite unevenly in pre-1920 cinema, and were perhaps not fully in place until the complex set of codes surrounding the cinematic articulation of 'the look' was developed in the 1920s and 1930s.

The look

If early cinema had already – by around 1920 – developed many, even most, of the narrative codes that were ultimately to constitute part of the armoury of the Institutional Mode of Representation, one area remained markedly distinct from those modes of narration more typical of the Institutional Mode. This is the cinematic look, exemplified by optical point-of-view and more especially by the editing conventions of eyeline matching and shot/reverse-shot (→NARRATIVE AND STRUCTURALISM: *Point-of-view*, p. 244; *Suture*, p. 246). Cinematic strategies whereby, for

example, identification with a character is set up through the subjectivity implied in shots that seem to be from his or her point-of-view were probably not an established feature of narrative cinema until well into the 1920s (→*Sunrise*, 1927). At this point, the device of optical point-of-view permits the integration into dominant narrative cinema of expressionistic devices such as marked camera angles, chiaroscuro lighting and certain kinds of mobile framing, because these could be justified in terms of a character's subjective state (→*Foolish Wives*, 1921). The cinematic articulation of the look consequently enhanced the potential for characterisation in narrative cinema.

References

David Bordwell and Kristin Thompson, *Film Art: An Introduction*, Reading, Massachusetts, Addison-Wesley, 1979
Noël Burch, 'How we got into pictures: notes accompanying *Correction Please*', *Afterimage* no. 8/9, Winter 1980/81
Noël Burch, 'Porter, or ambivalence', *Screen* vol. 19 no. 4, Winter 1978/79, pp. 91–95.

The Great Train Robbery (USA 1903 *p.c*– Edison Company; *d*– Edwin S. Porter; st b/w 12)

The complete film, a re-enactment of a real-life event and a pioneering western, is just under 12 minutes in length, and comprises only 13 shots plus the 'emblematic close shot' at the end of the film which portrays, according to some accounts, the leader of the bandit gang. *The Great Train Robbery* is already something of a departure from the tableau film in that it includes one virtual match on action, some mobile framing, and some rudimentary crosscutting. At the same time, the robbery itself is narrated in a single 2-minute static take (shot 6) which includes a good deal of detail which, being in long shot, is somewhat difficult to read (see *figs. 1a, b, c*).

The Pickwick Papers (USA 1912 *p.c*– Vitagraph; *d*– Larry Trimble; st b/w 13)

This film, based on the novel by Charles Dickens, seems to assume some prior knowledge on the part of its audience about the characters and events of the narrative. This would serve, no doubt, to bridge the narrative ellipses evident in this film version. The extract chronicles a practical joke involving an exchange of clothes which leads to a case of mistaken identity and finally to a narrowly-avoided duel. The literary origin of the film is evident in the large number of intertitles – nineteen – in the extract. Moreover, by comparison with other films of the same period, *The Pickwick Papers* has a rather 'primitive' appearance: the range of shots is limited, and editing is in general based

on the tableau, rather than on the continuity principle. However, the duel scene does include an early example of deep-focus cinematography, in which suspense is generated through the counterpoint of two independent sets of actions on different planes of depth within a single long take. This film highlights the non-linear nature of developments in modes of cinematic narration (←HISTORY: *Early film industry*, p. 5).

A Fool There Was (USA 1915 *p.c*– Fox Film Company; *d*– Frank Powell; st b/w 16)

In this extract an elderly man is spellbound and led astray by a femme fatale (Theda Bara), his wife and child have left him and he sinks into drunkenness and depravity. The film is interesting for its expressionistic lighting, which functions to construct narrative action in relation to characterisation. The wronged wife, for example, is associated with floods of bright 'natural' light, while the husband and his settings are typically chiaroscuro. Crosscutting, during a sequence in which the wife attempts to reclaim her husband from the clutches of the vamp, works both to highlight the contrast of character between the two women and to emphasise the poignancy of the melodrama (←HISTORY: *Box-office attractions*, p. 5).

The Birth of a Nation (USA 1915 *p.c*– Epoch Producing Corp./Reliance-Majestic; *d*– D. W. Griffith; st b/w 12 + 15).
Intolerance (USA 1916 *p.c*– Wark Producing Corp; *d*– D. W. Griffith; st b/w 10 + 13).

These extracts, from two of the earliest feature-length films in the history of cinema, illustrate the development of cinematic characterisation in relation to narrative action through close-ups, in this case of the faces of female characters. In *The Birth of a Nation* (Extract 2), characterisation functions quite directly in relation to action, in the crosscut sequence in which a group of rebels is attacked by marauding yankees and negroes while the Ku-Klux-Klan rides to the rescue. Sympathy for the rebels is solicited by close-ups, edited into action sequences involving the rebels, of virginally beautiful women portrayed as being 'at risk' from the enemy (←HISTORY: *Box-office attractions*, p. 5; AUTHORSHIP: *D. W. Griffith*, p. 137).

Easy Street (USA 1917 *p.c*– Mutual; *d*– Charles Chaplin; st b/w 5)
The Vagabond (USA 1916 *p.c*– Mutual; *d*– Charles Chaplin; st b/w 4)
The Pawnshop (USA 1916 *p.c*– Mutual; *d*– Charles Chaplin; st b/w 5)

These extracts (compiled together) adopt a theatrical style which is closer to the appearance of *The Pickwick Papers* than to that of the Griffith films. Framing is almost exclusively static and camera distance ranges very narrowly between long shot and medium long shot. Apart from some virtual match cuts in a chase sequence in *The* →

The classic narrative system

By the early to middle 1930s, the modes of representation now held to be characteristic of 'classic' narrative cinema were more or less consolidated and had already attained a large degree of dominance, certainly in Hollywood, but also in varying degrees in film industries elsewhere. By this time, of course, sound cinema was also established. The era of classic cinema may be regarded as a period in which the cinematic image remained largely subservient to the requirements of a specific type of narrative structure. This structure is that of the classic, sometimes also called the 'realist', narrative which calls forth certain modes of narration which are then put into effect by a limited set of cinematic codes (→NARRATIVE AND STRUCTURALISM: *The classic realist text*, p. 242).

The classic narrative structure

In the classic narrative, events in the story are organised around a basic structure of enigma and resolution. At the beginning of the story, an event may take place which disrupts a pre-existing equilibrium in the fictional world. It is then the task of the narrative to resolve that disruption and set up a new equilibrium (see Barthes, 1977). The classic narrative may thus be regarded as a process whereby problems are solved so that order may be restored to the world of the fiction. But the process of the narrative – everything that takes place between the initial disruption and the final resolution – is also subject to a certain ordering. Events in the story are typically organised in a relationship of cause and effect, so that there is a logic whereby each event of the narrative is linked with the next. The classic narrative proceeds step-by-step in a more-or-less linear fashion, towards an apparently inevitable resolution. The 'realist' aspects of the classic narrative are overlaid on this basic enigma-resolution structure, and typically operates on two levels: firstly, through the verisimilitude of the fictional world set up by the narrative and secondly through the inscription of human agency within the process of the narrative.

The world of the classic narrative is governed by verisimilitude, then, rather than by documentary-style realism (←AUTHORSHIP: *Documentary*, p. 190). The narration ensures that a fictional world, understandable and believable to the recipient of the story, is set up. Verisimilitude may be a feature of the representation of either, or preferably both, the spatial location of events in the narrative and the temporal order in which they occur. Temporal and spatial coherence are in fact preconditions of the cause-effect logic of events in the classic narrative (see Burch, 1973). In classic narrative, moreover, events are propelled forward through the agency of fictional individuals or characters. Although this is true also of other types of narrative, the specificity of the classic narrative lies in the nature of the human agency it inscribes, and also in the function of such agency within the narrative as a whole. The central agents of classic narrative are typically represented as fully-rounded individuals with certain traits of personality, motivations, desires and so on. The chain of events constituting the story is then governed by the motivations and actions of these characters. An important defining feature of the classic narrative is its constitution of a central character as a 'hero', through whose actions narrative resolution is finally brought about. These actions are rendered credible largely in terms of the kind of person the hero is represented to be (→NARRATIVE AND STRUCTURALISM: *Propp*, p. 234).

Finally, classic narrative may be defined by the high degree of closure which typically marks its resolution. The ideal classic narrative is a story with a beginning, a middle and an end (in that order), in which every one of the questions raised in the course of the story is answered by the time the narration is complete (see Barthes, 1975).

Classic codes of narrative cinema

Narratives may be communicated through various modes of expression, that is, stories can be told through a variety of media. The classic narrative is perhaps most often considered in its literary form, as a certain type of novel. However, stories may also be transmitted by word of mouth, in live theatre, on the radio, and in comic strips. Film is simply one narrative medium among many but the distinguishing features of film are its mode of production and consumption, and the specifically cinematic codes by which film narratives are constructed. Cinematic codes constitute a distinct set of expressive resources which can be drawn on for, among other things, telling stories (→NARRATIVE AND STRUCTURALISM: *Metz*, p. 229).

The classic narrative system would appear to make certain basic demands of these resources. Firstly, it demands that cinematic codes function to propel the narrative from its beginning through to its resolution, keeping the story moving along. Secondly, it is important that in the narration of fictional events the causal link between each event be clear. Thirdly, the narration called for would encompass the construction of a location, a credible fictional world, for the events of the story. Finally, it should be capable of constructing the individuated characters pivotal to the classic narrative, and of establishing and sustaining their agency in the narrative process.

Perhaps the foremost of the specifically cinematic codes is that of editing. Although editing is simply the juxtaposition of individual shots, this juxtaposition

---

Vagabond, the films are not edited for continuity. In all three extracts, the cinematic image is in fact subordinated to the requirements of the gag or the comic situation. For example, the matchcutting and consequent relatively coherent narrative space in *The Vagabond*, which is appropriate to the 'chase' motif, contrasts with the extended visual joke rendered in two very long static takes in *The Pawnshop*.

Foolish Wives (USA 1921 *p.c*– Universal; *d*– Erich von Stroheim; st b/w 11)

The extract from *Foolish Wives* demonstrates the nature of transformations which had already, by the early 1920s, taken place in codes of cinematic narration, particularly in codes relating to the cinematic articulation of the look. The first sequence, in which the Prince rejects his maid's offer of marriage and then takes money from her, is pivoted on an exchange and avoidance of looks between the two characters. In editing terms, this relay of looks operates through a counterpoint of point-of-view shots, eyeline matches and shot/reverse-shots. Narration works hand-in-hand with the function, crucial in this film, of characterisation. In the second sequence, both the editing, and also expressive *mise en scène* and marked camera angles, work together to construct a subjective point-of-view for the Prince which functions not to solicit any identification on the part of the spectator but rather as a comment from the 'narrator' on an aspect of the Prince's character which is central to the story – his misogyny (←HISTORY: *The origins of the studio system* p. 6).

Sunrise (USA 1927 *p.c*– Fox Film Corporation; *d*– F. W. Murnau; st b/w 12 + 16)

In Extract 2, in which the man takes his wife on a boat trip to the city and attempts to carry out his plan to murder her, tension is generated initially through subjectively-marked representations of the man's erotic and murderous fantasies, and then intensified in the narration of the boat trip itself. In the former, the man's subjectivity is narrated as it were impersonally, the fantasy being coded as such purely through expressionistic *mise en scène*. The boat trip, on the other hand, is set up in the interplay of looks between man and wife as the pinnacle of suspense. The repeated looks of the wife at her husband are not returned by him until the moment when he evidently decides not to carry out the planned murder (←HISTORY: *20th Century-Fox*, p. 18).

can take place according to a variety of principles. Editing in classic cinema works in conjunction with the basic demands of the classic narrative structure in highly circumscribed ways. First, the individual shots are ordered according to the temporal sequence of events making up the story. In this way, editing functions both to move the story along and also, through the precise juxtapositions of shots, to constitute the causal logic of narrative events (→*Stagecoach*). The specificity of classic editing lies in its capability to set up a coherent and credible fictional space, and often also to orchestrate quite complex relationships of narrative space and time.

The principles of classical editing have been codified in a set of editing techniques whose objective is to maintain an appearance of 'continuity' of space and time in the finished film; all learning film-makers have to master the rules of continuity editing. Continuity editing establishes spatial and temporal relationships between shots in such a way as to permit the spectator to 'read' a film without any conscious effort, precisely because the editing is 'invisible'. Despite the fact that every new shot constitutes a potential spatial disruption, and each gap of years, months, days and even minutes between narrated events a potential temporal disjuncture, an appearance of continuity in narrative space and time can be set up (→*Mildred Pierce*). The function of continuity editing is to 'bridge' spatial and temporal ellipses in cinematic narration, through the operation of such conventions as match on action, consistency of screen direction, and the 30° rule (see Burch, 1973). Coherence of fictional space is ensured by adherence to the 180° rule, whereby 'the line' is never crossed in the editing of shots taken from different set-ups in a single location. Since the 180° rule, in particular, depends on the hypothesis that screen direction signified direction in three-dimensional space, the credibility of the fiction is maintained through a form of editing which signifies verisimilitude (see Bordwell and Thompson, 1979).

In the classic narrative system editing is governed by the requirements of verisimilitude, hence the characteristic pattern in any one film sequence of establishing shot, closer shots which direct the gaze of the spectator to elements of the action to be read as significant, followed by further long-shots to re-establish spatial relations (→*His Girl Friday*). Since the classic narrative sets up fictional characters as primary agents of the story, it is not surprising that characters' bodies, or parts of their bodies, notably faces, figure so frequently in close shots. Close shots of this kind function also in relation to characterisation: personality traits are represented through costume, gesture, facial expression and speech (→*Klute*). At the same time, relationships between fictional protagonists are typically narrated through certain configurations of close shots, particularly those

Figs 8a, b

Figs 8c, d

Figs 8e, f

His Girl Friday (USA 1939 *p.c* – Columbia; *d* – Howard Hawks; sd b/w 19)

In the opening sequence of the film the heroine Hildy and her fiancé Bruce arrive at the newspaper office where Hildy formerly worked. Hildy's ex-husband Walter, the editor, tries to persuade her to return to her old job. Shots 1 and 2 of the film function in the classic manner as establishing shots: a tracking shot moves through a busy and crowded newspaper office. A virtually invisible lap dissolve introduces shot 2, in which the space of the office is further delineated, here in a closer shot but again with mobile framing. Hildy and Bruce are introduced into this same shot as they leave the lift adjacent to the office entrance. Shot 3 is a medium two-shot of Bruce and Hildy, shots 4, 5 and 6 a shot/reverse-shot figure (*figs. 8a, b, c, d, e, f*). The next five shots follow Hildy back through the office, re-establishing the space already introduced in shot 1, and show her entering Walter's room with a perfect match on action that moves her from one side of the door to another. This sequence demonstrates very clearly how the classic narrative system functions through cinematic codes to set up characterisation and organise a coherent narrative space (← AUTHORSHIP: *Howard Hawks*, p. 179).

Stagecoach (USA 1939 *p.c* – Walter Wanger Productions; *d* – John Ford; sd b/w 10)

The extract shows the final part of the stage's journey to Lordsburg, and includes a chase sequence in which the passengers are attacked by Indians. Since at this point in the narrative the character traits of the protagonists are already well established, the narration is free to focus more-or-less exclusively on action and suspense. Suspense is generated by the familiar device of crosscutting, which in this case initially functions also to establish narrative space. In the first segment of the actual chase, shots of the stagecoach and the Indians alternate, and it is only later that both groups are seen within one shot. Spectator identification with the passengers of the stage is sustained through two devices. The stage is placed first in the alternating sequence of shots in such a way that it is clear that it is the →

Figs 9a, b

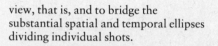

Figs 9c, d

where an exchange of looks between characters is implied (→*Marnie*). Here, editing is organised on the principle of the eyeline match, according to the direction of characters' gaze. The eyeline match also governs point-of-view in the shot/reverse-shot figure, which in fact reached the peak of its exploitation during the 1940s, at the height of the classic era of cinema. This method of organising the looks of protagonists, through a combination of *mise en scène* and editing, is a crucial defining characteristic of classic narrative cinema (see Browne, 1975/76).

The conventions of classical editing constitute a particular mode of address to the spectator. In accepting a certain kind of verisimilitude in the spatial and temporal organisation of the film narrative the spectator becomes witness to a complete world, a world which seems even to exceed the bounds of the film frame. In looking at the faces of characters in close-up, and in identifying with characters in the text

object of pursuit. Secondly, such point-of-view shots as are to be found in this sequence originate predominantly from the coach or its passengers rather than from the Indians *(figs. 9a, b, c, d)*. The main burden of narration falls here on the editing, which functions almost entirely to keep the story and the action moving along. Moreover, the specific form of editing – crosscutting – also generates suspense and excitement, while sustaining the spectator's identification with the passengers of the stagecoach (←AUTHORSHIP: *John Ford*, p. 184).

Mildred Pierce (USA 1945 *p.c* – Warner Bros; *d* – Michael Curtiz; sd b/w 10+18)

Extract 2 opens at the beginning of Mildred's second flashback, as she talks about the success of her restaurant business. The flashback is marked as such by conventionalised framing and editing quite prevalent in films of the 1940s, and a mark of narratives involving complex temporal relations. A close-up of Mildred dissolves very slowly into a long shot of one of her restaurants, and Mildred's direct speech then becomes voice-over for the image as her face fades from the screen. The temporal ellipsis referred to in the voice-over ('In three years I built up five restaurants') is marked by a series of discontinuous shots punctuated by brief dissolves *(figs. 10a, b, c, d, e, f, g)*. In the classic narrative system the dissolve is a conventional signifier of passage of brief but indefinite time. The voice-over, which is sustained throughout the montage sequence, functions simultaneously to mark the sequence as subjective, told from Mildred's point-of-

view, that is, and to bridge the substantial spatial and temporal ellipses dividing individual shots.

Marnie (USA 1964 *p.c* – Geoffrey Stanley Inc./Universal International; *d* – Alfred Hitchcock; sd col 20+20)

Extract 1 shows Marnie waking from a nightmare: her lover Mark then questions her. The segment in which Mark enters Marnie's room as she wakes up is constructed as a series of nine or ten alternating shot/reverse-shots. Since Marnie is not fully awake, however, and so does not see Mark, the shots of Mark are not strictly from her point-of-view, but those of Marnie are quite evidently from Mark's: as he moves closer to the bed, for example, the framing of the shots of Marnie contract from long shot to medium shot. In the next segment Marnie evades Mark's questions about her dream. Marnie's rival Lil passes by the bedroom door, looks into the next room and sees the book Mark has been reading: *The Sexual Aberrations of the Criminal Female*.

The extraordinarily high incidence of point-of-view shots in this extract is quite typical for a Hitchcock film. This is, of course, partly because the narratives of many of his films are actually organised around 'voyeuristic' situations. *Marnie* is no exception, and Mark's function as investigator of the enigma presented by Marnie is repeatedly condensed in the image by his gaze at her. Marnie is presented as a puzzle whose solution demands a close scrutiny, as she says to Mark: 'Stare – that's what you do' (see Mulvey, 'Visual pleasure and narrative cinema', 1975).

In this extract optical point-of-view

dominates the narration of a phase of an investigation. Classically, point-of-view functions to engage the spectator through identification with the look of a character. Here, however, identification is not simply with the character whose point-of-view dominates the sequence (Mark) but also, and perhaps more importantly, with the investigation which he is conducting. The solution to the enigma presented by Marnie is a necessary condition of narrative closure (←AUTHORSHIP: *Alfred Hitchcock*, p. 129).

River of No Return (USA 1954 *p.c* – 20th Century-Fox; *d* – Otto Preminger; sd col scope and standard 20). NB. The second half of this extract is in CinemaScope format)

This film is in CinemaScope, a widescreen format which pulled the traditional screen ratio of 1:1.33 out to 1:2.35. The Scope image is thus relatively wide in relation to its height. In *River of No Return*, as in other Scope films, a transformation in the shape of the screen image seems to have motivated an approach to composition, editing and narration rather different from that characteristic of the classic narrative system. In particular, long takes – often involving mobile framing – predominate, and in dialogue sequences two- and three-shots are much more common than shot/reverse-shots.

These variations on the classic narrative system have been hailed as conferring a greater 'realism' (in the Bazinian sense) upon the cinematic image (see Barr, 'CinemaScope before and after', 1974). So, for example, at the beginning of the second sequence of the →

Figs 10a, b, c

through taking on their implied point-of-view, the spectator identifies with the fictional world and its inhabitants, and so is drawn into the narration itself. Consequently, a resolution of the narrative in which all the ends are tied up is in certain ways pleasurable for the spectator.

Although classic narrative cinema moves towards the regulation of cinematic codes according to the requirements of a particular narrative structure, it is arguable that this objective can never be completely attained (see Guzzetti, 1975). Narrative and image in film are never entirely reducible to one another, if only because the demands of the classic narrative could in fact be met by a range of conventions of cinematic narration, of which the classic system is but one. Conventions, by their nature, are subject to change. Even if the classic narrative retains its dominance as a *structure*, its basic requirements could conceivably be met by *cinematic codes* different from those of classic cinema. And indeed, since the 1950s it appears that a rather wider range of cinematic codes has entered circulation in forms of cinema which still on the whole rely on a classic approach to narrative structure. This trend is exemplified by modes of narration characteristic of films on wide-screen formats (→*River of No Return*) and by the recent development of a New Hollywood cinema (→*Klute*).

Figs 10d, e

Figs 10f, g

References

Charles Barr, 'CinemaScope: before and after' in G. Mast and M. Cohen (eds.), *Film Theory and Criticism*, New York, Oxford University Press, 1974.

Roland Barthes, *The Pleasure of the Text*, New York, Hill and Wang, 1975; trans. Richard Miller.

David Bordwell and Kristin Thompson, *Film Art: An Introduction*, Reading, Massachusetts, Addison-Wesley, 1979.

Nick Browne, 'The spectator-in-the-text: the rhetoric of *Stagecoach*', *Film Quarterly* vol. 29 no. 2, 1975–76.

Noël Burch, *Theory of Film Practice*, London, Secker and Warburg, 1973.

Alfred Guzzetti, 'Narrative and the film image', *New Literary History* vol. 6 no. 2, 1975.

Laura Mulvey, 'Visual pleasure and narrative cinema', *Screen* vol. 16 no. 3, Autumn 1975.

Steve Neale, 'New Hollywood cinema', *Screen* vol 17 no. 2, Summer 1976.

Roland Barthes, 'Introduction to the structural analysis of narratives', in *Image-Music-Text*, London, Fontana, 1977; trans. Stephen Heath.

extract, several different sets of actions are dealt with in one single long take. Calder is in a store conversing with the storekeeper; he moves over to the window, picks up a rifle for Mark and exchanges some words with the boy. He then looks out of the window, moves forward and is joined from offscreen by the storekeeper; both men look out onto the street. Here the space of the store is established not by the classic method of giving an establishing shot and subsequent shots which break down the space, but through 'composition in width' and mobile framing. The extract as a whole may serve as demonstration of the potential which exists within the Institutional Mode of Representation for variation in the cinematic articulation of narratives which remain basically classical in structure (←AUTHORSHIP: '*Movie*' and mise en scène analysis, p. 151).

Klute (USA 1971 *p.c* – Warner Bros; *d* – Alan Pakula; sd col scope 24)

Klute is often regarded as an example of New Hollywood cinema, a recent variant of the classic narrative system in which a certain openness or ambiguity is admitted into the cinematic narration (see Neale, 'New Hollywood Cinema', 1976). *Klute* does in fact combine quite traditional elements of classic narrative cinema with a degree of openness which would certainly have been inadmissible in the classic era. The story takes off from the conventions of the classic 1940s film noir, in that it deals both with a mystery and the process of investigation which leads to the mystery's solution. The archetypal detective-hero is Klute, who falls in love with Bree, who herself becomes the object of the detective's enquiry.

The first part of the extract represents Bree both as a puzzle to be solved and as an object of the gaze. Klute's face is seen in close-up, silent, bearing a penetrating look, while Bree on the other hand is twice represented as object of the gaze of an unknown, and implicitly threatening, intruder. In the second part of the extract, the ambiguity of the narrative is foregrounded in a scene involving Bree and her therapist, in which Bree expresses some cynicism about her relationship with Klute. This is followed by an idyllic and romantic sequence with Bree and Klute together. Because Bree's cynical therapeutic voice-over continues into this second sequence, a degree of contradiction between sound and image becomes evident.

Alternative narrative systems

In classic cinema the organisation of the film image is subservient to the demands of the classic narrative structure. This structure calls forth certain modes of cinematic narration, which are then put into effect by the limited set of codes governing the Institutional Mode of Representation. Given this, any consideration of alternatives to classic narrative cinema demands a prior examination of the question of narrative structure. As outlined above, the defining features of classic narrative structure are:

1. Linearity of cause and effect within an overall trajectory of enigma-resolution.
2. A high degree of narrative closure.
3. A fictional world governed by spatial and temporal verisimilitude.
4. Centrality of the narrative agency of psychologically-rounded characters.

Classic narrative cinema tells stories structured in this manner through various codes of narration, some of them peculiar to cinema and others not. The foremost cinematically specific codes of classic narrative are editing according to the continuity system, in combination with a particular approach to the composition and framing of the image, and the construction of optical point-of-view (→ NARRATIVE AND STRUCTURALISM: *Point-of-view*, p. 244; *Suture*, p. 246).

At the same time, however, narrative and image constitute distinct levels of cinematic expression and so are not, in the final instance, reducible to one another; the possibility always exists of some degree of tension between them. Thus the cinematic codes characteristic of the IMR are by no means stable. On the contrary , the requirements of classic narrative structure could in fact be met by a range of cinematic codes. For example, films in the New Hollywood cinema category tend to retain a classic narrative structure, while at the same time mobilising cinematic codes rather different from those characteristic of classic narrative cinema.

But this begs the question of where classic narrative cinema ends and other systems of cinematic narrative begin, especially since departures from classic cinematic codes have become quite common in recent years, even within mainstream cinema. In considering this point, we might take up the distinction between narrative *structure* and its realisation through *cinematic codes*. A qualitative shift from dominant to alternative forms of narrative cinema may be said to take place when the underlying narrative structure no longer conforms to the classic model. A non-classic narrative structure might then operate according to an entirely different logic, and depart markedly from, or even overtly challenge, the dominant model.

Alternative narrative systems possess a number of structural features setting them apart from the classic system. Firstly, the narration of events in a story might not be organised according to any linear logic of cause and effect so, for example, a narrative may be interrupted at points by 'digressions' or appear to take unexpected turns. Secondly, narrative closure may be problematic or ambiguous; questions set up by a narrative might be left unanswered at the end of the story, say, or apparently significant matters 'left hanging'. Thirdly, a fictional world may be constructed according to principles other than those governing the impression of spatial and temporal verisimilitude so, for example, narrative action may seem to shift, without explanation or justification, between totally divergent places and/or times. Finally, a narrative may entirely lack human agency to move it along, or characters might appear contradictory or 'unconvincing', and in general not seem credible, psychologically-rounded individuals with whom it is possible to identify.

This approach to alternative narrative systems, by comparing them with the classic system, tends to define them in terms of what they are not. The outcome of this effectively negative definition is that the 'alternative' category becomes something of a miscellany, so that the range of available means of transgressing the classic narrative model becomes both wide and diverse. It is no surprise therefore to discover that there exists, alongside dominant forms of film narrative, a variety of alternative and even oppositional systems of cinematic narration. By definition these alternative systems tend to be something of a minority taste, certainly for cinema audiences in the West. But for various reasons many of them have taken quite prominent places in histories of cinema and/or in contemporary critical debates.

Three alternative approaches to film narrative will be considered here, each of which is distinct from the rest in terms both of its articulation of narrative structures and of the cinematic expression of those structures.

Art cinema

David Bordwell has argued that art cinema may be distinguished from classic cinema in terms of both its characteristic modes of production and consumption, and the formal features of the film texts themselves (Bordwell, 'Art cinema as a mode of film practice', 1979). In terms of its production, art cinema has generally been defined as a continental European, certainly a non-Anglophone phenomenon. It tends to offer itself, or is set up by film criticism, as a cinema of *auteurs*; directors are held to be creative individuals who stamp the marks of their personal genius on films bearing their names. Thus Bergman, Fellini, Truffaut, Antonioni and Dreyer, for example, are all characteristic art cinema directors.

European art cinema, according to Bordwell, also has its own institutional structures for the consumption of films, notably a distribution and exhibition circuit which is separate from that of dominant cinema and is supported by certain kinds of film criticism. Audiences usually see the films in special places – art house cinemas and film societies, in particular. This, among other things, ensures that such films are commonly approached with different expectations, and read differently, from more mainstream films. In general, audiences anticipate being challenged or 'made to think' by art cinema (←AUTHORSHIP: *Art cinema*, p. 116).

These institutional features are by no means unconnected with the formal traits of art cinema films. Bordwell points to a fundamental distinguishing mark of art cinema: its approach to narrative structure, in particular its tendency to eschew linear cause-effect relationships between narrative events. Rather, narratives are frequently motivated on the one hand by a realism of topic, setting or character, and on the other by an 'authorial expressivity' – a series of 'puzzling' or apparently unrelated events in the narrative may be understood or explained by reference to the artistic concerns of the director (← AUTHORSHIP: *Ingmar Bergman*, p. 116). Moreover, fictional characters in art cinema films often seem to lack 'defined desires and goals', and the relationship between character motivation and

Figs 11a, b, c

narrative events may not be immediately apparent. A looseness of causality may open up spaces for 'digressions' within the narrative, in the form, for example of expression by characters of their psychological states (as in Bergman and Antonioni), or perhaps of some commentary by characters on incidents in the story (as in early Godard) (←AUTHORSHIP: *Federico Fellini*, p. 118).

Art cinema may be marked, too, by violations of classic approaches to the construction of fictional time and space. Action may jump from one place to another with none of the conventional links of continuity, or time may appear to move backwards or even stand still. Generally speaking, though, the organisation of temporal and spatial relations in art cinema is not in fact completely unmotivated; simply that, rather than being motivated by a classic enigma-resolution trajectory,

it may be governed by subjective states, especially of characters. Here, instead of a verisimilitude of fictional time and space, a 'subjective verisimilitude' is constructed. The consequence of this is that in art cinema narrative closure is frequently problematic. A picaresque, fragmented, digressive, or loosely-structured narrative is conducive to open-endedness, or even ambiguity, in relation to either concrete events in the story and/or the story's ultimate resolution.

Art cinema may be quite diverse in its mobilisation of cinematic codes. An open-ended narrative can be cinematically constructed in a variety of ways. Fairly common in art cinema is a tendency to set aside editing conventions aimed at establishing the appearance of spatial continuity (through 'creative geography', say, or 'crossing the line') and of temporal continuity (through repetitions and 'stretch-

ing' time, by unpunctuated temporal ellipses, flashbacks or flashforwards). As Bordwell points out, some of these devices have in fact been taken up as formal devices in other types of cinema, New Hollywood cinema being a notable example of such appropriation. Consequently, in recent years there has been some convergence in outward appearance between art cinema films and mainstream films, principally because the latter has borrowed certain devices from the former (as, for example, in the films of Robert Altman). This would suggest that the relationship between these two types of cinema is undergoing a transformation. Whereas during the 1950s and 1960s the two types of cinema seemed to demand entirely different strategies of reading on the part of the spectator, this seems to be less true today (←AUTHORSHIP: *Art cinema*, p. 116)

Early Spring (Japan 1956 *p.c* – Shochiku/Ofuna; *d* – Yasujiro Ozu; sd b/w 10+12)

In the West, the Japanese film *Early Spring* has been assimilated institutionally into the canon of art cinema, and its Japanese director, Ozu, set up as an *auteur*. Although this is partly due to the 'differentness' of the cultural provenance of Ozu's films, the films do also exhibit many of the characteristic formal traits of art cinema (Bordwell, 1979).

Ozu's cinema is often noted for its rigorous infringements of classic codes of space and narrative logic. Spatial relationships are not primarily motivated, as they are in classic cinema, by a causal chain of narrative events. Thompson and Bordwell have suggested that the distinct character of spatial articulation in Ozu's films lies mainly in four areas (Thompson and Bordwell, 'Space and narrative in the films of Ozu', 1976).

1. *Intermediate spaces* Transitions within and between sequences are frequently marked by 'actionless spaces'. Transitions between sequences, furthermore, are repeatedly punctuated by bridging shots – of landscapes, for instance – which appear quite abstract, and are certainly not assimilable to the space of narrative action.
2. *360° shooting space* The construction of narrative space is predominantly through 360°, as opposed to the 180° space of the classic system.
3. *Hypersituated objects* As elements of *mise en scène*, objects in the pro-filmic space are repeatedly foregrounded to such an extent that they vie with narrative action for the spectator's attention.

4. *Graphic configurations* Transitions between shots are frequently governed by graphic matching rather than, say, matches on action.

An important consequence of this kind of organisation of space in films which retain a strong narrative thread is that the cinematic image is not in fact subordinated to the demands of the narrative, but retains a large degree of autonomy. Every scene in Extract 2 from *Early Spring* is constructed in 360° space. Thus in the first scene there is a virtual repetition of a figure composed of three shots: a two-shot of Sugi (the hero) screen left, and his manager screen right, lighting a cigatette; followed by a match on action (lighting cigarette), but from the other side of the 180° line, with the manager now screen left, facing right; followed by a medium close-up of Sugi, facing camera, taken from a 90° angle to shot 2, and therefore not a point-of-view shot *(figs. 12a, b, c)*. Despite the fact that the 180° rule, strictly adhered to in classic cinema, in no way governs the construction of *Early Spring*, the film is neither disorienting nor unreadable. The effect is rather that the fictional space of the film is brought forward in a peculiarly strong manner as an independent 'channel' alongside that of the narrative. In consequence, because the film image is never subordinated to the flow of the narrative, a relatively distanced relationship between text and spectator is perhaps rendered possible.

Ashes and Diamonds (Poland 1958 *p.c* – Kadr Unit, Film Adler; *d* – Andrzej Wajda; sd b/w 13)

The extract shows sequences from the beginning of the film. Maciek (Zbigniew Cybulski) shoots a man whom he has mistaken for Szczuka, a Communist

Party official. The incident represented is a reference to events which took place in Poland at the close of World War II and were centred in a struggle between two sets of forces: the nationalist partisans of the wartime Underground resistance movement, and the Polish Communists who were regarded by the partisans as outsiders installed by Moscow. None of this information comes through in the film's opening sequences, certainly to a spectator not versed in the history of Poland. The situation, in other words, is not laid out and explicated at the outset as it would be in a classic narrative film. While it is likely that a Polish audience armed with a prior historical knowledge would have little difficulty in understanding the initial situation, it is arguable that a degree of ambiguity nevertheless pervades the entire film, focusing on the main characters and the values they represent. Although Maciek and Szczuka are set up as adversaries, no thoroughgoing identification is made possible with either character, so that it is difficult to read the Communist/partisan struggle in black-and-white terms. The openness that results from this difficulty of identification with either main character, to the extent that it prevents spectators from being drawn into the action, arguably permits a relatively distanced, or at least reflective, attitude to the social and historical issues raised by the film, which may be said to be characteristic of art cinema in general.

It is perhaps worth noting, too, that *Ashes and Diamonds* was released in 1958, at a time when the formal gap between art cinema and mainstream Hollywood cinema was much wider than it seems today. In particular, character identification is quite frequently problematic in current →

Soviet cinema of the 1920s

A number of films made in the Soviet Union between around 1923 and 1930 have been written into cinema history as influential experiments in film language (←HISTORY: *Soviet cinema*, p. 34). In particular, the early films of S. M. Eisenstein have been taken up as innovations in a 'cinema of montage', a cinema in which particular meanings are produced through highly foregrounded, and often quite startling, juxtapositions of shots. The montage principle extends also to films by other Soviet directors, notably Dziga Vertov and Esfir Shub, whose work, however, differs somewhat from that of Eisenstein in operating within documentary rather than fictional narrative (←AUTHORSHIP: *S. M. Eisenstein*, p. 203; *Esfir Shub*, p. 206).

In montage cinema relationships between shots are governed mainly by compositional or graphic elements, or by rhythm and movement within shots, or by the 'tone' of shot content. In Eisenstein's system, a crucial objective of montage is to generate affect in the spectator (see Eisenstein, 'A dialectical approach to film form', 1949). Although all of Eisenstein's montage films are fictional narratives, the affective principle which underlies their editing is usually more important than any imperative to construct a coherent fictional space and time. Narrative flow, in other words, tends to be subordinated to film image.

The narrative opacity that results reinforces, though it comes about in part because of, the absence in Eisenstein's films of psychologically-rounded characters. None of Eisenstein's first three films (*Strike, Battleship Potemkin* and *October*) has an individual hero whose actions and motives form the pivot of the narrative. If there is any 'hero' in any of these films, it is the people, or the proletariat, as a group. Thus in their organisation these films depart from the classic model, not only as to the spatial and temporal relationships constructed, but also in the nature of character's agency. This does not result, however, in any lack of narrative closure, as might be the case for instance in art cinema. But while the questions posed by the narratives are set out very clearly and then dealt with and resolved without ambiguity, the actual process of narration does seem to demand a different relationship of spectator and text than that usually called forth by classic cinema (see Bordwell, 'The idea of montage in Soviet art and film', 1972).

In Soviet narrative cinema of this period there are 'alternative' systems of film narration which do not in fact operate according to the montage principle. These include the 'poetic' cinema made famous by Dovzhenko, and the eccentrism of the FEKS (Factory of the Eccentric Actor) and Lev Kuleshov. Poetic cinema is marked by a kind of plasticity of image which comes about partly through an artful composition of shots, but more particularly through shot-to-shot relationships governed by a play between on the one hand, spatial and temporal matching of the classic kind, and on the other infringement of the codes of verisimilitude of narrative space and/or time. For example, a distinguishing mark of poetic cinema is 'creative geography', in which a character's action is matched over two shots, while the setting in which the action takes place changes. In Soviet cinema, poetic strategies of this type may have the effect of 'foregrounding the device', making it difficult for the spectator to remain unaware of the process of cinematic narration. The exponents of eccentrism in cinema also aimed to foreground the narrative process, but by rather different means through, for example, highly stylised acting, gesture and make-up or a clearly 'artificial' *mise en scène* (Kuleshov's *The Adventures of Mr. West in the Land of the Bolsheviks* and the FEKS film *The Overcoat* are examples of this tendency. See Christie and Gillett, 1978).

Within their own historical context, montage cinema and poetic cinema are united by an intent to revolutionise both art and everyday life by bringing the two together. In this endeavour, many cultural workers of the period took their cue from the work on literary theory of the Formalists, adopting a deconstructive approach to the making and analysis of cultural products. In particular, the Formalists considered that the device of 'making-strange' *(ostranenie)*, by emphasising the artifice of the work, forced the reader to become aware of underlying assumptions which usually remained unquestioned in everyday life.

---

mainstream cinema in a way that it was not during the 1950s. Therefore the ambiguity of character and narrative that marks *Ashes and Diamonds*, even from today's vantage point, would certainly have been much more apparent when the film was first released.

Une Femme infidèle (France/Italy 1968 *p.c* – Les Films La Boetie (Paris)/Cinegai (Rome); *d* – Claude Chabrol; sd col 10)

Chabrol's films are renowned as *hommages* to the work of classic Hollywood director Alfred Hitchcock, to whom Chabrol explicitly acknowledges his debt. Chabrol's work, and critical accounts of it, highlight the extent to which art cinema has primarily been discussed as a cinema of *auteurs*.

In terms of their construction of narrative space and time, Chabrol's films in general, and *Une Femme infidèle* in particular, are narrated in a more-or-less classic manner. In this extract, a dinner scene with a tense exchange between husband and wife, done in shot/reverse-shot, is followed by a sequence in which the couple retires to bed, rendered in long takes with fluid mobile framing. However, although in Chabrol's work narratives are generally constructed basically according to the classic system, they do tend to be somewhat more 'open' in their trajectory than many mainstream films. For example, the extract includes, in the course of the couple's after-dinner conversation, a digression around a television set which appears to serve no cardinal function in the narrative.

Despite such minor variations on the classic model, the cinematic image in Chabrol's films generally works at the service of the narrative, so it may be argued that Chabrol's work is rather marginal in relation to the formal traits of art cinema outlined by Bordwell (1979). But these films are nonetheless still included in the category art cinema, which seems to indicate that art cinema institutions perform a vital function in determining which films are included in the canon (←AUTHORSHIP: *Art cinema*, p. 116).

SOVIET CINEMA

Battleship Potemkin (USSR 1925 *p.c* – Goskino; *d* – S. M. Eisenstein; st b/w 11)

The extract shows the famous 'Odessa steps sequence', constructed in this film as a pivotal moment in a fictionalised account of events which took place in Russia during the revolution of 1905. The film chronicles the progress of a single revolutionary action, the revolt of sailors aboard the cruiser Potemkin, its causes and its outcome. The story, then, is simple and unambiguous.

The Odessa steps sequence, which shows the massacre of citizens of Odessa who support the sailors, is commonly regarded as a *tour-de-force* of montage. For a full appreciation of how the montage operates, the sequence demands a shot-by-shot analysis (see Mayer, 1972). Overall, however, the impression given by the editing is one of constant movement. A sense of the chaos and confusion of the incident arises from a montage of shots showing movements (both of characters within shot and also of framing) in various screen directions. But within this overall movement, there are several   →

The General Line – more conventional cinematic narration

October – no individual heroes

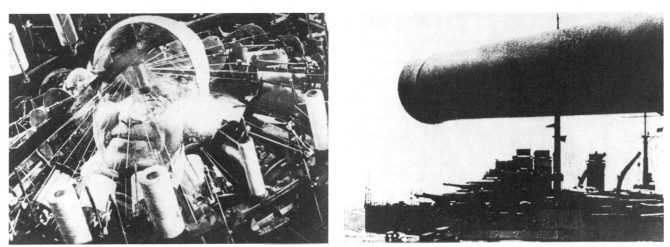

Man with a Movie Camera – Vertov's use of montage within documentary rather than the fictional narrative of Esfir Shub

'digressions' in the form of vignettes which serve both to halt the action and to emphasise the brutality of the soldiers. A nursemaid is shot in the belly and the child's pram rolls, unattended, down the steps. A small boy lying injured on the steps is carelessly trampled on in the soldiers' unremitting advance.

The specific relations of time set up in this sequence are very important for the film's narrative process. Basically, time is extended rather than elided. The incident is, as it were, stretched out and its various components, which may be inferred as taking place simultaneously in 'real time', are focused upon and opened up to contemplation. The centrality of the massacre within the film's overall narrative is underlined, and the maximum spectator affect generated.

The General Line (Old and New) (USSR 1929 *p.c* – Sovkino; *d* – S. M. Eisenstein/ G. V. Alexandrov; st b/w 12)

In this film Eisenstein's approach to cinematic narration appears to be rather more conventional than in his earlier films (e.g. *Battleship Potemkin*) because there is a central character and partly

because montage is not so evident. The extract, however, does include sequences in which montage remains an important component of the narrative process: the demonstration of the cream separator and the reaping competition.

The first sequence, which shows the heroine, Marfa Lapkina, demonstrating a new cream-separating machine to sceptical fellow-members of her agricultural co-operative, functions in part as a 'digression' from the main trajectory of the narrative. The beauty of the machine is dwelt upon, as are the sensual/erotic aspects of its operation. After an extended period of suspense during which narrative time is stretched by means of a series of cross cuts between Marfa, the machine and the onlookers, the whey begins to spurt out of the separator and several shots of jets of water are cut in. These function as metaphor rather than narrative, a process Eisenstein called *associational montage* (Eisenstein, 'A dialectical approach to film form', 1949, pp. 60–61). The montage in the reaping sequence operates in a similar manner in that the process of narration is again decelerated in order to privilege a moment in the narrative, which has the

double function of a lesson in the social and economic value of agricultural machinery and a reflection on the plastic qualities of the cinematic image.

Earth (USSR 1929/30 *p.c* – Ukrainfilm; *d* – Alexander Dovzhenko; st b/w 13)

The extract offers a demonstration of 'poetic' modes of organising relations of space and time in narrative film. Thus it includes several instances of creative geography; for example, at one point the father of the dead boy is transported between shots from his son's deathbed to a hilltop, while the spatial transition is bridged by a match on action. Here the verisimilitude of fictional space is opened to question by a foregrounding of the cinematic language used to articulate spatial relations. But at the same time the device is an economical way of effecting a spatial transition required by the narrative.

Later, there is a sequence of three identical shots showing the father sitting at a table grieving. Each of these fairly lengthy shots is punctuated by a slow fade out and in. Whereas in creative geography spatial coherence is broken, here it is the conventional articulation of narrative time which is infringed.

Counter-cinema

Counter-cinema may be defined as film practice which challenges dominant cinema, usually at the levels of both form and content. It sets out quite consciously to work against the conventions of classic narrative cinema and the relations between spectator and text proposed by its 'illusionism'. The anti-illusionist stance of counter-cinema is supported by an argument that the realism of classic narrative cinema is a mystification, that it deceives the spectator by obscuring the real relations of production of cinematic representations. Thus in order to break down this mystification, a transformation in cinema is demanded: one which calls not only for new contents for films but also for modes of cinematic representation entirely different from those of dominant cinema (←AUTHORSHIP: *Counter-cinema*, p. 192).

Counter-cinema, then, attempts a thoroughgoing subversion of all elements of the classic narrative system on a number of levels. These have been identified by Peter Wollen as follows:

Classic Cinema	Counter-cinema
Narrative transitivity	Narrative intransitivity
Identification	Estrangement
Transparency	Foregrounding
Single diegesis	Multiple diegesis
Closure	Aperture
Pleasure	Unpleasure
Fiction	Reality

This adds up to a cinema in which not only are linearity of causal relations between narrative events, narrative closure, spatial and temporal verisimilitude, and character identification eschewed by the process of film narration, they are also, in effect, negated (Wollen, 'Counter-cinema: *Vent d'est*', 1972). Although Wollen's dualities were drawn up in relation particularly to some of the films of Jean-Luc Godard, many or most of the characteristics he cites

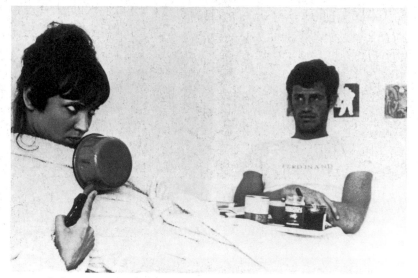

Pierrot le fou – the hybrid of art cinema and counter-cinema

also mark the work of other directors in the counter-cinema tradition, such as Jean-Marie Straub and Danièle Huillet. The strategies of audience address characteristic of counter-cinema have been dubbed 'Brechtian' on the grounds that they propose the critical and distanced attitude on the part of spectators which Brecht termed 'estrangement' *(Verfremdung)*.

The political objectives of counter-cinema may nevertheless sometimes be thwarted precisely by the difficulty of reading films which work so rigorously against conventional narrative codes, structures and modes of address. The line between estrangement as a kind of passionate and thinking detachment and estrangement as alienation in the worst sense is obviously thin. Because of this, it has often been suggested that counter-cinema demands a prior orientation of audiences towards an understanding of films that might, on unprepared viewing, seem hard to under-

stand. But at the same time, counter-cinema may be regarded as a matter of degree, with some films more transgressive of the classic model than others.

References

David Bordwell, 'Art cinema as a mode of film practice', *Film Criticism* vol. 4 no. 1, 1979.
David Bordwell, 'The idea of montage in Soviet art and film', *Cinema Journal* vol. 11 no. 2, 1972.
Ian Christie and John Gillett, *Futurism/Formalism/FEKS*, London, British Film Institute, 1978.
Sergei M. Eisenstein, 'A dialectical approach to film form', in *Film Form*, New York, Harcourt Brace, 1949.
David Mayer, *Sergei M. Eisenstein's Potemkin: a shot-by-shot Presentation*, New York, Grossman, 1972.
Kristin Thompson and David Bordwell, 'Space and narrative in the films of Ozu', *Screen* vol. 17 no. 2, Summer 1976, pp. 41–73.
Peter Wollen, 'Counter-cinema: *Vent d'est*', *Afterimage* no. 4, 1972.

Pierrot le fou (France/Italy 1965 *p.c* – Rome-Paris Films; *d* – Jean-Luc Godard; sd col scope 15)

Pierrot le fou may be regarded as a hybrid of art cinema and counter-cinema. Within Godard's *oeuvre*, it marks a move away from his New Wave period (←HISTORY: *French New Wave*, p. 40; AUTHORSHIP: *Jean-Luc Godard*, p. 134) towards a questioning as opposed to a celebration of cinema. In this film, the characteristically counter-cinematic moments are relatively few, and they are still readable, in the manner of art cinema, in terms of authorial expressivity.

However, the extract does incorporate elements which may, with hindsight, be regarded as embryonically counter-cinematic. These include numerous interruptions to the narrative in the form, for example, of shots of pulp novel covers and written intertitles/

extracts from Ferdinand's diary (narrative intransitivity), characters who are 'split', who comment on themselves and their own actions (estrangement), and direct address by characters to camera (foregrounding). The effect of these devices is to break the coherence of the film's fictional space, perhaps even implying some critique of the processes whereby, in classic narrative cinema, such coherence is constructed.

Tout va bien (France/Italy 1972 *p.c* – Anouchka Films/Vicco Films (Paris)/Empire Films (Rome); *d* – Jean-Luc Godard/Jean-Pierre Gorin; sd col 9+13)

This film, about a strike and occupation by workers at a food factory, is often regarded as a return to relatively conventional styles of cinematic narration, after a period of some four years during which Godard

and his associates experimented with increasingly rigorous approaches to counter-cinema (as, for example, in *Vent d'est*, 1969). If this is indeed so, it is nevertheless obvious that *Tout va bien* is not organised like any typical classic narrative film. For example, Extract 1 includes a sequence in which the factory building is shown in section, and twice revealed in its entirety by a slow and evenly-paced track right and then left. This emphasises, through *mise en scène*, the constructed nature of the film's fictional space, while simultaneously criticising the conventions of classic cinema in which mobile framing and tracking shots are given a payoff in the form of a narratively significant action. On the level of content, the constructed nature of the social relations of the factory is also highlighted.

Film Narrative and the Structuralist Controversy

Introduction

The impact of structuralist theory on film criticism during the 1970s was considerable, although to many sceptics and detractors the wholesale importation of French theories into British film culture was unwarranted, giving unjustifiable credence to new, untried disciplines because they were intellectually fashionable. Now that some of the dust has settled, it has become possible to reassess the influence of structuralism and semiology on film theory historically, testing the validity of arguments for and against.

Structuralism is a notoriously elusive and controversial concept. Anthologies and guides implicitly recognise this by beginning with an attempt to define the structuralist 'method' or 'activity'. Some definitions downplay its theoretical assumptions, or indeed suggest that the presence of such assumptions is detrimental to its credibility as a rigorous analytical approach. Other writers have disagreed, arguing that it 'was never conceived as an innocent science designed simply to provide a systematic analysis which is as inert as it is exhaustive. It requires a certain stance within history' (Coward and Ellis, 1977, p. 31). This latter premise informs the following discussion, which aims to point up the ideological implications of structuralist approaches to cinema in general, and the polemical edge of cinestructuralism in particular, not only as a critique of, and alternative practice to, the *auteur* method, but also as a radical reformulation of the process of cultural production.

Semiology: a general science of signs

The structuralist activity has been described in terms of two different, though related, modes of analysis. First, it may attempt to define the way in which the components of an art work or artefact derive their meaning from the culture within which this work is produced. This method originates in the *Course in General Linguistics*, a synthesis of students' notes taken from a series of lectures delivered by Ferdinand de Saussure at the University of Geneva between 1907 and 1911.

Saussure's work was based on a concept of language not as an instinctive or innate faculty but as a social institution, a 'language system' (*langue*) to which 'each single act of speech' (*parole*) has to conform. He argued that individual self-expression through language is neither spontaneous nor totally unrestricted, but that it takes place within a circumscribed network of linguistic conventions which could be seen as a contract signed by the members of a community, always eluding

the individual will (De George and De George, 1972, p. 66). Saussure went on to point out that in the case of a language system, the governing conventions are extremely arbitrary. There is no intrinsic relationship between a word (the 'signifier') and the concept, or idea which it designates (the 'signified') – a fact proved by differences among languages and by the very existence of different languages (De George and De George, 1972, p. 72).

Saussure speculated that his insights into the functioning of language might have a wider relevance beyond the specialised study of linguistic phenomena. Linguistics, he proposed, could become the prototype for a general science of signs, which he baptised 'semiology'. The linguistic system was, Saussure argued, peculiarly appropriate as a model for other sign systems because of the absence of any connection between signifier and signified. In many other sign systems (for instance, the rules of etiquette governing social behaviour) the connection, though in fact arbitrary, could easily appear to be self-evident. So by taking language as a paradigm, the semiologist could approach non-linguistic signs as also culturally determined, as the result of shared assumptions and conventions.

Structuralism: the rules of the system

Semiology, then, as formulated by Saussure, focuses on the relation between a signifier in a sign system and a signified in a culture. Structuralism, on the other hand, is concerned in early formulation with the interrelationship of the various signifiers within a sign system. It assumes that a signifier derives its meaning not only from its connection with the cultural signified, but also from its location within a sign system with its own internal logic. The aim of structural analysis is to reconstruct an object in such a way as to make clear the rules by which it functions. This enterprise may take the form of either the analysis of an already extant system (such as language or a cycle of myths) or the assemblage of a new system, for instance, a work of art. Thus artistic activity may also be seen as a variety of structuralism, in so far as both depend upon the reorganisation of raw material, which has in itself no inherent logic or sense, not in order to copy it, but to give it meaning. This analogy potentially allows for the demystification of notions of artistic creativity as a unique process separate from other forms of cultural production.

Semiology, structuralism and recent developments in film theory

Clearly, the two modes of analysis represented by semiology and structuralism are

closely connected. However, their concerns are in important respects not identical and recent developments in film theory can be seen to fall into two loosely defined groups depending on whether the issue of signification, the process whereby meaning is generated, is approached along the path of semiology, or that of structuralism.

The first path leads indirectly through the work of André Bazin via Jean Mitry to the early writings of Christian Metz. Its concerns derive from the semiological project of defining the relationship between signifier and signified – in the case of the cinema, between film image and that which it represents.

Though clearly akin to traditional debates within cinema aesthetics about film and reality, the semiological project differs in *starting out* from the belief that signifier and signified are not identical, and by addressing the question not of *whether* cinema is a purely mimetic art, faithfully recording the real world, but rather *how* and *why* it is able to create the illusion of doing so. How, for instance, is the impression of spatial depth constructed and sustained on a two-dimensional plane? Furthermore, why has cinema – with marginal exceptions in the avant-garde – remained committed to a realist aesthetic, and to producing with ever-increasing accuracy an image as close as possible to that perceived by the naked eye, when all the other arts have evolved a strong non-representational modernist tradition? Is this development inherent in the technology of photographic reproduction, and if not, what are the possible alternatives?

Attempts to find answers to these questions using semiological methods immediately encountered a major problem. The relation between signifier and signified, in the case of the sign system of the cinema, is evidently not, as in Saussure's linguistic model, a purely arbitrary one. An obvious resemblance and causal link exists between film image and object photographed.

Various solutions were proposed: adopting, for instance, C. S. Peirce's tripartite classification of signs, or distinguishing between the denotative and the connotative properties of the film image (→ *Metz*, p. 230). But the question remained of how to apply these categories with any degree of precision or indeed (a return to the old 'film and reality' disputes) how to establish the artifice which distinguishes the filmic signifier from its signified.

The difficulty led Metz, in an early essay, to conclude that the cinema lacked a Saussurian language system – a conclusion which appeared to block any attempt at a rigorous semiological analysis of film. Thus Metz proposed that critical examination should limit itself to the combination of images into sequences, in fact, to narrative (scc Stephen Heath, 'The work of Christian Metz', 1973) and Roland Barthes also suggested in an interview for *Cahiers du Cinéma* (1963) that 'for the moment the cinema appears to have chosen the . . . syntagmatic path, the syntagm being a . . . fragment of the narrative. This all seems to prove that there are possibilities of interchange between linguistics and the cinema provided we elect for a linguistics of the syntagm rather than a linguistics of the sign'.

This brings us to the second path traced by recent film theory – the structuralist study of narrative. Semiological analyses were directed at cinema as a specific means of expression, attempting to identify how film images function as a unique system of representation. By contrast, approaches to film narrative have frequently drawn upon research in other disciplines: Vladimir Propp's morphological analysis of Russian folk-tales for instance, the literary criticism of Roland Barthes or the work done by Claude Lévi-Strauss on North and South American myths. In doing so, some theorists have argued for the legitimacy of such comparisons on the grounds that there are certain universal narrative structures. But even for critics who do not accept this hypothesis, the analogies, particularly with the work of Propp and Lévi-Strauss on non-realist texts, can be instructive in suggesting how film narrative can be approached, despite its realist aesthetic, not as an authentic 'slice of life' but as a system with its own internal logic – a system which carefully sifts and organises its raw material in order to render it intelligible. The strengths of this method for understanding how film works and, more particularly, for exploring the central locus of the narrative cinema, Hollywood, will be discussed more fully below. But in order to appreciate its importance for film theory, it is necessary to consider the context within which it was adopted.

The historical background
The ascendancy of semiology and structuralism in French and British film criticism grew out of a growing dissatisfaction with the inadequacies of auteurism as a critical method. Indeed, the spate of work produced under the banner of *auteur*-structuralism strongly implies a period of overlap (← AUTHORSHIP: *Structuralism and auteur study*, p. 165).

In the pages of *Cahiers du Cinéma* a malaise about the continued viability of the *auteur* policy was apparent by the early 1960s. During this period the journal initiated a series of attempts to find alternatives to auteurism, exemplified by the interviews with Roland Barthes and Lévi-Strauss (no. 156, 1964), or the articles on methodology by Hoveyda (no. 126, 1961) and Comolli (no. 141, 1963). Besides the desire to find a more rigorous and theorised approach, there was a marked

La terra trema – the consummation of the neo-realist aesthetic

shift in the publication's attitude towards the Hollywood cinema. As a result of the successes of the French New Wave directors, the original polemical thrust of the *politique des auteurs* in playing off the vitality of Hollywood against the stagnation of the French film establishment began to appear redundant. In the course of the 1960s, *Cahiers* became more politicised, sharpening its critique of the ideological role of US culture, epitomised by Hollywood, in promoting American political influence abroad.

In Britain the intervention of structuralist theory into film studies took place in a rather different context. When *Screen*, the chief mediator of structuralism in this country, reorientated itself as a theoretical journal, it had a tentative programme: to go 'beyond subjective, taste-ridden criticism' and to try 'to develop more systematic approaches' (*Screen*, vol. 12, no. 1, 1971). From the outset, it saw itself as oppositional to two perceived forms of the British critical orthodoxy. First, the effusive, impressionistic, anti-intellectual writing of popular journalism (Barr, '*Straw Dogs, A Clockwork Orange* and the critics', 1971). Second, the more substantial critical tradition represented by the *Movie* group and, in particular, Robin Wood. *Movie*, which first appeared in 1962, pioneered the *auteur* approach in Britain and was instrumental in forcing a revaluation of the American cinema. Towards the end of the 1960s the basic premises behind this work were also beginning to be questioned, though for slightly different reasons than in France, and *Screen* provided a forum for the debates (← AUTHORSHIP: *British film criticism*, p. 165). Critics of *Movie*'s project conceded that the importance they placed on close attention to a text afforded the *Movie* writers valuable insights into its formal operations. But, partly because of their belief in the 'organic' unity of the work of art, a unity which was thought to defy dis-

section, and partly because it was thought that detailed textual analysis had wrongly been enshrined as a method in itself, the *Movie* position was felt by its critics to be under-theorised. Indeed, Wood strongly argued that theorisation was undesirable and that criticism should ideally be the articulation of a purely personal response. This argument raised the problem of the status of the critic. If the viewer-writer was enjoined to receptive and discriminating observation, was this a skill that could be acquired or was it an activity reserved for a receptive and discriminating élite? Moreover, the notion that the viewer should contemplate with a kind of hushed reverence the complete and self-contained art work, sensitively interpreting its inherent meaning, posited his or her role as the extremely passive one of receiving, consuming and (in the case of the critics) explaining a finished meaning already produced by somebody else.

Implications for film theory
In retrospect, the hopes voiced in some quarters that structuralism would magically transform film criticism into a discipline as accurate and systematic as the natural sciences seem unrealistic. Indeed they may well have been counterproductive, exposing the method to attacks that it overlooked the complexity and subtlety of the object of its attentions. However, few proponents of structuralism would claim that it can provide definitive or exhaustive accounts of an art work. In fact, one of Barthes' central postulates was that such definitive explanation is neither possible nor desirable. A text, he argued, 'is not a line of words releasing a single "theological" meaning (the "message" of the Author-God) but a multi-dimensional space in which a variety of writings, none of them original, blend and clash' (Barthes, 1977, p. 146). Confronted with such a text, the reader's task becomes that of production rather than of consumption: dismant-

ling and reassembling, literally 'rewriting' the text, in his or her own structuralist activity.

This recasting of the reader's role could be seen as a kind of liberation which aims at breaking down the division of labour between not only writer and reader but also reader and critic. To rewrite a text is seen as potentially inherent in the reading process, and not reserved for a professional élite. Moreover, by actively participating in the production of meaning, readers may begin to regard bodies of knowledge and beliefs as constructed rather than transcendental and to view themselves as the sites of these operations (→ *Narrative and audience*, p. 242). Such a redefinition of the critical activity unseats the author as the sole or even the primary source of meaning (a position which was already built into the work of Propp and Lévi-Strauss on cultural texts with no single identifiable author). The director-author becomes, in the structuralist view, not a great individual genius, but the *mediator* of many different voices, many different systems of cultural conventions, and the product, the art work, is regarded as a *text* which is no longer an organic whole but is able to accommodate contradiction: indeed, moments of paradox, opacity and resistance to interpretation are seen as a feature of the most interesting texts (→ *Barthes*, p. 238). The work of the reader is in part to focus upon those points at which meaning breaks down, rather than strenuously to attempt to account for every discrepancy in the cause of preserving the unity and consistency of the work of art.

A major achievement of the *auteur* method had been to force a reassessment of the commercial American cinema, previously dismissed out of hand by sociological critics. But with the growth of anti-American sentiment and of the suspicion that the *auteur* method had not paid sufficient attention to the political implications of the texts it celebrated, film writers found themselves once again threatened with the familiar impasse of left-wing criticism: the position which asserts that all art reflects the beliefs of the social system within which it is produced, and which is therefore forced to condemn Hollywood as the mirror of capitalist ideology. The structuralist mode of analysis, if properly negotiated, can open up a way out of this impasse. As the hypothesis of multiple and mutually incompatible voices within a text implies, many films may appear under scrutiny as not simply manipulative, but as embodying the contradictions of the culture from which they emerge, and may well include a subversive or critical discourse. This analysis sees the meaning of a text as generated out of the clash and counterpoint of diverse elements; and by positing that the whole is more than the sum of its parts holds out the possibility of investigating cultural production without lapsing into simple reductivism.

References
Charles Barr, '*Straw Dogs, A Clockwork Orange* and the critics', *Screen* vol. 13, no. 2, 1972.
Roland Barthes, Interview, *Cahiers du Cinéma* no. 147, 1963.
Roland Barthes, *Image-Music-Text*, London, Fontana, 1977; trans. Stephen Heath.
Rosalind Coward and John Ellis, *Language and Materialism*, London, Routledge and Kegan Paul, 1977.
Richard and Fernande De George (eds.), *The Structuralists from Marx to Lévi-Strauss*, New York, Doubleday Anchor, 1972.
Editorial, *Screen* vol. 12, no. 1, 1971.
Stephen Heath, 'The work of Christian Metz', *Screen* vol. 14, no. 3, Autumn 1973.

Bazin

Bazin's theory of film language
André Bazin's reputation rests upon a substantial body of film theory and criticism which shows him to have been a writer of impressive scope. His most influential work, however, was the essay entitled 'The evolution of the language of cinema' which revolutionised traditional thinking about the cinema to an extent perhaps difficult to appreciate in retrospect. Thomas Elsaesser has summarised the developments which preceded Bazin's intervention in contemporary film theory and which need to be taken into account in assessing its impact.

'In the 1920s the cinema, including the American cinema . . . enjoyed an enormous intellectual prestige, condensed in many a weighty volume on aesthetics and theory published during the decade. They unanimously hailed a new art which they assumed to have almost magical possibilities. . . The invention of sound at the end of the 1920s dashed this euphoria once and for all. Worried by the way the cinema was more forcefully developing in the direction of a realist-representational medium given over to narratives of dubious merit and originality, artists in the modernist vein came to regard the cinema as aesthetically reactionary, a throwback, in fact, to the nineteenth century. Film criticism throughout the 1930s did not recover from the blow' (Elsaesser, 'Two decades in another country', 1975, pp. 200–201).

Bazin wrote his article, then, at a moment when the artistic prestige of Hollywood had reached an all-time low, and it now seems clear that his work had a double polemical thrust. First, it aimed at rehabilitating certain products of the popular American cinema – an aspect of his thought which was to be seminal in the later authorship debates (← AUTHORSHIP: *The 'politique des auteurs'*, p. 119). Second, Bazin initiated a reassessment of the merits of the 'realist-representational' aesthetic which underpinned Hollywood's commitment to the narrative film.

Bazin's theory of film language rejected the conventional antithesis of silent versus sound cinema. In 'The evolution of the language of cinema' he proposed an alternative dichotomy based on two other 'fundamentally different conceptions of cinematographic expression' (Bazin, Vol. 1, 1958, p. 132) which both pre-dated and survived the coming of sound: 'directors who believe in the image and those who believe in reality'. The former favoured montage as a technique which allowed them to impose an interpretation on the events they portrayed. The effect of this, argued Bazin, was to *create* 'a meaning not objectively present in the images but derived purely from their juxtaposition'. This style was typified by the work of D. W. Griffith, Sergei Eisenstein and Alfred Hitchcock. The other kind of director, in contrast, would prefer long takes that preserved as far as possible the unity of time and space in order to *disengage* the 'deep structures' of reality and to *bring out* 'pre-existing relations'. Examples given by Bazin of practitioners of this approach included Erich von Stroheim, Jean Renoir and Orson Welles. Bazin made it clear that his sympathies lay with the latter method. The film image should, in his view, be evaluated 'according not to what it *adds* to reality but to what it *reveals* of it'.

The same ideas were elaborated, in even more emphatic terms, in another early essay on 'The ontology of the photographic image' (1945). Here, photography was praised as a 'process of mechanical reproduction from which man is excluded. . . All the other arts are based on the presence of man; only in photography do we take pleasure in his absence' (Bazin, Vol. 1, 1958, p. 15).

The anti-Bazin position
The philosophical premises behind Bazin's work have been traced back by John Hess to the tenets of Personalism which were espoused by a number of French Catholic intellectuals during the 1930s. Clearly, a connection can be seen between the Personalist ideals of spiritual fulfilment and an integrated, harmonious universe, and Bazin's call for an aesthetic which would preserve the continuity of experience.

Early criticism of Bazin, particularly that issuing from the left-wing film periodical *Positif*, objected to these moral and political assumptions and, more especially, to his failure to acknowledge their presence. His criterion of realism was a world portrayed as harmonious and unitary which was, it was pointed out, based on ideological premises just as much as the view of the world as discordant and contradictory that he rejected. More recent attacks on Bazin's work have, however, shifted the focus of attention away from his philosophy to its implications for his aesthetic and for his model of the interplay of style and meaning. His belief that the film image should ideally be the transparent mediator of a putative 'reality' with minimal human intervention has been attacked from the perspective of recent

Expressionistic devices and low camera angles in *Citizen Kane* – some of the trick effects condemned by Bazin

semiological theory. Bazin, it is held, denied that film is a culturally determined language system. For him, the relationship between signifier and signified in cinema was not arbitrary but intimate and existential. This hypothesis is evidenced in Bazin's celebrated analogies between the photograph and the death-mask or finger-print.

The signficance of Bazin's contribution

Bazin was, however, not only a theorist and aesthetician but also an exceptionally perceptive critic. His belief in the 'essence' of cinema as a natural, neutral process of registration did not prevent him from appreciating the signifying operations of individual films. That he could do so suggests the presence of interesting productive contradictions between his theoretical and critical work.

Opponents of Bazin have often dismissed as naively optimistic his belief that the cinema was evolving towards perfection (i.e. perfect mimesis). Certainly this strand in his writing could be seen as counter-productive in that it committed him to championing recent movements (Italian Neo-Realism and the development of deep-focus cinematography in Hollywood) as the culmination of film art. In this sense, Bazin's theoretical position was firmly enmeshed within history. Premature enthusiasm was perhaps under the circumstances almost inevitable and, looking back in 1958 on his article on William Wyler written ten years earlier, Bazin himself admitted that he had been rather too fulsome in his praise. His early death later that same year denied him the chance of revising the system in the light of the French New Wave and later anti-realist movements. Conversely, Bazin's receptiveness to recent trends bore fruitful results. It enabled him to break out of the stranglehold of the dogma, outlined by Elsaesser above, that film had gone into an irremediable decline since the advent of sound and to address the question of realism not as

a symptom of degeneracy but as a medium of expression within which it was possible to achieve the highest aesthetic excellence.

His insights into the construction of realism assure Bazin a place in the forefront of the semiological tradition in film analysis; his influence on Metz, for instance, is unmistakable. This may seem a provocative statement in view of his belief that the image should ideally produce an objective record of reality rather than the illusion of realism by means of a network of signs. However, and this is the nub of the contradiction in his thinking, he constantly stressed the actuality rather than the ideal. Perfect transparency was, he realised, precluded by the current limitations of film technology and might indeed never be possible. Consider his essay on photography, 'The ontology of the photographic image', which develops the carefully elaborated argument that it is an impartial, automatic process of registration but which ends with the rider: 'On the other hand, of course, cinema is also a language' (Bazin, Vol. 1, 1958). This contradiction is again found in one of Bazin's favourite images for the relation between film and reality: an *asymptote*, a curve which gradually approaches a straight line but which meets it only at infinity.

In his essay on Italian Neo-Realism, Bazin went as far as to claim that the need to enlist artifice to give the illusion of transparency generated a creative tension which was crucial to the work of art; true mimesis would result only in a flat and unheightened naturalism.

'We must beware of setting aesthetic refinement against a kind of crudeness, a kind of instant effectiveness of a realism satisfied just to show reality. Not the least of the merits of the Italian cinema will be, in my view, to have recalled once again that there is no "realism" in art which is not first and foremost profoundly "aesthetic" ... Realism in art can only be

achieved in one way – through artifice' (Bazin, 'Cinematic realism and the Italian school of the Liberation', Vol. 4, 1962, pp. 20–1.

Bazin's notion of realism was, then, rather more complex than is often admitted. Ideally he wanted the cinematographic image to have the status of an objective record: in actuality, though, he saw this as neither possible nor, in the last analysis, desirable. Positing that 'there is not one but several realisms' (Bazin, 'William Wyler, or the Jansenist of *mise en scène*', Vol. 1, 1958, p. 156), he set out to identify the very diverse methods by which these can be constructed. In doing so he opened up perspectives which were to become of central importance for film theorists.

References

Note: Quotations from Bazin in the text have been translated directly from:
André Bazin, *Qu'est-ce que le cinéma?* Vols. 1 and 4, Paris, Editions du Cerf, 1958 and 1962 (some of these articles have been translated by Hugh Gray, *What is Cinema?* Vols. 1 and 2, Berkeley, University of California Press, 1967 and 1971; 'William Wyler or the Jansenist of *mise en scène* is translated in Christopher Williams (ed.), *Realism and the Cinema*, London, Routledge and Kegan Paul/BFI, 1980, pp. 36–52).
André Bazin, *Orson Welles: a critical view*, London, Elm Tree Books, 1978; trans. Jonathan Rosenbaum.
Thomas Elsaesser, 'Two decades in another country', in Bigsby (ed.), *Superculture*, London, Paul Elek, 1975.
Gérard Gozlan, 'In praise of André Bazin', *Positif* no. 47, 1962 (trans. in part by Peter Graham in *The New Wave*, London, Secker and Warburg/BFI, 1968).
Brian Henderson, 'The long take', *Film Comment* vol. 7 no. 2, Summer 1971.
John Hess, 'World view as aesthetic', *Jump Cut* no. 1, June/July 1974.
Cesare Zavattini, 'A thesis on Neo-Realism' in Overby (ed.), *Springtime in Italy – a reader on Neo-Realism*, London, Talisman Books, 1978.

Citizen Kane (USA 1940 *p.c* – Mercury Productions/RKO; *d* – Orson Welles; sd b/w 25)

In his book on Orson Welles and the essay on the evolution of the language of cinema, Bazin cites this film as exemplary of the tendency towards the long take and staging in depth, techniques which, he believed, allowed the viewer to perceive the inner unity of events.

However, *Citizen Kane* manifests an abundance of the trick effects which are roundly condemned by Bazin in his article 'The virtues and limitations of montage'. Bazin acknowledges the presence of these elements in the film, but accounts for them as a counterpointing device to set off the sequences which employ long takes and deep-focus. Equally, however, it could be objected that in view of the profusion of other modes of representation, the long take could not be accurately described as the dominant feature of Welles's style.

Secondly, Bazin's opposition of the long take versus montage accounts for only one aspect of the film, suppressing the other myriad factors at work in producing meaning. For instance, although the scenes at the office of the *Inquirer* and in Xanadu are both in deep-focus, other elements such as, in the former case, specially constructed ceilings and low camera angles, convey an impression of cramped and old-fashioned accommodation and, together with the characterisation of the staff, a blinkered and traditionalist editorial policy. In the latter scene, vast rooms, high ceilings (often not visible), the towering statuary and mantelpiece which dwarf Kane and his wife, combined with the use of lighting and sound all build up an atmosphere of bleakness and solitude. Elements such as sound and music are usually ignored by Bazin, who concentrates on visual components.

Bazin's proposition that *Citizen Kane* gives viewers a sense of the ambiguity of reality, allowing them to perform their own interpretative activity, is also questionable. Whether ambiguity is an automatic function of staging in depth is in itself open to debate, but even if this premise is accepted, the lavish deployment of expressionistic devices in this extract creates a mood of portent rather than of openness and ambivalence. For example, lighting and camera positioning privilege Leland instead of Kane in the scene where the latter composes his 'declaration of principles'. Similarly, although staging in depth is used in the party scene, the cuts to Leland and placing in the foreground of his conversation with Bernstein amid the general revelry and euphoria again support his assertion that Kane will inevitably allow himself to be compromised. The weight given Leland's scepticism of these moments betrays a

fatality often seen by critics as characteristic of Welles's work – an element noted by Bazin who does not, however, find any incompatibility between this overwhelming sense of doom and what he describes as a liberal uncommitted *mise en scène*.

The Magnificent Ambersons (USA 1942 *p.c* – Mercury Productions/RKO; *d* – Orson Welles; sd b/w 12)

In discussing this film in terms of its 'luminous heterogeneous space', 'dramatic unity', and 'continuity of dramatic space', Bazin suppresses the dominant theme (much in evidence in this extract) of fragmentation and hostility. Certainly, much use is made of deep-focus (note, however, the crosscutting in the meal sequence to show the disintegration of the family gathering); but it creates not so much a 'heterogeneous space' as a battlefield where territories are demarcated, occupied, invaded and defended. A probing camera movement depicts George's incursion into Mrs. Johnson's home; Eugene Morgan is shut out behind a transparent glass door; the argument between George and Fanny, who prevents him from another intrusion, takes place on the staircase, a traditional locus in cinema of struggles for power and ascendancy.

What emerges is not Bazin's philanthropic vision of harmony but a critical portrait of social class and its patrician values of private ownership (cf. George's possessive attitude towards his mother) and property rights. It could therefore by argued that the meaning of a film should not be inferred from any one of its formal aspects considered in isolation (e.g. deep-focus), but is generated by the combination and organisation of a whole range of other signifying factors.

The Little Foxes (USA 1940–41 *p.c* – RKO-Goldwyn; *d* – William Wyler; sd b/w 15 + 20)

Bazin's article on Wyler describes him, curiously, as the 'Jansenist of *mise en scène*' probably referring to the virtues of self-discipline and asceticism advocated by this sect in opposition to the baroque indulgences of Jesuit doctrine and art. The title therefore appears to indicate a feature of Wyler's style but also contains an implicit value judgement since Jansenism is associated with two of France's greatest men of letters, Jean Racine and Blaise Pascal.

This double-edged significance is reflected in the argument itself; Wyler's is an 'intentionally self-effacing style' which aims at 'perfect neutrality and transparency', but he is, Bazin insisted, simultaneously an artist of the first order who, to achieve his purpose, makes

masterly use of a number of stylistic devices: the juxtaposition of two pieces of dramatic action which forces spectators to divide their attention between them; the employment of long focal length lenses (which Bazin contrasted with Welles's preference for distorting wide-angle lenses in *Citizen Kane*); the importance of the actors' looks as an index of the concealed under-currents crossing the screen; and a *mise en scène* that centres on the human figures and places them in tightly constructed geometrical formations to signify the tensions between them.

Obviously, this notion of a 'style without a style' seems incompatible with the presence of a distinctive touch in Wyler's work. However, Bazin was careful to stress that realism does not 'come naturally' but can only be created by careful planning and the deliberate adoption of aesthetic strategies that may cause considerable technical difficulties – for example, here the high lighting levels required by long focal length lenses. Moreover, these aesthetic strategies have not remained constant. Though, he believed, the striving for realism has existed in the cinema since its invention, each era developed its own methods and criteria of usage from Lumière's single-shot/fixed-camera technique through the invisible editing of the pre-war classics to Welles's and Wyler's sophisticated use of deep-focus.

Despite the labour which goes into producing the illusion of realism, it is essential, Bazin maintained, that the end result appear spontaneous and natural. Wyler's genius lay in his success in inventing a highly crafted style which nonetheless gave the impression of being 'style-less'.

How, if at all, can the notion of realism as an aesthetic *choice* be reconciled with Bazin's belief in neutrality? The effect, for instance, of the portrayal of Horace's death at the beginning of *The Little Foxes* extract requires a very idiosyncratic *mise en scène*. Deep space is used, but *not* deep-focus: thus Horace remains an indistinct blur as he dies in the far background of the image. The staging serves, as Bazin noted, to *conceal* the most significant event more properly than to reveal it. This casts doubt on his proposition that Wyler's is a transparent 'liberal and democratic' style which allows viewers to study the scene at their leisure, and could be used to argue that this is a distancing moment in the film since it causes a 'feeling of disquiet and almost the desire to push the immobile Bette Davis aside to see more clearly'. Another result is to confer upon Regina 'a privileged position of power in the dramatic geometry of space', to define her as the focus of interest (and perhaps sympathy?) at this point. Wyler uses immobile camera and severe *découpage* →

Exterior settings, non-professional actors and unscripted dialogue – *Paisà* – one of the first 'truly' neo-realist films

symbolically to reflect his theme of stasis and unnatural repression.

The Best Years of Our Lives (USA 1946 *p.c* – Goldwyn; *d* – William Wyler; sd b/w 20)

In 'The long take' Brian Henderson objects to what he sees as Bazin's false polarisation between the long take and montage styles. Only a very few film-makers work more or less exclusively with the sequence shot (a whole scene shot in a single take). Most 'long take' directors include some cuts within a scene and, because they are sparsely used, these cuts derive an exceptional signficance, often marking a shift of balance in the dramatic relations at stake.

In this extract the two cuts to Al in the bar scene (whose irruption into the long take Bazin tries to justify as a 'safety measure' in case the viewer forgets about Fred's phone call) could be seen as important punctuation marks, imposing tension and narrative development on an otherwise descriptive scene. This scene also illustrates the argument that Bazin's theory hinges solely on the visual properties of film and ignores the function of sound: the crux of the sequence lies precisely in the fact that we can see but not hear the decisive conversation. Arguably, the use of sound plays at least an equally instrumental role in creating tension as the composition of the image.

Paisà (Italy 1946 *p.c* – Organisation Films International/Foreign Film Productions (USA); *d* – Roberto Rossellini; sd b/w 20)

Paisà, made by Rossellini in 1946 following the international acclaim of *Rome, Open City*, was among the first films to be labelled neo-realist. For Bazin (writing in 1948) it was one of the most significant events in the history of the cinema since 1940 – the other was *Citizen Kane*. Both films, he believed, marked a 'decisive progress towards realism', though by very different routes. *Citizen*

Kane employed deep-focus and long takes in order to preserve continuity, but paradoxically had to sacrifice verisimilitude in other ways since the technical requirements of this shooting method virtually precluded the use of location shooting, natural light and non-professional actors. *Paisà* in contrast, incorporated all these features: unscripted dialogue, predominantly exterior settings and 'actors' recruited on the spot, as well as an unusual dramatic form. Instead of one self-contained narrative, the film consisted of six loosely-linked episodes, each set in a different part of Italy (moving from south to north with the Allied invasion) but sharing the common theme of the confrontation of people from different cultures thrown together by the fortunes of war.

In many respects *Paisà* therefore seems to respond to the demands of the non-realists (and of Bazin) for an unemphatic, contemplative style and a relaxed, open-ended narrative structure: the neo-realist movement was in part a reaction against the contrived and mannered melodramas and comedies, often called 'white telephone' films, popular during the Mussolini regime.

However, sequences such as the retrieval of the partisan's corpse and the parachute drop in the sixth and last episode depend heavily on suspense, reinforced in the former case by incidental music and extensive crosscutting between the groups of combatants. Though the events are, as Bazin points out, elliptically presented, they fall into a coherent pattern which hardly seems 'multiple and ambiguous'. Far from being undramatic or desultory the episode is orchestrated around a series of small climaxes that build up to a clearly-signalled conclusion.

In spite of certain broad resemblances in their use of narrative conventions, Bazin's conclusion that Welles and Rossellini share similar world-views and the same aesthetic conception of 'realism' seems quite extraordinary. *Paisà*'s

avoidance of star players, for instance, and its use of a *mise en scène* which focuses on the group rather than the individual, suggest an outlook and concerns that are very different from those of *The Magnificent Ambersons* or *Citizen Kane*. Bazin's claim suggests the weaknesses of his enduring belief that the form of a film is an invisible vehicle for, rather than itself constructing, a meaning.

La terra trema (Italy 1947 *p.c* – Universalia; *d* – Luchino Visconti; sd b/w 20)

La terra trema went even further than *Paisà* in paring down all dramatic residue and is often seen as the consummation of the neo-realist aesthetic. Note in this respect the preoccupation with social issues from a radical perspective (like several other film-makers of the period Visconti was concerned to expose the problems of the impoverished south, in this case Sicily); a cast which consists entirely of non-professional performers (fishermen recruited from the village where the story is set); dialogue improvised by the players along lines suggested by Visconti; the virtual avoidance of sound effects and music that are not motivated within the narrative world of the film; an extremely low-key scenario with minimal drama and suspense.

This extract is not subtitled, but apparently we are seeing it on the same terms as an Italian viewer since the fishermen speak a dialect that would not be understood even in other parts of Sicily: a laconic explanation and commentary are provided by a voice-over. It is interesting to consider whether, given, as Bazin noted, that the illusion of realism is the product of artifice, the converse also applies and the faithful observance of *verismo* (i.e. here the use of an esoteric dialect) has an estranging anti-realist effect.

In spite of its impeccably neo-realist approach and some images of remarkable

La strada – phenomenological realism

Umberto D – exploiting its melodramatic potential

beauty, *La terra trema* was a box-office disaster, and Bazin had to admit that the film which perhaps came the closest to his ideal ended up by thoroughly boring the public. He saw the reasons for this failure as lying partly in the exceptional length of the film (nearly three hours), but also, more crucially, in the total absence of drama, of 'emotional eloquence', which, he felt, was a 'wager which it might not be feasible to keep to, at least as far as the cinema is concerned'.

Umberto D (Italy 1951 *p.c* – Dear Films; *d* – Vittorio De Sica; sd b/w 10)

Umberto D reunited the team of Vittorio De Sica (director) and Cesare Zavattini (scriptwriter) who had previously worked together on *Sciuscià* and the highly successful *Bicycle Thieves*. According to Zavattini, who was perhaps the most celebrated propagandist and theorist of the neo-realist movement, the neo-realist approach to the cinema should renounce the relentless forward drive of the conventional narrative film in favour of a more leisurely pace which would savour every moment, however seemingly insignificant, for its own sake. Zavattini is often quoted as having wanted to make a film of a man to whom nothing happened. Yet his 'Thesis on Neo-Realism' indicates that he was aware of the risk of boredom involved in rejecting a strong narrative based on drama and suspense.

Umberto D clearly exploits the full melodramatic potential of a helpless old man and his dog. The joyful (and extremely coincidental) reunion of Umberto and his dog is underlined by incidental music, the chorus of barking which rises to a crescendo and a track in to Flike as he emerges from his van. The old man's acting performance at this point is also worth discussing, bearing in mind the neo-realists' belief that using non-professionals would increase authenticity. Note the use of editing in the begging sequence to suggest an

affectionate understanding between man and dog (a practice condemned by Bazin in 'The virtues and limitations of montage').

The powerful impetus of these sequences, deriving from the mythical theme of the *quest* (see also *Bicycle Thieves*) casts doubts on Zavattini's declared aim to defy narrative conventions. The events shown in the extract eventually lead to the man's despair and attempted suicide, so his life could not be said to be entirely devoid of incident! Bazin was aware that *Umberto D* deviated from the neo-realist model in a number of ways and his essays on De Sica have to argue long and hard in order to justify his approval of the aim behind the film. Though this work tried to give the impression of perfect spontaneity, it would, Bazin realised, be naive to accept it at face value: in striving to achieve the illusion of chance, De Sica employed meticulous planning.

As in the case of Wyler (see above) this contrived quality is explained away as a measure of expedience whose function is purely to sustain the drama (if the worker had found his bicycle in the middle of *Bicycle Thieves*, this would be the end of the film!). But it could be argued that these films' aura of inevitability blocks the neo-realist thrust towards penetrating social criticism, giving rise to a diffuse sentimentality and melodramatic fatalism.

La strada (Italy 1954 *p.c* – Ponti-De Laurentiis; *d* – Federico Fellini; sd b/w 9)

Though Fellini had been involved with the neo-realists, in particular as a scriptwriter and assistant director for Rossellini, he began making his own films (1950) just before the financial disaster of *Umberto D*, which was widely held to signal the end of the movement. Partly for tactical reasons connected with their struggle against the economic and political developments which were

stifling the new Italian cinema, Zavattini and his colleagues angrily condemned Fellini's work as betraying the ideals of Neo-Realism. Bazin's articles on these films were conceived as a riposte to their attacks and as an attempt to reintegrate Fellini within the movement.

Their dominant characteristic was seen as what Bazin called a *phenomenological realism*, by which he meant a *mise en scène* that observes and describes but without having recourse to explanation or interpretation. Phenomena do not function as the mediators of some higher meaning; instead, the relationship between meaning and appearance is reversed, so that appearance is constantly presented as a strange discovery, a 'quasi-documentary revelation'. Extended to the human figures, this approach breaks with the practice of affording privileged insight into their inner psychology. Gelsomina's unpredictable behaviour could be considered in this light (can it be 'explained' as feeble-mindedness?) and her clown make-up could perhaps be seen as a masking, distancing device.

The relatively traditional type of scenario used in Fellini's earlier films has, Bazin wrote, been discarded in *La strada* in favour of an amorphous series of chance events without any dramatic linkage; in his view, a revolution in narrative. Although this relaxed, contemplative *mise en scène* and meandering, almost picaresque plot structure appear compatible with Bazin's model of realism, it could be argued that these features lead precisely away from realism and towards Fellini's fascination with the inexplicable, bizarre and incongruous dimensions of experience.

Metz

Bazin's work on film language remained blocked by its inability to resolve the contradiction between film as record of reality and film as producer of meaning. The early writing of Christian Metz attempts to find a way around this contradiction whilst retaining certain basic tenets of Bazinian theory. Metz believed that the cinema should be regarded not as an automatic, 'objective' process of registration, but as a language: a means of communication which organises and encodes its raw material in accordance with a set of cultural conventions. He hoped to discover the rules that governed film language and to lay the groundwork for a semiotics of the cinema: a theory and taxonomy of film as a sign system. In doing so, he addressed two problems: that of determining where the artifice which qualifies the cinema as a language can be found; and that of distinguishing those features common to all films on which a systematic classification might be based. The answers he came up with were highly controversial.

The cinema: 'langue' or 'langage'?

This question, which forms the title of one of Metz's longest early essays, distinguishes between the two French words *langue* and *langage* (Metz, 1974). Although both terms can be translated into English as 'language', they designate slightly different concepts. *Langue* is spoken and written language in the restricted linguistic sense. *Langage* is a broader, generic term meaning any system of signs used for communication, including systems that may lack either the rigour (such as the language of flowers) or the subtlety (the language of computers) of *langue* proper. To see cinema as *langage* is relatively uncontroversial and even commonplace: Bazin, for example, had no doubt that cinema was *langage* (← p. 224). But to assimilate cinema to *langue* is more problematic. In addressing the question of whether cinema could be held to possess attributes analogous to verbal language, Metz applied criteria drawn from the work of the structural linguist André Martinet. According to Martinet, language (*langue*) is distinguished from less systematic communicative modes by what he called its 'double articulation'. Any linguistic utterance can be analysed first into smaller individually meaningful components, known as *morphemes* or *monemes*, and secondly into the distinctive but not in themselves meaningful *phonemes* which each moneme or morpheme contains. Thus the utterance 'I like Ike' contains three monemes, and these monemes, as it happens, between them require the use of only three phonemes. The number of phonemes in a language is strictly limited (most natural languages have about 30 to 40) but because of the way language is articulated they can be used to generate an infinite number of possible utterances.

What makes the second articulation possible (and to some extent the first as well) is the arbitrary nature of the linguistic sign, the absence of a natural or analogical relationship between an object and the sign that stands for it. The cinema, however, is founded on the photographic resemblance between image and object. Whereas a new sentence in language is simply a new combination of a finite number of reusable elements, each new film image is, strictly speaking, unique. It is also the case, Metz observed, that the cinema cannot be broken down into units smaller than the shot, and each shot is at least equivalent, in semantic content, to a sentence in language.

Metz concluded that there was no equivalent in the cinema of Martinet's second articulation (that between moneme and phoneme) and that even the first articulation (that between the utterance as a whole and its successive components) existed only as the level of the relations between large signifying units. Cinema therefore did not qualify as a *langue*, but it was a *langage*; more precisely it was a *langage*

fice which qualifies the cinema as a language. This was seen as residing in the organisation of images into a narrative structure. Reality itself 'does not tell stories' – film can thus be considered as *langage* to the extent that it imposes a narrative logic upon the events it portrays. The *grande syntagmatique* aimed, then, to identify and classify the segments of narrative, the autonomous shot and seven kinds of longer sequences called *syntagmas*, which, articulated together, produce the temporal and spatial variations which 'tell the story' of the film. Metz broke these down according to a simple taxonomy of binary oppositions which, he hoped, would be exhaustive (see Metz, 1974, pp. 119–146). He believed that by charting the frequency of the various syntagmas in different films, it would be possible to describe their style with greater precision than before and to pinpoint changes in film language over an historical period.

Criticisms of Metz

The *grande syntagmatique* has been attacked on a number of counts. Although

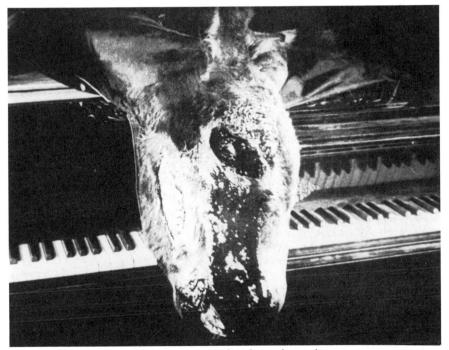

Un Chien Andalou – surrealist disruptions of traditional causality

d'art, an expressive mode adapted to the communication of one-way messages. The fact that cinema was merely a loosely structured *langage* did not mean that there was no scope for semiological analysis on the linguistic model, but it did imply, Metz considered, that any such analysis could most usefully be conducted at the level of what he called the *grande syntagmatique*, the articulation of successions of shots into meaningful sequence.

The 'grande syntagmatique'

It was in the elaboration of the notion of the *grande syntagmatique* that Metz found a reply to his first question about the arti-

the syntagmas appear to be clearly defined, in practice they are difficult to identify. The analyst is often confronted with a segment that either could fall into more than one of Metz's categories or does not seem to belong to any of them. Jack Daniel (1976) argues that a comparison of the successive versions of the system reveals it to be based on 'current observations' and that the impressive-looking diagram of 'successive dichotomies' is an unsuccessful attempt to impose a rigorous theoretical structure upon a random list of categories. The difficulties encountered by attempts to put the *grande syntagmatique* into practice lend weight to this objection. Moreover,

as suggested by the title 'grande syntagmatique of the image track', the breakdown into syntagmas is dictated by the
visual component of film. Difficulties arise
where there is asynchronous or overlapping sound which does not match the division of images. The analysis of *Citizen
Kane* (*Film Reader* 1, 1975) found this to
be a major drawback.

But some critics of Metz have made
more fundamental objections. Although
arguing for the importance of a structural
analysis of narrative, Metz ultimately begged the crucial question of how to
demarcate his field of study. In 'Notes
towards a phenomenology of the narrative' (1966), he explicitly discounted
formal or theoretical models of narrative
such as those of Greimas, Propp, Lévi-
Strauss or Barthes (→ p. 238) in favour of
a purely empirical definition based on
what 'even the naive consumer clearly
recognises' (Metz, 1974, p. 16). Narrative,
he concluded, 'represents one of the great
anthropological forms of perception'
(Metz, 1974, p. 28).

This definition was given a more
theoretical foundation in two articles written during the same period, 'Some points
in the semiotics of the cinema' and 'Problems of denotation in the fiction film'.
Again drawing on the work of a linguist,
this time Louis Hjelmslev, Metz distinguished between two levels of meaning in
a system of communication, *denotation*
and *connotation*. Denotation, in the
cinema, is the literal meaning of the spectacle; connotation encompasses all its
allusive, symbolic meanings (Metz, 1974,
p. 96). The artistic status of the cinema
resides in its connotative qualities, but it
is, Metz argued, through the procedures of
denotation that the cinema is *langage*. He
hoped that eventually the semiotic model
could be refined sufficiently to analyse both
these strata and their interplay in producing meaning. Meanwhile however it
should confine itself in the first instance to
the denotative level.

Critics found this theory of narrative
deficient because, despite his qualifications, narrative for the early Metz is what
we perceive it to be. His model thus
deliberately remains on the overt level at
which the film 'tells its story', excluding
visual subtleties such as 'framing, camera
movements and light "effects"' which he
saw as belonging to the realm of connotation. The classical *mise en scène* analysis
(← AUTHORSHIP: '*Movie* and *mise en
scène* analysis', p. 151) which examines
whether the story is underlined or (on
occasions) undermined by connotative
visual strategies is absent from the Metzian
system. It also excludes the possibility of
multiple levels of narrative signification,
where the deceptively calm surface of the
film may conceal all kinds of undercurrents
of repressed meanings (→ *Lévi-Strauss*
p. 232 and *Narrative and audience* p. 242).
Finally, it excludes a theory of the interaction between film and viewer. It is the

Adieu Philippine – a documentary on modern youth

viewer, according to Metz's 'Notes
towards a phenomenology of the narrative', who perceives, recognises, defines
narrative; on the contrary, argues more
recent theory, it is the narrative which in
part defines the viewer (→ *Narrative and
audience* p. 242). As critics have also pointed out, the *grande syntagmatique* is
designed for a specific type of film which
could be broadly described as realist. Since
each syntagma is defined by its logical,
temporal and/or spatial relationship to the
preceding and following one, Metz's
system presupposes that the film creates a
consistent, self-enclosed fictional world.
There is no provision for anti-realist juxtapositions of contradictory points of view
(e.g. *Tout va bien*) or surrealist disruptions of traditional causality (e.g. *Un
Chien Andalou*).

This bias was no accident. In Metz's
view, the evolution of film language went
hand in hand with the rise to ascendancy
of the realist narrative film. 'It so happens
that these (specifically cinematographic)
procedures were perfected in the wake of
the narrative endeavour ... It was in a
single movement that the cinema became
narrative and took over some of the
attributes of language' (Metz, 1974,
pp. 95–96). Thus Metz found a solution
for his second initial problem. The feature
common to all films and on which an
exhaustive classification could be based is,
he posited, *narrative* – indeed, narrative
and cinema are identified as one and the
same. In his essay on 'The modern cinema
and narrativity' (1966) he maintained that
even the apparently anti-narrative films of
the French New Wave could be assimilated
into the narrative tradition. The 'other
avant-garde' which, rather than experimenting with new modes of representation, works towards an abstract, non-
representational aesthetic, was given short

shrift by Metz, who deplored its 'gratuitous and anarchic images' and 'heterogeneous percussions' (Metz, 1974, p. 225).

Metz here echoed Bazin's belief in the
progressive improvement and refinement
of film language. But as critics argued, such
a system, while purporting to be comprehensive, can only account for a certain type
of film. And later debates within British
film criticism on the 'classic realist text' (→
Narrative and audience p. 243) questioned
the *endorsement* implicit in Metz's early
work of the direction in which the cinema
has developed. How true, it has been
asked, is that alleged inevitability of the
narrative film, the 'it-so-happens' which
underpins Metz's early argument?
Further, should an analytical model which
presents itself as neutral and descriptive
rather than prescriptive, support the domination of a single aesthetic, which, moreover, has been claimed in the course of
these debates to have a regressive, repressive ideological function?

Why read Metz?

In spite of the many problems posed by the
grande syntagmatique it remains an
important landmark in the history of film
theory. Devised (in 1966–67) at a moment
when a need was felt for an alternative to
auteurism (← *Introduction* p. 222) it initiated a series of attempts to find a rigorous
methodology for dissecting films. Whatever its defects, it was the first and arguably to date the only major classification
of narrative designed specifically for the
cinema, whereas the other structural
analyses discussed in this section were all
conceived originally for other narrative
media (myths, folktales, novels) and cannot be applied straightforwardly to film.

Metz himself has long since abandoned
the position taken up in these early essays.
His desire to revise the *grande syntag-*

matique was already evident in the copious errata and addenda sprinkled throughout the article when it was republished in *Essais sur la Signification au cinéma* in 1968. Like many of his contemporaries, he regarded his research as work in progress rather than as a closed-off, definitive system.

Bearing this in mind, it seems productive to approach the *Essais sur la Signification au cinéma* as a *heuristic* device, an aid to learning. In practical terms, applying the *grande syntagmatique* to individual films can point out their irregu-larities, ambiguities and unusual features. In theoretical terms, discussion of the basic premises of Metz's early work can promote awareness of the difficulties and advantages of attempting to construct a semiotics of the cinema.

References

Andrew Britton, 'Living historically', *Framework* no. 3, Spring 1976.
'Citizen Kane' (collective test) in *Film Reader* 1, 1975.
Jack Daniel, 'Metz's *grande syntagmatique*: summary and critique', *Film Form* vol. 1 no. 1, Spring 1976.
Steve Fagin, 'Introduction to syntagmatic analysis of *Citizen Kane*', *Film Reader* 1, 1975.
Colin MacCabe, *Godard: Images, Sounds, Politics*, BFI Cinema series, London, Macmillan, 1980.
Christian Metz, *Film Language*, New York, Oxford University Press, 1974; trans. Michael Taylor.
Screen vol. 14 no. 1/2, Spring/Summer 1973. Special double issue on cinema semiotics and the work of Christian Metz.
Kristin Thompson, 'Sawing through the bough', *Wide Angle* vol. 1 no. 3, 1976.
Nicole Zand, 'Le Dossier Philippine', *Cahiers du Cinéma* 148, 1963.

Adieu Philippine (France/Italy 1960–61 p.c – Unitec France/Alpha-Productions/Rome-Paris Films/Euro-International Films; d – Jacques Rozier; sd b/w 12)

The first attempts to develop a cinema semiotics operated on a general, theoretical level and seemed to exclude the detailed examination of individual texts. For this reason, the only example in Metz's first book of the structural analysis of a specific film occupies a unique place both within the evolution of his thought and within the history of cinema semiotics as a whole. Though aware that this work was then (1967) still very much in its infancy, Metz believed that the part of his programme concerned with narrative was 'sufficiently far advanced to be applied to the image track of an entire film' and that it was possible to make a 'complete inventory' (Metz's italics) using the eight basic categories outlined in the *grande syntagmatique* (Metz, 1974, p. 177).

For the early Metz narrative realism was the essence of the cinema, and even the apparent innovations of the French New Wave were for him no exception, despite some self-acknowledged difficulties with Godard's *Pierrot le fou* (Metz, 1974, pp. 217–9). *Adieu Philippine*, chosen, it seems, largely for reasons of personal taste and the availability of a shooting script and print, is described as a 'realist' film which presents few problems to a syntagmatic analysis. However, closer inspection reveals a number of points of resistance at which the film strains against the categories imposed on it by the *grande syntagmatique*. For example, the first syntagma is demarcated from the second by nothing more than Metz's imperial definition of the 'real action' of the film as 'individualised characters pursuing a definite goal' (Metz, 1974, p. 150) – a definition which is by no means self-evident. Similarly, the autonomous shot (syntagma 4) of Michel sitting idle in the television studio is identified as a directorial comment on the action ('this interpolative status . . . is "real" and not subjective') and thus defined as a 'displaced diegetic insert' (Metz, 1974,

p. 153). But the shot *could* be a subjective insert, representing the thoughts of either Michel (a three-quarter profile shot of him precedes it) or the two girls (a shot of them succeeds it).

Apparently a minor quibble, this illustrates a significant feature of Metz's analysis: the way in which he endows a sequence with a meaning which is deliberately held in abeyance by the film itself. The *grande syntagmatique* attempts to assimilate *Adieu Philippine* to the realist narrative tradition at the expense of contradictions which can be found in Rozier's film and also, perhaps, in even the most 'classical' conventional text.

Metz saw the film as primarily a documentary on modern youth. But Rozier's initial idea was to trace the history of a young man conscripted to fight in Algeria (1960–62 was, of course, the period of the Franco-Algerian war) and to show the 'disturbed side of his character'. Public pressures against such references to the Algerian question (witness the banning of Godard's 1960 film *Le Petit soldat* by the French Censor Board and the Minister of Information), dictated that the serious theme be masked by employing the structure of a musical comedy romance (see Nicole Zand, 'Le Dossier Philippine', 1963). A reading of *Adieu Philippine* which aims to pull out this political strand would need to point to the fact that Michel's departure for Algeria overarches the narrative (he discloses at the airfield that he is to be called up in a couple of months, and the film ends as he leaves for the army), as well as to the characters' growing malaise (is it only due to romantic rivalry?) and the eloquent silences: note (in the airfield sequence) Michel's poignantly unanswered questions to the girls reading his palm about where his imminent 'long journey' will take him ('où ça?', not translated in the subtitles) and what his life-line reveals. Metz's analysis, in contrast, collapses this scene together with the two preceding episodes, 'for alone they are treated too allusively for them to acquire any

autonomy', under the general rubric of 'Sunday outing' (Metz, 1974, p. 153). The effect is to privilege an account of the film as a documentary about 'youth and its flirtations' at the expense of the other meanings (for instance, the shadow of Algeria) which are struggling to emerge and are just as crucial as the things which are overtly said.

The point here is not to impose a 'more correct' reading, but to show that Metz's apparently objective, unimpeachable analysis and the conclusions he draws from it about the work's thematic concerns are the result of a series of *choices* which remain unacknowledged (probably even unconscious), laying early structural analyses such as this open to charges of presenting ideologically loaded readings in the guise of impartial science. Rather than passively discerning and describing *the* immanent and 'true' meaning, it is objected, critical inquiry actively produces *a* meaning in a process of interaction with the artistic text, and should therefore openly discuss, reflect upon and, if necessary, even call into question its own operations.

Tout va bien (France/Italy 1972 p.c – Anouchka Films/Vicco Films (Paris)/Empire Films (Rome); d – Jean-Luc Godard/Jean-Pierre Gorin; sd col 9+13)

Tout va bien represents an attempt by Godard/Gorin to develop an alternative strategy of political film-making that would be more accessible than the resolutely anti-narrative Maoist 'Dziga Vertov' films such as *Vent d'est* (1970). The decision to appropriate elements of 'mainstream' cinema such as international stars (Jane Fonda, Yves Montand) and a clearly-defined story (preferably with love interest) was in some respects a major compromise dictated by the dissolution of a militant audience in the aftermath of May '68 (see MacCabe, 1980, pp. 66–67). The film's ironic opening and closing sequences (not included in extracts) lay out the concessions enforced by the need to make the film commercially attractive, and the movie concludes with

→

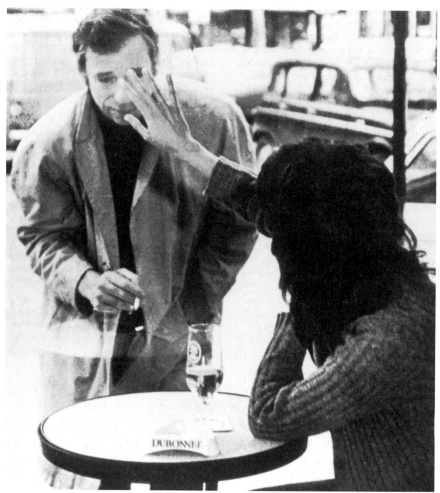

Tout va bien – 'a tale for the foolish one who still needs it'

a caption 'a tale for the foolish one who still needs it', which seems to question the indispensability of narrative.

Tout va bien is on one level a film about the conditions of political film-making and aims to problematise the sections in which the narrative is centred on the intellectual, middle-class couple. But Andrew Britton (1976) succeeds, by downplaying the importance of the framing sequences, in producing a reading that runs directly counter to the director's intentions. Britton sees the main concerns of the film as played out in the confrontation between Susan/ Fonda and Jacques/Montand, which focuses on the psychological development of 'two human individuals', the crisis in their personal relationship and their progress towards greater political consciousness (see also MacCabe, 1980, pp. 70–73).

This is where the value of a syntagmatic analysis comes in. The discipline of analysis foregrounds the fact that the central sections dealing with Susan, Jacques and the strike cannot be detached, as in Britton's account, from the overall structure of the film. Meanwhile, the difficulty of

demarcating and defining syntagmas brings out the extent to which the film deviates from the conventions of classical narrative (see Thompson, 1976). More particularly it demonstrates the way in which the film disrupts the traditional alignments of sound and image, appearance and reality – alignments which are assumed by Metz's *grande syntagmatique*. Note the overlapping sound combined with visual discontinuity between the penultimate and last syntagmas of extract I; or the indeterminate status of the 'radical song' in extract II, which could be classed as non-diegetic, but is allowed equal status with the framing interview sequences by Thompson, who sees the two stances taken up by the worker (submission and defiance) as two 'alternatives cut in together', neither of which is privileged as 'reality'.

Analysis of the film using Metz's categories can, therefore, be used to open up two sets of questions: firstly, to debate whether the use of narrative compromises the film or whether the text successfully resists being absorbed into the realist narrative tradition; and secondly, to reflect upon the usefulness of the *grande syntagmatique* itself.

Lévi-Strauss

The research of the French anthropologist Claude Lévi-Strauss into the myths of primitive North and South American tribal cultures was among the first structural analyses of narrative to attract the attention of British film critics. His influence can already be seen in some writing towards the end of the 1960s, preceding Metz who, though discussed at length in Peter Wollen's *Signs and Meaning in the Cinema* (1969 and 1972), had a necessarily limited impact until 1973–4 which saw the first English translation of *Essais sur la Signification au cinéma* and the *Screen* special issue on Metz and cinema semiotics (← *Metz* References p. 231).

The precise extent of Lévi-Strauss's contribution to recent film theory is difficult to assess. Often, partial and eclectic use (what Lévi-Strauss himself would call 'bricolage') is made of his concepts or methodology without explicitly citing his work. Moreover, because he has 'aroused excitement among many different brands of intellectual' (Leach, 1974, pp. 8–9), his ideas have also percolated into film culture indirectly through other disciplines. The picture is blurred still further by the somewhat confusing association of his name with some British *auteur*-structuralist criticism (→ p. 233 and AUTHORSHIP: *Structuralism and auteur study*, p. 179). However, despite these complications (or perhaps precisely because of them) it can be instructive to examine the work of Lévi-Strauss on myth in conjunction with other approaches to narrative. He shares common ground with a number of theorists: he drew on the work of Saussure and Propp, with which his own research is sometimes compared (see below *Propp* p. 234) and has in turn informed the writing of many of his contemporaries – Barthes for instance.

The structural study of myth

The project of much of Lévi-Strauss's work is to discover a hidden logic behind the apparently fantastic, inexplicable myths of primitive peoples. At first sight these myths appear rambling and arbitrary, and their surface themes seem to have little in common with the subject matter of contemporary Western narratives. Yet, Lévi-Strauss believed, they are driven by an internal dynamic equally powerful and consistent, and, at a deeper level, their concerns are not dissimilar to those of our culture. The bizarre dramatis personae of myth, which may bring together plants, animals, gods and/or human figures, function as symbols of the tribal sub-groups and the power relations between them; similarly, the narrative events illustrate tribal beliefs and taboos. The transformation of everyday experience into myth exemplifies, Lévi-Strauss argued, the universal and uniquely human faculty for symbolic interpretation (see Leach, 1974, Ch. 3 passim).

In this respect, myths are like language systems, operating according to a set of codes and conventions which, though not immediately obvious, are nonetheless present. As in Saussure's model of language (← *Introduction*, p. 222), each individual utterance (*parole*), in this case each single version of a myth, conforms to the overall symbolic system (*langue*), the language or group of myths and all the rules that govern its permutations. Just as language is the common feature of a linguistic family, binding its members together, so is myth; just as learning the language of its peers represents for the infant a process of integration into the social group, so are 'the novices of the society who hear the myths for the first time . . . being indoctrinated by the bearers of tradition' (Leach, 1974, p. 59). In order to understand these myths, it is necessary to learn the grammar of their language. By comparing a number of different versions, recurrent motifs should emerge from which, according to Lévi-Strauss, the underlying logical system and thence the meaning of the myths themselves could be inferred.

In attempting to disengage this meaning, he started from a major hypothesis about the social function of myths, namely that they 'express unconscious wishes which are somehow inconsistent with conscious experience . . . The hidden message is concerned with the resolution of unwelcome contradictions' (Leach, 1974, pp. 57–58). The embellishments, digressions and repetitions of the narrative all help to disguise these; conversely, the aim of a structural analysis should be to strip away the camouflage and to lay them bare. Here again, Lévi-Strauss insisted on the importance of juxtaposing as many variants as could be discovered. If we assume that the purpose of myth is to embody contradictions whilst repressing them from its surface, it is only by attending to their compulsive recurrence that we can force it to yield up its meaning.

Lévi-Strauss and British film culture
Lévi-Strauss's name was initially linked with the moment in British film theory known as *auteur*-structuralism, a phrase first used by the American writer Charles Eckert ('The English cine-structuralists', 1973) which purported to assess his influence on a group of British film critics. At once, however, it was vigorously contested on both sides of the Atlantic (Nowell-Smith, 'I was a star*struck structuralist', 1973; Henderson, 'Critique of cine-structuralism', 1973) as wrongly supposing first that these writers formed a cohesive 'school', and second that their work was part of a deliberate strategy to apply Lévi-Strauss's researches to the study of film. Soon afterwards, Eckert published an article in which he accepted these objections and retracted what he called his 'earlier fetishistic attachment to Lévi-Strauss's method' (Eckert, 'Shall we deport Lévi-Strauss?' 1974).

The attempt to connect Lévi-Strauss with an auteurist approach seems, in retrospect, curious given that a central premise of his work is that myths have no single creative source: this indeed is what allows him to consider myth as a collective cultural phenomenon. Thus, Lévi-Strauss claims to demonstrate, in a celebrated and much-quoted passage, 'not how men think in myths, but how myths operate (*se pensent* – literally 'think themselves') in men's minds without their being aware of the fact. And . . . it would perhaps be better to go still further and, disregarding the thinking subject completely, proceed as if the thinking process were taking place in the myths, in their reflection upon themselves and their interrelation' (Lévi-Strauss, 1970, p. 12). An *auteur*-structuralist such as Peter Wollen, however, even when he sees the director as an 'unconscious catalyst', synthesising contradictory elements into an 'unintended meaning' (Wollen, 1972, pp. 167–168), still differs from Lévi-Strauss in identifying the dominant voice as that of an individual *auteur* (← AUTHORSHIP: *Auteur-structuralism under attack*, p. 179). Eckert proposed as a suitable object of a structuralist analysis, not a group of films sharing the same *auteur* signature, but 'communal blocks' selected on the basis of studio, production unit, movement or genre (Eckert, 1973, p. 49). As Henderson pointed out, this argument seemed to promote a 'non-auteurist structuralism' (Henderson, 1973, p. 32) while blurring the more basic question of whether films could properly be considered as myths, whatever their organising principle.

How legitimate is it, then, to apply Lévi-Strauss's research into the structure of myth to a study of the cinema? In some ways, it is possible to see a mythical dimension to films, particularly in the constant return of generic texts to familiar patterns and their play upon viewer expectations, and to emulate Lévi-Strauss in comparing these films to individual utterances, formulated according to the conventions of a Saussurian language system. In establishing these processes, the ambition of *Mythologiques*, the series of books on American Indian myths written in the late 1960s, to discern beneath the trivial or absurd surface meaning of myth a hidden 'deep structure' which fulfils elemental needs within that culture, seems to promise an attractive alternative to both auteurism and the dismissive approach to popular cinema of sociological criticism (← *Introduction* pp. 222). On the other hand, there are obvious differences between the orally transmitted narratives of primitive tribes and the cultural products of an advanced industrial society. For example, in the case of myth, circumstances of origin are shrouded in mystery, while the opposite is usually true for the cinema, and consideration of the material conditions of production can inform and sometimes radically change our understanding of a film.

Will Wright's book on the western, *Sixguns and Society* (1975) was the first full-length structural study of the cinema to take Lévi-Strauss's work as its main 'idea and inspiration' (p. 16) (← GENRE: *The western*, p. 68). Surprisingly perhaps, in view of the affinities between an approach to families of myths as language systems and traditional film genre analysis it was also the first book to follow the *Mythologiques* in addressing itself to an entire corpus of films rather than a single text. For Wright, there is no doubt that 'the western, though located in a modern industrial society, is as much a myth as the tribal myths of the anthropologists' (Wright, 1975, p. 187). He sees it as performing a mythic function: disseminating 'simple and recognisable meanings which reinforce rather than challenge social understanding'. Wright claims that 'the structure of myth corresponds to the conceptual needs of social and self-understanding required by the dominant social institutions of that period', tracing a direct link between economic changes over some four decades of American history and transformations in the narrative structure of westerns (Wright, 1975, p. 14). The ambition of *Sixguns and Society* to trace the workings of myth through an entire genre forces Wright to confront a problem that analyses of individual films or *auteurs* were able to sidestep: faced with the sheer volume and diversity of our cultural production, how are we to distinguish the key texts from the insignificant ones? Wright proposes to resolve this problem by taking box-office receipts as a measure of mythic potency, contending that 'the (commercially) successful westerns correspond most exactly to the expectations of the audience, to the meanings the viewers demand from the myth' (Wright, 1975, p. 13).

There are a number of problems in Wright's method. For instance, a film's popularity could be due to myriad factors (stars, publicity, competing releases) that have little to do with its internal structure. Wright discounts this notion (pp. 13–14) but later himself cites precisely such a variable (technological innovation) to explain away the success of a film embarrassing to his theory (p. 30). Furthermore, in order to qualify as myths, his westerns must gross four million dollars, a constant figure which fails to take into account the effects of inflation over the forty years covered by the survey. In concentrating on big grossers, the 'chorus' of 'B' westerns is eliminated, and yet it is these which represent all the variants of the myth structures in Lévi-Strauss's schema. We also need to consider the impact of television on film-going patterns, the composition of cinema audiences (are they a representative social mix? have they changed over the decades?) and, perhaps the most fundamental question of all, whether a film's mythic power can simply be quantified in terms of bums on seats. Wright's book could, then, be used to consider the difficulties of defining our modern myths and of assessing the ambit and precise nature of their influence; and since he draws on the work of both Lévi-Strauss and Propp, to contrast these two different approaches.

The way in which Lévi-Strauss's ideas have been taken up at different moments for quite dissimilar purposes illuminates both the extent of his influence and the direction in which film theory has been moving. The problems involved in comparing myths to either *auteur* films or to popular narrative cinema raise important questions; in the one case, identification of the creative source(s) of an artistic text, and in the other, its ideological function for contemporary Western culture. Although it has been suggested here that the legitimacy of such comparisons remains to be established, a tentative approach to films as mythical objects, that is as strange and cryptic texts, allows us to stand back from fictional forms and to discern more clearly their codes and conventions.

References

Charles Eckert, 'The English cine-structuralists', *Film Comment* vol. 9 no. 3, May/June 1973.

Charles Eckert, 'Shall we deport Lévi-Strauss?', *Film Quarterly* vol. 27 no. 3, Spring 1974.

Brian Henderson, 'Critique of cine-structuralism', *Film Quarterly* vol. 26 no. 5, Autumn 1973 and vol. 27 no. 2, Winter 1973/74.

Edmund Leach, *Lévi-Strauss*, London, Fontana, 1974, Chs. 3 and 4.

Claude Lévi-Strauss, 'Overture' to *The Raw and the Cooked*, first volume of *Mythologiques*, London, Jonathan Cape, 1970; trans. John and Doreen Weightman.

Claude Lévi-Strauss, 'The structural study of myth', in R. and F. De George (eds.), *The Structuralists from Marx to Lévi-Strauss*, New York, Doubleday Anchor, 1972.

Geoffrey Nowell-Smith, 'I was a star*struck structuralist', *Screen* vol. 14 no. 3, Autumn 1973.

Peter Wollen, *Signs and Meaning in the Cinema*, London, Secker and Warburg/BFI, 1969 and 1972, Ch. 2 and postscript to 1972 edition.

Will Wright, *Sixguns and Society*, Berkeley, University of California Press, 1975.

Propp

Vladimir Propp's analysis of the narrative structure of Russian fairy tales predates Lévi-Strauss's *Mythologiques* by some forty years. But though his research is now recognised as 'pioneering' (Culler, 1975, p. 207) and of seminal importance for later work in this field, its impact was delayed for several decades. The Russian formalist school with which Propp was associated was already in a state of crisis when the single major book on which his international reputation rests was first published in 1928. As a result it languished untranslated until finally in 1958 the first English edition appeared, misleadingly entitled 'Morphology of the *Folk*tale'. It immediately generated enormous interest among folklorists, linguists, anthropologists and literary critics and inspired a number of studies drawing on his insights from the early sixties onwards.

Morphology of the Folktale

The initial and principal aim of Propp's research, stated clearly in the opening pages of his monograph, was a modest one: to find a reliable system of organising and categorising Russian fairy-tales. Starting with the observation that 'scholarly literature concerning the tale is not especially rich . . . : there are no general works on the tale' (Propp, 1968, p. 3), he diagnosed the root of the problem as the absence of a 'well-ordered classification, a unified terminology . . . and a methodology' (p. 4). In sharp and unfavourable contrast to the rigour of 'the physical and mathematical sciences', all previous attempts at a survey of the tale had been vitiated by random hypotheses, haphazard definitions and chaotic working methods. So, although Propp's work was to lead him to some provocative and influential conclusions he initially saw it as nothing more ambitious than a bid to lay the preliminary groundwork for further research. This of course was no mean task, and indeed, quite apart from his findings, was sufficient reason to attract the interest of film theorists anxious to displace erratic, impressionistic criticism with a more precise, systematic and detached approach.

One of the main sources of confusion and ambiguity in earlier studies of the tale was, Propp found, the researchers' assumption that their material should be classified according to its *theme*. The trouble was that often one tale incorporated either several of their themes at once or none of them. Propp also argued that this kind of taxonomy was fallacious, masking basic similarities between thematically dissimilar tales and lumping together quite different, but thematically related ones. He even asserted that 'the division of fairy tales according to themes is in general impossible' (p. 7). It was in establishing an alternative system of categorisation that Propp succeeded in making a major breakthrough. Rather than looking at the apparent subject-matter of his tales, he set out to discern their latent, 'skeleton' formation. This idea may have stemmed from an interest in the natural sciences: the primary meaning of the concept 'morphology' is, after all, 'the study of the form and structure of biological organisms', and his book is scattered with suggestive comparisons between the analysis of literary genres and that of 'minerals, plants and animals' (e.g. pp. 8, 11, 13, 102–103). This view of narrative as an autonomous object which obeys its own inner logic (rather than, for instance, the intentions of its author) was also to become extremely important within film criticism.

The raw material for Propp's investigation was a sequence of a hundred fairy-tales chosen, for the purposes of scientific objectivity, from an already existing collection. As a first step towards deciding how to classify them, he broke down the narrative of each one into its constituent parts (which he called *functions*). Each function represented a single action and, as the word implies, was defined in terms, not of the literal event taking place, but of the 'function' it performed within the overall development of the story. As a result, 'identical acts can have different meanings and vice versa'. For example, the same event, 'the prince builds a castle', could represent in one tale the *violation* of an interdiction which forbade this, in a second the *solution* of a difficult task and in a third the preparation of a *wedding*. Conversely, two different events involving different characters, 'a tsar gives an eagle to a hero' and 'a princess gives Ivan a ring', could both signify in their respective narratives the *provision of a magical agent* which would later enable the recipient to perform his/her difficult task. For Propp the actions were of cardinal importance; the actors who performed them remained subordinate, shadowy presences. Characters, he insisted, like functions, should be categorised not by their individual qualities, but exclusively in terms of the 'sphere of action' they occupied within the overall narrative structure (Chapter 6 passim). Thus the 'hero' would be identified as such not by his looks or his virtue but by the fact that he departed on a search, performed difficult tasks and so on. As with the functions, the spheres of action established by Propp were few, though not completely inflexible, numbering seven in all. The first conclusion about his tales was, then, that the 'functions of characters serve as stable, constant elements in a tale, independent of how and by whom they are fulfilled' (p. 21).

Clearly, a formal definition of a function will embrace a far wider range of events than a thematic one and thereby vastly reduce the number of categories required. Indeed, Propp found that 'the repetition of fundamental components . . . exceeds all expectations' (p. 24), managing to whittle down a potentially infinite number of narrative events to just thirty-one. Second conclusion: 'the number of functions known to the fairy-tale is limited' (p. 21). He also noted that certain kinds of function always occurred at the same stage of the narrative (an interdiction near the beginning; the punishment of the villain near the end) and that others were invariably combined in pairs or triads (interdiction/ violation; donor's test/hero's reaction/ provision of gift). Carrying these empirical observations further, he arrived at his third conclusion: with allowances for auxiliary, linking incidents and the omission and/or repetition of some functions, the sequence of events 'is always identical' (p. 22). These limitations on the number of main characters and functions, and on their position within the narrative, imposed, Propp argued, a homogeneity on the stories to such an extent that, despite the 'amazing multiformity, picturesqueness and colour' (p. 21) afforded by their surface texture and patterning, 'all fairy-tales are of one type in regard to their structure' (p. 23). This, his fourth conclusion, was perhaps the most unexpected and intriguing of all.

At the very end of his monograph, Propp entertained the idea that it might be possible to establish a universal narrative model. Quoting a colleague, he speculated that at some point in the future, 'the synthesis of time, that great simplifier', would enable scholars to discern a schema that applied not only to 'the poetic traditions of the distant past' but also to 'contemporary narrative literature with its complicated thematic structure and photographic reproduction of reality' (p. 116). Here, he raised the fascinating possibility that primitive, stylised narrative forms might be found to have the same basic armature as modern realist texts. However he was careful to withhold judgement on this score, stressing that his work accounted for only one genus of tale (p. 106) and repeatedly pointing out that comparative studies were the province of the historian (pp. 15–16; p. 107). As indicated above, he saw his own research as a necessary, but not sufficient precondition of an accurate and detailed cross-cultural study.

Propp and Anglo-American film theory

Propp attached great importance to 'proceeding from the material at hand to the consequences' (Propp, 1968, p. 5, p. 25), and indeed Dundes (in Propp, 1968, p. xii) sees this as a major difference between his empirical approach and the speculative path traced by Lévi-Strauss (although it is interesting that, from their opposing directions, they both arrive at the same conclusion: that the many narratives they examine are underpinned by a single basic structure). Paradoxically, then, any attempt to apply the *Morphology* to the cinema reverses a fundamental principle of Propp's method by starting *from* the working hypothesis that the model he found in the fairy-tale is also present in other narrative forms and by transferring it to (in most cases) a single, isolated text.

Sunset Boulevard – conforming to Propp's categories

This said, several analysts (Wollen 1976, Erens 1977, and Silverstone 1976) were surprised to find how easily the schema could be mapped on to their sample films. Can this compatibility be attributed to the skilful and selective choice of test cases? Or to ingenious distortions of the narratives to force them into the mould? It is notable and possibly more than coincidental that all the writers opted to work on classical Hollywood films (except for Silverstone, who, however, gives as his reasons for choosing a television series, its wide appeal and central role in contemporary culture). Could the model be extended to, for instance, a European art movie? Or are any basic similarities that do exist between fairy-tales and films confined to the popular media? Fell's article would seem to suggest that this is indeed the case. He found that 'breakdowns of pulp novel and film design in terms of Proppian distinctions are easy to accomplish' (Fell, 'Vladimir Propp in Hollywood', 1977, p. 22), demonstrating this with reference to *Kiss Me Deadly*, which he described and discussed as a movie in 'the conventionalised generic idiom'. But when he turned to three films all originating with a single creative source (the scriptwriter Jules Furthman) and directed by 'highly visible Hollywood figures' (Sternberg and Hawks), he encountered 'rather sobering discrepancies' (Fell, 1977, p. 23). Wollen (1976) and Erens (1977), on the other hand took highly-acclaimed films by celebrated directors (Hitchcock's *North by Northwest* and Wilder's *Sunset Boulevard*), and found them to conform to, rather than transcend, Propp's categories.

Fell also took issue with Propp's concept of character as inadequate to account for anything more subtle or complex than 'formularised behaviour' (Fell, 1977,

p. 22), echoing here a humanistic critical tradition which is generally antagonistic to Propp's work and the theorists who draw on it. These differences could be well illustrated by reading Wollen's account of *North by Northwest* which analysed the protagonist, Thornhill, as a shifting term (seeker or victim?) in the narrative equation, alongside that elaborated in an early essay by Robin Wood, who wrote of him as if he were a personal acquaintance ('he is brash, fast-talking, over-confident', Wood, 1965, p. 100). Recent film theory has reacted against this latter kind of approach, arguing that characters in a novel or film should be seen as components in a fictional system and not as 'real' human beings who can be psychoanalysed or evaluated as morally 'good' or 'bad'. In practice it is not so easy: the realist narrative film resists such detached scrutiny, even more tenaciously, perhaps, than realist literature, given its uniquely powerful mechanisms for sustaining the illusion of mimesis and inducing the audience to identify with the figures on the screen (→ *Narrative and audience* p. 242). Propp's work on narrative form is of value here in affording a more distanced perspective on the fictional world of cinema and the events and characters it encompasses. What it excludes, as Wood (among many others) countered in an article written over a decade later ('Levin and the jam', 1976), is any explanation of the fascination and pleasure, the 'tendency . . . to participate, to identify', the 'emotional involvement and satisfaction' offered by the realist narrative novel or film. It is this omission which has laid much film criticism deriving from the work of Propp and Lévi-Strauss open to accusations of impoverishing or betraying the 'aesthetic experience' and which theoretical work around the concept of pleasure (→ *Narrative and audience* p. 242) has been concerned to rectify.

Another controversial aspect of Propp's work is the emphasis he places upon the chronological order of his thirty-one functions. A number of commentators (Leach, 1974, Chs. 3 and 4, especially pp. 49–53; Dundes, in Propp, 1968, pp. xi–xii) have contrasted this with the approach of Lévi-Strauss, who, arguing that the linear sequence of events is just the 'apparent or manifest content', believes that the 'more important latent content' only emerges when key elements are isolated from the body of the narrative and rearranged into a new (achronological) matrix of binary oppositions. In his structural study of the western, Wright objects that Lévi-Strauss's 'denial of significance to the story itself is simply untenable', espousing Propp's view that 'the temporal order of events . . . is of central importance' (Wright, 1975, pp. 24–26). Hence he attempts a fusion of the two methods, plotting his narratives along two perpendicular axes: both thematic and temporal. However, he feels that Propp's insistence on events occurring in a 'rigid, unchangeable order in each tale' is 'unnecessarily restricting' (Wright, 1975, p. 25), introducing instead the notion of the 'narrative sequence', small clusters of events which, though each in itself invariable, could be combined in a multiplicity of ways (Wright, 1975, Ch. 4).

Claude Bremond, taking the argument even further, sees the belief that 'one function developed out of another with logical and artistic necessity' (Propp, 1968, p. 64) as a crippling constraint on the freedom of the narrator to take the story where s/he will. He proposes an alternative model, incorporating 'pivotal functions', points at which the tale could move in any one of several directions (see *Communications* 4, 1964). The problem here is that, as Bremond's increasingly labyrinthine diagrams bear out, the number of narrative possibilities soon multiply into an unwieldy network. Moreover, the tendency of Bremond's work leads away from Propp's structuralist thesis that 'the sequence of events has its own laws (and the short story too has similar laws, as do organic formations' (Propp, 1968, p. 22) back towards a reaffirmation of the autonomy of the artist in 'choosing his/her path' and producing an 'original creation' (Bremond, 1964). Culler points out in Propp's defence that his schema is not as restrictive as it first appears. A story may conform to his model in every respect and still, while it is unfolding, leave the audience uncertain of its outcome. It is often only in retrospect that we can identify the characters as hero, false hero, etc. and interpret the significance of each scene in the light of its place in the total structure (Culler, 1975, pp. 209–210).

These debates bring out a strand in Propp's work which connects with later theoretical writing on narrative. The *Mor-*

To Have and Have Not – 'princess' Slim and hero Morgan (Bogart)

phology drew attention to the 'two-fold quality of the tale': on the surface, multiform and spontaneous but, at a deeper level, uniform and subject to strict conventions. This concept was to be taken further by Barthes (→ *Barthes* p. 239) and, with specific reference to the cinema, Stephen Heath, who also sees a 'dual impulse' behind the classical narrative film. On the one hand, 'action is moulded in a *destiny*', governed by 'a stifling logic which *obliges* the film to do this or that' (Heath's italics); on the other, the viewer is allowed, by a process of self-deception or 'disavowal', to repress the knowledge of what is to come, to preserve the belief in infinite possibility and savour the illusion of uncertainty and/or suspense ('The work of Christian Metz', 1973, pp. 22–27; 'Lessons from Brecht', 1974, esp. pp. 121 ff.). The similarity with Propp's thinking is obvious but a new term has been introduced into the formulation: that of the audience. Thus although the *Morphology* appears deceptively simple (indeed, its critics claim, simplistic), it opens up an accessible path into difficult terrain (the study of the formal construction of narrative), and prepares the way for the more complex model of the 'realist text' developed by Barthes in *S/Z*.

References

Claude Bremond, 'Le message narratif', *Communications* 4, 1964, and 'La logique des possibles narratifs', *Communications* 8, 1966.
Claude Chabrol, review of *Kiss Me Deadly*, *Cahiers du Cinéma* no. 54. 1956.
Jonathan Culler, *Structuralist Poetics*, London, Routledge and Kegan Paul, 1975.
Raymond Durgnat, 'The apotheosis of va-va-voom', *Motion* no. 3, Spring 1962.
Patricia Erens, '*Sunset Boulevard*: a morphological analysis', *Film Reader* 2, 1977.
John L. Fell, 'Vladimir Propp in Hollywood', *Film Quarterly* vol. 30 no. 3, Spring 1977.
Sylvia Harvey, 'The absent family of film noir', in Kaplan (ed.), *Women in Film Noir*, London, British Film Institute, 1978.
Molly Haskell, 'Howard Hawks – masculine feminine', *Film Comment* vol. 10 no. 2, March/April 1974.
Stephen Heath, 'The work of Christian Metz', *Screen* vol. 14 no. 3, Autumn 1973; 'Lessons from Brecht', *Screen* vol. 15 no. 2, Summer 1974.
Edmund Leach, *Lévi-Strauss*, London, Fontana, 1974, Chs. 3 and 4, esp. pp. 49–53.
Vladimir Propp, *Morphology of the Folktale*, Austin and London, University of Texas Press, 1968; trans. Laurence Scott.
Alain Silver, '*Kiss Me Deadly* – evidence of a style', *Film Comment* vol. 11 no. 2, March/April 1975.
Roger Silverstone, 'An approach to the structural analysis of the television message', *Screen* vol. 17 no. 2, Summer 1976.
Peter Wollen, *Signs and Meaning in the Cinema*, London, Secker and Warburg/BFI, 1969, revised edition 1972.
Peter Wollen, '*North by North-West*: a morphological analysis', *Film Form* vol. 1 no. 1, 1976.
Robin Wood, *Hitchcock's Films*, London/New York, Zwemmer/Barnes, 1965.
Robin Wood, 'To Have (written) and Have Not (directed)', *Film Comment* vol. 9 no. 3, May/June 1973.
Robin Wood, 'Levin and the jam', in *Personal Views*, London, Gordon Fraser, 1976.
Robin Wood, 'Hawks de-Wollenised', in *Personal Views*, cit.
Robin Wood, *Howard Hawks*, London, Secker and Warburg/BFI, 1968, reprinted 1981.
Will Wright, *Sixguns and Society*, Berkeley, University of California Press, 1975.

Kiss Me Deadly (USA 1955 *p.c* –
Parklane Pictures; *d* – Robert Aldrich;
sd b/w 19)

In his Proppian analysis of this film,
Fell (1977) claims that, like its source, a
novel of the same name by Mickey
Spillane, it is a crude, routinely
conventional text. Other critics,
however, have been struck by its
formalistic visual style, and Claude
Chabrol's review for *Cahiers du Cinéma*
(1956) puts forward an auteurist reading
of the movie as a silk purse brilliantly
created by the director (Robert Aldrich)
out of 'the worst, most lamentable . . .
the most nauseous product of the genre
fallen into putrefaction'. Stylised film
noir conventions are much in evidence
(see Alain Silver, '*Kiss Me Deadly* –
evidence of a style', 1975) as, for
example, in the fragmented montage of
the pre-credit sequence, extreme camera
angles and the breaks of the 180° rule,
(← HISTORY OF NARRATIVE, p. 217),
low-key lighting, etc. Fell argues that the
use of the devices remains strictly within
the bounds of standardised formulae,
while for other critics, it veers towards
an excess that, in the view of one of
them, turns *Kiss Me Deadly* into a
'purely formal film . . (of) terrible
beauty' (Raymond Durgnat, 'The
apotheosis of va-va-voom', 1962).

Fell's moralistic condemnation of the
hero (or anti-hero) as 'sadistic,
manipulative, brutishly suspicious and
loutishly vulgar' is also open to debate.
In Proppian terms, Mike Hammer might
more suitably be considered as a
character-function in the 'hard-boiled'
detective genre. Durgnat describes
Aldrich's women as androgynous,
forceful, threatening, and Hammer as
'passive, sardonic and frigidly resistant'.
This sexual ambiguity is interesting in
relation to Fell's suggestion that Propp's
schema assumes stereotypical role-
playing (sexual or otherwise) and breaks
down where this is not present.

The first eight minutes of the film are
useful in discussion of Propp's opening
functions. The customary 'initial
situation' of his tales, the state of
equilibrium whose disruption and
restoration propels the Proppian
narrative, appears to be missing. How
right is Fell in seeing the first function as
'the hero leaves home'? Is Propp's
schema, centred as it is on the home and
the family, inappropriate to deal with
the 'absent family of film noir'? (see
Sylvia Harvey, 'The absent family of
film noir', 1978).

Fell argues that the thriller/detective
genre, with its theme of the quest and
'energetic, visibly active plots' is
particularly suitable for a morphological
analysis. In the light of the above
comments, it could be considered
whether the noir thriller lacks the
requisite stability and containment.
More generally, how correct are
'Proppian' critics such as Fell (1977) and
Erens (1977) in pointing to the potential
of his method as a means of inter- and
trans-generic comparisons? Are there
certain genres which strain against his
categories?

To Have and Have Not (USA 1944 *p.c*
– Warner Bros; *d* – Howard Hawks;
sd b/w 20)

Hawks's films, which in Robin
Wood's view exhibit 'a continual
tendency . . . to move towards myth'
and whose figures are, he argues,
elaborations on basic archetypes (Wood,
1968, pp. 26 ff.), could be used to
illuminate Propp's approach to
characterisation.

Frenchy is clearly a would-be
dispatcher and 'approaches the hero
with a request' three or four times.
Harry Morgan is, for Wood (1968,
p. 27) the vessel of 'a certain heroic
ideal'; here, however, his 'heroic
attributes', in particular his extreme
individualism, are posed as a problem.
Acting purely for oneself, in the style of
the fairytale prince, is no longer self-
evidently heroic, and becomes redefined
by the historical context (it is worth
noting that some critics see Morgan's
hesitation as a metaphor for America's
isolationism in the first years of the
Second World War).

The villains are soon unmasked:
Johnson, the minor villain, 'causes harm
or injury' (the attempt to cheat Morgan)
on a purely private level, and his
displacement early in the film by the
main villain in the bulky personage of
Captain Renard signals the progressive
compounding of personal conflicts by
political ones.

The princess is harder to identify.
Molly Haskell ('Howard Hawks –
masculine feminine', 1974) argues that
Slim is not simply a 'sought-for' person
but also a helper ('the peer comrade')
quoting Hawks's intention to make her
'a little more insolent' than Morgan/
Bogart. Interestingly, her 'sought-for'
status is shared, on another level, with
the Free French. Hélène de Bursac's
resemblance to Slim in physique and
dress is a kind of doubling. Robin Wood
('To Have (written) and Have Not
(directed)', 1973, p. 34) suggests that the
splitting of the female lead enables
Hawks to hold apart the two narrative
strands of love interest and the need for
political commitment. In structural
terms it could be argued that it is only
the presence of Hélène that releases Slim
from a straightforward (and more
passive) 'princess' role. This could
perhaps be an opportunity to examine
the 'spheres of action' open to women in
the classical narrative cinema. How
many of Propp's seven basic roles are
gender-specific?

Though Propp anticipated that a
single figure could occupy several
spheres of action, or conversely, that
several figures might share the same one
(Propp, 1968, pp. 80–81), Fell complains
that the splintering of functions in
Hawks's films resists Proppian analysis:
'when personae commit human mitosis
and divide into separate personalities,
they muddle the conventional formulae
by developing relationships with each
other' (Fell, 1977, p. 27). He also tends
to focus on details such as spittoons or
the location of hotel rooms, which
seems to miss Propp's point that such
features are surface variables peripheral
to the basic narrative structure. This
suggests that certain self-styled
'structuralist' criticism takes over only
the superficial trappings (terminology;
impressive-looking diagrams) of the
methodology it claims to employ.

Rio Bravo (USA 1959 *p.c* – Armada; *d*
– Howard Hawks; sd b/w 18)

For Robin Wood, this film is
remarkable for the way in which it
simultaneously draws on and transcends
western genre conventions and in
particular for Hawks's use of stock
characters. Wood's list of these seven
major western types (Wood, 1968, p. 36)
could be compared to Propp's seven
dramatis personae for correspondences
or mutations: the overlap would seem to
suggest an at least superficial
compatibility between Propp's model
and this particular genre, perhaps
because of its roots in tradition, history
and myth (in contrast to a film noir like
Kiss Me Deadly). *Rio Bravo* evidences a
number of significant variations on the
basic categories which Wood attributes
to Hawks's personal genius, whereas
Will Wright suggests that such variant
features as the emphasis on teamwork
and the attenuated evil of the villains are
due to historically determined changes
in the narrative structure of the genre as
a whole (see Wright, 1975, especially
Ch. 3 and the section on the
'Professional Plot').

It would be productive to examine
more closely the nature of these changes
as they affect the characters of *Rio
Bravo*. Fell (1977), following Wright
(1975), sees the fight between heroes and
villains as a contest of professional skills
rather than as a moral struggle between
good and evil; this could be compared
to Wood's reading (1968), which affirms
the conflict as an ethical one, though, for
him, it is largely internalised as the
search for self-awareness and respect. In
either case, the importance of the
villains (who do not appear in the
extract) is greatly diminished; it also
means that the hero becomes more →

Rio Bravo – popular structuralist fodder

complex and problematic. The
difficulties of assessing Chance, the
ostensible hero-figure, could be
discussed: are his heroic qualities (his
sense of superiority, his stoicism)
exaggerated in order to deride or to
revalidate them? Could a case be made
for Dude as victim-hero? Fell (1977)
notes that he displays heroic features (he
overcomes a misfortune, i.e. his
alcoholism and traumatic past) and
Wood (1968) accords him almost equal
status with Chance. The partial
doubling of the hero-role is significant.
Dude is able to win his fight to
rehabilitate himself only because he can
forget his unhappy romance, a pattern
which Chance, in starting an affair with
Feathers, could conceivably be seen as
set to repeat.

The portrayal of Feathers would
appear to discount this possibility.
However, as in *To Have and Have Not*,
the two narrative strands of love interest
and conquest of villainy are held almost
entirely separate, with the result that,
instead of linking heroic deeds to the
winning of the princess in the manner of
a Proppian fairy-tale, the film could be
interpreted as suggesting that Chance's
romantic liaison is a direct threat to his
activities as law-enforcer and leader of
the male group. Is the penultimate scene
in Feather's room simply a coda to the
main action, or could it be read as
signalling a new, but undeveloped
narrative departure? These issues have

of course been raised without recourse
to Propp's schema, but it is arguably a
helpful aid to isolating the film's
troubling (i.e. deviant) features.

Hawks's work is useful in comparing
different critical approaches, (e.g. Fell
(1977), Wright (1975), Wollen (1972)
and Wood (1968) (← AUTHORSHIP:
Howard Hawks, p. 179). The interest of
structuralist critics in his films is
noteworthy, and possible reasons (the
popularity of Hawk's films; his heavy
use of genre forms, etc.) could be
explored. Fell and Wood (see 'Hawks
de-Wollenised', 1976) both object that
structuralist analyses are too insensitive
and inflexible to account adequately for
the colour and detail of individual films:
this conclusion could be tested against
Wollen's account of Hawks's work and
Wright's interpretation of *Rio Bravo*,
bearing in mind the modesty of Propp's
original aim to provide a method of
classification rather than a total theory.

Barthes

Barthes' formulation of the realist aesthetic and the general reassessment of structuralist methodology epitomised by *S/Z*, first
published in France in 1970 and translated
into English in 1974, take up problems
which have already been raised here. In
particular, his work on the relationship
between reader and text was to become of
central importance for film theory.

Realism and narrative
The narrative dissected by Barthes in *S/Z*
– a novella, *Sarrasine*, written in 1830 by
Honoré de Balzac – is proposed as an
example of a realist text, albeit one which
conforms only imperfectly to the canons
of classic realism. Traditionally identified
with verisimilitude, the creation of a plaus-
ible and (if only potentially) familiar
world, realism is defined by Barthes in
rather broader terms: realist texts in his
view make up the greater part of Western
literature – and indeed *Sarrasine* itself,
with its unholy cast of degenerate
aristocrats and *demi-mondaines* and its
improbably melodramatic narrative, hardly seems the stuff of realism in the traditional sense. The commonsense equation
of realism with plausibility is discounted
in *S/Z*. Rather than assessing the credibility of Balzac's world-view, Barthes
traces from a post-structuralist perspective
a gradual and cumulative *structuring process* (← AUTHORSHIP: *Discursive activity*,
p. 189). The 'texture' of the realist text is,
for him, created by the interweaving of different *codes*, each less important in itself
than for the way in which they are combined. His 'slow-motion' reading of *Sarrasine* aims to show how the narrative is
put together. For – and this argument is
a throw-back to Barthes' early writing –
the art-work (or, in *Mythologies*, the
cultural artefact) should not be 'mythicised' as a spontaneously existing object,
or as one whose origins are attributable
only to the intuitive creation of genius, but
examined as a production in the throes of
being made.

Clearly, this relationship between realism and narrative is quite different from
that conceived by André Bazin (← *Bazin*
p. 224), who saw film as a neutral medium
for recording phenomena, and viewed
with suspicion any attempt to organise and
interpret what was for him a fundamentally ambiguous world. *S/Z* takes the
opposite view: that narrative is an ingred-
ient essential to the impression of realism.
For Barthes, reality itself is not something
passively revealed or reflected in art, but
an impression constructed with care and
artifice. Realism, as an aesthetic mode,
belongs to the realm of ideology, understood in the sense defined by Barthes' contemporary, the Marxist philosopher Louis
Althusser (→ *Narrative and audience*
p. 243), as 'relatively autonomous' from
'the real relations which govern the
existence of individuals'. It is therefore not

directly determined by 'the real' but is rather a system of representation with its own characteristic mode of operating (← AUTHORSHIP: *Structuralism and auteur study* p. 166); Lovell, 1980, pp. 29–31; Harvey, 1978, pp. 87–120).

Given this assumption, the point of reference of the realist text is not some putative, independently existing 'real world'. Instead, it is seen as the convergence of two sets of relations. On the one hand, the work is subject to its own tight *internal logic*, its *intra-textual economy*. Characters act consistently; the narrative 'obeys a principle of non-contradiction' (*S/Z* p. 156), though *snares* may be set for the reader by implanting misleading (but on no account retrospectively fallacious) information; actions follow predictable patterns so that, for instance, the disclosure that a character is asleep presupposes that at some future stage s/he will wake up (cf. the *code of actions*, or *proairetic code*, *S/Z* p. 18, and, especially, Appendix II, where these patterns are traced through in *Sarrasine* – and cf. *Propp* ← p. 234 in his work on the pairing of narrative functions); 'everything holds together' (*S/Z* pp. 181–182), that is, every detail, every action will play some – preferably more than one – functional role in the unfolding of the narrative, though ideally this functionality should not be too obvious (*S/Z* pp. 22–23); and all the main enigmas posed in the course of the story are resolved by the end. These, and the various other devices identified in *S/Z* as forming the intra-textual system illustrate the highly crafted and selective nature of the procedures through which the realist world is built up. On the other hand, the work depends on a set of *external relationships*, its position within a grid of other cultural texts; its *intertextuality*. Realism, Barthes argues, 'consists not in copying the real, but in copying a depicted copy of the real' (*S/Z* pp. 54–56). In *Sarrasine*, for example, Marianina's marvellous beauty can only be defined in terms, not of some ultimate, essential beauty, but of another cultural representation of it – 'the fabled imaginings of the Eastern poets' (*S/Z* pp. 32–34). However, inter-textual references can function not only when used within a realist aesthetic, as a guarantee of authenticity, but also, conversely, in modernist or proto-modernist texts (e.g. Flaubert) where the quotations are imperfectly assimilated, incongruous or contradictory, to produce the opposite effect, disrupting the illusions of unity and coherence instead of reinforcing it (Barthes, 'The realist effect', 1978, and ← AUTHORSHIP; *Frank Tashlin*, p. 175).

This definition of realism in terms of a work's formal operations rather than its subject-matter leads Barthes into a distinction between the realist and the modernist text. The *writerly* (*scriptible*) text is modernist, non-representational, 'a galaxy of signifiers, not a structure of signifieds', bereft of 'a narrative structure, a grammar or a logic', refusing definitive interpretation, opening up endless possibilities of meaning. The *readerly* (*lisible*) text is the other pole of the opposition: realist, representational, pre-eminently narrative, offering up only one, unequivocal meaning (*S/Z* pp. 3–7). Though Barthes' formulation is a little ambiguous, it appears that the 'writerly' and the 'readerly' should be seen not as global categories, but rather as the notional extremes of a spectrum on which all actual texts would be plotted at varying points in between. It would be exceptionally difficult, if not impossible, for a text to attain to either extreme – and indeed undesirable, for a totally 'readerly' text would be dull and pedestrian, while a totally 'writerly' one would be 'a text with no fertility, with no productivity, a sterile text' (*Le Plaisir du texte*, 1973, p. 53). *Sarrasine* would fall near the readerly end of the spectrum, but, for several reasons (the breakdown of meaning at important moments in the story, Balzac's immoderate 'excessive' use of certain techniques, such as an almost compulsive intertextuality) it does not for Barthes consistently and completely succeed in suppressing the artifice deployed in its own production and can therefore be shown to be an imperfectly realist text.

Barthes' discussion of *Sarrasine* emphasises the ways in which it deviates from the 'norms' of classic realism at the level of the means of representation. It has been objected that the significance (if any) of what is actually being represented is inadequately theorised by Barthes in *S/Z*, thus exposing him and those critics who draw on his ideas to accusations of formalism (see Britton, 'The ideology of *Screen*', 1978/79, pp. 18 ff). However, the concept of the 'readerly' text, understood as a paradigm, or model rather than as a real text, when imported (in a slightly modified form) into film studies as 'the classic realist text', enables provocative and revealing comparisons to be made between films conventionally regarded as realist and the implausible 'unreal' worlds of much Hollywood cinema (→ *The 'classic realist text'*, p. 242).

'S/Z' and film theory

In assessing the influence of *S/Z*, it is necessary to recall that it too, like *Sarrasine*, is subject to the principle of intertextuality. It was, along with much other writing on literature, film and the other arts, only one product of the intense theoretical speculation being generated in France at that time (see Harvey, 1978). *S/Z* appeared in 1970, the same year as the equally influential *Cahiers* collective text on Ford's *Young Mr. Lincoln* (← AUTHORSHIP: *Discursive activity*, p. 189) with which it shares a number of features. Moreover, as the ideas formulated by Barthes and others have been assimilated into British film culture, they have become diffused into a wider theoretical discourse whose precise point of origin is impossible to determine. For these reasons, it is both difficult and ultimately unhelpful to isolate the individual impact of *S/Z* on subsequent work. Less attention has been devoted to the specific features of its breakdown of narrative (e.g. the five codes) than to its more general propositions, and rigorously 'Barthesian' analyses are therefore not easy to identify. The tone of *S/Z* itself is speculative rather than prescriptive, indicating that it would be unwise to apply any of the techniques devised therein in a mechanical fashion to other texts, (though of course this has been done – see Lesage, 1976; Mayne, 1976; Welsch, 1978). For, in a very important sense *S/Z* is more a reflection on the difficulties, pleasures and aims of the reading experience than either a programme for establishing the structure of narrative or a close analysis of Balzac's novella. Its strategic importance, together with related work on film (e.g. *Cahiers* on *Young Mr. Lincoln*; Stephen Heath on *Touch of Evil* – cf. AUTHORSHIP p. 189 and p. 189) for British debates can be linked to its wealth of textual references: *S/Z* seems to prove that weighty theoretical deliberations need not be incompatible with the kind of attention to textual complexity which, for critics in the anglo-American tradition committed to empiricism, constitutes 'the life of a film' (Wood, 'Hawks de-Wollenised', 1976).

The structuralist method

A crucial aspect of *S/Z* is the critique it offers of early structuralist method. For instance, compared to the models considered above, *S/Z* appears extremely unsystematic. Its minimal unit (the 'lexie', usually translated as lexia) is 'a matter of convenience' (*S/Z* pp. 13–14) – compare for instance the lengthy deliberations of Metz (← p. 229) on precisely how to establish the minimal unit in a film; it claims to provide neither an exhaustive reading of *Sarrasine* (on the contrary) nor a universal narrative structure; and it refuses to offer its argument in a highly-organised, linear form.

These strategies are in sharp contrast to initial attempts by structuralist critics to understand the operations of narrative and other social sign systems. Their aim had been to develop exhaustive and immutable schemas; see Barthes' own earlier work on modern myth (*Mythologies*, 1957) and fashion journalism (*Système de la Mode*, 1967) and his bid to break down narrative into functional units on linguistic principles ('Introduction to the structural analysis of narratives', 1966). Such attempts to found a scientific poetics were a transitional stage, necessary in order to break with traditional criticism; by 1970, however, when *S/Z* was published, the problems of this approach were becoming apparent. Early structural analyses of film, like the *grande syntagmatique*, devised by Metz (← p. 229) in the mid-60s seemed either ignorant of or inexplicit about the assumptions behind their methods. The idea that culturally determined sign systems could be explained by an Olympian observer in a neutral metalanguage, supposedly immune from these very same determinants, began to seem questionable. Moreover, a model that claims to be universal has to work on the hypothesis that its basic material will always remain the same. But social systems are complex phenomena in a state of constant flux: as Coward and Ellis point out, a theory which 'does not eventually take account of this . . . inevitably declines into a sterile formalism, elaborating models whose only relevance is to a world that stands still' (Coward and Ellis, 1977, p. 26).

Finally, a need was felt to reassess not only the agent and tools performing the analysis on the one side, and the object(s) being analysed on the other, but also the *relationship* between the two. Reader and text were no longer seen as two discrete and stable entities, but instead as *processes*, both of which change and in turn are changed by each other in the course of their encounter (see Barthes' self-criticism in *Signs of the Times*, 1971, pp. 41–51). The practical consequences of these shifts of perspective in *S/Z* were threefold.

Method

The traditional critic would, according to Barthes, pose as a 'priest whose task is to decipher the writing of the (author-)god' (*S/Z* p. 174). Early structuralists would perhaps prefer to regard themselves as impartial scientists, but their claim to discern essential structures or processes would rest on a not dissimilar claim to provide a privileged insight into 'objective truths' about the text under scrutiny. *S/Z* in contrast is concerned throughout *not* to present itself as 'the discourse of knowledge'. The 'unsystematic' features referred to previously, the arbitrary division into lexias, the frequent digressions, the fragmented step-by-step commentary that replaces the tightly argued thesis we usually expect of a critical essay, are all meant to avoid 'structuring the text excessively . . . giving it that additional structure which would come from a dissertation and would close it' (*S/Z* p. 13). The prose style is dense, allusive and peppered with neologisms, colourful images and surprising comparisons: Barthes felt that 'the fact that *S/Z* may be subject to certain values of style in the traditional sense is important, for . . . to accept style is to refuse language as pure instrument' (*Signs of the Times*, 1971, p. 46). The purpose here was both to call into question the view of criticism as a 'neutral metalanguage' ('[a] refusal to turn language back on itself is the royal road of major ideological deception', *Signs of the Times*, p. 49) and to suggest a different mode of reading which does not have to proceed at a fixed speed or in terms of 'some continuous linear unfolding' (p. 48).

The difference of the text

In his 1966, 'Introduction to the structural analysis of narratives', Barthes, inspired by the work of Propp and Lévi-Strauss, had attempted to fashion 'a single descriptive tool', a hypothetical model which could be applied to 'different narrative species' in 'their historical, geographical and cultural diversity'. Analysis should, he argued here, concentrate on the ways in which individual narratives conform to and depart from this universal model (pp. 80–81). In the opening pages of *S/Z*, however, he distances himself from such an attempt 'to see all the world's stories . . . within a single structure', now holding it to be 'a task as

Le Gai savoir – the modernist text: 'a galaxy of signifiers'

exhausting . . . as it is ultimately undesirable'. The reason given for this change of heart is that by forcing a text into 'a great narrative structure', it 'thereby loses its difference' (*S/Z* p. 3). This statement is perhaps a surprising one, for it signals not only a break with previous structuralist approaches but also, in the view of some observers, a return to something closely resembling traditional, pre-structuralist criticism. Barthes' suggestion that each text is its own model would appear to reaffirm the uniqueness, the ineffability of the work of artistic genius.

However, Barthes uses the term *difference* in the sense formulated by his contemporary, Jacques Derrida, who, drawing in his turn on the theories of Ferdinand de Saussure (← *Introduction* p. 222), argued that linguistic signs are arbitrary, conventional, defined not by some essential property, but by the differences which distinguish them from other signs. The same is true, for Derrida, of signifying practices in general. Each work of literature *differs*, obviously, from other works; equally, however, it *defers* to them, i.e. relies on them for its distinctive meaning (Derrida, 1967). This formula-

tion draws a crucial distinction between traditional notions of 'uniqueness' or 'individuality', which are hermetic, essential qualities, and the concept of 'difference', which can only be assessed by matching a text against other social and cultural discourses. It is a distinction which has several consequences for critical method. For example, meaning cannot be established by considering a text in isolation, only by locating it within a network of differences and similarities (in relation to cinema, see Steve Neale on stereotyping, 'The same old story', 1979/80). Nor can meaning be assessed in terms of a definitive structural model in the manner of the earlier 'scientific' analyses. Because difference is determined within a cultural matrix which expands and changes shape through history, it is therefore itself also subject to historical change.

A work of art, then, should be seen not mechanistically, as a closed system, a completed, inert object which will always remain the same, but dynamically, as an endless process of rereading and rewriting. The uncovering of fresh information, the advent of later works may place a text in a new light. This model of the text proposes that it acquires its meaning(s) not primarily at the moment of production but at the various moments of reception. The author as originating source of meaning was steadily demoted if not altogether banished from the scene (← AUTHORSHIP: *Raoul Walsh*, p. 177) as attention was diverted to the function of the reader (→ *Narrative and audience*, p. 245). Barthes formulated this shift in a characteristic epigram: 'the birth of the reader must be at the cost of the death of the Author' (*Image-Music-Text*, 1977, p. 148).

Reader and text

Part of the project of *S/Z*, in conjunction with an assault on the myth of the author as only seat of creativity, was to argue for the emancipation of readers from the role of passive consumers traditionally assigned them by the 'culture industry': 'our literature is characterised by the pitiless divorce which the literary institution maintains between the producer of the text and its user ... Instead of gaining access ... to the pleasure of writing, (the reader) is left with no more than the poor freedom either to accept or reject the text' (*S/Z*

Littlest Rebel – raises questions of stereotyping

p. 4). This, Barthes believed, had not always been the case. Just as at one time the artist was seen not as creative genius but as a craftsman (← AUTHORSHIP: *Ingmar Bergman*, p. 116) so was his/her activity not a unique gift, but a skill which could be acquired, potentially at least, by anyone with the means, leisure and inclination to do so: 'There was a period when practising amateurs were numerous (at least within the confines of a certain class)' (*Image-Music-Text*, 1977, p. 162). This period came to an end when the privileged nobility was displaced through the rise of the middle class, and art within a capitalist economy became transformed into a commodity, produced by one sector of society, the talented élite, for another, the cultured but (supposedly) untalented consumers.

This division of labour, then, is not inevitable, and Barthes recalled in retrospect that 'what I tried to begin in *S/Z* was a kind of identification of the notions of writing and reading: I wanted to squash the two together' (*Signs of the Times*, 1971, p. 47). The reader should not consider him- or herself as the inferior of the 'creative' writer: rather than humbly, scrupulously attending to the text in order

to discern its 'singular, theological meaning', s/he should take up a less reverent attitude, seeking to *change* it by contributing to the process in which new meanings are generated: 'a form of work ... a labour of language' (*S/Z* pp. 10–11). However, this active reader was not 'free' to change the text(s) at will: the relationship between reader and text was conceived as a dialectical one, that is, not only does the reader act upon, produce the text (at least, ideally) but, equally, it acts upon, 'produces' him or her.

These formulations can be seen as a reaction against a long philosophical tradition, stemming from Descartes and other thinkers of the Enlightenment, which rested on a conception of the self as a unified, rational being. An important strand within structuralist theory, drawing on the psychoanalytical work of Freud and, more recently, Jacques Lacan (→ *Narrative and audience*, p. 246) holds this view to be a fallacy. In the same way that the text is not a pre-given, self-sufficient entity but an unstable, multiply determined and consistently developing process, so too, the argument runs, is the person who reads it. Our sense of identity is produced, and endlessly renewed by the intersection of systems of social conventions (language is seen as an exemplary case) which derive their peculiar power from the fact that they operate at a deep, unconscious level. At the same time, they allow the person concerned (or 'subject') to enjoy, on the conscious level, the illusion of being a consistent and autonomous 'human individual'. This is not, as the analogy drawn between text and reader might suggest, necessarily to deny any importance at all to conscious, rational elements, but rather to emphasise the

workings of the unconscious as a corrective strategy against the established and still dominant conception of the individual as a free agent fully aware and in control of him or herself (also ← AUTHORSHIP: *Structuralism and individualism*, p. 170).

The consequences of this shift for a theory of cinema are quite momentous. For, it is further maintained, one of these social systems, or discourses, which contribute to the formation of the human psyche is the artistic text. Each time we read a novel or view a film, we are perhaps, in a tiny way, reinforced (or, as the case may be, challenged) in our secure feeling of personal identity and all the preconceptions and prejudices that go with it. The difficult, but fascinating question remains of exactly how this happens, a question which has preoccupied recent theoretical writing on the cinema.

References

Roland Barthes, 'Introduction to the structural analysis of narratives', in *Communications 8*, 1966 (trans. by Stephen Heath in *Image-Music-Text*, London, Fontana, 1977).

Roland Barthes, *S/Z*, Paris, Editions du Seuil, 1970 (New York, Hill and Wang, 1974; trans. Richard Miller).

Roland Barthes, 'The realist effect', *Film Reader 3*, 1978; trans. Gerald Mead.

Roland Barthes, *Le Plaisir du texte*, Paris, Editions du Seuil, 1973 (*The Pleasure of the Text*, New York, Hill and Wang, 1975; trans. Richard Miller).

Roland Barthes, *Mythologies*, Paris, Editions du Seuil, 1957 (St. Albans, Paladin, 1973; trans. Annette Lavers).

Roland Barthes, *Système de la Mode*, Paris, Editions du Seuil, 1967.

Roland Barthes, *Image-Music-Text*, London, Fontana, 1977; selected and trans. by Stephen Heath.

Andrew Britton, 'The ideology of *Screen*', *Movie 26*, 1978/79.

Rosalind Coward and John Ellis, *Language and Materialism*, London, Routledge and Kegan Paul, 1977.

Jacques Derrida, *L'Ecriture et la différance*, Paris, Editions du Seuil, 1967 (*Writing and Difference*, London, Routledge and Kegan Paul, 1979; trans. A. Bass).

Sylvia Harvey, *May '68 and Film Culture*, London, British Film Institute, 1978.

Stephen Heath, 'A conversation with Roland Barthes', in *Signs of the Times*, Cambridge, 1971, pp. 41–51.

Julia Lesage, '*S/Z* and *Rules of the Game*', *Jump Cut* no. 12/13, December 1976.

Terry Lovell, *Pictures of Reality*, London, British Film Institute, 1980.

Judith Mayne, '*S/Z* and film criticism', *Jump Cut* no. 12/13, December 1976.

Steve Neale, 'The same old story', *Screen Education* 32/33, Autumn/Winter 1979/80.

Janice R. Welsch, 'Renoir through Lesage and Barthes', *Film Criticism* vol. 2 no. 2/3, Winter/Spring 1978.

Robin Wood, 'Hawks de-Wollenised', in *Personal Views*, London, Gordon Fraser, 1976.

Narrative and Audience

Introduction

An important shift in emphasis can be traced through the work of the past decade. Whereas the earlier research into narrative discussed above had analysed texts as autonomous, self-contained entities, theorists have increasingly argued that meaning is not immanent and pre-existing – instead it is created anew in every encounter between reader/viewer/listener and text. Attention has therefore been directed to a greater understanding of what happens in the course of this encounter. The change of focus is described succinctly in the Introduction to the 1976 *Edinburgh Film Festival Magazine*: 'The main problem of film criticism can no longer be restricted to the object cinema, as opposed to the operation cinema (a specific signifying practice which places the spectator)' (p. 4).

The difference between this new approach and the structural studies of narrative considered above can be seen quite clearly if we compare Metz's initial work on film language culminating in the *grande syntagmatique* (published in the mid 1960s ← p. 229) with his later but equally influential articles, 'The imaginary signifier' (1975) and 'History/Discourse – A note on two voyeurisms' (1975). In his earlier writing, Metz had tried to establish a method for classifying 'the object cinema', for identifying its components, breaking it down into segments. But his more recent work has aimed to define the *subjective* dimension of film-going, addressing itself to problems such as the effect produced upon us, the audience, by 'the operation cinema' and (a deceptively simple question) why we enjoy watching movies.

A similar direction has been pursued by Roland Barthes (← Barthes p. 238). His 'Introduction to the structural analysis of narratives' (1966) fashioned a 'descriptive tool' to dissect narrative into functional units with seemingly scientific precision. Even *S/Z* (1970), a transitional work, was still devoted primarily (though not exclusively) to the interplay of codes within the novella *Sarrasine*. But *The Pleasure of the Text* (1973) is a meditation on the actual experience of reading and the pleasures (cerebral, visceral and sometimes even erotic) which it provides. As the dates of the books and articles cited imply, all manner of shifts and changes in methodology have come in bewilderingly quick succession. This is, indeed, a 'runaway history', as Barthes himself acknowledged, 'marked by a very rapid acceleration' (*Signs of the Times*, 1971, p. 42). The evolution of post-structuralist theory in this country has been equally compressed: articles written within the space of only one or two years may put forward quite dissimilar ideas. Moreover, in many ways, the development has not always been straightforward and linear, one reason

being that translations of some of the most influential French sources have appeared erratically and out of chronological order. The strands are all the more difficult to untangle given that the debates have been conducted not in a couple of key books but in scattered articles, arguments and counter-arguments by a number of different writers (← AUTHORSHIP: *Structuralism: the French intellectual context*, p. 165). These cautionary remarks are intended partly to suggest that the corpus of film theory built up, mainly in *Screen*, in the course of the 1970s should not be seen as a simple monolith, although it may often appear as such to critics unfamiliar with or unfriendly to this kind of approach. Partly also as a caveat that the present project will, for reasons of space, also need to simplify and generalise – though, one hopes, without imposing too much of a spurious homogeneity on very diverse points of view.

Another factor which distinguishes this later work on narrative from the detached, quasi-scientific theories considered above is a felt need to redefine the ideological function of the popular cinema. Early structuralist work on cinema narrative was based on the principle that analysis should be impartial, assessing the text, Propp-like (← *Propp* p. 234), as if it were a biological organism. This work tended to content itself with dissecting films in order to discover their underlying formal structure, whilst neglecting to place them in their social context – this, indeed, is one of the most common criticisms levelled against Propp.

Under the pressure of political events and theoretical advances by Julia Kristeva, Barthes and others (see Harvey, 1978, and *Screen* Editorial, Spring 1974), it was increasingly felt that 'a theory of value' was needed, one which would provide some insight not just into the mechanical nuts-and-bolts structure of narrative, but also into its ideological effects. This argument informed the way in which approaches to narrative theory and analysis pioneered in France were mediated into British film culture. *Screen*, the main platform for these debates, had a consciously 'interventionalist' policy. Its aim was not only to describe but also to change its object of study (see for instance Stephen Heath's remarks on the desirable 'emphases and options' for *Screen*: Summer 1974, p. 126). Moreover, by the time that the semiotic/structuralist work of Metz and others had begun to make an impact in this country in the early 1970s, its interrogation of its own former specious objectivity was well under way. For instance, the *Screen* special issue on Metz (Spring/Summer 1973) contained not only translations of some of Metz's earlier essays, but an article by Julia Kristeva, 'The semiotic activity', which called many of their assumptions into question. So the primary concerns of the theoretical writing considered below are: first, to work towards

a greater understanding of the relationship between viewer and film; second, to assess the ideological implications of this process; and third, to do so not so much in the interests of scientific accuracy or high scholarly endeavour but rather with the political aim to develop 'a new social practice of the cinema' (see Introduction to the 1976 *Edinburgh Film Festival Magazine*).

The 'classic realist text'

Perhaps one of the more accessible routes into some difficult terrain is provided by Colin MacCabe's influential concept of *the classic realist text* (MacCabe, 'Realism and the cinema: notes on some Brechtian theses', 1974). MacCabe summarised this concept in the form of two theses: 1) 'The classic realist text cannot deal with the real as contradictory.' 2) 'In a reciprocal movement the classic realist text ensures the position of the subject in a relation of dominant specularity' (MacCabe, 1974, p. 12).

In the first of these theses, MacCabe addressed himself to the formal organisation of the text, its internal consistency and cohesion – characteristics which have also been identified by Barthes (← *Barthes* p. 238) as hallmarks of the 'readerly' work. The classic realist text might seem able to accommodate contradiction in the form of different discourses of viewpoints, usually assigned to various characters in the narrative, which vie for supremacy. But this apparent pluralism is actually, he argued, illusory; irreconcilable contradiction would threaten the inner stability of the text. This threat is neutralised by according the warring discourses unequal status, and arranging them in a hierarchy. The one at the top, the *dominant discourse*, acts as the Voice of Truth, over-ruling and interpreting all the others (← AUTHORSHIP: *Documentary* p. 190; HISTORY OF NARRATIVE: *The classic narrative system*, p. 212).

Taking as his first example the nineteenth-century novel, a form which has often been seen as the direct historical predecessor of mainstream cinema, MacCabe suggested that here the voice of truth is the 'narrative prose', the impersonal 'metalanguage' which constantly comments on and subsumes the 'object languages' of individual figures within the world of the fiction. He provided an analysis of George Eliot's *Middlemarch* to illustrate these strategies at work. While conceding that it was more difficult to detect the dominant discourse in classic cinema, MacCabe argued that the 'position of knowledge' offered in the novel by the 'narrative prose' was taken over in film by the 'narration of events' through *images*. Thus 'the camera shows us what happens – it tells the truth against which we can measure the other discourses' (MacCabe, 1974, p. 10). He supported this proposal by referring to scenes in *Klute* and (in the *Screen* Spring 1976 article) to *Days of Hope* where the 'erroneous' information purveyed on the soundtrack is played off against the 'truth' of what is seen (Mac-Cabe, '*Days of Hope* – a response to Colin McArthur', 1976). The commonsense assumption that we can 'trust the evidence of our own eyes' indicates how potent our confidence in the visual can be.

Clearly, this approach constitutes a break with the tradition within cinema aesthetics which conceives of the photographic image as an authentic record of the 'real world' (a view found for instance, in certain of Bazin's writings – ← p. 224). Instead, like Barthes (← p. 238), MacCabe insists that the realist narrative film bears no relation whatever to any 'essential reality', though it aims to give this impression. In its exclusive concern with the formal organisation of classic narrative in novel and film, examined as independent, self-contained entities, MacCabe's first proposition looks back to the earlier structuralist models considered above. But the second term in his definition of realism typifies the subsequent shift of film theory away from the internal features of the text and towards the process of interaction between text and reader/viewer. In classic cinematic narrative, according to this second proposition, not only does the image function as a guarantor of truth, but it is *seen* to do so by the viewer. His/her position is one of an overseer, of 'dominant specularity', which is however, illusory: a 'pseudo-dominance'. The hierarchy of discourses within the film favours a singular meaning, and the viewer, offered apparently unimpeded access to knowledge, is discouraged from working to create his/her own reading. S/he remains passive, placed 'outside the realm of contradiction and action – outside of production'. This 'petrification' of the viewer sustains the opposition between work/production and leisure/consumption (← *Barthes* p. 238) which is necessary in order to assure the 'reproduction of labour power' (MacCabe, 1974, pp. 21–27).

Althusser's theory of ideology

The thinking behind this assertion draws substantially on the writing of the Marxist philosopher Louis Althusser on ideology. His concept is a complex and controversial one, and has been amply debated elsewhere (see Thompson, 1978; Lovell, 1980). What is important, though, for the purposes of the present argument is that he recasts the classical Marxist model of economic base/ideological superstructure so as to propose for the latter a far more active role in society than had hitherto been generally allowed (← AUTHORSHIP: *Structuralism: the French intellectual context*, p. 165). For Althusser, ideology is 'relatively autonomous' of the economic base and determined by it only 'in the last instance'. Ideology takes the form of systems of representation which can have a political effectivity of their own. The political order is secured, in most societies,

not so much by coercion as by consent. The main agencies for organising and holding in place this consent are what Althusser calls the Ideological State Apparatuses. Of these the most important are institutions such as the education system, Church and family. Art, too, is seen as comprised within the apparatuses which contribute to the unconscious formation of individuals by 'interpellating' them in various ways, summoning them to take up their role in society (Althusser, 'Ideology and Ideological State Apparatuses', 1971). It is not a question here of the indoctrination of one class/sub-class by another (as some vulgar Marxist theories have it), since interpellation takes place at an unconscious level and in all men and women, but rather of a process of socialisation, an essential condition of communal existence within any economic order. In short, Althusser proposes that individuals are placed as social subjects in subtle and largely imperceptible ways – ways which simultaneously promote in them the impression of being consistent, rational and free human agents (for an account of this aspect of Althusser's thought, see Stephen Heath, 'Lessons from Brecht', 1974, pp. 113–115). A number of areas are still left grey by this theory of interpellation or subject positioning, especially as it was first taken up by MacCabe and others and applied to what was suggestively called 'the cinematic apparatus'. Many of these ambiguities and problems emerge sharply from the arguments around 'classic realism', as manifested in MacCabe's original article, as well as in the way some of his ideas were elaborated on by other writers and in the more common criticisms levelled against them.

One of the most potentially interesting and valuable aspects of Althusser's work for a theory of cinema is that it indicates a different way of conceiving its ideological function which avoids the twin pitfalls of, on the one hand, the reductionist model of Hollywood films as mirrors of the capitalist system which produced them (i.e. total and immediate determination) and on the other the essentialism involved in a belief in 'art for art's sake' (i.e. culture regarded as totally independent of its historical context). The formulation of 'relative autonomy' retains the notion of the long-term, ultimate determination of the economic ('in the last instance'), whilst resisting a notion of simple direct reflexivity. But the difficulty remains of understanding the precise workings of this intricate and highly mediated relationship between base and superstructure. An objection often made about some of the recent work on film narrative – the theory of 'classic realism' for instance – is that it tends indefinitely to postpone or to ignore altogether the moment of the 'last instance', so that the autonomy of the text, in principle 'relative', is effectively seen as absolute. This results in increasingly detailed sophisticated analyses of the

formal operations of texts which, however, fail to allow any significant role to the material conditions under which they were produced – a particularly questionable omission in the case of an industrial art-form like the cinema (see Harvey, 1978, for a discussion of these problems in connection with French film theory, or, for a more hostile view, Clarke et al, 1980).

Criticism of 'classic realism'

Other writers have argued that the concept of 'the classic text' is too ambitious in its aim to provide a prototype applicable to all realist narrative. Such a prototype completely disregards elements which may be extrinsic to the narrative proper but which nonetheless inflect and sometimes radically transform its meaning, such as generic conventions, institutional factors or its relation to other films (see McArthur '*Days of Hope*', 1975/76).

This case could be pressed further. It could be objected, for instance, that by downplaying the qualities of specific texts, by attending to formal structure, seen as a constant, rather than for instance to thematic content, which will vary far more widely, and by over-privileging 'sameness' at the expense of 'difference' (← *Barthes*, p. 240), this work fails to do justice to the subtlety of individual films. What then happens is that the model of classic realism becomes a grid within which each text is inserted a little too smoothly as yet another revamping of the same old pattern: MacCabe's readings (1974, 1976, and 1978/79) of films like *Klute*, *American Graffiti*, *Nashville* and *Padre Padrone* are arguably open to this stricture. Alternatively, a favoured film may be hailed as an exception which only serves to prove the rule (e.g. John Ellis on *A Matter of Life and Death* and its recalcitrance to the dominant British tradition in *Powell, Pressburger and Others*, 1978). To unmask a text as formally realist (whether it be classic or progressive in its content) is in a sense to denounce it as acting on the viewer in a repressive way. So some of this work on realism has tended to dismiss the mainstream narrative film wholesale as an ideological monolith, a purely manipulative 'Ideological State Apparatus' for 'the reproduction of labour power', and in doing so, arguably blocks off the possibility of a productive engagement with the popular cinema. Admittedly, the function of the mainstream film is now seen as actively reinforcing rather than passively reflecting dominant attitudes and beliefs. And in any case, MacCabe's category of classic realism avoids a charge of intellectual snobbery by spanning the high art/mass culture divide, 'lumping together *The Grapes of Wrath* and *The Sound of Music*' (MacCabe, 1974, p. 12). But even if it does not represent a simple hostility towards popular narrative forms it at times comes uncomfortably close to such a condemnation; what is needed perhaps, is a more flexible approach to the cinema, realist or

North by Northwest – a visual representation of reality?

Stagecoach – the camera assumes the spatial position of a character

otherwise, as a complex and highly differentiated cultural form.

These criticisms could provide a useful starting-point for debate, and many of them seem justified in retrospect. However, there is a danger involved in approaching the concept of realism in narrow terms of its theoretical 'correctness'. So it is important to bear it in mind that MacCabe's original formulation and subsequent work based on it form part of a movement in the development of film theory which many of the writers concerned have now left behind. The first *Screen* special issue on Brecht (where this article first appeared) was published in 1974, at a time when, leaving aside the odd

translation from the French of research by Metz (← p. 229), Gardies and others, British writers had scarcely begun to address themselves to the question of film narrative. So a beneficial effect of this work by MacCabe and others was to draw attention to the need for a greater understanding of this area. His comparative study of realism in novel and cinema exposed the glaring lack in film theory of the kind of precise critical concepts (omniscient narrator, *style indirect libre*, stream of consciousness, etc.) available to the analyst of literary prose. The MacCabe/McArthur exchange and concurrent research by other writers appear, then, not as fully-fledged theories, but as 'work in progress': ex-

ploratory attempts to come to grips with issues such as the kind of knowledge proffered by the realist cinema, the techniques it uses to regulate that knowledge and the relationship of the different characters within the narrative to knowledge and truth. These are among the matters which have been high on the agenda for subsequent theoretical inquiry.

Point-of-view in cinema

For instance, a notion which has become crucial to recent writing on the cinema is *point-of-view*, now recognised as one of the medium's major rhetorical figures. Technically speaking, this refers to a shot in which the camera assumes the spatial position of one of the characters within the narrative in order to show us what s/he sees (see Branigan, 'Formal permutations of the point-of-view shot', 1975); most directors use this device to varying extents, one of its acknowledged masters being Hitchcock (see Bellour, '*The Birds* – analysis of a sequence', 1972). It may (but not necessarily), intimate some notion of the person's inner state of mind (see Heath, 'Narrative space', 1976, and Metz, 'Current problems of film theory', 1973). It may even, perhaps, encourage the viewer to empathise with him or her, though again this need not be so: Nick Browne has examined in detail a sequence from *Stagecoach* (1939) which is dominated by point-of-view shots ascribed to a character whose prejudices we are clearly not invited to share (Browne, 'The spectator-in-the-text', 1975/76). Similarly, the most (in)famous example of sustained and systematic use of a single subjective point-of-view, *The Lady in the Lake*, is held by most critics to fail in its project to make the audience identify with the central figure (see Metz, 1973).

These difficulties indicate that much work still remains to be done on the way in which point-of-view is used to create a film narrative and to establish varying relationships between dramatis personae and audience (see *Film Reader* 4, 1979). However, recent research has opened up some fruitful fields of inquiry. If the use of point-of-view shots is linked to the discourses of different characters, are these subsumed, in the mainstream cinema, by an impersonal, dominant discourse comparable to the 'omniscient narrator' of realist prose (see Heath on *Touch of Evil*, 1975)? Can it be argued that certain texts resist or undermine this voice of authority, the case sometimes made for the modernism of filmmakers such as Dreyer or Bresson (see Nash, '*Vampyr* and the Fantastic', 1976, and Browne, 'Narrative and point-of-view', 1977)? Are some kinds of discourse consistently privileged over others? This third question has a particular purchase for an understanding of the status accorded the discourse of certain social groups: for example race, class or gender. Thus an important tendency within feminist film theory has been directed at the suppression of the woman's voice in the classical Hollywood cinema (see Rose, 'Paranoia and the film system', 1976/7 and Bellour, 1979), or its partial resistance in certain texts (see *Dorothy Arzner*, 1975, and *Women in Film Noir*, 1978).

Narrative and subject positions

So the basic groundwork laid by this early writing on realism has had far-reaching implications. However, the approaches outlined above could be seen as still primarily concerned (as indeed was Mac-Cabe's first proposition about the 'hierarchy of discourses' in the classical work) with the formal structures of narrative, considered as a self-contained entity. But perhaps even more influential has been the line of development presaged, and in part initiated by his second proposition: that the effect of these operations is to 'place' the *subject* in a fixed position of knowledge towards the text.

At first sight this seems a curious assertion. Surely sharp disagreement is perfectly possible between individuals even about what might seem the most unambiguously classic of realist texts; how then can one speak in such general terms of a single 'subject position'? In fact, an objection often made about this concept is that the 'viewing subject' it refers to is a meaningless abstraction, with no bearing on 'real' audiences in their social and historical diversity (see Coward, 'Class, "culture" and the social formation', 1977; Chambers et al, 'Marxism and culture', 1977/78). In considering criticisms in this vein, we need to take into account a key conceptual distinction. On the one hand, there is the empirical spectator whose interpretation of film will be determined by all manner of extraneous factors like personal biography, class origins, previous viewing experience, the variables of conditions of reception etc. On the other hand, the abstract notion of a 'subject-position', which could be defined as the way in which a film solicits, demands even, a certain closely circumscribed reading from a viewer by means of its own formal operations (Ellis, 1978). This distinction seems fruitful, inasmuch as it accepts that different individuals can interpret a text in different ways, while insisting that the text itself imposes definite limits on their room to manoeuvre. In other words, it promises a method which avoids the two extremes of an infinite pluralism which posits as many possible readings as there are readers, each equally legitimate, and an essentialism which asserts a single 'true' meaning. It would be, then, not altogether justified, simply to dismiss the work discussed below as a historical formalism, even if it might appear to be concerned exclusively with the subject as passively determined by the text rather than with the active input of individuals in creating and changing its meaning. Instead, these theories of subjectivity should perhaps be seen as a necessary step towards under-standing how these two processes interact in particular social contexts.

Renaissance space and the spectator

One of the most intriguing questions to have developed out of these debates is that of the function of space in the cinema. An important focus of interest has been the concept of *découpage*, i.e. the breakdown of the dramatic action into separate shots at the moment of filming and inversely, its reconstruction, on the editing table (and mentally, by the spectator in the cinema) into a coherent, logical space (see Burch, 1973). Some writers have examined how a narrative is generated out of the juxtaposition of these fragments (see Bellour, 'The obvious and the code', 1974/75, and the *Screen* issue on Ozu, Summer 1976). Others have investigated the historical emergence of certain conventions of editing (the so-called 'classical system') which eventually came to dominate film syntax (← HISTORY OF NARRATIVE: *Classic narrative system*, p. 212). However, a connected, though in significant ways quite different issue crucial to work on subjectivity pertains to another kind of spatial relationship: not between shots within the film, but between viewer and screen. For instance, how is the illusion of a three-dimensional area created and sustained on a flat plane, and how is the spectator situated vis-à-vis the events s/he sees? Perhaps because it is difficult to disengage oneself from the theoretical tradition that sees the photographic image as a neutral record of the 'real world', these problems have tended to be approached from a different discipline. The work of art historians has been utilised to trace through the emergence of a geometrical perspective system in another (and patently non-mechanical) medium of representation: painting.

The development of single perspective and deep space photography often seems an inevitable consequence of cinema technology, but in painting it is clearly neither a cultural nor an historical necessity. Many non-Western traditions employ multiple perspective just as, in the evolution of European art, the rise to dominance of the single perspective system took place at a particular historical moment. It was introduced in the early years of the fifteenth century in Italy (the period known as the *Quattrocento*) and was eventually abandoned towards the end of the nineteenth century by painters like Cézanne who explored different conceptions of space. So the use of three-dimensional perspective in painting did not become firmly established until the European Renaissance – and not, it has been suggested, by coincidence. This was a period of transition from the theocentric (i.e. God-centred) metaphysics of the Dark Ages to an anthropocentric (human-centred) view of the universe: dramatic changes which translated themselves into a new mode of artistic representation. In contrast to earlier conventions, Renaissance space required objects within the

Pre-Quattrocento perspective – XIV century mosaic (St Marks, Venice)

image to be set out in relation to a fixed point of reference. The viewer was, in a sense, implicit in a painting – it was organised *for* him or her in a way which both presupposed and perpetuated a vision of a logical and well-ordered world with man at its hub (see Heath, 'Narrative space', 1976).

Applying this line of argument to the cinema, theorists have noted that, despite the possibilities offered by distorting lenses, it depicts space in a manner very similar to Renaissance art. In fact the mechanical aid devised by *Quattrocento* painters to correct perspective errors (the *camera obscura*, or darkened chamber) was the forerunner of the modern camera used for still and motion photography (see Bordwell and Thompson, 1979, pp. 144-

145). This would seem to challenge the wide-spread notion that film technology has, thanks to scientific progress (the advent of sound, deep-focus cinematography and colour), moved steadily towards the ever more efficient and accurate reproduction of 'reality'. Rather, the end in view is the embodiment of specifically humanist values and beliefs (see Ogle, and Williams's response, *Screen Reader*, 1977). Indeed, for some writers cinema is already suffused with ideological assumptions at the level of the individual shot, that is, before the construction of narrative, by the very nature of its own machinery (see Baudry, 'Ideological effects of the basic cinematographic apparatus', 1974/75 and Bailblé, 'Programming the look', 1979/80). The organisation of components within the picture is not only informed by a particular world-view; it also demands of the spectator a certain complicity in these operations if s/he is to decipher its meaning.

Images into narrative

But film is unlike painting or still photography in one major respect: it provides not a single image but a series of images from ceaselessly shifting positions. It might seem at first that the cinema works upon the spectator quite differently from figurative art since, continually displaced within the fictional scene, s/he is unable to enjoy a fixed vantage-point. Indeed, paradoxically, these constant shot changes seem essential to the cinema's narrative system. Conversely, long static takes, as in, for instance, some of Chantal Akerman's films, far from providing a reassuringly secure viewing-position, appear to disrupt the illusion of reality (see Johnston, 'Towards a feminist film practice', 1976, and Heath 'Notes on suture', 1977/78): this finds expression in the impatience and/ or discomfort commonly felt by audiences when a shot is held a little 'too long'. The key to this puzzle could be seen as lying in the peculiar nature of film as narrative which, in contrast to the single image, depends heavily on duration and performance, the holding of the viewer over an extended period of time. This feat requires a delicate balancing act, the playing out of a tension between 'process (with its threat of incoherence, of the loss of mastery) and position (with its threat of stasis, fixity or of compulsive repetition, which is the same thing in another form)' (Neale, 1980, p. 26). Stability alone would soon lead to impatience and boredom, and what is needed is a perpetual oscillation between delicious instants of risk and repeated temporary returns to equilibrium. Some writers believe that the pleasurability of the cinema resides in precisely this process of limited risk (see Heath, 'Film performance', 1977). This model of the spectator's response to narrative contrasts sharply with MacCabe's more static formulation of 'dominant specularity (← *The 'classic realist text'*, p. 242).

It should be stressed that this theoretical work is not (primarily) concerned with any danger experienced by the characters in the fictional story, but, more crucially, with the threat posed to the viewer by the formal operations of the film: the threat, that is, of the loss of meaning and control. The concept which has been elaborated to explain how this happens is that of suture.

Suture

Originally used by surgeons to denote the stitching which joins the edges of a wound, the term 'suture' was borrowed in the 60s by the French neo-Freudian psychoanalyst Jacques Lacan and his associates as a means of understanding the relationship between the conscious and unconscious forces which produces the human subject (← AUTHORSHIP: *Structuralism and individualism*, p. 170). This relationship is seen in terms of an uneasy alliance between the two forms of psychic organisation called by Lacan the *Imaginary* and the *Symbolic*. The former, which is characterised by the unity it confers upon subject and object, bears a privileged relationship to vision: in early infancy, the child discovers its reflection in a mirror, its first apprehension of its body as unified. This moment (which Lacan calls the *mirror phase*) is central to the operation of the human psyche, providing the basis of our narcissistic relationship to the rest of the world, in which others are seen as versions of ourselves and we each experience ourselves as unified beings at the centre of the world (see MacCabe, 1976, p. 13).

However, the fact that the mind does not develop and function in a vacuum casts doubt on our assumption of total indiviual autonomy. Saussurian linguistics had opposed the notion that words have an already-given intrinsic meaning, insisting instead that they derive their signification only in the interplay of different, shifting combinations and contexts (← *Barthes* p. 238). In the same way, Lacanians argue, accounts of the 'human individual' such as those derived from ego-psychology, which see it as already and finally formed, fail to recognise that from birth onwards this individual must define its identity (and be defined) within and against systems of pre-existing cultural relations. Successful social interaction requires individuals to engage in a complex network of rules and conventions (described by Lacanians as 'entry into the Symbolic'). This process begins from earliest childhood, decisive stages being the learning of language, and the acquisition of a fixed (hetero-)sexual identity, which prepares the child for cultural 'normality'.

This argument suggests that the chief constraints at work in the evolution of the subject lie beyond our conscious control. Thus while manipulating the elementary codes essential to everyday activities like holding a conversation (or watching and understanding a film), we 'forget' the intricate symbolic structures which are necessary to any meaningful social activity. Yet

these structures are nonetheless present and, moreover, play a major role in shaping the unconscious. Because they originate within the culture as a whole, the unconscious should be seen less as a discrete entity than as a grey, shifting area between Self and Non-Self, the site where diverse and frequently conflicting sign systems coincide, and collide. For Lacanians our psychic life is a perpetual flux and reflux between the favoured realm of the Imaginary, which functions not as a temporary phase on the road to maturity, but as a recurring desire of the individual to seek and foster the wholeness of a unified ideal ego; and that, less congenial to us, of the Symbolic, which forces our acknowledgement of the morass of determinations at work in the constitution of the psyche. It is here that the concept of suture comes into play, understood as the constant striving of the ego to fill in these gaps, and to impose unity on the conflicting forces in the unconscious. These would otherwise challenge the coherence of a stable identity, and would lead, perhaps, if unchecked to mental illness, and an inability to negotiate 'normal' social relationships (← AUTHORSHIP: *Structuralism and individualism*, p. 170).

Psychoanalysis and film

What, then, is the relevance of this work for the study of the cinema? One of the most enduring problems facing film theory and criticism is the elusive quality of their own object. Images have a tangible existence on celluloid, yet this materiality is constantly belied by the conditions under which we receive them. On one level, there are the practical difficulties of access to facilities for studying actual films (though the advent of video technology should change this). But also, more fundamentally, the very nature of film seems to reside in a relentless flow of images, the pleasures and fascinations it offers stemming from a fleeting ephemerality which defies attempts to arrest and contain it. Empirical audience research is unable to account fully for the viewing experience, and for the relation between film narrative and spectator. The more or less vague, but cohesive and reasoned memory we retain from a visit to the cinema has little in common with the complex and subtle, barely perceptible processes that move us while we are actually watching a film. The sociological approach therefore appeared to be in itself inadequate; the insights it offered needed to be complemented by work on an altogether different plane.

The tools and methods of psychoanalysis offered film theorists a means of understanding the operations at a micro-level of the 'mental machinery' activated by the passage of images on screen. The idea of suture seemed a useful way of defining the minute shifts and revisions that take place in our state of mind throughout the viewing of a film: a constant movement of the spectator between the dual domains of the

Imaginary and the Symbolic, a movement which 'holds us in place' as we watch and enjoy the film. The concept is a difficult one, and has been used by various writers in slightly different ways (see Miller et al, 'Dossier on suture', *Screen*, Winter 1977/78), but the process has been described as something like this. At the beginning of each shot, the spectator enjoys a secure imaginary relationship to the film, a feeling bound up with the illusion of privileged control over and unmediated access to its fictional world. A moment later, though, this illusion is dispelled as s/he gradually becomes conscious of the image frame, and hence of the fact that the fictional space is after all narrowly circumscribed. This realisation stimulates the desire to see and find out more and the former illusion of the image as offering a 'window on the world' yields to an unpleasant perception of the film as artefact, a system of signs and codes that lie outside his/her control. However, this recognition is soon overcome by the advent of the next shot, which apparently restores the previous condition of the spectator's imaginary unity with the images and starts the cycle off again (Oudart, 'Cinema and suture', in 'Dossier on suture', 1977/78).

Another important aspect of the concept is its emphasis on the shot/reverse-shot pattern of narrative cinema and the involvement of the viewer in an intricate network of 'looks' (HISTORY OF NARRATIVE: *The look*, p. 211). The point-of-view shot unattached to a particular character draws the spectator into the text by positing him/her as the privileged observer of the image, in the place of an imagined character occupying the position of the camera (see Dayan, 'The tutor-code of classical cinema', 1974). In the following reverse-angle shot the point of origin of that look is assigned to a character within the fiction, thereby assuring that the viewer is not addressed directly by the film but remains safely outside it. In this way, s/he is, in topographical terms, right inside the fictional space, yet never actually part of the action.

It has been objected that this formulation tends to invest too much importance in a single rhetorical figure (the shot/reverse-shot) which, after all, is only one part of the total repertoire of film language: how for instance does suture function in sequences which feature no people, therefore no point-of-view shots? Certainly, it could be faulted for tending to equate suture with point-of-view cutting, and, as Stephen Heath suggested in a reply to these criticisms (Heath, 'Notes on suture', in 'Dossier on suture', 1977/78), it might be more useful to see suture as an effect of continuity editing in general, of which the shot/reverse-shot pattern would be one, but not the only, example. However, the most influential aspect of these ideas was less the precise mechanics of the process they aimed to describe than their model of the relationship ('separation in

Meet Me in St. Louis – 'film narrative . . . an interplay of looks'

identification' – Heath, 'Lessons from Brecht', 1974) of spectator to the events taking place on the screen.

Theories of the look

The concept of 'separation in identification' was echoed in contemporaneous theories of 'the look'. These also saw film narrative as a process generated primarily out of an interplay of looks: not only those exchanged between the characters on screen, epitomised by the point-of-view pattern, but also the look of the viewer, sitting in the cinema, at this fictional world, a look which the suturing process attempts to efface.

Metz was among those fascinated by the voyeuristic aspect of film viewing. In an essay first published in French in 1975 ('History/Discourse', 1976), he argued through this idea by comparing a visit to the cinema with a visit to the theatre. The performance of a play deliberately sets out to be a collective experience, an event which acknowledges the gathered populace implicitly or indeed sometimes even explicitly, as in direct asides to the audience. Thus 'actor and spectator are present to each other . . . (in) a ceremony which has a certain civic quality, engaging more than the private man'. Film, by contrast, 'is exhibitionistic and it is not . . . knows that it is being looked at and does not know . . . All the viewer requires – but he requires it absolutely – is that the actor should behave as though he is not being seen, and

so cannot see him, the voyeur'.

The peculiar nature of film as a not-quite performing art is reflected both in its conditions of production (the fact that, unlike the theatre, actors and audience are never physically present in the same place), and of its reception (the individual's immobility and sense of isolation from other spectators, the total darkness, the self-contained nature of the event, lack of interval to break up the narrative flow, etc.). In a striking image, Metz compared the cinema audience to fish gathered round the side of an aquarium, 'looking out' onto the fictional world, 'absorbing everything through their eyes and nothing through their bodies': the activity of looking becomes disproportionately important to the film-goer compared to the more integrated physical experience of theatre-going. Suggestively, he linked this difference to the much later historical origins of the cinema, which 'was born at a period when social life was strongly marked by the concept of the individual' and which 'belongs to the private man' (Metz, 'History/Discourse', 1976). His thinking is similar to some of the accounts mentioned above which link the development of film technology to changing conceptions of the world and our place in it.

In an influential article published around the same time, Laura Mulvey also focused on the drive to 'look' so important to visual pleasure in the cinema, but from a feminist perspective absent in Metz's

The Scarlet Empress – spectacle taking priority over narrative

work. Using a similar model of an uneasy and labile relationship between the forward drive of narrative and the potential of the static image to resist it, she proposed that in the classical Hollywood film these two functions were almost always gender-specific, reflecting and perpetuating the values of 'a world ordered by sexual imbalance' (Mulvey, 'Visual pleasure and narrative cinema', 1975). In other words, the active, narrative role of making things happen and controlling events usually fell to a male character, while the female star, often virtually peripheral to fictional events, remained more passively decorative. She functioned as the locus of masculine erotic desire, a spectacle to be looked at by both male characters and spectators, the latter, whatever their actual gender, being assumed and addressed as male by the operations of the film. The Sternberg/ Dietrich cycle has been seen as an extreme example of this tendency – Sternberg's celebrated remark that his films could well be projected upside-down was cited by Mulvey as evidence that for him spectacle tends to take priority over narrative.

Using Sternberg's and Hitchcock's work as contrasting examples, Mulvey's article analysed the way in which the figure of the woman could represent a 'trouble' within the classical narrative film (← AUTHORSHIP: *Alfred Hitchcock*, p. 128). On a simple level, those moments of enjoyable contemplation of the female body, if extended, constantly threatened to stall the

fictional flow, triggering the viewers' upleasant awareness of themselves as looking which the mechanisms of cinema are usually concerned to repress (← p. 247). In certain genres, such as the back-stage musical, which overtly employ the convention of the woman as showgirl, her spectacular performance of a song and/or dance anticipates this problem by 'matching' the look of the audience with that of male characters within the film, thus momentarily reconciling the tension between narrative and spectacle.

However, a more difficult and controversial strand in Mulvey's article examined in psychoanalytic terms the reason for the 'trouble' or threat represented by the female image in classic narrative cinema, with the aim of 'demonstrating the way the unconscious of patriarchal society has structured film form' (← AUTHORSHIP: *Feminism and counter-cinema*, p. 196). Drawing on Freudian theories of child development, this part of her argument placed great importance on the discovery of sexual difference: the moment at which the male child sees that his mother lacks a phallus, that she is 'castrated', and fears for the first time that he too might suffer such a dire fate. However, whilst classical psychoanalysis saw the 'castration complex' ahistorically, as universally necessary to the formation of the unconscious, feminist theorists began, in the course of the 1970s, to call this inevitability into question, reformulating the process as a

specific cultural phenomenon. At the same time, post-structuralist theories of representation and subject-positioning (← p. 245) provided concepts which could be appropriated as political weapons against the dominant system. For example, Saussure's hypothesis that 'in language there are only differences *without positive terms*' was taken over by Barthes, Derrida and other post-structuralists and applied to *all* sign systems (← *Barthes* p. 239). Put very simply, Mulvey's thesis was that the same ought to be true of representation of gender in the cinema. But, within patriarchal culture, the phallus becomes a privileged source of meaning, a 'positive term'. Instead of being defined by her own sexual attributes, her 'difference', 'woman' is perceived only negatively, as a lack: 'representation of the female form ... speaks castration and nothing else'. Mulvey saw the main project of the classical Hollywood narrative cinema as the generation of pleasures for the 'male' viewer which depended on deploying the body of the female star as a defence against the threat of castration she evokes (← AUTHORSHIP: *Raoul Walsh*, p. 177; HISTORY OF NARRATIVE: *Classic narrative system*, p. 212). Mulvey's article drew attention to the ideological implications of the interdependence of deep-seated psychic processes and the operations of narrative cinema, each feeding on and reinforcing the other. The problem she raised – without resolving it – was that of how to escape this

Dames – woman as indispensable element of spectacle

apparently vicious circle. Certainly, she made no bones about her own aims: 'It is said that analysing pleasure, or beauty, destroys it. That is the intention of this article . . . Not in favour . . . of intellectualised unpleasure, but to make way for a total negation of the ease and plenitude of the narrative fiction film . . . in order to conceive a new language of desire.' The precise form that this new language might take is left open. But in calling for it 'to free . . . the look of the audience into dialectics, passionate detachment', she seems to be calling for a viewer response which depends on radically different pleasures from the security of 'separation-in-identification' elicited by the classical cinema (← p. 247).

Conclusion
Much of the work on narrative and audience considered in this section has met, and in some quarters continues to meet, with considerable resistance. Critics in the empirical tradition, committed to close textual analysis, were suspicious of a high level of theoretical abstraction which often went unsupported by reference to specific films. To many, the writing seemed unnecessarily arcane: a weakness partly due to the difficulty of formulating new and unfamiliar ideas, and partly both the cause and the effect of a marginalised address to a small, mainly academic

readership. Others disliked what they perceived as an overall hostility towards mainstream cinema. In particular, the use of psychoanalysis to support an argument that images of women can only have a negative meaning within patriarchal culture appeared to block off the possibility of progressive feminist work within the rhetoric of the realist, representational (i.e. popular) film. Indeed, these approaches to narrative were often accompanied by a commitment to a different kind of filmmaking practice which would, in institutional terms, take place within a framework of independent production, distribution and exhibition and, in formal terms, set out to interrogate and subvert the conventions of dominant cinema (← AUTHORSHIP: *Counter-cinema*, p. 192; HISTORY OF NARRATIVE: *Counter-cinema*, p. 220). Although, in retrospect, many of these objections were justified, theoretical work evolved and changed in response to criticism. It was increasingly recognised that to see cinema in terms of polar oppositions – classic realist texts versus the avant-garde – was too schematic. This model ignores the extent to which a film's meaning and impact are historically variable and denies that specific texts always fall somewhere along a spectrum between the two extremes, combining in varying ratios features of traditional narrative with disruptive, contradictory elements (←

Barthes p. 238). Instead of rejecting wholesale the popular commercial cinema, writers and film-makers began to ask whether there might be a way of mobilising some of the pleasures of conventional narrative forms while at the same time calling them into question.

Similarly, the charge of over-abstraction receded as theory was put into practice, both explicitly, in informing textual analyses published in academic journals, and implicitly, in influencing the attitudes and priorities of teachers and journalists interested in this work. Many ideas which appear outrageous when they first surface are eventually assimilated in popularised (and vulgarised) form, transforming and being transformed by the critical orthodoxy until some new heterodoxy arrives to displace them. In film studies, this has already happened with the polemic for authorship, and is happening again with the theories of narrative examined here. Indeed this book is itself a part of that process.

References
Louis Althusser, 'Ideology and Ideological State Apparatuses', in *Lenin and Philosophy and other essays*, London, New Left Books, 1971; trans. Ben Brewster.
Claude Bailblé, 'Programming the look', *Screen Education* 32/33, Autumn/Winter 1979/80 (*Cahiers du Cinéma* 281, October 1977; 282, November 1977).

Woman as image, man as bearer of the look – *Under Capricorn, Lusty Men*

Roland Barthes, 'Introduction to the structural analysis of narratives', *Communications* 8, 1966 (*Image-Music-Text*, London, Fontana, 1977; trans. Stephen Heath).

Roland Barthes, *Le Plaisir du texte*, Paris, Editions du Seuil, 1970 (*The Pleasure of the Text*, New York, Hill and Wang, 1975; trans. Richard Miller).

Roland Barthes, *S/Z*, Paris, Editions du Seuil, 1970 (New York, Hill and Wang, 1974; trans. Richard Miller).

Jean-Louis Baudry, 'Ideological effects of the basic cinematographic apparatus', *Film Quarterly* vol. 28 no. 2, Winter 1974/75; trans. Alan Williams (*Cinéthique* 7/8, n/d).

Raymond Bellour, '*The Birds* – Analysis of a sequence', London, British Film Institute Education Dept., 1972 (reprinted 1981).

Raymond Bellour, 'The obvious and the code', *Screen* vol. 15 no. 4, Winter 1974/75.

Raymond Bellour, *L'Analyse du film*, Paris, Editions Albatros, 1979.

David Bordwell and Kristin Thompson, *Film Art*, Reading, Massachusetts, Addison-Wesley, 1979.

Edward Branigan, 'Formal permutations of the point-of-view shot', *Screen* vol. 16 no. 3, Autumn 1975.

Ben Brewster and Colin MacCabe, Editorial, *Screen* vol. 15 no. 1, Spring 1974.

Nick Browne, 'The spectator-in-the text: the rhetoric of *Stagecoach*', *Film Quarterly* vol. 29 no. 2, Winter 1975/76.

Nick Browne, 'Narrative point-of-view: the rhetoric of *Au hasard Balthazar*', *Film Quarterly* vol. 31 no. 1, Fall 1977.

Noël Burch, *Theory of Film Practice*, London, Secker and Warburg, 1973.

Simon Clarke et al, *One Dimensional Marxism: Althusser and the Politics of Culture*, London, Allison and Busby, 1980.

Iain Chambers et al, 'Marxism and culture', *Screen* vol. 18 no. 4, Winter 1977/78.

Rosalind Coward, 'Class, "culture" and the social formation', *Screen* vol. 18 no. 1, Spring 1977.

Daniel Dayan, 'The tutor-code of classical cinema', *Film Quarterly* vol. 28 no. 1, Fall 1974.

John Ellis, 'Watching death at work – an analysis of *A Matter of Life and Death*', in Ian Christie (ed.), *Powell, Pressburger and Others*, London, British Film Institute, 1978, esp. pp. 90 ff.

Film Reader 4, 1979, Point-of-view/Metahistory of film.

Hardy/Johnston/Willemen (eds.), *Edinburgh '76 Magazine: Psychoanalysis/Cinema/Avant-garde*, Edinburgh Film Festival, 1976.

Sylvia Harvey, *May '68 and Film Culture*, London, British Film Institute, 1978.

Stephen Heath, 'A conversation with Roland Barthes', *Signs of the Times*, Cambridge, 1971.

Stephen Heath, 'Lessons from Brecht', *Screen* vol. 15 no. 2, Summer 1974.

Stephen Heath, 'Film and system: terms of analysis', *Screen* vol. 16 no. 1/2, Spring/Summer 1975.

Stephen Heath, 'Narrative space', *Screen* vol. 17 no. 3, Autumn 1976, esp. pp. 93 ff.

Stephen Heath, 'Film performance', *Cinetracts* vol. 1 no. 2, 1977.

Stephen Heath, 'Notes on suture', *Screen* vol. 18 no. 4, Winter 1977/78.

Claire Johnston, 'Towards a feminist film practice' in Hardy/Johnston/Willemen (eds.), *Edinburgh '76 Magazine*, op. cit.

Claire Johnston (ed.), *Dorothy Arzner: towards a feminist critical strategy*, London, British Film Institute, 1975.

E. Ann Kaplan (ed.), *Women in Film Noir*, London, British Film Institute, 1978.

Terry Lovell, *Pictures of Reality*, London, British Film Institute, 1980.

Colin MacCabe, 'Realism and the cinema: notes on some Brechtian theses', *Screen* vol. 15 no. 2, Summer 1974.

Colin MacCabe, '*Days of Hope* – a response to Colin McArthur', *Screen* vol. 17 no. 1, Spring 1976.

Colin MacCabe, 'Principles of realism and pleasure', *Screen* vol. 17 no. 3, Autumn 1976.

Colin MacCabe, 'The discursive and the ideological in film', *Screen* vol. 19 no. 4, Winter 1978/79.

Colin McArthur, '*Days of Hope*', *Screen* vol. 16 no. 4, Winter 1975/76.

Christian Metz, 'Current problems of film theory: Christian Metz on Jean Mitry's *L'Esthétique et Psychologie du Cinéma Vol. II*', *Screen* vol. 14 no. 1/2, Spring/Summer 1973, esp. pp. 45 ff.; trans. Diana Matias.

Christian Metz, 'The imaginary signifier', *Screen* vol. 16 no. 2, Summer 1975, trans. Ben Brewster.

Christian Metz, 'History/Discourse – a note on two voyeurisms' in Hardy/Johnston/Willemen (eds.), *Edinburgh '76 Magazine*, op. cit.; trans. Susan Bennett.

Jacques-Alain Miller, Jean-Pierre Oudart, Stephen Heath, 'Dossier on suture', *Screen* vol. 18 no. 4, Winter 1977/78.

Laura Mulvey, 'Visual pleasure and narrative cinema', *Screen* vol. 16 no. 3, Autumn 1975.

Mark Nash, '*Vampyr* and the fantastic', *Screen* vol. 17 no. 3, Autumn 1976.

Stephen Neale, *Genre*, London, British Film Institute, 1980.

Patrick Ogle, 'Technological and aesthetic influences upon the development of deep-focus cinematography in the United States', *Screen Reader* 1, London, Society for Education in Film and Television, 1977.

Jacqueline Rose, 'Paranoia and the film system', *Screen* vol. 17 no. 4, Winter 1976/77.

Screen vol. 14 no. 1/2, Spring/Summer 1973 (special issue on Metz).

E. P. Thompson, *The Poverty of Theory*, London, Merlin, 1978.

Christopher Williams, 'The deep-focus question: some comments on Patrick Ogle's article', *Screen Reader* 1, op. cit.

Extract Information

The following film extracts are available for hire in the UK only from:
the BFI Film and Video Library, 81 Dean Street, London W1V 6AA   tel: 01-437-4355

A bout de souffle (Breathless)
France 1959 sd b/w 20

PRODUCTION
p.c – Société Nouvelle de Cinéma.
p – Georges de Beauregard.
d – Jean-Luc Godard. sc – Jean-Luc
Godard, from an idea by François
Truffaut. ph – Raoul Coutard. ed – Cécile
Decugis, Lila Herman. m – Martial Solal.

LEADING PLAYERS
Jean-Paul Belmondo (Michel Poiccard),
Jean Seberg (Patricia), Richard Balducci
(Tolmatchoff)

SYNOPSIS
*Michel Poiccard casually steals a car in
Marseilles and roars north for Paris. Pursued by the police, he finds a gun in the
glove compartment of the car and shoots
one of them. He leaves the car and arrives
in Paris penniless. After stealing some
money from an ex-girlfriend, he makes a
date with Patricia, an American who sells
New York Herald Tribunes, and visits a
man called Tolmatchoff at a travel agency.
The police also visit Tolmatchoff and
attempt to follow Michel. He stops admiringly in front of a picture of Humphrey
Bogart. The police are shaken off in the
Metro.*

Patricia returns to her flat to find Michel
in her bed. They make love and she tells
him that she is pregnant. The police net
tightens. Michel steals another car and
tries to sell it. He returns to Patricia with
enough money to leave Paris, but she is
reluctant to give up the world of literature
and journalism that attracts her and she
has already been questioned by the police.
She hides with Michel in a borrowed flat,
but next morning informs on him. Refusing protection from his friends, Michel is
fatally wounded by the police. As she looks
down on him dying, Michel calls her
'dégueulasse.' She asks one of the policemen what the word means.

Accident
UK 1967 sd col 20

PRODUCTION
p.c – Royal Avenue Chelsea. p – Joseph
Losey, Norman Priggen. d – Joseph
Losey. sc – Harold Pinter, from the novel
by Nicholas Mosley. ph – Gerry Fisher
(Eastman Color). ed – Reginald Beck. a.d
– Carmen Dillon. m – John Dankworth.

LEADING PLAYERS
Dirk Bogarde (Stephen), Stanley Baker
(Charley), Jacqueline Sassard (Anna),
Michael York (William), Vivien

Merchant (Rosalind), Delphine Seyrig
(Francesca), Ann Firbank (Laura).

SYNOPSIS
William, an Oxford undergraduate, is
killed in a car crash while driving with his
fiancée, Anna, an Austrian student, to see
his tutor Stephen. Stephen is first on the
scene of the crash and after he has taken
Anna into his house he recalls the events
leading up to the accident. As tutor to William and Anna, he is attracted to both of
them, although he is married with two
children and a third on the way. Later he
discovers that a colleague, Charley, is also
attracted to Anna and is already having an
affair with her. Stephen's wife Rosalind
goes to stay with her mother. Stephen goes
to London to be interviewed for a possible
television appearance and while there
looks up an old flame, Francesca. Both
meetings prove unsatisfactory.

*He returns home in the small hours after
his abortive day in London. First Charley
and then Anna appear on the stairs. They
all go into the kitchen while Stephen cooks
himself an omelette. Charley tells Stephen
that he has a letter for him from his wife,
Laura. Stephen ignores him, so Charley
reads the letter aloud. Laura has written
to tell Stephen how she feels about
Charley's affair with Anna. Stephen goes
upstairs alone and looks into the room
where Charley and Anna have been sleeping. Anna comes up and prepares to leave
while Charley is phoning for a taxi. She
goes downstairs and Charley talks to
Stephen about his desperation over the
affair. Stephen offers to let them stay in his
house while he is away for the weekend
but then they must leave. Stephen visits
Rosalind and tells her how Charley's marriage has broken under the strain, but is
shocked by her contemptuous dismissal of
the affair. He goes on to spend the weekend
at William's ancestral home, where by
tradition a rough indoor ball game is
played at house parties. Stephen is put in
goal and ends up smashing William's head
against the floor in a scrum.*

Anna decides to marry William and asks
Stephen to tell Charley, but before he can
do so the accident occurs. Anna leaves for
Austria; Charley cannot believe he has lost
her; Stephen goes to see Rosalind, who has
just given birth.

Adieu Philippine
France/Italy 1962 sd b/w 12

PRODUCTION
p.c – Unitec France/Alpha-Productions/
Rome-Paris Films/Euro-International

Films. p – Georges de Beauregard. d –
Jacques Rozier. sc. – Michèle O'Glor,
Jacques Rozier. ph – René Mathelin. ed –
Monique Bonnot, Claude Durand. m –
Jacques Denjean, Maxime Saury, Paul
Mattei.

LEADING PLAYERS
Jean-Claude Aimini (Michel), Yveline
Céry (Liliane), Stefania Sabatini (Juliette),
Vittorio Caprioli (Pachala).

SYNOPSIS
Michel Lambert, a young TV camera
assistant, meets two girls, Liliane and
Juliette, at the studio. To help his career
Liliane introduces him to Pachala, a producer of commercials in which she and
Juliette have acted. Pachala offers Michel
work as a cameraman on a commercial
about refrigerators. The film is a disaster
and Pachala disappears, leaving behind
large debts. After an argument in the
studio, when Michel walks in front of a
camera during transmission, he throws up
his job and goes off to Club Mediterranée
in Corsica to take a holiday before he is
called up for military service. Juliette and
Liliane follow him there and tell him that
Pachala is also on the island. All three set
off in a car to search for Pachala and the
money he owes them. En route Michel
plays the girls off against each other, sleeping first with Juliette and then with Liliane.
Arriving at Ajaccio, Pachala having disappeared again, Michel finds his call-up
papers have arrived and he returns to
France. As he sails away both girls wave
goodbye.

*This extract has been selected to exemp-
lify the syntagmatic types identified by
Christian Metz in the Grande Syntagmatique and also the Syntagmatic Study of
Jacques Rozier's Adieu Philippine. Copies
of both these articles are distributed with
the extract.*

(NB The extract is in two parts: the
first part consists of an uninterrupted run-
through of the extract; the second part is
a re-run, broken down with black spacing
into sequences, scenes, etc., as identified by
Metz in the Syntagmatic Study. This
should enable teachers to work through
Metz's categories with their students and
then to compare their own analysis.)

All That Heaven Allows
USA 1955 sd col 20+20

PRODUCTION
p.c – Universal-International. p – Ross
Hunter. d – Douglas Sirk. sc – Peg
Fenwick, from a story by Edna M. Lee
and Harry Lee. ph – Russell Metty

(Technicolor). ed – Frank Gross, Fred Baratta. a.d – Alexander Golitzen. cost – Bill Thomas.

LEADING PLAYERS

Jane Wyman (*Cary Scott*), Rock Hudson (*Ron Kirby*), Agnes Moorehead (*Sara Warren*), Conrad Nagel (*Harvey*), Gloria Talbott (*Kay Scott*), William Reynolds (*Ned Scott*), Donald Curtis (*Howard Hoffer*).

SYNOPSIS

Cary Scott, a wealthy New England widow, lives alone except for weekend visits from her two children. Her friend Sara Warren, worried by Cary's retreat from all social activities since her husband's death, invites her to a party at the Country Club. Ron Kirby, a forestry expert who has come to prune her trees, helps her with a heavy parcel and she invites him for coffee. Later Cary's children, Kay and Ned, arrive for the weekend and they discuss the eligibility of Harvey, Cary's escort, to the Country Club. At the Club Cary first rejects Howard, who suggests a weekend in New York, and then Harvey, who proposes marriage. (Ext. 1a, 16 mins.)

Gradually she falls in love with Ron. However, he is not acceptable to her children, friends, or social world.

One day she visits Ron's home. He proposes to her, but confused by gossip and social pressures, she first refuses, then breaks down and agrees. (Ext. 1b, 4 mins.)

Cary confides in Sara, who arranges a dinner party with friends to celebrate.

When Ron and Cary arrive, Howard makes a disparaging remark to her, Ron intervenes and they leave. Back home, Ned threatens to leave home for good if Cary marries Ron. The following morning Kay is in tears, having been taunted by her friends about her mother. Cary drives out to Ron's house and breaks off the engagement. (Ext. 2a, 12 mins)

She is again lonely and unhappy, and suffers from headaches.

She goes to the station to meet the children, but they don't arrive. Later while buying a Christmas tree she meets Ron, apparently with a younger woman. Back home, Kay and Ned arrive for Christmas – Kay announces her engagement and Ned that he intends to go to Paris to study. Their Christmas present for Cary arrives – a television set. (Ext. 2b, 8 mins.)

Cary realises that her sacrifice was pointless. One night, she hears that Ron has been seriously injured in an accident and goes to him.

Anatomy of a Murder
USA 1959 sd b/w 8

PRODUCTION

p.c – Carlyle. *p* – Otto Preminger. *d* – Otto Preminger. *sc* – Wendell Mayes, from the book by Robert Traver. *ph* – Sam Leavitt. *ed* – Louis R. Loeffler. *m* – Duke Ellington.

LEADING PLAYERS

James Stewart (*Paul Biegler*), Lee Remick (*Laura Mannion*), Ben Gazzara (*Lieutenant Frederick Mannion*), Arthur O'Connell (*Parnell McCarthy*), Eve Arden (*Maida*).

SYNOPSIS

Army lieutenant Frederick Mannion, held for the murder of a bartender who allegedly raped his wife, Laura, is defended by small-town lawyer Paul Biegler. Laura supports her husband's story and a lie-detector test, though inadmissable as evidence, verifies her account of the rape. A medical examination, however, finds bruises but no physical evidence of violation and Biegler, in his interviews with the Mannions, becomes aware that Mannion is a violently possessive husband of a not entirely faithful wife. The prosecuting attorney proposes that Laura was a willing partner in whatever happened – her bruises and her lover's death being the work of her jealous husband. To counter this, Biegler enters a plea of not guilty on the grounds of temporary insanity. His case is weak and witnesses are not forthcoming. Finally, after a hectic search for evidence, the dead man's daughter makes a last-minute appearance on the witness stand and her testimony virtually clinches the case in Mannion's favour.

The jury retire to consider their verdict. Biegler and his assistants Maida and McCarthy wait in his office while the jury is deliberating. The jury returns. As Biegler goes up the stairs into the courtroom, Laura tells him that she will wait for her husband in his car. The jury finds Mannion not guilty, by reason of his temporary insanity. When Biegler and McCarthy call on the Mannions to collect the legal fee, they find that they have disappeared.

(NB The credits, by Saul Bass, are appended to this extract.)

Angel Face
USA 1952 sd b/w 17

PRODUCTION

p.c – RKO Radio. *p* – Otto Preminger. *d* – Otto Preminger. *sc* – Frank Nugent, Oscar Millard, from a story by Chester Erskine. *ph* – Harry Stradling. *ed* – Frederick Knudtson. *a.d* – Albert S. D'Agostino, Carroll Clark. *m* – Dimitri Tiomkin.

LEADING PLAYERS

Robert Mitchum (*Frank*), Jean Simmons (*Diane*).

SYNOPSIS

Ambulance driver Frank Jessup is called out when the wealthy Mrs. Tremayne is found gassed. She recovers and claims that there was an attempt on her life. Frank becomes involved with her step-daughter, Diane; he throws over his fiancée and takes a job living-in as the Tremayne's chauffeur. He soon realises that Diane is devoted to her father and hates her step-mother.

Diane tells Frank how her step-mother tried to kill her one night by turning on the gas in her bedroom. Frank is sceptical, particularly when Diane refuses to tell her father or the police. He visits his ex-fiancée and makes a date with her. Later, Diane discovers him packing and preparing to leave the house. She persuades him to let her go with him. Then, knowing her step-mother is going out, she tampers with the car gears. However, her father decides, unknown to Diane, to accompany his wife; the car runs backwards over a cliff, and they are both killed. Diane, believing in the success of her plot, is playing the piano.

Frank and Diane stand trial together for murder, but a clever lawyer insists that they marry before the trial, plays for sympathy, and they are acquitted. When she finds that Frank means to have nothing more to do with her, Diane drives her car backwards over a cliff killing both of them.

Antonio das Mortes
Brazil 1969 sd col 10+11

PRODUCTION

p.c – Glauber Rocha/Produções Cinematográficas Mapa. *p* – Claude-Antoine Mapa, Glauber Rocha. *d* – Glauber Rocha. *sc* – Glauber Rocha. *ph* – Alfonso Beato (Eastman Color). *ed* – Eduardo Escorel. *a.d* – Glauber Rocha. *m* – Marlos Nobre, Walter Queiroz, Sérgio Ricardo.

LEADING PLAYERS

Mauricio do Valle (*Antonio das Mortes*), Odete Lara (*Laura*), Hugo Carvana (*Police Chief Mattos*), Othon Bastos (*The Teacher*), Joffre Soares (*Colonel Horacio*), Lorival Pariz (*Coirana*), Rosa Maria Penna (*Santa Bárbara – The Holy One*), Mário Gusmâo (*Antâo*), Vinicius Salvatori (*Mata Vaca*), Emanuel Cavalcanti (*Priest*), Sante Scaldaferri (*Batista*).

SYNOPSIS

Antonio das Mortes, legendary killer of bandits, recalls how he tracked down Lampiaõ, the last of the cangaceiros in 1940 in arid and poverty-stricken northeast Brazil. When he is told by Police Chief Mattos that a new bandit, Coirana, has appeared Antonio leaves the area.

Antonio waits outside the house belonging to the blind, tyrannical Colonel Horacio. Horacio's mistress, Laura, leans out of the window. Mattos recommends Antonio to the Colonel, who rules the village. There is an argument about the need for land reform, new industry and American aid, which the Colonel strongly opposes. Meanwhile, on a mountain ledge, Coirana's band of beatos (landless peasants) dance and sing. Back in the town, Mattos and the local teacher play billiards and laugh cynically about the long-promised economic boom. Antonio watches and listens in silence. In the mountains, Coirana, Santa Bárbara the Holy

One, and Oxosse (the Black St. George) discuss what must be done. Coirana wants to destroy the village but Oxosse says they must respect both God and the Government. He wants to return to Africa, but Coirana argues about living in the past. In the village billiard room Antonio and the teacher discuss Brazil's role in the war of 1945. Antonio says that he killed a hundred cangaceiros and now he is alone and needs to find a new enemy. (Ext. 1, 10 mins.)

While his followers chant, Coirana fights a ritualised duel with Antonio and receives a mortal wound. Antonio undergoes a crisis of conscience and comes to understand that his victim represents the oppressed peasantry. He joins them in their fight against the landowner who has brought in a band of killers (jaguncos), led by Mata Vaca, to deal with the beatos. Laura is having an affair with Mattos and wants him to kill the Colonel, but he cannot do it. When the Colonel finds out about the affair Laura kills Mattos in disgust.

Mata Vaca and his jaguncos dance wildly in front of the the beatos. In the town the priest, the teacher and Laura roll on the ground with Mattos's body. The jaguncos open fire; all are killed except the Holy One and Oxosse. Antonio, about to bury Coirana, stops as he hears the gun fire. He embraces Coirana's body. Mata Vaca taunts the Holy One and Oxosse, but is frightened off by the Holy One's stare. The Colonel screams for Laura, having dreamt that Antonio is going to murder him. Antonio chases the priest into the church, then goes to the mountain with the teacher. The Holy One gives Antonio her sword; the teacher attacks Oxosse, blaming him for the massacre, then tries to leave town. Antonio persuades him to stay and shows him Coirana's body. Finally he takes up Coirana's gun and sword. The Holy One and Oxosse arrive; she hands Antonio his rifle and hat. He follows the teacher back towards the town. (Ext. 2, 11 mins.)

In a final confrontation, Antonio, the teacher, the Holy One and Oxosse destroy the jaguncos, the Colonel and Laura. Antonio walks off alone, leaving the teacher with Laura's body.

Ashes and Diamonds
Poland 1958 sd b/w 13

PRODUCTION
p.c – Kadr Unit, Film Polski. p – Stanislaw Adler. d – Andrzej Wajda. sc – Andrzej Wajda, Jerzy Andrzejewski, from the novel by Jerzy Andrzejewski. ph – Jerzy Wojcik. ed – Halina Nawrocka. a.d – Roman Mann.

LEADING PLAYERS
Zbigniew Cybulski (*Maciek*), Adam Pawlikowski (*Andrzej*), Waclaw Zastrzezynski (*Szczuka*), Ewa Krzyzanowska (*Christina*), Bogumil Kobiela (*Drewnowski*).

SYNOPSIS
Outside a provincial Polish town on 7th May 1945, the first day of peace, Maciek and Andrzej, members of a nationalist underground unit, wait to ambush Szczuka, the new Communist District Secretary. A little girl asks them to open the nearby church door. As Adrzej lifts her to reach the key above the door, the signal comes. A car rounds the corner; they shoot at it. A young man escapes and runs to the church, but Maciek blasts him with a machine gun. Aflame, he falls into the church. Maciek and Andrzej abandon their guns and run off. Szczuka, their intended victim, arrives to find their bodies. A group of workers stop to look, and ask how long the fighting between the Poles will go on. All he can say is 'Don't lose heart'. In the town, Maciek and Andrzej meet Drewnowski, the town mayor's secretary and also a member of their unit, who reluctantly tells them about a victory banquet planned for that evening. They check into the hotel where the banquet is to be held. Maciek notices Christina, a young woman working behind the bar; he teases her and then asks to meet her later.

According to their orders, Maciek is to carry out the assassination of Szczuka and then join Andrzej in taking over a resistance group whose leader has been killed. Christina visits Maciek in his hotel room (next to Szczuka's) and awakens in him a longing for a new and peaceful life. Meanwhile the opportunist Drewnowski disgraces himself at the banquet, losing his chance of accompanying the mayor to Warsaw on important ministerial business. Maciek is torn: must he go on killing, even though he does not believe in the cause any more? Andrzej, however, will not accept a reversal, and Maciek confusedly shoots down Szczuka in the early hours of the morning. Leaving Christina, he sets out to join Andrzej. Drewnowski, beaten by Andrzej, tries to catch up with Maciek; Maciek flees from him, but runs into a military patrol, panics, and is shot trying to escape.

L'Atalante
France 1933 sd b/w 9

PRODUCTION
p.c – Gaumont. p – J. L. Nourez. d – Jean Vigo. sc – Jean Vigo, Albert Riéra, from a story by Jean Guinée. ph – Boris Kaufman, Louis Berger. ed – Louis Chavance. a.d – Francis Jourdain. m – Maurice Jaubert.

LEADING PLAYERS
Dita Parlo (*Juliette*), Jean Dasté (*Jean*), Michel Simon (*Père Jules*), Louis Lefebvre (*The Boy*).

SYNOPSIS
L'Atalante is a barge passing along the waterways of France, carrying with it a newly-married couple, Juliette and Jean, and crewed by Père Jules and a boy. After a while, the bride grows tired of the barge

and longs for the excitement of the town. She quarrels with her husband and later steals ashore; *L'Atalante* continues on its way without her.

Juliette wanders along the shore and into the town. On the boat, Jean moodily plays draughts with Père Jules. In despair, Jean dives into the river and imagines he sees his wife. Juliette also thinks of her husband as she wanders about the town. Jean finally expresses his frustration by running along an empty beach towards the distant horizon.

Juliette has her handbag stolen. She looks for the barge but cannot find it. In the end, Juliette is found and husband and wife are reconciled.

L'Avventura
Italy/France 1959 sd b/w 17

PRODUCTION
p.c – Cino Del Duca/Produzioni Cinematografiche Europee (Rome)/ Société Cinématographique Lyre (Paris). p – Amato Pennasilico. d – Michelangelo Antonioni. sc – Michelangelo Antonioni, Elio Bartolini, Tonino Guerra, from a story by Michelangelo Antonioni. ph – Aldo Scavarda. ed – Eraldo Da Roma. a.d – Piero Poletto. m – Giovanni Fusco.

LEADING PLAYERS
Gabriele Ferzetti (*Sandro*), Monica Vitti (*Claudia*), Lea Massari (*Anna*).

SYNOPSIS
Sandro, an architect who, having accepted easy success, is now resting on his laurels, joins Princess Patrizia's small yacht party cruising off the north-east coast of Sicily. The group includes Sandro's fiancée Anna and her friend Claudia. After bathing they go ashore to a volcanic island. A storm breaks. Anna grows desperate at the inadequacy of her relationship with Sandro and when the party leaves she is missing.

Having spent the night on the island, Claudia awakes and wanders over it looking for Anna. Sandro follows her and an incipient relationship is acknowledged between them. The search begins in earnest. The police and then Anna's father arrive. Claudia and Anna's father discuss Anna's disappearance. Claudia and Sandro's companions discover an ancient vase but it is accidentally dropped and smashed. Back on board the yacht Sandro again expresses his interest in Claudia.

At first separately and then together they visit places on the mainland where a strange girl is said to have been seen. After fighting the conventional feelings of shame and guilt and as hope fades that Anna will ever be found, Claudia and Sandro become lovers. One night he fails to return to her hotel room. She finds him wretchedly embracing another woman. Moved by compassion and the shared desolation of the search, Claudia forgives him.

Baby Doll
USA 1956 sd b/w 17

PRODUCTION
p.c – Newtown Productions. *p* – Elia
Kazan. *d* – Elia Kazan. *sc* – Tennessee
Williams, from the one-act plays *27
Wagons Full of Cotton* and *The
Unsatisfactory Supper* by Tennessee
Williams. *ph* – Boris Kaufman. *ed* – Gene
Milford. *a.d* – Richard Sylbert. *m* –
Kenyon Hopkins.

LEADING PLAYERS
Karl Malden (*Archie Lee Meighan*),
Carroll Baker (*Baby Doll Meighan*), Eli
Wallach (*Silva Vacarro*), Mildred
Dunnock (*Aunt Rose*).

SYNOPSIS
*Archie Lee, a middle-aged plantation
owner, attempts to supervise some blacks
repairing the roof of his decaying mansion.
Indoors he works away at a peep-hole in
the wall of the bedroom where his teenage
bride, Baby Doll, sleeps in her child's cot.
Baby Doll accuses him of being a Peeping
Tom. In their bedroom he reminds her that
it is the eve of her twentieth birthday, when
their marriage is to be consummated. She
retaliates by reminding him that the contract, agreed with her father, will be null
and void if he fails to provide her with a
decent home and complete suites of
furniture. She also threatens to get herself
a 'good paying' job when they are in town
since he seems unable to stave off his
creditors. While taking a bath, Baby Doll
mocks Archie again until they end up fighting. On the way to town, they quarrel
about Baby Doll's lack of interest in domesticity. While Archie is examined by the
doctor, Baby Doll enquires about a dental
receptionist's job she sees advertised.
Archie becomes agitated by her flirtations
with the dentist, and sends her back to the
car. In desperation he complains to some
bystanders of 'the torture a cold woman
inflicts on a man'. Baby Doll sees a van
which she guesses correctly belongs to
creditors reclaiming the hire-purchase
furniture. Enraged, she runs after it, followed by a weary Archie.*
    A fire destroys the cotton gin of their
neighbour Silva Vaccaro, a Sicilian immigrant, who is forced to bring his business
to Archie. Vaccaro, suspecting Archie of
arson, gets Baby Doll, by a mixture of
threats and flirtation, to sign an affidavit
breaking Archie's alibi. While Archie is in
town, Baby Doll, her latent sexuality
aroused, invites Vaccaro to rest in her cot.
When Archie returns, Vaccaro's men are
operating his mill, and he notices intimacy
between his wife and the Sicilian. Realising
his crime has been discovered, and suspecting seduction, Archie goes berserk and
chases Vaccaro with a gun. The police take
him away to cool off and Vaccaro, his
revenge complete, goes back to his plantation; Baby Doll is left in the decaying
mansion with her old Aunt Rose.

Baby Face Nelson
USA 1957 sd b/w 8

PRODUCTION
p.c – Fryman-ZS. *p* – Al Zimbalist. *d* –
Donald Siegel. *sc* – Irving Shulman,
Daniel Mainwaring. *ph* – Hal Mohr. *ed* –
Leon Barsche. *m* – Van Alexander.

LEADING PLAYERS
Mickey Rooney (*Nelson*), Carolyn Jones
(*Sue*), Cedric Hardwicke (*Doc Saunders*),
Chris Dark (*Jerry*), Ted De Corsia
(*Rocca*), Leo Gordon (*Dillinger*).

SYNOPSIS
In the early 1930s Lester Gillis leaves Joliet
prison. A waiting car takes him to town
where a powerful gangster, Rocca, offers
him money to murder a union leader who
is in his way. Gillis refuses, but when the
man is shot by somebody else the police
arrest Gillis on Rocca's information. Gillis
escapes from jail with the help of his girlfriend, Sue, finds Rocca and shoots him.
On Sue's suggestion he changes his name
to Nelson. Shot in a gun battle, Nelson
visits Doc Saunders' clinic where he
encounters one of Dillinger's men and is
introduced into the gang.
    *Nelson and Dillinger meet for the first
time, at night in a playground, where the
gang plans a robbery. They gain entry to
a depot where a large payroll is expected
by masquerading as plumbers. When the
payroll van arrives they hold it up and seize
the money. Nelson shoots down the
security men as they leave. When more
guards appear Nelson mows them down
too as the gang makes its escape. One of
the gangsters is injured. Out in the country
they abandon the plumbers' van and drive
off in a waiting car.*
    Later, after Dillinger's death, Nelson,
universally feared because of his hysterical
behaviour and total ruthlessness, becomes
America's Public Enemy Number 1. He
escapes the FBI several times but on
Thanksgiving Day, 1934, after a car chase,
he is mortally wounded. Sue gives him the
coup de grâce in a cemetery.

The Back of Beyond
Australia 1953 sd b/w 7
(w. **The Rival World**)

PRODUCTION
p.c – The Shell Film Unit, Australia. *d* –
John Heyer, Janet Heyer, Roland
Robinson. *sc* – John Heyer. *ph* – Ross
Wood. *m* – Sydney John Kay. *comm* –
Kevin Brennan.

SYNOPSIS
The Birdsville Track connecting Marree,
South Australia, with Birdsville Queens-
land, is one of the loneliest transport
routes in the world. Along the 330-mile
route, Tom Kruse maintains a bi-monthly
service with two trucks and a raft. He carries goods, mail and an occasional passenger, thereby providing a link between the
outside world and the few small outback

towns and cattle stations. Much of the
road is little more than a sand track, often
obscured by frequent dust storms. Where
the road meets the Cooper River, all the
goods are transferred from the truck to the
barge, which is powered by outboard
motor. On the other side, the journey is
completed by the second truck.
    *Night. A dingo howls. Jack the Dogger,
hunting wild dogs, is camping by the ruins
of the Lutheran Mission. Tom Kruse and
a local inhabitant join him, and talk about
how the country has dried up and changed
since the days when Father Vogelsang ran
the mission. The local man visits Vogelsang's grave and the church ruins, recalling
his warm and happy childhood in the living community, now only a parched
desert.*

La Baie des anges
France 1962 sd b/w 10

PRODUCTION
p.c – Sud-Pacifique Films. *p* – Paul
Edmond Décharme. *d* – Jacques Demy.
sc – Jacques Demy. *ph* – Jean Rabier. *ed* –
Anne-Marie Cotret. *a.d* – Bernard Evein.
m – Michel Legrand.

LEADING PLAYERS
Jeanne Moreau (*Jackie Demaistre*),
Claude Mann (*Jean Fournier*), Paul Guers
(*Caron*), Henri Nassiet (*Jean's father*).

SYNOPSIS
Jean Fournier is a young bank clerk from
a respectable middle-class family who
accepts the proposal of a friend to visit the
Casino at Enghien – although he disapproves of gaming. He returns with an enormous wad of notes, which he shows to his
father, who gives an interminable sermon.
Jean packs his bags and leaves. Intoxicated
by his initial success, he is impelled to go
where one can play for really high stakes.
On his first night at Nice, he meets Jackie
Demaistre at the tables and recognises her
as the woman he saw expelled from the
gaming room at Enghien for cheating. She
is strikingly beautiful and utterly committed to gambling, but invariably unlucky.
Jean offers her some chips, which she
gratefully accepts. Playing the same
chances as Jean, they have a fantastic success and, from that moment, they become
partners. Jean is bound to Jackie by the
love he feels, Jackie is bound to Jean by
the conviction that he is lucky. Their
newly-found affluence brings them a life of
luxury in the chi-chi hotels of the Côte
d'Azur. Alternately, they win enormous
sums and lose them again.
    *In their hotel bedroom, Jackie prepares
to leave for Paris, but first plans to visit
a friend to obtain money for the train
ticket. When she leaves, Jean goes down
to the beach, where Jackie later finds him.
She is unable to resist a final visit to the
Casino; Jean at first refuses to accompany
her, but then follows her. They gamble
together and hit a winning streak.*
    Although he is a slave to gambling fever,

Jean realises that they can never find happiness until they leave the tables. He proposes marriage but Jackie cannot tear herself away from her obsession and refuses. When they experience a run of bad luck, she leaves him. Jean knows where to find her and goes to the Casino to say goodbye. As he turns to leave, Jackie runs after him and throws herself into his arms.

Ballad of a Soldier
USSR 1959 sd b/w 9

PRODUCTION
p.c – Mosfilm. *d* – Grigori Chukhrai. *sc* – Valentin Yoshov, Grigori Chukhrai. *ph* – Vladimir Nikolayev, Era Savelyeva. *ed* – M. Tomofeieva. *a.d* – B. Nemechek. *m* – Mikhail Ziv.

LEADING PLAYERS
Vladimir Ivashov (*Alyosha*), Shanna Prokhorenko (*Shura*), Antonina Maximova (*Alyosha's Mother*), Nikolai Kryuchkov (*General*), Ievgeni Urbanski (*Invalid Soldier*).

SYNOPSIS
During World War II a young soldier, Alyosha, though very frightened, manages to destroy two enemy tanks. As a reward for his bravery, he is granted a brief leave to visit his mother. On the way home he meets a number of people affected by the war. In particular he meets and falls in love with Shura.

In one episode, Alyosha and Shura try to find Pavlov's wife to give her some promised soap from her husband at the front, but the family house is in ruins. They find Pavlov's wife living with another man in a flat. They refuse tea and leave without handing over the soap, but not before the wife has asked anxiously about Pavlov. They find Pavlov's father in an institution and give him the soap. The father tells Alyosha that his son's wife is working and sends her love.

As a result of a series of mishaps and his own generosity towards people, Alyosha is only able to reach home in time to give his mother a present and exchange a few words before it is time for him to return to the front.

Bande à part
France 1964 sd b/w 14 + 8

PRODUCTION
p.c – Anouchka Films/Orsay Films. *p. manager* – Philippe Dussart. *d* – Jean-Luc Godard. *sc* – Jean-Luc Godard, from the novel *Fool's Gold (Pigeon Vole)* by Dolores Hitchins and B. Hitchins. *ph* – Raoul Coutard. *ed* – Agnès Guillemot, François Collin. *m* – Michel Legrand.

LEADING PLAYERS
Anna Karina (*Odile*), Claude Brasseur (*Arthur*), Sami Frey (*Franz*), Louisa Colpeyn (*Madame Victoria*), Danièle Girard (*English Teacher*), Ernest Menzer (*Arthur's Uncle*).

SYNOPSIS
Arthur, scenting easy money, persuades his friend Franz to introduce him to his girlfriend, Odile, who knows about a pile of banknotes lying in a cupboard at home. The money apparently belongs to her Aunt Victoria's friend, Monsieur Stolz. Arthur immediately sets out, successfully, to impress Odile.

Arthur, Franz and Odile have a 'modern' conversation. They dance the Madison. Arthur walks Odile along the boulevard to a shooting gallery in the Place Clichy. They take the Metro. Odile does a musical number. Arthur meets his uncle. (Ext. 1, 14 mins.)

Soon Odile reluctantly agrees to the robbery. While looking to see how much money there is, she forgets to cover it up, so when the trio comes to steal it they find it gone. Arthur blames Odile and hits her; Odile is disillusioned and Franz disapproving. Arthur insists on returning the following day, knowing that his uncle too is now after the money. While searching for it, they are interrupted by Madame Victoria, but Arthur gags her and locks her in a cupboard. They fail to find the money and when they open the cupboard, Madame Victoria has apparently suffocated. Appalled, they run to their car, but Arthur, suspecting that the money must be hidden in the dog-kennel, tells the others to drive away.

He returns to the scene of the crime on the pretext of checking whether Madame Victoria is really dead. Franz and Odile, seeing the uncle heading for the house, return. Just as Arthur finds the money, his uncle arrives and they shoot one another dead. Franz and Odile, after witnessing Arthur's death, escape. Monsieur Stolz returns to find the money lying near the kennel, and Madame Victoria, who had only fainted, comes out to meet him. Franz and Odile head for South America on a liner. (Ext. 2, 8 mins.)

Barbarella
France/Italy 1967 sd col 1
(w. **Walk on the Wild Side**)

PRODUCTION
p.c – Marianne Productions (Paris)/Dino De Laurentiis (Rome). *p* – Dino De Laurentiis. *d* – Roger Vadim. *sc* – Terry Southern, from the book by Jean-Claude Forest. *ph* – Claude Renoir. *ed* – Victoria Mercanton. *ad* – Enrico Fea. *m* – Maurice Jarre. *lyrics* – Charles Fox, Bob Crewe. *cost* – Jacques Fonteray, Paco Rabanne.

LEADING PLAYERS
Jane Fonda (*Barbarella*), Anita Pallenberg (*Black Queen*), John Philip Law (*Pygar*), Milo O'Shea (*Durand-Durand*).

SYNOPSIS
Barbarella, sensuous astronaut in the year 4000, strips off her space suit in weightless conditions.

She is sent on a mission to find Durand-Durand, a scientist who has gone missing with a ray gun which could destroy the universe. Barbarella is saved from the attack of some female robots by a man who tells her that Durand-Durand is in the underground city of Sogo, which is built on a living lake of deadly liquid which lives off evil. Barbarella descends below ground and meets Pygar, who has large white wings and was blinded by the tyrannical Black Queen of Sogo. Barbarella restores his will to fly and he carries her to the gates of Sogo. There they are captured by the Chief Guard who delivers them to the Queen. Pygar is crucified by his wings and Barbarella is thrown into a cage of pecking birds. A handsome rebel rescues her and she repays him with sex, but Barbarella is soon captured again. The Chief Guard decides to kill her through an excess of pleasure but the machine is not powerful enough for Barbarella and she escapes. She realises that the Chief Guard is Durand-Durand, now a raving madman who plans to conquer the universe. The Queen liberates the living liquid which destroys Durand-Durand and the entire city. Barbarella is saved as the liquid only consumes evil, and she rescues Pygar. They fly away together, along with the Black Queen, whom Pygar forgivingly saves.

Barrier
Poland 1966 sd b/w 10

PRODUCTION
p.c – Kamera Film Unit, Film Polski. *p* – Stanislaw Zylewicz, Ryszard Straszewski. *d* – Jerzy Skolimowski. *sc* – Jerzy Skolimowski. *ph* – Jan Laskowski. *ed* – H. Prugar. *a.d* – Roman Wolyniec, Z. Straszewski. *m* – Krzysztof Komeda.

LEADING PLAYERS
Jan Nowicki (*He, The Student*), Joanna Szczerbic (*She, The Girl*), Tadeusz Lomnicki (*The Doctor*), Zdzislaw Maklakiewicz (*Magazine Seller*).

SYNOPSIS
The barrier of the title is that between the generations. A young medical undergraduate decides to give up his studies, hoping that marriage to a rich girl will provide him with substantial means for good living, which, as a doctor, he could achieve only through self-denial and hard work over many years. His attitude brings him into conflict with the older generation.

He and She, in a restaurant, give a magazine seller a new marketing idea. Their friends arrive and dancing commences. He refuses to sell his family sabre, and talks to a religious-portrait vendor. There is a musical demonstration, followed by the veteran's chorus. He cashes some savings which he has won from fellow students.

Battleship Potemkin
USSR 1925 st b/w 11

PRODUCTION
p.c – Goskino. *p* – Yakov Bliokh. *d* –

Sergei M. Eisenstein. *sc* – Sergei M. Eisenstein, from an outline by Nina Agadzhanova. *ph* – Edward Tisse. *ed* – Sergei M. Eisenstein. *a.d* – Vasili Rakhals.

LEADING PLAYERS
Alexander Antonov (*Vakulinchuk*), Vladimir Barsky (*Captain Golikov*), Grigori Alexandrov (*Lieutenant Giliarovski*).

SYNOPSIS
A notorious incident which occurred during the 1905 uprising in Russia. The sailors of the Russian flotilla, moored off Odessa, mutiny against their officers. The people of Odessa, sympathetic to the sailors, are brutally massacred by Cossack soldiers on the marble steps leading down to the harbour.
Yawls go out to the Potemkin with food. The people of Odessa, from all classes, watch and wave on the steps. The sailors meet the boats. Suddenly, Cossack soldiers advance on the crowd. The people begin to run in terror. A child is shot and trampled in the ensuing panic. Its mother is shot walking up the steps carrying her dead child. As chaos and panic increase, the cavalry attacks the crowd. Then the guns of the Potemkin come to the support of the people.

The Beguiled
USA 1970 sd col 20

PRODUCTION
p.c – Universal/Malpaso. *p* – Donald Siegel. *d* – Donald Siegel. *sc* – John B. Sherry, Grimes Grice, from the novel by Thomas Cullinan. *ph* – Bruce Surtees (Technicolor). *ed* – Carl Pingitore. *a.d* – Alex Golitzen. *m* – Lalo Schifrin.

LEADING PLAYERS
Clint Eastwood (*John McBurney*), Geraldine Page (*Martha Farnsworth*), Elizabeth Hartman (*Edwina Dabney*), Jo Ann Harris (*Carol*), Darleen Carr (*Doris*), Pamelyn Ferdin (*Amy*).

SYNOPSIS
A wounded Unionist soldier, Corporal John McBurney, is found in the woods near the Farnsworth Seminary for Young Ladies. Martha Farnsworth and Edwina Dabney, the two teachers in charge of the school, decide to take him in and nurse him back to health before handing him over to the Confederate troops. McBurney encourages the attention of Edwina, who is openly attracted to him, but is in fact more interested in Carol, a precocious student.
While the girls prepare for bed, Martha invites McBurney for a glass of wine, and tentatively suggests that he stay at the school. All three women – Martha, Edwina and Carol – wait for McBurney in their respective rooms. While she waits Martha dreams of being in a bed with McBurney, Edwina and Carol. McBurney goes up the stairs, deliberating which room to go into, but is then led by Carol to her

room. They are heard by Edwina, who bursts into Carol's room, discovers McBurney and pushes him down the stairs. Martha decides that his leg must be amputated, so severe are his injuries.
When he regains consciousness and finds his leg has been cut off, McBurney raids the wine-cellar and drunkenly terrorises the women. Martha, with the help of Amy, prepares a dish of poisoned mushrooms. McBurney eats the mushrooms, dies and is buried in the woods outside the school.

Belle of the Nineties
USA 1934 sd b/w 5
(w. **I'm No Angel**)

PRODUCTION
p.c – Paramount Publix. *p* – William LeBaron. *d* – Leo MacCarey. *sc* – Mae West. *ph* – Karl Struss. *ed* – Leroy Stone. *a.d* – Hans Dreier and Bernard Herzbrun. *m* – Arthur Johnston. *lyrics* – Sam Coslow. *cost* – Travis Banton.

LEADING PLAYERS
Mae West (*Ruby Carter*), Roger Prior (*Tiger Kid*).

SYNOPSIS
The story is about a nineteenth-century showgirl, Ruby Carter, who despite her toughness falls in love with a boxer whose trainer does his best to break up the affair. Ruby travels to another town to work for a villainous theatre manager against whom she holds her own. She is reconciled to the boxer; they become involved in robbing and killing the manager, at the same time as he is committing arson and attempting murder himself. Consequently they are acquitted by the jury.
Mae West performs a musical number, 'My American Beauty'.

Bend of the River (Where the River Bends)
USA 1952 sd col 10

PRODUCTION
p.c – Universal-International. *p* – Aaron Rosenberg. *d* – Anthony Mann. *sc* – Borden Chase. *ph* – Irving Glassberg (Technicolor). *ed* – Russell Shoengarth. *a.d* – Bernard Herzbrun, Nathan Juran. *m* – Hans J. Salter.

LEADING PLAYERS
James Stewart (*Glyn McLyntock*), Arthur Kennedy (*Cole Garrett*), Julia Adams (*Laura Baile*), Rock Hudson (*Trey Wilson*), Jay C. Flippen (*Jeremy Baile*).

SYNOPSIS
Glyn McLyntock, a reformed Missouri raider, is the guide for a wagontrain of Midwestern pioneers seeking new farmlands in Oregon. En route, Glyn rescues another raider, Cole Garrett, from hanging. Cole decides to join the pioneers.
The pioneers take a paddlesteamer as far as some rapids and then set off across country. They locate a suitable spot and

start preparing the land and building a settlement. When badly-needed stores fail to arrive from Portland Glyn and Jeremy Baile go into town to investigate. They discover Portland has become a gold-rush city and that their supplies are lying on the quayside, now worth far more than the pioneers originally paid for them. Glyn hires some men to load the goods onto the steamer.
During the cross-country trek to the settlement they are attacked by men from Portland, but Glyn organises an ambush and they are successfully repelled. Later they are approached by prospectors from a nearby mining camp who offer large amounts of money for the stores. Glyn and Baile refuse the offer, but later, with the connivance of Cole, Baile is injured, Glyn beaten up and left to walk back to Portland. Their wagons are taken on to the miners' camp. Glyn manages to follow the wagons, kills Cole and diverts the supplies back to the settlement.

Berlin, Symphony of a Great City
Germany 1927 st b/w 10

PRODUCTION
p.c – Fox-Europa Film. *d* – Walter Ruttmann. *sc* – Walter Ruttmann, Karl Freund, from an idea by Carl Mayer. *ph* – Karl Freund, Reimar Kuntze, Robert Baberske, Laszlo Schäffer. *ed* – Walter Ruttmann. *m* – (Original music – Edmund Meisel).

SYNOPSIS
Ruttmann wanted to create a 'symphony of a great city', using patterns of movement. The film shows how the city wakes up in the morning, how the streets are first deserted and are gradually filled with people going to work, at first singly and then in larger and larger crowds. The description continues through the day from the time typewriters are uncovered and machines begun to the later evening when people are out enjoying themselves.
The extract shows the period between 8 am and noon, through scenes of city life – workers building roads, a wedding party arriving in taxis, a prostitute early at work, a street fight between two men. Military manoeuvres take place on a parade ground, and there is a street-corner gathering listening to a soap-box orator. Inside luxury hotels page boys take care of luggage, while outside midday traffic jams build up.

The Best Years of Our Lives
USA 1946 sd b/w 20

PRODUCTION
p.c – Samuel Goldwyn Productions. *p* – Samuel Goldwyn. *d* – William Wyler. *sc* – Robert E. Sherwood, from the novel *Glory for Me* by Mackinlay Kantor. *ph* – Gregg Toland. *ed* – Daniel Mandell. *a.d* – Perry Ferguson and George Jenkins. *m* – Hugo Friedhofer. *cost* – Irene Sharaff.

LEADING PLAYERS
Myrna Loy (*Milly Stephenson*), Fredric March (*Al Stephenson*), Dana Andrews (*Fred Derry*), Teresa Wright (*Peggy Stephenson*), Cathy O'Donnell (*Wilma Cameron*), Hoagy Carmichael (*Butch Engle*), Harold Russell (*Homer Parrish*).

SYNOPSIS
Three men of different ranks in the three different Services meet up on their return flight home at the end of the Second World War. Homer Parrish, a naval engineer who has lost his hands, finds the embarrassment of his family and girlfriend unbearable and goes out to 'Butch's Place', the bar his uncle owns. There he meets up with Fred, an airforce captain, whose newly-wed wife is now working in a nightclub and is therefore not at home. Later, they are joined by Al, sergeant in the army, who is unable to settle down for a quiet evening with his wife and his now grown-up children. They all get drunk together and the women end up putting the men to bed. Al is immediately taken back by his bank to deal with loans to ex-servicemen; Fred fails to find a job and when money runs out he is forced to take a job at the soda fountain in the store where he worked before the war; Homer is unable to come to terms with his disability and accept Wilma's love. Fred's marriage deteriorates and Peggy, Al's daughter lets herself become involved with him.

Al meets Fred in 'Butch's Place' and they discuss Fred's relationship with Peggy. Finally Fred agrees to break off his association with her and goes to the telephone at the front of the bar. In the meantime, Homer comes in and asks Al to watch his newly-acquired skill at playing the piano with his hooks. As he plays, Al gazes anxiously at the telephone booth where Fred is talking to Peggy. (Ext. 1a, 6 mins.)

When Fred comes to Homer's defence in a fight, he loses his job. Homer is persuaded to accept Wilma's love, and marries her. Fred walks out on his wife when he discovers her with a former boyfriend.

Fred, having left his wife, and without a job, spends his last hours before leaving town musing about his past flying experiences in the cockpit of a junked bomber. However, when he manages to get the offer of a job breaking up the bombers for prefab building material, he goes, after all, to act as best man at Homer's wedding. There he sees Peggy for the first time since their separation. Once the wedding ceremony is over and the room clears, they are left together to be reunited. (Ext. 1b, 14 mins.)

Beyond a Reasonable Doubt
USA 1956 sd b/w 15

PRODUCTION
p.c – RKO Radio. *p* – Bert Friedlob. *d* – Fritz Lang. *sc* – Douglas Morrow. *ph* – William Snyder. *ed* – Gene Fowler Jr. *a.d* – Carroll Clark. *m* – Herschel Burke Gilbert. *lyrics* – Alfred Perry.

LEADING PLAYERS
Dana Andrews (*Tom Garrett*), Joan Fontaine (*Susan Spencer*), Sidney Blackmer (*Austin Spencer*), Philip Bourneuf (*Thompson*).

SYNOPSIS
Newspaper proprietor Austin Spencer, an opponent of capital punishment, bases his case on the risk that an innocent man may be tried and sentenced to death on the strength of circumstantial evidence. When a burlesque dancer is found strangled in a ravine near town he persuades Tom Garrett, a novelist who is engaged to his daughter Susan, to join him in a highly risky scheme designed to test his theory.

Garrett and Spencer arrive at the burlesque club where they see a dancer performing; Garrett later contrives a meeting with her. At a tailor's Garrett buys an overcoat similar to that worn by the man last seen with Patti Gray, the murdered club dancer. Spencer photographs Garrett in the coat. Garrett and Susan, his fiancée, have an argument when she discovers he has taken the dancer out. Tom and Spencer smear body make-up on the upholstery of Tom's car. Spencer asks Garrett if he wants to continue with the experiment; Tom says he is too deeply involved to back out.

Garrett is eventually arrested for the murder of Patti Gray. Proof that the incriminating evidence has been deliberately planted will be produced by Spencer only after Garrett has been tried and convicted. At the height of the trial, Spencer is killed in a motor accident. The authorities refuse to accept Garrett's story. He is found guilty, and sentenced to death. Susan desperately tries to find additional evidence to clear him, but just before he is pardoned Susan realises that he really is Patti Gray's killer, and long-lost husband. Susan reveals her knowledge to the authorities before a pardon can be given.

The Big Heat
USA 1953 sd b/w 13

PRODUCTION
p.c – Columbia. *p* – Robert Arthur. *d* – Fritz Lang. *sc* – Sydney Boehm, from the novel by William P. McGivern. *ph* – Charles Lang. *ed* – Charles Nelson. *a.d* – Robert Peterson.

LEADING PLAYERS
Glenn Ford (*Dave Bannion*), Gloria Grahame (*Debby Marsh*), Jocelyn Brando (*Katie Bannion*), Alexander Scourby (*Mike Lagana*), Lee Marvin (*Vince Stone*), Adam Williams (*Larry Gordon*).

SYNOPSIS
A policeman, Duncan, commits suicide. Dave Bannion, a colleague, suspects that the case is more complicated than it appears. This is confirmed when a girl who has given him information is brutally murdered. His superiors order him off the case, but Bannion continues his investiga-

tions unofficially. A bomb planted in his car kills his wife and he resigns from the police force to avenge her murder. He is convinced that Mike Lagana, a racketeer who controls the city administration, is responsible, but he at first makes little progress in getting evidence.

Vince Stone, one of Lagana's henchmen, and Larry, another cohort, are greeted by Debby, who is Vince's girlfriend. She mimics the way they respond to their boss when he arrives. Lagana warns Larry that he is getting careless, and that the murder of the nightclub girl has given them unwelcome publicity. A clue about his wife's murderers takes Bannion to a wrecked car lot but the man in charge claims to know nothing. His secretary, however, is more helpful, and tells Bannion about a man called Larry from a club called 'The Retreat'. Bannion arranges with his brother-in-law to call Larry at 'The Retreat' while he, Bannion, is there watching, but the ruse doesn't work. While he is waiting, Bannion sees Vince burn a woman with a cigarette. Bannion intervenes and forces Vince to leave. He refuses Debby's offer to buy him a drink.

Debby is disfigured when Vince throws scalding coffee in her face. Later, she comes to Bannion with information which leads him to his wife's murderer and the discovery that Duncan left evidence against Lagana in a letter which his widow is using to blackmail him. She has instructed her lawyers to open it only in the event of her death. Bannion finds that he cannot kill Mrs. Duncan in cold blood, but Debby does it and is then shot by Stone.

The Big Sky
USA 1952 sd b/w 15

PRODUCTION
p.c – Winchester Pictures. *p* – Howard Hawks. *d* – Howard Hawks. *sc* – Dudley Nichols, from the novel by A. B. Guthrie Jr. *ph* – Russell Harlan. *ed* – Christian Nyby. *a.d* – Albert S. D'Agostino, Perry Ferguson. *m* – Dimitri Tiomkin.

LEADING PLAYERS
Kirk Douglas (*Jim Deakins*), Dewey Martin (*Boone Caudill*), Arthur Hunnicutt (*Zeb*), Elizabeth Threatt (*Teal Eye*).

SYNOPSIS
In 1830 two tough Kentucky mountaineers, Jim Deakins and Boone Caudill, join a group of traders on an expedition from St. Louis up the Mississippi into unknown territory. They have a cargo, mainly of whisky, which they plan to exchange for furs with the Blackfoot Indians. In case the Indians prove difficult, they also have Teal Eye, the chief's daughter, on board as a hostage. As well as natural hazards the expedition has to contend with the problems caused by her presence and with the opposition of the regular fur-trading company, who kidnap Teal Eye and stir up the hostile Crow

Indians. Jim and Boone rescue Teal Eye, to whom they are both attracted, the expedition beats off the Crow Indians and finally reaches Blackfoot territory.

After three days of trading, Teal Eye appears and gives Jim a token signifying that they are brother and sister. Boone follows her to her tent and surrenders his knife to her. Boone reappears and discovers that the drums and dancing are to celebrate his 'wedding' to Teal Eye. Believing that Boone will not want to stay with her Teal Eye requests that he pays for her, thereby leaving him free to go. Zeb, one of the traders, arranges a payment of rifles and horses, and the expedition sets off South. Boone leaves Teal Eye, which causes a rift between himself and Jim. At their first stop, Boone throws away the scalp which has sustained his bitterness towards Indians, and decides to go back to Teal Eye. The friendship between Jim and Boone is reestablished.

The Birds
USA 1963 sd col 18

PRODUCTION
p.c – Alfred Hitchock/Universal-International. *p* – Alfred Hitchcock. *d* – Alfred Hitchcock. *sc* – Evan Hunter, from the story by Daphne du Maurier. *ph* – Robert Burks (Technicolor). *ed* – George Tomasini. *a.d* – Robert Boyle. *cost* – Edith Head.

LEADING PLAYERS
Tippi Hedren (*Melanie Daniels*), Rod Taylor (*Mitch Brenner*), Suzanne Pleshette (*Annie Hayworth*), Jessica Tandy (*Lydia Brenner*), Veronica Cartwright (*Cathy Brenner*).

SYNOPSIS
A chance meeting in a San Francisco pet shop impels Melanie Daniels, a wealthy playgirl, to track down Mitch Brenner, a lawyer, to his mother's home in Bodega Bay. She finds out a little about the Brenner family from Annie Hayworth, a school teacher who evidently loves Mitch, then crosses to the Brenner house by boat. On the way a seagull swoops and pecks her head. Mitch invites her for dinner and to his sister Cathy's birthday thc following day, and Melanie stays with Annie overnight. During the evening the conversation is interrupted by a gull hurling itself against the door. Melanie recalls that Mitch's possessive mother, Lydia, has been worried by her chickens' refusal to eat. A group of gulls attack the children at Cathy's party; and in the evening hundreds of sparrows force their way down the chimney of the Brenner's house and wreck the living room. Next day Lydia discovers a local farmer pecked to death by birds and she starts to worry about Cathy's safety. Melanie goes back to the school to bring her home. While she is there an army of crows attack the school. Eventually the whole community is besieged. Melanie is trapped in a phone booth until rescued by

Mitch, and Annie is savaged to death on her front porch.

The Brenners and Melanie board up the house. Lydia becomes hysterical when Mitch says that he doesn't know what will happen or what they should do. Melanie looks after Cathy while they wait for the attack, but as soon as it begins Cathy runs to her mother. The birds almost succeed in breaking in but are rebuffed and eventually go away. The Brenners fall asleep from exhaustion but Melanie hears a sound upstairs and goes to investigate. She finds the attic full of birds and is severely injured before Mitch rescues her. Mrs. Brenner pulls herself together to help Mitch nurse Melanie, and they decide they must try to get her to a hospital in San Francisco. Taking advantage of a calm period, they leave the house. Mitch drives Melanie, Lydia and Cathy towards San Francisco, leaving the birds in sole possession of Bodega Bay.

(NB An extract chosen to illustrate Raymond Bellour's article *The Birds: analysis of a sequence*, obtainable in English from BFI Education, is also available. The extract consists of the sequence in which Melanie crosses the bay by boat to take a surprise gift of two love-birds to Mitch's house, and is attacked by a gull on her return. It includes titles which indicate Bellour's breakdown of the sequence into smaller units, or 'sets', called A and B.)

The Birth of a Nation
USA 1915 st b/w 12+7

PRODUCTION
p.c – Epoch Producing Corp. *p* – D. W. Griffith. *d* – D. W. Griffith. *sc* – D. W. Griffith and Frank Woods, from the novel *The Clansman* by Rev. Thomas Dixon Jr. *ph* – G. W. Bitzer. *ed* – D. W. Griffith.

LEADING PLAYERS
Henry B. Walthall (*Colonel Ben Cameron*), Mae Marsh (*Flora Cameron*), Miriam Cooper (*Margaret Cameron*), Josephine Crowell (*Mrs. Cameron*), Spottiswoode Aitken (*Dr. Cameron*), André Beranger (*Wade Cameron*), Lillian Gish (*Elsie Stoneman*).

SYNOPSIS
Dr. Cameron and his five children, Ben, Wade, Duke, Flora and Margaret, live in the South and are friendly with Austin Stoneman and his daughter Elsie who live in the North. The Camerons visit the Stonemans, but their trip is cut short by signs of the impending civil war. Shortly after they arrive home the war commences. Ben becomes a colonel. Wade is killed.

During the last days of the Confederacy Duke is also killed. Ben leads an attempt to break through to a cut-off food train. He is wounded and his forces are demolished, but his bravery is cheered by the Union soldiers when he reaches their trenches, which are littered with bodies. (Ext. 1, 12 mins.)

Ben is taken prisoner and is sent to the

hospital where Elsie Stoneman is a nurse. They fall in love and when he is sentenced to death, Elsie goes to see President Lincoln and arranges a pardon. After the war is over, and Lincoln has been assassinated, Austin Stoneman who has a fanatical hatred of the South becomes powerful in politics. He disenfranchises white men and gives the vote to the newly-freed black slaves. Crime and disorder result, and the blacks attack whites and demand marriage to white women. Flora Cameron dies trying to defend herself from an attempted rape by a black man. Ben becomes the leader of the Ku Klux Klan. The Cameron home is pillaged, and the family flee to a log cabin. Silas Lynch, black governor of the state and a protegé of Austin Stoneman's, abducts Elsie Stoneman and is about to rape her.

The cabin where the Camerons are hiding is under attack from armed black soldiers, while in the town whites are tarred and feathered. Ben Cameron arrives at the head of a column of hundreds of Ku Klux Klan men, who rescue Elsie and set out for the log cabin. There, the white men are about to kill the white women to prevent them falling into the hands of the black men. The Klan disarms the blacks, and have a celebratory parade. They are cheered by grateful white families. (Ext 2, 7 mins.)

Blackmail
UK 1929 sd b/w 10

PRODUCTION
p.c – British International Pictures. *p* – John Maxwell. *d* – Alfred Hitchcock. *sc* – Benn W. Levy, Charles Bennett, Alfred Hitchcock, from the play by Charles Bennett. *ph* – Jack Cox. *ed* – Emile de Ruelle. *a.d* – Wilfred C. Arnold, Norman Arnold. *m* – Campbell and Connelly.

LEADING PLAYERS
Anny Ondra (*Alice White*), Sara Allgood (*Mrs. White*), John Longden (*Frank Webber*), Charles Paton (*Mr. White*), Donald Calthrop (*Tracy*), Cyril Ritchard (*The Artist*).

SYNOPSIS
Alice White, sweetheart of Frank Webber, a London detective, kills in self-defence an artists who attempts to seduce her in his studio.

She escapes from the studio and returns home. The artist's landlady discovers the body and informs the police, who assign Frank Webber to the case. At home, Alice is subjected to conversation about the murder, with the word 'knife' recurring again and again.

Frank's investigations lead him to suspect that Alice is somehow involved, and he learns the truth when Tracy, a shady character who saw Alice come out of the studio, begins to blackmail him. Frank turns the tables on the blackmailer by contriving to get him suspected of the murder. Fleeing from the police, Tracy crashes through the dome of the British Museum, having been cornered on the roof at the end of a chase. Meanwhile, a conscience-stricken Alice has gone to Scotland Yard to confess. Frank, returning to the Yard to report the death of Tracy, now accepted by the police as self-evidently the murderer, breaks into Alice's conversation before she confesses. The pair depart with all obstacles to their marriage removed.

Blacula
USA 1972 sd col 12

PRODUCTION
p.c – American International Pictures. *p* – Joseph T. Naar. *d* – William Crain. *sc* – Joan Torres, Raymond Koenig. *ph* – John Stevens (colour by Movielab). *ed* – Allan Jacobs. *a.d* – Walter Herndon. *m* – Gene Page. *cost* – Ermon Sessions, Sandy Stewart.

LEADING PLAYERS
William Marshall (*Mamuwalde/Blacula*), Vonetta McGee (*Tina*), Denise Nicholas (*Michelle*), Thalmus Rasulala (*Gordon Thomas*), Gordon Pinsent (*Lieutenant Peters*).

SYNOPSIS
Castle Dracula, Transylvania, 1780. A visiting black prince, Mamuwalde, hopes to enlist the Count's support for his mission to end the slave trade, but he is vampirised and cursed with the title Blacula. His wife is immured. Nearly two centuries later the coffin of Blacula/Mamuwalde is taken to Los Angeles by two antique dealers. Blacula is resurrected and attacks them both. Later at one of their funerals he sees Tina, the exact likeness of his former wife, and tries to follow her, but she runs off. A forensic scientist, Dr. Thomas, begins to be suspicious and demands an autopsy on one of the antique dealers. Meanwhile, Blacula has vampirised two women, a taxidriver and a photographer.

He goes to see Tina at her flat. He tells her that they have been together before, about the visit to Dracula's castle, and about his vampirism and her reincarnation. He wants her to go with him. She admits that she is drawn, but is afraid. He declares that he will not harm her, that he wants her to come to him of her own free will. He turns to leave but she calls him back and they embrace. (Ext. 1a, 3 mins.)

Dr. Thomas is now certain that there is an outbreak of vampirism in Los Angeles. Two vampires are destroyed, one by a stake, one by the rising sun. A special police alert is called. The vampire's lair is discovered and they are all killed except Blacula. Tina agrees to act as a decoy to lead the police to Blacula, but he metamorphoses into a bat and escapes. Tina eludes the police and finds him in an underground electrical power station. The police pursue them.

Tina is shot and in order not to lose her again Blacula vampirises her. There is a verbal confrontation between Dr. Thomas and Blacula. Carnage follows, in which numerous policemen are killed. They discover a coffin, open it, and stake the vampire that Tina has now become. With his wife finally lost, Blacula no longer has any reason to live. He staggers up the staircase into the sunlight and disintegrates. (Ext. 1b, 9 mins.)

Blow for Blow (Coup pour coup)
France/West Germany 1972 sd col 10

PRODUCTION
p.c – MK2 Productions/Cinema Services (Paris)/WDR (Cologne). *d* – Marin Karmitz. *ph* – André Dubreuil (Eastman Color). *m* – Jacky Moreau.

SYNOPSIS
The film is a fictional reconstruction of a successful strike to get better pay and conditions in a clothing factory, based on a number of factory occupations in France since 1968. It opens with scenes on the assembly line, while a woman's voice-over explains conditions of work – the speed-ups, the lousy pay, the role of the foremen, the female supervisor and management. The women are driven to sabotage to gain a moment's respite; one woman breaks into screams of rage under the strain. She and two others identified as trouble-makers are summarily dismissed and the women immediately stop work and lock Boursac, the boss, in his office. The union representatives get him released and negotiate paltry wage increases, which the women reject. They organise an occupation; food is brought in from outside and there are problems with children when husbands can't manage.

The factory owner, Boursac, makes arrangements over the phone with police to send in provocateurs to attack the occupation. Meanwhile the strikers prepare for the night. An old woman recounts incidents from the 30s. Police vans gather in nearby streets. The women construct barricades. A woman writes about her experiences – how she now feels a solidarity with the other factory workers and how her life has been changed by the experience of the occupation. Other women discuss picket duty and how they will not give in. Finally, the provocateurs storm the factory gates but the women repel their attack and a victory speech is made. On television Boursac, the factory manager and the union leader give their views of the strike.

Boursac sneaks into his office again, but is discovered by the women and sequestered in a glass office. Other factories strike in sympathy. The local authorities are afraid of further escalation and compel Boursac to give in to the women's demands. The women talk of their new-found sense of solidarity and power.

Le Bonheur
France 1965 sd col 11

PRODUCTION
p.c – Parc Film/Mag Bodard. *d* – Agnès Varda. *sc* – Agnès Varda. *ph* – Jean Rabier, Claude Beausoleil (Eastman Color). *ed* – Janine Verneau. *a.d* – Hubert Monloup. *m* – Mozart.

LEADING PLAYERS
Jean-Claude Drouot (*François*), Claire Drouot (*Thérèse*), Sandrine Drouot (*Gisou*), Olivier Drouot (*Pierrot*), Marie-France Boyer (*Emilie*).

SYNOPSIS
François, a simple young carpenter living at Fontenay, is happy – happy with his wife Thérèse, happy with his children Gisou and Pierrot, and happy in his work. While away from home on a job, at Vincennes, he meets and falls in love with Emilie, a post-office clerk. Later, Emilie is transferred to Fontenay.

A bride-to-be leaves Thérèse's house with the wedding-dress Thérèse has made. The wedding group is photographed leaving the church. François calls on Emilie to deliver some shelving. François and Thérèse are seen at the wedding reception and later at home François calls again on Emilie. While Thérèse is shopping, François goes to the post-office to give Emilie a telegram.

François and Emilie become lovers. François, who still loves his wife, is happier than ever. During one of their favourite outings, a weekend picnic in the country he attempts to explain his feelings to Thérèse. Later she is found drowned. Once he has overcome his grief, François marries Emilie and resumes his happy family life and his weekend picnics in the country.

Born to Kill (Deadlier than the Male)
USA 1947 sd b/w 15

PRODUCTION
p.c – RKO Radio Pictures. *p* – Herbert Schlom. *d* – Robert Wise. *sc* – Eve Green and Richard Macaulay, from the novel *Deadlier than the Male* by James Gunn. *ph* – Robert de Grasse. *ed* – Les Millbrook. *a.d* – Albert S. D'Agostino and Walter E. Keller. *m* – Paul Sawtell. *cost* – Edward Stevenson.

LEADING PLAYERS
Lawrence Tierney (*Sam Wild*), Claire Trevor (*Helen Brent*), Walter Slezak (*Albert Arnett*), Philip Terry (*Fred Grover*), Audrey Long (*Georgia Staples*), Elisha Cook Jr. (*Marty Waterman*), Esther Howard (*Mrs. Kraft*), Isabel Jewell (*Laury Palmer*).

SYNOPSIS
Helen Brent talks to her lawyer about her newly-obtained divorce, and then returns to her lodgings. There she talks about men with her landlady Mrs. Kraft and her neighbour Laury Palmer. Laury tells her

that she is going out with a former boy-friend, Danny, in order to make her new one jealous. That night Helen goes to a casino where she sees Sam Wild, Laury's new boyfriend. He is furious with Laury and Danny, follows them home and murders them both. Helen discovers their bodies and realises that Sam is probably the killer but is unwilling to jeopardise her forthcoming marriage to the rich Fred Grover by any involvement with the police. She decides to leave town. On the railway platform she meets Sam and during their journey they discuss their lives.

Irresistably attracted to him, but unprepared to leave Fred, Helen is confused when Sam turns up at the house of Georgia, her foster sister, where she is staying. When Sam realises that Georgia is rich and that Helen is dependent on her for money, Sam becomes engaged to the impressionable Georgia, and despite declarations of mutual love between Sam and Helen, he marries Georgia. His friend Marty is best man. In the meantime Mrs. Kraft has hired a seedy detective, Arnett, to track down Laury's murderer. He turns up at the wedding and Helen appears to give him a clue implicating Sam. Sam becomes frustrated by Georgia's refusal to let him control the newspaper she owns, and the passion between Sam and Helen re-emerges. Helen agrees to pay Arnett off. Sam persuades Marty to try and kill Mrs. Kraft and he lures her to a deserted beach, but Sam kills Marty, whom he jealously and wrongly believes has double-crossed him with Helen. Mrs. Kraft escapes, but Helen threatens to kill her if she talks. Helen is rejected by Fred, and in revenge against Sam she calls the police. She tries to destroy Georgia's faith in Sam in front of her, but Sam remembers Helen's role in calling the police and kills her. He is fatally wounded by the police.

Born Yesterday
USA 1950 sd b/w 19

PRODUCTION
p.c – Colombia. *p* – S. Sylvan Simon. *d* – George Cukor. *sc* – Albert Mannheimer, from the play by Garson Kanin. *ph* – Joseph Walker. *ed* – Charles Nelson. *a.d* – Harry Horner. *m* – Frederick Hollander.

LEADING PLAYERS
Judy Holliday (*Billie Dawn*), William Holden (*Paul Verrall*), Broderick Crawford (*Harry Brock*).

SYNOPSIS
Harry Brock, a scrap-iron tycoon, comes to Washington intending to buy congressmen's support for a bill which will enable him to extend his activities. He brings with him his mistress, Billie Dawn, an ex-chorus girl of phenomenal ignorance. Billie seems likely to disgrace him in front of his new acquaintances, so Brock hires Paul Verrall, a young writer, to educate her.
In the hotel, Brock and Billie play cards.

Billie wins ostentatiously, putting Brock in a fury. Paul comes round with some newspapers and books for the benefit of Billie's education. Next morning, Paul takes Billie to see the Lincoln Memorial and other important sites and she starts to find out about the principles of democracy. After going to a concert with Paul, she talks about her father.

Soon she is reading Tom Paine, and accuses Brock of fascism. Brock, enraged by this startling change, hits her. This clarifies the confusion in Billie's mind. Although in a position to expose Brock and his crooked lawyer, she decides instead to curb his activities by exerting control over the junkyards of which she is the nominal owner. After professing their love Paul and Billie go off together, taking documents about Brock's crooked dealings with them.

Boudu sauvé des eaux
France 1932 sd b/w 11

PRODUCTION
p.c – Michel Simon/Jean Gehret. *p* – Michel Simon, Jean Gehret. *d* – Jean Renoir. *sc* – Jean Renoir, from the play by René Fauchois. *ph* – Marcel Lucien Asselin. *ed* – Suzanne de Troyes. *a.d* – Hugues Laurent, Jean Castanier. *m* – Raphaël, Johann Strauss.

LEADING PLAYERS
Michel Simon (*Boudu*), Charles Grandval (*Monsieur Lestingois*), Marcelle Hainia (*Madame Lestingois*), Séverine Lerczinska (*Anne-Marie*).

SYNOPSIS
When he throws himself into the Seine in a fit of melancholy after losing his dog, the magnificently scruffy tramp Boudu is rescued by an antiquarian bookseller, Monsieur Lestingois. Far from being grateful, Boudu insists that his rescuer is now responsible for him. The kindly Lestingois does his best, but his task is not made easy by Boudu's total disregard of the proprieties.
Boudu makes nonsense of civilised living-habits during a meal with Monsieur and Madame Lestingois. Later he has a conversation with the maid in which – despite his frightfulness – he manages to exhibit a curiously sexual allure.

Boudu's anti-social behaviour has Madame Lestingois on the verge of hysteria. Lestingois and the maid Anne-Marie, who are prevented from spending their nights together because Boudu insists on sleeping in the corridor between their rooms, become cross and frustrated. Nobody demurs when Madame Lestingois declares that the tramp must go. After a visit to the barber, however, a rejuvenated Boudu has little difficulty in seducing her. Then, while Madame Lestingois languishes hopefully, Boudu turns his attentions to Anne-Marie, who is being consoled by Lestingois – and the double adultery is discovered. But Boudu has just

won a fortune with a lottery ticket given him by Lestingois, so Anne-Marie agrees to marry him, and this seems the best solution for all concerned. After the marriage, however, as the wedding party sails down the river in a punt, Boudu accidentally upsets it. The others scramble ashore, but Boudu, suddenly rediscovering his liberty, drifts downstream and disappears. While the others mourn his supposed death, he changes his clothes with a scarecrow, and sets happily out on the road again as a tramp.

Breathless
(*see* A bout de souffle)

The Brides of Dracula
UK 1960 sd col 14

PRODUCTION
p.c – Hammer/Hotspur. *p* – Anthony Hinds. *d* – Terence Fisher. *sc* – Jimmy Sangster, Peter Bryan, Edward Percy. *ph* – Jack Asher (Technicolor). *ed* – Jim Needs, Alfred Cox. *a.d* – Bernard Robinson, Thomas Goswell. *m* – Malcolm Williamson.

LEADING PLAYERS
Peter Cushing (*Van Helsing*), Yvonne Monlaur (*Marianne*), Freda Jackson (*Greta*), David Peel (*Baron Meinster*), Martita Hunt (*Baroness Meinster*), Andrée Melly (*Gina*), Mona Washbourne (*Frau Lang*), Henry Oscar (*Lang*), Norman Pierce (*Landlord*).

SYNOPSIS
Marianne Daniello, a teacher on her way to the Badstein Girls' Academy, sets free the chained-up Baron Meinster, not knowing that he is a vampire. Later she gets frightened and runs away from the Meinster chateau, to be found next morning by Dr. Van Helsing, who has been summoned by the local priest to investigate vampirism in the district. The Baron goes to visit Marianne at the Academy, but is interrupted when about to vampirise her. Instead, he vampirises Gina, another teacher. Van Helsing, exploring the chateau, finds the tormented Baroness, the Baron's mother, and agrees to stake her.
He orders that the coffin containing Gina's body be kept in the stables. As Marianne watches over the coffin its lid springs open and Gina, now a vampire, bursts out. She advances towards Marianne and is about to take her to the Baron who is hiding out at the Old Mill when Van Helsing rushes in. Gina vanishes and Van Helsing carries Marianne up to the house and explains that the Baron is a vampire. He gives her a cross to wear for protection. Van Helsing arrives at the Old Mill, and finds an empty coffin. He throws his cross at three female vampires to ward them off, but as he is about to retrieve it the Baron arrives. There is a fight, the Baron throttles Van Helsing into unconsciousness and vampirises him. Van Helsing comes to, finds the bite marks on

his neck and cauterises the wound with a red-hot poker. Meanwhile, at the Academy, Marianne prepares for bed. She removes the cross. The Baron crashes in through the window and takes her to the Mill. There is a fight between Van Helsing and the Baron, in which Van Helsing eventually destroys the vampire by catching him in the cruciform shadow of the arms of the windmill. As Marianne and Van Helsing walk away together, the Mill goes up in flames.

(NB The trailer for *The Brides of Dracula* is appended to this extract.)

The Bridge on the River Kwai
UK 1957 sd col 11

PRODUCTION
p.c – Horizon. p – Sam Spiegel. d – David Lean. sc – Pierre Boulle, from the novel by Pierre Boulle. ph – Jack Hildyard (CinemaScope and Technicolor), ed – Peter Taylor. a.d – Donald M. Ashton. m – Malcolm Arnold.

LEADING PLAYERS
William Holden (*Shears*), Alec Guinness (*Colonel Nicholson*), Jack Hawkins (*Major Warden*), Sessue Hayakawa (*Colonel Saito*).

SYNOPSIS
A batallion of British war prisoners under the command of Colonel Nicholson is employed by the Japanese on the 'death railway'. Their specific task to to build a bridge over the River Kwai, a vital link in Japanese military communications. When the officers are ordered to work alongside the men, Nicholson cites the Geneva Convention and refuses to comply as a matter of principle. He is subjected by Colonel Saito, the Japanese commandant, to brutal imprisonment. Nicholson stands firm and wins a moral triumph. He then takes charge of the building operations, determined to restore the men's morale and to demonstrate to the Japanese the invincibility of the British soldier. He believes the bridge will be a symbol of British achievement, and in driving his men ruthlessly he wholly loses sight of the fact that he is now aiding the enemy. Meanwhile, a small British commando force, led by Major Warden and joined by Shears, an American sailor who has previously escaped from the camp, is breaking through the jungle. Their mission is the destruction of the Kwai bridge.

Walking with Colonel Saito on the bridge, Nicholson notices a wire. he calls Saito's attention to this, and then examines the wire, which leads him to the detonator. The sabotage party try to prevent him from cutting the wire, but by now the Japanese have been alerted. In the fighting that follows, Shears and Saito are killed. Shears dies accusing Nicholson of treachery. Nicholson is hit by mortar fire, and falls on the plunger – blowing up the bridge just as a train passes over it.

(NB This extract is standard reduced from Scope.)

Brighton Rock
UK 1947 sd b/w 13

PRODUCTION
p.c – Associated British. p – Roy Boulting. d – John Boulting. sc – Graham Greene and Terence Rattigan, from the novel by Graham Greene. ph – Harry Waxman. ed – Peter Graham Scott. a.d – John Howell. m – Hans May. cost – Honoria Plesch.

LEADING PLAYERS
Richard Attenborough (*Pinkie Brown*), Herminone Baddeley (*Ida Arnold*), William Hartnell (*Dallow*).

SYNOPSIS
Placards announce the arrival in Brighton of Kolley Kibber, a journalist on a circulation stunt. Pinkie Brown, the neurotic and sadistic 17-year-old leader of a gang, recognises Kolley as the man responsible for the death of their former leader. Kolley sees Pinkie and realises that his life is in danger. He goes to Ida Arnold, a concert artist, for protection. She takes him on a ghost train on the pier but he is killed by Pinkie.

At the inquest the verdict is faked. Spicer, a member of Pinkie's gang, gives him an alibi by taking Kolley's promotional visiting cards to various locations after he has been killed. At one of these, Rose, a waitress, is puzzled by her customer's lack of resemblance to the press pictures. Pinkie realises the possible consequences and arranges to meet Rose who falls in love with him. Spicer begins to lose his nerve and Pinkie tries to get him killed in a fight with a rival gang at the racetrack. The plan goes wrong; Spicer escapes and Pinkie is slashed with a razor. Ida wins £250 and uses it to start investigations into Kolley's death. Scared, Pinkie decides that the only way to stop Rose ever testifying against him is to marry her. He causes Spicer's death by hurling him over some bannisters in a fit of rage, and later marries Rose in a dingy registry office. He plans to kill her in a mock 'suicide pact', but Ida arrives with the police in time to prevent this. Pinkie falls off the pier and is drowned, and Rose is left with a record he made for her on their wedding day. On it, he describes his disgust for her, but the needle sticks after the first three words of 'I love you is what you want me to say . . .'.

Bringing Up Baby
USA 1938 sd b/w 8

PRODUCTION
p.c – RKO Radio. p – Howard Hawks. d – Howard Hawks. sc – Dudley Nichols, Hagar Wilde, from a story by Hagar Wilde. ph – Russell Metty. ed – George Hively. a.d – Van Nest Polglase, Perry Ferguson. m. – Roy Webb. cost – Howard Greer.

LEADING PLAYERS
Cary Grant (*David Huxley*), Katharine Hepburn (*Susan*).

SYNOPSIS
David is a young professor in prehistoric zoology. On the evening of a climax in his career and just before his marriage to his co-worker he meets irresponsible Susan Vance, who falls in love with him.

He phones his fiancée to try to explain a mix-up to her, and then a delivery boy brings the 'interclosterclavicle' vital to the reconstruction of a brontosaurus. As he is unwrapping it, Susan phones requesting his help with her tame leopard, Baby. Feigning hysteria, she coaxes him to her flat. David is uneasy with Baby but Susan tricks him into agreeing to help her take Baby to her country home in Connecticut. En route they hit a car-load of chickens, much to Baby's delight. Susan blithely justifies everything to a feather-covered David.

In Connecticut David meets Susan's aunt, who turns out to be the Mrs. Random whose financial aid he has been trying to obtain for his scientific work through her secretary Mr. Peabody. He attempts to preserve an appearance of dignity and extricate himself from the embarrassing situation caused by Susan's infatuation, but to no avail. Susan's dog runs off and buries the precious bone. Baby escapes, and another leopard, less tame, is mistaken for Baby and freed from the cage in which it is being taken to be killed. Susan and David get locked in gaol before the situation is finally sorted out.

British Sounds
UK 1969 sd col 10

PRODUCTION
p.c – Kestrel Productions, for London Weekend TV. p – Irving Teitelbaum, Kenith Trodd. d – Jean-Luc Godard. sc – Jean-Luc Godard. ph – Charles Stewart (Eastman Color). ed – Elizabeth Kozmian.

SYNOPSIS
The film is divided into two parts, each consisting of three well-defined sections. Part One identifies two areas of revolutionary confrontation – the point of production (illustrated by the BMC car assembly plant at Abingdon) and the situation of women in capitalist society. There is also a caricature commentary on bourgeois ideology.

A naked woman walks between two rooms while a female voice-over describes the social problems of women – the difficulties of only complaining about the little things and not the essential problems; the position of the working-class women workers as the exploited of the exploited. This section is followed by a right-wing student leader delivering a speech on the necessity of keeping wages low until such time as the employers decide they ought to be raised, the need to curb permissiveness in society, etc.

Part Two deals with the need for political organisation and class consciousness. In 'Workers' Sounds' militant workers discuss their roles within the profit system, while 'Student Sounds' shows students at Essex University designing posters and attempting to politicise a Beatles song. Finally in Part Three, 'Sounds of Revolution', a blood-stained hand is seen reaching out towards a red flag. The film ends with a succession of fists punching through a paper Union Jack.

Broken Arrow
USA 1950 sd col 10

PRODUCTION
p.c – 20th Century-Fox. *p* – Julian Blaustein. *d* – Delmer Daves. *sc* – Michael Blankfort, from the novel *Blood Brother* by Elliot Arnold. *ph* – Ernest Palmer (Technicolor). *ed* – J. Watson Webb Jr. *a.d* – Lyle Wheeler and Albert Hogsett. *m* – Hugo Friedhofer.

LEADING PLAYERS
James Stewart (*Tom Jeffords*), Jeff Chandler (*Cochise*), Debra Paget (*Conseeahray*), Basil Ruysdael (*General Howard*).

SYNOPSIS
Captain Tom Jeffords, a Scout in the US army during the wars against the Apache Indians, led by Cochise, is travelling to Tucson. He spots some circling buzzards whose prey turns out to be a wounded Indian boy. Although at first distrustful, the Indian allows Jeffords to remove the shot from his wounds. As a result of Jeffords's attention, the boy recovers and the two are about to part when an Apache war party appears and seizes Jeffords. The boy defends his white friend and the boy's father eventually allows Jeffords to be released.

Jeffords persuades Cochise to allow the US mail riders to pass unmolested through Apache country, although the struggle against the US military would be maintained. General Howard, sent by the President to make peace with the Apache, is taken to Cochise by Jeffords. Peace terms are successfully concluded and the majority of Apache chieftains agree to a three-month armistice. Meanwhile, Jeffords has fallen in love with Conseeahray, an Indian girl, and through Cochise's intervention is able to marry her. The truce is broken by dissidents and renegades on both sides, and during an ambush by a gang of Indian-haters Conseeahray is killed and Jeffords badly wounded. Jeffords wants to avenge the death of his wife, but is persuaded against revenge killing by both General Howard and Cochise.

Brute Force
USA 1947 sd b/w 20

PRODUCTION
p.c – Universal-International. *p* – Mark Hellinger. *d* – Jules Dassin. *sc* – Richard Brooks, from a story by Robert Patterson. *ph* – William Daniels. *ed* – Edward Curtiss. *a.d* – Bernard Herzbrun and John F. Decuir. *m* – Miklós Rózsa. *cost* – Rosemary Odell.

LEADING PLAYERS
Burt Lancaster (*Joe Collins*), Hume Cronyn (*Captain Munsey*), Charles Bickford (*Gallagher*).

SYNOPSIS
Six men are imprisoned in cell R-17 of Westgate Penitentiary. Joe Collins is their acknowledged leader. Captain Munsey, the sadistic and ambitious head guard, stirs up trouble among the prisoners, hoping to discredit the warden, whose job he covets. When Joe learns that his girlfriend Ruth has refused to undergo an operation until he is at her side he determines to break out of prison. He draws up a plan with Gallagher, who runs the prison newspaper, to take effect when he is assigned to work on a drainpipe outside the walls.

One of Gallagher's men tries to take a message to Joe, but he is picked up by Munsey and beaten unconscious when he refuses to reveal the plan. Later, the prison doctor warns Joe of Munsey's suspicions but he decides to go ahead regardless. The warden resigns. Munsey is appointed, and the prisoners crowd in the yard. Violence erupts throughout the prison and Gallagher's men throw bombs at the guard's tower. Joe and his men run from the drainpipe, and although wounded, Joe climbs the tower to open the gate. Gallagher tries to smash the gate open with a truck, but jams it shut instead. Before he dies Joe throws Munsey from the tower.

Buck and the Preacher
USA 1971 sd col 16

PRODUCTION
p.c – E & R Productions/Belafonte Enterprises. *p* – Joel Glickman. *d* – Sidney Poitier. *sc* – Ernest Kinoy, from a story by Ernest Kinoy and Drake Walker. *ph* – Alex Phillips. *ed* – Pembroke J. Herring. *m* – Benny Carter. *cost* – Guy Verhille.

LEADING PLAYERS
Sidney Poitier (*Buck*), Harry Belafonte (*Preacher*), Ruby Dee (*Ruth*), Enrique Lucero (*Indian Chief*).

SYNOPSIS
Buck, a former Union cavalryman, is dedicated to the task of guiding black wagontrains to California and of protecting them from a marauding gang led by Deshay, who is determined to stop this exodus of cheap labour from the South. One wagontrain is destroyed. Buck manages to escape the gang and later steals a horse from a fake preacher. Preacher makes inquiries about Buck and learns from Deshay about a $500 reward on his head. He finds Buck, who is very suspicious. Next morning, Preacher tries to leave but is surrounded by the Indians Buck has set out to meet. He watches Buck bargain for safe passage for the wagontrain through Indian territory. In the meantime, however, it is raided by Deshay who burns the supplies and takes the money belonging to the pioneers. The survivors determine to keep going and Preacher decides to help Buck track down Deshay, which they do in a brothel. After a shoot-out they discover the money has already been spent. The sherriff and the remainder of Deshay's gang ride out after them.

Buck and Preacher try to raid an Express Office but all the paper money has been banked, and gold is too heavy to carry on the horses. Although the posse is in hot pursuit, they decide to raid a bank. Ruth, Buck's wife, brings them guns but they find the back door is locked. Ruth makes her way into the bank and surreptitiously unlocks the door. Buck and Preacher surprise the occupants and take the money. As they ride away the alarm is given and the posse closes in but at the last minute the Indians arrive to confront their pursuers. Buck talks to the Indian chief and tries to persuade him to give the wagontrain guns. The chief speaks of the Indians' long history of oppression and exploitation: the guns are needed for their own battle. Buck argues that Indians and blacks are brothers and have the same enemies. The chief points out that Buck was in the US cavalry that rode against the Indians and is adamant in his refusal.

The Indians offer to assist the black wagontrains by providing food, however. After a final shoot-out in the rocks, in which the crucial shots are fired by the Indians who have been watching, Deshay's men are defeated and the party continues West.

Build My Gallows High
(see Out of the Past)

Butch Cassidy and the Sundance Kid
USA 1969 sd col 18

PRODUCTION
p.c – Campanile Productions/20th Century-Fox/A Newman Foreman Presentation. *p* – John Foreman. *d* – George Roy Hill. *sc* – William Goldman. *ph* – Conrad Hall (Panavision and Colour by DeLuxe). *ed* – John C. Howard, Richard C. Meyer. *a.d* – Jack Martin Smith, Philip Jefferies. *m* – Burt Bacharach. *lyrics* – Hal David. *cost* – Edith Head.

LEADING PLAYERS
Paul Newman (*Butch Cassidy*), Robert Redford (*The Sundance Kid*), Katharine Ross (*Etta Place*).

SYNOPSIS
Butch Cassidy wanders round a bank, noting the locks, alarm system and heavily-protected safes. He asks what has happened to the old bank. The doorman tells him that people kept robbing it. Butch sug-

gests ruefully that that was a small price to pay for beauty. Meanwhile, the Sundance Kid is playing cards. He is accused of cheating and told to leave until the other player realises who he is dealing with, and backs down. The Kid gives a demonstration of his shooting skills, without causing injury. (Ext. 1a, 6 mins.)

They decide to undertake a double hold-up of the Union Pacific Railroad. The first robbery is successful, but on the return journey, the authorities are ready for them and Butch and the Kid find themselves being pursued by a highly-skilled posse, who relentlessly track them day and night.

Butch and the Kid scramble up a rocky escarpment in their attempts to evade the posse. The trackers follow them relentlessly. When they reach the top they find themselves trapped with the posse behind them and a raging river torrent below. Butch decides that their only chance of escaping is to jump into the river. The pair make their way back to Etta Place's house. She tells them that the pursuers are led by Baltimore and Lefours and that the posse has been brought together by Harriman of the Union Pacific Railroad with the specific aim of bringing Butch and the Kid in, dead or alive. Butch suggests that they go away to Bolivia; they invite Etta along. She agrees to go but vows that she'll do anything for them except watch them die. They all leave together. (Ext. 1b, 12 mins.)

In Bolivia the three live well from bank-robbing. One day, however, they see Lefours in a cafe, and Etta decides to return to the States. After some 'straight' work as payroll guards, Butch and the Kid are eventually taken by surprise in a small mountain village, and ringed by troops. Butch suggests starting a new life in Australia and they rush out from their cover to meet a hail of bullets.

(NB This extract is standard reduced from Scope. Part 1a is also available compiled with *The Sting*.)

The Cabinet of Dr. Caligari (Das Cabinett des Dr. Caligari)
Germany 1919 st b/w 11

PRODUCTION
p.c – Decla-Bioscop. *p* – Erich Pommer. *d* – Robert Wiene. *sc* – Carl Mayer, Hans Janowitz, from a story by Hans Janowitz. *ph* – Willy Hameister. *a.d* – Hermann Warm, Walter Röhrig.

LEADING PLAYERS
Werner Krauss (*Dr. Caligari*), Conrad Veidt (*Cesare*), Friedrich Feher (*Francis*), Lil Dagover (*Jane*), Hans Heinz von Twardowski (*Alan*).

SYNOPSIS
A man tells the story of how a fair with side shows and a merry-go-round moved to a small town in Germany. The weird bespectacled Dr. Caligari advertises a somnambulist called Cesare. Caligari is haughtily treated by a local official. Next

morning, the man is found murdered in his room.

Two students, Francis and Alan, both in love with Jane, enter Caligari's tent. He tells them that Cesare will answer questions about the future. When Alan asks how long he will live Cesare answers 'Until dawn'. They return home and a shadow falls over Alan's bed.

The next day Francis learns that his friend has been stabbed in the same way as the official. He becomes suspicious of Caligari and persuades Jane's father to help him investigate. They attend the examination of a criminal who frantically denies that he is the murderer. Francis continues to watch Caligari's tent, but although he thinks he can see the somnambulist in his coffin-like box, at that moment Cesare is breaking into Jane's room. He carries her away over roofs and roads until he dies of exhaustion. Francis returns to Caligari's tent with two policemen, and they find that the figure in the box is a dummy. Caligari escapes and seeks shelter in a lunatic asylum. Francis follows and demands to see the director, but is horror-struck when he finds that Caligari and the director are the same person. The following night Francis and three members of the medical staff search Caligari's office and find a book about an 18th century show-man who committed several murders through the agency of a hypnotised medium. The records show that when a somnambulist was entrusted to the director's care he could not resist the temptation of trying to recreate the experiment. Francis confronts Caligari with this information and he collapses into madness. Then, however, we realise that it is Francis who is telling the story – and that he himself is an asylum inmate. Caligari approaches and Francis rushes towards him. Once he has been subdued Caligari contemplatively says 'At last now I can understand the nature of his madness. He thinks I am that mystic Caligari. Now I see how he can be brought back to sanity again'.

Das Cabinett des Dr. Caligari
(*see* The Cabinet of Dr. Caligari)

Calcutta
France 1968 sd col 10

PRODUCTION
p.c – Nouvelle Edition de Films. *p* – Elliot Kastner. *d* – Louis Malle. *sc* – Louis Malle. *ph* – Etienne Becker. *ed* – Suzanne Baron.

SYNOPSIS
An episodic documentary of the sights and sounds of Calcutta. Various aspects of its turbulent life are shown and the problems posed by numerous immigrants to the city from Pakistan and Bihar are outlined.

The insoluble problem of the insanitary slum districts. If some people are moved and given better housing by the muni-

cipality, the space left will immediately be filled by other immigrants. The insanitary living conditions are described and shown in detail : excrement from cows blocks the open sewers, pigs root in the dirt, garbage has not been collected for several months.

Le Caporal épinglé
(*see* The Vanishing Corporal)

Carmen Jones
USA 1954 sd col 10

PRODUCTION
p.c – 20th Century-Fox. *p* – Otto Preminger. *d* – Otto Preminger. *sc* – Harry Kleiner, from the stage play by Oscar Hammerstein II. *ph* – Sam Leavitt (CinemaScope and Colour by DeLuxe). *ed* – Louis R. Loeffler. *a.d* – Edward L. Ilou. *m* Georges Bizet. *lyrics* – Oscar Hammerstein II. *cost* – Mary Ann Nyberg.

LEADING PLAYERS
Harry Belafonte (*Joe*), Dorothy Dandridge (*Carmen*), Pearl Bailey (*Frankie*), Olga James (*Cindy Lou*), Joe Adams (*Husky*).

SYNOPSIS
Cindy Lou visits her fiancé, Joe, at an army parachute factory before he leaves to train as a pilot. Joe takes her to the canteen. Carmen is there, refusing to go out with any of the men who ask her. Only Joe appears to be not interested in her. Carmen makes advances to him, and Cindy Lou gets uneasy, but when the other workers have returned to the factory, Joe re-assures her and asks her to marry him.

Carmen becomes involved in a fight and Joe is obliged to escort her to a nearby jail. On the way Carmen persuades him to let her stop at her grandmother's house and there she seduces him. She later escapes and Joe is sent to prison for negligence. Although offered a trip to Chicago by a boxer friend, Carmen waits for Joe and after he is released they go to Chicago together. The lovers hide out in a tenement room, but soon Carmen is bored and penniless. They quarrel and Carmen starts seeking her boxer friend. Joe strangles her in a jealous rage and then waits for the Military Police to come and arrest him.

(NB This extract is standard reduced from Scope.)

Catch Us If You Can
UK 1965 sd b/w 14

PRODUCTION
p.c – Bruton Film Productions. *p* – David Deutsch. *d* – John Boorman. *sc* – Peter Nichols. *ph* – Manny Wynn. *ed* – Gordon Pilkington. *m* – Dave Clark.

LEADING PLAYERS
Dave Clark (*Steve*), Barbara Ferris (*Dinah*), Lenny Davidson (*Lenny*), Rick Huxley (*Rick*), Mike Smith (*Mike*), Denis Payton (*Denis*), David Lodge (*Louis*),

Robin Bailey (*Guy*), Yootha Joyce (*Nan*), David de Keyser (*Zissell*).

SYNOPSIS

Steve, Lenny, Rick, Mike and Dennis, freelance stuntman, are working on a television commercial for meat at Smithfield Meat Market in London. Steve, and the commercial's star, Dinah, decide to get away from it all.

They take the white E-type Jaguar that is being used as a prop in the film and drive away from Smithfield, through the City and West End. They go skin-diving at the Oasis, visit the Botanical Gardens at Kew and then decide to go to Devon where Dinah hopes to buy an island just off the coast. Zissell, an executive of the advertising company, schemes to recapture them.

Heading for Devon, they encounter a group of beatniks, and then get mixed up in an army exercise which results in the destruction of the car. A middle-aged couple, Guy and Nan, give them a lift to Bath and invite them to stay at their elegant home. Zissell issues to the media a story that Steve has kidnapped Dinah. Guy and Nan persuade their visitors to go to an Arts Fancy Dress Ball. Zissell's henchmen and the police converge on the scene but Steve and Dinah escape, and make their way to a farm run by Louis, former leader of their London youth club. Steve is depressed to find that Louis is interested only in getting publicity out of the situation, and even further disillusioned to discover that Dinah's island is only an island when the tide is high. They find that Zissell is waiting for them but Steve refuses to play a part in the press stunt that Zissell has lined up, and leaves Dinah to face the photographers alone.

Cat People
USA 1942 sd b/w 15

PRODUCTION

p.c – RKO Radio. *p* – Val Lewton. *d* – Jacques Tourneur. *sc* – DeWitt Bodeen. *ph* – Nicholas Musuraca. *ed* – Mark Robson. *a.d* – Albert S. D'Agostino and Walter E. Keller. *m* – Roy Webb. *cost* – Renié.

LEADING PLAYERS

Simone Simon (*Irena Dubrovna*), Kent Smith (*Oliver Reed*), Tom Conway (*Dr. Louis Judd*), Jane Randolph (*Alice Moore*), Jack Holt (*Commodore*), Alan Napier (*Carver*).

SYNOPSIS

Irena, a Serbian-born fashion artist living in New York, is haunted by the fear that she is descended from a race of cat-women who, when physically aroused, turn into panthers. Oliver Reed falls in love with her and tries to convince her that her fears are groundless. They marry, but Irena is afraid to consummate the marriage. Oliver persuades her to visit Dr. Judd, a psychiatrist, but he is unable to help. Irena grows worse and Oliver confides his problems to Alice, a girl at work.

One evening, in order to avoid quarrelling with Irena about Alice, Oliver leaves their flat and returns to the office. Before beginning work, he goes for a coffee. Meanwhile, Irena calls the office to check that Oliver is there, but the phone is answered by Alice who has been working late but is about to leave. Alice then meets Oliver by chance in the café, and Irena follows her when she leaves. Alice, aware that she is being followed, begins to run and manages to catch a bus. Irena later returns home shaken and covered in mud. After a visit to a museum, Irena follows Alice back to her hotel and down to the swimming pool. Alice, hearing the noise of a growling animal, leaps into the pool and begins to scream for help, but Irena appears from the shadows and calmly turns on the light.

Later, Oliver tells Irena that he intends to divorce her. Judd visits Irena, armed, and tries to make love to her. She turns into a panther and kills him. Wounded by Judd, Irena dies at the Central Park Zoo while trying to free a caged panther.

Charlie Chaplin's Burlesque on 'Carmen'
USA 1916 st b/w 15

PRODUCTION

p.c – Essanay. *p* – Jesse J. Robbins. *d* – Charlie Chaplin. *sc* – Charlie Chaplin, from the story by Prosper Merimée and the opera by H. Meilhac, L. Halevy and Georges Bizet. *ph* – Roland H. Totheroh. *a.d* – E. T. Mazy.

LEADING PLAYERS

Charlie Chaplin (*Darn Hosiery*), Edna Purviance (*Carmenita*).

SYNOPSIS

Charlie is the newly-appointed captain of a fortress around which a gang of smugglers are carrying on their illegal trade. Knowing he is new they try to bribe him not to interfere with them, and when this fails they persuade one of their girls, Carmenita, to lure him from his post. Carmenita succeeds, and Charlie is arrested as a confederate of the smugglers.

He fights at great length with his guard and finally disposes of him. He goes to Carmenita, but she turns him down now that he is out of a job, and leaves for Seville with another of her admirers, a bullfighter. Charlie follows them, and stabs Carmenita, so that if he cannot have her, no-one shall. He then stabs himself. The matador appears and mourns over their bodies. When the matador has gone, Charlie sits up and reveals that the dagger was only a toy and that he and Carmenita are both unharmed.

The Childhood of Maxim Gorky
USSR 1938 sd b/w 11

PRODUCTION

p.c – Children's Film Studio. *d* – Mark Donskoy. *sc* – I. Gruzdev, from *The Autobiography of Maxim Gorky – Vol. 1: Childhood. ph* – Pyotr Yermolov. *a.d* – I. Stepanov. *m* – Lev Schwartz.

LEADING PLAYERS

Alyosha Lyarsky (*Alexei Pjeshkov/ Maxim Gorky*), V. C. Massalitinova (*Grandmother*), M. G. Troyanovsky (*Grandfather*).

SYNOPSIS

Wide-eyed and silent, little Alexei (Maxim Gorky) travels with his mother to the small town where her family lives in dire poverty. The film shows the boy's life with the family, and his reactions to their arguments, misunderstandings, small joys and great misfortunes. This home – sometimes cruel, sometimes kindly, often strange and fascinating – leaves an indelible impression on the boy.

Gorky and his cousin are involved in a fight, in which a prized tablecloth belonging to Gorky's grandmother gets dipped in a vat of dye. After church, Alexei witnesses his cousin being brutally whipped by his grandfather.

Later, he leaves his grandparents' house to make his own way in the world.

Citizen Kane
USA 1941 sd b/w 25

PRODUCTION

p.c – Mercury Productions/RKO. *p* – Orson Welles. *d* – Orson Welles. *sc* – Herman J. Mankiewicz, Orson Welles. *ph* – Gregg Toland. *ed* – Robert Wise, Mark Robson. *a.d* – Van Nest Polglase. *m* – Bernard Herrmann. *cost* – Edward Stevenson.

LEADING PLAYERS

Orson Welles (*Charles Foster Kane*), Joseph Cotton (*Jedediah Leland*), Everett Sloane (*Bernstein*), Dorothy Comingore (*Susan Alexander*), Paul Stewart (*Raymond, The Reporter*).

SYNOPSIS

A fictional biography. Kane, an aged millionaire, dies in his palatial retreat, Xanadu, uttering the word 'Rosebud'. Outstanding stages in Kane's public life are shown in a newsreel that is being compiled, but the producer is dissatisfied. He commissions a reporter to go and find out about the 'real' Kane, suggesting that he could start by trying to discover the significance of that dying word. In a series of interviews between the reporter and Kane's associates, aspects of Kane's life are unfolded in flashback. As a boy, when his mother inherits a legacy he is taken away from his parents' humble log-cabin home to be educated privately. Later he discovers that his inherited wealth includes a newspaper *The Inquirer*, and he decides it would be 'fun' to run it personally.

Kane and Jedediah Leland, a friend from student days, arrive to take over the paper, and Kane issues his own 'declaration of principles' for the newspaper. He buys up the staff of a rival newspaper, holding a party to celebrate. He goes off to Europe and returns married to the President's niece. The reporter then goes to see Leland, who tells him about the development of marriage. In flashback we see the marriage change from infatuation to indifference. (Ext. 1a, 20 mins.)

The scandal of his affair with a singer, Susan Alexander, ruins his political career. He divorces his first wife, marries Susan, and unsuccessfully attempts to make her into an opera star.

In the cavernous rooms of Xanadu, Kane and Susan are at home. Susan is bored. She does jig-saw puzzles to pass the time. With car-loads of house-guests they go for a picnic on the beach. (Ext. 1b, 5 mins.)

Kane dies in lonely splendour. The reporter concludes that no single word can explain a man's life. A clue, which he does not see, is given in a shot of a child's sledge, embellished with the word 'Rosebud', being thrown onto a fire with Kane's other bric-à-brac.

Cleopatra Jones
USA 1973 sd col 12

PRODUCTION
p.c – Warner Bros. *p* – William Tennant, Max Julien. *d* – Jack Starrett. *sc* – Max Julien, Sheldon Keller, from a story by Max Julien. *ph* – David Walsh (Panavision and Technicolor). *ed* – Allan Jacobs. *a.d* – Peter Wooley. *m* – J. J. Johnson.

LEADING PLAYERS
Tamara Dobson (*Cleopatra Jones*), Bernie Casey (*Reuben*), Brenda Sykes (*Tiffany*), Antonio Fargas (*Doodlebug*), Dan Frazer (*Detective Crawford*), George Reynolds (*Fireplug*), Theodore Wilson (*Pickle*), Shelley Winters (*Mommy*).

SYNOPSIS
Cleopoatra Jones, a black CIA narcotics agent, supervises the destruction of vast opium fields in Turkey, thus provoking the outrage of Mommy, the white head of a drugs racket in Los Angeles.

Cleo arrives at B and S House, a hostel for ex-drug addicts run by her lover Reuben, to find that it has been raided and closed down by the police as a result of pressure from Mommy. Cleo is berated by a young black woman for not being around at the time of the raid. Reuben tells the woman that Cleo is a powerful friend. He is then called to help a young addict with withdrawal symptoms. Cleo observes the kids arming themselves, and begs Reuben to keep them passive for 72 hours so that she can investigate the raid. When she leaves B and S House, snipers attack her from the opposite building. She dashes across to its entrance, and guns down an apparently elderly couple leaving the lift armed with machine guns. She goes to visit Doodlebug, a black drugs racketeer and is shown in by his white English butler. Doodlebug is proclaiming his indepen-

dence of Mommy to his followers, Fireplug and Pickle, when Cleo arrives and grills him. Doodlebug is sarcastic about B and S House, and describes the pusher who supplied dope to a boy arrested in the raid. Tiffany, Doodlebug's mistress, appears and demands to be taken shopping. Cleo says that she is going to prove that Doodlebug and Mommy were behind the raid.

Cleo enlists the help of two karate experts, and uses her own exceptional powers on a motor-bike to escape various dangers. Doodlebug is gunned down after a row with Mommy but Tiffany escapes. The corrupt cop who planted dope in B and S House is uncovered. In a final show-down Mommy has Cleo and Tiffany in her power and intends to feed them into a car-crushing machine. The two karate experts arrive in the nick of time. Cleo leaves Mommy splayed out in the mud.

(NB This extract is standard reduced from Scope.)

Les Coeurs verts
(*see* Naked Hearts)

Comin' Thro' the Rye
UK 1923 st b/w 11
(w. **Sally in Our Alley**)

PRODUCTION
p.c – Hepworth Picture Plays. *p* – Cecil M. Hepworth. *d* – Cecil M. Hepworth. *sc* – Blanche McIntosh, from the novel by Helen Mathers. *ph* – Geoffrey Faithfull.

LEADING PLAYERS
Alma Taylor (*Helen Adair*), Shayle Gardner (*Paul Vasher*), Eileen Dennes (*Sylvia Fleming*).

SYNOPSIS
By stealing some letters, and substituting others the beautiful vamp Sylvia Fleming manages to come between the young lovers Paul Vasher and Helen Adair. Sylvia and Paul are married and have a child.

Paul and Sylvia return to his estate after an absence. At a vicarage tea party Sylvia meets Helen and attempts a reconciliation with her, but she is rebuffed. When the two women are alone, however, it becomes clear that Sylvia's hatred for Helen has not weakened. Her life with Paul becomes poisoned by these feelings. Later, Sylvia is taken ill and asks Paul to send for Helen. At first Helen is unwilling, but Paul persuades her to see the dying Sylvia. When she is at her bedside Sylvia begs for forgiveness. Helen is still uneasy but she reconciles herself for the sake of Sylvia's child.

Un Condamné à mort s'est echappé
(*see* A Man Escaped)

Coogan's Bluff
USA 1968 sd col 20

PRODUCTION
p.c – Universal. *p* – Donald Siegel. *d* – Donald Siegel. *sc* – Herman Miller, Dean

Riesner, Howard Rodman, from a story by Herman Miller. *ph* – Bud Thackery (Technicolor). *ed* – Sam E. Waxman. *a.d* – Alexander Golitzen, Robert C. MacKichan. *m* – Lalo Schifrin. *cost* – Helen Colvig.

LEADING PLAYERS
Clint Eastwood (*Walt Coogan*), Lee J. Cobb (*McElroy*), Susan Clark (*Julie*), Tisha Sterling (*Linny Raven*), Don Stroud (*Ringerman*).

SYNOPSIS
Deputy Sheriff Walt Coogan arrives in New York from Arizona to bring back an escaped killer being held in custody. He is not allowed to use his traditional western methods and is frustrated by the New York police department's red tape. Ringerman, his prisoner, is in hospital following a drug overdose, but Coogan bluffs the hospital into releasing Ringerman and gets him as far as the airport. There he is tricked by Linny Raven, Ringerman's girl, and Ringerman escapes. Coogan is taken off the case but continues to pursue his prisoner.

He makes contact with Julie, Linny's probation officer, who invites him to her flat for dinner. While she is preparing the meal, Coogan rifles through a filing cabinet and finds Linny's address. After leaving Julie's flat he traces Linny to 'The Pigeon-Toed Orange Peel' – a disco haunted by freaks and dope-smokers. Linny takes Coogan home; they make love. Afterwards, she takes him down to a pool-hall, where Ringerman is supposed to be. It is a set-up and Coogan is brutally beaten, but escapes before the police arrive. After cleaning up at his hotel, he returns to Linny's flat and threatens to beat her up if she refuses to lead him to Ringerman.

Eventually she co-operates, and reveals where Ringerman is hiding out. There is a chase. Coogan catches him, makes a citizen's arrest and is subsequently authorised to take him back to Arizona.

Coup pour coup
(*see* Blow for Blow)

The Covered Wagon
USA 1923 st b/w 9

PRODUCTION
p.c – Famous Players-Lasky. *d* – James Cruze. *sc* – Jack Cunningham, from the novel by Emerson Hough. *ph* – Karl Brown. *ed* – Dorothy Arzner.

LEADING PLAYERS
Lois Wilson (*Molly Wingate*), J. Warren Kerrigan (*Will Banion*), Alan Hale (*Sam Woodhull*), Charles Ogle (*Jesse Wingate*).

SYNOPSIS
A band of pioneers travelling in covered wagons embark upon a 2,000-mile journey across the desert to Oregon from Westport Landing (now Kansas City).

The wagontrain sets off enthusiastically, but after two weeks discontent and hard-

ship have set in. Some of the wagons turn back. Molly Wingate wants to ride Will Banion's horse but he refuses, although he loves her, saying that it is too wild for her. Sam, Will's rival, eggs her on, and she defies Will and mounts. Immediately the horse runs away with her and Will grabs Sam's horse to rescue her. When she is safe Sam picks a fight with Will for taking his horse, but one of the old men stops them. An old lady dies, a baby is born, and the train sets out once more. (Ext. 1a, 5 mins.)

After many more dangers, and much rivalry between Molly's two suitors, the wagons arrive at the point where the trail divides, one route leading to California.

An army courier brings news of the discovery of gold in California. Some of the settlers decide to head that way rather than to Oregon, despite Molly's father's attempts to stop them. As the wagontrain splits, Sam tells Molly that as he knows she will never marry him, he will see to it that she doesn't marry Will, who has already gone ahead towards California, either. (Ext. 1b, 4 mins.)

Will finds gold, disposes of Sam, and joins Molly in Oregon.

Cowboy
USA 1957 sd col 14

PRODUCTION
p.c – Phoenix Productions. *p* – Julian Blaustein. *d* – Delmer Daves. *sc* – Edmund H. North, from *On the Trail* by Frank Harris. *ph* – Charles Lawton Jr. (Technicolor). *ed* – William A. Lyon, Al Clark. *a.d* – Cary O'Dell. *m* – George Duning.

LEADING PLAYERS
Glenn Ford (*Tom Reece*), Jack Lemmon (*Frank Harris*), Anna Kashfi (*Maria Vidal*).

SYNOPSIS
Frank Harris, a hotel employee, is in love with the daughter of a rich Mexican rancher and prepared to go to any lengths to join her. Hard-bitten cattle-driver Tom Reece accepts Harris as his partner on the next trip to Mexico in return for a loan.

Tom and Frank arrive for the beginning of the cattle drive. Tom provides Frank with a horse, which he learns to ride, but only after much difficulty. The drive begins and Tom is consistently hard on Frank, keeping him up to the mark. One evening the cowhands fool round the fire with a rattlesnake, until an accident is caused and one man killed.

Frank is depressed to realise that the cowhands are self-seeking and unprepared to unite in danger and he is disillusioned when he finds that his girl has married someone else. On the return trip Tom saves Frank's life during an Indian attack, but only at the cost of stampeding the herd. Frank, bitter and only interested in the herd, which he part owns, is not grateful. Later, the cattle panic in the train to Chicago, and are only calmed when Tom and

Frank enter the wagons, at the risk of their lives. Saving the animals together, they reach a new understanding of each other.

Le Crime de Monsieur Lange
France 1935 sd b/w 11

PRODUCTION
p.c – Obéron. *p* – André Halley des Fontaines. *d* – Jean Renoir. *sc* – Jacques Prévert, from an idea by Jean Renoir & Jean Castanier. *ph* – Jean Bachelet. *ed* – Marguerite Renoir. *a.d* – Jean Castinier, Robert Gys. *m* – Jean Weiner. *lyrics* – Joseph Kosma.

LEADING PLAYERS
René Lefèvre (*Lange*), Jules Berry (*Batala*), Florelle (*Valentine*), Nadia Sibirskaia (*Estelle*), Maurice Baquet (*Charles*).

SYNOPSIS
Monsieur Lange is employed in a 'pulp' publishing house where he and other employees are exploited by the vile, lecherous proprietor, Batala. In his spare time Lange writes western stories whose hero, 'Arizona Jim' is the expression of all his daydreams. Batala buys the right to these stories, swindling Lange in the process, but his creditors are on his heels and he runs away. Lange is happily in love with Valentine, a laundress who works in the courtyard.

Batala is involved in a train crash, and is believed to have been killed. Lange and Valentine spend the night together. In the morning there is chaos in the printing works when Batala's creditors converge at the news of his death. They are persuaded by Lange and the other employees to join in running the business on a co-operative basis. Lange tears down a poster advertising Batala publications from the front of a window where Charles, the concierge's son, is lying in bed with a broken leg. Charles is in love with Estelle, another laundress. Estelle is planning to leave because she is pregnant by Batala, but her baby dies.

The co-operative has a great success with 'Arizona Jim'. Just as they are all celebrating their good fortune, Batala re-appears, dressed as a priest. He survived the crash and changed clothes with one of the dead, and is determined to cash in on the firm's new found prosperity. Lange shoots Batala and flees with Valentine to the frontier. In a café Valentine tells the whole story to some workmen who have recognised them. They agree to help the couple escape.

The Criminal
UK 1960 sd b/w 20

PRODUCTION
p.c – Merton Park Studios. *p* – Jack Greenwood. *d* – Joseph Losey. *sc* – Alun Owen, from a story by Jimmy Sangster. *ph* – Robert Krasker. *ed* – Reginald Mills.

a.d – Scott MacGregor. *m* – Johnny Dankworth.

LEADING PLAYERS
Stanley Baker (*Johnny Bannion*), Sam Wanamaker (*Mike Carter*), Patrick Magee (*Chief Warder Barrows*), Kenneth Cope (*Kelly*).

SYNOPSIS
Underworld king Johnny Bannion has almost finished a three-year prison sentence, during which he has planned the biggest robbery of his career – a £40,000 race-course take. On the day before he is due out, Kelly a prisoner he has a grudge against, comes into his cell block. Despite a warning from Chief Warder Barrows, Bannion arranges for Kelly to be beaten up. The Chief Warder seems to revel in the noise the prisoners create to cover the beating-up.

On Bannion's release, his partner Mike Carter fixes up a fence for the planned race-course job. Bannion's 'coming-out' party is abruptly terminated by the arrival of his ex-girlfriend, Maggie, who later tips off the police when the robbery is carried out. Bannion, the only person who knows where the £40,000 is hidden, is sentenced to fifteen years imprisonment, but is confident that his new girl, Suzanne, will wait for him. The gang uses contacts inside the prison to try to learn where the money is hidden, but they fail, and then plan Bannion's escape, using Suzanne as bait. Bannion falls into the trap and leads them to the field where the money is buried. Carter shoots Bannion before he discoveres the exact location of the banknotes, and as Bannion dies the gang begins to dig frantically.

Crossfire
USA 1947 sd b/w 14

PRODUCTION
p.c – RKO/Dore Schary. *p* – Adrian Scott. *d* – Edward Dmytryk. *sc* – John Paxton, from the novel *The Brick Foxhole* by Richard Brooks. *ph* – J. Roy Hunt. *ed* – Harry Gerstad. *a.d* – Albert S. D'Agostino and Alfred Herman. *m* – Roy Webb.

LEADING PLAYERS
Robert Young (*Captain Finlay*), Robert Mitchum (*Sergeant Peter Keeley*), Robert Ryan (*Monty Montgomery*), Gloria Grahame (*Ginny Tremaine*), George Cooper (*Arthur Mitchell*), Steve Brodie (*Floyd Bowers*).

SYNOPSIS
A Jewish man named Joseph Samuels is found murdered. Police captain Finlay learns that a woman and three GIs – Montgomery, Mitchell and Floyd – had been drinking with him at a bar. Montgomery tells Finlay that he left Mitchell with Samuels. While searching for Mitchell the police pick up Keeley, a friend of Mitchell's. Keeley, refusing to believe in Mitchell's guilt, finds him and hides him.

Keeley tries to help Mitchell recall what

happened on the evening Samuels was killed. *Mitchell describes in a flashback how they got talking in a bar, and later adjourned to Samuel's flat where they were joined by Montgomery and Floyd. Mitchell began to feel dazed, and left halfway through the evening, just as Montgomery started to pick a quarrel. He walked around for some time and eventually met Ginny in a dance hall and took the key of her apartment to go and sleep it off. He was woken by a man arriving, full of fictitious stories about his relationship with Ginny.*

Another GI turns up and says that Floyd, now in hiding, has communicated with him. At Floyd's hide-out Montgomery urges him to stick to their claim that they left Samuels alive. When Keeley calls, Montgomery hides. He overhears Floyd altering his story and later strangles him. When this murder is revealed, Finlay and Mitchell's wife prevail upon Keeley to surrender Mitchell, after which they go to Ginny to try to confirm his alibi. Ginny refuses, but the stranger re-appears and backs up Mitchell's story. Finlay lays a trap for Montgomery and tricks him into incriminating himself. Montgomery is killed trying to escape.

Cry of the City
USA 1948 sd b/w 10

PRODUCTION
p.c – 20th Century-Fox. *p* – Sol. C. Siegel. *d* – Robert Siodmak. *sc* – Richard Murphy, from a novel by Henry Edward Helseth. *ph* – Lloyd Ahern. *ed* – Harmon Jones. *a.d* – Lyle Wheeler and Albert Hogsett. *m* – Alfred Newman. *cost* – Bonnie Cashin.

LEADING PLAYERS
Victor Mature (*Lieutenant Candella*). Richard Conte (*Martin Rome*), Fred Clark (*Lieutenant Collins*), Shelley Winters (*Brenda*), Betty Garde (*Mrs. Pruett*), Debra Paget (*Teena Riconti*), Hope Emerson (*Rose Given*).

SYNOPSIS
Lieutenant Candella is investigating the murder of a policeman. The prime suspect is Martin Rome, who has been badly wounded. By systematically using his women and his family, Rome secures his escape from the prison hospital. He kills a bent lawyer and finds some jewels from a robbery in his safe.

With the assistance of Brenda, a former girlfriend, Rome gets his wounds treated by an unlicensed doctor. After he has been patched up, Brenda takes him to Rose Given, a masseuse who was involved in the jewel robbery. Rome tells her that she can have the jewels in exchange for $5,000 cash and a safe passage out of the country. Rose agrees and then tries to force Rome to hand over the key to the locker in which the jewels have been hidden. Rome, however, hasn't brought the key with him.

Later he double-crosses Rose, and in the subsequent affray Candella is seriously wounded. Although very weak, he leaves the hospital and hunts Rome down to a deserted church. Rome tries to escape but Candella shoots him down.

Cuba Si!
France 1961 sd b/w 10

PRODUCTION
p.c – Films de la Pléiade. *p* – Pierre Braunberger. *d* – Chris Marker. *sc* – Chris Marker. *ph* – Chris Marker. *ed* – Eva Zora. *m* – E. G. Mantici and J. Calzada.

SYNOPSIS
A personal documentary about Cuba, shot in January 1961 during celebrations of the second anniversary of the Revolution but much influenced by the European and American press coverage of the counter-revolutionary attack the following April. Impoverished families are moved from slums to sanitary, modern dwellings. Holiday crowds fill villa gardens that were once the exclusive domain of industrial millionaires.

There are scenes showing a street procession that turns gradually into a carnival conga, an artist painting a mountainside and men dealing with a fire in the cane fields. Meanwhile, on the coast, soldiers tensely wait for the imminent invasion. Reports from Western newspapers prophesy doom for Cuba and Castro. The invasion begins, and war-evacuees, the injured and the dead, are shown along with convoys of lorries. Castro directs operations, and the attack is successfully repelled.

The Curse of Frankenstein
UK 1957 sd col 9

PRODUCTION
p.c – Hammer. *p* – Anthony Hinds. *d* – Terence Fisher. *sc* – James Sangster, from the book by Mary Shelley. *ph* – Jack Asher (Eastman Color). *ed* – James Needs. *a.d* – Ted Marshall. *m* – James Barnard.

LEADING PLAYERS
Peter Cushing (*Baron Victor Frankenstein*), Christopher Lee (*The Creature*), Robert Urquhart (*Paul Krempe*), Hazel Court (*Elizabeth*).

SYNOPSIS
The brilliant Baron Victor Frankenstein, aided by Paul Krempe, begins the creation of a monster out of parts of bought or stolen corpses. Paul is disgusted, however, when Victor murders a great scientist in order to use his brain, and he tries to dissuade Victor from proceeding with the experiment. In a struggle with Victor, Paul damages the brain, but Victor insists on completing his creation.

In his laboratory Victor is ready to begin his attempt to create life. The inert monster lies in a tank of water, attached to torts of bubbling coloured liquids, and an electrically-operated wheel. Victor begins to work the dials. Meanwhile, Paul walks up and down in his room, restless. In the laboratory the process speeds up and Frankenstein can barely keep up with it. He goes upstairs to Paul to ask for help in operating the apparatus, but Paul refuses. Meanwhile in the laboratory the monster takes its first breath. Victor threatens Paul and he reluctantly agrees to help. As Victor returns to his laboratory he hears the sound of movement. When he opens the door he is confronted by a hideous creation which tries to strangle him. Paul arrives just in time to save Victor from death. Paul insists the creature be destroyed but Victor lays the blame for its behaviour on its damaged brain, and therefore on Paul. He says he will operate on its brain the following day and will keep his creation alive for three months in order to complete his experiments.

Later the creature escapes and commits a series of brutal murders. The monster is destroyed but Victor is condemned to death. Paul, by now in love with Victor's wife, refuses to corroborate his plea that the guilt is the Creature's, and allows him to go to the guillotine.

La Dame aux camélias
(see *The Lady of the Camellias*)

The Damned
UK 1961 sd b/w 19

PRODUCTION
p.c – Hammer/Swallow. *p* – Anthony Hinds. *d* – Joseph Losey. *sc* – Evan Jones, from the novel *The Children of Light* by H. L. Lawrence. *ph* – Arthur Grant (HammerScope). *ed* – Reginald Mills. *a.d* – Don Mingaye. *m* – James Bernard.

LEADING PLAYERS
MacDonald Carey (*Simon Wells*), Shirley Ann Field (*Joan*), Viveca Lindfors (*Freya*), Alexander Knox (*Bernard*), Oliver Reed (*King*), Walter Gotell (*Major Holland*), James Villiers (*Captain Gregory*).

SYNOPSIS
Simon Wells, an American tourist, picks up Joan on the promenade at Weymouth. It turns out that she is a decoy for her brother King's gang of motorcycle hoodlums. They beat up and rob Simon, who is later helped by Bernard, a scientist and his friend Freya, a sculptress. Later Simon meets Joan again and they go off on a boat, eventually coming in to land near Freya's cliff-top studio where they hide. The studio adjoins a barbed wire enclosure which contains Bernard's highly secret research project. King appears at the studio, there is a chase, which ends when Simon, Joan and King fall over the cliff into the sea. The three are rescued by some strange, cold-blooded children, who are kept sealed off from the world and whose only outside contact is with Bernard and his staff through television monitors.

Bernard talks to the children via the television monitor, telling them that he knows about their secret hide-out and the people they have hidden there. When he tells them that the adults will die if they stay with them, the children argue with him and start throwing things at the television screen. Meanwhile at the cave Simon, Joan and King decide to escape, taking the children with them. The two men overcome the guards patrolling the children's living quarters. Using a Geiger counter taken from one of the guards Simon discovers that the children are radioactive. Although recognising the danger, Simon, Joan and King take the children out of their underground world into the open. Guards appear and the children are recaptured. King escapes in Freya's car with one of the children. Bernard allows Simon and Joan to leave in a boat. He explains to Freya how the children's mothers were all accidentally exposed to radiation and how he hopes that the children would provide the basis of a new civilisation after a nuclear holocaust. He asks her to forget all that she has seen, she refuses and he shoots her. Meanwhile King, suffering from radiation sickness, crashes into the harbour, the little boy having earlier been snatched from the car by the guards. Joan and Simon, both dying, head back towards the children's cave.

(NB This extract is in Scope and needs an anamorphic lens.)

Dance, Girl, Dance
USA 1940 sd b/w 18

PRODUCTION
p.c – RKO Radio. *p* – Harry E. Edington and Erich Pommer. *d* – Dorothy Arzner. *sc* – Tess Slesinger, Frank Davis, from a story by Vicki Baum. *ph* – Russell Metty. *ed* – Robert Wise. *a.d* – Van Nest Polglase and Al Herman. *m* – Edward Ward. *choreo* – Ernst Matray.

LEADING PLAYERS
Maureen O'Hara (*Judy*), Louis Hayward (*Jimmie Harris*), Lucille Ball (*Bubbles*), Virginia Field (*Elinor Harris*), Ralph Bellamy (*Steve Adams*), Maria Ouspenskaya (*Madame Basilova*).

SYNOPSIS
Judy and Bubbles are both members of Madame Basilova's dancing troupe. Judy, refined and romantic, is dedicated to a 'classy' ballet career, but Bubbles, an extrovert entertainer, is prepared to exploit her sexuality.

Madame Basilova tries to get work for her troupe in a burlesque hall act. Bubbles is inexplicably absent, so Judy takes her place, but the manager is unimpressed. Suddenly Bubbles turns up, and does a hula dance. This persuades the manager to hire her alone, despite her pleas on behalf of the rest of the girls. (Ext. 1a, 5 mins.)

Judy tries to get an introduction to Steve Adams, director of a ballet company. This is delayed by Madame Basilova's death, and a number of misunderstandings. Bubbles brings Judy into her burlesque act ostensibly to add a touch of class, but

really to make the male audience impatient. Meanwhile, both Judy and Bubbles, in their different ways, have become involved with Jimmie Harris, an irresponsible and recently divorced millionaire. Bubbles cons him into marriage when he is very drunk.

Judy hears this news just as she is about to go into her ballet routine. Combined with a pent-up feeling of disgust for the male burlesque audience, it causes her to stop in the middle of her performance and tell the jeering, heckling men how she and other women regard them. She marches off – and gets a resounding ovation, which makes Bubbles furious. A fight breaks out on stage between them, and they end up in the night court. Judy insists on her part as instigator of the brawl. Steve Adams turns up, but she refuses to allow him to pay her fine, and is sent to prison. Jimmie is reunited with his wife and proposes to annul his marriage to Bubbles. The following morning Judy's fine is paid by Steve Adams. He makes her a ballerina and, by implication, his future wife. (Ext. 1b, 13 mins.)

Day of Wrath (Vredens Dag)
Denmark 1943 sd b/w 9

PRODUCTION
p.c – Palladium Films. *p* – Carl Dreyer. *d* – Carl Dreyer. *sc* – Carl Dreyer, Paul Knudsen, Mogens Skot-Hansen, from the novel *Anne Pedersdotter* by Johanssen Wiers Jenssens. *ph* – Carl Andersson. *ed* – Edith Schlussel and Ann-Marie Petersen. *a.d* – Eric Aaes and Lis Fribert. *m* – Paul Schierbeck. *cost* – K. Sandt Jensen, Olga Thomsen and Lis Fribert.

LEADING PLAYERS
Thorkild Roose (*Absalon Pedersson*), Preben Lendorff Rye (*Martin*), Lisbeth Movin (*Anne Pedersdotter*), Anna Svierkier (*Marthe Herloff*).

SYNOPSIS
In 17th-century Denmark Pastor Absalon Pedersson signs a decree for the trial for witchcraft of Marthe, a peasant woman. Marthe is finally caught in Absalon's own house. She has taken refuge there because his newly-married wife Anne is the daughter of a woman he saved from a similar accusation. Martin, Absalon's son by a former marriage returns from the seas. The Pastor's mother makes no attempt to hide her hatred of her new daughter-in-law.

After torturing Marthe the priests announce that she has made a voluntary confession of witchcraft. Walking in the country, Martin and Anne see the wood being gathered for the stake at which Marthe is to burn. Absalon goes to visit Marthe in the dungeon, but she turns him out. Anne watches through the window as the fire is being prepared. Martin leaves the crowd and comforts Anne when Marthe curses Absalon as she is lowered onto the flames.

The memory of what he has done haunts Absalon. Anne falls in love with Martin, finds new strength, and begins to defy her mother-in-law, whose suspicion of her deepens. Absalon's self-torture makes him admit he has wronged Anne by marrying her. She tells him that she wishes him dead because she loves his son. He dies of a seizure. At the funeral her mother-in-law denounces her as a witch. Deserted by Martin, whose conscience has never been at rest over his love for her, Anne finds that she is unable to swear on oath that she did not kill her husband through witchcraft. The implication is that she will die as Marthe did.

The Day the Earth Caught Fire
UK 1961 sd b/w 9

PRODUCTION
p.c – Melina. *p* – Val Guest. *d* – Val Guest. *sc* – Wolf Mankowitz, Val Guest. *ph* – Harry Waxman (DyaliScope). *ed* – Bill Lenny. *a.d* – Tony Masters. *m* – Stanley Black.

LEADING PLAYERS
Edward Judd (*Peter Stenning*), Janet Munro (*Jeannie*), Leo McKern (*Bill Maguire*).

SYNOPSIS
Fleet Street is startled by reports of strange phenomena all over the world – blizzards in New York, floods in the Sahara, tornadoes in Russia. Official explanations are guarded and contradictory. Two *Daily Express* journalists – Peter Stenning, a reporter, and Bill Maguire, a science correspondent – discover that the climatic upheavals began after an American nuclear test at the South Pole and a Russian explosion at the North Pole.

Following a disagreement with his editor, Stenning offers to resign but is interrupted by a phone call from Jeannie, a telephonist at the Meteorological Office. They meet and she tells him that the combined explosions have shifted the orbit of the Earth, which is now racing towards the sun. She asks him not to use the information. Stenning tells Maguire and they both go to the paper's editor. The news is printed. Later, Stenning goes to Jeannie's flat, and sees her being arrested for passing on the information to him.

Temperatures rise. Water is at a premium. Emergency measures fail to curb panic and looting. Scientific consultations result in a desperate plan to save the world: all nations are to unite in exploding four super-bombs in an effort to restore the earth to its proper orbit. On detonation day, in a deserted London, Stenning dictates a final story pondering the future of mankind. Two front pages are printed, one bearing the headline 'World Saved', the other 'World Doomed'.

(NB This extract is standard reduced from Scope.)

Deadlier than the Male
(*see* Born to Kill)

Dead of Night
UK 1945 sd b/w 15

PRODUCTION

p.c – Ealing Studios. *p* – Michael Balcon. *d* – Alberto Cavalcanti (*The Christmas Party* and *The Ventriloquist's Dummy*), Charles Crichton (*The Golfing Story*), Basil Dearden (*The Hearse Driver* and the linking story), Robert Hamer (*The Haunted Mirror*). *sc* – John V. Baines, Angus MacPhail, from stories by E. F. Benson, Angus MacPhail, John V. Baines, H. G. Wells. *ph* – Jack Parker, H. Julius. *ed* – Charles Hassey. *a.d* – Michael Relph. *m* – Georges Auric.

The Haunted Mirror sequence: *d* – Robert Hamer. *sc* – John V. Baines, Angus MacPhail, from a story by John V. Baines.

LEADING PLAYERS

Googie Withers (*Joan Cortland*), Ralph Michael (*Peter Cortland*).

SYNOPSIS

Walter Craig is summoned to Pilgrim's Farm on business; when he arrives he finds that he is already familiar with the layout of the house, although he has never been there before. Eliot Foley, the owner of the house, also seems familiar to him, as do his guests. He gradually realises that the house and all the people in it are part of his recurring dream/nightmare which always ends in disaster. Dr. Van Straaten, a psychiatrist who is one of the guests, is sceptical of Craig's story and seeks a rational explanation but the others are more sympathetic. Each tells of a strange incident in which they have been involved.

Joan Cortland tells how she gave a large antique mirror to her fiancé as a birthday present. That evening, while dressing for a celebration dinner he looks into it and sees a totally different room with a blazing log fire and a four-poster bed reflected. At dinner he is sullen and broody. When pressed by Joan for an explanation, he tells her about his experiences. She laughs off the story, but that night he sees the strange room in the mirror again. In the following weeks Joan prepares for the wedding, but one day Peter announces that he wants to call the whole thing off; he thinks he's going mad. Joan makes him stand in front of the mirror with her and her power dispels the image. The wedding takes place and the couple settle down, Peter seeming to be no longer troubled by the mirror. However, when Joan goes to visit her mother, Peter looks into the mirror and again sees the strange room reflected.

Joan feels her husband is being 'invaded' by the mirror. She discovers that it belonged to a sensual but tyrannical old man who strangled his wife in a fit of jealousy and then cut his throat in front of the mirror. Later Peter attempts to strangle her in the same way but she breaks the spell by smashing the mirror. The other guests also tell stories, but at the end of the last one Craig's nightmare starts to happen. Left alone with Van Straaten, he finds himself compelled to murder the psychiatrist. The characters from the other stories come to life and prevent his escape. Craig then awakes struggling on his bed, with the telephone ringing. He answers it; Eliot Foley is on the line and wants Craig to call on business. The address is Pilgrim's Farm . . .

The Defiant Ones
USA 1958 sd b/w 11

PRODUCTION

p.c – Lomitas-Curtleigh Productions. *p* – Stanley Kramer. *d* – Stanley Kramer. *sc* – Nathan E. Douglas, Harold Jacob Smith. *ph* – Sam Leavitt. *ed* – Frederic Knudtson. *a.d* – Fernando Carrere. *m* – Ernest Gold.

LEADING PLAYERS

Tony Curtis (*John 'Joker' Jackson*), Sidney Poitier (*Noah Cullen*), Theodore Bikel (*Max Muller*), Lon Chaney (*Big Sam*).

SYNOPSIS

John 'Joker' Jackson is a 'nigger-hating' white, Noah Cullen a touchy, proud black, but as members of a chain gang, they are manacled together. When the truck carrying the gang back from work overturns they escape, still chained together, with a twelve-hour start on Sheriff Max Muller and the State Police. Arguing all the way, they cross a river, fall into a clay pit, break into a small store, and are caught.

The Sheriff and his men talk about running the convicts in. Meanwhile the crowd is setting up a lynching for them. A man named Big Sam intervenes, and takes Jackson and Cullen to his barn. Cullen sings the blues. Big Sam cuts their ropes and watches them run off, still manacled together.

A woman who is attracted to Jackson at last unshackles them. She promises to help them escape, but gives Cullen directions which will lead him straight into a swamp. Jackson discovers this, flings her aside, and follows Cullen to warn him, but is wounded by the woman's son. He saves Cullen from the swamp but, weakened by loss of blood, can't board the train when they reach it. Cullen refuses to abandon him. The posse catches up with them to find Cullen waiting for them with Jackson cradled in his arms.

Destiny (Der müde Tod)
Germany 1921 st b/w 20

PRODUCTION

p.c – Decla-Bioscop. *p* – Erich Pommer. *d* – Fritz Lang. *sc* – Fritz Lang, Thea von Harbou. *ph* – Erich Nilzschmann, Fritz Arno Wagner, Hermann Saalfrank. *a.d* – Walter Röhrig, Hermann Warm, Robert Herlth.

LEADING PLAYERS

Lil Dagover (*Young Woman/Zobeide/ Fiametta/Liang*), Walter Janssen (*Young Man/Frank/Giovanfrancesco/Tiao Tsien*), Bernhard Goetzke (*Death*), Karl Platen (*The Apothecary*).

SYNOPSIS

A young couple's honeymoon in a small German town is disrupted when the husband disappears with an ominous stranger.

Learning that the stranger owns the land next to the graveyard, the distraught wife hurries there, only to see her husband among a procession of ghosts passing through the huge wall surrounding the plot. Treated for shock by an apothecary, she is about to drink poison when she is precipitated into a vision. She confronts the stranger, who is Death incarnate, and begs for the life of her husband. Death, weary with his onerous duties, offers her three chances to save his life, each represented by a guttering candle. (Ext. 1a, 10 mins.)

Arabian Tale: Zobeide, sister of the cruel Caliph, is secretly in love with Frank, an 'infidel' who risks death each time he visits her. One day the Caliph's spies follow Zobeide's maid and she carries a message to Frank; an ambush is set and Frank is caught, buried up to his neck and left to die.

Venetian Tale: Fiametta is engaged to the vicious Girolamo but loves Giovanfrancesco. During the carnival she invites Girolamo to visit her and hires a Moor to stab him with a poisoned dagger, but the suspicious Girolamo redirects the letter to his rival, who dies in his place. (Ext. 1b, 10 mins.)

Chinese Tale: A Hi, a magician, is summoned to entertain the Emperor on his birthday and travels to the palace by magic carpet with his friends, the young lovers Liang and Tiao Tsien. The Emperor is pleased with A Hi's gifts of a miniature army and a magic horse, but demands to keep Liang too. When she refuses he imprisons Tiao Tsien. Liang snatches A Hi's wand, accidentally turning him into a cactus, and escapes with Tiao Tsien, using the wand to erect obstacles in their wake. The Emperor despatches his archer on the magic horse. The couple use the last of the wand's power to turn themselves into a statue and a tiger but the archer releases an arrow that kills Tiao Tsien. With all three candles extinguished, Death offers the wife a final chance to save her husband by bringing him another life in exchange within the hour. Coming to her senses as the apothecary dashes the poison from her lips, the girl vainly begs him, a beggar and old people in a hospital to give up their lives for her husband's sake. The commotion in the hospital starts a fire which traps a baby. As the wife enters the burning building she hopes that the baby's life will serve her purpose, but at the last minute she lowers the baby to safety and surrenders her own life in order to join her husband.

The Devil Rides Out
UK 1967 sd col 20

PRODUCTION
p.c – Hammer. p – Anthony Nelson-Keys. d – Terence Fisher. sc – Richard Matheson, from the novel by Dennis Wheatley. ph – Arthur Grant (Technicolor). ed – Spencer Reeve. a.d – Bernard Robinson. m – James Bernard. choreo – David Toguri.

LEADING PLAYERS
Christopher Lee (Duc de Richleau), Charles Gray (Mocata), Nike Arrighi (Tanith), Leon Greene (Rex Van Ryn), Patrick Mower (Simon Aron), Sarah Lawson (Marie Eaton), Paul Eddington (Richard Eaton), Rosalyn Landor (Peggy Eaton).

SYNOPSIS
Nicholas and Rex discover that Simon, son of a friend of theirs, is getting involved in black magic, and that he and a young woman, Tanith, are about to undergo a ritual baptism. After various dangers they manage to extricate Simon and Tanith from the coven and hide them with friends, Richard and Marie Eaton.

Mocata, head of the coven, finds the house. Fixing Marie with his eyes, he tries to persuade her that Simon and Tanith are good friends of his, and says that magic is the power of one mind over other minds. Bemused, she tells him where Simon and Tanith are, and he turns his mental focus on them. Peggy, Marie's daughter, arrives and breaks his concentration. He leaves, warning that 'something' will be back. (Ext. 1a, 8 mins.)

Later that day, Nicholas returns from researches in the British Museum, and takes command.

Tanith is gagged and bound and taken to a distant cottage, to be guarded by Rex. Mocata tries to will Rex to set her free. Meanwhile, Richard protests at Nicholas's elaborate arrangements for the night – a magic pentangle in which everyone must stay until daybreak. Standing inside it they see and hear a series of illusions: Rex's voice at the door, a giant tarantula. Simon is made thirsty by Mocata, and Nicholas has to knock him out to prevent him from breaking the pentangle. The Angel of Death appears, Simon regains consciousness and looks up into its face. Nicholas uses his last weapon, the Zu Sama incantation, which has the power to alter space and time. Tanith has convulsions. By now it is morning and they can leave. Rex arrives with Tanith, apparently dead, in his arms. (Ext. 1b, 12 mins.)

Peggy has disappeared. Nicholas locates Mocata's hideaway through Tanith's spirit. Tanith, working through Marie, breaks Mocata's will power and destroys the coven. Next morning both Peggy and Tanith are safe and well, as the Zu Sama has changed time for them.

Diamonds of the Night
Czechoslovakia 1964 sd b/w 9

PRODUCTION
p.c – Ceskoslovensky Film. d – Jan Nemec. sc – Arnost Lustig, Jan Nemec, from the novel Darkness Has No Shadows by Arnost Lustig. ph – Jaroslav Kucera. ed – Miroslav Hájek. a.d – Oldrich Bosák.

LEADING PLAYERS
Ladislav Jansky (The First), Antonin Kumbera (The Second), Ilse Bischofová (The Woman).

SYNOPSIS
Two Jewish boys jump from a train taking them to a Nazi concentration camp. They evade the bullets of their pursuers and escape into a thick forest. As they trudge wearily through woods, swamps and rocky clearings, a jumble of memories, fantasies and premonitions flash through the younger boy's mind. Next day, hungry and exhausted, they come upon a lonely farmhouse.

Standing in the rain, the boys observe a woman bringing food from the farmhouse to a man who is ploughing a field. They watch the woman go back inside, then one of the boys follows her and asks for food. She gives them bread and milk. They depart, watched by the woman.

Some time later they are hunted by an armed posse of elderly villagers, the local contingent of the German Home Guard. The boys are caught and locked up in an inn where the old men excitedly celebrate their success in the presence of the starving boys. Eventually they take the boys outside and form a firing squad, but at the last moment suddenly let the boys go. With the ironic applause and laughter of the old men ringing in their ears, the boys plod on.

Dirty Harry
USA 1971 sd col 15

PRODUCTION
p.c – Warner Bros/Malpaso. p – Don Siegel. d – Don Siegel. sc – Harry Julian Fink, Rita M. Fink, Dean Reisner, from a story by Harry Julian Fink and Rita M. Fink. ph – Bruce Surtees (Panavision and Technicolor). ed – Carl Pingitore. a.d – Dale Hennessey. m – Lalo Schifrin.

LEADING PLAYERS
Clint Eastwood (Harry Callahan), Harry Guardino (Lieutenant Bressler), John Vernon (The Mayor), Andy Robinson (Scorpio).

SYNOPSIS
A sniper kills a young woman while she is swimming in a roof-top pool. Inspector Harry Callahan arrives, and finds an empty cartridge and a note on the roof of an adjacent skyscraper. The note, read by the Mayor in his City Hall office, says that 'Scorpio' will kill others unless a payment of $100,000 is made. Callahan is brought in to give an account of his investigation, but is constantly interrupted by his superior officer. The Mayor wants to pay the $100,000, but Callahan disagrees. Later, while having a hot-dog in a lunch diner, Callahan sees a bank robbery taking place. He tells the diner's owner to phone the police, but the bank-raiders pour onto the street. Callahan goes out, and kills or wounds all the raiders with his Magnum 44. He sees a wounded man who is about to pick up a gun from the pavement, and dares him to take a chance on whether or not the Magnum has any bullets left. The raider plays safe, and Callahan shows that it is empty.

A new recruit is assigned to work on the Scorpio case with Callahan, and learns that Callahan got his nickname of 'Dirty Harry' from the rough jobs he has to do, as well as from his unorthodox methods. As the $100,000 has not been paid, Scorpio kills a young black boy. He evades a trap set by Callahan and kidnaps a young girl, demanding $200,000 for her release. The Mayor decides to pay. Callahan, carrying the money, is almost killed by Scorpio, but manages to wound him with a flick-knife. Later he tracks Scorpio to a football stadium and tortures him until he reveals where the kidnapped girl is being held. She is traced, but has been dead for some time. Scorpio, however, is allowed to go free because the evidence Callahan has obtained is deemed inadmissable. Taken off the case, Callahan undertakes private surveillance. Eventually, after Scorpio has hi-jacked a busload of school children, Callahan kills him in a quarry. As he watches Scorpio's body drift in the quarry pond, he throws his police badge in after it.

(NB This extract is standard reduced from Scope.)

Dr. Mabuse der Spieler: I – Der Spieler/Ein Bild der Zeit
Germany 1921 st b/w 10+10

PRODUCTION
p.c – Decla-Bioscop/Ullstein-Uco Film/Ufa. p – Erich Pommer. d – Fritz Lang. sc – Fritz Lang, Thea von Harbou, from the novel by Norbert Jacques. ph – Carl Hoffman. a.d – Otto Hunte, Stahl-Urach. cost – Vally Reinecke.

LEADING PLAYERS
Rudolf Klein-Rogge (Dr. Mabuse), Paul Richter (Edgar Hull), Aud Egede Nissen (Cara Carozza), Gertrud Welcker (Countess Told), Alfred Abel (Count Told), Bernhard Goetzke (von Wenk).

SYNOPSIS
Dr. Mabuse steals a secret Dutch-Swiss trade agreement. News of its theft causes share prices to fall on the Stock Exchange. Mabuse buys them up, then arranges the discovery of the lost agreement. Once Exchange prices have risen again, Mabuse

sells, making a massive profit. At the Folies Bergère nightclub, Cara Carozza dances and is rapturously applauded by the clientele. Mabuse arrives and learns from a note left by Cara that Edgar Hull is in the audience. (Ext. 1, 10 mins.)

Mabuse's scheme is to make more money by hypnotising rich gamblers into losing vast sums at cards. Hull, playboy son of a wealthy industrialist, is one of Mabuse's proposed victims. To help Mabuse, Cara contrives a romantic involvement with Hull. Aware of something amiss, Hull agrees to assist state attorney von Wenk, who is investigating Mabuse. Hull provides von Wenk with the secret password to various clubs. At one of these, von Wenk meets the bored and beautiful Countess Told.

Von Wenk goes to another club, in disguise. Using a secret password he is admitted to a gambling room. Mabuse is there, also in disguise. He is aware of von Wenk's real identity because of a tip-off from Cara. Mabuse unsuccessfully attempts to hypnotise von Wenk at the card table. When Mabuse leaves, von Wenk follows him to the Exelsior Hotel, but he manages to give von Wenk the slip. Von Wenk takes a taxi to continue the chase, but the cab is driven by one of Mabuse's henchmen, who drugs him. Later von Wenk finds himself adrift at sea in a small dinghy. (Ext. 2, 10 mins.)

Mabuse's henchmen try to kill von Wenk. They fail, and Hull is killed instead. Cara is arrested for complicity, but refuses to reveal anything about Mabuse. At a soirée Mabuse, now enamoured of the Countess Told, hypnotises the Count into cheating at cards, and then kidnaps the Countess.

Dr. Mabuse der Spieler: II – Inferno/ Ein Spiel von Menschen unserer Zeit
Germany 1921 st b/w 13

PRODUCTION
p.c – Decla-Bioscop/Ullstein-Uco Film/ Ufa. *p* – Erich Pommer. *d* – Fritz Lang. *sc* – Fritz Lang, Thea von Harbou, from the novel by Norbert Jacques. *ph* – Carl Hoffman, *a.d* – Otto Hunte, Erich Kettelhut, Karl Vollbrecht. *cost* – Vally Reinecke.

LEADING PLAYERS
Rudolf Klein-Rogge (*Dr. Mabuse*), Paul Richter (*Edgar Hull*), Aud Egede Nissen (*Cara Carozza*), Gertrud Welcker (*Countess Told*), Alfred Abel (*Count Told*), Bernhard Goetzke (*von Wenk*).

SYNOPSIS
Mabuse becomes psychiatric consultant to Count Told, who is distraught about his apparent cheating at cards. Mabuse, angered by the Countess's rejection of his advances, uses his hypnotic powers to make the Count put von Wenk off his wife's track. Under the power of Mabuse, Told commits suicide. Mabuse is mistakenly informed that Cara is about to

betray him and sends her poison which she obediently takes. Von Wenk's suspicions are aroused by Told's death.

Mabuse suggests that von Wenk should attend a demonstration of hypnotism to be given by a man named Weltman. Weltman (Mabuse in disguise) involves von Wenk in the demonstration and is able to instruct the hypnotised von Wenk to take a car and drive into a quarry. Von Wenk obeys, but is rescued just in time by his men, who have followed him.

Mabuse plans to abscond with the Countess, but finds his house surrounded by the police. In the shoot-out, all of Mabuse's gang is either killed or arrested and the Countess is rescued, but Mabuse escapes to his counterfeiting plant. He realises too late that the exits and entrances are self-locking. When von Wenk finds him, he is completely insane.

Dr. Strangelove, or How I Learned to Stop Worrying and Love the Bomb
UK 1963 sd b/w 18

PRODUCTION
p.c – Hawk Films. *p* – Stanley Kubrick. *d* – Stanley Kubrick. *sc* – Stanley Kubrick, Terry Southern, Peter George, from the novel *Red Alert* by Peter George. *ph* – Gilbert Taylor. *ed* – Anthony Harvey. *a.d* – Peter Murton. *m* – Laurie Johnson.

LEADING PLAYERS
Peter Sellers (*Group Captain Lionel Mandrake/President Muffley/Dr. Strangelove*), George C. Scott (*General 'Buck' Turgidson*), Sterling Hayden (*General Jack D. Ripper*), Peter Bull (*Ambassador de Sadesky*).

SYNOPSIS
Convinced that a Communist plot is poisoning the 'vital fluids' of the free world, General Ripper, the demented commander of a US air force base, launches an all-out attack on Russia, and seals off his base. President Muffley summons his general staff and the Russian ambassador to the Pentagon war room and tells the Soviet Premier Kissov the news over the hot-line. The aircraft cannot be recalled because their radios respond only to a code signal known soley by Ripper, so Muffley offers to help the Russians shoot down the US planes.

The Russian ambassador discloses the existence of the USSR's supreme weapon called the Doomsday Device, which is triggered off by any nuclear explosion. Meanwhile, US land forces are attacking Ripper's base. The occupants believe that they are fighting cunningly-disguised Communist invaders. Ripper explains his theory of 'fluoridisation', the process by which the Communists are poisoning the free world's vital fluids, to Mandrake, an RAF officer. The base has to surrender. Ripper is inconsolable and to keep the radio code safe, he commits suicide. The bombs fly nearer to their target. One of

them is badly damaged by a missile, and has its radio shot away, but flies on.

Mandrake works out the radio code and the bombers are recalled, except the one with no radio. The Texan pilot of this plane is determined to complete his mission. The President's German physicist adviser, Dr. Strangelove, calculates that if the worst happens a selected few can take to the deep shelters from which emergence could be possible in a few hundred years. The bomb is released, mushroom clouds darken the world, and Vera Lynn is heard singing 'We'll meet again' on the soundtrack.

Don Quixote
France/UK 1933 sd b/w 25

PRODUCTION
p.c – Vandor-Nelson-Webster. *p* – Constantin Geftman. *d* – G. W. Pabst. *sc* – Paul Morand and Alexander Arnoux, from the novel by Miguel De Cervantes. *ph* – Nicolas Farkas, Paul Portier. *ed* – Hans Oser. *a.d* – Andrei Andreiev. *m* – Jacques Ibert. *cost* – M. Pretzfelder.

LEADING PLAYERS
Feodor Chaliapine (*Don Quixote*), George Robey (*Sancho Panza*), Oscar Asche (*Captain of the Police*).

SYNOPSIS
Don Quixote, a country squire whose blood is fired by tales of knightly valour, sets out on a career as knight-errant in an age when knight-errantry has long since disappeared. He takes his servant, Sancho Panza, a man of common sense and earthy appetites with him. In a village, a shabby little troupe of actors performs a play in which a knight fights against a giant. The valiant Don Quixote rushes to the knight's rescue. To humour the old man, the actor who plays the king ceremoniously knights Don Quixote, who chooses the sluttish village girl Dulcinea as the lady of his dreams. Later, Don Quixote mistakes the dust raised by a flock of sheep for an evil spirit, and charges into them. Next, he liberates a gang of prisoners in chains who show their gratitude by stoning him. The police set out to put an end to the knight's activities. In a lenient mood, a Duke decides to cure Don Quixote's madness by playing along with his fantastic ideas. He invites Don Quixote to his court, where he meets a masked knight who challenges him to a tournament in which the loser has to renounce his knighthood. Unfortunately, Don Quixote wins. He discovers that his opponent is only his niece's fiancé, and leaves, deeply hurt.

Don Quixote believes giant spectres are waving eerie arms and cursing the peaceful countryside. He valiantly charges them at full tilt, but they turn out to be windmills. Sadly battered, the knight is taken home in a cage by police. When he arrives he sees the Inquisition burning his books. Robbed of the illusions which gave him life, Don

Quixote expires in the arms of his faithful Sancho.

Don't Look Now
UK/Italy 1973 sd col 15

PRODUCTION
p.c – Casey Productions (London)/ Eldorado Films (Rome). *p* – Peter Katz. *d* – Nicholas Roeg. *sc* – Allan Scott, Chris Bryant, from the short story by Daphne du Maurier. *ph* – Anthony Richmond (Technicolor). *ed* – Graeme Clifford. *a.d* – Giovanni Soccol. *m* – Pino D'Onnagio.

LEADING PLAYERS
Julie Christie (*Laura Baxter*), Donald Sutherland (*John Baxter*), Hilary Mason (*Heather*), Clelia Matania (*Wendy*), Nicholas Salter (*Johnny Baxter*), Sharon Williams (*Christine Baxter*).

SYNOPSIS
Laura Baxter is reading while her husband John works with slides of the stained-glass window of the church he is to repair in Venice. Their son Johnny is cycling round the garden while their daughter runs around the pond wearing a red mac. John spills water over a slide and a strange red blob appears to spread over it. He runs into the garden, and finds Christine drowning. He tries to revive her by artificial respiration, but fails. (Ext. 1a, 7 mins.)

After the funeral, Laura accompanies John to Venice, where they meet a pair of elderly sisters, one blind, who claims that she can 'see' Christine.

John and Laura get lost one evening and argue about which is the right direction. John is puzzled by a sense of knowing the place. Screams are heard as another murder – one of a series currently terrorising Venice – is discovered. They emerge into crowded, well-lit streets. Next day, John is working on the church, high up. He sees the two sisters meet Laura by chance and works on abstractedly. Hearing how Christine died Heather, the blind sister, tells Laura that John has 'the gift'. Laura asks about the possibility of contacting the dead, and the sisters invite them back to tea. John refuses to go. Meanwhile, the two sisters cackle with laughter in their hotel. Laura blames John for Christine's death. He walks off. (Ext. 1b, 8 mins.)

Laura goes to the séance alone. She is warned that John is in danger, but has to return to England because her son has had an accident. Meanwhile, John has a near-fatal fall while working on the church. Afterwards he is convinced that he sees Laura dressed in black mourning clothes and travelling along a canal in a hearse with the two sisters. He instigates a police search for Laura. She returns from England but misses him both at the police station and the sisters' hotel. He follows a small figure in red who is reminiscent of Christine but turns out to be an ugly

dwarf, who fatally stabs him. His vision of Laura with the sisters on the gondola-hearse is finally realised.

Double Indemnity
USA 1944 sd b/w 23

PRODUCTION
p.c – Paramount. *p* – Joseph Sistrom. *d* – Billy Wilder. *sc* – Billy Wilder, Raymond Chandler, from the novel by James Cain. *ph* – John Seitz. *ed* – Doane Harrison. *a.d* – Hans Dreier, Hal Pereira. *m* – Miklós Rózsa. *cost* – Edith Head.

LEADING PLAYERS
Barbara Stanwyck (*Phyllis Dietrichson*), Fred MacMurray (*Walter Neff*), Edward G. Robinson (*Barton Keyes*), Porter Hall (*Mr. Jackson*), Jean Heather (*Lola Dietrichson*), Tom Powers (*Mr. Dietrichson*), Byron Barr (*Nino Zachetti*).

SYNOPSIS
Walter Neff staggers wounded into his office in the early hours of the morning to record a confession for his superior, Keyes, which tells of his fatal involvement with Phyllis Dietrichson. A series of flashbacks shows how he first meets her when he calls to remind her husband about the renewal of his car insurance. On a second visit when her husband is out, she asks about the possibility of taking out life insurance for him, but without his knowing. Walter realises her designs and walks out.

Walter arrives back at his flat, declaring in voice-over his intention to keep clear of Phyllis Dietrichson and her evil temptations. But despite considerable antagonistic banter, when she arrives he is finally overcome by passion and refuses to let her leave. He elaborates a complex murder plan, through which they could claim the maximum insurance on a double indemnity clause, which operates in the case of a fatal fall from a moving train. (Ext. 1a, 10 mins.)

The murder is carried out and everything goes according to plan, but at the last moment before the insurance claim goes through, Keyes's sixth sense tells him something is wrong and he sets an investigation going which puts relations between Walter and Phyllis under a great strain. In the meantime Phyllis's step-daughter, Lola, comes to Walter in great distress, saying that Phyllis, who had been her sick mother's nurse, left a window open which caused her mother's death, and that Phyllis has also seduced Nino, her Italian boyfriend, away from her. When it becomes clear that Keyes is going to crack the case, Walter goes to confront Phyllis.

Phyllis prepares for Walter's visit and hides a gun under some cushions. Walter arrives and declares that he is through with her and intends to kill her. She pulls a gun on him first, but only wounds him. She suddenly realises that she does love Walter when she finds herself unable to fire a second shot. Despite her passionate declarations, Walter shoots and kills her

while she is embracing him. He sees Nino outside the house and explains Phyllis's role in his estrangement from Lola and sends him back to her. Walter returns to Keyes's office and starts his confession. The flashback ends when Keyes arrives and overhears Walter's last words. Keyes calles for an ambulance and the police, Walter tries to escape, but collapses at the lift. Keyes lights a cigarette for him. (Ext. 1b, 13 mins.)

Dracula
USA 1931 sd b/w 10

PRODUCTION
p.c – Universal. *d* – Tod Browning. *sc* – Garrett Fort, from the play by Hamilton Deane and John Balderston, based on the novel by Bram Stoker. *ph* – Karl Freund. *ed* – Milton Carruth, Maurice Pivar. *a.d* – Charles D. Hall. *m* – Tchaikovsky.

LEADING PLAYERS
Bela Lugosi (*Count Dracula*), David Manners (*Renfield*), Helen Chandler (*Mina Seward*).

SYNOPSIS
Count Dracula, apparently dead for 500 years, in fact retains his power to rise from the grave each night and assume different forms.

Renfield, an English lawyer, arrives at Dracula's ruined castle and is unnerved by the eeriness of the place and Dracula's strange manners. Dracula welcomes his guest and they discuss the lease of Carfax Abbey and his arrangements for returning to England. Renfield pricks his finger and draws blood as they talk, but Dracula's approach is stopped short when he sees the cross round Renfield's neck. He gives Renfield some wine and leaves him for the night. Renfield sees three women in white standing before him, and collapses on the floor. Dracula returns and crouches over him menacingly.

Renfield returns to England by boat, having been driven insane by his experiences. Dracula goes too, having arranged to be smuggled aboard, along with three boxes of earth. The boxes are delivered to Carfax Abbey. Dracula travels fast, since he can transform himself into a bat, a wolf, or a cloud of mist. Renfield is taken to an asylum run by a Dr. Seward, next to Carfax Abbey. Dracula changes one of Seward's relatives, Lucy Weston, into a vampire, and then turns his attention to Seward's daughter, Mina. Van Helsing, a scientist called in by John Harker, Mina's fiancée, discovers that Dracula is a vampire and tries to counteract his influence. By now Dracula is assisted by the mad Renfield. Dracula kidnaps Mina and takes her to Carfax Abbey. When Renfield escapes from the asylum, Van Helsing and Harker follow him and discover Dracula, who strangles Renfield then becomes insensible as the sun rises. Van Helsing drives a stake through his heart. Mina recovers.

Dracula

UK 1957 sd col 16

PRODUCTION

p.c – Hammer. *p* – Anthony Hinds. *d* – Terence Fisher. *sc* – Jimmy Sangster, from the novel by Bram Stoker. *ph* – Jack Asher (Eastman Color). *ed* – James Needs, Bill Lenny. *a.d* – Bernard Robinson. *m* – James Bernard.

LEADING PLAYERS

Peter Cushing (*Dr. Van Helsing*), Christopher Lee (*Count Dracula*), John Van Eyssen (*Jonathan Harker*), Carol Marsh (*Lucy*), Valerie Gaunt (*Vampire Woman*).

SYNOPSIS

Jonathan Harker begins reading aloud from his diary an account of his arrival at Dracula's castle, ostensibly to take up the post of librarian. The coach-driver leaves him at the village refusing to go any further. As he approaches the castle Jonathan is struck by the lack of birds singing and the abnormal coldness. Inside, he finds a fire burning, supper laid out for him, and a note from Count Dracula promising his return in the evening. He reads about vampirism, and is suddenly confronted by a beautiful woman begging him to help her get away. Dracula arrives suddenly, she vanishes and he shows Harker to his room. Dracula is interested in a photograph of Lucy, Harker's fiancée. Despite being locked in, Harker sits down to continue his diary. His entry concludes 'with God's help I will end his reign of terror for ever'. (Ext. 1a, 11 mins.)

Harker fails in his mission, and is vampirised. His friend, Van Helsing, finds his tomb, stakes him, and notices that Lucy's photograph is missing. He hurries back to England, to find that Lucy is already ill.

Lucy is in bed, restless. She gets up and opens the window onto the balcony, removes her cross, then lies back in bed. Meanwhile, Van Helsing listens to a recording he has made of his researches into vampirism. To it he adds an account of how a victim of vampirism is unable to relinquish the practice and suffers an addiction as if to drugs. Eventually the victim will appear to die, but in fact will pass into the state of the undead. He declares that Dracula must be found and destroyed. Meanwhile, Dracula enters Lucy's room. Her face exhibits desire and terror. (Ext. 1b, 5 mins.)

Lucy's sister, Mina, asks Van Helsing to help, but Lucy frustrates his attempts. Later, Lucy is apparently killed by Dracula, but her grave is found empty. Van Helsing finds her and puts her to rest. Dracula visits Mina and abducts her. There is a frantic chase across Europe. Finally, Van Helsing confronts Dracula in his castle's library and destroys him with the help of the first daylight and a makeshift cross. With Dracula dead, Mina is saved.

Dracula, Prince of Darkness

UK 1965 sd col scope 23

PRODUCTION

p.c – Hammer. *p* – Anthony Nelson-Keys. *d* – Terence Fisher. *sc* – John Sansom, from an idea by John Elder, based on characters created by Bram Stoker. *ph* – Michael Reed (TechniScope and Technicolor). *ed* – Chris Barnes. *a.d* – Don Mingaye. *m* – James Bernard.

LEADING PLAYERS

Christopher Lee (*Dracula*), Barbara Shelley (*Helen*), Francis Matthews (*Charles*), Suzan Farmer (*Diana*), Charles Tingwell (*Alan*), Philip Latham (*Klove*).

SYNOPSIS

Two English couples, Alan and Helen, Charles and Diana, are holidaying in the Carpathians. After warnings from a local Abbot, Father Sandor, they are brought to Count Dracula's castle by a driverless carriage. Despite Helen's misgivings they go in.

Charles, who has gone to investigate upstairs, calls to Alan. Helen screams as a sinister shadow moves towards them. It is an ancient servant, Klove, who has come to invite them in to dinner, on instructions from his dead master that the castle should always be ready to receive visitors. As they sit down to eat, Klove lugubriously adds 'My master's hospitality is renowned'. Helen is still frightened, but the others think everything has been satisfactorily explained and drink a toast to the Count, at which the lights flicker and the curtains stir in a mysterious breeze. That night Charles and Diana joke about the lumpy beds and anticipate Helen's complaints. Meanwhile Helen senses an evil presence and declares to Alan 'There will be no morning for us'. Helen suddenly awakes, convinced someone has called her. Alan, seeing Klove dragging an old trunk down the corridor, goes to investigate and finds steps leading to a cellar which is set out with satanic paraphernalia and houses Dracula's tomb. He is stabbed by Klove, then strung up by his ankles over the tomb, which Klove sprinkles with Dracula's ashes. He cuts Alan's throat, the dripping blood gives life back to the ashes, and Dracula is gradually reformed. Meanwhile Klove goes to fetch Helen, who is horrified by the sight of Alan's body. She is vampirised by Dracula.

Next morning Charles and Diana escape from Helen and Dracula, saved by Diana's cross. Father Sandor takes them in. Klove drives Dracula's and Helen's coffins to the monastery. Diana is bitten by Helen, but saved by Father Sandor, who cauterises the bite. Helen is caught and staked, and Dracula captures Diana. They are pursued by Sandor and Charles back to the castle, where Dracula eventually drowns.

(NB This extract is in Scope and needs an anamorphic lens.)

Each Dawn I Die

USA 1939 sd b/w 10

PRODUCTION

p.c – Warner Bros. *p* – Hal B. Wallis. *d* – William F. Keighley. *sc* – Norman Reilly-Raine, Warren Duff, Charles Perry, from the novel by Jerome Odlum. *ph* – Arthur Edeson. *ed* – Thomas Richards. *a.d* – Max Parker. *m* – Max Steiner.

LEADING PLAYERS

James Cagney (*Frank Ross*), George Raft (*Stacey*), Jane Bryan (*Joyce*), George Bancroft (*John Armstrong*), Stanley Ridges (*Meuller*).

SYNOPSIS

While investigating a construction company fraud, Frank Ross, a journalist, finds that the District Attorney is implicated in the racket. He is given the go-ahead by his editor to write a feature on what he has discovered. Ross is later kidnapped and knocked unconscious. A bottle of whisky is poured over him and he is placed in a moving car. There is an accident and three people are killed. Ross pleads his innocence but is found guilty of manslaughter and sentenced to an indefinite period of hard labour. En route to the prison Ross finds himself sitting next to Stacey, a long-time ganster; they take an instant dislike to each other and a fight breaks out.

In prison, Ross saves Stacey's life. Stacey then agrees to help Ross by tracing the men who framed him. Ross helps him escape in order to do this. After pressure from Joyce, Ross's girlfriend, Stacey honours the agreement and tracks down the man who 'fingered' Ross. It transpires that this man is in prison. Stacey gives himself up and is also returned to gaol. Stacey is seriously wounded in a riot, but before dying he forces the man who framed Ross to confess, within hearing distance of the Governor. Ross is cleared of murder and released.

Early Spring

Japan 1956 sd b/w 10 + 12

PRODUCTION

p.c – Shochiku/Ofuna. *p* –Shizuo Yamanouchi. *d* – Yashujiro Ozu. *sc* – Yashujiro Ozu, Kogo Noda. *ph* – Yushun Atsuta. *ed* – Yoshiyasu Hamamura. *ad* – Tatsuo Hamada. *m* – Takanobu Saito. *cost* – Yuji Nagashima.

LEADING PLAYERS

Chikage Awashima (*Masako*), Ryo Ikebe (*Sugiyama*), Keiko Kishi (*Goldfish*), Chishu Ryu (*Onodera*).

SYNOPSIS

Early in the morning the office workers from Tokyo who live together in cramped conditions converge on the railway station and a group of friends meet. In town, an observer sees his fellow workers as an anonymous mass. Work begins in a room where every space is utilised. During the lunch hour the office group decides to go on a communal hike that Sunday. (Ext. 1, 10 mins.)

Sugiyama, a young office worker bored with his wife, embarks on an unsatisfactory affair with the office flirt. Later, he becomes disillusioned with the relationship which causes arguments with his wife.

He is called into the manager's office and offered a transfer to the firm's provincial branch in Osaka. At a party a group of men discuss Sugiyama's affair. His lover comes in and there is an argument, during which she angrily leaves the room. The young man visits a sick friend who talks about his joyous reaction when he learnt that he has been hired by his company. (Ext. 2, 12 mins.)

The young man moves to Osaka. Away from the bustle of Tokyo he ponders his life and is reconciled to a forgiving wife.

Earth
USSR 1930 st b/w 13

PRODUCTION
p.c – Ukrainfilm (Kiev). *d* – Alexander Dovzhenko. *sc* – Alexander Dovzhenko. *ph* – Danylo Demutsky. *a.d* – Vasili Krichevsky.

LEADING PLAYERS
Mikola Nademsky (*Grandfather Semion Trubenko*), Stepan Shkurat (*Opanas Trubenko*), Semion Svashenko (*Vasili Trubenko*), Yulia Solntseva (*Orisya Trubenko*), Nikolai Mikhailov (*Father Gerasim*).

SYNOPSIS
The young peasants of a Ukrainian village want to buy a tractor. The kulaks of the community fear their strength and unity, and one of them kills the young village chairman, Vasili.

The villagers and the family mourn Vasili. On the hills, his father confronts a man: 'You murdered my son!' The priest is turned from the door and the father requests a modern burial for his son – a burial by the young people with songs of the new life. This is agreed.

Easy Rider
USA 1969 sd col 15

PRODUCTION
p.c – Pando Company, in association with Raybert Productions. *p* – Peter Fonda. *d* – Dennis Hopper. *sc* – Peter Fonda, Dennis Hopper, Terry Southern. *ph* – Laszlo Kovacs (Technicolor). *ed* – Donn Cambren. *a.d* – Jerry Kay. *m* – Steppenwolf, The Byrds, The Band, Holy Modal Rounders, Fraternity of Man, The Jimi Hendrix Experience, Little Eva, The Electric Prunes, The Electric Flag, Roger McGuinn.

LEADING PLAYERS
Peter Fonda (*Wyatt*), Dennis Hopper (*Billy*), Antonio Mendoza (*Jesus*), Jack Nicholson (*George Hanson*).

SYNOPSIS
After selling a large quantity of cocaine, Wyatt and Billy conceal their money in Wyatt's petrol tank, throw away their watches and set off on their motorcycle odyssey across America. They aim to reach New Orleans in time for the Mardi Gras carnival.

Wyatt and Billy stop at an isolated farmhouse to mend Wyatt's bike. They join the farmer, his Mexican wife and children for lunch. They continue their journey picking up a hitch-hiker on the way. At nightfall they camp in a cave.

They stop at a small Texas town, where they are jailed. Their cell-mate George Hanson, an alcoholic civil rights lawyer, secures their release and decides to accompany them to Orleans. They set up camp outside a small town, but during the night Hanson is clubbed to death by a party of local vigilante townsmen. Wyatt and Billy continue the journey and eventually reach New Orleans. After visiting the carnival they leave, vaguely heading for Florida, but are both shot down by a passing lorry-driver.

Easy Street
USA 1917 st b/w 5
(w. **The Pawnshop** and **The Vagabond**)

PRODUCTION
p.c – Lone Star-Mutual. *p* – Charlie Chaplin. *d* – Charlie Chaplin. *sc* – Charlie Chaplin. *ph* – Rolland Totheroh, William C. Foster.

LEADING PLAYERS
Charlie Chaplin (*Tramp*), Edna Purviance (*Mission Worker*), Eric Campbell (Big Eric).

SYNOPSIS
Charlie wanders into a mission and becomes a reformed character. He joins the police.

As a new recruit he is assigned to patrol Easy Street, renowned for its invincible bully, Big Eric. Although the bully is insensible to blows, he is outwitted by Charlie's deft footwork and quick thinking.

The Eclipse
(*see* L'Eclisse)

L'Eclisse (The Eclipse)
Italy/France 1962 sd b/w 15

PRODUCTION
p.c – Interopa Film/Cineriz (Rome)/Paris Film Production. *p* – Robert and Raymond Hakim. *d* – Michelangelo Antonioni. *sc* – Michel Antonioni, Tonino Guerra, Elio Bartolini, Ottiero Ottieri, from a story by Michelangelo Antonioni and Tonino Guerra. *ph* – Gianni Di Venanzo. *ed* – Eraldo Da Roma. *s.d* – Piero Poletto. *m* – Giovanni Fusco.

LEADING PLAYERS
Monica Vitti (*Vittoria*), Alain Delon (*Piero*), Francisco Rabal (*Riccardo*).

SYNOPSIS
It is summer in Rome. Vittoria, an attractive and independent young woman who works as a translator has decided that she must finish her relationship with Riccardo. She is not entirely sure why, but feels that a nagging sensation of 'incompleteness' makes the break necessary. Bewildered, Riccardo presses her for a more specific reason, but Vittoria does not respond, and leaves.

Vittoria is uncertain of her future plans, and decides to seek the advice of her mother, an imprudent woman with a passion for gambling on the Stock Exchange. She goes there and finds her mother discussing business with Piero, a young stockbroker's agent and notices his more than usual interest in her. That night Vittoria enjoys herself with some friends and feels free and relaxed for the first time since her life with Riccardo. Returning to Rome after a brief trip to Verona, her mind is filled with thoughts of Piero. On the pretext of seeing her mother, Vittoria returns to the Stock Exchange. But now the atmosphere is different; shares have dropped drastically, ruining some people and causing great losses to others, including her mother. Piero and Vittoria leave the Stock Exchange and go to her mother's flat. He tries to make advances but is foiled by the arrival of Vittoria's mother. Piero and her mother start to talk about business, Vittoria feels unwanted and leaves. That evening Piero stands up an old girlfriend and drives to Vittoria's flat. She refuses to let him in. During their conversation his car is stolen. Next day, Piero hears that the car has been found in a lake and he goes with Vittoria to the scene of the accident. They see a hand in the wreckage that is dragged from the lake – the thief died in the crash. Stunned, Vittoria turns to Piero, but he is only concerned with the time he has wasted and the cost of repairs. On the way home Piero suggests going to his flat and although Vittoria at first refuses, the following day she accepts his invitation. They go to Piero's parents' house and as there is no one there, the two make love. After the Stock Exchange closes the next day, the couple revive the happy moments of their previous meetings. They discuss their future and make a date for the next day, but it seems unlikely that their relationship will be free from problems.

8½ (Otto e mezzo)
Italy 1962 sd b/w 14

PRODUCTION
p.c – Cineriz. *p* – Angelo Rizzoli. *d* – Federico Fellini. *sc* – Federico Fellini, Ennio Flaiano, Tullio Pinelli, Brunello Rondi, from a story by Federico Fellini and Ennio Flaiano. *ph* – Gianni Di Venanzo. *ed* – Leo Catozzo. *a.d* – Piero Gherardi. *m* – Nino Rota.

LEADING PLAYERS
Marcello Mastroianni (*Guido Anselmi*), Claudia Cardinale (*Claudia*), Anouk Aimée (*Luisa Anselmi*), Guido Alberti (*Pace, The Producer*).

SYNOPSIS
Guido Anselmi, a successful film director, is embarking on a costly and ambitious picture without any idea of what he wants to say. Nightmares and nervous exhaustion drive him to seek refuge at a health spa near the film's location. He is followed first by Carla, his amiably vulgar mistress, and then by his long-suffering wife, Luisa. He escapes from them, the production executives and hopeful actresses who pursue him, by retreating into sexual fantasies and childhood memories. As a schoolboy he watches a huge lecherous creature, La Saraghina, emerge from her concrete pillbox and dance for money. In another memory his dead mother intrudes into a fetishistic interlude with his mistress. He fantasises about a harem where he controls all the women he has known with a whip. He has a vision of an ideal woman, pure and innocent.

Claudia comes into the theatre where Guido is. In her white dress she looks the ideal of purity that Guido has imagined. Inspired, he takes her into the courtyard and starts to talk about the film. She turns out to be a hard, opportunistic actress. The producer drives up and announces the go-ahead on the film. Guido returns to the film set, a gigantic missile ramp. He is hounded by reporters and hangers-on. When called upon to speak to the gathering, he is so confused that he retreats under a table in terror.

A travelling band of clowns comes to his aid. Joined by the entire film crew plus mistresses and hangers-on, they form a procession which encircles the set.

El
Mexico 1952 sd b/w 10

PRODUCTION
p.c – Nacional Film. *p* – Oscar Dancigers. *d* – Luis Buñuel. *sc* – Luis Buñuel, Luis Alcoriza, from the novel *Pensamientos* by Mercedes Pinto. *ph* – Gabriel Figueroa. *ed* – Carlos Savage. *a.d* – Edward Fitzgerald. *m* – Luis Hernández Breton.

LEADING PLAYERS
Arturo de Cordova (*Francisco*), Delia Garcés (*Gloria*), Luis Beristain (*Raúl*).

SYNOPSIS
Don Francisco, a handsome bachelor in his early forties, is a wealthy landowner and pillar of the church. One day he is struck by the sight of a beautiful woman, Gloria, in the church. He becomes obsessed by her and returns to the church every day in the hope of seeing her again. Eventually, he discovers that she is engaged to Raúl, an old friend of his, and manages to affect an introduction. Gloria is swept off her feet, and while Raúl is away, she breaks off her engagement and marries Francisco. But, right from the start, things go wrong. Francisco, who has never loved or even slept with a woman before, is pathologically jealous, and accuses her of infidelity on the slightest provocation. Back at home after the honeymoon, Francisco beats Gloria with increasing cruelty, keeping her virtually a prisoner, and even threatens to kill her. Unable to stand it any longer, Gloria finally escapes, and Francisco's mind gives way completely. Gloria is married to Raúl and Francisco enters a monastery in retreat.

Years later, Gloria tells Raúl in flashback how on one occasion Francisco shot her with blank cartridges, and on another tried to push her from a high building. He sees her return home with Raúl, and accuses her of infidelity. She says she doesn't want to go on living with him, and leaves the room. Later Francisco breaks down and asks his servant's advice about Gloria. Afterwards, on his way upstairs, weaving from side to side, he picks up a stair rod and starts to bang rhythmically with it. Gloria, hearing the noise, locks her bedroom door.

Raúl and Gloria visit the monastery where Francisco is, accompanied by their small son. They leave without seeing Francisco, after being told by the Father Superior that Francisco is now cured, protected from the past by his faith. Francisco, who is aware of their visit, assures the Father Superior that he has indeed regained his serenity, then walks away down the garden with the same zigzag weaving gait that heralded his breakdown all those years past.

Emitai
Senegal 1972 sd col 15

PRODUCTION
p.c – Films Domirev. *p* – Paulin Soumanou Vieyra. *d* – Ousmane, Sembene. *sc* – Ousmane Sembene. *ph* – Michel Remaudeau. *ed* – Gilbert Kikoïne.

LEADING PLAYERS
Robert Fontaine (*Commandant*), Michel Remaudeau (*Lieutenant*), Pierre Blanchard (*Colonel*).

SYNOPSIS
The action of the film based on an actual event, takes place towards the end of World War II. The Diola people of Casamance, Southern Senegal, worship several gods, represented by fetishes. The colonial power, France, presses all able-bodied male villagers into military service, leaving the women to plant and harvest the rice. To oppose the French the chiefs refuse to pay the taxes – in the form of rice – demanded by them.

The Governor of Southern Senegal receives a telegram saying that the rice must be seized by force and sent to the troops. A lieutenant is instructed to take a machine-gun platoon to the village, with Sergeant Badgi, a native of the area, as his guide. Meanwhile the Diola women carry away the rice harvest, transporting it up the river by canoe, and pass on warning signals through horn calls and drums. The French platoon is on the march, singing military songs, but Badgi stops to listen to the Diola signals. (Ext. 1a, 7 mins.)

The elders consult Bakine, the Earth Father. Djmeko, chief of the fetishists, decides to mount an attack on the French. It fails. The platoon kills large numbers of the Diola men and takes the women as hostages. The Commander demands sixty pounds of rice from each inhabitant.

The elders decide to call up the gods. A cockerel's throat is slit, and blood and water are sprinkled on the ground, while the elders chant and beat drums. The blurred figures of the gods are seen dancing. One of the elders, supporting the wounded Djmeko, summons the fetishes. They condemn Djmeko's rebellious stance over the rice. Djmeko challenges them; then accepting his own death, but predicting the end of the gods too, he collapses. (Ext. 1b, 8 mins.)

Eventually the chiefs capitulate. The men are used to carry the rice away, but at a certain point they stop and refuse to go further. At the same time the Commander learns that the war is over. But discipline has to be maintained, and the troops open fire, killing the men.

The End of St. Petersburg
USSR 1927 st b/w 14

PRODUCTION
p.c – Mezhrabpom-Russ. *d* – Vsevolod I. Pudovkin. *sc* – Nathan Zarkhi. *ph* – Anatoli Golovnya. *a.d* – Sergei Kozlovsky.

LEADING PLAYERS
A. P. Chistyakov (*A Worker*), Vera Baranovskaya (*His Wife*), Ivan Chuvelyov (*A Peasant*).

SYNOPSIS
A peasant leaves a Russian village where food is scarce, drifts into St. Petersburg, and endeavours to get work at a factory. An agitation for better conditions is in progress. Ignorant of the true state of affairs, he becomes a blackleg. When his eyes are opened, he attacks his employer and is flung into prison.

War is declared, and speeches are made to instil patriotism into the crowds. The peasant, along with other prisoners, is released from jail and forced to enlist. At the front, cold and wounded soldiers sleep in trenches and trudge through waist-high mud and water. The stock market booms and the capitalists oppose peace while devastation and suffering increases on the front.

The people revolt, attack the Winter Palace, overthrow the Kerensky Government and establish Revolutionary Councils. St. Petersburg becomes Leningrad.

The Entertainer
UK 1960 sd b/w 10

PRODUCTION
p.c – Woodfall/Holly. p – Harry Saltzman. d – Tony Richardson. John Osborne, Nigel Kneale, from the play by John Osborne. ph – Oswald Morris. ed – Alan Osbiston. a.d – Ralph Brinton. m – John Addison. choreo – Honor Blair.

LEADING PLAYERS
Laurence Olivier (Archie Rice), Joan Plowright (Jean Rice), Roger Livesey (Billy Rice), Brenda de Banzie (Phoebe Rice), Alan Bates (Frank), Albert Finney (Mick).

SYNOPSIS
Archie Rice, a third-rate song, dance and patter man, is the star of a limp girlie show in a half-empty seaside theatre. Jean, Archie's daughter by his first marriage, returns to her family after failing as a teacher and quarelling with her fiancé, but she finds no solace. Archie is busy trying to get a new show together while his present one crumbles around him; his second wife, Phoebe, has been reduced to drunkenness and hysteria by his sarcasm. Archie's father, Billy, a retired music hall artist, surveys the menage with dignity and contempt. The knowledge that Archie's son Mick is with the Army in the Middle East hangs over the family.

On stage, Archie does one of his numbers – 'Thank God we're normal'. Jean and Billy return home, Jean has an argument with Phoebe, but Archie and Billy interrupt the row. Phoebe is further upset when she discovers Billy eating the cake she bought specially for Mick's return. Archie temporarily lightens the atmosphere by pursuading Jean to play the piano and Phoebe to sing.

News comes that Mick has been taken prisoner. Archie gets embroiled in a sexual adventure with Tina Lapford, a teenage beauty queen. He promises Tina a part in his new show if her parents will put up the money. The Lapfords are enthusiastic until Billy tells them that Archie is an undischarged bankrupt. They pull out, but by then Archie has signed various cheques. The family hears that Mick has been killed at Suez. After the funeral, Archie exploits Billy's remorse and sets up a new show which combines nudes with nostalgia, and has the old man as partner and star. This fails too, when the old man finds the strain of a comeback too great and dies in the wings. Bankrupt, facing imprisonment and shorn of every illusion, Archie walks towards Jean across a deserted, barren stage.

Eroica
Poland 1957 sd b/w 8

PRODUCTION
p.c – Kadr Film Unit. p – Stanislaw Adler. d – Andrzej Munk. sc – Jerzy Stefan Stawinski. ph – Jerzy Wojcik. ed – Jadwiga Zaicek, Miroslawa Garlicka. a.d – Jan Grandys. m – Jan Krenz.

LEADING PLAYERS
Edward Dziewenski (Dzidzius), Tadensy Lomnicki (Zawistowski), Jozef Kostecki (Zak).

SYNOPSIS
The film consists of two stories, separate in themselves but complementary in theme. Part I: *Scherzo alla Polacca*. During the Warsaw uprising in September 1944, Dzidzius, a disenchanted volunteer, leaves his patrol and returns to his wife, whom he finds entertaining a Hungarian officer. Hungary offers to help the insurgents, and against his will Dzidzius crosses the German lines with messages for his superiors. He arrives safely, but by chance rather than through the exercise of caution. His superiors refuse offer of help from Hungary. Back with his wife, Dzidzius finds he prefers the discomforts of the Resistance to her company, and leaves to rejoin his patrol. Part II: *Ostinato lugubre*. Two arrivals at a German prisoner-of-war camp for Polish resistance fighters find that only one man – Zawistowski – has ever escaped, but that his achievement has supported the officers' morale ever since. Zak, a highly-strung prisoner, is particularly inspired by Zawistowski's escape. In fact, Zawistowski has not escaped at all, and lies hidden in the roof.

Zak attempts to escape from the prisoner-of-war camp but his rather feeble attempt is foiled by some passing peasant women. The other officers admire his attempt but Zak is scornful of them and refuses the award for attempted escapes. He retreats into his specially-created hideaway.

Later, Zak commits an extravagantly dramatic suicide. Zawistowski also dies, and his body is smuggled from the camp in an old boiler to uphold the morale of the prisoners.

Eva (Eve)
France/Italy 1962 sd b/w 17

PRODUCTION
p.c – Paris Film (Paris)/Interopa Film (Rome). p – Robert and Raymond Hakim. d – Joseph Losey. sc – Hugo Butler, Evan Jones, from the novel by James Hadley Chase. ph – Gianni Di Venanzo. ed – Reginald Beck, Franca Silvi. a.d – Richard Macdonald, Luigi Scaccianoce. m – Michel Legrand. cost – Pierre Cardin.

LEADING PLAYERS
Jeanne Moreau (Eve Olivier), Stanley Baker (Tyvian Jones), Virna Lisi (Francesca Ferrara).

SYNOPSIS
Tyvian Jones lives in Venice on the success of his first novel, newly-filmed and ostensibly based on his experiences as a Welsh pit boy. In fact, he was never a miner, and the book was written by his brother, now dead. Tyvian has just announced his engagement to Francesca, a successful young screenwriter, when he meets Eve, a provocative Frenchwoman who openly equates love with money. She alternately tantalises and humiliates him, until he is obsessively in love with her. Eventually, she agrees to spend a weekend with him, provided that they stay in the most expensive hotel in Venice and he stakes her at the gambling tables.

Tyvian and Eve are together at the hotel. While he gets drunk, she meets future clients. They visit his villa, but do not go inside. Later, he admits to her that his brother wrote the novel. Eve demands payment for her services. When he has given her money she throws it back at him as insufficient, saying 'You need it worse than I do'.

Tyvian returns to Francesca and marries her. On their honeymoon, Eve telephones and Tyvian cannot resist seeing her again. Francesca finds them together, and commits suicide. After the funeral Tyvian goes to Eve's flat with murderous intent, but ends up begging her to take him back. She drives him out with a whip. Two years later Tyvian is still in Venice, earning a seedy living as a guide to wealthy tourists. He sees Eve planning a cruise with her latest admirer, and begs her to see him when she returns. She ignores him.

Eve
(see Eva)

The Evil of Frankenstein
UK 1963 sd col 13

PRODUCTION
p.c – Hammer. p – Anthony Hinds. d – Freddie Francis. sc – John Elder (Anthony Hinds). ph – John Wilcox (Eastman Color). ed – James Needs. a.d – Don Mingaye. m – Don Banks.

LEADING PLAYERS
Peter Cushing (Baron Frankenstein), Sandor Eles (Hans), Kiwi Kingston (The Creature).

SYNOPSIS
Baron Frankenstein is denounced by a priest and forced to flee after patiently pursuing his life-creating experiments with corpses brought from a local body-snatcher.

He returns with Hans his assistant to his abandoned castle and laboratory which was smashed up several years previously by the local populace. Hans asks what happened, and Frankenstein explains the purpose of his experiment, and how a night of thunderstorms offered him all the energy he needed to 'create the spark of life'. In flashback we see the creature's body suspended horizontally, attached to wires along which energy hums and crackles. Eventually an eye blinks and Frankenstein sets the creature free, recording its behaviour. It falls down the laboratory steps, burns itself on a gas light, refuses cooked food, but eats raw meat. Next morning Frankenstein awakes to find the creature gone. A trail of bandages leads him to the creature who is gnawing on the last carcase of a ravaged flock of sheep. The villagers arrive with a policeman, who arrests Frankenstein. The creature is shot but escapes up onto some rocks where it falls out of sight. There the flashback ends.

Later Frankenstein and Hans discover the body of the creature preserved in a glacier. They thaw it out, take it to the castle, and try reviving it during an electrical storm; but the brain is damaged. Zoltan the Mesmerist is in the district, and Frankenstein persuades him to reactivate the Creature's brain through hypnosis. Zoltan however, arranges that the Creature will obey only his orders, and commands it to steal all the gold it can find, and punish the Burgomaster and Police Chief. The Creature murders them both. Frankenstein, furious at this misuse of his Creature, throws Zoltan out. Zoltan orders the Creature to kill Frankenstein, but the Creature revolts and kills Zoltan. Frankenstein is jailed but escapes. Eventually he and the Creature are trapped together inside the laboratory. It catches fire, and the whole castle explodes.

Eyes Without a Face (Les Yeux sans visage)
France/Italy 1959 sd b/w 11

PRODUCTION
p.c – Champs-Elysées Productions (Paris)/Lux (Rome). *p* – Jules Borkon. *d* – Georges Franju. *sc* – Jean Redon, from his novel. *ph* – Eugene Schuftan. *ed* – Gilbert Natot. *a.d* – Auguste Capelier. *m* – Maurice Jarre.

LEADING PLAYERS
Pierre Brasseur (*Professor Genéssier*), Alida Valli (*Louise*), Edith Scob (*Christiane*), François Guerin (*Jacques*).

SYNOPSIS
Professor Genéssier, a surgeon, feels himself to be responsible for the disfigurement of his daughter Christiane's face in a car accident. He attempts to repair the damage by grafting another young girl's face onto Christiane's. The operation fails and the girl dies. Her body is dumped in the river. Later, Genéssier identifies it as that of his daughter, and the body is buried.

After the funeral, Genéssier drives home past the clinic. Passing through the kennels where he keeps his dogs, he goes to see Christiane. He finds that she knows about her supposed death and funeral. He argues that it is less risky this way, and urges her to get into the habit of wearing a mask. His assistant, Louise, brings her mask and tries to comfort her, saying how much she hopes that the Professor will succeed in restoring her face. Christiane accuses her father of having caused the accident and of trying to subordinate everything to his will. Later, she wanders through the

house, dials her former fiancé's number, and wanders on again.

Another girl is forcibly recruited, and her body disposed of after the operation. The new face soon starts to deteriorate, and yet another girl is brought in to be operated on. This one is really a police decoy, planted as a result of the suspicions of Christiane's ex-fiancé. When she is strapped to the operating table, Genéssier is urgently summoned to the hospital by Inspector Parot. Christiane, her mind unhinged, frees the decoy, stabs Louise with a scalpel, and releases her father's caged birds and dogs. On his return, the dogs kill Genéssier. Christiane walks into the night, the freed birds perching on her arms.

(NB There are no sub-titles on this print.)

A Face in the Crowd
USA 1957 sd b/w 17

PRODUCTION
p.c – Newtown. *p* – Elia Kazan. *d* – Elia Kazan. *sc* – Budd Schulberg, from his story *Your Arkansas Traveller*. *ph* – Harry Stradling, Gayne Rescher. *ed* – Gene Milford. *a.d* – Richard Sylbert, Paul Sylbert. *m* – Tom Glazer.

LEADING PLAYERS
Andy Griffith (*Lonesome Rhodes*), Patricia Neal (*Marcia Jeffries*), Anthony Franciosa (*Joey Kiely*), Walter Matthau (*Mel Miller*), Marshall Nielan (*Senator Fuller*).

SYNOPSIS
Marcia Jeffries, roving reporter for a small Arkansas radio station, discovers Lonesome Rhodes, a young down-and-out with a guitar and humorous homespun philosophy, in a gaol. She arranges for Rhodes to be given his own radio show; within weeks he is the station's main asset. He soon has a television show, and his power over his audience grows. Rhodes goes to New York with Marcia and his self-appointed agent, Joey Kiely and sends his sponsor's sales soaring. He becomes a national idol, with enormous influence over his public. Rhodes asks Marcia to marry him, but then suddenly marries a little majorette, part of his adoring public.

Rhodes is invited to coach Senator Fuller, a right-wing isolationist presidential candidate, in the art of projecting a good television personality. Having tasted political power, Rhodes promotes Fuller on a new television show called 'Lonesome Rhodes's Cracker Barrel' which is billed as 'the voice of grass-roots wisdom'. It is watched with anxiety by Marcia, and with disgust by Mel Miller, a writer who hopes to expose Rhodes.

Appalled by Rhodes's megalomaniacal dreams, Marcia destroys him by leaving the sound on one night at the end of his show so that his public learn of his contempt for their gullibility. Rhodes is left alone with his empty fantasies of power.

The Fall of the Romanov Dynasty
USSR 1927 st b/w 20

PRODUCTION
p.c – Sovkino and the Museum of the Revolution. *d* – Esfir Shub. *ed* – Esfir Shub.

SYNOPSIS
This film was constructed entirely from newsreel and archive material, including some footage from the Royal family's home movies. It opens by showing the role of priests, landowners and bourgeoisie who comprise the Duma – the supposed representatives of the people – and of the police in upholding the rule of the Romanovs during the Czarist period.

The luxurious indolence of the ruling class is shown by the Royal family's home movies of the Czar dancing a mazurka while on a sea-trip. This is contrasted with the work of peasants and industrial labourers. Nicholas II celebrates the 300th anniversary of the Romanov dynasty. International war-mongers, led by the European heads of state, perfect war technology which will pit the working class against itself in the name of nationalism.

War is declared and millions are slaughtered. A hard winter threatens starvation; unrest among the people grows. Soldiers join workers on strike. Revolutionary activity and a mutiny leads to the formation of the provisional government. Lenin's proclamations encourage workers to struggle against the provisional government's attempts to continue the war, and to persist in demanding peace and bread. Revolutionary activity continues against Kerensky's counter-revolutionary government and with the aim of gaining power for the Soviets and uniting soldiers, peasants and workers.

(NB Intertitles are in Russian but an English transcript is provided.)

Fanatic
UK 1965 sd col 18

PRODUCTION
p.c – Hammer/Seven Arts. *p* – Anthony Hinds. *d* – Silvio Narizzano. *sc* – Richard Matheson, from the novel *Nightmare* by Anne Blaisdell. *ph* – Arthur Ibbetson (Technicolor). *ed* – John Dunsford. *m* – Wilfred Josephs.

LEADING PLAYERS
Tallulah Bankhead (*Mrs. Trefoile*), Stefanie Powers (*Patricia*), Peter Vaughan (*Harry*), Yootha Joyce (*Anna*), Donald Sutherland (*Joseph*).

SYNOPSIS
Patricia Carroll, arriving from America to marry Alan Glentower, decides to make a courtesy visit to Mrs. Trefoile, whose son, Stephen, now dead, was once her fiancé. She drives out to her house in the country, which is staffed by Anna the housekeeper, Anna's lecherous husband Harry and the imbecile general help, Joseph. Mrs. Tre-

foile greets Patricia warmly and clearly expects her for a long stay. Out of politeness Patricia agrees to stay for just one night. She is amused by the old woman's little quirks – the absence of mirrors, interminable religious services, orders to remove lipstick and bright red jumpers, the flavourless food and the blunt questions about her virginity.

Patricia and Mrs. Trefoile walk to the church, where Mrs. Trefoile prays for the souls of Stephen and Patricia. As they return Mrs. Trefoile makes it clear that she believes there should only be one marriage in a lifetime and that Patricia must be preserved unsullied if Stephen is not to be contaminated beyond redemption. Patricia tells the horrified Mrs. Trefoile that not only does she not consider herself to be Stephen's wife, but even had Stephen not committed suicide, she wouldn't have married him. Patricia runs back to the house and starts to pack, but finds herself locked in. She regards the situation as a joke until Mrs. Trefoile appears with a gun and orders Anna to drag Patricia up to a remote attic room. The following morning Anna and Mrs. Trefoile appear and Anna starts to tear up Patricia's clothes. There is a struggle during which Patricia is stabbed in the shoulder with a pair of scissors. She staggers from the bathroom and sinks down among the shredded remnants of her clothes.

During the ensuing days Patricia is starved, roughly handled by Anna, and subjected to endless bible readings by Mrs. Trefoile, who hopes that Patricia will repent her sin of wanting to marry another man. Patricia makes several attempts to escape but all end in failure. Mrs. Trefoile discovers Harry with Patricia as she tries to seduce him in order to steal back her car keys, and murders him in the cellar. Alan, meanwhile, arrives in time to prevent Mrs. Trefoile sacrificing Patricia in front of the portrait of her son. As they leave to call the police, Anna discovers Harry's body and stabs Mrs. Trefoile in front of Stephen's portrait.

The Far Country
USA 1954 sd col 20

PRODUCTION
p.c – Universal-International. *p* – Aaron Rosenberg. *d* – Anthony Mann. *sc* – Borden Chase, from the novel by Ernest Haycox. *ph* – William Daniels (Technicolor). *ed* – Russell Schoengarth. *a.d* – Bernard Herzbrun, Alex Golitzen. *m* – Joseph Gershenson. *cost* – Jay Morley Jr.

LEADING PLAYERS
James Stewart (*Jeff Webster*), Ruth Roman (*Ronda Castle*), Corrine Calvet (*Renée Vallon*), Walter Brennan (*Ben Tatem*), John McIntyre (*Mr. Gannon*), Jay C. Flippen (*Rube*), Henry Morgan (*Ketchum*).

SYNOPSIS
After herding cattle from Wyoming, Jeff Webster and his partner Ben Tatem arrive in Seattle; the Sheriff tries to arrest Jeff for a murder he did not commit. On board a ship to Skagway, Jeff takes refuge in a cabin occupied by Ronda Castle, a gambling-saloon owner. In Skagway he falls foul of Gannon, the town boss, who confiscates his herd. Ronda hires Jeff to take some goods into Dawson, where she is establishing another saloon. During the night Jeff rides back into Skagway and reclaims his herd; he is followed from Skagway by Renée Vallon, who warns him that Gannon is determined to get him.

In Dawson, one of Gannon's henchmen murders a prospector. Rube, the Marshall, tries to arrest him, but Jeff intervenes in order to prevent more killing. Humiliated, Rube hands in his badge. Jeff and Ben sell the herd and buy a goldmining stake. As they are leaving Dawson, they are attacked by Gannon's men. Jeff is seriously wounded; Ben is killed. While Jeff is being nursed back to health by Ronda, Gannon so terrorises the rest of the prospectors that they decide to move on, abandoning everything to Gannon. Jeff seeks a show-down with Gannon and kills him and his gang in a gunfight. He decides to stay on in Dawson and try to establish law and order.

Farewell, My Lovely
USA 1944 sd b/w 10

PRODUCTION
p.c – RKO Radio. *p* – Adrian Scott. *d* – Edward Dmytryk. *sc* – John Paxton, from the novel by Raymond Chandler. *ph* – Harry J. Wilde. *ed* – Joseph Noriega. *a.d* – Albert S. D'Agostino and Carroll Clark. *m* – Roy Webb.

LEADING PLAYERS
Dick Powell (*Phillip Marlowe*), Claire Trevor (*Mrs. Grayle*), Anne Shirley (*Anne Grayle*), Otto Kruger (*Jules Amthor*), Mike Mazurki (*Moose Malloy*).

SYNOPSIS
Phillip Marlowe is relating to the police how he became involved in the Moose Malloy affair. He tells how Moose, a tough, slow-witted, ex-convict, appeared in his office late one evening asking him to trace Velma, a girl he last saw 8 years before. He takes Marlowe to a seedy bar where Velma once worked, but no-one there will reveal her present whereabouts. Marlowe visits the widow of the former owner of the bar, who tries to conceal a photo of Velma. Marlowe obtains the photo and leaves. Looking back through the door he sees the woman making a phone call.

Marlowe is engaged by another man, Marriott, to accompany him to a lonely spot, where Marriott is to buy back from some crooks a jade necklace stolen from a Mrs. Grayle. When they reach the spot, Marriott is murdered and Marlowe knocked unconscious. Through Mrs.

Grayle, who is attracted to him, Marlowe gets on the track of Jules Amthor, but is kidnapped, beaten and taken to a 'rest home'. He escapes and continues his investigations aided by Ann, Mrs. Grayle's stepdaughter. Amthor is later found dead, murdered, it is later revealed, by Moose. It also transpires that Mrs. Grayle, who is in fact Velma, killed Marriott. In a gunbattle she is shot by her husband, who then kills Moose.

Farrebique
France 1947 sd b/w 10

PRODUCTION
p.c – L'Ecran Français/Les Films Etienne Lallier. *p* – Jacques Girard. *d* – Georges Rouquier. *sc* – Georges Rouquir, from an idea by C. Blanchard. *ph* – André A. Danton. *ed* – Madeleine Gug, Jacqueline Jacoupy. *m* – Henri Sauguet.

SYNOPSIS
Farrebique is the name of a family farm situated in an isolated area of Central France. It is run by a hard-working peasant family who do most of the work on the farm themselves, and who still largely observe traditional customs and ways of dressing. The family eat soup one autumn morning and discuss the necessity of repairs to the farmhouse.

They leave the dinner table to go about their various tasks of baking bread, ploughing and sowing. That evening the cattle are fed and milked while the children do their homework.

Winter, spring and summer follow. The old man takes the eldest son and heir to the farm to task for not making improvements, but eventually electricity is installed with the help of a neighbour. The younger son who is hardworking and tends to be the innovator in the family breaks his leg which puts a stop to the building plans. Later, the old man dies and the oldest son takes over Farrebique. He pays off the younger son who is now free to leave the farm and marry.

Fear Eats the Soul
West Germany 1973 sd col 10

PRODUCTION
p.c – Tango Film. *p* – Christian Hohoff. *d* – Rainer Werner Fassbinder. *sc* – Rainer Werner Fassbinder. *ph* – Jürgen Jürges. *ed* – Thea Eymèsz.

LEADING PLAYERS
Brigitte Mira (*Emmi Kurowski*), El Hedi Ben Salem (*Ali*), Barbara Valentin (*Barbara*), Irm Hermann (*Krista*), Rainer Werner Fassbinder (*Eugen*).

SYNOPSIS
Emmi, a 60-year-old cleaner, takes shelter from the rain in a bar frequented by Moroccan immigrant workers. As a dare, Ali, one of the young Moroccans asks Emmi to dance and then offers to see her home. Emmi invites him in for coffee; he

stays the night and later moves in with her. The landlord's son calls after reports from the neighbours about Ali's presence in the flats. In order to avoid an unpleasant scene Emmi tells him that she and Ali are to be married shortly. Gruber departs appeased and when Emmi tells Ali what she has said, he agrees that it's a good idea. When Emmi visits her daughter Krista and her husband to tell them the news they react with disbelief.

Emmi and Ali celebrate with a few friends in the Moroccan bar, while Barbara and another bar-hostess look on, predicting the failure of the marriage. After the wedding ceremony Emmi phones Krista and arranges for all the family to come over on the following Saturday. Emmi and Ali have an uncomfortable meal in an expensive restaurant. At the family gathering Emmi announces her marriage and presents Ali. The news is received in shocked silence until one of the sons kicks in the television and the family hurriedly departs. Later, when Emmi sends Ali to buy some margarine the local grocer deliberately misunderstands him. Emmi has a fierce argument with the shopkeeper, who orders her out of his shop.

The social pressures increase until Emmi eventually breaks down and decides to leave Munich and take a holiday with Ali. On their return, the situation has drastically altered. Emmi is once again needed – her son needs her to look after his children so that his wife can go back to work, a neighbour needs some of her cellar space, the grocer needs her custom. Her workmates draw her back into their circle when they close ranks against a new immigrant worker. Emmi begins to treat Ali as an object. In desperation Ali turns to Barbara, the hostess in the bar and Ali moves out of Emmi's flat despite her pleas. Emmi visits him in the bar and they dance together again. Ali suddenly collapses in agony. In hospital, the doctor tells Emmi that his illness is endemic to immigrant workers and his case is fairly hopeless.

La Femme infidèle
France/Italy 1968 sd col 10

PRODUCTION
p.c – Les Films la Boétie (Paris)/Cinegai (Rome). *p* – André Genovès. *d* – Claude Chabrol. *sc* – Claude Chabrol. *ph* – Jean Rabier (Eastman Color). *ed* – Jacques Gaillard. *a.d* – Guy Littaye. *m* – Pierre Jansen.

LEADING PLAYERS
Stéphane Audran (*Hélène Desvallées*), Michel Bouquet (*Charles Desvallées*), Maurice Ronet (*Victor Pegala*), Serge Bento (*Bignon*).

SYNOPSIS
*Charles, Hélène and their young son Michel live just outside Paris in a luxurious mansion. They are shown together, an apparently happy family. After Michel has gone to bed, Charles and Hélène have din-*ner, watch television, and then go to bed themselves. The following day Charles drops Hélène off in Paris.*

A general change in Hélène and her frequent visits to Paris lead Charles to suspect that she has a lover. He hires a private detective, Bignon, to confirm his suspicions. Bignon reports that Hélène is having an affair with a writer, Victor Pegala. One afternoon, Charles calls on Victor, and pretends to be a broad-minded husband curious to see his wife's latest conquest. Charles cannot maintain the façade however, and in a violent fit of jealousy he murders Victor. He meticulously cleans up the flat and dumps the body in a stagnant pond. When the police call on Hélène in the course of their investigations into Victor's disappearance, having found her name and address in an address book, she feigns indifference. Later she finds evidence that implicates Charles in her lover's murder. She burns it. A renewed tenderness grows up between the couple, as the police persistently continue their research.

Une Femme mariée
France 1964 sd b/w 13

PRODUCTION
p.c – Anouchka Films/Orsay Films. *d* – Jean-Luc Godard. *sc* – Jean-Luc Godard. *ph* – Raoul Coutard. *ed* – Agnès Guillemot, Françoise Collin. *m* – Beethoven, Claude Nougaro.

LEADING PLAYERS
Macha Méril (*Charlotte*), Bernard Noël (*Robert*), Philippe Leroy (*Pierre*), Roger Leenhardt (*Himself*), Rita Maiden (*Madame Céline*).

SYNOPSIS
Charlotte pays her daily visit to her actor lover Robert. She promises that she will make up her mind about leaving her husband, then goes by a roundabout route by car and taxi before picking up her schoolboy son, Nicholas. She takes Nicholas to the private airfield where her husband, Pierre has just flown in from Germany with Roger Leenhardt. They all go home for dinner; Pierre makes love to Charlotte. Next day Charlotte phones her doctor, who confirms that she is pregnant. Robert rings to arrange their afternoon meeting at Orly airport cinema. He tells her that he is due to start touring the provinces. Charlotte listens to her maid, Madame Céline, talk about sex, then visits a swimming pool and hears two young girls discuss love. She goes to see her doctor, admits that she doesn't know whether Robert or Pierre is the father of the baby, and asks for advice.

She takes a taxi to the airport, and meets Robert in the cinema as arranged. They go to a hotel and make love. Robert talks about acting and love. Charlotte explains why she cannot reach a decision about leaving Pierre. Robert declares that in that case the affair is over; Charlotte appears to agree.*

Le Feu follet
France/Italy 1963 sd b/w 12

PRODUCTION
p.c – Nouvelles Editions de Films/Arco Film. *d* – Louis Malle. *sc* – Louis Malle, from the novel by Pierre Drieu la Rochelle. *ph* – Ghislain Cloquet. *ed* – Suzanne Baron. *a.d* – Bernard Evein. *m* – Erik Satie.

LEADING PLAYERS
Maurice Ronet (*Alain Leroy*), Léna Skerla (*Lydia*), Yvonne Clech (*Madamoiselle Farnoux*), Hubert Deschamps (*d'Averseau*).

SYNOPSIS
Alain, a thirtyish playboy, spends the night with Lydia, a friend of his estranged American wife. Next morning, she drives him back to the private clinic where he is undergoing a cure for alcoholism.

He has lunch at the clinic and is chided by another patient for his night's absence. Alain leaves an abstract discussion involving some patients. From a balcony he observes some scenes of everyday life outside the clinic: a woman shakes dishclothes, a car drives into the hospital. Alain goes back inside, and watches a billiard game before returning to the secure retreat of his room. He wanders around looking at himself in the mirror, observing the photographs on the walls, clipping a piece about a dead girl from a newspaper, chain-smoking, wearing funny hats, scribbling in a meaningless diary, and taking a revolver from a drawer. Finally his attention is again drawn to what is going on outside, and from his window he observes a girl with a violin case walking along the sunlit street.

Alain's doctor urges a reunion with his wife and more 'positive living'. He goes to Paris for the day, half-heartedly hoping that by reviving his past he might find a reason for staying alive, but his former friends disappoint him. Dubourg has retreated into Egyptology and a respectable family life; Jeanne is lost in drugs; Solange is now a society hostess, involved in bitchy dinner parties and promiscuous affairs. Alain's disgust starts him drinking again. After a bout of drunken self-analysis, he is taken back to the clinic by one of Solange's guests. Next morning Solange calls to invite him to lunch. Alain cables his wife, packs his belongings, finishes the book he is reading, and shoots himself.

La Fiancée du pirate
France 1969 sd col 20

PRODUCTION
p.c – Cythère Films. *p* – Claude Makovski. *d* – Nelly Kaplan. *sc* – Nelly Kaplan, Claude Makovski. *ph* – Jean Badal (Technicolor). *ed* – Gerard

Pollicand, Nelly Kaplan, Noëlle Boisson, Suzanne Lang-Willar. *a.d* – Michel Landi, Patrick Lafarge, Jean-Claude Landi. *m* – Georges Moustaki.

LEADING PLAYERS
Bernadette Lafont (*Marie*), Georges Géret (*Gaston Duvalier*), Michel Constantin (*André*), Julien Guiomar (*Le Duc*), Francis Lax (*Emile*), Claire Maurier (*Irène*).

SYNOPSIS
Marie, the village drudge, is exploited by everyone. When her mother is killed by a hit-and-run driver, Marie inherits a small shack in the woods outside the village, and a few hundred francs. She uses the money to buy food, wine and cigarettes, to make up her face for the first time, and to hold a wake.

After the wake, Marie organises the village men, by now very drunk, to help her bury her mother. She carefully measures out the spot for the grave and after much drunken ribaldry the body is eventually buried. The priest arrives anxious because no proper Christian burial has been given, but is ignored by Marie and leaves. The following morning Marie appears at the farm where she is employed and refuses to work for Irène, her employer. At the village shop the men appear one by one to order drinks to relieve their hangovers. It is suggested that Marie has put a spell on them. The wife of one of the farm workers appears in tears, saying that Marie has seduced her husband. The villagers chase through the village to Marie's hut. Marie arrives before them and bolts the door, but her pet goat is locked outside and in frustration the villagers shoot the animal. (Ext 1a, 10 mins.)

Marie starts to make her living as the village prostitute. She realises that the services she can offer are in scarce supply and is able therefore to continually put up her price. She uses the money to buy a vast range of consumer goods.

Finally, Marie takes all the things she has bought and decorates the trees outside her home with them. She sets fire to her shack, watches it burn and then goes to the church where the villagers are attending mass. Marie places her tape-recorder on a high and inaccessible ledge at the back of the church and leaves it to play back the incriminating conversations she had with the local men who were her clients. The villagers run to Marie's hut and, not finding her, destroy everything which Marie has left behind. Meanwhile, Marie walks away from the village. (Ext 1b, 10 mins.)

Fires Were Started (I Was a Fireman)
UK 1943 sd b/w 6
(w. **Song of Ceylon**)

PRODUCTION
p.c – Crown Film Unit. *p* – Ian Dalrymple. *d* – Humphrey Jennings. *sc* – Humphrey Jennings. *ph* – C. Pennington-Richards. *ed* – Stewart McAllister. *a.d* – Edward Carrick. *m* – William Alwyn.

LEADING PLAYERS
Commanding Officer George Gravett (*Sub-Officer Dykes*), Fireman Philip W. Dickson (*Walters*), Fireman Fred Griffiths (*Johnny Daniels*), Fireman Johnny Houghton (*Rumbold*), Fireman William Sansom (*Barrett*).

SYNOPSIS
During the heavy air-raids in 1940 a dockside Auxiliary Fire Service sub-station spends the day servicing its equipment. It is expected that the full moon will bring night raiders.

In the control room the operators are ready and waiting. The firemen stand around in the rest room or play billiards. A newcomer plays 'One Man went to Mow' on the piano and all the men join in, making each chorus appropriate to the next man to come into the room. Their singing is interrupted by the siren.

The firemen take two trailer pumps to deal with a blaze at a warehouse. The fire turns out to be serious, so Local Control, then District Control and finally, Brigade Headquarters are all called on for more apparatus. A bomb cuts the water-mains, and water has to be pumped from the river. Two firemen are rescued from the roof of the warehouse by extension ladder, but a third is killed when the roof collapses. The fire is eventually brought under control, and an ammunition ship which it had threatened is able to sail safely from the dock.

A Fool There Was
USA 1914 st b/w 10

PRODUCTION
p.c – The Box-Office Attractions Company. *p* – William Fox. *d* – Frank Powell. *sc* – Frank Powell, from the play by Porter Emerson Browne and a poem by Rudyard Kipling.

LEADING PLAYERS
Theda Bara (*The Vamp*), Edward Jose (*Schulyer, The Husband*), Mabel Frenyar (*The Wife*).

SYNOPSIS
A seductive vamp reduces Schulyer, a middle-aged man, to helpless drunkenness. Scandals are caused, his business declines and his wife leaves him.

The vamp has left Schulyer. He staggers drunkenly around in his darkened house in a state of abject misery, opening yet more bottles of alcohol. His secretary comes in, draws the curtains, and seeing the state of his employer, resigns. Schulyer replies that rats always leave a sinking ship. Meanwhile the vamp entertains a new, younger lover, drinks and gambles with friends. Schulyer's secretary goes to see his abandoned wife who promises to go to him. The vamp hears about this and arrives at Schulyer's house soon after his wife. He is overcome with passion and clings drunkenly to her. His wife leaves in disgust. At a party that night Schulyer rants and rages as the vamp dances with her other lovers. The wife has a change of heart after putting her daughter to bed, and resolves to take their daughter to see Schulyer in one last attempt to change his mind. At first this seems successful, but then the vamp comes downstairs in a nightgown with her hair loose. Yet again the husband fawns over her, and spurns his sad family in favour of the vamp.

Foolish Wives
USA 1922 st b/w 11

PRODUCTION
p.c – Universal Super Jewel. *p* – Carl Laemmle. *d* – Erich von Stroheim. *sc* – Erich von Stroheim. *ph* – Ben Reynolds, William Daniels. *ed* – Erich von Stroheim, Arthur D. Ripley. *a.d* – E. E. Sheeley, Richard Day. *m* – (Original music – Sigmund Romberg). *cost* – Western Costuming Co., Richard Day, Erich von Stroheim.

LEADING PLAYERS
Erich von Stroheim (*'Prince' Sergei Karamazin*), Dale Fuller (*Maruschka, The Maid*), Cesare Gravina (*The Artist*), Malvina Polo (*The Artist's Daughter*).

SYNOPSIS
Three adventurers – two Russian 'Princesses' and their cousin the 'Prince' – live on their wits in a luxurious villa overlooking the sea in Monte Carlo during the First World War. The Prince survives by seducing, then blackmailing, rich foolish wives.

While the Prince is at breakfast his maid agitatedly asks when he is going to fulfil his promise to marry her. He evades giving her a direct answer and manages to calm her down. He goes to the slums to see a poor Italian artist who supplies him with counterfeit banknotes. The Prince sees the artist's daughter, who is beautiful but simple-minded and sickly.

A new American ambassador comes to Monte Carlo with his pretty young wife. The Prince plans to seduce her and use her to put the forged banknotes into circulation. Although she is not totally indifferent to his attentions his attempts fail. He comes to love her and writes her a note threatening suicide. In answer she comes to his villa. The Prince's maid becomes jealous and sets the house on fire, but they are rescued just in time. The husband learns what has happened, confronts the Prince in the gaming room and demands a duel. On the night it is to take place the Prince arranges to see the artist's daughter, who has aroused his sexual desires. The noises awakens the artist, who kills the Prince and throws the body into a sewer. Meanwhile, the Princesses are arrested by the police.

Foreign Correspondent
USA 1940 sd b/w 8

PRODUCTION
p.c – Walter Wanger Productions. *p* –
Walter Wanger. *d* – Alfred Hitchcock.
sc – Charles Bennett, Joan Harrison. *ph* –
Rudolph Maté. *ed* – Otho Lovering,
Dorothy Spencer. *a.d* – William Cameron
Menzies, Alexander Golitzen. *m* – Alfred
Newman.

LEADING PLAYERS
Joel McCrea (*Johnnie Jones/Huntley
Haverstock*), Laraine Day (*Carol Fisher*),
Herbert Marshall (*Stephen Fisher*),
George Sanders (*Herbert Folliott*), Albert
Basserman (*Van Meer*).

SYNOPSIS
Just prior to World War II, Johnnie Jones,
a hard-headed tough crime reporter works
for the *New York Globe*.

*He is assigned by his editor to investi-
gate the chances of an outbreak of war in
Europe, and goes to Amsterdam with the
false identity of Huntley Haverstock. He
sets about reporting the Amsterdam Peace
Conference and meets Van Meer, a Dutch
diplomat who has memorised a secret
clause in an Allied Treaty with his country.
Van Meer appears to be killed by an assassin posing as a photographer. Jones chases
after him in a taxi which contains Carol
Fisher, the daughter of the head of a pacifist group and Folliott, an English reporter.
The car they are following suddenly seems
to vanish in the landscape. Jones notices
that the arms of a windmill are turning
against the wind and goes to investigate
while the others call the police. He finds
the car inside the windmill, but at that
moment a plane lands outside.*

Jones is nearly trapped inside the windmill but manages to escape. Jones realises
that Van Meer has been kidnapped rather
than killed and that Carol's father is actually the nazi who masterminded the plot.
Jones returns to London and narrowly
avoids being pushed off Westminster
Cathedral. When war is declared, Stephen
Fisher and Carol – who is disillusioned
with her romance with Jones – take the last
plane from London to America. Jones is
also aboard. The plane is mistaken by a
German ship and attacked. Fisher saves
Carol by keeping a wing of the plane
afloat, but sacrifices his own life doing this,
knowing that he would have been arrested
in America. They are rescued by an American ship, but the neutral captain insists
that Jones cannot wire his story to the
Globe. Carol eventually succeeds in making a personal call, however. She places the
telephone receiver behind her back as she
and Jones talk to the captain and they
thereby manage to explain their exploits
to Jones's editor. On their arrival in New
York Jones marries Carol and becomes
the paper's top European foreign correspondent.

Fort Apache
USA 1948 sd b/w 20

PRODUCTION
p.c – Argosy Pictures/RKO Radio. *p* –
John Ford, Merian C. Cooper. *d* – John
Ford. *sc* – Frank Nugent, from the story
Massacre by James Warner Bellah. *ph* –
Archie J. Stout. *ed* – Jack Murray. *a.d* –
James Basevi. *m* – Richard Hageman.
cost – Michael Myers, Ann Peck.

LEADING PLAYERS
Henry Fonda (*Lieutenant Colonel Owen
Thursday*), John Wayne (*Captain Kirby
York*), Shirley Temple (*Philadelphia
Thursday*), John Agar (*Lieutenant
Michael O'Rourke*), Ward Bond
(*Sergeant Major O'Rourke*), George
O'Brien (*Captain Sam Collingwood*),
Miguel Inclan (*Cochise*).

SYNOPSIS
Lieutenant Colonel Owen Thursday is sent
to take command of Fort Apache, which
is isolated in the middle of Arizona. He is
bitter because he has been demoted from
his Civil War rank of General. Thursday
has little knowledge of Indian warfare, and
stubbornly refuses to take advice from
veteran Indian fighters like Captain York
and Captain Collingwood. Thursday
insists on maintaining strict discipline,
thereby antagonising the troops; he also
tries to prevent the friendship between his
daughter, Philadelphia, and Lieutenant
O'Rourke, the son of a non-commissioned
officer. An ambitious man, he thinks he
can enhance his reputation by making a
deal with the Apache Indians who, resent-
ing the corrupt tactics of the local agent,
have left the settlement. Captain York is
sent to arrange a meeting between
Thursday and Cochise, the Apache leader.

*At dawn the troops set out from Fort
Apache for the meeting with Cochise.
Cochise is prepared to make honourable
peace terms, but Thursday finds this
demeaning and breaks off the meeting. He
arrogantly orders Cochise to go back to the
reservation or take the consequences. York
questions Thursday's battle strategies, but
is accused of cowardice and sent to guard
the supply wagons. The remaining troops
charge into the valley and are massacred.
Only York and his small detachment
survive.*

The 400 Blows
(*see* Les Quatre cents coups)

Frankenstein
USA 1931 sd b/w 7

PRODUCTION
p.c – Universal. *p* – Carl Laemmle Jr. *d* –
James Whale. *sc* – Garrett Fort, Francis
Edward Faragoh, Robert Florey, from the
play by Peggy Webling, adapted from the
novel by Mary Shelley. *ph* – Arthur
Edeson. *ed* – Clarence Kolster. *a.d* –
Charles D. Hall.

LEADING PLAYERS
Boris Karloff (*The Monster*), Colin Clive
(*Dr. Frankenstein*), Edward Van Sloan
(*Professor Waldman*), Dwight Frye
(*Fritz*).

SYNOPSIS
Dr. Frankenstein is obsessed with the idea
of creating life in his laboratory by means
of a revolutionary new ray. He steals
bodies from graves, robs the hangman's
gibbet, and gradually assembles a body of
giant proportions. His hunchback henchman steals a preserved abnormal brain
from a medical school. During a thunderstorm the Creature comes to life.

*Three days later, Frankenstein tells a
colleague, Professor Waldman, that they
must have patience and wait to see how
the Creature develops. The Professor tells
him that the brain he used in the Creature
was that of a criminal. The Creature comes
in and for the first time Frankenstein lets
the daylight fall on him. He stretches out
his hand towards it longingly, but remains
quiet when the window is closed. When a
servant carrying a flaming torch enters the
Creature becomes frantic and has to be
shut up in a dungeon. Frankenstein lures
him out to give him a tranquilising injection, and is half-strangled in the process.
The Creature collapses.*

The Creature becomes a monster, more
animal than human, and escapes into the
countryside. Frankenstein's health begins
to suffer, much to the consternation of his
fiancée Elizabeth. Frankenstein and
Elizabeth marry, but the celebrations are
interrupted by the news that the Monster
has murdered Waldman and drowned a
child. Next he makes a vicious attack on
Elizabeth. The local populace scour the
countryside with torches and dogs looking
for the Monster. Frankenstein is captured
by the Monster and taken to an old mill.
They struggle and Frankenstein is thrown
from the roof to the crowds below. The
people then set fire to the mill. The Monster is trapped and burnt alive. Frankenstein is nursed back to health by his wife
and the past is forgotten.

French Can-Can
France/Italy 1955 sd col 16

PRODUCTION
p.c – Franco London Film–Jolly Film. *p* –
Louis Wipf. *d* – Jean Renoir. *sc* – André-
Paul Antoine, Jean Renoir. *ph* – Michel
Kelber (Technicolor). *ed* – Boris Lewyn.
a.d – Max Douy. *m* – George Van Parys.
choreo – G. Grandjean.

LEADING PLAYERS
Jean Gabin (*Danglard*), Françoise Arnoul
(*Nini*), Maria Felix (*La Belle Abbesse*),
Jean-Roger Caussimon (*Baron Walter*).

SYNOPSIS
*An exotic entertainer, La Belle Abbesse, is
dancing in a fashionable nightclub in Paris
in the 1880s. Backstage Danglard, the
club's impresario and her lover, is encour-*

aging a whistler who is about to make his debut. Her act over, La Belle Abbesse persuades Danglard and some of her friends including Baron Walter, Danglard's financial backer, to go to a dance hall called The White Queen in a poorer part of Paris. Danglard discovers Nini, a laundry girl and talented amateur dancer, and arouses the jealousy of Baron Walter by the way he dances with La Belle Abbesse. Next morning, Danglard awakes to find his creditors calling for him. Out of pique, Baron Walter has refused to meet the debts he has acquired in the running of the nightclub.

Later the baron relents and even agrees to finance the building of a new music-hall, the Moulin Rouge, where Nini will star. La Belle Abbesse's jealousy later causes him to withdraw his support, but a Balkan prince who is desperately in love with Nini offers his help. Nini, now happily in love with Danglard, rehearses for the opening, but on the first night she discovers that he is now interested in a newer discovery, a singer. She refuses to go on, but Danglard argues that she has to choose between the theatre and love as she is unlikely to achieve happiness in both. Nini dances the first Can-Can.

Frenzy
Sweden 1944 sd b/w 15

PRODUCTION
p.c – Aktiebolagel Svenskfilmindustri. p Carl Anders Dymling. d – Alf Sjöberg. sc – Ingmar Bergman. ph – Martin Bodin. ed – Oscar Rosander. a.d – Arne Akermark. m – Hilding Rosenberg.

LEADING PLAYERS
Stig Jarrel (Caligula), Alf Kjellin (Jan-Erik Widgren), Mai Zetterling (Bertha), Olof Winnderstran (The Headmaster), Costa Cederlund (Pippi), Hugo Bjorne (The Doctor).

SYNOPSIS
Early one morning at a Swedish high school a prowling teacher catches a boy who is late, but another teacher, himself a latecomer, has a kind word for him. During school assembly the Latin master, nicknamed Caligula, appears an evil figure and in class he seizes sadistically on any weakness displayed. The boys react volubly on his departure. Caligula goes to a tobacconist's shop nearby and flirts with Bertha, the assistant.

An older pupil, Jan-Erik Widgren, sees Bertha drunk in the street and takes her home. She is frightened of an unknown man and prevails on him to stay with her. His studies suffer through their relationship, and Caligula's hateful behaviour drives him to the brink of despair. One day when he goes to see Bertha he finds her drunk. She says the man has visited her again, forced her to drink and tormented her with horrifying stories. Jan-Erik is disgusted and leaves her, but later realises that Bertha's tormentor is his teacher. On Caligula's next visit she has a heart attack. Shortly afterwards Jan-Erik arrives and notifies the police. Caligula is arrested but he is released when the doctor diagnoses heart failure. He tells the headmaster that he only visited the girl in order to induce her to leave Jan-Erik alone, and that she died of her consequent excitement. Jan-Erik tells him to his face – in front of the headmaster – that he tortured Bertha to death. Jan-Erik is expelled from the school, and fleeing from the reproaches of his parents, moves into Bertha's room. The headmaster visits him there and says that he does not believe in Jan-Erik's guilt but that he cannot prevent his expulsion. Caligula comes too: a broken man, he confesses to Jan-Erik and says that his actions were not intentional. Jan-Erik leaves Caligula in Bertha's room.

Frenzy
UK 1972 sd col 15

PRODUCTION
p.c – Universal. p – Alfred Hitchcock. d – Alfred Hitchcock. sc – Anthony Shaffer, from the novel Goodbye Piccadilly, Farewell Leicester Square by Arthur La Bern. ph – Gil Taylor (Technicolor). ed – John Jympson. a.d – Robert Laing. m – Ron Goodwin. cost – Dulcie Midwinter.

LEADING PLAYERS
Jon Finch (Richard Blaney), Alec McCowen (Inspector Oxford), Barry Foster (Bob Rusk), Barbara Leigh-Hunt (Brenda Blaney), Anna Massey (Barbara Milligan), Vivien Merchant (Mrs. Oxford), Bernard Cribbens (Forsythe), Billie Whitelaw (Hetty Porter).

SYNOPSIS
London is being terrorised by a series of 'necktie murders'. Richard Blaney, his RAF career and marriage both over, works behind the bar in a Covent Garden pub but is dimissed after taking a free drink. He visits Brenda, his ex-wife, to tell her but refuses her offer of money. His friend, Bob Rusk, a wholesale fruitier, offers sympathy but later visits Brenda and strangles her. Blaney is immediately suspected by the police. He meets his girlfriend, Barbara, and they go to a Bayswater hotel. The police trace them, but the couple escape and are later spotted by Johnny Porter, an old RAF friend of Blaney's, who lets Blaney spend the night in his Hilton suite. Later that night Rusk meets Barbara, takes her to his flat and murders her.

Having concealed Barbara's body in a sack of potatoes, Rusk loads the sack onto a lorry and returns to his flat. There he discovers that his monogrammed lapel pin is missing. With horror he realises that Barbara must have torn it off during the struggle. Rusk returns to the lorry to search for the pin, but while he is looking the lorry starts its journey. He eventually finds Barbara's body, the missing pin clutched in her hand. In order to release it he has to break her fingers. The lorry pulls in at a café and Rusk gets off. The lorry continues its journey and Barbara's body begins to fall out of the back. Police stop the lorry.

Blaney is arrested, tried, found guilty and sent to prison. He manages to get himself transferred to the prison hospital and escapes. He goes straight to Rusk's flat and there discovers the latest necktie victim. Inspector Oxford appears and finds Blaney, but Rusk returns dragging a large trunk. When he sees the two men he realises that he has been caught.

Freud (Freud – The Secret Passion)
USA 1962 sd b/w 10

PRODUCTION
p.c – Universal-International. p – Wolfgang Reinhardt. d – John Huston. sc – Charles Kaufman, Wolfgang Reinhardt, from a story by Charles Kaufman. ph – Douglas Slocombe. ed – Ralph Kemplen. a.d – Stephen B. Grimes. m – Jerry Goldsmith and Henk Badings.

LEADING PLAYERS
Montgomery Clift (Sigmund Freud), Susannah York (Cecily Koertner), Larry Parks (Dr. Joseph Breuer), Susan Kohner (Martha Freud).

SYNOPSIS
Doctor Sigmund Freud, a young neurologist in Vienna in 1885, is in conflict with his colleagues about the nature of hysteria. He goes to Paris to study under Professor Charcot who has demonstrated by hypnosis that some hysterical symptoms are mentally induced. Encouraged by Martha Bernays, whom he later marries, and by Dr. Joseph Breuer, Freud returns to Vienna and continues to use hypnosis to treat hysterical patients.

Freud and Breuer try to cure Cecily Koertner, a young woman who broke down completely after her father's death. By using hypnosis they make her relive the moments leading up to the time when she saw her father's corpse. At first she is not truthful, but Freud makes her repeat the incident, questioning her closely. Finally, she does tell the truth, and when she recovers from her hypnotic state her symptoms are temporarily relieved. Cecily feels a deep hatred of Freud however, and resents the knowledge of herself she now has to live with.

Freud also treats Carl von Schlosser, a youth who has made a homicidal attack on his father. Freud realises that the boy's hatred of his father springs from incestuous love of his mother. Horrified, he drops the case, but after the boy has died in an asylum Freud begins to understand a similar neurosis in himself. While trying to find a way into his own unconscious, Freud perseveres with Cecily using analysis rather than hypnosis. He uncovers Cecily's repressed desire for her father and finally cures her of her physical symptoms. He also traces the incident in his own childhood memories which forms the foundation of his feelings of guilt towards his father. Freud is now able to formulate his theory of sexuality in infancy and expounds it in a lecture. Most of the audience is hostile and not even Breuer is convinced, but Freud is more determined than ever to go on with his research.

Freud – The Secret Passion
(*see* Freud)

From Russia with Love
UK 1963 sd col 20

PRODUCTION
p.c – Eon Productions. *p* – Harry Saltzman, Albert R. Broccoli. *d* – Terence Young. *sc* – Richard Maibaum, Joanna Harwood, from the novel by Ian Fleming. *ph* – Ted Moore (Technicolor). *ed* – Peter Hunt. *a.d* – Syd Cain. *m* – John Barry. *lyrics* – Lionel Bart.

LEADING PLAYERS
Sean Connery (*James Bond*), Daniela Bianchi (*Tatiana Romanova*), Bernard Lee (*M*), Lois Maxwell (*Miss Moneypenny*), Lotte Lenya (*Rosa Klebb*), Robert Shaw (*Grant*).

SYNOPSIS
During the pre-credit sequence a man wearing a rubber mask of Bond's face is killed by an agent practising his skills. The titles which follow are superimposed on the body of a belly dancer. (Ext. 1a, 5 mins.)

SPECTRE, an international crime syndicate, has decided to get James Bond and the Lektor, a secret Russian coding machine, by using Tatiana Romanova, a patriotic Russian cipher clerk, as bait.

Bond jokes with Miss Moneypenny, secretary to the all-powerful M, at the headquarters of the British Secret Service. He hears about Tatiana's offer to defect with the Lektor from M and is given a briefcase of self-defence gadgets. (Ext. 1b, 4 mins.)

Bond arrives in Istanbul and makes contact with Kerim Bey, a local ally. (Ext. 1c, 1 min.)

Bond and Kerim make plans, and escape several attempts on their lives.

Whilst on a ferry-trip Bond tape-records Tatiana's description of the Lektor. She is more interested in talking about their relationship. The tape is played back to a gathering of experts at secret service headquarters. (Ext. 1d, 3 mins.)

Bond and Tatiana escape with the Lektor on the Orient Express but they have to fight off Grant, a SPECTRE agent sent to kill Bond and steal the Lektor.

They are pursued by a SPECTRE helicopter which Bond eventually manages to destroy. (Ext. 1e, 3 mins.)

In Venice Bond steals a boat. SPECTRE agents try to blast it out of a canal but once again Bond manages to escape.

Finally, Bond encounters Rosa Klebb, former head of the Russian Secret Service, but now the brains behind SPECTRE. Klebb tries to kill Bond with a poisoned

knife blade attached to her shoe, but she is shot by Tatiana. (Ext. 1f, 2 mins.)

Bond and Tatiana relax together on a Venetian canal. (Ext. 1g, 2 mins.)

Funny Face
USA 1956 sd col 20

PRODUCTION
p.c – Paramount. *p* – Roger Edens. *d* – Stanley Donen. *sc* – Leonard Gershe. *ph* – Ray June (VistaVision and Technicolor). *ed* – Frank Bracht. *a.d* – Hal Pereira, George W. Davis. *m* – George and Ira Gershwin. *lyrics* – George and Ira Gershwin. *choreo* – Eugene Loring and Fred Astaire. *cost* – Edith Head.

LEADING PLAYERS
Audrey Hepburn (*Jo Stockton*), Fred Astaire (*Dick Avery*), Kay Thompson (*Maggie Prescott*), Michel Auclair (*Emile Flostre*), Robert Flemyng (*Paul Duval*).

SYNOPSIS
Maggie Prescott, the editor of *Quality* magazine, wants a fashion photograph with an 'intellectual' setting. She and her staff invade a Greenwich Village bookshop and turn the place upside down getting their pictures despite resistance from Jo Stockton, a saleswoman. Afterwards, Dick Avery, the photographer, helps Jo clear up. She talks about her dream of going to Paris to meet Professor Flostre, the founding father of Empathicalism. Later, when Maggie is looking for a new model Dick remembers Jo. He persuades her to become a model as a means of reaching Paris. In Paris, Dick and Jo fall in love.

One day Jo fails to turn up for dress fitting with Paul Duval, the designer. Dick eventually finds her in a club expounding the philosophy of Empathicalism. (Ext. 1a, 5 mins.)

On the eve of the fashion show Jo and Dick finally meet Flostre, but Dick distrusts him and the two men quarrel.

Dick and Maggie are worried that Jo might not appear at the show and go to Flostre's salon disguised as Empathicalists. They find Jo there but again there is an argument. Dick hits Flostre, then leaves, saying he is going to return to New York. Jo is left to revive the unconscious Flostre. When he comes round Jo discovers that he is less interested in discussing Empathicalism than in having an amorous adventure. Jo hits him over the head with a statue. (Ext. 1b, 15 mins.)

Jo models the clothes at the show believing that Dick has returned to New York. He turns back at the airport, however, and is reunited with Jo.

(NB This extract is standard reduced from Scope.)

The Gay Divorcee
USA 1934 sd b/w 20

PRODUCTION
p.c – RKO Radio. *d* – Mark Sandrich.

sc – George Marion Jr., Dorothy Yost, Edward Kaufman, from the musical by Dwight Taylor. *ph* – David Abel. *ed* – Frank Sullivan. *m* – Cole Porter, Mack Gordon, Harry Revel, Con Conrad, Herb Magidson.

LEADING PLAYERS
Fred Astaire (*Guy Holden*), Ginger Rogers (*Mimi*), Alice Brady (*Aunt Hortense*), Edward Everett Horton (*Egbert*), Erik Rhodes (*Tonetti*), Eric Blore (*The Waiter*).

SYNOPSIS
Guy and Egbert watch dancers in a nightclub. When they realise that they have no money with them, Guy has to dance in order to prove that he is a famous professional and therefore creditworthy. Next day they sail for England. At the customs Guy meets and falls for Mimi, the niece of Hortense, an old flame of Egbert's. Mimi goes off with Hortense and Egbert, who is a lawyer, to arrange her divorce. Guy cannot forget Mimi.

Mimi is having dinner with her Aunt Hortense but runs off when Guy appears. He chases and catches up with her and they dance a romantic pas-de-deux to the song 'Night and Day'. (Ext. 1a, 6 mins.)

Later they argue and part again. Egbert arranges for himself, Mimi and Hortense to go to a Brighton Hotel, where a co-respondent will provide Mimi with grounds for divorce. Guy agrees to go along, not knowing that Mimi is to be there. Through a misunderstanding, Mimi thinks Guy is her co-respondent, but this is sorted out.

Guy decides to spend the night in Mimi's rooms in order to protect her from Tonetti, the real co-respondent. They hear 'The Continental' playing and sneak out and join the couples on the dance floor. The dance develops into a big production number. (Ext. 1b, 14 mins.)

Eventually there is a showdown with Mimi's husband, who at first says he does not intend to give her a divorce, but after evidence of his own two-timing is produced he agrees. Mimi and Guy dance over the tables.

The General Line (The Old and the New)
USSR 1929 st b/w 12

PRODUCTION
p.c – Sovkino. *d* – S. M. Eisenstein and G. V. Alexandrov. *sc* – S. M. Eisenstein and G. V. Alexandrov. *ph* – E. Tisse, V. Nilsen, V. Popov. *ed* – S. M. Eisenstein. *a.d* – V. Kovrigin, V. Rakhals.

LEADING PLAYERS
Marfa Lapkine (*Marfa*), Kostya Vasiliev (*Tractor Driver*), Vasya Buzenkov (*Young Komsomol*), Chukhmarev (*The Kulak*).

SYNOPSIS
Marfa, a peasant girl, lives in a typical village in Russia just after the Revolution. The people are backward, illiterate and

poor. She humbly begs the rich kulaks of the village to lend her a horse to plough her miserable plot of land, but they spurn her. She yokes her cow to the plough but it soon dies. A commissar is sent by the Soviet Government to organise a village co-operative, and Marfa, who has resolved that the terrible conditions shall not go on, appeals to the peasants to join the co-operative. At first they are suspicious and derisive.

A new mechanical milk separator arrives for the co-operative and the villagers assemble to see a demonstration. They watch, doubting each process, but are amazed when the separated cream pours from the machine. Co-op membership increases . (Ext. 1a, 6 mins.)

The village begins to prosper, but Marfa still has to fight against the few peasants who steal, the kulaks, and the local bureaucracy. Gradually, however, these problems are overcome.

It is harvest time and the peasants are cutting the wheat. Two men show off their strength, each trying to get ahead of the other, while the peasants watch and cheer. The wheat is cut easily with the aid of a mechanical reaper from the neighbouring village and the villagers applaud. (Ext. 1b, 6 mins.)

The old fences which divide the small plots of land are broken down by a tractor, and the co-operative is triumphant.

A Generation
Poland 1954 sd b/w 15

PRODUCTION
p.c – Film Polski. *p* – Ignacy Taub. *d* – Andrzej Wajda. *sc* – Bohdan Czeszko, from his novel. *ph* – Jerzy Lipman. *ed* – Czeslaw Raniszewski. *a.d* – Roman Mann. *m* – Andrzej Markowski. *cost* – Jerzy Szeski.

LEADING PLAYERS
Tadeusz Lomnicki (*Stach*), Urszula Modrzynska (*Dorota*), Ryszard Kotas (*Jacek*).

SYNOPSIS
In Warsaw in 1942 three teenage boys play a game with a knife, then graduate to a train game which results in one getting wounded, one lost, and one killed by a German sentry. Stach, the wounded boy, later gets employment as an apprentice in a woodwork shop. There he finds friends and encouragement, and also a cache of arms hidden by the Polish Resistance.

He asks about joining the Resistance and is taken to meet Dorota, the leader of the local group, at a church. They talk while a wedding is taking place. Later, Dorota explains the aims of the Resistance movement at a meeting of young people and they swear allegiance. Next day Jacek, a friend of Stach's, sees crowds staring at bodies hanged by the Germans. He is frightened and turns down Stach's offer of a place in the Fighting Youth. As Stach is driving a lumber truck into the yard he sees a group of people being taken to a concentration camp by Germans. He is warned against the German sentry at the gate. Stach is called into the sentry's office, accused of stealing, beaten, and thrown out on the verge of tears.

On the day of the Ghetto rising, the Resistance group helps some fighters escape through a sewer. Dorota and Stach realise that they are in love, but soon afterwards Dorota is arrested. Stach takes over her duties in the Fighting Youth group and young people rally around his leadership.

Gentlemen Prefer Blondes
USA 1953 sd col 15

PRODUCTION
p.c – 20th Century-Fox. *p* – Sol. C. Siegel. *d* – Howard Hawks. *sc* – Charles Lederer, from the novel by Anita Loos. *ph* – Harry J. Wild (Technicolor). *ed* – Hugh S. Fowler. *a.d* – Lyle Wheeler, Joseph C. Wright. *m* – Jule Styne and Leo Robin, Hoagy Carmichael and Harold Adamson. *choreo* – Jack Cole. *cost* – Travilla.

LEADING PLAYERS
Jane Russell (*Dorothy*), Marilyn Monroe (*Lorelei Lee*), Charles Coburn (*Sir Francis Beekman/Piggy*), Elliott Reid (*Malone*), Tommy Noonan (*Gus Esmond*), George Winslow (*Henry Spofford III*).

SYNOPSIS
Two former showgirls Lorelei and Dorothy are on a trip to Paris paid for by Lorelei's millionaire fiancé, Gus Esmond.

The two women walk along the gangway to the ship, accompanied by wolf-whistles from the Olympic team, who happen to be travelling to Europe on the same ship. Malone, a private detective, is told by Gus's father to find compromising evidence which will prevent Lorelei from marrying his son. On board, Lorelei is naively excited by her cabin and thrilled to receive a letter of credit from Gus, once its function has been explained to her. While Gus and Lorelei go through a tearful farewell, Dorothy organises a party for the relay team. (Ext. 1a, 5 mins.)

When the boat sails, Lorelei sets about finding a rich husband for Dorothy, who seems more interested in the Olympic team.

While they exercise Lorelei checks the passenger list for a rich suitor for Dorothy. Meanwhile, Dorothy goes to the swimming pool where the team are practising and sings 'Anyone Here for Love!' about the tragedy of their wasted sex appeal. Lorelei has decided on Mr. Henry Spofford for Dorothy and blackmails the head waiter into placing him on their table. Unfortunately Henry Spofford turns out to be a small, if precocious, child. At the bar Dorothy learns that Sir Francis Beekman (Piggy) owns a diamond mine but it is too late to prevent Lorelei from overhearing the information. Lorelei imagines Piggy's head transformed into an enormous diamond. (Ext. 1b, 10 mins.)

Malone ingratiates himself with Dorothy but she repudiates him when she discovers him photographing Lorelei and Piggy together. Lorelei and Dorothy drug Malone and retrieve the photograph, which Lorelei then uses as a means of persuading Piggy to give her his wife's tiara. In Paris Dorothy and Lorelei find that the letter of credit has been cancelled through Malone's intervention and they are reduced to working as singers in a café. Piggy tells the police that his wife's tiara has been stolen. Eventually Gus and his father come to Paris, and Malone finds out the truth about Piggy, while Dorothy, disguised as Lorelei, makes a covert declaration of love for Malone. Everything is sorted out and on the ship back to New York there is a double wedding: Lorelei marries Gus and Dorothy marries Malone.

The Ghost That Never Returns
USSR 1929 st b/w 16+15

PRODUCTION
p.c – Sovkino. *d* – Abram Room. *sc* – Valentin Turkin, from the story *Le Rendez-vous qui n'a pas eu lieu* by Henri Barbusse. *ph* – Dmitri Feldman. *a.d* – Victor Aden.

LEADING PLAYERS
B. Ferdinandov (*José Real*), Olga Zhizneva (*Clemence*), L. Yurenev (*Senior Warden*).

SYNOPSIS
New inmates are brought to a modern prison in South America. The cells are organised in five circular tiers, with a guard watching from a rotating desk in the centre. The new prisoners are workers from the oilfields. One recognises José Real, a workers' leader who is serving a life sentence. He escapes his guards and rushes to tell José news of a forthcoming strike. The new prisoner is chased along the corridors until he is cornered and jumps to his death. José encourages the prisoners to revolt. They pelt the guard at the rotating desk with their plates and cups until he frenziedly telephones the ape-like governor in his office. The governor orders that the prisoners should be subdued with water-cannons. Although they fight back order is eventually restored. (Ext. 1, 16 mins.)

Knowing that José was behind this latest revolt, they offer him a day's parole – intending that an agent will shoot him at the end of twenty-four hours.

Alone in his cell José imagines himself speaking to a group of workers. Their interest grows, but as they decide to take action they disappear and José is left by himself again. On the last morning before his parole José makes a minute examination of his cell, staring obsessively at the walls, the floor and the toilet. At exactly seven o'clock the warders come in and taken him with them. The other prisoners watch him leaving, shout him warnings and wish him good luck. Outside the

*prison wall José picks a flower and sud-
denly realises that he is free.* (Ext. 2,
15 mins.)

José squanders his hours of freedom,
but despite the police agents who follow
him he reaches his family. Rather than
returning to prison José leads an armed
revolt against the oil companies.

Gilda
USA 1946 sd b/w 24

PRODUCTION
p.c – Columbia. *p* – Virginia Van Upp.
d – Charles Vidor. *sc* – Marion Parsonnet,
from a story by E. A. Ellington. *ph* –
Rudolph Maté. *ed* – Charles Nelson. *a.d* –
Stephen Goosson, Van Nest Polglase. *m* –
M. Stoloff and Marlin Skiles. *cost* – Jean
Louis.

LEADING PLAYERS
Rita Hayworth (*Gilda*), Glenn Ford
(*Johnny Farrell*), George Macready
(*Ballin Mundson*), Joseph Calleia
(*Obregon*), Stevan Geray (*Uncle Pio*), Joe
Sawyer (*Casey*).

SYNOPSIS
Johnny Farrell, a professional gambler, is
rescued from a hold-up on the Buenos
Aires waterfront by Ballin Mundson, the
proprietor of an exclusive but illegal gambling house. Mundson employs Farrell and
gives him responsibility for running the
Casino. The men become good friends.

*Before Mundson leaves on a business
trip he and Johnny drink a toast to 'the
three of us' (Mundson, Johnny and Mundson's walking stick/stiletto, which saved
Johnny's life). On Mundson's return,
Johnny goes to the house and finds that he
has brought back a wife, the beautiful
Gilda. Mundson observes the hostility
between Johnny and Gilda. It is clear that
they already know each other.* (Ext. 1a,
8 mins.)

Johnny is made responsible for Gilda,
just as he is responsible for all Ballin's
other possessions. Members of the international tungsten cartel, over which Mundson has gained total control, become
restless and suspicious and demand the restoration of their rights. Mundson fakes
suicide to avoid a confrontation – and
because he wrongly suspects Gilda and
Johnny of having an affair.

*Johnny marries Gilda, but only as an act
of revenge. After the ceremony he takes her
to a hotel suite and makes her prisoner. A
member of the tungsten cartel tells Johnny
how Mundson defrauded them. Gilda goes
to visit Johnny to try and discover what
he is doing and why, but she is rejected.
When she tries to go out with other men
her attempts are thwarted by the intervention of Johnny's cohorts.* (Ext. 1b, 8 mins.)

Finally, Gilda manages to escape to
Montevideo where she sings in a nightclub.

*Gilda returns to Buenos Aires to get her
marriage to Johnny annulled on the advice
of Langford, a lawyer she has met in Montevideo. When they arrive at the hotel she*
discovers that Langford has been hired by
Johnny to bring her back. At the casino,
while Obregon, a secret service officer,
talks to Johnny about the tungsten cartel,
Gilda appears on the dance floor, sings 'Put
the Blame on Mame' and goes into a strip
routine. Johnny has her dragged away and
hits her across the face.* (Ext. 1c, 8 mins.)

Obregon persuades Johnny to give up
documents relating to the illegal cartel and
tells him also that Gilda's infidelities were
only imagined. Johnny and Gilda are
reconciled. Mundson returns to revenge
himself on them, but is killed by Pio, the
Casino's old retainer.

G-Men
USA 1935 sd b/w 15

PRODUCTION
p.c – Warner Bros. *p* – Hal B. Wallis. *d* –
William Keighley. *sc* – Seton I. Miller,
from the book *Public Enemy No. 1* by
Gregory Rogers. *ph* – Sol Polito. *ed* – Jack
Killifer. *a.d* – John J. Hughes. *m* – Leo F.
Forbstein.

LEADING PLAYERS
James Cagney (*Brick Davies*), Margaret
Lindsay (*Kay McCord*), Robert
Armstrong (*Jeff McCord*), Lloyd Nolan
(*Hugh Farrell*), Noel Madison (*Durfey*),
William Harrigan (*McKay*), Edward
Pawley (*Danny Leggett*).

SYNOPSIS
Brick Davies has been put through law
school by McKay, a big-time racketeer,
but is determined to remain honest and is
consequently without work.

*The McKay mob are playing cards when
Durfey appears needing money to help him
get over the state line. Brad Collins, one
of the gang, watches Durfey leave with the
money and sees him being arrested by
Buchanan. He shoots the G-man. Learning
of Buchanan's murder, Davies decides to
join the Federal Police, but he first goes to
McKay and explains why he intends to
give up his studies.* (Ext. 1a, 8 mins.)

He is accepted as a G-man recruit.

*During his training Davies proves him-
self to be an excellent marksman. Because
of his underworld connections he is able
to give vital assistance in tracing those
involved in a bank robbery and pinpoints
Danny Leggett as one of the men with rifles
on the raid. Davies also learns that Leggett
was in some way involved in the murder
of Buchanan and asks for a transfer to New
York, but his transfer request is refused.
Davies encounters Kay McCord, sister of
the FBI agent in charge of training recruits.*
(Ext. 1b, 8 mins.)

As a result of the information provided
by Davies, Leggett is captured, but he is
later rescued by friends at a railroad
station. A G-man is killed during the
shoot-out and there is pressure to arm the
FBI and make murder a Federal (as
opposed to a State) offence. Davies is
assigned to Chicago where he is instrumental in the recapture of Leggett. Meanwhile, the rest of the mob are hiding out
at McKay's summer lodge. The G-men
surround the house, there is a bloody
shoot-out and out of the mob only Brad
Collins survives. Collins kidnaps Kay
McCord, but Davies successfully rescues
her with the help of a former girlfriend.

The Goddess
USA 1958 sd b/w 13

PRODUCTION
p.c – Columbia. *p* – Milton Perlman. *d* –
John Cromwell. *sc* – Paddy Chayefsky.
ph – Arthur J. Ornitz. *ed* – Carl Lerner.
a.d – Edward Haworth. *m* – Virgil
Thompson. *cost* – Frank L. Thompson.

LEADING PLAYERS
Kim Stanley (*Emily Ann Faulkner*), Lloyd
Bridges (*Dutch Seymour*), Steve Hill (*John
Tower*), Betty Lou Holland (*The
Mother*), Burt Brinckerhoff (*Lewis*).

SYNOPSIS
Emily Ann Faulkner's childhood is lonely
and unhappy: her father is dead, her
mother a frustrated Southern Belle turned
religious fanatic. She dreams of success in
Hollywood as an escape from the cheapness and squalor she resents.

*A boyfriend, Lewis, comes into the shop
where she works and makes a date for that
evening. Later he calls for her and as they
drive to the movies Emily expresses all her
discontents to Lewis. On the way back
Lewis tries to kiss her but she rebuffs him.
He drives her to her home but, anxious to
hold on to him as a boyfriend, Emily Ann
eventually allows him to kiss her.*

Some years later she marries John
Tower, a neurotic soldier she encounters
lying drunk in a gutter who happens to be
the son of a screen star. The marriage turns
out disastrously. Emily Ann gets a divorce,
abandons her small daughter, and leaves
for Hollywood. As starlet Rita Shawn she
experiences another unhappy marriage
with ex-prizefighter Dutch Seymour, but
finally becomes a star. She has a nervous
breakdown during which she clings to her
mother and her mother's brand of religious
fanaticism. The confidence her conversion
gives her is, however, short-lived. Sodden
with drink and drugs and under the care
of a formidable secretary-nurse she returns
home to her mother's funeral which is
attended by Tower and her daughter.
Screaming 'I want to die' she attempts to
throw herself in the grave. She is brought
back to bed by her secretary and visited by
Tower. He leaves her and tells his daughter
that 'Your mother never had a chance'.

The Godfather
USA 1971 sd col 19

PRODUCTION
p.c – Alfran Productions. *p* – Albert S.
Ruddy. *d* – Francis Ford Coppola. *sc* –
Mario Puzo, Francis Ford Coppola, from
the novel by Mario Puzo. *ph* – Gordon
Willis (Technicolor). *ed* – William

Reynolds, Peter Zinner, Marc Laub, Murray Solomon. *a.d* – Warren Clymer. *m* – Nino Rota. *cost* – Anna Hill Johnstone.

LEADING PLAYERS
Marlon Brando (*Don Vito Corleone*), Al Pacino (*Michael Corleone*), James Caan (*Sonny Corleone*), Robert Duvall (*Tom Hagen*), Al Lettieri (*Sollozzo*), Lenny Montana (*Luca Brasi*), Victor Rendina (*Philip Tattaglia*), John Cazale (*Fredo Corleone*), Diane Keaton (*Kay Adams*).

SYNOPSIS
In August 1945 Don Corleone agrees to help a Sicilian defend the honour of his daughter. In the meantime the wedding reception for Connie, Don Corleone's own daughter, is in full swing. The Godfather joins the family for a wedding photograph but refuses to have it taken until Michael, his youngest son, arrives. (Ext. 1a, 7 mins.)

A plea for help comes from a singer who has been refused a part in a Hollywood film. The obdurate producer wakes up to find the head of his favourite racehorse in his bed. Sollozzo, a leading member of the powerful Tattaglia family, proposes that the Corleones collaborate with them in the drugs racket.

Tom Hagen, the Godfather's adopted son, argues that narcotics are the thing of the future. The Godfather discusses the matter with Sollozzo and his associates who offer a 30% deal for financial, legal and political protection. The Godfather refuses this because the drugs are not popular with politicians. While Michael and Kay, his girlfriend, go Christmas shopping, Luca Brasi, the Corleone strong arm man, gets ready for a visit to the Tattaglias. They suspect his motives, however, and he is stabbed through the hand with a stiletto and then brutally garotted. Tom is picked up by two other members of the family and taken off in their car for a 'chat'. On his way home the Godfather stops to buy fruit and is shot down on the street. Fredo, his second son, who was driving him home, weeps over his body. (Ext. 1b, 12 mins.)

The Godfather survives. While he is recovering in hospital Michael who until now has kept his distance from the family's underworld activities, executes revenge. While Michael is lying low in Sicily – where he marries – Sonny is gunned down in counter-revenge. Michael's new wife is killed by a car bomb intended for him. Michael returns home to find an uneasy truce between the two families, presided over by the Godfather. Michael marries Kay, and when the Godfather dies, takes over headship of the family and eliminates all their enemies.

Gold Diggers of 1933
USA 1933 sd b/w 20

PRODUCTION
p.c – Warner Bros. *p* – Hal. B. Wallis. *d* – Mervyn LeRoy. *sc* – Erwin Gelsey and James Seymour, from the play by Avery Hopwood. *ph* – Sol Polito. *ed* – George Amy. *m* – Harry Warren. *lyrics* – Al Dubin. *choreo* – Busby Berkeley.

LEADING PLAYERS
Dick Powell (*Brad*), Joan Blondell (*Carol*), Ruby Keeler (*Polly*), Ginger Rogers (*Fay*), Aline MacMahon (*Trixie*).

SYNOPSIS
As Fay performs 'We're in the Money' in a Broadway show, the police enter and begin to take the scenery away – it is the Depression and the management is heavily in debt. Next morning Fay calls on Carol and Polly and tells about a new show. As they get ready for the audition Polly overhears Brad singing 'In the Shadows' in a nearby apartment. A producer, Barney, arrives and hires Carol, Polly and Fay. He also overhears Brad and asks him to come over and play. Brad has an idea for a number about the forgotten men who fought in the war but cannot now get a job. Barney is moved by this, but reveals that the show's backer has just pulled out. Brad says that he can provide the money. During a run-through of 'Pettin' in the Park', Brad shows the male singer how to do it, but cannot be persuaded to take over the part himself. However, on the opening night, the singer is taken ill and Brad goes on. The press reveal that Brad comes from a rich Boston family. His brother and an associate, Peabody, arrive to rescue him and to break up his involvement with Polly. However, when they appear at the apartment they mistake Carol for Polly. Carol goes on a spending spree with the two men and her friend Trixie, finally getting them drunk and making it look as if they spent the night with them. Next morning Trixie gets $10,000 out of Peabody in return for silence but Carol doesn't want any money as she has fallen in love with Brad's brother. The newspapers announce the marriage of Brad and Polly.

Backstage everybody gets ready for the show. The curtain rises for 'The Shadow Waltz' sung by Brad and Polly. The finale of the show, 'Forgotten man', is announced backstage. As Carol is about to go on stage Brad's brother appears with a detective, who tries to arrest Polly and get her marriage annulled. When the detective is revealed as a fake, however, Brad's brother is reconciled to Polly. He gives them a large cheque and then makes it up with Carol. The show ends with 'Remember my Forgotten Man'.

La Grande illusion
France 1937 sd b/w 11

PRODUCTION
p.c – Réalisations d'Art Cinématographique. *p* – Frank Rollmer, Albert Pinkovitch. *d* – Jean Renoir. *sc* – Charles Spaak, Jean Renoir. *ph* – Christian Matras. *ed* – Marguerite Renoir. *a.d* – Eugène Lourié. *m* – Joseph Kosma.

LEADING PLAYERS
Jean Gabin (*Maréchal*), Pierre Fresnay (*de Boeldieu*), Erich von Stroheim (*Von Rauffenstein*), Marcel Dalio (*Rosenthal*).

SYNOPSIS
Three French officers of different ranks are thrown together as prisoners of war during World War I. Boeldieu, one of the three, is an aristocrat, while Maréchal and the Jewish Rosenthal are working-class.

All three are taken to new prison accommodation in a German fortress. An escape project involving the construction of a ladder and discussion of a cross-country route is cut short by a German search party. Boeldieu has a conversation with Rauffenstein, who is the head of the fortress, and an aristocratic career officer much like himself. A friendship develops and they discuss the role of their class in the world of the future.

The three French officers unite in efforts to escape but the class barrier comes between them. Finally, Boeldieu gives up his life to help the others to get away. They have a long and difficult trek across country but are befriended by a young German peasant woman. Maréchal falls in love with her and when they leave he promises to return after the war. Finally, they cross the border into Switzerland.

The Grapes of Wrath
USA 1940 sd b/w 10

PRODUCTION
p.c – 20th Century-Fox. *p* – Darryl F. Zanuck. *d* – John Ford. *sc* – Nunnally Johnson, from the novel by John Steinbeck. *ph* – Gregg Toland. *ed* – Robert Simpson. *a.d* – Richard Day, Mark-Lee Kirk. *m* – Alfred Newman. *cost* – Gwen Wakeling.

LEADING PLAYERS
Henry Fonda (*Tom Joad*), Jane Darwell (*Ma Joad*), John Carradine (*Casey*), Charley Grapewin (*Grampa Joad*), Dorris Bowden (*Rosasharn*), Russell Simpson (*Pa Joad*), Zeffie Tilbury (*Grandma Joad*).

SYNOPSIS
After serving a prison sentence Tom Joad returns to his Oklahoma dustbowl home to find his family have been evicted and are preparing to move to California. The Joad family, plus Casey, a one-time preacher, load their possessions onto a broken-down lorry and set off. During the long and arduous journey Grampa dies.

Before crossing the Arizona desert the men bathe in the Colorado river. Grandma Joad becomes very sick and Rosasharn's husband shows signs of regretting the move. Once across the desert the guards tell the family that they must unload the lorry for an inspection. Ma Joad pleads with them to waive the inspection because of the need to get Grandma Joad to a doctor. The guards let them through and the family arrive in a rich and luxurious California which at first sight seems to fulfil all their hopes. Ma tells the story that Grandma is dead and had, in fact, died before they crossed the desert.

Once in California, the Joads are faced with intolerable conditions of labour exploitation on the fruit farms. Casey tries to organise a strike but is murdered during a skirmish with the law; Tom kills a Deputy. The family flees and eventually settles in a Government camp but Tom is forced to become a fugitive. As he leaves Ma Joad he vows to continue Casey's fight. The remaining members of the family prepare to load up the lorry once again and continue the search for a new home.

The Great Man
USA 1956 sd b/w 10

PRODUCTION
p.c – Universal-International. *p* – Aaron Rosenberg. *d* – José Ferrer. *sc* – Al Morgan and José Ferrer, from the novel by Al Morgan. *ph* – Harold Lipstein. *ed* – Sherman Todd, Al Joseph. *a.d* – Richard H. Riedel, Eric Orbom. *m* – Herman Stein.

LEADING PLAYERS
José Ferrer (*Joe Harris*), Dean Jagger (*Philip Carleton*), Keenan Wynn (*Sid Moore*), Julie London (*Carol Larson*).

SYNOPSIS
Joe Harris, a radio commentator, is assigned the job of arranging a memorial programme to Herb Fuller, America's best-loved radio and television personality. His investigations tell him about a very different man to the national hero: unfaithful to his wife, sadistic to his mistresses, obsessive in his need for a hold over his co-workers. Joe's disillusion is complete when Paul Beaseley, the owner of the small provincial radio station, tells how he gave Fuller his first job and was rewarded by vandalism and treachery. Joe decides to go through with his radio programme only when he hears a recording of Fuller's stirring appeal from the warfront for blood donations, but is once more sickened when he learns that the broadcast was not made by Fuller, who never went near the battlefront.

The sponsors try to persuade Joe to go ahead with his radio programme and to distort the true facts. They listen in a nearby office while Joe begins his programme in the usual way. During the course of transmission, however, Joe decides to tell the real story about Herb Fuller and begins to disclose the unsavoury facts. The sponsors are angry and try to stop the programme, but on reflection they realise that as Joe will become a public hero overnight his integrity can be turned into a saleable commodity. They decide to promote him as their new champion of truth.

The Great Road
USSR 1927 st b/w 20

PRODUCTION
p.c – Sovkino and the Museum of the Revolution. *d* – Esfir Shub. *ed* – S. I. Mitskevich.

SYNOPSIS
This film, reconstructed entirely from newsreel and archive material, was made to celebrate the October Revolution. The masses have already overthrown Czar Alexander III and despite Western capitalist intervention they also seek to overthrow Kerensky's provisional government. Soldiers fraternise at the front as peace talks are held with Austria. The entire capitalist world blockades and attacks the first republic of working people in support of the counter-revolutionaries. The Japanese occupy the Ukraine, and General Kornilov advances on Moscow. In Germany the monarchy of Wilhelm II collapses after the Berlin Revolution. The representatives of the defeated meet the victors at Versailles and the capitalist countries share the spoils. Meanwhile, the struggle for communism throughout the world is spurred on by the Soviet example, but the new socialist state suffers sabotage from the White Guards and is beset by starvation. The West continues to attack but Chapayev and Trotsky gain victories and in 1922 the Red Army secures peace.

Inspired by Lenin's presence reconstruction proceeds apace. After he dies the struggle continues both in the USSR and capitalist countries, including the USA. In the new socialist state cultural standards are raised, women move towards emancipation, progress is made to agricultural self-sufficiency and hydro-electric power stations, homes and factories are built – all according to Lenin's philosophy.
(NB Intertitles are in Russian but an English transcript is provided.)

Greed
USA 1923 st b/w 9

PRODUCTION
p.c – Goldwyn Company. *d* – Erich von Stroheim. *sc* – Erich von Stroheim, from the novel *McTeague* by Frank Norris. *ph* – Ben Reynolds, Billy Daniels. *ed* – Rex Ingram, June Mathis. *a.d* – Cedric Gibbons, Erich von Stroheim.

LEADING PLAYERS
Gibson Gowland (*McTeague*), Zasu Pitts (*Trina*), Jean Hersholt (*Marcus Schouler*), Dale Fuller (*Maria*).

SYNOPSIS
The burly young McTeague starts his working life pushing an ore cart in a Californian gold mine at the turn of the century. When his alcoholic miner father dies in a brothel McTeague's mother becomes determined that McTeague must escape the mines and apprentices him to a travelling charlatan dentist. McTeague's strength makes him a good tooth extractor and after a few years he opens a practice in San Francisco. Business thrives and McTeague becomes friends with Marcus Schouler who works in a nearby dog hospital. Schouler is engaged to Trina and when she breaks a tooth on a picnic he brings her to be treated by McTeague, who falls in love with her. When McTeague confesses his infatuation Schouler agrees to give her up in order to prove what friends they are.

McTeague goes on a picnic with Trina's German immigrant family, and the two wander off to sit by themselves on a sewer. It begins to rain so McTeague and Trina hide in a small hut. He kisses her passionately and ignores her protestations.

Their courtship continues and on the day before their wedding Trina finds that she has won $5,000 with a lottery ticket bought from Maria, McTeague's charwoman. Schouler is furious that he has lost the chance of a fortune as well as his girlfriend. The McTeagues settle down to married life and all seems well until Schouler tells the authorities that McTeague is not a licensed dentist. They are forced to auction all their possessions but Trina insists that the lottery money cannot be touched. McTeague begins to drink heavily. Not content with the $5,000, Trina wants a second hoard and begins to save every penny she can. McTeague beats her in order to get money for drink and bites her fingers which subsequently have to be amputated. Trina goes mad with grief when she discovers that McTeague has used some of the saved housekeeping money, and cashes her lottery ticket into gold pieces. At night she sleeps with them next to her naked skin. McTeague requests some money for food but she refuses and he leaves hungry. Trina gets a job as a charwoman so that she can save still more, but one night McTeague breaks in and demands cash to buy back his beloved concertina, sold by Trina. When she argues he beats her to death and takes the gold pieces. McTeague becomes an outlaw hunted by a sheriff's posse which includes his old enemy Schouler, who has seen McTeague's 'wanted' poster. The posse gives up when they realise that McTeague has headed for Death Valley but Schouler follows doggedly, crazed by the thought of the lottery. By the time he finally catches up with him in some desolate salt flats Schouler has no water left. McTeague has a water bottle tied to his mule but Schouler shoots the animal when it starts to move off and it crushes the canteen as it falls. The men begin to fight and McTeague beats Schouler to the ground with the butt of his gun. Schouler dies, but as he does McTeague realises that his enemy has managed to handcuff them together so that he is now tethered to a body in the middle of a desert.

La Guerre est finie
France/Sweden 1966 sd b/w 20

PRODUCTION
p.c – Sofracima/Europa Film. *d* – Alain
Resnais. *sc* – Jorge Semprun. *ph* – Sacha
Vierny. *ed* – Eric Pluet. *a.d* – Jacques
Saulnier. *m* – Giovanni Fusco.

LEADING PLAYERS
Yves Montand (*Diego*), Ingrid Thulin
(*Marianne*), Geneviève Bujold (*Nadine*),
Dominique Rozan (*Jude*), Françoise
Bertin (*Carmen*), Michel Piccoli (*Customs
Inspector*), Jean Bouise (*Ramon*).

SYNOPSIS
Diego is a Spanish revolutionary living in
exile in Paris. He is a member of an
organisation working to bring revolution
to Spain. Returning from one of his visits
to Spain he is stopped at the frontier and
asked to verify his identity. Diego is
illegally using the passport of a Frenchman, but when the police telephone the
man's home his daughter Nadine acts as
though Diego were her father. In Paris he
tries to warn Juan, a fellow-member of the
group, that he is in danger, but he had
already left the city. At Nadine's home
Diego finds that she is impressed by his
status as a revolutionary, but he leaves her
and returns to Marianne, the woman with
whom he has been living for several years.
Next day, Diego reports to the group on
the situation created by a series of arrests
in Madrid. The group leaders are planning
a general strike for Spain but Diego feels
disillusioned.
*Diego and Marianne are stopped by the
police for driving without lights but are
allowed to continue on their way. They go
to the station where Marianne leaves a bag
of plastic explosives in a luggage locker.
Back in the car they discuss the likelihood
of a revolution in Spain. They drive to the
river where Marianne says she wants to
have a child and they contemplate returning to Spain to live a normal life. Diego
later meets Nadine, who takes him to meet
a group of student revolutionaries. Their
assessment of the situation in Spain is very
different from Diego's. He leaves and goes
to an older revolutionary's flat where he
is told of the sudden death of Ramon,
another member of the group. Diego then
departs for Barcelona, in Ramon's place.*
Meanwhile, Nadine has discovered that
the police are likely to be waiting when he
arrives. Marianne arranges to fly to
Barcelona to warn him, but as she leaves
Paris Diego is already crossing the frontier
into Spain.

The Gunfighter
USA 1950 sd b/w 11

PRODUCTION
p.c – 20th Century-Fox. *p* – Nunnally
Johnson. *d* – Henry King. *sc* – William
Bowers and William Sellers, from a story
by William Bowers and André de Toth.
ph – Arthur Miller. *ed* – Barbara

McClean. *a.d* – Lyle Wheeler and Richard
Irvine. *m* – Alfred Newman.

LEADING PLAYERS
Gregory Peck (*Jimmy Ringo*), Skip
Homeier (*Hunt Bromley*), Jean Parker
(*Molly*), Helen Westcott (*Ringo's Wife*).

SYNOPSIS
Jimmy Ringo is a gunfighter past his
prime: a tried, disappointed hero, he is the
target of every small-time sharp-shooter
who wants to gain a reputation as the man
who killed Jimmy Ringo. He rides into
Cheyenne with three fame-seeking pursuers at his heels to visit his wife and son
and try to persuade them to follow him to
a new, peaceful life. But he cannot shake
off the past.
*At the barber-shop Hunt Bromley, one
of the townsfolk, learns that Jimmy Ringo
is in town. Bromley goes into the bar and
unsuccessfully attempts to provoke Ringo.
Ringo's wife is visited by a friend, Molly,
and they talk about Ringo. His wife feels
that it is too late to start again. As they
talk the Ringo boy escapes from his bedroom where his mother has put him in
order to keep him out of harm's way.
Meanwhile, Ringo's pursuers near the
town.*
Ringo's old friend, the Marshal, orders
him out of town. His wife relents and
agrees to try to start a new life with him
on condition that he first serves a year's
trouble-free 'probation'. Ringo happily
prepares to ride on his way, but he is shot
in the back by one of the three pursuers.

The Guns of Navarone
UK 1961 sd col 14

PRODUCTION
p.c – Open Road. *p* – Cecil F. Ford. *d* – J.
Lee Thompson. *sc* – Carl Foreman, from
the book by Alistair MacLean. *ph* –
Oswald Morris (CinemaScope and
Technicolor). *ed* – Alan Osbiston,
Raymond Poulton, John Smith, Oswald
Hafenrichter. *s.d* – Geoffrey Drake. *m* –
Dimitri Tiomkin.

LEADING PLAYERS
Gregory Peck (*Mallory*), David Niven
(*Miller*), Anthony Quinn (*Andrea*),
Stanley Baker (*Brown*), Anthony Quayle
(*Franklin*), James Darren (*Pappadimos*),
Irene Papas (*Maria*), Gia Scala (*Anna*).

SYNOPSIS
During 1943 a British force on an island
off Turkey is under imminent threat of
German bombardment. The only escape is
by sea, but the route is dominated by the
giant guns of Navarone which are set into
a cliff and impregnable to air attack. A sabotage group of sixteen men led by Major
Franklin is sent to Navarone. The others
include Mallory, a mountaineer; Miller,
an explosives specialist; Andrea, a Greek
officer, and two trained killers, Brown and
Pappadimos. Franklin breaks his leg while
they are scaling the sheer cliff which is the
only unguarded approach and Mallory

takes over command. They contact Maria,
one of the local resistance group, and
Anna, who has become dumb after
Gestapo torture. The Germans are alerted
to their presence and the whole group is
rounded up. Andrea tricks the guard and
they all escape with the exception of
Franklin, who is left with false information
which he believes to be true.
*The saboteurs force their way into the
fort in an effort to destroy the guns. Miller
discovers that his explosives have been
tampered with, and suggests that one of
the group must be responsible. Suspicion
falls on Anna and it is established that she
is a spy. Miller goads Mallory to shoot her,
but before he can do so Maria does it.*
Mallory and Miller sabotage the guns
while the others stage diversions. As the
British destroyers approach the straits a
gigantic explosion shatters the cliff. Pappadimos and Brown are killed but the
others watch from the sea.
(NB This extract is standard reduced
from Scope.)

Hamlet
UK 1913 st b/w 22

PRODUCTION
p.c – Hepworth Manufacturing
Company. *p* – Cecil Hepworth. *d* – Hay
Plumb, from the play by William
Shakespeare.

LEADING PLAYERS
Walter Ringham (*King of Denmark*),
Johnston Forbes-Robertson (*Hamlet*),
S. A. Cookson (*Horatio*), J. H. Barnes
(*Polonius*), Alexander Scott-Gatty
(*Laertes*), Percy Rhodes (*Ghost of
Hamlet's father*), Grendon Bentley
(*Fortinbras*), Montague Rutherford
(*Rosencrantz*), E. A. Ross (*Guildenstern*),
Adeline Bourne (*Queen of Denmark*),
Gertrude Elliot (*Ophelia*).

SYNOPSIS
An early film version of Shakespeare's
play.
*The ghost of Hamlet's father appears on
the battlements.* (Ext. 1a, 6 mins.)
*Hamlet's 'To be or not to be' soliliquy;
the 'Get thee to a nunnery' scene with
Ophelia; preparations for the visiting
players' performance.* (Ext. 1b, 7 mins.)
*The sword fight between Hamlet and
Laertes from near the end of the play.*
(Ext. 1c, 9 mins.)

A Hard Day's Night
UK 1964 sd b/w 12

PRODUCTION
p.c – Proscenium Films. *p* – Walter
Shenson. *d* – Richard Lester. *sc* – Alun
Owen. *ph* – Gilbert Taylor. *ed* – John
Jympson. *a.d* – Ray Simm. *m* – The
Beatles. *cost* – Julie Harris.

LEADING PLAYERS
John Lennon, Paul McCartney, George
Harrison, Ringo Starr, Wilfred Brambell

(*Grandfather*), Victor Spinetti (*Television Director*).

SYNOPSIS

Hotly pursued by fans, the Beatles embark on a train for London where they are to do a television show. They are accompanied by their harassed manager Norm, his assistant Shake, and Paul's grandfather.

They arrive at a hotel for a press conference and go in through a trick entrance to avoid the screaming fans outside. After answering some routine questions at the press conference as zanily as possible, they make their escape and go to the television theatre for a rehearsal. While the technicians are preparing the stage around them they sing 'If I Fell in Love with You'. The director comes in and makes a fuss, saying that Paul's grandfather has been interfering with his work. Fed up with it all, the Beatles run down the fire escape onto a large field. They race about and play games with 'Can't Buy Me Love' on the soundtrack, until the owner of the field asks them to leave.

Later, they sneak out to a twist club instead of staying in their hotel. Ringo disappears, spurred on by grandfather who points out the dangers of being a teenagers' idol. A frantic search ensues, but eventually all four turn up at the studio. The show is successfully completed and they dash off to their next engagement.

The Harder They Fall
USA 1956 sd b/w 13

PRODUCTION

p.c – Columbia. *p* – Philip Yordan. *d* – Mark Robson. *sc* – Philip Yordan, from the novel by Budd Schulberg. *ph* – Burnett Guffey. *ed* – Jerome Thoms. *a.d* – William Flannery. *m* – Hugo Friedhofer.

LEADING PLAYERS

Humphrey Bogart (*Eddie Willis*), Rod Steiger (*Nick Benko*), Jan Sterling (*Beth Willis*), Mike Lane (*Toro Moreno*), Jersey Joe Walcott (*George*).

SYNOPSIS

Toro Moreno, a famous boxer from Argentina, arrives in New York. He is met by boys working for boxing promoter Nick Benko and driven off. Benko and his boys arrive at the gym and wait anxiously for Eddie Willis, an unemployed sports writer who has been offered the job of promoting Toro. Willis finally turns up and Benko calls Toro into the ring. During a short work-out with a sparring partner Toro proves to be totally vulnerable. Willis is against promoting him, but Benko is insistent, saying 'I can get millions who can box, but Toro can fill a stadium'. Interested by the challenge, as well as the lucrative offer Benko makes him, Willis agrees to act as press agent for Toro.

A series of fixed fights and cleverly-engineered press publicity puts Toro in line for the title. Thinking, wrongly, that

he has killed a man in the ring, Toro threatens to quit. Willis tells him the truth about the way he has been used and convinces him that he must meet the champion, Brannen, if he is to make any money at all out of his boxing career. Toro fights Brannen and is mercilessly beaten. Willis begins to feel sickened by his own part in the racket which has earned him his wife's disgust and finally revolts when he hears that Benko's accountants have reduced Toro's share in the purse to less than $50. Willis gives Toro his own share of the spoils and puts him on a plane to Buenos Aires. He then returns home to his wife and writes a savage denunciation of the fight racket.

The Haunted Palace
UK 1963 sd col 20

PRODUCTION

p.c – Alta Vista. *p* – Roger Corman. *d* – Roger Corman. *sc* – Charles Beaumont, from the poem by Edgar Allan Poe and the novel *The Strange Case of Charles Dexter Ward* by H. P. Lovecraft. *ph* – Floyd Crosby (Panavision and Pathé-Color). *ed* – Ronald Sinclair. *a.d* – Daniel Haller. *m* – Ronald Stein.

LEADING PLAYERS

Vincent Price (*Joseph Curwen/Charles Dexter Ward*), Debra Paget (*Ann Ward*), Lon Chaney (*Simon*), Frank Maxwell (*Dr. Willett*), Leo Gordon (*Ezra Weeden*), Elisha Cook (*Smith*).

SYNOPSIS

In 1765 in Arkham, New England, Joseph Curwen, a local aristocrat, is burned alive by the villagers for practising black magic. As he dies he promises revenge. 110 years later his great-grandson Charles Dexter Ward and his wife Ann arrive at the palace they have inherited. They are immediately struck by Charles's likeness to a portrait of Curwen. Perturbed by the strangeness of the palace, they agree to leave.

By the next morning, however, Charles has changed his mind and talks of staying longer. He suggests that Ann goes home alone but she refuses. They walk into the village, which seems to be deserted but suddenly they see some little girls whose eye-sockets are covered in flesh. At supper the local doctor explains the history of Arkham and how the villagers believe that Joseph Curwen was a warlock whose experiments to produce a new race resulted in a generation of mutants. During a thunderstorm that night Charles goes outside and stands under the tree where Joseph was burned. He hears voices and later, prompted by Simon, the family retainer, he gazes at the portrait. Simon brings him a book of black magic, but Joseph has difficulty in supressing Charles's identity. (Ext. 1a, 10 mins.)

Ann's presence keeps Charles fighting, but during a period of Joseph's control the grave of his mistress, Hester, is opened.

Joseph tries unsuccessfully to bring her back to life.

Next day Charles is back in control and agrees to leave Arkham. Simon contrives to leave him alone with the portrait and Joseph completes his possession of Charles's body. He tells Simon and Janis, an assistant, that he must get revenge before carrying on with his work. Ann tries to help him but he repulses her. In Arkham Ezra Weeden argues that another burning is necessary. Joseph unbolts the door to the attic where Weeden keeps his mutant son. Later, the mutant kills Weeden and Joseph appears at Weeden's funeral in order to savour his revenge. (Ext. 1b, 10 mins.)

Joseph is ready to resume his grand satanic project and to use Ann as the female sacrificial victim, when the villagers arrive. Their destruction of the portrait gives Charles control again. He escapes the burning mansion with Ann, but as he leans against the oak tree the transformation looks set to begin again.

(NB This extract is standard reduced from Scope.)

Hearts of the World
USA 1918 st b/w 28

PRODUCTION

p.c – Artcraft/D. W. Griffith Productions for the Allied Governments. *p* – D. W. Griffith. *d* – D. W. Griffith. *sc* – M. Gaston de Tolignac (D. W. Griffith). *ph* – G. W. Bitzer. *ed* – James Smith, Rose Smith.

LEADING PLAYERS

Lillian Gish (*The Girl*), Robert Harron (*The Boy*), Adolphe Lestina (*The Grandfather*).

SYNOPSIS

A French boy and girl fall in love in a small village in 1914. They are excitedly planning their wedding when news of war comes and the boy has to enlist. The girl sadly folds away her wedding dress.

Orders are given at the German headquarters, while in the village the lovers lisen to the town crier. The soldiers leave. The boy says goodbye to his parents and exchanges photographs with his fiancée. His letters are full of determination but he soon finds himself defending a trench within sight of his home. The girl's grandparents, with whom she lives, are killed in the bombardment of the village. Deranged with grief she wanders onto the battlefield with her wedding dress in her arms, looking for her lover. By the time she finds him he is wounded and unconscious, but she lies down beside him and goes to sleep.

In the morning she awakes and, recovering her senses, runs for help. While she is away, however, the boy is carried away in an ambulance and the girl is distraught on her return. Once well, the boy is sent on a dangerous mission behind enemy lines. The girl has to fight off a murderous jack-booted German in a ruined inn before the

Allied Forces arrive to rescue her. Eventually, the boy and girl are reunited.

High Sierra
USA 1941 sd b/w 14

PRODUCTION
p.c – Warner Bros. *p* – Jack L. Warner, Hal B. Wallis. *d* – Raoul Walsh. *sc* – John Huston and W. R. Burnett, from a novel by W. R. Burnett. *ph* – Tony Gaudio. *ed* – Jack Killifer. *a.d* – Ted Smith. *m* – Adolph Deutsch. *cost* – Milo Anderson.

LEADING PLAYERS
Ida Lupino (*Marie*), Humphrey Bogart (*Roy Earle*), Alan Curtis (*Babe*), Arthur Kennedy (*Red*), Joan Leslie (*Velma*), Henry Travers (*Pa*), Elizabeth Risdon (*Ma*). Donald MacBride (*Big Mac*).

SYNOPSIS
Earle is released from prison having served only part of a life sentence for bank robbery. He knows he has only been released through the good offices of Big Mac, who wants him to rob a hotel. With a car provided by Big Mac, Earle goes out to Shaw's Camp to meet with the other members of the gang. En route he meets the Goodhue family and is attracted to the granddaughter, Velma, who has a club foot. At the Camp Earle is disturbed to find that the young gangsters, Babe and Red, have brought a woman, Marie, with them. He orders her back to Los Angeles but she persuades him to allow her to stay.

Red, Babe and Mendoza, a fourth member of the gang, play cards, while Marie looks on. They discuss details of the robbery including the layout of the hotel and the getaway route across the Sierra mountains. Earle warns the novice gangsters about talking too much. Later, driving back from the hotel, Earle meets the Goodhue family again and hears about their lack of money to pay for an operation to cure Velma's club foot. Velma shows Earle the stars. He then drives into Los Angeles to see big Mac, who is ill and bemoans the fact that there are no more good guys left – they're either dead or in Alcatraz. Earle talks to Big Mac's doctor about the cost of curing a club foot.

Later, Earle goes to see the Goodhues again and arranges to finance Velma's operation. The robbery takes place, but a policeman is accidentally shot and Babe and Red are killed when their car crashes. Big Mac dies before Earle and Marie get to him with the jewels. On the run, Earle and Marie drive to the Goodhues' and see Velma dancing with her boyfriend. They leave and separate – Marie going to Las Vegas to avoid identification. Earle is spotted, however, and there is a chase through the mountains. Marie hears the news on the radio and goes to Earle but he is shot and killed by a police marksman.

His Girl Friday
USA 1939 sd b/w 19

PRODUCTION
p.c – Columbia. *p* – Howard Hawks. *d* – Howard Hawks. *sc* – Charles Lederer, from the play *The Front Page* by Ben Hecht and Charles MacArthur. *ph* – Joseph Walker. *ed* – Gene Haylick. *a.d* – Lionel Banks. *m* – Morris W. Stoloff. *cost* – Kalloch.

LEADING PLAYERS
Cary Grant (*Walter Burns*), Rosalind Russell (*Hildy Johnson*), Ralph Bellamy (*Bruce Baldwin*), Gene Lockhart (*Sheriff Hartwell*), John Qualen (*Earl Williams*).

SYNOPSIS
Star reporter Hildy Johnson returns to the *Morning Post* office to tell her ex-husband Walter Burns, the editor of the paper, that she is about to marry Bruce Baldwin, an insurance agent, and devote all her energies to being an Albany housewife.

During their fast-talking repartee, Hildy eventually convinces a disbelieving Walter that she really is leaving for Albany that day. In order to play for time while devising a way of preventing his star reporter's departure Walter offers to take Hildy and Bruce out for lunch. (Ext. 1a, 14 mins.)

He makes a bargain with Hildy: in exchange for an interview with Earl Williams, a condemned prisoner, he promises to take out a large insurance policy with Bruce. Hildy keeps her side of the bargain, but Walter tries to sabotage the marriage plans by arranging for Bruce's arrest on fictitious theft charges. Hildy bails him out.

Hildy goes to collect her things from the press room while Bruce waits outside. The other reporters read Hildy's story on the Earl Williams case with admiration and discuss whether she'll be able to give up the newspaper business. Hildy appears determined to do just that, phones up Walter, tells him she's through and tears up her article. As she is leaving the alarm bells ring, signalling that Earl Williams has escaped. Hildy immediately chases after the Sheriff and brings him down with a flying rugby tackle. (Ext. 1b, 5 mins.)

Hildy gets an exclusive story from the Sheriff, and goes back to the press room to write it up. She sees Earl Williams at the window and persuades him to hide in a roll-top desk. While the other reporters batter at the press room door, Hildy and Walter try to devise ways of smuggling Williams out of the building in order to get his exclusive escape story. Bruce arrives but is ignored by Hildy who is engrossed in writing her article. Chaos follows as Bruce's mother also appears, having earlier been kidnapped by one of Walter's underworld friends, and Molly (Earl's girlfriend) jumps out of the window to prevent the reporters discovering Earl's hiding place. Hildy and Walter are arrested for obstructing justice but Walter manages to secure their release by accusing the Sheriff and

mayor of forestalling the Governor's reprieve for Earl. Bruce is alarmed but Walter tells him not to worry and gives him his watch as a wedding present. Hildy, Bruce and Bruce's mother set off together, but Walter arranges to have their train stopped at the first station and Bruce arrested for stealing his watch.

The Hound of the Baskervilles
UK 1959 sd col 16

PRODUCTION
p.c – Hammer. *p* – Anthony Hinds. *d* – Terence Fisher. *sc* – Peter Bryan, from the story by Arthur Conan Doyle, *ph* – Jack Asher (Technicolor). *ed* – James Needs. *a.d* – Bernard Robinson. *m* – James Bernard.

LEADING PLAYERS
Peter Cushing (*Sherlock Holmes*), André Morrell (*Dr. Watson*), Christopher Lee (*Sir Henry Baskerville*), David Oxley (*Sir Hugo Baskerville*), Francis De Wolff (*Dr. Mortimer*).

SYNOPSIS
The legend of the hound of the Baskervilles is explained. The cruel Sir Hugo Baskerville and his friends torture a servant who had objected to Sir Hugo's design on his daughter by throwing him out of a window and holding him over a fire. The girl escapes through a window and out onto Dartmoor, but Sir Hugo gives chase with his pack of hunting hounds. She takes refuge in a ruined abbey. Sir Hugo's hounds and horse become frightened as they approach the place but Sir Hugo goes on alone and stabs the girl on the altar. As he does a terrible howling is heard, and something leaps at the now terrified man. At this point it becomes clear that the legend is being read to Sherlock Holmes and Dr. Watson by a Dr. Mortimer. Holmes is impatient, but makes some accurate deductions about Mortimer who explains that he wants them to ivestigate the recent death of Sir Charles Baskerville in similar circumstances to those surrounding his ancestor. Mortimer hopes that Holmes will help him dissuade Sir Henry Baskerville, who has just inherited the estate, from going to Dartmoor.

Dr. Watson is sent on ahead to question the Baskerville servants and Stapleton, a tenant farmer. Directions given by Cecile, Stapleton's daughter, nearly cause Watson to get lost in a bog. Watson meets Holmes on the moor where he is doing some secret investigating and shortly afterwards an escaped convict is found dead on the moor, wearing an old coat of Sir Henry's. Holmes persuades Stapleton to take him down a local tin-mine. The roof collapses, apparently accidentally, but Holmes manages to survive. Cecile entices Sir Henry to the ruined abbey, where he is attacked by a hound. Holmes and Watson rescue him and reveal that the Stapleton's are descendants of Sir Hugo and that with the connivance of Dr. Mortimer they have been trying to reactivate the legend as a means of regaining their inheritance.

The Hour of the Furnaces: Part I
Argentina 1968 sd b/w 11

PRODUCTION
p.c – Solanas Productions/Grupo Ciné-Liberacion. p – Edgardo Pallero. d – Fernando E. Solanas. sc – Octavio Getino, Fernando E. Solanas. ph – Juan Carlos De Sanzo. ed – Fernando E. Solanas.

SYNOPSIS
Neocolonialism and Violence, the first part of a three-film series, has thirteen sections. The first five deal with 'false histories' of Argentina; the country's natural resources; the daily violence produced by starvation; Buenos Aires as a 'white city' and the beef-rich oligarchy.

The sixth section 'The System' suggests that Argentina's problem lies in the difficulty of recognising the enemy. An extract from a Joris Ivens documentary shows Vietnamese children re-enacting their war against America, but for the Argentinians 'It is more difficult ... neo-colonialism speaks our language'. While a military parade marches through the streets a narrator lists factors which make neo-colonial domination possible, including the agrarian oligarchy, the industrial bourgeoisie and the armed forces, and states that missionaries and monetary loans have the same colonialist function. Various dignitaries arrive at the airport, including the Kennedy family, de Gaulle and Prince Philip. A speech by Kennedy explains how military strength is necessary to maintain the stability of the dollar. The seventh section is entitled 'Political Violence', and states that change through democratic elections is impossible because of the frequency of military coups. A tank patrols the streets and people are forced into their houses by a water-cannon. (Ext. 1a, 5 mins.)

Section eight looks at racism in Argentina.

The ninth section examines under-development and dependency. A narrator explains how the capitalist neo-colonial countries take far more out of Argentina than they put in. Aid replaces more direct exploitation in some cases but the result is the same. Sequences from a slaughter house are intercut with advertising images and while music plays a voice announces Argentina's foreign debt. The section ends with a list of foreign corporations operating in Argentina. (Ext. 1b, 6 mins.)

The remaining four sections of Part I show cultural violence, 'cultural cosmopolitanism', ideological warfare, and the choice that the peoples of Latin America must make.

House of Bamboo
USA 1955 sd col 10

PRODUCTION
p.c – 20th Century-Fox. p – Buddy Adler.
d – Samuel Fuller. sc – Harry Kleiner. ph – Joe MacDonald (CinemaScope and colour by DeLuxe). ed – James B. Clark. a.d – Lyle Wheeler, Addison Hehr. m – Leigh Harline.

LEADING PLAYERS
Robert Ryan (*Sandy Dawson*), Robert Stack (*Eddie Spanier*), Shirley Yamaguchi (*Mariko*), Cameron Mitchell (*Griff*), Brad Dexter (*Captain Hanson*).

SYNOPSIS
A US Military Police sergeant is sent to Tokyo to investigate the illegal activities of an armed gang of dishonourably discharged ex-US servicemen. Posing as Eddie Spanier, an ex-convict from the States, he manages to establish contact with Sandy Dawson, the gang leader, and with Mariko, the Japanese wife of a one-time member of the gang who was left fatally wounded after a raid. Spanier is accepted into the gang and, unaware of his real identity, Mariko agrees to work with him.

Mariko moves in with Eddie, but while shopping in the market she is shunned by her neighbours. She returns to Eddie and tells him that she must leave. She hurriedly returns a few minutes later just before a member of the gang appears with a message from Sandy Dawson. The gang meet and are briefed on a raid on a gravel factory. The raid is successful but Eddie is wounded; Sandy countermands his own rule that any injured man should be killed by the gang rather than be left to be taken prisoner and Eddie is helped away. After the raid Sandy has Mariko brought to his house and informs her and Eddie that they are to live with him from now on.

When he learns the details of a planned raid Eddie alerts the police. Suspecting that he has been betrayed, Dawson calls the raid off and subsequently murders Griff, his former lieutenant, mistakenly believing him to be responsible for the betrayal. When Dawson is told by a police spy that Eddie is the informer he plans an elaborate revenge. The plan misfires and in trying to escape Dawson is trapped in a roof-top fun fair. Finally, he is shot by Spanier.

(NB This extract is standard reduced from Scope.)

How Green Was My Valley
USA 1941 sd b/w 10

PRODUCTION
p.c – 20th Century-Fox. p – Darryl F. Zanuck. d – John Ford. sc – Philip Dunne, from the novel by Richard Llewellyn. ph – Arthur Miller. ed – James B. Clark. a.d – Richard Day and Nathan Juran. m – Alfred Newman. cost – Gwen Wakeling.

LEADING PLAYERS
Walter Pidgeon (*Mr. Gruffydd*), Maureen O'Hara (*Angharad Morgan*), Donald Crisp (*Mr. Morgan*), Roddy McDowall (*Huw Morgan*), Anna Lee (*Bronwen Morgan*), Sara Allgood (*Mrs. Beth Morgan*).

SYNOPSIS
Huw Morgan looks back 50 years to his boyhood in a Welsh mining village. He describes the apparently idyllic life of the Morgan family – mother, father, four adult sons who are all miners, their daughter Angharad, and the small Huw. The men arrive home and hand their wages to Mrs. Morgan. After washing they all sit down to eat together, and once the meal is over the brothers receive their pocket money. Huw goes to the sweetshop to buy toffee and on his return meets Bronwen, who is engaged to one of his brothers.

Gradually, however, their lives are disrupted by misfortune and labour troubles. Ivor, Angharad's husband, is killed in a pit accident; all four Morgan sons are sacked when cheap scab labour is hired from nearby valleys. Although in love with Mr. Gruffydd, the minister, Angharad marries the mine-owner's son. Mr. Morgan is trapped in the pit after an explosion, and dies before Mr. Gruffydd and Huw can rescue him.

I Am a Fugitive from a Chain Gang
USA 1932 sd b/w 20

PRODUCTION
p.c – Warner Bros. p – Morgan Wallis.
d – Mervyn LeRoy. sc – Howard J. Green, Brown Holmes, from the book *I Am a Fugitive from a Georgia Chain Gang* by Robert E. Burns. ph – Sol Polito. ed – Wiliam Holmes. a.d – Jack Okey. m – Leo F. Forbstein. cost – Orry-Kelly.

LEADING PLAYERS
Paul Muni (*James Allen*), Glenda Farrell (*Marie Woods*), Helen Vinson (*Helen*), Noel Francis (*Linda*), Preston Foster (*Pete*).

SYNOPSIS
James Allen returns from the war and decides to look for work on a construction site. He travels the country but finds the Depression has made permanent work impossible to get. In a doss-house Allen meets Pete, also unemployed, who invites him to share a free handout at a local hamburger joint. While waiting for the meal, Pete attempts to hold the owner up but the police appear. Allen is arrested trying to escape and sentenced to a long period of hard labour. (Ext. 1a, 10 mins.)

Conditions on the chain gang are exceptionally brutal, but eventually Allen manages to escape. He gets to Chicago and finds a job with an engineering company. After a period of hard work and study he qualifies as a surveyor. His landlady finds out about Allen's past and blackmails him into marrying her. The marriage is not successful and when Allen demands a divorce, she goes to the police and he is re-arrested.

Allen is refused a pardon but he is told that if he is a model prisoner for nine months, his case will be reconsidered. It is, but again his pardon is refused. Unable to face the prospect of indefinitely working on the chain gang, Allen again escapes but is doomed to spending the rest of his life on the run – which means that he has to turn to crime to support himself. (Ext. 1b, 10 mins.)

I Basilischi
(*see* The Lizards)

If . . .
UK 1968 sd b/w + col 14

PRODUCTION

p.c – Memorial Enterprises. *p* – Michael Medwin, Lindsay Anderson. *d* – Lindsay Anderson. *sc* – David Sherwin, from the scenario *Crusaders* by David Sherwin and John Howlett. *ph* – Miroslav Ondricek (Eastman Color). *ed* – David Gladwell. *a.d* – Jocelyn Herbert. *m* – Marc Wilkinson. *cost* – Shura Cohen.

LEADING PLAYERS

Malcolm McDowell (*Mick Travers*), David Wood (*Johnny*), Richard Warwick (*Wallace*), Robert Swann (*Rowntree*), Christine Noonan (*The Waitress*), Anthony Nicholls (*General Denson*).

SYNOPSIS

A new term begins at public school; the boys settle in and Mick Travers drinks vodka with his friends.

One afternoon while the rest of the school are watching a college rugby match, Mick and Johnny steal a motorbike and ride to a roadside café. They have coffee and Mick kisses the waitress. She slaps his face, but they then play a fantasy game. (Ext. 1a, 7 mins.)

On their return Mick, Johnny and Wallace are beaten by the head of house for their general negative attitude towards the school. During a Cadet Corps field exercise Mick shoots the college chaplain. As a punishment he is given the task of clearing out a junk room where a stock of forgotten guns and ammunition is discovered.

Speech day at the school. Boys, teachers and parents gather in the chapel to listen to a speech by General Denson, a national hero and old boy of the school. Smoke begins to seep through the floorboards as he speaks and the congregation stampedes. As they leave the chapel they are gunned down by Mick and his friends. The headmaster steps forward to reason with the rebels, but is himself shot down. The remaining parents start to shoot back. (Ext. 1b, 7 mins.)

I'm No Angel
USA 1933 sd b/w 12
(w. **Belle of the Nineties**)

PRODUCTION

p.c – Paramount Publix. *p* – William LeBaron. *d* – Wesley Ruggles. *sc* – Mae West, from story suggestions by Lowell Bretano. *ph* – Leo Tover. *ed* – Otho Lovering. *m* – Harvey Brooks. *lyrics* – Gladys Du Bois, Ben Ellison.

LEADING PLAYERS

Mae West (*Tira*), Cary Grant (*Jack Clayton*), Gertrude Michael (*Alicia Hatton*).

SYNOPSIS

Tira performs in a small-town circus as a side-show vamp and lion-tamer.

She is presented to the show-ground crowd as a great sexual attraction. When she appears she parades before them exchanging repartee with the ogling male audience, then sings a suggestive number, 'Sister Honky Tonk'. (Ext. 1a, 8 mins.)

She is associated with Slick, a professional pick-pocket, but has a room in town where she shakes down male visitors. Slick is jealous and knocks out one of her admirers. They leave him for dead. The police track down Slick and in order to get money for his defence Tira agrees to put her head into a lion's mouth, a dangerous feat which will draw crowds to the ailing circus.

She successfully performs the lion act. One day her brave display attracts the rich 'silk hats' in the audience to her dressing-room after the show. Among them are Kirk Lawrence and his fiancée, Alicia Hatton, who tries to patronise Tira, to no avail. (Ext. 1b, 4 mins.)

Tira soon becomes intimate with Kirk. His friend, Jack Clayton, tries to persuade her to break off the relationship, but becomes involved with her himself. After a series of misunderstandings over Slick and attempts by the circus owner to sabotage the affair which result in a breach-of-promise court action Tira and Clayton are finally united.

The Informer
USA 1935 sd b/w 14

PRODUCTION

p.c – RKO Radio. *p* – John Ford. *d* – John Ford. *sc* – Dudley Nichols, from the novel by Liam O'Flaherty. *ph* – Joseph H. August. *ed* – George Hively. *a.d* – Van Nest Polglase, Charles Kirk. *m* – Max Steiner. *cost* – Walter Plunkett.

LEADING PLAYERS

Victor McLaglen (*Gypo Nolan*), Heather Angel (*Mary McPhillip*), Preston Foster (*Dan Gallagher*), Margot Grahame (*Katie*), Wallace Ford (*Frankie McPhillip*), D'Arcy Corrigan (*The Blind Man*).

SYNOPSIS

In Dublin in 1922 Gypo Nolan, a powerful but stupid Irishman is dismissed from the revolutionary party. He is left without money and with friends, but he retains the love and loyalty of his girl, Katie. Gypo's former best friend Frankie McPhillip is wanted by the police for political murder and a bounty of £20 has been placed on his head. Goaded by poverty, Gypo betrays him.

The police come to McPhillip's house and shoot him in front of his family. Gypo

receives his money, but as he is leaving the police headquarters he nearly strangles a blind man whom he thinks might be also on the wanted list. He gets drunk at a pub. Katie finds him but leaves angrily when she discovers where his new found wealth comes from. Still drunk, Gypo goes to McPhillip's wake but while he is there he drops some coins which he feels are evidence of his crimes. His subsequent storm of denials arouse the suspicions of Gallagher and Mulholland, members of the party.

Gallagher offers Gypo reinstatement if he can discover McPhillip's betrayer and Gypo accordingly accuses Mulligan, who was known to have a grievance against the dead man. While Mulligan is being captured Gypo continues his drinking spree but is tailed by Mulholland who keeps a record of his expenditures. Finally, Gypo presents what is left of the money to Kate. At his trial Mulligan is proved to have a perfect alibi and when the record of Gypo's expenditures are read out it is he who is put into the death cell. He manages to get away and hides in Katie's rooms while she goes to plead in vain with Gallagher. Gypo manages to escape from his hide-out but is badly wounded. He goes to church where McPhillip's family are praying and pleads for, and obtains, their forgiveness just before he dies.

In the Heat of the Night
USA 1967 sd col 17

PRODUCTION

p.c – Mirisch. *p* – Walter Mirisch. *d* – Norman Jewison. *sc* – Stirling Silliphant, from the novel by John Ball. *ph* – Haskell Wexler (colour by DeLuxe). *ed* – Hal Ashby. *a.d* – Paul Groesse. *m* – Quincy Jones.

LEADING PLAYERS

Sidney Poitier (*Virgil Tibbs*), Rod Steiger (*Bill Gillespie*), Warren Oates (*Sam Wood*), Quentin Dean (*Delores Purdy*), Larry Gates (*Eric Endicott*).

SYNOPSIS

Sam Woods, a policeman patrolling the small cotton town of Sparta, Mississippi finds the body of Colbert, a rich Northern industrialist who was planning to build a factory in the town. Gillespie, the local police chief, orders Woods to search for the killer, and he arrests a solitary black man that he discovers in the station waiting room. Back at the police station, however, it emerges that the man is Virgil Tibbs, Philadelphia's number one homicide expert. The antagonism between Gillespie and Tibbs is further exacerbated when Tibbs quickly proves the innocence of a newly arrested suspect in the Colbert case.

The mayor tells Gillespie that it would be useful to have Tibbs working on the case: he might find the murderer, but he could also be a scapegoat. Gillespie goes to the station where Tibbs is waiting for a train north, and persuades him to stay. Together they drive to a garage where Tibbs picks up a car. The black owner is amused by Tibbs's intention to stay in a (white) hotel and offers him accommodation with his family, which he accepts. After talking to Colbert's widow Tibbs begins to suspect Endicott, a local plantation owner and boss of Sparta. Tibbs and Gillespie go to a meeting with Endicott in the orchid house of his mansion, but he objects to being questioned by a black man and slaps Tibbs across the face. Tibbs slaps him back. Later, the mayor tells Gillespie that the last police chief would have immediately shot Tibbs.

Despite the mayor's desire to be rid of him and the harassment of a local vigilante group, a sense of mutual understanding begins to develop between Tibbs and Gillespie. Tibbs continues his investigations, which lead to the sex-obsessed teenager Delores Purdy, who accuses Wood of the murder. This proves to be false, but through the help of a black abortionist Tibbs is present when Delores's boyfriend Ralph Henshaw is confronted by her brother. Henshaw admits to the murder, which he committed to get the money to pay for an abortion for Delores. The case satisfactorily solved, Gillespie drives Tibbs to the station and the two men shake hands warmly before parting.

Intolerance
USA 1916 st b/w 10+13

PRODUCTION
p.c – Wark Producing Corporation. *p* – D. W. Griffith. *d* – D. W. Griffith. *ph* – G. W. Bitzer. *ed* – James Smith, Rose Smith.

LEADING PLAYERS
Lillian Gish (*Woman Who Rocks Cradle*), Howard Gaye (*Jesus*), Lillian Langdon (*Mary*), Constance Talmadge (*Mountain Girl*), Elmer Clifton (*The Rhapsode*), Seena Owen (*Princess Beloved*), Mae Marsh (*The Dear One*), Robert Harron (*The Boy*).

SYNOPSIS
Four intertwined stories illustrate the history of intolerance – the struggle of the Pharisees against Jesus; the war between the Catholics and the Huguenots in 16th-century France; the fall of Babylon after betrayal by the high priests, and the social and moral intolerance and the struggle between labour and capital in the early years of the 20th century. The narrative is punctuated by a woman rocking the 'cradle of destiny'.

In the modern story a boy and his Dear One walk home but she refuses him a kiss as she has promised her father and God that no man will come into her room. At first he is angry, but he asks her to marry him and they then kiss contendedly. The story of Jesus and the adulterous woman is shown; Jesus demands that 'He who is without sin should cast the first stone' at the woman. The Pharisees disperse angrily. Back in the current period girls are herded out of brothels while campaigners and lecherous men smile self-satisfiedly. (Ext. 1a, 8 mins.)

The boy is in court accused of murder. The Dear One tries to signal encouragement to him, while the lawyers give evidence about a gun. (Ext. 1b, 2 mins.)

The armies of Cyrus attack the walled city of Babylon with battering rams, arrows and high towers which they use to attempt to scale the walls. The Babylonians respond with boiling oil and a tank-like machine which spouts fire. At first thanks are given but when night falls the walls collapse. (Ext. 2, 13 mins.)

I Remember Mama
USA 1948 sd b/w 8

PRODUCTION
p.c – RKO Radio. *p* – George Stevens, Harriet Parsons. *d* – George Stevens. *sc* – DeWitt Bodeen, from the play by John Van Druten, based on the novel *Mama's Bank Account* by Kathryn Forbes. *ph* – Nick Musuraca. *ed* – Robert Swink. *a.d* – Albert S. D'Agostino, Carroll Clark. *m* – Roy Webb.

LEADING PLAYERS
Irene Dunne (*Mama*), Barbara Bel Geddes (*Katrin*), Oscar Homolka (*Uncle Chris*), Philip Dorn (*Papa*), Cedric Hardwicke (*Mr. Hyde*), Rudy Vallee (*Dr. Johnson*).

SYNOPSIS
Katrin types the last lines of her autobiography and sits back to think about her Norwegian immigrant family and, in particular, Mama, the centre of the Hanson household. She remembers how every Saturday night the family crowded around the table to watch Mama split up Papa's wages to pay different bills. The children announce their special needs for money and are given it, and Nels, Katrin's brother, says that he would like to go to college. The 'little bank' – a tin where emergency money is kept – is fetched, but the family is distressed to realise that there is still not enough to cover all of Nel's expenses. One by one the family offer small sacrifices – Papa will give up tobacco, the daughters will earn a little babysitting – until there is enough. With a sigh of relief, the mother says her ritual refrain 'Now we won't have to go to the bank'.

The money in the 'big bank' is never touched, but is a comforting reassurance for all the family as the Hansons struggle to get along on Papa's slender earnings. Mama guides her children and her three eccentric sisters through life, resourcefully sorting out their problems. In order to help Katrin achieve her ambition to be a writer Mama writes to a famous woman novelist and her encouragement is such that Katrin sells a story to a magazine. Eventually, she discovers Mama's guilty secret – there was never any bank account. It was Mama's invention to give her family a feeling of security in times of stress.

The Italian Straw Hat
France 1927 st b/w 13

PRODUCTION
p.c – Films Albatros. *d* – René Clair. *sc* – René Clair, from the play by Eugène Labiche and Marc Michel. *ph* – Maurice Desfassiaux, Nicholas Roudakoff. *a.d* – Lazare Meerson.

LEADING PLAYERS
Albert Préjean (*The Groom*), Olga Tschechowa (*Madame de Beauperthuis*), Marise Maia (*The Bride*), Yvonneck (*Nonancourt*), Jim Gérald (*Beauperthuis*).

SYNOPSIS
A young bridegroom is on his way to church when his pony eats the Italian straw hat of a married woman who is entertaining a lover behind a bush. Unfortunately for everyone the hat was a gift from the woman's husband and its loss threatens the secrecy of her affair with a fierce army officer. He demands that the hat is immediately replaced.

The wedding party assembles but the bridegroom is forced to make an excuse and go in search of the hat. The mayor of the town arrives to officiate but the groom is still absent. Infuriated, the bride's father initiates a search for his future son-in-law. He eventually discovers him in a hat shop and brings him back to the wedding. Meanwhile, the officer rages as he waits for a replacement for the hat and composes threatening notes. The wedding finally starts, but the party is uneasy and when the officer's valet enters with a message the bridegroom is forced to bring the mayor's speech to a sudden end.

The woman's husband arrives looking for her and her lover but they escape. It is discovered that the deaf uncle of the bride has brought her an Italian straw hat as a wedding present.

It's Gift
USA 1933 sd b/w 10

PRODUCTION
p.c – Paramount. *p* – William LeBaron. *d* – Norman McLeod. *sc* – Jack Cunningham, from a story by Charles Bogle (W. C. Fields) and J. P. McEvoy. *ph* – Henry Sharp. *a.d* – Hans Dreier, John B. Goodman

LEADING PLAYERS
W. C. Fields (*Harold Bissonette*), Jean Rouverol (*Mildred Bissonette*), Julian Madison (*John Dursten*), Kathleen Howard (*Amelia Bissonette*), Tom Bupp (*Norman Bissonette*).

SYNOPSIS
Harold Bissonette is surrounded by a dominating wife, a moody teenage daughter and a barely-controllable son.

He cannot shave without interruption in the morning, is bullied at the breakfast table and accused of being inconsiderate by his daughter. Nevertheless, he declares he is master of the house – in a low voice.

Harold dreams of owning an orange farm in California and when his wealthy Uncle Bean dies leaving him his money he immediately sells his grocery shop and sets off for California with his family. When they arrive they find that the orange ranch is derelict. Mildred bitterly reproaches her husband and leaves with the children. Harold is approached by a developer who wants to build a race-track grandstand on the site of his land. They bargain and Harold gets enough money to buy the orange grove of his dreams.

Ivan the Terrible: Part I
USSR 1945 sd b/w 15

PRODUCTION
p.c – Studio Cinema Centrale–Alma Ata Studios. *d* – S. M. Eisenstein. *ph* – Edward Tisse, Andrei Moskvin. *a.d* – Isaac Shpinel. *m* – Prokofiev. *lyrics* – V. Lougovsky. *cost* – Leonid Naumova.

LEADING PLAYERS
Nikolai Cherkasov (*Ivan the Terrible*), Ludmila Tselikovskaya (*Tsarina Anastasia*), Serafima Birman (*Euphrosinia*).

SYNOPSIS
In 1564 the 34-year-old Ivan is crowned Tsar at a majestic ceremony, but his speech disturbs the foreign ambassadors and provokes the resentment of the Boyars, scheming and treacherous noblemen. Ivan aims to create a new, powerful and united state and to subdue the enemies on Russia's borders. Later, Ivan marries Anastasia but the wedding is disrupted by a riot engineered by the Boyars. Ivan calms the crowds and receives emissaries from the Khan of Kazan who have come to bring a declaration of war. The Tsar attacks Kazan and clashes with prince Kurbsky but is eventually successful in overthrowing the Mongolians who have oppressed the Russians for centuries. On his return Ivan falls seriously ill and calls the Boyars to swear allegiance to his son Dimitri. Ivan's aunt, Euphrosinia, is jealous of him and anxious to see her own son on the throne.

Ivan addresses his courtiers and prepares for an allegiance with Elizabeth I of England. He receives messages about the continued plotting of the Boyars and about his wife who is ill. Euphrosinia tricks Ivan into giving a poisoned cup to his wife, who dies. As he mourns at her funeral bier further reports about the Boyars are brought.

The Tsar's followers are reduced to a faithful few and he decides on the device of retiring from the capital to Alexandrov, where he surrounds himself with trusted servants and guards. He waits there until a huge procession of people arrives to plead for his return to power. He goes back to Moscow, his rule stronger than ever before.

I Was a Fireman
(*see* Fires Were Started

Jalsaghar (The Music Room)
India 1958 sd b/w 10

PRODUCTION
p.c – Satyajit Ray Productions. *p* – Satyajit Ray. *d* – Satyajit Ray. *sc* – Satyajit Ray from a story by Tarashankar Banerjee. *ph* – Subrata Mitra. *ed* – Dulal Dutta. *a.d* – Banshi Chandragupta. *m* – Ustad Vilayat Khan.

LEADING PLAYERS
Chabi Biswas (*Bishamber Rai*), Pinaki Sen Gupta (*Khoka, His Son*), Padma Devi (*His Wife*), Tulsi Lahari (*Estate Manager*), Kali Sarkar (*Servant*), Ganga Pada Basu (*Mahim Ganguly*).

SYNOPSIS
The impoverished landowner Bishamber Rai reflects on his past life and how he let his estate decay while pursuing music and dancing, his main interests in life. Five years earlier he had found himself in competition with the nouveau riche moneylender, Ganguly, over the music concerts they had planned for their sons' initiation ceremonies. To finance his own, Rai sells his wife's jewellery. On another occasion Rai's wife and son leave to visit her family. Rai determines to hold as lavish a New Year's concert as his neighbour, who had recently acquired a new music room. Despite warnings about the coming monsoons, Rai sends for his wife and son.

The day of the New Year concert. A storm is brewing and Rai enquires if the boat bringing his wife and son has been sighted yet. It has not. When the concert begins Rai leaves the music room and wanders restlessly about the house watching the storm. News comes that the boat has foundered and a servant brings the drowned body of his son. By the following morning the estate is submerged beneath the flood waters of the river.

Rai is roused from these memories by an invitation to another of Ganguly's concerts. He decides to spend his remaining money on one final extravagant concert on his own – but then rides wildly into the country and is thrown from his horse and killed.

The James Brothers (The True Story of Jesse James)
USA 1956 sd col 10

PRODUCTION
p.c – 20th Century-Fox. *p* – Herbert Swope Jr. *d* – Nicholas Ray. *sc* – Walter Newman, from a screenplay by Nunnally Johnson. *ph* – Joe MacDonald (CinemaScope and Eastman Color). *ed* – Robert Simpson. *a.d* – Lyle R. Wheeler and Addison Hehr. *m* – Leigh Harline. *cost* – Mary Wills.

LEADING PLAYERS
Robert Wagner (*Jesse James*), Jeffrey Hunter (*Frank James*), Hope Lange (*Zee*), Agnes Moorehead (*Mrs. Samuel*), Alan Hale (*Cole Younger*), Alan Baxter (*Remington*), John Carradine (*Reverend Jethro Bailey*).

SYNOPSIS
At the end of the Civil War, Jesse and Frank James form a band of outlaws which carries out a series of bank and train robberies. Jesse sets up house with his lover Zee in a town where his real identity is not known, but a railroad company hires the Pinkerton Detective Agency to track Jesse down. The James's family homestead is surrounded and Jesse's younger brother is killed; Jesse takes personal revenge on a local farmer who had informed the law. Frank and Jesse decide to attempt a raid on the bank at Northfield.

The gang is on the outskirts of the town and Jesse checks final details with each member of the party. Frank is uneasy and wants to call the raid off, but Jesse is determined to go through with it. The raid is not successful, but Frank and Jesse escape by riding through a shop window. Only they and one other gang member survive.

Frank and Jesse quarrel and part but are later reconciled. Jesse decides to abandon his life as an outlaw, but as he and Zee are preparing to move house Jesse is shot by his cousin Bob Ford.

(NB This extract is standard reduced from Scope.)

The Jazz Singer
USA 1927 st + sd b/w 12

PRODUCTION
p.c – Warner Bros. *d* – Alan Crosland. *sc* – Alfred A. Cohn, from the play by Samson Raphaelson. *ph* – Hal Mohr. *ed* – Harold McCord. *m* – *Blue Skies* by Irving Berlin.

LEADING PLAYERS
Al Jolson (*Jakie Rabinowitz/Jack Robin*), May McAvoy (*Mary Dale*), Warner Oland (*Cantor Rabinowitz*), Eugenie Besserer (*Sara Rabinowitz*).

SYNOPSIS
Jakie Rabinowitz's love of jazz is continually getting him in trouble with his father, a cantor at the synagogue. A crisis occurs when he is found singing in a café the night he is supposed to take on his family heritage by singing the Kol Nidre for the first time. Despite his mother's protests, his father beats him and Jakie runs away to sing, changing his name to Jack Robin. He is eventually spotted by a successful musical comedy actress, whose faith in him is responsible for his engagement on Broadway.

He arrives home and hears his father rehearsing in a neighbouring synagogue. His mother is overwhelmed to see him again and he gives her a diamond pendant.

Jack notices that his portrait has been removed but his mother says that it has been broken. He tells her about his big show and taps out 'Blue Skies' on the piano. In the first dialogue of the film, Jack promises to buy his mother a house in the Bronx. He then demonstrates how he might jazz up 'Blue Skies', at which point his father enters crying 'Stop!'. The film reverts to intertitles as an argument takes place about Jack's using the voice God gave him in the theatre. Jack tries to smooth over the conflict by giving his father a new prayer shawl for his birthday, but the old man is adamant. Jack leaves again, this time, his mother fears, for good.

Jack is a great success with the theatre company and is in love with his actress-discoverer, who joins him in the production. On the night of the opening his mother comes to say that his father is severely ill, and he must return home to sing Kol Nidre in the synagogue. Torn between conflicting loyalties, Jack finally decides to go home. His father dies happy, listening to his son chanting. Jack's sweetheart stands by him in his choice.

(NB This extract should be projected at sound speed throughout.)

Jeanne Eagels
USA 1957 sd b/w 10

PRODUCTION
p.c – Columbia. p – George Sidney. d – George Sidney. sc – Daniel Fuchs, Sonya Levien, John Fante, from a story by Daniel Fuchs. ph – Robert Planck. ed – Viola Lawrence, Jerome Thoms. a.d – Ross Bellah. m – George Duning.

LEADING PLAYERS
Kim Novak (Jeanne Eagels), Jeff Chandler (Sal Satori), Agnes Moorehead (Madame Neilson), Virginia Grey (Elsie Desmond).

SYNOPSIS
Jeanne Eagels attracts the attention of Sal Satori, owner of a carnival, and uses him to help her achieve her ambition to become a great actress. Her only experience is as a side-show dancer, but when Sal takes Jeanne to New York she persuades Madame Neilson to train her and manages to get the starring part in the play Rain, originally intended for an actress named Elsie Desmond.

Jeanne is preparing to make her entrance on the opening night when Elsie Desmond takes her by the shoulder and threatens her. Shaken, Jeanne goes on stage and still manages to give a rapturously received performance. Next day she learns that Elsie Desmond has publicly ascused her of stealing the play. She goes to see Elsie, only to find that the actress has just committed suicide by leaping from the window of her top-floor apartment. While examining the photographs and newspaper clippings that litter the flat, Jeanne is approached by the police and asked whether she can explain the suicide.

During the next decade Jeanne becomes a celebrated star of stage and screen. At the same time, however, she develops an addiction to drink and drugs which eventually ruins her career. She dies in a seaside carnival at the age of 35.

Johnny Guitar
USA 1954 sd col 11

PRODUCTION
p.c – Republic. p – Herbert J. Yates. d – Nicholas Ray. sc – Philip Yordan, from the novel by Roy Chanslor. ph – Harry Stradling. ed – Richard L. Van Enger. a.d – James Sullivan. m – Victor Young. lyrics – Peggy Lee and Victor Young. cost – Sheila O'Brien.

LEADING PLAYERS
Joan Crawford (Vienna), Sterling Hayden (Johnny Guitar), Mercedes McCambridge (Emma Small), Scott Brady (Dancing Kid), Ward Bond (John McIvers), Ben Cooper (Turkey Ralston), John Carradine (Tom).

SYNOPSIS
Johnny Guitar wants to forget his past as a notorious gunman and earn a quiet living playing the guitar at the remote gambling house owned by the beautiful, strong-willed Vienna. On Johnny's first evening a troop of irate ranchers, led by venomous-tongued Emma Small, arrive with the body of Len Small, Emma's banker brother who was killed in a stage hold-up that afternoon. They insist that stage was held up by the Dancing Kid, a local outlaw who is known to frequent Vienna's place, and his gang, and demand that Vienna helps to capture them. In the course of the argument it is revealed that months earlier Vienna learned the route of a new railroad from a surveyor she 'exchanged confidences' with. She staked a claim to enough land to build an entire town, and built her gambling house despite the fury of the neighbouring ranchers whose lands are threatened by the railroad. Rancher Emma Small's hatred is additionally fuelled by her twisted desire for the Dancing Kid, who had been discarded by Vienna. After witnesses, including Johnny Guitar, have refused to give any testimony that would link the Kid and his gang with the hold-up, Vienna, the Dancing Kid and his gang are given twenty-four hours to get out of the territory. Enraged at being ordered to leave and at Vienna's refusal to resume their former relationship, the Kid robs the local bank while the townsfolk are attending Len Small's funeral. Vienna happens to be in the bank at the time closing her account. Emma Small uses this coincidence to accuse Vienna of being involved in the robbery.

Vienna lights the lamps in her gambling house. Two members of the Dancing Kid's gang, Tom and the badly wounded Turkey, arrive looking for sanctuary. Tom persuades her to hide them both. When the posse arrives, Vienna is playing the piano. They search the premises, interrogating her about the bak robbery and her own part in it, but she protests her innocence and they find nothing. Emma insists that Vienna must be implicated because of her association with the Kid. As Vienna confronts the posse Turkey's unconscious body rolls out from its hiding place. Emma eventually persuades Turkey to betray Vienna in order to save himself and then incites the posse to hang them both. The Marshal intervenes and in the ensuing struggle Tom is killed. As Vienna and Turkey are dragged off by the posse Emma sets fire to the gambling house by shooting at the lamps. She exults as it burns and the posse rides off with its victims.

Johnny rescues Vienna from being hanged, but Emma forces Vienna into a duel. Vienna, however, is faster on the draw and she kills Emma with Johnny's gun. The Dancing Kid is taken into the custody of the law while McIvers and the remaining ranchers take Emma Small's body away. Vienna and Johnny leave to start a new life together.

Judex
France/Italy 1963 sd b/w 10

PRODUCTION
p.c – Comptoir Français du Film (Paris)/Filmes (Rome). d – Georges Franju. sc – Jacques Champreux, Francis Lacassin, from the films by Louis Feuillade. ph – Marcel Fradetal. ed – Gilbert Natot. a.d – Robert Giordani. m – Maurice Jarre. cost – Christiane Courcelles.

LEADING PLAYERS
Channing Pollock (Judex), Francine Bergé (Diana Monti), Théo Sarapo (Moralès), Michel Vitold (Favraux), Edith Scob (Jacqueline).

SYNOPSIS
Judex is a righter of wrongs, a Zorro silhouette in a wide romantic black cape. He has notified crooked banker Favraux that he will be punished unless his ill-gotten fortune is turned over to the poor. When the warnings go unheeded the avenger appears at a party for the banker's daughter where all the guests are dressed as birds. The banker is apparently struck dead.

That night Diana Monti, an adventuress disguised as a nun, and her assistant, Moralès, break into Favraux's house to steal incriminating documents. In Judex's stronghold Favraux awakes from a drugged sleep, stuns his jailer and makes a telephone call to his house. Jacqueline, Favraux's daughter, goes downstairs to answer the phone and discovers the intruders. Favraux is recaptured while phoning and Jacqueline is chloroformed by the intruders after she has learned their identity. Judex's hounds, however, prevent Monti and Moralès from getting Jacqueline out of the grounds. Judex carries her back into the house unconscious.

On learning the truth about her father Jacqueline renounces her tainted inheritance. Diana Monti tries to blackmail her. Eventually, thanks partly to the prowess of Daisy, a good-natured circus acrobat, all wrongs are righted and Judex and Jacqueline are happily united.

Jules et Jim
France 1961 sd b/w 12

PRODUCTION
p.c – Films du Carosse/SEDIF. *d* – François Truffaut. *sc* – François Truffaut, Jean Gruault, from the novel by Henri-Pierre Roché. *ph* – Raoul Coutard (FranScope). *ed* – Claudine Bouché. *m* – Georges Delerue.

LEADING PLAYERS
Jeanne Moreau (*Catherine*), Oskar Werner (*Jules*), Henri Serre (*Jim*), Sabine Haudepin (*Sabine*).

SYNOPSIS
Jules and Jim first meet as young men in Montparnasse in 1907; Jules is Austrian, Jim French. They share each other's confidences, read and translate each other's poems and visit each other's houses. On a trip to Provence they discover a statue of a girl with a smile which disturbs and enchants them both. Later they meet Catherine, who has the statue's fascinating smile. It is Jules who notices the resemblance and who first falls in love with Catherine. One night when the three are together, Catherine asks Jim to come and see her the next day as she must speak to him. Jim arrives half an hour late for their meeting and finding no Catherine assumes she has not waited and leaves. Next day, Jules phones Jim and tells him Catherine arrived two hours late. He adds that Catherine has agreed to marry him and that they are leaving the next day for Austria. Jim turns for comfort to his childhood girlfriend Gilberte, who is gentle and faithful – everything that Catherine is not. Time passes, but Jules and Kim continue to correspond. Jim learns that Catherine has had a baby girl. He is about to leave to see them when the war breaks out. Jules and Jim are called up and fight on opposite sides. After the Armistice, Jim goes to see Jules and Catherine.

Jim arrives by train. Catherine and her daughter Sabine meet him. They take him to the chalet where he and Jules are reunited. They talk about plants, about the war, about insects, about future possibilities. Jules and Catherine seem to be idyllically happy. They all run across the fields and Jim rolls in the grass with Sabine. Later, Jules tells Jim that he is unable to hold Catherine, that she has left him once already and will no doubt do so again.

Soon Jim has also become Catherine's lover. She tells him she wants to bear his child and his name. Jules accepts the situation as this way he will not lose her entirely. But Catherine finds out about Gilberte and renews her relationship with an old flame, Albert. Finally they all return together to France, Jules still secretly in love with Catherine. Jim has decided that he wants to marry Gilberte. He explains this to Catherine, who seems to take the news calmly. She proposes a last drive with Jim and Jules before she says goodbye. Leaving Jules at the side of the road, she drives her car off a bridge into a river.

(NB This extract is standard reduced from Scope.)

Kameradschaft
Germany/France 1931 sd b/w 26

PRODUCTION
p.c – Nero (Berlin)/Gaumont-Franco (Aubert). *p* – Seymour Nebenzal. *d* – G. W. Pabst. *sc* – Ladislaus Vajda, Karl Otten, Peter Martin Lampel, Fritz Eckhardt, from a story by Karl Otten. *ph* – Fritz Arno Wagner, Robert Baberske. *ed* – Hans Oser. *a.d* – Ernö Metzner, Karl Vollbrecht.

LEADING PLAYERS
Alexander Granach (*Kasper*), Fritz Kampers (*Wilderer*), Daniel Mendaille (*Pierre*), Ernst Busch (*Kaplan*), Elisabeth Wendt (*Françoise*).

SYNOPSIS
The story is based on an actual French mining disaster in the 1920s. The introductory section exposes economic and political conditions in a mining area near the French-German border. Unemployed German miners try their luck in France, but there is no work there either. Tension grows between the French and Germans.

As the French miners are about to finish their work, smoke begins to filter through the mine. Terrific fires start to rage and many men are burnt to death. There is an explosion which is seen throughout the town and at the station where a woman frantically tries to disembark, but the train pulls out. The townspeople panic and rush towards the mine. They are kept back at the gates by guards but an old miner sneaks in on the running-board of an ambulance and cautiously descends into the pit by a vertical shaft to look for his son. The lift which should have carried the rescuers fails to work and there is new panic in the mine as the walls and roof begin to collapse. Many miners are buried. The woman on the train dashes out at the next station leaving her belongings behind. In the German mine the workers hear about the disaster as they are in the showers and after a heated discussion they decide to help. The director reluctantly allows them equipment and they drive through the town to the mine, calling goodbye to their worried families.

Deep in the pit three miners remove the iron fence which has marked the boundary between French and German shafts since the Treaty of Versailles. The German rescuers open a door to see the old man and his boy with the pit ponies. Suddenly the roof begins to fall and the mine is completely flooded. Rescue operations continue deep in the pit. A German follows some noises to where a Frenchman is trapped. Seeing the gas-masked German the Frenchman is transported back to the war and fights his rescuer until the latter manages to knock him out. Wounded Germans are cared for in a French hospital. Spokesmen of both sides simultaneously condemn the recent war, extol the fraternity of all workers and insist on unity between France and Germany. The official attitude is different, however, and a French and a German official, separated by a new iron fence in the shafts, exchange protocols ratifying the re-establishment of the frontier.

The Killers
USA 1946 sd b/w 12

PRODUCTION
p.c – Mark Hellinger Productions/ Universal. *p* – Mark Hellinger. *d* – Robert Siodmak. *sc* – Anthony Veiller, from the short story by Ernest Hemingway. *ph* – Elwood 'Woody' Bredell. *ed* – Arthur Hilton. *a.d* – Jack Otterson, Martin Obzina. *m* – Miklos Rózsa. *lyrics* – Jack Brooks. *cost* – Vera West.

LEADING PLAYERS
Burt Lancaster (*Swede*), Ava Gardner (*Kitty Collins*), Edmond O'Brien (*James Reardon*), Albert Dekker (*Jim Colfax*), Phil Brown (*Nick Adams*).

SYNOPSIS
Two strangers arrive in Brentwood and after looking at a filling-station cross the road and go into the diner opposite. They taunt the owner when he attempts to serve them and finally imprison his cook and another customer at gunpoint. They explain that they have come to kill 'Swede' Lunn, who works in the petrol station and usually eats in the diner in the evenings. The owners assures them that the Swede will not come as it is after six, his usual time. Eventually they believe him and leave. As soon as he is freed, Nick Adams, the customer, races to warn Swede but although he arrives before the strangers he cannot persuade him to take any action. Swede says there is nothing he can do and that he is being threatened because he once did something wrong. Nick leaves, bewildered, and almost immediately the killers arrive at the house and shoot Swede as he lies on his bed.

Local police are casual about an investigation, but James Reardon, an insurance agent, becomes interested when a green handkerchief with an embossed harp is found in Swede's effects. He interviews the beneficiary of a small life insurance policy left by Swede – the maid in an Atlantic City hotel who had stopped him from jumping out of a window years before. Next Reardon meets a detective, Sam Lubinsky, who tells him Swede had been seeing Kitty Collins, racketeer Jim Colfax's girl, and had gone to prison in her stead when she was convicted of stealing. An old thief who had been Swede's cellmate in prison tells how they were summoned by Colfax to take part in a hold-up after their release. Kitty was at the meeting with Colfax, but still interested in Swede. Reardon reads in a newspaper how one of the hold-up men wore a green handkerchief with a harp. He then discovers that after the robbery Swede learnt that the others meant to doublecross him and vanished with the money. Kitty joined him in Atlantic City, but soon left him. Later, Swede was seen by Colfax working at a petrol station and two days later he was killed. Reardon now hunts out Colfax and the rest of the gang and arranges to meet Kitty. It transpires that from the start Kitty and Colfax were in partnership to doublecross Swede and the other participants in the hold-up.

The Killers
USA 1964 sd col 10

PRODUCTION
p.c – Universal-International. *p* – Donald Siegel. *d* – Donald Siegel. *sc* – Gene L. Coon, from the story by Hemingway. *ph* – Richard L. Rawlings (Pathé-Color, print by Technicolor). *ed* – Richard Belding. *a.d* – Frank Arrigo, George Chan. *m* – Johnny Williams. *cost* – Helen Colvig.

LEADING PLAYERS
Lee Marvin (*Charlie*), Angie Dickinson (*Sheila Farr*), John Cassavetes (*Johnny North*), Ronald Reagan (*Browning*), Clu Gulagher (*Lee*), Claude Akins (*Earl Sylvester*).

SYNOPSIS
Charlie and Lee, two hired killers, arrive at the Sage House of the Blind where Johnny North works as an instructor. Although warned, North makes no attempt to escape and is killed. On the train Charlie is disturbed and pensive; he is unable to understand why North made no effort to save his life. He connects North with a million dollar robbery staged some years earlier; Charlie and Lee decide to go to Miami to question Johnny's old partner, Earl Sylvester.

By talking to him and a crook named Mickey, North's story is pieced together. Once an ace racing driver, North had fallen in love with Sheila Farr, who was already involved with a middle-aged protector – Browning. After a serious crash, North became a mechanic; Sheila found him and persuaded him to join Browning's bank robbery team as driver. She and North doublecrossed Browning and went off with the money. Charlie and Lee continue the investigation and learn from cross-examining Sheila that she and Browning had in turn doublecrossed North, leaving him so shattered that he was a 'dead man already'. Charlie and Lee set off to find Browning taking Sheila with them. In the ensuing gunfight Lee is killed, Charlie kills Sheila and Browning, but is himself wounded. He dies in the street as he tries to escape with the money.

A Kind of Loving
UK 1962 sd b/w 14+10

PRODUCTION
p.c – Vic/Waterhall. *p* – Joseph Janni. *d* – John Schlesinger. *sc* – Willis Hall, Keith Waterhouse, from the novel by Stan Barstow. *ph* – Denys Coop. *ed* – Roger Cherrill. *a.d* – Ray Simm. *m* – Ron Grainer.

LEADING PLAYERS
Alan Bates (*Vic Brown*), June Ritchie (*Ingrid*), Thora Hird (*Mrs. Rothwell*), Bert Palmer (*Mr. Brown*), Gwen Nelson (*Mrs. Brown*), Malcolm Patton (*Jim Brown*), James Bolam (*Jeff*).

SYNOPSIS
Vic Brown, a young draughtsman in a northern factory, longs to escape from the boredom of his workaday life.

One day at the factory he exchanges glances with Ingrid Rothwell, a local girl of 19 who also works there, but then carries on looking through a pornographic magazine with his friends. After work Vic and Ingrid meet on the bus and though embarrassed begin to talk. They arrange to go to the pictures together. Back home Vic's younger brother finds the magazine but Vic takes it away from him saying that marriage involves something different. (Ext. 2, 10 mins.)

Ingrid and Vic soon get engaged, but Vic is uneasy about the relationship, unsure that it is what he really wants.

At breakfast one morning his mother scolds him about his courting. He and his father set off for work. They walk across the railway bridge and talk about work, about being free to travel and about Ingrid. Vic meets Ingrid in a cafe. As Ingrid chatters on Vic observes the other couples there. Later they sit on the hill, uneasy and unsure after trying to make love. Ingrid saves a seat in the works cafeteria for Vic but he avoids her. Upset, she waylays him as he comes home from an evening spent with one of his mates. They make a date and separate. (Ext. 1, 14 mins.)

The couple finally make love at Ingrid's house while her mother is away. At the firm's annual dance Ingrid tells Vic that she is pregnant. Vic grudgingly marries her. They set up home with Ingrid's mother, but there is a great deal of conflict. When Ingrid is rushed to hospital with a miscarriage Mrs. Rothwell fails to tell Vic. Later, after a drunken scene with Mrs. Rothwell, Vic leaves the house for good. He gets very little sympathy from his own family and after thinking about his marriage he persuades Ingrid to leave her mother and look for a home with him.

King Kong
USA 1933 sd b/w 16

PRODUCTION
p.c – RKO Radio. *p* – David O. Selznick. *d* – Ernest B. Schoedsack, Merian C. Cooper. *sc* – James Creelman, Ruth Rose, from a story by Edgar Wallace and Merian C. Cooper. *ph* – Edward Lindon, Verne Walker, J. O. Taylor. *ed* – Ted Cheeseman. *a.d* – Carroll Clark, Al Herman. *m* – Max Steiner. *cost* – Walter Plunkett.

LEADING PLAYERS
Fay Wray (*Ann Darrow*), Robert Armstrong (*Denham*), Bruce Cabot (*Driscoll*).

SYNOPSIS
After great difficulty in finding a girl to star in an unusual and dangerous role, Denham, a film producer, eventually selects Ann Darrow and sets out on an expedition to a mysterious tropical island. As the ship nears the land the natives aboard become restless and speak of a Beast God known as Kong who lives there. On the island the film unit find a native village surrounded by a high wall, outside of which the villagers periodically leave a human sacrifice to appease the wrath of their menacing God. The natives spirit Ann away from the party, intending her as a bride for the monster. While attempting to rescue the girl, the crew are suddenly confronted with Kong. He is a giant ape fifty feet high, with a strange half-human intelligence in his features. He snatches up the girl and flees back into the wilderness. Denham, his friend Driscoll and half of the crew pursue Kong into the jungle. They start to cross a chasm on a log but Kong upsets it, hurling all the party except Denham and Driscoll to their deaths. Denham returns for help and Driscoll discovers Kong in his cave. A pterodactyl seizes Ann and while Kong attacks the reptile, Driscoll rescues the girl. Kong pursues them but they manage to leave the island after capturing him with the help of a gas bomb.

'King' Kong becomes a show piece in New York. At the theatre where he is being displayed he breaks loose from his chains and escapes to terrorise the city. He seizes Ann through the window of her hotel and carries her to the top of the Empire State Building after wrecking an elevated train. The police organise aeroplanes to attack him and they start to swoop and fire on him after he has put Ann down on a ledge. He catches one plane and hurls it in flames to the ground before the gunfire has any effect on him.

King Kong is finally killed by shots from the aeroplanes.

King Kong Versus Godzilla
Japan 1963 sd col 23

PRODUCTION
p.c – Toho. *p* – John Beck (US dubbed version). *d* – Inoshiro Honda/Thomas Montgomery (US version). *sc* – Shin-Ichi Sekizawa/Paul Mason, Bruce Howard (US version). *ph* – Hajime Koizumi (TohoScope and Eastman Color). *ed* – Peter Zinner. *m* – Peter Zinner.

LEADING PLAYERS

Michael Keith (*Eric Carter*), James Yagi (*Yataka Omura*), Tadao Takashima (*O. Sakurai*), Mie Hama (*Fumiko Sakurai*), Yu Fujiki (*Kinzaburo Furue*).

SYNOPSIS

Reports of large ice floes breaking up and heading towards Japan are investigated by a United Nations submarine, which perishes when it strikes a radioactive iceberg. The crew of an observation helicopter watch the explosion and see Godzilla – a huge fire-breathing Tyrannosaurus – emerge from the ice. Simultaneously, a team are investigating reports of a giant god seen on a remote Pacific island. It turns out to be King Kong. They capture him and tow him away on a raft, but King Kong escapes and sets off for Japan, keen to fight his old enemy Godzilla. Their first encounter is brief and King Kong retreats.

King Kong towers over Tokyo and the decision is made to evacuate the city. Fleeing crowds frantically cram themselves into trains. King Kong picks up a train carriage in his hand and gently plucks out Fumiko, a beautiful young woman. Later, he is cornered on the top of a building where he has retreated with Fumiko. A team of scientists put him to sleep with gas bombs and the lulling sounds of drums. He falls to the ground and Fumiko escapes unharmed. Other scientists report that it is impossible to use atomic weapons on Godzilla and they decide to pit the two giants against each other. The sleeping King Kong is transported to Japan by a cluster of hot air balloons directed by a helicopter. Godzilla is waiting for King Kong and the battle commences. At first King Kong seems to be losing but he is rejuvenated by an electrical storm, and the battle turns in his favour. At the height of the contest there is an earthquake and both monsters fall into the sea. Godzilla disappears from sight but King Kong emerges triumphant and is seen swimming off into the distance. On television an announcer wishes him luck.

(NB This extract is from the US dubbed version and is standard reduced from Scope.)

Kiss Me Deadly
USA 1955 sd b/w 18

PRODUCTION

p.c – Parklane Pictures. *p* – Robert Aldrich. *d* – Robert Aldrich. *sc* – A. I. Bezzerides, from the novel by Mickey Spillane. *ph* – Ernest Laszlo. *ed* – Mike Luciani. *a.d* – William Glasgow. *m* – Frank Devol.

LEADING PLAYERS

Ralph Meeker (*Mike Hammer*), Albert Dekker (*Dr. Soberin*), Maxine Cooper (*Velda*), Cloris Leachman (*Christina Bailey*), Nick Dennis (*Nick Gellis*), Gaby Rogers (*Lily Carver*).

SYNOPSIS

A desperate woman wearing only a raincoat and with bare feet flags down the car of Mike Hammer, a private detective, in the middle of the night. A radio newscast says that she has escaped from a nearby mental home. She tells him her name is Christina. Mike does not give her away when they pass through a roadblock. After she has discussed his character and relationship to women, Christina tells him that if anything should happen, to 'remember' her. She hands a letter to the pump attendant when they stop for petrol. Shortly afterwards their car is rammed and they are seized. (Ext. 1a, 8 mins.)

Mike and Christina are tortured and disposed of, apparently dead, in a feigned car accident. Mike survives to be interrogated by the police and warned off further investigation. Later, he tracks down Christina's ex-flatmate, Lily Carver.

He finds her hiding on the stairs of her apartment building, smuggles her out and takes her to his flat where she acts seductively towards him. After asking Nick, his mechanic, to check his car for him Mike goes to see Velda, his girlfriend and partner, who ridicules his pursuit of 'the great whatsit' for which he ruthlessly uses people. As he leaves, however, she agrees to talk to one of his leads to try and get information for him. (Ext. 1b, 10 mins.)

Nick is killed when someone removes the jack from the car he is working underneath. Mike persuades Velda to go after further information, but both Mike and Velda are captured. Mike is taken to a beach house, drugged and tortured. He manages to escape and now understands the clue Christina left in a letter she posted to him shortly before the accident; 'Remember me' is a reference to a Christina Rossetti poem and eventually leads him to retrieve from the morgue attendant a key she had swallowed. The key opens a locker in a tennis club containing a box of what appears to be radioactive material. The police confirm his suspicions and he returns to the beach house to rescue Velda. In another room the girl he knew as Lily Carver shoots her lover – who has master-minded the theft and is about to desert her – in order to gain possession of the box. She opens it, causing an atomic explosion.

Kiss Me, Stupid
USA 1964 sd b/w scope 18

PRODUCTION

p.c – Mirisch/Phalanx. *p* – Billy Wilder. *d* – Billy Wilder. *sc* – Billy Wilder, I. A. L. Diamond, from the play *L'ora della fantasia* by Anna Bonacci. *ph* – Joseph LaShelle (Panavision). *ed* – Daniel Mandell. *a.d* – Robert Luthardt. *m* – André Previn. *songs* – George Gershwin. *lyrics* – Ira Gershwin. *choreo* – Wally Green. *cost* – Bill Thomas.

LEADING PLAYERS

Dean Martin (*Dino*), Kim Novak (*Polly The Pistol*), Ray Walston (*Orville J. Spooner*), Cliff Osmond (*Barney Millsap*).

SYNOPSIS

Orville J. Spooner, piano teacher, and Barney Millsap, local garage owner, have for many years collaborated in an unsuccessful song-writing team in the backwater town of Climax, Nevada. When pop singer and noted womaniser, Dino, has to make a detour to Climax in order to get petrol Barney sabotages his car and persuades him to stay the night at Orville's house. The jealous Orville is fearful of introducing Dino to Zelda, his wife, so Barney suggests replacing her for the night with Polly, hostess at the local bar, The Belly Button. He persuades Orville to provoke Zelda into leaving in a huff.

Polly the Pistol has a terrible cold and is not amused by her bottom-slapping customers. Barney arrives with his strange assignment, to which she agrees despite her cold. (Ext. 1a, 3 mins.)

A sympathy begins to develop between Polly and Orville while Dino is sleeping in the spare bedroom.

While they prepare for Dino's awakening Polly learns her role as Zelda. Orville cooks a meat sauce and Polly tells him something of her near-marriage to a hula-hoop seller who ran out on her. They hastily feign a domestic row as Dino appears but end up in an embrace. Polly tries to put on a dumb blonde act to help Orville but takes an increasingly strong dislike to Dino's lecherous egotism. She follows Orville to the kitchen and complains about Dino. Orville unthinkingly replies that it is a good thing she is not his real wife or he'd throw Dino out. Polly threatens Dino with a macaroni shampoo; Orville brings out an enormous bottle of Chianti, makes suggestive jokes about their wedding anniversary and says Dino is to be his wife's present. (Ext. 1b, 15 mins.)

Later, Orville throws Dino out for molesting his 'wife'. Meanwhile, Zelda returns full of forgiveness. Seeing what is going on she repairs to The Belly Button, gets drunk and has to be carried to Polly's caravan to sleep. Dino turns up at the bar and is mistakenly directed to Polly's caravan for comfort. Orville and Polly spend the night together as husband and wife and Zelda, long a fan of Dino's, succumbs to his advances after gaining a promise that he will use one of Orville's songs on his next TV show.

(NB This extract is in Scope and needs an anamorphic lens.)

Klute
USA 1971 sd col scope 24

PRODUCTION

p.c – Warner Bros. *p* – Alan J. Pakula and David Lange. *d* – Alan J. Pakula. *sc* – Andy K. Lewis, Dave Lewis. *ph* – Gordon

Willis (Panavision and Technicolor). *ed* – Carl Lerner. *a.d* – George Jenkins. *m* – Michael Small.

LEADING PLAYERS
Jane Fonda (*Bree Daniel*), Donald Sutherland (*John Klute*), Charles Cioffi (*Cable*), Roy Scheider (*Frank Ligourin*), Dorothy Tristan (*Arlyn Page*).

SYNOPSIS
John Klute, a young policeman and friend of the Gruneman family, is asked to investigate the disappearance of Tom Gruneman. Klute goes to see Cable, Tom's employer. They discuss their only lead, an obscene letter apparently written by Tom to Bree Daniel, a prostitute and would-be actress. Bree gets a call and goes out to meet a client. Afterwards she returns to her flat and settles down for the night but when she turns out the light she gets a telephone call from a heavy breather. Next morning Klute calls on her, but she refuses to talk to him and denies knowing Tom Gruneman. (Ext 1a, 12 mins.)

Klute moves into the basement of the house where she lives, taps her phone and using the tapes of her calls blackmails her into helping him track down a client who once beat her up. One prostitute named Jane McKenna apparently committed suicide after seeing this man, while another, Arlyn Page, became a drug addict. Klute and Bree visit Arlyn, but get no information and scare her heroin dealer away.

Upset by this meeting, Bree rushes into a nearby discotheque. Klute follows and finds her with Frankie, her former pimp. Klute visits Cable and tells him that Gruneman is not the man who beat up the prostitutes. Klute leaves and Cable plays a tape-recording of Bree. Klute goes to Bree's flat, finds her in a drugged state and puts her to bed. Later Bree talks to her psychiatrist about her motivation in returning to Frankie, her wish to be left alone and her feelings about Klute. He, meanwhile, looks through Jane McKenna's belongings. (Ext 1b, 12 mins.)

By now Klute knows that his employer, Cable, wrote the obscene letter and suspects that he is the murderer. Cable catches up with Bree at a garment factory and plays a tape recording of their first meeting to her. He blames her 'kind' for his corruption and tries to kill her, but Klute arrives just in time. The film concludes with Bree's voice-over explaining to her psychiatrist that she is going back to the country with Klute, but suggests that she may be back. The phone is left ringing in her empty room.

(NB This extract is in Scope and needs an anamorphic lens.)

Knuckle-Men (Terminal Island)
USA 1973 sd col 17

PRODUCTION
p.c – Dimension Pictures. *p* – Charles S. Swartz. *d* – Stephanie Rothman. *sc* – Jim Barnett, Charles S. Swartz, Stephanie Rothman. *ph* – Daniel Lacambre (Metrocolor). *ed* – John O'Connor. *a.d* – Jack Frisk. *m* – Michael Andres.

LEADING PLAYERS
Ena Hartman (*Carmen Sims*), Marta Kristen (*Lee Phillips*), Don Marshall (*A. J. Thomas*), Phyllis Davis (*Joy Lang*), Barbara Leigh (*Bunny Campbell*), Sean David Kenney (*Bobby Farr*), Tom Selleck (*Dr. Milford*), Clyde Ventura (*Dylan*).

SYNOPSIS
In California at some time in the future convicted murderers are sent to Terminal Island to fend for themselves. The island is ringed with mines and anti-escape devices. Carmen Sims arrives at the camp and is immediately and violently brought to heel by Monk, the side-kick of the camp's sadistic and autocratic ruler Bobby. She realises that along with Lee, Joy and Bunny, the other women at the camp, she is expected to become a slave, sexually servicing the men and performing hard labour.

Joy and Carmen are working. Joy calls the doctor to attend to Carmen's blistered hands, but he is sent away by Monk. That evening Monk comes into the women's tent and reads out the night-shift roster. The following day while the men are queueing for food there is a fierce argument between two of the prisoners which ends in the violent death of one of them. His body is unceremoniously thrown into the sea from the cliff top. (Ext. 1a, 9 mins.)

Eventually the four women are abducted by a radical breakaway group who operate within a more egalitarian structure.

The rebel group are constantly on the run. Carmen objects to being treated as a prisoner and is told that she must pull her weight like everyone else. Lee suggests that the constant running is futile and that if they cut off the snake's head – Bobby – the body would die too. Lee and Joy work out a way of making gunpowder using plants, charcoal and saltpetre, while Carmen suggests using wild berries to make poison. Pestered by one of the group, Joy uses a swarm of bees to gain her revenge. (Ext. 1b, 8 mins.)

Bobby captures Bunny. Using her as bait he lures guards who have come to the island with provisions onto the beach, where they are overpowered and killed. The rebels launch a final attack in which Bobby and most of his followers are destroyed, leaving the survivors to establish an alternative, pastoral and utopian community.

The Ladykillers
UK 1955 sd b/w 9

PRODUCTION
p.c – Ealing Studios. *p* – Michael Balcon. *d* – Alexander Mackendrick. *sc* – William Rose. *ph* – Otto Heller (Technicolor). *ed* – Jack Harris. *a.d* – Jim Morahan. *m* – Tristram Carey.

LEADING PLAYERS
Alec Guinness (*Professor Marcus*), Peter Sellers (*Harry Robinson*), Katie Johnson (*Mrs. Wilberforce*).

SYNOPSIS
Mrs. Wilberforce, a vague old lady, takes in Professor Marcus as a lodger believing that he and his friends are keen amateur musicians. In fact, they are planning a robbery.

The Professor photographs the arrival of money at a station while the gang waits in his room. Mrs. Wilberforce's invitation to tea is refused but when she asks for help in giving her parrot, General Gordon, his medicine, one of the gang is sent. The bird escapes and the whole gang becomes involved in a chase for him until the Professor returns and deftly picks him off the fence. Later, the robbery begins. A security van is halted by a staged traffic hold-up and the money taken. The taxi with the trunk containing the stolen money arrives at the station and it is put aboard a train.

The money is hidden in Mrs. Wilberforce's house. When she discovers it the gang realises it is necessary to kill her. They cannot agree who should do it, however, and fall out over the issue. The result is internecine warfare, and with Marcus's death the gang ceases to exist. The police disbelieve the old lady's story and she is left wondering what to do with £60,000.

(NB The film is in colour but this extract is in black and white.)

The Lady of the Camellias (La Dame aux camélias)
France 1910 st b/w 19

PRODUCTION
p.c – Film D'Art. *d* – André Calmettes, from the stage play, adapted from the novel by Alexandre Dumas.

LEADING PLAYERS
Sarah Bernhardt (*Marguérite Gautier*), Lou Tellegen (*Armand Duval*).

SYNOPSIS
Marguérite Gautier, a popular and beautiful courtesan, is in the early stages of consumption. She nonetheless continues her 'round of pleasure'.

She is welcomed warmly at a salon but she collapses while dancing and is attended to by the men present, to the consternation of the ladies. (Ext. 1a, 3 mins.)

She meets Armand Duval and they fall passionately in love. They are blissfully happy, but Armand's father is shocked to find his son in the company of a woman of her reputation and suspects that his heir is being exploited. He makes Marguérite promise that she will give up Armand and never explain why.

Marguérite leaves Armand and goes to live with Count Varville. Armand sees the note she has left and collapses in despair in the arms of his father. Months later Marguérite and Armand meet accidentally at the card table. Her despair has aggra-

vated her consumption. Armand throws the money he has won in Marguérite's face and Varville challenges him to a duel. When Armand's father hears of this he recants and asks for Marguérite's forgiveness. The lovers are reconciled, but Marguérite is now very ill and dies in Armand's arms. (Ext. 1b, 16 mins.)

The Last Laugh (Der letzte Mann)
Germany 1924 st b/w 13

PRODUCTION
p.c – Ufa. *p* – Erich Pommer. *d* – F. W. Murnau. *sc* – Carl Mayer. *ph* – Karl Freund. *a.d* – Robert Herlth, Walter Röhrig.

LEADING PLAYERS
Emil Jannings (*The Porter*), Maly Delschaft (*His Daughter*), Emilie Kurz (*housekeeper*), Hans Unterkirchen (*Hotel Manager*).

SYNOPSIS
A proud old porter wears a splendid uniform to usher guests through the revolving doors of a majestic hotel. All the tenants of the tenement block where he lives are awed by the uniform, especially the female ones. One day the manager of the hotel sees him struggling under the burden of a heavy trunk.

He calls the porter to his office. On the way he fearfully wonders what his future is. The manager gives him a letter saying that they have decided not to dismiss him but to give him a post more suitable to his years. The manager turns away and the porter attempts to demonstrate his strength by hoisting a huge trunk onto his shoulders. He collapses under its weight and has to be helped to his feet. His elegant coat is taken from him and he is presented with the crumpled white jacket of the attendant of the men's lavatory. The porter staggers away with a pile of towels.

The other tenants hear about his ignominious fall and laugh. Even his own relatives throw him out onto the street. The porter falls prey to self-pity and sits alone in the dark lavatory until a nightwatchman comes in and tenderly wraps him in a blanket. A final title of the film says 'Here the story should really end for, in real life, the forlorn old man would have little to look forward to but death. The author took pity on him, however, and has provided a quite impossible epilogue'. In this, the porter is dining in the grill room of the hotel. As he tries to cope with the intricate dishes in front of him, amused guests show each other a newspaper which carries a report of how an American millionaire bequeathed everything to the last person present at his death: the lavatory attendant. The newly-rich porter showers money on the worthy and unworthy alike and then, in a final triumph, leaves the hotel with the nightwatchman in a fine carriage.

The Last Stage
Poland 1947 sd b/w 8

PRODUCTION
p.c – Film Polski. *d* – Wanda Jakubowska. *sc* – Wanda Jakubowska, Gerda Schneider. *ph* – Borys Monastyrski. *ed* – R. Pstrokowska. *a.d* – R. Mann, C. Piaskowski. *m* – R. Palester.

LEADING PLAYERS
Huguette Faget (*Michèle*), W. Bartowna (*Helena*), T. Gorecka (*Eugenia*), B. Fijewska (*Anielka*), N. Winogradowa (*Nadia*), B. Drapinska (*Marta*).

SYNOPSIS
A new consignment of prisoners is due at Auschwitz concentration camp.

The train stops, the people are herded out and families are separated. The Commander arrives and as he delivers orders he hears Marta translating to the crowd. He singles her out to be an interpreter, but she is still herded away with the others. Details, clothing, valuables are taken; the women are given uniforms and tattoos. As the guards sort out the jewellery Marta is shown the crematorium.

The new prisoners see the latest batch departing in lorries for the 'last stage' of their journey to the gas chambers, while the commanders discuss methods of speeding up the massacre. When a Red Cross commission visits the camp the Nazi's clean up certain sections. Eugenia, a prisoner-doctor, shouts out the truth; she is tortured and killed. Marta hears that the Nazis intend to destroy all trace of Auschwitz as the Allied Forces approach and becomes determined to tell the outside world about the camp. She escapes with a male prisoner and gives information to two men from an underground radio station. They are captured and Marta is forced to watch her comrade's torture and death. Marta herself is about to be hanged when a Soviet air raid disperses the Nazis in terror.

Last Tango in Paris
Italy/France 1972 sd col 17

PRODUCTION
p.c – P. E. A. Cinematografica (Rome)/Les Artistes Associés (Paris). *p* – Alberto Grimaldi. *d* – Bernardo Bertolucci. *sc* – Bernardo Bertolucci, Franco Arcalli. *ph* – Vittorio Storaro (Technicolor). *ed* – Franco Arcalli. *a.d* – Ferdinando Scarfiotti. *m* – Gato Barbieri.

LEADING PLAYERS
Marlon Brando (*Paul*), Maria Schneider (*Jeanne*), Jean-Pierre Léaud (*Tom*).

SYNOPSIS
A middle-aged American, Paul, and Jeanne, a young French woman, meet in an apartment they are both interested in renting. They immediately have sex and part. She goes to meet her boyfriend, Tom, who wants to make a film about her.

Jeanne makes a second visit to the flat where she discovers the stranger moving furniture in. He has her help him arrange it and they again have sex. He refuses to hear her name and says he wants to forget the outside world. (Ext. 1a, 4 mins.)

Their meetings and sex are intercut with Paul's arrangements for his wife's funeral. Flashbacks show his discovery of her suicide, arguments with his mother-in-law and a talk with his wife's lover.

Paul visits his dead wife in the funeral parlour and alternately weeps over and harangues her. (Ext. 1c, 6 mins.)

Jeanne continues to be involved in her boyfriend's film, in which she has to enact her past. She tries to discover the stranger's name and past, but he repulses her attempts to get close to him.

In frustration she agrees to marry Tom but immediately rushes back to the flat in the pouring rain wearing the wedding dress which is one of the costumes for the film. As she is going up in the lift she passes Paul, who races up the stairs. She lifts up her skirt and declares she cannot leave him. He carries her over the threshold and is amused by her screams when she finds a dead rat on the bed. As he gives her a bath she declares she has fallen in love with somebody. He sneers at this, but stops when she declares that he is the person. (Ext. 1b, 7 mins.)

Nonetheless, he brutally rejects her. When she comes back to the flat she is heartbroken to find it empty. She eventually meets Paul again by accident. He has changed, and looks smarter than before. They go to a dance hall and get drunk. She is disillusioned with him and leaves him, but he follows her home. She shoots him with a gun which belonged to her father.

Laura
USA 1944 sd b/w 9

PRODUCTION
p.c – 20th Century-Fox. *p* – Otto Preminger. *d* – Otto Preminger. *sc* – Jay Dratler, Betty Reinhardt, Samuel Hoffenstein, from a novel by Vera Caspary. *ph* – Joseph LaShelle. *ed* – Louis Loeffler. *a.d* – Lyle Wheeler, Leland Fuller. *m* – David Raksin. *cost* – Bonnie Cashin.

LEADING PLAYERS
Gene Tierney (*Laura Hunt*), Clifton Webb (*Waldo Lydecker*), Dana Andrews (*Mark McPherson*), Vincent Price (*Shelby Carpenter*).

SYNOPSIS
Detective Mark McPherson is investigating the death of career woman Laura Hunt. He talks to her fiancé, Shelby Carpenter, and to Waldo Lydecker, a radio personality who is Laura's mentor and seems to regard her as his personal property. Gradually, Mark becomes obsessed with the mysterious Laura.

He enters her apartment, searches through her things, pours himself a drink and then stares wistfully at a large portrait of the dead woman. Waldo arrives and argues with Mark. Suddenly the door opens and Laura appears, having been in the country.

It is established that the body in Laura's apartment is that of Diane Redfern, a model once involved with Shelby. Shelby admits having invited Diane to the apartment in order to kill her but denies the murder. Mark also suspects the jealous Waldo and Ann Treadwell, an older woman in love with Shelby, but Mark is most suspicious of Laura despite the fact that he is by now in love with her. Later, however, he discovers the murder weapon in a clock given to Laura by Waldo: in a jealous rage Waldo had tried to kill Laura but accidentally shot Diane instead. Mark goes to arrest him but Waldo has already set off for Laura's to 'finish the job'. He arrives as Laura is listening to his pre-recorded radio broadcast, but Mark bursts in in time to save her.

The Lavender Hill Mob
UK 1951 sd b/w 10

PRODUCTION
p.c – Ealing Studios. *p* – Michael Balcon. *d* – Charles Crichton. *sc* – T. E. B. Clarke. *ph* – Douglas Slocombe. *ed* – Seth Holt. *a.d* – William Kellner. *m* – Georges Auric.

LEADING PLAYERS
Alec Guinness (*Holland*), Stanley Holloway (*Pendlebury*), Sidney James (*Lackery*), Alfie Bass (*Shorty*).

SYNOPSIS
Mr. Holland, an elderly bank official, has dreamed for years of stealing some of the gold bullion which he handles daily. When he meets Pendlebury and they think of a way of getting the gold out of the country his dreams look like coming true. They enlist the aid of two professional crooks, steal the gold, and get it to France by transforming it into worthless-looking souvenirs of the Eiffel Tower. Everything goes according to plan until six of the souvenirs are sold by mistake to some English schoolgirls. One of them refuses to return hers.

Holland and Pendlebury follow the schoolgirl. She goes to a police exhibition and gives it to a policeman friend. A detective notices them eyeing the tower, remembers that they were the witnesses in the bullion case and places it in some nitric acid to test for gold. It registers positive. Holland grabs the tower and a chase ensues. They escape in a police car using the car radio to put the police off the scent. They engineer a crash, putting all police radios out of action. The correction of the fault leads to Pendlebury's capture but Holland manages to escape.

He has a brief but pleasant sojourn in South America before the police catch up with him.

The Leather Boys
UK 1963 sd b/w 10

PRODUCTION
p.c – Raymond Stross Productions. *p* – Raymond Stross. *d* – Sidney J. Furie. *sc* – Gillian Freeman, from the novel by Eliot George. *ph* – Gerald Gibbs (CinemaScope). *ed* – Reginald Beck. *a.d* – Arthur Lawson. *m* – Bill McGuffie.

LEADING PLAYERS
Rita Tushingham (*Dot*), Colin Campbell (*Reggie*), Dudley Sutton (*Pete*), Gladys Henson (*Gran*).

SYNOPSIS
Two London working-class teenagers, Dot and Reggie, marry soon after Dot leaves school. Signs of conflict appear during their honeymoon at a holiday camp: Dot wants to enjoy the camp entertainment, Reggie prefers bed. At home in their flat Dot is more interested in hairstyles than in cooking or housework. Reggie seeks refuge from squalor and quarrels at his grandmother's house, where he shares a room with Pete, a fellow motor-cycling enthusiast.

Reggie and Pete see Dot with another boy in a café. Reggie has a row with Dot in the course of which she says she is pregnant. Later, Dot goes to Gran's house to see if Reggie is living with anyone. When she finds he is sharing a room with Pete she goes to the workshop where the boys are working on their motor-bikes and accuses them of being a 'couple of queers'.

As they roar round the country in their leather jackets a close camaraderie develops between the two boys. During a ton-up race to Edinburgh Reggie makes it up with Dot but when he returns to the flat he finds another man in her bed. Pete proposes that he and Reggie sail to New York but a chance encounter in a dockside pub reveals that Pete has a homosexual past. Reggie leaves him.

(NB This extract is standard reduced from Scope.)

Legend of the Werewolf
UK 1974 sd b/w + col 18

PRODUCTION
p.c – Tyburn. *p* – Kevin Francis. *d* – Freddie Francis. *sc* – John Elder. *ph* – John Wilcox (Eastman Color). *ed* – Henry Richardson. *a.d* – Jack Shampan. *m* – Harry Robinson. *cost* – Mary Gibson.

LEADING PLAYERS
Peter Cushing (*Paul Cataflanque*), Ron Moody (*Zoo Keeper*), David Rintoul (*Etoile*), Hugh Griffith (*Maestro Pamponi*), Roy Castle (*Photographer*).

SYNOPSIS
In Central Europe in the mid-19th century travelling showman Maestro Pamponi stumbles across a strange boy – half-human half-wolf – who has grown up among wolves. At first Pamponi uses the child, Etoile, as the main attraction in his

show but the boy grows into a seemingly normal young man. One night, however, Etoile's wolf instincts are aroused by a full moon and he kills Pamponi's assistant. Terrified, Etoile runs off to Paris where he gets a job as a zoo keeper and falls in love with Christine, who works in the nearby brothel. Believing Christine to be a servant-girl, Etoile climbs into her room. He discovers her entertaining a local dignitary and attacks him. Christine explains how her poverty led to prostitution, Etoile offers marriage but she refuses. The dignitary is murdered and other men, all clients of the brothel, are discovered savaged in a similarly brutal way.

At the morgue, police pathologist, Paul Cataflanque, and Inspector Gerard are baffled. Paul suspects the deaths were caused by animals but he discovers the wolves at the zoo are too old to inflict such damage.

When the next full moon brings another series of attacks Paul suspects Etoile. Armed with a pistol loaded with silver bullets, Paul finds him and tries to gain his trust. Others arrive and wound Etoile but he manages to return to his lair. Inspector Gerard follows him and kills him with a silver bullet. The werewolf's features gradually revert back to those of the young zoo attendant.

(NB This extract illustrates a single sequence at four stages of production. It shows black and white rushes, with the original 'floor' sound, recorded on the set; a black and white rough cut of the sequence, still with the original 'floor' sound; a black and white fine cut, with post-sync (re-recorded) sound; the colour sequence as it appears in the finished film, with music.)

Letter from an Unknown Woman
USA 1948 sd b/w 23

PRODUCTION
p.c – Rampart/Universal-International. *p* – John Houseman. *d* – Max Ophüls. *sc* – Howard Koch, from a story by Stefan Zweig. *ph* – Franz Planer. *ed* – Ted J. Kent. *a.d* – Alexander Golitzen. *m* – Daniel Amfitheatrof. *cost* – Travis Banton.

LEADING PLAYERS
Joan Fontaine (*Lisa Berndle*), Louis Jourdan (*Stefan Brand*), Mady Christians (*Frau Berndle*), Art Smith (*John*).

SYNOPSIS
Stefan, who is about to leave town in order to avoid a duel, returns home to find a letter which begins 'By the time you read this letter I may be dead'. He starts to read and in flashback we see a young girl watching as Stefan's possessions are moved into an apartment in her block. Lisa listens to Stefan playing the piano. After a brief meeting with Stefan, Lisa describes in voice-over how from that moment she was in love with him, and began to prepare herself for him by learning about music and

dances. *She learns about his friends –
mostly women – and listens at night to his
piano playing. One day Lisa contrives to
get into his apartment and wanders
through it. As she comes out she sees her
mother kissing a stranger.* (Ext. 1a,
13 mins.)

Lisa leaves Vienna when her mother re-
marries and goes to live in a small army
town. She almost becomes engaged to a
young officer, but instead returns to
Vienna, gets a job in a shop and spends
her evenings waiting at a street corner for
a glimpse of Stefan.

*Eventually he sees her and buys her a
white rose; they drive through the snow
to the Winter Gardens, take several rides
on the scenic merry-go-round, and talk
about their childhoods. They then dance
to the music of an all-woman band. Stefan
plays the piano for Lisa. They return to
Stefan's apartment.* (Ext. 1b, 10 mins.)

The following morning Stefan leaves for
Milan and Lisa does not see him for many
years, during which time she has his son
and marries a rich man who is prepared
to accept the child as his own. Lisa and
Stefan meet again at the opera. Aware of
the consequences for her marriage, Lisa
goes again to Stefan's flat, having first sent
her son to the country. Stefan does not
remember her and while he chatters on
Lisa silently leaves. Her son dies of typhus
and Lisa also catches the disease, but
before she dies she writes the letter to
Stefan. Stefan finishes reading, and instead
of fleeing sets out to almost certain death
in a duel with Lisa's husband.

Der letzte Mann
(*see* The Last Laugh)

The Lighthouse by the Sea
(Rin-Tin-Tin)
USA 1925 st b/w 12

PRODUCTION
p.c – Warner Bros. *d* – Malcolm St. Clair.
sc – Darryl F. Zanuck, from the play by
Owen Davis. *ph* – Lyman Broening.

LEADING PLAYERS
Rin-Tin-Tin, Louise Fazenda (*Flora*),
William Collier Jr. (*Albert Dorn*),
Douglas Gerrard (*Doggett*).

SYNOPSIS
Albert, a young man, is shipwrecked on
the coast of Maine with his dog, Rin-Tin-
Tin. He finds a new home with old Caleb
Cole, a blind lighthouse keeper, and his
daughter Flora. Two smugglers, Doggett
and Cavanna, plan to extinguish the lighthouse lamp in order to facilitate their
smuggling. Flora and Albert are kidnapped
and Caleb is knocked unconscious.

*Rin-Tin-Tin fights with Doggett's bull-
dog and defeats him. Doggett beats up
Albert and leaves him on the ground.
When he recovers Albert returns to the
lighthouse and goes in, tying Rin-Tin-Tin
up outside. Caleb comes out and wanders
to the edge of the cliff. Rin-Tin-Tin frees

himself and barks to attract Albert's attention. They reach Caleb just in time.*

The smugglers are captured, Albert
becomes lighthouse keeper and marries
Flora.

The Lineup
USA 1958 sd b/w 18

PRODUCTION
p.c – Columbia. *p* – Jaime Del Valle. *d* –
Don Siegel. *sc* – Stirling Silliphant, from
the TV series by Lawrence L. Klee. *ph* –
Hal Mohr. *ed* – Al Clark. *a.d* – Ross
Bellah.

LEADING PLAYERS
Eli Wallach (*Dancer*), Robert Keith
(*Julian*), Warner Anderson (*Lieutenant
Guthrie*), Emile Meyer (*Inspector Al
Quine*), Mary Laroche (*Dorothy
Bradshaw*), Richard Jaekel (*Sandy
McLain*), Cheryl Callaway (*Cindy*).

SYNOPSIS
A nationwide dope ring smuggles heroin
from the Orient using objects carried by
innocent passengers. Dancer and Julian
arrive in San Francisco to retrieve a consignment from three unsuspecting carriers
who are passengers on a newly-docked
ship. The first, a seaman, is killed by
Dancer after he discovers what he has
smuggled and demands a cut. The second
parcel is retrieved from a Mr. Saunders,
but only after Dancer has killed a Chinese
servant who attempts to obstruct him. The
third passenger is Mrs. Bradshaw. Dancer
learns that her daughter, Cindy, has used
the heroin to powder her doll's face.
Knowing that the truth will not be
accepted by the boss, Dancer takes the
mother and child prisoner intending to
present them to the boss in support of his
story.

*Dancer arrives at the pick-up point, a
marine museum; his explanation about the
missing heroin is not accepted. Enraged,
Dancer pushes the pick-up man from the
balcony onto the ice-rink below. Dancer
is spotted by the police as he leaves the
museum, chased through San Francisco
and eventually trapped. He attempts to
escape using Cindy as a shield but is shot
and falls to his death.*

Little Caesar
USA 1930 sd b/w 11

PRODUCTION
p.c – First National Pictures. *p* – Darryl F.
Zanuck. *d* – Mervyn LeRoy. *sc* – Francis
Edwards Faragoh, from the novel by
W. R. Burnett. *ph* – Tony Gaudio. *ed* –
Ray Curtiss. *a.d* – Anton Grot. *m* – Erno
Rapee.

LEADING PLAYERS
Edward G. Robinson (*Caesar Enrico
Bandello*), Douglas Fairbanks Jr. (*Joe
Massara*), William Collier Jr. (*Tony
Passa*), Glenda Farrell (*Olga Strassof*),
Stanley Fields (*Sam Vettori*).

SYNOPSIS
Desperately ambitious to be a 'somebody', small-time hoodlum Caesar Enrico
Bandello persuades his friend Joe Massara,
whose ambition is to be a dancer, to move
to Chicago with him. Rico goes to work
for gang boss Vettori, while Joe gets a job
in The Bronze Peacock, a local nightclub
used by the underworld. At a meeting of
gangsters Rico is impressed by the legendary Diamond Pete Montana, but Montana
warns Vettori that hot-headed gunmen
like Rico could cause them problems with
the new crime commissioner McClure.
Vettori plans a hold-up of The Peacock,
but Rico has his own ideas about the raid
and quarrels with Vettori. Rico browbeats
Joe, who is keen to quit the racket, into
taking part in the hold-up. During it
McClure is killed by Rico and Tony, the
childlike driver, breaks down.

*Rico returns from the raid and hides
while detectives begin to investigate the
killing. After they have left Rico demands
a larger share of the proceeds of the raid
and assumes leadership of the gang from
a dismayed Vettori. Meanwhile, Tony has
an emotional scene with his mother and
changes his mind about the gang. He
refuses to accept his share of the money,
and says he is going to talk to a priest. Rico
arranges that Tony is shot on the steps of
the church.*

Despite the gulf that now exists between
them, Joe warns Rico that Arnie Lorch, a
racketeer who used the Peacock as a front,
is planning to kill him. Rico forces Lorch
to leave town, but is unable to persuade
Joe to join his gang. Olga, Joe's lover and
dancing partner, convinces him that their
only way out is to go to the police. Rico
discovers this and confronts his old friend,
but cannot bring himself to kill him.
Otero, a lieutenant of Rico's, wounds Joe,
and during their escape Otero is killed by
the police. Rico goes into hiding, but leaves
incensed when he reads newspaper reports
planted by the police saying he is a coward.
He dies in a police ambush.

The Littlest Rebel
USA 1936 sd b/w 11

PRODUCTION
p.c – 20th Century-Fox. *p* – Darryl F.
Zanuck. *d* – David Butler. *sc* – Edwin
Burke, Harry Tugend, from the play by
Edward Peple.

LEADING PLAYERS
Shirley Temple (*Virgie Cary*), John Boles
(*Captain Herbert Cary*), Jack Holt
(*Colonel Morrison*), Bill Robinson (*Uncle
Billy*), Steppin Fetchit (*Willie Best*) (*James
Henry*).

SYNOPSIS
Virgie Cary, daughter of a rich Southern
family, is having a birthday party.

*Carriages arrive accompanied by the
song 'Still Longing for the Old Plantation'.
Two slaves, Uncle Billy and James Henry,
serve Virgie and her guests at tea. Virgie*

solves the problem of there being no more ice cream by having Uncle Billy hand her own unfinished portion to Master Harold – much to James Henry's consternation. The adults arrive to watch the children and Virgie has Uncle Billy entertain her guests with a tap dance while James Henry plays the harmonica. Virgie then excuses herself from the party to receive a deputation of black children, one of whom presents her with a black doll. Although much older than Virgie, the child is confused and forgets her words. Virgie graciously accepts the gift and promises to save the black children some cake. The party is then unceremoniously broken up with the announcement of the Civil War. Uncle Billy tries to explain what war is to Virgie but adds that no-one seems to know why it happens. (Ext. 1a, 8 mins.)

Virgie's father, Herbert, becomes a captain in the Confederate cause. The family estate gets cut off behind Yankee lines, but as his wife is dying he makes a secret visit. The Yankees arrive before he can escape, however, and Captain Cary is forced to hide in a loft in the slave quarters. Virgie and Uncle Billy perform a tap-dance to distract Colonel Morrison's attention.

Virgie leads a troop of black children on a mock military parade with James Henry in the rear. Yankees arrive headed by Colonel Morrison. While the others hide Vergie shoots her catapult at him and defiantly marches up and down singing 'Dixie'. (Ext. 1b, 3 mins.)

Their efforts fail, but the Yankee Colonel Morrison's heart has been won by Virgie and he tries to help his father and daughter escape. They are caught and both Morrison and Cary are condemned to hang. Uncle Billy and Virgie make a visit to Washington and win a reprieve from Abraham Lincoln for the two men. Virgie is happily reunited with her father.

The Little Foxes
USA 1941 sd b/w 15+20

PRODUCTION
p.c – RKO-Samuel Goldwyn Productions. *p* – Samuel Goldwyn. *d* – William Wyler. *sc* – Lillian Hellman, from her play. *ph* – Gregg Toland. *ed* – Daniell Mandell. *a.d* – Stephen Goosson. *m* – Meredith Wilson.

LEADING PLAYERS
Bette Davis (*Regina Giddens*), Herbert Marshall (*Horace Giddens*), Teresa Wright (*Alexandra Giddens*), Patricia Collinge (*Birdie Hubbard*), Dan Duryea (*Leo Hubbard*), Charles Dingle (*Ben Hubbard*), Carl Benton Reid (*Oscar Hubbard*).

SYNOPSIS
In a Southern town in 1900 Ben and Oscar Hubbard and their sister Regina, who is unhappily married to an invalid banker, hope to make their fortune in a cotton mill deal. Regina sends her daughter Alexandra to fetch Horace, her husband, home from

a sanatorium. When he arrives she tries to use his reluctance as a means of demanding a larger share of the deal than her brothers. Oscar's son Leo, who works in a bank, reveals that a large number of bonds are lying in Horace's bank-box and they arrange that he should 'borrow' them. Unexpectedly, Horace fetches the box from the bank and guesses what has happened.

Regina arrives home to find Horace in her part of the house. He reveals her brothers' removal of the bonds. At first Regina excitedly plans to blackmail them with the theft but she is outraged when Horace tells her that he is going to alter his will in Alexandra's favour and say he lent the bonds to her brothers. During the quarrel that ensues, Horace has an attack and drops the medicine on which his life depends. Regina refuses to move when he asks for the second bottle and he is forced to attempt to climb the stairs to fetch it himself. He collapses. Regina waits calmly for a few minutes and then screams for help. (Ext. 1a/2a, 10 mins.)

Regina's brothers arrive with Leo, who is horrified to see the bank-box while waiting downstairs for news about Horace. When Regina arrives she tells them she knows of Leo's theft and demands a 75% share in their business deal in exchange for the bonds. (Ext. 1b, 5 mins.)

Regina announces Horace's death and continues bargaining for a larger share in the deal. Alexandra overhears much of this conversation and her doubts about her father's death are confirmed. She demands a private conversation with Regina, who refuses and continues to argue with her brothers. They finally accept that she has won and go, joking that they will get even on the next deal. Alexandra says there is now nothing to discuss and that she is going to leave her mother. Suddenly worried by the thought of staying in the house alone with her husband's corpse, Regina attempts a last minute reconciliation, but it is too late. Alexandra walks out of the house to join her journalist admirer. (Ext. 2b, 10 mins.)

Live in Peace
(*see* Vivere in pace)

The Lizards (I Basilischi)
Italy 1963 sd b/w 16

PRODUCTION
p.c – 22 Dicembre/Galatea. *d* – Lina Wertmuller. *sc* – Lina Wertmuller. *ph* – Gianni Di Venanzo. *ed* – Ruggero Mastroianni. *m* – Ennio Morricone.

LEADING PLAYERS
Toni Petruzzi (*Antonio*), Stefano Sattaflores (*Francesco*), Sergio Farrannino (*Sergio*), Luigi Barbieri (*Antonio's Father*), Rosanna Santoro (*Rosanna*), Rosetta Palumbo (*Rosetta*).

SYNOPSIS
Antonio is supposed to be studying law but he and his friends Francesco and Sergio lounge about the small Italian town where they live trying to make dates with the heavily-chaperoned girls and fantasising about 'Long Legs', the sexy ex-chorus girl wife of the local baron who is incarcerated in his home.

Antonio and Francesco dawdle in the street waiting for a sight of two attractive girls. They desultorily discuss opening a youth club and organising a party. Joined by Sergio, they wander up and down the street discussing a woman doctor until eventually the girls appear. Francesco follows one of them through the town; she stops, they chat briefly and cautiously about who her cousin prefers – Antonio or Sergio. Antonio wonders about the possibility of setting up a co-operative to produce salami. He returns to his room, finds he cannot concentrate on his studies and goes out to join Francesco and Sergio on the edge of town, where they discuss 'Long Legs'. They walk into town, see the two girls, follow them to church and wait for them to reappear. They come out and Francesco is told that Rosanna's cousin has chosen Antonio. The three wander off and meet a barber who is returning to the town after experiencing various misfortunes in Rome.

Antonio's rich aunt and uncle arrive and he triumphantly sets off with them to escape provincial life. A marriage is arranged for Antonio's elder brother, Long Legs finally leaves, Antonio's friend visits a prostitute, and an old woman, tired of being bullied by her daughter-in-law, slips quietly over a balcony to her death. When Antonio comes back to visit he is full of talk about the city, but he keeps delaying his return until everyone knows that he will never escape.

Lonely are the Brave
USA 1962 sd b/w 6

PRODUCTION
p.c – Universal-International/Joel. *p* – Edward Lewis. *d* – David Miller. *sc* – Dalton Trumbo, from the novel *Brave Cowboy* by Edward Abbey. *ph* – Phil Lathrop (Panavision). *ed* – Leon Barsha. *a.d* – Alexander Golitzen, Robert E. Smith.

LEADING PLAYERS
Kirk Douglas (*Jack Burns*), Gena Rowlands (*Jerri Bondi*), Walter Matthau (*Sheriff Johnson*), Michael Kane (*Paul Bondi*).

SYNOPSIS
Jack Burns, an itinerant cowboy, is resting on the ground near his horse, Whisky, somewhere on the prairie. Suddenly the peace is shattered by the sound of jets flying overhead. Jack and Whisky move on. Later they come across some wired-off land and a sign saying that it is privately owned. Jack cuts the wire and continues

his journey but when he and Whisky try to cross a highway they have to contend with a stream of fast moving cars.

Jack learns that his friend Paul Bondi is in prison for giving assistance to illegal immigrants from Mexico. He gets himself imprisoned so that he and Paul can break out together but Paul refuses to come. Jack breaks out alone, calls in to say goodbye to Paul's wife, whom he loves, and heads back to the hills with Whisky. The sheriff organises a pursuit by jeep and helicopter. Jack refuses to abandon Whisky although he could make better speed on foot but still manages to elude his pursuers. Before he can make his final escape into Mexico he has to cross a main highway. In a confusion of rain and headlights Whisky shies and is run down. Jack is killed.

(NB This extract is standard reduced from Scope.)

The Long and the Short and the Tall
UK 1960 sd b/w 10

PRODUCTION
p.c – Michael Balcon/Associated British. *p* – Michael Balcon. *d* – Leslie Norman. *sc* – Wolf Mankowitz, from the play by Willis Hall. *ph* – Erwin Hillier. *ed* – Gordon Stone. *a.d* – Terence Verity, Jim Morahan. *m* – Stanley Black.

LEADING PLAYERS
Laurence Harvey (*Private Bamforth*), Richard Harris (*Corporal Johnstone*), Richard Todd (*Sergeant Mitchem*), Ronald Fraser (*Lance Corporal MacLeish*), David McCallum (*Private Whitaker*), Kenji Takaki (*Tojo*).

SYNOPSIS
A British patrol is on a special assignment in Japanese territory during the Second World War. They capture a lone Japanese scout, Tojo. Sergeant Mitchem, the leader, refuses to kill the scout in cold blood, but Corporal Johnstone wants him shot right away.

A search of Tojo reveals that he has British cigarettes with him. A group of soldiers start to attack him but Private Bamforth appears from guard duty and claims that he gave him the cigarettes. Feelings cool slightly, but heat up again when it is discovered that Tojo's cigarette case is also British-made.

During the subsequent argument, Whitaker, posted on guard duty, panics and shoots the prisoner. The sound of the shot attracts a Japanese patrol. Only Johnstone and Whitaker survive to be taken prisoner. When Whitaker is searched, Tojo's water canteen is found in his pocket. The cycle of suspicion and hatred begins again.

Lord of the Flies
UK 1963 sd b/w 10

PRODUCTION
p.c – Allen-Hodgdon Productions/Two Arts. *p* – Lewis Allen. *d* – Peter Brook, from the novel by William Golding. *ph* – Tom Hollyman, Gerald Feil. *ed* – Peter Brook, Gerald Feil, Jean-Claude Lubtchansky. *m* – Raymond Leppard.

LEADING PLAYERS
James Aubrey (*Ralph*), Tom Chapin (*Jack*), Hugh Edwards (*Piggy*).

SYNOPSIS
When their plane crashes a party of English schoolboys find themselves stranded on an uninhabited tropical island. At first they attempt to preserve discipline by electing a chief, Ralph, and agreeing to obey rules, but their society soon begins to fall apart. Jack, the choir leader and Ralph's main rival, turns his choirboys into hunters.

They kill a pig, but in the enthusiasm they neglect the fire which it was their job to tend. As a result when a plane passes overhead there is no smoke to attract its attention. There is an angry exchange between Piggy, Jack and Ralph, but they all ravenously eat the pig.

Some of the boys claim to have seen a nameless beast and terror spreads amongst them. Simon discovers that it is only the corpse of a parachutist blowing in the wind. He returns to tell the others, but they are engaged in a primitive ritual dance to celebrate the killing of a pig. Simon is mistaken for the nameless beast and they kill him. Ralph, Piggy and one or two others find themselves belonging to a tiny minority outside Jack's tribe. The hunters kill Piggy by toppling a boulder onto him. Ralph becomes a terrified outcast fleeing for his life. With the hunters in close pursuit, he finally falls in exhaustion at the feet of a British naval commander who has come to rescue the boys.

The Lost World
USA 1925 st b/w 13

PRODUCTION
p.c – First National Pictures. *p* – Earl Hudson. *d* – Harry O. Hoyt. *sc* – Marion Fairfax, from the novel by Sir Arthur Conan Doyle. *ph* – Arthur Edeson, Homer Scott, Fred Jackman. *ed* – George McGuire. *a.d* – Milton Menasco.

LEADING PLAYERS
Bessie Love (*Paula White*), Lloyd Hughes (*Ed Malone*), Lewis Stone (*Sir John Roxton*), Wallace Beery (*Professor Challenger*), Arthur Hoyt (*Professor Summerlee*).

SYNOPSIS
Professor Challenger takes Edward Malone, Paula White, Professor Summerlee and Sir John Roxton down the Amazon in an attempt to prove his belief that prehistoric animals exist there.

The explorers discover an isolated plateau, where they watch a variety of prehistoric animals. When a volcano causes a forest fire they flee, and eventually reach their camp with the help of their pet monkey.

After more adventures they return to England, taking a live brontosaurus with them. This escapes in London causing widespread panic and breaking down Tower Bridge. It is last seen swimming seawards.

Lotna
Poland 1959 sd col 13

PRODUCTION
p.c – Kadr Film Unit. *p* – Stanislaw Adler. *d* – Andrzej Wajda. *sc* – Wojciech Zukrowski, Andrzej Wajda, from a novel by Wojciech Zukrowski. *ph* – Jerzy Lipman (Agfacolor). *ed* – Janina Niedzwiecka, Lena Deptula. *a.d* – Roman Wolyniec. *m* – Tadeusz Baird. *cost* – Lidia Grys, Jan Banucha.

LEADING PLAYERS
Jerzy Pichelski (*Captain Chodakiewicz*), Adam Pawlikowski (*Lieutenant Wodnicki*), Jerzy Moes (*Ensign Grabowski*), Mieczyslaw Loza (*Sergeant Major Laton*), Bozena Kurowska (*Ewa*).

SYNOPSIS
In the autumn of 1939 German tanks are advancing across the Polish border but the only Polish answer to the sophisticated German war machine is a disorganised infantry and detachments of the proud Polish cavalry. One of these, led by Captain Chodakiewicz, comes across a deserted country estate, where the bedridden owner presents him with Lotna, a beautiful white mare. As the Polish troops are surrounded, the captain leads an attack against the German infantry.

The cavalry makes rapid progress until they are confronted by a squadron of German tanks, which decimate horses and riders. The survivors eventually regroup and Lotna returns, dragging the captain's dead body. He is buried.

Lieutenant Wodnicki and Ensign Grabowski had already drawn lots for Lotna in the event of the captain being killed and Grabowski now takes the mare. The squadron rests in a village, where Grabowski meets Ewa, a young schoolteacher he knew as a boy. They marry, but as the village is celebrating the wedding, the Polish infantry passes by in disordered retreat. Next morning Lotna runs from cover during an air raid and Grabowski is killed attempting to get a her back. The wounded are left in a village. Lieutenant Wodnicki leads a desperate attack against the advancing Germans but the squadron, now reduced to a handful of men, disbands. Sergeant Major Laton finds Lotna standing by the prostrate lieutenant. He takes the mare but he rides her too hard and she breaks a leg. He destroys his ceremonial sword, shoots Lotna, and he and Wodnicki bury her beneath pine branches. They then walk towards the frontier.

Louisiana Story
USA 1948 sd b/w 9

PRODUCTION
p.c – Robert Flaherty Productions. p – Robert Flaherty. d – Robert Flaherty. sc – Frances Flaherty, Robert Flaherty. ph – Richard Leacock. ed – Helen van Dongen. m – Virgil Thomson.

LEADING PLAYERS
Joseph Boudreaux (*Alexander*), Lionel Le Blanc (*Father*).

SYNOPSIS
Twelve-year-old Alexander Napoleon Ulysses Latour lives with his parents near the Bayou marshlands and forests of Louisiana. The animal life and lush vegetation of the swamp are shown and then Alexander appears paddling a boat through the waters. He sees a racoon and goes after it. While he is in the tall grasses with his shotgun he hears a great noise. Water rises into the sky and birds fly off frightened as the wheels of a tractor plough through the marshland. The boy watches quietly, then runs to his boat and paddles off.

Alexander is fascinated by the intruders who have come to drill for oil, and their enormous derricks. Although fearful he goes aboard the rig and makes friends with them. The oil is trapped after a terrible battle with escaped steam, which fills the area with slippery mud, and the men leave. Alexander feels lonely, but continues with his life of hunting and fishing.

Love Happy
USA 1949 sd b/w 10+24

PRODUCTION
p.c – Lester Cowan Production. p – Lester Cowan. d – David Miller. sc – Frank Tashlin, Mac Benoff, from a story by Harpo Marx. ph – William Mellor. ed – Basil Wrangell, Al Joseph. a.d – Gabriel Scognamillo. m – Ann Ronell.

LEADING PLAYERS
Harpo Marx (*Harpo*), Chico Marx (*Faustino*), Groucho Marx (*Sam Grunion*), Ilona Massey (*Madame Egilichi*).

SYNOPSIS
In the pre-credit sequence Sam Grunion, a nearsighted private eye, introduces himself and recalls the famous case of the missing Romanoff diamonds. (Ext. 1a, 1 min.)

In flashback we see the poverty-stricken cast of *Love Happy*, a closed Broadway show, who are fed by the pilfering activities of Harpo.

Harpo is stealing food from people's shopping baskets as they leave an exclusive food store when he accidentally descends to the shop's storeroom on a ramp. After stuffing vast quantities of food into his coat Harpo notices the manager of the shop caressing a tin of sardines. Although he doesn't know that the tin contains diamonds, Harpo becomes curious and exchanges it for a tin of real sardines. (Ext. 2a, 5 mins.)

Madame Egilichi and her gang, who have smuggled the diamonds, arrange that the police arrest all vagrants corresponding to Faustino's description.

After a chase through the theatre Harpo is brought to Madame Egilichi's apartment by the police. She says that he is not the man, but persuades the police to leave him with her by feigning interest in his welfare. She then deliberately sends Harpo into a stupor by flaunting her beauty, and sets her cohorts to search him. They pull an amazing selection of items from his overcoat pockets including a large musical box, the legs of a shop window dummy, a doormat, a barber's pole, a block of ice and a dog. (Ext. 2b, 5 mins.)

Hoping to gain possession of the can Madame Egilichi backs the show on opening night. Grunion is setting off for the show when a man threatens to kill him unless he can produce the diamonds. Meanwhile Maggie, Love Happy's singer, is innocently wearing the diamonds which have been given to her by Harpo. A trio of Madame Egilichi's thugs grab her and demand the diamonds. Harpo sees them and after a long game of charades finally manage to communicate the danger to Faustino, the show's pianist. Harpo and Faustino break into the dressing room where the thugs are holding Maggie and another chorus girl. Harpo begins a frantic chase across rooftops and past neon signs with some fake diamonds. Meanwhile, Faustino discovers the real diamonds inside his piano during his performance and joins in the chase. Eventually Faustino and Harpo defeat the thugs, Harpo walks off with the diamonds without realising their true value and Grunion leaves in the loving embrace of Madame Egilichi. The flashback ends and it is revealed that Grunion is now married to Madame Egilichi. (Ext. 1b, 23 mins.)

Love is My Profession
France/Italy 1958 sd b/w 9

PRODUCTION
p.c – Iéna-UCIL (Paris)/Incom (Rome). p – Raoul J. Lévy. d – Claude Autant-Lara. sc – Jean Aurenche, Pierre Bost, from the novel by Georges Simenon. ph – Jacques Natteau. ed – Madeleine Gug. a.d – Max Douy. m – René Cloerec.

LEADING PLAYERS
Jean Gabin (*Gobillot*), Edwige Feuillère (*Vivane*), Brigitte Bardot (*Yvette*), Nicole Berger (*Jeanine*).

SYNOPSIS
After failing in her first attempt at robbery, Yvette Maudet seeks out André Gobillot, an elderly lawyer. Gobillot takes the case, wins it for Yvette, and drifts into a casual affair with her. She accepts his protection although she is infatuated with Mazetti, a young student. Gobillot's involvement with her increases. He becomes indifferent to his wife's unhappiness and the loss of his professional reputation.

He installs Yvette in an apartment of her own where Mazetti cannot trace her and employs Jeanine, a young girl, as a maid for Yvette. The two women meet in the new apartment and when Gobillot arrives, Yvette pretends to be the maid. Master, mistress and maid have a drink together.

While Gobillot is absent on business Yvette is again drawn to Mazetti and Gobillot returns to find her gone. He goes to the police who direct him to a hotel, where he finds her stabbed to death by Mazetti.

Loving
USA 1970 sd col 13

PRODUCTION
p.c – Brooks Ltd. p – Don Devlin. d – Irvin Kershner. sc – Don Devlin, from the novel *Brooks Wilson Limited* by J. M. Ryan. ph – Gordon Willis (Eastman Color). ed – Robert Lawrence. a.d – Walter Scott Herndon. m – Bernardo Segáll. lyrics – William B. Dorsey. cost – Albert Wolsky.

LEADING PLAYERS
George Segal (*Brooks Wilson*), Eva Marie Saint (*Selma Wilson*), Sterling Hayden (*Lepridon*), Keenan Wynn (*Edward*), Nancie Phillips (*Nelly*), Janis Young (*Grace*).

SYNOPSIS
Brooks Wilson has reached crisis points in his life with his wife, his mistress and with his career as a commercial artist. On the day of his appointment with Lepridon, a trucking tycoon whose account he badly needs, Wilson spends the morning getting drunk at the Illustrators' Club.

After his drinking bout he arrives on the site of the half-completed Lepridon building to submit his ideas for the Lepridon truck advertising campaign. Lepridon is not impressed by Wilson's drawings, preferring photographs, but Wilson prevents a final refusal by inventing a personal history of trucking. He returns home, where he rows with his wife and daughters.

Later at a party he learns that he has got the account, but tells neither his wife, who wants a new house, nor Grace, his mistress, who wants him to get a divorce. He goes instead for a drunken romp in the children's playroom with Nelly, a neighbour. Their antics are watched on a closed-circuit television by the party guests until stopped by Nelly's enraged husband. Brooks, without his trousers, is left to face his angry wife in the snow. She beats him with her handbag. Her anger does not subside even when he reveals that he has won the Lepridon account.

The Lusty Men
USA 1952 sd b/w 15

PRODUCTION
p.c – Wald-Krasna Productions. p – Jerry

Wald and Norman Krasna. *d* – Nicholas Ray. *sc* – Horace McCoy and David Dortort, from a story by Claude Stanush. *ph* – Lee Garmes. *ed* – Ralph Dawson. *a.d* – Albert S. D'Agostino, Alfred Herman. *m* – Roy Webb.

LEADING PLAYERS
Susan Hayward (*Louise Merritt*), Robert Mitchum (*Jeff McCloud*), Arthur Kennedy (*Wes Merritt*), Frank Faylen (*Al Dawson*), Walter Coy (*Buster Burgess*).

SYNOPSIS
Jeff McCloud, a one-time rodeo champion, rides a bull at a rodeo and is thrown. Later he leaves the empty stadium and hitches back to the ranchhouse where he was born. There he meets Wes Merritt, a ranch-hand, and his wife, Louise, who are hoping one day to have enough money to buy the place. Jeff drives back with them to the Jackhammer Ranch where he works.

To earn the necessary money Wes persuades Jeff to teach him the technique of rodeoing. They subsequently join the professional rodeo circuit on a 50–50 profit-sharing basis. Wes is very successful and he refuses to quit the circuit when he has earned enough to buy the ranch. Louise asks Jeff to persuade Wes to leave rodeoing, but this results in Wes accusing Jeff of being a hanger-on. Jeff is determined to disprove this and enters the rodeo to show that he is still capable of top-class rodeoing. He does, but during the bull-riding event Jeff meets with a fatal accident. This sobers Wes, he is reconciled with Louise and they leave together to buy the ranch.

M
Germany 1931 sd b/w 16

PRODUCTION
p.c – Nero Films. *p* – Seymour Nebenzal. *d* – Fritz Lang. *sc* – Fritz Lang, Thea von Harbou. *ph* – Fritz Arno Wagner, Karl Vash. *a.d* – Emil Hasler, Karl Vollbrecht.

LEADING PLAYERS
Peter Lorre (*Hans Becker/M*), Ellen Widmann (*Frau Beckmann*), Gustav Gründgens (*Schränker*), Otto Wernicke (*Lohmann*).

SYNOPSIS
A German town is being terrorised by a child murderer and there is a public outcry about the ineffectiveness of the police in tracking him down. When a little girl, Elsie Beckmann, disappears and is later found dead the government puts pressure on the police to bring the murderer to justice without further delay. Led by Inspector Lohmann, the police begin an intensive combing of the underworld. Fearing that their livelihood is being endangered, criminals decide to find the murderer themselves, and they enlist the help of the beggars of the town. Each beggar is given territory to watch and gradually the nets close in on the murderer. Lohmann suspects that the killer may be an ex-

inmate of an asylum and Becker, the murderer, is finally tracked down. Before the police have time to catch him, however, the beggars see him about to kill another child and chase him to the attic of an office building. The criminals ransack the entire building in an attempt to find him. When they do they take him to an old distillery to pass judgement.

The police hear about the wrecking of the office building. One man is caught but won't talk until he is told that he is in the hands of the murder squad. Terrified, he explains that they were looking for the child murderer. A great crowd has gathered at the distillery and a mock trial is organised. Becker at first hysterically denies the charges and tries to escape, but as he becomes more desperate he appeals for a counsel and a proper court trial by the police. In an agony of terror he describes the torment of not being able to control his actions. The criminal 'judge' responds that he has condemned himself by his words.

The police arrive and take Becker away just as the criminals get ready to lynch him.

Macao
USA 1952 sd b/w 12

PRODUCTION
p.c – RKO Radio. *p* – Alex Gottlieb. *d* – Joseph von Sternberg. *sc* – Bernard C. Shoenfeld and Stanley Rubin, from a story by Bob Williams. *ph* – Harry J. Wild. *ed* – Samuel E. Beetley, Robert Golden. *a.d* – Albert S. D'Agostino, Ralph Berger. *m* – Anthony Collins.

LEADING PLAYERS
Robert Mitchum (*Nick Cochran*), Jane Russell (*Julie Benson*), William Bendix (*Lawrence Trumble*), Thomas Gomez (*Lieutenant Sebastian*), Gloria Grahame (*Margie*), Brad Dexter (*Halloran*).

SYNOPSIS
Nick Cochran, an ex-GI escaping from a criminal charge in the United States, Julie Benson, a nightclub singer and Lawrence Trumble, a detective posing as a salesman, enter Macao, the Portuguese colony south of Hong Kong. Trumble intends to capture Halloran, the owner of Macao's leading nightclub, who is wanted for murder in New York and has already killed three detectives sent to Macao. Cochran and Trumble's identities become confused when Julie steals Cochran's wallet while kissing him and Halloran begins to believe that it is Cochran who is the detective.

Julie is hired to sing in Halloran's club and while she does so Nick plays dice, encouraged by Halloran. (Ext. 1a, 5 mins.)

Margie, Halloran's girlfriend and the dice-girl at his club, is jealous of Julie. Trumble exploits the confusion of identities by offering Cochran a large diamond to dispose of, hoping that this will lure Halloran beyond Macao's borders. Halloran recognises the gem as one of his own from a failed smuggling mission and plans

to murder Cochran like the other men he has suspected of being detectives.

Nick is imprisoned at Halloran's house, but Margie helps him to escape. Halloran's men chase Nick across rooftops to the harbour. Trumble attempts to hand Cochran a gun, but is knifed as he does so. (Ext. 1b, 7 mins.)

Before he dies Trumble promises that the criminal charges against Cochran will be dropped if he delivers Halloran to the authorities waiting outside Macao's three-mile off-shore limit. After a vicious battle Cochran succeeds and leaves with Julie.

Machine Gun Kelly
USA 1958 sd b/w 15

PRODUCTION
p.c – El Monte. *p* – Roger Corman. *d* – Roger Corman. *sc* – R. Wright Campbell. *ph* – Floyd Crosby. *ed* – Ronald Sinclair. *a.d* – Daniel Haller. *m* – Gerald Fried.

LEADING PLAYERS
Charles Bronson (*Machine Gun Kelly*), Susan Cabot (*Flo*), Morey Amsterdam (*Fandango*), Wally Campo (*Maize*), Bob Griffin (*Vito*), Barboura Morris (*Lynn*).

SYNOPSIS
Machine Gun Kelly's dexterity in dismantling, assembling and using a machine gun covers an inferiority complex and a morbid superstition about death. Kelly and Flo, his girlfriend, hold up a bank and make a successful getaway. After transferring the money to another accomplice, they meet at a designated point to divide the spoils. Fandango, the accomplice, tries to hold out on some of the money. As a punishment the gang does not include him in on the take.

Kelly and a crony are in the middle of a fight when Flo disturbs them. They discuss another proposed bank raid and later work out the plans in great detail. On the day of the raid everything goes as planned until Kelly is paralysed by the sight of a coffin. The gangsters scatter and Flo and Kelly flee to her mother's house.

During their stay there, Flo learns that George, one of the members of their ex-gang, has joined another and plans to kill Kelly for the failure of their last hold-up. She warns Kelly and encourages him to kill George, which he does. Finding bank robberies too dangerous, Kelly and Flo kidnap a steel executive's little girl and her nurse. Ransom arrangements are made and Kelly persuades Fandango to join them once again. Fandango picks up the ransom money and is followed by one of Kelly's henchmen. He then goes to the hide-out and the police, who were tipped off by him, close in. Kelly kills Fandango and then Flo, but is afraid to fight the police and gives himself up.

Madigan
USA 1968 sd col 20

PRODUCTION
p.c – Universal. *p* – Frank P. Rosenberg.

d – Don Siegel. *sc* – Henri Simoun, Abraham Polonsky, from the novel *The Commissioner* by Richard Dougherty. *ph* – Russell Metty (TechniScope and Technicolor). *ed* – Milton Shifman. *a.d* – Alexander Golitzen, George C. Webb. *m* – Don Costa.

LEADING PLAYERS

Richard Widmark (*Detective Daniel Madigan*), Henry Fonda (*Commissioner Russell*), Inger Stevens (*Julia Madigan*), Harry Guardino (*Detective Rocco Bonaro*), Steve Inhat (*Barney Benesch*), Don Stroud (*Hughie*).

SYNOPSIS

Detectives Dan Madigan and Rocco Bonaro prepare a surprise attack on Benesch, a well-known criminal who has holed up in a New York apartment with a young girl. They arrest him, but by using the girl as a diversion Benesch takes their guns, locks them on the roof and escapes. They unsuccessfully give chase. (Ext. 1a, 10 mins.)

There is a row at headquarters because Benesch is wanted for murder. Commissioner Russell, a dedicated follower of the rules, gives Madigan and Bonaro three days to bring Benesch in. Madigan also has problems with Julia, his wife, who complains bitterly about not seeing enough of him and their lack of money.

Madigan meets Julia in a hotel room where she is getting ready for a party. They quarrel when he says that he will have to leave early in order to continue the search for Benesch. Later, Madigan takes Julia down to the hotel lobby and arranges for a colleague to take her to the party. Two patrolmen spot Benesch in the street and try to stop him, but he pulls out a gun, kills one man and seriously wounds the other. Meanwhile, Madigan and Rocco have picked up Hughie, who supplies Benesch with girls. They come across the scene of Benesch's attack and it is learned that the gun used to kill the policeman belonged to Madigan. (Ext. 1b, 10 mins.)

They eventually track Benesch down, but in the subsequent shoot-out Madigan is killed by Benesch.

(NB This extract is standard reduced from Scope.)

The Magnificent Ambersons
USA 1942 sd b/w 12

PRODUCTION

p.c – Mercury Productions. *p* – Orson Welles. *d* – Orson Welles. *sc* – Orson Welles, from the novel by Booth Tarkington. *ph* – Stanley Cortez. *ed* – Robert Wise, Jack Moss, Mark Robson. *a.d* – Mark-Lee Kirk. *m* – Bernard Herrmann. *cost* – Edward Stevenson.

LEADING PLAYERS

Joseph Cotten (*Eugene Morgan*), Dolores Costello (*Isabel Amberson*), Tim Holt (*George Amberson*), Agnes Moorehead (*Fanny Minnafer*), Anne Baxter (*Lucy Morgan*), Ray Collins (*Jack Amberson*), Charles Phipps (*Uncle John*).

SYNOPSIS

A spoilt only child, George Minnafer Amberson is brought up in the aristocratic traditions of the proud and imperious Amberson family. Eugene Morgan, a car designer and rejected suitor of George's mother, Isabel, is a friend of the family. He is now a widower, with a daughter, Lucy.

At a dinner party in the Amberson's house George says that all automobiles are a useless nuisance. Eugene replies calmly, then leaves. Isabel and George's uncle both reproach George for his outburst. Later Fanny, Isabel's spinster sister, reveals to George that several people know about the scandal of Isabel's romance with Eugene. George visits a Mrs. Johnston to ask exactly how many. She tells him to leave her house. When Eugene arrives to take Isabel for a drive George tells him he is not wanted and shuts the door in his face. Later George's uncle explains to Isabel what has happened, but Fanny prevents George from overhearing the conversation.

After the death of his father George obstinately crushes his mother's hopes of marrying Eugene, her first and only true love, even though he himself loves Lucy. George and his mother travel to Europe and on their return she is dying. Her death is followed by financial ruin for George, who has to work in order to support himself and his aunt. When he is involved in a serious accident Lucy and Eugene go to him and all three are reconciled.

Mahanagar
India 1963 sd b/w 9

PRODUCTION

p.c – R.D. Bansal Productions. *p* – R.D. Bansal. *d* – Satyajit Ray. *sc* – Satyajit Ray, from the novel by Narendra Nath Mitra. *ph* – Subrata Mitra. *ed* – Dulal Dutta. *a.d* – Dulal Dutta. *ad* – Bansi Chandragupta. *m* – Satyajit Ray.

LEADING PLAYERS

Madhabi Mukherjee (*Arati Majumder*), Anil Chatterjee (*Subrata Majumder*), Haradhan Banerjee (*Mr. Mukherjee*), Haren Chatterjee (*Subrata's Father*), Vicky Redwood (*Edith Simmons*).

SYNOPSIS

Subrata Majumder, a bank accountant in Calcutta, hardly earns enough to support his elderly parents, his wife, his sister and his son. He persuades his wife Arati to take a job and once she overcomes her initial nervousness she is very successful at it and enjoys her work. Subrata's parents are shocked that his wife is working and his father refuses to speak to him. A strain is put on the relations between husband and wife.

Arati comes home from work to find her son slightly unwell. Subrata has decided to find an extra part-time job and asks Arati to give up work. She agrees unwillingly and the next morning takes a letter of resignation he has written out for her, but when she goes to give it to her boss he begins to talk about promotion. Meanwile Subrata has arrived at work to find the bank has crashed and he is redundant. He phones Arati to give her the news and she summons up the courage to demand a rise from Mr. Mukherjee.

Arati discovers that her friend Edith has been unjustly sacked and hands in her resignation as a protest. She meets Subrata and they set out together to find work, equal in their unemployment.

Major Dundee
USA 1964 sd col 24

PRODUCTION

p.c – Jerry Bresler Productions. *p* – Jerry Bresler. *d* – Sam Peckinpah. *sc* – Harry Julian Fink, Oscar Saul, Sam Peckinpah, from a story by Harry Julian Fink. *ph* – Sam Leavitt (Panavision, Eastman Color by Pathé, print by Technicolor). *ed* – William A. Lyon, Don Starling, Howard Kunin. *a.d* – Al Ybarra. *m* – Daniele Amfitheatrof. lyrics – Ned Washington. *cost* – Tom Dawson.

LEADING PLAYERS

Charlton Heston (*Major Amos Dundee*), Richard Harris (*Captain Benjamin Tyreen*), Senta Berger (*Teresa Santiago*), Warren Oates (*O. W. Hadley*), Michael Pate (*Sierra Carriba*).

SYNOPSIS

Towards the end of the Civil War a small band of Apache led by Sierra Carriba attacks a US Cavalry post and massacres almost the entire force. They escape into Mexico. Major Dundee, a Federal Officer in charge of Benlin, a fort used to house Confederate prisoners, determines to avenge the massacre. He augments his tiny force with a motley collection of thieves and renegades, a group of black volunteers and some Confederate prisoners led by Captain Tyreen, who agrees to serve under Dundee's command only until the Apache are taken or destroyed. Tyreen makes it clear that he intends to kill Dundee once the mission is accomplished.

As it moves out of Fort Benlin the regiment strikes up three different songs – the Federal troops sing 'The Battle Hymn of the Republic', the Confederates 'Dixie' and the remainder 'My Darling Clementine'. (Ext. 1a, 3 mins.)

After trailing the Apache for many miles the disparate collection of men achieve a semblance of unity.

It is discovered that O. W. Hadley, a Confederate, has deserted. He is brought back. Tyreen asks that he be handed over to the Confederates for punishment, but Dundee insists on a rule-book firing squad execution. As Hadley turns to curse Dundee Tyreen shoots him. The regiment is again disunited. (Ext. 1b, 9 mins.)

The troops arrive at a Mexican village. Both Dundee and Tyreen are attracted to

Teresa Santiago, a widow. Dundee is hit in the thigh by an arrow while bathing with Teresa behind his own lines. He is forced to seek medical help in Durango, where he sinks into a drunken stupor. He is rescued by Tyreen and the hunt for Carriba is resumed.

The Apache attack and are routed by Dundee's men. The approach of the French cavalry prevents a final confrontation between Tyreen and Dundee. The regiment prepares to flee to Texas but is stopped at the river border by a group of French troops. They fight and Tyreen makes a lone charge into the midst of the pursuing French. He is hacked down, but Dundee and the few survivors escape across the Rio Grande into the United States. (Ext. 1c, 12 mins.)

(NB This extract is standard reduced from Scope.)

The Maltese Falcon
USA 1941 sd b/w 9

PRODUCTION
p.c – Warner Bros. *p* – Hal B. Wallis. *d* – John Huston. *sc* – John Huston, from the novel by Dashiell Hammett. *ph* – Arthur Edeson. *ed* – Thomas Richards. *a.d* – Robert Haas. *m* – Adolph Deutsch. *cost* – Orry-Kelly.

LEADING PLAYERS
Humphrey Bogart (*Sam Spade*), Mary Astor (*Brigid O'Shaughnessy*), Peter Lorre (*Joel Cairo*), Sydney Greenstreet (*Caspar Gutman*).

SYNOPSIS
The mysterious and beautiful Miss Wonderly employs the detective agency of Archer and Spade to shadow a man named Thursby. When Archer is killed Sam Spade determines to find the murderer who has by now also killed Thursby. Spade confronts Miss Wonderly, who admits that her real name is Brigid O'Shaughnessy and says that the killer is also threatening her in an attempt to find the Maltese Falcon, a fabulously jewelled statuette now disguised with a layer of black enamel. Spade is attracted to O'Shaughnessy and agrees to help her.

Spade arrives back at his office where a workman is removing Archer's name from the door. A gardenia-scented card announces the arrival of Joel Cairo who offers Spade $5,000 for the Maltese Falcon, no questions asked. Cairo pulls a gun on Spade and demands to search his office for the bird. Spade knocks Cairo out and then frisks him. Among his effects he finds several passports all in Cairo's name, but of different nationalities. When Cairo comes round he gives Spade a retainer and his address. Spade hands Cairo back his gun. Cairo immediately holds up the detective again and searches his office.

Cairo leads Spade to his employer, Caspar Gutman, 'the Fatman' who is masterminding the search. Spade realises that Brigid is a psychopathic liar and that she is as deeply involved in the search for the Maltese Falcon as the others. Eventually the bird falls into Spade's hands and he contrives to bring the whole group together to find out what is really going on. When the bird is produced they realise that it is in fact a fake and the disappointed Gutman and Cairo flee. Spade sends the police after them and then confronts Brigid and demands the truth. Brigid confesses that she killed Archer. She pleads with Spade to let her go and says that she is in love with him. Spade falters momentarily, but still turns her over to the police.

The Manchurian Candidate
USA 1962 sd b/w 20

PRODUCTION
p.c – M.C. Productions. *p* – George Axelrod, John Frankenheimer. *d* – John Frankenheimer. *sc* – George Axelrod, from the novel by Richard Condon. *ph* – Lionel Lindon. *ed* – Ferris Webster. *m* – David Amram.

LEADING PLAYERS
Frank Sinatra (*Bennett Marco*), Laurence Harvey (*Raymond Shaw*), Janet Leigh (*Rosie*), Angela Lansbury (*Raymond's Mother*).

SYNOPSIS
Bennett Marco, a major in Army Intelligence, is troubled by recurring nightmares of the Korean War in which he sees Raymond Shaw, a former comrade, murder two other soldiers. Marco mentions his worries to supervisors, who conclude that he is exhausted and give him sick leave. He suffers an anxiety attack on a New York-bound train and is comforted by a young woman named Rosie. She helps him again after he visits Shaw's apartment and is attacked by Shaw's servant, who was formerly the patrol's Korean guide. Marco meets Shaw and learns of Shaw's hatred for his mother and reactionary stepfather and that another member of their patrol has written to Shaw complaining of nightmares similar to Marco's. Military superiors are dubious about the origin of these dreams since Shaw holds the Congressional Medal of Honour but they authorise Marco to investigate. He discovers that the entire patrol was brainwashed in Korea and that Shaw is under the supervision of a Communist agent who uses playing cards to trigger Shaw's hypnotic obedience. The hypnotic bond is tested when Shaw murders his employer, his new wife and his father-in-law. Shaw's American contact is his own mother, who intends to profit by her son's condition and make her husband President. Shaw becomes suspicious of himself and tries to fight his hypnosis. Marco realises that Shaw has been programmed to assassinate a presidential nominee at a Madison Square Gardens rally.

Marco tells Shaw that the hold on him is broken and that when he gets to the rally he is to phone Marco. Shaw is briefed by his mother on how he is to carry out the assassination and leaves to take up his position in a lighting booth in the hall. Marco is watching the rally on television but he goes to the hall when the deadline for the killing approaches and Shaw has not phoned. He discovers Shaw's position and starts fighting his way towards him. At the moment when he is supposed to shoot the presidential nominee Shaw swings his gun round and kills his mother and stepfather, who are in the audience, instead. As Marco reaches him, he justifies what he has done and then shoots himself. Marco talks sadly and bitterly to Rosie about Shaw.

Mandingo
USA 1975 sd col 14

PRODUCTION
p.c – Dino De Laurentiis. *p* – Dino De Laurentiis. *d* – Richard Fleischer. *sc* – Norman Wexler, from the play by Jack Kirkland and the novel by Kyle Onstott. *ph* – Richard H. Kline (Technicolor). *ed* – Frank Bracht. *m* – Maurice Jarre. *lyrics* – Hi Tide Harris and Maurice Jarre. *cost* – Ann Roth.

LEADING PLAYERS
James Mason (*Warren Maxwell*), Susan George (*Blanche*), Perry King (*Ham Maxwell*), Richard Ward (*Mem*), Brenda Sykes (*Ellen*), Ken Norton (*Mede*), Ji-Tu Cumbuka (*Cicero*), Ben Masters (*Charles*).

SYNOPSIS
Plantation owner Warren Maxwell has two ambitions left – to own a mandingo (mixed-blood) slave prize-fighter and to have a grandson. His son, Ham, is sent to woo Blanche, his cousin and to go to a slave auction. On an overnight stop Ham is offered the sexual services of Ellen, a young virgin slave.

At the auction Ham buys Mede, a pure-bred mandingo. Another slave to be sold is Cicero, a noted agitator. Cicero talks to Mem, the Maxwell family retainer, about black oppression and teaches him to read a passage from the Bible. Ham discovers what is going on and discusses an appropriate punishment for Mem with his father. That night as Ham beds down with another slave woman he refuses to pray for Mem. Next morning Ham walks away as a slave is set to whip Mem. Ham's cousin, Charles, accuses the slave of not doing the job properly and takes over himself. Ham indignantly rushes back to defend his property. (Ext. 1a, 7 mins.)

Ham and Blanche marry, but Ham is disgusted to learn that she is not a virgin. He buys Ellen as a bed companion. His relationship with Blanche deteriorates further when she sees him putting all his interest into training Mede.

Ham, crippled by a horse as a child, watches admiringly as Mede chops down trees. Mede is then submitted to a hot water treatment to harden his skin. Later

Ham enviously watches Mede in a trial fight. Mem rubs Mede down and criticises his willingness to become a white man's fighting animal. (Ext. 1b, 3 mins.)

Mede is again confronted with his role when he helps track down Cicero, who has led a slave uprising.

Ellen tells Ham that she is pregnant and says she fears that he will no longer want her. When Ham reassures her she asks if she can keep the baby. Ham agrees but gets angry when she asks for the child's freedom if it is a boy. Ellen sobs and Ham gives in. (Ext. 1C, 4 mins.)

Blanche takes to drink. When Ham is absent at a prize-fight she whips Ellen into a miscarriage. Later Blanche threatens to accuse Mede of rape if he does not have sex with her and eventually she becomes pregnant. The identity of the father is not discovered until the child is born. The doctor lets it bleed to death. Ham gives Blanche a poisoned drink and then tries to force Mede into a vat of boiling water. Mede refuses, but falls in when he is shot by Ham. Mem shoots Warren Maxwell dead.

A Man Escaped (Un Condamné à mort s'est echappé)
France 1956 sd b/w 12

PRODUCTION
p.c – SNE Gaumont/Nouvelle Edition de Films. *p* – Robert Sussfeld. *d* – Robert Bresson. *sc* – Robert Bresson, from the true story of André Devigny. *ph* – L. H. Burel. *ed* – Raymond Lamy. *a.d* – Pierre Charbonnier. *m* – Mozart.

LEADING PLAYERS
François Leterrier (*Lieutenant Fontaine*), Charles Leclainche (*Jost*), Maurice Beerblock (*Blanchet*).

SYNOPSIS
It is 1943 in Lyons in occupied France and three French prisoners are being driven to the Montluc fortress prison by an SS officer. Lieutenant Fontaine, who is not handcuffed, makes his first escape attempt by jumping from the car as it slows down before a traffic obstruction. He is recaptured at once and led back to the car. On arrival at the prison Fontaine is brutally beaten and thrown handcuffed into a cell, half dead. He is woken during the night but feigns weakness. Later he is allowed to wash and contacts the other prisoners. With the help of three men in the yard outside his cell window he obtains a pin with which he manages to undo his handcuffs.

Over a period of months Fontaine plans a careful escape with help of his fellow prisoners. He learns from a tragically unsuccessful attempt by Orsini, a prisoner who was denounced by his own wife. Fontaine dismantles his cell door with the help of an iron spoon which he has sharpened on the stone floor. He makes the necessary ropes from his bed-springs, his blankets and a parcel of shirts and pyjamas received from his family. With all his plans made, he procrastinates until he is sentenced to

death after an interview with the Gestapo. Then, however, Jost, a sixteen-year-old boy known to have worked for the Germans, is put into his cell. Fontaine is faced with the problem of deciding whether to kill him or trust him. Finally, they escape together.

The Man from Laramie
USA 1955 sd col 12

PRODUCTION
p.c – Columbia. *p* – William Goetz. *d* – Anthony Mann. *sc* – Philip Yordan, Frank Burt, from a story by Thomas T. Flynn. *ph* – Charles Lang (CinemaScope and Technicolor). *ed* – William Lyon. *a.d* – Cary Odell. *m* – George Duning.

LEADING PLAYERS
James Stewart (*Will Lockhart*), Arthur Kennedy (*Vic Hansbro*), Donald Crisp (*Alec Waggoman*), Cathy O'Donnell (*Barbara Waggoman*), Alex Nicol (*Dave Waggoman*), Aline MacMahon (*Kate Canaday*).

SYNOPSIS
Will Lockhart comes to a small New Mexican town looking for the man who sold repeating rifles to a group of Apaches who killed his brother, a cavalry man. Lockhart quickly comes into conflict with Dave Waggoman, the weak and vicious son of Alec Waggoman, a local cattle baron. Alec has persuaded his foreman and foster-son Vic Hansbro to keep Dave out of trouble on the understanding that it will be Hansbro who inherits the ranch. The cattle baron is distrustful of Lockhart and uncertain whether to employ him on his ranch or force him out of the territory. Meanwhile, however, Lockhart is jailed for a murder he did not commit. He is released through the intervention of Kate Canaday, a rival rancher, and goes to work for her.

Kate sends Lockhart to round up her stray cows from Waggoman land. He is spotted by Dave Waggoman who attempts to shoot Lockhart but is himself wounded. With the aid of his men Waggoman captures Lockhart and in revenge shoots him in the hand. Still in a frenzy, Waggoman signals the Indians to come and collect the rifles he has obtained for them. Vic Hansbro discovers him doing this and, after a quarrel, Hansbro shoots Waggoman.

Alec suspects Lockhart of killing his son but after an attempt is made on his own life he realises Hansbro is the murderer and that he had been working with Dave in a gun-running enterprise. Hostile Apaches kill Hansbro and Lockhart returns to Laramie with his mission accomplished.

(NB This extract is standard reduced from Scope.)

The Man in the White Suit
UK 1951 sd b/w 18

PRODUCTION
p.c – Ealing Studios. *p* – Michael Balcon.

d – Alexander Mackendrick. *sc* – Roger Macdougall, John Dighton, Alexander Mackendrick. *ph* – Douglas Slocombe. *ed* – Bernard Gribble. *a.d* – Jim Morahan. *m* – Benjamin Frankel.

LEADING PLAYERS
Alec Guinness (*Sidney Stratton*), Joan Greenwood (*Daphne Birnley*), Cecil Parker (*Alan Birnley*).

SYNOPSIS
Sidney Stratton, a laboratory dishwasher at a textile mill, is secretly at work on the invention of a new fabric that will never get dirty and never wear out.

His employer, Alan Birnley, arrives in time to see one of Stratton's experiments. He decides to give Stratton money and facilities to develop his invention. News of the manufacture of the suit leaks out, causing consternation among the clothing manufacturers. The most powerful figure in the industry comes to see Birnley, who eventually agrees to suppress the invention. Stratton refuses to co-operate and attempts to escape, but is accidentally knocked out and taken to hospital.

He goes to the clothing industry trade unionists but is imprisoned by them too. In a final chase he is cornered by both parties. It is discovered that the fabric is not everlasting after all – it comes to pieces as they all tear at Stratton's white coat and trousers. Stratton walks away, humiliated, but determined to find the fault in his formula and start again.

Man with a Movie Camera
USSR 1928 st b/w 18

PRODUCTION
p.c – VUFKU (Ukraine). *d* – Dziga Vertov. *ph* – Mikhail Kaufman. *ed* – Dziga Vertov, Yelizaveta Svilova.

SYNOPSIS
A cameraman films city life, an editor puts the film together and people watch it in a cinema. All of these activities are intercut with experiments with film form, including superimposition of images, montage, the splitting of images on the screen and the tilting of the two parts, and various angled and tracking shots.

The cameraman appears to stand like a giant on the top of a building and then seems to be inside a glass of beer. Customers in a bar drink bottles of beer, but montage makes it seem as though the bottles are disappearing because a woman at a fairground is shooting them away. The cinema audience watches film of trains and laughs as the camera and tripod do a 'dance' apparently unaided by the cameraman. Shots of trams are overlaid on each other to give complex patterns and the cameraman towers over a vast, milling crowd.

Marnie
USA 1964 sd col 20+20

PRODUCTION
p.c – Geoffrey Stanley Inc/Universal-

International. *p* – Alfred Hitchcock. *sc* –
Jay Presson Allen, from the novel by
Winston Graham. *ph* – Robert Burks
(Technicolor). *ed* – George Tomasini. *a.d.*
– Robert Boyle. *m* – Bernard Herrmann.

LEADING PLAYERS
Sean Connery (*Mark Rutland*), Tippi
Hedren (*Marnie*), Martin Gabel (*Sidney
Strutt*), Louise Latham (*Bernice Edgar*).

SYNOPSIS
*A woman walks along a deserted railway
platform, goes into a hotel room and
assumes an entirely new appearance.
Meanwhile her employer, Strutt, discovers
that he has been robbed and reports the
theft to the police.* (Ext. 1a, 3 mins.)

The woman is Marnie, a compulsive
and expert thief who takes office jobs,
establishes herself as a reliable worker and
then steals the contents of the safe.

*Marnie applies for work in Mark Rut-
land's publishing company and is
employed on the insistence of Mark. He
observes that she becomes excessively
upset after spilling red ink on her blouse.
Marnie agrees to do some work for him
on Saturday morning. When a storm
breaks, terrifying her, Mark takes her in
his arms.* (Ext. 2, 20 mins.)

Alarmed by Mark's attentions, Marnie
makes off with money from the office safe.
He discovers the theft, follows and catches
her and presents her with an ultimatum:
either she marries him or he will turn her
over to the police. On their honeymoon
cruise Marnie tells Mark that she will kill
herself if he touches her. He forces her to
submit, whereupon she attempts suicide in
the ship's swimming pool.

*Marnie has a nightmare. Mark comes
into her room and encourages her to describe her dream, but Marnie refuses. They
play a word association game which ends
when Marnie breaks down crying for help.
Later Strutt appears at a party given by
Mark, having been invited by Lil, Mark's
increasingly suspicious sister. Marnie
wants to run, but Mark forces her to stay
and they bluff their way through the meeting. Mark pays Strutt off.* (Ext. 1b,
17 mins.)

The following day Marnie goes hunting
on her beloved horse Forio. There is an
accident and she is forced to shoot the
horse. Marnie goes to the safe at Rutland's
but is unable to take the money. Mark,
who has followed her to the office, takes
her to her mother's home and forces her
to confront the causes of the trauma. It
transpires that Marnie's mother was a
prostitute and that as a child Marnie killed
one of her sailor clients. Her history
revealed, Marnie and Mark leave together.

La Marseillaise
France 1937 sd b/w 5

PRODUCTION
p.c – Société de Production et
Exploitation du film 'La Marseillaise'. *p* –
A. Zwoboda. *d* – Jean Renoir. *ph* –
Bourgoin, A. Douarinou, Maillois, Jean-
Pierre Alphen, Jean Louis. *ed* –
Marguerite Renoir.

LEADING PLAYERS
Pierre Renoir (*Louis XVI*), Lise Delamare
(*Marie Antoinette*), Louis Jouvert
(*Roederer*), Andrex (*Arnaud*), Ardisson
(*Bonnier*).

SYNOPSIS
In a prologue a duke informs Louis XVI
that the Bastille has fallen. *Provence, 1790:*
A poor tenant farmer is on trial for catching a pigeon. He pleads that he was defending his crops, but is sentenced to hang. His
friends release him and he escapes into the
mountains where he meets two other
outlaws, Arnaud and Bonnier. They see a
château burning and realising the revolution has begun return to town. *Marseilles,
October 1790:* The king makes concessions to the revolutionaries but is himself
dominated by his court aristocrats. At a
stormy meeting the revolutionaries express
their anger that the town's forts are still
commanded by aristocratic officers. A
wine barrel 'Trojan Horse' is wheeled into
a fort and its officer capitulates. *Coblenz,
1792:* Exiled aristocrats dream of returning to France in the wake of the German
troops of the Duke of Brunswick. With
some surprise the aristocrats find they can
no longer recall the finer points of their
court dance. *April, 1792:* Two French
soldiers stationed near the border watch
refugees streaming by. Demoralised by
poor supplies, they suspect their officers of
treasonable sympathies with the
Austrians. Respectable men without debts
are sought to march to face the Prussian
troops. Bonnier has debts but his mother
arranges for him to go. In Paris the battalion is taunted by a group of aristocrats
and fights break out but they are interrupted by rain.

*Meanwhile, at court Louis XVI allows
himself to be swayed by Marie Antoinette
and accepts the bloodthirsty ultimatum
issued by the Duke of Brunswick.*

Bonnier and his lover go to the shadow
theatre and watch a political satire.
August, 1792: Revolutionary troops mass
in readiness for an attack on the Tuileries
which is defended by loyalist soldiers and
Swiss mercenaries. The king is persuaded
to leave the palace. Though many of the
guards change allegiance the remainder
offer a savage resistance. Bonnier dies in
the arms of his lover. The reactionaries
push their way into the streets until stopped by reinforcements which include a
Parisian militia, who then march away to
defeat the Prussians.

Marty
USA 1955 sd b/w 20

PRODUCTION
p.c – Harold Hecht/Burt Lancaster
Productions. *p* – Harold Hecht. *d* –
Delbert Mann. *sc* – Paddy Chayefsky. *ph*
– Joseph LaShelle. *ed* – Alan Crosland Jr.
a.d – Edward S. Haworth, Walter
Simonds. *m* – Roy Webb.

LEADING PLAYERS
Ernest Borgnine (*Marty*), Betsy Blair
(*Clara*), Joe Mantell (*Angie*), Esther
Minciotti (*Mrs. Pilletti*), Augusta Ciolli
(*Catherine*), Karen Steele (*Virginia*).

SYNOPSIS
Marty, a 34-year-old Italian-American
butcher in the Bronx, fears he will never
get married because he is not the type to
attract women. One evening Marty and a
friend go to Waverly Hall Ballroom.

*At the dance hall Clara, a charming but
plain school teacher, is deserted by her
escort who goes off with a better-looking
woman. Marty and Clara dance. Meanwhile Marty's mother tries to persuade her
sister to come and live with her and leave
her married son and daughter-in-law
alone. Marty and Clara leave the dance
hall together.*

Although a close attachment springs up
between Marty and Clara, his friends are
not impressed with Clara's looks. Marty's
mother also becomes jealous, feeling that
her relationship with Marty is threatened.
It seems that the pressures of family and
friends will force Marty back into his usual
aimless, unsatisfied life but suddenly he
realises how much Clara means to him,
asserts his independence and rings her up
to make another date.

Masculin-Féminin
France/Sweden 1966 sd b/w 10

PRODUCTION
p.c – Anouchka Films/Argos-Films
(Paris)/Svensk Filmindustri/Sandrews
(Stockholm). *d* – Jean-Luc Godard. *sc* –
Jean-Luc Godard, from the stories *La
Femme du Paul* and *Le Signe* by Guy de
Maupassant. *ph* – Willy Kurant. *ed* –
Agnès Guillemot. *m* – Francis Lai.

LEADING PLAYERS
Jean-Pierre Léaud (*Paul*), Chantal Goya
(*Madeleine*), Catherine-Isabelle Duport
(*Catherine*), Marlène Jobert (*Elizabeth*),
Michel Debord (*Robert*).

SYNOPSIS
The film is divided into 15 numbered acts
and includes captions, interviews, jokes
and a parody of a Bergman film. Paul
returns to Paris after doing his military
service and meets Madeleine, who finds
him work on the magazine where she is
employed. Her ambition is to succeed as
a pop singer. Paul and his friend Robert
spend much of their time signing petitions
on behalf of political prisoners in Brazil,
painting pro-Vietcong slogans on US army
cars and putting up election posters.

*Act 2: Paul and Robert have a discussion
in a café. Paul tries to put himself in
Robert's place, but finds it does not help.
Act 3: The voice of Catherine, a flatmate
of Madeleine's, is heard talking about the
sexual situation of women. Paul follows
Madeleine into the washroom and they*

interview each other about the centres of their respective worlds. Act 4: Paul and Robert meet Madeleine, Catherine and Elizabeth, who also shares their flat, in the street.

Paul loses his lodgings and moves in with Madeleine, Catherine and Elizabeth. Madeleine rows with Paul over Elizabeth, but he suddenly dies, having fallen from the window of a new apartment he is buying with inherited money. Madeleine is left pregnant and considering an abortion.

Metropolis
Germany 1926 st b/w 10 + 10 + 14 + 19

PRODUCTION
p.c – Ufa. *p* – Erich Pommer. *d* – Fritz Lang. *sc* – Fritz Lang, Thea von Harbou, from the novel by Thea von Harbou. *ph* – Karl Freund, Günther Rittau. *a.d* – Otto Hunte, Erich Kettelhut, Karl Vollbrecht. *cost* – Aenne Willkomm.

LEADING PLAYERS
Brigitte Helm (*Maria/The Robot*), Alfred Abel (*John Fredersen*), Gustave Fröhlich (*Freder Fredersen*), Rudolf Klein-Rogge (*Rotwang*), Heinrich Georg (*The Foreman*).

SYNOPSIS
In the year 2000 workers live in misery underground the vast city of Metropolis while the rulers live in luxury on the surface.

The city and its machines. A whistle blows and the day shift files back to the workers' city. Above ground, the sons of the leaders are frolicking in pleasure grounds when Maria, a young girl, appears surrounded by the children of the workers proclaiming 'These are your brothers'. Shocked, Freder Fredersen, the son of the tyrant of Metropolis, follows her to the depths of the earth. (Ext. 2a, 8 mins.)

Freder sees the workers struggling with their machines. The temperature rises and a machine overheats. As the workers fall, Freder imagines the exploding machine to be the god Moloch eating slaves. (Ext. 1a/2b, 2 mins.)

The injured are dragged away while Freder races across elevated freeways to interrupt his father who is in a meeting. Freder describes his horror at the accident but his father is more appalled by the fact that his son was allowed to visit the depths. Freder asks what will happen if the workers rise up against the leaders. (Ext. 1b, 8 mins.)

Freder again goes to the underground zone. He takes the place of a worker who collapses and is swept along with the rest when they proceed to a secret chamber deep below the city. There the saintly Maria exhorts them to patiently wait for the saviour who will change their lives. Meanwhile, Fredersen is shown the secret chamber by his inventor Rotwang and overhears Maria's speech; he then instructs Rotwang to disguise his latest invention – a robot – as Maria. Rotwang kidnaps Maria.

Freder searches for her and is captured too. Rotwang makes the robot Maria come to life and gives it instructions to lead the workers in a fruitless revolt. Escaping, Freder sees the robot Maria in his father's arms and collapses. In a delirious dream he imagines the robot performing a sensuous dance in front of a crowd of ogling men, the statues of the seven deadly sins coming alive and Death swinging his scythe. (Ext. 3, 14 mins.)

Maria manages to escape but not in time to prevent the workers, incited by the robot, from destroying the machines.

The real Maria and Freder save the workers' children from floods caused by the uprising. When the foreman tells the workers about their children's danger, they turn on the robot Maria and burn her as a witch. Freder arrives and thinks that they are burning the real Maria, but then sees her on a cathedral roof being chased by Rotwang. Freder struggles with Rotwang, who falls to his death. Maria and Freder kiss and then Fredersen, the workers' foreman and Freder ('The head, hands and heart of Metropolis') shake hands in reconciliation. (Ext. 4, 19 mins.)

A Midsummer Night's Dream
USA 1935 sd b/w 12

PRODUCTION
p.c – Warner Bros. *p* – Max Reinhardt. *d* – Max Reinhardt, William Dieterle. *sc* – Charles Kenyon, Mary McCall Jr., from the play by William Shakespeare. *ph* – Hal Mohr. *ed* – Ralph Dawson. *a.d* – Anton Grot. *m.* – Mendelssohn. *cost* – Max Ree.

LEADING PLAYERS
James Cagney (*Bottom*), Dick Powell (*Lysander*), Mickey Rooney (*Puck*), Anita Louise (*Titania*).

SYNOPSIS
A film version of Shakespeare's play.

A unicorn and some fairies materialise as Puck and a fairy discuss Titania's little Indian boy. Titania awakes, Oberon arrives and demands the child. Titania refuses. Enraged, Oberon calls on Puck to make Titania fall in love with the first creature she sees on waking up.

Mildred Pierce
USA 1945 sd b/w 10 + 18

PRODUCTION
p.c – Warner Bros. *p* – Jerry Wald. *d* – Michael Curtiz. *sc* – Ranald MacDougall, Catherine Turney, from the novel by James Cain. *ph* – Ernest Haller. *ed* – David Weisbart. *a.d.* – Anton Grot. *m* – Max Steiner. *cost* – Milo Anderson.

LEADING PLAYERS
Joan Crawford (*Mildred Pierce*), Jack Carson (*Wally*), Zachary Scott (*Monty Beragon*), Eve Arden (*Ida*), Bruce Bennett (*Bert Pierce*), Ann Blyth (*Veda Pierce*), Jo Ann Marlowe (*Kay Pierce*), Lee Patrick (*Mrs. Biederhof*).

SYNOPSIS
A shooting takes place in a beach house at night. Mildred Pierce is found standing on a bridge by a policeman and told that her husband is dead. At the police station she begins to tell her story in flashback. She describes her separation from her first husband because of their disagreement over their elder daugher, Veda, and how she secretly takes a job as a waitress in order to buy expensive clothes and piano lessons for Veda. Gradually Mildred becomes more financially independent and plans to open her own restaurant.

Mildred's husband, Bert, comes to take the children on an outing. Mildred demands a divorce. In her new restaurant, preparations are interrupted by Monty Beragon, a bankrupt playboy, who persuades Mildred to go swimming from his beach house. She spends the evening with him. On her return she finds that Kay, her other daughter, has fallen serious ill. The doctor fights for Kay's life but she dies. (Ext. 1, 10 mins.)

Mildred's restaurant chain is a huge success. Wally, an old friend, harangues her about allowing Monty to draw cheques on her business. Veda arrives with Monty and is given her birthday present, a car. Mildred quarrels with Monty about his influence on Veda and ends the relationship, paying him off with a last cheque. (Ext. 2a, 8 mins.)

Veda despises her mother's 'common' involvement with business and so Mildred finally marries Monty to give Veda the aristocratic background she desires.

Mildred learns that her business has collapsed because of Monty's treachery. She returns to Veda's 21st birthday party but finds that Veda and Monty have left for the beach house. There Veda declares that Monty is going to divorce Mildred and marry her. A shot is fired – it appears that Mildred has killed Monty. Back in the present Veda is brought before her mother in the police station. She gives away her own guilt by accusing her mother of betrayal. A final flashback reveals the truth: Veda shot Monty when he laughed at her pretensions and Mildred was trying to cover up for her daughter. Mildred is reunited with her first husband. (Ext. 2b, 10 mins.)

The Miracle Worker
USA 1962 sd b/w 12

PRODUCTION
p.c – Playfilms. *p* – Fred Coe. *d* – Arthur Penn. *sc* – William Gibson, from his play. *ph* – Ernest Caparros. *ed* – Aram Avakian. *a.d* – George Jenkins. *m* – Laurence Rosenthal.

LEADING PLAYERS
Anne Bancroft (*Annie Sullivan*), Patty Duke (*Helen Keller*), Victor Jory (*Captain*

Keller), Inga Swenson (*Kate Keller*), Andrew Prine (*James Keller*).

SYNOPSIS

An illness suffered in infancy has left Helen Keller deaf, blind and dumb. Her parents have petted and spoiled her but given her no methodical training. She is becoming unmanageable and they are thinking of sending her to an asylum when, as a last resort, they write to a school for the blind in Boston. The school sends a young ex-pupil, Annie Sullivan, herself half-blind, to teach the child.

At lunchtime on Annie's first day in the Keller household Helen walks round the table helping herself from everyone's plates and stuffing the food into her mouth with her hands. Annie disagrees violently with the family's attitude that this is the easiest way out. When they are left alone in the dining room, Annie's efforts to make Helen eat off her own plate result in her throwing the spoon across the room and viciously attacking Annie. The family wait outside in the garden. At last Annie comes out, dishevelled and exhausted, and announces that Helen has eaten her lunch off a plate with a spoon and folded her napkin afterwards. As she leaves to go to her room the maid reminds her that dinner will soon be ready.

Annie insists on having Helen completely to herself in a small garden house away from the family. The Kellers allow her only two weeks there. In that time she succeeds in 'house training' Helen but the child still has no conception of language. Annie patiently teaches her to spell words with her hands, but she does not connect them in her mind with the objects they represent. After a violent argument with the family during which Helen flings water over her teacher, Annie drags the child outside to refill the jug. The pump water running over her fingers awakens a memory in Helen. She tries to say the only word she knew as a baby – 'Water'. More important still, she at last associates the word with the letters Annie is spelling into her hand.

Mr. and Mrs. Smith
USA 1941 sd b/w 7

PRODUCTION

p.c – RKO Radio. *p* – Harry E. Edington. *d* – Alfred Hitchcock. *sc* – Norman Krasna. *ph* – Harry Stradling. *ed* – William Hamilton. *a.d* – Van Nest Polglase, L. P. Williams. *cost* – Irene.

LEADING PLAYERS

Carole Lombard (*Ann Smith*), Robert Montgomery (*David Smith*), Gene Raymond (*Jeff Custer*), Philip Merivale (*Mr. Custer*), Lucile Watson (*Mrs. Custer*).

SYNOPSIS

David, a successful New York lawyer, and his wife Ann are a happy if slightly eccentric couple. One of their rules for domestic bliss is that in the event of a quarrel neither is to leave the bedroom until they have made it up. After a three-day bedroom session David arrives at his office to cope with the work that has piled up. His first visitor is a man who says that his marriage is not legal. Ann hears the news too, but believes that David will hurry home for a new ceremony. Instead he takes her to a nightclub. Earlier David had told Ann that given the opportunity he would rather have been a bachelor. He really loves her but she does not realise this and throws him out of the flat. Ann resumes her maiden name and David goes to live at his club. After trying to heal the breach without success, David asks the help of his partner Jeff Custer. Ann retains Jeff as legal adviser and is soon considering marrying him.

David is following Ann in a taxi. She arrives at his office to see Jeff and meet his parents. David pursues her into the office and disrupts the interview. Jeff attempts to mollify his parents in another room, to the accompaniment of the office plumbing system.

Later David follows Ann and Jeff on holiday and tries to regain her affection. After an argument David offers to fight Jeff, but Jeff refuses. Ann sends him on his way and is reunited with David.

Mr. Deeds Goes to Town
USA 1936 sd b/w 20

PRODUCTION

p.c Columbia. *p* – Frank Capra. *d* – Frank Capra. *sc* – Robert Riskin, from the story *Opera Hat* by Clarence Budingham Kelland. *ph* – Joseph Walker. *ed* – Gene Havlick. *a.d* – Stephen Goosson. *m* – Howard Jackson. *cost* – Samuel Lange.

LEADING PLAYERS

Gary Cooper (*Longfellow Deeds*), Jean Arthur (*Mary*), George Bancroft (*MacWade*), Lionel Stander (*Cornelius Cobb*), Douglas Dumbrille (*John Cedar*), H. B. Warner (*Judge Walker*).

SYNOPSIS

Mr. Deeds, who has never stirred from the backwoods town where he was born and where he makes a living writing poetry for postcards, inherits $20,000,000 from an uncle he has never seen. He is brought to New York and is immediately surrounded by crooks and parasites but is saved by his native common sense. Mary, a woman reporter, is assigned to his story. She gains his confidence and fills the front pages with the antics of the 'Cinderella Man' as she calls him. Not suspecting that Mary is the author of these articles that hurt him so much, he continues to see her and they fall in love. She tells her editor she will not continue and decides to tell Deeds the truth, but the news is broken to him from another source. Disillusioned, he decides to give his money away to bring happiness to those who are suffering from the slump. He develops a scheme to put farmers back on the land in smallholdings and works at it feverishly. Meanwhile, other relatives of the dead man have Deeds arrested on the grounds of insanity. Disgusted with everything he refuses to plead.

The court re-assembles and the Judge pronounces sentence – that Deeds should be sent to an institution. Mary rises to defend him and, demanding that he somehow be made to speak for himself, confesses her love for him. Spurred on by her admission Deeds takes the stand and gains the sympathy of the court by showing that the evidence brought against him is only evidence of the 'humanity' of humanity. He wins the case and is united with Mary.

Moana
USA 1926 st b/w 10

PRODUCTION

p.c – Famous Players-Lasky/Paramount. *p* – Robert J. Flaherty, Frances Hubbard Flaherty. *d* – Robert J. Flaherty, Frances Hubbard Flaherty. *sc* – Robert J. Flaherty, Frances Hubbard Flaherty. *ph* – Robert J. Flaherty, Bob Roberts. *ed* – Robert J. Flaherty, Frances Hubbard Flaherty.

LEADING PLAYERS

Ta'avale (*Moana*), Fa'angase (*Moana's Fiancée*), Tu'ungaita (*Moana's Mother*), Tama (*Moana's Father*).

SYNOPSIS

The film shows the idyllic life of the Samoans – children growing up absorbing crafts and culture from their parents, learning how to climb palm trees and making dresses from palm leaves. It also documents the customs, ceremonies and taboos which shape Samoan life.

The experience of education before manhood culminates in a trial of pain, when the youth, Moana, undergoes the traditional tattooing ceremony. He is helped by his mother and fiancée and encouraged by a tribal dance as he endures the sharp bone needles.

Morgan a Suitable Case for Treatment
UK 1966 sd b/w 14

PRODUCTION

p.c – Quintra. *p* – Leon Clore. *d* – Karel Reisz. *sc* – David Mercer, from his play. *ph* – Larry Pizer, Gerry Turpin. *ed* – Victor Proctor. *a.d* – Philip Harrison. *m* – John Dankworth.

LEADING PLAYERS

David Warner (*Morgan*), Vanessa Redgrave (*Leonie*), Robert Stephens (*Napier*).

SYNOPSIS

Morgan Delt, artist and schizophrenic, has been shipped off to Greece while his rich wife Leonie negotiates a divorce. Inconveniently, he returns on the day of the hearing. Morgan realises that he is both creator and prisoner of his semi-serious fantasy identification with the zoo gorilla, the noble savage. Despite her susceptibility to Morgan, Leonie has determined on a 'sensible' second marriage to art dealer Charles Napier. Morgan camps outside her house in a car; shaves a hammer and sickle on the rug; wires up the house so that Charles and Leonie embrace to the background accompaniment of an American rocket take-off; manufactures a bomb which blows up his mother-in-law. In between he takes refuge with his own mother, a Communist who regards him as a class traitor and whose favourite diversion is a visit to Marx's tomb in Highgate Cemetery. Morgan persuades his mother's friend, wrestler Wally Carver, to join him in kidnapping Leonie and taking her off to a lonely lake. But the idyll falls flat: Morgan's Tarzan fantasies are answered only by Leonie's sulks and her parents come to her rescue. Sent to prison after this adventure, Morgan gets out on the day of Leonie's wedding.

Morgan invades the reception in his gorilla suit, causing havoc, and escapes, appropriating a motor cycle which he drives into a river. He emerges in a scrap yard and experiences a ceremonial Marxist execution by Napier, Leonie and friends. Later, Leonie discovers Morgan gardening in an asylum.

Mother
USSR 1926 st b/w 12

PRODUCTION
p.c – Mezhrabpom-Russ. *d* – Vsevolod Pudovkin. *sc* – Nathan Zarkhi, from the novel by Maxim Gorky. *ph* – Anatoli Golovnya. *ed* – Vsevolod Pudovkin. *a.d* – Sergei Kozlovksy.

LEADING PLAYERS
Vera Baranovskaya (*Mother*), A. P. Christyakov (*Father*), Nikolai Batalov (*Son*).

SYNOPSIS
At the time of the uprising in 1905 a woman lives with her husband, a drunken reactionary, and her son, who is involved in the revolutionary movement. The son supports the strikers in the factory where he and his father work, but the older man is bribed by the bosses. During a fight between the strikers and blacklegs the father is killed.

The mother remembers that her son has a parcel of guns, gathers them up and hides them under the floorboards. Mourners come to see the body of the father. The police arrive to arrest the son, but cannot find anything incriminating in the house. Hoping to save her son, the mother gives up the guns to the police but he is still sent to prison.

The mother realises what she has done and begins to help the strikers by hiding leaflets for them. One day there is a march to the prison and at the same time a revolt inside. Several prisoners are shot by the wardens but some escape, including the

son who finds his mother heading the demonstration. The police disperse the demonstrators, the son is shot and the mother is trampled to death by the Cossacks.

Moulin Rouge
UK 1952 sd col 20

PRODUCTION
p.c – Romulus. *p* – John Huston. *d* – John Huston. *sc* – Anthony Veiller and John Huston, from the book by Pierre La Mure. *ph* – Oswald Morris (Technicolor). *ed* – Ralph Kemplin. *a.d* – Paul Sheriff. *m* – Georges Auric. *cost* – Marcel Vertes.

LEADING PLAYERS
José Ferrer (*Toulouse-Lautrec/His Father*), Colette Marchand (*Marie*), Suzanne Flon (*Myriamme*), Zsa Zsa Gabor (*Jane Avril*), Katherine Kath (*La Goulue*), Claude Nollier (*Comtesse de Toulouse-Lautrec*), Walter Crisham (*Valentin Le Desosse*).

SYNOPSIS
Toulouse-Lautrec makes his drawings of activities at the Moulin Rouge and sketches some of the famous figures there – Jane Avril, La Goulue, Valentin Le Desosse.

Lautrec wanders through the streets of Montmartre, thinking of his crippling childhood accident and of his first sweetheart who said 'No girl will marry you – ever'. A girl implores Lautrec to protect her from the police, who try to arrest her and caution Lautrec that she is Marie Charlet, a prostitute. Marie becomes his mistress and despite her insistence on her love for him, her lying and deceit finally lead to her being turned out by Lautrec. Later he meets her in a sordid café and she drunkenly confesses that she only stayed with him for his money which she gave to her lover. Lautrec prepares to commit suicide but as he waits for the gas to overcome him he looks at his paintings and decides to live for Art. He devotes himself to designing a poster for the Moulin Rouge and becomes famous overnight when copies of his posters are plastered all over Paris. Orders pour in, but so do complaints. Lautrec's father denounces his son but Lautrec is happy in his work and seeks out the wild night life of Paris, painting in the brothels, the circus and the Moulin Rouge. Through his friend Jane Avril, Lautrec meets Myriamme, a model, and falls deeply in love with her. Remembering Marie, he tries to stay cold and invulnerable. Convinced that she can never win his love, Myriamme consents to marry an old admirer. Distraught, Lautrec searches for her and seeks forgetfulness in brandy. His delicate health breaks down and he is finally brought home in a state of collapse. Lautrec returns to his ancestral château to die. His mother tries to rally him with the news that he is the first artist to have a collection of his paintings exhibited in the Louvre while still alive, but Lautrec lies

awaiting the end and dreaming of the Moulin Rouge. He sees all his old friends, Chocolat, La Goulue, Valentin and Jane Avril come to greet him as, smiling, he dies.

Der müde Tod
(*see* Destiny)

The Mummy
UK 1959 sd col 20

PRODUCTION
p.c – Hammer. *p* – Michael Carreras. *d* – Terence Fisher. *sc* – Jimmy Sangster. *ph* – Jack Asher (Technicolor). *ed* – James Needs, Alfred Cox. *a.d* – Bernard Robinson. *m* – Frank Reizenstein.

LEADING PLAYERS
Peter Cushing (*John Banning*), Christopher Lee (*Kharis, The Mummy*), Yvonne Furneaux (*Isabel/Ananka*), Eddie Byrne (*Inspector Mulrooney*), George Pastell (*Mehemet*).

SYNOPSIS
A family of British archaeologists, Stephen Banning, his brother and his son John, open the tomb of Princess Ananka, despite warnings from an Egyptian named Mehemet. Back in England they are pursued by Kharis who was mummified alive and set to guard Ananka's tomb. Stephen and his brother are killed. Mehemet next directs Kharis to kill John, but the Mummy is halted by the appearance of John's wife Isabel, who is the exact likeness of Ananka.

Mulrooney, a local police inspector, warns John against doing any 'private police work'. John goes to visit Mehemet who, thinking John is dead, is trying to set Kharis at rest. John and Mehemet argue about Egyptian religions. John dismisses Carnak, worshipped by Kharis and Mehemet, as a third-rate deity. Mehemet prays to Carnak and prepares Kharis to punish 'the last desecrator'. Mulrooney, hoping to catch the Mummy, takes Isabel into the grounds while John awaits the Mummy in his library. A poacher and a policeman are killed and Mulrooney is knocked out. Mehemet lets the Mummy into the house and it is in the process of strangling John when Isabel enters and commands it to stop. It does so at once. Mehemet orders the Mummy to kill her, but instead it kills him and then walks off into the woods with Isabel. By now Mulrooney has recovered and the police arrive with some of the villagers. They follow Kharis to a swamp. John gets Isabel to command it to put her down. It does so and the police and villagers open fire.

The Music Room
(*see* Jalsaghar)

My Darling Clementine
USA 1946 sd b/w 14

PRODUCTION
p.c – 20th Century-Fox. *p* – Darryl F.

Zanuck. *d* – John Ford. *sc* – Samuel G. Engel, Winston Miller, from a story by Sam Hellman, based on the book *Wyatt Earp, Frontier Marshall* by Stuart N. Lake. *ph* – Joseph P. MacDonald. *ed* – Dorothy Spencer. *a.d* – James Basevi, Lyle H. Wheeler. *m* – Cyril Mockridge. *cost* – René Hubert.

LEADING PLAYERS
Henry Fonda (*Wyatt Earp*), Cathy Downs (*Clementine Carter*), Victor Mature (*Doc Holliday*), Linda Darnell (*Chihuahua*).

SYNOPSIS
Wyatt Earp becomes the Marshall of Tombstone to avenge the murder of one of his brothers. He suspects the Clanton family of the killing but has no evidence. As Marshall, Earp is drawn into the life of the town. He is forced to confront the gunman Doc Holliday, but a strange friendship develops between the two men after Earp fails to kill the consumptive Holliday when he is having a coughing fit. Earp meets Clementine, Doc's former fiancée from the east.

On a Sunday morning Earp leaves the barber's shop and sits on the verandah. He is invited to the dance the town is holding to celebrate the building of the church. At first he declines, but later when Clementine appears he escorts her to the dance. In the meantime Doc Holliday has decided to marry Chihuahua, a glamorous bar girl.

Wyatt gets proof that it was the Clantons who killed his brother and he and his remaining brothers meet and fight the Clantons at the OK Corral. Wyatt leaves town with the help of Doc, promising Clementine that he will be back.

My Sister Eileen
USA 1955 sd col 15 + 5

PRODUCTION
p.c – Columbia. *p* – Fred Kohlmar. *d* – Richard Quine. *sc* – Blake Edwards and Richard Quine, from the play by Joseph Fields and Jerome Chodorov, adapted from stories by Ruth McKenney. *ph* – Charles Lawton Jr. (CinemaScope and Technicolor). *ed* – Charles Nelson. *a.d* – Walter Holscher. *m* – Morris Stoloff, George Duning. *lyrics* – Jule Styne and Leo Robin. *choreo* – Bob Fosse.

LEADING PLAYERS
Janet Leigh (*Eileen Sherwood*), Betty Garrett (*Ruth Sherwood*), Jack Lemmon (*Bob Baker*), Bob Fosse (*Frank Lippencott*), Tommy Rall (*Chick Clark*).

SYNOPSIS
Blonde, beautiful scatter-brain Eileen and her older sister Ruth arrive in New York from Columbus, Ohio hoping to become, respectively, an actress and a writer. They rent a scruffy basement. Ruth meets Bob Baker, an attractive magazine editor, and pretends that her stories about a man-chased heroine are based on her own life rather than her sister's.

Rick, their neighbour in the apartment block, has his athletics practice interrupted by Helen, his girlfriend, who explains that her mother is coming to stay. They sheepishly ask Eileen and Ruth if Rick can stay with them for a few days so that Helen's mother won't realise that they share a flat. Eileen agrees, much to Ruth's irritation and tells her sister that she has invited Frank, a soda-fountain operator, and Chick, his smooth-talking journalist friend, to dinner. Eileen and Ruth sing 'There's Nothing Like Love'. (Ext. 1a, 5 mins.)

Eileen, Ruth, Frank and Chick go to a nightclub.

As usual, Frank and Chick direct all their attention to Eileen, and treat Ruth as a mother-confessor. Ruth is horrified to see Bob Baker arrive and tries to hide under the table, but he finds her there. She persuades Eileen, Chick and Frank to leave the nightclub with her. (Ext. 1b, 5 mins.)

They get drunk and perform 'Give Me a Band and My Baby' on a deserted bandstage. (Ext. 1c/2, 5 mins.)

To get Eileen alone Chick inveigles Ruth to Brooklyn to cover the arrival of a Brazilian cadet training ship. Ruth returns home pursued by the cadets who initiate a gigantic conga line which ends in a riot and jail. After many confusions Bob admits his love for Ruth and Frank proposes to Eileen. The Brazilian cadets arrive to apologise to the Sherwood sisters, Ruth inadvertently mentions the word conga and the dance starts again.

(NB These extracts are standard reduced from Scope.)

Naked Hearts (Les Coeurs verts)
France 1966 sd b/w 20

PRODUCTION
p.c – Films Raoul Ploquin/Sodor Films. *p* – Raoul Ploquin. *d* – Edouard Luntz. *sc* – Edouard Luntz. *ph* – Jean Badal. *ed* – Suzanne Sandberg, Colette Kouchner. *m* – Serge Gainsbourg, Henri Renaud.

LEADING PLAYERS
Gerard Zimmerman (*Zim*), Erick Penet (*Jean-Pierre*), Marise Maire (*Jacqueline*), Françoise Bonneau (*Patricia*).

SYNOPSIS
Zim is imprisoned for stealing petrol from parked cars. Among his fellow prisoners is another juvenile, Jean-Pierre, a petty thief. Zim and Jean-Pierre are released on the same day and they explore Paris together. Nearing home, they stop at a local café where they meet up with a gang. Jean-Pierre's mother receives him coldly and sends Zim away when he arrives the following day to ask Jean-Pierre to join him in looking for work. Zim spends a fruitless day and ends up at the café where one of the gang unsuccessfully tries to persuade him to help him to steal a car.

Jean-Pierre has spent the day at the café. When he catches the eye of a factory girl passing by one of the gang bets him that he cannot pick her up. Jean-Pierre accepts the bet and finds the girl waiting for him outside. The leader of the gang suggests that they all go for a walk on some wasteland and the girl agrees to accompany them. The leader tells the girl that she must choose one of them as her lover. Unenthusiastically she picks Jean-Pierre and they have sex under the surveillance of the others. With the exception of Zim, the others also have sex with her.

The gang is picked up by the police and taken before the magistrate who releases them with a warning. Zim finds a job on a building site. At a dance Zim is attracted to Pat, a smart ambitious girl. Jean-Pierre sees the girl from the café sitting miserably by herself and attempts to excuse himself for what happened. A group of wealthy youths arrive at the dance and Pat deserts Zim for one of them. Later, however, Zim finds her waiting for him. Zim persuades Jean-Pierre to join him at the building site, but he finds the discipline too great and goes back to his life at the café. One day, as Zim goes to meet Pat he see her driving off with her smart boyfriend. Jean-Pierre finally persuades his girl to go out with him, but they are accosted by the gang and she walks off accusing him of arranging the incident. The gang meets two boys from the reform school and raid a store. Later the boys break into another store and are shot by the owner. Eventually Zim is given a place in a trade school. When he visits Jean-Pierre he sees him being taken away by the police for attempting to steal a car.

Nanook of the North
USA 1922 st b/w 7

PRODUCTION
p.c – Revillon Frères. *d* – Robert J. Flaherty. *ph* – Robert J. Flaherty. *ph* – Robert J. Flaherty. *ed* – Robert J. Flaherty.

LEADING PLAYERS
Nanook, Nyla, Allee, Rainbow, Conayou.

SYNOPSIS
After several days' trek Nanook, his wife Nyla and the rest of their Eskimo family arrive at a trading station. They barter furs for goods and Nanook listens to music from a gramophone. The traders explain that the sounds come from a record, but Nanook, who is familiar with the songs of whales, tries to eat it. The nomadic family continue on their travels searching for food. A group of Eskimo men fight and eventually kill a walrus.

Nanook builds an igloo, first testing the snow to check that it is packed firmly enough. He cuts blocks and then builds walls including an ice window for illumination. The family moves its belongings inside. Nanook teaches his small son to shoot with a bow and arrow.

Days later, a blizzard makes building impossible and it begins to look as though the family will perish, but they find a deserted igloo left by another group and sleep inside it until the storm fades away.

Nazarin
Mexico 1958 sd b/w 16

PRODUCTION
p.c – Producciones Barbachano Ponce
S.A. *p* – Manuel Barbachano Ponce. *d* –
Luis Buñuel. *sc* – Julio Alejandro, Luis
Buñuel, from the novel by Benito Pérez
Galdós. *ph* – Gabriel Figueroa. *ed* –
Carlos Savage. *a.d* – Edward Fitzgerald.

LEADING PLAYERS
Francisco Rabal (*Nazarin*), Margo Lopez
(*Beatriz*), Rita Macedo (*Andara*), Noe
Murayama (*El Pinto*).

SYNOPSIS
Mexico 1900. The dictator Porfirio Diaz
reigns, supported by the landowning class,
a military clique and a conservative clergy.
In a slum district filled with beggars,
whores and thieves, Nazarin, a humble
priest, lives near two women, Beatriz and
Andara. Beatriz has attempted to commit
suicide and Andara, a flamboyant prostitute, has killed another woman in a brawl.
Both go to the priest for help and refuge.
Deprived of his clerical garb by the church
authorities, Nazarin takes to the road dressed like a simple workman to live a Christ-
like life among the poor. He is accompanied by the faithful Beatriz and by
Andara, who is now a fugitive from justice.
Nazarin asks for work on the railway, but
his humble offer to work just for his keep
leads to a clash between workers and
employers in which several workers are
killed. In a village where he cures a sick
child, hysterical women acclaim him as a
witchdoctor rather than a priest and in a
town struck by cholera, two dying lovers,
still in the grip of passion, refuse the religious comfort he offers them. Finally,
Nazarin, Beatriz and Andara are captured
in a small village and imprisoned.

*The prisoners are brought out for the
day's march, during which a guard has to
restore order after Nazarin has been
humiliated by the other prisoners. Beatriz
realises the nature of her love for Nazarin
and throws a fit. Further humiliated in the
jail, Nazarin forgives an attacker but
despises him. The beating is stopped by
another prisoner who befriends Nazarin
and in conversation questions the value of
either of their lives. The church arranges
for Nazarin to be escorted separately by
a guard in plain clothes. Beatriz returns to
her former way of life and Nazarin overcomes some of his doubts and accepts a
pineapple from a trader, choosing man's
charity over God's comfort.*

Never Weaken
USA 1921 st b/w 18
(w. **The Soilers**)

PRODUCTION
p.c – Hal Roach. *d* – Fred Newmeyer,
Sam Taylor.

LEADING PLAYERS
Harold Lloyd (*Harold*), Mildred Davies
(*Mildred*).

SYNOPSIS
*Harold is in love with the girl who works
for an osteopath in the next office to his
in a skyscraper. He dangles a ring for her
on a fishing rod. When she is sacked
because there are not enough patients
Harold determines to find some. He persuades a friendly acrobat to pretend to hurt
himself by falling and to be 'cured' by
Harold's fake osteopathic manipulations.
Harold then distributes the osteopath's
business cards to the amazed crowd. The
plan goes wrong when Harold mistakes a
man who has really had an accident for his
friend and rushes back to the osteopath's
office. There he sees his girlfriend hugging
another man and saying that he can marry
her. Devastated, Harold decides to kill
himself and ties the trigger of his gun to
the door handle, intending that the janitor
will shoot him when he opens it. Before
this can happen, however, Harold is lifted
out of his open office window by a girder
from the massive building works opposite.
At first he believes that he is in heaven and
imagines that a statue is an angel, but he
soon realises the danger and attempts to
climb back down to the ground. After
several terrifying incidents he eventually
finds his way to the ground. There, his girlfriend explains that the man he saw her
with is her brother, a clergyman, and that
she was saying that he could conduct their
wedding ceremony. Delighted, Harold
leads her to sit next to him on a girder from
the building site and only just avoids them
both being whisked up the half-built
skyscraper.*

New Babylon
USSR 1929 st b/w 13

PRODUCTION
p.c – Sovkino. *d* – Grigori Kozintsev,
Leonid Trauberg. *sc* – Grigori Kozintsev,
Leonid Trauberg. *ph* – Andrei Moskvin
and Yevgeni Mikhailov. *ed* – Grigori
Kozintsev and Leonid Trauberg.

LEADING PLAYERS
Yelena Kuzmina (*Louise, A Shop
Assistant*), Pyotr Sobolevsky (*Jean, A
Soldier*), David Gotman (*Department
Store Proprietor*).

SYNOPSIS
Paris 1877. A sale is in progress at New
Babylon, an opulent department store
where Louise, an overworked shop
assistant, is employed. Customers flock to
buy lace, haberdashery, fans and Oriental
curiosities. Later, many of them go to a
ball where a journalist frantically tries to
tell the revellers that the French army has
been defeated by the Germans. Nobody
listens. As the cabaret continues the Germans are seen riding towards Paris and the
poor of Paris fraternise with the French
soldiers. Louise meets and falls in love with
Jean, a peasant soldier, who is mainly concerned to return to his village. The government surrenders but the people take up
arms and build barricades, setting up the
revolutionary Paris Commune. Louise is in
the forefront of the fight and persuades
Jean to join in.

*The 49th, and last, day of the Com-
mune. The Communards remove cobbles
from the streets to build the barricades and
ransack the New Babylon store. Meanwhile the rich enjoy a picnic at Versailles.
A French soldier opens fire and the battle
begins while an old man plays revolutionary songs on a piano that has been used
as part of a barricade. A woman takes up
a gun from a dead man and kills the
soldiers as they advance.*

The Commune is crushed and the Communards executed. Jean digs Louise's
grave.

New Face in Hell
USA 1967 sd col 20

PRODUCTION
p.c – Universal. *p.* – Edward J. Montagne.
d – John Guillermin. *sc* – Philip Reisman
Jr., from the story by Philip Reisman Jr.
and Edward J. Montagne. *ph* – Loyal
Griggs (TechniScope and Technicolor). *ed*
– Sam Waxman. *a.d* – Alexander
Golitzen, Philip Harrison. *m* – Neal Hefti.

LEADING PLAYERS
George Peppard (*P. J. Detweiler*),
Raymond Burr (*William Orbison*), Gayle
Hunnicutt (*Maureen Preble*), Coleen Gray
(*Betty Orbison*), Jason Evers (*Jason
Grenoble*).

SYNOPSIS
*In the credit sequence P. J. Detweiler, a
down-and-out private eye, is involved in
a seedy co-respondent deal. The husband's
henchmen beat him up to make it look
real, for which they give him an extra $50.
P.J. tries to throw the money back in their
faces, but they merely hit him again.
Finally he stoops down and picks up the
note. (Ext. 1a, 4 mins.)*

His next job comes when he is hired by
tycoon William Orbison as bodyguard to
his mistress, Maureen Preble.

*P.J. arrives at Maureen Preble's house.
She tells him that someone is trying to
murder her. (Ext. 1b, 5 mins.)*

It seems that the murder attempts have
been engineered by Orbison's wife Betty
and her family, who fear that Orbison
might leave Maureen his money. After two
further attempts on Maureen's life have
been made, Orbison decides to take the
whole family and Maureen to an island in
the West Indies. He disregards P.J.'s protests that this will put Maureen in greater
danger.

*Orbison, his wife, her family, Maureen
Preble and P.J. arrive at the island and the
party is met by the governor. The Chief
Inspector of Police checks up on P.J. (Ext.
1c, 5 mins.)*

P.J. kills a prowler, who turns out to be
Jason Grenoble – Orbison's business
manager. With the matter apparently
closed P.J. is dismissed but he decides to
investigate further when he learns that the

gun Grenoble had been carrying was not loaded. He discovers that Grenoble was blackmailing Orbison.

P.J. realises that he had been set up to kill Grenoble. He confronts Orbison, who is about to shoot him when Maureen arrives. She shoots Orbison and runs off. P.J. chases her and tells her he knows of her involvement in the scheme to get rid of Grenoble. The police arrive, but while attempting to escape, Maureen is shot by the wounded Orbison, who in turn is shot by P.J. Later, in a friend's bar, P.J. takes his revenge on the man who set him up as co-respondent in the opening scenes of the film. (Ext. 1d, 6 mins.)

(NB Apart from the opening credits this extract is standard reduced from Scope.)

A New Leaf
USA 1970 sd col 18

PRODUCTION
p.c – Paramount/Aries/Elkins Productions. p – Florence Nerlinger. d – Elaine May. sc – Elaine May, from the short story *The Green Heart* by Jack Ritchie. ph – Gayne Rescher (Colour by Movielab). ed – Fredric Steinkamp, Donald Guidice. a.d – Warren Clymer. cost – Anthea Sylbert.

LEADING PLAYERS
Walter Matthau (*Henry Graham*), Elaine May (*Henrietta Lowell*), Jack Weston (*Andrew McPherson*), George Rose (*Harold*), William Redfield (*Beckett*), James Coco (*Uncle Harry*), Graham Jarvis (*Bo*).

SYNOPSIS
During the pre-credit sequence an 'operation' is carried out on a sports car belonging to Henry Graham, a pedantic, wealthy and middle-aged batchelor. Henry continues his blasé social round and ignores his lawyer's attempts to contact him. When he finally does, he tells Henry that he is bankrupt. (Ext. 1a, 6 mins.)

Harold, his faithful butler, exhorts him to marry a rich wife. Henry borrows money from his Uncle Harry on the understanding that unless he is married and the loan is returned within six weeks, he will lose all his assets.

Henry looks for marital possibilities, but the women he meets are either too passionate or too philanthropic. Finally, at an afternoon tea party his attention is drawn to Henrietta Lowell, a socially gauche but wealthy botanist. When she embarrasses everyone by upsetting two cups of tea Henry seizes the opportunity and stands up for her against the hostess. He insists on driving her home, but his car breaks down. They watch the sunset and she tells him her botanical obsessions. The breakdown van rescues them the next morning and he promises to see her again. (Ext. 1b, 12 mins.)

Henry woos and wins Henrietta despite the efforts of her lawyer, who is exploiting her financially, to stop the marriage. On their honeymoon she discovers a new species of fern while Henry reads books on poison, intending to murder her. When they return Henry takes over her household and dismisses the servants. Henrietta's untidiness drives Henry to distraction but she appears not to notice and names her botanical discovery after him. They go on a field trip together and when their canoe overturns Henry prepares to leave her to drown. The sight of another specimen of the fern makes him forget his intention and as he rescues her he resigns himself to a lifetime of marriage.

Die Nibelungen: II – Kriemhilds Rache
Germany 1924 st b/w 20

PRODUCTION
p.c – Decla-Bioscop/Ufa. p – Erich Pommer. d – Fritz Lang. sc – Thea von Harbou, from a 13th-century poem and Norse sagas. ph – Carl Hoffman and Günther Rittau. a.d – Otto Hunte, Erich Kettelhut, Karl Vollbrecht. cost – Paul Gerd Guderian, Anne Willkomm, Heinrich Umlauff.

LEADING PLAYERS
Margarete Schön (*Kriemhild*), Theodor Loos (*King Gunther*), Hans Adalbert von Schlettow (*Hagen Tronje*), Rudolph Klein-Rogge (*Attila*).

SYNOPSIS
In part one Siegfried seized the legendary Nibelung gold and pledged to marry Kriemhild, but was killed by Hagen, the jealous servant of Gunther, Kriemhild's brother. In part two Hagen hides the Nibelung gold as Attila the Hun's servant arrives to ask the grief-stricken Kriemhild to marry his master. She does and eventually bears a son. When her husband offers her any favour she wants she asks for the presence of her brother and then demands Hagen's death. Attila refuses to kill a guest, however.

Kriemhild secretly orders her troops to massacre everyone in Gunther's party while he is dining with Attila, but Hagen is alerted to the impending massacre and kills Attila's son. A major battle takes place, during which Gunther's men barricade themselves inside Attila's castle causing many more deaths. Supported by the now-crazed Attila, Kriemhild orders that the castle should be set on fire to drive out Gunther and Hagen. Attila tries to make Hagen reveal the whereabouts of the gold, but he will not. Kriemhild kills him and Gunther and then dies, her vengeance appeased. Attila takes her body in his arms and allows the flames to engulf them both.

Nightcleaners
UK 1975 sd b/w 10+12

PRODUCTION
p.c – Berwick Street Collective. p – Berwick Street Collective. d – Berwick Street Collective.

SYNOPSIS
An experimental documentary about the strike of a group of night office cleaners in south London.

Women talk about their daily routines and the lack of sleep that night-work imposes. Images of the cleaners at work are intercut with comments from their employers and black leader inserted between some shots to give a blank screen. The soundtrack is made up of a montage of different voices and the sound of a tinkling piano. Later, a narrator comments about the theoretical relationship between sexuality and capitalism, while a cleaner works alone in a high office block. The cleaners discuss the effect of their work on their health. (Ext. 1, 10 mins.)

The voice of a male trade unionist is heard discussing the difficulties of action while shots of the cleaners' faces are shown. The cleaners' employer explains that he believes that unions can 'go too far'. The women complain about their union's apparent lack of interest. Members of a women's liberation group talk about the financial problems of setting up a union branch with the cleaners. (Ext. 2, 12 mins.)

Nosferatu, eine Symphonie des Grauens
Germany 1922 st b/w 10+20

PRODUCTION
p.c – Prana film. d – F. W. Murnau. sc – Henrik Galeen, from the novel *Dracula* by Bram Stoker. ph – Fritz Arno Wagner. a.d – Albin Grau. cost – Albin Grau.

LEADING PLAYERS
Max Schreck (*Nosferatu*), Alexander Granach (*Renfield*), Gustav von Wangenheim (*Jonathan Harker*), Greta Schröder-Matray (*Mina*), John Gottowt (*Professor Van Helsing*).

SYNOPSIS
Jonathan Harker is sent to Transylvania by Renfield, an estate agent, to close a property deal with Nosferatu (Count Dracula). The villagers are full of foreboding when he tells them where he is going and the regular coach driver refuses to take him there. He makes the last stage of the journey in what appears to be a phantom coach. He is met by Nosferatu, who is fascinated when Harker cuts his finger while slicing some bread. The next morning Harker finds two mysterious bite wounds on his neck. (Ext. 1, 10 mins.)

The Count quickly closes the deal for a house situated directly opposite Harker's home in Bremen. Reading about vampires, Jonathan begins to realise the truth. Meanwhile, Harker's wife, Mina, is subject to evil dreams and forebodings.

Coffins belonging to Nosferatu, filled with earth and live rats, are loaded onto a ship bound for Bremen. Meanwhile, Professor Van Helsing lectures his biology students about carnivorous plants 'the vampires of the vegetable kingdom' and Renfield, who is under Nosferatu's influ-

ence, is confined to a lunatic asylum. In Bremen Mina waits on the beach for the return of her husband. Sailors on the ship carrying the coffins start to die, until only the first mate and captain remain. The mate determines to open the coffins with an axe, but throws himself overboard when Nosferatu rises up out of one of them. The captain lashes himself to the wheel and the ship drifts slowly towards Bremen. Harker is reunited with Mina and Renfield exults as the ship arrives. (Ext. 2a, 13 mins.)

Bremen is struck by the same plague that killed the sailors.

Mina learns that in order to destroy Nosferatu a virgin must freely offer herself to him and make him stay with her until daybreak. Renfield escapes from the asylum and is pursued by a mob of townspeople. Mina sends her husband to fetch Van Helsing and then lures Nosferatu to her room; he takes her blood. She keeps him by her until Nosferatu is destroyed by the morning sunlight. (Ext. 2b, 7 mins.)

Nothing but the Best
UK 1964 sd col 9

PRODUCTION
p.c – Domino. *p* – David Deutsch. *d* – Clive Donner. *sc* – Frederic Raphael, from a short story by Stanley Ellin. *ph* – Nicolas Roeg (Eastman Color). *ed* – Fergus McDonell. *a.d* – Reece Pemberton. *m* – Ron Grainer.

LEADING PLAYERS
Alan Bates (*Jimmy Brewster*), Denholm Elliott (*Charlie Prince*), Harry Andrews (*Mr. Horton*), Millicent Martin (*Ann Horton*), Pauline Delany (*Mrs. March*), Godfrey Quigley (*Coates*).

SYNOPSIS
Jimmy Brewster is an ambitious young clerk in Horton's, a smart London estate agents and auctioneers, where he is in daily contact with a world of money and privilege which he is determined to gatecrash. At a dance hall he picks up a girl and engineers her return to his lodgings where they meet his loving landlady, Mrs. March. Next morning at work he meets his boss's daughter, Ann Horton.

A chance meeting with Charlie Prince, a seedy man with expensive tastes, a public-school accent and a record which includes dismissal from Horton's for forgery, gives him his opportunity to make it big. Brewster installs Prince at his lodgings, advances him money, borrows his clothes, and takes a crash course from him in speaking the right language, playing the right games, and assimilating the right background. Brewster is making rapid progress, both in his job and with Ann, when a racing win gives Prince the chance to break up the arrangement. Since the departure of Prince means the loss of his wardrobe and also of his monthly allowance cheques, Brewster strangles him

with his Old Etonian tie, packs the body away in a trunk and dumps it in the cellar. Brewster bundles his working-class parents off to Australia and is soon set for a partnership and marriage to Ann. He even survives the discovery that Charlie was in fact Anne's black sheep brother, and the reappearance of the trunk - minus corpse. Mrs. March has stowed the body away in her cellar and is quite prepared to share Brewster with his wife. On Brewster's return from his honeymoon, however, he discovers that Mrs. March's house is being demolished, and that his former landlady has decamped to South Africa. Brewster is left awaiting – or not awaiting – discovery.

October
USSR 1928 st b/w 17

PRODUCTION
p.c – Sovkino. *d* – S. M. Eisenstein, G. Alexandrov. *sc* – S. M. Eisenstein, G. Alexandrov. *ph* – Edward Tisse. *ed* – S. M. Eisenstein. *a.d* – V. Kovrigin.

LEADING PLAYERS
Nikandrov (*V. I. Lenin*), Boris Livanov (*Minister Tereshchenko*), V. Popov (*Kerensky*), E. Tisse (*The German*).

SYNOPSIS
St. Petersburg, 1917. Kerensky's Provisional Government has taken power after the abdication of the Tsar, but there is little difference between the old and new regimes. Food prices soar and the war continues. At a frontier railway station crowds wait with banners for Lenin's return to Russia from exile abroad.

A demonstration demanding bread, land and peace is marching through St. Petersburg towards the Government offices across a great bridge. Suddenly shots ring out as machine-guns scatter the crowds and the great bridge is swung upwards to cut off the workers' part of the town.

Kerensky is cheered by hysterical women and prosperous men and secretly toys with the imperial crown. Korniloff and his Cossacks are travelling towards the capital to smash the Revolution. Kerensky does nothing, but a Red Guard and a worker change the points at a railway junction, bringing the Cossacks' train to a standstill. The two men advance and ask the Cossacks 'What are you fighting for?' They do not really know and gradually they are brought over to the side of the Revolution. Lenin enters the Congress of Soviets with his face bandaged, as he is still in hiding. The Congress is divided about whether to seize power. Finally a young soldier jumps up and says 'The 12th Army is with the Bolsheviks' and the Bolsheviks win the day. Kerensky prepares to flee for his life. Red Guards and sailors march to storm the Winter Palace and two messengers convey the ultimatum: twenty minutes in which to surrender or the Winter Palace will be shelled. The cruiser

Aurora signals midnight by a shot, and there is a rush over the barricades that surround the Palace. The Red Guards capture the ministers of the Provisional Government and the Bolshevik Government takes their place.

Odds Against Tomorrow
USA 1959 sd b/w 16 + 19

PRODUCTION
p.c – Harbel. *p* – Robert Wise. *d* – Robert Wise. *sc* – John O. Killens, Nelson Gidding, from the novel by William McGivern. *ph* – Joseph Brun. *ed* – Dede Allen. *a.d* – Leo Kerz. *m* – John Lewis. *cost* – Anna Hill Johnstone.

LEADING PLAYERS
Harry Belafonte (*Johnny Ingram*), Robert Ryan (*Earle Slater*), Ed Begley (*Dave Burke*), Shelley Winters (*Lorry*), Will Kuluva (*Bacco*), Lois Thorne (*Eadie*), Kim Hamilton (*Ruth*).

SYNOPSIS
Dave Burke, an ex-policeman who was dismissed on corruption charges, devises a plan to rob a small provincial bank. As he needs two partners he approaches Slater, who is embittered and financially dependent on Lorry, the woman he lives with, and Johnny Ingram, a black nightclub singer whose gambling has resulted in massive debts to an Italian gangster mob led by Bacco.

Ingram is singing in a nightclub when he is told that Bacco wants to see him. He goes instead to the club manager and asks in vain for a loan. Bacco and his henchmen appear and make a final demand for their money. Ingram pulls a gun but is overpowered. Threats are made against his ex-wife, Ruth, and his daughter, Eadie. Meanwhile, Slater refuses Burke's deal because it would involve working with a black man. Ingram arrives at Ruth's flat to take Eadie out for the day and is introduced to the predominantly white PTA Steering Committee meeting there. He makes a cynical remark about their work and leaves with Eadie. In Central Park he spots two of Bacco's heavies watching them. They leave only when he involves a policeman. (Ext. 1a, 12 mins.)

Ruth finds Ingram asleep in her flat. She wakes him and they have an argument about black politics. Ruth represents an integrationist position, saying Johnny will never change the world, while he denigrates her white do-gooding friends. Eadie comes in, woken by the angry voices, and the row ends unresolved. (Ext. 1b, 4 mins.)

Slater accepts Burke's proposal as his only way to financial independence.

Burke is explaining the robbery to Ingram at his flat when Slater arrives and the two meet for the first time. Slater's attitude to Ingram becomes increasingly racist and Burke is forced to intervene to prevent a fight. (Ext. 2a, 3 mins.)

Ingram changes into a waiter's suit,

replacing the real black waiter, and gains entrance to the bank. The robbery goes according to plan until Slater refuses to give the car keys to Ingram as planned and hands them to Burke, who is shot by police when he leaves the bank. Slater runs off pursued by Ingram and is trapped on top of a gas-tank. The two shoot it out and eventually blow themselves up. (Ext. 2b, 16 mins.)

Oh! For a Man!
(see Will Success Spoil Rock Hunter?)

The Old and the New
(see The General Line)

On a Clear Day You Can See Forever
USA 1970 sd col 17

PRODUCTION
p.c – Paramount. p – Howard W. Koch. d – Vincente Minnelli. sc – Alan Jay Lerner, from the musical play by Burton Lane and Alan J. Lerner. ph – Harry Stradling. ed – David Bretherton. choreo – Howard Jeffrey.

LEADING PLAYERS
Barbra Streisand (Daisy Gamble), Yves Montand (Dr. Marc Chabot), Larry Blyden (Warren Pratt), John Richardson (Robert Tentrees).

SYNOPSIS
Daisy Gamble, a chain-smoker, is worried that her addiction may jeopardize the employment chances of Warren Pratt, her fiancé. She gatecrashes a lecture on hypnotism given by Dr. Marc Chabot.

Later, Daisy arrives in Chabot's office to ask if he will help her stop smoking. He agrees, but while under hypnosis Daisy goes back to a previous 19th-century incarnation when she was Lady Melinda Tentrees. She recollects how she first met Robert Tentrees.

Chabot is surprised that Daisy succumbs to hypnosis so readily and astonished at her amazing power of extra-sensory perception. In subsequent sessions Chabot gradually pieces together Melinda's story – her marriage to Robert Tentrees and his subsequent abandonment of her when she is brought to trial for treason after he has used her powers to further his business interests. Chabot finds himself falling in love with Melinda and Daisy falls in love with Chabot. When she realises that his interest in her has merely been a means of reaching Melinda she refuses to talk to him anymore. Chabot harasses Daisy in order to find out about Melinda but stops when he realises that they are fated to meet, reincarnated, in the 21st century.

(NB This extract is standard reduced from Scope.)

Once Upon a Time in the West
Italy 1968 sd col 18 + 15

PRODUCTION
p.c – Rafran Cinematografica/San Marco. p – Fulvio Morsella. d – Sergio Leone. sc – Sergio Leone, Sergio Donati, from a story by Dario Argento, Bernardo Bertolucci and Sergio Leone. ph – Tonino Delli Colli (TechniScope and Technicolor). ed – Nino Baragli. a.d – Carlo Simi. m – Ennio Morricone. cost – Carlo Simi.

LEADING PLAYERS
Henry Fonda (Frank), Claudia Cardinale (Jill McBain), Jason Robards (Cheyenne), Charles Bronson (Harmonica), Frank Wolff (McBain), Gabriele Ferzetti (Morton).

SYNOPSIS
Three men arrive at a station and wait, guns ready. When a train arrives they prepare to meet someone, but nobody is seen to get off. As the train pulls out Harmonica comes into view on the far side of the track. After a short exchange, Harmonica guns the three men down. (Ext. 1a, 14 mins.)

Jill arrives from a high-class New Orleans brothel to start a new life as the wife of McBain, who owns Sweetwater farm just outside Flagstone. When she arrives at Sweetwater she finds that the whole McBain family has been mysteriously murdered. She stays at the farm and searches for the motive. The townspeople mistakenly suspect Cheyenne, a local outlaw, of the murders but he appears and refutes the accusation. Later Harmonica arrives, saves Jill's life and disappears again. Meanwhile, Frank, the murderer of the McBain family, is working in uneasy partnership with Morton, a crippled railroad entrepreneur whose dream is to extend his railroad to the Atlantic. Sweetwater is crucial to this project as the only watering point in the desert through which the railway has to pass.

On a train Morton describes his plan for continuing the railroad. Frank discusses how working for Morton has shown him the potential of money and power. Morton, however, is not unduly disturbed by Frank's implied threat, maintaining that money will always be more powerful than violence. (Ext. 1b, 4 mins.)

Frank forces Jill to sell the Sweetwater farm, but the rigged auction is disrupted when Harmonica produces Cheyenne, who has a $5,000 price on his head, and uses him to outbid Frank. Jill is further confused when Harmonica saves Frank from being murdered by his own men, who have been bought by Morton. Harmonica returns to Sweetwater to wait for Frank.

Cheyenne and Jill remain in the kitchen, while Harmonica and Frank take up their positions for the final shoot-out. Harmonica reveals how Frank murdered his brother. Frank is killed and Harmonica returns to the house, but refuses to stay. Cheyenne also leaves. Jill takes fresh water down to the men building the railroad. (Ext. 2, 15 mins.)

(NB These extracts are standard reduced from Scope.)

On Dangerous Ground
USA 1951 sd b/w 15

PRODUCTION
p.c – RKO Radio. p – John Houseman. d – Nicholas Ray. sc – A. I. Bezzerides, from the novel Mad With Much Heart by Gerald Butler. ph – George E. Diskant. ed – Roland Gross. a.d – Albert S. D'Agostino and Ralph Berger. m – Bernard Herrmann.

LEADING PLAYERS
Robert Ryan (Jim Wilson), Ida Lupino (Mary Malden), Ward Bond (Walter Brent), Charles Kemper (Bill Daly), Ed Begley (Captain Brawley), Richard Irving (Bernie), Cleo Moore (Myrna).

SYNOPSIS
Jim Wilson, a lonely, tough police detective, is becoming brutalised by his job, detesting all criminals and achieving results only by savage handling of suspects.

Wilson forces Myrna, the girlfriend of Bernie, a small-time crook, to reveal his hiding-place. They discover him in a waterfront hotel and Wilson brutally forces him to divulge the required information. The following day Wilson is reprimanded by Captain Brawley for his unnecessarily violent questioning and sent on a case out of town.

The little daughter of Brent, a farmer, has been found murdered. Brent resents Wilson's arrival because he means to achieve his own revenge. The killer is a disturbed teenager, Danny Malden. Danny's blind sister, Mary, pleads with Wilson to bring her brother in unharmed, but Brent's interference results in Danny fleeing in panic through the snow-covered countryside. He loses his grip as he tries to scale some rocks and falls to his death. At first Mary believes Wilson has betrayed her trust and he heads back to New York. On the way, however, he realises the desolation that awaits him there and returns to Mary.

On the Waterfront
USA 1954 sd b/w 15

PRODUCTION
p.c – Horizon. p – Sam Spiegel. d – Elia Kazan. sc – Budd Schulberg, from articles by Malcolm Johnson. ph – Boris Kaufman. ed – Gene Milford. a.d – Richard Day. m – Leonard Bernstein.

LEADING PLAYERS
Marlon Brando (Terry Malloy), Eva Marie Saint (Edie Doyle), Karl Malden (Father Barry), Lee J. Cobb (Johnny Friendly), Rod Steiger (Charley Malloy).

SYNOPSIS
Terry Malloy is asked to call Joey up to the roof tops where he is seized by Friendly's mob and thrown off because of his impending testimony against Friendly for

his corrupt running of the longshoremen's union. Terry has not known what was planned, and is disturbed by the murder.

Terry has invited Edie, Joey's sister, for her first drink in a bar. He talks about his experience as a prize-fighter and asks why Father Barry, a priest, is stirring up trouble among the longshoremen. Edie is angered by his fatalistic acceptance of things and his individualistic philosophy. He says he wishes he could help her to get to the bottom of her brother's death, but he can't. She leaves. (Ext. 1a, 6 mins.)

At the docks the longshoremen fight for work and Father Barry offers his church as a meeting place for those dissatisfied with the way the union is run. Terry is sent to spy on this meeting and helps Edie escape when some of the men there are beaten up by Friendly's mob. The relationship between Terry and Edie is gradually cemented, but after Kayo Dugan, who was also prepared to testify, is 'accidentally' crushed by a craneload of whisky, Terry confesses to Father Barry and Edie about his role in Joey's death.

Friendly expresses his distrust of Terry and warns Charley, Terry's brother, to straighten him out or have him eliminated. Charley tries to make excuses for him but is forced to agree. He talks to Terry, and tries to persuade him to take on a job for Friendly to prove his loyalty, but Terry is reluctant. He remembers his prize-fighting past which ended in a crooked fight for Friendly's benefit. In desperation Charley pulls a gun on Terry, but then lets him go. Charley is driven off to his own execution. (Ext. 1b, 9 mins.)

When Terry discovers that his brother has been murdered, he prepares to gun down Friendly, but Father Barry persuades him to testify instead. As a result Terry is refused work at the docks and is brutally beaten up by Friendly's henchmen. The rest of the men refuse to go to work without Terry and he heroically staggers in at the head of the workforce having broken Friendly's authority.

Otto e mezzo

(see 8½)

Orphée

France 1950 sd b/w 12

PRODUCTION
p.c – André Paulvé-Films du Palais Royal. *p* – Emile Darbon. *d* – Jean Cocteau. *sc* – Jean Cocteau. *ph* – Nicolas Hayer. *ed* – J. Sadoul. *a.d* – D'Eaubonne. *m* – Georges Auric.

LEADING PLAYERS
Jean Marais (*Orpheus*), François Périer (*Heurtebise*), Maria Casarès (*The Princess*), Edouard Dermithe (*Cégeste*).

SYNOPSIS
Orpheus, a successful and envied French poet, encounters Death, an elegant and mysterious Princess who travels in a luxurious Rolls Royce driven by Heurtebise, one of the many living dead who serve her. Her lethal agents are two motor-cyclists and her headquarters a deserted villa. She receives instructions in code from a radio.

The police arrive at the Café des Poètes. While Orpheus is being given preferential treatment, Cégeste, a drunken young poet, is run down by the cyclists. The Princess enlists Orpheus's help in taking him away. They listen to the code on the radio and the motor-cyclists appear. At the house the cyclists take Cégeste upstairs and Orpheus is led into a room. He sees the Princess raise Cégeste and the party goes through a mirror. Orpheus tries to do the same, but falls, awakening in the street. After crossing some dunes, he finds Heurtebise waiting with the car. They drive off.

Orpheus becomes fascinated by the radio messages and, determined to discover their secret, neglects his wife, Eurydice, who turns in despair to the Bacchantes, members of a women's dancing club. The Princess, enamoured of Orpheus, disobeys orders and has her cyclists run down Eurydice. Orpheus goes down to the Shades to recover her, guided by the sympathetic Heurtebise. There, the Princess is being judged for her disobedience by a Supreme Tribunal, which allows Orpheus to take Eurydice providing he never looks at her again. Back in the real world, Eurydice decides to die again and forces Orpheus to look at her. The Bacchantes descend on the house and in the brawl that follows Orpheus is shot. The Princess is waiting for him in the Shades. As she is arrested by her cyclists she orders Heurtebise to bring Orpheus back to life.

Our Man in Havana

UK 1959 sd b/w 11

PRODUCTION
p.c – Kingsmead. *p* – Carol Reed. *d* – Carol Reed. *sc* – Graham Greene, from his novel. *ph* – Oswald Morris (CinemaScope). *ed* – Bert Bates. *a.d* – John Box. *m* – Hermanos Deniz Cuban Rhythm Band.

LEADING PLAYERS
Alec Guinness (*Jim Wormold*), Noel Coward (*Hawthorne*), Burl Ives (*Dr. Hasselbacher*), Maureen O'Hara (*Beatrice*), Ernie Kovacs (*Segura*), Paul Rogers (*Carter*), Ralph Richardson (*C*).

SYNOPSIS
Jim Wormold, manager of a vacuum cleaner agency in Havana, allows himself to be persuaded to join the British Secret Service in order to earn enough money to gratify his teenage daughter's ambition to own a horse. Hawthorne, head of the Caribbean network, gives Wormold a code number, a very basic training in sending messages in invisible ink and then leaves him to his own devices. Wormold has no idea how to recruit a spy ring, nor indeed what he would do with it if he had one, but his new-found affluence encourages him to invent what he cannot find, including plans for some mysterious military installations in the mountains – actually a caricature of a new vacuum cleaner. The London office is delighted with his progress and send him a secretary called Beatrice. Inevitably, the elaborate web of deception begins to trap innocent people, and he is even invited to join 'the other side' by police chief Segura.

Wormold gets Segura drunk in order to get his revolver from him. He then goes to meet Carter, another spy whom Wormold has decided he must kill, and they go off to a nightclub together. Wormold has misled Carter about the name of the club so Carter cannot arrange for them to be followed. Wormold persuades Carter to come with him to a brothel. When they reach the entrance he shoots Carter.

Wormold's best friend, Dr. Hasselbacher, is murdered and he himself narrowly escapes being poisoned at a banquet. Realising that reality has caught up with him in a terrifying manner, he allows himself to be deported, returns to London and is rewarded with an OBE.

(NB This extract is standard reduced from Scope.)

Out of the Past (Build My Gallows High)

USA 1947 sd b/w 21

PRODUCTION
p.c – RKO Radio. *p* – Warren Duff, Robert Sparks. *d* – Jacques Tourneur. *sc* – Geoffrey Homes (Daniel Mainwaring), from his novel *Build My Gallows High*. *ph* – Nicholas Musuraca. *ed* – Samuel E. Beetley. *a.d* – Albert S. D'Agostino and Jack Okey. *m* – Roy Webb.

LEADING PLAYERS
Robert Mitchum (*Jeff Bailey*), Jane Greer (*Kathy Moffat*), Kirk Douglas (*Whit Sterling*), Rhonda Fleming (*Meta Carson*), Steve Brodie (*Fisher*), Virginia Huston (*Ann Miller*).

SYNOPSIS
Jimmy, a deaf mute who helps Jeff Bailey run a small garage in Bridgeport, California, tells him a stranger is looking for him. Later, Jeff gets a message to go to Lake Tahoe to see Whit Sterling.

He picks up Ann, his girlfriend, and as they drive through the night he tells her in flashback about his previous dealings with Whit. As a New York private eye, he and his partner Fisher had been hired by Whit, a successful gambler and crook, to trace his mistress, Kathy Moffat, who had run off with $40,000 of his money. Jeff traces Kathy to Acapulco, where he waits knowing that she will eventually appear. When he finds her, she denies taking the money and declares that she hates Whit. Jeff believes her, they start an affair and run away together. (Ext. 1a, 14 mins.)

On the run from Whit, Jeff and Kathy hide out in San Francisco, living a shadowy existence in seedy cinemas and out-of-the-

way clubs. When they begin to feel safer, they venture into more public places but Jeff is spotted by Fisher at a racetrack. He and Kathy split up and hide separately until Jeff feels that he has shaken Fisher off his trail. They meet again, but Fisher suddenly appears, having followed Kathy, not Jeff. Fisher offers a deal – he will forget everything in return for a share of the money Kathy is supposed to have stolen. The two men fight, until Kathy kills Fisher. While Jeff is bending over the body she flees, leaving behind her bank book in which Jeff sees an entry showing a deposit of $40,000. Shattered, he drifts to Bridgeport. The flashback ends as Ann and Jeff reach Whit's estate. (Ext. 1b, 7 mins.)

Inside, Jeff finds Kathy re-established as Whit's mistress. Whit offers him the job of retrieving some incriminating tax documents from a lawyer's office in San Francisco and he accepts. Jeff starts work, but the lawyer is murdered. He realises that Kathy is trying to frame him for the crime and for Fisher's death. Jeff escapes the police net and returns to Tahoe, where he demands that Whit turn Kathy over to the police. Kathy shoots Whit and later, at a roadblock, Jeff. She is herself killed in a shoot-out with the police. Jimmy, the mute, tells Ann that Jeff always loved Kathy so that she will not grieve too much.

Paisà
Italy 1946 sd b/w 20

PRODUCTION
p.c – Organisation Films International/ Foreign Film Productions. *p* – Roberto Rossellini, Rod E. Geiger, Mario Conti. *d* – Roberto Rossellini. *sc* – Federico Fellini, Roberto Rossellini, Sergio Amidei. *ph* – Otello Martelli. *ed* – Eraldo Da Roma. *m* – Renzo Rossellini.

LEADING PLAYERS
Dale Edmonds (*Dale*), Cigolani (*Cigolani*), Lorena Berg (*Maddalena*).

SYNOPSIS
A film in six episodes which take place during the Allied advance through Italy. 1: *Sicily*. Carmela, an Italian, volunteers to guide an American patrol along the coast. She is left in a ruined castle with Joe, a GI. Joe uses his lighter and is shot by a German patrol. Before being caught by the Germans, Carmela manages to fire Joe's rifle to warn his comrades. When they arrive they assume that Carmela killed Joe. 2: *Naples*. A drunken black American soldier falls asleep and his boots are stolen. Some days later, he finds the boots in a shelter where whole families and dozens of children live crowded together. Horrified, the American drops the boots and rushes away. 3: *Rome*. Francesca, a prostitute, brings home an American soldier who seems indifferent to her charms. He tells her how he treasures the memory of a girl who welcomed him six months before when Rome was liberated. Francesca gradually remembers that she was the girl.

4: *Florence*. Harriet, an American nurse, loves a Florentine painter. She realises that he is in fact 'Lupo' a partisan leader. When she hears that he has been wounded, she crosses the lines to find him. While attending to another wounded man, she hears him say 'Lupo is dead; things are going badly today'. 5: *Monastery*. Three American army chaplains are invited to celebrate the Liberation in a Franciscan monastery. The meal is made possible by American provisions. The half-starved monks look forward to the feast, but they then discover that only one of the chaplains is a Catholic. The guests dine alone while the monks do penance for the two souls who have strayed from the path of truth. 6: *Po Valley*. Partisans and soldiers are fighting together in marshlands surrounded by the enemy and out of supplies and ammunition. Cigolani, a partisan, takes Dale, an American, to a house where they are fed and given food for the whole band. Next day the entire family except the baby are slaughtered by the Nazis as a reprisal. Following an air attack by the British the Nazis send a gunboat down the river. The survivors are taken prisoner and the Allies separated from their partisan comrades, who are tied hand and foot and thrown into the river. Horrified, Dale attacks the Nazis and is machine-gunned down.

Les Parapluies de Cherbourg (The Umbrellas of Cherbourg)
France/West Germany 1963 sd col 10

PRODUCTION
p.c – Parc Film/Madeleine Films (Paris)/ Beta Film (Munich). *p* – Mag Bodard. *d* – Jacques Demy. *sc* – Jacques Demy. *ph* – Jean Rabier (Eastman Color). *ed* – Anne-Marie Cotret. *a.d* – Bernard Evein. *m* – Michel Legrand.

LEADING PLAYERS
Catherine Deneuve (*Geneviève*), Nino Castelnuovo (*Guy*), Anne Vernon (*Madame Emery*), Ellen Farner (*Madeleine*), Marc Michel (*Roland Cassard*).

SYNOPSIS
A musical in which every word is sung. Guy and Geneviève are in love and plan to marry, but are prevented from doing so by Geneviève's mother, Madame Emery, who keeps an umbrella shop. Guy gets his call-up papers, but before leaving Cherbourg he sleeps with Geneviève. She hears very little from Guy after he leaves and though pregnant by him she eventually marries Roland Cassard, a rich young diamond merchant. Guy returns home to his elderly godmother, Elise, and her young companion, Madeleine, and it emerges that he had not written because he had been lying wounded in hospital. Elise dies and Guy turns to Madeleine for comfort.

June 1959. Guy completes the arrangement for the purchase of a new garage and returns to meet Madeleine at a café. Guy

asks Madeleine if she would like to marry him. December 1963. Madeleine finishes decorating the Christmas tree and then takes their son François out to see the shops. As they leave Geneviève pulls into the garage for petrol. She follows Guy into the office where they talk nervously to each other. Geneviève asks if Guy wants to see their daughter, Françoise. Guy refuses and as Geneviève leaves Madeleine returns with their son.

Pather Panchali
India 1955 sd b/w 9

PRODUCTION
p.c – Government of West Bengal. *d* – Satyajit Ray. *sc* – Satyajit Ray, from the novel by Bibhut Bhusan Bandopadhaya. *ph* – Subrata Mitra. *ed* – Dulal Dutta. *a.d* – Banshi Chandragupta. *m* – Ravi Shankar.

LEADING PLAYERS
Kanu Banerjee (*Harihar, The Father*), Karuna Banerjee (*Sarbojaya, The Mother*), Uma Das Gupta (*Durga, The Daughter*), Subir Banerjee (*Apu, The Son*), Chunibala (*The Aunt*).

SYNOPSIS
In a Bengal village Harihar, a would-be writer, and his harassed and nagging wife Sarbojaya try to raise their children, Apu who is six and Durga, an adolescent, as well as supporting their aunt, an aged hanger-on. Harihar leaves for the town in order to make money and for some time nothing is heard from him. A friend of Durga's is married.

Apu brings a letter announcing his father's return. Durga makes offerings to the Gods and prays for a husband, then runs out into the fields as a storm threatens. Apu follows her and watches as she dances in the lashing rain. Their mother finds some fruit on a path, blown down by the storm, and guiltily hides it under her sari. Apu and Durga shelter under a tree. Durga sneezes.

Durga develops a fever and dies. Harihar eventually returns, but finding his daughter dead and his home in ruins, he decides that his remaining family should leave the village and seek a better life in the city.

The Pawnshop
USA 1916 st b/w 5
(w. **Easy Street** and **The Vagabond**)

PRODUCTION
p.c – Lone Star-Mutual. *p* – Charlie Chaplin. *d* – Charlie Chaplin. *sc* – Charlie Chaplin. *ph* – Rolland Totheroh, William C. Foster.

LEADING PLAYERS
Charlie Chaplin (*The First Assistant*), Edna Purviance (*The Daughter*), Henry Bergman (*The Pawnbroker*), John Rand (*The Clerk*), Eric Campbell (*The Thief*).

SYNOPSIS

Two pawnshop assistants are competing for the favours of the pawnbroker's daughter. The first assistant gets into trouble with the boss, but avoids being sacked by arousing his sympathy. As soon as the pawnbroker's back is turned the assistants start fighting. When the boss's daughter appears the first assistant pretends to be hurt and is invited into the kitchen, where he larks about until the pawnbroker comes in. Customers enter the shop, one of whom is a thief who pretends to pawn his umbrella and then announces his interest in buying the shop. He is introduced to the boss, while the first assistant attends to a man with an alarm clock.

After examining the clock with a stethoscope he attacks it with a hammer and a drill, opens it up with a tin opener, sniffs suspiciously at the contents and scrutinises them through a watchmaker's glass. Then he pulls out the entire works and tries to oil them. Finally he sweeps the ruins of the alarm clock into the client's hat and hands it back to him with an apologetic shrug.

The thief breaks into the safe, unaware that the first assistant, fleeing from his boss's wrath, is hiding in a nearby chest. The assistant opens the chest and hits the thief with a rolling pin. All is forgiven and the boss's daughter leaves with the first assistant.

La Peau douce
France 1964 sd b/w 10

PRODUCTION

p.c – Films du Carosse/SEDIF. *d* – François Truffaut. *sc* – François Truffaut, Jean-Louis Richard. *ph* – Raoul Coutard. *ed* – Claudine Bouché. *m* – Georges Delerue.

LEADING PLAYERS

Jean Desailly (*Pierre Lachenay*), Françoise Dorléac (*Nicole Chomette*), Nelly Bénédetti (*Franca Lachenay*).

SYNOPSIS

Aged 43 and married with a small daughter, Pierre Lachenay runs a successful literary magazine in Paris. On a lecturing trip to Lisbon, he meets a young air hostess, Nicole, and has a brief but happy affair with her.

Back in Paris Pierre arrives home with a record for his daughter. He and his wife have an argument over a paper he has mislaid. Pierre drives off to the airport. As he is sending a telegram to Nicole, he suddenly sees her. He returns home and makes love to his wife. Later on, he meets Nicole when she returns from a flight. They go to a nightclub where Pierre watches Nicole dance. They try to find a room for the night but are unsuccessful. Eventually they spend the night at Nicole's place.

Pierre seizes the opportunity of a lecture at Rheims to arrange to spend a couple of days with Nicole in the country. The need for concealment keeps Nicole hanging about while he fulfils his lecturing commit-

ments and the weekend is not an unqualified success. Meanwhile, Pierre's wife accidentally discovers that he lied about the trip and begins to suspect his infidelity. Faced by her jealous rage, Pierre leaves her, determined to marry Nicole. A few days later he takes Nicole to see the flat he has chosen for them, but she is not interested in marriage and walks out. Humiliated and alone, Pierre tries to ring his wife, but having found proof of his affair she has already left for the restaurant where she knows he will be and shoots him dead.

Peeping Tom
UK 1959 sd col 10

PRODUCTION

p.c – Michael Powell (Theatre). *p* – Michael Powell. *d* – Michael Powell. *sc* – Leo Marks. *ph* – Otto Heller (Eastman Color). *ed* – Noreen Ackland. *a.d* – Arthur Lawson. *m* – Brian Easdale.

LEADING PLAYERS

Carl Boehm (*Mark*), Anna Massey (*Helen*), Maxine Audley (*Mrs. Stephens*).

SYNOPSIS

Mark Lewis is a film studio focus-puller who takes pornographic photographs for a newsagent in his spare time. During his childhood his sadistic father used him as a guinea-pig in studying the psychology of fear. This has warped his personality so that he has become obsessed with a lust to murder and at the same time photograph the fear on his victim's face. His first subject is a prostitute whom he follows to her room and kills, recording the entire murder with his camera; his second is Vivian, an extra at the studios, whose murder he shoots in a deserted film set; and his third is a model whom he arranges to meet at the newsagent's. While these murders are taking place Mark meets Helen Stephens, who rents a flat in his house for herself and her blind mother. Despite her mother's instinctive dislike of Mark, Helen penetrates his reserve and they fall in love.

Helen, visiting Mark's room for the first time, see a film of his father's experiments which records the young Mark's terror.

One night she accidentally switches on his projector and watches, horrified, the film he has made of Vivian's murder. As he struggles with his impulse to add Helen to his list of victims, the police arrive. Mark switches on the recorded screams of his childhood and films his own suicide.

The Pickwick Papers
USA 1913 st b/w 13

PRODUCTION

p.c – Vitagraph. *d* – Larry Trimble.

LEADING PLAYERS

John Bunny (*Mr. Pickwick*), Sidney Hunt (*Mr. Snodgrass*), James Pryor (*Mr. Tupman*), Fred Hornby (*Mr. Winkle*), Arthur Ricketts (*Mr. Jingle*), Arthur

White (*Dr. Slammer*), Minnie Raynor (*Mrs. Budger*).

SYNOPSIS

This version of *The Pickwick Papers* is adapted from only two incidents in the novel.

The Corresponding Society of the Pickwick Club, composed of Mr. Pickwick, Mr. Snodgrass, Mr. Tupman and Mr. Winkle, is ready to set off on travels which they are to report to the rest of the club members. Mr. Picwick takes a cab to meet his friends but he has a disagreement with the driver, who attacks him when they reach their destination. Mr. Pickwick is saved by the intervention of a stranger, Mr. Jingle, who then travels with them to Rochester and dines with them. A ball is taking place in the inn where they stay and Mr. Tupman and Mr. Jingle decide to go to it. Mr. Jingle has no suitable clothes so he borrows some from Mr. Winkle, who has fallen asleep. At the ball Mr. Jingle offends a Dr. Slammer and is challenged to a duel, but as the challenge is delivered to the owner of the clothes Mr. Jingle was wearing, it is Mr. Winkle who has to face the irate Dr. Slammer next morning. Luckily the mistake in identity is discovered just in time, but Mr. Jingle disappears before he can be brought to account.

Mr. Pickwick is informed by Mr. Jingle's servant that he is planning to elope with a pupil from a nearby girls' school and follows him there, only to find that the information was false. Mr. Pickwick is locked up and accused of behaving improperly, but he is rescued by his friends. Once again Mr. Jingle cannot be found.

Pierrot le fou
France/Italy 1965 sd col scope 15

PRODUCTION

p.c – Rome-Paris Films. *p* – Georges de Beauregard. *d* – Jean-Luc Godard, from the novel *Obsession* by Lionel White. *ph* – Raoul Coutard (*TechniScope and Eastman Color*). *ed* – Françoise Colin. *m* – Antoine Duhamel.

LEADING PLAYERS

Jean-Paul Belmondo (*Ferdinand*), Anna Karina (*Marianne*), Dirk Sanders (*Marianne's Brother*), Raymond Devos (*The Man on the Pier*), Graziella Galvani (*Ferdinand's Wife*).

SYNOPSIS

Ferdinand is bored with his secure, monotonous married life in Paris. He snatches at the escape offered by a chance meeting with Marianne, a girl he had known some years before, who presents him with the possibility of an exciting, violent life – involvement with gangs, guns and death. She also has a brother in the south of France whom she wants to visit. Ferdinand, whom she calls Pierrot, drives away with her.

Ferdinand and Marianne are at an idyl-

lic seashore retreat. Ferdinand writes, but Marianne is restless; they try unsuccessfully to have a serious conversation. Back at the house Marianne is increasingly bored and discontented with the simple life and wants to return to her 'gangster movie'. They go and entertain some American tourists on the quayside.

A chance encounter takes Marianne back to violence. She telephones Ferdinand to rescue her, but she has gone by the time he arrives. When he traces her, she involves him in a showdown between the gangs. He discovers that her 'brother' is not really a brother at all and that Marianne intended his betrayal. Ferdinand returns to the retreat, where he shoots Marianne and her 'brother', straps dynamite to his head, and lights the fuse. By the time he changes his mind it is too late.

(NB This extract is in Scope and needs an anamorphic lens.)

The Plague of the Zombies
UK 1966 sd col 24

PRODUCTION
p.c – Hammer. *p* – Anthony Nelson-Keys. *d* – John Gilling. *sc* – Peter Bryan. *ph* – Arthur Grant (Technicolor). *ed* – Chris Barnes. *a.d* – Don Mingaye. *m* – James Bernard.

LEADING PLAYERS
André Morrell (*Sir James Forbes*), Diane Clare (*Sylvia*), Brook Williams (*Dr. Peter Tompson*), Jacqueline Pearce (*Alice*), John Carson (*Squire Hamilton*).

SYNOPSIS
Sir James Forbes, Professor of Medicine, receives a letter from a former pupil, Dr. Peter Tompson, about a mysterious fatal malady affecting the village in Cornwall where he now practises. Sir James and his daughter Sylvia go to investigate and find Alice, Peter's wife, sick and the villagers very frightened. James and Peter decide to exhume the body of the most recently dead villager, but find the grave empty.

Alice describes Squire Hamilton, leader of the local hunt, to Sylvia while the two men wash up. Later Sylvia sees Alice leave the house, apparently in a trance. Following her to some old tin mines, she suddenly finds herself surrounded by wild huntsmen. They take her back to Hamilton Manor and are about to cut cards for her when the Squire appears and apologises. Sylvia goes back past the old tin mines, where a zombie suddenly appears carrying Alice's body, which he throws to the ground. Sylvia sees that Alice's throat has been cut. (Ext. 1a, 16 mins.)

The Squire visits Sylvia. He manages to engineer an accident in which her finger is cut and covertly collects some of the blood. Sylvia realises that Squire Hamilton is creating zombies in order to work a disused but rich tin mine.

Sir James and Peter watch over Alice's grave, but are lured away by a trick. They rush back and see Alice rise up out of her grave as a zombie. Sir James strikes her head off with a shovel. Peter faints and has a nightmare in which zombies emerge from open graves and encircle him. He wakes from the nightmare and tells Sir James about it. (Ext. 1b, 8 mins.)

Sir James places Sylvia in Peter's care and goes to investigate Hamilton Manor. During a scuffle with one of Hamilton's men Peter starts a fire. Meanwhile, Sylvia, in a trance, goes to the Manor, where the squire is preparing a voodoo ritual. Sylvia is about to be sacrificed when the fire spreads to the mines. The zombies go berserk and attack Hamilton. Sir James and Peter rescue Sylvia just before the mine explodes.

Portrait of a Mobster
USA 1961 sd b/w 10

PRODUCTION
p.c – Warner Bros. *d* – Joseph Pevney. *sc* – Howard Browne, from a book by Harry Grey. *ph* – Eugene Polito. *ed* – Leo H. Shreve. *a.d* – Jack Poplin. *m* – Max Steiner.

LEADING PLAYERS
Vic Morrow (*Dutch Schultz*), Leslie Parrish (*Iris Murphy*), Peter Breck (*Frank Brennan*), Ray Danton (*Legs Diamond*), Norman Alden (*Bo Wetzel*).

SYNOPSIS
Two callow safe-breakers, Dutch Schultz and Bo Wetzel, force their way into Legs Diamond's apartment to demand he take them into his mob. Eventually Diamond is persuaded and gives them their first assignment – to take over John Murphy's brewery. This leads to Murphy's death.

Diamond is angry with Dutch after the killing of Murphy and Dutch and Bo quit Diamond's mob. Dutch starts up on his own in order to show Diamond 'how an outfit should be run' and begins to keep a scrap-book with press cuttings about himself. He dresses up in new clothes and goes to Murphy's wake, where he chats up his daughter Iris. In a speakeasy poolroom he declares his intention of imitating the organisation of the big boys by putting all the small operations on his payroll. His ultimate aim is 'to take over every brewery in the Bronx'. Later his lawyer introduces him to a rich politician who will be his backer.

Gang warfare breaks out and Dutch is attacked while out for a drive with Iris. As a result of this and family pressure Iris leaves him for her policeman lover, Frank Brennan. Dutch eventually guns down Diamond in the street. Iris overhears that Frank is on Dutch's payroll and leaves him in disgust, but when Dutch asks her to come and live with him, she does. A special prosecutor is appointed to deal with the gangs. A meeting of gangsters is called by the Mafia who propose instituting their own police force to control 'trigger happy punks'. Dutch rejects the idea outright. He is brought to court but the judge, who has been bribed, only fines him. Prohibition ends and times look hard for the bootleggers but Dutch still refuses to do a deal with the Italians, partly for racial reasons. Iris finally learns that it was Dutch who killed her father and leaves him for good. At last Dutch is prepared to come to terms with the Mafia, although they insist on the elimination of Bo, his lifelong friend. Dutch disappears to the lavatory when the gunmen come for Bo, but he suddenly finds the attack turned on him as well. He escapes but Bo shoots him by mistake.

Il posto
Italy 1961 sd b/w 10

PRODUCTION
p.c – The Twenty Four Horses. *p* – Alberto Soffientini. *d* – Ermanno Olmi. *sc* – Ermanno Olmi. *ph* – Lamberto Caimi. *ed* – Carla Colombo. *a.d* – Ettore Lombardi.

LEADING PLAYERS
Sandro Panzeri (*Domenico Cantoni*), Loredana Detto (*Antonietta*).

SYNOPSIS
Sixteen-year-old Domenico is sent to Milan from his parents' flat in the suburbs to look for his first job. The big, solid industrial concern where he goes for an interview offers security but the interviews and exams he must pass to get the job are difficult.

Later that day Domenico is lunching in a milk-bar when he notices Antonietta, another examination candidate. They window-shop together and talk about wages, conditions of work and the future. They run back for their interview; he takes her hand as they cross the street. He is chastised by an old man for running across the grass in a park.

Domenico and Antonietta both pass their examinations. She becomes a typist in the main office while Domenico is sent to an outside section as a messenger boy until there is a vacancy for a clerk. Hoping to see Antonietta again, he goes to the office dance, but she fails to arrive. One of the clerks dies, making room for Domenico. The dead man's things are moved out and Domenico proudly arrives with an armful of papers, clips and pastepots. His fellow clerks move forward from the back of the room and Domenico, now secure in his job, takes his seat at the back in the darkest corner.

The Prisoner
UK 1955 sd b/w 12

PRODUCTION
p.c – London Independent Producers/A Facet Production. *p* – Vivian A. Cox. *d* – Peter Glenville. *sc* – Bridget Boland, from her play. *ph* – Reg Wyer. *ed* – Freddie Wilson. *a.d* – John Hawkesworth. *m* – Benjamin Frankel.

LEADING PLAYERS

Alec Guinness (*The Cardinal*), Jack Hawkins (*The Interrogator*), Wilfrid Lawson (*The Cell Warder*), Gerard Heinz (*The Doctor*).

SYNOPSIS

In a nameless totalitarian state somewhere in Europe, a cardinal – formerly a resistance leader during the enemy occupation – is considered by the authorities as a menace to their new regime. He is arrested, charged with treason and handed over to an interrogator, whose job it is to extract confessions. The interrogator does not believe in torture or drugs but in the methods of modern psychology; he aims subtly to break down the cardinal's resistance and make him confess what is not true.

The interrogator moves into the prison so that he can observe the cardinal at close quarters. The cardinal occupies himself cleaning the floor of his cell. An attempt is made to destroy his sense of time by feeding him irregularly and cutting his cell off from the light. The cardinal begins to crack under the pressure. The interrogator confronts the cardinal again and once a doctor has given the cardinal a sedative feels that he now has the cardinal in his control.

Later, the interrogator resorts to confronting the cardinal with the anaesthetised body of his mother. This device fails to break him, but the cardinal reveals that he never loved her. The interrogator seizes his chance and sends the cardinal into solitary confinement, where darkness and solitude at last break his will. He begs to see the interrogator and confesses that he became a priest not through a sense of vocation but to escape from a squalid childhood and satisfy his pride. The interrogator persuades him that the only way of expiation is to sign the confession. The cardinal does so. He is tried and sentenced to death, then reprieved to face a heavier penalty – to return to the people whose guide he once was and who are now angry and bewildered by his confession. In a moment of revulsion the interrogator resigns.

Psycho
USA 1960 sd b/w 13

PRODUCTION

p.c – Shamley. *p* – Alfred Hitchcock. *d* – Alfred Hitchcock. *sc* – Joseph Stefano, from the novel by Robert Bloch. *ph* – John L. Russell. *ed* – George Tomasini. *a.d* – Joseph Hurley, Robert Clatworthy. *m* – Bernard Herrmann.

LEADING PLAYERS

Anthony Perkins (*Norman Bates*), Janet Leigh (*Marion Crane*), John Gavin (*Sam Loomis*), Vera Miles (*Lila Crane*), Martin Balsam (*Milton Arbogast*).

SYNOPSIS

Marion Crane, secretary to a real-estate agent, is involved in a seedy affair with Sam Loomis, owner of a hardware shop. One day she yields to a momentary temptation and absconds with $40,000 of her employer's money. After a long drive she stops at the lonely, run-down Bates Motel. Norman Bates, its withdrawn, intense young proprietor, gives her supper, talks to her and sees her into her cabin. That night Marion is brutally stabbed to death – apparently by Bates's maniacally possessive mother who lives in a large house which over-shadows the motel. Bates cleans up the blood, bundles Marion's body into her car and drives it into a nearby swamp. Marion's sister, Lila, and Sam hire an insurance investigator, Arbogast, to enquire into her whereabouts. Arbogast tracks her to the motel.

Arbogast arrives at the motel and finds Norman in the office. Gradually he gets the story of Marion's visit out of the nervous and reluctant Norman, but he gets nowhere when he wants to meet Mrs. Bates and is forced to leave. Arbogast phones Lila and Sam to report on his progress and tells them he is determined to return to the motel to make another attempt to meet Mrs. Bates. He does so immediately and finding no-one in the office, goes up to the house, lets himself in and starts to climb the stairs. A door opens on the landing and a figure in a long dress rushes out and stabs him to death. He falls back down the stairs.

Bates again makes use of the swamp to dispose of the body. Lila and Sam visit the motel, but they get separated and Sam is knocked out by Bates, who is dressed as his mother. Bates is arrested and a psychiatrist explains that he became psychotic after discovering his mother was having an affair and killed her. The psychiatrist leaves, and Norman, his own personality now completely subsumed, determines to remain completely silent and motionless.

The Public Enemy
USA 1931 sd b/w 16

PRODUCTION

p.c – Warner Bros. *d* – William A. Wellman. *sc* – Harvey Thew, from the story *Beer and Blood* by Kubec Glasmon and John Bright. *ph* – Dev Jennings. *ed* – Edward M. McCormick. *a.d* – Max Parker. *m* – David Mendoza. *cost* – Earl Luick.

LEADING PLAYERS

James Cagney (*Tom Powers*), Edward Woods (*Matt Doyle*), Beryl Mercer (*Ma Powers*), Donald Cook (*Mike Powers*), Leslie Fenton (*Nails Nathan*), Robert Emmett O'Connor (*Paddy Ryan*).

SYNOPSIS

A sequence pointing out the evils of Prohibition is followed by the credits in which each of the main characters is introduced. There is a further prologue emphasising that what is to be shown is an honest prediction of an environment, not the glorification of a hoodlum and criminal.

1909: Scenes from working-class urban Chicago – the stockyards, beer parlours, the Salvation Army marching through the streets. Two young boys, Tom Powers and Matt Doyle, emerge from a beer hall, take a swig from the pails of beer they are carrying and have a bantering conversation with two girls. (Ext. 1a, 5 mins.)

They graduate to working in a small-time gang and in 1915 they go out on their first big job – a raid on a fur store. There is a chase and a policeman is killed. 1917: The United States enters the war and Mike, Tom's upright and law-abiding brother, enlists.

1920: Following the introduction of Prohibition the liquor stores advertise that all stock must be sold. There is mayhem in the streets as everyone rushes to buy and Paddy Ryan explains to Tom and Matt that Prohibition will mean good profits. Tom and Matt steal whisky from a bonded warehouse and are fitted for new suits with their share of the take. They are next seen arriving at a hotel in their large new chauffeur-driven car; inside they expertly pick up two young women. After a meeting with Ryan and Mr. Leehman, the owner of a large brewery, Tom and Matt are given jobs 'encouraging' speakeasy owners to take the Leehman beer. (Ext. 1b, 11 mins.)

Mike returns from the war. He is told about Tom's illegal activities and the two brothers quarrel at a family reunion supper. The death of Nails Nathan in a riding accident precipitates a gangland war between Ryan's mob and a rival gang led by Schemer Burns. Matt and Ryan are killed; Tom undertakes a one-man attack on Schemer and his gang, but is himself seriously wounded. In hospital, Tom is reconciled with his family, but he is later kidnapped by Schemer's gang. Mike receives a telephone call which promises that Tom will be sent home. When he answers a ring at the door some minutes later, Tom's body, swathed in bandages, falls into the hall.

The Pumpkin Eater
UK 1964 sd b/w 14

PRODUCTION

p.c – Romulus/Jack Clayton. *p* – James Woolf. *d* – Jack Clayton. *sc* – Harold Pinter, from the novel by Penelope Mortimer. *ph* – Oswald Morris. *ed* – James Clark. *a.d* – Edward Marshall. *m* – Georges Delerue.

LEADING PLAYERS

Anne Bancroft (*Jo*), Peter Finch (*Jake*), James Mason (*Conway*), Maggie Smith (*Philpot*).

SYNOPSIS

Jo, a single parent with seven brawling youngsters, marries Jake, an affluent and promiscuous screenwriter. Jo's hunger for permanence, domesticity and the strictest morality causes disruption despite the strong physical and emotional ties between them. She survives the short intrusion of Jake's mistress, Philpot, by burying herself even more firmly in her children.

The extract begins in flashback. Walking across Hampstead Heath, Jo's children tell her that Philpot had fainted into Jake's arms the day before. Questioned by Jo, Jake denies this. Jo and Jake arrive back from the cinema in time to hear Philpot leaving the house. Jo asks Jake about his relationship with Philpot. That night Jo throws all the clothes Philpot has left behind into the rubbish bin. The film returns to the present, with Jo leaving her flat and going to Harrods. Inside the shop she is overwhelmed by her feelings and breaks down. She is taken home.

The two eldest children go away to school. Increasing pressures lead her to seek psychiatric aid. She refuses to accompany Jake on location in Morocco and feels alienated at the party celebrating his return. Conway, the least endearing of the guests, makes a pass at her. He also sends her flowers later when she is recovering from a mutually agreed sterilisation operation. Confused and desperate, she accepts Conway's invitation to meet for tea at the Zoo. There, he vindictively pours out the details of Jake's affair with his wife, Beth. Horrified, Jo comes to blows with Jake, then goes to bed with Giles, her ex-husband. Jake ignores her at his father's funeral and she retreats to an old love-nest in a converted windmill. Jake comes to see her with the children.

The Quatermass Experiment
UK 1955 sd b/w 21

PRODUCTION
p.c – Hammer. *p* – Anthony Hinds. *d* – Val Guest. *sc* – Richard Landau and Val Guest, based on the television series by Nigel Kneale. *ph* – Jimmy Harvey. *ed* – James Needs. *a.d* – J. Elder Wills.

LEADING PLAYERS
Brian Donlevy (*Quatermass*), Jack Warner (*Lomax*), Margia Dean (*Judith Carroon*), Richard Wordsworth (*Victor Carroon*).

SYNOPSIS
A rocket ship, launched as part of Professor Quatermass's space programme, crashes in southern England narrowly missing a courting couple. Two of its original three-man crew have vanished completely, while the third, Victor Carroon, staggers out, apparently in a state of severe shock. An examination of the rocket and of film taken during the flight reveals very little. Quatermass concludes that some mysterious force entered the rocket during its flight, vapourising two of the crew and taking possession of Carroon's body.

Judith, Victor's wife, arrives at the clinic where her husband is being nursed. Unhappy with Quatermass's insensitive attitude Judith decides to abduct Victor. Her scheme goes according to plan until Victor and the detective she has hired are

about to leave the hospital room; Victor becomes entranced by a cactus plant and suddenly smashes it with his bare fist. In the lift Victor attacks and kills the detective. Unaware of anything amiss, Judith drives off with her husband. In the car his strange staring frightens her but it is not until Victor struggles out of the car that she sees his arm is mutating and begins to scream. (Ext. 1a, 8 mins.)*

Victor starts to lose his human form and take on the shape of a monstrous vegetable growth.

After spending the night on a barge, Victor wakes to find a little girl playing with her doll on the bank. She invites him to join in the tea-party she is having with her doll, but Victor dashes the doll from her arms and staggers away. (Ext. 1b, 3 mins.)

The creature that Victor has become wanders around London, looking increasingly fungoid and feeding on the blood of its human and animal victims. Quatermass and Inspector Lomax organise a search.

A general alert is put out for the 'thing'. The recording of a BBC television programme about the restoration of Westminster Abbey is disrupted when a technician falls dead from some scaffolding. The programme continues until one of the TV cameras picks up the monster, now an enormous size, wrapped around the scaffolding. Quatermass decides to electrocute it and power from all over London is diverted to the Abbey. The electric shock successfully kills the monster, and Quatermass leaves the Abbey making plans to re-activate his rocket programme. (Ext. 1c, 10 mins.)

Quatermass II
UK 1957 sd b/w 19

PRODUCTION
p.c – Hammer. *p* – Anthony Hinds. *d* – Val Guest. *sc* – Nigel Kneale, Val Guest, from the television play by Nigel Kneale. *ph* – Gerald Gibbs. *ed* – James Needs. *a.d* – Bernard Robinson. *m* – James Bernard.

LEADING PLAYERS
Brian Donlevy (*Quatermass*), John Longden (*Lomax*), Bryan Forbes (*Marsh*), William Franklyn (*Brand*), Tom Chatto (*Broadhead*).

SYNOPSIS
Returning from a meeting in London at which the authorities have refused to support his rocket project, Professor Qartermass sees a man's face marked by a peculiar abrasion which appeared while he and his wife picnicked on Wynerton Flats, a desolate and isolated area of land near Carlisle.

Next day Marsh, one of his research assistants, tells him that radar has picked up objects falling on Wynerton Flats. Quatermass decides to investigate and drives out to the Flats with Marsh. They find the area deserted, until in a distant valley they see an exact reconstruction of Quatermass's moon life-support research

project. Marsh examines the ruins of a deserted village and discovers numerous meteorite-like objects. He picks one up; it explodes in his face leaving a V-shaped scar on his cheek. Alarm sirens go off in the plant and Quatermass and Marsh find themselves surrounded by silent armed soldiers. They take Marsh with them and order Quatermass out of the area. Quatermass drives to the nearest village, but there is no police station and no-one at the community centre there can help him. (Ext. 1a, 9 mins.)*

Quatermass realises that Wynerton Flats is the prototype of a police state that invaders from outer space are planning to extend over the whole country. Officials tell him that the complex is a government research project investigating the manufacture of synthetic foods for the third world.

Quatermass talks to Willie Broadhead, a campaigning MP, about the research plant. Broadhead has managed to get onto an official inspection tour of the plant and Quatermass's request to go too is granted. When the group arrives at the Wynerton Flats plant the guide, who has V-shaped marks on his wrists, becomes agitated when Quatermass and Broadhead want to go for an exploratory tour alone. Broadhead goes off to investigate and the group is taken into one of the domes. Quatermass realises it is a trap and manages to escape. As he runs through the plant calling for Broadhead he sees the MP stagger from one of the domes, blackened and dying. (Ext. 1b, 10 mins.)

Quatermass goes to the police, but the Commissioner has himself already been taken over. At a dance for the plant workers Quatermass tells them that the plant is run by aliens, but no-one believes him until a meteorite crashes into the hall and a young woman picks it up and is immediately marked with a V-shaped scar. The guards rush in, drag the woman away and kill a journalist who questions what is going on. Quatermass gets inside the plant to the control centre disguised as a guard. Meanwhile the workers form themselves into a vigilante group and break into the plant. There is a pitched battle between the workers and the guards which ends when the workers fire on the domes.

Les Quatre cents coups (The 400 Blows)
France 1958 sd b/w 20

PRODUCTION
p.c – Les Films du Carosse, SEDIF. *d* – François Truffaut. *sc* – François Truffaut. *ph* – Henri Decae (DyaliScope). *ed* – Marie-Josèphe Yoyotte. *a.d* – Bernard Evein. *m* – Jean Constantin.

LEADING PLAYERS
Jean-Pierre Léaud (*Antoine Dionel*), Claire Maurier (*Antoine's Mother*), Albert Rémy (*Antoine's Father*), Patrick Auffay (*René*), Guy Decomble (*The Schoolmaster*).

SYNOPSIS

Antoine Doinel is a twelve-year-old Parisian boy who comes from a home background of indifference, quarrels and infidelity.

One day, while playing truant with his friend René, Antoine sees his mother kissing a stranger. That evening he tries to forge an absence note to take to school the next day. When his teachers press for a reason for his non-attendance Antoine blurts out that his mother has died. Later, however, both his parents arrive at the school. Antoine decides to leave home and spends the night at a printing works.

Antoine and his friend René are forbidden to come to school for a week. Unable to return home, Antoine hides at René's house until the two decide to steal a typewriter and go on a trip to the sea, which Antoine has never seen. They find the machine impossible to sell, however, and Antoine is caught as he tries to return it. Exasperated, his father takes him to a police station, from which he is sent to a reform school. Antoine's mother tells him that his father is no longer interested in his future. The following day Antoine escapes and runs across the country until he suddenly reaches the sea.

(NB This extract is standard reduced from Scope.)

Racket Busters
USA 1938 sd b/w 20

PRODUCTION

p.c – Warner Bros. *d* – Lloyd Bacon. *sc* – Robert Rossen, Leonardo Bercovici. *ph* – Arthur Edeson. *ed* – James Gibbon. *a.d* – Esdras Hartley. *m* – Adolph Deutsch. *cost* – Howard Shoup.

LEADING PLAYERS

Humphrey Bogart (*Pete Martin*), George Brent (*Denny Jordan*), Gloria Dickson (*Nora Jordan*), Allen Jenkins (*Skeets Wilson*), Walter Abel (*Thomas Allison*), Henry O'Neill (*The Governor*), Oscar O'Shea (*Pop*).

SYNOPSIS

Pete Martin, New York City's leading racketeer, sweeps the board in the city elections. Meanwhile, Thomas Allison is sworn in as special prosecutor with responsibility for cleaning up the city. Martin establishes his headquarters, from where he intends to 'organise' all the truck drivers and commission merchants. (Ext. 1a, 6 mins.)

Allison cannot get far because all the potential witnesses against Martin are afraid of retribution, but Martin does meet opposition from a few truck drivers, among them Denny Jordan and Skeets Wilson.

Nora, Denny's pregnant wife, meets him and Skeets at the truck garage. They are about to leave when a car-load of Martin's men appear and put up posters advertising their organisation. Denny hears Pop, the long-standing secretary of the Truckers'

Association, making a speech about solidarity amongst the truckers and persuading them not to go to the meeting arranged by Martin's men. There is a fight and Pop is knocked to the floor; Denny goes to his defence and the racketeers leave. (Ext. 1b, 5 mins.)

Later, Denny is desperate for money to pay for medical care for Nora and robs Martin's office. Martin learns of this and froces Denny to join his association. With the truckers safely 'associated', Martin sets about recruiting the commission merchants. During this campaign Pop gives evidence to the special prosecutor and is later found murdered. Denny is ostracised by his fellow truckers and Nora decides to leave him. Finally he is thrown into prison by Allison for witholding evidence.

Martin successfully calls a general strike of truckers and food delivery to the city is paralysed. Skeets tries to get the men back to work. Allison decides to release Denny in the hope that he will prove his honesty and help Skeets. The truckers rally to Denny and return to work. Denny chases and captures Martin, who is subsequently given a maximum prison sentence. (Ext. 1c, 9 mins.)

Rancho Notorious
USA 1952 sd col 20

PRODUCTION

p.c – Fidelity Pictures-RKO Radio. *p* – Howard Welsch. *d* – Fritz Lang. *sc* – Daniel Taradash, from a story by Sylvia Richards. *ph* – Hal Mohr (Technicolor). *ed* – Otto Ludwig. *a.d* – Robert Priestly. *m* – Emil Newman. *cost* – Don Loper.

LEADING PLAYERS

Marlene Dietrich (*Altar Keane*), Arthur Kennedy (*Vern Haskell*), Mel Ferrer (*Frenchy Fairmont*), Gloria Henry (*Beth*).

SYNOPSIS

Beth, the fiancée of cowboy Vern Haskell, is raped and murdered during a hold-up in a small town. He swears revenge.

The posse which had been trailing Beth's killer turns back but Vern continues the search alone. His only clue is the name Chuck-a-Luck, which he eventually links with a saloon singer, Altar Keane. Vern is arrested after a fight, but one of the men in the sheriff's office remembers Altar and suggests that Vern might trace her in Virginia City. (Ext. 1a, 9 mins.)

There he finds that Altar was last heard of in association with Frenchy Fairmont, a gunfighter. Vern helps Frenchy to break out of prison and is taken by Frenchy to Chuck-a-Luck, an isolated ranch run by Altar as a hideout for wanted men.

At the ranch they find outlaws relaxing while Altar sings. Vern notices that she is wearing a brooch that he gave to Beth. (Ext. 1b, 6 mins.)

Altar is attracted to Vern, who joins in the outlaws' activities.

After a bank robbery Vern returns to Chuck-a-Luck with Altar's cut of the tak-

ings. He persuades her to dress up for him in her finest clothes, including the brooch. He then forces Altar to reveal who gave her the brooch and explains how Beth lost it. (Ext. 1c, 5 mins.)

Before Vern can kill the outlaw who murdered Beth he is caught with Altar and Frenchy in a gun battle at the ranch. Altar is killed while saving Frenchy's life. Vern and Frenchy ride away from the ranch together.

Rashomon
Japan 1950 sd b/w 16

PRODUCTION

p.c – Daiei. *p* – Jingo Minoru. *d* – Akira Kurosawa. *sc* – Shinobu Hashimoto, Akira Kurosawa, from two stories, *Rashomon* and *In a Grove* by Ryunosuke Akutagawa. *ph* – Kazuo Miyagawa. *a.d* – So Matsuyama. *m* – Fumio Hayasaka.

LEADING PLAYERS

Toshiro Mifune (*Tajomaru, The Bandit*), Masayuki Mori (*Takehiro, The Samurai*), Machiko Kyo (*Masago, Takehiro's Wife*), Takashi Shimura (*The Woodcutter*), Minoru Chiaki (*The Priest*), Kichijiro Ueda (*The Servant*).

SYNOPSIS

Japan, 1200 years ago: a time of civil war and famine. Three men, a woodcutter, a servant and a Buddhist priest shelter from torrential rain under a ruined city gate. The priest and the woodcutter are disturbed by a recent event, which the servant goads the woodcutter into explaining. He repeats the story told that morning by a bandit, Tajomaru, who confessed to the murder of Takehiro, a samurai, and the rape of Masago, the samurai's wife.

Tajomaru is dozing beneath a tree on a hot summer's day when he sees Takehiro and Masago passing by. Feeling aroused by the woman, Tajomaru lures the samurai with a false story of buried treasure, ties him up and then rapes Masago in front of him. At first she resists, but later she succumbs.

Masago says that she cannot live with both men knowing her shame, that they must fight a duel and that she will belong to the winner. After a fierce battle Tajomaru kills Takehiro, but by then Masago has fled. Tajomaru takes Takehiro's horse and belongings and sells his sword at an inn. Later, he is found by the police. The priest and woodcutter disagree violently with this story, since Masago has been found and has told a very different version of events. According to her, after she was raped Tajomaru taunted her by revealing his identity. When he left, she untied her husband who treated her with contempt. She fainted, and on coming round found her dagger in her husband's breast. Takehiro contributes his version through a medium: after the attack, Tajomaru tried to soothe Masago, who begged him to kill her husband. Disgusted, Tajomaru asked Takehiro whether they should kill her, but she ran off. Finally, the woodcutter tells his own story: the husband refused to risk his life for his wife and she had to goad the men into a duel in which her husband was killed. At that moment the three men discover a baby abandoned near the gate. The servant strips the quilts from the child, despite the woodcutter's protests, and justifies himself by accusing the latter of having himself stolen the missing dagger. The priest takes the baby, but the woodcutter offers to bring up the child with his own six children, saying that one more will not make any difference to his poverty. The man's sincerity satisfies the priest who regains a little of his lost faith in humanity.

Rebel Without a Cause
USA 1955 sd col scope 24

PRODUCTION
p.c – Warner Bros. p – David Weisbart. d – Nicholas Ray. sc – Stewart Stern, Irving Schulman, from a story by Nicholas Ray. ph – Ernest Haller (CinemaScope and Warnercolor). ed – William Ziegler. a.d – Malcolm Bert. m – Leonard Rosenman.

LEADING PLAYERS
James Dean (Jim), Natalie Wood (Judy), Jim Backus (Jim's Father), Ann Doran (Jim's Mother), Sal Mineo (Plato), Corey Allen (Buzz).

SYNOPSIS
In the credit sequence, Jim, a rebellious youth who has just moved into town with his neurotic mother and weak father, falls down drunk among the rubbish in the street, where he finds a clockwork toy. After wrapping it in paper he lies down beside it to sleep. He is taken to the police station, where Plato and Judy, two other disturbed teenagers who will eventually become Jim's friends, are already being held. (Ext. 1a, 3 mins.)

Jim is collected by his parents and taken to their middle-class home. The next morning Jim meets Judy and offers her a lift, but she declines, preferring to be with the gang led by Buzz, her boyfriend. A mutual antagonism develops between the two boys and they fight.

Jim's father, dressed in a frilly apron, fusses over his son's bruises while evading his questions about the courage necessary to be a man. When he cannot get a direct answer Jim leaves to go to the Chicken Run, where he is expected to compete against Buzz by driving a car towards a cliff edge at full speed to see who will be the last one to jump out. Plato, Judy and Buzz and his gang are already there and while Buzz and Jim test their car doors Judy and Plato discuss Jim's qualities. Buzz tells Jim he likes him, but cannot answer Jim's question 'So why do we do this?' Judy gives the signal and the run begins. Buzz's coat is caught on his door handle and he is killed when his car goes over the cliff. The crowd of onlookers panics and leaves. Jim, brought closer to

Judy by Buzz's death, drives Plato and Judy home. Plato wants Jim to stay the night and have breakfast at his house but Jim gently declines. (Ext. 1b, 14 mins.)

Jim's father is sleeping in an armchair, waiting for his son's return. His mother comes downstairs and Jim tells them about the Chicken Run and Buzz's death. A family row ensues because Jim wants to take responsibility and go to the police, against his parents' wishes. His mother wants to leave town. Jim asks his father to stand up to her; when he is unable to do so, Jim attacks him violently then pushes his mother aside and runs out of the house. (Ext. 1c, 6 mins.)

Fearing Jim will go to the police, Buzz's friends track him to a deserted mansion where he hides out with Judy and Plato, who is armed with his father's gun. Before Jim can intervene, Plato opens fire, hitting one of the youths. Summoned by the shots, police close in and order the gun-crazed youngster to surrender. Jim reassures Plato and brings him out to where the police are waiting. Plato makes a sudden nervous movement which is mistaken by a policeman who fires at him.

(NB This extract is in Scope and needs an anamorphic lens.)

La Règle du jeu (The Rules of the Game)
France 1939 sd b/w 9 + 10

PRODUCTION
p.c – La Nouvelle Edition Française. p – Claude Renoir. d – Jean Renoir. sc – Jean Renoir, Carl Koch. ph – Jean Bachelet. ed – Marguerite Renoir. a.d – Eugène Lourié, Max Douy. m – Mozart, Monsigny, Saint-Saëns.

LEADING PLAYERS
Marcel Dalio (Robert, Marquis de La Chesnaye), Nora Gregor (Christine, Marquise de La Chesnaye), Jean Renoir (Octave), Gaston Modot (Schumacher), Mila Parély (Geneviève de Marras), Roland Toutain (André Jurieux), Julien Carette (Marceau), Paulette Dubost (Lisette).

SYNOPSIS
A house-party assembles at La Colinière, a château belonging to the wealthy Marquis de La Chesnaye, a collector of mechanical toys. Among the guests are Geneviève, the Marquis's mistress whom he wants to leave, Octave, a mutual friend, and the young aviator André Jurieux who is in love with Christine, the Marquis's wife. Lisette, Christine's maid, prefers the town to the country life of her husband, Schumacher, the gamekeeper at La Colinière. When his gamekeepers capture a notorious poacher, Marceau, the Marquis decides to take him into the château as a valet.

The party goes hunting and Schumacher gives instructions to the beaters. They advance in a line, the animals are forced out into the open and then shot by the

waiting hunters. The hunt over, everybody returns to the château. The Marquis and Geneviève separate themselves off and Geneviève berates him for ending their affair. As she kisses him they are accidentally observed by Christine who is looking at the countryside through binoculars. (Ext. 1a, 9 mins.)

That night there is a fancy dress masquerade. André manages to get Christine on her own. She says she loves him and they discuss going away together. Marceau and Lisette are discovered by Schumacher, who chases Marceau upstairs, causing chaos amongst all the guests. The Marquis surprises André and Christine and this leads to a fight. Geneviève becomes hysterical and is led off to her room. Octave spirits Christine away and they talk together. The Marquis tells one of his servants to restrain Schumacher. (Ext. 2, 10 mins.)

Schumacher and Marceau are both dismissed. Feeling disillusioned with both André and her husband, Christine decides that she is in love with Octave. She asks him to take her away and Octave, who has been secretly in love with her for many years, agrees. Later, however, he decides that he is too old and too poor for her and tells André that Christine is hoping to run away with him instead. Christine borrows a coat from Lisette and goes to wait in a greenhouse for Octave. Schumacher and Marceau see her there and think that Lisette is keeping an assignment with another man. When André arrives the jealous Schumacher shoots him. In the early morning light the Marquis assists Christine back to the château and declares to the guests that Schumacher fired by mistake at a man he thought to be a poacher. The guests, however, prefer to believe the Marquis responsible for the removal of a rival.

The Revenge of Frankenstein
UK 1958 sd col 20

PRODUCTION
p.c – Hammer. p – Anthony Hinds. d – Terence Fisher. sc – Jimmy Sangster, from the character created by Mary Shelley. ph – Jack Asher (Technicolor). ed – James Needs. m – Leonard Salzedo.

LEADING PLAYERS
Peter Cushing (Dr. Frankenstein), Francis Matthews (Dr. Hans Kleve), Michael Gwynn (Karl).

SYNOPSIS
After narrowly escaping being guillotined for his experiments, Baron Frankenstein arrives in Carlsberg, where under the alias of Dr. Stein he builds up a lucrative and fashionable medical practice and starts a poor people's hospital.

Frankenstein examines the daughter of a countess whose mother is keen for her to make a match with the doctor and then goes to his hospital. He keeps three members of the medical council of Carlsberg waiting while he does his rounds and tells a pickpocket that his arm will have to be amputated. He refuses the doctors' invitation to join their council and continues with his work. Later, however, Dr. Kleve, one of the council members, goes to Frankenstein's rooms and reveals that he knows his real identity. He demands to become his assistant. Although initially suspicious, Frankenstein agrees and takes Kleve to his underground laboratory where he demonstrates elaborate experiments with the amputated limbs of his hospital patients. He then unveils his artificial 'perfect human' and explains that his crippled assistant Karl has given permission for Frankenstein to transfer his brain into a new body.

The operation takes place, but a nurse at the clinic allows the new 'Karl' to escape before the primeval instincts have been eradicated from the body. Karl kills a janitor, rapes a girl and embarks on a cannibalistic expedition which eventually brings him to a party that Frankenstein is attending. Learning the truth, the patients at the clinic turn on Frankenstein and nearly beat him to death. But his young assistant, Kleve, performs an experiment already demonstrated to him by his master. Frankenstein emerges in London as Dr. Frank of Harley Street.

The Revolt of Mamie Stover
USA 1956 sd col scope 20

PRODUCTION
p.c – 20th Century-Fox. *p* – Buddy Adler. *d* – Raoul Walsh. *sc* – Sydney Boehm, from the novel by William Bradford Hine. *ph* – Leo Tover (CinemaScope and colour by DeLuxe). *ed* – Louis Loeffler. *a.d* – Lyle R. Wheeler, Mark-Lee Kirk. *m* – Hugo Friedhofer. *cost* – Charles Le Maire, Travilla.

LEADING PLAYERS
Jane Russell (*Mamie Stover*), Richard Egan (*Jimmy Blair*), Agnes Moorehead (*Bertha Parchman*), Richard Coogan (*Captain Eldon Sumac*), Michael Pate (*Harry Adkins*).

SYNOPSIS
San Francisco, 1941. During the credit sequence a police car draws up at a dockside. Mamie gets out, walks towards a waiting ship, stops, turns and looks into camera. (Ext. 1a, 2 mins.)

On board and bound for Hawaii, Mamie becomes friendly with Jimmy Blair, a writer. She asks him to 'dress her up and teach her how to behave', but he refuses. When they dock Jimmy is met by his fiancée and Mamie becomes a hostess and high-class prostitute in The Bungalow, a nightclub for US servicemen. Later, a relationship develops between Jimmy and Mamie, despite the restrictive rules of The Bungalow. He wants her to go straight but she wants to go on on making money. Jimmy enlists after Pearl Harbour and asks Mamie to marry him when the war is over.

She agrees, but he makes her promise to stop being a hostess. She tries, but is persuaded by the offer of more money.

Mamie has a drink with a captain, who agrees to teach her how to play golf. Later at the club surrounded by hula-hula girls she sings 'Keep your eyes on the hands'. Meanwhile, Jimmy is seen at the battlefront reading a letter from her in which she says that she had given up working at The Bungalow. Mamie bargains for a higher cut of the profits at a photography session. Taking advantage of the panic caused by the bombing of Pearl Harbor, she buys up real estate cheaply and becomes very wealthy. At the golf course the captain tells Mamie that they are two of a kind and is cynical about the chances of Jimmy ever marrying a girl like her. She hits him and leaves. A soldier returning from Hawaiian leave shows Jimmy and the rest of his company a pin-up picture of Flaming Mamie. As Jimmy looks at the photograph there is an air-raid and he is hit. Given ten days leave, he goes to The Bungalow to see Mamie. He accuses her of being only interested in money and leaves. In San Francisco Mamie is met at the dockside by the police, who agree to take her out to the airport and are incredulous when she says she has made a fortune and given it all away. (Ext. 1b, 18 mins.)

(NB This extract is in Scope and needs an anamorphic lens.)

Richard III
UK 1911 st b/w 6

PRODUCTION
p.c – F. R. Benson Co-operative Company. *p* – Frank R. Benson, from the play by William Shakespeare. *ph* – Will G. Barker.

LEADING PLAYERS
Frank Benson (*Richard III*), Alfred Brydone (*Edward IV*), Cathleen Yorke (*Edward, Prince of Wales*), Hetty Kenyon (*Richard, Duke of York*), Murray Carrington (*Duke of Clarence*), Violet Fairbrother (*Elizabeth*).

SYNOPSIS
An early version of Shakespeare's play.
The Battle of Bosworth.

Rin-Tin-Tin
(*see* The Lighthouse by the Sea)

Rio Bravo
USA 1959 sd col 18

PRODUCTION
p.c – Armada Productions. *p* – Howard Hawks. *d* – Howard Hawks. *sc* – Jules Furthman, Leigh Brackett, from a short story by B. H. McCampbell. *ph* – Russell Harlan (Technicolor). *ed* – Folmer Blangsted. *a.d* – Leo K. Kuter. *m* – Dimitri Tiomkin. *lyrics* – Paul Francis Webster. *cost* – Marjorie Best.

LEADING PLAYERS
John Wayne (*John T. Chance*), Dean Martin (*Dude*), Ricky Nelson (*Colorado*), Walter Brennan (*Stumpy*), Ward Bond (*Pat Wheeler*), Angie Dickinson (*Feathers*), John Russell (*Nathan Burdette*), Pedro Gonzalez-Gonzalez (*Carlos*), Estelita Rodriguez (*Consuela*).

SYNOPSIS
When Sheriff John T. Chance arrests Joe Burdette for murder the prisoner's brothers blockade the small Texan border town of Rio Bravo. Determined to free Joe before the arrival of the State Marshall, Nathan Burdette hires extra gunmen. The Sheriff has only two deputies to help him: the old and crippled Stumpy and Dude, an alcoholic. Pat Wheeler, a wagontrain master, comes into town.

Chance and Dude return from an inspection tour of the town and are met at the hotel by Carlos, who is alarmed by Wheeler's attempt to enlist help from the townspeople. Chance interrupts Wheeler at a card game to warn him against actively trying to organise support for him. Wheeler suggests that one of his men, Colorado, could help, but when asked Colorado says that he prefers to mind his own business. Chance notices that the pack of cards which the players had been using is missing its aces. He sees Feathers, a professional gambler, leaving the table after winning some money and immediately assumes that she is the card cheat. He confronts her and tells her to leave on the next coach out of town. She insists on her innocence and tells him he will have to search her for the cards to establish her guilt. Colorado accuses one of the card players, finds the missing cards and tells Chance that he should apologise to Feathers, which he grudgingly does. (Ext. 1a, 11 mins.)

Posted at the edge of town to disarm strangers, Dude is captured by Burdette's men, who then ride into town and hold up Chance. Colorado intervenes and saves Chance. Nathan Burdette offers to exchange Dude for Joe and the Sheriff agrees. During the exchange there is a shoot-out in which Chance, Stumpy, Dude and Colorado use dynamite to force the Burdette gang to surrender.

Dude and Stumpy jokingly discuss the Sheriff's relationship with Feathers. Chance goes to visit her and finds her dressed in black net stockings and a scanty, revealing costume. After much banter he orders her not to go downstairs to the bar and tosses her stockings out of the window onto the heads of Stumpy and Dude who are walking in the street below. (Ext. 1b, 7 mins.)

The Rise and Fall of Legs Diamond
USA 1959 sd b/w 13

PRODUCTION
p.c – United States Productions. *p* – Milton Sperling. *d* – Budd Boetticher. *sc* – Joseph Landon. *ph* – Lucien Ballard. *ed*

– Folmar Blangsted. *a.d* – Jack Poplin. *m* – Leonard Rosenman.

LEADING PLAYERS
Ray Danton (*Legs Diamond*), Karen Steele (*Alice*), Elaine Stewart (*Monica*), Jesse White (*Leo Bremer*), Warren Oates (*Eddie Diamond*), Robert Lowery (*Arnold Rothstein*).

SYNOPSIS
Jack 'Legs' Diamond and his brother arrive in New York City. Legs befriends Alice Shiffer, a dancing teacher. He robs a jewellery shop, is caught and jailed. On his release he determines to rob only those who cannot call the police – other thieves and gangsters. He works his way up the hierarchy of a gangland boss, Arnold Rothstein, and becomes known as 'the man who can't be killed'. Eventually he murders Rothstein and takes over his protection racket. Other gangland leaders try to kill him, but he survives the attack.

Legs arrives at the Hotsy Totsy Club and the assembled gang leaders reluctantly agree to pay him the protection money he demands. He also tells them that he wants the club for himself. Later Alice comes into the club; she has become an alcoholic and Legs calls her a lush. Legs refuses to pay his brother Eddie's hospital fees because he does not want any vulnerable points through which he could be attacked. At the pinnacle of his success Legs suggests that he and Alice go on a long European tour. At each stop on their journey they go to the movies and there, through a succession of Movie News Reviews, they learn about the abolition of Prohibition, followed by the imprisonment of Al Capone and the declaration of a war against crime. On their return to the States they find the Hotsy Totsy Club has been closed down. Mafia executives explain to Legs that the old order is over, dead bodies on the streets are now considered bad public relations and that there is need for a new nationwide syndicate whose methods are more subtle. Legs doggedly insists on his share of the take for protection, but they laugh in his face.

Legs is deserted by his friends, including Alice. Alone, his legendary powers demystified, he is murdered by two gunmen of the crime syndicate

The Rival World
UK 1955 sd col 16
(w. **The Back of Beyond**)

PRODUCTION
p.c – Shell Film Unit. *p* – Stuart Legg. *d* – Bert Haanstra. *ph* – Sidney Beadle, Ronald Whitehouse, Han Van Gelder (Eastman Color). *ed* – Bert Haanstra. *m* – James Stevens, Pierre Henri.

SYNOPSIS
The rival world is the terrifying kingdom of insects. Four-fifths of all animal life consists of insects, and many of the world's most horrible diseases can be traced, directly or indirectly, to their presence.

The destruction of food and vegetable products by members of the insect world is shown. Locusts must be combatted by scientific methods both on the ground and in the air and an aeroplane flies through a massive swarm of locusts, discharging insecticide.

River of No Return
USA 1954 sd col scope and standard 20

PRODUCTION
p.c – 20th Century-Fox. *p* – Stanley Rubin. *d* – Otto Preminger. *sc* – Frank Fenton, from a story by Louis Lanz. *ph* – Joseph LaShelle (CinemaScope and colour by DeLuxe). *ed* – Louis Loeffler. *a.d* – Lyle Wheeler, Addison Hehr. *m* – Lionel Newman. *lyrics* – Ken Darby. *choreo* – Jack Cole.

LEADING PLAYERS
Robert Mitchum (*Matt Calder*), Marilyn Monroe (*Kay Weston*), Rory Calhoun (*Harry Weston*), Tommy Rettig (*Mark*).

SYNOPSIS
During the gold rush of 1875, widower Matt Calder is released from prison after serving a sentence for shooting a man in the back. With his 10-year-old son, Mark, who knows nothing of his father's past, Matt plans to work his farm, which borders on a raging torrent known as the 'river of no return'. One morning they see a raft out of control and rescue Kay, an ebullient saloon singer, and Harry Weston, her gambler husband, who are hurrying to Council City to register a gold claim Harry has won in a card game. Matt tells them that they will never make it by river. After a fight Harry takes Matt's gun and only horse and continues his journey alone. Indians attack the farm and Matt, Mark and Kay escape by raft. During the hazardous river journey Matt and Kay have an argument and Kay reveals that she knows why Matt had been in prison. Mark overhears and rejects his father's explanations for the incident.

Matt, Mark and Kay arrive in Council City. Kay goes across to the saloon to try to persuade them to apologise to Matt. Harry pulls a gun on Matt and is about to kill him but is himself shot in the back by Mark. Father and son are reconciled and Kay goes back to the Golden Nugget saloon to resume her career as a singer. Matt appears while she is singing, tosses her over his shoulder and takes her back to the farm.

(NB This extract comprises two versions of the same sequence: the first is standard reduced from Scope, the second is in Scope and needs an anamorphic lens.)

The Roaring Twenties
USA 1939 sd b/w 9

PRODUCTION
p.c – Warner Bros. *p* – Mark Hellinger and Hal B. Wallis. *d* – Raoul Walsh. *sc* – Jerry Wald, Richard Macauley, Robert Rossen, from a story by Mark Hellinger. *ph* – Ernie Haller. *ed* – Jack Killifer. *a.d* – Max Parker. *m* – Leo F. Forbstein.

LEADING PLAYERS
James Cagney (*Eddie Bartlett*), Priscilla Lane (*Jean Sherman*), Humphrey Bogart (*George Hally*), Gladys George (*Panama Smith*), Jeffrey Lynn (*Lloyd Hart*), Frank McHugh (*Danny Green*).

SYNOPSIS
The film opens with a fake newsreel account of the 20s. Then, three soldiers at the front during the First World War are shown arguing about their plans for the future. Back in New York they all drift into crime, one of them, Lloyd, covertly as a lawyer. The other two, Eddie and George, get involved in the bootleg liquor business. Eddie falls in love with Jean Sherman, who wants to be a musical comedy star, and gets her a job at a club run by Panama Smith.

The narrator announces '1924' and explains that bootlegging has become big business and the arrival of the lightweight machine gun has increased gang warfare. Eddie and George are engaged in a raid on a warehouse belonging to their rival Nick Brown. Eddie sends Danny, an old friend, outside to watch for trouble. When he warns them that the relief watchman is arriving they lure him into a trap. George realises he is his former army sergeant and shoots him. Back in Panama's club, Jean is singing 'It had to be you', giving meaningful looks at Lloyd. Panama tries to encourage Lloyd's interest in Jean. When Eddie and George arrive, Lloyd complains that Eddie has been avoiding talking about business. George warns him to stop fooling around with his collection of taxi cabs, which Eddie defends as protection for his old age. George goes on to warn Eddie about Lloyd's interest in Jean.

George and Eddie quarrel about the way to handle Nick Brown. Lloyd insists that Jean tells Eddie of their affair. Danny's body is delivered at the club with a note of warning from Nick Brown. George and Jean both leave Eddie, and he is bankrupted by the Wall Street crash. George buys up his business, leaving him one taxi cab. Lloyd is now crusading against the racketeers. George's gang delivers a warning threat to Jean, who seeks out Eddie's help. He confronts George and shoots him, but is himself fatally wounded by one of George's gang. He dies in the street in Panama's arms.

Room at the Top
UK 1958 sd b/w 15

PRODUCTION
p.c – Remus. *p* – John and James Woolf. *d* – Jack Clayton. *sc* – Neil Paterson, from the novel by John Braine. *ph* – Freddie Francis. *ed* – Ralph Kemplen. *a.d* – Ralph Brinton. *m* – Mario Nascimbene.

LEADING PLAYERS

Laurence Harvey (*Joe Lampton*), Simone Signoret (*Alice Aisgill*), Heather Sears (*Susan Brown*), Ambrosine Phillpotts (*Mrs. Brown*), Donald Wolfit (*Mr. Brown*), John Westbrook (*Jack Wales*), Allan Cuthbertson (*George Aisgill*).

SYNOPSIS

Working-class and ambitious, Joe Lampton arrives in Warley to take up a secure but poorly-paid post in the Borough Treasurer's Office. He fastens his attentions on Susan Brown, daughter of a local industrial magnate.

Joe argues with the upper-class war hero Jack Wales who is waiting for Susan outside a dress shop. At the dog track Joe discusses his method of grading women and then offers to join the local drama society. During a rehearsal the cast and Jack Wales are amused by Joe's mistaken pronunciation. Later Joe takes Alice Aisgill, an older French woman and member of the cast, for a drink. They drive past the Brown's palatial house and Joe talks about Susan. He phones her for a date but the call is cut short by Susan's mother. In the pub after another rehearsal Alice's husband appears and humiliates her in front of Joe and her friends.

Brown sends Susan abroad and Joe turns for solace to Alice who falls in love with him. Susan returns from her holiday shortly after the lovers have quarrelled and is seduced by Joe, who then goes back to Alice. Susan realises she is pregnant. Brown fails to buy Joe off, but finally forces him to agree to give up Alice and marry Susan. Deserted and heartbroken, Alice goes on a drinking bout that culminates in a fatal car accident. Joe disappears and is beaten unconscious by a gang of toughs for making a drunken pass at a girl, but is rescued in time for his wedding.

Rosemary's Baby
USA 1968 sd col 20

PRODUCTION

p.c – Paramount/William Castle Enterprises. *p* – William Castle. *d* – Roman Polanski. *sc* – Roman Polanski, from the novel by Ira Levin. *ph* – William Fraker (Technicolor). *ed* – Sam O'Steen, Bob Wyman. *a.d* – Joel Schiller. *m* – Krzysztof Komeda. *cost* – Anthea Sylbert.

LEADING PLAYERS

Mia Farrow (*Rosemary Woodhouse*), John Cassavetes (*Guy Woodhouse*), Ruth Gordon (*Minnie Castevet*), Sidney Blackmer (*Roman Castevet*), Maurice Evans (*Hutch*), Ralph Bellamy (*Dr. Sapirstein*).

SYNOPSIS

Rosemary Woodhouse and her actor husband Guy move into a rambling apartment block in New York. Their lives become increasingly involved with their next door neighbours, Roman and Minnie Castevet. Rosemary becomes pregnant

and the Castevets arrange for her to be looked after by their friend, the celebrated gynaecologist Abe Sapirstein. After several months of constant pain and the mysterious death of her friend Hutch, Rosemary begins to make connections between Guy's rapid success (he steps into a leading part when the chosen actor suddenly becomes blind), the Castevet's solicitude and their strange circle of friends. A cryptic deathbed message from Hutch convinces her that she and the unborn child are the object of a witches' plot and that Roman Castevet is the son of a notorious 19th-century Satanist. When Rosemary learns that Sapirstein is also implicated, she seeks help from her former doctor, but he delivers her back to Sapirstein. The baby is born, but Rosemary is told that he died at birth.

Guy laughingly discounts her theory that he, the Castevets and Sapirstein are all witches. That night, Rosemary finds a passage leading from their airing cupboard. She takes a knife and goes through into the next apartment, where she finds Guy, the Castevets and their friends celebrating the birth of her baby. She goes over to the child and is at first repelled by his strange eyes, but eventually accepts him.

The Rules of the Game
(*see* La Règle du jeu)

Saddled with Five Girls
Czechoslovakia 1967 sd b/w 10

PRODUCTION

p.c – Svabík-Procházka. *d* – Evald Schorm. *sc* – Iva Hercíková, Evald Schorm, from a story by Iva Hercíková. *ph* – Jan Curík. *m* – Frantisek Belfin, Carl Maria Weber.

LEADING PLAYERS

Andrea Cunderlíková (*Natasha*), Jana Krupicková (*Zdena*), Lucie Zulová (*Jana*), Dana Matejková (*Jirina*), Martin Vedra (*Petr*).

SYNOPSIS

Five schoolgirls are interested in making friends with Petr, the new boy tenant of a tower museum. One of the girls, Natasha, has a family that is relatively wealthy and because of this she is envied by the others. She in turn is jealous of their comradeship and the fun they have together.

One day Natasha is left at the zoo by the other four girls. She manages to get into the tower and finds Petr there. The custodian interrupts their talk with a cry of 'Sodom and Gomorrah!' They arrange a date and afterwards at a party at her flat Natasha tells the girls. They celebrate with mixed feelings.

At an appointed time the four girls lock Natasha in the school cloakroom. They write a letter to Petr as if from Natasha, revealing the most passionate sentiments. Petr is shocked and Natasha at first considers drowning herself, but she decides

that she will no longer try to win the other girls' favour.

A Sailor-Made Man
USA 1921 st b/w 10

PRODUCTION

p.c – Associated Exhibitors. *p* – Hal Roach. *d* – Fred Newmeyer. *sc* – Hal Roach, Sam Taylor. *ph* – Walter Lundin.

LEADING PLAYERS

Harold Lloyd (*The Boy*), Mildred Davis (*The Girl*), Noah Young (*Rough-House O'Rafferty*), Dick Sutherland (*Maharajah of Khaipura Bhandanna*).

SYNOPSIS

The boy, a wealthy idler, is told by the girl's father to do some work if he wants to marry his daughter. He joins the navy and has a rough time on board ship. When they reach an Oriental port the boy finds the girl has arrived in her yacht. She is kidnapped by a Maharajah.

The boy sets out to save her and is chased over an Arab palace. After a series of adventures he finds her and makes a successful rescue attempt.

The grateful father allows their marriage.

The St. Valentine's Day Massacre
USA 1967 sd col scope 18

PRODUCTION

p.c – Los Altos/20th Century-Fox. *p* – Roger Corman. *d* – Roger Corman. *sc* – Howard Browne. *ph* – Milton Krasner (Panavision and colour by DeLuxe). *ed* – William B. Murphy. *a.d* – Jack Martin Smith, Philip Jefferies. *m* – Fred Steiner.

LEADING PLAYERS

Jason Robards (*Al Capone*), George Segal (*Peter Gusenberg*), Ralph Meeker (*Bugs Moran*), Jean Hale (*Myrtle*), Clint Ritchie (*Jack McGurn*), Michèle Guayini (*Patsy Lelordo*), Reed Hadley (*Hymie Weiss*), John Agar (*Dion O'Bannion*), Alex D'Arcy (*Aiello*).

SYNOPSIS

Chicago 1928. A voice-over gives details of the careers and biographies of the members of the two opposing gangs led by Capone and Moran.

Capone is introduced by the narrator as the unchallenged leader of Chicago's underworld. The leading members of Capone's gang meet in a plush red velvet boardroom, are similarly described and their eventual deaths foretold. Capone explodes during a report on the state of business in the stockyards, rages about Bugs Moran's gradual takeover of Capone territory and says he wants Moran killed before Moran kills him. A flashback shows how Hymie Weiss attempted to murder Capone. A convoy of cars passes slowly by the restaurant where Capone is eating, each with machine guns blazing. The restaurant is almost destroyed. The flashback ends and Capone insists that Moran is likely to do something as crazy again. Jack McGurn, a young member of the gang, is given the job of dealing with Moran. The film then introduces Moran, leader of Chicago's North Side mob, who is being warned by members of his gang not to continue his five-year-long battle with Capone for control of the bootleg business. A flashback shows the killing of O'Bannion, the previous leader of the North Side gang, in his flower shop and his lavish gangland funeral. Moran outlines his plan to murder Patsy Lelordo, Capone's Mafia contact, and have him replaced by Aiello, who is prepared to be Moran's ally.

Capone hears the news of Lelordo's murder and personally disposes of Aiello by ritualistically cutting his throat. When McGurn's plans are almost complete Capone goes off to Florida to establish his alibi. On 14 February 1929 seven of Moran's men are lured to a garage and machine-gunned by Capone's men who are disguised as policemen. Moran himself is delayed by a chance phone call and escapes.

(NB This extract is in Scope and needs an anamorphic lens.)

Sally in Our Alley
UK 1913 st b/w 5
(w. **Comin' thro' the Rye**)

PRODUCTION
p.c – Hepworth Manufacturing Co. d Cecil Hepworth.

LEADING PLAYERS
Chrissie White (Sally), Cecil Mannering (Jack), Alec Worcester (The Curate).

SYNOPSIS
Sally, a coster, is loved by another coster, Jack, but also secretly admired by a young curate. Jack finds the curate at Sally's house bandaging her finger, which she has pricked while sewing. He is furiously jealous and storms out to a pub where he gets drunk. Egged on by his friends, he attacks the curate.

There is a fight, but Sally separates the two men. At first she won't be reconciled with Jack but eventually she forgives him. Later they visit the curate to ask for the banns to be published. He tries to appear happy but becomes gloomy when they have gone. Jack and Sally are married and the curate watches them leave the church.

Salt of the Earth
USA 1953 sd b/w 10

PRODUCTION
p.c – Independent Productions Corporation/International Union of Mine, Mill and Smelter Workers. p – Paul Jarrico. d – Herbert J. Biberman. sc – Michael Wilson, Herbert J. Biberman. ph – Simon Lazarus. m – Sol Kaplan.

LEADING PLAYERS
Rosaura Revueltas (Esperanza Quintero), Juan Chacon (Ramon Quintero), Will Geer (The Sheriff).

SYNOPSIS
Esperanza, the wife of Ramon, a Mexican-American mineworker, tells the story of the miner's lives – the unequal working hours and housing conditions they suffer in comparison with the Anglo workers and the growing unrest against the Delaware Zinc Corporation. An accident in the mine precipitates a strike. The wives form a Ladies' Auxiliary to aid the strikers and try to make connections between conditions at home and at work.

The Ladies' Auxiliary supports the miners' strike in several ways including a letter-writing campaign. Food supplies arrive from other unions. At a union meeting a court injunction against the pickets is announced and it seems as though the strike is defeated until one of the wives suggests that the women should take over the picket line to evade the injunction. Esperanza supports this and suggests that they should have a vote on the idea. Eventually the motion is passed and the women go to the picket lines, to the amusement of the Sheriff and his men. The women beat back his men when they try to remove them. Esperanza, who has been kept out of the picket line by Ramon, finally hands him their baby and joins in. The women re-form their picket after a tear gas attack and others from the surrounding neighbourhood join in singing songs of solidarity.

Esperanza's confidence grows through the success of this strategy and she is finally imprisoned with other women, leaving the men to care for the children. On her return home she has a bitter quarrel with Ramon, who, feeling redundant in the organisation of the strike, goes off hunting with other disgruntled husbands. At the last moment, however, the men decide to stand by their responsibilities and arrive home in time to defeat the company's final plot of eviction. As the Sheriff's men remove the family furniture from the front door, Ramon organises friends and neighbours to return it through the back door. Attempts to break the strike are abandoned and Ramon and Esperanza are reunited.

Le Samourai (The Samurai)
France/Italy 1967 sd col 15

PRODUCTION
p.c – Filmel/CICC (Paris)/Fida Cinematografica (Rome). p – Eugène Lépecier. d – Jean-Pierre Melville. sc – Jean-Pierre Melville, from the novel The Ronin by Joan McLeod. ph – Henri Decaë (Eastman Color). ed – Monique Bonnot, Yolande Maurette. a.d – François de Lamothe. m – François de Roubaix.

LEADING PLAYERS
Alain Delon (Jeff Costello), Nathalie Delon (Jane Lagrange), Cathy Rosier (Valérie), Jacques Leroy (The Gunman), Jean-Pierre Posier (Oliver Rey), Catherine Jourdan (The Hat-Check Girl).

SYNOPSIS
Jeff Costello, a professional gunman, lies on the bed smoking in a sparsely furnished room where a caged bird sings. A quotation appears on the screen from the Bushido, book of the samurai: 'No deeper loneliness than the samurai's. None but the tiger's in the jungle . . . perhaps . . .'. Saturday 4 April 6.30 pm. Jeff gets up from the bed, hides a roll of banknotes, puts on a white trench coat and trilby and leaves. He steals a car, drives out to a small village garage where the car's number plates are changed and buys a revolver. Later he goes to see Jane Lagrange, his girlfriend, and establishes an alibi. He then goes to a seedy hotel room where a group of men are playing cards and arranges to come in on the game at 2 am. Jeff goes to an exclusive club, puts on white gloves and walks through to the back office where he kills the proprietor. He passes Valérie, the club's pianist, who says nothing. The barman and the hat-check girl watch him as he leaves the club.

The police pick up Jeff as a suspect, but none of the nightclub staff will identify him and Jane backs up his alibi. At the pay-off point Jeff is shot and wounded by another gunman. Having dressed his wound, he goes back to the nightclub and asks Valérie, who fascinates him, to put him in touch with his anonymous employer. She says she might. At his flat he is confronted by the gunman again but this time he offers Jeff his money and another contract. Jeff accepts, but forces the name of his boss out of the gunman. Successfully evading the police, Jeff goes to the home of Olivier Rey, the man who ordered the killing, and shoots him. The second contract is to kill Valérie, and he goes to the nightclub, puts on his white gloves and aims his revolver at her. The waiting police shoot him down and discover that his gun was not loaded.

The Samurai
(see Le Samourai)

The Satanic Rites of Dracula
UK 1973 sd col 15

PRODUCTION
p.c – Hammer. p – Roy Skeggs. d – Alan Gibson. sc – Don Houghton. ph – Brian Probyn (Technicolor). ed – Chris Barnes. a.d – Lionel Couch. m – John Cacavas.

LEADING PLAYERS
Christopher Lee (D. D. Denham/Count Dracula), Peter Cushing (Professor Lorrimer Van Helsing), Michael Coles (Inspector Murray), Joanna Lumley (Jessica Van Helsing), Barbara Yu Ling (Chin Yang).

SYNOPSIS
A government agent has provided information on the activities of a witches' coven

which involves a minister, military leaders, a landowner and a Nobel prize-winning scientist. Professor Van Helsing is called in by Inspector Murray of Scotland Yard and listens to tapes of the coven's rituals. He identifies them as belonging to the cult of vampirism. Later he visits the scientist involved and finds him at work on Black Death bacilli. Van Helsing is shot and when he recovers finds the scientist dead and the bacilli gone. Meanwhile Inspector Murray and Jessica, Van Helsing's grand-daughter, visit Pelham House where the rites took place. Jessica finds a cellar containing a coffin, and various vampirised young women chained to the walls.

Van Helsing prepares himself for confrontation with Dracula by melting down a silver cross to make a silver bullet. Jessica and Inspector Murray watch Pelham House from nearby fields, but suddenly find themselves under fire from snipers and are captured. Van Helsing arrives at the Denham tower block, erected over the site of Dracula's grave, where he is asked to state the purpose of his visit to a TV camera. Murray regains consciousness under the watchful eyes of a Chinese woman, Chin Yang. Van Helsing at last gains access to D. D. Denham, an industrial millionaire who, as he suspected, is Dracula himself. Van Helsing and Dracula discuss their long conflict and Dracula announces his preparation of a political machine. Van Helsing declares his intention to thwart Dracula's new plans, and draws a pistol loaded with the silver bullet. He is overpowered by Dracula's allies and taken prisoner. Meanwhile Murray has managed to escape and brutally stakes Chin Yang. He then uses a cross to keep the other chained vampires at bay until he can reach the stop-cock of the sprinkler system and destroy them by water.

Murray, Van Helsing and Jessica manage to escape just before Pelham House goes up in flames. Dracula is impaled on a hawthorn bush and crumbles to dust.

Saturday Night and Sunday Morning
UK 1960 sd b/w 11

PRODUCTION
p.c – Woodfall. *p* – Harry Saltzman, Tony Richardson. *d* – Karel Reisz. *sc* – Alan Sillitoe, from his novel. *ph* – Freddie Francis. *ed* – Seth Holt. *a.d* – Ted Marshall. *m* – Johnny Dankworth.

LEADING PLAYERS
Albert Finney (*Arthur*), Shirley Anne Field (*Doreen*), Hylda Baker (*Aunt Ada*), Norman Rossington (*Bert*).

SYNOPSIS
In the pre-credit sequence of the film Arthur Seaton works in a factory at his machine. He delivers a voice-over monologue on his attitude to life which involves refusing to 'let the bastards grind you down'. (Ext. 1a, 2 mins.)

Arthur spends his days at a factory bench, his Saturday evenings at the local pubs, and his Saturday nights with Brenda, wife of another factory worker. He is determined to make the most of the money he earns and to let no-one tell him how to spend it. Arthur refuses to become either simply a unit on the factory books, or to follow his father in letting television rule his evenings.

At home Arthur talks to his Aunt Ada and her son Bert. When Ada and Bert go home Arthur meets Doreen, a younger and more sexually inhibited woman, for a date. Later, Arthur and Bert go fishing and discuss their attitudes to the world. Next morning, Arthur rides through the streets on his way to the factory. (Ext. 1b, 9 mins.)

A sense of responsibility touches Arthur when Brenda becomes pregnant. He takes her to see his Aunt Ada, hoping for helpful advice about an abortion, but without success. Meanwhile Doreen wants marriage and Jack, Brenda's husband, learns of her affair with Arthur. Jack's soldier brother and a friend waylay Arthur after an evening at a fair and give him a severe beating-up. Arthur decides to become engaged to Doreen and they visit a housing estate together, but it seems that he will remain the same obstinate and independent man at heart.

Sawdust and Tinsel
Sweden 1953 sd b/w 15

PRODUCTION
p.c – Sandrew Productions. *p* – Rune Waldekranz. *d* – Ingmar Bergman. *sc* – Ingmar Bergman. *ph* – Sven Nykvist, Hilding Bladh. *ed* – Carl-Olov Skeppstedt. *a.d* – Bibbi Lindström. *m* – Karl-Birgir Blomdahl. *cost* – Mago.

LEADING PLAYERS
Harriet Andersson (*Anna*), Ake Grönberg (*Albert*), Hasse Ekman (*Frans*), Anders Ek (*Frost*), Gudrun Brost (*Alma*).

SYNOPSIS
As the wagons of the Circus Alberti move slowly along, one of the drivers tells Albert, the circus owner, of a past incident involving the humiliation of Frost, an elderly clown, and his wife Alma. In flashback the film shows Alma bathing naked in front of a regiment of soldiers until the distraught Frost tries to drag her away. The flashback ends and the wagons enter a town. With rain pouring down, the circus tents are erected.

Since the circus is in an impoverished state Albert visits Sjuberg, the manager of the local theatre, to try and borrow some costumes. The request is granted, due mainly to the presence of Albert's beautiful young mistress, Anna, who successfully repulses the advances of Frans, a neurotic young actor in Sjuberg's company. Albert's wife, Agda, and their small son live in the same town and while visiting her Albert senses the peaceful and orderly atmosphere in which they live and is seized

by remorse. Feeling that Albert has spurned her, Anna visits Frans and, tempted by a worthless trinket he offers her, submits to his demands. Returning to their caravan, Albert forces Anna to tell him the truth; grief-stricken, he gets drunk and mercilessly taunts Frost. During the evening performance Frans shouts indecent remarks at Anna during her equestrienne act and is challenged to a fight by Albert. Albert is soundly beaten and humiliated and unsuccessfully attempts to commit suicide. The circus must go on, however, and Anna silently rejoins Albert as the wagons move off.

Scarface
USA 1932 sd b/w 14

PRODUCTION
p.c – Caddo Company. *p* – Howard Hughes and Howard Hawks. *d* – Howard Hawks. *sc* – Ben Hecht, from the novel by Armitage Trail. *ph* – Lee Garmes, L. William O'Connell. *ed* – Edward Curtis. *a.d* – Harry Oliver. *m* – Adolph Tandler, Gus Arnheim.

LEADING PLAYERS
Paul Muni (*Tony 'Scarface' Camonte*), Karen Morley (*Poppy*), George Raft (*Guino Rinaldo*), Vince Barnett (*Angelo*), Ann Dvorak (*Cesca*).

SYNOPSIS
A gangland leader, Johnny Lovo, arranges to have 'Big Louis' Costillo, his chief competitor, eliminated. Tony 'Scarface' Camonte, Costillo's bodyguard, is chosen to do the killing and is rewarded with a high position in Lovo's gang and a cut of the profits. Supervised by Scarface, Lovo's gang launches a reign of terror and with his help Lovo succeeds Costillo as President of the 'First Ward Social Club'. Scarface decides that Lovo is too soft and prepares to take over the gang leadership. Despite Lovo's warnings not to get involved in other areas of the city, Scarface smashes up a beer joint in their rival O'Hara's territory and subsequently commissions Rinaldo to kill O'Hara.

Having just murdered O'Hara, Rinaldo comes into Scarface's flat wearing a rose in his button-hole. Poppy, Lovo's girl-friend, arrives and Scarface shows her over the place, pointing out the steel shutters at the windows and the Cook's Tours sign outside which says 'The World is Yours'. He tries to impress her with his shirts and his new interior sprung mattress. He is about to kiss her when his secretary, Angelo, appears to say that the police are downstairs. Poppy slips out through a back door and Scarface goes with the police, who want to question him in connection with the O'Hara murder. As he leaves he tells Rinaldo to arrange a writ of habeus corpus for him. Later, Scarface meets Poppy in a restaurant. As Angelo struggles with a telephone call, a convoy of cars passes by with machine guns blazing.

Scarface organises reprisals and establishes his supremacy. He goes on holiday with Poppy but returns suddenly when told that Cesca, his sister, has gone to live with a man. In a rage Scarface goes to the flat, finds Rinaldo there and shoots him, only to discover that he and Cesca were already married. The police close in and Cesca is killed by a stray bullet. Scarface is heart-broken and emerging from the flat is taken prisoner by the police. He is shot as he attempts to escape.

The Scarlet Empress
USA 1934 sd b/w 11

PRODUCTION
p.c – Paramount. p – Adolph Zukor. d – Josef von Sternberg. sc – Josef von Sternberg, from a diary of Catherine II. ph – Bert Glennon. a.d – Hans Dreier. m – Tchaikovsky, Mendelssohn, Wagner. cost – Travis Banton.

LEADING PLAYERS
Marlene Dietrich (Sophia Frederica, later Catherine II), John Lodge (Count Alexei), Sam Jaffe (Grand Duke Peter), Louise Dresser (Empress Elizabeth).

SYNOPSIS
Princess Sophia Frederica of Anhalt-Zerbst is chosen as the bride of Grand Duke Peter, nephew and heir of the Russian Empress. Sophia and her mother are escorted to Moscow by Count Alexei, who tells them that Peter is a handsome youth but wins Sophia's love himself. When they arrive Sophia meets the domineering Empress who gives her the Russian name Catherine, and Peter, who is an imbecile.

The grand wedding of Catherine and Peter is watched by the Empress, Count Alexei and the Russian court and is followed by a wedding feast presided over by the Empress. Count Alexei drinks a toast to Catherine and Peter and the couple retire to the bridal chamber. Outside the people pray for an heir.

The wedding over, Catherine determines to avoid Peter and to have as good a time as is possible. Peter is fully occupied with his mistress, Countess Elizabeth, and his toy soldiers. Catherine meets Alexei and accepts a miniature portrait from him. She is amazed to learn that no-one would be surprised if she took a lover, and that the Empress has many. The Empress sends Catherine's mother home and humiliates Catherine by attaching her to her personal staff to be taught deportment. She also warns her against Alexei, whom she says is a notorious heart-breaker. When she discovers Peter spying on her the Empress reprimands him and dismisses Elizabeth from court. Catherine leaves her room by a secret passage and meets Alexei who is on his way to the Empress. Catherine throws Alexei's portrait out of her window, then she goes out into the garden to retrieve it and is made love to by a handsome young officer who does not recognise her. All Russia

rejoices when a son is born to Catherine. The Empress dies and Peter begins a tyrannical reign and plots to replace Catherine with Countess Elizabeth. Catherine, who has the support of the people and the army, overthrows Peter and becomes Empress.

Schatten
(see Warning Shadows)

The Searchers
USA 1956 sd col 32

PRODUCTION
p.c – C. V. Whitney. p – Merian C. Cooper. d – John Ford. sc – Frank S. Nugent, from the novel by Alan LeMay. ph – Winton C. Hoch (VistaVision and Technicolor). ed – Jack Murray. a.d – Frank Hotaling and James Basevi. m – Max Steiner.

LEADING PLAYERS
John Wayne (Ethan Edwards), Jeffrey Hunter (Martin Pawley), Vera Miles (Laurie Jorgensen), Natalie Wood (Debbie Edwards), Henry Brandon (Scar).

SYNOPSIS
Texas 1868. Ethan Edwards, an unrepentant Confederate, belatedly returns from the Civil War to the ranch he owns with his brother Aaron. The homecoming is disturbed by Ethan's dislike of Martin Pawley, a part-Cherokee boy Aaron and his wife have brought up with their three children. The following morning, Sam Clayton, who is a priest and a captain in the Texas Rangers, arrives with a posse seeking help in tracking down cattle rustlers. After a suggestion that Comanche Indians might be in the area, Ethan replaces Aaron in the posse, which then rides off watched by Martha. (Ext. 1a, 14 mins.)

Finding the missing cattle killed by Comanche arrows, the men realise that they have been tricked by the Indians who have meanwhile killed Aaron, Martha and their son and carried off their two daughters Lucy and Debbie. Ethan, Martin and Brad Jorgensen, who is in love with Lucy, continue to trail the Comanche after the rest of the posse turns back. Brad is killed when he hysterically attacks the Indian camp after finding Lucy's body. The posse returns, but Martin insists on continuing the search with Ethan, despite the protests of his sweetheart, Brad's sister Laurie. In a letter to Laurie Brad describes how he accidentally married an Indian woman named Look, who ran away when she realised their mission was to track down Scar, leader of the Comanche.

Martin and Ethan examine an arrow of stones left by Look. Snow wipes out all other traces. Martin's letter continues, explaining how Ethan killed a buffalo herd to deprive the Indians of food. The sounds of a cavalry charge lead them to a decimated Indian camp where they find Look's body and visit female captives of the Indians who have been deranged by their experiences. Ethan insists that the

women are no longer 'white'. Martin and Ethan inspect the dead but fail to find Debbie. (Ext. 1b, 7 mins.)

The search continues for several more years.

Ethan and Martin hear news of Scar in New Mexico and hire a local guide to take them to his camp. While the guide attempts to trade, Ethan and Scar spar verbally. Eventually Scar takes them to his tent where they see that Debbie is one of his wives. Ethan and Martin retreat from the camp. That night Debbie arrives and tells Martin to leave, saying that the Indians are her people. Ethan aims his gun at Debbie and orders Martin to stand clear but Martin shields her. Before Ethan can shoot, Scar wounds him with a poisoned arrow. In the confusion Debbie disappears and Martin and Ethan escape to a cave where Ethan tells Martin that he is going to leave him all his property since he now regards him as blood kin. Martin hotly denies this and wishes Ethan dead. Ethan replies 'That'll be the day'. (Ext. 1c, 11 mins.)

The Indians are routed by a cavalry charge. Ethan relents and takes Debbie home. After chasing off another suitor, Martin resumes his romance with Laurie.

Sergeant Rutledge
USA 1960 sd col 16

PRODUCTION
p.c – John Ford/Warner Bros. p – Willis Goldbeck, Patrick Ford. d – John Ford. sc – James Warner Bellah, Willis Goldbeck. ph – Bert Glennon (Technicolor). ed – Jack Murray. a.d – Eddie Imazu. m – Howard Jackson.

LEADING PLAYERS
Woody Strode (Braxton Rutledge), Jeffrey Hunter (Lieutenant Cantrell), Constance Towers (Mary Beecher), Willis Bouchey (Major Fosgate), Juano Hernandez (Skidmore).

SYNOPSIS
1881. Braxton Rutledge, war hero and sergeant in one of the two black cavalry regiments formed after the Civil War, is on trial for raping and killing a white woman, 16-year-old Lucy Dabney, and for the murder of her father, the post's commanding officer. Various witnesses tell of Rutledge's friendship with Lucy and how he was seen leaving the Dabney house.

Lieutenant Cantrell, Rutledge's defence, takes the stand. A flashback shows him leaving with a patrol of the 9th Cavalry for the railroad station, where they discover the wounded Rutledge and roughly overpower him. Mary Beecher, who is also waiting at the station, objects to the way he is treated and testifies to his gallant protection of her against the Apache. Rutledge is searched and his Freedom Papers – he was born in slavery – are read aloud. Rutledge reports on the signs he has seen of a large Indian raiding party and Cantrell decides that they must take Rutledge and

Mary with them and track the Indians down. Alone with some of the black soldiers, Rutledge tells them that they should no longer call him 'top soldier' and asserts the need to keep the rest of the regiment clear of the 'white woman business' he has walked into. (Ext. 1a, 8 mins.)

The patrol finds the body of Chris Hubble, son of the post's store owner, badly mutilated by Apache. An ambush by the Indians gives Rutledge the chance to escape, but as he follows their trail he sees them murder Mary Beecher's father and begin to set up another trap for the patrol. Rutledge turns back and warns the patrol, who decimate the Indians.

Back in the courtroom Rutledge breaks down while describing how the 9th Regiment was both a home to him and his self-respect. The court recesses and the trial board go to a back room to play poker and drink whisky. When they return Cantrell recalls Mary Beecher to the stand. A flashback shows her and Cantrell talking at night about her father while the black soldiers sing 'Captain Buffalo'. Rutledge stands silhouetted against the skyline as Cantrell explains that Captain Buffalo is a legendary black soldier of the 9th Regiment and that Rutledge's men are singing to give him courage. (Ext. 1b, 8 mins.)

Another battle follows, but again the Indians are defeated. Cantrell looks at the dead bodies of the Indians and discovers Lucy's gold cross attached to the headband of one of the Apache, who is also wearing a jacket with Chris Hubble's initials. Back at the trial, suspicion is switched from Rutledge to the dead boy. Rutledge testifies that when he entered Major Dabney's quarters he found the girl's dead naked body. As he stooped to cover it with a blanket, the officer burst into the room and jumping to conclusions opened fire. In self-defence Rutledge returned the fire killing the officer. The dead Chris Hubble seems guilty, but a hysterical testimony by his father reveals that he is the true killer.

Sergeant York
USA 1941 sd b/w 12 + 10

PRODUCTION
p.c – Warner Bros. *p* – Jesse L. Lasky, Hal B. Wallis. *d* – Howard Hawks. *sc* – Abem Finkel, Harry Chandlee, Howard Koch, John Huston, from *War Diary of Sergeant York* edited by Sam B. Cowan, *Sergeant York and his People* by Sam B. Cowan, and *Sergeant York – Last of the Long Hunters* by Tom Skeyhill. *ph* – Sol Polito, Arthur Edeson. *ed* – William Holmes. *a.d* – John Hughes. *m* – Max Steiner.

LEADING PLAYERS
Gary Cooper (*Alvin C. York*), Walter Brennan (*Pastor Rosier Pile*), Joan Leslie (*Gracie Williams*), George Tobias (*Pusher*), Charles Esmond (*The German Major*).

SYNOPSIS
In the Cumberland Mountains, Tennessee, Alvin C. York, a strong young mountain dweller, scratches out a meagre existence from the impoverished soil, supporting his mother, brother and sister. He dreams of owning more fertile land and marrying his childhood friend, Gracie Williams.

York wins a turkey-shooting contest. He also wins all five shots on the beef contest and gets the whole beef, which he raffles off again for money to buy the land he so desperately wants but finds it has already been sold. At the dance, he feeds his anger with drink and goes out into the rain thinking of murder. By the church his gun is struck by lightning. He walks into the service and kneels at the altar, a converted man. (Ext. 1, 12 mins.)

America enters the First World War and York is called up. He thinks war is wrong and applies for exemption but it is denied. He is a model soldier and because of his brilliant marksmanship his superior officers offer him promotion. He declines, but changes his mind after some leave and becomes a corporal. Overseas, his division is swept into the battle of Argonne.

On 8 October 1918 York and sixteen others are despatched to silence the enemy guns. Sent to get the Germans from behind, York launches a one-man attack, picking off 20 Germans one by one until the rest surrender. Once in line, one of the prisoners throws a grenade killing York's sergeant, Pusher. York angrily shoots the offender and threatens the commander of the German troops as he single-handedly marches back the 132 prisoners. (Ext. 2, 10 mins.)

Although hailed as the outstanding hero of the war, York refuses to make any capital out of it and returns to his home. Tennessee presents him with a fine house and a farm; he marries Gracie and leads the life he dreamed of.

The Set-Up
USA 1949 sd b/w 15

PRODUCTION
p.c – RKO Radio. *p* – Richard Goldstone. *d* – Robert Wise. *sc* – Art Cohn, from a poem by Joseph Moncure March. *ph* – Milton Krasner.

LEADING PLAYERS
Robert Ryan (*Stoker Thompson*), Audrey Totter (*Julie Thompson*), George Tobias (*Tiny*), Alan Baxter (*Little Boy*), Hal Fieberling (*Tiger Nelson*).

SYNOPSIS
Stoker Thompson, an ageing one-time boxing champion, refuses to retire despite the pleas of his wife, Julie. He constantly hopes for a big match which will bring him a cash prize and re-establish his former reputation. Stoker is billed to fight Tiger Nelson, a much younger man. He is unaware that Tiny, his manager, has accepted a bribe from Tiger's manager Little Boy to ensure that Stoker 'lies down' after

the second round. Tiny, convinced that Stoker cannot win the fight, doesn't bother to tell Stoker about the arrangement.

During the fight Stoker is told by Tiny that the bout has been fixed, but although taking a lot of punishment Stoker refuses to 'lie down' and Tiger is eventually counted out. While Stoker is being cleaned up in the changing room, Little Boy and his cronies appear and threaten him. Stoker tries to escape from the hall, but he is trapped in a side alley where he is severely beaten and the fingers of his right hand broken. Julie later finds him lying in the road.

The Seven Samurai
Japan 1954 sd b/w 10

PRODUCTION
p.c – Toho. *p* – Shojiro Motoki. *d* – Akira Kurosawa. *sc* – Akira Kurosawa, Shinobu Hashimoto, Hideo Oguni. *ph* – Asaichi Nakai. *ed* – Fumio Yanoguchi. *a.d* – Takashi Matsuyama. *m* – Fumio Hayasaka.

LEADING PLAYERS
Takashi Shimura (*Kambei, The Samurai Leader*), Toshiro Mifune (*Kikuchiyo, The Crazy Samurai*), Yoshio Inaba (*Gorobei*), Ko Kimura (*Katsushiro*).

SYNOPSIS
In Japan in the 16th century a group of villagers decide to hire professional soldiers to defend them from the annual raid by brigands, who carry off the harvest and the village girls. After various recruiting difficulties, they manage to acquire seven impoverished samurai, led by the veteran Kambei. Overcoming the villagers' initial fear of them, the samurai organise their defences.

The samurai and the villagers wait for the brigands to attack. They appear and fight in the rain and mud. The bandits are wiped out but four of the samurai are also killed. The following day, village life returns to normal. The three remaining samurai watch and then prepare to leave and resume their wandering.

The Seventh Seal
Sweden 1957 sd b/w 10

PRODUCTION
p.c – Svensk Filmindustri. *p* – Allan Ekelund. *d* – Ingmar Bergman. *sc* – Ingmar Bergman. *ph* – Gunnar Fischer. *ed* – Lennart Wallen. *a.d* – P. A. Lundgren. *m* – Erik Nordgren. *cost* – Manne Lindholm.

LEADING PLAYERS
Gunnar Björnstrand (*The Squire*), Bengt Ekerot (*Death*), Nils Poppe (*Joseph*), Max von Sydow (*The Knight*), Bibi Andersson (*Mary*).

SYNOPSIS
Against the background of the sea the Biblical quotation of the 'Seventh Seal' is read. The knight and his squire sleep on

the rocky beach and the knight wakes and prays. Death appears and the knight challenges him to a game of chess. They begin. The knight and the squire ride up the beach and along the road; the squire tries to break his knight's pensive mood with a bawdy song and then with talk of omens and superstitions. They stop to ask directions of a figure sitting in the road, but examining him closer the squire finds the figure's head is a skull. When the knight asks 'Did he show you the way?' the squire replies 'He was most eloquent ... yet gloomy'. They come across the wagon where Mary, Joseph and their child sleep. The flies wake Joseph and he goes outside, talks with the horse, juggles and then sees a vision of the Virgin Queen with her tiny babe. He runs to tell his wife, who pays little attention to his story.

The knight knows that Death must win the chess game, but his challenge gives him precious time to allay his doubts about God. In their progress through the countryside the two men meet many examples of fear, superstition, cruelty and suffering, but the knight finds true peace and goodness in a family of strolling players whom they help on their way. At last they reach the knight's castle where his wife waits for him. But now the game is over and Death has won. After upsetting the pieces in order to give the little family time to escape, the knight and those he has met on his journey are led off by Death.

The Seven Year Itch
USA 1955 sd col 10

PRODUCTION
p.c – 20th Century-Fox. A Feldman Group Production. p – Charles K. Feldman and Billy Wilder. d – Billy Wilder. sc – Billy Wilder and George Axelrod, from the play by George Axelrod. ph – Milton Krasner (CinemaScope and colour by DeLuxe). ed – Hugh S. Fowler. a.d – Lyle Wheeler, George W. Davis. m – Alfred Newman.

LEADING PLAYERS
Marilyn Monroe (The Girl), Tom Ewell (Richard Sherman), Evelyn Keyes (Helen Sherman).

SYNOPSIS
With his family packed off to the beach away from the New York heat, respectable publisher Richard Sherman has fantasies of sexual adventure. A glamorous new tenant in his apartment block nearly knocks him out by dropping a flower pot on him from her balcony. Fantasising about her as a femme fatale, he invites her down for a drink. She turns out to be a dumb blonde who works as a model. As she comes in Richard's wife rings up and asks him to send their son's canoe paddle to the beach.

The girl goes back to her apartment and returns with potato chips and a bottle of champagne in which Richard gets his finger stuck when he attempts to open it.

She declares that she is relieved to hear he is married, because that way things can't get 'drastic' and he can't propose to her. Richard tries to fulfil his fantasy by playing Rachmaninov, but she is dismissive of classical music and crunches noisily on her potato chips. She discovers US Camera magazine and proudly shows him a nude photograph of herself. Then she gets him to play 'Chopsticks' with her on the piano. Again Richard's fantasies of grand passion take over, but he ends up pulling both of them off the piano stool onto the floor.

Later, Richard's wife tells him that she has met a writer friend of theirs, Tom McKenzie. Jealous, he takes the blonde to the movies in revenge. Her electric fan is broken so she innocently asks to stay in his air conditioned flat for the night. Next morning Tom McKenzie arrives to collect the canoe paddle. Richard accuses Tom of having an affair with his wife. Tom points out that there is a blonde in Richard's kitchen. A fight breaks out, but eventually Richard comes to his senses.

(NB This extract is standard reduced from Scope.)

Shadow of a Doubt
USA 1943 sd b/w 15

PRODUCTION
p.c – Universal. p – Jack H. Skirball. d – Alfred Hitchcock. sc – Thornton Wilder, Alma Reville, Sally Benson, from a story by Gordon McDonell. ph – Joseph Valentine. ed – Milton Carruth. a.d – John B. Goodman, Robert Boyle, A. Gausman, L. R. Robinson. m – Dimitri Tiomkin. cost – Vera West.

LEADING PLAYERS
Joseph Cotten (Uncle Charlie), Teresa Wright (Young Charlie), Macdonald Carcy (Jack Graham), Patricia Collinge (Emma Newton), Henry Travers (Joseph Newton).

SYNOPSIS
Charles Oakley, who is being pursued by detectives for the robbery and murder of three wealthy widows, decides to visit his sister in California where he believes he can hide safely. He sends a telegram informing her and her family when he will be arriving. Meanwhile, his niece Charlie, named after her uncle, feels that her family is getting into a rut and needs someone to wake them up. She suddenly remembers her uncle and sends him a telegram asking him to come and visit them. When she arrives at the telegram office to send her message, she learns of her uncle's intended visit.

His niece is attracted to him at first, but gradually her instincts tell her that something is wrong with popular, handsome Uncle Charlie. After a number of incidents she begins to realise he is a wanted murderer whose description appears in almost every daily paper. A meeting with Jack Graham, one of the detectives who is shadowing her uncle, finally convinces

her. Once Oakley realises that his niece has guessed his secret he tries to kill her but an attempt to push her out of a train finally brings about his own death in front of an oncoming locomotive. Young Charlie is distraught, but finds relief in the arms of Jack Graham, who advises her to say that her uncle has met with an accident. Unaware of the true facts, her mother gives her brother a wonderful funeral and, with the exception of young Charlie, the whole family continues to believe that Uncle Charlie was a fine man who met with an untimely death.

Shadows
USA 1959 sd b/w 6

PRODUCTION
p.c – Cassavetes-McEndree-Cassel. p – Maurice McEndree. d – John Cassavetes. ph – Erich Kollmar. ed – Len Appelson, Maurice McEndree. m – Charles Mingus.

LEADING PLAYERS
Lelia Goldoni (Lelia), Ben Carruthers (Ben), David Pokitellow (David), Dennis Sallas (Dennis), Tom Allen (Tom).

SYNOPSIS
Hugh, a young black nightclub singer, lives in a flat in Manhattan with Ben, his light-skinned brother, and Lelia, his sister, who can both pass for white. Lelia moves in literary and artistic circles in a constant search for her own identity while Ben, similarly trying to find himself, aimlessly roams the streets with his two white friends, Tom and Dennis.

Lelia and David, a friend of hers, are sitting around in the Fountain Service Restaurant with Ben, Tom and Dennis. Finally Ben, Tom and Dennis go off to the Museum of Modern Art.

Lelia meets and falls in love with Tony, a weak, handsome young man who seduces her. She is shocked and confused by her first sexual experience. When he learns she is a mulatto, Tony leaves Lelia with feelings of superiority mixed with shame and guilt. He tries to renew contact with her later but Hugh throws him out of the flat. Lelia accepts the advances of a black man and after submitting him to a barrage of insults allows him to take her to a dance. Hugh is persuaded by his manager, Rupe, to accept a third-rate engagement in a nightclub. They quarrel but for the sake of friendship Hugh finally accepts the job. Ben and his friends are beaten up by a rival group. Tom and Dennis decide to change their aimless way of life and depart, leaving Ben still wrestling with the problem of his identity.

Shaft
USA 1971 sd col 19

PRODUCTION
p.c – MGM/Shaft Productions. p – Joel Freeman. d – Gordon Parks. sc – Ernest Tidyman, John D. F. Black, from the novel by Ernest Tidyman. ph – Urs Furrer

(Metrocolor). *ed* – Hugh A. Robertson. *a.d* – Emanuel Gerard. *m* – Isaac Hayes.

LEADING PLAYERS
Richard Roundtree (*John Shaft*), Moses Gunn (*Bumpy Jonas*), Charles Cioffi (*Vic Androzzi*), Christopher St. John (*Ben Buford*), Tommy Lane (*Leroy*), Sherri Brewer (*Marcy*).

SYNOPSIS
John Shaft, a black private detective, walks towards his Greenwich Village office. He stops at a shoe-shine shop, where he is told that two men are looking for him. Coming out of the shop he is stopped by Vic Androzzi, a police officer, and a young trainee policeman. Vic wants to know if Shaft has heard anything of possible gangland trouble, Shaft refuses to say. As he starts to walk away the young cop asks where he is going; Shaft replies 'To get laid'. At his office building Shaft sneaks up on a man answering to the description given to him in the shoe-shine shop. He forces him upstairs to the office at gunpoint where another man is waiting. There is a fight; Shaft hurls one of the men out of the window and forces the other to admit that they had been sent by Bumpy Jonas, a wealthy Harlem racketeer. (Ext. 1a, 11 mins.)

The police take Shaft in and threaten to suspend his licence if he does not co-operate. Shaft resists the threat.

Bumpy and Leroy arrive at Shaft's office and let themselves in. Leroy mutters about the death of his man. Shaft appears and although angered at Bumpy's way of operating agrees to trace the gangland boss's kidnapped daughter Marcy in return for a high fee. Bumpy implies that Ben Buford and his black militant group might be involved. (Ext. 1b, 8 mins.)

Shaft traces Buford and his group, but while they are talking there is a machine gun attack and only Buford and Shaft escape alive. Shaft assures Buford that the attack was not set up by him and the two go to visit Bumpy. Bumpy denies having organised the attack, saying he only intended that Shaft should get together with Ben in order to use the black militant army in Marcy's rescue. Ben agrees to allow the use of his men in the operation at a price of $10,000 per head. It is by now clear to Shaft and the police that Marcy has been kidnapped by the Mafia, who are anxious to move in on Bumpy's successful underworld operations. Shaft traces Marcy to a hotel, the Mafia kidnappers are overcome and she is rescued.

Shane
USA 1952 sd col 20+20

PRODUCTION
p.c – Paramount. *p* – George Stevens. *d* – George Stevens. *sc* – A. B. Guthrie Jr., from the novel by Jack Schaefer. *ph* – Loyal Griggs (Technicolor). *ed* – William Hornbeck, Tom McAdoo. *a.d* – Hal Pereira, Walter Tyler. *m* – Victor Young.

LEADING PLAYERS
Alan Ladd (*Shane*), Jean Arthur (*Marion Starrett*), Van Heflin (*Joe Starrett*), Brandon De Wilde (*Joey Starrett*), Jack Palance (*Wilson*), Emile Meyer (*Rufus Ryker*), Elisha Cook Jr. (*Torrey*).

SYNOPSIS
The knight-errant gunfighter Shane mysteriously appears at Joe Starrett's smallholding, one of a small group on a lonely plain. Ryker, a local cattle baron arrives with his gang to warn Starrett to keep off the land, which he wants to keep open and unfenced for cattle grazing. (Ext. 1a, 8 mins.)

Shane is befriended by Joe and his wife Marion and idolised by their son Joey. He stays at the smallholding and works for his keep.

Shane gives Joe a lesson in shooting and gun skills. (Ext. 1b, 3 mins.)

The conflict between Ryker and the homesteaders is brought to a head when Ryker brings in Wilson, a sinister professional gunfighter.

Wilson provokes a confrontation with Torrey, another of the homesteaders, and guns him down. (Ext. 1c, 6 mins.)

Torrey is buried.

At the funeral many of the homesteaders decide to move on. (Ext. 1d, 3 mins.)

Joe tries to dissuade them, but to no avail.

Joe decides to tackle Wilson himself, but Shane realises that Joe would have no chance against the professional and intervenes. He knocks Joe out, goes into town and shoots Wilson and Ryker. He then rides away. (Ext. 2, 20 mins.)

She Wore a Yellow Ribbon
USA 1949 sd col 27

PRODUCTION
p.c – Argosy Pictures. *p* – John Ford, Merian C. Cooper. *d* – John Ford. *sc* – Frank S. Nugent, Laurence Stallings, from the story *War Party* by James Warner Bellah. *ph* – Winton C. Hoch, Charles P. Boyle (Technicolor). *ed* – Jack Murray. *a.d* – James Basevi. *m* – Richard Hageman.

LEADING PLAYERS
John Wayne (*Captain Nathan Brittles*), Joanne Dru (*Olivia Dandridge*), John Agar (*Lieutenant Flint Cohill*), Ben Johnson (*Sergeant Tyree*), Harry Carey Jr. (*Lieutenant Pennell*), Victor McLaglen (*Sergeant Quincannon*).

SYNOPSIS
Just after the battle of Little Big Horn Captain Nathan Brittles sets out on his last mission before his retirement. His patrol, whose purpose is to find and contain the Indians who have murdered the paymaster and are amassing for a large attack, is encumbered by the eastern-born Olivia Dandridge and her aunt who are not 'army' enough to stay at the western fort for the winter.

As the party nears the boarding-point for the stagecoach it sees Indians ransacking the place. The cavalry drives them off but there are several casualties and that evening they bury Trooper Smith, who had previously been a Confederate general, with full military honours. Lieutenants Cohill and Pennell almost become involved in a fight over Olivia, but are stopped by Captain Brittles. The three men watch the Indians kill a trader who had been selling them repeating rifles. The next morning the troops retreat to the fort leaving Cohill to guard a river crossing and to hold the Indians back. (Ext. 1a, 22 mins.)

Brittles cannot go back for him because he will be a civilian by the next midnight.

Captain Brittles' troops give him a silver watch in a ceremony before they leave without him. (Ext. 1b, 5 mins.)

Pennell sets out the next day with the troops to rescue Cohill. Brittles leaves the fort, rejoins his command and gives orders for them to wait while he rides into the Indian camp. There he talks to Old Pony That Walks. He no longer controls the young braves led by Red Shirt and advises Brittles that he cannot stop the coming war. Brittles waits until night, then he and his unit stampede the Indians' pony herd and prevent the war. His retirement now a fact, Brittles rides westward but is stopped by Sergeant Tyree, who brings him news of his appointment as head of civilian scouts with the rank of colonel. They return to the fort, where Brittles goes to the graves of his family.

La signora senza camelie
Italy 1953 sd b/w 12

PRODUCTION
p.c – Produzioni Domenico Forges Davanzati/ENIC. *p* – Domenico Forges Davanzati. *sc* – Michelangelo Antonioni, Suso Cecchi D'Amico, Francesco Maselli, P. M. Pasinetti, from a story by Michelangelo Antonioni. *ph* – Enzo Serafin. *ed* – Eraldo Da Roma. *a.d* – Gianni Polidori. *m* – Giovanni Fusco.

LEADING PLAYERS
Lucia Bosé (*Clara Manni*), Andrea Cecchi (*Gianni Franchi*), Gino Cervi (*Ercole Borra*), Ivan Desny (*Nardo Rusconi*).

SYNOPSIS
Clara is discovered in a shop by a film producer, Gianni Franchi, and made the star of a 'B' picture. Next day, on the set of the film, Gianni proposes to her, overrides her doubts and whisks her off on honeymoon. When they return he decides that 'B' pictures are not good enough for his wife and refuses to let her finish the film. Left with nothing to do, Clara confides in the director, Ercole. Gianni decides that Clara should star in a big production of *Joan of Arc*. When it is booed at the Venice Film Festival Clara flees from the cinema and is approached by Nardo, who had a small part in the film. She turns him down. *Joan of Arc* is taken off in Rome

and Gianni is pressed by his backers for their money.

Nardo meets Clara in a hotel and again asks her for a date. She refuses and goes to ask Gianni for a part in his new film, but he offers her an insignificant role. Clara begins to realise that she has been foolish in hoping to become a great actress. She meets a producer of 'B' pictures and agrees to star in a film. Gianni releases her from her contract and she phones Nardo and arranges a date. Clara is photographed with the producer and cast of the new film. Gianni, who has been hovering in the background, leaves.

Gianni attempts suicide and Clara drops Nardo. In an effort to sort out their lives Gianni and Clara agree to finish the 'B' picture they were working on before their honeymoon. Clara, however, refuses to go to the opening and goes away with Nardo, who wants a liaison with no ties. She leaves a note for Gianni saying that she loves Nardo, but he leaves her after Gianni has telephoned. Gianni again refuses Clara a star part in his new film so finally she submits to Nardo on his own terms and signs up with a third-rate producer.

The Silence
Sweden 1963 sd b/w 12

PRODUCTION
p.c – Svensk Filmindustri. *p* – Ingmar Bergman. *d* – Ingmar Bergman. *sc* – Ingmar Bergman. *ph* – Sven Nykvist. *ed* – Ulla Ryghe. *a.d* – P.A. Lundgren. *cost* – Marik Vos.

LEADING PLAYERS
Ingrid Thulin (*Ester*), Gunnel Lindblom (*Anna*), Jörgen Lindström (*Johan*), Birger Malmsten (*Cafe Waiter*).

SYNOPSIS
Ester, her sister Anna and Anna's ten-year-old son Johan are returning to Sweden after a holiday. Ester has a serious lung disease. They travel through a strange country and break their journey at a town where the streets are narrow, the people are always hurrying and tanks clatter round corners. Their vast hotel is empty except for a troupe of Spanish dwarf entertainers and an elderly waiter. There is tension between the sisters: Ester, given to self-abuse and alcohol, regards her younger sister with a mixture of responsibility and suppressed lesbian desire; Anna lustful almost to nymphomania, resents Ester's dominance. Johan vacillates uneasily between the two and spends his time wandering around the corridors of the hotel. Restless in the sultry heat, Anna goes out into the town where, aroused by the sight of an amorous couple in a variety theatre, she rushes to pick up a waiter in a cafe.

Ester watches the street through a window and turning back into the room switches on the radio. Anna and Johan discuss going home. Anna goes to leave but instead she sends Johan into the corridor

and defiantly relates the details of her pick-up to her sister, while the waiter stands outside in the corridor. Anna goes out and they embrace passionately. Johan watches as they struggle with the door of an empty bedroom and then go in. The boy listens at the door and then wanders off through the corridors once again.

Ester, learning where Anna is from Johan, knocks on the door. Anna unlocks it, but begins making love in front of her sister. She breaks off to scream hysterically at Ester until she goes out. Next day, Anna departs with Johan leaving the dying Ester in the care of an elderly waiter whose language she cannot understand.

The Soilers
USA 1923 st b/w 7
(w. **Never Weaken**)

PRODUCTION
p.c – Hal Roach and Pathé Exchange.
d – Edwin Miles Farman.

LEADING PLAYERS
Stan Laurel (*Bob*), James Finlayson (*Snacknamara*).

SYNOPSIS
A parody of the dramatic film *The Spoilers*. Bob Canister, an innocent gold prospector in Alaska, is turned off his claim by the burly Snacknamara.

Bob interrupts Snacknamara opening a safe and they start to fight, but are continually interrupted by a fey cowboy from the next room. The fight, which uses all the Western clichés, moves through the cowboy's room and out into the dance hall where, finally, Bob wins. As he staggers out of the saloon, he is invited upstairs by the cowboy who drops a flowerpot on his head when he refuses. The street cleaners take him away in their van.

Some Like It Hot
USA 1959 sd b/w 12

PRODUCTION
p.c – Ashton/Mirisch. *p* – Billy Wilder. *d* – Billy Wilder. *sc* – Billy Wilder, I. A. L. Diamond, from a story by R. Thoeren and M. Logan. *ph* – Charles Lang J. *ed* – Arthur Schmidt. *a.d* – Ted Haworth. *m* – Adolph Deutsch. *cost* – Orry-Kelly.

LEADING PLAYERS
Marilyn Monroe (*Sugar*), Tony Curtis (*Joe*), Jack Lemmon (*Jerry*), Joe E. Brown (*Osgood Fielding*).

SYNOPSIS
Joe and Jerry, two unemployed musicians, accidentally observe the St. Valentine's Day massacre and decide they must make a rapid escape from Chicago.

They answer an advertisement for girl musicians and, dressed as two matronly women musicians, join the band which is on its way to Florida. While searching for somewhere to adjust Jerry's false bosom they discover Sugar, a beautiful singer, having a secret drink from a flask which

she keeps in her garter. Later, the flask falls to the floor when the band is rehearsing and is pounced on by the manager and assumed to be Sugar's. She has been in trouble before for drinking, but Jerry saves her by saying the flask is his.

When they arrive, Jerry, still disguised, is picked up by a millionaire, Osgood Fielding. Joe, now in love with Sugar, pretends to be an inhibited millionaire and entertains her on Osgood's yacht. Their hotel, however, is the scene of a gathering of gang bosses, among them Spats Colombo, organiser of the massacre. Spats and his men are slaughtered on the orders of a more powerful racketeer and Joe and Jerry are identified as witnesses. They escape gangsters and police and taking Sugar with them they put hastily to sea in Osgood's motor boat. Joe and Sugar are united and Jerry is proposed to by the doting Osgood. Jerry reveals that he is in fact a man, but Osgood is not the least deterred.

Song of Ceylon
UK 1934 sd b/w 7
(w. **Fires Were Started**)

PRODUCTION
p.c – GPO Film Unit for Ceylon Tea Marketing Board. *p* – John Grierson. *d* – Basil Wright. *sc* – Basil Wright, John Grierson. *ph* – Basil Wright. *m* – Walter Leigh.

SYNOPSIS
Section I: The islanders make a pilgrimage to the top of Adams Peak to celebrate the ascension of Buddha and their release by him from the fearful worship of a devil. Section II: The culture and economy of the island is shown: women carrying wood and drawing water, priests receiving wood from the faithful, elephants at work, fishermen in their boats, pottery, wood-carving and the building of houses with mud and wood, the reaping of rice, with all the men working in one man's field until it is reaped, women beating the rice from the husks and children being instructed in native dances.

Images of Ceylonese at work in the fields. The soundtrack tells how the British dispose of the products of this labour.

Section III: The new perspectives due to the coming of modern commercial and industrial practices. Section IV: The continuity of life and tradition. Buddha is still the teacher of the islanders, protecting them from the evils of dark forests where they once worshipped the devil.

Spare the Rod
UK 1961 sd b/w 9

PRODUCTION
p.c – Bryanston/Weyland. *p* – Victor Lyndon. *d* – Leslie Norman. *sc* – John Cresswell, from the novel by Michael Croft. *ph* – Paul Beeson. *ed* – Gordon

Stone. *a.d* – George Provis. *m* – Laurie Johnson.

LEADING PLAYERS

Max Bygraves (*John Saunders*), Donald Pleasance (*Jenkins*), Geoffrey Keen (*Gregory*), Betty McDowall (*Miss Collins*).

SYNOPSIS

A pre-credit sequence shows tough and aggressive children making their way to the playground of an East London school and then rushing in when the whistle blows. (Ext. 1a, 3 mins.)

John Saunders, an ex-naval gunnery instructor, arrives at the Worrel Street School for his first day's teaching there. He meets Gregory, an embittered woodwork master, who believes in treating trouble-makers harshly and advises John to use his cane freely. Jenkins, the ill and disillusioned headmaster, condones Gregory's methods. John, however, says that he prefers to win the confidence of mutinous pupils.

Jenkins takes John to his class and advises him to hold his class of fourteen-year-olds down if he values his sanity. John makes an attempt to be friendly to his class and attempts to let them decide on their own monitors, but the situation gets out of hand and when Jenkins returns he makes his own choice. (Ext. 1b, 6 mins.)

Miss Collins, a progressive fellow teacher, backs John's idealism. He achieves some success and survives the attempt of a girl in his class to seduce him but is forced eventually into caning Harkness, his favourite pupil. When it transpires that John chastised Harkness unjustly, he promises Mrs. Harkness to put things right. Later, however, Gregory is locked in the lavatory all night and Harkness is blamed. Gregory thrashes him mercilessly. John promptly intervenes and Jenkins insists that, whatever the true facts of the matter, he resign. Fed up, John is tempted to give up teaching altogether but the regard shown him at the end of the term by his pupils, two black parents and Miss Collins gives him second thoughts.

Spartacus
USA 1960 sd col 28

PRODUCTION

p.c – Bryna/Universal-International. *p* – Edward Lewis. *d* – Stanley Kubrick. *sc* – Dalton Trumbo, from the novel by Howard Fast. *ph* – Russell Metty (Super Technirama-70 and Technicolor). *ed* – Robert Lawrence, Robert Schultz, Fred Chulak. *a.d* – Alex North. *cost* – Peruzzi, Vallès, Bill Thomas.

LEADING PLAYERS

Kirk Douglas (*Spartacus*), Laurence Olivier (*Marcus Crassus*), Jean Simmons (*Varinia*), Charles Laughton (*Gracchus*), Peter Ustinov (*Batiatus*), John Gavin (*Julius Caesar*), Tony Curtis (*Antonius*) John Dall (*Glabrus*).

SYNOPSIS

Epic music and poetic commentary open the film. (Ext. 1a, 5 mins.)

Batiatus buys some slaves for his gladiator training school. Spartacus is among them.

A gladiator fight is set up for the amusement of Marcus Crassus and his party. Spartacus is chosen as one of the combatants, but he loses. His opponent goes berserk, attacks the Romans and is eventually killed by Crassus. (Ext. 1b, 3 mins.)

Spartacus meets Varinia, a woman slave.

Towards the end of his training Spartacus is taunted by a guard about Varinia, who has just been sold. Spartacus attacks and kills him. The incident provokes a riot and the slaves break out, overcoming their guards and the soldiers. The movement of the slave army is discussed in the Senate in Rome. Gracchus arranges for Glabrus to take a section of the Roman garrison to quell the revolt, leaving Julius Caesar in charge of the remaining troops. (Ext. 1c, 4 mins.)

Spartacus decides to lead the slaves out of Italy and pay Tigranes, a pirate chief, to provide ships. When they arrive at the coast Spartacus and the slaves find the pirates have been bought off by Rome and that there are no ships.

Spartacus addresses the slave army explaining that the pirates have betrayed them and they are trapped between three armies. Meanwhile Crassus addresses the Romans, promising the restoration of law and order. (Ext. 1d, 4 mins.)

The slaves realise they have to fight.

All the armies line up and the battle starts. The slaves are massively outnumbered and eventually defeated. (Ext. 1e, 12 mins.)

Spartacus and Antonius, Crassus's ex-body servant are taken to Rome, where Varinia and Spartacus's new-born child are taken into the household of Crassus. Crassus cannot force Varinia's love so he takes revenge by ordering that Spartacus and Antonius must fight to the death. Antonius loses and is killed by Spartacus, who is then crucified.

(NB This extract is standard reduced from Scope.)

Squibs Wins the Calcutta Sweep
UK 1922 st b/w 30

PRODUCTION

p.c – Welsh, Pearson and Co. *d* – George Pearson. *sc* – Hugh E. Wright and George Pearson. *ph* – Emile Lauste.

LEADING PLAYERS

Betty Balfour (*Squibs*), Hugh E. Wright (*Sam Hopkins*), Fred Groves (*P. C. Lee*), Annette Benson (*Ivy*), Betram Burleigh (*The Weasel*).

SYNOPSIS

Squibs, a Piccadilly flower-seller, and her drink-prone father win £60,000 when their horse comes first in the Calcutta Sweep at the Derby.

Their whole street celebrates with open-air dancing. Squibs spreads happiness through the neighbourhood, helping those in need and upsetting the prim charity workers. Squibs's fiancé is upset now that she has money and a visit to her future in-laws is almost a disaster. Weasel, the husband of Squibs's sister and a hunted killer, is pursued by a detective in Paris and goes into hiding, growing increasingly morbid. The last scene shows Squibs and her father looking over the new house they have just bought.

Stagecoach
USA 1939 sd b/w 10

PRODUCTION

p.c – Walter Wanger Productions. *p* – Walter Wanger. *d* – John Ford. *sc* – Dudley Nichols, from the story *Stage to Lordsburg* by Ernest Haydox. *ph* – Bert Glennon, Ray Binger. *ed* – Dorothy Spencer, Walter Reynolds. *a.d* – Alexander Toluboff. *m* – Richard Hageman, Frank Harling, John Leipold, Leo Shuken. *cost* – Walter Plunkett.

LEADING PLAYERS

Claire Trevor (*Dallas*), John Wayne (*Ringo Kid*), John Carradine (*Hatfield*), Thomas Mitchell (*Dr. Josiah Boone*), Andy Devine (*Buck*), Donald Meek (*Peacock*).

SYNOPSIS

Geronimo and his Apache braves are out in force. A stagecoach loads up with an assortment of characters for the journey to Lordsburg: Lucy Mallory, a respectable and dignified woman, soon to have a baby and anxious to rejoin her husband; Dr. Josiah Boone, an alcoholic; Hatfield, a bombastic actor, and Dallas, a prostitute who is scorned by the other passengers. Shortly after setting off, the stage picks up a sheriff and the Ringo Kid, a young outlaw in his custody who is privately determined to get to Lordsburg to avenge the killing of his relations. He agrees to being placed on parole by the sheriff, who is riding with the driver, and strikes up a friendship with Dallas. All goes well on the journey at first, but then the cavalry escort fails to arrive. Lucy's baby is born in a roadside cabin, with assistance from Dr. Boone.

The stage travellers remain cheerful until they come to the remains of a burned camp, evidence of Apache activity. Since they have come too far to turn back, they continue across the river and over the plains. The Apaches who are watching from the hills suddenly give chase and open fire. There is a long race across the plains. When the stage driver is hit Ringo climbs out and rides the lead horse, but just as all seems lost the cavalry appear and rescue the stage.

In Lordsburg, Ringo kills his enemies but the charges against him are dropped by the sheriff. Ringo then persuades Dallas to marry him.

The Stars Look Down
UK 1939 sd b/w 9

PRODUCTION
p.c – Grafton Films. *p* – Isadore Goldsmith. *d* – Carol Reed. *sc* – J. B. Williams, from the novel by A. J. Cronin. *ph* – Mutz Greenbaum, Henry Harris. *ed* – Reginald Beck. *a.d* – James Carter.

LEADING PLAYERS
Michael Redgrave (*David Fenwick*), Margaret Lockwood (*Jenny Sunley*), Emlyn Williams (*Joe Gowlan*).

SYNOPSIS
When the owner of the mine which is the livelihood of the village of Sleesdale decides to work the unsafe Scupper Flats, Robert Fenwick, an experienced miner, persuades the other men to strike.

Drinking hot water, the Fenwick family discuss the strike and the pit. Robert's wife, Martha, disapproves of the strike and of their son David's desire to go to university and get away from the mines. Anger builds up in the village when a miner is refused credit by the butcher. The miners pillage the shop and the police make arrests. Young Joe Gowlan, the butcher's son, steals from the till when the others leave for the police station. (Ext. 1a, 7 mins.)

The miners win, and Scupper Flats is not re-opened.

David Fenwick goes to university and makes a speech about the need for public ownership of the coal industry at the debating society. (Ext. 1b, 2 mins.)

Two years later, he meets Joe Gowlan who is by now a prosperous and unscrupulous businessman. David falls in love with Jenny, Joe's former girlfriend and in order to support her becomes a schoolmaster in Sleesdale. Jenny, however, is bored and discontented. Joe returns to Sleesdale to negotiate a coke contract, which will mean re-opening the Scupper Flats. David puts the men's case to the union but he is defeated because Joe has convinced the committee that David's opposition is due to his personal quarrel with Joe. Almost as soon as the work has begun at Scupper Flats the flood waters break through and David's father and brother are among the many dead. David is vindicated and he dedicates his life to fighting for the miners' cause.

Stella Dallas
USA 1938 sd b/w 14

PRODUCTION
p.c – Goldwyn Productions. *p* – Merritt Hulburd. *d* – King Vidor. *ph* – Rudolph Maté. *ed* – Sherwood Todd. *m* – Alfred Newman.

LEADING PLAYERS
Barbara Stanwyck (*Stella Dallas*), John Boles (*Stephen Dallas*), Anne Shirley (*Laurel Dallas*), Barbara O'Neil (*Helen*), Alan Hale (*Ed Munn*), Tim Holt (*Richard*).

SYNOPSIS
Stella, the daughter of a mill-hand, marries Stephen Dallas, the manager. They have an adored daughter, Laurel, but Stephen becomes increasingly conscious of the social gap between them and sees Stella's friends, particularly Ed Munn, a brash racecourse tout, as a bad influence on his wife and daughter. When Stephen is transferred to New York he and Stella separate. Meanwhile, Stephen starts seeing Helen Morrison, to whom he was once engaged, again. During the summer vacation Laurel visits Helen's luxurious house.

On her return from Helen's Laurel is upset when Stella invites Ed Munn to dinner. Stella says she has let the maid go in order to buy Laurel a fur coat. Laurel rejects the offer, since none of the girls she met at Helen's had one, but asks for a little house with a garden. Laurel describes Helen to Stella in romantic terms and shows her mother a photograph. She is upset when Stella marks it with greasy fingers and rushes from the room, but reappears to help her mother with her hair. (Ext. 1a, 4 mins.)

Fearing that her daughter is being lured away from her, Stella takes her to a fashionable resort where Laurel meets Dick Grosvenor. After spending most of the holiday in bed with a cold, Stella appears in an absurdly extravagant dress which makes her a figure of ridicule for Laurel's friends. Laurel demands that they leave. On the train home, Stella overhears two girls comparing her to an overdressed Christmas tree. Stella secretly visits Helen and offers to divorce Stephen so that they can make a home for Laurel.

Laurel refuses to go, saying that her place is with her mother. Believing that Stephen and Helen can provide a 'better' life for Helen, Stella appears at her most blowzy and pretends that she is going to marry Ed Munn. The following day the heartbroken Laurel returns to Helen's home. Some time later when Laurel is marrying Dick Grosvenor, Stella stands outside the house in the rain and watches the ceremony through the window until moved on by the police. Stella walks away triumphant. (Ext. 1b, 10 mins.)

The Sting
USA 1973 sd col 9
(w. **Butch Cassidy and the Sundance Kid**)

PRODUCTION
p.c – Universal. *p* – Tony Bill, Michael Phillips, Julia Phillips. *d* – George Roy Hill. *sc* – David S. Ward. *ph* – Robert Surtees (Technicolor). *ed* – William Reynolds. *m* – Scott Joplin, adapted by Marvin Hamlisch. *cost* – Edith Head.

LEADING PLAYERS
Paul Newman (*Henry Gondorff*), Robert Redford (*Johnny Hooker*), Eileen Brennan (*Billie*).

SYNOPSIS
Johnny Hooker seeks out Henry Gondorff, an ace confidence trickster. He wants to learn the 'big time' so that he can 'take' Doyle Lonnegan, an influential racketeer, who has been responsible for the death of Johnny's former mentor.

Johnny arrives at Billie's 'joy house' to look for Gondorff, who is hiding out there as a mechanic in charge of the roundabout. He discovers Gondorff in a drunken stupor. Hooker drags Gondorff under a shower, and later they talk. (Ext. 1a, 5 mins.)

Their conversation continues while Gondorff repairs the roundabout. Hooker is impatient and doubtful about Gondorff but finally he realises that Gondorff is testing him, and intends to do what he can to help. (Ext. 1b, 4 mins.)

They decide to exploit Lonnegan's weakness for gambling and construct a fake off-track betting club in which the roles of operatives and customers are played by a specially gathered troupe of con-men. Hooker then contacts Lonnegan. Acting as a disaffected employee of Gondorff's, he persuades him that he has a friend who runs a Western Union office that can hold up the racing results until they have placed their bets. They do a series of test runs which persuade Lonnegan of the truth of Hooker's claims. Finally, he is ready to place an enormous bet. The climax of this elaborate con-trick is a simulated FBI raid the moment Lonnegan has laid his bet, resulting in the mock death of Hooker and Gondorff. This serves to separate Lonnegan, who fears police attention, from his money, and leaves the pair of tricksters celebrating their revenge.

(NB This extract is compiled with *Butch Cassidy and the Sundance Kid*, Ext. 1a.)

La Strada
Italy 1954 sd b/w 9

PRODUCTION
p.c – Ponti-De Laurentiis. *p* – Dino De Laurentiis, Carlo Ponti. *d* – Federico Fellini. *sc* – Federico Fellini, Tullio Pinelli, Ennio Flaiano, from a story by Federico Fellini and Tullio Pinelli. *ph* – Otello Martelli. *ed* – Leo Cattozzo. *a.d* – Mario Ravasco. *m* – Nino Rota. *cost* – M. Marinari.

LEADING PLAYERS
Giulietta Masina (*Gelsomina*), Anthony Quinn (*Zampano*), Richard Basehart (*Il Matto*).

SYNOPSIS
Gelsomina, a half-witted peasant girl, is hired by Zampano, a travelling street entertainer who does a strong-man act. Brutal and taciturn, Zampano teaches Gelsomina as he would teach an animal and

also seduces her. In her crazed way she tries to establish a human relationship with him but he always rejects her.

Gelsomina visits a sick boy. Other children ask her to make him laugh, but a nun chases them all out. Zampano talks with the hostess of a wedding banquet about marriage and about her first husband. She offers him her first husband's clothes and they go upstairs. After the banquet Gelsomina waits for them, goes to the barn and sings to herself. When she falls down a hole she tells herself that she will spend the night there. At dawn she tries to tell Zampano that she is leaving him and goes off alone. When a small band appears by the roadside Gelsomina follows them into town.

Zampano tracks her down and beats her. They join a circus and Zampano is imprisoned for attacking Il Matto, a tightrope walker. Il Matto convinces Gelsomina that Zampano needs her and she waits for his release. On the road again Zampano accidentally kills Il Matto and as a result Gelsomina loses her already feeble grasp on sanity. Zampano leaves her. Years later he hears of her death and acknowledges his dependence on her.

A Streetcar Named Desire
USA 1951 sd b/w 10

PRODUCTION
p.c – Group Productions. *p* – Charles K. Feldman. *d* – Elia Kazan. *sc* – Tennessee Williams, from his play. *ph* – Harry Stradling. *ed* – David Weisbart. *a.d* – Richard Day. *m* – Alex North.

LEADING PLAYERS
Vivien Leigh (*Blanche DuBois*), Marlon Brando (*Stanley Kowalski*), Kim Hunter (*Stella Kowalski*).

SYNOPSIS
Blanche, the refined daughter of a once well-to-do family, comes to stay with her sister Stella and Stella's husband Stanley. She is horrified by her sister's apartment, Stella and Stanley's undisguised physical love, and his vulgarity.

While Blanche is dressing Stanley brings in her trunk. Stella tries to coax Stanley into treating her sister gently. Stanley, however, turns out Blanche's trunk and displays the finery to the dismay of Stella. Finally, Stella goes out and Blanche comes into the room to find Stanley and her disarrayed things. She flirts and fishes for compliments, but Stanley calls her bluff. Stella comes in to make peace, but Blanche cajoles her outside.

Blanche's relationship with Mitch, a shy middle-aged suitor and her one prospect of marriage, is wrecked when Stanley reveals her dubious past, including how she lost her job as a schoolteacher because of the men she took back to her room. Finally, Stanley rapes Blanche while Stella is having a baby in hospital. Blanche is pushed over the edge into madness.

Stromboli
Italy 1949 sd b/w 20

PRODUCTION
p.c – Be-Ro (Bergman-Rossellini) Film. *p* – Roberto Rossellini. *d* – Roberto Rossellini. *sc* – Roberto Rossellini, Art Cohn, Sergio Amidei, Gianpaolo Callegari and Renzo Cesana, from a story by Roberto Rossellini. *ph* – Otello Martelli. *ed* – Roland Gross. *m* – Renzo Rossellini.

LEADING PLAYERS
Ingrid Bergman (*Karin*), Mario Vitale (*Antonio*), Renzo Cesana (*Priest*), Mario Sponza (*The Lighthouse Keeper*).

SYNOPSIS
Karin, a stateless refugee interned in Italy, wishes only to reach America. When her plans fall through she marries an Italian fisherman and ex-soldier from Stromboli in order to escape re-internment. Karin is bitterly unhappy from the moment of her arrival on the island. She finds Stromboli inhospitable, her husband Antonio insensitive and the villagers suspicious and sullen.

Karin talks to the priest about her unhappiness but his only advice is that she should have courage and be patient. She flirts harmlessly with another man on the sea shore but Antonio hears about the incident and beats her. The following day Karin watches the slaughter of tunny fish which sickens and disgusts her.

Karin's life becomes more and more intolerable and she finally leaves Antonio. After persuading a lighthouse keeper to give her money she sets off across the island. Her path leads her to the volcano and after a terrible night on its slopes she decides to return to her husband.

Student Nurses
USA 1970 sd col 13

PRODUCTION
p.c – New World Pictures. *p* – Charles S. Swartz. *d* – Stephanie Rothman. *sc* – Don Spencer, from a story by Charles S. Swartz and Stephanie Rothman. *ph* – Steven Larner (Colour by Movielab). *ed* – Stephen Judson. *a.d* – David Nichols. *m* – Clancy B. Grass III.

LEADING PLAYERS
Elaine Giftos (*Sharon*), Karen Carlson (*Phred*), Brioni Farrell (*Lynn*), Barbara Leigh (*Priscilla*), Reni Santoni (*Victor Charlie*), Richard Rust (*Les*), Lawrence Casey (*Jim Casper*).

SYNOPSIS
The interrelated stories of four student nurses – Phred, Sharon, Lynn and Priscilla – who share a flat. Phred has to confess to Dr. Jim Casper that she has administered the incorrect dosage to a patient. No harm results and they agree to meet later.

The four nurses swop scarves and blouses and discuss where they are going while Jim impatiently waits outside their flat. Finally Sharon, Lynn and Priscilla leave. Jim enters and finds Phred alone. (Ext. 1a, 4 mins.)

Sharon, who has stood out against the inhuman treatment of a patient who tried to rape her, is set to nurse a young terminally ill patient, Greg, with whom she forms a sympathetic understanding. Priscilla picks up Les, a hippy vegetarian who walks in and out of her life as he pleases. Lynn witnesses a performance of political street theatre and fails to offer medical aid when one of the participants is injured after a fascist-inspired street fight. Priscilla, having taken LSD with Les after a rock concert, discovers that she is pregnant.

Priscilla tells the other three about her situation. She is interviewed by a hospital doctor, but her request for an abortion is turned down. One of the senior nurses explains that the hospital is afraid of publicity in the case of its own nurses and urges Priscilla to find a safe alternative. Sharon and Lynn prepare to help Jim perform the abortion at their flat. Phred arrives and is hysterically angry at what they are doing. While Jim performs the operation, Priscilla has visions from past LSD experiences and Phred makes love to a friend of Jim's in revenge. She later tells him their relationship is over. (Ext. 1b, 9 mins.)

In the meantime, Lynn has offered her services to Victor Charlie, leader of the guerrilla group. Sharon spends a night with Greg in his hospital bed and then has to face his sudden death in her absence the next day. Lynn arrives at their graduation ceremony dressed in guerrilla uniform.

Sullivan's Travels
USA 1941 sd b/w 16

PRODUCTION
p.c – Paramount. *p* – Paul Jones. *d* – Preston Sturges. *sc* – Preston Sturges. *ph* – John F. Seitz. *ed* – Stuart Gilmore. *a.d* – Hans Dreier, Earl Hedrick. *m* – Leo Shuken and Charles Bradshaw.

LEADING PLAYERS
Joel McCrea (*John L. Sullivan*), Veronica Lake (*The Girl*), Robert Warwick (*Mr. Lebrand*).

SYNOPSIS
John L. Sullivan is a successful director of film comedies, but he passionately wants to make serious dramas about the downtrodden. His producers argue that he knows nothing about trouble or poor people. To try to persuade them he dresses in a tramp's outfit and sets out to see the world of the less fortunate.

The studio sends a luxurious land yacht to follow him in case of need. He shakes it off and gets a job but is forced to leave by the attentions of his widowed employer. He goes back to Hollywood and meets an actress who can't get a job. He says he can introduce her to a director who may be able to help her and takes her to his own house. When she discovers his identity the girl persuades him to take her with him on his travels and they hop a freight train out of town. They sleep on the floors of dosshouses, eat at soup kitchens and eventually decide the experiment is over. Sullivan goes out with $1,000 to give to all the poor people he can find but he is beaten up, robbed and put on a freight train. The tramp who robbed him is run over by an express and thought to be Sullivan. Sullivan, having lost his memory, beats up a man and is sent to prison. Here he reads a newspaper report of his own death, confesses to the murder of Sullivan, is taken to court, identified and freed. Having seen how the prisoners enjoyed a comedy film Sullivan decides to make more comedies rather than the intended drama.

Summer with Monika
Sweden 1952 sd b/w 15

PRODUCTION
p.c – Svensk Filmindustri. *d* – Ingmar Bergman. *sc* – Per Anders Fogelström and Ingmar Bergman, from the novel by Per Anders Fogelström. *ph* – Gunnar Fischer. *ed* – Tage Holmberg, Gösta Lewin. *a.d* – P. A. Lundgren, Nils Svenwall. *m* – Erik Nordgren.

LEADING PLAYERS
Harriet Andersson (*Monika*), Lars Ekborg (*Harry*), Georg Skarstedt (*Harry's Father*).

SYNOPSIS
A chance meeting between Harry, an errand boy at a crockery shop, and Monika, a wild, restless girl who works in a greengrocer's shop, develops into a love affair. After a row with her father, Monika goes off with Harry on a motorboat to the Stockholm skerries.

Harry and Monika are enjoying their summer idyll and go to a local dance. Monika later announces that she is probably pregnant, but she is carefree and untroubled about the future. Harry, however, starts thinking about getting a good job and earning money. Monika begins to show signs of restlessness and Harry suggests that they ought to return to Stockholm so that Monika can be looked after properly.

They get married and set up home in a small flat. Monika finds married life and babyminding tedious. Harry learns that Monika has been unfaithful and they agree to part, with Harry taking the child.

Sunrise
USA 1927 st b/w 12 + 16

PRODUCTION
p.c – Fox Film Corporation. *p* – William Fox. *d* – F. W. Murnau. *sc* – Carl Meyer, from the story *Die Riese nach Tilsit* by Hermann Sudermann. *ph* – Charles Rosher, Karl Struss. *ed* – Katherine Hilliker, H. H. Caudwell. *a.d* – Rochus Gliese.

LEADING PLAYERS
George O'Brien (*The Husband*), Janet Gaynor (*The Wife*), Margaret Livingstone (*The City Girl*).

SYNOPSIS
An intertitle states that this tells the story of every man and woman. A city girl comes to stay in a lakeshore village and sets out to lure a young farmer away from his wife.

The city girl makes up and smokes. She has a peasant woman clean her shoes, then sets out to call for the young farmer. The farmer's wife sets the table for supper. He comes to the table but when he hears the vamp's whistle he goes out, leaving his wife alone and disconsolate. While she plays with their child her husband meets the city girl on the marshes. She kisses him and suggests drowning his wife so that he could sell his farm and go with her to the city. Then, dancing erotically before him, she calls up a vision of city night-life. (Ext. 1, 12 mins.)

The young man goes home racked by guilt and desire.

Next morning his wife is overjoyed at the prospect of a boat trip with her husband and leaves their child in the care of a neighbour. As they are about to set off their dog breaks free and swims to join them. Angry, the young man takes the dog back and ties him up again. As they row out over the lake his behaviour becomes more and more strange and troubled. His wife is increasingly anxious. Finally, he stops rowing and approaches her with the intention of pushing her into the water. Her piteous expression brings him to his senses and he rows hurriedly to the other side of the lake. As soon as they touch land his wife runs off and leaps aboard a passing trolley-bus. He follows and tries to reassure her. They get off the bus and wander miserably into the street, oblivious of the hooting traffic. (Ext. 2, 16 mins.)

The farmer begs his wife's forgiveness and they are reconciled. They perform a peasant dance together, to the delight of the other dancers. When they cross the lake again the boat capsizes and the wife is presumed drowned. The husband turns murderously upon the city girl when she comes to find him, but news arrives that his wife has been found alive and they are reunited.

Sweet Charity
USA 1968 sd col 25

PRODUCTION
p.c – Universal. *p* – Robert Arthur. *d* – Bob Fosse. *sc* – Peter Stone, from the musical play by Neil Simon, Cy Coleman and Dorothy Fields, adapted from the screenplay *Notti Di Cabiria* by Federico Fellini, Tullio Pinelli and Ennio Flaiano. *ph* – Robert Surtees (Panavision 70 and Technicolor). *ed* – Stuart Gilmore. *a.d* – Alexander Golitzen, George C. Webb. *m* – Cy Coleman. *lyrics* – Dorothy Fields. *choreo* – Bob Fosse. *cost* – Edith Head.

LEADING PLAYERS
Shirley MacLaine (*Charity Hope Valentine*), Sammy Davis Jr. (*Big Daddy*), Ricardo Montalban (*Vittorio Vitale*), John McMartin (*Oscar*), Barbara Bouchet (*Ursula*), Dante D'Paulo (*Charlie*).

SYNOPSIS
Charity Hope Valentine, a hostess at the seedy Fandango Ballroom, dreams of love, marriage and a respectable future. Her fiancé Charlie persuades her to withdraw her savings from the bank, but when they meet in Central Park he grabs her handbag, pushes her in the lake and disappears. Charity returns to the club.

Hostesses in the ballroom welcome a customer and perform their 'Big Spender' number. Later, Charity, who has abandoned all hopes of seeing Charlie again, walks home. She witnesses an argument between an Italian film star Vittorio Vitale and his girlfriend, Ursula. Vitale asks Charity to go to the Pompeii Club with him, where fashionable nightclubbers perform 'The Aloof'. (Ext. 1a, 16 mins.)

Charity returns to Vittorio's luxurious apartment with him.

Charity sings 'If My Friends Could See Me Now'. The evening is interrupted by the arrival of Ursula. Charity is unceremoniously bundled into a closet in order to avoid provoking her jealousy. (Ext. 1b, 9 mins.)

Charity decides to better herself, but when she visits an employment agency she is told that her educational deficiencies make her unsuitable for office work. While trapped in the agency's lift she meets Oscar, a shy insurance agent, who asks Charity for a date, thinking she works in a bank. When Oscar proposes Charity is forced to reveal her real profession. Oscar decides to marry her anyway but is so appalled by Charity's Fandango friends that he abandons her at the registry office. Charity spends the night on a bench in Central Park but is cheered by a band of smiling flower children.

(NB This extract is standard reduced from Scope.)

A Taste of Honey
UK 1961 sd b/w 11

PRODUCTION
p.c – Woodfall. *p* – Tony Richardson. *d* – Tony Richardson. *sc* – Shelagh Delaney, Tony Richardson, from the play by Shelagh Delaney. *ph* – Walter Lassally. *ed* – Antony Gibbs. *a.d* – Ralph Brinton. *m* – John Addison.

LEADING PLAYERS
Rita Tushingham (*Jo*), Dora Bryan (*Helen*), Murray Melvin (*Geoffrey*), Robert Stephens (*Peter*), Paul Danquah (*Jimmy*).

SYNOPSIS
Thrown out by their Salford landlady, Helen and her schoolgirl daughter Jo escape through the basement window leav-

ing the rent unpaid and take another dingy furnished room. Helen goes to the local pub to meet her latest boyfriend, Peter, leaving Jo alone. Wandering by the dockyards, Jo meets Jimmy, a black sailor. She accepts a cheap ring from him and wears it around her neck. Helen, meanwhile, decides to marry Peter.

Jo goes off to Blackpool with her mother, Peter and some of their friends. Feeling out of things Jo has a row with Peter and is sent home. Arriving back she meets Jimmy and spends the night with him. The next day she watches him sail off on the boat he works on.

Helen returns, gives Jo a preoccupied goodbye kiss and a warning against marrying her sailor and drives off with her new husband to the bungalow he has bought. Jo finds herself a job in a shoe shop and moves into a big bare room of her own. She meets Geoffrey, a homeless young homosexual, who moves in and takes over the cooking, cleaning and decoration. When Jo discovers that she is to have Jimmy's baby, Geoffrey visits the clinic with her and offers her marriage. But Jo does not appear to want the baby and Geoffrey goes to tell Helen her daughter is pregnant. Having been abandoned by her husband, the still self-absorbed Helen comes back to Jo and drives Geoffrey out. Jo and Helen face each other in a room that now seems as bleak as all the others they have known.

Taste the Blood of Dracula
UK 1969 sd col 21 + 16

PRODUCTION
p.c – Hammer. *p* – Aida Young. *d* – Peter Sasdy. *sc* – John Elder, based on the character created by Bram Stoker. *ph* – Arthur Grant (Technicolor). *ed* – Chris Barnes. *a.d* – Scott MacGregor. *m* – James Bernard.

LEADING PLAYERS
Christopher Lee (*Dracula*), Geoffrey Keen (*William Hargood*), Linda Hayden (*Alice Hargood*), Peter Sallis (*Samuel Paxton*), Anthony Corlan (*Paul Paxton*), Isla Blair (*Lucy Paxton*), John Carson (*Jonathan Secker*), Martin Jarvis (*Jeremy Secker*), Ralph Bates (*Lord Courtley*), Roy Kinnear (*Weller*).

SYNOPSIS
In a pre-credit sequence Weller is ejected from a coach where he has been trying to sell nicknacks. He comes across Dracula staked and dying in agony. (Ext. 1a / 2a, 3 mins.)

After the credits, in England three fathers, Hargood, Paxton and Secker, seem anxious about their daughters' chastity. Alice Hargood is in trouble for flirting with Paul Paxton. Her father tells his wife that he will be making his usual charity trip into the East End that evening. (Ext. 1b, 6 mins.)

The fathers go to a brothel, meet Lord Courtley and then visit Weller who encourages them to buy Dracula's cloak,

ring, name-bracelet and a phial of dried blood.

The three fathers arrive at a deserted chapel. Courtley startles them by pretending to be an effigy on a tomb. He puts on Dracula's cloak and drinks his reconstituted blood, commanding them to do likewise. Frightened and disgusted, they attack and kill him with their canes. Back in the chapel, Dracula rises from Courtley's body. (Ext. 2b, 13 mins.)

Hargood takes to drink.

Paul and Alice are having a party in the garden when Hargood comes home drunk and hits Alice. She runs away, straight into Dracula's arms and is vampirised. Under Dracula's influence she stands up to her father and kills him with a spade. (Exh. 1c, 5 mins.)

Alice disappears for a while, but then reappears at her father's funeral and makes contact with Lucy, Paul's sister.

Lucy meets Alice in her garden and is persuaded by her to get into a driverless carriage. During a nightmarish ride Alice talks enthusiastically about a man she has met, but Lucy is frightened. When they reach the chapel Dracula vampirises Lucy. (Ext. 1d, 7 mins.)

Paxton and Secker discover Lucy in a tomb at the chapel. Secker wants to stake her, but Paxton shoots him. He is then killed by the awakened Lucy. Eventually Paul goes to the chapel and still has enough influence over Alice to get her help in trapping Dracula, who is destroyed by the rising sun.

Teen Kanya
(*see* Two Daughters)

Tell England
UK 1930 sd b/w 17

PRODUCTION
p.c – British Instructional at Welwyn Studios. *p* – Bruce Woolfe. *d* – Anthony Asquith and Geoffrey Barkas. *sc* – Anthony Asquith, from the novel by Ernest Raymond. *ph* – Jack Parker, Stanley Rodwell, James Rogers. *ed* – Mary Field.

LEADING PLAYERS
Carl Harbord (*Edgar Doe*), Tony Bruce (*Rupert Ray*), Fay Compton (*Mrs. Doe*), Dennis Hoey (*The Padre*).

SYNOPSIS
Edgar Doe and Rupert Ray, boyhood friends, enlist in the British army at the outbreak of the war in 1914.

While they patriotically discuss the war, generals plan the landing on the beaches of Gallipoli. Despite heavy fire from the Turkish on the shore, the men are sent out from the troop-ships and massive slaughter ensues. Further down the coast the devastation is repeated.

The horrors of war begin to dampen Doe and Ray's enthusiasm and Doe, the more idealistic of the two, is unhinged by the months of inactivity followed by the

slaughter of his men by a Turkish mortar. He quarrels with Ray, now a captain, and breaks down. His self-confidence returns when he is chosen to lead a raid on the Turkish trenches. Though wounded, he manages to put the trench mortar post out of action single-handed. Soon after his death the British withdraw from Gallipoli.

Terminal Island
(*see* Knuckle-Men)

La terra trema
Italy 1947 sd b/w 20

PRODUCTION
p.c – Universalia. *p* – Salvo D'Angelo. *d* – Luchino Visconti. *sc* – Luchino Visconti, from the novel *I Malavoglia* by Giovanni Verga. *ph* – G. R. Aldo. *ed* – Mario Serandrei. *m* – Willi Ferrero.

SYNOPSIS
Acitrezza, Sicily. The fishing boats return at dawn and the fishermen go to bargain at the market where the wholesalers who own the boats band together to keep the prices low. The older men accept the situation, but 'Ntoni, the eldest son of the Valastro family, seizes their scales and throws them into the sea. A fight breaks out and the police are called. (Ext. 1a, 5 mins.)

'Ntoni is taken to prison but released a few days later to general jubilation. He decides that the fishermen must fight their employers and the middle-men. When no-one else will support the family they mortgage their house to buy their own boat. Many of the village elders disapprove and Mara, a bricklayer who has been courting Nicola, 'Ntoni's sister, leaves her, believing that she is now too good for him.

'Ntoni and his brothers set out in their boat. A woman rings the church bell to warn of a coming storm and the Valastro women wait anxiously on the shore for the boat's return. (Ext. 1b, 6 mins.)

The boat is wrecked in the storm destroying the Valastros' entire livelihood and the mortgage company forecloses on the loan. Another sister, Lucia, allows herself to be seduced by the village policeman and is driven out by the rest of the family, while Cola, a brother, emigrates illegally under the wing of a racketeer.

The Valastros pack up their belongings and leave the home that their family have occupied for generations. Mara and Nicola speak again, but the romance is as impossible now that the family is ruined as it was when it seemed that they could become rich. (Ext. 1c, 7 mins.)

The family moves into their new home and rehangs the family portrait and the image of Christ, 'Ntoni sets out to sea in a boat owned by a wholesaler, just as he did before his revolt. (Ext. 1d, 2 mins.)

The Terror
France 1925 st b/w 10

PRODUCTION
d – Edward José. *sc* – Gérard Bourgeois.

LEADING PLAYERS
Pearl White (*Hélène*), Robert Lee (*Roger Durand*).

SYNOPSIS
A complete episode from a Pearl White serial film.

Professor Lorfeuil is working on a new discovery, radiominium, at a château in France. He is haunted by the fear of failure and refuses to confide his theories to his assistant, Roger Durand. The professor's daughter Hélène has fallen in love with Roger despite her father, who is planning to marry her to a prince. Hélène overhears the professor order Roger not to have anything to do with his daughter while she is under his roof. While out riding she goes to Roger's lodgings and climbs onto his balcony. She tells him that she knows about his promise but reminds him that she is not now under her father's roof.

They Drive by Night
USA 1940 sd b/w 23

PRODUCTION
p.c – Warner Bros. *p* – Mark Hellinger. *d* – Raoul Walsh. *sc* – Richard Macauley and Jerry Wald, from the novel *Long Haul* by A. I. Bezzerides. *ph* – Arthur Edeson. *ed* – Thomas Richards. *a.d* – John Hughes. *m* – Adolph Deutsch. *cost* – Milo Anderson.

LEADING PLAYERS
George Raft (*Joe Fabrini*), Ann Sheridan (*Cassie Hartley*), Ida Lupino (*Lana Carlsen*), Humphrey Bogart (*Paul Fabrini*), Alan Hale (*Ed Carlsen*), Gale Page (*Pearl Fabrini*), Charles Wilson (*Mike Williams*), Charles Halton (*Farnsworth*).

SYNOPSIS
The trucking business of the Fabrini brothers is always on the verge of disaster – haunted by Farnsworth, a loan shark who chases them for back installments on their truck, and exploited by Mike Williams, a haulage agent.

The Fabrinis' truck crashes after swerving to avoid a school bus. While waiting for a new wheel to be sent up by Williams, Joe meets Cassie, a sharp-talking waitress. Williams tries to doublecross the brothers by arranging for another truck driver to pick up their load and putting Farnsworth on their trail. (Ext. 1a, 9 mins.)

Joe meets Ed Carlsen, a former truck driver who is now head of a large freight fleet. Ed tips Joe to buy a consignment of cheap lemons, which he sells at a large profit. The brothers use the money to pay off Farnsworth and buy another load. Then, however, Paul falls asleep at the wheel on a long haul and the truck crashes. Paul loses an arm and the truck and its load are written off. Ed hears about the accident and offers Joe a job, which he accepts. Lana Carlsen, Ed's wife, becomes infatu-ated with Joe, but he doesn't return her affections.

Joe goes to dinner with his brother, who is very depressed about his inability to get work, and Pearl, his wife. The following evening Joe goes to Ed Carlsen's house-warming party. Ed gets very drunk and after driving him home, Lana leaves him in the garage with the door closed and the engine running. (Ext. 1b, 4 mins.)

The death is pronounced as accidental and at Lana's request Joe takes over the business. Her hopes of marrying him are shattered when he introduces her to Cassie who is now his fiancée. Desperate, Lana tells the district attorney that Joe forced her to murder her husband. At the trial, Lana breaks down, is declared insane and Joe is freed. He returns to the garage, where the drivers insist that he continues as manager.

They Live by Night
USA 1948 sd b/w 6

PRODUCTION
p.c – RKO Radio. *p* – John Houseman. *d* – Nicholas Ray. *sc* – Charles Schnee, from the novel *Thieves Like Us* by Edward Anderson. *ph* – George D. Diskant. *ed* – Sherman Todd. *a.d* – Darrell Silvera, Michael Yates. *m* – Leigh Harline.

LEADING PLAYERS
Farley Granger (*Bowie*), Cathy O'Donnell (*Keechie*), Howard Da Silva (*Chicamaw*), Jay C. Flippen (*T-Dub*), Helen Craig (*Mattie*).

SYNOPSIS
Bowie, a naive youth sentenced for an accidental killing, escapes from prison with Chicamaw, a one-eyed killer, and T-Dub, an experienced bank robber. After a desperate flight Bowie is injured in a car accident and they are forced to hide at a service station run by Chicamaw's mercenary brother and his daughter, Keechie.

Bowie and Keechie fall in love and are about to leave on a bus when Bowie proposes. They get off the bus and go to a tawdry registry office where they buy a ring for $5 and are married for $20. Later, they hire a car and drive off together.

The newly married couple are continually forced to flee from the law. Chicamaw tracks them down and compels Bowie to participate in a robbery in which Chicamaw and T-Dub are killed. The two fugitives move on but Keechie is pregnant and is obliged to take refuge with Mattie, T-Dub's embittered sister-in-law, who turns informant in exchange for her husband's release from prison. Bowie walks into the police trap and is killed.

This Land is Mine
USA 1943 sd b/w 15

PRODUCTION
p.c – RKO Radio. *p* – Jean Renoir. *d* – Jean Renoir. *sc* – Dudley Nichols, Jean Renoir. *ph* – Frank Redman. *ed* – Frederic Knudtson. *a.d* – Albert S. D'Agostino, Walter E. Keller. *m* – Lothar Perl.

LEADING PLAYERS
Charles Laughton (*Albert Lory*), Maureen O'Hara (*Louise Martin*), George Sanders (*George Lambert*), Walter Slezak (*Major von Keller*), Una O'Connor (*Mrs. Lory*), Kent Smith (*Paul Martin*).

SYNOPSIS
The Nazis enter a small French town and take over. Major von Keller's hopes for a peaceful occupation are increased by the fact that many of the high-ranking town officials are collaborators. Albert Lory, a well-meaning but cowardly schoolteacher dominated by his possessive mother, is one of those resigned to the occupation. When Nazi food shipments are blown up and German soldiers killed, von Keller takes hostages, among them Lory. In an attempt to save her son Mrs. Lory tells Lambert, the railway supervisor, that Paul, one of his employees is the real saboteur.

Lambert tells the mayor he plans to betray Paul, who is seen drinking with German soldiers – apparently collaborating. Paul is later shot in a chase in a goods yard and Lory is released from prison. Paul's sister Louise, with whom he is secretly in love, accuses Lory of causing the death of her brother. In an argument with his mother Lory discovers that she betrayed Paul in order to get him released.

In an attempt to clear his name Lory becomes involved in the murder of Lambert. At his trial, Lory denounces collaborators and urges resistance. He is acquitted by the jury, but is later re-arrested by the Nazis.

Throne of Blood
Japan 1957 sd b/w 10

PRODUCTION
p.c – Toho. *p* – Akira Kurosawa and Sojiro Motoki. *d* – Akira Kurosawa. *sc* – Hideo Oguni, Shinobu Hashimoto, Ryuzo Kikushima, Akira Kurosawa, from the play *Macbeth* by William Shakespeare. *ph* – Asaichi Nakai. *a.d* – Yoshiro Murai. *m* – Masaru Sato.

LEADING PLAYERS
Toshiro Mifune (*Taketoki Washizu*), Isuzu Yamada (*Asaji*), Minoru Chiaki (*Yoshiaki Miki*), Takamaru Sasaki (*Tsuzuki*).

SYNOPSIS
A re-telling of Shakespeare's *Macbeth*. Two samurai, Washizu and Miki, who are under the command of Tsuzuki, Lord of the Cobweb Forest, meet an old woman who prophesies that Washizu will one day have command of Cobweb Castle, but that Miki's son will succeed him.

Washizu's soldiers enjoy the tranquillity of their life. His wife, Asaji tries to persuade him to take over Cobweb Castle but Washizu is reluctant, wanting to remain loyal to his lord. Asaji insists that Miki will tell the old woman's prophesies to Tsuzuki, forcing him to destroy Washizu. She suggests that Miki may have already betrayed him and at that moment the watch reports the approach of soldiers. It is, however, only Tsuzuki paying a private visit in order to discuss strategy for the destruction of a rival. Later, back in their room, Washizu mocks his wife for her unfounded suspicions, but Asaji manages to revive his fears and outlines how he might murder Tsuzuki.

Washizu murders Tsuzuki and becomes Lord of Cobweb Castle. Asaji insists that he kill Miki and his son. Miki is assassinated, but his son escapes to join Inui, a rival lord. Using the trees of the forest as camouflage, Inui's army surrounds Washizu who is finally shot to death by the arrows of his own men.

To Have and Have Not
USA 1944 sd b/w 20

PRODUCTION
p.c – Warner Bros. p – Howard Hawks. d – Howard Hawks. sc – Jules Furthman, William Faulkner, from the novel by Ernest Hemingway. ph – Sidney Hickox. ed – Christian Nyby. a.d – Charles Novi. m – Franz Waxman. cost – Milo Anderson.

LEADING PLAYERS
Humphrey Bogart (Harry Morgan), Walter Brennan (Eddie), Lauren Bacall (Slim), Dolores Moran (Hélène de Bursac), Walter Molnar (Paul de Bursac), Walter Sande (Johnson), Marcel Dalio (Frenchy), Dan Seymour (Captain Renard).

SYNOPSIS
After the fall of France, Martinique becomes a centre for the Free French, despite the Vichy 'loyalists' who are in control. An American, Harry Morgan, manages to remain totally uninvolved in politics and continues to make a living by hiring out his boat for fishing trips.

Harry returns from a trip with Johnson, a client. Frenchy, the hotel manager, asks Harry to help some patriots but he refuses. In his hotel room he meets Slim, a beautiful drifter who lives on the gifts she receives from admirers and petty larceny. Later in the hotel Harry sees Slim steal a wallet from Johnson and demands that she return it. Frenchy appears with the patriots, but again Harry refuses to help them. (Ext. 1a, 10 mins.)

Harry's attitude to Slim changes when he realises that Johnson was about to leave without paying him. Before Harry can demand his money Johnson is killed during a shoot-out between the police and the French patriots. Slim and Harry are both taken to the police station, and treated roughly.

After being questioned by Captain Renard, Slim and Harry leave the police station to go into a bar. Neither has any money but Slim hustles a bottle for them, which she takes to Harry's room. Harry makes the decision to get involved with the Free French. (Ext. 1b, 10 mins.)

Following instructions, Harry picks up two patriots, Paul and Hélène de Bursac, but during the operation they are attacked by a Vichy patrol boat and Paul is wounded. They all return to the hotel where Slim is now working as a singer. Harry successfully removes the bullet from Bursac's shoulder. Renaud imprisons Eddie, an old man befriended by Harry, and then goes to arrest Harry. With Slim's assistance, however, the police are overcome and Renard is forced at gunpoint to release Eddie and issue a harbour pass for his boat. Harry and Slim set off with their suitcases to start a new life.

To Kill a Mockingbird
USA 1962 sd b/w 15

PRODUCTION
p.c – Brentwood. p – Alan Pakula. d – Robert Mulligan. sc – Horton Foote, from the novel by Harper Lee. ph – Russell Harlan. ed – Aaron Stell. a.d – Alexander Golitzen, Harry Bumstead. m – Elmer Bernstein.

LEADING PLAYERS
Gregory Peck (Atticus Finch), Mary Badham (Scout Finch), Phillip Alford (Jem Finch), John Megna (Dill Harris), Frank Overton (Sheriff Heck Tate), James Anderson (Bob Ewell), Robert Duvall (Boo Radley), Brock Peters (Tom Robinson).

SYNOPSIS
Maycomb, Alabama, 1932. Widowed lawyer Atticus Finch defies local opposition by undertaking to defend Tom Robinson, a black accused of assaulting and raping a white girl, Mayella Ewell. Meanwhile Atticus's children Scout and Jem terrify themselves and their new friend, six-year-old Dill Harris, with exaggerated stories of Boo Ridley, a mentally retarded neighbour they have never seen.

Atticus tries to cope with his tomboy seven-year-old daughter, Scout, on her first day at school. A mad dog is killed by Atticus in the street. On another day a hostile and drunken white farmer frightens the children who are left inside the car while Atticus visits his black client's shanty and later Jem becomes fearful when left alone.

The night before Tom's trial, the children find Atticus sitting guard outside the gaol. Scout's innocent chatter unwittingly shames a group of angry farmers out of a lynching attempt. It emerges from Atticus's strong defence not only that Tom is innocent of the charges preferred against him, but that Mayella's father, Bob Ewell, himself beat up his daughter when he found her making advances to Tom. The jury none the less find Tom guilty and after the trial he is killed while attempting to escape. Bob Ewell takes his revenge on Atticus by attacking Scout and Jem in a wood, but Boo Radley, who has been secretly leaving gifts for the children in a tree trunk, saves their lives by killing their assailant. The sheriff decides that Ewell fell on his own knife and this time there is no trial.

The Tomb of Ligeia
UK 1964 sd col 10

PRODUCTION
p.c – Alta Vista/A Roger Corman Production. p – Pat Green. d – Roger Corman. sc – Robert Towne, from the story by Edgar Allan Poe. ph – Arthur Grant (CinemaScope and Eastman Color). ed – Alfred Cox. a.d – Colin Southcott. m – Kenneth V. Jones.

LEADING PLAYERS
Vincent Price (Verden Fell), Elizabeth Shepherd (Rowena/Ligeia), John Westbrook (Christopher Gough), Oliver Johnston (Kenrick).

SYNOPSIS
1821. While attending the funeral of his wife, Ligeia, Verden Fell outrages the parson by suggesting that she is not dead. A black cat screeches and Ligeia's eyes open in the coffin. Months pass and the beautiful Lady Rowena meets Fell and finds herself drawn to him despite his strange manner. When she tries to kiss him a black cat scratches her face. Later the same cat steals Fell's dark glasses, luring Rowena into the abbey's perilous bell-tower. Rowena jilts her admirer, Christopher, and marries Fell. She falls prey to strange phenomena: saucers of milk and dead foxes which appear and disappear on her bed and dreams in which she kisses Fell but finds herself embracing Ligeia.

During a dinner party at the abbey, the subject of Mesmer and his powers comes up. Fell says he will demonstrate hypnotism, using Rowena as a subject. He succeeds dramatically and Rowena sings a song she had forgotten but which her mother sang to her as a child. She is then briefly possessed by Ligeia's personality but immediately comes to herself and collapses. As she is put to bed she pleads with Fell to stay with her but he refuses. She falls asleep and dreams that her maid gives her a bouquet of flowers, but as she looks it turns into a bleeding fox's mask. She flees in dream-like slow motion through hazy corridors, pursued by the black cat.

Christopher engages gravediggers to disinter Ligeia, but finds only a wax effigy. Rowena turns into Ligeia's double and Fell attacks the black cat in a frenzy. He throws Ligeia into an altar of flames, but the cat now takes yet another form of Ligeia and it and Fell destroy each other as the abbey catches fire. Christopher finds Ligeia's double which turns back into Rowena. He carries her to safety.

(NB This extract is standard reduced from Scope.)

Tom Brown's Schooldays
UK 1951 sd b/w 7 + 7 + 10

PRODUCTION
p.c – George Minter. *p* – Brian Desmond Hurst. *d* – Gordon Parry. *sc* – Noel Langley, from the novel by Thomas Hughes. *ph* – C. Pennington-Richards. *ed* – Kenneth Heeley-Ray. *a.d* – Frederick Pusey. *m* – Richard Addinsell.

LEADING PLAYERS
John Howard Davies (*Tom Brown*), Robert Newton (*Dr. Arnold*), Diana Wynyard (*Mrs. Arnold*), John Charlesworth (*East*).

SYNOPSIS
Eleven-year-old Tom Brown is sent to Rugby School, which is under the headship of Dr. Arnold. He is looked after by East, a slightly older worldly-wise pupil.

East takes Tom around the school and introduces him to the matron and the porter. In class he is the subject of a teacher's lecture on the severity of the school's corporal punishments. (Ext. 1a, 2 mins.)

East shows Tom the birching tower and Tom observes a rugby match between his house and the rest of the school. At a crucial moment in the game Tom valiantly jumps in to save his house from certain defeat and is congratulated by the captain and the rest of the team. (Est. 1b/2a/3a, 5 mins.)

Tom is writing a letter home when East tells him that it would not really be proper for them to stay friends now that Tom's introductory period is over, but he wishes him luck. (Ext. 2b/3b, 2 mins.)

An older boy demands that Tom performs some errands for him as his fag. Later that evening, with the encouragement of East, Tom manages to withstand the customary initiation of new boys – having to sing a song while standing on a table and being pelted with food. The boys applaud when Tom finishes. (Ext. 3c, 3 mins.)

Tom offends Flashman, the school bully and is subjected to ear-twisting, blanket-tossing and 'roasting' by the fire. But he refuses to 'peach' and somehow survives. Next term, Tom is asked to look after a sickly, fatherless new boy, Arthur. Tom, East and Arthur join a paper chase only open to Seniors and accidentally witness a fight between Flashman and a young farmer. Flashman is thrown into the river and rescued by the three boys. As a result of the escapade, Arthur becomes ill. When Dr. Arnold calls the boys to his study, Flashman tries to blame Tom for the disaster but he is expelled instead. Arthur recovers; East regains the faith in prayer he lost when his mother died.

To New Shores
(*see* Zu neuen Ufern)

Topaz
USA 1969 sd col 20

PRODUCTION
p.c – Universal. *p* – Alfred Hitchcock. *d* – Alfred Hitchcock. *sc* – Samuel Taylor, from the novel by Leon Uris. *ph* – Jack Hildyard (Technicolor). *ed* – William H. Ziegler. *m* – Maurice Jarre. *cost* – Edith Head.

LEADING PLAYERS
Frederick Stafford (*André Devereaux*), John Vernon (*Rico Parra*), Karin Dor (*Juanita De Cordoba*), Michel Piccoli (*Jacques Granville*), Roscoe Lee Browne (*Philippe Dubois*), Per-Axel Arosenius (*Boris Kusenov*), John Forsythe (*Michael Nordstrom*).

SYNOPSIS
Boris Kusenov, a distinguished Soviet official, decides to defect. He and his family are spirited away to Washington by US Intelligence agent Michael Nordstrom.

Needing to follow up information given by Kusenov, Nordstrom asks André Devereaux, a French agent, to make contact with Uribe, a member of the Cuban delegation to the United Nations who is known to be willing to talk, but will not give information to Americans. André goes to Philippe Dubois, a florist from Martinique, who agrees to try and meet Uribe and photograph some trade pact documents. Posing as a journalist, Dubois goes to the hotel where the Cuban delegation is staying. Uribe agrees to help, but says that the documents are kept in a briefcase in the office of Rico Parra, the head of the delegation. Dubois succeeds in getting an interview with Parra and while he takes photographs of Parra on the balcony, Uribe removes the case. Parra discovers the theft and goes to Uribe's room where he sees Dubois photographing the documents. Dubois escapes through an open window and manages to pass the camera to André.

André gets information about Russian missile installations in Cuba through Juanita, his mistress, who is the widow of a Cuban revolutionary hero. Although recognised as the man to whom Dubois passed the camera, André is allowed to go free. Juanita's agents talk under torture and she is killed by Parra. André leaves for Washington with the film hidden in a volume of poetry. Nordstrom then asks André to go to Paris to investigate Kusenov's disclosure that high French officials are involved in a Russian spy ring called Topaz. André eventually realises that Jacques Granville, a distinguished government official, is the head of Topaz. There is insufficient evidence to arrest Granville and he is allowed to leave for the East, but commits suicide instead.

Top Hat
USA 1935 sd b/w 25

PRODUCTION
p.c – RKO Radio. *p* – Pandro S. Berman. *d* – Mark Sandrich. *sc* – Dwight Taylor, Allan Scott, from the play *The Girl Who Dared* by Alexander Farago and Aladar Laszlo. *ph* – David Abel. *ed* – William Hamilton. *a.d* – Van Nest Polglase. *m* – Irving Berlin. *lyrics* – Irving Berlin. *choreo* – Hermes Pan. *cost* – Bernard Newman.

LEADING PLAYERS
Fred Astaire (*Jerry Travers*), Ginger Rogers (*Dale Tremont*), Edward Everett Horton (*Horace Hardwick*), Helen Broderick (*Marge Hardwick*), Erik Rhodes (*Alberto Beddini*).

SYNOPSIS
Horace Hardwick, the just-married friend of tap dancer Jerry Travers, tries to persuade him that he should also find a wife. Jerry demurs and launches into the song and dance number 'No Strings', thereby disturbing the sleep of Dale Tremont, who has the room beneath. She goes upstairs to complain. (Ext. 1a, 6 mins.)

Next morning, Jerry replaces the hansom cab driver who is taking her to a riding lesson and engages in banter with her. While she is out on her horse there is a thunderstorm and Dale is forced to shelter in a deserted bandstand. Jerry arrives and they perform 'Isn't it a Lovely Day' in the rain. (Ext. 1b, 10 mins.)

Dale mistakenly believes that it is Jerry rather than Horace who has married her friend Madge and determines to have nothing to do with him.

Jerry and Dale meet again at a dance in a hotel on the Lido, Venice, and they perform 'Cheek to Cheek.' At the end of the number, Jerry proposes. Dale slaps his face. (Ext. 1c, 9 mins.)

Dale immediately marries Beddini, another suitor, but the service is not conducted by a real clergyman. Jerry disturbs them on their wedding night by tap dancing in the upstairs room and when Beddini rushes up to complain, Jerry slips out with Dale to explain the situation to her. Their gondola drifts out to sea, but they end up safely at the Venice carnival and dance the 'Piccolino'.

Torn Curtain
USA 1966 sd col 15

PRODUCTION
p.c – Universal. *p* – Alfred Hitchcock. *d* – Alfred Hitchcock. *sc* – Brian Moore. *ph* – John F. Warren (Technicolor). *ed* – Bud Hoffman. *a.d* – Frank Arrigo. *m* – John Addison. *cost* – Edith Head.

LEADING PLAYERS
Paul Newman (*Professor Michael Armstrong*), Julie Andrews (*Sarah Sherman*), Hansjörg Felmy (*Heinrich Gerhard*), Wolfgang Keiling (*Hermann Gromek*), Ludwig Donath (*Professor Gustav Lindt*), Mort Mills (*Farmer*), Carolyn Conwell (*Farmer's Wife*).

SYNOPSIS
Professor Michael Armstrong, a nuclear physicist, receives a telegram while in Copenhagen attending a scientific convention. Sarah, his assistant and fiancée col-

lects a book for Armstrong; when he gets it, he immediately locks himself in a toilet, where he locates and deciphers a message. Sarah is anxious when Armstrong announces that he is leaving for Stockholm. When she learns that he is in fact booked on a flight for East Berlin, she follows him and on arrival learns that Armstrong is apparently defecting to the East. Meanwhile Armstrong manages to shake off Gromek, the security guard assigned to follow him.

Armstrong goes to a remote farmhouse and makes contact with the farmer, who is actually an American agent. It emerges that Armstrong has defected in order to work with Lindt, a German professor who possesses vital scientific information wanted by scientists in the West. He finds that Gromek has traced him but after a long hard struggle Armstrong and the farmer's wife manage to kill him.

Armstrong goes to Leipzig with Sarah to meet some scientists and eventually manages to elicit the vital information from Lindt just before Gromek's body is discovered and the alarm raised. An escape organisation takes them back to East Berlin and from there they are smuggled back to Sweden.

Touch of Evil
USA 1958 sd b/w 14

PRODUCTION
p.c – Universal-International. *p* – Albert Zugsmith. *d* – Orson Welles. *sc* – Orson Welles, from the novel *Badge of Evil* by Whit Masterson. *ph* – Russell Metty. *ed* – Virgil Vogel, Aaron Stell. *a.d* – Alexander Golitzen, Robert Clatworthy. *m* – Henri Mancini. *cost* – Bill Thomas.

LEADING PLAYERS
Charlton Heston (*Mike Vargas*), Janet Leigh (*Susan Vargas*), Orson Welles (*Hank Quinlan*), Joseph Celleia (*Pete Menzies*), Marlene Deitrich (*Tanya*).

SYNOPSIS
Mike Vargas, special narcotics investigator for the Mexican Ministry of Justice, is honeymooning with his American wife, Susan, in the frontier town of Los Robles when a time bomb explodes in the car of the town's boss. Hank Quinlan, detective in charge of the case, reluctantly obeys orders to co-operate with Vargas. Quinlan believes that a young Mexican, Sanchez, is guilty of the murder and plants evidence to frame him. Discovering this, Vargas seeks to expose Quinlan. The outraged Quinlan, who has routinely framed suspects ever since he failed to bring his wife's murderer to justice, retaliates by enlisting the help of racketeer Uncle Joe Grandi, who is seeking to discredit Vargas so that his brother will not go to prison. Grandi sends a gang to the isolated American motel where Susan Vargas is staying to set her up as an apparent drug addict. To cover his tracks, Quinlan kills Grandi in the hotel room to which Susan has been

brought, but Quinlan's devoted partner, Menzies, discovers Quinlan's cane in the room and is pressured by Vargas to expose him.

Quinlan visits Tanya, a fortune teller. Meanwhile, outside the house Vargas is preparing recording equipment with Menzies. Tanya tells Quinlan he has no future and Menzies goes in and persuades him to come out. Vargas follows them as they walk among the oil rigs, taping the conversation. Quinlan gives himself away before he realises that Vargas is there and shoots and wounds Menzies. Vargas discloses himself but before Quinlan can shoot him, Menzies shoots Quinlan and then dies. The rest of the police arrive bringing Susan Vargas who is reunited with her husband. Tanya pronounces a valediction on Quinlan.

Tout va bien
France/Italy 1972 sd col 9 + 13

PRODUCTION
p.c – Anouchka Films/Vicco Films (Paris)/Empire Films (Rome). *p* – J. P. Rassan. *d* – Jean-Pierre Gorin, Jean-Luc Godard. *sc* – Jean-Pierre Gorin, Jean-Luc Godard. *ph* – Armand Marco (Eastman Color). *ed* – Kenout Peltier. *a.d* – Jacques Dugied.

LEADING PLAYERS
Yves Montand (*Jacques*), Jane Fonda (*Susan DeWitt*), Vittorio Caprioli (*The Factory Boss*).

SYNOPSIS
Susan DeWitt is an American journalist living in Paris reporting to an American broadcasting company. While researching a programme on French employers she goes to visit the Salumi sausage factory, accompanied by her lover, Jacques, a former nouvelle vague filmmaker who now feels it more honest to make publicity films.

Strikers have occupied the factory and on the roof a banner proclaims an indefinite strike. Susan and Jacques are treated roughly by the workers when they try to get an interview with the managing director and are locked in with him. A tracking shot shows the layout of the film studio set in cross-section, while on the soundtrack the workers sing a song. The boss addresses the camera interview-style from behind his desk and gives his view of the strike, revolution and capitalism. (Ext. 1, 9 mins.) Susan and Jacques are more irritated by his complacency than by their sequestration.

The managing director sleeps while Susan and Jacques pace the room. Outside, women workers talk about sexism at work and at home, the need to historicise the workers' struggle and the unions' failings. Later the boss does exercises and Susan polishes her report on the strike while the workers await the outcome of talks. Susan and Jacques are brought out to talk to the workers and are seen doing the same work

as the strikers. The workers describe the pleasure they feel in turning their power against the system. (Ext. 2, 13 mins.)

By next morning, union and management have come to an agreement. Susan and Jacques return to their everyday routines, but Susan finds it increasingly difficult to express her ideas in the format of conventional radio broadcasting. When the radio station turns down her report on the strike she leaves her job and quarrels with Jacques. A supermarket where Susan is shopping is invaded by activists who distribute merchandise free until rounded up by police. In the evening Susan and Jacques meet for a drink, newly aware of the changes through which they and society are passing.

The Treasure of the Sierra Madre
USA 1947 sd b/w 11

PRODUCTION
p.c – Warner Bros. *p* – Henry Blanke. *d* – John Huston. *sc* – John Huston, from the novel by B. Traven. *ph* – Ted McCord. *ed* – Owen Marks. *a.d* – John Hughes. *m* – Max Steiner.

LEADING PLAYERS
Humphrey Bogart (*Dobbs*), Walter Huston (*Howard*), Tim Holt (*Curtin*).

SYNOPSIS
Tampico, Mexico, 1920. Dobbs and Curtin, two tramps, meet Howard who reminisces longingly about gold prospecting. He tells them that he knows where gold can be found and offers to form a partnership provided that they can pay for a share of the necessary equipment. At the same time, however, Howard warns that the discovery of gold breeds mistrust and inevitably leads to trouble. The trip begins badly, with the three prospectors only just managing to survive a train ambush by bandits but once they reach the appointed spot they find the promised gold. Almost immediately the dust-like gold begins to affect Dobb's temper and he accuses the others of coveting his share. A man called Cody arrives and demands to be made a partner. The prospectors decide to kill him, but before they can do so he is shot in the mêlée which follows the arrival of the bandits who ambushed the train. After they have been fought off, Dobbs, Curtin and Howard begin their journey back to the city. Howard saves the life of an Indian boy and is virtually forced to stay in his village, leaving Dobbs and Curtin to go on alone. Dobbs suggests that they take Howard's gold with them, but Curtin refuses. He considers shooting Dobbs but cannot bring himself to do it; Dobbs, however, has no such qualms, shoots Curtin and leaves him for dead.

Dobbs is lying in the dirt. He picks himself up and staggers with his mules to a small dirty waterhole where he drinks voraciously. Looking up, he sees the bandits watching him. They knock him out, take his shoes, hat and mules, impatiently tearing the sacks of gold dust off their backs. At market the brand on the mules is recognised only by a small boy and the thieves are surrounded by silent villagers.

Howard is summoned from the village to treat a wounded white man, and discovering it is Curtis, goes with him to look for Dobbs. They find his body and frantically scrabble for the gold dust which is by now being scattered on the winds.

Triumph of the Will
Germany 1934 sd b/w 10 + 10

PRODUCTION
p.c – N.S.D.A.P. p – Walter Traut and Walter Groskopf. d – Leni Riefenstahl. p – Sepp Allgeier. ed – Leni Riefenstahl. m – Herbert Windt.

SYNOPSIS
The official film record of the 6th Nazi Party Congress held 4–10 September 1934 in Nuremberg, Germany.

The opening of the film shows the plane carrying Hitler flying down through the clouds to Nuremberg. At the airport Hitler is welcomed by enthusiastic crowds; he drives through streets which are lined with saluting people. (Ext. 1, 10 mins.)

Hitler and two Nazi Party leaders walk up through a large assembly of German troops, salute the tomb of the unknown soldier and march back. Bugles sound and the troops start their march past. Hitler speaks, the crowd salutes, there is a gun salute and Hitler inspects the troops. (Ext. 2, 10 mins.)

(NB These extracts are not subtitled.)

The True Story of Jesse James
(see The James Brothers)

Twelve Angry Men
USA 1957 sd b/w 20

PRODUCTION
p.c – Orion-Nova. p – Henry Fonda, Reginald Rose. d – Sidney Lumet. sc – Reginald Rose. ph – Boris Kaufman. ed – Carl Lerner. a.d – Robert Markell. m – Kenyon Hopkins.

LEADING PLAYERS
Henry Fonda (Juror No. 8), Lee J. Cobb (Juror No. 3), Ed Begley (Juror No. 10), E. G. Marshall (Juror No. 4), Jack Warden (Juror No. 7), Martin Balsam (Juror No. 1).

SYNOPSIS
A 12-man jury adjourns to consider its verdict on a youth accused of killing his father. It seems an open and shut case.

In the jury room a preliminary show of hands includes, to everyone's surprise, one vote of 'not guilty'. The others explain why they think the boy is guilty and the dissenter, Juror No. 8, says that while he is not convinced of the man's innocence, he is equally unsure of his guilt. He gives the reasons for his doubts and then pro-

duces a knife exactly like the murder weapon, hitherto believed to be unique.

The subsequent discussions bring to the surface other issues which throw doubt on the prisoner's guilt and the evidence of key witnesses is shown to be inadequate. One by one the jurymen admit to doubts. Among the last to change their opinions are a man with deep racial prejudice and a sadist. Finally, everyone's conviction is shaken and the accused is acquitted.

Two Daughters (Teen Kanya)
India 1961 sd b/w 16

PRODUCTION
p.c – Satyajit Ray Productions. p – Satyajit Ray. d – Satyajit Ray. sc – Satyajit Ray, from three stories The Postmaster, Samapti and Monihari by Rabindranath Tagore. ph – Soumendou Roy. ed – Dulal Dutta. a.d – Bansi Chandra Gupta. m – Satyajit Ray.

LEADING PLAYERS
Anil Chatterjee (Nandalal, The Postmaster), Chandana Banerjee (Ratan), Soumitra Chatterjee (Amulya), Aparna Das Gupta (Mrinmoyee).

SYNOPSIS
Part 1: The Postmaster. Nandalal, the new postmaster in a remote village, is looked after by Ratan, an orphan girl. When he discovers her desire to improve herself he begins to give her a rudimentary education.

Ratan learns to read and write while Nandalal gets into the post office routine. After a musical evening in the village he has a bout of malaria which develops into a sustained attack. Ratan nurses him through it. When he recovers he requests a transfer and failing to obtain it, resigns. Ratan is too deeply hurt by his desertion to say goodbye and is left to work for the new postmaster, who plays the clarinet.

Part 2: Samapti. When Amulya, a student, returns to his native village after passing his examinations his mother announces that she has found him a bride. Amylya rejects his mother's choice but offers to marry the village tomboy, Mrinmoyee. Recovering from her initial consternation, his mother arranges the marriage, but Mrinmoyee causes a scandal by running away on her wedding night. Leaving his rebellious bride with her own mother, Amulya goes to Calcutta. His humiliating rejection of her gradually chastens Mrinmoyee and when Amulya is finally called home she has become a loving wife.

Two-Lane Blacktop
USA 1971 sd col 20

PRODUCTION
p.c – Universal/Michael Laughlin Enterprises. p – Michael S. Laughlin. d – Monte Hellman. sc – Rudolph Wurlitzer, Will Corry, from a story by Will Corry. ph – Jack Deerson (Technicolor). ed –

Monte Hellman. m – Billy James. cost – Richard Bruno.

LEADING PLAYERS
James Taylor (The Driver), Warren Oates (G.T.O.), Laurie Bird (The Girl), Dennis Wilson (The Mechanic).

SYNOPSIS
The driver and mechanic of a souped-up '55 Chevrolet drive through the South West living on money made in racing bets. They acquire a passenger when a young girl slips silently into their car outside a diner. The two men pay her little attention, although the girl is evidently drawn to the driver.

The driver of a gleaming new Pontiac G.T.O. picks up a hitch-hiker and spins a long fantasy about how he acquired the car. He passes the Chevvy pulled in by the side of the road. Later, both cars stop at a garage and after a great deal of fencing a challenge is issued with the first car to reach Washington D.C. collecting the pink slips denoting ownership of both cars. En route, G.T.O. picks up another hitch-hiker.

G.T.O. is soon in trouble: his car threatens to break down and in order to give him a rest the mechanic drives it into the nearest town. The Pontiac is repaired by the mechanic and G.T.O. is driven out of town and left fast asleep in his car. He catches up with the Chevvy and accepts a challenge to a racetrack meeting. The team with the Chevvy win the bet, but the girl leaves with G.T.O. The driver and his mechanic set out in pursuit and overtake the pair at a diner. The girl abruptly terminates their discussion about future travelling arrangements by leaving with a young motorcyclist. With the contest tacitly cancelled G.T.O. continues on his way and the driver and mechanic resume racing.

Two Rode Together
USA 1961 sd col 13

PRODUCTION
p.c – Columbia/John Ford/Shpetner. p – Stan Shpetner. d – John Ford. sc – Frank Nugent, from the novel Comanche Captive by Will Cook. ph – Charles Lawton Jr. (Technicolor). ed – Jack Murray. a.d – Robert Peterson. m – George Duning.

LEADING PLAYERS
James Stewart (Guthrie McCabe), Richard Widmark (Lieutenant Jim Gary), John McIntyre (Major Frazer).

SYNOPSIS
Lieutenant Jim Gary and his troop escort Marshall Guthrie McCabe to see their commanding officer. McCabe is surprised to be hailed by the settlers as some kind of saviour. The commanding officer explains that he wants McCabe to go into the camp of hostile Indians to get back the sons and daughters of the settlers who have been taken prisoner over the years. After

a lengthy haggle, McCabe agrees provided the reward is high enough.

McCabe rides to the Indian camp with Gary. Only four prisoners are found and only one boy and one girl, Elena, who has been the squaw of the chief's rival, Stonecalf, are brought back. McCabe waits for Stonecalf to pursue the party and shoots him. At the fort, the horrified settlers refuse to accept the boy, now a young brave, and he is handed over to a grief-demented woman willing to regard him as her son. The boy knifes her and a lynching follows. Too late it is discovered that he was the brother of Marty Purcell, the girl Gary loves. McCabe persuades Elena to withstand the disapproval of the officers' wives at a dance and takes her to Tascosa. Finding his job as Marshall has been appropriated, they take the stage to California.

Ugetsu Monogatari
Japan 1953 sd b/w 10

PRODUCTION
p.c – Daiei. *p* – Masaichi Nagata. *d* – Kenji Mizoguchi. *sc* – Matsutaro Kawaguchi, Giken Yoda, from Giken Yoda's adaptation of two stories *Asaji Ga Yado* and *Jasei No In* from the classic collection by Akinari Ueda. *ph* – Kazuo Miyagawa. *ed* – Kenji Mizoguchi. *a.d* – Kisaku Ito. *m* – Fumio Hayasaka.

LEADING PLAYERS
Masayuki Mori (*Genjuro*), Machiko Kyo (*Princess Wakasa*), Sakae Ozawa (*Tobei*), Mitsuko Mito (*Ohama*), Kinuyo Tanaka (*Miyagi*).

SYNOPSIS
Japanese villagers in the 16th century are at the mercy of the marauding troops serving rival warlords. Genjuro, a potter and chief of one of the village families, Tobei, his farmer brother-in-law who dreams of becoming a samurai, and their families are forced to flee the village.

Genjuro and Miyagi, his wife, return to their kiln and hide while soldiers contemptuously examine it. He realises that his pots have baked themselves in his absence and determines to profit from the wars by setting off with Miyagi, their son, and Tobei and his wife to sell pots in a nearby city. While Ohama, Tobei's wife, is rowing the party across a lake she sees what she thinks is a ghost but is actually a fisherman who has been mortally injured by pirates. Frightened, Genjuro puts Miyagi and their son ashore, but Ohama insists on staying with Tobei. The remaining three set off again, waving goodbye to Miyagi.

In the town Genjuro sells his pots at a great profit. Tobei acquires samurai armour and by a trick achieves military command. The neglected Ohama is raped by a gang of soldiers and becomes a prostitute in a geisha house. Genjuro is approached by the beautiful Lady Wakasa

and her nurse and invited to their castle. Enchanted by Wakasa, Genjuro becomes her lover, forgetting his former life. Meanwhile, Miyagi is killed. Tobei meets Ohama again and they are reconciled after a violent quarrel. A wandering monk warns Genjuro that he is living with ghosts and he returns to the castle with cabalistic signs painted on his back by the monk. After fighting with the ghosts, he finds himself in the ruins of a derelict castle. Disconsolately he returns and believes he is greeted by Miyagi. Genjuro's son comforts him and Miyagi's ghost exhorts him to return to his work. Tobei and Ohama arrive back at the village and, also released from their dreams, continue with everyday life.

Ulzana's Raid
USA 1972 sd col 20

PRODUCTION
p.c – Universal. A Carter De Haven/ Robert Aldrich Production. *p* – Carter De Haven. *d* – Robert Aldrich. *sc* – Alan Sharp. *ph* – Joseph Biroc (Technicolor). *ed* – Michael Luciano. *a.d* – James Vance. *m* – Frank DeVol.

LEADING PLAYERS
Burt Lancaster (*McIntosh*), Bruce Davison (*Lieutenant Garnett DeBuin*), Jorge Luke (*Ke-Ni-Tay*), Richard Jaeckel (*Sergeant*), Joaquin Martinez (*Ulzana*), Karl Swenson (*Rukeyser*), Gladys Holland (*Mrs. Rukeyser*).

SYNOPSIS
When news reaches a US cavalry fort that a troop of Apaches, led by Ulzana, have left their reservation for a murderous raid on the surrounding homesteads, Lieutenant Garnett DeBuin, an idealistic young officer, is given command of a small detachment to pursue the Indians. DeBuin is accompanied by two scouts, McIntosh, an ageing Indian-fighter, and Ke-Ni-Tay, a young Apache.

DeBuin is inexperienced and uncertain how he should tackle Ulzana. Meanwhile Ulzana's warriors attack Mrs. Rukeyser and her son who are on their way to the fort. The trooper escorting Mrs. Rukeyser flees, then in response to her cries for help returns, shoots her and takes the boy. The Indians shoot his horse and the soldier then shoots himself. The boy is left sitting by his mother's body. The main Indian party reaches the Rukeyser homestead, and lures Mr. Rukeyser out of his barricaded home. His mutilated body is later found by DeBuin and the troopers. That evening DeBuin tries to learn why Ulzana is so cruel from Ke-Ni-Tay. DeBuin then talks to McIntosh who says that he does not hate the Apache, but who is scared of them.

At the next ransacked homestead, DeBuin finds the body of a young farmer, Riordan, and rescues Riordan's wife who has been raped by the Apache. McIntosh

suggests that half the troop, under his own command, escort Mrs. Riordan back to the fort, distracting the Indians and enabling DeBuin to surprise Ulzana by arriving in the middle of the attack with fresh troops. The plan is followed, but DeBuin arrives too late and finds the soldiers dead and McIntosh mortally wounded. Ke-Ni-Tay kills Ulzana. McIntosh insists that he be left to die.

Umberto D
Italy 1952 sd b/w 10

PRODUCTION
p.c – Dear Films. *p* – Vittorio De Sica, Giuseppe Amato, Carlo Rizzoli. *d* – Vittorio De Sica. *sc* – Cesare Zavattini and Vittorio De Sica, from a story by Cesare Zavattini. *ph* – G. R. Aldo. *ed* – Eraldo Da Roma. *a.d* – Virgilio Marchi. *m* – Alessandro Cicognini.

LEADING PLAYERS
Carlo Battisti (*Umberto D*), Maria Pia Casilio (*Maria*), Lina Gennari (*The Landlady*), Alberto Albani Barbieri (*The Landlady's Lover*).

SYNOPSIS
Umberto D is a retired civil servant with no family and few friends who lives on an inadequate pension. His chief companion is his dog. Because he owes rent his landlady allows lovers to use his room as a meeting place. Only the landlady's maid, Maria, who is pregnant by a soldier, is sympathetic to Umberto's problems. When he gets a chill Umberto saves money by spending a week in hospital only to find his dog sent to a pound and his room in chaos due to building alterations.

After rescuing his dog Umberto confronts the landlady out walking with her middle-aged and well-off fiancé. After an altercation with them about his rent – he must pay it all or get out – Umberto declares to indifferent onlookers that he has always paid his way. Later he meets an old friend who is sympathetic but who shies away at the hint of a loan. In despair, Umberto tries to beg but he is too hesitant. While trying to get his dog to beg for him, another old colleague appears and Umberto glosses over his behaviour. They talk uneasily until his friend's bus moves off into the darkness.

Umberto comes to feel that suicide is the only solution. Finally he decides to throw himself under a train with the dog in his arms, but at the last moment the dog runs away. Realising that he has betrayed the trust of the only creature he loves Umberto decides that all that matters is to retain the dog's affection.

The Umbrellas of Cherbourg
(see Les Parapluies de Cherbourg)

Under Capricorn
UK 1949 sd col 15

PRODUCTION
p.c – Transatlantic Pictures. *p* – Sidney Bernstein. *d* – Alfred Hitchcock. *sc* – James Bridie from the play by John Celton and Margaret Linden and the novel by Helen Simpson. *ph* – Jack Cardiff (Technicolor). *ed* – A. S. Bates. *a.d* – Thomas N. Morahan. *m* – Richard Addinsell.

LEADING PLAYERS
Ingrid Bergman (*Lady Henrietta Flusky*), Joseph Cotten (*Sam Flusky*), Michael Wilding (*Charles Adare*), Margaret Leighton (*Milly*), Cecil Parker (*The Governor*).

SYNOPSIS
Sydney, 1831. Charles Adare arrives in Australia as guest of his uncle, the Governor of the colony. He meets Sam Flusky, an ex-convict who is now a respectable citizen and recognises his broken-down wife Henrietta as a childhood friend from Ireland whose elopement with Flusky, the family groom, resulted in her brother being shot dead and Flusky being deported for the crime. Henrietta waited for his release. Adare tries to help Henrietta regain her interest in life but is thwarted by the jealous housekeeper, Milly. Milly insinuates to Flusky that Adare and Henrietta are lovers, but when Flusky refuses to believe her she leaves the house. Henrietta recovers.

Adare is dining with the Fluskys when an invitation to the Governor's ball arrives. He persuades Henrietta to let him take her and although Sam will not agree to go he gives Henrietta the keys of the house, previously held by Milly and promises her a new dress for the occasion. As Adare and Henrietta are about to leave for the ball Flusky suggests that a ruby necklace would finish Henrietta's dress perfectly. He is holding one behind his back in readiness, but when Adare says the dress needs no embellishment he stuffs it in his pocket. Adare and Henrietta are almost refused entry at Government House because Adare has written the invitation himself, being out of favour with his uncle. Henrietta's beauty and charm carry the day, however, and she is taken in to supper by the infatuated Governor. Milly returns to Flusky's house and inflames his jealously by insisting that there is something dishonest in Henrietta's relationship with Adare. Sam goes to the ball and shames Henrietta by insisting on telling the Governor about his past and she hastily leaves.

Henrietta explains to Adare that she loves Flusky and cannot leave him. Flusky returns and after an argument, shoots and wounds Adare. In order to save Flusky from trial as a second offender, Henrietta confesses that it was she who killed her brother. When Milly tries to poison Henrietta, Flusky at last understands her tricks. Adare recovers, forces all charges against Flusky and Henrietta to be drop-ped and returns to Ireland, leaving them together.

Underworld USA
USA 1960 sd b/w 22

PRODUCTION
p.c – Globe Enterprises. *p* – Samuel Fuller. *d* – Samuel Fuller. *sc* – Samuel Fuller, from articles by Joseph F. Dineen. *ph* – Hal Mohr. *ed* – Jerome Thomas. *a.d* – Robert Peterson. *m* – Harry Sukman. *cost* – Bernice Pontrelli.

LEADING PLAYERS
Cliff Robertson (*Tolly Devlin*), Beatrice Kay (*Sandy*), Larry Gates (*John Driscoll*), Richard Rust (*Gus*), Dolores Dorn (*Cuddles*), Paul Dubov (*Gela*), Gerald Milton (*Gunther*), Allan Greuner (*Smith*).

SYNOPSIS
Tolly, a young boy already involved in petty crime, sees his father killed and swears vengeance. After an adolescence spent in a series of reformatories and prisons, Tolly discovers that Gela, Gunther and Smith, big-time syndicate bosses running, respectively, drugs, labour and vice rackets ordered his father's death. Tolly meets Cuddles, a woman who has become dangerous to the syndicate and is trying to extricate herself. He pretends to be a cop and gets Sandy, an old family friend, to shelter her and then uses the heroin she has refused to handle as a means of meeting Gela.

Tolly shows the heroin to Gus, one of Gela's henchmen, and claims that he unwittingly broke into one of the syndicate's safes. Gela decides to use him as a pick-up man in the drugs racket. Cuddles learns that Tolly is not a cop, but is still grateful to him. Gela holds a business meeting; it transpires that the police chief is paid more in bribes than the leaders of the labour racket. Meanwhile John Driscoll, Federal Crime Commissioner, explains the workings of the syndicate to his men and the difficulty of getting anyone to testify against it. Mencken, a syndicate bookmaker, is prepared to testify about bribes given to police chief Fowler, but Fowler shoots himself. Tolly hears how the syndicate operates like any other business, paying taxes and contributing to charities when asked. Connors, the syndicate's head, tells Gela, Gunther and Smith that as long as they continue this tactic they will 'win the war'. Gus is told to kill Mencken's daughter, which he does. Tolly finds Cuddles getting drunk and, trading on her love for him, tries to persuade her to testify.

Connors wants Tolly to crack Driscoll's safe. With Driscoll's co-operation he steals planted evidence implying that his three old enemies are collaborating with the commission and Connors has them killed. Before he can get out of the syndicate, however, Connors orders Tolly to kill Cuddles. Tolly confronts Connors and shoots him, but is then himself killed by one of Connors' bodyguards.

The Vagabond
USA 1916 st b/w 4
(w. **Easy Street** and **The Pawnshop**)

PRODUCTION
p.c – Lone Star-Mutual. *p* – Charlie Chaplin. *d* – Charlie Chaplin. *sc* – Charlie Chaplin, from a story by Charlie Chaplin and Vincent Bryan. *ph* – William C. Foster, Rolland Totheroh.

LEADING PLAYERS
Charlie Chaplin (*The Vagabond*), Edna Purviance (*The Girl*), John Rand (*The Trumpeter*), Albert Austin (*The Trombonist*), James T. Kelley (*Bandsman*), Frank J. Coleman (*Bandsman*).

SYNOPSIS
A vagabond violinist tries to compete with a German band in a bar and goes round with his hat reaping the harvest of their efforts until they see what is going on and he has to leave quickly.

The vagabond sees a girl washing her clothes outside a gypsy caravan. It transpires that as a child she was kidnapped by the gypsies and maltreated by their leader. Her mother, a society woman, has never ceased to grieve for her. The vagabond plays his violin to the girl, who becomes so excited that she upsets a washtub. The gypsy leader whips the girl but the vagabond seizes a club, knocks out several of the gypsies and flees with her. The couple camp in idyllic surroundings and when the girl goes to fetch some water she meets a young artist who has set up his easel near the spring. He asks to paint her portrait and they fall in love at first sight. Later, when the artist's portrait of the girl goes on display her mother recognises her long-lost daughter. Meanwhile, the vagabond has been trying in vain to recover lost ground with the girl. The mother and the artist arrive in a chauffeur-driven car to fetch the girl. They offer the vagabond money for what he has done, but he rejects it and sadly watches them drive off.

The Vanishing Corporal (Le Caporal épinglé)
France 1961 sd b/w 15

PRODUCTION
p.c – Les Films du Cyclope. *p* – René Vuattoux. *d* – Jean Renoir. *sc* – Jean Renoir, Guy Lefranc, from the novel by Jacques Perret. *ph* – Georges Leclerc. *ed* – Renée Lichtig. *a.d.* – Wolf Witzmann. *m* – Joseph Kosma.

LEADING PLAYERS
Jean-Pierre Cassell (*The Corporal*), Claude Brasseur (*Pater*), Guy Bedos (*Le Bègue*), Claude Rich (*Ballochet*).

SYNOPSIS
After the fall of France in 1940, a corporal and his friends Pater and Ballochet find

themselves in a German detention camp. Their first escape attempt fails and they are shipped to Germany, where the corporal and Pater are separated from Ballochet. After another unsuccessful attempt Pater refuses to try again. The corporal escapes with Penche-à-Gauche; on their recapture they meet Ballochet who is now living in comfort as an interpreter, despite his total lack of German. The corporal is tempted to share Ballochet's ivory tower until a romantic encounter with a German girl, daughter of his dentist, brings back his determination to escape. Ballochet's incompetence as an interpreter is exposed and when they next meet he confesses his cowardice to the corporal and sets out on a desperate bid for freedom. He is killed.

The corporal, Pater and another prisoner, Le Bègue, leave the dentist's house disguised as civilians. When Le Bègue's odd dress draws the attention of some plainclothes German police he runs from the other two, making it possible for them to continue the escape by joining a funeral procession. Pater and the corporal board a train full of Germans, but Pater gives them away by speaking French in reply to a drunken German. Before they can be arrested, however, an air raid forces everybody to flee from the train. Pater and the corporal meet a French soldier and his German wife who run a farm together. They give the two escapers food and direct them to the frontier. Pater and the corporal arrive in Paris and go their separate ways.

Verboten!
USA 1958 sd b/w 15

PRODUCTION
p.c – Globe Enterprises for RKO Radio. *p* – Samuel Fuller. *d* – Samuel Fuller. *sc* – Samuel Fuller. *ph* – Joseph Biroc. *ed* – Philip Cahn. *a.d* – John Mansbridge. *m* – Harry Sukman, from themes by Wagner and Beethoven. *cost* – Bernice Pontrelli, Harry West.

LEADING PLAYERS
James Best (*Sergeant David Brent*), Susan Cummings (*Helga Schiller*), Torn Pittman (*Bruno Eckhart*), Harold Daye (*Franz*).

SYNOPSIS
Towards the end of the Second World War, US army sergeant David Brent is wounded in a small Bavarian town. He is found by Helga Schiller, a German girl, who takes him to her home. In order to be able to marry her David gets discharged from the army and takes a job in the American Military Government Office in Rothbach, Helga's home town. In Rothbach the Werewolf organisation – a movement of ex-Hitler Youth which aims to destroy the American occupation – has begun to emerge under the direction of Bruno, an ex-Nazi and old friend of Helga's. Franz, Helga's brother, becomes a key member of the organisation.

David loses his temper and starts a fight at a Werewolf demonstration and is sub- *sequently suspended by his commandant. He worries about having to return to America without Helga, who is now pregnant. While sympathising with David, Bruno implies that Helga only married him for the food and clothes he could obtain. David returns home and confronts her with the rumour. She admits it was true at first. David promises to feed Helga until their child is born, but says that he will then return to America with the baby.*

Helga becomes aware that her brother Franz is involved in the Werewolf movement and insists that he accompany her to the Nuremberg Trials. Franz is appalled and tells David about a planned Werewolf meeting. He informs the military and the group is wiped out.

Viridiana
Spain/Mexico 1961 sd b/w 20

PRODUCTION
p.c – Uninci, S.A./Films 59 (Madrid)/ Gustavo Alatriste (Mexico). *p* – R. Munôz Suay. *d* – Luis Buñuel. *sc* – Luis Buñuel, Julio Alejandro. *ph* – José F. Aguayo. *ed* – Pedro Del Rey. *a.d* – Francisco Canet.

LEADING PLAYERS
Silvia Pinal (*Viridiana*), Francisco Rabal (*Jorge*), Fernando Rey (*Don Jaime*).

SYNOPSIS
Viridiana, who is about to take her religious vows, is sent home to make her last contact with the outside world. Don Jaime, her uncle, is struck by her resemblance to his wife who died on their wedding night thirty years before and begs her to try on the wedding dress he treasures. Reluctantly, she does so. He persuades Ramona, his servant, to give Viridiana a sleeping draught, intending to seduce her to ensure she will not leave him. He finds he cannot have sex with her, but next morning he lies to Viridiana. When she leaves for the bus, he hangs himself. His death binds Viridiana to the estate, which she shares with Don Jaime's illegitimate son, Jorge. Jorge begins to modernise the house and brings a woman friend to share his bed; Viridiana installs a band of beggars in the outbuildings, hoping to expiate the guilt she feels for her uncle's death by putting them to work and guiding them in prayer.

Viridiana conducts an angelus with the beggars while Jorge supervises the renovation of the estate. Jorge calls Viridiana 'a bloodless bigot' and then seduces his maidservant in an attic. The next day, when Jorge and Viridiana go off to town, the beggars stage a feast which turns into an orgy in the main house. Jorge and Viridiana return.

One of the beggars rapes Viridiana. Humiliated and disillusioned, she abandons her faith and joins Jorge and Ramona, now his mistress, in a game of cards.

Viva Zapata!
USA 1952 sd b/w 10

PRODUCTION
p.c – 20th Century-Fox. *p* – Darryl F. Zanuck. *d* – Elia Kazan. *sc* – John Steinbeck. *ph* – Joe MacDonald. *ed* – Barbara McLean. *a.d* – Lyle Wheeler, Leland Fuller. *m* – Alex North. *cost* – Travilla.

LEADING PLAYERS
Marlon Brando (*Zapata*), Jean Peters (*Josefa*), Anthony Quinn (*Eufemio*), Joseph Wiseman (*Fernando*), Arnold Moss (*Don Nacio*), Alan Reed (*Pancho Villa*), Florenz Ames (*Senor Espejo*).

SYNOPSIS
In Mexico during the wars of liberation at the beginning of this century Zapata, a revolutionary leader, is outlawed for trying to help the Morelos Indians reclaim the land taken from them by the tyrannical President Diaz and goes into hiding. He is approached by Fernando Aquirre, who brings news of the emergence of an opponent to Diaz called Madero. Zapata orders that Madero should be investigated.

Zapata visits Señor Espejo to ask for his daughter Josefa's hand in marriage, but it is refused because he lacks wealth and substance. As he leaves he is captured by government troops and led out of the town. The party is gradually joined by hundreds of peasants silently coming down from the hills. The procession is eventually halted by Eufemio and his band of armed, mounted followers. The captain sees that he is surrounded and cuts Zapata free. Rebellion is declared.

The insurgence is successful and Zapata becomes a general and marries Josepha. Although Diaz has fled the country, Zapata is suspicious of Madero's reluctance to return the land to the Indians. Madero is killed and Zapata is persuaded to become President. He becomes disillusioned with his new role, however, and returns to the mountains to continue the fight against the Federal troops. Zapata is eventually lured into a trap and murdered.

Vivere in pace (Live in Peace)
Italy 1947 sd b/w 12

PRODUCTION
p.c – Lux Pao. *p* – Carlo Ponti. *d* – Luigi Zampa. *sc* – Suso D'Amico, Aldo Fabrizi, Piero Teleiu, Luigi Zampa. *ph* – Carlo Montuori. *ed* – Louis Wipf. *a.d* – Ino Battelli. *m* – Nino Rota.

LEADING PLAYERS
Aldo Fabrizi (*Uncle Tigna*), Gar Moore (*Ronald*), Mirella Monti (*Silvia*), John Kitzmiller (*Joe*), Heinrich Bode (*Hans*).

SYNOPSIS
The German army has passed by an Italian mountain village leaving only a single officer with a telephone. The peace is disturbed when two escaped Americans, a journalist and Joe, who is black, are given

shelter by Uncle Tigna at his farm and treated as members of the family.

The family and the Americans are eating together when Hans, the German officer, knocks at the door, paying a routine visit. They send Joe to hide in the wine cellar, but Hans is homesick and lingers at the farm drinking and talking. Joe gets drunk in the wine cellar and starts singing loudly. To cover the noise the family start a wild party. Angered by this activity, Joe breaks down the cellar door. Hans and Joe, both drunk, stare silently at each other. Suddenly, they laugh and embrace. Everyone joins in. The music and dancing continues.

Later, the German passes out at his post. Fearing reprisals when he wakes and remembers, the villagers take to the mountains. The sound of joyful chimes from the church proclaims the arrival of the American army, but Uncle Tigna, who returns home alone to make peace with the officer, is shot by retreating German troops.

Vredens Dag
(*see* Day of Wrath)

The Wages of Fear
France/Italy 1953 sd b/w 10 + 16

PRODUCTION
p.c – Filmsonor/CICC/Vera Film. *p* – Louis Wipf. *d* – Henri-Georges Clouzot. *sc* – Henri-Georges Clouzot, from the novel by Georges Arnaud. *ph* – Armand Thirard. *ed* – Madeleine Gug, Henri Rust. *a.d* – René Renoux. *m* – Georges Auric.

LEADING PLAYERS
Yves Montand (*Mario*), Charles Vanel (*Jo*), Vera Clouzot (*Linda*), Folco Lulli (*Luigi*), Peter Van Eyck (*Bimba*).

SYNOPSIS
A collection of down-and-out foreigners are surviving on credit in a small Central American town which has grown up around an American controlled oilfield. The manager of the field offers $2,000 to any drivers prepared to take two truckloads of nitro-glycerine over 300 miles of primitive roads to the site of an oilwell fire knowing that any serious jolt will set off an explosion. Mario, a young Corsican, Luigi, an Italian bricklayer, and Bimba, a silent German, are picked for the trip. Jo, a middle-aged gangster on the run, disposes of the fourth man and takes his place as Mario's partner.

Bimba and Luigi carefully ease the truck off the newly-built road platform as Mario and Jo drive round a bend. Looking over the site, Jo wants to turn back, but Mario insists they continue. Jo guides the truck back as Mario drives, stopping at the very edge. He looks frantically for Jo, who seems to have disappeared, but finally spots him climbing up the side of the hill. As Jo watches from the distance, Mario carefully eases the truck out, putting branches beneath the wheels to keep it from skidding on the wet cement. As the truck pulls onto the road the entire platform collapses behind it. (Ext. 1, 10 mins.)

Mario hates Jo for losing his nerve and tension rises as the drivers face appalling obstacles.

Bimba and Luigi are stopped by a boulder blocking the road and Bimba prepares to blow it up. Mario and Jo arrive and lend their assistance until Bimba sends the men out of range and continues the job himself. Finishing, Bimba lights the fuse and runs. The men watch fearing that the trucks will be hit by the rocks hurtling around them, but as the dust clears, they see that all is well and the boulder is gone. The men celebrate together. (Ext. 2, 16 mins.)

In the last stages, the truck driven by Luigi and Bimba blows up. Jo wades into an oil-filled crater left by the explosion to guide Mario across. He slips and Mario drives over him, crushing his leg. Jo dies before Mario reaches the oilwell, delivers the load and receives the money. Returning, happy and incautious, Mario crashes over a precipice.

Wagonmaster
USA 1950 sd b/w 10

PRODUCTION
p.c – Argosy Pictures Corporation. *p* – John Ford and Merian C. Cooper. *d* – John Ford. *sc* – Frank Nugent and Patrick Ford. *ph* – Bert Glennon. *ed* – Jack Murray. *a.d* – James Basevi. *m* – Richard Hageman. *cost* – Wes Jeffries, Adele Parmenter.

LEADING PLAYERS
Ben Johnson (*Travis Blue*), Joanne Dru (*Denver*), Harry Carey Jr. (*Sandy Owens*), Ward Bond (*Elder Wiggs*), Charles Kemper (*Uncle Shiloh Clegg*), Alan Mowbray (*Dr. A. Locksley Hall*), Jane Darwell (*Sister Ledyard*).

SYNOPSIS
A Mormon wagontrain is setting out westward to establish a new settlement on the Utah-Arizona border. Brother Wiggs, the wagonmaster, persuades two wandering horse-traders, Travis and Sandy, to act as guides. En route the waggontrain meets an itinerant medicine show that has run out of water. Brother Wiggs allows its members to join the wagontrain until they reach the California track.

After a trek across the desert the Mormons eventually reach water. That evening there is a dance, but the merrymaking is disrupted by the appearance of a gang of outlaws led by Uncle Shiloh.

The outlaws join the wagontrain. The company is halted by Indians who are friendly when they realise that the white men are Mormons. A feast of friendship is arranged, but the peace is disrupted when one of the Clegg gang rapes an Indian girl; to appease the Indians the wagonmaster publicly flogs him. The outlaws subsequently take control of the wagontrain and force the Mormons to hide them from an inquisitive posse. Uncle Shiloh and his gang are eventually gunned down by Travis and Sandy and the Mormons are able to cross the mountains to the fertile valley.

Walk on the Wild Side
USA 1962 sd b/w 9
(w. **Barbarella**)

PRODUCTION
p.c – Famous Artists. *p* – Charles K. Feldman. *d* – Edward Dmytryk. *sc* – John Fante, Edmund Morris, from the novel by Nelson Algren. *ph* – Joe MacDonald. *ed* – Harry Gerstad. *a.d* – Richard Sylbert. *m* – Elmer Bernstein. *cost* – Charles LeMaire.

LEADING PLAYERS
Laurence Harvey (*Dove Linkhorn*), Jane Fonda (*Kitty Twist*), Capucine (*Hallie*).

SYNOPSIS
Dove Linkhorn sets out to hitch-hike to New Orleans to find Hallie, his past love. En route he meets Kitty Twist who is on the run from an orphanage. Kitty persuades Dove to share the drainpipe she sleeps in, then tries to steal his wallet.

Kitty and Dove emerge from the pipe to start the days travelling and jump a train. Kitty is scornful of Dove's ignorance about hitch-hiking and undertakes to teach him what she knows. After they have left the train and he has bought her breakfast she gets them a lift on the back of a lorry. She begins to make advances to Dove but he tells her he is only interested in Hallie.

Dove parts company from Kitty when she steals a crucifix from Teresina Vidveri, the owner of a café. He takes a job with Teresina who helps him compose an advertisement for Hallie who now lives in the Doll House, a brothel run by Jo Courtney, to whom she has a lesbian attachment. Tension is created between Jo and Hallie when Dove, not realising Hallie's circumstances, proposes marriage. After a quarrel with Jo Hallie promises to send Dove away. He, however, offers to forget the past and persuades Hallie to run away with him. Her escape is prevented by Jo who threatens Dove with prosecution for immorality with a minor and produces Kitty Twist, a recent addition to the brothel. Dove is beaten up by Oliver, Jo's henchman, and Schmidt, her despised, legless husband. Teresina persuades Kitty to help Hallie escape so she can go to Dove who is badly injured, but Hallie is followed by Jo, and Schmidt, aiming at Dove, shoots her dead before the police arrive.

Wanda
USA 1970 sd col 15

PRODUCTION
p.c – Foundation for Filmmakers. *d* – Barbara Loden. *sc* – Barbara Loden. *ph* – Nicholas T. Proferes (Colour by Kodachrome). *ed* – Nicholas T. Proferes.

LEADING PLAYERS
Barbara Loden (*Wanda*), Michael Higgins (*Mr. Dennis*).

SYNOPSIS
After borrowing money for her bus fare, Wanda arrives late at the law court where she passively acquiesces to her husband's demand for a divorce. She leaves the Appalachian mining town where she has been staying, is picked up by a passing motorist in a bar and spends the night with him at a motel. The following day she is abandoned by him.

Wanda goes into a cinema, falls asleep and eventually wakes to find the cinema deserted and her money stolen. She goes into a nearby bar to use the washroom and disturbs Mr. Dennis, who is in the middle of robbing the till. He takes her with him; they eat and go to a cheap hotel. They are in bed when Mr. Dennis orders Wanda to go out for some food. She returns with hamburgers covered with onions and ketchup, although Mr. Dennis had specified 'no garbage'. He slaps her face.

Wanda and Mr. Dennis fall into a routine of car journeys by day and cheap hotels by night, until Mr. Dennis decides to rob a large city bank. Wanda is supposed to drive the getaway car, but she gets lost and finally arrives at the bank to find Mr. Dennis shot dead by the police. Grief-stricken, she wanders off and hysterically rejects a young soldier who tries to pick her up. She ends up at a bar in the middle of a crowd of raucous drinkers.

Warning Shadows (Schatten)
Germany 1923 st b/w 10

PRODUCTION
p.c – Pan-Film/Dafu Film Verlieh. *d* – Arthur Robison. *sc* – Rudolf Schneider, Arthur Robison, from an idea by Albin Grau. *ph* – Fritz Arno Wagner. *ed* – Arthur Robison. *a.d* – Albin Grau. *cost* – Albin Grau.

LEADING PLAYERS
Fritz Kortner (*The Husband*), Ruth Weyher (*The Wife*), Alexander Granach (*The Shadowgraph Showman*), Gustav von Wangenheim (*The Lover*), Fritz Rasp (*The Manservant*).

SYNOPSIS
A strolling juggler presents a shadow play at the house of a count who is exasperated by his wife's favours to her four courtiers. *The showman hypnotises the entire party and the shadow play begins, with the shadows acting out the inclinations of each member of the party. In the play, the wife leaves, followed down the halls by her lover. Enraged, the count follows, sees their embrace and begins to hunt the lover with rope in his hand. Two servants find him struggling with the rope.* Mad with jealousy the count compels the courtiers to stab his wife and then rests his head on the lover's chest to weep bitterly over what has happened. The halluci-

nation ends with the courtiers throwing the count out of the window in a fury. The shadows return to their owners who, awakened from their collective nightmare, are cured.

Warning Shot
USA 1966 sd col 20

PRODUCTION
p.c – Bob Banner Associates. *p* – Buzz Kulik. *d* – Buzz Kulik. *sc* – Mann Rubin, from the novel *711 – Officer Needs Help* by Whit Masterson. *ph* – Joseph Biroc (Technicolor). *ed* – Archie Marshek. *a.d* – Hal Pereira, Roland Anderson. *m* – Jerry Goldsmith. *cost* – Edith Head.

LEADING PLAYERS
David Janssen (*Sergeant Tom Valens*), Ed Begley (*Captain Roy Klodin*), Keenan Wynn (*Sergeant Ed Musso*), Sam Wanamaker (*Frank Sanderman*), Lillian Gish (*Alice Willows*), George Grizzard (*Walt Cody*).

SYNOPSIS
On duty outside a Los Angeles apartment block looking out for a psychopathic killer, Detective Sergeant Tom Valens sees a man coming towards him in the fog. When challenged he appears to draw a gun. Valens shoots in self-defence. When the body is identified Valens is told that he has killed James Ruston, a well-respected doctor. The gun he was supposed to have drawn cannot be found and Valens is suspended until the inquest is over. Meanwhile, citizens demonstrate against the police. At the inquest the evidence against Valens mounts up. After the first day's hearing Ed Musso finds Valens in a bar and tries to make him admit that he has made a mistake.

Valens is suspended from service and given time to try and clear himself. He goes back to the apartment block and talks to two other residents, Alice Willows and Walt Cody, but learns nothing. He again draws a blank when he investigates Ruston's gambling activities and frequent visits to Mexico. Working on a hint dropped by Alice Willows in connection with the death of her dog, he goes to the pets' cemetery with Walt Cody and in the grave finds the missing gun which is actually a toy used for smuggling heroin. He confronts Cody with this and accuses him of being Ruston's contact. When Cody draws a gun Valens shoots him.

The Way We Were
USA 1973 sd col scope 10

PRODUCTION
p.c – Rastar Productions. *p* – Ray Stark. *d* – Sydney Pollack. *sc* – Arthur Laurents, from his novel. *ph* – Harry Stradling Jr. (Panavision and Eastman Color). *ed* – Margaret Booth. *m* – Marvin Hamlisch.

LEADING PLAYERS
Barbra Streisand (*Katie Morosky*), Robert Redford (*Hubbell Gardiner*), Bradford

Dillman (*J.J.*), Lois Chiles (*Carol Ann*), Patrick O'Neal (*George Bissinger*).

SYNOPSIS
Katie Morosky, the Jewish President of the Young Communist League at Eastern University, campaigns relentlessly for the issues she believes in, much to the amusement of a group of wealthy and carefree WASP students. Hubbell Gardiner, a member of this set, is the golden boy of the campus, talented both as an athlete and as a writer. Katie is contemptuous of his political apathy but strongly attracted to him. They dance together at their 1937 Graduation Ball.

Seven years later, Katie goes to a New York nightclub with her boss from the radio studio. She sees Hubbell sitting bolt upright on a bar stool, evidently very drunk. She remembers their college days and in flashback he is shown excelling at numerous sporting activities while she works as a waitress, studies in her room or prints political posters. Hubbell's girlfriend, Carol Ann, relaxes in her sorority house. (Ext. 1a, 5 mins.)

Still in flashback, Katie walks home in her waitress's uniform and sees Hubbell drinking alone. He calls her over and asks her to have a drink with him to celebrate the sale of one of his short stories. He tells her she has no sense of humour; she responds by asking whether he smiles all the time. He ties up her shoelace. (Ext. 1b, 5 mins.)

An affair gradually develops between Katie and Hubbell after their nightclub meeting in New York but the relationship is strained and when Hubbell is invited to write a script for a producer friend in Hollywood, Katie objects and they split up. Later they are reconciled and Katie moves out to Hollywood. She becomes pregnant and is involved in the HUAC witchhunt. The film of Hubbell's proves to be a disastrous compromise. When Katie learns that he has co-operated with the Committee she decides that they should separate once the baby is born. Some years later they meet by chance in New York – Katie is still a political activist, Hubbell is writing scripts for television. They chat briefly and part.

(NB This extract is in Scope and needs an anamorphic lens.)

Weekend
France/Italy 1967 sd col 10

PRODUCTION
p.c – Camacico/Copernic/Lira Films (Paris)/Ascot Cineraid (Rome). *p* – Ralph Baum, Philipe Senné. *d* – Jean-Luc Godard. *sc* – Jean-Luc Godard. *ph* – Raoul Coutard (Eastman Color). *ed* – Agnès Guillemot. *m* – Antoine Duhamel.

LEADING PLAYERS
Mireille Darc (*Corinne*), Jean Yanne (*Roland*), Jean-Pierre Kalfon (*Leader of*

the FLSO), Jean-Pierre Léaud (*Saint-Just/
Man in Phone Booth*), Blandine Jeanson
(*Emily Brontë/Girl in Farmyard*).

SYNOPSIS

Corinne and Roland, a young French
bourgeois couple, have plotted for some
time to kill each other, but pause in hostili-
ties to make a weekend trip to Corinne's
mother in the hope that they will benefit
from her husband's will. On the road the
couple ignore a trail of wrecked cars and
mutilated bodies, while in the country they
encounter a series of real, imaginary and
historical characters – a young blood-
stained woman abusing a tractor driver
who has just killed her rich fiancé in a
crash, a young man granting wishes, but
not the materialist fantasies for which the
couple ask, Saint-Just, Emily Brontë dressed as Alice in Wonderland and two dustmen from Africa.

*Corinne and Roland collect garbage in
the countryside while the dustmen eat their
lunch. Romand asks for some food; he
receives a crumb. Corinne asks for food
and receives it on condition that she kisses
the dustman; he then hits her, demonstrating the attitude of the capitalist West to
the Third World. Quoting from Franz
Fanon, the dustmen define the evils of the
capitalist bourgeoisie and state their belief
that liberation will not be achieved with
patience and pacifism, but with violence,
aggression and guerrilla warfare. Corinne
and Roland sit in the garbage with bored,
uncomprehending faces.*

Arriving at Oinville, they murder Corinne's mother when she refuses to give them
money. On the way home they are kidnapped by a group of revolutionaries.
Roland is killed and eaten by Corinne who
joins the group.

What's New Pussycat?
USA/France 1965 sd col 12

PRODUCTION

p.c – Famous Artists/Famartists. *p* –
Charles K. Feldman. *d* – Clive Donner. *sc*
– Woody Allen. *ph* – Jean Badal
(Technicolor). *ed* – Fergus McDonell. *a.d*
– Jacques Saulnier. *m* – Burt Bacharach.
lyrics – Hal David. *cost* – Mia
Fonssagrives, Vicki Tiel.

LEADING PLAYERS

Peter Sellers (*Fritz Fassbender*), Peter
O'Toole (*Michael James*), Romy
Schneider (*Carol Werner*), Woody Allen
(*Victor Shakapopolis*).

SYNOPSIS

Michael James, the editor of a fashion
magazine, is in love with Carol Werner but
is distracted by the many beautiful girls he
meets in the course of his work. He con-
sults psychiatrist Fritz Fassbender about
this problem, but the doctor has romantic
troubles of his own, complicated by the
aggressive jealousy of his wife, Anna.
Michael's friend, Victor, is also in love

with Carol but she is only interested in
Michael. Hearing that her parents are
about to visit her, Carol determines to
bring Michael up to scratch. He is equally
anxious to have a last fling before he marries her.

*Michael meets Victor in a café where he
is playing chess with a girl who immediately starts making eyes at him. Later,
Michael visits Carol who tries to force him
to discuss marriage but only succeeds in
driving him away. At the strip club where
Victor works, Michael meets Fritz Fassbender who pretends to have a scientific
interest in the strippers. Victor helps the
strippers with their costumes, with disastrous results. Michael joins in the dancing, while Fassbender watches, fascinated.*

Michael meets Liz, a suicidal stripper
who writes beat verse. Through Fassbender he also becomes involved with a
fellow patient, the coldly beautiful Renée.
Meanwhile, Carol is trying to make him
jealous by encouraging Victor, but by the
time her parents arrive the situation has
deteriorated, with misunderstandings on
both sides. Declaring a temporary truce,
they have an enjoyable evening out with
Carol's parents and Michael decides to
marry and settle down. But before Carol
and Michael finally manage to marry
everyone is involved in a wild chase in and
out of the bedrooms of a country hotel.

Where the River Bends
(*see* Bend of the River)

Why We Fight – The American
People
(*see* Why We Fight – War Comes to
America)

Why We Fight – Prelude to War (War
Comes to America)
USA 1942 sd b/w 19

PRODUCTION

p.c – US War Department. *p* – Frank
Capra. *d* – Frank Capra. *sc* – Eric Knight,
Anthony Veiller. *ed* – William Hornbeck.
m – Dimitri Tiomkin.

SYNOPSIS

An extract from the first of the *Why We
Fight* series.

*The history of the ending of America's
neutrality at the beginning of World
War II. Congress and ordinary people in
the streets argue about the sale of muni-
tions to the Allies and the embargo is
finally lifted. Meanwhile, the narrator suggest that the Sino-Japanese War 'threatens
America's interests in the Pacific'. Dead
Chinese children are shown, while opinion
poll figures demonstrate an increased popular sympathy for China: the Assistant
Secretary for State explains the new
embargo of the sale of goods to Japan.
American families listen to radio reports
of the Nazi invasions of France and the*

*French surrender. Hitler visits the Eiffel
Tower to the soundtrack accompaniment
of a sad popular song: 'The Last Time I
Saw Paris'. The narrator expresses fears
about a fascist fifth column in South
America; the first lottery for the draft takes
place and finally there is a slow, dramatic
build-up to the bombing of Pearl Harbor
and America's declaration of war.*

Why We Fight – War Comes to
America
(The American People)
USA 1945 sd b/w 12

PRODUCTION

p.c – US War Department. *p* – Frank
Capra. *d* – Anatole Litvak. *sc* – Anthony
Veiller. *ed* – William Hornbeck. *m* –
Dimitri Tiomkin.

SYNOPSIS

An extract from the seventh of the *Why
We Fight* series.

*Scenes of American soldiers fighting
around the world and of the different parts
of the United States and class backgrounds
they come from. The landing of the pil-
grims is re-enacted, and parts of the
Declaration of Independence and the poem
on the Statue of Liberty recited. The narrator says 'We are an inventive people' and
lists American contributions to technology. Different American racial and eth-
nic groups are enumerated and shown
making particular contributions to American life. The extract ends with images of
American power – machinery, hydro-
electric dams, pylons and freeways – and
American children.*

Why We Fight – War Comes to
America
(*see* Why We Fight – Prelude to War)

Wild River
USA 1960 sd col scope or standard 10

PRODUCTION

p.c – 20th Century-Fox. *p.* – Elia Kazan.
d – Elia Kazan. *sc* – Paul Osborn, from the
novels *Mud on the Stars* by William
Bradford Huie and *Dunbar's Cove* by
Borden Deal. *ph* – Ellsworth Fredericks
(CinemaScope and colour by DeLuxe). *ed*
– William Reynolds. *a.d* – Lyle R.
Wheeler, Herman A. Blumenthal. *m* –
Kenyon Hopkins. *cost* – Anna Hill
Johnstone.

LEADING PLAYERS

Montgomery Clift (*Chuck Glover*), Lee
Remick (*Carol*), Jo Van Fleet (*Ella
Garth*), Albert Salmi (*Hank Bailey*), Jay
C. Flippen (*Hamilton Garth*), James
Westerfield (*Cal Garth*).

SYNOPSIS

Chuck Glover, a Tennessee Valley
Authority agent, is sent to a small Southern
town to deal with Ella Garth, an old
woman who refuses to leave her island
although it is soon to be flooded as part

of the TVA Scheme. Chuck attempts to reason with her, but she refuses to change her mind.

Carol, Ella Garth's young widowed granddaughter, walks down to the river with Chuck. He talks to some of Ella's black workers about leaving the island. As Chuck departs by raft, Carol suddenly scrambles aboard. Together they go to the house where she used to live before her husband died. She asks him to stay the night with her. Next morning they part by the river.

Chuck manages to persuade Ella's black workers to leave the island by offering them jobs on the mainland. Chuck's insistence that they be paid the same wages as the white workers leads to local hostility which culminates in a violent attack on Chuck and Carol. Eventually Chuck is forced to have Ella evicted and although a new house is found for her, she dies shortly after the move. Chuck, Carol and her two children leave together.

(NB This extract is available in standard reduced from Scope or in Scope which needs an anamorphic lens.)

Wild Strawberries
Sweden 1957 sd b/w 18

PRODUCTION
p.c – Svensk Filmindustri. *p* – Allan Ekelund. *d* – Ingmar Bergman. *sc* – Ingmar Bergman. *ph* – Gunnar Fischer. *ed* – Oscar Rosander. *a.d* – Gittan Gustafson. *m* – Erik Nordgren.

LEADING PLAYERS
Victor Sjöström (*Professor Isak Borg*), Ingrid Thulin (*Marianne*), Bibi Andersson (*Sara*), Gertrud Fridh (*Fru Isak Borg*), Ake Fridell (*Her Lover*).

SYNOPSIS
Professor Isak Borg, a grand old man of medicine, is to receive an honorary degree from the University of Lund. He decides to drive from Stockholm by car taking Marianne, his daughter-in-law, with him. She tells him that he is selfish and hard under his remote and humorous charm.

Borg dozes off. In his dream he talks to the girlfriend of his youth. She leaves him to look after a baby and takes it into a house where Borg watches her playing the piano and dining with another man. Borg is taken into another part of the house and is examined before an audience. He is unable to use the microscope or to recognise the Hippocratic oath. A patient whom he diagnoses as dead breaks into mocking laughter. He is shown his wife being seduced in a forest, after which he wakes to find himself in the car again.

The drive continues. An irrepressible girl hiker, Sara, reminds Borg of how he lost his first love through a combination of selfishness and idealism while a quarrelling couple make him think of his later, tragic marriage where his love and understanding proved inadequate.

Will Success Spoil Rock Hunter? (Oh! For a Man!)
USA 1957 sd col scope 6

PRODUCTION
p.c – 20th Century-Fox. *p* – Frank Tashlin. *d* – Frank Tashlin. *sc* – Frank Tashlin, from the play by George Axelrod. *ph* – Joe MacDonald (CinemaScope and Eastman Color). *ed* – Hugh S. Fowler. *a.d* – Lyle R. Wheeler, Leland Fuller. *m* – Charles LeMaire.

LEADING PLAYERS
Jayne Mansfield (*Rita Marlow*), Tony Randall (*Rock Hunter*), Betsy Drake (*Jenny*), Joan Blondell (*Violet*), John Williams (*LaSalle Jr.*), Mickey Hargitay (*Bobo*).

SYNOPSIS
In order to maintain his position in a New York advertising agency Rockwell Hunter develops an idea for a lipstick promotion which entails getting the endorsement of Hollywood film star Rita Marlow. Rita agrees on the condition that Rock assumes the mantle of the 'great lover' in order to make Bobo, her estranged boyfriend, jealous. Jenny, Rock's fiancée, becomes jealous and attempts to improve her physique with body-building exercises.

Rock has had to borrow Bobo's suit after having his own torn off by a mob of girls. Rita instructs Rock in his role and produces a pair of built-up shoes for him but he has difficulty in learning to walk in them. Rock later returns to Jenny's flat to find that she has collapsed after excessive exercise.

After a series of mishaps and confusions Rita is reunited with her first true love, Georgie Schmidlapp. Rock's fame leads to his promotion but he soon realises that success isn't everything and resigns as president of the agency to start a chicken farm with Jenny.

(NB This extract is in Scope and needs an anamorphic lens.)

Winchester '73
USA 1950 sd b/w 15

PRODUCTION
p.c – Universal-International. *p.* – Aaron Rosenberg. *d* – Anthony Mann. *sc* – Robert L. Richards and Borden Chase, from a story by Stuart N. Lake. *ph* – William Daniels. *ed* – Edward Curtiss. *a.d* – Bernard Herzbrun, Nathan Juran. *m* – Joseph Gershenson.

LEADING PLAYERS
James Stewart (*Lin McAdam*), Shelley Winters (*Lola Manners*), Dan Duryea (*Waco Johnnie Dean*), Stephen McNally (*Dutch Henry Brown*), Millard Mitchell (*High Spade*).

SYNOPSIS
At a shooting contest Lin McAdam wins a Winchester repeating rifle, the most prized gun in the west. The rifle is stolen by Dutch Henry Brown, who in turn loses it in a poker game to an Indian trader; it then passes to an Indian chief, a cowardly young man, an outlaw and finally back to Dutch Henry. Meanwhile, Lin has been pursuing Dutch Henry, who is in fact his brother, in order to avenge the murder of their father.

Lola, the girlfriend of the psychotic Waco Johnnie, finds a photograph of Lin and Dutch Henry. Meanwhile, Lin rides into Tascosa with High Spade where they meet Lola in the saloon. As a bank robbery is carried out, Lin spots Dutch Henry and gives chase. He stops at a rocky outcrop where he is shot by Lin and plunges to his death. Lin reclaims his Winchester and rides back into Tascosa.

Woman in a Dressing Gown
UK 1957 sd b/w 10

PRODUCTION
p.c – Godwin-Willis-Lee-Thompson Production. *p* – Frank Godwin and J. Lee-Thompson. *sc* – Ted Willis, from his TV play. *ph* – Gilbert Taylor. *ed* – Richard Best. *a.d* – Robert Jones. *m* – Louis Levy.

LEADING PLAYERS
Yvonne Mitchell (*Amy*), Anthony Quayle (*Jim*), Sylvia Syms (*Georgie*), Andrew Ray (*Brian*), Carole Lesley (*Hilda*).

SYNOPSIS
Sunday morning at the council flat of Amy and Jim Preston, a middle-aged married couple. The kitchen and the living room are in a shambles. Amy burns the breakfast and makes the mess worse when she tries to clear up. Their teenage son, Brian, comments on the state of the flat but Jim smiles wearily and Amy asks whether mess matters as long as they're happy. Jim leaves saying he is going to work and telephones Georgie, a woman he works with.

Georgie, a calm, orderly woman, is a total contrast to Amy. Gradually the attraction between her and Jim develops into an affair. Jim decides to leave Amy, but she insists that all three of them should meet to discuss the situation. Amy gets very drunk and the meeting is a disaster. Jim leaves with Georgie, but returns almost immediately, deciding that he cannot leave Amy.

The Woman on the Beach
USA 1947 sd b/w 22

PRODUCTION
p.c – RKO Radio. *p* – Jack Gross, Will Price. *d* – Jean Renoir. *sc* – Jean Renoir and Frank Davis, from the novel *None So Blind* by Mitchell Wilson. *ph* – Leo Tober and Harry Wild. *ed* – Roland Gross, Lyle Boyer. *a.d* – Albert S. D'Agostino and Walter E. Keller. *m* – Hanns Eisler.

LEADING PLAYERS
Joan Bennett (*Peggy Butler*), Robert Ryan (*Lieutenant Scott Burnett*), Charles Bickford (*Ted Butler*), Nan Leslie (*Eve Geddes*).

SYNOPSIS

Scott Burnett, a coast guard, is patrolling a lonely stretch of beach when he meets Peggy Butler near the hulk of a wrecked ship. He continues along the beach to the shipyard to meet Eve, his fiancée. Scott suggest that they get married immediately, but Eve wants to wait. He rides back along the beach and again meets Peggy: this time he helps her carry driftwood back to her house. Peggy's husband Ted, a blind painter, appears and makes Scott promise to visit them again on the following day (Ext. 1a, 15 mins.)

Scott becomes fascinated by Peggy and convinced that Ted is not really blind, but watching their meetings. He attempts to prove his theory by leading Ted to a cliff's edge, but Ted falls and narrowly escapes death.

Scott apologises for his obsession. Ted shows Scott his paintings, but a portrait of Peggy is missing. When Scott leaves, Ted and Peggy quarrel about the painting. Scott returns to his office but is tormented by memories of a wartime torpedo accident and Peggy. He rushes from his office and rides along the beach to the wrecked ship where he finds Peggy waiting for him. (Ext. 1b, 7 mins.)

The hostility between the two men grows and they quarrel violently on a fishing expedition. During the struggle both men fall overboard. Eve sends a rescue boat. Ted later burns his house and all his paintings and returns to New York with Peggy, leaving Scott to go back to Eve.

The Wonderful Country

USA 1959 sd col 13

PRODUCTION

p.c – D.R.M. *p* – Chester Erskine. *d* – Robert Parrish. *sc* – Robert Ardrey, from the novel by Tom Lea. *ph* – Floyd Crosby, Alec Philips (Technicolor). *ed* – Michael Luciano. *a.d* – Harry Horner. *m* – Alex North.

LEADING PLAYERS

Robert Mitchum (*Martin Brady*), Julie London (*Ellen Colton*), Gary Merrill (*Major Colton*), Pedro Armendariz (*Cipriano Castro*).

SYNOPSIS

Martin Brady, an American-born gunman wanted for killing his father's murderer, crosses the Rio Grande on a gun-running expedition for Cipriano Castro, a provincial Mexican dictator. Arriving in Puerto, Texas, he breaks a leg and is forced to stay there for two months. Colton, an American army major in the Texas Rangers asks Brady to help form a joint US-Mexican battalion against the Apaches.

Brady arrives at an outdoor party and meets Ellen Colton. The captain of the Rangers warns Brady to keep out of trouble, motioning towards Ellen, who is dancing with her estranged husband. Ellen turns down another man's invitation to dance so she can talk with Brady, who forces her to admit that she loves him but warns her that he doesn't want trouble. He then leaves abruptly. The man Ellen refused to dance with starts to abuse Brady drunkenly, picks a fight with his companion who is standing by and knocks him down with a broken bottle. Brady, attracted by the uproar, shoots him. Ellen is watching as he realises what he has done and makes hastily for the Rio Grande. In return for fetching his horse from the American side the Mexicans order Brady to carry a message to one of their fellow conspirators. Before he leaves he is told that both men involved in the fight are dead. He rides off alone across the plains and through villages, finally arriving at the place where he is to deliver the message.

Castro holds him responsible for the failure of his earlier mission and Brady finds himself a virtual prisoner. When at last he escapes, he encounters the Coltons again. Major Colton is killed by the Apaches and Brady is briefly reunited with Ellen, but has to flee from Castro's new gunman, Rascon. He kills Rascon in battle, lays down his gun and returns hopefully to American territory.

World of Apu

India 1958 sd b/w 13

PRODUCTION

p.c – Satyajit Ray Productions. *p* – Satyajit Ray. *d* – Satyajit Ray. *sc* – Satyajit Ray, from the novel by Bibhut Bhusan Bandopadhaya. *ph* – Subrata Mitra. *ed* – Dulal Dutta. *a.d* – Bansi Chandragupta. *m* – Ravi Shankar.

LEADING PLAYERS

Soumitra Chatterjee (*Apu*), Sharmila Tagore (*Aparna*), Shapan Mukerjee (*Pulu*), S. Aloke Chakravarty (*Kajole*).

SYNOPSIS

Apu has left university and is living in poverty while trying to become a writer. Pulu, an old friend, invites him to the wedding of his cousin Aparna at a distant village.

Pulu and Apu travel by boat to Aparna's wedding quoting poetry and discussing their ideas. They are welcomed by Aparna's family who are in the midst of preparations for the wedding. The bridegroom arrives and is found to be mad. The family despairs. Pulu approaches Apu to ask if he will save the family by marrying Aparna. Apu reluctantly agrees and a marriage between Aparna and Apu takes place.

The couple return to Calcutta and Apu takes on a job there. The marriage is idyllically happy and when Aparna dies giving birth to a child Apu is shattered. He refuses to see his new-born son and wanders through the country in search of peace. Five years later, Pulu returns from abroad to find the boy an uncontrollable savage.

He seeks out Apu and persuades him to return to his son. On seeing the boy, Apu loves him. He tries to win the boy's friendship and after much difficulty succeeds. The two of them leave for Calcutta.

Written on the Wind

USA 1956 sd col 15

PRODUCTION

p.c – Universal-International. *p* – Albert Zugsmith. *d* – Douglas Sirk. *sc* – George Zuckerman, from the novel by Robert Wilder. *ph* – Russell Metty (Technicolor). *ed* – Russell F. Schoengarth. *a.d* – Alexander Golitzen, Robert Clatworthy. *m* – Frank Skinner. *lyrics* – Victor Young and Sammy Cahn. *cost* – Jay Morley Jr., Bill Thomas.

LEADING PLAYERS

Rock Hudson (*Mitch Wayne*), Lauren Bacall (*Lucy Hadley*), Robert Stack (*Kyle Hadley*), Dorothy Malone (*Marylee Hadley*), Robert Keith (*Jasper Hadley*).

SYNOPSIS

Kyle Hadley, the irresponsible son of oil tycoon Jasper Hadley, marries Lucy Moore, a secretary in his father's organisation, after a whirlwind courtship. Jasper hopes that Lucy will prove a steadying influence in Kyle's life. Mitch Wayne, an old friend of the Hadley family, also welcomes the bride. Only Marylee, Kyle's spoilt and restless sister, resents the newcomer.

Kyle learns from a doctor that he may be sterile, while Marylee drives to a garage and picks up a petrol pump attendant. At Kyle's request Mitch and Lucy go to a country club, where they find him drunk. They take him back to the Hadley mansion. While Jasper is talking to Mitch about his feelings of failure as a father and husband, the police arrive with Marylee and the petrol pump attendant, who have been arrested at a motel. Mitch deals with the police and they leave. Upstairs, Marylee undresses in front of a photograph of Mitch while playing loud, frenetic music. Jasper starts to climb the stairs, has a heart attack and tumbles to his death.

Encouraged by Marylee, Kyle accuses Lucy of having an affair with Mitch. When Lucy tells Kyle that she is pregnant by him, he refuses to believe her and hits her, causing a miscarriage. Later, Kyle shoots himself during a quarrel with Mitch. Marylee threatens to tell the police that Mitch shot Kyle unless he promises to go away with her. Mitch refuses and at the inquest Marylee tells the truth, freeing Mitch and Lucy to start a new life together.

The Wrong Man

USA 1956 sd b/w 7

PRODUCTION

p.c – Warner Bros. *p* – Alfred Hitchcock. *d* – Alfred Hitchcock. *sc* – Maxwell Anderson and Angus McPhail, from *The True Story of Christopher Emmanuel*

Balestrero by Maxwell Anderson. *ph* – Robert Burks. *a.d* – Paul Sylbert. *ed* – George Tomasini. *m* – Bernard Herrmann.

LEADING PLAYERS

Henry Fonda (*Manny Balestrero*), Vera Miles (*Rose Balestrero*), Anthony Quayle (*O'Connor*), Harold J. Stone (*Lieutenant Bowers*).

SYNOPSIS

Manny Balestrero, a bass player at New York's Stork Club, arrives home shortly before dawn. His wife, Rose, has toothache and is worried about the cost of the dental work. Manny says he will find out if they can borrow the money against her insurance policy. At the insurance office Manny doesn't notice the perturbation caused by his appearance. The clerk informs the police and when he returns later Manny is arrested. He learns that he answers the description of a man who has committed a number of hold-ups in the neighbourhood.

The police take Manny to a liquor store and make him parade in front of the owner and then to a supermarket where the shopkeeper encourages his assistant to take a good look at him. Manny looks increasingly worried as they set off for the next shop.

Rose worries when her husband doesn't come home. The detectives learn that Manny is desperately in need of money. When they ask him to print the words the hold-up man used the writing is similar and contains the same mis-spelling. Frank O'Connor, Manny's attorney urges him to establish an alibi for the date of the insurance office robbery. Manny was on holiday at the time and recalls the names of several people but a tedious search reveals that they have all either died or do not recall him. He finally remembers that he was treated by a dentist on the date of the second robbery. O'Connor believes that the dentist's testimony might vindicate him. Rose, meanwhile, sinks into complete hopelessness and is sent to a mental hospital. Manny's trial opens but is ruled a mis-trial on a technical point. While Manny awaits re-trial, a man who resembles Manny is caught after a hold-up. The thief confesses to the other hold-ups and Manny is released. He hurries to tell Rose the news.

X – the Unknown
UK 1956 sd b/w 7

PRODUCTION

p.c – Hammer. *p* – Anthony Hinds. *d* – Leslie Norman. *sc* – Jimmy Sangster. *ph* – Gerald Gibbs. *ed* – James Needs. *m* – James Bernard.

LEADING PLAYERS

Dean Jagger (*Dr. Adam Royston*), Edward Chapman (*Peter Elliot*), Leo McKern (*Inspector McGill*), Anthony

Newley (*Private Webb*), Kenneth Cope (*Private Lancing*).

SYNOPSIS

Soldiers are using a Geiger counter on a deserted Scottish moor as part of an army exercise, the object of which is to find a planted piece of radioactive material. As the platoon are preparing to return to base Private Lancing points out that he hasn't had a turn with the Geiger counter. He starts on the exercise but finds signs of radioactivity in a place other than where it is expected. While the officers investigate, a soldier is left to guard the spot. A crack appears in the ground, there is a sudden violent explosion and a large fissure is left in the moor.

Casualties from the blast are later found to be suffering from severe radiation burns and Dr. Adam Royston, a scientist at a nearby atomic research station, is called in to investigate. A series of inexplicable deaths follow: two soldiers guarding the seemingly bottomless fissure are killed and a doctor dies when the hospital's radium-store is plundered. The army try to concrete over the fissure, but Royston realises that it contains an 'unknown thing' which feeds on radiation. He decides to move the research centre's cobalt phial to a safer place, but the unknown thing attacks the station before the phial can be moved and absorbs the radiation from the cobalt. Now doubled in size, the unknown thing is finally lured out and destroyed.

Yangtse Incident
UK 1957 sd b/w 18

PRODUCTION

p.c – A Wilcox-Neagle Production. *p* – Herbert Wilcox. *d* – Michael Anderson. *sc* – Eric Ambler, from the book by Laurence Earl. *ph* – Gordon Dines. *ed* – Basil Warren. *a.d* – Ralph Brinton. *m* – Leighton Lucas.

LEADING PLAYERS

Richard Todd (*Lieutenant Commander Kerans*), William Hartnell (*Leading Seaman Frank*), Akim Tamiroff (*Colonel Peng*).

SYNOPSIS

19 April, 1949. With the permission of the Chinese Government, HMS *Amethyst*, a Royal Navy frigate, sails up the Yangtse with supplies for the British Embassy in Nanking. Half-way up the river the ship is shelled by shore batteries of the Chinese People's Liberation Army and, badly crippled, runs aground on a sandbank. Heavy gunfire frustrates a rescue attempt by a destroyer. With her captain dead and most of the crew badly injured, Lieutenant Commander John Kerans is sent from Nanking to organise the evacuation of the crew to the safety of the shore and later takes command of the *Amethyst*.

Kerans and Leading Seaman Frank, who is dressed as an officer much to the amuse-

ment of the crew, set off to negotiate with the Chinese. In the conference room Colonel Peng, the local communist leader, says that the ship will be allowed to leave only if the Navy formally apologises for interfering in Chinese waters and communicating with the Kuomintang. Kerans refuses, but the Chinese seem unperturbed and offer to supply the ship with food. (Ext. 1a, 8 mins.)

Negotiations continue but there is no break in the deadlock. Kerans determines to escape.

After careful preparations the Amethyst slips anchor and starts down river. Despite heavy shore-fire Kerans successfully guides the ship to the open sea where, amidst celebrations, the Amethyst rejoins the fleet. A message to the Amethyst from the King is seen on the screen. (Ext. 1b, 10 mins.)

Les Yeux sans visage
(*see* Eyes Without a Face)

The Young Chopin
Poland 1951 sd b/w 12

PRODUCTION

p.c – Film Polski. *d* – Alexander Ford. *sc* – Alexander Ford. *ph* – Jaroslaw Tuzar. *ed* – Christine Tunis. *a.d* – Roman Mann. *m* – Chopin, Bach, Mozart, Paganini.

LEADING PLAYERS

Czeslaw Wollejke (*Chopin*), Aleksandra Slaska (*Konstancia Gladkowska*), J. Kurnakowicz (*Professor Elsner*).

SYNOPSIS

While still a student, Chopin joins a radical movement opposing the aristocracy which pays homage to Russia at the expense of Poland.

Chopin visits a dance hall with his fellow students and discusses the revolution. The students realise a traitor is among them, get him drunk and then lead him out of the dance hall to be executed.

In Warsaw Chopin falls in love with the singer Konstancia Gladkowska. After great difficulties he gains a grant from the authorities, gives a farewell concert, and sets out on a successful tour of Europe. His fame grows, but he is increasingly troubled by a chest complaint. Hearing of the uprising in Warsaw, he hurries home. Despite his deteriorating health he continues to compose in Paris, where the remnants of the Polish national army are received. Chopin meets some of his old friends. They walk the streets, seething with insurrection, looking forward to the time when Poland will be free again.

The Young One
Mexico 1960 sd b/w 13

PRODUCTION

p.c – Olmeca Films, S.A. *p* – George P. Werker. *d* – Luis Buñuel. *sc* – Luis Buñuel, H. B. Addis, from a story by Peter

Matthieson. *ph* – Gabriel Figueroa. *ed* – Carlos Savage. *a.d* – Jesús Bracho.

LEADING PLAYERS
Zachary Scott (*Miller*), Kay Meersman (*Evalyn*), Bernie Hamilton (*Travers*).

SYNOPSIS
An aged handyman dies on a small lonely island in the American South. Miller, the game warden, has designs on the old man's innocent 13-year-old daughter Evalyn. Travers, a black jazz musician fleeing an unjust rape charge, lands on the island.

Travers works at patching up his boat, chatting to Evalyn as he does so. Miller appears and there is an ugly exchange between him and Travers, with Travers holding Miller at bay with a rifle. The exchange continues when Miller returns to his shack and Travers follows him. Travers plays his clarinet but he is interrupted when Miller produces a hand grenade. That night Miller assaults Evalyn.

Miller and Travers are in conflict until Evalyn persuades Miller that Travers has not molested her. Jackson, a boatman, brings the Reverend Fleetwood to the island to take Evalyn to a children's home and Miller learns of the rape charge connected with Travers. Travers is seized by Miller and Jackson, but learning of Evalyn's lost innocence the Reverend Fleetwood warns Miller that he believes Travers innocent, but has no doubt about Miller's own culpability. Stricken with fear and conscience, Miller affirms his intentions of marrying Evalyn and assists Travers in his flight to freedom.

The Young Stranger
USA 1957 sd b/w 10

PRODUCTION
p.c – RKO Radio. *p* – Stuart Miller. *d* – John Frankenheimer. *sc* – Robert Dozier, from his TV play *Is This Our Son?* *ph* – Robert Planck. *ed* – Robert Swink, Edward Biery Jr. *a.d* – Albert S. D'Agostino, John B. Mansbridge. *m* – Leonard Rosenman.

LEADING PLAYERS
James McArthur (*Hal*), Kim Hunter (*Helen*), James Daly (*Tom Ditmar*), James Gregory (*Shipley*), Whit Bissell (*Grubbs*), Jess Silver (*Jerry*).

SYNOPSIS
The Ditmar's adolescent son, Hal, gets into trouble with the police for hitting a cinema manager.

The cinema manager withdraws charges at the police station, but Hal shows no gratitude. On the way home he sees his friend Jerry and they have a sudden, although friendly, fight. Over a meal at home Tom Ditmar reproaches Hal for his surly conduct at the police station. Hal reacts violently and walks out of the room, leaving his father and mother sitting apart.

It transpires that Hal believes that his father does not love or trust him and he is concerned that his story of the incident be believed. He becomes obsessed with making his father understand that he hit the cinema manager in self-defence. In order to do this, he strikes the manager again and ends up back in the police station. This time, however, parents and son are reconciled through the intervention of an understanding detective.

Zéro de conduite
France 1933 sd b/w 10

PRODUCTION
p.c – Argui Films. *p* – J-L. Nounez. *d* – Jean Vigo. *sc* – Jean Vigo. *ph* – Boris Kaufman. *ed* – Jean Vigo. *a.d* – Jean Vigo, Henri Storck, Boris Kaufman. *m* – Maurice Jaubert.

LEADING PLAYERS
Jean Dasté (*Huguet*), Le Nain Delphin (*The Principal*), Léon Larive (*The Chemistry Master*), Louis Lefebvre (*Caussat*), Gilbert Pruchon (*Colin*), Constantin Kelber (*Bruel*), Gérard de Bédarieux (*Tabard*).

SYNOPSIS
The narrow, repressive discipline and sordid living conditions in a small French boarding school lead a number of boys to revolt.

One of the schoolboys has been insolent in class and is reported to the principal. He refuses to apologise and instead insults him, provoking an uprising and a riotous pillow fight which turns into a strange, almost religious ritual. The boys tie one of the masters to his bed and hurl boots, old tin cans and other assorted missiles from the rooftops at the dignitaries who are assembling for the school speech day. Finally, the rebellious boys sing as they disappear over the rooftops.

Zu neuen Ufern (To New Shores)
Germany 1937 sd b/w 19

PRODUCTION
p.c – Ufa. *p* – Bruno Duday. *d* – Detlef Sierck (Douglas Sirk). *sc* – Detlef Sierck, Kurt Heuser, from the novel by Lovis H. Lorenz. *ph* – Franz Weihmayr. *ed* – Milo Harbich. *a.d* – Fritz Maurischat. *m* – Ralph Benatzky. *cost* – Arnold Richter.

LEADING PLAYERS
Zarah Leander (*Gloria Vane*), Willy Birgel (*Sir Albert Finsbury*), Herbert Hübner (*Music Hall Proprietor*), Jakob Tiedtke (*Wells Snr.*), Robert Dorsay (*Bobby Wells*).

SYNOPSIS
In Victorian England Albert Finsbury, a dissolute aristocrat, forges a promissory note from an associate, Wells, to clear his debts before leaving London for a military posting in New South Wales. When Wells's father threatens prosecution, Gloria Vane, a singer with whom Finsbury was having an affair, takes the blame for the forgery to protect his reputation.

Wells Snr. decides to go ahead with the prosecution when he realises that Gloria is not a 'lady'. Gloria is tried before an unsympathetic court and, in spite of Bobby Wells's efforts to intercede on her behalf, is found guilty and sentenced to transportation and seven years in Parramatta, a women's prison in Sydney. (Ext. 1a, 8 mins.)

From prison Gloria smuggles a note to Finsbury asking him to intercede for her. Finsbury, who has been made adjutant to the governor of the colony and is courting his daughter Mary, is reluctant to jeopardise his position and makes only an indirect and futile attempt to help. Encouraged by fellow prisoners, Gloria enlists in a scheme enabling convicts to gain release by contracting marriages with local settlers and becomes engaged to a young farmer, Henry Hoyer. She abandons Hoyer before the marriage, however, and goes in search of Finsbury, only to discover he is engaged to Mary. She takes a job as a singer in a music hall.

Finsbury visits the music hall with some friends, but when he learns that Gloria is one of the acts he decides to leave. As she begins to sing, however, he is drawn by her haunting song to stay. The audience finds the song too tragic and Gloria is jeered off the stage. Finsbury visits her backstage and tries to justify himself and get her to leave with him. Finsbury returns to his room, where he is haunted by Gloria's words and her song. (Ext. 1b, 11 mins.)

On the day of his marriage to Mary, Finsbury shoots himself. Gloria has meanwhile lost her job and is about to return voluntarily to jail. But Hoyer, who has been searching for her, finds her praying in a church near the prison. He proposes marriage and she accepts.

(NB This extract is not subtitled, but a transcript is included.)

Extract Category Listings

These extract category listings have been devised to assist teachers more easily to locate extracts which they might wish to use in order to raise questions about particular critical areas for discussion.

The intention is not that these categories be regarded as absolute and fixed; extracts have a variety of possible uses and can be used to serve as illustrative material in a number of critical areas, not just those suggested here.

(* indicates problematic or mixed category)

1. Bazin: Deep-Focus Techniques and Realism
2. Blacks in the Cinema
3. CinemaScope
4. Comedy
5. Directors
6. Directors, Women
7. Documentary, Realism and Politics
8. Genres:
    Film Noir/Gangster/Crime Film
    Horror
    Melodrama Musical
    Science Fiction
    Western
9. Narrative: Film Openings, Film Endings, Film Openings and Endings
10. National cinemas and movements
    Britain – 60s Social Realism
    Czechoslovakia
    France – French New Wave
    Germany – German Expressionism
    Italy – Italian Neo-Realism
    Japan
    Latin-American Cinema
    Poland
    Sweden
    USSR
    Hollywood, 1900–1930
    Hollywood in the 30s
    Hollywood in the 40s
    Hollywood in the 50s
    Hollywood in the 60s
    Hollywood in the 70s
11. Notions of *Mise en Scène*
12. Social Realism in Hollywood
13. Stars
14. Studios
    Britain:
        Ealing
        Hammer
    Hollywood:
        Columbia
        Paramount
        RKO
        Twentieth Century-Fox
        Universal
        Warner Brothers
15. Subversion and Counter-Cinema
16. Surrealism in the Cinema
17. The Treatment of Women in Hollywood
18. Television Material

1. Bazin:
Deep-Focus Techniques and Realism
(Film titles referred to in 'The Evolution of Film Language' in *What is Cinema?* Volume 1, University of California Press, 1971.)

The Russian Orthodoxy:
Battleship Potemkin (Eisenstein 1925)
The General Line (Eisenstein/Alexandrov 1929)

Silent Film-Makers Anticipating Deep-Focus Techniques:
Foolish Wives (Stroheim 1922)
Nanook of the North (Flaherty 1922)
Nosferatu (Murnau 1922)
Sunrise (Murnau 1927)

American Classics:
Frankenstein (Whale 1931)
I am a Fugitive from a Chain Gang (Leroy 1932)
The Informer (Ford 1935)
Scarface (Hawks 1932)
Stagecoach (Ford 1939)

Deep-Focus Breakthrough:
Best Years of Our Lives (Wyler 1946)
Citizen Kane (Welles 1941)
La Grande illusion (Renoir 1938)
Little Foxes (Wyler 1941)
The Magnificent Ambersons (Welles 1942)
La Règle du jeu (Renoir 1939)

2. Blacks in the Cinema
(Comprehensive listing, arranged alphabetically.)
Blacula (Crain 1972)
Buck and the Preacher (Poitier 1971)
Cleopatra Jones (Starret 1973)
The Defiant Ones (Kramer 1958)
In the Heat of the Night (Jewison 1967)
The Littlest Rebel (Butler 1936)
Mandingo (Fleischer 1975)
Odds Against Tomorrow (Wise 1959)
Sergeant Rutledge (Ford 1960)
Shaft (Parks 1971)
To Kill a Mocking Bird (Mulligan 1962)

3. CinemaScope
(Comprehensive listing.)
The Damned (Losey 1961)
Kiss Me, Stupid (Wilder 1964)
Klute (Pakula 1971)
Pierrot le fou (Godard 1965)
Rebel Without a Cause (Ray 1955)
The Revolt of Mamie Stover (Walsh 1956)
River of No Return (Preminger 1945) – Scope and standard compilation
The St. Valentine's Day Massacre (Corman 1967)
The Way We Were (Pollack 1973)
Wild River (Kazan 1960) – Scope and standard versions available separately
Will Success Spoil Rock Hunter (Tashlin 1957)

4. Comedy
(Comprehensive listing arranged alphabetically.)
The Blood Donor (TV) – Hancock (Wood)
Born Yesterday (Cukor 1950)
Boudu sauvé des eaux (Renoir 1932)
Bringing up Baby (Hawks 1938)
Carmen – Charlie Chaplin's Burlesque on 'Carmen' (Chaplin 1916)
Le Crime de Monsieur Lange (Renoir 1935)
Dr. Strangelove (Kubrick 1963)
Easy Street (Chaplin 1917)
His Girl Friday (Hawks 1939)
It's a Gift – W. C. Fields (McLeod 1933)
Kiss Me, Stupid (Wilder 1964)
The Lavender Hill Mob (Crichton 1951)
Love Happy – Marx Brothers (Miller 1949)
Mae West Compilation: Belle of the Nineties/I'm No Angel (McCarey/Ruggles 1934/35)
Man in the White Suit (MacKendrick 1951)
Mr. Deeds Goes to Town (Capra 1936)
Never Weaken – Harold Lloyd (Newmeyer & Taylor 1921)
A New Leaf (May 1970)
Nothing but the Best (Donner 1964)
The Pawnshop (Chaplin 1916)
La Règle du jeu (Renoir 1939)
A Sailor-Made Man – Harold Lloyd (Newmeyer 1921)
The Seven Year Itch (Wilder 1955)
The Soilers – Laurel & Hardy (Farman 1923)
Some Like It Hot (Wilder 1959)
Steptoe & Son (TV) (Wood 1964)
Till Death Do Us Part (TV) – Alf Garnet (Main-Wilson 1966)
The Vagabond (Chaplin 1916)
The Vanishing Corporal (Le Caporal épinglé (Renoir 1961)
What's New Pussycat? (Donner 1965)
Will Success Spoil Rock Hunter (Tashlin 1957)

5. Directors
(Select listing arranged alphabetically by director and chronologically by film title.)

ALDRICH, Robert
Kiss Me Deadly (1955)
Ulzana's Raid (1972)

ANTONIONI, Michelangelo
La Signora Senza Camelie (1953)
L'Avventura (1959/60)
L'Eclisse (1962)

ARZNER, Dorothy
Dance, Girl, Dance (1940)

BERGMAN, Ingmar
Summer with Monika (1952)
Sawdust & Tinsel (1953)
Seventh Seal (1957)

MURNAU, F. W.
Nosferatu (1922)
The Last Laugh (1924)
Sunrise (1927)

OLMI, Ermanno
Il posto (1961)

OPHULS, Max
Letter from an Unknown Woman (1948)

OZU, Yasujiro
Early Spring (1956)

PAKULA, Alan
Klute (1971)

PECKINPAH, Sam
Major Dundee (1964)

POLANSKI, Roman
Rosemary's Baby (1968)

POLLACK, Sydney
The Way We Were (1973)

POWELL, Michael
Peeping Tom (1959)

PREMINGER, Otto
Laura (1944)
Angel Face (1952)
River of No Return (1954)
Carmen Jones (1954)
Anatomy of a Murder (1959)

PUDOVKIN, Vsevolod
Mother (1926)
The End of St. Petersburg (1927)

RAY, Nicholas
They Live by Night (1948)
On Dangerous Ground (1951)
The Lusty Men (1952)
Johnny Guitar (1954)
Rebel Without a Cause (1955)
The James Brothers (The True Story of
    Jesse James) (1956)

RAY, Satyajit
Pather Panchali (1955)
Jalsagar (The Music Room) (1958)
The World of Apu (1958)
Two Daughters (1961)
Mahanagar (1963)

RENOIR, Jean
Bondu sauvé des eaux (1932)
Le Crime de Monsieur Lange (1935)
La Marseillaise (1937)
Le Grande illusion (1937)
La Règle du jeu (1939)
This Land is Mine (1943)
Woman on the Beach (1947)
French Can-Can (1955)
The Vanishing Corporal (Le Caporal
    épinglé) (1961)
Study Unit No. 8: Renoir

RESNAIS, Alain
La Guerre est finie (1966)

RIEFENSTAHL, Leni
Triumph of the Will (1934)

ROCHA, Glauba
Antonio das Mortes (1969)

ROEG, Nicholas
Don't Look Now (1973)

ROSSELLINI, Roberto
Paisà (1946)
Stromboli (1949)

ROTHMAN, Stephanie
Student Nurses (1970)
Knucklemen (1973)

SEMBENE, Ousmane
Emitai (1972)

SHUB, Esfir
The Fall of the Romanov Dynasty (1927)
The Great Road (1927)

SIEGEL, Donald
Baby Face Nelson (1957)
The Lineup (1958)
The Killers (1964)
Coogan's Bluff (1968)
Madigan (1968)
The Beguiled (1970)
Dirty Harry (1971)

SIRK, Douglas
Zu neuen Ufern (1937)
All That Heaven Allows (1955)
Written on the Wind (1956)

SOLANAS, Ferdinand
Hour of the Furnaces (1968)

STERNBERG, Joseph von
The Scarlet Empress (1934)
Macao (1952)

STROHEIM, Erich von
Foolish Wives (1922)
Greed (1923)

STURGES, Preston
Sullivan's Travels (1941)

TASHLIN, Frank
Will Success Spoil Rock Hunter (1957)

TOURNEUR, Jacques
Cat People (1942)
Out of the Past (Build My Gallows High)
    (1947)

TRUFFAUT, François
Les quatre cents coups (1958)
Jules et Jim (1961)
La peau douce (1964)

VARDA, Agnès
Le Bonheur (1965)

VERTOV, Dziga
Man with a Movie Camera (1928)

VIGO, Jean
L'Atalante (1934)
Zéro de conduite (1933)

VISCONTI, Luchino
La terra trema (1947)

WAJDA, Andrzej
A Generation (1954)
Ashes and Diamonds (1958)
Lotna (1959)
Study Unit No. 7: Polish Cinema

WALSH, Raoul
The Roaring Twenties (1939)
They Drive by Night (1940)
High Sierra (1941)
The Revolt of Mamie Stover (1956)

WATKINS, Peter
Culloden (TV 1964)

WELLES, Orson
Citizen Kane (1941)
The Magnificent Ambersons (1942)
A Touch of Evil (1958)
Study Unit No. 9: Orson Welles

WERTMÜLLER, Lina
The Lizards (1963)

WILDER, Billy
Double Indemnity (1944)
Seven Year Itch (1955)
Some Like It Hot (1959)
Kiss Me, Stupid (1964)

WYLER, William
The Little Foxes (1941)

6. Directors, Women
(Comprehensive listing, arranged
alphabetically.)

ARZNER, Dorothy
Dance, Girl, Dance (1940)

JAKUBOWSKA, Wanda
The Last Stage (1947)

KAPLAN, Nelly
La Fiancée du pirate (1969)

LODEN, Barbara
Wanda (1970)

MAY, Elaine
A New Leaf (1970)

RIEFENSTAHL, Leni
Triumph of the Will (1936)

ROTHMAN, Stephanie
Knucklemen (1973)
Student Nurses (1970)

SHUB, Esfir
The Fall of the Romanov Dynasty (1927)
The Great Road (1927)

VARDA, Agnès
Le Bonheur (1965)

WERTMÜLLER, Lina
The Lizards (1963)

7. Documentary, Realism and Politics
(Select listing, arranged alphabetically
within sub-categories.)

Documentary
Back of Beyond (Heyer 1953)
Calcutta (Malle 1968)

Cuba Si! (Marker 1961)
Farrebique (Rouquier 1947)
Fires Were Started (I Was a Fireman)
 (Jennings 1943)
Moana (Flaherty 1923/4)
Nanook of the North (Flaherty 1922)
The Rival World (Haanstra 1955)
Song of Ceylon (Wright 1934)

Documentary re-enactments of Fictional
Documentaries:
(with actual participants and/or actors)
Battle of Algiers (Pontecorvo 1965)
Cathy Come Home (TV) Loach 1966)
Coup our coup (Karmitz 1972)
Culloden (TV) (Watkins 1964)
In Two Minds (TV) (Loach 1966)
Salt of the Earth (Biberman 1953)
*Stromboli (Rossellini 1949)
La terra trema (Visconti 1947)

Formal Experiment and Political
Documentary:
Berlin (Ruttman 1927)
British Sounds (Godard 1969)
The Fall of the Romanov Dynasty (Shub
 1927)
The Great Road (Shub 1927)
Hour of the Furnaces (Solanas 1968)
Man with a Movie Camera (Dziga-Vertov
 1929)
The Nightcleaners (Berwick Street
 Collective 1975)
Triumph of the Will (Riefenstahl 1936)

8. Genres
(Comprehensive listing arranged
 alphabetically in sub-categories.)

FILM NOIR
Beyond a Reasonable Doubt (Lang 1956)
*The Big Heat (Lang 1953)
Crossfire (Dmytryk 1947)
Cry of the City (Siodmak 1948)
Deadlier than the Male (Born to Kill)
 (Wise 1947)
Double Indemnity (Wilder 1944)
Farewell My Lovely (Dmytryk 1944)
Gilda (Charles Vidor 1946)
*High Sierra (Walsh 1941)
The Killers (Siodmak (1946)
*The Killers (Siegel (1964)
Kiss Me Deadly (Aldrich 1955)
Laura (Preminger 1944)
Maltese Falcon (Huston 1941)
*Mildred Pierce (Curtiz 1945)
*On Dangerous Ground (Nicholas Ray
 1951)
Out of the Past (Build My Gallows High)
 (Tourneur 1947)
*The Set-Up (Wise 1949)
They Drive by Night (Walsh 1940)
They Live by Night (Ray 1948)
*Woman on the Beach (Renoir 1947)

GANGSTER/CRIME FILM
Gangster:
Baby Face Nelson (Siegel 1957)
G-Men (Keighley 1935)
The Godfather (Coppola 1971)
The Harder They Fall (Robson 1956)
The Lineup (Siegel 1958)
Little Caesar (LeRoy 1930)
Machine Gun Kelly (Corman 1958)
Odds Against Tomorrow (Wise 1959)

Portrait of a Mobster (Pevney 1961)
The Public Enemy (Wellman 1931)
Racket Busters (Bacon 1938)
The Rise and Fall of Legs Diamond
 (Boetticher 1959)
The Roaring Twenties (Walsh 1939)
The St. Valentine's Day Massacre
 (Corman 1967)
Scarface (Hawks 1932)
Underworld USA (Fuller 1960)
The Death of a Gangster – Film Study
 Extract Compilation
Police Movie:
Coogan's Bluff (Siegel 1968)
Dirty Harry (Siegel 1971)
*In the Heat of the Night (Jewison 1967)
Madigan (Siegel 1968)
New Face in Hell (Guillermin 1967)
Shaft (Parks 1971)

Foreign antecendents/derivations:
A bout de souffle (Breathless) (Godard
 1959)
Bande à part (Godard 1964)
M (Lang 1931)
The Samurai (Melville 1967)

HORROR
*The Birds (Hitchcock 1963)
Blacula (Crain 1972)
The Cabinet of Dr. Caligari (Wiene 1919)
Cat People (Tourneur 1942)
Dead of Night (Hamer 1945)
Don't Look Now (Roeg 1973)
Dracula (Browning 1930)
Frankenstein (Whale 1931)
*King Kong (Schoedsack/Cooper 1933)
King Kong Versus Godzilla (Honda 1963)
Legend of the Werewolf and teachers
 resource pack (Francis 1974)
Nosferatu (Murnau 1922)
Peeping Tom (Powell 1959)
Rosemary's Baby (Polanski 1968)
The Tomb of Ligeia (Corman 1964)
Les Yeux sans visage (Eyes Without a
 Face) Franju 1959)

HAMMER HORROR
The Brides of Dracula (Fisher 1960)
The Curse of Frankenstein (Fisher 1957)
The Damned (Losey 1961)
The Devil Rides Out (Fisher 1967)
Dracula (Fisher 1957)
Dracula Prince of Darkness (Fisher 1965)
The Evil of Frankenstein (Francis 1963)
Fanatic (Narizzano 1965)
The Hound of the Baskervilles (Fisher
 1959)
The Mummy (Fisher 1959)
The Plague of the Zombies (Gilling 1966)
The Revenge of Frankenstein (Fisher
 1958)
The Satanic Rites of Dracula (Gibson
 1973)
Taste the Blood of Dracula (Sasdy 1969)

MELODRAMA
(Select listing, arranged alphabetically
within sub-categories.)

Hollywood:
The Birth of a Nation (Griffith 1915)
Foolish Wives (Stroheim 1922)
Hearts of the World (Griffith 1918)
Intolerance (Griffith 1916)

Sunrise (Murnau 1927)
All That Heaven Allows (Sirk 1955)
Angel Face (Preminger 1952)
Baby Doll (Kazan 1956)
I Remember Mama (Stevens 1948)
Johnny Guitar (Ray 1954)
Letter from an Unknown Woman
 (Ophuls 1948)
The Little Foxes (Wyler 1941)
The Magnificent Ambersons (Welles
 1942)
Marnie (Hitchcock 1964)
Mildred Pierce (Curtiz 1945)
On Dangerous Ground (Ray 1951)
Rebel Without a Cause (Ray 1955)
Shadow of a Doubt (Hitchcock 1943)
Stella Dallas (King Vidor 1938)
A Streetcar Named Desire (Kazan 1951)
The Way We Were (Pollack 1973)
Written on the Wind (Sirk 1956)

European Developments:
Fear Eats the Soul (Fassbinder 1973)
La Femme infidèle (Chabrol 1968)
Stromboli (Rossellini 1949)
The Umbrellas of Cherbourg (Les
 Parapluies de Cherbourg) (Demy
 1963)
Woman on the Beach (Renoir 1947)

THE MUSICAL
Carmen Jones (Preminger 1954)
Funny Face (Donen 1956)
The Gay Divorcee (Sandrich 1934)
Gentlemen Prefer Blondes (Hawks 1953)
Gold Diggers of 1933 (LeRoy 1933)
My Sister Eileen (Quine 1955)
On a Clear Day You Can See Forever
 (Minnelli 1970)
Sweet Charity (Fosse 1968)
Top Hat (Sandrich 1935)
The Umbrellas of Cherbourg (Les
 Parapluies de Cherbourg) (Demy
 1963)
Study Unit 16: The Musical

SCIENCE FICTION
*The Birds (Hitchcock 1963)
*The Damned (Losey 1961)
The Day the Earth Caught Fire (Guest
 1961)
Dr. Strangelove (Kubrick 1963)
Dr. Who (TV) (Nation 1964)
The Lost World (Hoyt 1924)
*King Kong Versus Godzilla (Honda
 1963)
Metropolis (Lang 1926)
The Quatermass Experiment (Guest 1955)
Quatermass II (Guest 1957)
X – The Unknown (Norman 1956)

THE WESTERN
Bend of the River (Mann 1952)
*The Big Sky (Hawks 1952)
Broken Arrow (Daves 1950)
Buck and the Preacher (Poitier 1972)
Butch Cassidy and the Sundance Kid (Roy
 Hill 1969)
The Covered Wagon (Cruze 1923)
Cowboy (Daves 1957)
The Far Country (Mann 1954)
The Gunfighter (King 1950)
The James Brothers (Ray 1956)
Johnny Guitar (Ray 1954)
Lonely are the Brave (Miller 1962)
The Lusty Men (Ray 1952)

Major Dundee (Peckinpah 1964)
The Man from Laramie (Mann 1955)
My Darling Clementine (Ford 1946)
Once Upon a Time in the West (Leone 1968)
Rancho Notorious (Lang 1952)
Rio Bravo (Hawks 1959)
River of no Return (Preminger 1954)
The Searchers (Ford 1956)
Sergeant Rutledge (Ford 1960)
Shane (Stevens 1952)
She Wore a Yellow Ribbon (Ford 1949)
Stagecoach (Ford 1939)
Two Rode Together (Ford 1961)
Wagonmaster (Ford 1950)
The Wonderful Country (Parrish 1959)
Study Unit No. 12 : The Western

9. Narrative:
Openings and Endings
of Films

OPENINGS
(Comprehensive listing, arranged alphabetically.)
A bout de Souffle (Breathless) (Godard 1959)
All That Heaven Allows – extract 1 (Sirk 1955)
Ashes and Diamonds (Wajda 1958)
Baby Doll (Kazan 1956)
Broken Arrow (Daves 1950)
Butch Cassidy and the Sundance Kid – part a) of the extract (Roy Hill 1969)
Carmen Jones (Preminger 1954)
The Criminal (Losey 1960)
Deadlier than the Male (Born to Kill) (Wise 1947)
Dirty Harry (Siegel 1971)
Dracula (Fisher 1957)
Each Dawn I Die (Keighley 1940)
L'eclisse – extract 1 (Antonioni 1962)
Farewell My Lovely (Dmytryk 1944)
La Femme infidèle (Chabrol 1968)
French Can-Can (Renoir 1955)
The Godfather – part a) of the extract (Coppola 1971)
Hancock (TV) (Wood 1965)
The Harder they Fall (Robson 1956)
His Girl Friday – part a) of the extract (Hawks 1939)
Hound of the Baskervilles (Fisher 1959)
I Am a Fugitive from a Chain Gang – part a) of the extract (LeRoy 1932)
I Remember Mama (Stevens 1948)
The Killers (Siodmak 1946)
The Killers (Siegel 1964)
Kiss Me Deadly – part a) of the extract (Aldrich 1955)
Louisiana Story (Flaherty 1948)
Love Happy – Marx Brothers – extract 1 (Miller 1949)
The Lusty Men (Ray 1952)
Madigan – part a) of the extract (Siegel 1968)
A Man Escaped (Bresson 1956)
Marnie – extract 1, part a) (Hitchcock 1964)
Moulin Rouge (Huston 1952)
A New Face in Hell – part a) of the extract (Guillermin 1967)
A New Leaf – part a) of the extract (May 1970)
Nothing But The Best (Donner 1964)

Once Upon a Time in the West – extract 1, part a) (Leone 1968)
The Pickwick Papers (Trimble 1913)
The Public Enemy – part a) of the extract (Wellman 1931)
Racket Busters – part a) of the extract (Bacon 1938)
The Revolt of Mamie Stover – part a) of the extract, pre-credit sequence (Walsh 1956)
The Samurai (Melville 1967)
Saturday Night and Sunday Morning – part a) of the extract (Reisz 1960)
Sawdust and Tinsel (Bergman 1953)
The Seventh Seal (Bergman 1957)
Shadow of a Doubt (Hitchcock 1943)
Shaft – part a) of the extract (Parks 1971)
Shane – part a) of extract 1 (Stevens 1952)
Softly Softly (TV) (Lewis 1966)
Spare the Rod – part a) of the extract (Norman 1961)
Spartacus – part a) of the extract (Kubrick 1960)
Taste the Blood of Dracula – part a) of the extract (Sasdy 1969)
To Have and Have Not – extract 1, part a) (Hawkes 1944)
Triumph of the Will – extract 1 (Riefenstahl 1936)
Up the Junction (TV) (Loach 1965)
Warning Shadows (Robinson 1922)
Woman in a Dressing Gown (Thompson 1957)
Woman on the Beach – part a) of the extract (Renoir 1947)
X – the Unknown (Norman 1956)

ENDINGS
(Comprehensive listing, arranged alphabetically.)
Anatomy of a Murder (Preminger 1959)
Bande à part – extract 2 (Godard 1964)
The Birds (Hitchcock 1963)
Blacula (Crain 1972)
The Brides of Dracula (Fisher 1960)
The Bridge on the River Kwai (Lean 1957)
Brute Force (Dassin 1947)
The Damned (Losey 1961)
Dance, Girl, Dance – part b) of the extract (Arzner 1940)
Don Quixote (Pabst 1933)
Double Indemnity – part b) of the extract (Wilder 1944)
L'eclisse – part b) of the extract (Antonioni 1962)
8½ (Otto e Mezzo) (Fellini 1962/3)
La Fiancée du pirate – part b) of the extract (Kaplan 1969)
Gold Diggers of 1933 (LeRoy 1933)
The Great Man (Ferrer 1956)
The Little Foxes – extract 2, part b) (Wyler 1941)
Love Happy – Marx Brothers – extract 1, part b) (Miller 1949)
Major Dundee – part c) of the extract (Peckinpah 1964)
The Manchurian Candidate (Frankenheimer 1962)
Man with a Movie Camera (Dziga-Vertov 1929)
Mildred Pierce – extract 2, part b) (Curtiz 1945)
Morgan, A Suitable Case for Treatment (Reisz 1966)
The Mummy (Fisher 1959)

Nazarin (Buñuel 1958)
A New Face in Hell – part d) of the extract (Guillermin 1967)
Die Nibelungen : Part II Kriemhild's Revenge (Lang 1924)
Odds Against Tomorrow – extract 2, part b) (Wise 1959)
The Revolt of Mamie Stover – part b) of the extract (Walsh 1956)
Richard III (Frank Benson 1911)
Rio Bravo – part b) of the extract (Hawks 1959)
River of No Return (Preminger 1954)
Rosemary's Baby (Polanski 1968)
Sally In Our Alley (Hepworth 1913)
The Set-Up (Wise 1948)
The Seven Samurai (Kurosawa 1954)
Softly Softly (TV) (Lewis 1966)
Stella Dallas – part b) of the extract (King Vidor 1938)
Touch of Evil (Welles 1958)
The Vanishing Corporal (Le Caporal épinglé) (Renoir 1961)
Wild Strawberries (Bergman 1957)
Yangste Incident (Anderson 1957)

OPENINGS AND ENDINGS
(Comprehensive listing, arranged alphabetically.)
L'eclisse – extracts 1 & 2 (Antonioni 1962)
Love Happy – Marx Brothers – extract 1, parts a) & b) (Miller 1949)
A New Face In Hell – parts a) and d) (Guillermin 1967)
The Revolt of Mamie Stover – parts a) & b) (Walsh 1956)
Softly Softly (TV) (Lewis 1966)

10. National cinemas and movements
(Comprehensive listing, arranged alphabetically.)

BRITAIN
Blackmail (Hitchcock 1929)
The Bridge on the River Kwai (Lean 1957)
The Brides of Dracula (Fisher 1960)
Brighton Rock (Boulting 1947)
British Sounds (Godard 1968)
Catch Us If You Can (Boorman 1965)
Cathy Come Home (TV) (Loach 1966)
Comin' Thro' The Rye (Hepworth 1923)
Coronation Street (TV) (Shaw 1964)
The Criminal (Losey 1960)
The Curse of Frankenstein (Fisher 1957)
The Damned (Losey 1961)
The Day The Earth Caught Fire (Guest 1961)
Dead of Night (Hamer 1945)
The Devil Rides Out (Fisher 1967)
Don Quixote – w. France (Pabst 1933)
Don't Look Now – w. Italy (Roeg 1973)
Dracula (Fisher 1957)
Dracula Prince of Darkness (Fisher 1965)
The Entertainer (Richardson 1960)
The Evil of Frankenstein (Francis 1963)
Fanatic (Narizzano 1965)
From Russia With Love (Young 1963)
The Guns of Navarone (Lee-Thompson 1961)
Hamlet (Plumb 1913)
A Hard Day's Night (Lester 1964)
Hound of the Baskervilles (Fisher 1959)
If . . . (Anderson 1968)
A Kind of Loving – Extract 1 (Schlesinger 1962)

The Ladykillers (Mackendrick 1955)
The Lavender Hill Mob (Crichton 1951)
The Leather Boys (Furie 1963)
Legend of the Werewolf (Francis 1974)
The Long and the Short and the Tall
 (Norman 1960)
Lord of the Flies (Brook 1963)
The Man in the White Suit (Mackendrick
 1951)
Morgan, A Suitable Case for Treatment
 (Reisz 1966)
Moulin Rouge (Huston 1952)
The Mummy (Fisher 1959)
Nothing But the Best (Donner 1964)
Our Man in Havana (Reed 1959)
Peeping Tom (Powell 1959)
Plague of the Zombies (Gilling 1966)
The Prisoner (Glenville 1955)
The Pumpkin Eater (Clayton 1964)
The Quatermass Experiment (Guest 1955)
Quatermass II (Guest 1957)
Room at the Top (Clayton 1958)
Sally in our Alley (Hepworth 1913)
The Satanic Rites of Dracula (Gibson
 1973)
Saturday Night and Sunday Morning
 (Reisz 1960)
Spare the Rod (Norman 1961)
Squibbs Wins the Calcutta Sweep
 (Pearson 1922)
The Stars Look Down (Reed 1939)
Taste the Blood of Dracula (Sasdy 1969)
A Taste of Honey (Richardson 1961)
Tell England (Asquith/Barkas 1930)
Tom Brown's Schooldays (Parry 1951)
Tomb of Ligeia (Corman 1964)
Under Capricorn (Hitchcock 1949)
Up the Junction (TV) (Loach 1965)
Woman in a Dressing Gown (Lee-
 Thompson 1957)
X – the Unknown (Norman 1956)
Yangste Incident (Anderson 1957)

BRITAIN – 60S SOCIAL REALISM
Cathy Come Home (TV) (Loach 1966)
Coronation Street (TV) (Pauline Shaw
 1964)
In Two Minds (TV) (Loach 1966)
A Kind of Loving (Schlesinger 1962)
The Leather Boys (Furie 1963)
Nothing But the Best (Donner 1964)
The Pumpkin Eater (Clayton 1964)
Room at the Top (Clayton 1958)
Saturday Night and Sunday Morning
 (Reisz 1960)
Spare the Rod (Norman 1961)
A Taste of Honey (Richardson 1961)
Woman in a Dressing Gown (Lee-
 Thompson 1957)

CZECHOSLOVAKIA
Diamonds of the Night (Nemec 1964)
Saddled with Five Girls (Schorm 1967)

FRANCE
A bout de souffle (Breathless) (Godard
 1959)
Adieu Philippine (Rozier 1961)
L'Atalante (Vigo 1933)
La Baie des anges (Demy 1962)
Bande à part (Godard 1964)
Le Bonheur (Varda 1965)
Boudu sauve des eaux (Renoir 1932)
Calcutta (Malle 1968)

Le Crime de Monsieur Lange (Renoir
 1935)
Cuba Si! (Marker 1961)
Don Quixote – w. Britain (Pabst 1933)
Eva (Losey 1962)
Farrebique (Rouquier 1947)
Le Femme infidèle (Chabrol 1968)
Une Femme mariée (Godard 1964)
Le Feu follet (Malle 1963)
La Fiancée du pirate (Kaplan 1969)
French Can-can (Renoir 1955)
La Grande illusion (Renoir 1937)
La Guerre est finie (Resnais 1966)
The Italian Straw Hat (Clair 1927)
Judex (Franju 1963)
Jules et Jim (Truffaut 1961)
Lady of the Camellias (La Dame aux
 camélias) (Carmettes 1912)
Love is My Profession (Autant-Lara 1958)
A Man Escaped (Bresson 1956)
La Marseillaise (Renoir 1937)
Masculin-Féminin (Godard 1966)
Naked Hearts (Luntz 1966)
Orphée (Cocteau 1950)
La peau douce (Truffaut 1964)
Les Quatres cents coups (Truffaut 1958)
Pierrot le fou (Godard 1965)
The Samurai – w. Italy (Melville 1967)
Terror (Jose 1925)
Tout va bien – w. Italy (Godard/Gorin
 1972)
The Umbrellas of Cherbourg (Les
 Parapluies de Cherbourg) (Demy
 1963)
The Vanishing Corporal (La Caporal
 épinglé) (Renoir 1961)
The Wages of Fear (Clouzot 1953)
Weekend (Godard 1967)
Les Yeux sans visage (Eyes Without a
 Face) (Franju 1959)
Zéro de conduite (Vigo 1933)

French New Wave:
A bout de souffle (Godard 1959)
Adieu Philippine (Rozier 1961)
La Baie des anges (Demy 1962)
Bande à part (Godard 1964)
Le Bonheur (Varda 1965)
Une Femme mariée (Godard 1964)
Le Feu follet (Malle 1963)
La Guerre est Finie (Resnais 1966)
Jules et Jim (Truffaut 1961)
Masculin-Féminin (Godard 1966)
La peau douce (Truffaut 1964)
Pierrot le fou (Godard 1965)
Les Quatres cents coups (Truffaut 1958)
The Umbrellas of Cherbourg (Les
 Parapluies de Cherbourg) (Demy
 1963)

GERMANY
Berlin (Ruttman 1927)
Zu neuen ufern (Sirk 1937)
Fear Eats the Soul (Fassbinder 1974)
Triumph of the Will (Reifenstahl 1934)

German Expressionism
The Cabinet of Dr. Caligari (Wiene 1919)
Dr. Mabuse – Der Spieler: Part I (Lang
 1921)
Dr. Mabuse – Der Spieler: Part II (Lang
 1921)
Kameradschaft (Pabst 1931)
The Last Laugh (Murnau 1924)
M (Lang 1931)

Metropolis (Lang 1926)
Der Müde Tod (Destiny) (Lang 1921)
Die Nibelungen: Part I – Siegfried (Lang
 1923)
Die Nibelungen: Part II – Kriemhild's
 Revenge (Lang 1924)
Warning Shadows (Robinson 1923)

ITALY
L'avventura (Antonioni 1959/60)
L'eclisse (Antonioni 1962)
8½ (Fellini 1962)
Last Tango in Paris – w. France
 (Bertolucci 1972)
The Lizards (Wertmüller 1963)
Once Upon a Time in the West (Leone
 1968)
Paisà (Rossellini 1946)
Il posto (Olmi 1961)
La Signora Senza Camelie (Antonioni
 1953)
La strada (Fellini 1954)
Stromboli (Rossellini 1949)
La terra trema (Visconti 1947–48)
Umberto D (De Sica 1952)
Vivere in pace (Zampa 1947)

Italian Neo-Realism:
The Lizards (Wertmüller 1963)
Paisà (Rossellini 1963)
Il posto (Olmi 1961)
La Signora Senza Camelie (Antonioni
 1953)
La strada (Fellini 1954)
Stromboli (Rossellini 1949)
La terra trema (Visconti 1947)
Umberto D (De Sica 1952)
Vivere in pace (Zampa 1947)

JAPAN
Early Spring (Ozu 1956)
King Kong Versus Godzilla (Honda 1963)
Rashomon (Kurosawa 1951)
The Seven Samurai (Kurosawa 1957)
Throne of Blood (Kurosawa 1957)
Ugetsu Monogatari (Mizoguchi 1953)

LATIN-AMERICAN CINEMA
Antonio das mortes (Brazil: Rocha 1969)
Hour of the Furnaces (Argentina: Solanas
 1968)

POLAND
Ashes and Diamonds (Wajda 1958)
Barrier (Skolimowski 1966)
Eroica (Munk 1957)
A Generation (Wajda 1954)
The Last Stage (Jakubowska 1947)
Lotna (Wajda 1959)
The Young Chopin (Ford 1951)

SWEDEN
Frenzy (Sjoberg 1944)
Sawdust and Tinsel (Bergman 1953)
The Seventh Seal (Bergman 1957)
The Silence (Bergman 1963)
A Summer with Monika (Bergman 1952)
Wild Strawberries (Bergman 1957)

USSR
Ballad of a Soldier (Chukrai 1959)
Battleship Potemkin (Eisenstein 1925)
The Childhood of Maxim Gorky
 (Donskoi 1938)
Earth (Dovzhenko 1929/30)

The End of St. Petersburg (Pudovkin 1927)
The Fall of the Romanov Dynasty (Shub 1927)
The General Line (Eisenstein/Alexandrov 1920)
The Ghost That Never Returns (Room 1929)
The Great Road (Shub 1927)
Ivan the Terrible – Part I (Eisenstein 1945)
Man with a Movie Camera (Vertov 1929)
Mother (Pudovkin 1929)
New Babylon (Kozintsev/Trauberg 1929)
October (Eisenstein/Alexandrov 1927)

HOLLYWOOD 1900–1930
(Comprehensive listing, arranged chronologically.)
The Pickwick Papers (Trimble 1913)
A Fool There Was (Powell 1914)
The Birth of a Nation (Griffith 1915)
Carmen (Charlie Chaplin's Burlesque on 'Carmen') (Chaplin 1916)
Intolerance (Griffith 1916)
The Pawnshop (Chaplin 1916)
The Vagabond (Chaplin 1916)
Easy Street (Chaplin 1917)
Hearts of the World (Griffith 1918)
Never Weaken – Harold Lloyd (Newmeyer and Taylor 1921)
A Sailor-Made Man – Harold Lloyd (Newmeyer 1921)
Foolish Wives (Stroheim 1922)
Nanook of the North (Flaherty 1922)
The Covered Wagon (Cruze 1923)
The Soilers – Stan Laurel (Farman 1923)
Moana (Flaherty 1923/24)
The Lost World (Hoyt 1924)
Lighthouse by the Sea – Rin-Tin-Tin (Mal St. Clair 1925)
The Jazz Singer (Crosland 1927)
Sunrise (Murnau 1927)

HOLLYWOOD IN THE 30S
Little Caesar (LeRoy 1930)
Dracula (Browning 1931)
Frankenstein (Whale 1931)
The Public Enemy (Wellman 1931)
Scarface (Hawks 1932)
I Am a Fugitive from a Chain Gang (LeRoy 1932)
King Kong (Schoedsack & Cooper 1933)
Gold Diggers of 1933 (LeRoy 1933)
It's a Gift (McLeod 1933)
Mae West Compilation: Belle of the Nineties/I'm No Angel (1935/34)
The Scarlet Empress (Sternberg 1935)
Top Hat (Sandrich 1935)
A Midsummer Night's Dream (Reinhardt/Dieterle 1935)
The Informer (Ford 1935)
G-Men (Keighley 1935)
The Littlest Rebel (Butler 1936)
Mr. Deeds goes to Town (Capra 1936)
The Gay Divorcee (Sandrich 1937)
Stella Dallas (King Vidor 1937)
Racket Busters (Bacon 1938)
Bringing up Baby (Hawks 1939)
Destry Rides Again (Marshall 1939)
His Girl Friday (Hawks 1939)
Each Dawn I Die (Keighley 1939)
The Roaring Twenties (Walsh 1939)
Stagecoach (Ford 1939)

HOLLYWOOD IN THE 40S
Citizen Kane (Welles 1940)
Foreign Correspondent (Hitchcock 1940)
The Grapes of Wrath (Ford 1940)
They Drive by Night (Walsh 1940)
Dance, Girl, Dance (Arzner 1940)
Sergeant York (Hawks 1941)
High Sierra (Walsh 1941)
Mr. and Mrs. Smith (Hitchcock 1941)
Sullivan's Travels (Sturges 1941)
How Green Was My Valley (Ford 1941)
The Little Foxes (Wyler 1941)
The Maltese Falcon (Huston 1942)
The Magnificent Ambersons (Welles 1942)
Cat People (Tourneur 1942)
Shadow of a Doubt (Hitchcock 1943)
This Land is Mine (Renoir 1943)
Laura (Preminger 1944)
Farewell My Lovely (Dmytryk 1944)
Double Indemnity (Wilder 1944)
To Have and Have Not (Hawks 1945)
The House on 92nd Street (Hathaway 1945)
Mildred Pierce (Curtiz 1945)
The Killers (Siodmak 1946)
My Darling Clementine (Ford 1946)
The Best Years of our Lives (Wyler 1946)
Gilda (Charles Vidor 1946)
The Treasure of Sierra Madre (Huston 1947)
Brute Force (Dassin 1947)
Crossfire (Dmytryk 1947)
Woman on the Beach (Renoir 1947)
Deadlier than the Male (Born to Kill) (Wise 1947)
Out of the Past (Build My Gallows High) (Tourneur 1947)
Louisiana Story (Flaherty 1948)
They Live by Night (Ray 1948)
Cry of the City (Siodmak 1948)
The Set-Up (Wise 1948)
Fort Apache (Ford 1948)
I Remember Mama (Stevens 1948)
Letter from an Unknown Woman (Ophuls 1948)
Love-Happy – Marx Brothers (Miller 1949)
She Wore a Yellow Ribbon (Ford 1949)
Under Capricorn (Hitchcock 1949)

HOLLYWOOD IN THE 50S
Born Yesterday (Cukor 1950)
The Gunfighter (King 1950)
Broken Arrow (Fuller 1950)
Wagonmaster (Ford 1950)
Winchester '73 (Mann 1950)
A Streetcar Named Desire (Kazan 1951)
Gambling House (Tetzlaff 1951)
On Dangerous Ground (Ray 1951)
Angel Face (Preminger 1952)
Bend of the River (Mann 1952)
The Big Sky (Hawks 1952)
Macao (von Sternberg 1952)
The Lusty Men (Ray 1952)
Rancho Notorious (Lang 1952)
Viva Zapata! (Kazan 1952)
Shane (Stevens 1952)
The Big Heat (Lang 1953)
Gentlemen Prefer Blondes (Hawks 1953)
Johnny Guitar (Ray 1954)
Carmen Jones (Preminger 1954)
On the Waterfront (Kazan 1954)
River of no Return (Preminger 1954)
The Far Country (Mann 1954)

The Man from Laramie (Mann 1955)
Marty (Delbert Mann 1955)
My Sister Eileen (Quine 1955)
Kiss Me Deadly (Aldrich 1955)
All That Heaven Allows (Sirk 1955)
Rebel Without a Cause (Ray 1955)
The Seven Year Itch (Wilder 1955)
House of Bamboo (Fuller 1955)
Baby Doll (Kazan 1956)
The Harder They Fall (Robson 1956)
The Great Man (Ferrer 1956)
Beyond a Reasonable Doubt (Lang 1956)
The Scarchers (Ford, 1956)
The James Brothers (Ray 1956)
The Revolt of Mamie Stover (Walsh 1956)
Funny Face (Donen 1956)
Written on the Wind (Sirk 1956)
The Wrong Man (Hitchcock 1956)
Cowboy (Daves 1957)
A Face in the Crowd (Kazan 1957)
Jeanne Eagels (Sidney 1957)
Paths of Glory (Kubrick 1957)
Baby Face Nelson (Siegel 1957)
Will Success Spoil Rock Hunter (Tashlin 1957)
Twelve Angry Men (Lumet 1957)
The Young Stranger (Frankenheimer 1957)
The Goddess (Cromwell 1958)
The Defiant Ones (Kramer 1958)
Touch of Evil (Welles 1958)
Machine Gun Kelly (Corman 1958)
The Lineup (Siegel 1958)
Verboten (Fuller 1958)
Shadows (Cassavetes 1959)
Anatomy of a Murder (Preminger 1959)
Odds Against Tomorrow (Wise 1959)
Rio Bravo (Hawks 1959)
The Rise and Fall of Legs Diamond (Boetticher 1959)
The Wonderful Country (Parrish 1959)
Some Like It Hot (Wilder 1959)
Spartacus (Kubrick 1960)

HOLLYWOOD IN THE 60S
Sergeant Rutledge (Ford 1960)
Wild River (Kazan 1960)
Psycho (Hitchcock 1960)
Underworld USA (Fuller 1960)
Portrait of a Mobster (Pevney 1961)
Two Rode Together (Ford 1961)
The Manchurian Candidate (Frankenheimer 1962)
Freud, The Secret Passion (Huston 1962)
Lonely are the Brave (Miller 1962)
The Miracle Worker (Penn 1962)
To Kill a Mocking Bird (Mulligan 1962)
Walk on the Wild Side/Barbarella (Dmytryk/Vadim 1962/67)
The Birds (Hitchcock 1963)
The Haunted Palace (Corman 1963)
Major Dundee (Peckinpah 1964)
Kiss Me, Stupid (Wilder 1964)
The Killers (Siegel 1964)
Marnie (Hitchcock 1964)
Torn Curtain (Hitchcock 1966)
Warning Shot (Kulik 1966)
In the Heat of the Night (Jewison 1967)
New Face in Hell (Guillermin 1967)
The St. Valentine's Day Massacre (Corman 1967)
Coogan's Bluff (Siegel 1968)
Rosemary's Baby (Polanski 1968)
Sweet Charity (Fosse 1968)
Madigan (Siegel 1968)

Butch Cassidy and the Sundance Kid (Roy Hill 1969)
Topaz (Hitchcock 1969)
Easy Rider (Hopper 1969)

HOLLYWOOD IN THE 70S
Loving (Kershner 1970)
The Beguiled (Siegel 1970)
On a Clear Day You Can See Forever (Minnelli 1970)
Dirty Harry (Siegel 1971)
The Godfather (Coppola 1971)
Klute (Pakula 1971)
Shaft (Parks 1971)
Blacula (Crain 1972)
Two Lane Blacktop (Hellman 1972)
Ulzana's Raid (Aldrich 1972)
Butch Cassidy and the Sundance Kid/The Sting (Roy Hill 1969/73)
Cleopatra Jones (Starrett 1973)
The Way We Were (Pollack 1973)
Mandingo (Fleischer 1975)

11. Notions of *Mise en Scène*
Film titles referred to in: Brian Henderson, 'The Long Take', *Film Comment*, Summer, 1971; Victor Perkins: *Film as Film*, Penguin, 1972; Charles Barr: 'On Cinemascope' in Mast & Cohen eds. *Film Theory and Criticism*, OUP, 1974, and abridged in *Film: A Montage of Theories*, ed. R. Dyer McCann, Dutton, 1966; *Movie Reader*, November Books, 1972.

BRIAN HENDERSON in 'The Long Take':
Boudu sauvé des eaux (Renoir 1932)
Citizen Kane (Welles 1940)
Le Crime de Monsieur Lange (Renoir 1935)
La Grande illusion (Renoir 1937)
Letter from an Unknown Woman (Ophuls 1948)
The Magnificent Ambersons (Welles 1942)
La Règle du jeu (Renoir 1938)
Touch of Evil (Welles 1958)

VICTOR PERKINS in 'Film as Film':
Anatomy of a Murder (Preminger 1959)
Carmen Jones (Preminger 1954)
The Far Country (Mann 1954)
Letter from an Unknown Woman (Ophuls 1948)
Marnie (Hitchcock 1964)
Psycho (Hitchcock 1960)

VICTOR PERKINS in 'Film as Film' (Cont.):
River of No Return (Preminger 1954)
L Règle du jeu (Renoir 1938)
Ugetsu Monogatari (Mizoguchi 1953)

VICTOR PERKINS' counter examples:
Battleship Potemkin (Eisenstein 1925)
The Bridge on the River Kwai (Lean 1957)
The Criminal (Losey 1960)
Moulin Rouge (Huston 1952)

CHARLES BARR on 'CinemaScope':
River of No Return ('Scope & Standard) (Preminger 1954)
Wild River ('Scope & Standard) (Kazan 1960)

'Movie Reader' on *Mise en Scène*:
Anatomy of a Murder (Preminger 1959)

La Baie des anges (Demy 1962)
The Birds (Hitchcock 1960)
The Blue Angel (von Sternberg 1930)
Carmen Jones (Preminger 1954)
The James Brothers (Ray 1956)
Laura (Preminger 1944)
They Live by Night (Ray 1948)
The Lusty Men (Ray 1952)
Marnie (Hitchcock 1964)
Peeping Tom (Powell 1959)
Psycho (Hitchcock 1960)
The Scarlet Empress (von Sternberg 1934)

Other extracts useful for discussing *Mise en Scène*:
All That Heaven Allows (Sirk 1955)
Baby Doll (Kazan 1956)
Beyond a Reasonable Doubt (Lang 1956)
The Big Heat (Lang 1953)
Dead of Night (Hamer 1945)
Don't Look Now (Roeg 1975)
La Femme infidèle (Chabrol 1968)
The Godfather (Coppola 1971)
Klute (Pakula 1971)
Legend of the Werewolf and teachers' resource pack (Francis 1974)
Macao (von Sternberg 1952)
Mandingo (Fleischer 1975)
On a Clear Day You Can See Forever (Minnelli 1970)
On Dangerous Ground (Ray 1951)
Pierrot le fou (Godard 1965)
The Revolt of Mamie Stover (Walsh 1956)
Rio Bravo (Hawks 1959)
St. Valentine's Day Massacre (Corman 1967)
Sergeant Rutledge (Ford 1960)
They Live by Night (Ray 1948)
Underworld USA (Fuller 1960)
Written on the Wind (Sirk 1956)

12. Social Realism in Hollywood
(Films consciously offering themselves as dealing with social reality and employing a realist aesthetic – a select listing, arranged chronologically.)

Foolish Wives (Stroheim 1921)
I Am a Fugitive from a Chain Gang (LeRoy 1932)
The Grapes of Wrath (Ford 1940)
Salt of the Earth (Biberman 1953)
Marty (Delbert Mann 1955)
A Face in the Crowd (Kazan 1957)
Twelve Angry Men (Lumet 1957)
The Young Stranger (Frankenheimer 1956)
The Goddess (Cromwell 1958)
The Defiant Ones (Kramer 1958)
To Kill a Mocking Bird (Mulligan 1962)
*In the Heat of the Night (Jewison 1967)

13. Stars
(Comprehensive listing of titles arranged chronologically under select listing of stars.)

ANDREWS, Julie:
Torn Curtain (Hitchcock 1966)

ASTAIRE, Fred/ROGERS, Ginger:
Gay Divorcee (Sandrich 1934)
Top Hat (Sandrich 1935)
Funny Face (Donen 1957)

BACALL, Lauren:
To Have and Have Not (Hawks 1945)
Written on the Wind (Sirk 1956)

BALL, Lucille:
Dance, Girl, Dance (Arzner 1940)

BELMONDO, Jean-Paul:
A bout de souffle (Breathless) (Godard 1959)
Pierrot le fou (Godard 1965)

BERGMAN, Ingrid:
Under Capricorn (Hitchcock 1949)
Stromboli (Rossellini 1949)

BOGARDE, Dirk:
Accident (Losey 1967)

BOGART, Humphrey:
The Maltese Falcon (Huston 1941)
Racket Busters (Bacon 1938)
The Roaring Twenties (Walsh 1939)
They Drive by Night (Walsh 1940)
High Sierra (Walsh 1941)
To Have and Have Not (Hawks 1945)
The Treasure of the Sierra Madre (Huston 1948)

BRANDO, Marlon:
A Streetcar Named Desire (Kazan 1951)
Viva Zapata! (Kazan 1952)
On the Waterfront (Kazan 1954)
The Godfather (Coppola 1971)
Last Tango in Paris (Bertolucci 1972)

BRONSON, Charles:
Machine Gun Kelly (Corman 1958)
Once Upon a Time in the West (Leone 1968)

CAGNEY, James:
The Public Enemy (Wellman 1931)
G-Men (Keighley 1935)
Each Dawn I Die (Keighley 1939)
The Roaring Twenties (Walsh 1939)

CHAPLIN, Charlie:
Carmen (Charlie Chaplin's burlesque on 'Carmen') (Chaplin 1916)
Easy Street (Chaplin 1916)
The Pawnshop (Chaplin 1916)
The Vagabond (Chaplin 1916)

CHRISTIE, Julie:
Don't Look Now (Roeg 1973)

CLIFT, Montgomery:
Wild River (Kazan 1960)
Freud, The Secret Passion (Huston 1962)

COOPER, Gary:
Mr. Deeds goes to Town (Capra 1936)
Sergeant York (Hawks 1941)

CONNERY, Sean:
From Russia with Love (Young 1963)
Marnie (Hitchcock 1964)

CRAWFORD, Joan:
Mildred Pierce (Curtiz 1945)
Johnny Guitar (Ray 1954)

CUSHING, Peter:
The Curse of Frankenstein (Fisher 1957)

Dracula (Fisher 1957)
Hound of the Baskervilles (Fisher 1959)
The Revenge of Frankenstein (Fisher 1958)
The Mummy (Fisher 1959)
The Evil of Frankenstein (Francis 1963)
The Satanic Rites of Dracula (Gibson 1973)
Legend of the Werewolf (Francis 1974)
The Baron Frankenstein – Film Study
    Extract Compilation (1957–1969)

DAVIS, Bette:
Little Foxes (Wyler 1941)

DEAN, James
Rebel Without a Cause (Ray 1955)

DIETRICH, Marlene:
Scarlet Empress (von Sternberg 1934)
Destry Rides Again (Marshall 1939)
Rancho Notorious (Lang 1952)
Touch of Evil (Welles 1959)

DOUGLAS, Kirk:
Out of the Past (Build My Gallows High)
    (Tourneur 1947)
The Big Sky (Hawks 1952)
Paths of Glory (Kubrick 1957)
Spartacus (Kubrick 1960)
Lonely are the Brave (Miller 1962)

EASTWOOD, Clint:
Coogan's Bluff (Siegel 1968)
The Beguiled (Siegel 1970)
Dirty Harry (Siegel 1971)

FONDA, Henry:
Grapes of Wrath (Ford 1940)
My Darling Clementine (Ford 1946)
Fort Apache (Ford 1948)
The Wrong Man (Hitchcock 1956)
Twelve Angry Men (Lumet 1957)
Madigan (Siegel 1968)
Once Upon a Time in the West (Leone 1969)

FONDA, Jane:
Walk on the Wild Side/Barbarella
    (Dmytryk/Vadim 1962/1967)
Klute (Pakula 1971)
Tout va bien (Godard/Gorin 1972)

GRAHAME, Gloria:
Crossfire (Dmytryk 1947)
The Big Heat (Lang 1953)

GRANT, Cary:
Bringing up Baby (Hawks 1938)

GUINNESS, Alec:
The Lavender Hill Mob (Crichton 1951)
The Ladykillers (Mackendrick 1955)
The Prisoner (Glenville 1955)
The Bridge on the River Kwai (Lean 1957)
Our Man in Havana (Reed 1959)

HAYWORTH, Rita:
Gilda (Charles Vidor 1946)

HEPBURN, Audrey:
Funny Face (Donen 1956)

HEPBURN, Katharine:
Bringing up Baby (Hawks 1938)

HESTON, Charlton:
Touch of Evil (Welles 1958)
Major Dundee (Peckinpah 1965)

HOLLIDAY, Judy:
Born Yesterday (Cukor 1950)

HUDSON, Rock:
All That Heaven Allows (Sirk 1955)
Written on the Wind (Sirk 1956)

KARLOFF, Boris:
Frankenstein (Whale 1931)
Targets (Bogdanovich 1968)

LANCASTER, Burt:
The Killers (Siodmak 1946)
Brute Force (Dassin 1947)

LEE, Christopher:
The Curse of Frankenstein (Fisher 1957)
Dracula (Fisher 1957)
The Mummy (Fisher 1958)
Dracula Prince of Darkness (Fisher 1965)
The Devil Rides Out (Fisher 1967)
Taste the Blood of Dracula (Sasdy 1969)
The Satanic Rites of Dracula (Gibson 1973)

LUPINO, Ida:
They Drive by Night (Walsh 1940)
High Sierra (Walsh 1941)

LORRE, Peter:
M (Lang 1931)
The Maltese Falcon (Huston 1941)

MANSFIELD, Jayne:
Will Success Spoil Rock Hunter (Tashlin 1957)

MARVIN, Lee:
The Big Heat (Lang 1953)
The Killers (Siegel 1964)

MARX, The Brothers:
Love Happy (Miller 1949)

MATTHAU, Walter:
A Face in the Crowd (Kazan 1957)
Lonely are the Brave (Miller 1962)
A New Leaf (May 1970)

MITCHUM, Robert:
Out of the Past (Build My Gallows High)
    (Tourneur 1947)
Crossfire (Dmytryk 1947)
The Lusty Men (Ray 1952)
Macao (Sternberg 1952)
Angel Face (Preminger 1953)
River of No Return (Preminger 1954)
The Wonderful Country (Parrish 1959)

MONROE, Marilyn:
Gentlemen Prefer Blondes (Hawks 1953)
River of No Return (Preminger 1954)
The Seven Year Itch (Wilder 1955)
Some Like It Hot (Wilder 1959)

MONTAND, Yves:
The Wages of Fear (Clouzot 1953)
La Guerre est finie (Resnais 1966)
On a Clear Day You Can See Forever
    (Minnelli 1970)

MOREAU, Jeanne:
Jules et Jim (Truffaut 1961)
Eva (Losey 1962)
La Baie des anges (Demy 1962)

NEWMAN, Paul:
Torn Curtain (Hitchcock 1966)
Butch Cassidy and the Sundance Kid (Roy Hill 1969)
Butch Cassidy and the Sundance Kid/The Sting (Roy Hill 1969/1973)

NICHOLSON, Jack:
Easy Rider (Hopper 1969)

NOVAK, Kim:
Jeanne Eagels (Sidney 1957)
Kiss Me, Stupid (Wilder 1964)

PECK, Gregory:
The Gunfighter (King 1950)
The Guns of Navarone (Lee Thompson 1961)
To Kill a Mockingbird (Mulligan 1963)

POITIER, Sidney:
The Defiant Ones (Kramer 1958)
In the Heat of the Night (Jewison 1967)
Buck and the Preacher (Poitier 1972)

PRICE, Vincent:
The Haunted Palace (Corman 1963)
The Tomb of Ligeia (Corman 1964)

REDFORD, Robert:
Butch Cassidy and the Sundance Kid (Roy Hill (1969)
Butch Cassidy and the Sundance Kid/The Sting (Roy Hill 1969/1973)
The Way We Were (Pollack 1973)

ROBINSON, Edward G:
Little Caesar (LeRoy 1930)
Double Indemnity (Wilder 1944)

ROUNDTREE, Richard:
Shaft (Parks 1971)

RUSSELL, Jane:
Macao (von Sternberg 1952)
Gentlemen Prefer Blondes (Hawks 1953)
The Revolt of Mamie Stover (Walsh 1956)

RUSSELL, Rosalind:
His Girl Friday (Hawks 1939)

RYAN, Robert:
Crossfire (Dmytryk 1947)
Woman on the Beach (Renoir 1947)
Cry of the City (Siodmak 1948)
The Set-Up (Wise 1948)
On Dangerous Ground (Ray 1951)

SELLERS, Peter:
The Ladykillers (Mackendrick 1955)
Dr. Strangelove (Kubrick 1963)
What's New Pussycat? (Donner 1965)

SINATRA, Frank:
The Manchurian Candidate
    (Frankenheimer 1962)

STANWYCK, Barbara:
Stella Dallas (King Vidor 1937)
Double Indemnity (Wilder 1944)

STEIGER, Rod:
On the Waterfront (Kazan 1954)
Run of the Arrow (Fuller 1956)
The Harder They Fall (Robson 1956)
In the Heat of the Night (Jewison 1967)

STEWART, James:
Destry Rides Again (Marshall 1939)
Winchester '73 (Mann 1950)
Broken Arrow (Daves 1950)
Bend of the River (Mann 1952)
The Far Country (Mann 1954)
The Man From Laramie (Mann 1955)
Anatomy of a Murder (Preminger 1959)
Two Rode Together (Ford 1961)

STREISAND, Barbra:
On a Clear Day You Can See Forever
(Minnelli 1970)
The Way We Were (Pollack 1973)

SUTHERLAND, Donald:
Klute (Pakula 1971)
Don't Look Now (Roeg 1973)

TEMPLE, Shirley:
The Littlest Rebel (Butler 1936)

VITTI, Monica:
L'avventura (Antonioni 1959/60)
L'eclisse (Antonioni 1962)

WAYNE, John:
Stagecoach (Ford 1939)
Fort Apache (Ford 1948)
She Wore a Yellow Ribbon (Ford 1949)
The Searchers (Ford 1956)
Rio Bravo (Hawks 1959)

WEST, Mae:
Belle of the Nineties/I'm No Angel
(McCarey/Ruggles 1935/34)

14. Studios

Britain:
(Comprehensive listing, arranged
chronologically.)

EALING
Dead of Night (Hamer 1945)
The Lavender Hill Mob (Crichton 1951)
The Man in the White Suit (MacKendrick
1951)
The Ladykillers (MacKendrick 1955)

HAMMER
The Quatermass Experiment (Guest 1955)
X – the Unknown (Norman 1956)
The Curse of Frankenstein (Fisher 1957)
Quatermass II (Guest 1957)
Dracula (Fisher 1957)
The Revenge of Frankenstein (Fisher
1958)
The Hound of the Baskervilles (Fisher
1959)
The Mummy (Fisher 1959)
The Brides of Dracula (Fisher 1960)
The Damned (Losey 1961)
The Evil of Frankenstein (Francis 1963)
Dracula Prince of Darkness (Fisher 1965)
Fanatic (Narizzano 1965)
The Plague of the Zombies (Gilling 1965)
The Devil Rides Out (Fisher 1967)
Taste the Blood of Dracula (Sasdy 1969)
The Satanic Rites of Dracula (Gibson
1973)

Hollywood:
(Select comprehensive listing arranged
chronologically under listing of studios.)

COLUMBIA
Mae West Compilation: Belle of the
Nineties/I'm No Angel (McCarey
1935/Ruggles 1934)
Mr. Deeds goes to Town (Capra 1936)
His Girl Friday (Hawks 1939)
Double Indemnity (Wilder 1944)
Mildred Pierce (Curtiz 1945)
Gilda (Charles Vidor 1946)
Born Yesterday (Cukor 1950)
The Big Heat (Lang 1953)
The Man from Laramie (Mann 1955)
My Sister Eileen (Quine 1955)
The Harder they Fall (Robson 1956)
Jeanne Eagels (Sidney 1957)
The Goddess (Cromwell 1958)
The Lineup (Siegel 1958)
Anatomy of a Murder (Preminger 1959)
Two Rode Together (Ford 1961)
Klute (Pakula 1971)

PARAMOUNT
The Scarlet Empress (von Sternberg 1934)
Shane (Stevens 1952)
Funny Face (Donen 1956)
Rosemary's Baby (Polanski 1968)
A New Leaf (May 1970)
On a Clear Day You Can See For Ever
(Minnelli 1970)

RKO
King Kong (Schoedsak and Cooper 1933)
The Gay Divorcee (Sandrich 1934)
The Informer (Ford 1935)
Top Hat (Sandrich 1935)
Bringing up Baby (Hawks 1938)
Dance, Girl, Dance (Azner 1940)
Mr. and Mrs. Smith (Hitchcock 1941)
Cat People (Tourneur 1942)
This Land is Mine (Renoir 1943)
Farewell My Lovely (Dmytryk 1944)
Deadlier than the Male (Born to Kill)
(Wise 1947)
Crossfire (Dmytryk 1947)
Out of the Past (Build My Gallows High)
(Tourneur 1947)
Woman on the Beach (Renoir 1947)
They Live by Night (Ray 1948)
The Set-up (Wise 1948)
Wagonmaster (Ford 1950)
On Dangerous Ground (Ray 1951)
Angel Face (Preminger 1952)
Macao (von Sternberg 1952)
Rancho Notorious (Lang 1952)
Beyond a Reasonable Doubt (Lang 1956)
The Young Stranger (Frankenheimer
1957)
Machine Gun Kelly (Corman 1958)
Verboten (Fuller 1958)

TWENTIETH CENTURY-FOX
A Fool There Was (Powell 1914)
Sunrise (Murnau 1927)
The Littlest Rebel (Butler 1936)
Grapes of Wrath (Ford 1940)
How Green Was My Valley (Ford 1941)
Laura (Preminger 1944)
The House on 92nd Street (Hathaway
1945)
My Darling Clementine (Ford 1946)
Cry of the City (Siodmak 1948)

Broken Arrow (Daves 1950)
The Gunfighter (King 1950)
Viva Zapata! (Kazan 1952)
Gentlemen Prefer Blondes (Hawks 1953)
Carmen Jones (Preminger 1954)
River of No Return (Preminger 1954)
House of Bamboo (Fuller 1955)
The Seven Year Itch (Wilder 1955)
The James Brothers (Ray 1956)
The Revolt of Mamie Stover (Walsh 1956)
Will Success Spoil Rock Hunter (Tashlin
1957)
Wild River (Kazan 1960)
The St. Valentine's Day Massacre
(Corman 1967)
Butch Cassidy and the Sundance Kid +
Campanile Production (Roy Hill 1969)

UNIVERSAL
Foolish Wives (Stroheim 1921)
Dracula (Browning 1931)
Frankenstein (Whale 1931)
Destry Rides Again (Marshall 1939)
Shadow of a Doubt (Hitchcock 1943)
The Killers (Siodmak 1946)
Brute Force (Dassin 1947)
I Remember Mama (Stevens 1948)
Bend of the River (Mann 1952)
The Far Country (Mann 1954)
All That Heaven Allows (Sirk 1955)
The Great Man (Ferrer 1956)
Written on the Wind (Sirk 1956)
Touch of Evil (Welles 1958)
Spartacus (Kubrick 1960)
Lonely Are the Brave (Miller 1962)
The Birds (Hitchcock 1963)
Marnie (Hitchcock 1964)
Torn Curtain (Hitchcock 1966)
New Face in Hell (Guillermin 1967)
Coogan's Bluff (Siegel 1968)
Madigan (Siegel 1968)
Sweet Charity (Fosse 1968)
Topaz (Hitchcock 1969)
The Beguiled (Siegel 1970)
Two-Lane Blacktop (Hellman 1971)
Frenzy (Hitchcock 1972)
Ulzana's Raid (Aldrich 1972)
The Sting – compiled with Butch Cassidy
and the Sundance Kid (Roy Hill 1973)

WARNER BROTHERS
The Jazz Singer (Crosland 1927)
Little Caesar (LeRoy 1930)
The Public Enemy (Wellman 1931)
I Am a Fugitive from a Chain Gang
(LeRoy 1932)
Gold Diggers of 1933 (LeRoy 1933)
G-Men (Keighley 1935)
The Roaring Twenties (Walsh 1939)
Each Dawn I Die (Keighley 1940)
They Drive by Night (Walsh 1940)
High Sierra (Walsh 1941)
The Maltese Falcon (Huston 1941
Sergeant York (Hawks 1941)
Racket Busters (Bacon 1942)
To Have and Have Not (Hawks 1944)
Rebel Without a Cause (Ray 1955)
The Wrong Man (Hitchcock 1956)
Sergeant Rutledge with John Ford (Ford
1960)
Portrait of a Mobster (Pevney 1961)
Dirty Harry with Malpaso (Siegel 1971)
Cleopatra Jones (Starrett 1973)

15. Subversion and Counter-Cinema
(Select listing arranged alphabetically in sub-categories.)

The Avant-Garde View:
The Cabinet of Dr. Caligari (Wiene 1919)
Day of Wrath (Dreyer 1943)
Man with a Movie Camera (Dziga-Vertov 1929)

Godard, the Exemplum:
Bande à part (Godard 1964)
British Sounds (Godard 1969)
Une Femme marièe (Godard 1964)
Masculin-Féminin (Godard 1966)
Pierrot le fou (Godard 1965)
Two Or Three Things I Know About Her (Godard 1966)
Weekend (Godard 1967)
Tout va bien (Godard/Gorin 1972)

Comolli's Category 'E':
All That Heaven Allows (Sirk 1955)
Fear Eats the Soul (Fassbinder 1974)
On a Clear Day You Can See Forever (Minnelli 1970)
Rancho Notorious (Lang 1952)
Stromboli (Rossellini 1949)
Will Success Spoil Rock Hunter (Tashlin 1957)
Written on the Wind (Sirk 1956)

Feminist Applications:
Dance, Girl, Dance (Arzner 1940)
La Fiancée du pirate (Kaplan 1969)
The Heartbreak Kid (May 1972)
Knucklemen (Rothman 1972)
A New Leaf (May 1970)
The Revolt of Mamie Stover (Walsh 1956)
Student Nurses (Rothman 1970)

Third World practice:
Hour of the Furnaces (Solanas 1968)
Antonio das mortes (Rocha 1969)
Emitai (Sembene 1972)

16. Surrealism in the Cinema
(Select listing, arranged alphabetically.)
L'Atalante (Vigo 1933)
Don't Look Now (Roeg 1973)
8½ (Fellini 1962/63)
El (Buñuel 1952)
La Fiancée du pirate (Kaplan 1969)

Judex (Franju 1963)
King Kong (Schoedsack & Cooper 1933)
Lotna (Wadja 1959)
Nazarin (Buñuel 1958)
On a Clear Day You Can See Forever (Minnelli 1970)
Orphée (Cocteau 1950)
Plague of the Zombies (Gilling 1966)
Sawdust and Tinsel (Bergman 1953)
The Tomb of Ligeia (Corman 1964)
Viridiana (Buñuel 1961)
Les Yeux sans visage (Eyes Without a Face) (Franju 1959)
Zéro de conduite (Vigo 1933)

17. The Treatment of Women in Hollywood
(Select listing of films directed by men, arranged alphabetically.)
Angel Face (Preminger 1952)
All That Heaven Allows (Sirk 1955)
Baby Doll (Kazan 1956)
The Beguiled (Siegel 1970)
The Big Heat (Lang 1953)
Born Yesterday (Cukor 1950)
Bringing up Baby (Hawks 1938)
Cleopatra Jones (Starrett 1973)
Cry of the City (Siodmak 1948)
Deadlier than the Male (Born to Kill) (Wise 1947)
Destry Rides Again (Marshall 1939)
Double Indemnity (Wilder 1944)
A Fool There Was (Powell 1914)
Foolish Wives (Stroheim 1921)
Funny Face (Donan 1956)
Gentlemen Prefer Blondes (Hawks 1953)
Gilda (Charles Vidor 1946)
Hearts of the World (Griffith 1918)
High Sierra (Walsh 1941)
His Girl Friday (Hawks 1939)
Intolerance (Extract 1) (Griffith 1916)
It's a Gift (McLeod 1934)
King Kong (Schoedsack & Cooper 1933)
Kiss Me Deadly (Aldrich 1955)
Kiss Me Stupid (Wilder 1964)
Klute (Pakula 1971)
Laura (Preminger 1944)
Letter from an Unknown Woman (Ophuls 1948)
The Little Foxes (Wyler 1941)
The Littlest Rebel (Butler 1936)
Loving (Kershner 1970)
Macao (von Sternberg 1952)

Mildred Pierce (Curtiz 1945)
My Darling Clementine (Ford 1964)
Out of the Past (Build My Gallows High) (Tourneur 1947)
Rancho Notorious (Lang 1952)
The Revolt of Mamie Stover (Walsh 1956)
Rio Bravo (Hawks 1959)
River of No Return (Preminger 1954
Scarface (Hawks 1931)
The Scarlet Empress (von Sternberg 1934)
The Seven Year Itch (Wilder 1955)
Some Like It Hot (Wilder 1959)
Stella Dallas (King Vidor 1938)
Sunrise (Murnau 1927)
Such Good Friends (Preminger 1971)
Sweet Charity (Fosse 1968)
They Drive by Night (Walsh 1940)
To Have and Have Not (Hawks 1944)
Underworld USA (Fuller 1960)
Walk on the Wild Side (Dmytryk 1962)
The Way We Were (Pollack 1973)
What's New Pussycat? (Donner 1965)
Will Success Spoil Rock Hunter (Tashlin 1957)
Written on the Wind (Sirk 1956)
The Dumb Blonde Stereotype – Film Study Extract Compilation

18. TV Material
(Comprehensive listing, arranged alphabetically.)
The Blind Man (Whatham 1966)
The Blood Donor – Hancock (Wood 1965)
Cathy Come Home (Loach 1966)
Coronation Street (Pauline Shaw 1964)
Culloden (Watkins 1964)
Dr. Who (Martin 1964)
Face to Face – Lord Reith (Burnett 1960)
The Forsyte Saga – The Indian Summer Of A Forsyte (Giles 1966)
In Two Minds (Loach 1966)
Softly Softly – It Doesn't Grow On Trees (Lewis 1966)
Steptoe & Son (Wood 1964)
Television Materials – Vox Pop (1958); Dr IQ (1952), (Wood) TV Commercials
Till Death Us Do Part – Alf Garnett (Main Wilson 1966)
Up the Junction (Loach 1965)
Z Cars – Incident Reported (Rose 1962)

Index

Page numbers in *italic* refer to the illustrations